Western Civilizations

Their History & Their Culture

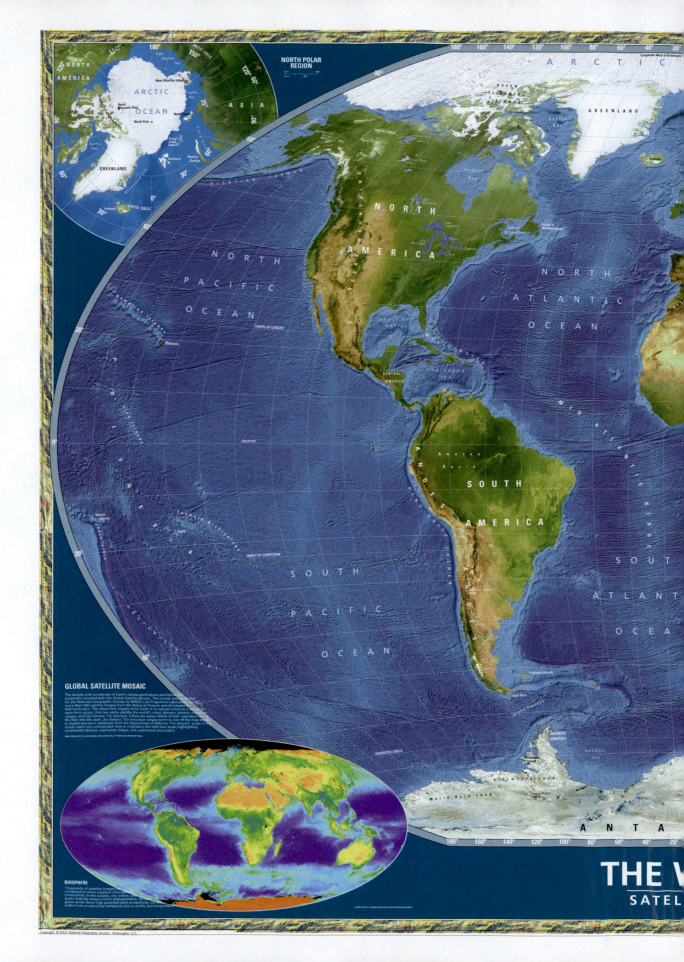

NORTH POLAR REGION

GLOBAL SATELLITE MOSAIC

The beauty and complexity of Earth's landscapes—oceans and beneath the oceans—is revealed with the Global Satellite Mosaic. The mosaic was prepared for the National Geographic Society by NASA's Jet Propulsion Laboratory from more than 500 satellite images from the National Oceanic and Atmospheric Administration. The cloud-free images show Earth in its natural colors as it would be seen from space. One can easily identify the world's major glaciers, deserts, mountain ranges, and rain forests. For example, follow the green ribbon of lush vegetation along the Nile into the stark, dry Sahara. The mountain ranges seem to rise off the map thanks to digital elevation databases from the Department of Defense. The deepest areas of the ocean realm are colored dark blue in contrast to the light blue areas highlighting continental shelves, submarine ridges, and undersea mountains.

BIOSPHERE

Thousands of satellite images were combined to show a picture of biosphere productivity. In the oceans, red, yellow, and green indicate waters rich in phytoplankton. On the continents, green areas show high-potential plant productivity, tan areas suffer from productivity limitations due to aridity and temperature.

THE W

SATEL

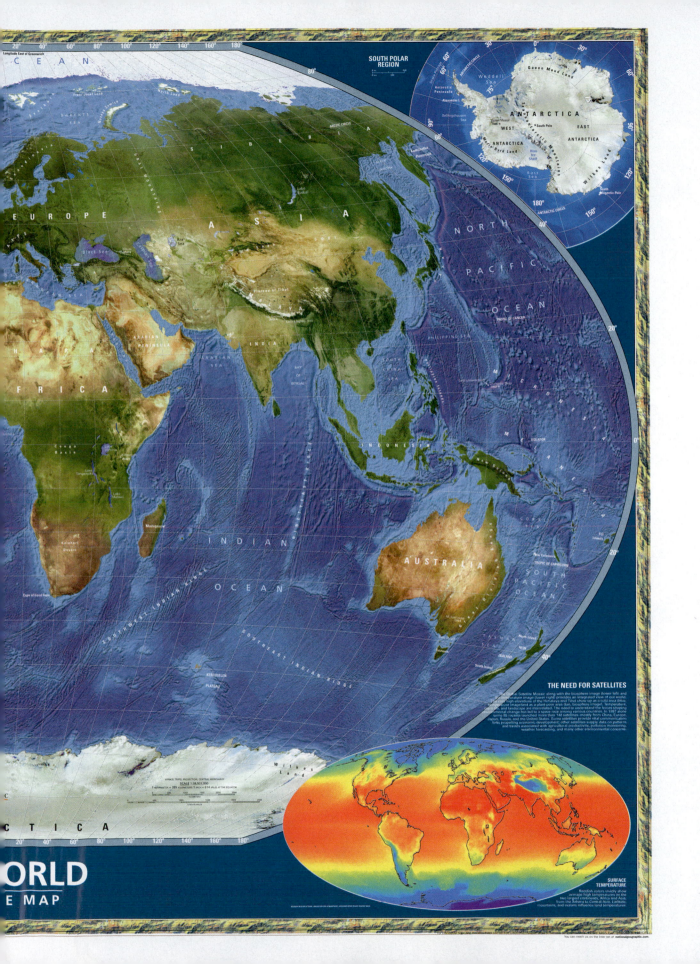

SOUTH POLAR
REGION

ANTARCTICA

THE NEED FOR SATELLITES

The Global Satellite Mosaic along with the biosphere image (lower left) and
the temperature image (lower right) provides an integrated view of our world.
Although high elevations of the Himalaya and Tibet show up as a cold area (blue,
lower right), they are imagined as a plant poor area (tan, biosphere image). Temperature,
rainfall, and landscape are interrelated. The need to understand the forces shaping
environmental change has led to a space race among various countries. In 1997 alone
some 85 rockets launched more than 140 satellites—mostly from China, Europe,
Japan, Russia, and the United States. Some satellites provide vital communication
links propelling economic development; other satellites supply data on pattern
and trends associated with agricultural productivity, pollution monitoring,
weather forecasting, and many other environmental concerns.

ORLD
E MAP

SURFACE
TEMPERATURE
Reddish colors vividly show
average high temperatures on the
two largest continents, Africa and Asia,
from the Sahara to Central Asia. Latitude,
mountains, and oceans influence land temperatures.

Western Civilizations
Their History & Their Culture

BRIEF FIFTH EDITION
VOLUME ONE

❯ **JOSHUA COLE**
University of Michigan, Ann Arbor

❯ **CAROL SYMES**
University of Illinois, Urbana-Champaign

W. W. NORTON & COMPANY
Independent Publishers Since 1923

W. W. NORTON & COMPANY has been independent since its founding in 1923, when William Warder Norton and Mary D. Herter Norton first published lectures delivered at the People's Institute, the adult education division of New York City's Cooper Union. The firm soon expanded its program beyond the Institute, publishing books by celebrated academics from America and abroad. By midcentury, the two major pillars of Norton's publishing program—trade books and college texts—were firmly established. In the 1950s, the Norton family transferred control of the company to its employees, and today—with a staff of four hundred and a comparable number of trade, college, and professional titles published each year—W. W. Norton & Company stands as the largest and oldest publishing house owned wholly by its employees.

Editor: Justin Cahill
Editorial Assistants: Angie Merila, Funto Omojola
Managing Editor, College: Marian Johnson
Project Editor: Linda Feldman
Managing Editor, College Digital Media: Kim Yi
Media Project Editor: Rachel Mayer
Media Editor: Carson Russell
Associate Media Editor: Alexander Lee
Assistant Media Editor: Lexi Malakhoff
Marketing Manager, History: Sarah England Bartley

Production Manager: Ashley Horna
Design Director: Lissi Sigillo
Designer: Jen Montgomery
Photo Editor: Mike Cullen
College Permissions Specialist: Elizabeth Trammell
Composition: Cenveo® Publisher Services
Cartographers: Mapping Specialists
Manufacturing: Transcontinental

Permission to use copyrighted material is included in the Credits section of this book.

The Library of Congress has cataloged the full edition as follows:

Names: Cole, Joshua, 1961- author. | Symes, Carol, author.
Title: Western civilizations : their history & their culture / Joshua Cole,
    Carol Symes.
Description: 20th edition. | New York : W. W. Norton & Company, [2020] |
    Includes index.
Identifiers: LCCN 2019030137 | ISBN 9780393418750 (cloth)
Subjects: LCSH: Civilization, Western—Textbooks. |
    Europe—Civilization—Textbooks.
Classification: LCC CB245 .C56 2020 | DDC 909/.09821—dc23
LC record available at https://lccn.loc.gov/2019030137

This edition: ISBN 978-0-393-41895-8

W. W. Norton & Company, Inc., 500 Fifth Avenue, New York, NY 10110
wwnorton.com

W. W. Norton & Company Ltd., 15 Carlisle Street, London W1D 3BS
1 2 3 4 5 6 7 8 9 0

About the Authors

JOSHUA COLE (PhD, University of California, Berkeley) is Professor of History at the University of Michigan, Ann Arbor. He has published work on gender and the history of population sciences, colonial violence, and the politics of memory in nineteenth- and twentieth-century France, Germany, and Algeria. His first book was *The Power of Large Numbers: Population, Politics, and Gender in Nineteenth-Century France* (2000), and he recently published a second book, *Lethal Provocation: The Constantine Murders and the Politics of French Algeria* (2019).

CAROL SYMES (PhD, Harvard University) is Associate Professor of History at the University of Illinois, Urbana-Champaign, where she has served as Director of Undergraduate Studies in History and has won numerous teaching awards. Her main areas of study include the history of medieval Europe, cultural history, and the history of media and communication technologies. Her first book, *A Common Stage: Theater and Public Life in Medieval Arras* (Cornell University Press, 2007), won four national awards. She is the founding executive editor of *The Medieval Globe*, the first academic journal to promote a global approach to medieval studies.

Brief Contents

MAPS xxiii

PRIMARY SOURCES xxv

PREFACE xxvii

MEDIA RESOURCES FOR
INSTRUCTORS AND STUDENTS xxxiii

ACKNOWLEDGMENTS xxxvii

CHAPTER 1 Early Civilizations 2

CHAPTER 2 Peoples, Gods, and Empires:
1700–500 B.C.E. 40

CHAPTER 3 The Civilization of Greece,
1000–400 B.C.E. 78

CHAPTER 4 The Greek World Expands,
400–150 B.C.E. 114

CHAPTER 5 The Civilization of Ancient
Rome 148

CHAPTER 6 The Transformation of
Rome 182

CHAPTER 7 Rome's Three Heirs,
500–950 216

CHAPTER 8 The Expansion of Europe,
950–1100 252

CHAPTER 9 The Consolidation of Europe,
1100–1250 292

CHAPTER 10 The Medieval World,
1250–1350 332

CHAPTER 11 Rebirth and Unrest,
1350–1453 366

CHAPTER 12 Innovation and Exploration,
1453–1533 400

CHAPTER 13 The Age of Dissent and Division,
1500–1564 436

CHAPTER 14 Europe in the Atlantic World,
1550–1660 468

CHAPTER 15 European Monarchies and
Absolutism, 1660–1725 508

CHAPTER 16 The New Science of the
Seventeenth Century 538

APPENDIX: RULERS OF PRINCIPAL
STATES A1

FURTHER READINGS A6

GLOSSARY A22

TEXT CREDITS A58

PHOTO CREDITS A61

INDEX A64

Contents

MAPS   xxiii

PRIMARY SOURCES   xxv

PREFACE   xxvii

MEDIA RESOURCES FOR INSTRUCTORS AND STUDENTS   xxxiii

ACKNOWLEDGMENTS   xxxvii

Chapter 1 › EARLY CIVILIZATIONS   2

Before Civilization   4

The Building Blocks of Civilization   6

Urban Development in Mesopotamia   9

The Culture of Sumer   12

Competing Viewpoints: The Flood: Two Accounts   14

The First Empires?   17

The Development of Civilization in Egypt   21

Analyzing Primary Sources: The Code of Hammurabi   22

Interpreting Visual Evidence: The Narmer Palette   28

Egyptian Culture and Society   31

Analyzing Primary Sources: The Instruction of Ptah-Hotep   33

Conclusion   37

Chapter 2 › PEOPLES, GODS, AND EMPIRES, 1700–500 B.C.E.   40

Indo-European Languages and Peoples   42

The New Kingdom of Egypt   44

Interpreting Visual Evidence: Remembering Hatshepsut   46

Transnational Networks of the Late Bronze Age   49

Aegean Civilization: Minoan Crete, Mycenaean Greece   51

The States of the Early Iron Age   56

Analyzing Primary Sources: The Diplomacy of the Mycenaeans and the Hittites   57

The Revival of the Assyrian Empire   62

The Rise of the Persians   66

The Development of Hebrew Monotheism   70

Competing Viewpoints: Two Perspectives on Imperial Rule   72

Conclusion   75

Chapter 3 › THE CIVILIZATION OF GREECE, 1000–400 B.C.E.   78

From Chaos to Polis   80

Analyzing Primary Sources: The Obligations of Hospitality: The Encounter of Odysseus and Nausicaa   82

The Culture of Archaic Greece, 800–500 B.C.E.   83

Interpreting Visual Evidence: The Ideal of Male Beauty   87

Portraits of Three Poleis   89

Analyzing Primary Sources: Songs of Sappho   90

The Challenge of the Persian Wars   97

The Golden Age of Classical Greece   100

"The Greatest War in History" and Its Consequences   105

The Failure of Athenian Democracy   108

Competing Viewpoints: Two Views of Socrates   110

Conclusion   112

Chapter 4 › THE GREEK WORLD EXPANDS, 400–150 B.C.E.   114

The Downfall of the Greek Polis   116

Analyzing Primary Sources: Xenophon Describes an Ideal Leader   117

Reimagining the Polis: The Artistic and Intellectual Response   118

Interpreting Visual Evidence: Reconstructing an Ideal of Female Beauty   121

The Rise of Macedonia   122

The Conquests of Alexander, 336–323 B.C.E.   124

The Hellenistic Kingdoms   127

Analyzing Primary Sources: Alexander Puts Down a Mutiny   128

From Polis to Cosmopolis   132

Hellenistic Worldviews   134

Analyzing Primary Sources: A Jewish Response to Hellenization   137

The Scientific Revolution of Antiquity   138

Competing Viewpoints: Debating the Education and Role of Women   142

Conclusion   145

Chapter 5 › THE CIVILIZATION OF ANCIENT ROME   148

Rome's Early Influences   150

The Triumph of the Early Republic   151

The Essence of Roman Identity   154

Analyzing Primary Sources: Polybius Describes the Romans' Worship of Their Ancestors   156

From Republic to Empire   157

The Consequences of Imperialism   160

"Restoring the Republic": The Struggle for Power   162

Analyzing Primary Sources: Antony and Cleopatra   166

The Principate and the *Pax Romana*, 27 B.C.E.–180 C.E.   167

Making the World Roman   171

Competing Viewpoints: Two Views of Augustus's Rule   172

Interpreting Visual Evidence: Roman Urban Planning   178

Conclusion   179

Chapter 6 › THE TRANSFORMATION OF ROME   182

The Challenge of Christianity   184

The Challenge of Imperial Expansion   189

Analyzing Primary Sources: The Prosecution of a Roman Citizen   190

Competing Viewpoints: The Development of an Imperial Policy toward Christians   192

The Conversion of Christianity   195

Interpreting Visual Evidence: The Power of the Invincible Sun   199

Shifting Centers and Moving Frontiers   203

The Shaping of a New Worldview   207

Classical Learning and the Christian Life   210

Analyzing Primary Sources: Roman or Barbarian?   212

Conclusion   214

Chapter 7 › ROME'S THREE HEIRS, 500–950   216

Justinian's Imperial Ambitions   218

The Roman Empire of Byzantium   220

Competing Viewpoints: Debating the Power of Icons   224

Muhammad and the Teachings of Islam   227

Analyzing Primary Sources: A Sura from the Qur'an   229

The Widening Islamic World   230

The Conversion of Northwestern Europe   235

Interpreting Visual Evidence: The Ship Burial of Sutton Hoo   238

The Empire of Charlemagne   242

Disputed Legacies and New Alliances   247

Conclusion   250

Chapter 8 › THE EXPANSION OF EUROPE, 950–1100   252

A Tour of Europe around the Year 1000   254

The Agricultural Revolution of the Medieval Warm Period   259

The Growth of Towns and Trade   261

Violence, Lordship, and Monarchy   266

Interpreting Visual Evidence: The Graphic History of the Bayeux Tapestry   269

Religious Reform and Papal Power   271

Analyzing Primary Sources: A Miraculous Reliquary   274

Crusading Causes and Outcomes   276

Competing Viewpoints: Preaching the First Crusade: Two Accounts   278

Analyzing Primary Sources: An Arab Aristocrat Encounters the Crusaders   284

The Culture of the Muslim West   285

Conclusion   289

Chapter 9 › THE CONSOLIDATION OF EUROPE, 1100–1250   292

The Making of Medieval Monarchies   294

Continuing the Crusades   303

Interpreting Visual Evidence: Picturing Legal Transactions   304

Unity and Dissent in the Western Church   308

Analyzing Primary Sources: The Canons of the Fourth Lateran Council   312

An Intellectual Revolution   315

Competing Viewpoints: Two Conversion Experiences   316

Courts, Cities, and Cathedrals   322

Analyzing Primary Sources: Illicit Love and the Code of Chivalry   327

Conclusion   330

Chapter 10 › THE MEDIEVAL WORLD, 1250–1350   332

The Mongol Empire and the Reorientation of the West   334

Competing Viewpoints: Two Travel Accounts   340

The Extension of European Commerce and Settlement   342

Ways of Knowing and Describing the World   344

Papal Power and Popular Piety   347

Interpreting Visual Evidence: Seals: Signs of Identity and Authority 348

Struggles for Sovereignty   352

Analyzing Primary Sources: A Declaration of Scottish Independence   356

From the Great Famine to the Black Death   359

Competing Viewpoints: Responses to the Black Death   362

Conclusion   364

Chapter 11 › REBIRTH AND UNREST, 1350–1453   366

Life after the Black Death   368

Analyzing Primary Sources: Why a Woman Can Write about Warfare   373

The Beginnings of the Renaissance in Italy   374

Interpreting Visual Evidence: Realizing Devotion 377

The End of the Eastern Roman Empire   379

Warfare and Nation Building   383

Analyzing Primary Sources: The Condemnation of Joan of
Arc by the University of Paris, 1431   387

Challenges to the Roman Church   391

Competing Viewpoints: Council or Pope?   394

Conclusion   398

Chapter 12 › INNOVATION AND EXPLORATION, 1453–1533   400

Renaissance Ideals—and Realities   402

Competing Viewpoints: Printing, Patriotism, and the Past   404

Analyzing Primary Sources: Leonardo da Vinci Applies for a Job   411

The Renaissance North of the Alps   413

The Politics of Christian Europe   418

New Targets and Technologies of Conquest   423

Europeans in a New World   427

Interpreting Visual Evidence: America as an Object of Desire   429

Analyzing Primary Sources: A Spanish Critique of New World
Conquest   432

Conclusion   434

Chapter 13 › THE AGE OF DISSENT AND DIVISION, 1500–1564   436

Martin Luther and the Reformation in Germany   438

Interpreting Visual Evidence: Decoding Printed Propaganda   442

The Many Forms of Protestantism   446

The Domestication of Reform   452

Competing Viewpoints: Marriage and Celibacy: Two Views   454

The Reformation in England   456

Analyzing Primary Sources: The Six Articles of the English Church   458

The Rebirth of the Roman Catholic Church   460

Analyzing Primary Sources: The Demands of Obedience   463

Conclusion   465

Chapter 14 › EUROPE IN THE ATLANTIC WORLD, 1550–1660   468

The Emergence of the Atlantic World   470

Analyzing Primary Sources: Enslaved Native Laborers at Potosí   474

Conflict and Competition in Europe and the Atlantic World   477

The Thirty Years' War and Its Outcomes   484

Analyzing Primary Sources: The Devastation of the Thirty Years' War   486

Analyzing Primary Sources: Cardinal Richelieu on the Common People of France   491

The Crisis of Kingship in England   492

An Age of Doubt and the Art of Being Human   495

Competing Viewpoints: Debating the English Civil War   496

Interpreting Visual Evidence: The Execution of a King   498

Analyzing Primary Sources: Montaigne on Cannibals   501

Conclusion   506

Chapter 15 › EUROPEAN MONARCHIES AND ABSOLUTISM, 1660–1725   508

Population and Climate in the Absolutist Age   510

Absolutism's Goals and Opponents   511

The Absolutism of Louis XIV   512

Interpreting Visual Evidence: The Performance and Display of Absolute Power at the Court of Louis XIV   514

Competing Viewpoints: Absolutism and Patriarchy   516

Alternatives to Absolutism   518

War and the Balance of Power, 1661–1715   522

The Remaking of Central and Eastern Europe   525

Analyzing Primary Sources: The Siege of Vienna (1683)   528

Autocracy in Russia   530

Analyzing Primary Sources: The Revolt of the *Streltsy* and Peter the Great   532

Conclusion   535

Chapter 16 › THE NEW SCIENCE OF THE SEVENTEENTH CENTURY 538

The Intellectual Origins of the Scientific Revolution   540

The Copernican Revolution   542

Tycho's Observations and Kepler's Laws   544

New Heavens, New Earth, and Worldly Politics: Galileo   545

Determining the Age of the Earth: The Origins of Geology and the
Environmental Sciences   547

Interpreting Visual Evidence: Astronomical Observations and the
Mapping of the Heavens   548

Analyzing Primary Sources: Galileo on Nature, Scripture, and Truth   550

Methods for a New Philosophy: Bacon and Descartes   552

Competing Viewpoints: The New Science and the Foundations of Certainty   554

"And All Was Light": Isaac Newton   559

Analyzing Primary Sources: Gassendi on the Science of Observation and the
Human Soul   560

Conclusion   564

APPENDIX: RULERS OF PRINCIPAL STATES   A1

FURTHER READINGS   A6

GLOSSARY   A22

TEXT CREDITS   A58

PHOTO CREDITS   A61

INDEX   A64

Maps

The Growth of Agriculture   7
The Fertile Crescent   13
Ancient Egypt and the Eastern Mediterranean   25

Migrations of the Bronze Age, 2000–1400 B.C.E.   43
Egypt and Its Neighbors, c. 1400 B.C.E.   50
Mycenaean Greece   55
Phoenician Colonization   58
The Hebrew Kingdoms, c. 900 B.C.E.   62
The Persian Empire under Darius I,
      521–486 B.C.E.   69

Greek Colonization, c. 550 B.C.E.   84
The Peloponnesus   94
Ionia, Lydia, and the Persian Empire   96
The Persian Wars with Greece   99
The Peloponnesian War   107

The Campaigns of Alexander   127
The Hellenistic World   129

The Further Expansion of Rome, 264–44 B.C.E.   159
The Roman Empire at Its Greatest Extent,
      97–117 C.E.   170

Judea and Galilee in the Time of Jesus   185
Paul's Missionary Journeys   187
Diocletian's Division of the Empire, c. 304 C.E.   196
The Migrations of Rome's Frontier Peoples   205

The Mediterranean World under Justinian,
      527–565   219
The Expansion of Islam to 750   231
The Empire of Charlemagne in 814   243
Patterns of Viking Activity and Settlement,
      c. 800–1100   248

Europe, c. 1000   257
Medieval Trade Routes   262

The Byzantine Empire, c. 1025   277
The Routes of the Crusaders, 1096–1204   282

Henry II's Empire and the Kingdom of France,
      1180–1223   297
The Holy Roman Empire and Central and Eastern
      Europe, c. 1200   299
The "Reconquest" of Spain, 900–1250   301
The Crusader States   303
The Spread of Universities   321

The States of the Mongol Empire   335
The Medieval World System, c. 1300   338
European Outbreaks of the Black Death,
      1347–1350   361

The Growth of the Ottoman Empire   382
The Phases of the Hundred Years' War   385
The Great Schism, 1378–1417   392

The Spread of Printing   403
The States of Italy, c. 1494   406
The Expansion of Muscovite Territory
      to 1505   419
Overseas Exploration in the Fifteenth and Sixteenth
      Centuries   426

The European Empire of Charles V, c. 1526   445
Confessional Differences, c. 1560   447

The Atlantic World and the Triangular
      Trade   475
Population Density, c. 1600   478
The Netherlands after 1609   482
Europe at the End of the Thirty Years'
      War   487

Europe after the Treaty of Utrecht (1713)   526
The Growth of the Russian Empire   534

Primary Sources

Competing Viewpoints: The Flood: Two Accounts   14

Analyzing Primary Sources: The Code of Hammurabi   22

Interpreting Visual Evidence: The Narmer Palette   28

Analyzing Primary Sources: The Instruction of Ptah-Hotep   33

Interpreting Visual Evidence: Remembering Hatshepsut   46

Analyzing Primary Sources: The Diplomacy of the Mycenaeans and the Hittites   57

Competing Viewpoints: Two Perspectives on Imperial Rule   72

Analyzing Primary Sources: The Obligations of Hospitality: The Encounter of Odysseus and Nausicaa   82

Interpreting Visual Evidence: The Ideal of Male Beauty   87

Analyzing Primary Sources: Songs of Sappho   90

Competing Viewpoints: Two Views of Socrates   110

Analyzing Primary Sources: Xenophon Describes an Ideal Leader   117

Interpreting Visual Evidence: Reconstructing an Ideal of Female Beauty   121

Analyzing Primary Sources: Alexander Puts Down a Mutiny   128

Analyzing Primary Sources: A Jewish Response to Hellenization   137

Competing Viewpoints: Debating the Education and Role of Women   142

Analyzing Primary Sources: Polybius Describes the Romans' Worship of Their Ancestors   156

Analyzing Primary Sources: Antony and Cleopatra   166

Competing Viewpoints: Two Views of Augustus's Rule   172

Interpreting Visual Evidence: Roman Urban Planning   178

Analyzing Primary Sources: The Prosecution of a Roman Citizen   190

Competing Viewpoints: The Development of an Imperial Policy toward Christians   192

Interpreting Visual Evidence: The Power of the Invincible Sun   199

Analyzing Primary Sources: Roman or Barbarian?   212

Competing Viewpoints: Debating the Power of Icons   224

Analyzing Primary Sources: A Sura from the Qur'an   229

Interpreting Visual Evidence: The Ship Burial of Sutton Hoo   238

Interpreting Visual Evidence: The Graphic History of the Bayeux Tapestry   269

Analyzing Primary Sources: A Miraculous Reliquary   274

Competing Viewpoints: Preaching the First Crusade: Two Accounts   278

Analyzing Primary Sources: An Arab Aristocrat Encounters the Crusaders   284

Interpreting Visual Evidence: Picturing Legal Transactions   304

Analyzing Primary Sources: The Canons of the Fourth Lateran Council   312

Competing Viewpoints: Two Conversion Experiences   316

Analyzing Primary Sources: Illicit Love and the Code of Chivalry   327

Competing Viewpoints: Two Travel
Accounts 340

Interpreting Visual Evidence: Seals: Signs of Identity
and Authority 348

Analyzing Primary Sources: A Declaration of
Scottish Independence 356

Competing Viewpoints: Responses to the Black
Death 362

Analyzing Primary Sources: Why a Woman Can
Write about Warfare 373

Interpreting Visual Evidence: Realizing
Devotion 377

Analyzing Primary Sources: The Condemnation
of Joan of Arc by the University of Paris,
1431 387

Competing Viewpoints: Council or Pope? 394

Competing Viewpoints: Printing, Patriotism,
and the Past 404

Analyzing Primary Sources: Leonardo da Vinci
Applies for a Job 411

Interpreting Visual Evidence: America as an Object
of Desire 429

Analyzing Primary Sources: A Spanish Critique of
New World Conquest 432

Interpreting Visual Evidence: Decoding Printed
Propaganda 442

Competing Viewpoints: Marriage and Celibacy: Two
Views 454

Analyzing Primary Sources: The Six Articles of the
English Church 458

Analyzing Primary Sources: The Demands of
Obedience 463

Analyzing Primary Sources: Enslaved Native
Laborers at Potosí 474

Analyzing Primary Sources: The Devastation of the
Thirty Years' War 486

Analyzing Primary Sources: Cardinal Richelieu on
the Common People of France 491

Competing Viewpoints: Debating the English Civil
War 496

Interpreting Visual Evidence: The Execution of a
King 498

Analyzing Primary Sources: Montaigne on
Cannibals 501

Interpreting Visual Evidence: The Performance and
Display of Absolute Power at the Court of Louis
XIV 514

Competing Viewpoints: Absolutism and
Patriarchy 516

Analyzing Primary Sources: The Siege of Vienna
(1683) 528

Analyzing Primary Sources: The Revolt of the
Streltsy and Peter the Great 532

Interpreting Visual Evidence: Astronomical
Observations and the Mapping of the Heavens 548

Analyzing Primary Sources: Galileo on Nature,
Scripture, and Truth 550

Competing Viewpoints: The New Science and the
Foundations of Certainty 554

Analyzing Primary Sources: Gassendi on the Science
of Observation and the Human Soul 560

Preface

THIS BRIEF FIFTH EDITION of *Western Civilizations* is a landmark in a long and continuing journey. Since the original publication of the Full Edition in 1941, this book has been assiduously updated by succeeding generations of historians who have kept it at the forefront of the field in both scholarship and pedagogical innovation. Our newest edition carries this legacy forward, further honing the tools we have developed to empower students—our own and yours—to engage effectively with the themes, sources, and challenges of history. It presents a clear and concise narrative of events that unfolded over many thousands of years, supplemented by a compelling selection of primary sources and striking images. At the same time, it features a unified program of pedagogical elements that guide students from understanding core content to reading and analyzing historical sources and, finally, to developing a sophisticated sense of the ways that historians reconstruct the past on the basis of those sources. This framework, and a brand-new set of activities built around select sources from each chapter, helps students to read and interpret historical evidence on their own, encouraging them to become active participants in the learning process and helping them to think historically.

The wide chronological and geographical scope of this book offers an unusual opportunity to trace historical trends across several interrelated regions—western Asia, the Middle East, North Africa, and Europe—whose cultural diversity has been constantly reinvigorated and renewed. Our increasing awareness that no region's history can be isolated from global processes and connections has merely heightened the need for a richly contextualized and broad-based history such as that represented in *Western Civilizations*. In this edition, we have accordingly supplemented this rich narrative with a new focus on human mobility. From the ancient world to the recent past, societies and cultures have always been shaped by people in motion. Migrations—both voluntary and coerced—are fundamental to understanding human history and have profound implications for the development of the world economy, for cultural exchange among the world's regions, and for the history of political institutions and their development. Indeed, the study of human mobility has emerged as one of the most vital and important fields of history in recent years. Today's students are deeply interested and invested in the relationship between globalization and population movements, and in the ways that mobility is related to social conflict, environmental changes, and contemporary disagreements about national and ethnic identity. It is important that students be able to put these contemporary discussions in historical context and to see their own concerns and aspirations reflected in the historical curriculum.

As in previous editions, we have continued to balance the coverage of political, social, economic, and cultural phenomena with extensive treatment of gender, race, sexuality, daily life, material culture, art, science, and popular culture. Our history is also attentive to the latest developments in historical scholarship. The title of this book asserts that there is no single and enduring "Western civilization" whose inevitable march to domination can be traced chapter by chapter through time. This older paradigm, strongly associated with the curriculum of early twentieth-century American colleges and universities, no longer conforms to what we know about the human past. It was also overly reliant on the nationalist histories of only a few countries, notably England, France, and Germany. In this book, we therefore pay much closer attention to central and eastern Europe, as well as to Europeans' near neighbors in Asia, Africa, and the Atlantic world, with a particular focus on European and Muslim relations throughout the Mediterranean and Middle East. No history of Western civilizations can be coherent if it leaves out the intense conflicts, extraordinary ruptures, and dynamic changes that took place within and across all of these territories. Indeed, smoothing out the rough edges of the past does students no favors. Even an introductory text such as this one should present the past as it appears to the historians who study it: as a complex panorama of human effort, filled with possibility and achievement but also fraught with discord, uncertainty, accident, and tragedy.

Pedagogical Features

In our continuing effort to promote the active study of history, this book is designed to reinforce your course objectives by helping your students to master core content while challenging them to think critically about the past. Those familiar with the previous Brief Edition of *Western Civilizations* will find here a student-friendly new design, with the narrative presented in an easy-to-read single column format. The design introduces new pedagogical tools inspired by instructor and student feedback, including bolded key terms with definitions in the margins as well as marginal review flags that offer guidance for students as they review. Moreover, the design includes a beloved set of features from the previous edition: a consistent pedagogical structure that supports each chapter. As we know from long experience, many students in introductory survey courses find the sheer quantity of information overwhelming, and so we have provided guidance to help them navigate through the material and to read in meaningful ways.

At the outset of each chapter, the **Before You Read This Chapter** feature offers two key windows into the material to be covered: *Story Lines*, which allow the student to become familiar with the primary narrative threads that tie the chapter's elements together, and *Core Objectives*, which alert the student to the primary teaching points in the chapter. The student is then reminded of these teaching points upon completing the chapter, in the **After You Read This Chapter** section, which revisits the material in four key ways. First, the *Chronology* presents a brief timeline of major developments in the period under study. The second, *Reviewing the Objectives*, asks the reader to reconsider the *Core Objectives* by answering a pointed question about each one. Third, *Peoples, Ideas, and Events in Context* summarizes some of the particulars that students should retain from their reading, through questions that allow them to relate individual terms to the major objectives and story lines. These key terms now appear in bold type in the body of the chapter along with the new marginal definitions mentioned above. Finally, *Thinking About Connections* allows for more open-ended reflection on the significance of the chapter's main themes, drawing students' attention to issues that connect it to previous chapters and to their own historical present. Together, these pedagogical features serve to enhance the student's learning experience by breaking down the process of reading and analysis into manageable tasks.

A second package of pedagogical features is designed to capture students' interest and to compel them to think about what is at stake in the construction and use of historical narratives. Each chapter opens with a vignette that showcases a particular person or event representative of the era as a whole. Within each chapter, an expanded program of illustrations and maps has been enhanced by the addition of *Questions for Analysis* that urge the reader to explore the historical contexts and significance of these images in a more analytical way. The historical value of visual artifacts is further emphasized in another feature we have introduced: ***Interpreting Visual Evidence.*** This section provides a provocative departure point for analytical discussions about the key issues raised by visual sources, which students often find more approachable than texts. Once this conversation has begun, students can further develop their skills with the ***Analyzing Primary Sources*** feature, which offers close readings of primary texts accompanied by thought-provoking interpretive questions. The diversity of Western civilizations is also illuminated through a look at ***Competing Viewpoints*** in each chapter, in which specific debates are presented through paired primary source texts. The bibliographical *Further Readings*, located at the end of the book, has also been brought up to date.

A Tour of Chapters and the Newest Revisions

This Brief Fifth Edition of *Western Civilizations* benefits from updates to two recent revisions of the parent Full Edition of the book. In the first of these, the Full Nineteenth Edition, we focused on two primary themes. First, we updated and reorganized the presentation of material on central and eastern Europe in order to provide a richer account of Europe's diverse political and social histories. Second, we developed a theme on environmental history in both volumes, with special attention to the ways that human society has been shaped by—and affected—the physical world. The highlight of this reorganization was the inclusion of new sections on environmental history in multiple chapters in order to apply recent work in this rapidly evolving field to every period.

In the more recent revision, the Full Twentieth Edition, we made a number of exciting updates, many of which were imported into this Brief Fifth Edition. Highlights include:

In Chapter 1, the challenges of locating and interpreting historical evidence drawn from nontextual sources (archaeological, anthropological, mythic) is a special focus. In keeping with our new emphasis on mobility, this chapter includes a more detailed account of Paleolithic-era human migration from Africa into Europe and Asia, with expanded consideration of the Neolithic Revolution as an early example of large-scale human impact on the natural world. It also reflects recent scholarship on the earliest "empires" of Mesopotamia, whose alleged strength may have been more the result of propaganda than of real power, and offers a more explicit discussion of Sumerian religion and the relationship between gods and earthly rulers. There is also new treatment of cultural and economic exchanges between the Egyptians and the Nubians of Sudan.

Chapter 2 includes a revised map of Bronze Age migrations and a careful discussion of the ways that modern concepts of identity may not be applicable to the development of transnational networks in this era. Evidence gathered from recently deciphered inscriptions and new climatological research enhances the discussion of the factors leading to the collapse of this civilization, including the raids of the Sea Peoples and the mass movement of refugees fleeing famine and violence. Boasting a new *Analyzing Primary Sources* excerpt from Emily Wilson's recent translation of *The Odyssey*, Chapter 3 builds on previous narratives of migration in its discussion of guest-friendship as a key social institution for a changing world. Public participation in Athenian political life is considered with added depth, and the existing content has been reorganized to better frame and signpost the section on "The Challenge of the Persian Wars."

Chapter 4 provides a glimpse into Alexander the Great's journey through the Hindu Kush from the perspective of locals as well as that of the king's army. It includes new information on Alexander's half-brother and successor, Philip II, and provides a grassroots account of the Greek diaspora that led to the development of a common Hellenistic culture encompassing the eastern Mediterranean and western Asia. New images depict fresh examples of Hellenistic art. A new question in *Thinking About Connections* encourages students to analyze the 2018 agreement between Greece and Macedonia in light of this chapter's narrative.

In Chapter 5, the differences between Roman and Hellenistic societies are sharpened through a detailed discussion of Roman identity, social structures, and governing practices. A new comparison of Pompey and Caesar offers insight into Roman notions of class, distinguishing between the experiences of immigrant and patrician families. A new image of a wooden tablet from Roman Britain features the earliest known Latin writings by a woman. In Chapter 6, discussion of the early development and spread of Christianity offers a fresh consideration of Paul's missionary travels and the degree to which they depended on Roman infrastructure and rapid mobility. The chapter also includes a more detailed reflection on how the army's domestication led to the decentralization of power in Roman society.

Both the *Core Objectives* and *Reviewing the Objectives* features of Chapter 7 have been revised to better reflect the aims and learning outcomes of the chapter. *Story Lines* has also been amended to more clearly address the expansion of Islam and the interrelated causes that drove this process. Students are prompted to consider the role of gender in the representation of power, and a new image encourages them to think critically about notions of femininity and motherhood as represented in Christian icons. This chapter also pays new attention to the central role of women in the silk industry, both in China and Byzantium. Chapter 8 includes a brand-new discussion of piracy in the medieval Mediterranean and its effects on migration and pilgrimage. Women's contributions to the Crusades and their motivations for participation are another new feature, as is a more extended discussion of daily life in the crusader states of the Levant and the interactions between Christians and Muslims in these territories.

In Chapter 9, a revised and very timely discussion of Magna Carta also pays attention to the ways that King John of England and his successors attempted to resist its demands. The discussion of emerging vernacular languages and forms of identity has been enriched with new segments on German-speaking lands and varieties of popular entertainment. Themes of migration and religion are accentuated through an exploration of the Muslim and Jewish communities of Spain, and the precarious legal status of Jews elsewhere in Europe, where pogroms and other forms of persecution were becoming more frequent. Chapter 10 includes a new discussion of Mansa Musa, the sultan of the West African empire of Mali and the richest man in the world at the time—and perhaps of all time. The map and discussion of "The Medieval World System, c. 1300" have been revised to reflect new research on the close connections between sub-Saharan Africa and Western civilizations.

Chapter 11's discussion of "Life after the Black Death" has been revised to reflect very recent scholarship on the lasting impact of the plague, and the enormous social and economic upheavals that reshaped Europe and its neighbors during the late fourteenth and early fifteenth centuries. Chapter 12 offers a new consideration of Ivan the Great's conquests and the political consolidation of medieval Rus'. Meanwhile, an enhanced account of Portuguese colonial initiatives and the beginnings of the West African slave trade bring the history of Western civilizations into the orbit of the Atlantic world.

In Chapter 13, two key sections have been revised and reorganized for added clarity, while the causes of the Protestant revolution and the spread of dissent are tied more clearly to contemporary political developments. The chapter also discusses the growing power that states claimed to exert over the daily lives and moral choices of their citizens. Chapter 14 features a new discussion of indentured servitude and other forms of unfree labor in the Americas.

Chapter 15 features a new section, "Population and Climate in the Absolutist Age," which addresses the social and economic consequences of Jewish expulsions, the impact of the Wars of Religion and the Thirty Years' War, as well as the effects of the "Little Ice Age" on the lives of working people. A Dutch painting, *Winter Landscape with Ice Skaters*, accompanies this discussion. The newly titled subsection "Administration and Finance" has been thoroughly revised to explain the institutional consolidation of power under Louis XIV and the mercantilist ideology of finance minister Jean-Baptiste Colbert.

We have retained the emphasis on intellectual and cultural history in Chapter 16, on the scientific revolution, and in Chapter 17, on the Enlightenment. In Chapter 16, a beautiful new image depicting Tycho Brahe's earth-centered universe and its accompanying caption elaborate on the differences between Brahe's understanding of the cosmos and that of his contemporary, Johannes Kepler. In Chapter 17, meanwhile, we have continued to present the Enlightenment more clearly in its social and political context with a new section, "Population, Commerce, and Consumption." This new passage emphasizes the relationship between demographic change, economic development, and colonial expansion as the background to the century's intellectual breakthroughs. We have added to our coverage of women in the Enlightenment with a new image highlighting female literacy in the eighteenth century.

Chapters 18 and 19 cover the political and economic revolutions of the late eighteenth and early nineteenth centuries. The beginning of Chapter 18 has been revised to clarify the stages of the French Revolution and the Napoleonic Empire. A new critical thinking caption for the portrait of Louis XVI considers how the king's attachment to the monarchy's absolutist powers came under pressure in the late eighteenth century. Chapter 19 includes a new *Competing Viewpoints* that ties in to the volume's new theme on migration. This feature contrasts the experience of Agricol Perdiguier, a carpenter and member of a laborer's confraternity, with that of Franz Rehbein, a farmworker struggling to meet the challenges of the new mechanized agriculture made possible by industrialization.

An extended new section in Chapter 20, "Revolutions, Migration, and Political Refugees," discusses the connections between the spread of nationalism and the increase in the number of political refugees who moved through Europe and to other regions of the globe. A parallel theme is also covered in a new *Competing Viewpoints* in Chapter 22: a speech by Lord Curzon, which praised British imperialism in India, is contrasted with a new passage by Henry Polak, which described the treatment of Indian migrants at the British colony in Natal, South Africa. New questions prompt students to reflect on the understandings of race and agency present in these sources and identify the benefits of British India for the Empire as they were understood by each of the authors. The chapter's section on imperialism, population movements, and global environmental change now has its proper context within the larger theme of migration in history and connects as well with the earlier treatment of the Columbian exchange in Chapter 14. Chapter 23, meanwhile, offers a completely revised section on "Global Economics," which now includes a discussion of migration flows from Europe to the Americas and the imposition of trade barriers and tariffs by European states. It provides an overview of the growing interdependence of global economies and the advantages and disadvantages that countries faced by participating in the gold standard. A new *Analyzing Primary Sources* feature includes an excerpt from Booker T. Washington's "The Man Farthest Down," in which he argues that the progress of human society ought to be understood through the lives of the working classes.

Chapter 24 contains a new extended section titled "Total War, Economic Blockade, and Population Displacement." The section discusses the civilian toll caused by new technologies and military tactics, defines the term "total war," and discusses the massive displacement of civilian populations during the fighting. A passage from Lenin's *What Is to Be Done?*, formerly presented in Chapter 23, has been moved to this chapter where it is more directly relevant. In Chapter 25, a revised section on the fascist myth of the "March on Rome," which claims that Mussolini took power in Italy by force, explains how his rise to power conformed entirely with the provisions of the Italian constitution.

Chapter 27 continues its emphasis on decolonization and the Cold War, and a new subsection, "The Displaced," offers an extensive discussion of the mass migrations, deportations, and expulsions that accompanied the end of the Second World War. Continuing the discussion of political refugees in earlier periods of history, this section also discusses the formation of the United Nations Relief and Rehabilitation Administration (UNRRA) in 1943, and its subsequent supersession by the UN International Refugee Organization in 1947.

Chapter 29 brings both volumes to a close in a wide-ranging discussion that connects current events in Europe and the world to the deeper past. The theme of population mobility is reinforced by a new *Analyzing Primary Sources* feature that allows students to examine the text of the United Nations statement from 1951 on the protection of refugees. This final chapter discusses the economic and political turbulence of the first decades of the twenty-first century—the threat of terrorism, the global financial crisis of 2008, and the rise of populist political parties in Europe that challenge the goal of European integration—as an indication that the global order that emerged in the aftermath of the Second World War is now being transformed into something else whose contours remain as yet unclear. The conclusion invites students to place these very contemporary debates within the context of Europe's broader history, allowing them to connect what they have learned from the past to the world in which they themselves live.

Media Resources for Instructors and Students

History becomes an immersive experience for students using Norton's digital resources with *Western Civilizations*. The comprehensive ancillary package includes tools for teaching and learning that reinforce the *Core Objectives* from the narrative while building on the history skills introduced in the pedagogy throughout the book. This Brief Fifth Edition features a groundbreaking suite of resources, including InQuizitive, Norton's award-winning formative adaptive system, which helps students master core content; and a brand-new library of History Skills Tutorials to guide students in analysis and interpretation. Norton is unique in partnering exclusively with subject matter experts who teach the course to author these and other resources listed below. As a result, instructors have all the course materials they need to successfully manage their Western Civilizations course, whether they are teaching face-to-face, online, or in a hybrid setting.

Student Resources

+ **Norton Ebooks** provide an enhanced reading experience at a fraction of the cost of a print textbook. Students are able to have an active reading experience and can take notes, bookmark, search, highlight, and even read offline. As an instructor, you can even add your own notes for students to see as they read the text. Norton Ebooks can be viewed on—and synced among—all computers and mobile devices. Norton Ebooks are born accessible, which means we keep all learners in mind during the entire production process. Features such as built-in text-to-speech and advanced keyboard navigation, along with embedded videos with synchronized closed captions, save instructors valuable time in setting up their course and ensure that the ebooks they assign meet the latest accessibility requirements.

+ **InQuizitive** is a groundbreaking, formative adaptive learning tool that improves student understanding of the core objectives in each chapter. Students receive personalized quiz questions on the topics with which they need the most help. Questions range from vocabulary and concepts to interactive maps and primary sources that challenge students to begin developing the skills necessary to do the work of a historian. Engaging, gamelike elements motivate students as they learn. As a result, students come to class better prepared to participate in discussions and activities.

+ **New! History Skills Tutorials** combine video and interactive assessments to teach students how to analyze sources. Three overview tutorials provide start-of-the-semester introductions to "Analyzing Primary Sources," "Analyzing Images," and "Analyzing Maps." Developed by Stacey Davis (Evergreen State), a library of tutorials for each chapter asks students to interpret a document, image, or map from their reading—with guided questions and explanatory author videos—and then relate that source to a key chapter theme. These tutorials give students the opportunity to practice and hone their critical analysis skills every week of the semester, and since each tutorial builds from a source, image, or map in each chapter, students can get the most from their textbooks.

+ The **Student Site** includes additional resources and tools to ensure students come to class prepared and ready to actively participate in discussions and activities: Office Hour Videos, iMaps, and Online Reader.

Instructor Resources

RESOURCES FOR YOUR LMS

Easily add high-quality Norton digital resources to your online, hybrid, or lecture course. Get started building your course with our easy-to-use coursepack files; all activities can be accessed right within your existing learning management system, and many components are customizable.

+ **InQuizitive** is Norton's award-winning, easy-to-use adaptive learning tool that personalizes the learning experience for students and helps them master—and retain—key learning objectives.

+ **History Skills Tutorials** are interactive, online modules that provide practice and a framework for analyzing primary source documents, images, and maps.

+ **Primary Source Exercises** assess students' ability to analyze supplemental sources that are not included in the text, with questions for analysis.

+ **Chapter Review Quizzes** can be assigned for a more summative assessment to see what students have understood from their reading. Customize the length or wording from the questions to suit your course needs. Quizzes include page references.

+ **Author Videos** on both *Core Objectives* and *Past and Present* feature topics from the reading.

+ **Online Reader** offers hundreds of additional Primary Sources and supplemental Media Analysis Worksheets.

+ **Interactive iMaps** for each chapter allow students to view layers of information on each map with printable accompanying Map Worksheets for offline labeling practice and quizzing.

+ **Flashcards** for each chapter, which can be flipped, printed, or downloaded, align key terms and events with brief descriptions and definitions.

+ **Chapter Outlines** provide students with an opportunity to see at a glance what will be covered in the chapter.

OTHER INSTRUCTOR RESOURCES

+ **Interactive Instructor's Guide** is the ultimate teaching guide for the Western Civilizations course. The Interactive Instructor's Guide features a series of videos created by the authors, where they discuss best practices for teaching the most challenging concepts in each chapter. The IIG also includes the robust Instructor's Manual, which is designed to help instructors prepare lectures and exams. It contains detailed chapter outlines, general discussion questions, document discussion questions, lecture objectives, interdisciplinary discussion topics, and recommended reading and film lists.

- **Test Bank** contains more than 2,000 multiple-choice, true/false, and essay questions. This edition of the Test Bank has been completely revised for content and accuracy. All test questions are now aligned with Bloom's Taxonomy for greater ease of assessment.

- **Lecture PowerPoint Slides** are ready-made presentations that provide comprehensive outlines of each chapter, as well as discussion prompts to encourage student comprehension and engagement. They can easily be customized to meet your presentation needs.

- **Graphic content** includes all of the art from the book available in JPEG and PowerPoint format for instructor use. Alt-text is provided for each item.

- **StoryMaps** break complex maps into a sequence of annotated PowerPoint slides. There are ten maps that include topics such as the Silk Road, the Spread of the Black Death, and Population Growth and the Economy.

Acknowledgments

In working on this Brief Fifth Edition, we continue to be very grateful for the expert assistance and support of the Norton team, especially that of our editor, Justin Cahill. Linda Feldman, our fabulous project editor, has driven the book beautifully through the manuscript process. Funto Omojola has cheerfully handled many aspects of the project, including sourcing document excerpts and managing complex map revisions, with a keen eye for detail, and Angie Merila helped bring the project over the finish line. Meanwhile, Mike Cullen and Dena Betz did an excellent job of clearing many of the exact images we specified. Ashley Horna has efficiently marched us through the production process, masterfully orchestrating the many permutations of this text, both print and electronic. The wonderful Carson Russell has been tirelessly developing the book's fantastic e-media, particularly in developing, with Stacey Davis (Evergreen State), the new suite of History Skills Tutorials, as well as revisions to the successful InQuizitive course. Alexander Lee and Alexandra Malakhoff have ably managed many other electronic ancillary materials. Finally, we want to thank Sarah England Bartley and social science specialists Julie Sindel and Emily Rowan for spearheading the marketing and sales campaign for the revision.

We are also indebted to the numerous expert readers who commented on various chapters, thereby strengthening the book as a whole. We are thankful to our families for their patience and advice, and to our students, whose questions and comments over the years have been essential to the framing of this book. And we extend a special thanks to, and hope to hear from, all the teachers and students we might never meet: their engagement with this book will frame new understandings of our shared past and its bearing on our future.

REVIEWERS

Brief Fourth and Full Eighteenth Edition Reviewers

Matthew Barlow, John Abbott College
Ken Bartlett, University of Toronto
Bob Brennan, Cape Fear Community College
Jim Brophy, University of Delaware
Keith Chu, Bergen Community College
Geoffrey Clark, SUNY Potsdam
Bill Donovan, Loyola University Maryland
Jeff Ewen, Sussex County Community College
Peter Goddard, University of Guelph
Paul Hughes, Sussex County Community College
Michael Kulikowski, Penn State University
Chris Laney, Berkshire Community College

James Martin, Campbell University
Derrick McKisick, Fairfield University
Dan Puckett, Troy University
Major Ben Richards, U.S. Military Academy
Bo Riley, Columbus State Community College
Kimlisa Salazar, Pima Community College
Sara Scalenghe, Loyola University Maryland
Suzanne Smith, Cape Fear Community College
Bobbi Sutherland, Dordt College
David Tengwall, Anne Arundel Community College
Pam West, Jefferson State Community College
Julianna Wilson, Pima Community College
Margarita Youngo, Pima Community College

Full Nineteenth Edition Consultants

Dawn L. Gilley, Northwest Missouri State University
Andrzej S. Kamiński, Georgetown University
Adam Kożuchowski, University of Warsaw
Peter Kracht, University of Pittsburgh Press
Eulalia Łazarska, Łazarski University
Krzysztof Łazarski, Łazarski University
John Merriman, Yale University
Daria Nałęcz, Łazarski University
Andrzej Novak, Jagiellonian University
Nicoletta Pellegrino, Regis College
Endre Sashalmi, University of Pécs
Robert Schneider, Indiana University

Full Nineteenth Edition Reviewers

Ken Bartlett, University of Toronto
Keith Chu, Bergen Community College
Bruce Delfini, SUNY Rockland Community College
Paul Fessler, Dordt College
Peter Goddard, University of Guelph
Bonnie Harris, San Diego State University
Anthony Heideman, Front Range Community College
Justin Horton, Thomas Nelson Community College
Catherine Humes, John Abbott College
Leslie Johnson, Hudson Valley Community College
Megan Myers, Howard Community College
Craig W. Pilant, County College of Morris
Christopher Thomas, J. Sargeant Reynolds Community College
Rebecca Woodham, Wallace Community College

Brief Fifth and Full Twentieth Edition Reviewers

Antonio Acevedo, Hudson County Community College
Seth Armus, St. Joseph's College
Ben Beshwate, Cerro Coso College
Robert S. Boggs, North Greenville University
Vivian Bouchard, Vanier College
Edward Boyden, Nassau Community College
Jan Bulman, Auburn University at Montgomery
Julien Charest, Cegep John Abbott College

Keith Chu, Bergen Community College
Eric Cimino, Molloy College
Emily Dawes, Midlands Technical College
Patrice Laurent Diaz, Montgomery County Community College
John Diffley, Springfield Technical Community College
Nicole Eaton, Boston College
Greg Eghigian, Pennsylvania State University
Daniel Ferris, Miles Community College
Bryan Givens, Pepperdine University
Abbie Grubb, San Jacinto College
Ingo Heidbrink, Old Dominion University
Ke-chin Hsia, Indiana University Bloomington
Nicole Jacoberger, Nassau Community College
Leslie Johnson, Leslie C. Johnson
Stephen Julias, Rockland Community College
Lisa Keller, Purchase College
Andrew Keitt, University of Alabama at Birmingham
Deborah Kruger, Butler County Community College
John P. Lomax, Ohio Northern University
Anthonette McDaniel, Pellissippi State Community College, Knoxville, Tennessee
Stan Mendenhall, Illinois Central College
Alexander Mikaberidze, Louisiana State University-Shreveport
Marisa Balsamo Nicholson, Long Island University Post
Thomas Ort, Queens College, City University of New York
David Parnell, Indiana University Northwest
Betsy Pease, Concordia University Wisconsin
Hannah C. Powers, Thomas Nelson Community College
Nicole Rudolph, Adelphi University
Shannan Schoemaker-Mason, Lincoln Land Community College
Michael Shanshala, Michael Shanshala
Jennifer Sovde, State University of New York at Canton
Chris Vicknair, Brother Martin Highschool
Kevin Wolfe, Trident Technical College
Dirk Yarker, Texas Southmost College
Margarita Youngo, Pima Community College

Western Civilizations

Their History & Their Culture

1

Early Civilizations

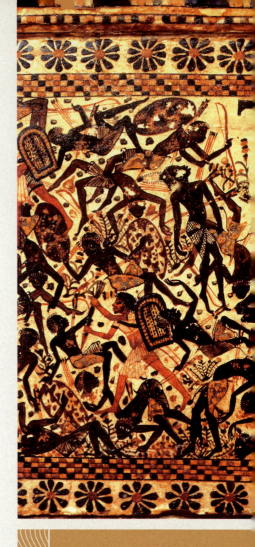

BEFORE YOU READ THIS CHAPTER

THERE WAS A TIME, the story goes, when all the peoples of the earth shared a common language and could accomplish great things. Together, they aspired to build a city with a tower reaching to the sky. But their god was troubled by this, so he destroyed their civilization by making it impossible for them to understand each other's speech.

We know this as the legend of Babel. It's a story that probably circulated among peoples of the ancient world for thousands of years before it became part of the Hebrew book we call by its Greek name, Genesis: "the beginning." This story lets us glimpse some of the conditions in which the first civilizations arose, and it also reminds us of the challenges that make it hard to study them. We no longer speak the same languages as those ancient peoples, just as we no longer have direct access to their experiences or beliefs.

Such foundational stories are usually called *myths*, but they are really an early form of history. For the people who told them, the stories helped to make sense of the present by explaining the past. The fate of Babel conveyed a crucial message: human beings are powerful when they share a common goal, and what enables human interaction is civilization. To the peoples of the ancient world, the characteristic benefits of civilization—stability and safety, government, art, literature, science—were always products of city life. The very word *civilization* derives from the Latin word *civis*, "city." Cities, however, became possible only as a result of

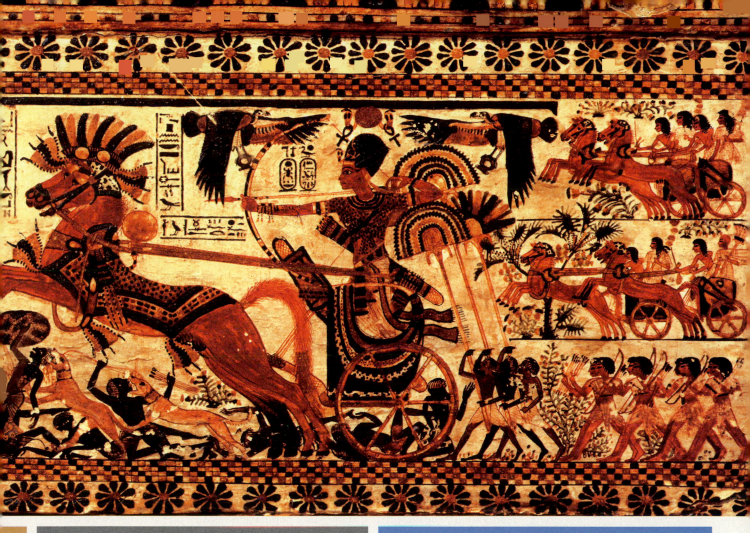

STORY LINES

> To study the earliest civilizations, historians interpret evidence from a diverse array of sources, many of them environmental, visual, and archaeological.

> All civilizations emerge as the result of complex historical processes specific to a time and place, yet all share certain defining features.

> Prominent individuals can achieve power through the use of force, but maintaining power requires legitimacy.

> Those individuals wielding power in ancient Mesopotamia and Egypt responded in different ways to the challenge of establishing legitimacy.

CORE OBJECTIVES

> **UNDERSTAND** the challenges involved in studying the distant past and the crucial importance of interdisciplinary methods and unconventional sources.

> **DEFINE** the key characteristics of civilization.

> **IDENTIFY** the factors that shaped the earliest cities.

> **EXPLAIN** Hammurabi's tools for governing the cities of his empire.

> **DESCRIBE** the main differences between the Mesopotamian and Egyptian civilizations.

innovations that began around the end of the last Ice Age, about thirteen thousand years ago, and that came to fruition some eight thousand years later. The history of civilization is therefore a short one. Within the study of humanity, which reaches back to the genus *Homo* in Africa, some 1.7 million years ago, it is merely a blip on the radar screen. Even within the history of *Homo sapiens*, the species to which we belong and that evolved about forty thousand years ago, civilization is a very recent development.

The study of the earliest civilizations is both fascinating and difficult. Historians still do not understand why cities should have developed in the region between the Tigris and Euphrates Rivers, in what is now Iraq. Once developed, however, the basic patterns of urban life quickly spread to other parts of the ancient world, both by imitation and by conquest. A network of trading connections linked these early cities, but intense competition for resources made alliances fragile and warfare frequent. Then, around the middle of the second millennium B.C.E. ("Before the Common Era," equivalent to the Christian dating system B.C., "Before Christ"), some rulers of independent cities started to make broader claims to power over their citizens and other states. How this happened—and how we know that it happened—is the subject of Chapter 1.

Before Civilization

More than nine thousand years ago, a town began to develop at Çatalhöyük (*CHUH-tal-hih-yik*) in Anatolia (now south central Turkey). Over the next two thousand years, it grew to cover an area of thirty-three acres, within which some eight thousand inhabitants lived in more than two thousand separate houses. If this seems small, consider that Çatalhöyük's population density was actually twice that of today's most populous city: Mumbai, India. It was so tightly packed that there were hardly any streets. Instead, each house was built immediately next to its neighbor and generally on top of another house.

The people of Çatalhöyük developed a highly organized and advanced society. They wove wool cloth; they made kiln-fired pottery; they painted elaborate scenes on the walls of their houses; they made weapons and tools of razor-sharp obsidian, imported from the nearby Cappadocian mountains. They honored their ancestors with religious rites and buried their dead beneath the floors of their houses. Settled agriculturalists, they grew grains, peas, and lentils and tended herds of domesticated sheep and goats. But they also hunted and gathered fruits and nuts, like their nomadic ancestors, and their society was egalitarian, another feature common to nomadic societies: both men and women did the same kinds of work. But despite their relatively diverse food supply, their life spans were very short. Men died, on average, at the age of thirty-four. Women, who bore the additional risks of childbirth, died around age thirty.

The basic elements of life in Çatalhöyük are common to all early civilizations. But how and why did such settlements emerge? And how do we access information about this remote past? The era before the appearance of written records, around 3200 B.C.E., is far longer than the eras we are able to document—and no less important. But it requires special ingenuity to identify, collect, and interpret the evidence of the distant past. In fact, historians have only just begun to explore the ways that

New sources of information about the remote past

climatology, neuroscience, and evolutionary biology can augment the older findings of paleontology, archaeology, and historical anthropology.

SOCIETIES OF THE STONE AGE

Primates with human characteristics originated in Africa 4 to 5 million years ago, and toolmaking hominids—our distant ancestors—evolved approximately 2 million years ago. Because these early people made most of their tools out of stone, all human cultures before the fourth millennium B.C.E. (the thousand years ending in 3000 B.C.E.) are designated as belonging to the Stone Age. This vast expanse of time is divided into the Paleolithic ("Old Stone") and the Neolithic ("New Stone") Eras, with the division falling around 11,000 B.C.E.

Long before modern humans made their appearance, human activities had already begun to leave traces on the landscape. Humans in Africa were kindling and controlling fire 164,000 years ago, and using it to make tools. The Neanderthals, a hominid species that flourished about 200,000 years ago, made jewelry, painted on the walls of caves, and buried their dead in distinctive graves with meaningful objects such as horns (to make music) and flowers. Scientists have recently discovered that Neanderthals were also capable of speech and that they began interbreeding with *Homo sapiens* around sixty thousand years ago. How and why Neanderthals became extinct, around forty thousand years ago, is a matter of intense debate.

Archaeology has shown that, about this time, the pace of human development and movement began to accelerate dramatically. Around 40,000 B.C.E., human populations in Africa expanded and began to migrate into Europe and Asia, suggesting that people were better nourished as a result of new technologies. In many places, the subspecies *Homo sapiens sapiens* began to produce finely crafted and more effective tools such as fishhooks, arrowheads, and sewing needles made from wood, antler, and bone. The most astonishing evidence of these developments was produced by such tools: cave paintings like those at Lascaux and Chauvet

CAVE PAINTINGS FROM LASCAUX. These paintings, which date to between 10,000 and 15,000 B.C.E., show several of the various species of animals that were hunted by people of the Ice Age. The largest animal depicted here, a species of long-horned cattle known as the *aurochs*, is now extinct.

(France)—some of which may be thirty thousand years old. These amazing scenes were purposefully painted in recesses where acoustic resonance is greatest, and were probably experienced as part of multimedia musical ceremonies. This is further evidence for the development of language and other sophisticated forms of communication.

Still, the basic patterns of human life altered very little during this era. Since virtually all human societies were bands of a few dozen people who moved incessantly in search of food, these groups left no continuous archaeological record. Yet we can discern some of the social and economic structures that make these subsistence societies different from those that can be called "civilizations." Early humans had no domestic animals to transport goods, so they could have no significant material possessions aside from basic tools. And because they could not accumulate goods over time, the distinctions of rank and status created by disparities in wealth could not develop. Hierarchical structures were therefore uncommon. When conflicts arose, or resources became scarce, the solution probably was to divide and separate.

Patterns of early human life: 1) constantly mobile, 2) few material possessions, 3) no hierarchy

The Building Blocks of Civilization

What changes enabled some hunter-gatherer societies to settle and build civilizations? Around 11,000 B.C.E., developments brought about by changes in the climate led to the growth of managed food production, which in turn fostered settlements that could trade with each other. For the first time, it became possible for individuals and communities to accumulate and store wealth on a large scale. The results were far-reaching. Societies became more stable and human interactions more complex. Specialization developed, along with distinctions of status and rank. Both the rapidity and the radical implications of these changes have given this era its name: the **Neolithic Revolution**.

THE BEGINNINGS OF HUMAN IMPACT ON THE ENVIRONMENT

The artists who executed the cave paintings at Lascaux and Chauvet were conditioned to survive in harsh conditions. Before 11,000 B.C.E., daytime temperatures in the Mediterranean basin averaged about 60°F (16°C) in summer and about 30°F (–1°C) in winter. These are very low compared with today's temperatures: in the city of Marseilles, not far from Lascaux, they average about 86°F (30°C) in summer and 52°F (11°C) in winter. This means that cold-loving reindeer, elk, wild boar, bison, and mountain goats abounded in regions now famous for their beaches and vineyards. But as the glaciers receded with the warming climate, these species retreated with them, to Scandinavia. Some humans also migrated north with the game, but others stayed behind to create a very different world.

Within a few thousand years after the end of the Ice Age, peoples living in the eastern Mediterranean accomplished the most momentous transformation in human history: from food gathering for subsistence to intensive cultivation of land. The warmer, wetter climate now allowed wild grains to flourish, greatly increasing the food supply and making permanent settlements possible. People then began to domesticate animals and cultivate plants. Stable settlements grew into cities. This

Neolithic Revolution The "New" Stone Age, which began around 11,000 B.C.E., saw new technological and social developments, including managed food production, the beginnings of permanent settlements, and the rapid intensification of trade.

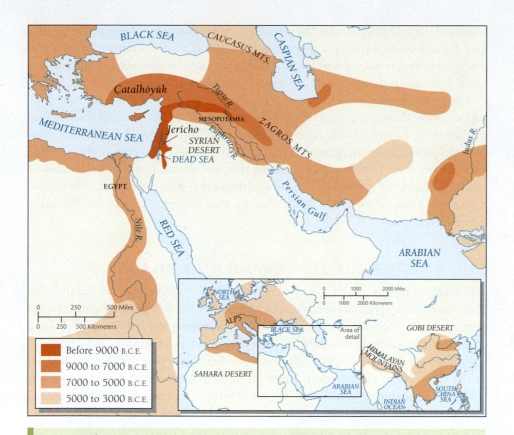

The map legend reads:

- Before 9000 B.C.E.
- 9000 to 7000 B.C.E.
- 7000 to 5000 B.C.E.
- 5000 to 3000 B.C.E.

THE GROWTH OF AGRICULTURE. Examine the chronology of agriculture's development in this region. › **What areas began cultivating crops first, and why?** › **In what period did agriculture spread the most rapidly, and why?** › **How might rivers have played a crucial role in the exchange of farming technologies?**

process took several thousand years, but it still deserves to be called "revolutionary." In a relatively short time, these peoples fundamentally altered patterns of existence that were millions of years old.

As humans began to alter the environment, some scholars posit the beginning of a new epoch: the **Anthropocene** (from the Greek word for "human," *anthropos*). During this epoch—our epoch—slow-moving geological and natural climatological fluctuations have been overtaken by large-scale human efforts to alter the Earth's ecosystems. We will be paying close attention to this process and its intensification throughout the following chapters.

The changes of this period produced new surpluses of food, but they also produced new challenges and inequalities. For example, well-nourished women in sedentary communities can bear more children than women in hunter-gatherer groups, and so women became increasingly sequestered from their male counterparts, who in turn gave up an equal role in child care. The rapid increase in population was countered by the rapid spread of infectious diseases, while dependence on carbohydrates resulted in earlier deaths. Eventually, increased fertility and birthrates outweighed these limiting factors, and by about 8000 B.C.E. human populations were beginning

Anthropocene The current geological epoch, characterized by human impact on the environment. Some scientists argue that it began as early as the Neolithic Revolution.

to exceed the wild food supply. They therefore had to increase cultivation of the land and devise ways of storing grain between harvests. With deliberate cultivation and storage, humans could support larger populations and also compensate for disasters (such as flooding) that might inhibit natural reseeding.

Even more important, stable and predictable surpluses of food were needed to support more domestic animals. This brought a host of additional benefits, not only guaranteeing a more reliable supply of meat, milk, leather, wool, bone, and horn, but also providing animal power to pull carts and plows. However, it also resulted in a pattern of environmental engineering that had devastating and unsustainable effects. In 2015, for example, a team of environmental scientists calculated that the number of trees on earth has diminished by over 50 percent since the Neolithic Revolution began.

THE EMERGENCE OF TOWNS AND VILLAGES

Emergence of cities as administrative and commercial centers

The accelerating changes of this epoch, exemplified by towns such as Çatalhöyük, also resulted in the simultaneous rise of trade and warfare: signs of increased competition among societies. Thousands of new settlements grew up between 7500 and 3500 B.C.E. Some can be classified as cities: centers of administration and commerce with relatively large populations, often protected by walls. One of these was Jericho, in the territory between modern Israel and Jordan. Jericho first emerged as a seasonal, grain-producing settlement; but by 6800 B.C.E. its inhabitants were undertaking a spectacular building program to protect their stored surplus of food. Many new dwellings were placed on stone foundations and a massive dressed stone wall was constructed around the western edge of the settlement. It included a circular tower whose remains still reach to a height of thirty feet: a powerful expression of its builders' wealth, technical prowess, and ambitions.

Jericho was sustained by the intensive cultivation of recently domesticated strains of wheat and barley grown by farmers who were skilled irrigation engineers. Jericho's inhabitants also produced some of the earliest known pottery, which enabled them to store grain, wine, and oils more effectively. Pottery revolutionized cooking, too: for the first time, it was possible to produce nourishing stews and porridges, as well as fermented beverages such as beer. Pottery production was not only vital to ancient civilizations, it is vital to those who study them: as this technology spread throughout Eurasia, identifiable regional styles developed. By studying these different varieties, archaeologists can trace the movements of goods and people over time and space.

NEW ECONOMIES AND SOCIETIES

Jericho and Çatalhöyük illustrate the impact that stored agricultural surpluses have on human relations. In these settled societies, significant differences began to arise in the amount of wealth individuals could stockpile for themselves and their heirs. Dependence on agriculture also made it more difficult for individuals to split from the community when disputes arose. The result was a much more stratified society, with more opportunities for a few powerful people to become dominant. The new reliance on agriculture also meant a new dependence on the land, the seasons, and the weather, which led to new speculations about the supernatural. Different life forces were believed to require special services and gifts, and the regular practice of ritual and sacrifice ultimately produced a priestly caste of individuals or families who seemed able to communicate with these forces. Spiritual leadership was allied to more worldly forms of power, including the capacity to lead war bands, to exact tribute from other settlements, to construct defenses, and to resolve disputes. Through their command of the community's resources, certain clans could establish themselves as a ruling class.

Trade was another important element in the development of early settlements. By 5000 B.C.E., both local and long-distance routes linked settlements throughout the region. Exotic and luxury goods were the most frequent objects of exchange, and long-distance trade also accelerated the exchange of ideas and information. And because status was enhanced by access to high-prestige goods, local elites sought to monopolize trade by organizing and controlling the production of commodities within their own communities and regulating their export. Certain people could now devote at least a portion of their labor to pursuits other than food production: making pottery or cloth, manufacturing weapons or tools, building houses and fortifications, or facilitating trade. The elites who exploited the labor of others eventually became specialized themselves, as full-time speculators and organizers, with the leisure and resources to engage in intellectual, artistic, and political pursuits. The building blocks of civilization had been laid.

Mesopotamia A region between the Tigris and Euphrates Rivers (corresponding roughly to present-day Iraq and Syria) where Sumerian civilization emerged.

Urban Development in Mesopotamia

The Greeks called it **Mesopotamia**, "the Land between Rivers." This land received only about eight inches (20 centimeters) of rainfall per year, its soils are sandy, and summer temperatures regularly exceed 110°F (43°C). The two rivers supplying water—the Tigris and the Euphrates—are noted for their unpredictability: both are prone to flooding, and the Tigris was likely to change its course from year to year. It was in this challenging environment that the first urban society, the civilization of Sumer, flourished.

THE UBAID CULTURE

The earliest cities were founded by the Ubaid peoples, so called because of their settlement at al-Ubaid (now in Iraq) around 5900 B.C.E. During this era, the headwaters of the Persian Gulf extended at least a hundred miles farther inland than they do today, so some Ubaid settlements bordered on fertile marshlands, which were developed into irrigation systems. Ubaid farmers also constructed dikes and levees to control the flooding of the rivers and to direct excess water into canals. Despite their hostile environment, Ubaid communities were soon producing surpluses sufficient to support the typical occupations of Neolithic village life.

Yet there is also evidence of something quite new in Ubaid settlements: central structures that served religious, economic, and administrative functions. Starting out as shrines, these structures soon became impressive temples built of dried mud brick, like the bricks in the story of Babel. Unlike the plentiful stone used at Jericho, the scarcity of stone here meant that builders had to be more resourceful. Each large settlement had such a temple, from which a priestly class acted as managers of the community's stored wealth.

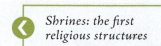

Shrines: the first religious structures

URBAN LIFE IN URUK, 4300–2900 B.C.E.

After about 4300 B.C.E., some Ubaid settlements developed into larger, more prosperous, and more organized communities. The most famous of these, Uruk, is considered the first **Sumerian** city-state. Its scale is exemplified by the White Temple at Uruk, built between 3500 and 3300 B.C.E. This massive platform looms nearly forty feet above the landscape, its four corners oriented toward the cardinal points of the compass. Atop the platform stands the temple itself, dressed in brick and originally painted a brilliant white.

Such temples were eventually constructed in every Sumerian city, reflecting the central role that ritual played in urban life. Uruk in particular seems to have owed its rapid growth to its importance as a religious center, eventually enclosing a population of forty thousand people within massive brick walls. The villages and towns of Sumer, although a mere fraction of the size, also grew rapidly, their teeming economic activity attracting waves of immigrants, just as the larger cities did. Trade routes expanded dramatically, binding the peoples of Mesopotamia to the Mediterranean and bringing foods from as far away as Scandinavia and China. To manage this increasingly complex economy, the Sumerians invented the technology on which most historians rely: writing.

THE DEVELOPMENT OF WRITING

In 4000 B.C.E., the peoples of Mesopotamia were already using clay tokens to keep inventories. Within a few centuries, they developed the practice of placing tokens inside hollow clay balls and inscribing, on the outside of each ball, the shapes of all the tokens it contained. By 3300 B.C.E., scribes had replaced these balls with flat clay tablets on which they impressed symbols representing tokens. These tablets made keeping the tokens themselves unnecessary, and they could be archived for future reference or sent to other settlements as receipts or requests for goods.

Sumerians The ancient inhabitants of southern Mesopotamia (modern Iraq and Kuwait) whose sophisticated civilization emerged around 4000 B.C.E.

Writing thus evolved as a practical recording technology. And because it existed to represent real things, its system of symbols—called *pictograms*—was also realistic: each pictogram resembled the thing it represented. Over time, however, a pictogram might not only symbolize a physical object but also an idea associated with that object. For example, the symbol for a bowl of food, a *ninda*, might be used to express something more abstract, such as "nourishment" or "sustenance." Pictograms also came to be associated with particular spoken sounds, or *phonemes*. Thus when a Sumerian scribe needed to employ the sound *ninda*, even as part of another word, he would use the symbol for a bowl of food to represent that phoneme. Later, special marks were added to the symbol so that a reader could tell whether the writer meant it to represent the object itself, or an abstract concept, or a sound.

Around 3100 B.C.E., Sumerian scribes also developed a specialized tool for writing, a stylus made of reed. Because this stylus leaves an impression shaped like a wedge (in Latin, *cuneus*), this script is called **cuneiform** (*kyoo-NAY-i-form*). With it, symbols could be impressed more quickly into clay. But the symbols became more abstract; eventually they barely resembled pictograms at all. Meanwhile, symbols were invented for every phonetic combination in the Sumerian language, reducing the number of pictograms from about 1,200 to 600. Whereas the earliest pictograms could have been written and read by anyone, writing and reading now became specialized skills accessible only to a small, educated minority.

Cuneiform proved remarkably durable. For over two thousand years it remained the principal writing system of antiquity, even in societies that did not speak Sumerian. It was still being used as late as the first century C.E. ("Common Era," equivalent to the traditional Christian dating by A.D., for *Anno Domini*, "in the year

CUNEIFORM WRITING. The image on the left shows a Sumerian clay tablet from about 3000 B.C.E. Here, standardized pictures are beginning to represent concepts as well as things: notice the symbol *ninda* ("bowl of food") at the top. On the right, carvings on limestone from about 2600 B.C.E. reveal the evolution of cuneiform into more abstract forms. › **Why would such abstract pictograms have been easier to reproduce quickly than the earlier, more realistic images?**

of the Lord"). Tens of thousands of clay tablets still survive, which makes it possible for us to know a great deal more about the Sumerians than we do about any other human society before this time. We can better understand the social structures that shaped their lives, their attitudes toward their gods, and their changing political circumstances.

The Culture of Sumer

The great centers of Sumerian civilization shared a common culture and language. But they also competed for natural resources and sources of labor, rivalries that could lead to warfare. Water rights and access to arable land and trade routes were frequently at stake.

Much of the economic production of each city passed through great temple warehouses, where priests redistributed the city's produce. During the third millennium B.C.E., these great temples also began to control the production of textiles, employing thousands of enslaved people, mostly women and children. Temple elites began to play a key role in long-distance trade as both buyers and sellers of goods. Each Sumerian city therefore had its own gods and an aristocracy from which priests were drawn.

As much as half of the remaining population may have consisted of families who farmed only enough land to sustain themselves. The rest were dependents of the temple who worked as artisans or as agricultural laborers; many were slaves. Most were prisoners of war from other Sumerian city-states whose bondage was limited to three years. But foreigners could be held indefinitely and were the property of their owners. They could be beaten, branded, bought, and sold like any other merchandise. Perhaps the only positive thing to say about slavery in antiquity is that anyone could become a slave. It was not until the beginning of the modern era that slavery became closely linked to new ideas about race (see Chapter 14).

Lugals consolidate power through military prowess and create dynasties

Epic of Gilgamesh One of the world's oldest epics, which circulated orally for nearly a millennium before being written down.

THE EARLY DYNASTIC PERIOD, 2900–2500 B.C.E.

Around 2900 B.C.E., competition for resources intensified and warfare among cities became more frequent. As a result, a new type of military leadership began to emerge. Historians call this era the Early Dynastic Period because it was dominated by powerful dynasties—families who held and handed down power to their members—each headed by a war leader known as a *lugal*, a "big man." Unlike the priestly rulers of the Uruk Period, lugals did not see themselves as faithful servants of a city's god. Rather, they believed that success in battle had earned them the right to exploit the city's wealth.

The most striking expression of this development is the **Epic of Gilgamesh**, a series of stories recited over many generations and eventually written down on cuneiform tablets: the first literary monument in world history. It recounts the exploits of a lugal named Gilgamesh, who probably lived in Uruk sometime around 2700 B.C.E. Gilgamesh earns his reputation through the military conquest of uncivilized—non-Sumerian—tribes. But he becomes so powerful that his own people complain that he keeps their sons away at war and shows no respect for

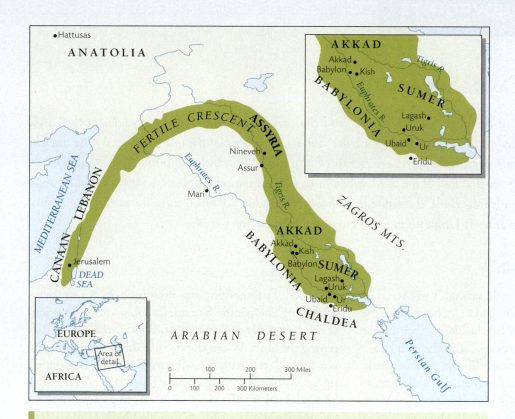

the nobles, carousing with their wives and compromising their daughters; he also disrespects the priesthood and commits acts of sacrilege. So the people of Uruk pray to the gods for retribution, and the gods fashion a wild man named Enkidu to challenge Gilgamesh.

The confrontation between Gilgamesh and Enkidu reveals the core values of Sumerian society. Gilgamesh is a creature of the city; Enkidu is his uncivilized Other, like the hunter-gatherers who still subsisted in unclaimed wilderness lands between cities. But then Enkidu has a sexual encounter with a beguiling woman and this urban initiation civilizes him, allowing him to befriend Gilgamesh. Together they have many adventures. But Enkidu is eventually killed by the goddess Inanna, who punishes the friends for mocking her powers. Gilgamesh, distraught with grief, searches for a magical plant that will revive his friend. He finds it at the bottom of a deep pool, only to have it stolen from him by a water snake. He becomes "The One Who Looked into the Depths," the name by which his story was known to Sumerians. The larger message seems to be that not even civilization can shield humans from the forces of nature and the inevitability of death.

The Flood: Two Accounts

One of the oldest stories in the world tells of a great flood that devastated the lands and peoples of the earth, an event that can be traced to the warming of the earth's climate at the end of the last Ice Age. Many ancient cultures told versions of this story; two of these are excerpted below. The first, included in the Epic of Gilgamesh, was written down during the first half of the third millennium B.C.E., making it at least 1,500 years older than the similar account in the Hebrew Bible. But both are probably the products of much older storytelling traditions. The hero of the Sumerian story is Utnapishtim; the hero of the Hebrew story is Noah.

The Epic of Gilgamesh

Utnapishtim spoke to Gilgamesh, saying: "I will reveal to you, Gilgamesh . . . a secret of the gods. . . . The hearts of the Great Gods moved them to inflict the Flood. Their Father Anu uttered the oath (of secrecy). . . . [But the god] Ea . . . repeated their talk [to me, saying]: 'O man of Shuruppak, son of Ubartutu: Tear down the house and build a boat! . . . Spurn possessions and keep alive living beings! Make all living beings go up into the boat. The boat which you are to build, its dimensions must measure equal to each other: its length must correspond to its width. Roof it over like the Apsu.' I understood and spoke to my lord, Ea: 'My lord, thus is the command which you have uttered. I will heed and will do it.' . . . On the fifth day I laid out her exterior. It was a field in area, its walls were each 10 times 12 cubits in height. . . . I provided it with six decks, thus dividing it into seven (levels). . . . Whatever I had I loaded on it. . . . All the living beings that I had I loaded on it. I had all my kith and kin go up into the boat, all the beasts and animals of the field and the draftsmen I had go up.

I watched the appearance of the weather—the weather was frightful to behold! I went into the boat and sealed the entry. . . . All day long the South Wind blew . . . , submerging the mountain in water, overwhelming the people like an attack. . . . Six days and seven nights came the wind and flood, the storm flattening the land. When the seventh day arrived . . . [t]he sea calmed, fell still, the whirlwind and flood stopped up. . . . When a seventh day arrived, I sent forth a dove and released it. The dove went off, but came back to me, no perch was visible so it circled back to me. I sent forth a swallow and released it. The swallow went off, but came back to me, no perch was visible so it circled back to me. I sent forth a raven and released it. The raven went off, and saw the waters slither back. It eats, it scratches, it bobs, but does not circle back to me. Then I sent out everything in all directions and sacrificed (a sheep). I offered incense in front of the mountain-ziggurat. . . .

The gods smelled the savor . . . and collected like flies over a sacrifice. . . . Just then Enlil arrived. He saw the boat and became furious. . . . 'Where did a living being escape? No man was to survive the annihilation!' Ea spoke to Valiant Enlil, saying . . . 'How, how could you bring about a Flood without consideration?

SUMERIAN RELIGION

During the Uruk Period, Sumerians had identified their gods with the capricious forces of nature. During the Early Dynastic Period, however, many societies came to imagine their gods as resembling the lugals who now lorded over them. From either perspective, humans exist merely to work for their gods or rulers: this was, indeed, why the gods had created people in the first place. There was thus a reciprocal relationship: gods and lugals depended on their servants to honor and sustain them; and in return, they occasionally bestowed gifts and favors.

Charge the violation to the violator, charge the offense to the offender, but be compassionate lest (mankind) be cut off, be patient lest they be killed.' Enlil went up inside the boat and, grasping my hand, made me go up. He had my wife go up and kneel by my side. He touched our forehead and, standing between us, he blessed us. . . ."

Source: Maureen Gallery Kovacs, trans., *The Epic of Gilgamesh*, Tablet XI (Stanford, CA: 1985, 1989), pp. 97–103.

The Book of Genesis

The Lord saw that the wickedness of humankind was great in the earth and . . . said, "I will blot out from the earth the human beings I have created . . . for I am sorry I have made them." But Noah found favor in the sight of the Lord. . . . God saw that the earth was corrupt and . . . said to Noah, "I have determined to make an end to all flesh. . . . Make yourself an ark of cypress wood, make rooms in the ark, and cover it inside and out with pitch. . . . Make a roof for the ark, and put the door of the ark in its side. . . . For my part I am going to bring a flood on the earth, to destroy from under heaven all flesh. . . . But I will establish a covenant with you, and you shall come into the ark, you, your sons, your wife, and your sons' wives with you. And of every living thing you shall bring two of every kind into the ark, to keep them alive with you. . . . Also take with you every kind of food that is eaten." . . . All the fountains of the great deep burst forth, and the windows of the heavens were opened. . . . The waters gradually receded from the earth. . . . At the end of forty days, Noah opened a window of the ark . . . and sent out the raven, and it went to and fro until the waters were dried up from the earth. Then he sent out the dove from him, to see if the waters had subsided from the face of the ground, but the dove found no place to set its foot, and it returned. . . . He waited another seven days, and again sent out the dove [which] came back to him . . . and there in its beak was a freshly plucked olive leaf, so Noah knew the waters had subsided from the earth. Then he . . . sent out the dove, and it did not return to him anymore. . . . Noah built an altar to the Lord . . . and offered burnt offerings. And when the Lord smelled the pleasing odor, the Lord said in his heart, "I will never again curse the ground because of humankind . . . nor will I ever again destroy every living creature as I have done." . . . God blessed Noah and his sons.

Source: Genesis 6:5–9:1, *The New Oxford Annotated Bible* (Oxford: 1994).

Questions for Analysis

1. What are the similarities and differences between these two accounts? Does one seem to derive from the other? Why or why not?

2. What do these differences or similarities reveal about the two societies that told these stories?

3. How did the geography and climate of Mesopotamia affect the Sumerian version of the story?

Some lugals therefore claimed to be the gods' representatives on earth, reigning as kings with special responsibilities and privileges. But kings were also obliged to honor the gods through offerings, festivals, and massive building projects. Kings who neglected these duties, or who exalted themselves at the expense of the gods, were likely to bring disaster on themselves and their people. And even kings could not evade death, when the human body returned to clay and the soul crossed into the underworld, a place of silent darkness.

Lugals: "big men" (or war leaders) who often claimed gods' representation on earth

SUMERIAN SCIENCE AND TECHNOLOGY

Because neither their gods nor their environment were predictable, Sumerians cultivated a high degree of self-reliance and ingenuity. These qualities made them the most technologically innovative people of the ancient world. For example, despite the fact that their land had no mineral deposits, the Sumerians became skilled metallurgists. By 6000 B.C.E., a number of cultures throughout Eurasia had learned how to produce weapons and tools from copper, but Mesopotamia itself has no copper. By the Uruk Period (4300–2900 B.C.E.), however, trade routes were bringing copper ore into Sumer, where it was processed into weapons and tools.

Shortly before 3000 B.C.E., perhaps starting in eastern Anatolia (now Turkey), people also discovered that copper could be alloyed with arsenic (or later, tin) to produce bronze. Bronze is almost as malleable as copper, and it pours more easily into molds; when cooled, it also maintains its rigidity and shape better than copper. For almost two thousand years, until about 1200 B.C.E. and the development of techniques for smelting iron (see Chapter 2), bronze was the strongest metal known to humans—the most useful and, in war, the most deadly. Like the ancient Greeks, we call this period the Bronze Age.

Invention of the wheel fosters military conquest and commercial growth

Along with writing and bronze, the invention of the wheel was a fundamental technological achievement of this era. The Sumerians were using potter's wheels by the middle of the fourth millennium B.C.E. and could quickly produce high-quality clay vessels. By around 3200 B.C.E., they were also using two- and four-wheeled chariots and carts drawn by donkeys. (Horses were still unknown in Mesopotamia.) Wheeled carts dramatically improved productivity, and chariots gave warriors a tremendous advantage over armies on foot: the earliest depiction of their use, dating from 2600 B.C.E., shows one trampling an enemy. While the use of the wheel in pottery-making may have led to its adaptation for vehicles, a connection between these related uses is not inevitable. The ancient Egyptians, too, were using the potter's wheel by at least 2700 B.C.E., but they did not use the wheel for transport until a millennium later, when they learned the technique from Mesopotamia. In the Western Hemisphere, wheeled vehicles were unknown until the sixteenth century C.E., although the Incas had a sophisticated system of roads and probably used iron rollers to move huge blocks of stone for building projects. These two points of comparison help to explain why the wheel was probably invented by nomadic peoples living on the steppes of what is now Russia. By contrast, sedentary civilizations that can rely on the manpower of thousands, or that can transport heavy cargo by water, do not feel the same necessity for invention.

The Sumerians, then, can be credited with innovations that made the most of their scarce resources. An example is the seed drill, in use for two millennia before it was depicted on a stone tablet of the seventh century B.C.E. Strikingly, this technology was unknown to any other Western civilization until the sixteenth century C.E., when Europeans adopted it from China; it would not be in general use until the nineteenth century of our era.

TIMEKEEPING, TRADE, AND TRAVEL

Other impressive Sumerian inventions derived from the study of mathematics. In order to construct their elaborate irrigation systems, farmers had developed sophisticated measuring and surveying techniques as well as the art of mapmaking. Agricultural needs may also lie behind the lunar calendar the Sumerians invented, which consisted of twelve months, six lasting thirty days and six lasting twenty-nine days. Since this produced a year of only 354 days, the Sumerians eventually began to add a month to their calendars every few years in order to predict the recurrence of the seasons with sufficient accuracy. This Sumerian practice of dividing time has lasted to the present day, not only in our notions of the thirty-day month (which corresponds approximately with the phases of the moon) but also in our division of the hour into sixty minutes, each comprising sixty seconds. Mathematics also contributed to Sumerian architecture, enabling them to build domes and arches thousands of years before the Romans would adopt and spread these architectural forms throughout the West.

Sumerian technology depended not only on ingenuity but also on the spread of information and raw materials through trade. Because their homeland was almost completely devoid of many natural resources, Sumerian pioneers traced routes up and down the rivers and into the hinterlands of Mesopotamia, following the tributaries of the Tigris and the Euphrates. They blazed trails across the deserts toward the west, where they influenced the Egyptians. By sea, they traded with the peoples of the Persian Gulf and, directly or indirectly, with the civilizations of the Indus Valley (modern Pakistan and India). And, along with merchandise, they carried ideas: stories, art, the use of writing, and the whole cultural complex that arose from their way of life. The elements of civilization, which had fused in their urban crucible, would thus come together in many other places throughout the world.

A SUMERIAN PLOW WITH A SEED DRILL. Seed drills control the distribution of seed and ensure that it falls directly into the furrow made by the plow. By contrast, the method of sowing seed practiced elsewhere in the world—and as late as the nineteenth century in Europe and the Americas—was to broadcast the seed by throwing it out in handfuls. Sumerian-style plows were developed during the third millennium B.C.E. and were still being used in the seventh century B.C.E., when this black stone tablet was engraved. › **Think about what you have learned about the Sumerians and their environment. Why would they have developed this technology?**

The First Empires?

Sumerian inscriptions and other writings suggest that competition among Mesopotamian cities reached a new level around 2500 B.C.E., as ambitious lugals vied to magnify themselves and their domains.

Yet no Sumerian lugal was able to impose centralized rule on his city, much less control the settlements that he conquered. As a result, Sumer remained a collection of interdependent but mutually suspicious and vulnerable states whose rulers were unable to forge any lasting structures of authority. This would ultimately make them vulnerable to a new style of rulership imposed from the north, in the person of Sargon the Akkadian.

SARGON AND THE AKKADIAN REALM, 2350–2160 B.C.E.

The Akkadians were the predominant people of central Mesopotamia. Their Sumerian neighbors to the south had greatly influenced them, and they had adopted cuneiform script along with many other elements of Sumerian culture. Yet the

Akkadians preserved their own Semitic language, which was part of the linguistic family that includes Hebrew, Arabic, Aramaic, Ethiopic, and Assyrian. Although Sumerians tended to regard the Akkadians as uncivilized, they feared the ruler whom the Akkadians called "great king": Sargon. Indeed, Sargon's inscriptions suggest that he was ambitious to subject the cities of Sumer to his authority.

The success of his efforts could not have matched some of his more extravagant claims, but Sargon does appear to have consolidated certain powers at his capital city, Akkad, by around 2350 B.C.E. He also appears to have installed Akkadian-speaking governors in the cities under his control, where they would collect tribute and work to impose his will. Sargon was thus attempting to knit the independent cities of Mesopotamia into a larger political unit: what we now call an empire, a word derived from the Latin *imperium,* "command." This would have enabled him to manage and exploit the network of trade routes crisscrossing the region and to extend his influence from Ethiopia to India.

Although Sargon's imperialism was probably more aspirational than actual, it does seem to have had an effect on Sumerian religion and culture. Sargon took steps to merge the Akkadian and Sumerian divinities, so that, for example, the Akkadian fertility goddess Ishtar became identified with the Sumerian goddess Inanna. He also tried to lessen the rivalry of Sumerian cities by appointing a single Akkadian high priest or priestess, often a member of his own family, to preside over several temples. His own daughter Enheduanna (*en-he-doo-AH-nah*) was high priestess of both Uruk and Ur, and her hymns in honor of Ishtar/Inanna are the earliest surviving works by a named author in world history.

The precedent that Enheduanna and her father established would continue even after Sargon's dynasty ended: for several centuries thereafter, the kings of Sumer continued to appoint their daughters as high priestesses of Ur and Uruk. And by about 2200 B.C.E., most people in central and southern Mesopotamia would have been able to converse in the language of either the Sumerians or the Akkadians. Indeed, the two civilizations became virtually indistinguishable except for these different languages.

THE DYNASTY OF UR AND THE AMORITES, 2100–1800 B.C.E.

After the death of Sargon's son and heir, Naram-Sin, Akkadian rule in the region dissolved. Around 2100 B.C.E., however, a new dynasty came to power in Ur under a king called Ur-Nammu and his son Shulgi. Ur-Nammu was responsible for the construction of the great **ziggurat** at Ur, which originally rose seventy feet (over twenty-one meters) above the surrounding plain, as well as for many other architectural marvels. Shulgi continued his father's work, raiding lands up to the Zagros Mountains northeast of Ur and demanding massive tribute payments; one collection site accounted for 350,000 sheep per year. Shulgi then built state-run textile production facilities to process the wool. He also promulgated a code of law, calling for fair weights and measures, the protection of widows and orphans, and limitations on the death penalty for crimes.

While there was no mechanism for actually enforcing this code, Shulgi's commercial expansion of his realm and his patronage of art and literature established a pattern that influenced other rulers in the region for centuries to come. It also

ziggurats Temples constructed under the Dynasty of Ur in what is now Iraq, beginning around 2100 B.C.E.

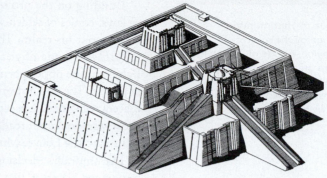

influenced newcomers known as the Amorites, a Semitic people (like the Akkadians) who (unlike the Akkadians) had largely been nomads and warriors. But now, some Amorite leaders began to gain control of Mesopotamia's ancient cities.

THE EMPIRE OF HAMMURABI

In 1792 B.C.E., a young Amorite chieftain named Hammurabi (*hah-muh-RAH-bee*) became the ruler of **Babylon**, an insignificant city in central Mesopotamia. While Babylon was precariously wedged among a number of more powerful cities, its site on the Tigris and Euphrates had great potential. Hammurabi turned this situation to his advantage, recognizing that military intelligence, diplomacy, and strategic planning might accomplish what his small army could not.

A rich archive of tablets found at the city of Mari (which eventually fell under his rule) testifies to his clever manipulation of his more powerful adversaries: for Hammurabi used writing itself as a weapon. He did not try to confront his mightier neighbors head on. Rather, through letters and embassies, double-dealing and cunning, he induced his stronger counterparts to fight each other. While other rulers exhausted their resources in costly wars, Hammurabi fanned their mutual hatred and skillfully portrayed himself as a friend and ally to all sides. Meanwhile, he quietly strengthened his kingdom, built up his army, and, when the time was right, fell on his depleted neighbors. By such policies, he transformed his small state into what historians call the Old Babylonian Empire.

Under Hammurabi's rule, Mesopotamia achieved a new degree of political integration that reached from the Persian Gulf into Assyria. The southern half of the region, formerly Sumer and Akkad, would henceforth be known as Babylonia. To help unify these territories, Hammurabi introduced another innovation, promoting the worship of the little-known patron god of Babylon, Marduk, and making him the ruler-god of his entire empire. Although he also paid homage to the ancient gods of Sumer and Akkad, Hammurabi made it clear that all his subjects now owed allegiance to Marduk.

The idea that political power derives from divine approval was nothing new, but Hammurabi's genius was to use Marduk's divine supremacy to legitimize his own claim to rule, in Marduk's name, because he was king of Marduk's home city. Hammurabi thus became the first known ruler to launch wars of aggression justified in the name of his primary god. This set a precedent for colonial expansion that would become a characteristic feature of Western civilizations and that lies behind nearly all imperial ventures down to the present day.

THE ZIGGURAT OF UR. Built around 2100 B.C.E., this great temple is the best-preserved structure of its kind. It is located at Nasiriyah, in what is now Iraq. Archaeological investigations (see diagram) reveal that its central shrine, the most sacred part of the temple, was reached by climbing four sets of stairs and passing through a massive portal.

Babylon Ancient city between the Tigris and Euphrates Rivers, which became the capital of Hammurabi's empire in the eighteenth century B.C.E. and continued to be an important administrative and commercial capital under many subsequent imperial powers, including the Neo-Assyrians, Chaldeans, Persians, and Romans.

Building on the precedents of past rulers, Hammurabi also issued a collection of laws, copies of which were inscribed on stone pillars and set up in public places throughout his realm. The example that survives is an eight-foot-tall pillar or *stele* (*STEH-leh*) made of gleaming black basalt, erected in the central marketplace of Babylon. The upper portion shows Hammurabi consulting with Shamash, the god of justice. The phallic form on which the laws were inscribed would have been immediately recognizable as a potent symbol of Hammurabi's authority, obvious even to those who could not read the laws themselves. (It still makes a strong impression on visitors to the Louvre Museum in Paris.)

Hammurabi's decision to represent himself as a lawgiver was symbolically important—even if, like previous rulers, he had no effective mechanism for policing his state or enforcing these laws. By collecting legal precedents, Hammurabi declared himself to be (as he stated in the code's preamble) "the shepherd of the people, the capable king"—not a mere lugal ruling through fear and caprice. This was setting a new standard of kingship and expressing a new vision of empire as a union of peoples subject to the same laws.

LAW AND SOCIETY IN HAMMURABI'S CODE

The **Code of Hammurabi** reveals a great deal about the structure and values of Babylonian society. The organization of its 282 pronouncements offers insight into the kinds of litigation that Hammurabi and his officials regularly handled and also suggests the relative importance of these cases. It begins with legislation against false testimony (fraud or lying under oath) and theft, followed by laws regulating business deals; laws regulating the use of public resources, especially water; laws relating to taverns and brothels, most of which appear to have been run by women; laws relating to debt and slavery; many laws dealing with marriage, inheritance, divorce, and widows' rights; and, finally, laws punishing murder, violent assault, and even medical malpractice. What emerges is a fascinating picture of a complex urban society that required more formal legislation than the accumulated customs of previous generations.

WOMEN AND TEXTILES. Women were the predominant producers of textiles throughout the ancient world. Even upper-class women were almost continuously engaged in spinning thread and weaving cloth for their households. Here, a servant fans an elegant lady at work with her spindle.

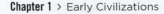

Most of these laws appear to be aimed at free commoners, who made up the bulk of the population. Above them was an aristocratic class, tied to the king's court and active in its bureaucracy, that controlled a great deal of any community's wealth: these were the palace officials, temple priests, high-ranking military officers, and rich merchants. Indeed, even legally free individuals were probably dependents of the palace or the temple in some way, or leased land from the estates of the powerful. They included laborers and artisans, small-scale merchants and farmers, and the minor political and religious officials.

At the bottom of Babylonian society were slaves, who were far more numerous than they had been in the older civilizations of Sumer or Akkad. Many, indeed, had become slaves not because of war but through trade: either sold as payment for debts or to the profit of a family with too many children, or because they had been forced to sell themselves on the open market. Others had been enslaved in punishment for certain offenses. Slaves in the Old Babylonian Empire were treated much more harshly than in previous civilizations and were more readily identifiable as a separate group: whereas free men in Babylonia wore long hair and beards, male slaves were shaved and both male and female slaves were branded.

Slavery in Babylonian society

The division among classes in this society was therefore very marked. As Hammurabi's code indicates, an offense committed against a nobleman carried a far more severe penalty than did the same crime committed against a commoner or slave; nobles were also punished more severely than were commoners for crimes they committed against other nobles. Marriage arrangements also reflected class differences, with bride-prices and dowries depending on the status of the parties involved. That said, Hammurabi's code also reveals the relatively high status of women in Babylonian society, who enjoyed certain important protections under the law, including the right to divorce abusive or indigent husbands. Indeed, if a husband divorced a wife "without cause," he was obliged to provide financial support for her and their children. However, a wife who went around the city defaming her spouse was subject to severe punishment. And a woman would risk death, as would her lover, if she were caught in adultery. The sexual promiscuity of husbands, by contrast, was protected under the law.

HAMMURABI'S LEGACY

Hammurabi died around 1750 B.C.E. Although the imperial powers he had wielded were not sustainable, he had created a durable state. For another two centuries, Babylon continued to play a significant role in Mesopotamia until invaders from the north sacked the capital and occupied it. But even then, and for another thousand years thereafter, Babylon remained the region's most famous and prominent city.

Hammurabi's legacy also extended well beyond Babylonia, because he had shaped a new conception of kingship. Unifying state religions became an increasingly important technique that kings used to annex and subjugate diverse territories and peoples. Hammurabi had also demonstrated the effectiveness of writing as a political tool. Diplomacy and the keeping of archives would be essential to all subsequent empires. So would the claim that rulers should be the arbiters of justice.

The Development of Civilization in Egypt

At about the time that Sumerian civilization was transforming Mesopotamia, another civilization was taking shape in a different part of the world and in very different ways. Unlike the Sumerians, the Egyptians did not have to wrest survival from a hostile and unpredictable environment. Instead, their land was renewed every year by the flooding of the Nile River. The fertile black soil that was left behind every summer made theirs the richest agricultural region in the entire Mediterranean world.

The Code of Hammurabi

The laws of Hammurabi, published on the authority of this powerful king and set up in central places throughout the Old Babylonian Empire, were influenced both by the needs of an urban society and by older ideas of justice and punishment common among Semitic peoples. In its entirety, the code comprises 282 laws, beginning and ending with statements of Hammurabi's devotion to the gods, his peacekeeping mission, and his sense of his duties as king. The following excerpts are numbered so as to show the order in which these provisions appear on the stele that publicizes them.

When the god Marduk commanded me to provide just ways for the people of the land in order to attain appropriate behavior, I established truth and justice as the declaration of the land. I enhanced the well-being of the people.

* * *

1. If a man accuses another man and charges him with homicide but cannot bring proof against him, his accuser shall be killed.

2. If a man charges another man with practicing witchcraft but cannot bring proof against him, he who is charged with witchcraft shall go to the divine River Ordeal, he shall indeed submit to the divine River Ordeal; if the divine River Ordeal should overwhelm him, his accuser shall take full legal possession of his estate; if the divine River Ordeal should clear that man and should he survive, he who made the charge of witchcraft against him shall be killed; he who submitted to the divine River Ordeal shall take full legal possession of his accuser's estate.

3. If a man comes forward to give false testimony in a case but cannot bring evidence for his accusation, if that case involves a capital offense, that man shall be killed.

* * *

6. If a man steals valuables belonging to the god or to the palace, that man shall be killed, and also he who received the stolen goods from him shall be killed.

7. If a man should purchase silver, gold, a slave, a slave woman, an ox, a sheep, a donkey, or anything else whatsoever, from a son of a man or from a slave of a man without witnesses or a contract—or if he accepts the goods for safekeeping—that man is a thief, he shall be killed.

8. If a man steals an ox, a sheep, a donkey, a pig, or a boat—if it belongs either to the god or to the palace, he shall give thirtyfold; if it belongs to a commoner, he shall replace it tenfold; if the thief does not have anything to give, he shall be killed.

* * *

15. If a man should enable a palace slave, a palace slave woman, a commoner's slave, or a commoner's slave woman to leave through the main city-gate, he shall be killed.

* * *

53. If a man neglects to reinforce the embankment of the irrigation canal of his field and then a breach opens and allows the water to carry away the common irrigated area, the man in whose embankment the breach opened shall replace the grain whose loss he caused.

* * *

104. If a merchant gives a trading agent grain, wool, oil, or any other commodity for local transactions, the trading agent shall collect a sealed receipt for each payment in silver that he gives to the merchant.

* * *

128. If a man marries a wife but does not draw up a formal contract for her, she is not a wife.

129. If a man's wife should be seized lying with another male, they shall bind them and throw them into the water; if the wife's master allows his wife to live, then the king shall allow his subject [i.e., the other male] to live.

* * *

142. If a woman repudiates her husband, and declares, "You will not have marital relations with me"—her circumstances shall be investigated by the authorities of her city quarter, and if she is circumspect and without fault, but her husband is wayward and disparages her greatly, that woman will not be subject to any penalty; she shall take her dowry and she shall depart for her father's house.

Source: Martha T. Roth, ed., *Law Collections from Mesopotamia and Asia Minor* (Atlanta: 1995), pp. 76–135 (excerpted).

Questions for Analysis

1. On the basis of these excerpts, what conclusions can you draw about the societal values of the Old Babylonian Empire? For example, what types of crimes are punishable by death, and why?

2. In what ways does the Code of Hammurabi exhibit the influences of the urban civilization for which these laws were issued? What are some characteristics and consequences of urbanization? What, for example, do we learn about economic developments?

3. Examine the photographs of the stele preserving the code. What is the significance of the image that accompanies the laws, Hammurabi's conference with the enthroned god Shamash? What is the significance of the stele itself as the medium that conveyed these laws to the people?

THE CODE OF HAMMURABI. The laws of Hammurabi survive on an eight-foot column made of basalt. The top quarter of the column depicts the Babylonian king (standing, at left) being vested with authority by Shamash, the god of justice. Directly below are the cuneiform inscriptions that are the law code's text.
› How would the very format of these laws send a powerful message about Hammurabi's kingship?

Egypt's distinctive civilization rests on this fundamental ecological fact. It also explains why ancient Egypt was a narrow, elongated kingdom, running along the Nile north from the First Cataract (a series of rapids near the ancient city of Elephantine) toward the Mediterranean Sea for a distance of more than six hundred miles (some 965 kilometers). Outside this narrow band of territory—fourteen miles (twenty-three kilometers) at the widest—lay uninhabitable desert. This contrast between the fertile Nile valley and the desiccated land beyond deeply influenced the Egyptian worldview, in which the Nile itself was the center of the cosmos and the lands beyond were hostile.

In many respects, ancient Egyptian civilization enjoyed a remarkable continuity. Its roots date back to 5000 B.C.E. at least, and Egypt continued to thrive as an independent and distinctive entity even after it was conquered by Alexander the Great in 331 B.C.E. (see Chapter 4) and then subsumed into the Roman Empire after 30 B.C.E. (see Chapter 5). The defining element of this civilization would be the pervasive influence of a powerful, centralized, bureaucratic state headed by pharaohs (*FARE-ohs*) who were regarded as living gods. No other civilization in world history has ever been governed so steadily, for so long.

For convenience, historians have traditionally divided ancient Egyptian history into distinctive "kingdoms" and "periods." Following ancient chroniclers, modern historians have also tended to portray these Old, Middle, and New Kingdoms as characterized by unity and prosperity, punctuated by chaotic interludes known as Intermediate Periods. Like all attempts at periodization, these divisions do not capture the complexities or real pace of historical development.

PREDYNASTIC EGYPT, c. 10,000–3100 B.C.E.

Predynastic Egypt refers to the period before the emergence of the pharaohs and their royal dynasties, an era for which archaeological evidence is scarce. Many predynastic settlements were destroyed by the waters of the Nile and are now buried under layers of silt. The first known permanent settlement, situated at the southwestern edge of the Nile Delta (near the modern town of Merimde Beni Salama: see the map on page 25), dates to approximately 4750 B.C.E. It was a farming community that may have numbered as many as sixteen thousand residents, which means that some Egyptian communities were much larger than those of Mesopotamia at the same time. By around 3500 B.C.E., evidence shows that the Egyptian economy rapidly became more diversified and that the residents of the delta had extensive commercial contacts with the Sinai Peninsula, the eastern Mediterranean, and the upper reaches of the Nile some several hundred miles to the south. This northern area is known as Lower Egypt, because it was downstream. Comparable developments were also occurring upstream and, by the end of this Predynastic Period, Egyptian culture was more or less uniform from the southern edge of the delta throughout the vast length of the Nile known as Upper Egypt.

Although settlements in Lower Egypt were more numerous, it was in Upper Egypt that the first Egyptian cities developed. By 3200 B.C.E.—when the Sumerian city of Uruk had been thriving for a thousand years—important communities such as Nekhen, Naqada, This, and Abydos had all developed high degrees of occupational and social specialization. They had encircled themselves with sophisticated fortifications and built elaborate shrines to honor their gods. Indeed, as in Mesopotamia, a

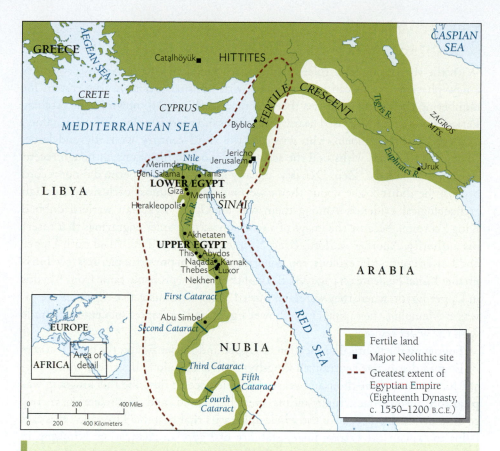

ANCIENT EGYPT AND THE EASTERN MEDITERRANEAN. Notice the peculiar geography of ancient Egypt and the role played by the Nile River. Identify the Nile on the map. › **In what direction does the Nile flow?** › **How did the lands on either side help to isolate Egyptian culture from outside influences?** › **Consider how the Nile helped forge Egypt into a unitary state under a powerful centralized government. Yet how might Egypt's relationship to the Nile be potentially hazardous as well as beneficial?**

city's role as the center of a prominent religious cult attracted travelers and encouraged the growth of industries. And compared with travel in Mesopotamia, travel in Egypt was relatively easy: the Nile bound cities together, and the lack of competition for resources fostered peace.

It was due to the Nile, therefore, that the region south of the delta was able to forge a cultural and political unity, despite its enormous length. The Nile fed Egypt and was a conduit for people, goods, and information. Centralizing rulers could project their power quickly and effectively up and down its course. Within a remarkably short time, then, just a century or two after the first cities' appearance in Upper Egypt, they had banded together in a confederacy under the leadership of the city of This. The pressure exerted by this confederacy in turn forced the towns of Lower Egypt to adopt their own form of political organization. By 3100 B.C.E., the rivalry between these regions had given rise to the two nascent kingdoms of Upper and Lower Egypt.

Importance of the Nile River in Egyptian society

THE POWER OF THE PHARAOH, c. 3100–c. 2686 B.C.E.

With the rise of powerful rulers in these two kingdoms, Egyptian history enters a new phase, one that can be chronicled with unusual precision. The system for numbering the ruling dynasties that emerged in this era—known as the Archaic Period—was actually devised nearly three thousand years later by a historian named Manetho (*mahn-EH-thoh*), who wrote in the third century B.C.E. By and large, Manetho's work has withstood the scrutiny of modern historians, although recent research has added a "Zero Dynasty" of early kings whom Manetho did not record because he didn't know about them; we know them almost exclusively through archaeological evidence. Among them was an Upper Egyptian warlord dubbed King Scorpion, because the image of a scorpion accompanies engravings that assert his authority. Another warlord, King Narmer, appears to have ruled both Upper and Lower Egypt. His exploits, too, come down to us in powerful pictures (see *Interpreting Visual Evidence* on page 28). Both of these kings probably came from Abydos in Upper Egypt, where they were later buried. Their administrative capital, however, was at Memphis, the capital city of Lower Egypt and an important center for trade with the wider region.

Following the political unification of Upper and Lower Egypt, the basic features of Egypt's distinctive centralized kingship took shape along lines that would persist for the next three thousand years. The title used to describe this kingship was **pharaoh**, a word that actually means "great household" and thus refers not merely to an individual ruler but to the whole apparatus that sustained his rule. This fact helps to explain the extraordinary stability of Egyptian civilization. Kingship in Mesopotamia was a form of personal rule, and even the empires of Sargon and Ur-Nammu scarcely survived another generation or two after their deaths. But in Egypt, the office of the pharaoh was durable enough to survive the deaths of many individual successors, facilitating the peaceful transition of power to new rulers and withstanding the incompetence of many.

This was partly accomplished by the efficiency of palace bureaucracy, but it was also a function of the pharaoh's close identification with the divine. Like the seasons, the pharaoh died only to be born again, renewed and empowered. Egyptian rulers thus laid claim to a sacred nature quite different and more powerful than that governing Sumer. By the end of the Second Dynasty, which coincides with the end of the Archaic or Early Dynastic Period (2686 B.C.E.), the pharaoh was not just the ruler of Egypt, he *was* Egypt: a personification of the land, the people, and their gods.

THE OLD KINGDOM, c. 2686–2160 B.C.E.

Because few written documents of the **Old Kingdom** survive, historians have to rely on surviving funerary texts from the tombs of the elite. These sources have tended to convey the impression that Egyptians were obsessed with death; and they also tell us little about the lives of ordinary people. Further complicating the historian's task is the early Egyptians' own belief in the unchanging, cyclical nature of the universe.

pharaoh The title borne by the rulers of ancient Egypt. The pharaoh was regarded as the divine representative of the gods and the embodiment of Egypt itself.

Old Kingdom During this period, c. 2686-2160 B.C.E., the pharaohs of ancient Egypt controlled a powerful and centralized bureaucratic state with vast human and material resources.

However, the surviving inscriptions and art of the Third Dynasty (c. 2686–2613 B.C.E.) do tell us a great deal about the workings of the "great household" that undergirded the vast power of the pharaoh who, as the embodiment of Egypt, was the intermediary among the land, its people, and their gods. Hence, all the resources of Egypt belonged to him. Long-distance trade was entirely controlled by pharaohs, as were systems of taxation and conscripting labor. To administer these, the pharaohs installed provincial governors, many of whom were members of the royal family.

Old Kingdom pharaohs kept tight control over their lesser officials, to prevent them from establishing local roots in the territories they administered. Writing was therefore critical to communication and the management of Egypt's wealth. This dependence on writing gave rise to a whole class of scribal administrators who enjoyed the power, influence, and status that went along with literacy: a skill few people could command, since few could master the intricate writing Egyptian system (see below). Even a child just beginning his scribal education was considered worthy of great respect because the training was so difficult. But it carried great rewards. According to the author of a document called "The Satire of the Trades," the beginning student should persevere because, in the end, he would be so much better off than everyone else.

THE POWER OF WRITING

Among the many fascinating facets of ancient Egyptian culture is the system of pictographic writing. Called **hieroglyphs** (*HI-eroh-glifs*) or "sacred carvings" by the Greeks, these elaborate symbols remained completely mysterious to modern scholars until the nineteenth century, when a Frenchman named Jean François Champollion deciphered them with the help of history's most famous decoding device, the Rosetta Stone. This stele preserves three versions of the same decree issued by one of the Ptolemaic rulers of Egypt in 196 B.C.E. (see Chapter 3), written in ancient Greek, demotic (a later Egyptian script), and hieroglyphs—still in use after more than three thousand years. Becuse he could read the text in Greek, Champollion was eventually able to translate the demotic and hieroglyphic texts as well.

The development of hieroglyphic writing in Egypt dates to around 3200 B.C.E., about the time when pictograms began to appear in Mesopotamia. But the two scripts are so different that they probably developed independently, and the uses of writing certainly developed far more quickly in Egypt. And unlike Sumerian cuneiform, Egyptian hieroglyphs never evolved into a system of simplified phonograms. Instead, the Egyptians developed a faster, cursive script for representing hieroglyphs, called *hieratic*, which they employed for everyday business. They also developed a shorthand version that scribes could use for rapid note-taking.

Little of this hieratic script remains, however, owing to the perishable nature of its written support: papyrus. Produced by hammering, drying, and processing river reeds, papyrus was much lighter, easier to write on, and more transportable

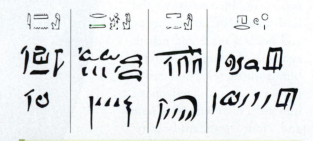

EGYPTIAN WRITING. Egyptian scribes used a variety of scripts: hieroglyphs for inscriptions and religious texts (top row), a cursive hieratic script for administrative documents (middle row), and a more informal shorthand for note-taking (bottom row). › **What are the relationships among these three forms of writing?**

The Narmer Palette

The Narmer Palette (c. 3100 B.C.E.) is a double-sided carving made of green siltstone. Palettes were used to grind pigments for the making of cosmetics, but the large size (sixty-three centimeters; over two feet) of this one is unusual. It was discovered in 1897 by archaeologists excavating a temple dedicated to the god Horus at Nekhen, the capital of Upper Egypt. Found nearby were other artifacts, including the so-called Narmer Macehead, thought to depict the marriage of Narmer, king of Upper Egypt, to a princess of Lower Egypt.

On the left, dominating the central panel, Narmer wears the White Crown of Upper Egypt. He wields a mace and seizes the hair of a captive kneeling at his feet. Above the captive's head is a cluster of lotus leaves (a symbol of Lower Egypt) and a falcon representing the god Horus, who may be drawing the captive's life force (*ka*) from his body. The figure behind Narmer is carrying the king's sandals; he is depicted as smaller because he is an inferior. The two men in the lower panel are either running or sprawling on the ground, and the symbols above them indicate the name of a defeated town. On the right, the other side of the palette shows Narmer as the chief figure in a procession. He now wears the Red Crown of Lower Egypt and holds a mace and a flail, symbols of conquest. Behind him is the same servant carrying his sandals, and in front of him are a man with long hair and four standard-bearers. There are also ten headless corpses. Below, the entwined necks of two mythical creatures (serpopards, leopards with serpents' heads) are tethered to leashes held by two

men. In the lowest section, a bull tramples the body of a man whose city Narmer is destroying.

Questions for Analysis

1. This artifact has been called "the first historical document in the world," but scholars are still debating its meanings. For example, does it represent something that actually happened? Or is it political propaganda? In your view, is this proof that Narmer has united the two kingdoms? Why or why not?

2. Do the two sides of the palette tell a coherent story? If so, on which side does that story begin?

3. What might be significant about the site where the palette was found? Should the palette be interpreted as belonging with the mace, found nearby? If so, how might that change your interpretation of the palette's significance?

A. Narmer wearing the White Crown of Upper Egypt.

B. Narmer wearing the Red Crown of Lower Egypt.

than the Sumerians' clay tablets. When sewn together into scrolls, papyrus also made it possible to record and store large quantities of information in a rolled, portable package. Production of this versatile writing material remained one of Egypt's most important industries and exports into the Middle Ages. Yet even in the arid environment of Egypt, papyrus is fragile and subject to decay. Compared with the huge volume of papyrus documents that would have been produced, therefore, the quantity that survives is small, and this significantly limits our understanding of Old Kingdom Egypt.

The origins of the ancient Egyptian language in which these texts were written have long been a matter of debate. It can be plausibly linked to both the Semitic languages of western Asia and a number of African language groups. Whatever its origins, the Egyptian language has enjoyed a long history. Eventually, it became the tongue known as Coptic, which is still used today in the liturgy of the Coptic Christian church, in Ethiopia.

IMHOTEP AND THE STEP PYRAMID

One of the greatest administrators in the history of Egypt exemplifies both the skills and the possibilities for advancement that a talented scribe could command. Imhotep (*im-HO-tep*) rose through the ranks to become the right-hand man to Djoser (*ZOH-ser*), a pharaoh of the Third Dynasty (c. 2686–2613 B.C.E.). Imhotep's expertise embraced medicine, astronomy, and mathematics; above all, he was an architect. It was Imhotep who designed the Step Pyramid, the first extant building in history constructed entirely of dressed stone. It was not only to be the final resting place of Djoser but an expression of his transcendent power as pharaoh.

Built west of the administrative capital at Memphis, the Step Pyramid towers over the desert to a height of two hundred feet (sixty-one meters). Its design was based on an older form of burial monument, the *mastaba*, a low rectangular structure built entirely of brick with a flat top and sloping sides. Imhotep probably began with this model in mind, but he radically altered it by stacking one smaller mastaba on top of another and constructing each entirely of limestone. Surrounding this structure was a huge temple and mortuary complex whose buildings served two purposes. First and foremost, they would provide Djoser's *ka*, his spirit or life force, with a home and sustenance in the afterlife. Second, the design of the buildings, with their immovable doors and labyrinthine passageways, would (it was hoped) thwart tomb robbers.

Imhotep set a precedent to which all other pharaohs would aspire. The pyramids on the plain of Giza, built during the Fourth Dynasty (2613–2494 B.C.E.), are a case in point. The Great Pyramid itself, built for the pharaoh Khufu (*KOO-foo*; called *Cheops* by the Greeks), was originally 481 feet high and 756 feet along each side of its

THE ROSETTA STONE. This famous stone, carved in 196 B.C.E., preserves three translations of a single decree in three different forms of writing: hieroglyphs (top), demotic Egyptian (middle), and classical Greek (bottom). **› Why would scholars be able to use the classical Greek text to decipher the hieroglyphic and demotic scripts?**

base (147 by 235 meters) and was constructed from more than 2.3 million limestone blocks, enclosed a volume of about 91 million cubic feet (2.6 million cubic meters). Originally, the entire pyramid was encased in gleaming white limestone and topped by a gilded capstone, as were the two massive but slightly smaller pyramids built for Khufu's successors. During the Middle Ages, the Muslim rulers of nearby Cairo had their builders strip off the pyramid's casing stones and used them to construct their new city. (The gold capstones had probably disappeared already.) But in antiquity, these pyramids would have glistened brilliantly by day and glowed by night, making them visible for miles. The Greek historian Herodotus (*heh-RAH-duh-tuhs*), who toured Egypt more than two thousand years after the pyramids were built, estimated that it must have taken a hundred thousand laborers twenty years to build the Great Pyramid.

Once thought to have been the work of slaves, the pyramids were in fact raised by tens of thousands of peasants. Some workers may have been conscripts, but most probably participated willingly, since these projects glorified the living god who served as their link to the cosmic order. Still, the investment of human and material resources required to build the pyramids put strains on Egyptian society. Control over the lives of individual Egyptians increased, and the number of administrative officials employed by the state grew ever larger. So too did the contrast between the lifestyle of the pharaoh's splendid court at Memphis and that of Egyptian society as a whole. A gap was opening between the pretensions of the pharaohs and the continuing loyalties of Egyptians to their local gods and local leaders.

THE END OF THE OLD KINGDOM

Perhaps as a result of these disparities, the Fifth and Sixth Dynasties of the Old Kingdom (2494–2181 B.C.E.) witnessed the slow erosion of pharaonic power.

STEP PYRAMID OF PHARAOH DJOSER. This monument to the pharaoh's power and divinity was designed by the palace official Imhotep around 2650 B.C.E.

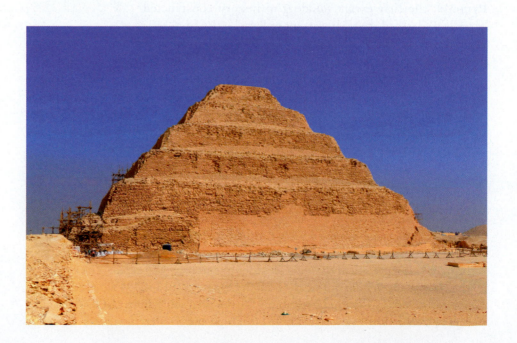

Although pyramid construction continued, the monuments of this period are less impressive in design, craftsmanship, and size. Meanwhile, the priesthood of the sun god Ra at Nekhen, which was also the center of worship for the great god Horus and the place where Narmer's unification of Egypt was memorialized, began to assert its own authority. Ultimately, it declared that the pharaoh was not a god, but merely the god's earthly son. This was a blow to the heart of the pharaoh's political power. A more practical threat was the growing power of the pharaoh's provincial governors, whose increased authority had enabled them to become a hereditary local nobility. Some of these nobles became so influential that one Sixth Dynasty pharaoh even married into their ranks.

It appears that the extraordinarily costly building efforts of the Fourth Dynasty had overtaxed the economy, while the channeling of resources to the royal capital at Memphis increased shortages and resentments in the provinces. Other evidence points to changing climatic conditions that may have disrupted the regular inundations of the Nile, leading to famine. Meanwhile, small states were beginning to form to the south in Nubia, perhaps in response to Egyptian aggression. With better organization and equipment, the Nubians may even have restricted Egyptian access to precious-metal deposits around the First Cataract, further crippling the Egyptian economy.

As a result of these developments, local governors and religious authorities began to emerge as the only effective guarantors of stability and order. By 2160 B.C.E., the beginning of what historians call the First Intermediate Period, Egypt had effectively ceased to exist as a unified entity. The central authority of the pharaoh in Memphis collapsed, and a more ancient distribution of power reemerged: a northern center of influence was opposed by a southern regime headquartered at Thebes, with families from each region claiming to be the legitimate pharaohs of all Egypt.

The First Intermediate Period: Egyptian central authority collapses

Compared with the centralized authority of the Old Kingdom, this looks like chaos. But redistribution of power always leads to the opening of new opportunities. In Egypt, wealth became much more widely and evenly distributed than it had been, as did access to education and possibilities for personal advancement. Resources that the pharaoh's court at Memphis had once monopolized now remained in the provinces, enabling local elites to emerge as both protectors and as patrons. The result was a much wider and more rapid dispersal of cultural forms and goods throughout Egyptian society. Many of these arts and luxuries—including elaborate rites for the dead—had been developed originally at the pharaoh's court and limited to it. Now, however, they became available to Egyptian society at large.

Egyptian Culture and Society

The unique environment of Egypt and the special benefits it conferred on its inhabitants were construed as divine gifts that made Egyptians superior to all other civilizations. For Egyptians, it was simply self-evident that their country—nurtured by the Nile and guarded by the deserts and seas that surrounded it—was the center of the universe.

RELIGION AND WORLDVIEW

Unlike the peoples of Mesopotamia, who were constantly faced with new and terrible challenges—both environmental and political—the Egyptians experienced existence as predictably repetitive. This was mirrored in their perception of the cosmos. At the heart of Egyptian religion lay the myth of the gods Osiris and Isis, not only brother and sister but husband and wife. Osiris was, in a sense, the first pharaoh: the first god to hold kingship on earth. His brother Seth, however, wanted the throne for himself. So Seth betrayed and killed Osiris, sealing his body in a coffin. But their loyal sister Isis retrieved the corpse and managed to revive it long enough to conceive her brother's child, the god Horus. Enraged by this, Seth seized Osiris's body and hacked it to pieces, spreading the remains all over Egypt. Still undeterred, Isis sought the help of Anubis, the god of the afterlife. Together they reassembled and preserved the scattered portions of Osiris's body, thus inventing the practice of mummification. Then Horus, with the help of his mother, managed to defeat Seth.

Osiris was thereby avenged, and revived as god of the underworld. Like Egypt itself, he could not be killed; and the cycle of his death, dismemberment, and resurrection was reflected in the yearly renewal of life along the Nile.

PHARAOH MENKAURE AND HIS QUEEN, KHAMERERNEBTY II. A sculpture from the Fourth Dynasty, c. 2500 B.C.E., shows this queen as her husband's royal partner.

LIFE AND DEATH IN ANCIENT EGYPT

In addition to embodying Egypt's continual regeneration, Osiris exemplified the Egyptian attitude toward death, which was very different from the Sumerians' rather bleak view. For the Egyptians, death was a rite of passage to be endured on the way to an afterlife that was more or less like earthly existence, only better. Yet the journey was full of dangers because the individual's ka had to roam the Duat, the underworld, searching for the House of Judgment. There, Osiris and forty-two other judges would decide the ka's fate. If successful and judged worthy, the deceased would enjoy immortality as an aspect of Osiris.

Egyptian funerary rites emulated the example set by Isis and Anubis, who had carefully preserved the parts of Osiris's body and enabled his afterlife. This is why the Egyptians developed their sophisticated techniques of embalming, whereby many of the body's organs were removed and treated with chemicals—except for the heart, which played a key role in the ka's final judgment. A portrait mask was then placed on the mummy before burial, so that the deceased would be recognizable. To sustain the ka, food, clothing, utensils, weapons, and other items of vital importance would be placed in the grave along with the body.

"Coffin texts," or books of the dead, also accompanied the body and were designed to speed the ka's journey. They contained special instructions, including magic spells and incantations, that would help the ka travel through the underworld and prepare for the final test. They also described the "negative confession" the ka would

The Instruction of Ptah-Hotep

Egyptian literature often took the form of "instructions" to or from important personages, offering advice to those in public life. This document declares itself to be the advice of a high-ranking official of the Old Kingdom to his son and successor, perhaps composed around 2450 B.C.E. However, the earliest surviving text dates from the Middle Kingdom period.

Be not arrogant because of your knowledge, and be not puffed up because you are a learned man. Take counsel with the ignorant as with the learned, for the limits of art cannot be reached, and no artist is perfect in his skills. Good speech is more hidden than the precious greenstone, and yet it is found among slave girls at the millstones.

. . . If you are a leader commanding the conduct of many seek out every good aim, so that your policy may be without error. A great thing is *ma'at*, enduring and surviving; it has not been upset since the time of Osiris. He who departs from its laws is punished. It is the right path for him who knows nothing. Wrong-doing has never brought its venture safe to port. Evil may win riches, but it is the strength of *ma'at* that endures long, and a man can say, "I learned it from my father." . . . If you wish to prolong friendship in a house which you enter as master, brother, or friend, or anyplace that you enter, beware of approaching the women. No place in which that is done prospers. There is no wisdom in it.

A thousand men are turned aside from their own good because of a little moment, like a dream, by tasting which death is reached. . . . He who lusts after women, no plan of his will succeed. . . . If you are a worthy man sitting in the council of his lord, confine your attention to excellence. Silence is more valuable than chatter. Speak only when you know you can resolve difficulties. He who gives good counsel is an artist, for speech is more difficult than any craft.

Source: Nels M. Bailkey, ed., *Readings in Ancient History: Thought and Experience from Gilgamesh to St. Augustine*, 5th ed. (Boston: 1995), pp. 39–42.

Questions for Analysis

1. According to Ptah-Hotep, what are the most important attributes of a man engaged in public life? What are the most dangerous pitfalls and temptations he will encounter?

2. Why does Ptah-Hotep emphasize the importance of acting in accordance with *ma'at*, the principle of truth, order, and justice?

3. Recall what you have learned about the changes in Egyptian politics and society. What might indicate that Ptah-Hotep lived during the prosperous Fifth Dynasty of the Old Kingdom? How might these instructions have resonated differently with later readers of the Middle Kingdom?

ma'at Egyptian term for the serene order of the universe, with which the individual soul (*ka*) must remain in harmony. The power of the pharaoh was linked to *ma'at*, insofar as it ensured the prosperity of the kingdom.

make before the court of Osiris: a formal denial of offenses committed in life. The god Anubis would then weigh the deceased's heart against the principle of *ma'at*: truth, order, justice. Because *ma'at* was envisioned as a goddess wearing a plumed headdress, a feather from this headdress would be placed in the scales, along with the heart, at the time of judgment; only if the heart was light (empty of wrongdoing) and in perfect balance with the feather would the ka achieve immortality.

Throughout the era of the Old Kingdom, the privilege of undergoing these preparations (and thus of ensuring immortality) was reserved for the royal family alone. By the time of the Middle Kingdom, it was becoming possible for many Egyptians to ensure that their bodies would participate in these rituals, too. This manner of confronting death was inherently life-affirming, bolstered by confidence in the resilience of nature and the renewal of creation. Binding together the endless cycle was *ma'at*, the serene order of the universe with which the individual must remain in harmony, and against which each person's ka would be weighed after death. Embodying *ma'at* on earth was the pharaoh. For most of the third millennium, thanks to a long period of successful harvests and peace, the Egyptians were able to maintain their belief in this perfectly ordered paradise and the pharaoh that ensured it. But when that order broke down, so did their confidence in the pharaoh's power.

EGYPTIAN SCIENCE

Given the powerful impression conveyed by the pyramids, it may seem surprising that the ancient Egyptians lagged far behind the Mesopotamians in science, mathematics, and the development of new technologies. Only in the calculation of time did the Egyptians make notable advances, because their close observation

FUNERARY PAPYRUS. This scene, inscribed on a papyrus scroll dating from the Thirtieth Dynasty (380–343 B.C.E.), shows the heart of the princess for whom this book was prepared being weighed in a balance (left) before the god Osiris. On the other side of the balance (right) are the symbols for life (the *ankh*) and the feather of the goddess Ma'at.

of the sun led them to develop a solar calendar that was far more accurate than the Mesopotamian lunar calendar. Whereas the Sumerians invented our means of dividing and measuring the day, the Egyptian calendar is the direct ancestor of the calendar adopted for Rome by Julius Caesar in 45 B.C.E. (see Chapter 5) and later corrected by Pope Gregory XIII in 1582 C.E.: this is the calendar we use today. The Egyptians also devised some effective irrigation and water-control systems, but they did not adopt labor-saving devices like the wheel until much later, perhaps because the available pool of peasant manpower was virtually inexhaustible.

THE SOCIAL PYRAMID

The social pyramid of Old Kingdom Egypt was extremely steep. At its apex stood the pharaoh and his extended family. Below them was a class of nobles whose primary role was to serve as priests and officials of the pharaoh's government; scribes were usually recruited and trained from among the sons of these families. All of these Egyptian elites lived in considerable luxury. They owned extensive estates, exotic possessions, and fine furniture. They kept dogs and cats and monkeys as pets, and hunted and fished for sport.

But most Egyptians lived in crowded conditions in simple mud-brick dwellings. During a period of prosperity, master craftsmen might improve their own conditions and those of their families but they did not constitute anything like a middle class. Other skilled professionals—potters, weavers, masons, merchants—also enjoyed some measure of respect as well as a higher standard of living. The vast majority of Egyptians, however, were peasant laborers. Beneath them were slaves, typically captives from foreign wars.

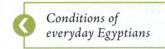
Conditions of everyday Egyptians

And yet this Egyptian hierarchy does not appear to have been particularly oppressive. Commoners' belief in the pharaoh's divinity made them willing subjects, as did the material benefits of living in a stable, well-governed society. Even slaves had certain legal rights, including the ability to own, sell, and bequeath personal property. Unfortunately, though, the written laws and records produced by the lugals of Mesopotamia do not have any Old Kingdom parallels. The Egyptians of this era apparently had no need for written laws beyond what was customary in their communities or what was proclaimed as law by their pharaoh. This makes it difficult for historians to reconstruct their lives in any detail.

THE STATUS OF WOMEN

Although we have no formal law codes to consult, there is evidence that Egyptian women enjoyed unusual freedoms by the standards of the ancient world. Female commoners were recognized as persons in their own right and were allowed to initiate lawsuits (including suits for divorce), to defend themselves in court and to act as witnesses, to possess property of their own, and to dispose of it. And they could do all of this without the permission of a male guardian, as was typically required in most Western societies until the twentieth century. Women were not allowed to undergo formal scribal training, but surviving personal notes exchanged between high-born ladies suggest that some could read and even write.

FOOD FOR THE JOURNEY OF THE KA. These wooden models show peasants plowing, grinding grain, baking bread, brewing beer, and slaughtering a steer. Bread and beer were the staple foods of ancient Egypt; beef was too expensive for ordinary consumption, but cattle were frequently sacrificed as funeral offerings. Such models were placed in Middle Kingdom tombs to provide food for the afterlife.

Middle Kingdom Following the First Intermediate Period of dynastic warfare, this period of ancient Egyptian history (c. 2055-1650 B.C.E.) began with the reassertion of pharaonic rule under Mentuhotep II.

Normally, women were barred from holding high office, apart from that of priestess. But queens were often represented as the partners of their royal husbands and were certainly instrumental in ruling alongside them: note the proud, confident bearing of Queen Khamerernebty II (*kah-mehr-en-EB-tee*; see image on page 32). And occasionally, a woman from the royal family might assume pharaonic authority for a time, as Queen Nimaathap may have done for her son Djoser, before he came of age. Some women may even have ruled in their own right; this was certainly the case during the New Kingdom (see Chapter 2).

Among the peasantry, gender divisions were less clearly defined—as is the case in most rural societies. Women often worked in the fields alongside men and carried out a number of vital tasks in the community. Whatever their status, though, women did not enjoy sexual equality. Although most Egyptians practiced monogamy, wealthy men could and did keep a number of lesser wives, concubines, and female slaves; and any Egyptian man, married or not, enjoyed freedoms that were denied to women, who were subject to severe punishments under the law if they were viewed as guilty of any misconduct.

THE WIDENING HORIZONS OF THE MIDDLE KINGDOM, 2055–c. 1650 B.C.E.

After the disruption of Old Kingdom authority around 2160 B.C.E., warfare between two competing pharaonic dynasties would continue for more than a century. Then, in 2055 B.C.E., the Theban king Mentuhotep (*men-too-HO-tep*) II conquered the northerners and declared himself the ruler of a reunited Egypt. His reign marks the beginning of Egypt's **Middle Kingdom** and the reestablishment of a central government, this time based in Thebes rather than Memphis. The head of this new government was Mentuhotep's chief supporter, Amenemhet (*ah-meh-NEHM-het*), who actually seized power after the king's death and established himself and his descendants as Egypt's Twelfth Dynasty. This succession of remarkable pharaohs remained in power for nearly two hundred years and began to expand Egypt's influence and capacity for trade with its neighbors. This brought Egypt into closer contact with the land of Nubia (present-day Sudan), whose sandy soil contained numerous rich gold deposits. This was the gateway to the rest of Africa and provided a foothold for Egyptian expansion farther down the Nile, as well as to the coast of the Red Sea in what is now Somalia. Recent archaeological discoveries have revealed an enormous trove of funerary texts in the Meroitic language of this region: the oldest known writing system of sub-Saharan Africa. These are still being deciphered, but they shed an especially bright light on the high status of women in Nubia, a matrilineal society in which both men and women traced their ancestry through the female line.

Meanwhile, diplomatic relations with the smaller principalities of Palestine and Syria led to decisive Egyptian political and economic dominance in this region. These lands were not incorporated into Egypt; instead, Amenemhet constructed the Walls of the Prince in Sinai, to guard against incursions by foreigners. These huge fortifications symbolize a marked shift in the Egyptian outlook on the world. The placid serenity of *ma'at* and the devotion to the pharaoh that had built the pyramids had been challenged, and Egyptians could no longer disregard the world beyond their borders. Unlike their Old Kingdom ancestors, the Egyptians of the Middle Kingdom began to turn outward.

Although continuing to enjoy a position as divine representative on earth, the pharaohs of the Middle Kingdom represented themselves as good shepherds, tenders of their flock. Only by diligently protecting Egypt from a hostile world could a pharaoh provide the peace, prosperity, and security desired by his subjects; his alignment with *ma'at* was now clearly conditional, and it had to be earned.

Portraits of the great pharaohs of the Twelfth Dynasty mirror this new status, as does the literature of the Middle Kingdom. Among the most popular of the new literary forms were manuals ostensibly written by or for kings, detailing the duties and perils of high office and offering advice for dealing with difficult situations. *The Instruction of Ptah-Hotep* (see **Analyzing Primary Sources**, on page 33), attributed to a court official of the Old Kingdom, achieved a wide readership—much as Machiavelli's *The Prince* (see Chapter 12) has become a "self-help" book for business executives and politicians in our own time. Other examples of this genre are bleakly pragmatic. A pharaoh must trust no one: not a brother, not a friend, not intimate companions. He must crush the ambitions of local nobles with ruthless ferocity. He must always be on the lookout for trouble. In return for his exertions on behalf of his people, he should expect neither gratitude nor reward; he should expect only that each year will bring new dangers and more pressing challenges. Reading between the lines, we discern that Egyptian elites' sense of their own superiority had been diminished. They were being drawn into a much wider world that they could not control.

Conclusion

Whereas the story of Babel records the loss of a shared language, this chapter shows that people of the distant past can still communicate with us. The remains of their daily

NUBIAN STELE. In 2017–2018, an enormous necropolis (literally, a "city of the dead") was discovered along the Nile in the ancient land of Nubia (now Sudan). Dating from the seventh to fourth centuries B.C.E., it includes more than a hundred tombs and over eighty brick pyramids and other monuments built by the people of Meroë, whose written language (known as Meroitic) is one of the oldest in Africa. One of these monuments is a stone stele or upright slab with an inscription honoring Ataqeloula, the matriarch of a powerful family.

lives, their written records, and their very bodies make it possible for historians to piece together evidence and to make sense of it. And every year, new sources come to light, meaning that we have to be ready to revise—constantly—our understanding of the past.

Although this chapter has emphasized the differences between the early civilizations of Mesopotamia and Egypt, it is worth noting some significant similarities. Both developed the fundamental technologies of writing at about the same time, and this facilitated political alliances, long-distance trade, and the transmission of vital information to posterity. During the third millennium B.C.E., both underwent

AFTER YOU READ THIS CHAPTER

CHRONOLOGY

11,000 B.C.E.	Neolithic Revolution begins
7500–5700 B.C.E.	Çatalhöyük flourishes
6800–3000 B.C.E.	Jericho flourishes
4300–2900 B.C.E.	The rise of Uruk in Sumer
c. 3200 B.C.E.	Development of writing
c. 3100 B.C.E.	King Narmer unites Upper and Lower Egypt
2900–2500 B.C.E.	Early Dynastic Period in Sumer
c. 2700 B.C.E.	Reign of Gilgamesh
c. 2686–2160 B.C.E.	Old Kingdom of Egypt
c. 2650 B.C.E.	Imhotep engineers the Step Pyramid for King Djoser
c. 2350 B.C.E.	Sargon of Akkad consolidates power in Sumer
2160–2055 B.C.E.	First Intermediate Period in Egypt
2100–2000 B.C.E.	Ziggurat of Ur constructed
2055–c. 1650 B.C.E.	Middle Kingdom of Egypt
c. 1792–1750 B.C.E.	Reign of Hammurabi

REVIEWING THE OBJECTIVES

> The study of the distant past is challenging because written sources are rare. What other sources of information do historians use?

> All civilizations require the same basic conditions for survival and share certain characteristics. What are they?

> The cities of Mesopotamia remained largely independent from one another yet shared a common culture. Why was this the case?

> Hammurabi's efforts created a new precedent for governance in Mesopotamia. How did he achieve this?

> The civilizations of ancient Mesopotamia and Egypt differ in profound ways. What were the major causes of their differences?

a process of political consolidation and a melding of spiritual and political leadership. Both engaged in massive building and irrigation projects, and both commanded material and human resources on an enormous scale. Although they had some contact with each other, they had few significant political or cultural interactions. This relative isolation was about to change, however. The next millennium would see the emergence of large-scale, land-based empires that would transform life in Mesopotamia, Egypt, and their Mediterranean neighbors. These are the developments we examine in Chapter 2.

 Go to **INQUIZITIVE** to see what you've learned—and learn what you've missed—with personalized feedback along the way.

PEOPLE, IDEAS, AND EVENTS IN CONTEXT

❯ What fundamental changes associated with the **NEOLITHIC REVOLUTION** made early civilizations possible? Why is this considered to be the beginning of a new epoch, the **ANTHROPOCENE**?

❯ What new technologies allowed the **SUMERIANS** to master the environment of **MESOPOTAMIA**? How did these technologies contribute to the development of a new, urbanized society?

❯ By contrast, why did the Nile River foster a very different civilization and enable the centralized authority of the **PHARAOH**?

❯ How do the differences between **CUNEIFORM** and **HIEROGLYPHS** reflect the different circumstances in which they were invented and the different uses to which they were put?

❯ In what ways are the **EPIC OF GILGAMESH** and the **CODE OF HAMMURABI** rich sources of information about the civilizations of Sumer and **BABYLON**?

❯ How do the **ZIGGURATS** of Mesopotamia and the pyramids of Egypt exemplify different forms of power, different ideas about the gods, and different beliefs about the afterlife?

❯ Why was the worldview of ancient Egyptians, which was strongly reflected in the concept of *MA'AT* during the **OLD KINGDOM**, altered in significant ways by the time of the **MIDDLE KINGDOM**?

THINKING ABOUT CONNECTIONS

❯ How do the surviving sources of any period limit the kinds of questions that we can ask and answer about the distant past? In your view, have sources for this early era been undervalued? For example, if writing had not been developed in Mesopotamia and Egypt, what would we still be able to know about the civilizations of these two regions?

❯ What features of ancient civilizations do modern civilizations share? What might be the implications of these shared ideas, social structures, and technologies?

❯ In particular, what lessons can we draw from humans' tendency to manipulate their environment? How should knowledge of the distant past influence current debates over sustainability and climate change?

2

Peoples, Gods, and Empires, 1700–500 B.C.E.

BEFORE YOU READ THIS CHAPTER

ACCORDING TO HESIOD, a Greek poet who flourished during the eighth century B.C.E., all of human history falls into five ages. The dawn of time was a golden age, when men lived like gods. Everything was good then, food was plentiful, and work was easy. The next age was silver, when men took gods for granted, killed one another, and lived in dishonor. So the gods destroyed them, sending a mighty flood that spared only the family of Deucalion, the son of wily Prometheus, who built an ark. Then came the age of bronze, when everything was made of bronze—houses and armor and weapons and tools. Giants fought incessantly from huge strongholds, causing destruction so great that no man's name survives. The time following was short but bright, a heroic age, the time of men who traveled with Theseus and fought with Achilles and sailed with Odysseus, men whose names will live forever. But Hesiod's own age was iron: a dull age, a time of tedium and strife and petty feuds.

Hesiod's periodization captures an understanding of history that reflects actual developments. The stories he knew told of a time before cities and the need for agriculture. They recalled a time when the human race was saved by one legendary hero: the Sumerian Utnapishtim, the Hebrew Noah, or the Greek Deucalion. They chronicled the wars of an age we still call Bronze, when enormous palaces (abandoned by Hesiod's day) had been built. And they remembered the race of warriors whose glory was measured by their abiding fame. Thanks to new archaeological finds, linguistic

STORY LINES

> During the second millennium B.C.E., new peoples migrated into Eurasia, spreading a related set of Indo-European languages that are the ancestors of several modern language groups.

> In Egypt, the rise of the Eighteenth Dynasty fostered imperial expansion beyond the Nile Valley for the first time.

> During the Late Bronze Age, an interconnected network of alliances bound societies together in new ways. But this civilization was eventually destroyed by the raids of mysterious Sea Peoples.

> In the wake of these invasions, both oppressive new empires and smaller-scale states emerged.

> In the Iron Age, the worship of Yahweh among the Hebrews, and of Ahura-Mazda among the Persians, fostered a new view of the world: one in which a single creator god ruled over all peoples.

CORE OBJECTIVES

> **DESCRIBE** the impact of new migrations and settlements on ancient civilizations.

> **DEFINE** the differences between Egypt's New Kingdom and the previous Old and Middle Kingdoms.

> **EXPLAIN** the workings of transnational networks during the Late Bronze Age.

> **IDENTIFY** the new empires and kingdoms that emerged during the Iron Age.

> **UNDERSTAND** the historical importance of monotheism.

discoveries, and efforts at decoding the historical record, we can both confirm and correct Hesiod's perspective on the past.

In the second millennium B.C.E., Western civilizations were transformed by the arrival of new peoples and the emergence of extensive land-based empires built up through systematic military conquest. These migrations and conquests caused enormous upheaval, but they also led to intensified cultural contact and economic integration in a network that not only encompassed the Mediterranean but extended from Scandinavia to China.

Yet this extraordinary system proved more fragile than its participants could have imagined. Around 1200 B.C.E., a wave of mysterious invasions led to the destruction of nearly every established Mediterranean civilization. As a result, around the turn of the first millennium B.C.E., we enter a world organized along profoundly different lines. In this Iron Age, iron would slowly replace bronze as the primary component of tools and weapons. New and more brutal empires would come to power, while new ideas about the divine and its relationship to humanity would emerge. Two of the Western world's most enduring religious traditions—Judaism and Zoroastrianism (*zoh-roh-AHS-tree-an-ism*)—were born, fundamentally altering conceptions of ethics, politics, and the natural world.

Indo-European Languages and Peoples

In 1786, a British judge serving in India made a discovery that transformed the prevailing understanding of history. While studying Sanskrit, the ancient language of South Asia, Sir William Jones discovered that it shares its grammar and vocabulary with ancient Greek and Latin, to an extent inexplicable by sheer coincidence. His interest piqued, he then examined the early Germanic and Celtic languages of Europe and the Old Persian language of Mesopotamia: they, too, shared marked similarities. He concluded that all of these languages must have evolved from a common source.

Within another generation, the ancient language whose existence Jones had hypothesized, and the later languages derived from it, would be labeled **Indo-European**, reflecting a wide distribution from India to Ireland. The biblical story of mankind's shared language, the story of the Tower of Babel, turns out to be partly true.

Since then, scholars have greatly enlarged our understanding of Indo-European languages and their speakers. Yet much remains controversial. Was the original form of the language spoken by a single population at some point in time? If so, when and where? How did it spread? At the moment, we have no clear answers. It is certain, however, that Indo-European linguistic forms began to appear in western Asia and the eastern Mediterranean shortly after 2000 B.C.E. Around this same time, a group of Indo-European speakers also moved into the Aegean basin, where the resulting language became an early form of Greek. Other Indo-European speakers went east; some may have reached western China.

These new immigrants and settlers did not wipe out existing cultures; rather, they built on established patterns of urban life and organization. But their collective impact was enormous.

IMMIGRANTS IN ANATOLIA

By 1900 B.C.E., a nomadic people called the Assyrians had become caravan merchants whose extensive trade networks stretched across Anatolia and

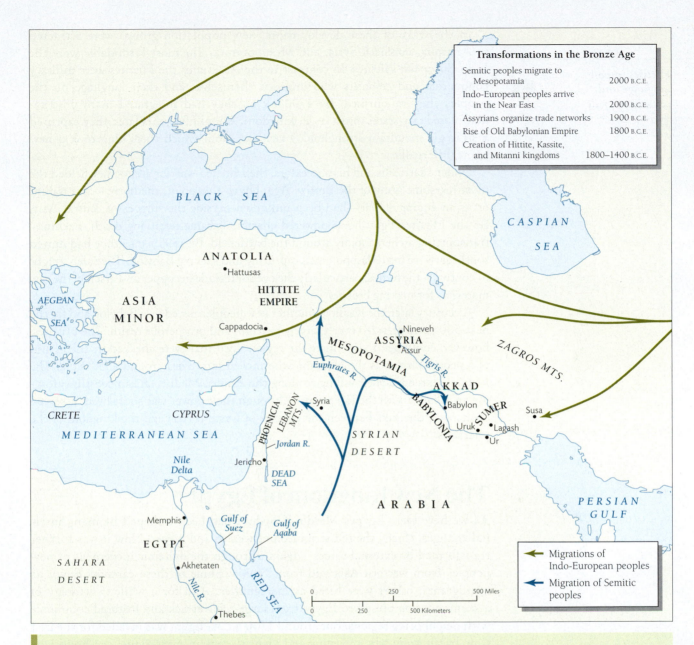

Transformations in the Bronze Age

Semitic peoples migrate to Mesopotamia	2000 B.C.E.
Indo-European peoples arrive in the Near East	2000 B.C.E.
Assyrians organize trade networks	1900 B.C.E.
Rise of Old Babylonian Empire	1800 B.C.E.
Creation of Hittite, Kassite, and Mitanni kingdoms	1800–1400 B.C.E.

Migrations of Indo-European peoples

Migration of Semitic peoples

MIGRATIONS OF THE BRONZE AGE, 2000–1400 B.C.E. Notice the geographical relationships among the older centers of Mesopotamia and Egypt, and among newer civilizations such as Babylonia, Assyria, Phoenicia, and the Hittite Empire. **› Which of these emerging cultures was most likely to come into contact with Egypt, and why? › Where did the Indo-European peoples come from? › What was the impact of Indo-European settlements?**

Mesopotamia. They did not seek military dominance over the region; instead, they relied on the protection of local rulers and, in turn, made these rulers rich. They also served as advisers and officials, marrying into important urban families. In the process, they carried Mesopotamian civilization and its trappings into far-flung regions of the world.

In the wake of these developments, new population groups were attracted to Anatolia, northern Syria, and Mesopotamia. The most formidable were the Indo-European Hittites. In contrast to the Assyrians, the Hittites were military conquerors and colonists who imposed themselves and their language on the peoples they vanquished. By 1700 B.C.E., they had integrated many Hittite-dominated city-states into a larger kingdom. About fifty years later, they captured a strategic mountain stronghold, Hattusas, from which their king took a new name, Hattusilis.

Under Hattusilis and his successors, the Hittites' warrior aristocracy fielded the most fearsome army of the Bronze Age. Up to this point, the horse—as a mount or as an engine of war—had been unknown outside the steppes of central Asia. So the Hittites' light, horse-powered chariots became terrifying death machines, transporting archers rapidly around the battlefield. By 1595 B.C.E., they had moved southeastward into Mesopotamia, capturing and sacking Babylon. They also sought to control trade routes, particularly the overland trade in copper and arsenic: the raw materials for making bronze.

A century later, the Kassites, another new people, moved into Babylon and for the next 500 years presided over a largely peaceful and prosperous realm. The Hittites, however, continued to dominate the region until they were checked by the arrival of a people known as the Mitanni, who moved into Syria around 1550 B.C.E. The Mitanni extended their influence along the eastern Mediterranean coastline, forging an alliance with the Egyptians. Although their power was short-lived, it served to increase the links between the peoples of western Asia and the kingdom of the pharaohs.

The New Kingdom of Egypt

As we have seen, Egypt's Middle Kingdom had been reshaped by many internal changes, chiefly the redistribution of wealth and power. Now it was further transformed by external forces—again, through the dynamic movement of new peoples from western Asia and from Nubia. Some of these came to Egypt as immigrants; others were hired as mercenaries. And for a while, a strategy of accommodation preserved Egypt from large-scale attack and fostered commerce with neighboring regions. But around 1700 B.C.E., Egypt was invaded for the first time by an army whose origins and identity remain mysterious; the Egyptians called them simply Hyksos (*HIHK-sohs*), "rulers of foreign lands." From their power base in the eastern delta of the Nile, the Hyksos began to project their authority over Lower Egypt.

With this conquest, the central authority of the pharaohs once again dissolved and Egypt entered what historians call the Second Intermediate Period (c. 1650–1550 B.C.E.). Significantly, however, the Hyksos did not destroy the machinery of pharaonic government but instead took steps to legitimize their rule in accordance with *ma'at*. Some Hyksos rulers even incorporated the name of the sun god Ra into their own names. In Upper Egypt, by contrast, Hyksos power was weak. Here, a pharaonic regime maintained a tenuous independence at the capital city of Thebes, under the suzerainty (overlordship) of the foreigners to the north.

The Hyksos established Lower Egypt as a significant power, filling the vacuum left by the Hittites. Meanwhile, their conquest weakened Egyptian dominion over the peoples of Nubia, who were able to establish the independent kingdom of Kush with its capital at Meroë (*MEH-ro-hay*). As we noted in Chapter 1, the Meroitic language is the oldest sub-Saharan language to be preserved in writing, and it reflects the strength of the kingdom's culture and identity. Kush therefore posed a much greater threat to the Egyptian dynasty in Upper Egypt than to the Hyksos—but it also provided an additional incentive to the pharaohs, who were determined to reunify Egypt. Ultimately, they succeeded. By the end of the sixteenth century B.C.E., the pharaoh Ahmose had driven out the Hyksos, establishing the Eighteenth Dynasty and the New Kingdom.

THE PHARAOHS OF THE EIGHTEENTH DYNASTY

The Eighteenth Dynasty: Egyptian power at its height

Under the Eighteenth Dynasty, Egyptian civilization reached the height of its magnificence and power. Although many Egyptian traditions were renewed and strengthened, the dynamism of the New Kingdom—particularly its new focus on imperial expansion—changed the very fabric of Egyptian life, which had never looked far beyond the narrow world of the fertile Nile Valley.

Striking developments took place during this period. Most important was the rise of an aristocracy whose wealth was acquired through warfare and the winning of lands (with slaves to work them), which they received from pharaoh as rewards for their service. The Eighteenth Dynasty itself was forged in battle, something that had not been true of a ruling family since the time of King Narmer, over a millennium and a half earlier (see Chapter 1). Ahmose himself, the pharaoh who expelled the Hyksos, had been reared by the warrior queen Ahhotep, who had ruled Upper Egypt. His eventual successor, Thutmose I (c. 1504–1492 B.C.E.), was the son of an unknown warrior who married Ahmose's powerful daughter.

Under Thutmose's leadership, the Egyptians subdued the Nubians to the south, seizing control of their gold mines. They also penetrated beyond their northeastern frontier, driving deep into Palestine and Syria. By the time of his death, Thutmose could claim to rule the land from beyond the Nile's Fourth Cataract in the south to the banks of the Euphrates in the north. Never had Egypt so clearly declared its imperial ambitions, and it would sustain a strong military presence in this wider region for the next four hundred years.

THE LEGACY OF HATSHEPSUT

The early death of Thutmose's son and successor could have resulted in a crisis for the Eighteenth Dynasty. Instead, it led to one of the most remarkable reigns in Egypt's history, for Thutmose II (1492–1479 B.C.E.) passed the power of pharaoh to his sister, wife, and co-ruler **Hatshepsut** (*HAHT-shep-soot*; 1479–1458 B.C.E.). Such brother–sister unions were common in the Egyptian royal family, although pharaohs customarily kept a harem of subsidiary wives and concubines for the production of children. However, Thutmose II and Hatshepsut did conceive at least one child together, Neferure (*neh-feh-RUH-reh*), who acted as queen while her mother ruled as pharaoh. As such, Hatshepsut was routinely portrayed on monuments with the masculine figure and ceremonial beard characteristic of pharaohs. She did not pretend to be a man; inscriptions almost always indicate her gender, and she claimed

Hatshepsut (1479–1458 B.C.E.) As a pharaoh during the New Kingdom, she launched several successful military campaigns and extended trade and diplomacy. She was an ambitious builder who probably constructed the first tomb in the Valley of Kings.

Remembering Hatshepsut

The pharaohs of Egypt's New Kingdom were obsessed with self-representation and carefully controlled their public images. The visual language they used was an iconography (vocabulary of images) intended to make each successive pharaoh look as much like his predecessors as possible: godlike, virile, authoritative—even when the pharaoh was a woman. So many statues and portraits of Hatshepsut survive that nearly every major museum in the world has at least one. (The Metropolitan Museum of Art in New York has a whole room for them.) But many of these images show signs of having been defaced (images A and B) during the reign of her successor, Thutmose III, who was also her nephew and stepson. Until very recently, scholars assumed that Hatshepsut must have usurped his powers and that this was his revenge. Yet the evidence clearly shows that Hatshepsut was Egypt's legitimate ruler. Why, then, would Thutmose III or his heirs have tried to efface her memory?

On the facing page, the two unblemished steles (images C and D) depict Hatshepsut and Thutmose III. In the stele on the left (image C), they sit back to back

A. Defaced head of Hatshepsut.

B. Defaced statue of Hatshepsut.

on matching thrones, under the protection of the gods. In the stele on the right (image D), Thutmose III wears a warrior's crown, while Hatshepsut wears the Double Crown of Upper and Lower Egypt and wields a mace.

to be the most beautiful woman in the world. But it was important to Egyptians that she use the conventional iconography of power to locate herself firmly within a long history of dynastic rule.

Hatshepsut's statecraft proved crucial to the continuing success of Egypt. With her stepson/nephew Thutmose III (the son of one of her brother's lesser wives), she even launched several successful military campaigns and extended trade and diplomacy. The arts also flourished, setting standards that would be emulated for a thousand years. Indeed, Hatshepsut was one of the most ambitious builders in Egyptian history, which is saying something. Her own mortuary temple was probably the first tomb constructed in the Valley of the Kings.

Yet after Hatshepsut's death in 1458 B.C.E., her legacy was called into question. At some point late in her nephew's reign, attempts were made to remove her name from inscriptions and to destroy her images (see *Interpreting Visual Evidence*, above). Scholars used to assume that Thutmose himself resented his stepmother/aunt's power over him. But more recent research has suggested that the culprit was his son, Amenhotep II (1427–1400 B.C.E.), who was thereby blocking the claims of royal

Questions for Analysis

1. Bear in mind that few Egyptians could read the hieroglyphs accompanying these images. How might they have "read" the relationship between these two royal relatives? Does this visual evidence support the hypothesis that Thutmose was slighted by Hatshepsut? Why or why not?

2. What can these images tell us about gender roles? What else would we need to know before making a judgment about masculine and feminine characteristics in ancient Egypt?

3. Given that Hatshepsut was Egypt's legitimate pharaoh, what might have motivated either Thutmose III or his son Amenhotep II to deface her image many years after her death?

C. Stele of Hatshepsut and Thutmose.

D. Stele of Thutmose and Hatshepsut from the Red Chapel at Karnak.

rivals, possibly the descendants of Hatshepsut's daughter Neferure. In either case, the near erasure of Hatshepsut's legacy caused her to be neglected by historians until the late twentieth century.

RELIGIOUS CHANGE AND POLITICAL CHALLENGES

The great conquests of the Eighteenth Dynasty brought mind-boggling riches to Egypt. Much of this wealth went to glorify the pharaohs, for whom grand temples, tombs, and other monuments were erected. Another significant portion went to the military aristocracy that made such conquests possible. But the lion's share went to the gods as offerings of thanks. As the temples became wealthy and powerful, so too did their priests. And no temple complex was so wealthy as that of Amon at Thebes.

Thebes was not only the capital of New Kingdom Egypt but the place most sacred to Amon (or Amun), god of creation. He therefore played an important role in the Eighteenth Dynasty's self-image, and is evoked in the dynastic name Amenhotep ("Amon Is Pleased"). Amon had come into new prominence when the political center of gravity shifted to Thebes and he had become identified as another manifestation of the sun god Ra; as Amon-Ra he was the divine force behind the triumph over the Hyksos. As a result, his priests at Thebes became a formidable political and economic force. Eventually, the priesthood of Amon surpassed even the military aristocracy in importance and influence.

THE REIGN OF AKHENATEN (1352–1336 B.C.E.)

These factors are important when we consider the reign of Amenhotep IV, who inherited the vast, well-governed kingdom assembled by his predecessors. This young pharaoh showed an early inclination toward worship of the sun—but not in the figure of Amon. Instead, Amenhotep exalted Ra as a discrete divinity and replaced the traditional iconography of this god as a falcon (or a falcon-headed man) with the symbol *Aten*, the hieroglyph representing the sun's rays. He then changed his own name to **Akhenaten** (*AH-ken-AH-ten*), "He Who Is Profitable to the Aten," and built a new capital to honor the god. Located halfway between Memphis in the north and Thebes in the south, it was called Akhetaten ("The Horizon of the Aten").

Akhenaten's theology: a departure ❯

Although the priests of Thebes exalted Amon-Ra, they had still worshiped all the other gods in the Egyptian pantheon. But Akhenaten's theology was closer to monotheism because, unlike traditional Egyptian deities, the Aten could not be imagined as taking on human or animal form. If this were not controversial enough, Akhenaten also celebrated his new religion by representing himself in a very unconventional way. In a complete departure from the divine virility of his ancestors—which even his ancestor Hatshepsut had emulated—Akhenaten had himself pictured as a normal human being with distinctive features: a family man enjoying the company of his wife, Nefertiti, and their children. This emphasis on his own humanity was an extension of his theology, which honored the life force within every being. But it was very dangerous to the ideology of royal power. The pharaoh was not supposed to be an approachable man with a quirky personality. He was supposed to be a god on earth.

Akhenaten's spiritual revolution therefore had enormous political implications. Indeed, some scholars have suggested that it was part of a cunning attempt to undermine the influence of Amon's priests, to the pharaoh's benefit. Whatever the motives behind it, Akhenaten did not succeed in converting many Egyptians to his new religion. The priesthood of Amon, not surprisingly, also put up strenuous resistance. To make matters worse, Akhenaten did not balance his spiritual enthusiasm with attention to Egypt's security or empire. This cost him the support of his nobility and may have led to his deposition.

AKHENATEN, HIS WIFE NEFERTITI, AND THEIR CHILDREN. The Aten is depicted here as a sun disk, raining down power on the royal family. ❯ **What messages might this image have conveyed to contemporary Egyptians? ❯ How does this depiction of the pharaoh differ from earlier precedents?**

Akhenaten was ultimately succeeded by one of his younger sons, Tutankhaten ("Living Image of Aten"), a child of nine whose name was quickly changed to reflect his advisers' restoration of the god Amon and his priesthood to positions of power. He thus became Tutankhamun (1333–1324 B.C.E.), the famous boy king whose sumptuous tomb was discovered in 1922. After his early death, he was succeeded by Horemheb, a general unrelated to the royal family and who reigned as the last pharaoh of the Eighteenth Dynasty for nearly three decades. When he died, he passed his office to another general. This was Ramses, the founder of the Nineteenth Dynasty, who would restore Egypt to glory.

Transnational Networks of the Late Bronze Age

Bronze Age history must be understood within the context of what we might call international relations. Yet it is more accurate to call the political and economic networks of this period *transnational*, because this web of alliances transcended any idea of national identity or national boundaries—both of which are modern concepts.

This Late Bronze Age was also an age of superpowers. The great pharaohs of the Eighteenth Dynasty had transformed Egypt into a conquering state and the Hittites had created an empire out of the disparate city-states of Anatolia. The Assyrians controlled trade, and the Kassite kingdom of Babylonia remained a significant force. In addition to these imperial entities, numerous smaller states also flourished and extended their influence westward into the Mediterranean. Holding it all together was a network of trade routes that created an interdependent Afro-Eurasian world.

TRANSNATIONAL DIPLOMACY

Although warfare remained a fundamental mode of interaction, a balance of power among the larger empires gradually helped to stabilize the region and encourage trade. The archives discovered by archaeologists at Akhenaten's abandoned capital of Akhetaten (modern el-Amarna) provide us with a clear picture of this process. By the fourteenth century B.C.E., a wide-ranging correspondence was forging alliances and understandings among rulers and elites. This is reflected in the letters' vocabulary: the most powerful rulers address one another as "brother," whereas lesser princes and chieftains show their deference to the pharaoh, the Hittite king, and other sovereigns by using the term "father." Breach of this protocol could cause great offense. When an Assyrian king presumed to address the Hittite ruler as "brother," he received a stern rebuke: "What is this about 'brotherhood'? Were you and I born of the same mother? Far from it!"

Rulers of this period also exchanged lavish gifts and entered into marriage contracts with each other. Professional envoys journeyed back and forth among the centers of power, conveying treasures and handling politically sensitive missions. Some of these emissaries were also merchants, sent to explore the possibility of trading opportunities.

TRANSNATIONAL TRADE

Indeed, it was trade that allowed smaller communities to become integral parts of this transnational network. Seaside ports became powerful merchant city-states and centers for the exchange of dazzling commodities. A single vessel's cargo might

Bronze Age The name given to the era 3200–1200 B.C.E., characterized by the discovery of techniques for smelting bronze (an alloy of copper and tin), which was then the strongest known metal.

contain scores of distinct items originating anywhere from the interior of Africa to the Baltic Sea, as demonstrated by the contents of a merchant ship discovered at Uluburun off the Turkish coast in 1982. At the same time, the region was supplied with goods brought in over land, via contacts reaching into China.

Transnational trade fosters exchange of culture and technology ›

Long-distance trade was not only the basis for a new economy but the conduit for art, ideas, and technology. In the past, such influences had spread slowly and unevenly; now, the societies of the Late Bronze Age could keep abreast of all the latest developments and commodities. Egyptians delighted in Canaanite glass, Greeks prized Egyptian amulets, and the merchants of Canaan were eager for Greek pottery and wool. This trend was particularly marked in large coastal towns. At Ugarit, on the coast of modern-day Syria, the swirl of commerce and the multiplicity of languages spoken by traders even propelled the development of

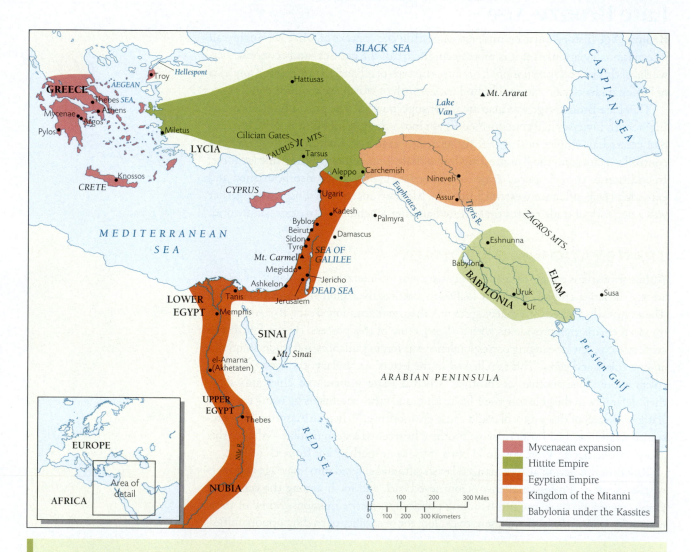

EGYPT AND ITS NEIGHBORS, c. 1400 B.C.E. › What is the major change on this map compared with the previous map of Bronze Age civilizations (page 43)? › What factors appear to shape patterns of conquest and settlement in the eastern Mediterranean? › What developments would have enabled trade to flourish during this period?

a simpler form of written communication. In contrast to cuneiform, the Ugaritic alphabet consisted of about thirty symbols representing the sounds of consonants (vowels had to be inferred). This system was far more easily mastered and more flexible than cuneiform, and it became the model for the development of all modern alphabets.

The search for markets, resources, and trade routes also promoted greater understanding among cultures. After a great battle between Egyptians and Hittites near Kadesh (c. 1275 B.C.E.), the pharaoh Ramses II realized that more was to be gained through peaceful relations than through warfare. The treaty he established with the Hittites fostered geopolitical stability in the region and allowed further economic exchanges to flourish. But greater integration also meant greater mutual dependence. If one economy suffered, the effects of that decline were sure to be felt elsewhere. And the farther this transnational system spread, the more fragile it became. Many of the new markets depended on emerging societies in regions far less stable, where civilization was new.

Aegean Civilization: Minoan Crete, Mycenaean Greece

Like Hesiod, many ancient Greek poets celebrated a heroic age when great men mingled with gods and powerful kingdoms contended for wealth and glory. For a long time, modern scholars dismissed these stories as fables. Tales of the Athenian hero Theseus and the Minotaur, the Trojan War, and the wanderings of Odysseus were not regarded as reflecting any historical reality. Greek history was assumed to begin in 776 B.C.E., when the first recorded Olympic Games occurred. Greece in the Bronze Age was considered a primitive backwater that played no significant role in the Mediterranean world or in the later, glorious history of classical Greece.

But in the late nineteenth century, an amateur archaeologist named Heinrich Schliemann became convinced that these legends were really historical accounts. Using the epic poems of the *Iliad* and the *Odyssey* as his guide, he found the site of Ilium (Troy) near the coast of northwest Anatolia. He also identified a number of once-powerful citadels on the Greek mainland, including the home of the legendary king Agamemnon at Mycenae (*MY-seh-nee*).

Soon afterward, the British archaeologist Sir Arthur Evans took credit for discovering the remains of a great palace at Knossos (*kuh-NOHS-ohs*) on the island of Crete: a vast complex that predated any of the major citadels on the Greek mainland. He dubbed its magnificent culture (which no modern person had known to exist) "**Minoan Crete**," after King Minos, the powerful ruler whom the ancient Greeks had described as dominating the Aegean, and the man for whom the legendary engineer Daedalus had designed the Labyrinth.

Although some of their conclusions have been proven false, the discoveries of Schliemann and Evans forced scholars to revise, entirely, the early history of Western civilizations. It is now clear that Bronze Age Greece—or, as it is often termed, **Mycenaean Greece**—was an important player in this integrated Mediterranean world during the second millennium B.C.E.

Minoan Crete A sea empire based at Knossos on the Greek island of Crete and named for the legendary King Minos. The Minoans dominated the Aegean for much of the second millennium B.C.E.

Mycenaean Greece Describes the civilization of Bronze Age Greece from 1600 B.C.E. to 1200 B.C.E., when territorial kingdoms such as Mycenae formed around a king, a warrior caste, and a palace bureaucracy.

THE MINOAN THALASSOCRACY

In the fifth century B.C.E., the Athenian historian Thucydides wrote that King Minos of Crete had ruled a *thalassocracy*, an empire of the sea. We now know that Thucydides was correct, and that a very wealthy civilization began to flourish on the island of Crete around 2500 B.C.E. For about a millennium, the Minoans controlled shipping around the central Mediterranean and the Aegean, and may have exacted tribute from many smaller islands. At its height between 1900 and 1500 B.C.E., Minoan civilization was the contemporary of Egypt's Middle Kingdom and the Hittite Old Kingdom. But unlike them, it was virtually unassailable by outside forces, protected by the surrounding sea. Astonishingly, neither the great palace at Knossos nor the other palaces on the island were fortified, so secure were they from attack.

Thanks to its strategic position, Crete was not only a safe haven but a nexus of vibrant economic exchange. Knossos was also a production center for textiles, pottery, and metalwork. Minoan merchants traded these for a range of exotic goods from Egypt, southwest Anatolia, and Cyprus. Through Cyprus, the Minoans had further contacts with the Levantine coast (modern-day Lebanon and Syria). Artistic influences also traveled along these routes; among much else, Minoan-style fresco paintings appear regularly in the Nile Delta and the Levant.

Traces of the bright colors and graceful lines of these paintings are still evident on the ruined walls of Knossos. Endowed with indoor plumbing, among other luxuries, it covered several acres and comprised hundreds of rooms joined by an intricate web of winding hallways that inspired the story of the Labyrinth, at the center of which lurked the terrible Minotaur, a creature half man and half bull. These legends, too, reflect historical realities: the Minoans worshiped a god in the form of a bull or bull-man, and they devised an elaborate but lethal ritual sport known as bull-leaping: similar to bullfighting but involving an element of athletic dance.

Minoan Crete: a haven for trade ❯

MINOAN FRESCO, c. 1500 B.C.E. A stylized representation of bull-leaping, painted into the plaster of a wall at Knossos. ❯ **Is this fresco likely to represent real practices?** ❯ **Why or why not?**

Despite all these fascinating remains, Minoan culture remains mysterious because its language has yet to be decoded. Its script is called Linear A, to distinguish it from the Linear B used in Mycenaean Greece—a script that *has* been deciphered. Although Linear A and Linear B represent different languages, their formal relationship reflects the close ties between Minoan Crete and the mainland of Greece. Yet the nature of that relationship is still debated. The Minoans were clearly much more sophisticated and originally may have dominated their Greek neighbors. One story told of the Greek hero Theseus describes how the young Athenian was sent to Crete as a hostage, intending to free Athens from the heavy tribute imposed by King Minos. Given what we have already learned about the close relationship between myth and history, it is probable that this story preserves ancient memories.

LINEAR A TABLET FROM KNOSSOS. Unlike cuneiform, whose characters are formed using the wedge-shaped tip of a reed, Linear A was inscribed with a sharp stylus that incised fine lines in clay or soft stone.

MYCENAEAN GREECE

Since Linear B was deciphered in the early 1950s, new research shows that the Indo-Europeans whose language became Greek entered the region in several waves after the turn of the second millennium, dominating and displacing the indigenous inhabitants. By 1500 B.C.E., their huge citadels dotted the Greek landscape, ruled by warriors whose epitaphs boast of their martial prowess and who were buried with their weapons.

In 2015, American archaeologists excavating near one of these citadels—at Pylos in southwestern Greece—discovered an extraordinarily rich grave with all of its contents intact. Known as the tomb of the Griffin Warrior, from the decorative motifs of this mythical beast carved on an ivory plaque, it contained the body of a man in his early thirties who was buried with his sword and dagger, as well as combs, a mirror, jewelry, and other items: all made of ivory, silver, gold, bronze, and all beautifully fashioned. Many of these items came from Minoan Crete, and because the tomb was dug *before* the building of the great palace citadel at Pylos, it allows us to glimpse the process of cultural transfer that was shaping a new civilization on the Greek mainland. Analysis of ancient DNA (aDNA) extracted from the warrior's teeth and bones may soon yield even more information about him, while radiocarbon analysis could assist in dating the burial.

This grave, and the close relationship between the writing systems of Crete and the mainland, reveal that Mycenaean society was decisively influenced by Minoan cultural, religious, and political models. Its citadels, copying the great palaces of Crete, were both centers of government and warehouses for the storage of goods and agricultural surpluses, of which careful records were kept. (Thousands of Linear B tablets testify to this.) Some Mycenaean rulers carved out territorial kingdoms with as many as a hundred thousand inhabitants, dwarfing the city-states of the later classical age. (Hesiod imagined them to have been built by giants.) Indeed, their massive size was not really suited to the Greek landscape; nor were the war chariots that the Mycenaean elites adopted from their contem-

 Mycenaean Greece: evidence of cultural exchange

THE GRAVE OF THE GRIFFIN WARRIOR AT PYLOS. The contents of this Mycenaean tomb, discovered in 2015, reveal the extent of the connections between Mycenaean Greece and Minoan Crete. This photograph shows a bronze mirror in its original location.

poraries on the plains of Anatolia, despite the fact that they were highly impractical on rocky terrain.

The Mycenaean Greeks came to play a central role in Bronze Age networks. By about 1400 B.C.E., they had subjugated Crete, taking over Knossos and remaking it as a Mycenaean center. When the pharaoh Amenhotep III mentions a place called "Keftiu" in his correspondence, he is probably negotiating with Crete's Mycenaean conquerors. In western Anatolia, not far from fabled Troy, at least one Mycenaean king exercised enough influence for a Hittite ruler to address him as "my brother." This evidence suggests that the Mycenaeans earned prestige as warriors and mercenaries, just as the Greeks' heroic poems attest.

The basic political and commercial unit of the Mycenaean world—a powerful king and war leader, a warrior aristocracy, a palace bureaucracy, a complex economy, large territorial kingdoms—differs markedly from the tiny, self-contained Greek city-states we will study in Chapter 3. However, we can trace some features of this later civilization back to the Mycenaeans, including the Greek language. Linear B tablets record a social group with considerable political rights, the *damos*; this may be the precursor of the *demos*, the urban citizens who sought political empowerment (*democracy*) in many Greek cities. The tablets also record the names of several gods familiar from the later period, such as Zeus, Poseidon, and Dionysos. Although later Greeks such as Hesiod knew little about these Mycenaean ancestors in fact, the impact of the stories they told about them was considerable.

THE SEA PEOPLES AND THE END OF THE BRONZE AGE

For many years, historians have guessed that the collapse of Mycenaean civilization was caused by factors such as drought, disease, and social unrest. Indeed, new climatological research shows that sustained arid conditions could have led to decreased crop yields and famine. The devastating consequences are clear: the civilization of Mycenaean Greece ceased to exist around the end of the thirteenth century B.C.E. And because Greece was an integrated part of a transnational network, the effects of its demise were felt throughout the region.

Thereafter, a wave of devastation swept from north to south, caused by a group of people so thoroughly destructive that they obliterated everything in their path. We might know nothing about them were it not for a narrow victory by the pharaoh Ramses III around 1176 B.C.E. In the monument commemorating his triumph, near the modern city of Luxor on Egypt's West Bank, these invaders are called the "Sea Peoples." From the description of their battle gear, it seems that many were from the Aegean. Most notable were the Philistines who, after their defeat, withdrew to populate the coast of the region named after them: Palestine. In 2018, another inscription describing the Sea Peoples was finally deciphered, and it indicates that one group in their confederation was a powerful new kingdom called Mira, which had begun its rise by conquering Troy.

The "Sea Peoples": what we know

MYCENAEAN GREECE. › What stands out about the geography of Greece? › How might this dry, mountainous country surrounded by the sea determine the nature of Greek civilization and economic interests? › How might geography have allowed Mycenaean culture to spread so widely?

This new evidence lends weight to older hypotheses that the Sea Peoples' arc of destruction began in the northern Aegean and was another of the factors contributing to the collapse of Mycenaean Greece. Disruption of northern commercial networks would have devastated the Mycenaean kingdoms, which could not support their enormous populations without trade. Suddenly faced with an apocalyptic combination of overpopulation, famine, and violence, bands of desperate refugees would have fled the Aegean basin. Meanwhile, the damage to commerce had a domino effect that devastated the economy of the Hittites, whose ancient kingdom rapidly disintegrated. Along the Mediterranean coast we find other evidence of rapid decline. The king of Ugarit wrote a letter to a "brother" king on the island of Cyprus, begging for immediate aid because he had sent all his own warriors to help the Hittites. It is poignant that we have his letter only because the clay tablet on which it was written was baked hard in the fire that destroyed his palace. The letter was never sent.

The desperation of refugees fleeing famine and violence, combined with the raids of the Sea Peoples, destroyed the Western civilizations that had flourished for more than two thousand years. The devastation was not total; not all cities disappeared and trade did not cease entirely. But the Hittite Empire was eradicated and the great cities of the eastern Mediterranean lay in ruins, while new groups—sometimes contingents of Sea Peoples like the Philistines—populated the coast. The citadels of Mycenaean Greece were depopulated by as much as 90 percent over the next century, and Greece entered into a period of cultural and economic isolation that would last for two hundred and fifty years.

The victorious Egyptians survived; but with their trading partners diminished or dead, their civilization suffered. The Assyrians, the original architects of the networks that had undergirded the transnational system, had to fight for their very existence. In Babylon, the peaceful and prosperous rule of the Kassites withered. In the vacuum left behind, new political configurations took shape as a new metallurgical technology began to supplant the use of bronze. Out of the ashes arose the phoenix of the Iron Age.

The States of the Early Iron Age

With the destruction of transnational networks, the geopolitical map of the ancient world changed significantly. In Anatolia, a patchwork of small kingdoms grew up within the territories once controlled by the Hittites. Similar developments took place in the Levant, the eastern Mediterranean coastline that today comprises Israel, Lebanon, and parts of Syria. For centuries, this region had been controlled either by the Egyptians or the Hittites. With the collapse of these empires, new states began to emerge there, too. They were small, but they had a huge impact on the history of Western civilizations.

THE PHOENICIANS

One of the most influential peoples is usually called by their Greek name: the **Phoenicians**. They are also known as Canaanites and were speakers of a Semitic language closely related to Hebrew. Each Phoenician city on the coast of the Levant had its own hereditary royal government, and every Phoenician's first loyalty was to his own city. In the Phoenicians' overseas colonies, however, a new type of political system emerged in which power was shared among a handful of elite families. This aristocratic form of government would become a model for many other Western societies, including those of classical Greece and Rome (see Chapters 3 and 5).

During the Late Bronze Age, most Phoenician cities had been controlled by Egypt. But the erosion of Egyptian imperial power after 1200 B.C.E. gave these cities the opportunity to forge a new independence and to capitalize on their commercial advantages. One Phoenician city was a clearinghouse for papyrus, the highly prized

Phoenicians A Semitic people known for their trade in exotic purple dyes and other luxury goods, they originally settled in present-day Lebanon around 1200 B.C.E. and from there established commercial colonies throughout the Mediterranean, notably Carthage.

The Diplomacy of the Mycenaeans and the Hittites

Around 1260 B.C.E., the powerful Hittite king Hattusilis III sent the following letter to a "King of Ahhiyawa," identifiable as a leader of the Mycenaean Greeks, who often called themselves Akhaiwoi, Achaeans. This fascinating document exemplifies the tangle of close ties that bound powerful men together within the transnational system of the Late Bronze Age, as well as the problems and misunderstandings that could arise from the misbehavior of the men under their command. The events referenced here all occurred in western Anatolia (Turkey), a region controlled partly by the Hittites and partly by the Greeks, the same region in which Troy (Ilium) was located. (See the map on page 55.)

I have to complain of the insolent and treacherous conduct of one Tawagalawas. We came into contact in the land of Lycia, and he offered to become a vassal of the Hittite Empire. I agreed, and sent an officer of most exalted rank to conduct him to my presence. He had the audacity to complain that the officer's rank was not exalted enough; he insulted my ambassador in public, and demanded that he be declared vassal-king there and then, without the formality of an interview. Very well: I order him, if he desires to become a vassal of mine, to make sure that no troops of his are found in Iyalanda when I arrive there. And what do I find when I arrive in Iyalanda?—the troops of Tawagalawas, fighting on the side of my enemies. I defeat them, take many prisoners . . . scrupulously leaving the fortress of Atriya intact out of respect for my treaty with you. Now a Hittite subject, Piyamaradus by name, steals my 7,000 prisoners, and makes off to your city of Miletus. I command him to return to me: he disobeys. I write to you: you send a surly message unaccompanied by gift or greeting, to say that you have ordered your representative in Miletus, a certain Atpas, to deliver up Piyamaradus. Nothing happens, so I go fetch him. I enter your city of Miletus, for I have something to say to Piyamaradus, and it would be well that your subjects there should hear me say it. But my visit is not a success. I ask for Tawagalawas: he is not at home. I should like to see Piyamaradus: he has gone to sea. You refer me to your representative Atpas: I find that both he and his brother are married to daughters of Piyamaradus; they are not likely to give me satisfaction or to give you an unbiased account of these transactions . . . . Are you aware, and is it with your blessing, that Piyamaradus is going round saying that he intends to leave his wife and family, and incidentally my 7,000 prisoners, under your protection while he makes continual inroads on my dominion? . . . Do not let him use Achaea [in Greece] as a base for operations against me. You and I are friends. There has been no quarrel between us since we came to terms in the matter of Ilios [the territory of Troy]: the trouble there was my fault, and I promise it will not happen again. As for my military occupation of Miletus, please regard it as a friendly visit. . . . [As for the problems between us], I suggest that the fault may not lie with ourselves but with our messengers; let us bring them to trial, cut off their heads, mutilate their bodies, and live henceforth in perfect friendship.

Source: Adapted from Denys Page, *History and the Homeric Iliad* (Berkeley: 1959), pp. 11–12.

Questions for Analysis

1. Reconstruct the relationship between Hattusilis III and the Achaean king, on the basis of the references to people and places in this letter. What picture emerges of their interactions and of the connections between the Hittite Empire and Mycenaean Greece?

2. Why is Hattusilis so concerned about the disrespect that the Achaeans have shown to him? Reading between the lines, what do you think he wanted to accomplish by sending this letter?

3. On the basis of this letter, what can you deduce about the standards of behavior expected of civilized participants in the transnational system of the Late Bronze Age? Within this code of conduct, what sanctions or penalties could be imposed on individuals or their nations?

Egyptian writing material. Hence the Greek name for this city, Byblos, became the basis for the Greek word *biblon*, meaning "book." (The Bible is so called from the plural *bibloi*, "the books.")

Another valuable commodity associated with the Phoenicians gave them their name: a rare purple dye derived from the shells of snails culled from the Levantine coast. According to the Greeks, those who supplied this rich dye were *phoinikeoi*, the "purple people." The Phoenicians also became expert metalworkers, ivory carvers, and shipbuilders.

PHOENICIAN COLONIES AND CULTURAL INFLUENCE

Phoenician expansion

The Phoenicians were aggressive migrants and colonists. By the end of the tenth century B.C.E., they had planted settlements from one end of the Mediterranean to the other, and their merchants had even begun to venture out into the Atlantic Ocean. We have good evidence that they traveled as far as Cornwall (southwest Britain) during this period. The Greek historian Herodotus later claimed that Phoenician merchant-explorers even circumnavigated Africa. At the end of the ninth century B.C.E.,

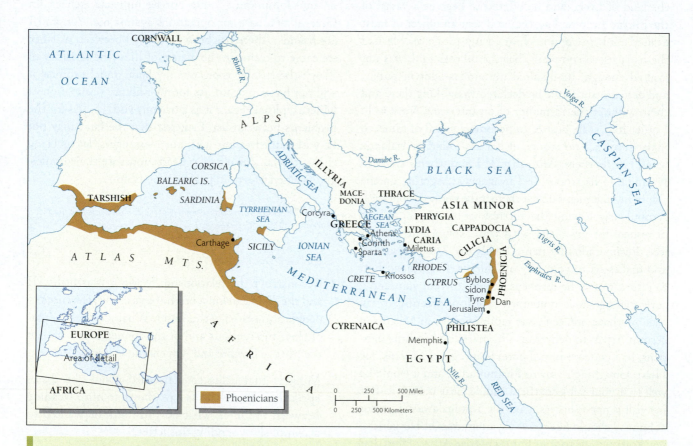

PHOENICIAN COLONIZATION. Compare this map with the more detailed one of the Hebrew kingdoms on page 62. **What part of the Mediterranean was the homeland for the Phoenician city-states? › Where did Phoenicians establish colonies? › Why would overseas colonization be of such crucial importance to Phoenician city-states? › What does their westward colonization imply about the Phoenicians' aims and about the different opportunities available in the western Mediterranean?**

Phoenicians from the city of Tyre established Carthage in modern-day Tunisia (North Africa). Carthage would ultimately become the preeminent power in the western Mediterranean; centuries later, it became the arch-rival of Rome (see Chapter 5).

The widespread colonial and mercantile efforts of the Phoenicians influenced cultures across the Mediterranean. Among their early trading partners were the Greeks, whom the Phoenicians reintroduced to seafaring and urban life after the collapse of the Mycenaean citadels. Without question, however, the most important contribution of the Phoenicians was their alphabet.

As we noted earlier, a thirty-character alphabet had evolved at Ugarit by the end of the Bronze Age. Around 1100 B.C.E., the Phoenicians refined this writing system down to twenty-two characters in order to further facilitate communication and accounting among their trading partners. The Greeks remained aware of their debt to the Phoenicians because their legends ascribe the invention of the alphabet to Cadmus, a Phoenician who settled in Greece. Their debt is also clear in the close relationship between the names of letters in Greek (alpha, beta, gamma, delta . . .) and Phoenician letter names (aleph, bayt, gimel, dalet . . .), and from the obvious similarities in letter shapes.

THE PHILISTINES

Southward along the Levantine coast from Phoenicia lay the land of the **Philistines**, descendants of the Sea Peoples defeated by Ramses III (see the map on page 62). Their bad reputation is the result of their dominance over their pastoral neighbors, the herdsmen known as the Hebrews. Because the Hebrews used writing as an effective weapon, the Philistines became the great villains of the Hebrew scriptures. Accordingly the word *philistine* has come to mean a boorish, uncultured person. And because the Philistines do not appear to have recorded their own outlook on the world, almost everything we know about them comes from the work of archaeologists or has to be sifted through the bad press of their detractors.

We know little about their language, but their material culture, behavior, and organization all exhibit close affinities with Mycenaean Greece. For example, the Philistines introduced grapevines and olive trees to the Levant from the Aegean basin. With the profits from these industries, they created powerful armies that dominated the region in the twelfth and eleventh centuries B.C.E. They also established a monopoly over metalsmithing, making it virtually impossible for their enemies to forge competitive weaponry.

Philistine power was based in five great strongholds, the so-called Pentapolis (Greek for "five cities"): Gaza, Ashkelon, and Ashdod on the coast; and the inland cities of Ekron and Gath. (Again, these citadels are strikingly similar to the fortified palaces of Mycenaean civilization.) From these strongholds, the Philistines dominated the surrounding countryside by organizing agricultural production and controlling trade routes.

THE EVOLUTION OF THE ALPHABET. This table shows how the shapes of letters changed as the Phoenician alphabet was adapted by the Hebrews, the Greeks, and eventually the Romans (from whom our modern alphabet derives).

HEBREW	PHŒNICIAN	ANCIENT GREEK	LATER GREEK	ENGLISH
א	✗✗	◁ △△△	A ᴧ	A
ב	ᕼ	∆ ∆	B	B
ג	∧∧	∧ᒐ∧c	Γ	G
ד ד	◁◁	△△▽ᑫ	ᗞ	D
ה ה ה	ᖵ	ᖴᖵ ᕮᖴᕮ	Ε Ϲ	E
ו	ᒎ	ᒉ ᖴ		F
ז	Ɀ	∑ ∑ I	Z	Z
ח	ᕼ	ᗷ ᗷ		H
ט	⊕	⊙⊗⊕◈·□	Θ	Th
י	⟆	ᒆ ᒉ	◖ I	I
כ ך	ᖔ ᖔ	ꓘ ꓘ Ӄ	K	K
ל	ᒫ ᒷ	∧√ᒋ	ᐱ	L
מ ם	ᒻ	ꙧ ꙧ Ꙣ	M	M
נ ן	ᒻᒻ	ꓬ ꓬ ᒹ	Ν	N
ס	Ꙙ Ꙙ	‡ ᕤ	Ξ	X
ע	○	⊙○◇□	○	O
פ ף	ᒉ	ᒉ Γ	Π	P
צ ץ	ᕝ	Ꝗ		Q
ק	ꟼ φ φ	ꟼφφ ꓑꓑꓑ	Ρ	R
ר ר	ꙡꙡ ꟺꟺ	ꙧꟺ ꙧᗰᗶ ᗶᑕ	∑ Ϲ	S
ת	✝✝ᒆ	⊤· ✝	Τ	T
°ץ	ꙮꙮ	OMITTED NOT BEING IN GREEK		ᴛ₃

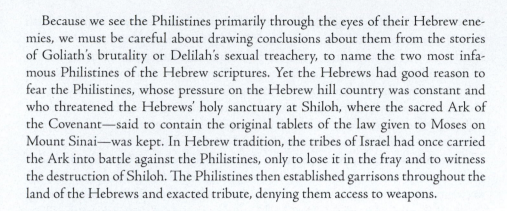

Philistines Descendants of the Sea Peoples who fled to the region that now bears the name Palestine, after their defeat at the hands of pharaoh Ramses III.

Hebrews Originally a pastoral people divided among several tribes, they were briefly united under the rule of David and his son, Solomon, who promoted the worship of a single god, Yahweh, and constructed the first temple at the new capital city of Jerusalem.

Using the Hebrew Bible as a primary source

Because we see the Philistines primarily through the eyes of their Hebrew enemies, we must be careful about drawing conclusions about them from the stories of Goliath's brutality or Delilah's sexual treachery, to name the two most infamous Philistines of the Hebrew scriptures. Yet the Hebrews had good reason to fear the Philistines, whose pressure on the Hebrew hill country was constant and who threatened the Hebrews' holy sanctuary at Shiloh, where the sacred Ark of the Covenant—said to contain the original tablets of the law given to Moses on Mount Sinai—was kept. In Hebrew tradition, the tribes of Israel had once carried the Ark into battle against the Philistines, only to lose it in the fray and to witness the destruction of Shiloh. The Philistines then established garrisons throughout the land of the Hebrews and exacted tribute, denying them access to weapons.

THE HEBREWS AND THEIR SCRIPTURES

The central feature of **Hebrew** culture, their conception of and relationship to their god, will be discussed toward the end of this chapter. In this section, we focus our attention on the historical development of Hebrew society. In reconstructing this early history, we are indebted to an unusual textual source already mentioned: a series of scriptures ("writings") that comprise mythology, laws and ritual practices, genealogical records, books of prophecy, proverbs, poetry, and royal chronicles. These are collectively known as the Hebrew Bible or (among Christians) the Old Testament.

These multiple books were composed at different times for different purposes and were only gradually assembled over many centuries, mostly by unknown authors, copyists, and editors. Some are clearly derived from ancient oral traditions; others respond to immediate challenges. Like any historical source, then, each has to be placed in a specific context and analyzed carefully.

The first five books of the Hebrew Bible are traditionally attributed to the Hebrew leader Moses. But many of the materials in these books were borrowed from other cultures, including the stories of the creation and the flood (as we saw in Chapter 1). The story of Moses's childhood draws on a legend told about the Akkadian king Sargon the Great. The laws and rituals of the patriarchs can be found in other traditions, too. Meanwhile, the story of the exodus from Egypt is fraught with contradictions. Although the later Book of Joshua claims that the Hebrews who returned from Egypt conquered and expelled the native Canaanites, archaeological and linguistic evidence suggests that the Hebrews were essentially Canaanites themselves. They may have merged with scattered refugees from Egypt in the aftermath of the Sea Peoples' invasions, but for the most part they had been continuously resident in Canaan for centuries. In sum, these first five books constitute a retrospective history whose purpose was to justify Hebrew traditions and claims to territory.

Among the other writings included in the Hebrew Bible are a group of texts that record events of the more recent past, the period we are considering now. These "historical books" are more straightforwardly verifiable, even if many details are difficult to confirm. According to the Book of Judges, the Hebrews were herdsmen who had just begun to establish permanent settlements around the time of the Philistines' arrival in the Levant. They had organized themselves into twelve tribes: clans whose families owed each other mutual aid and protection in times of war, but who frequently fought over cattle and grazing rights. Each tribe was ruled by a patriarch known as a judge, who acted as a war leader, high priest, and settler of disputes. By the middle of the twelfth century B.C.E., these tribes occupied two major territories, with those in the south calling themselves the tribes of Judah, and those in the north the tribes of Israel.

THE STRUGGLE FOR HEBREW UNITY

The Hebrew tribes thus had few occasions to work together and little experience of organized activity. This made them highly vulnerable to the power of the Philistines. Faced with the threat of extinction, the Hebrews appear to have put up desperate resistance from their bases in the hilly interior. To counter the Philistine threat effectively, however, they needed a leader. Accordingly, around 1025 B.C.E., an influential judge called Samuel selected a king, Saul, to lead the tribes of Israel against the Philistines. However, Saul proved to be an ineffective war leader. So Samuel withdrew his support from Saul and threw it behind a young man in Saul's entourage, Saul's son-in-law David, a warrior from Judah. Waging his own independent military campaigns, David achieved one triumph after another over the Philistines—that is, according to the chroniclers who wrote their accounts under David's patronage.

These same books reveal that David was a man on the make. When Saul drove him from his court, he became an outlaw and a mercenary in Philistine service. It was as a Philistine mercenary, in fact, that David fought against Saul in the climactic battle in which Saul was killed. Soon thereafter, David himself became king, first over the tribes of Judah, his home territory, and later over Saul's territory of Israel as well.

THE CONSOLIDATION OF A HEBREW KINGDOM

Around 1000 B.C.E., David strove to strengthen his authority within and beyond his kingdom. He took advantage of Egypt's decline to expand his territory southward, eventually confining the Philistines to an inconsequential narrow strip of coastal land. David also defeated the neighboring Moabites and Ammonites, extending his control to the Dead Sea. By the time of his death in 973 B.C.E., his kingdom stretched from the middle Euphrates in the north to the Gulf of Aqaba in the south, and from the Mediterranean coast into the Syrian deserts.

As David's power and prestige grew, he was able to impose on his subjects a highly unpopular system of taxation and forced labor. His goal was to build a glorious capital at Jerusalem, a Canaanite settlement that he made the central city of his realm. It was a shrewd choice, because Jerusalem had no previous affiliation with any of the twelve tribes or the ancient rivalries that divided them. It was also a geographically strategic choice, lying between the southern tribes of Judah (David's people) and the northern tribes of Israel.

David also exalted the city as a religious center by making Jerusalem the resting place of the Ark of the Covenant and elevating the priesthood of the Hebrew's chief god, Yahweh. By these measures, he sought to forge a new collective identity centered on his own family and its connections to Yahweh. To this end, he also encouraged the writing of histories and prophecies that would affirm this identity and his central role in forging it.

David promotes Hebrew identity based on worship of Yahweh

Sidon

PHOENICIA

Tyre

Litani R.

Dan

SEA OF GALILEE

Megiddo

Yarmuk R.

KINGDOM
OF ISRAEL

Samaria

Jordan R.

Zarqa R.

Shechem

MEDITERRANEAN SEA

Shiloh

Bethel

Ekron

Jericho

Ashdod

Jerusalem

Ashkelon

DEAD SEA

Gaza

Gath

Hebron

PHILISTAEA

KINGDOM
OF
JUDAH

Hasa R.

0   25   50 Miles

0   25   50 Kilometers

EUROPE

AFRICA

Area of detail

THE HEBREW KINGDOMS, c. 900 B.C.E. Notice the scale of the map and consider the comparatively small size of the Hebrews' world. **›** **What advantages did the Philistines and Phoenicians possess, geographically and otherwise?** **›** **Why did they present such a challenge to the Hebrews?** **›** **What political and religious consequences might have resulted from the division of the kingdom after the death of King Solomon, given the location of Jerusalem?**

THE REIGN OF KING SOLOMON (973–937 B.C.E.)

Continuing his father's policies, David's son Solomon built a great temple complex at Jerusalem to house the Ark. This visible support of Yahweh's cult was approved by the chronicles included in the Bible, which portray Solomon's reign as a golden age. Yet Solomon could be a ruthless and often brutal ruler. According to his own chroniclers, Solomon kept an enormous harem of some three hundred wives and seven hundred concubines, many of them drawn from subject or allied peoples. To finance his expensive tastes and projects, which recall the grand style of ancient Mesopotamian rulers, Solomon instituted oppressive taxation and imposed customs duties on the lucrative caravan trade that passed through his country. With the help of the Phoenician king of Tyre, Solomon also constructed a commercial fleet whose ships plied the waters of the Red Sea and beyond, trading—among other commodities—the gold and copper mined by Solomon's slaves.

This new wealth was bought at a high price. Solomon maintained a large standing army of unwilling conscripts from his own people. To undertake his ambitious building projects, he also required his subjects to perform forced labor four months out of every year. This level of oppression was too much for many Israelites, and the northern tribes seethed with rebellion against the royal capital.

Within a decade or so of Solomon's death, the fragile monarchy split in two. The dynasty descended from David continued to rule the southern kingdom of Judah with its capital at Jerusalem, but the ten northern tribes banded together as the kingdom of Israel, with their capital at Shechem. Archaeology, combined with accounts in the Bible, reveal that the cult of Yahweh was not yet dominant in either the north or the south, so major religious differences made reunification even more difficult. In the meantime, the changing political situation of the larger region made the Hebrew kingdoms increasingly vulnerable.

The Revival of the Assyrian Empire

The Assyrians had long played an important role in spreading trade and promoting urban settlements. But like other great powers, their civilization had been devastated by the Sea Peoples. For several centuries afterward, they struggled for survival.

Then, in the ninth century B.C.E., a brilliant but brutal ruler laid the foundations of what historians call the **Neo-Assyrian Empire**.

Under the leadership of Assurnasirpal II (*ah-sur-NAH-sur-PAHL*; 883–859 B.C.E.), the Assyrians began to conduct aggressive military campaigns against their neighbors on an annual basis. Those whom they defeated either had to pay tribute or face the full onslaught of the Assyrian war machine, which acquired a deserved reputation for savagery.

Yet Assurnasirpal and his successors inspired stiff resistance. The northern kingdom of Israel formed an alliance with other small states to halt Assyrian expansion. This coalition ultimately forced the Assyrians to settle for smaller victories against the Armenians to the northwest and the Medes to the northeast. Thereafter, a cycle of violent oppression and rebellion continued until the reign of a military commander who took the name Sargon II (722–705 B.C.E.). He claimed to be the direct successor of Sargon of Akkad, the great king of Sumer and the first great king in Mesopotamian history, nearly 1,500 years earlier (see Chapter 1).

Like the Hebrews, Sargon II and his successors skillfully deployed history as a political tool. Eventually, they extended the frontiers of the Neo-Assyrian Empire from western Iran to the shores of the Mediterranean; briefly, they even subjugated parts of Egypt. Sargon himself put an end to the kingdom of Israel in 722 B.C.E., enslaving and deporting most of the population, and he terrified the southern kingdom of Judah into remaining a loyal and quiet vassal. By the seventh century B.C.E., Assyria was the unrivaled power of the ancient region.

NEO-ASSYRIAN GOVERNMENT AND ADMINISTRATION

The Neo-Assyrian Empire was a military dictatorship, built on the ability of its army to spread terror and oppress both enemies and subjects alike. At its head was a hereditary monarch regarded as the earthly representative of the Assyrians' patron god, Assur. Supporting the empire's centralized authority was an extensive bureaucracy whose administrators formed the highest class in Neo-Assyrian society and exercised local authority on behalf of the king. They maintained lines of transport and communication, the engines of imperial hegemony, and supervised the construction of an extensive network of roads that served these needs for centuries. The Neo-Assyrian state also deployed a system of spies and messengers to report on the activities of subjects and provincial governors. Provincial governors collected tribute, recruited for the army, and administered the king's law.

Not surprisingly, for a people so mindful of historical precedent, the Neo-Assyrians modeled their laws on the Code of Hammurabi—although many of their penalties were much more severe. The harshest punishments were reserved for practices deemed detrimental to human reproduction: the penalties for same-sex relations and abortion were particularly severe. Neo-Assyrian law was also rigidly patriarchal, which entailed substantial revision of the women's rights granted in Hammurabi's code. Now, only husbands had the power of divorce and they were legally permitted to inflict a variety of penalties on their wives, ranging from corporal punishment to mutilation and death.

Neo-Assyrian Empire (883–859 B.C.E. to 612–605 B.C.E.) Assurnasirpal II laid the foundations of this oppressive empire through military campaigns in the name of its principal god, Assur. The empire eventually stretched from the Mediterranean Sea to western Iran.

Neo-Assyrian administrators serve as local authorities within the empire

THE ASSYRIAN MILITARY–RELIGIOUS ETHOS

The Assyrians' religious, political, and military ideology had taken shape during the long centuries when they fought for survival, and it then became the foundational ethos for their empire's relentless conquests. Its two fundamental tenets were the waging of holy war and the exaction of tribute through terror.

The Neo-Assyrians were convinced that their god demanded the constant expansion of his worship through military conquest. Essentially, their army belonged to Assur, and all who did not accept Assur's supremacy were his enemies. Ritual humiliation of a defeated city's gods was therefore a regular feature of conquest. Statues of conquered gods would be carried off to the Neo-Assyrian capital, where they would remain as hostages. Meanwhile, an image of Assur himself—usually represented as a sun disk with the head and shoulders of an archer—would be installed in the defeated city, and the conquered people would be required to worship him. Although conquered peoples did not have to abandon their previous gods altogether, they were made to feel their gods' inferiority. The Assyrians were therefore strict henotheists, meaning that they acknowledged the existence of other gods but believed that one god should be the supreme deity of all peoples.

Rather than defeating their foes once, the Assyrians raided their vanquished foes each year. This strategy kept the Neo-Assyrian military machine primed for battle, but it did little to inspire loyalty among subject peoples. Neo-Assyrian imperial battle tactics became notoriously savage—even by the standards of ancient warfare, in which the mutilation of prisoners, systematic rape, and mass deportations were commonplace. Moreover, the Neo-Assyrian army was not a seasonal army of part-time warriors or peasant conscripts, but a massive standing force of more than a hundred thousand soldiers. And because the Assyrians had mastered iron-smelting techniques on a large scale, they could equip their fighting men with high-quality iron weapons that overwhelmed opponents still reliant on bronze.

The organization of this army also contributed to its success. At its core were heavily armed and armored shock troops, equipped with a variety of thrusting weapons and bearing tall shields for protection. They were the main force for crushing enemy infantry in the field. To harass enemy infantry and break up their formations, the Assyrians deployed light skirmishers with slings and javelins, and they combined archery and chariotry as never before. They also developed the first true cavalry force in the West, with mounted warriors

NEO-ASSYRIAN ATROCITIES. Judean captives whose city had fallen to the Neo-Assyrian king Sennacherib (704–681 B.C.E.) are shown being impaled on stakes. This triumphal carving comes from the walls of Sennacherib's palace at Nineveh. **› What was the purpose of advertising these captives' fates?**

wielding bows or heavy lances. They even trained a highly skilled corps of combat engineers to undermine city walls and to build siege engines, battering rams, and battle towers.

THE LEGACY OF NEO-ASSYRIAN POWER

The successors of Sargon II continued these military policies while devoting great energy to promoting an Assyrian cultural legacy. Sargon's immediate successor, Sennacherib (*sen-AH-sher-ib*; 704–681 B.C.E.), rebuilt the ancient Assyrian city of Nineveh, fortifying it with a double wall for a circuit of nine miles. He constructed an enormous palace there, decorated with marble, ivory, and exotic woods; and he ordered the construction of a massive irrigation system, including an aqueduct that carried fresh water to the city from thirty miles away. His son rebuilt the conquered city of Babylon along similar lines and was also a patron of the arts and sciences. His grandson Assurbanipal (*ah-sur-BAHN-ih-pahl*; r. 669–627 B.C.E.) was perhaps the greatest of all the Neo-Assyrian kings. For a time, he ruled the entire delta region of northern Egypt and also enacted a series of internal reforms, seeking ways to govern his empire more peacefully.

By Neo-Assyrian standards, Assurbanipal was an enlightened ruler, and one to whom we owe a tremendous debt. Like Sargon II, he had a strong sense of the rich traditions of Mesopotamian history and laid claim to them. But he did this much more systematically: he ordered the construction of a magnificent library at the great capital of Nineveh, where all the cultural monuments of Mesopotamian literature were to be copied and preserved. This library was also an archive for the correspondence and official acts of the king. Fortunately, this trove of documentation has survived. Our knowledge of history, not to mention all modern editions of the *Epic of Gilgamesh*, derive from the library at Nineveh.

 Assurbanipal's library at Nineveh: a cultural legacy

When Assurbanipal died in 627 B.C.E., the Neo-Assyrian Empire appeared to be at its zenith. Its borders were secure, its kings had adorned their capitals with magnificent artwork, and the hanging gardens of Babylon were already famous: artificial slopes whose cascading flowers and trees were fed by irrigation systems that pumped water uphill, an amazing marriage of engineering and horticulture.

ASSURBANIPAL FEASTING WITH HIS WIFE IN A HANGING GARDEN. Even in this peaceful, domestic scene, the severed head of the king's recently defeated enemy, the king of Elam, can be seen hanging from the pine tree on the left.

The collapse of this empire is therefore all the more dramatic for its suddenness. Within fifteen years of Assurbanipal's reign, Nineveh lay in ruins. An alliance had formed between the Indo-European Medes of Iran and the Chaldeans, a Semitic people who controlled the southern half of Babylonia. By 605 B.C.E., the Chaldeans had occupied Babylon itself and destroyed the last remnants of Neo-Assyrian power on the upper Euphrates. In 586 B.C.E., they captured Jerusalem, destroyed the Temple, and deported the population of Judah to Babylon. Meanwhile, the Medes retired to the Iranian Plateau to extend their dominion there.

The Rise of the Persians

In the sixth century B.C.E., the **Persian Empire** emerged as the successor state to the Neo-Assyrian kings and the Chaldeans. Once the Persians had thrown off the Chaldeans' dominance, they in turn would construct the largest empire known to the world up to that time.

THE PERSIAN EMPIRE OF CYRUS THE GREAT

The Persians came to power relatively suddenly, under an extraordinary prince named Cyrus, who became the ruler of a single tribe in 559 B.C.E. Shortly thereafter, Cyrus made himself ruler of all the Persians and then, around 549 B.C.E., challenged the lordship of the Medes and began to claim dominion over lands stretching from the Persian Gulf to eastern Anatolia.

This brought the Persians into close contact with the kingdom of Lydia. The Lydians had attained great prosperity as producers of gold and silver specie (money): the first people in antiquity to use precious-metal coinage as a medium of exchange for goods and services. When Cyrus came to power, the Lydians' king was Croesus (*CREE-suhs*). Distrusting his new neighbor, Croesus decided to launch a preventive strike against the Persians. According to the Greek historian Herodotus, he took the precaution of asking the oracle of Apollo at Delphi whether this strategy was a good one, and was told that if he attacked the Persians he would destroy a great nation. The oracle's pronouncement was both ambiguous and true: the nation Croesus destroyed was his own. Cyrus defeated his forces in 546 B.C.E.

Cyrus then invaded Mesopotamia in 539 B.C.E., striking so quickly that he took Babylon without a fight. Once he was in Babylon, the entire Chaldean Empire was his for the taking. Yet his own imperial policies proved very different from those of his predecessors. Cyrus freed the Hebrews who had been held captive in Babylon since 586 B.C.E. and sent them back to Jerusalem, helping them to rebuild their temple and allowing them to set up a semi-independent vassal state. Cyrus also allowed other conquered peoples considerable self-determination,

AN EARLY LYDIAN COIN. Probably struck during the reign of Croesus, this coin was one of many that facilitated long-distance trade by making wealth portable.

especially with respect to cultural and religious practices—a marked reversal of Neo-Assyrian and Chaldean policies. When he died in battle, in 530 B.C.E., Persian expansion continued; his son conquered Egypt in 525 B.C.E. Two hundred years later, the young Alexander the Great would emulate many of Cyrus's policies and build an empire sustained by many of the same strategies (see Chapter 4).

Cyrus's new approach to conquered peoples: religious and cultural toleration

THE CONSOLIDATION OF PERSIAN RULE

Cyrus's son Cambyses II was a warrior like his father, but his death left the Persian Empire a poorly organized collection of rapid conquests. After a short period of civil war, the aristocratic inner circle that had served both him and his father settled on a collateral member of the royal family as the new king.

This was Darius, whose long reign of thirty-five years (521–486 B.C.E.) consolidated his predecessors' military gains by improving the administration of the Persian state. Darius divided the empire into provinces, each of which was administered by an official called a *satrap*. Although satraps enjoyed extensive powers, they owed fixed tributes and absolute loyalty to the central government. Adhering to the tolerant policy of Cyrus, Darius allowed the various peoples of the empire to retain most of their local customs while enforcing a standardized central currency and a system of weights and measures. Beyond this, he had little interest in imposing onerous taxes, martial law, or the Persians' own religious practices on subject peoples. After centuries of Neo-Assyrian and Chaldean tyranny, the light hand of Persian rule was welcomed throughout the empire's far-reaching lands.

Darius was also a great builder. He erected a new royal residence and ceremonial capital that the Greeks called Persepolis ("Persia City"). He ordered a canal dug from the Nile to the Red Sea to facilitate trade, and installed irrigation systems on the Persian plateau and on the fringe of the Syrian desert to increase agricultural production. Most important, Darius expanded the existing Assyrian road system to enhance trade and communications throughout his huge realm. The most famous artery was the Royal Road, stretching 1,600 miles from Susa, near the Persian Gulf, to Sardis (the former Lydian capital) near the Aegean. Government couriers along this road constituted the first postal system, carrying messages and goods in relay stages from one post to another. Each post was a day's horseback ride from the next, where a fresh horse and rider would be ready to carry the dispatches brought by the postman before him. An extensive imperial spy network also used this postal system and was the "eyes and ears of the king."

Darius expands network of roads

Darius was an extraordinarily gifted administrator, but as a military strategist he made an enormous mistake when he attempted to extend Persian hegemony into Greece. Cyrus's conquest of Lydia had made Persia the ruler of some long-established Greek-speaking cities on the western coast of Anatolia, a region called Ionia. But these cities resisted even the easy terms of Persian rule, desiring instead to model themselves on the self-governing city-states that had come into being across the Aegean. Consequently, between 499 and 494 B.C.E., the Greeks of Asia waged a war for independence and briefly gained the support of troops from Athens, who burned the Persian administrative center at Sardis.

Darius quelled this uprising and then sent a force to punish Athens and serve notice of Persian dominion over all Greek states. But, at the battle of Marathon in

A CYLINDRICAL SEAL OF DARIUS THE GREAT (521–486 B.C.E.). Seals were used in place of signatures to authenticate documents and correspondence. The cylindrical matrix (right) was rolled in soft wax to create an impression. This finely wrought example shows the king in a chariot, hunting lions with a bow. A winged representation of the god Ahura-Mazda rises above the scene.

490 B.C.E., the Athenians' victory dealt Darius the only major setback of his reign. And when his son and successor, Xerxes (*ZEHRK-zees*), attempted to avenge this humiliation in 480 B.C.E., a resistance led by both Athens and Sparta forced him to retreat and abandon his plans. (We will discuss these events at greater length in Chapter 3.)

The Persians were thus compelled to recognize that they had reached the westward limits of their expansion. Thereafter, they concentrated on their Asian possessions and used money and diplomacy to keep the Greeks in check. This was not difficult, because the Greeks' hasty union in the face of Persian hegemony was shortlived, and they were too embroiled in wars with one another to pose any threat to Persia.

In general, the richness of their culture and the tolerance they exhibited served the Persians well in maintaining their enormous empire. Unlike the Neo-Assyrian or Chaldean rulers, the Persians could count on the loyalty and even the affection of their subjects. In fact, their imperial model—the accommodation of local institutions and practices, consistent administration through a trained bureaucracy, and rapid communications between center and periphery—would be adopted by the great and lasting empires of all subsequent Western civilizations.

THE LEGACY OF ZOROASTRIANISM

The Persians' political and cultural achievements were paralleled by a spiritual one: **Zoroastrianism**. Along with Buddhism and Judaism, this important religion was one of the three major universal faiths before Christianity and Islam. Its founder was Zarathustra, known to the Greeks as Zoroaster, a Persian who probably lived shortly before 600 B.C.E. Zarathustra sought to eradicate polytheism, animal sacrifice, and magic. That is, he wanted to redefine religion as an ethical practice common to all people, rather than a set of rituals and superstitions that caused divisions among them.

> *Legacies of Persian rule* ▸

Zoroastrianism One of the three major universal faiths of the ancient world, alongside Judaism and Christianity, it was derived from the teachings of the Persian Zoroaster around 600 B.C.E. Zoroastrianism teaches that there is one supreme god in the universe, Ahura-Mazda (Wise Lord), but that his goodness will be constantly assailed by the forces of evil until the arrival of a final "judgment day."

Zoroastrianism teaches that there is one supreme god, whom Zarathustra called Ahura-Mazda, "Wise Lord." Ahura-Mazda is the essence of truth and righteousness; there is nothing wrathful or wicked about him, and his goodness extends to everyone, not just to one people or tribe. How, then, can there be evil and suffering in the world? Because, Zarathustra posited, there is a counter-deity, Ahriman, treacherous and malignant, who rules the forces of darkness. Yet Zarathustra also posited that Ahura-Mazda must be vastly stronger than Ahriman.

Later teachers and priests of Zoroastrianism, the magi (*MAHJ-eye*), placed greater emphasis on the equality of these divine forces: they insisted that Ahura-Mazda and Ahriman are evenly matched, engaged in a desperate and eternal struggle for supremacy. According to them, light will not triumph over darkness until the Last Day, when the forces of Ahura-Mazda vanquish those of Ahriman forever. This vision of the universe has proved enormously influential, informing the developing theologies of Christianity and Islam—not to mention the plots of our own science fiction, fantasy literature, and action films.

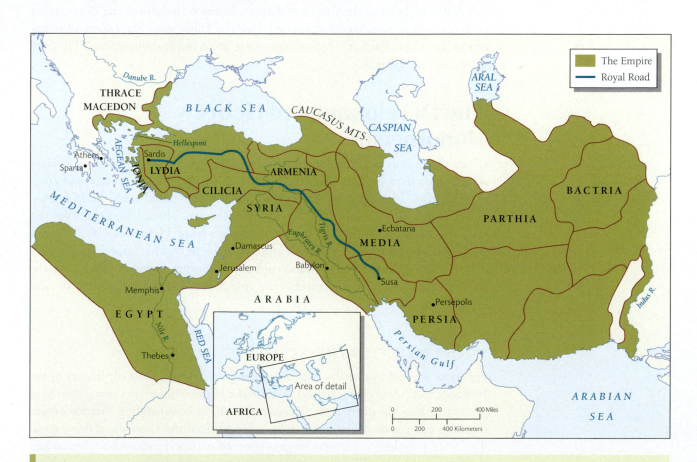

THE PERSIAN EMPIRE UNDER DARIUS I, 521–486 B.C.E. Consider the location of the Persian heartland and the four administrative centers of Persepolis, Susa, Ecbatana, and Sardis. **› What older kingdoms and empires did the Persian Empire contain? › Why is the Royal Road especially noted on this map? › How did Darius I successfully rule such a large and complex empire?**

The Persian imperial dynasty's support of Zarathustra's teachings helps to explain the tolerance of Persian rule. Unlike the Neo-Assyrians, the Chaldeans, or even the Egyptians, the Persian kings saw themselves as presiding over an assemblage of different nations whose customs and beliefs they were prepared to tolerate. Whereas Mesopotamian potentates characteristically called themselves "true king," Persian rulers took the title "king of kings" or "great king," thereby recognizing the legitimacy of other kings who ruled under their canopy.

Unlike other ancient religions, then, Zoroastrianism did not exalt the power of a godlike king or support any particular political regime. It was a personal religion, making private, spiritual demands as opposed to public, ritual ones. It posits that individuals possess free will and can choose to sin or not to sin; they are not compelled by an array of conflicting gods to act in particular ways. Zoroastrianism thus urges its adherents to choose good over evil, to be truthful, to love and help one another to the best of their powers, to aid the poor, and to practice generous hospitality. Those who do so will be rewarded in an afterlife, when the dead are resurrected on Judgment Day and consigned either to a realm of joy or to the flames of despair. In the scriptures of the Zoroastrian faith, known as the Avesta (compiled, like the Bible, over the course of many centuries), the rewards for righteousness are great but not immediate. They are spiritual, not material.

The Development of Hebrew Monotheism

Of all the important developments of the Iron Age, perhaps none is of greater significance than monotheism: the belief in a single god, the creator and ruler of all things. This development is traditionally associated with the Hebrews, but even the Hebrews were not always monotheists. Those who argued for the exclusive worship of Yahweh were a minority within Hebrew society, albeit a vocal and assertive one. How the Hebrews came to regard Yahweh as the only divine being in the universe, and to root their identity in such an exclusive religious outlook, is a phenomenon that can only be understood within its historical context.

FROM MONOLATRY TO MONOTHEISM

For those who advocated the exclusive worship of Yahweh, the early history of the Hebrews was full of embarrassments. Even the Hebrew scriptures reveal their propensity to worship many gods. Yahweh himself, in commanding that his people "have no other gods before me," clearly acknowledged the existence of other gods. The older, polytheistic Hebrew religion honored nature spirits such as Azazel and the Canaanite deity El, whose name is an important element in many Hebrew place-names (e.g., Bethel) and soon became a synonym for "god." The temple built by Solomon at Jerusalem had even included altars dedicated to Ba'al and his wife Asherah, a fertility goddess. Later Hebrew kings continued such practices, overriding the protests of religious purists devoted to Yahweh.

By the beginning of the first millennium, however, the Hebrews living under the rule of David began to promote monolatry, meaning that they exalted one god without denying the existence of others. Although the legendary prophet Moses is often credited as the first promoter of Yahweh's cult sometime around the middle of the second millennium B.C.E., the ascendancy of Yahweh really took place much later, under the influence of the Levites, a tribe who claimed unique priestly authority over Yahweh's worship and sought to enhance their own power and prestige by discrediting other gods.

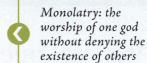

Monolatry: the worship of one god without denying the existence of others

The success of their campaign rested on the Levites' skilled use of writing. As we have frequently noted, the written word was especially potent in the ancient world because its mastery was rare. In an age of constant threats to Hebrew religious and political sovereignty, the literacy of the Levites thus helped to preserve and promote Yahweh's worship. So did the political supremacy of David's dynasty, which bolstered its own legitimacy by allying itself with the Levites. The result was a centralized cult situated in the new royal capital of Jerusalem, which attempted to link the political and the religious identity of the Hebrews with the acknowledgment of Yahweh as the supreme god.

Nevertheless, the worship of other Hebrew gods actually increased during the eighth and seventh centuries B.C.E., perhaps in reaction to the austere morality demanded and imposed by the Yahwists. One of these, Jeremiah (c. 637–587 B.C.E.), railed against "foreign" cults and warned of the disastrous consequences that would arise if Yahweh's people did not remain faithful to him. The Yahweh of this era was still imagined as a conventional god, possessing a physical body and portrayed as capricious and irascible. Further, he was not omnipotent; his power was largely confined to the territory occupied by the Hebrews.

Still, some of the Hebrews' most important contributions to subsequent Western religions crystallized during this period. One was a theology of Yahweh's transcendence: the teaching that God is not part of nature but exists outside of it. God can therefore be understood as entirely separate from the operations of the natural world. Complementing this principle was the belief that Yahweh had appointed humans to be the rulers of nature by divine mandate. In the Book of Genesis, when Yahweh orders Adam and Eve to "replenish the earth and subdue it, and have dominion over . . . every living thing," his injunction stands in striking contrast to other accounts of creation in which humans are made to serve the gods. Finally, Hebrew religious thought was moving toward the articulation of universal ethics—a universal theory of justice and righteousness. According to the Babylonian flood story, for example, a particularly petulant god destroys humanity because their noise deprives him of sleep. In Genesis, by contrast, Yahweh sends a flood in punishment for human wickedness but saves Noah and his family because "Noah was a just man."

The Hebrews honored Yahweh during this era by subscribing to certain moral precepts and taboos. The Ten Commandments as they now appear in Exodus 20:3–17 may not yet have existed in that exact form, but they certainly reflect earlier ethical injunctions against murder, adultery, lying, and greed. In addition, the Hebrews observed an array of ritual practices unusual in the ancient world, such as the circumcision of male infants, adherence to strict dietary laws, and refraining from labor on the seventh day of the week.

Two Perspectives on Imperial Rule

These two inscriptions exemplify two very different attitudes toward imperial power and two very different methods of achieving it. The first glorifies the victories of the Assyrian king Esarhaddon in Syria and is one of the most important records of his reign (681–669 B.C.E.). The second commemorates the taking of Babylon by the Persian king Cyrus the Great (c. 559–530 B.C.E.), whose empire came to encompass and surpass that of the Assyrians.

The Stele of King Esarhaddon at Senjirli, c. 680 B.C.E.

To Assur, father of the gods, lover of my priesthood, Anu mighty and preeminent, who called me by name, Ba'al, the exalted lord, establisher of my dynasty, Ea, the wise, all-knowing . . . Ishtar, lady of battle and combat, who goes at my side . . . all of them who determine my destiny, who grant to the king, their favorite, power and might . . . the king, the offering of whose sacrifices the great gods love . . . their unsparing weapons they have presented him as a royal gift . . . [he] who has brought all the lands in submission at his feet, who has imposed tribute and tax upon them; conqueror of his foes, destroyer of his enemies, the king, who as to his walk is a storm, and as to his deeds, a raging wolf; . . . the onset of his battle is powerful, he is a consuming flame, a fire that does not sink: son of Sennacherib, king of the universe, king of Assyria, grandson of Sargon, king of the universe, king of Assyria, viceroy of Babylon, king of Sumer and Akkad . . . I am powerful, I am all-powerful, I am a hero, I am gigantic, I am colossal, I am honored, I am magnified, I am without an equal among all kings, the chosen one of Assur . . . the great lord [who], in order to show to the peoples the immensity of my mighty deeds, made powerful my kingship over the four regions of the world and made my name great.

. . . Of Tirhakah, king of Egypt and Kush, the accursed . . . without cessation I slew multitudes of his men, and him I smote five times with the point of my javelin, with wounds, no recovery. Memphis, his royal city, in half a day . . . I besieged, I captured, I destroyed, I devastated, I burned with fire. . . . The root of Kush I tore up out of Egypt and not one therein escaped to submit to me.

Source: Daniel David Luckenbill, ed., *Ancient Records of Assyria and Babylonia*, vol. 2 (Chicago: 1926-27), pp. 224-27.

Inscription Honoring Cyrus, c. 539

He [the god Marduk] scanned and looked (through) all the countries, searching for a righteous ruler who would lead him. (Then) he pronounced the name of Cyrus, king of Anshan [Persia], declared him to be the leader

Yet the moral standards imposed by Yahweh on the Hebrew community were not binding when the Hebrews dealt with outsiders. Lending at interest, for example, was not acceptable among Hebrews but was quite acceptable between a Hebrew and a non-Hebrew. Such distinctions applied also to more serious issues, such as the killing of civilians in battle. When the Hebrews conquered territories in Canaan, they took "all the spoil of the cities, and every man they smote with the sword . . . until they had destroyed them." Far from having any doubts about such a brutal policy, the Hebrews believed that Yahweh had inspired the Canaanites to resist so that the Hebrews could slaughter them: "For it was the Lord's doing of the world. . . . And he (Cyrus) did always endeavor to treat according to justice the black-headed [people] whom he (Marduk) made him conquer. Marduk, the great lord, a protector of his people/worshipers, beheld with pleasure his good deeds and his upright mind, (and therefore) ordered him to march against his city Babylon. He made him set out on the road to Babylon, going at his side like a real friend. His widespread troops—their number, like the water of a river, could not be established—strolled along, their weapons packed away. Without any battle, he made them enter his town Babylon, sparing Babylon any calamity. He delivered into his hands Nabonidus, the king who did not worship him. All the inhabitants of Babylon as well as of the entire country of Sumer and Akkad, princes and governors (included), bowed to him and kissed his feet, jubilant that he (had received) the kingship, and with shining faces. Happily they greeted him as a master through whose help they had come (again) to life from death (and) had all been spared damage and disaster, and they worshiped his name.

I am Cyrus, king of the world, great king, legitimate king, king of Babylon, king of Sumer and Akkad, king of the four rims (of the earth), son of Cambyses, great king, king of Anshan, grandson of Cyrus, great king, king of Anshan, descendent of Teispes, great king, king of Anshan, of a family (which) always (exercised) kingship; whose rule Bel and Nebo love, whom they want as king to please their hearts.

When I entered Babylon as a friend and (when) I established the seat of the government in the palace of the ruler under jubilation and rejoicing. . . . My numer-

ous troops walked around Babylon in peace, I did not allow anybody to terrorize (any place) of the (country of Sumer) and Akkad. I strove for peace in Babylon and in all his (other) sacred cities. . . . I abolished the . . . [yoke] which was against their (social) standing, I brought relief to their dilapidated housing, putting (thus) an end to their (main) complaints. . . . All the kings of the entire world from the Upper to the Lower Sea, those who are seated in throne rooms, (those who) live in other (types of buildings as well as) all the kings of the West living in tents, brought their heavy tributes and kissed my feet in Babylon.

Source: Excerpted from James B. Pritchard, ed., *Ancient Near Eastern Texts Relating to the Old Testament*, 3rd ed. (Princeton, NJ: 1969), pp. 315–16.

Questions for Analysis

1. Both of these inscriptions constitute propaganda, but of different kinds. How do they differ? What audience(s) are they addressing? What function(s) does each inscription serve?

2. Each of these rulers claims to have a close relationship with the divine. How do those relationships differ? What do those differences reveal about their attitudes to kingship and its sources of power?

3. Both of these kings boast of their royal lineage and their connections to past rulers. How different or similar are these perspectives? What do they reveal about these kings' awareness of history?

to harden their hearts that they should come against Israel in battle, in order that they should be utterly destroyed, and should receive no mercy but be exterminated" (Joshua 11:20).

With the political fragmentation of the fragile Hebrew kingdom after Solomon's death, important regional distinctions arose within Yahweh's cult. The rulers of the northern kingdom of Israel discouraged their citizens from participating in ritual activities at Jerusalem—at least according to the Jerusalem-based Yahwists who shaped the biblical tradition and who wanted to represent their own Judah as the favored kingdom. The erosion of a cohesive Hebrew identity

was further accelerated by the Neo-Assyrians who, under Sargon II, absorbed the northern kingdom as a province and enslaved nearly twenty-eight thousand Hebrews.

This Neo-Assyrian threat was the whetstone on which the Yahwist prophets sharpened their demands for an exclusive monotheism. These prophets were practical political leaders as well as religious figures, and most of them understood that military resistance to the Neo-Assyrians was futile. So if the Hebrews were to survive as a people, they had to emphasize the one thing that separated them from everyone else: the worship of Yahweh and the denial of all other gods. The prophets' insistence that Yahweh alone should be exalted was thus an aggressive reaction to the equally aggressive promotion of Assur by the Neo-Assyrians.

The foremost Hebrew prophets of this era were Amos and Hosea, who preached in the kingdom of Israel before it fell to the Neo-Assyrians in 722 b.c.e.; Isaiah and Jeremiah, who preached in Judah before its fall to the Chaldeans in 586 b.c.e.; and Ezekiel and the "second Isaiah" (the Book of Isaiah had at least two different authors), who continued to preach "by the waters of Babylon" during the Hebrews' exile there. Despite some differences in emphasis, these prophets' messages consistently emphasize three core doctrines:

1. Yahweh is the ruler of the universe. He even makes use of all peoples to accomplish his purposes. The gods of other nations are false gods. There has never been and never will be more than this one god.

2. Yahweh is exclusively a god of righteousness. He wills only the good, and all evil in the world comes from humanity, not from him.

3. Because Yahweh is righteous, he demands ethical behavior from his people. Over and above ritual and sacrifice, he requires that his followers "seek justice, relieve the oppressed, protect the fatherless, and plead for the widow."

THE GODDESS ASHERAH. The Canaanite fertility goddess, Asherah, was the wife of the god Ba'al (or his father, El), but she also figures in some inscriptions as the wife of the Hebrew god Yahweh. One Hebrew king placed an image of her in the Temple of Yahweh at Jerusalem. **› Why might this be viewed as controversial—then or now?**

JUDAISM TAKES SHAPE

The Yahwists made it possible for the Hebrews to survive under Neo-Assyrian domination through their insistence on monotheism as the cornerstone of Hebrew identity, and they enjoyed political and religious triumph under King Josiah (621–609 b.c.e.) of Judah, who was a committed monotheist and whose court employed prominent prophets, including Jeremiah. Josiah presided over the redrafting and revision of the "Law of Moses" to bring it into line with current policies, and it was during his reign that the Book of Deuteronomy was "discovered" and hailed as Moses's "Second Law." Deuteronomy is the most stridently monotheistic book of the Hebrew Bible, and it was probably composed at this time to lend weight to this new political program.

But within a generation of Josiah's death, the Chaldeans under Nebuchadnezzar conquered Jerusalem, destroyed the Temple, and carried thousands of Hebrews off to Babylon in 587/586 B.C.E. This Babylonian Captivity brought many challenges, paramount among them the maintenance of the Hebrews' hard-won religious identity. The leading voices in defining that identity continued to be the Yahwists, who would also spearhead the return to Jerusalem two generations later, after Cyrus captured Babylon and liberated the Hebrews. Among the Yahwists, the prophet Ezekiel stressed that salvation could be found only through religious purity, which meant ignoring all foreign gods and acknowledging only Yahweh. Kingdoms and states and empires came to nothing in the long run, Ezekiel said. What mattered for those living in exile was the creature God had made in his image—man—and the relationship between God and his creation.

This period of captivity and exile was therefore decisive in forging a universal religion that transcended politics. Just as Yahweh existed outside creation, so the people who worshiped him could exist outside a Hebrew kingdom. In Babylon, the worship of Yahweh therefore became something different; it became **Judaism**, a religion that was not tied to any particular political system or territory, for there was neither a Hebrew ruling class nor a Hebrew state after 586 B.C.E. Outside of Judah, Judaism flourished and became the crucial factor in the emergence of a new Jewish identity. This was an unparalleled development in the ancient world: the survival of a religion that had no political power to back it and no holy place to ground it.

When Cyrus conquered Babylon and allowed the Hebrews to return to their lands, Jerusalem became once again the central holy place of their religious life— although many Hebrews remained and flourished in Persia, while others had long since settled in Egypt. Thereafter, Judaism would be promulgated by a new generation of Jews, particularly the prophet Ezra, who is credited with bringing the strict interpretation and application of the Torah from Persia to Jerusalem; and Nehemiah, the Persian-appointed governor of Judea who began the process of rebuilding the Temple. Eventually, the monotheistic religion that emerged from these historical processes would become common to the worldview of all Western civilizations.

Judaism The religion of the Hebrews as it developed in the centuries after the establishment of the Hebrew kingdoms under David and Solomon, especially during the period of Babylonian Captivity.

Conclusion

The centuries between 1700 and 500 B.C.E. were an epoch of empires. Although the two great powers of the second millennium were New Kingdom Egypt and the Hittite Empire in Anatolia, a host of lesser empires also coalesced during this period, including Minoan Crete, Mycenaean Greece, and the trading empire of the Assyrians. All were sustained by a sophisticated network of trade and diplomacy. But between 1200 and 1000 B.C.E. the devastation wrought by the Sea Peoples destroyed this integrated civilization. These invasions cleared the way for the emergence of many new, small states, including those of the Phoenicians, the Philistines, the Hebrews, and the Lydians. Many crucial cultural and economic developments were fostered by these small states, including alphabetic writing, coinage, mercantile colonization, and monotheism. But the dominant states of the Iron Age continued to be great land empires centered in western Asia: first that of the Neo-Assyrians, then briefly the Chaldeans, and finally the Persians.

Yet the empires of the early Iron Age were quite different from those that had dominated the ancient world a thousand years before. These new powers were much more highly unified. They had capital cities, centrally managed systems of communication, sophisticated administrative structures, and ideologies that justified their aggressive imperialism. They commanded armies of unprecedented size, and they demanded from their subjects a degree of obedience impossible for any Bronze Age emperor to imagine or enforce. Their rulers declared themselves the chosen instruments of their god's divine will.

At the same time, we can trace the emergence of more personalized religions. Zoroastrian dualism and Hebrew monotheism added an important new emphasis on

AFTER YOU READ THIS CHAPTER

CHRONOLOGY

1900–1500 B.C.E.	Minoan civilization flourishes
1800–1400 B.C.E.	Formation of the Hittite Empire
1792 B.C.E.	Rise of Babylon under Hammurabi
1650–1550 B.C.E.	Hyksos invasion of Egypt and Second Intermediate Period
1600–1200 B.C.E.	Mycenaean civilization flourishes
1550–1075 B.C.E.	New Kingdom of Egypt established
C. 1200 B.C.E.	Invasions of the Sea Peoples begin
1100–1000 B.C.E.	Philistine dominance in Palestine
1000–973 B.C.E.	Hebrew kingdom consolidated
924 B.C.E.	Israel and Judah divided
883–859 B.C.E.	Neo-Assyrian Empire founded
722 B.C.E.	Kingdom of Israel destroyed
612–605 B.C.E.	Fall of the Neo-Assyrian Empire
586 B.C.E.	Fall of the kingdom of Judah
539–486 B.C.E	Persian Empire consolidated

REVIEWING THE OBJECTIVES

❯ The settlement of Indo-European peoples in the Near East had marked effects on the older civilizations there. What were some major consequences?

❯ Egypt's New Kingdom differed profoundly from the Old and Middle Kingdoms that preceded it. Why was this the case?

❯ The civilizations of the Late Bronze Age were bound together by transnational networks. What were the strengths and fragilities of these relationships?

❯ What kingdoms and empires emerged in the ancient world after the devastation caused by the Sea Peoples?

❯ Monotheism was a significant historical development of the first millennium B.C.E. Why is it so important?

ethical conduct, and both pioneered the development of authoritative written scriptures that advanced religious teachings. Zoroastrianism, despite its radical reimagining of the cosmos, proved fully compatible with imperialism and became the driving spiritual force behind the Persian Empire. Judaism, by contrast, was forged in the struggle to resist the imperialism of the Neo-Assyrians and Chaldeans. Both systems of belief would exercise enormous influence on future civilizations. In particular, they provided the models on which Christianity and Islam would ultimately erect their own traditions, just as models of imperial governance forged in this period would become the template for future empires. In Chapter 3, we will look at the ways in which the city-states of ancient Greece both built on and departed from these models.

 Go to **INQUIZITIVE** to see what you've learned—and learn what you've missed—with personalized feedback along the way.

PEOPLE, IDEAS, AND EVENTS IN CONTEXT

❯ How did the Hittite Empire integrate the cultures of **INDO-EUROPEANS** with the older civilizations of this region?

❯ What do the reigns of **HATSHEPSUT** and **AKHENATEN** tell us about the continuities and limitations of pharaonic power?

❯ What factors produced the transnational networks of the Late **BRONZE AGE**?

❯ How did the civilizations of **MINOAN CRETE** and **MYCENAEAN GREECE** differ from one another and from neighboring civilizations?

❯ In what ways do the **PHOENICIANS**, the **PHILISTINES**, and the **HEBREWS** exemplify three different approaches to state building at the beginning of the first millennium B.C.E.?

❯ What was new about the **NEO-ASSYRIAN EMPIRE**? How do its methods of conquest and its military-religious ethos compare with those of the **PERSIAN EMPIRE** that followed it?

❯ How and why did monotheism develop in the Hebrew kingdoms? In what ways might **JUDAISM** have been influenced by **ZOROASTRIANISM**?

THINKING ABOUT CONNECTIONS

❯ In the religions of Akhenaten, the Persians, and the Hebrews, we see a rejection of polytheism. What cultural factors may have contributed to this? What would you consider to be the long-term effects of monotheism as a motivating force in history?

❯ What patterns of success or failure appear to be emerging when we consider the empires that flourished in the Iron Age, particularly those of the Assyrians and the Persians? Are similar patterns visible in other periods of history, including our own?

The Civilization of Greece, 1000–400 B.C.E.

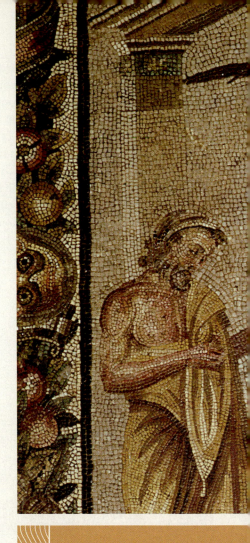

BEFORE YOU READ THIS CHAPTER >

IN THE FIFTH CENTURY B.C.E., a Greek-speaking subject of the Persian Empire began to write a book. He had been to Egypt and the African coast, the Greek colonies of Italy, the wilds of Thrace, and all over the Aegean. He had collected stories about peoples even farther afield, in Ethiopia, India, and the Black Sea. We have already met this traveler, Herodotus (c. 484–c. 425 B.C.E.), who marveled at the pyramids (see Chapter 1) and told how the king of Lydia lost his power (see Chapter 2). His motive was to write a history of recent events, as he put it, "with the aim of preventing the great and wonderful deeds of both Greeks and barbarians from losing their glory; and in particular to examine the causes that made them fight one another."

Herodotus's fascination with the Persians and Egyptians underscores the extent to which all Greek-speakers regarded themselves as different. While they struggled to cooperate politically, they were able to forge a common language and culture distinct from those whom they called *barbarians*: peoples whose speech, to Greek ears, sounded like gibberish ("bar-bar-bar"). Greeks also valued individual liberty, participatory government, artistic innovation, and confidence in the powers of the human mind. Our own civilization would be unimaginable without the political experiments and cultural achievements of ancient Greece.

> The emergence of democracy in the ancient Greek world was dependent on specific historical circumstances, which included reliance on slavery and the exclusion of women from public life. It therefore differs markedly from the political system(s) described as democratic today.

> Although the various Greek *poleis* did not share a common political structure, they shared a strong sense of identity and were united by their language and culture.

> The Athenians' empire and their leadership in the Persian Wars enabled them to dominate the Mediterranean and also, through the use of writing, to influence our understanding of their role in history.

> The cultural achievements of the fifth century B.C.E. glorified the individual male citizen and his role in the community.

CORE OBJECTIVES

> **DESCRIBE** the factors that led to the emergence of the Greek polis.

> **EXPLAIN** the importance of hoplite warfare and its effects on democracy and military tactics.

> **DEFINE** the key differences among the poleis of Athens, Sparta, and Miletus.

> **IDENTIFY** the ways in which Athenian culture, philosophy, and art reflect democratic ideals.

> **UNDERSTAND** the impact of the Persian and Peloponnesian Wars on Greek civilization.

aristocracy From the Greek word meaning "rule of the best," a new type of social class based on wealth rather than one's birth or achievements in warfare. These men saw their wealth as a reflection of their superior qualities and tended to emulate the heroes of old.

Homer (fl. Eighth century B.C.E.) A Greek rhapsode credited with merging centuries of poetic tradition in the epics known as the *Iliad* and the *Odyssey*.

Increased trade leads to development of a new social class based on wealth

From Chaos to Polis

By the end of the twelfth century B.C.E., Mycenaean civilization had vanished (see Chapter 2). Except at Athens, the great citadels of the mainland kingdoms had been destroyed. The population sharply declined and settlements moved inland, cutting themselves off from trade and communication. The use of writing also declined, to such an extent that the knowledge of Linear B disappeared.

The harsh realities of life in this era profoundly shaped the new civilization that emerged from it, which would emphasize male political equality, modest display, and self-sufficiency: the principles basic to early democracies. This new reality also had long-term effects on religion and philosophy, because the hardships of daily life contrasted sharply with the stories of a heroic and opulent past. Although worship of their gods continued to be central to Greek civic life, the power of individual human beings was celebrated, too—so long as excessive pride, *hubris*, did not anger the gods.

HOMER AND THE HEROIC TRADITION

Around 1000 B.C.E., the disruption of the transnational networks that had contributed to the isolation of Greece was alleviated by a period of relative peace. Standards of living improved and increased contact fostered trade. New techniques made Greek pottery a sophisticated and sought-after commodity that could be exchanged for luxury goods from abroad. The personal fortunes of those who engaged in commerce increased accordingly, leading to a new form of social status based on wealth, rather than on warfare or noble birth—as had been the case in the distant past. Members of this new economic class justified their preeminence as a reflection of their own superior qualities as *aristoi* ("best men"). Yet wealth in itself was not sufficient to this **aristocracy**, the "rule of the best." They were also expected to emulate the heroes of old, whose stories lived in the prodigious memories of the singers of tales.

These guardians of a rich oral history were part poets and part *rhapsodes* ("weavers of songs"). The most famous is the legendary **Homer**, credited with having woven together the stories we know as the *Iliad* and the *Odyssey*. They crystallized around 800 B.C.E., at about the time when Hesiod was working on shorter lyrics about daily life (see Chapter 2), and they constitute vast encyclopedias of Bronze Age lore. They tell of the days when Agamemnon ruled in Mycenae and launched an expedition to conquer Troy, whose prince Paris had taken Helen, the ravishing wife of Agamemnon's brother, Menelaus of Sparta. They tell of Achilles and his Trojan rival, Hector; they tell of Odysseus the wayfarer.

Like the much older Epic of Gilgamesh (Chapter 1), these Greek epics preserve long-standing traditions. As a result, they are of tremendous value to historians but they also offer significant analytical challenges. Although the events described in them date from the late Bronze Age, the society they reflect is more like that of Homer's contemporaries, half a millennium later. Treating these epics as sources, therefore, requires the historian to work like an archaeologist, carefully peeling back layers of meaning.

For example, Homer depicts a world in which competition and status are of paramount importance, just as they were to the aristocrats of his own day. Through the exchange of gifts and hospitality, men sought to create strong ties of guest friendship (*xenia, zeh-NEE-ah*) and to construct networks of influence that would support their ambitions. Indeed, it is almost impossible to overestimate the importance of guest friendship as a sacred institution, as illustrated by the encounter between the wandering Odysseus and the young princess Nausicaa (see page 82).

However, the practice of guest friendship and the shared sense of a common culture among aristocratic households did not lessen the competition that frequently led to violence. (The Trojan War, after all, was caused because Paris violated the holy ties of guest friendship by seducing the wife of his host.) It also led to competition over the epic past, as fledgling aristocratic clans vied to claim descent from one or another legendary hero. A hero cult might begin when an important family claimed an impressive Mycenaean tomb as that of their own famous ancestor, someone named in the *Iliad* and said to come from that place. They would then develop a tradition of practicing sacrifices and other rites at the tomb. This devotion would extend to their followers and dependents; eventually, an entire community might come to identify with the famous local hero. The heroic ideal thus became a deeply ingrained feature of Greek society, as did the stories the epics preserved and propagated.

THE RISE OF THE POLIS

The ninth century B.C.E. saw dramatic changes throughout the Aegean. Contacts between Greeks and Phoenicians intensified, and the Greeks adopted the Phoenician alphabet, since the Linear B of the Mycenaeans had become obsolete. The Phoenicians also pointed the way to the revival of a lost art among the Greeks: seafaring. After the devastation of the Late Bronze Age, Greek vessels hugged the shoreline and traveled only short distances. By the tenth century, however, Greeks were copying Phoenician designs for merchant vessels to travel throughout the Mediterranean. As commercial activity increased, Greek communities began to move back to the shores of the sea and to outlying islands, as well as to the western coast of Anatolia, which they called Ionia.

These developments were also sparked by dramatic growth of the Greek population, which placed heavy demands on the environmental resources of a mountainous country with limited agricultural land. As smaller villages grew into towns, inhabitants of rival communities came into more frequent contact and some degree of cooperation among them became necessary. But long centuries of isolation did not make such cooperation easy: each community treasured its autonomy, celebrated its own rituals, and honored its own heroes. How could disparate communities unite?

The solution was the ***polis***, the root from which we derive *politics*. To the Greeks, the polis was a social grouping of people who shared an identity—"the Athenians," "the Spartans," or "the Thebans"—rather than a place. Membership in the polis came to be so essential that Aristotle would later define man as "a political animal": someone whose identity depends on the polis.

Most *poleis* (the plural of *polis*) combined legal institutions with informal customs that could differ widely. They were usually organized around a social center known as the *agora* ("marketplace"), where business was conducted in the open air. Surrounding this was the urban settlement, the *asty*, and beyond the *khora*, "land." The khora of a large polis might support several other towns or smaller poleis, as

Greeks draw on Phoenician culture: (1) Alphabet

(2) Seafaring

The Obligations of Hospitality: The Encounter of Odysseus and Nausicaa

Before the emergence of the Greek poleis, relations among communities depended largely on the personal connections made among leading families of different settlements. Often founded on the exchange of gifts or hospitality, the resulting bonds of guest friendship imposed serious obligations on those involved in such relationships—and on their heirs. Most such friendships were formed between men, but in the following excerpt from the Odyssey, *we watch as the shipwrecked Odysseus, naked and frightened, is rescued by a young princess, Nausicaa (now-SIC-ah-ah), whose name means "Ship-Burner." As a woman who gives him a new life, she becomes his second mother, despite her youth.*

"What is this country I have come to now?
Are all the people wild and violent, or good, hospitable,
    and god-fearing?
I heard the sound of female voices. Is it nymphs, who fre-
    quent the craggy mountaintops, and river streams and
    meadows lush with grass? Or could this noise I hear be
    human voices? I have to try to find out who they are."
Odysseus jumped up from out the bushes.
Grasping a leafy branch he broke it off to cover up his
    manly private parts.
Just as a mountain lion trusts its strength, and beaten
    by the rain and wind, its eyes burn bright as it attacks
    the cows or sheep, or wild deer, and hunger drives it
    on to try the sturdy pens of sheep—so need impelled
    Odysseus to come upon the girls with pretty hair,
    though he was naked.

All caked with salt, he looked a dreadful sight.
They ran along the shore quite terrified, some here,
    some there. But Nausicaa stayed still.
Athena made her legs stop trembling and gave her
    courage in her heart. She stood there.

***

His words were calculated flattery.
"My lady, please! Are you divine or human?
If you are some great goddess from the sky, you look
    like Zeus' daughter Artemis—you are as tall and
    beautiful as she.
But if you live on earth and are a human, your mother
    and your father must be lucky, your brothers also—
    lucky three times over.
Their hearts must be delighted, seeing you, their flour-
    ishing new sprout, the dancers' leader.

well as numerous villages; for example, all the free male residents of the territory of Attica were citizens of Athens. Thus the vast majority of Athenian citizens were farmers who might come to the asty and agora only at certain times of the year.

The Greeks described this process of urbanization as the "bringing together of dwellings" (*synoikismos,* synoecism). Polis formation could also come about through the conquest of one settlement by another and/or through the gradual alliance of neighboring communities. Some poleis took shape around fortified hilltops, such as the Athenian acropolis (literally, "the high *polis*"). Other communities grew around a temple precinct. In many Greek cities, however, temples may have been a *consequence* of polis formation rather than a cause, as elites competed with one another to exalt their poleis and glorify themselves.

And that man will be luckiest by far, who takes you home with dowry, as his bride.

***

I am in awe of you, afraid to touch your knees. But I am desperate. I came from Ogygia, and for twenty days storm winds and waves were driving me, adrift until yesterday some god washed me up right here, perhaps to meet more suffering. I think my troubles will not end until the gods have done their all. My lady, pity me.

Battered and wrecked, I come to you, you first—and I know no one else in this whole country.

Show me the town, give me some rags to wear, if you brought any clothes when you came here."

***

Then white-armed Nausicaa replied, "Well, stranger, you seem a brave and clever man; you know that Zeus apportions happiness to people, to good and bad, each one as he decides.

Your troubles come from him, and you must bear them.

But since you have arrived here in our land, you will not lack for clothes or anything a person needs in times of desperation.

I will show you the town. The people here are called Phaeacians, and I am the daughter of the great King Alcinous, on whom depends the strength and power of our people."

And then she called her slaves with braided hair. "Wait, girls! Why are you running from this man?

Do you believe he is an enemy?

No living person ever born would come to our Phaeacia with a hostile mind, since we are much beloved by the gods.

Our island is remote, washed round by sea; we have no human contact. But this man is lost, poor thing. We must look after him.

All foreigners and beggars come from Zeus, and any act of kindness is a blessing.

So give the stranger food and drink, and wash him down in the river, sheltered from the wind."

Source: From *The Odyssey*, translated by Emily Wilson (New York: 2018), pp. 201–203.

Questions for Analysis

1. Read Nausicaa's response to Odysseus carefully. Does she know that he is trying to flatter her? What does she mean when she says that his troubles come from the god Zeus?

2. Who seems to have the most power in this encounter? Explain your reasoning.

3. Does the initial description of Odysseus strike you as humorous? Why might the poet want to portray him as slightly ridiculous?

The Culture of Archaic Greece, 800–500 B.C.E.

Scholars associate the Archaic ("early") Period of Greek history with the emergence of the polis and the renewed use of writing, which the Greeks would put to a wide variety of uses. The Athenians, in particular, used writing as a way of establishing their cultural dominance over other Greek poleis by controlling the inscription of the Homeric canon, promoting the work of poets and dramatists, and fostering the writing of prose histories. It is therefore important to bear in mind that much of what we know about this period derives from the work of authors who wrote from this Athenian perspective: these include the Ionian-born Herodotus, who spent much of his later life in

Athens; the historians Thucydides (c. 460–395 B.C.E.) and Xenophon (430–354 B.C.E.); and the philosophers Plato (c. 428–348 B.C.E.) and his pupil Aristotle (384–322 B.C.E.).

Greeks draw on Phoenician culture: (3) Patterns of colonial settlements

COLONIZATION AND PANHELLENISM

During the eighth and seventh centuries B.C.E., small-scale Greek trading ventures gradually developed into full-fledged mercantile settlements that followed the example of the Phoenicians. Many larger poleis competed to establish trading colonies, with Athens and Corinth being particularly successful. Although each new colony was an independent entity, it sustained strong familial and emotional ties to its mother polis; even if it had no formal obligations to that polis, it was often called to support it and could become entangled in its political and military affairs. At the same time, these Greek colonies were also unified by their shared language and heritage, creating a Panhellenic ("all-Greek") culture that stretched from the Black

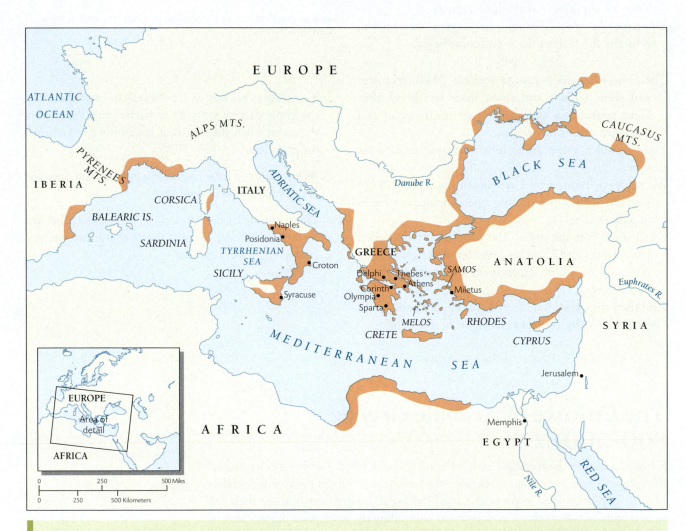

GREEK COLONIZATION, c. 550 B.C.E. Compare this map with that on page 58. › How do you account for the differences in Greek and Phoenician patterns of colonization? › Were Greek colonies likely to compete with Phoenician colonies? › Where were such conflicts most likely to erupt?

Sea (parts of modern Romania, Ukraine, and Russia) to the southern coastlines of modern France and Spain.

This process of colonization permanently altered the cultural geography of the Mediterranean. The western shores of Anatolia (modern Turkey) would remain a stronghold of Greek culture for the next two thousand years. So many Greeks migrated to southern Italy that later Romans called the region Magna Graecia, "Greater Greece," and Greek-speaking communities would survive there into the twentieth century. By the fourth century b.c.e., more Greeks lived in Magna Graecia than in Greece itself.

Motives for migration and colonization varied. A polis such as Corinth was blessed by its strategic location on the land bridge between Attica and the Peloponnesus (*pel-oh-poh-NEE-suhs*), the peninsula of mainland Greece, but cursed by the poverty of its land. Trade therefore became the lifeblood of the ruling aristocracy, which bankrolled the ambitious planting of colonies up the coast of the Adriatic and into Sicily. Other poleis, confronted by growing populations and political unrest, sponsored new colonies as outlets for unwanted multitudes.

Colonial expansion intensified Greek contacts with other cultures. Phoenician pottery brought new artistic motifs and mythological figures into Greece, while Egyptian artists profoundly influenced early Greek sculptural representations (see **Interpreting Visual Evidence** on page 87). However, these contacts also sharpened Greeks' awareness of their own identity as Hellenes: the Greeks' name for themselves. Hellenism did not usually lead to greater political cooperation, but it did encourage the establishment of Panhellenic festivals, such as the Olympic Games, as well as shared holy sites.

Colonization helps crystallize Hellenic identity

The most important of these was the temple of Apollo at Delphi, home to the oracle of the sun god. Suppliants would offer gifts to the shrine and then wait while the god spoke through his priestess, whose mysterious answers to their questions would be translated into enigmatic Greek by an attending priest. The resulting advice was essentially a riddle that called for further interpretation on the part of the recipient—who often misconstrued it. As we saw in Chapter 2, Croesus of Lydia thought he was following the oracle's advice when he attacked the Persians; but the great nation she had promised that he would destroy was his own.

At the Olympic Games, Greeks honored the king of the gods, Zeus, near his giant temple at Olympia. Greek historians dated events by olympiads, the four-year periods between games. Only Hellenes were permitted to participate in these sacred athletic contests, and all wars among Greeks ceased while they took place. A victory brought great prestige and the victor would be catapulted to a position of social and political power in his polis. As a result, these games increased competition among poleis. Yet they also strengthened the Greeks' belief in their superior culture.

HARNESSING THE POWER OF THE HORSE

Horses are now common on all continents except Antarctica, but in antiquity they could be found only on the Eurasian steppes. From this region, wild horse populations were gradually domesticated and interbred to yield the modern horse (*Equus caballus*). This animal's global spread testifies to its extraordinarily close relationship with humans, who in turn became dependent on it: as a source of milk, meat, hides; as a draft animal; as the engine that powered chariots; and finally as a mount. Horses were first harnessed for riding on the plains of western Asia and, as we will see, they became crucial to the armies of the Persian Empire.

A CHARIOTEER AND HIS TEAM RACING AT THE OLYMPIC GAMES. Chariot racing was the most prestigious and expensive event at the Olympics, since only the very wealthy could afford to maintain and transport a racing team. All the glory of a win accordingly went to the owner, not the charioteer or trainer. Since women were forbidden to compete at the Olympics, sponsoring a team was the only way that a woman could claim an Olympic victory.

 Consequences of hoplite revolution in politics

They also became essential to the new Greek aristocracy in the course of the eighth century B.C.E. Whereas Homeric heroes had ridden into battle on chariots, their later imitators were *hippeis* ("horsemen") constituting the first cavalries. Chariots, while virtually useless on the rocky terrain of Greece, were still beautifully adapted to a new type of sporting event: the first four-horse chariot race is attested at Olympia in 680 B.C.E., and chariot racing would become wildly popular in the Roman Empire, too. And since breeding, raising, and training horses was expensive, owning a horse—or a team of horses—was the ultimate sign of wealth and status.

HOPLITE WARFARE: A MILITARY AND POLITICAL REVOLUTION

Common men, fighting on foot, had played a very minor role in ancient warfare. But just as new cavalries were being formed by the aristocracy, a revolution in military tactics was making their dominance ineffective. The defense of a polis increasingly required a standing militia, not just a band of elite warriors. Able-bodied citizens who could afford to equip themselves for battle became known as **hoplites**, from the large round shield (*hoplon*) each carried. The shield was one element in a *panoply* (complete hoplite outfit) consisting of a spear, short sword, breastplate, helmet, and sometimes leather greaves and wrist-guards.

In battle, hoplites stood shoulder to shoulder in a close formation called a *phalanx*, several columns across and several rows deep, with each hoplite carrying his shield on the left arm to protect the unshielded right side of the man next to him. In his right hand, he carried a spear or sword, so that an approaching phalanx presented

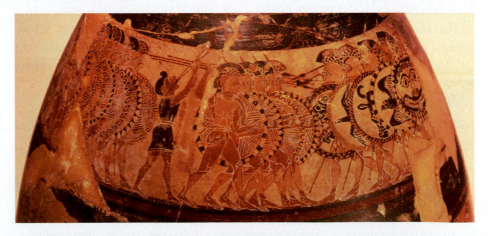

HOPLITE INFANTRY ADVANCING INTO COMBAT. This Corinthian vase, dating from around 650 B.C.E., displays the earliest known depiction of hoplites fighting in a phalanx formation.

The Ideal of Male Beauty

The Greek word *kouros* ("young man" or "youth") is now applied to a whole series of life-size statues from the Archaic Period. The one shown here comes from Anavyssos in Attica and was made between 540 and 515 B.C.E. (It is now in the National Archaeological Museum of Athens.) Although scholars used to believe that such statues were meant to represent the god Apollo, further research has shown that most were made to commemorate the dead, especially young warriors who had fallen in battle. This one appears to be walking forward, smiling, but his eyes are closed. The accompanying inscription reads: "Stop and show your pity here for Kroisos, now dead, who once fighting in the foremost ranks of battle was destroyed by raging Ares."

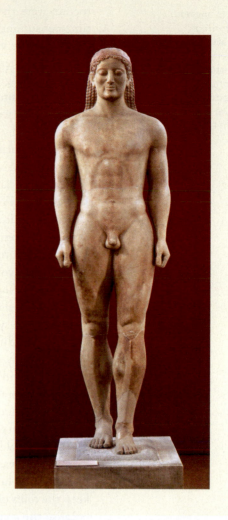

Questions for Analysis

1. What aspects of the body does the kouros emphasize? If this is intended to be a model of Greek manhood, what values would it convey to contemporary youths?

2. Is this a representation of the young man as he was when living or in death? How do your conclusions about the ideal of male beauty change if this is a glorification of death?

---

a nearly impenetrable wall of armor and weaponry. If a man in the front rank fell, the one behind him stepped up to take his place, each soldier aiding the assault by leaning with his shield into the man in front.

This tight formation relied on a single shared skill: the will to stay together. As long as the phalanx remained intact, it was nearly unbeatable. But like the polis itself, it could fall apart if its men were not committed to a common goal. The "hoplite revolution" was therefore bound up with a parallel revolution in politics. As a polis came to need the resources of more and more citizens, it had to offer them a larger share in political power. Any free man who could afford the requisite panoply thus became a man with political and social standing.

ARISTOCRACY, TYRANNY, AND DEMOCRACY

Until the sixth century B.C.E., the aristocratic classes controlled most Greek poleis. Struggles for influence among competing families were therefore commonplace,

hoplite A Greek foot-soldier armed with a spear or short sword and protected by a large round shield (*hoplon*). In battle, hoplites stood shoulder to shoulder in a close formation called a *phalanx*.

democracy In ancient Greece, this form of government allowed a class of propertied male citizens to participate in the governance of their polis; but it excluded women, slaves, and citizens without property from the political process.

and these rivalries affected polis government at every level, not least because aristocrats were the only members of society who could afford to hold unpaid and time-consuming political offices.

The aristocrats also cultivated a distinctive lifestyle. Participating in politics was part of this lifestyle. So too was the *symposium*, literally "drinking party": an intimate gathering at which elite men would enjoy wine, poetic competition, performances by trained dancers and acrobats, and the company of *hetaeras* (courtesans) who provided witty conversation, music, and the promise of sex. Respectable women were excluded, as they were from most other aspects of social life (see page 103). So too were nonaristocratic men. The symposium was thus an arena for the display of aristocratic masculinity.

The glorification of male sexuality was another important aspect of this homosocial culture. Typically, a man in his late twenties, who had just begun to make his career in political life, would take as his lover and protégé an aristocratic youth in his early to midteens. The two would form an intimate bond that included sexual intercourse. This intimate relationship could benefit both partners and their families, and it allowed the younger to make valuable connections and alliances. Many later philosophers, including Plato, argued that true love could exist only between two such equal men. Sexual relationships between men of unequal status were considered illicit.

A complex system of values and practices thus shaped aristocratic identity. As a result, it was difficult for those outside this elite world to participate fully in public life. Eventually, in many poleis, the circle of the aristocratic elite tightened further, and smaller and smaller groups dominated higher offices. This meant that even many aristocrats were left on the outside, looking in. For them, one remedy lay close at hand: they could form an alliance with the rising class of hoplites, who resented their exclusion from political power. Occasionally, with the backing of the hoplites, a single aristocrat would succeed in setting up an alternative form of government, a *tyranny*.

A tyrant was not necessarily an abusive ruler. If he sought the support of the hoplite class, he would have to extend it further political rights while striving to keep the reins of power in his own hands. This was an inherently unstable situation because the continuance of tyranny became an obstacle to even greater power for the hoplites, who would then work to overthrow it. For this reason, tyrannies rarely lasted for more than two generations and could drive the transition from aristocracy to a more participatory form of government: **democracy**.

Our ideas and practices of democracy are quite different from those of the ancient Greeks. Indeed, the philosopher Aristotle dismissed this form of government as "mob rule" because it gave too much power to the *demos*, a word meaning "neighborhood" or "affinity group." He saw it as a system too easily controlled by a particular faction, under the influence of a demagogue ("leader of the *demos*"). Our ideal of democracy is closer to what Aristotle would call a polity, direct governance by the polis as a whole.

THE POWER OF POETRY

Although aristocrats admired the heroic ideals of an earlier age, they also expressed their own unique culture in newer poetic forms. The most characteristic is the lyric, a series of rhythmic verses sung to the music of the lyre. Because these songs were composed orally, even improvised, few survive. Those that do are valuable sources because they reveal the immediate interests of their audiences and are often politically charged, sexually explicit, or daringly subversive. For example, Archilochus of Paros (c. 680–640 B.C.E.) flouts the conventions of epic poetry by mocking his own failures on the battlefield: "Some barbarian hefts my shield, since I had to abandon it / . . . but I escaped, so it scarcely matters / . . . I can get another just as good." So much for the heroic ideal of returning either with one's shield or on it! In another lyric, Archilochus berates his faithless (female) lover and his even more faithless (male) lover, with whom she has an affair.

Given the male domination of Greek culture, it is therefore surprising that the most famous poet of this age was a woman, Sappho (*SAF-foh*; c. 620–550 B.C.E.), who lived in the polis of Mytilene on the island of Lesbos. Sappho composed songs for a wide array of occasions and moods: songs of courtship and marriage, longing and desire, loss and old age. Sometimes her lyrics seem addressed to men, but more often they are passionately dedicated to women: both those whom Sappho loved and the historical women who occupy the margins of masculine epic.

In one song, Sappho compares herself with Agamemnon, who was able to return from Troy only after he prayed to Hera; Sappho now prays that her beloved, too, will arrive safely with the goddess's help. In another, she imagines a scene not included in the *Iliad*, the joyous wedding of Hector and his bride, Andromache—made more poignant by listeners' foreknowledge of the legendary couple's terrible fate (Hector's death at the hands of Achilles and Andromache's rape and enslavement at the hands of the victorious Greeks). The intimacy of lyric thus reveals what few other sources from antiquity are able to convey: the distinctive feelings and desires of individuals who were often at odds with the dominant culture of their time.

Portraits of Three Poleis

There were some one thousand poleis, and about most of them we know almost nothing. But at least we can survey some of the features that, with variations, they held in common. Here, we examine three interesting examples: Athens and Sparta, on the Greek mainland; and Miletus, on the Ionian coast of Anatolia.

ATHENS

In Greek, the name of this city, **Athens**, is the same as that of its patron goddess Athena, the wise and warlike daughter of Zeus. When the Athenians first came together to form a polis, theirs was a distinctly agricultural economy. Indeed, Athenian elites regarded commerce as disreputable: a mentality that persisted even when the city's excellent harbors and orientation toward the Aegean made Athens famous as a mercantile center.

In the early centuries, aristocratic dominance over the polis rested on monopolization of elected offices and control of the city's council, the Areopagus (*ah-ree-OP-ah-guhs*). By the early seventh century B.C.E., those who came to wield executive authority in Athens were called *archons* ("first men"). Ultimately, nine archons presided over the entire governance of the polis. Although each served for only one year, all became lifetime members of the Areopagus. And because the Areopagus appointed the archons, it could ensure that power remained in the hands of its own future membership.

Athens The Greek polis with the most markedly democratic form of government, achieved through a series of political struggles during the sixth century B.C.E. Athens would become the preeminent naval power of ancient Greece and the exemplar of Greek culture.

Songs of Sappho

Although Sappho of Lesbos (c. 620–550 B.C.E.) was a prolific poet and skilled musician, we know very little about her life and only a few examples of her extraordinary verse survive. Of the nine books collected in the third century B.C.E., we now have just one complete lyric and a series of fragments, some consisting of only two or three words, often preserved because they were quoted admiringly by other authors. In an astonishing discovery, though, a papyrus scroll containing a previously unknown part of a poem was identified as recently as 2004 (see below). Another papyrus fragment, discovered in 2014, contains parts of two more lyrics: one on unrequited love, addressed to Aphrodite, and another that mentions Sappho's two brothers.

Fragment 16

Some say thronging cavalry, some say foot soldiers,
others call a fleet the most beautiful of
sights the dark earth offers, but I say it's whatever you
    love best.
And it's easy to make this understood by
everyone, for she who surpassed all human
kind in beauty, Helen, abandoning her husband—that
    best of
men—went sailing off to the shores of Troy and
never spent a thought on her child or loving
parents: when the goddess seduced her wits and left her
    to wander,
she forgot them all, she could not remember
anything but longing, and lightly straying
aside, lost her way. But that reminds me now: Anactória,
she's not here, and I'd rather see her lovely
step, her sparkling glance and her face than gaze on
all the troops in Lydia in their chariots and glittering
    armor.

Source: Jim Powell, trans., *The Poetry of Sappho* (New York: 2007), pp. 6–7.

A Newer Fragment (2004)

Live for the gifts the fragrant-breasted Muses
send, for the clear, the singing, lyre, my children.
Old age freezes my body, once so lithe,
rinses the darkness from my hair, now white.
My heart's heavy, my knees no longer keep me
up through the dance they used to prance like fawns in.
Oh, I grumble about it, but for what?
Nothing can stop a person's growing old.
They say that Tithonus was swept away
in Dawn's passionate, rose-flushed arms to live
forever, but he lost his looks, his youth,
failing husband of an immortal bride.

Source: Lachlan Mackinnon, trans., *Times Literary Supplement*, July 15, 2005.

Questions for Analysis

1. How does Sappho use stories from the older tradition she has inherited to address her own concerns? How does the perspective of this female poet transform masculine ideas about heroism, beauty, warfare, aging?

2. What are the challenges of working with such fragmentary sources as these? If these were the only pieces of evidence to survive from Archaic Greece, what conclusions could you draw about this society and its values?

THE ATHENIAN PNYX, WITH A VIEW OF THE ACROPOLIS. The Athenian assembly, the *ekklesia*, met on the sloping hill of the Pnyx. A speaker standing on the *bema* ("stepping-stone"; to the right) would have to make himself heard by all the citizens gathered in front of this platform, and all proceedings would have been plainly visible to noncitizens and foreigners in the agora at the foot of the hill (to the left). Overlooking it all was the temple of the city's patron goddess, Athena, on the crest of the Acropolis. › **Why would this particular site be the focal point of political activity? › How is the relative openness of Athenian democracy symbolized by this chosen site?**

As this small group consolidated power, deep economic and social divisions developed. A significant proportion of the population fell into slavery through debt, while struggles among aristocratic families destabilized society and fomented cycles of revenge. This situation eventually inspired Athenians' first attempt to promulgate a set of written laws. In 621 B.C.E., an aristocrat named Drakon sought to regulate violence through harsh punishments: hence our term *draconian* to describe any severe penalty or regime. The negative effects of this policy ultimately led both aristocrats and hoplites to support the election of the poet Solon as the sole archon for one year, in 594 B.C.E., and they gave him sweeping powers. Solon was an aristocrat but had made his fortune as a merchant, so he was not allied with any one interest group. After his laws were enacted, he went into self-imposed exile for a decade so that he could not be forced to change his law code.

Solon's reforms laid the foundations for the later development of Athenian democracy. He forbade the practice of debt slavery and set up a fund to buy back citizens who had been sold abroad. He encouraged the cultivation of olives and grapes, spurring cash-crop farming and urban industries such as oil and wine production, and the manufacture of pottery storage jars and decorative drinking cups. He also broadened the rights of political participation and set up courts in which a range of citizens served as jurors and to which any Athenian might appeal.

 Solon's reforms

Most significantly, he based eligibility for political office on property qualifications, making it possible for someone not born into the aristocracy to gain access to power. Moreover, he convened an Athenian assembly, the *ekklesia* (*eh-KLAY-see-a*) and gave it the right to elect archons. Now all free-born Athenian men over the age of eighteen could participate in government. Even those who were not eligible for citizenship were able to see the workings of government for themselves, since the assembled citizens met on the slopes of the Pnyx (*pNIX*), a hill visible from the central marketplace and overlooked by the sacred precincts of the acropolis.

Solon's reforms initially met with resistance and, in the resulting decades of controversy, an aristocrat named Peisistratos (*pi-SIS-trah-tohs*) succeeded in establishing a tyranny in 546 B.C.E. In a somewhat ironic move, Peisistratos then proceeded to institute Solon's reforms. He also launched a massive campaign of public-works projects, including the collection and copying of Homer's epics. But the apparent mildness of his rule was undergirded by the persistent intimidation of Athenian citizens and the ruthless crushing of any dissent. His sons were less able to control the various factions that threatened their rule. One was assassinated, and the other was ousted with the help of the Spartans in 510 B.C.E.

The following period of Spartan-sponsored oligarchy ("rule of the few") was brief. Two generations of increasing access to power had left the Athenian demos with a taste for self-government. For the first time in recorded history, a group of citizens can be credited with the overthrow of a regime: they rallied behind Cleisthenes (*CLIE-sthen-ees*), an aristocrat who was able to build a coalition within the ekklesia and, by these democratic means, to check the power of the oligarchs in 508–507 B.C.E. Then, by reorganizing the Athenian population into ten voting districts, Cleisthenes suppressed traditional loyalties that had tied each demos to certain aristocratic families. He further strengthened the powers of the Athenian assembly and extended the machinery of democratic government throughout Attica. He also introduced the practice of ostracism, whereby Athenians could decide each year whether they wanted to banish someone for a decade and, if so, whom. This, Cleisthenes hoped, would prevent the return of a tyranny.

The result of these struggles made the governance of Athens more populist than that of any other Greek polis (at least, that we know of). In the meantime, Athens had become the principal exporter of olive oil, wine, and pottery in the Greek world. It was poised to assume the role it would claim for itself during the fifth century B.C.E.

SPARTA

Located in the mountainous Peloponnesus, the polis of **Sparta** took shape when four villages (and ultimately a fifth) combined to form a single entity. Perhaps as a relic of this process, Sparta retained a dual monarchy throughout its history, with two royal families and two lines of succession: a situation that often led to competition among their respective supporters.

According to our only written accounts—all authored by Athenians and therefore requiring careful analysis—Spartan control over the surrounding region of Laconia began with the conquest of Messenia, one of Greece's few agriculturally rich territories. Around 720 B.C.E., the Spartans subjugated and enslaved the indigenous people there, the *helots*, who now became an unfree population forced to work under Spartan lordship. Around 650 B.C.E., however, the helots revolted, gaining support from several neighboring poleis and briefly threatening Spartan hegemony.

Sparta A Greek polis based in the southern part of the Peloponnesus. Around 650 B.C.E., Spartan rulers militarized their society in order to prevent rebellions and to protect Sparta's superior position in Greece.

Determined to prevent another uprising and to protect its superior position, Sparta became the most militarized polis in Greece. Within a few generations, everything was oriented to the maintenance of its hoplite army—a force so superior that the Spartans confidently left their city unfortified. At a time when Athenian society was becoming more democratic and citizens spent more time legislating than fighting, Spartan society was becoming increasingly devoted to an older aristocratic ideal of perpetual warfare.

The Spartan system made every male citizen a professional soldier of the phalanx. At birth, every Spartiate child was examined by officials who determined whether it was healthy enough to raise; if not, the infant was abandoned in the mountains. This was a custom observed elsewhere in the ancient world, but only in Sparta was it institutionalized. If deemed worthy of upbringing, the child was placed at age seven in the polis-run educational system. Boys and girls trained together until age twelve, participating in physical drills and competitions. Boys then went to live in barracks. Girls continued their training until they became the mates of eligible Spartiate males, usually around the age of eighteen. But for most of their married lives, couples lived apart, so their personal interests would not compete with those of the polis.

Barracks life was designed to accustom youths to physical hardship. At age eighteen, the young man who survived this training would try for membership in a brotherhood whose sworn comrades lived and fought together. Failure to gain acceptance would mean that the young man would lose his rights as a citizen. If accepted, however, he remained with his brotherhood until he was thirty. Between the ages of twenty and thirty he was also expected to mate with a Spartiate woman—but occasions for this were few, a fact that partially accounts for the low birthrate among Spartan citizens. After age thirty, a Spartiate male could opt to live with his family, but was still required to remain on active military duty until he was sixty.

All Spartiate males over the age of thirty were members of the citizens' assembly, the *apella*, which voted on matters proposed by a council, the *gerousia* (*gher-oo-SEE-ah*; "assembly of elders"), consisting of twenty-eight senior citizens and the two kings. Its members were elected for life but had to be over the age of sixty before they could stand for office. Meanwhile, five *ephors* (overseers), elected annually, supervised the educational system and acted as guardians of Spartan tradition. In the latter role, ephors could even remove an ineffectual king from command of the army while on campaign. They also supervised the Spartan "secret service," the *krypteia*, recruiting agents from among the most promising young Spartiates. Agents spied on citizens, but their main job was to infiltrate the helot population and identify potential troublemakers.

This Spartan polity hinged on its precarious relationship with the helots, who outnumbered the Spartiates ten to one. In wartime, helots accompanied the Spartans on campaign as shield bearers, spear carriers, and baggage handlers. At home, however, they were a constant security concern. Every year the Spartans ritually declared war on them as a reminder that they would not tolerate dissent. Moreover, the constant threat of unrest at home meant that the polis was notoriously reluctant to commit its army abroad.

This also inevitably limited the Spartans' contact with the outside world. Indeed, Spartiates were forbidden to engage in commerce, nor did they farm their own

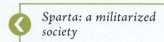

Sparta: a militarized society

lands, as many Athenians did. Economic activity in the Spartan state fell either to the helots or the free residents of other Peloponnesian cities who were known as *perioikoi* (*per-ee-OY-koi*; "those dwelling around"). The perioikoi enjoyed certain rights within Spartan society, and some grew rich handling its business concerns. But unlike the residents of Attica, in the hinterland of Athens, the perioikoi exercised no political rights.

The Spartans styled themselves as the protectors of the "traditional customs" of Greece, by which they meant aristocratic dominance and a strict observance of older heroic ideals. In this role, Sparta tried to prevent the establishment of tyrannies in neighboring states and moved to overthrow them when they arose: hence their willing intervention in the affairs of Athens under the Peisistratids. Indeed, Sparta's stern defense of tradition made it an object of admiration throughout the Greek world, even though few Greeks had any desire to live as the Spartans did.

The fatal flaw in the Spartan system was demographic. There were many ways to lose the status of Spartiate, but only one way to become one—and the Spartan birthrate simply could not keep pace with the demand for trained warriors. As a result, the number of Spartiates declined from perhaps ten thousand in the seventh century B.C.E. to only about a thousand by the middle of the fourth century B.C.E. Another flaw is historical: because the Spartans placed little value on writing, almost everything we know about them (including the summary offered here) must be gleaned from the negative propaganda of their Athenian rivals.

MILETUS AND THE IONIAN REVOLUTION IN THOUGHT

Across the Aegean lay the Greek cities of Ionia, a narrow strip of the Anatolian coast. Here, **Miletus** was the foremost commercial and cultural power. Long a part of the Greek world, it had also been shaped by Mesopotamian and Egyptian influences. It was therefore a crucible of hybrid cultures that produced important forms of art and modes of thought.

The relationship between the Ionian Greeks and the interior kingdom of Lydia—which, like Ionia, was absorbed into the Persian Empire in the sixth century (Chapter 2)—was fraught. It was through the Ionians that the Lydian invention of coinage was introduced to the Greek world, where it revolutionized trade by making wealth portable while also introducing a host of new ethical problems. The Ionians, in turn, played a crucial role in Hellenizing western Asia when the major poleis banded together to form the Ionian League, a political and cultural confederation. Its aim was to insulate Ionian Greeks from the growing power of the Persians.

The Milesians founded many colonies, especially in and around the Black Sea. They were also active in Egypt, where the main Greek trading outposts were all Milesian. These colonial efforts, combined with its advantageous position for trade with the rest of Asia, brought Miletus extraordinary wealth. At the same time, it also became a center for speculative thinking, what the Greeks called *philosophia* ("love of wisdom"). A series of intellectuals (now known as the pre-Socratics, because they came before Socrates) raised new and vital questions about the relationship among the natural world (the *kosmos*), the gods, and men. Often, their explanations moved the influence of the gods to the margins or removed it altogether, something that other Greeks regarded as blasphemous. For example, Milesian philosophers sought physical explanations for the movements of the heavens and did not presume that heavenly bodies were divine. By making human observation the starting point for their knowledge, they began to formulate more scientific explanations for the workings of the universe.

Stimulated by the cultural diversity of their city, Milesian philosophers also began to rethink their place in the cosmos. Hecataeus (*heck-ah-TAY-us*) set out to expand their horizons by mapping the world, traveling extensively and studying the customs and beliefs of other cultures. Xenophanes (*zee-NOFF-uh-nees*) posited that all human knowledge is conditioned by human experience: he observed that the Thracians (north of Greece) believed that the gods had blue eyes and red hair, just as

Milesian philosophers rethink their place in the world

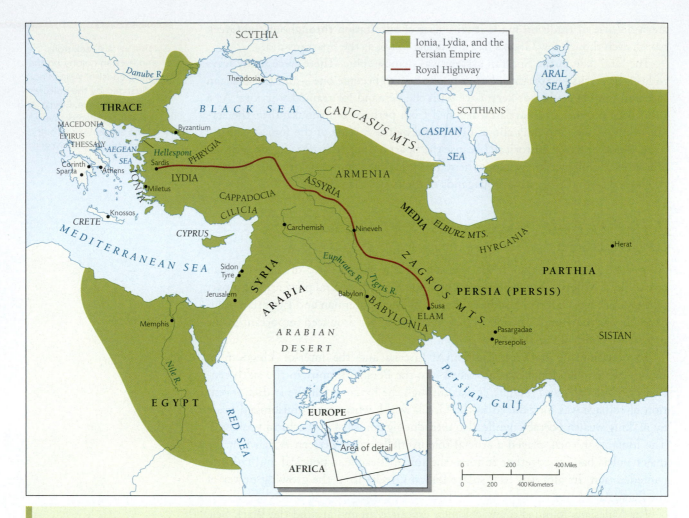

SCYTHIA

THRACE

MACEDONIA
EPIRUS
THESSALY

Corinth
Sparta   Athens

CRETE   Knossos

Danube R.

Theodosia

BLACK SEA

CAUCASUS MTS.

Byzantium

AEGEAN
SEA
Hellespont   PHRYGIA
Sardis

IONIA   LYDIA
Miletus

CAPPADOCIA

CILICIA

CYPRUS

ARMENIA

ASSYRIA

Carchemish

Nineveh

SCYTHIANS

CASPIAN

SEA

MEDIA   ELBURZ MTS.   HYRCANIA

ZAGROS

Euphrates R.   *Tigris R.*

MEDITERRANEAN SEA

Sidon
Tyre

SYRIA

Jerusalem

ARABIA

BABYLONIA

PERSIA (PERSIS)

Babylon

Susa
ELAM

ARAL
SEA

Herat

PARTHIA

SISTAN

Memphis

ARABIAN
DESERT

Pasargadae
Persepolis

Nile R.

EGYPT

RED
SEA

Persian Gulf

EUROPE

Area of detail

AFRICA

Legend:
- Ionia, Lydia, and the Persian Empire
- Royal Highway

0   200   400 Miles
0   200   400 Kilometers

IONIA, LYDIA, AND THE PERSIAN EMPIRE. During the seventh and sixth centuries B.C.E., the Greek cities of the Ionian coast were the cultural and commercial leaders of Greece. But during the fifth century B.C.E., after the Persians conquered Lydia, they lost this position to Athens. **› Where are Ionia, Lydia, and Miletus on this map? › How does Ionia's geographical position help to explain the change in its fortunes? › How might this change have influenced Ionian attitudes toward the Persian Empire?**

the Thracians did, whereas Ethiopians portrayed the gods as dark skinned and curly haired, as they were. He concluded that human beings always make gods in their own image, not the other way around. If horses could fashion images of the gods, Xenophanes argued, the gods would look like horses.

These and other theories formed a distinctive strand in Greek philosophy, yet would continue to be regarded as disturbing and dangerous—dangerous enough to warrant the later execution of Socrates in Athens, where the struggle between religion and philosophy would ultimately be fought. Meanwhile, the Persian conquest of Lydia had made Miletus and its sister cities subject to that great empire. Soon, Ionian resistance to Persian rule would trigger the greatest clash the Greek world had yet known.

The Challenge of the Persian Wars

The profound significance of Greek experiments with new forms of governance and new ideas about the world can be seen with particular clarity if we compare the Greek poleis with the empires and kingdoms of the Bronze Age, in which the typical political regime was a monarchy supported by a powerful priesthood. In this context, cultural achievements were mainly instruments to enhance the prestige of rulers, and economic life was controlled by palaces and temples. By contrast, the core values of the Greeks were the primacy of the human male and the principles of competition, individual achievement, and human freedom and responsibility. In his history, Herodotus records a conversation between a Greek and a Persian, who expresses surprise that the Greeks should raise spears against the benign rule of his emperor. The Spartan retorts, "You understand how to be a slave, but you know nothing of freedom. Had you tasted it, you would advise us to fight not only with spears but with axes." How the Greeks came to turn those spears on each other within a few generations of their united victory over the Persians is a story worthy of one of their own tragedies.

The two major wars fought between the uneasily unified Greeks and the vast Persian Empire were understood as defining events by those who witnessed and looked back on them. Persia was the largest and most efficient state the world had ever seen, capable of mustering more than a million armed men. The Greeks remained a collection of disparate communities, fiercely competitive. An exceptionally large polis, such as Athens or Sparta, might put ten thousand hoplites in the field; but the vast majority of Greek states could only provide a few hundred each. So the threat of Persian conquest loomed large on the Greek horizon.

THE IONIAN REVOLT (499–494 B.C.E.)

For the first time in the history of Western civilizations, we can follow these unfolding events through the narrative of a contemporary historian, Herodotus. And luckily for us, Herodotus was uniquely qualified to probe the long-term and more immediate causes of the **Persian Wars**. Raised in the Ionian polis of Halicarnassus, he was a product of the hybrid culture discussed previously. He was also a keen observer of human nature and human diversity. He regarded both the Greeks and the Persians as great peoples. Yet as a Greek himself—albeit one born within the Persian dominion—he was not impartial. Indeed, his surviving account reflects many of the intellectual currents of mid-fifth-century Athens, where he spent the better part of his career, as well as many Athenian prejudices. This is something to bear in mind when reading his work.

Herodotus wanted to show that war between the Persians and Greeks could be traced back to long-standing cultural differences, but his narrative also shows that the catalyst was a political conflict in Miletus. In 501 B.C.E., the city was governed by Aristagoras (*EHR-is-STAG-or-uhs*), a tyrant who owed his power to the backing of the Persian emperor, **Darius**. But Aristagoras apparently came to believe that his days as the emperor's favorite were numbered. So he turned abruptly from puppet to patriot, rousing the Milesians and the rest of Ionia to revolt against Persian rule. As a safeguard, he also sought military support from the sympathetic poleis on the Greek mainland. The Spartans refused to send their army abroad, but Athens

Persian Wars
(490–479 B.C.E.) In 501 B.C.E., the Persian emperor Darius sent an army to punish Athens for its political alliance with Miletus, sparking the first of the Persian Wars. Despite being heavily outnumbered, Athenian hoplites defeated the Persian army at the plain of Marathon. In 480 B.C.E. Darius's son Xerxes invaded Greece but was defeated at sea and on land by combined forces of Athens and Sparta.

Darius (521–486 B.C.E.) The Persian emperor whose conflict with Aristagoras, the Greek ruler of Miletus, ignited the Persian Wars.

 Cause of the Persian Wars

A MODERN REPLICA OF AN ATHENIAN TRIREME. As the name suggests, a trireme had three banks of oars on each side, one hundred and seventy oars in total. In battle, rowers could help power a ship forward, turn it, and keep it on course in a chase, even when sailing into the wind. In favorable winds, the sails were hoisted for added speed. **> How did this new military technology build on some of the same strategies as hoplite warfare?**

and Eretria (*er-eh-TREE-uh*), on the island of Euboea (*you-BOY-ah*), agreed to send twenty-five ships and crews. This small force managed to capture the old Lydian capital of Sardis (by then a Persian administrative center) and burn it to the ground. Then the Athenians and Eretrians went home, leaving the Ionians to their own devices. In 494 B.C.E., the rebellious poleis were finally overwhelmed by the vastly superior might of Persia.

Darius realized, however, that so long as his Greek subjects in Ionia could cast a hopeful eye to their neighbors across the Aegean, they would forge alliances with them. He therefore decided to launch a preemptive strike against Athens and Eretria, to teach these upstart poleis a lesson. In the summer of 490 B.C.E., a punitive expedition of twenty thousand soldiers crossed the Aegean. Their forces sacked and burned Eretria to the ground, sending its population into captivity in Persia. They then crossed the narrow strait to Attica, landing on the plain of Marathon, approximately twenty-six miles from Athens.

THE BATTLE OF MARATHON AND ITS AFTERMATH

When the Persians landed in Attica, the Athenians called on the only polis that could conceivably help them: Sparta. But the Spartans responded that they were celebrating a religious festival. Only the small, nearby polis of Plataea offered the Athenians aid. The Athenian and Plataean hoplites would have to engage the mighty Persian forces on their own. Heavily outnumbered and without effective cavalry to counter that of the Persians, the Athenian phalanx took a position between two hills blocking the main road to the polis. After a standoff of several days, the Athenian general Miltiades (*mil-TIE-uh-dees*) received word that the Persians were watering their horses and that the infantry was vulnerable to attack. So Miltiades led a charge that smashed the Persian force, resulting in crippling losses. In an almost unbelievable victory, the Athenians had defeated the world's major imperial power. It was a vindication of hoplite tactics and a tremendous boost to Athenian confidence.

Yet the Athenian politician Themistocles (*the-MIS-toh-klees*) warned that the Persians would retaliate with an even larger force. So when the Athenians discovered a rich vein of silver ore in the Attic countryside, a few years later, Themistocles persuaded them to finance a fleet of two hundred triremes, state-of-the-art warships.

XERXES' INVASION

Darius the Great died in 486 B.C.E. and was succeeded by his son **Xerxes** (*ZERK-sees*), who almost immediately began preparing a massive invasion of Greece to avenge his father's shame. Supported by a fleet of six hundred ships, this grand army (which numbered at least one hundred and fifty thousand men and may have been

Xerxes (519?–465 B.C.E.) Xerxes succeeded his father, Darius, as Great King of Persia. Seeking to avenge his father's shame and eradicate future threats to Persian hegemony, he launched his own invasion of Greece in 480 B.C.E. but was defeated by an allied Greek army in 479 B.C.E.

THE PERSIAN WARS WITH GREECE. Imagine that you are the Persian emperor Xerxes, planning the conquest of Greece in 480 B.C.E. › **What are the two possible routes that you could take to attack Greece?** › **What geographical considerations would dictate your military strategy?** › **Bearing in mind that Xerxes' attempt failed, what would you do differently?**

as large as three hundred thousand) set out from Sardis in 480 B.C.E., crossing the Hellespont, the narrow strait separating Europe from Asia. Unlike his father, who had dispatched talented generals against Athens, Xerxes led this campaign himself.

Many Greek poleis capitulated immediately. But Athens, Sparta, Corinth, and some thirty other cities hastily formed the Hellenic League, an unprecedented alliance. In August of 480 B.C.E., a major Persian offensive was held at bay when the outnumbered Greek allies, under the military leadership of Sparta, confronted Xerxes at the mountain pass of Thermopylae (*ther-MO-puh-lie*). For three days, they valiantly held off the Persian multitude. Meanwhile, a Greek fleet led by Athens and guided by

The Hellenic League: an unprecedented alliance of Greek poleis

GREEK FORCES DEFEAT THE PERSIANS. This detail from a bowl commemorating the defeat of Xerxes' army depicts an Athenian hoplite poised to strike a deathblow to his Persian opponent. The artist has carefully delineated the differences between the enemies' dress and weaponry. To the Greeks, the Persian preference for trousers over short tunics seemed particularly barbaric and effeminate.

Themistocles engaged a Persian flotilla. The Spartans' defense of Thermopylae ultimately failed, but their sacrifice allowed the new Athenian warships to inflict heavy losses on the Persians.

However, these engagements left Athens without any men to defend the city. Themistocles therefore persuaded the entire population to abandon Athens for the island of Salamis. From there, the Athenians watched the Persians torch their city. Time, however, was on their side. Xerxes' massive army depended on his damaged fleet for supplies, and the Persians' military tactics—heavy reliance on cavalry and chariots—were not adapted for the rocky terrain of Greece. Bad weather also made sailing the Aegean in autumn a risky business.

In late September, the vastly superior Persian fleet sailed into the straits of Salamis, believing that the Athenians were preparing to flee the island. The report turned out to be false, but so confident was Xerxes of his victory that he had a throne placed on the headland above the bay, where he would have a good view. Instead, he watched as the battle-ready Athenian triremes demolished the Persian fleet. This was the turning point of the war. When the allied Greek army met the Persians on favorable terrain the next spring—an open plain near Plataea—the Greeks prevailed. The small, fractious poleis had defeated the mightiest army of the known world.

The Golden Age of Classical Greece

During the half-century after the Persian Wars, Athens enjoyed a meteoric rise in power and prestige, becoming the premier naval power of the eastern Mediterranean. Athens also emerged as leader of the Delian League, a group of poleis whose representatives met on the sacred island of Delos and pledged to continue the war against Persia. This era simultaneously witnessed the greatest achievements in Athenian culture and politics. These were complicated, however, by its increasingly awkward relationship with its allies, which began to feel more like Athenian subjects than free poleis.

PERICLEAN ATHENS

In the decades before the Persian Wars, political reforms in Athens had continued to encourage experiments in democracy, including the practice of selecting major officeholders by lot. Only one key position was now filled by traditional voting: the office of *strategos*, or general. And because a man could be elected strategos year after year, this office became the career goal of Athens' most ambitious leaders.

Meanwhile, new voices were demanding a greater role in government. Most prominent were the *thetes* (*THAY-tees*), the lowest class of free men and the class that provided the triremes' rowers: the backbone of the all-important Athenian fleet. Like the hoplites who had achieved citizenship because they were indispensable to the defense of the poleis, the thetes wanted higher status and equal representation. The man who emerged to champion their cause was **Pericles** (*PEHR-eh-klees*), an aristocrat from one of Athens' most prestigious families.

Pericles made the enfranchisement of the thetes the main plank of his political platform. He also advocated a foreign policy oriented away from cooperation with Sparta. In 462–461 B.C.E. he was elected strategos and immediately used his position to secure the ostracism of his rival, Cimon. He then pushed through reforms that gave every Athenian citizen the right to propose and amend legislation, not just to vote yes or no in the assembly. And by paying an average day's wage for attendance, he made it easier for poorer citizens to participate. Through such measures, the thetes and other free men of modest means became a dominant force in politics—and loyal to the man who had made that dominance possible.

ATHENIAN THEATER: A MIRROR OF THE POLIS

Pericles glorified Athens with an ambitious scheme of public building and lavish festivals honoring the gods. The most important of these was the Dionysia, a spring feast devoted to the god Dionysos, which became a celebration of Athenian democratic ideals. From the beginning, therefore, drama was closely connected to the political and religious life of the state that sponsored it. Indeed, the very format of classical tragedy replicates the tensions of democracy, showcasing conflict among opposing perspectives. This format was perfected under the great tragedian Aeschylus (*AY-skihl-uhs*; 525–456 B.C.E.) and his younger contemporary, Sophocles (496–406 B.C.E.). Their dramas made use of two or (eventually) three professional actors, each of whom could play numerous roles, and a chorus of Athenian citizens that represented collective opinion and could comment on the action.

Although Aristotle would later declare that the purpose of tragedy was to inspire pity and fear and so purge these emotions through *katharsis* ("purification"), this definition does not capture either the variety or impact of Athenian tragedy. Tragedies were almost always set in the distant or mythical past, but they were intended to address the cutting-edge issues of their day. The very earliest of all surviving tragedies, Aeschylus' *Persians*, dramatizes events of the playwright's own lifetime; we know for certain that he fought at Marathon, because he had this fact proudly recorded on his tomb. Performed for the first time in 472 B.C.E., this contemporary tragedy tells the story of the great Athenian victory at Salamis—but through the eyes of the defeated Xerxes, who thus becomes its tragic hero.

Even when the subject matter was derived from the epics of Homer, the fundamental themes of tragedy—justice, the conflicting demands of personal desire and public duty, the unforeseen consequences of human actions, the brutalizing effects of power—addressed problems of immediate concern. For example, *Oedipus at Colonus*, one of Sophocles' later tragedies, used the story of the mythical king of Thebes to comment bitterly on Athens' disastrous war with Sparta (to be discussed later in this chapter). Similarly, *The Trojan Women* of Euripides (485–406 B.C.E.), presented in 415 B.C.E., marks the Athenians' tragic march toward defeat in this war. By looking back at the capture, rape, and enslavement of Troy's defeated women, Athenians were forced to look at the dreadful consequences of their own imperial policies.

Comedy was even more obviously a genre of political commentary and social satire, and could deal more openly with current events: sexual scandals, political corruption, moral hypocrisy, popular fads. Aristophanes (*EHR-ih-STOFF-ah-nees*; c. 446–386 B.C.E.), the greatest of Athenian comic playwrights, lampooned

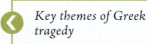

Key themes of Greek tragedy

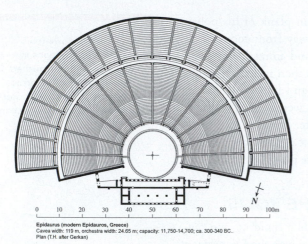

Epidaurus (modern Epidauros, Greece)
Cavea width: 119 m, orchestra width: 24.65 m; capacity: 11,750-14,700; ca. 300-340 BC..
Plan (T.H. after Gerkan)

THE THEATER AT EPIDAUROS. Greek dramas were invariably presented in the open air, usually at dawn. Since these were civic spectacles, theaters had to be large enough to accommodate all citizens. Most, like this one at Epidauros (right), took advantage of the natural slope of a hill. The plan for the theater is shown above (left). The acting area would have been backed by a high wall, the *skene*, which housed stage machinery and enhanced the acoustics. A trained actor standing in the *orchestra* would have been plainly audible even to those seated in the top tier. **› How would the size and setting of such a theater enhance the political character of the plays performed within it?**

everything from the philosophy of Socrates to the tragedies of his contemporary Euripides, and was an especially outspoken critic of Athenian warmongers and their imperialist aims. He regularly savaged the powerful figures whom he saw as leading Athens to its doom, and he was repeatedly dragged into court to defend himself against the demagogues he attacked. But the power and popularity of comic theater were such that politicians never dared to shut it down for long. It was too much an expression, and outcome, of Athenian ideals.

A NEW SCIENCE OF HISTORY

Even though the Greeks of this age were becoming more dependent on writing for legal and commercial transactions, they valued highly the arts of memory, poetry (which was always intended to be sung and enjoyed in performance), and oral debate. Now, though, the rise of functional literacy in Athens encouraged the emergence of prose as a distinct literary form. Herodotus found a ready market for his histories in Athens. His younger contemporary Thucydides (*thoo-SID-ih-dees*) used his time in exile to write a masterful—and scathingly critical—history of the war between his polis and Sparta, in which he himself had fought.

The emergence of prose writing, a new literary form

Between them, these two historians developed a new approach to the study of the past, emphasizing the need to collect and interpret multiple sources and focusing on human agency as the driving force of history—rather than divine intervention. In different ways, they both conceived the historian's role as distinct from that of a storyteller. The word *historia* would continue to mean both "story" and "history," but the historian's task was to investigate and critically reflect on the events of his own time, as well as to illuminate those of the past.

ART AND ARCHITECTURE

The visual artists of classical Greece revealed the same range of talents as poets did in their dramas. Athenian sculptors in particular were drawn to the challenges of representing the human form accurately while celebrating an ideal of physical beauty. Perhaps the most striking development in fifth-century Greek sculpture was the new attention paid to the crafting of naturalistic figures, both clothed and nude. This is a trend already discernible in the figure of the kouros examined on page 86, and in the successive refinements of the sculptor's art made in the previous century. Scholars have long wanted to link the innovation of naturalism to the victories over the Persians in those key decades, for Greeks regarded the Persian male's preference for trousers, fondness for jewelry, and luxurious long hair as proofs of effeminacy (see the bowl on page 100). Greek men, by contrast, took pride in sculpting their physiques through exercise, and participating in athletic contests in the nude. A Greek might have said that only barbarians and women covered their shameful bodies in constricting clothes; free men celebrate their individuality in the care of the body and its representation.

The Athenians also made exceptional contributions to architecture in this period. All Greek temples sought to create an impression of harmony, but the Parthenon of Athens, built between 447 and 438 B.C.E., is generally considered the finest example. Construction of this stunning and structurally ambitious building was urged on the Athenians by Pericles as a tribute to their patron goddess, Athena Parthenos ("Athena the Virgin"), and as a symbol of their own power, confidence, and genius.

THE DAILY LIFE OF ATHENS: MEN, WOMEN, AND SLAVES

Toward the end of his famous funeral oration, which Thucydides quotes in his history, Pericles addresses only a few brief remarks to the women of Athens who mourn their fallen fathers, husbands, and sons at the end of the first year of the disastrous war with Sparta. He urges them to do three things: rear more children for Athens and its wars, show no more weakness than is "natural to their sex," and attract no attention to themselves. His remarks reveal widely held attitudes toward women in classical Greece, although they may not reflect complex historical realities.

The growth of democracy did not lead to greater equality between the sexes; in fact, it had the opposite result. In the Bronze Age of Mycenaean Greece, women were viewed as possessing extraordinary funds of courage and wisdom, as well as beauty and virtue. They were prized for their shrewd advice on political and military matters, and they played an active role in the world. Sometimes, elite women ruled kingdoms in their own right. But as aristocratic ideals gave way to more democratic ones, Greek women increasingly spent their lives in the confinement of home.

The importance of the hoplite infantry encouraged men to train together and develop close relationships, something that was also sanctioned by the political system. At the same time, that spirit of equality discouraged the political agency of women. Instead, the production of children to supply the infantry became the female imperative. Public spaces were largely restricted to male activities, whereas

THE SHRINE OF ATHENA IN THE PARTHENON. This is a replica of the statue of Athena that once stood inside the Parthenon dedicated to her. Made of gold and ivory and designed by the great sculptor Phidias, who was updating a more archaic style, the statue stood forty feet high and was visible to viewers outside the temple and some distance away. The statue was reflected in a shallow pool of water located in front of it.

inner domestic spaces were reserved for female endeavors, such as child care and weaving. Respectable women lived largely in the seclusion of a house's courtyard, rarely venturing forth from there.

In Athens, girls could be legally married at age fourteen, usually to husbands more than twice their age. A girl's father arranged her marriage and provided a dowry for her support. Shortly after a wife entered her new home, a regular schedule of childbirth would begin. The average young wife would bear between four and six children before she died, usually around the age of thirty-five. Her place might then be taken by another, younger woman.

Because women seldom ventured beyond their neighborhoods, slaves did whatever shopping or marketing the household required. Even at home, women were expected to withdraw into private rooms if visitors arrived. But they were not supposed to sit around idly, and their main occupation—true of all women, from royalty to slaves—was the spinning and weaving of cloth. And since women's work was basically menial, men looked down on it, even though their own livelihoods and comfort depended on it.

Some evidence suggests that husbands were not encouraged to form emotional attachments to their wives, although many certainly did. In a revealing passage, Herodotus talks of a certain Lydian king who "fell in love with his own wife, a fancy that had strange consequences." By contrast, an Athenian orator remarked that "we have prostitutes for pleasure, concubines for daily physical needs, and wives to bear us legitimate children and be our faithful housekeepers." However, these perspectives are offset by a range of archaeological and material evidence that testify to women's valued social roles, the affection of their husbands and children, and even their wider economic and legal powers.

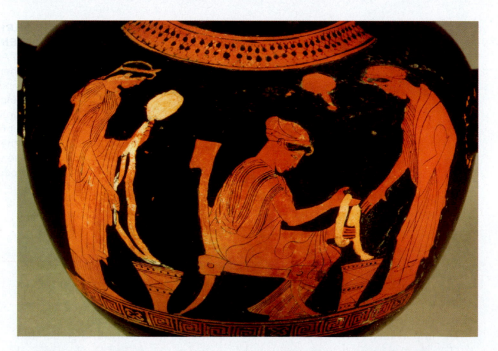

WOMEN AND WEAVING. Wool working and weaving were gender-specific activities throughout the ancient world, in which women of all social ranks were expected to participate. On this red-figure vase, dating from 460 to 450 B.C.E., we see the woman on the left carding wool, and the two women on the right preparing fibers for spinning into threads, which could then be woven into cloth.

In addition to depending on the labor and fertility of women, Athenians were as reliant on slaves as Spartans were on helots. Without slavery, none of the Athenian accomplishments in politics, thought, or art would have been possible. The Athenian ideal of dividing and rotating governmental duties depended on slaves who worked in fields, businesses, and homes while free men engaged in politics. In fact, the Athenian democratic system began to function fully only with the expansion of Athenian mining and commerce around 500 B.C.E., which enabled the Athenians to buy slaves in larger numbers. Freedom and slavery were thus aligned, an inescapable contradiction of this democracy. It seems likely that there were only about a hundred thousand Athenians: of these, only a fraction—somewhere between thirty thousand and sixty thousand men—were eligible for citizenship and could take part in political life. Nearly as many of the city's residents were enslaved, with an additional population of some ten thousand resident foreigners (known as *metics*).

 Rise of Athenian democracy linked to spread of slavery

Although widespread, Athenian slavery was modest in scale. Slaves did not ordinarily work in teams or in factories; the only exceptions were the state-owned silver mines, where large numbers toiled in miserable conditions. Most slaves were owned in smaller numbers by a wide range of Athenian families, including the relatively poor. As domestic servants and farm laborers, slaves might be considered trusted members of the household, although their masters were legally empowered to beat them or abuse them; concubines and sex workers (of both genders) were often drawn from among this class of slaves. Yet slaves could never be entirely dehumanized as they were in modern slaveholding societies: the misfortune of becoming a slave through debt was a reality of Athens' recent past, and the real possibility of being enslaved in war became a widespread consequence of Athens' overreaching ambitions.

"The Greatest War in History" and Its Consequences

Ultimately, Athens' foreign policy and imperial ambitions undermined its civic and cultural achievements. Since the 470s B.C.E., as we noted previously, Athens had begun crushing those allies who attempted to break from its control. By the early 440s B.C.E., its only rival for supremacy in the Greek world was Sparta. Rather than attempting to maintain a balance of power, however, Pericles determined on a more aggressive policy: he made a formal peace with Persia to ensure that available military resources would be directed toward any future Spartan opposition. But this undermined the sole purpose of the Delian League, which had been the defense of Greece against Persian aggression. Athens now had no justification for compelling the league members to maintain their allegiance. Many remained loyal nonetheless, paying their contributions and enjoying the economic benefits of warm relations with Athens. Others, however, did not, and Athens found itself increasingly having to force its reluctant allies back into line, often installing Athenian garrisons and planting Athenian colonists—who retained their Athenian citizenship—to ensure continued loyalty.

In the context of recent history and long-standing Greek values, such behavior was disturbing. The Delian League had been established to preserve Greek independence. Now Athens itself was becoming an oppressive power. Foremost among its critics were the Corinthians, whose own economic standing was threatened by Athenian dominance. The Corinthians were close allies of the Spartans, who were the dominant power in what historians call the Peloponnesian League. The Greeks called it simply the "Spartans and their allies." When war finally erupted between Athens and Sparta, Thucydides—himself an Athenian—ascribed it to the growing power of Athens and the anxiety this inspired in other poleis. No modern historian has improved on Thucydides' thesis. Yet for the Athenians and their leaders, there could be no question of relinquishing their empire. For Sparta and its Peloponnesian allies, meanwhile, the prospect of relinquishing their own independence was equally unthinkable. Two very different ideas of Greek superiority were about to fight to the death.

THE PELOPONNESIAN WAR BEGINS

When the Athenians and Spartans found themselves at war in 431 B.C.E., both sides believed a conclusion would come quickly—a delusion common to many of history's pivotal wars. Instead, the **Peloponnesian War** dragged on for twenty-seven years. Thucydides, writing in exile, recalled that he knew from the time of its outbreak that it was going to be "the greatest war in history," amounting to the first world war, as it would involve the entire Mediterranean. He also meant that it was the worst, so devastating to both sides that it partially destroyed the Greeks' proud heritage of independence. By the time Athens was forced to concede defeat, all the poleis were weakened to such an extent that they could not withstand outside threats.

Athens knew that it could not defeat Sparta on land; and neither Sparta nor its allies had a fleet capable of facing the Athenians at sea. Pericles therefore developed a bold strategy: he would pull the entire population of Attica within the walls of Athens and not attempt to defend the countryside. For sustenance, Athenians would rely on supplies shipped in by its fleet, which would also be deployed to ravage the coasts of the Peloponnesus.

The Spartans duly plundered the farms and pastures of Attica. Meanwhile, the Athenians inflicted significant destruction on Spartan territory in a series of raids and by encouraging rebellion among the helots. The advantage appeared to be on Athens' side, but in 429 B.C.E. the crowded conditions of the besieged city gave rise to a typhus epidemic that killed over a third of the population, including the aged Pericles.

Pericles' death revealed that he had been the only man capable of managing the political forces he had unleashed. His successors were mostly demagogues who played to the worst instincts of people. The most successful of these was Cleon, a particular target of Aristophanes' ridicule, who refused a Spartan offer of peace in 425 B.C.E. and continued the war until his own death in battle four years later. It was under Cleon that Thucydides was given the impossible task of liberating a city under Spartan control; his failure in 423 B.C.E. led to his exile.

After the death of Cleon, a truce with Sparta was negotiated by an able Athenian named Nikias. But Athens continued to pursue a "dirty war" by preying on poleis that might support the Spartans. This led to atrocities such as the destruction of Melos, an island colonized by the Spartans but which had maintained its neutrality. When the inhabitants of Melos refused to compromise this position by accepting Athenian rule, Athens had the entire male population slaughtered and every woman and child sold into slavery.

Thereafter, Athens' policy of preemptive warfare proved destructive even to itself. In 415 B.C.E., a charismatic young aristocrat named Alkibiades (*al-kih-BY-uh-dees*) convinced the Athenians to attack the powerful Greek city of Syracuse in Sicily, which was allegedly harrying Athenian allies in the western Mediterranean. The expedition failed disastrously, ending with the death or enslavement of thousands of Athenian warriors.

The scale bar reads:
```
        50          100 Miles
0
        50          100 Kilometers
0
```

THRACE

BLACK SEA

Byzantium

SEA OF MARMARA

MACEDONIA

Mt. Olympus

CHALCIDICE

SAMOTHRACE

LEMNOS

THRACIAN SEA

EPIRUS

CORCYRA

THESSALY

Hellespont

ARGINUSAE

LESBOS

AEGEAN

AETOLIA

SEA

EUBOEA

Delphi BOEOTIA

Thebes Eretria

CHIOS

IONIAN SEA

Gulf of Corinth

ACHAEA

Megara Athens

Corinth ATTICA

ANDROS

SAMOS

Argos

PERSIA

PELOPONNESUS

Mt. Ithome

Mt. Parnon

MESSENIA   Sparta

Pylos   LACONIA

Mt. Taygetus

CYCLADES

DELOS NAXOS

Miletus

MEDITERRANEAN

MELOS

SEA

SEA OF CRETE

RHODES

CRETE

Legend:
- Sparta and allies
- Athens and allies
- Neutral Greek states
- • City
- ▲ Selected mountain
- △ Other mountains

Inset map:
EUROPE
Area of detail
AFRICA

THE PELOPONNESIAN WAR. This map shows the patchwork of colonies and alliances that bound together the supporters of Sparta and Athens at the outbreak of the Peloponnesian War. **›** Which side had the geographical advantage? **›** Which neutral powers might have been able to tip the balance by entering the war on one side or the other? **›** What strategic and military choices did geography impose on the two combatants and their allies?

News of the Syracusan disaster shattered Athens. Many political leaders were driven from the polis as scapegoats, and in 411 B.C.E. a hastily convened assembly of citizens voted democracy out of existence, replacing it with an oligarchy of four hundred members, many of whom had been present at this vote. The remains of the Athenian fleet, then stationed at Samos on the Ionian coast, responded by declaring a democratic government in exile under the leadership of none other than Alkibiades. The oligarchy proved to be brief, and democracy was restored to Athens by 409 B.C.E. But a pattern of self-destruction had been established, making it difficult for anyone to believe in the possibility of restored greatness.

The Failure of Athenian Democracy

The Spartans, too, despaired of bringing the war to an end. Even weakened, the Athenian fleet was still invincible. Finally, Sparta turned to the Persians, who were hungry to avenge themselves on Athens and agreed to supply the gold and expertise necessary to train an effective Spartan navy. Meanwhile, the Athenians were turning against each other, making the Spartans' task easier. In 406 B.C.E., a rare naval victory at Arginusae (ar-gen-NOO-sign) ended in a sudden storm that prevented the Athenian commanders from rescuing the sailors whose ships had been wrecked. A firestorm of protest was fanned by demagogues who insisted on making an example of those generals brave enough to return. One of these was Pericles' son, who was executed, thereby dying a victim of his father's policies. Through such measures, the Athenians killed or exiled the last of their able commanders.

The poorly led Athenian fleet was destroyed in 404 B.C.E. Without ships, the Athenians could neither feed themselves nor defend their city. The Spartans sailed the Aegean unopposed, installing pro-Spartan oligarchies to rule former Athenian allies. Finally, they besieged Athens, which surrendered after months of starvation and disease. Corinth and Thebes, remembering the ruthless treatment of Melos, called for Athens' annihilation. The Spartans refused, but imposed harsh terms: the dismantling of Athens' defensive walls, the scrapping of its fleet, and the acceptance of an oligarchy under Spartan supervision. These so-called Thirty Tyrants confiscated private property and murdered their political opponents. Their excesses drove committed democrats to plan a desperate coup, averted only through the intervention of the Spartan kings. By the end of 401 B.C.E., Athens had restored a semblance of democratic governance, but it was never more than a shadow of its former self.

With its victory, Sparta succeeded Athens as the arbiter of the Greek world. But this was a thankless job, made worse by the losses the Spartans themselves had suffered during the war and the fact that they were even more aggressive in their control of the Aegean than the Athenians had been. Ironically, indeed, the Spartans found themselves in a position they had avoided throughout their history. They also faced a reinvigorated Persian Empire, which had increased its naval presence in the Aegean.

These were the circumstances in which the Athenian philosopher Socrates (469–399 B.C.E.) attempted to reform his city's ethical and political traditions. To understand something of his accomplishments, and to assess the reasons for his trial and execution at the hands of his fellow citizens, we must trace the development of philosophical speculation in the half-century before his birth.

THE PYTHAGOREANS AND THE SOPHISTS

After the Persian conquest of Ionia in 546 B.C.E., many Milesian philosophers fled to southern Italy. Philosophical speculation thus continued in the Greek "far west." A major proponent was Pythagoras (pi-THAG-or-ahs), who founded a community in the Italian city of Croton. Pythagoras and his followers regarded the speculative life as the highest good, but they believed that one must be purified of fleshly desires to achieve this. Just as the essence of life lay in the mind, they believed that the essence of the universe was to be found, not in the natural world, but in the study of abstracts; and so they concentrated on mathematics and musical theory. The Pythagoreans established the key properties of odd and even numbers and also proved an old Babylonian hypothesis in geometry, known today as the Pythagorean theorem. Even though they shunned the material world, they still exhibited the characteristic Greek quest for regularity and predictability in that world.

Meanwhile, philosophy in mainland Greece was more attuned to questions of ethics and politics. The increasing power of individual citizens begged the question of how a man should conduct himself, in public and private life, so as to embrace "the beautiful and the good"—or at least to advance himself by the use of his wits. To answer this question, a new group of teachers arose. They were known as the Sophists, a term meaning "wise men."

Unlike the Milesian philosophers or the Pythagoreans, the Sophists made a living by selling their knowledge. Their teachings are best exemplified by Protagoras (*pro-TAG-or-ahs*), an older contemporary of Socrates. His famous dictum, "Man is the measure of all things," means that goodness, truth, and justice are relative concepts, adaptable to the needs and interests of human beings. In other words, values are not unchanging moral imperatives. Instead, Protagoras declared that no one could know whether the gods existed or, if they did, what they wanted. He concluded, consequently, that there could be no absolute standards of right and wrong. Empirical facts, established by the perceptions of the senses, were the only source of knowledge. And because each man experienced the world in a different way, there could be only individual truths valid for the individual knower.

Such teachings struck many as dangerous. Sophists such as Protagoras made everyday life a subject for philosophical discussion, but their relativism could too easily degenerate into a conviction that the wise man (or the wise state) was the one best able to manipulate others and gratify individual desires. In both personal and collective terms, this conviction could rationalize monstrous acts of brutality—such as those committed by Athens in the case of Melos. Indeed, the lessons of the Peloponnesian War went a long way toward demonstrating the disastrous consequences of this self-serving logic: if justice is merely relative, then neither individual morality nor society can survive. This ethical conviction led to the growth of a new philosophical movement grounded in the theory that absolute standards *do* exist and that human beings can determine what these are through the exercise of reason. The initiator of this trend was Socrates.

THE LIFE AND THOUGHT OF SOCRATES

Socrates was not a professional teacher, as the Sophists were. He may have trained as a stonemason, and he certainly had some sort of livelihood that enabled him to maintain his status as a citizen and hoplite. Having fought in three campaigns as part of the Athenian infantry during the war with Sparta, he was both an ardent patriot and a sincere critic of Athenian policy. His method of instruction was conversation: through dialogue with passersby, he submitted every presumed truth to rigorous examination in order to establish a firm foundation for further inquiry. Everything we know about Socrates' teachings

SOCRATES AS THE IDEAL EDUCATED MAN. This image of Socrates features on a Roman funerary monument known as the Sarcophagus of the Muses, made in the second century C.E. The sarcophagus advertises its owner-occupant's desire to be viewed (even in death) as a highly cultivated man, the companion of the Nine Muses of Greek mythology and the companion of Socrates, who taught that the practice of philosophy helped to prepare the soul for immortality.

Two Views of Socrates

Most people regard Socrates as the sage thinker who challenged the prevailing prejudices of his day. During his own time, however, he was not so universally admired. In the first excerpt, from Aristophanes' comedy The Clouds, *the protagonist, Strepsiades, goes to Socrates and his "Thought Shop," asking that Socrates make him and his son, Pheidippides, orators capable of winning lawsuits and growing rich. Aristophanes implies throughout that Socrates is a charlatan who teaches word games and tricks for hire.*

In the second excerpt, according to his pupil Plato, Socrates spent the last days of his life in conversation with his friends and followers, some of whom urged him to escape from captivity and live in exile. In the dialogue Crito, *a young aristocrat argues that the very laws that have condemned Socrates are unjust, and that by choosing to obey them Socrates is giving them legitimacy they do not deserve. But halfway through the debate, Socrates turns the tables on him.*

Socrates as a Sophist

STREPSIADES: See that he [Pheidippides] learns your two Arguments, whatever you call them—oh yes, Right and Wrong—the one that takes a bad case and defeats Right with it. If he can't manage both, then at least Wrong—that will do—but that he must have.

SOCRATES: Well, I'll go and send the Arguments here in person, and they'll teach him themselves.

STREPSIADES: Don't forget, he's got to be able to argue against any kind of justified claim at all.

RIGHT: This way. Let the audience see you. . . .

WRONG: Sure, go wherever you like. The more of an audience we have, the more soundly I'll trounce you.

RIGHT: What sort of trick will you use?

WRONG: Oh, just a few new ideas.

RIGHT: Yes, they're in fashion now, aren't they, [*to the audience*] thanks to you idiots. . . . [*to Pheidippides*] You don't want to be the sort of chap who's always in the agora telling stories about other people's sex lives, or in the courts arguing about some petty, filthy little dispute. . . .

WRONG: People here at the Thought Shop call me Wrong, because I was the one who invented ways of proving anything wrong, laws, prosecutors, anything. Isn't that worth millions—to have a really bad case and yet win? . . . Suppose you fall in love with a married woman—have a bit of fun—and get caught in the act. As you are now, without a tongue in your head, you're done for. But if you come and learn from me, then you can do whatever you like and get away with it . . . and supposing you do get caught with someone's wife, you can say to him. . . . "What have I done wrong? Look at Zeus; wasn't he always a slave of his sexual passions? And do you expect a mere mortal like me to do any better than a god?" . . .

STREPSIADES [*to Socrates*]: I wonder if you'd accept a token of my appreciation? But my son, has he learned that Argument we were listening to a moment ago?

comes from the writings of younger men who considered themselves his pupils and participated in these conversations. The most important of these followers was Plato.

According to Plato, Socrates sought to show that all supposed certainties are merely unexamined prejudices inherited from others. Socrates always said that he himself knew nothing, because this was a more secure place from which to begin the learning process. He sought to base his speculations on sound definitions of key concepts—justice, virtue, beauty, love—that he and his pupils could arrive at only

SOCRATES: Yes, he has.

STREPSIADES: Holy Fraud, how wonderful!

SOCRATES: Yes, you'll now be able to win any case at all.

Socrates and the Laws of Athens

SOCRATES: I should like you to consider whether we are still satisfied on this point: that the really important thing is not to live, but to live well.

CRITO: Why, yes.

SOCRATES: And that to live well means the same thing as to live honorably, or rightly?

CRITO: Yes.

SOCRATES: Then in light of this agreement we must consider whether or not it is right for me to try to get away without an official pardon. If it turns out to be right, we must make the attempt; if not, we must let it drop. . . .

CRITO: I agree with what you say, Socrates. . . .

SOCRATES: Well, here is my next point, or rather question. Ought one to fulfill all one's agreements, provided they are right, or break them?

CRITO: One ought to fulfill them.

SOCRATES: Then consider the logical consequence. If we leave this place without first persuading the polis to let us go . . . are we or are we not abiding by our just agreements?

CRITO: I can't answer your question, Socrates. I am not clear in my mind.

SOCRATES: Look at it this way. Suppose that while we were preparing to run away (or however one should describe it), the Laws of Athens were to come and confront us with this question: "Now, Socrates, what are you proposing to do? Can you deny that by this act which you are contemplating you intend, so far as you have the power, to destroy us, the Laws, and the whole polis as well? Do you imagine that a city can continue to exist and not be turned upside down, if the legal judgments which are pronounced in it have no

force but are nullified and destroyed by private persons?"— How shall we answer this question, Crito, and others of the same kind? . . . Shall we say, "Yes, I do intend to destroy the Laws, because the polis has wronged me by passing a faulty judgment at my trial"? Is this to be our answer, or what?

CRITO: What you have just said, by all means, Socrates.

SOCRATES: Then supposing the Laws say, "Was there provision for this in the agreement between you and us, Socrates? Or did you pledge to abide by whatever judgments the polis pronounced? . . . [I]f you cannot persuade your country you must do whatever it orders, and patiently submit to any punishment it imposes, whether it be flogging or imprisonment. And if it leads you out to war, you must comply, and it is right that you should do so; you must not give way or retreat or abandon your position. Both in war and in the law courts you must do whatever your city and your country commands."

Source: Plato, *Crito*, excerpted (with modifications) from *The Last Days of Socrates*, trans. Hugh Tredennick (New York: 1969), pp. 87–91.

Questions for Analysis

1. Socrates actually refused to teach the art of "making the weaker argument defeat the stronger." But in *The Clouds*, Aristophanes shows him teaching how "to win any case at all." Why were the powers of persuasion considered potentially dangerous in democratic Athens? Why would Aristophanes choose to represent Socrates in this way?

2. How do the arguments of Plato's Socrates compare with those of Aristophanes' character?

Source: Aristophanes, *The Clouds*, trans. Alan H. Sommerstein (New York: 1973), pp. 148–50, 154, 159–60 (slightly revised).

by investigating their own assumptions. And he focused his attention on practical ethics rather than the study of the physical world (as the Milesians did) or mathematical abstractions (as the Pythagoreans did). He urged his listeners to reflect on the principles of proper conduct, both for their own sakes and for that of society as a whole. He taught that one should consider the meaning and consequences of one's actions at all times and be prepared to take responsibility for them. According to one of his most memorable sayings, "The unexamined life is not worth living."

It is bitterly paradoxical that Socrates, the product of Athenian democracy, should have been put to death by democratic processes. In 399 B.C.E., shortly after the end of the Peloponnesian War, Athens was reeling from both the shock of defeat and violent internal upheavals. It was then that a democratic faction decided that Socrates was a threat to the state. A democratic court agreed, condemning him to death for denying the gods, disloyalty to the polis, and "corrupting the youth." Although his friends made arrangements for him to flee the city and evade punishment, Socrates insisted on abiding by the laws and remaining in prison, proving himself true to his own principles and setting an example for future citizens. He died calmly by the prescribed method: self-administered poison.

According to Socrates, the goal of philosophy is to help human beings understand and *apply* standards of absolute good, rather than master a series of mental tricks that facilitate personal gain at the expense of others. The circumstances of his death, however, show that it is difficult to translate this philosophy into principles that can be widely accepted. This would be the task of Plato, who would lay the groundwork for all subsequent Western philosophy (see Chapter 4).

Conclusion

There are many striking similarities between the civilization of ancient Greece and our own—and many stark differences. Perhaps the most salient example of both is

AFTER YOU READ THIS CHAPTER

CHRONOLOGY

800–400 B.C.E.	Rise of the *polis*
c. 750 B.C.E.	Homeric epics transcribed
725–650 B.C.E.	Hoplite tactics become standard
c. 600 B.C.E	Militarization of Sparta
600–500 B.C.E.	Emergence of the Milesian School (pre-Socratic philosophy)
594 B.C.E.	Solon's reforms in Athens
546 B.C.E.	Cyrus of Persia conquers Lydia and controls the Greek cities of Ionia
510 B.C.E.	Overthrow of the Peisistratid tyranny in Athens
499–494 B.C.E.	Ionian Revolt
490 B.C.E.	Battle of Marathon
480 B.C.E.	Battles of Thermopylae and Salamis
478 B.C.E.	Formation of the Delian League
431 B.C.E.	Peloponnesian War begins
404 B.C.E.	Defeat of Athens by Sparta
399 B.C.E.	Death of Socrates

REVIEWING THE OBJECTIVES

❯ The Greek polis was a unique form of government. What factors led to its emergence?

❯ Hoplite warfare had a direct effect on the shaping of early democracy. How?

❯ Poleis could develop in very different ways. What are some of the reasons for this?

❯ In what ways did Athenian culture, philosophy, and art reflect democratic ideals?

❯ The Persian and Peloponnesian Wars affected Greek civilization in profound ways. Describe some of the consequences of Athens' victory in the former and its defeat in the latter.

the concept of democracy, which the people of ancient Greece would have defined as a rule by a class of privileged male citizens supported by slavery. In theory and in practice, this amounted to only a small percentage of the population in Athens, and in Sparta the vast majority were subject to the rule of an even smaller class of Spartiates. Moreover, the growth of Athenian power meant, increasingly, the exploitation of other poleis, a ruinous policy of preemptive warfare, and greater intolerance and paranoia. Socrates was not the only man put to death for expressing his opinions. Finally, the status of women in this "golden age" was lower than it had been in earlier periods of Greek history, and women had far fewer personal rights than in any of the ancient societies we have studied so far.

And yet the enduring importance of Greek civilization has given us the essential vocabulary we have inherited from it: not only the word *democracy* but also *politics, philosophy, theater, history.* The very notion of humanity comes to us from the Greeks. For them, the fullest development of one's potential should be the aim of existence: every free man is the sculptor of his own monument. Indeed, the concept of freedom—in Greek, *eleutheria*—did not exist in any other ancient language, including Hebrew. This work of growing from childishness to personhood is what the Greeks called *paideia*, from which our term *pedagogy is* derived. The Romans called it *humanitas.* How this and other ideas came to be disseminated beyond Greece, to be adopted by the peoples and places of a much wider world, is the subject of Chapter 4.

 Go to **INQUIZITIVE** to see what you've learned—and learn what you've missed—with personalized feedback along the way.

PEOPLE, IDEAS, AND EVENTS IN CONTEXT

> How did the epics of **HOMER** transmit the values of the Bronze Age to the **ARISTOCRACY** of the new Greek **POLEIS**?

> How did the spread of Greek culture transform the Mediterranean, even as the adoption of **HOPLITE** military tactics transformed Greek politics?

> Compare and contrast the historical circumstances that led to the development of **ATHENS**, **SPARTA**, and **MILETUS**. What were the main differences among them?

> What were the different motives for the invasions by **DARIUS** and **XERXES**? By what methods did the Greek poleis manage to emerge victorious from the **PERSIAN WARS**?

> What were the triumphs and limitations of **DEMOCRACY** in **PERICLEAN ATHENS**?

> How did the **PELOPONNESIAN WAR** transform Athens and affect the balance of power in the Mediterranean?

THINKING ABOUT CONNECTIONS

> The trial and execution of Socrates can be seen as a referendum on the relationship between the individual and the state. What does this incident reveal about the limitations of personal power and individual rights? To what degree was this incident a product of Athenian losses during the Peloponnesian War? To what extent does it reflect long-term trends in the Greek world?

> We like to think that we can trace our democratic ideals and institutions back to Athens, but does this mean that the failings of Athenian democracy also mirror those of our own? What parallels can you draw between the cultures of fifth-century Athens and today's United States? What are some key differences?

4

The Greek World Expands, 400–150 B.C.E.

WHEN THE YOUNG ALEXANDER OF MACEDONIA set out for Persia in 334 B.C.E., he brought two favorite books. The first was a copy of the *Iliad* that his teacher Aristotle had given him. The second was the *Anabasis*, "The Inland Expedition," by an Athenian called Xenophon (*ZEN-oh-fon*; 430–354 B.C.E.). Both choices are significant. The *Iliad* recounts a much earlier Greek assault on Asia, and its hero is Achilles—consummate warrior, favorite of the gods, a man who inspired passionate loyalty: a figure with whom Alexander identified. The *Anabasis* was a more practical choice. Its author had been one of ten thousand Greek mercenaries hired by a Persian prince to overthrow his older brother, the Great King. The attempted coup failed, but Xenophon's book made the prince, Cyrus, another role model for Alexander. It also told, in detail, how Persians fought and lived, how they were governed, and what an army of hoplites could accomplish on Persian terrain.

As a student of history, Alexander recognized that the golden age of the Greek polis had ended in the war of attrition between Athens and Sparta (Chapter 3). The fifty years prior to his own birth in 356 B.C.E. had merely continued this downward trend. Social and economic problems were mounting. Faith in the ideals of democracy was compromised. Increasingly, the wealthy withdrew from politics altogether, while free citizens were reduced to debt slavery. As the poleis decayed, a new generation of intellectuals argued about what had gone wrong, and they tried to imagine a better future. One of these was Aristotle, a pupil of Plato and Alexander's own teacher.

BEFORE YOU READ THIS CHAPTER ❯

STORY LINES

> After the Peloponnesian War, divisions within and among the Greek poleis made them vulnerable to the ambitions of King Philip II of Macedonia and his son, Alexander.

> Alexander's conquest of the Persian Empire and Egypt merged the civilizations of antiquity under Greco–Macedonian rule. Even after his death, a shared language and culture continued to bind these civilizations together in a new Hellenistic ("Greek-like") world.

> Ease of travel, trade, and communication spurred a mass migration of Greeks and fostered urbanization on an unprecedented scale. The resulting cosmopolitan culture challenged traditional social, economic, and political norms, giving rise to new classes, forms of wealth, and technological innovations.

> The unique art forms and intellectual inquiries of Greece were thus disseminated throughout this world, and transformed by it.

CORE OBJECTIVES

> **EXPLAIN** the reasons for Macedonia's rise to power and its triumph over the Greek poleis.

> **DESCRIBE** Alexander's methods of conquest, colonization, and governance.

> **IDENTIFY** the three main Hellenistic kingdoms and their essential differences.

> **DEFINE** the main characteristics of the Hellenistic world.

> **UNDERSTAND** how new philosophies and artistic movements reflect the historical changes of this era.

No one would have been able to predict that the era of greatest Greek influence lay ahead. For rather suddenly, the stalemate of the weakened poleis was shattered by the rise of a tiny kingdom on their northern borders. Beginning in the reign of King Philip II, Macedonia came to control the Greek mainland. Then, under Philip's remarkable son, a united Greek and Macedonian army extended Greek values and governance from Egypt to the frontier of India. This personal empire of Alexander could not last; but a cultural empire built upon it did. For more than a thousand years, a Hellenistic ("Greek-like") civilization united the disparate lands and peoples of a vast region, forming the basis of the more lasting Roman Empire and mirroring, in uncanny ways, the globalized culture of our own time.

The Downfall of the Greek Polis

The Peloponnesian War had left the Spartans a dominant power, but they showed little talent for maintaining their preeminence. At home, they remained deeply divided; abroad, they showed even less restraint than the Athenians had, in subduing cities that should have been allies. In 395 B.C.E., a significant portion of Greece—including such former enemies as Athens, Argos, Corinth, and Thebes—aligned themselves against Sparta. After years of stalemate, the Spartans could win the war only by turning once again to the Persians, who brokered a peace that left Sparta in control. This pattern of violence, temporarily halted by Persia, was repeated time and again over the next fifty years.

THE STRUGGLE FOR DOMINANCE

After the war, the Spartans punished their most dangerous rival, Thebes, by occupying the city for four years. This subjugation was intended as an act of humiliation, and when the Thebans regained their autonomy, they retaliated by electing a military genius, Epaminondas (*eh-pa-min-OHN-das*; c. 410–362 B.C.E.), as their *strategos*.

For decades, poleis had been experimenting with improvements to the hoplite phalanx, adding skirmishers and archers to enhance its effectiveness. Epaminondas went further: he formed an elite unit known as the Sacred Band, made up of 150 pairs of male couples: devoted lovers, pledged to fight to the death for each other's honor. Epaminondas also trained a corps of lighter, fast-moving infantry. When the Theban and Spartan armies met at Leuctra in 371 B.C.E., Epaminondas defied convention by placing his best troops (the Sacred Band) on the left side of his formation and stacking this phalanx fifty rows deep, making a narrow wedge of ten men abreast whose hidden depth of strength he further disguised under a barrage of arrows and javelin attacks. The weight of the Theban left drove through the Spartan right flank, breaking it in two and collapsing it. After the victory, Epaminondas and his army marched through Spartan territory, freeing the helots.

Almost overnight, Epaminondas had reduced Sparta and launched what has been called the Theban Hegemony. But as Theban power grew, so did the animosity of other poleis. When the Thebans and Spartans squared off again in 362 B.C.E., the Athenians even allied with their old enemies. Although Thebes again won, Epaminondas fell in battle. Athens then attempted to establish a naval alliance, but quickly reverted to abusing its allies. Greece was reduced to a constellation of petty warring states.

The Theban Sacred Band

Xenophon Describes an Ideal Leader

In his history of "The Inland Expedition" undertaken by the Ten Thousand, Xenophon (430–354 B.C.E.) mourns the death of Cyrus the Younger, whom he believes would have made a better Great King of Persia than the brother he challenged, Artaxerxes II. The following description of the prince's character and leadership became very famous in its time, often circulating as a separate booklet. It is likely to have influenced the young Alexander.

Thus then died Cyrus, a man who, of all the Persians since Cyrus the elder, was the most princely and the most worthy of rule, as is agreed by all who appear to have had personal knowledge of him. In the first place, while he was yet a boy, and when he was receiving his education with his brother and other youths, he was thought to surpass them all in everything. For all the sons of the Persian nobles are educated at the gates of the king, where they may learn many a lesson of virtuous conduct, but can see or hear nothing disgraceful. Here the boys see some honored by the king, and others disgraced, and hear of them, so that in their very childhood they learn to govern and to obey.

Here Cyrus, first of all, showed himself most remarkable for modesty among those of his own age, and for paying more ready obedience to his elders than even those who were inferior to him in station; and next, he was noted for his fondness for horses, and for managing them in a superior manner. They found him, too, very desirous of learning, and most assiduous in practicing, the warlike exercises of archery, and hurling the javelin. When it suited his age, he grew extremely fond of the chase, and of braving dangers in encounters with wild beasts. On one occasion, he did not shrink from a she-bear that attacked him, but, in grappling with her, was dragged from off his horse, and received some wounds, the scars of which were visible on his body, but at last killed her. The person who first came to his assistance he made a happy man in the eyes of many.

When he was sent down by his father, as satrap of Lydia and Great Phrygia and Cappadocia, and was also appointed commander of all the troops whose duty it is to muster in the plain of Castolus, he soon showed that if he made a league or compact with anyone, or gave a promise, he deemed it of the utmost importance not to break his word. Accordingly the states that were committed to his charge, as well as individuals, had the greatest confidence in him; and if anyone had been his enemy, he felt secure that if Cyrus entered into a treaty with him, he should suffer no infraction of the stipulations. When, therefore, he waged war against Tissaphernes, all the cities, of their own accord, chose to adhere to Cyrus in preference to Tissaphernes, except the Milesians; but they feared him, because he would not abandon the cause of the exiles; for he both showed by his deeds and declared in words that he would never desert them, since he had once become a friend to them, not even though they should grow still fewer in number, and be in a worse condition than they were.

Whenever anyone did him a kindness or an injury, he showed himself anxious to go beyond him in those respects; and some used to mention a wish of his that he desired to live long enough to outdo both those who had done him good, and those who had done him ill, in the requital that he should make. Accordingly to him alone of the men of our days were so great a number of people desirous of committing the disposal of their property, their cities, and their own persons.

Source: Excerpted from Xenophon, *Anabasis*, ed. M. I. Finley, in *The Portable Greek Historians* (New York: 1959), pp. 383–84.

Questions for Analysis

1. According to Xenophon, what are the attributes of a great leader? How would Alexander have applied these attributes to his own situation?

2. What seems to be Xenophon's attitude toward the Persians? How might his portrayal of them have been influenced by his travels among them? How might it have been colored by his attitude toward his own countrymen?

3. In what ways does Cyrus the Younger appear to have followed the example of his ancestor, Cyrus the Great (page 66)?

SOCIAL AND ECONOMIC CRISES

Meanwhile, individual poleis were riven by internal turmoil. Struggles between democrats and oligarchs worsened. Incessant warfare profoundly affected economic and social infrastructures. Many ordinary people were homeless or enslaved. Farmlands throughout Greece were ravaged. The destruction was particularly devastating because of the long time it takes grapevines and olive trees to mature: forty or fifty years in the latter case. So when an invading army cut down an olive grove, it was destroying a staple crop for two generations. Even arable land was exhausted and less productive. As a result, prices rose around 50 percent while standards of living declined and taxes increased. In Athens, the wealthiest citizens now became the patrons of public theaters and buildings, as well as sponsors who maintained roads and warships.

To support themselves, many men turned to mercenary service. The Greek states in Sicily and Italy began to hire warriors from the mainland. So, as we have noted, did Cyrus, the brother of the Persian emperor, who hired a force of ten thousand men in an attempt to seize the throne in 401 B.C.E. Cyrus was killed in battle; shortly thereafter, the troops' Spartan general was murdered by imperial agents. The army—marooned in a hostile country—had to fight its way out under elected leaders, one of whom was Xenophon. Finally, they reached the Black Sea and made their way back to Greece, where many (including Xenophon) settled in Sparta. Despite these hardships, this episode was a stunning demonstration of what a professional Greek army could achieve, and it would fire Alexander's imagination.

Reimagining the Polis: The Artistic and Intellectual Response

We might take 399 B.C.E., the year of Socrates' execution, as the end of an era. The polis, the engine of innovation in the Greek world, had broken down. This had a profound impact on the arts, philosophy, and political thought.

THE ARTS OF THE FOURTH CENTURY

As we observed in Chapter 3, the painters and sculptors of the fifth century B.C.E. were already working to achieve a heightened appearance of realism. During the fourth century B.C.E., this experimentation continued: painters and sculptors tried to render both objects and people as they actually looked—for better or for worse—and to convey the illusion of movement. They also grew bolder in their use of sophisticated techniques, such as casting full-size statues in bronze, which combined high levels of artistry with metallurgy. The era's most famous sculptor, Praxiteles (*prak-SIT-el-ees*), was bold, too, in his choice of subjects, and widely regarded as the first artist to create full-size female nudes, which sparked controversy (see *Interpreting Visual Evidence* on page 121).

The forms and functions of drama also changed considerably. Tragedy and comedy were no longer mounted as part of public festivals but were financed by private patrons who exercised greater control over performances. As a result, playwrights did not have the freedom for political and social critique. Aristophanes' biting,

BRONZE YOUTH. This lithe statue, dating from the years 340–330 B.C.E., was found in the sea near Marathon and has been identified as a work by the master sculptor Praxiteles (or one of his pupils). Compare this male nude with the one discussed in Chapter 3. **› How might changes in the style of sculpture parallel cultural changes in society at large?**

satirical wit gave way to a milder, less provocative style resembling early television sitcoms. This "New Comedy" relied on mistaken identities, tangled familial relationships, and humorous breaches of etiquette. Similar trends toward escapism and frivolity were also apparent in a new literary genre: the prose novel, in which star-crossed lovers undergo perilous adventures before reuniting happily ever after. These pleasant fictions targeted an increasingly literate audience of women.

PHILOSOPHY AFTER SOCRATES: THE SCHOOLS OF PLATO AND ARISTOTLE

The work of Socrates was advanced by his most talented student, **Plato**. Born to an aristocratic family around 429 B.C.E., the young Plato witnessed the persecution, trial, and death of his mentor. For the next fifty years, until his own death around 349 B.C.E., he strove to vindicate Socrates by constructing a philosophical system based on his teacher's precepts. He did this by founding an informal school called the Academy and by writing a series of dramatic dialogues that feature Socrates as the central character.

Plato (429–349 B.C.E.) Student of Socrates who dedicated his life to transmitting his teacher's legacy through the writing of dialogues on philosophical subjects, in which Socrates himself plays the major role.

PLATO AND ARISTOTLE IN THE SCHOOL OF ATHENS. Although many artistic representations of Plato and Aristotle were made in antiquity, the image that best captures the essential difference between their philosophies is this one, the focal point of a fresco by the Renaissance painter Raphael (1483–1520 C.E.; discussed further in Chapter 12). Plato is the older man (center left), who points with his right hand to the heavens; Aristotle is the younger man (center right), gesturing with an open palm to the earth. › **How does this double portrait reflect these philosophers' teachings and perspectives?**

The longest and most famous dialogue is now known by its Latin title, the *Republic*. In it, Plato argues—through the character of Socrates—that social harmony is more important than individual liberty or equality. He imagines a polis in which farmers, artisans, and traders are governed by a superior group of "guardians" chosen in their youth for their intelligence and character. These prospective guardians would serve the polis first as soldiers, living together without private property. Those found to be the wisest would then receive more education, and a few would ultimately become "philosopher-kings." These enlightened rulers would then choose the next generation of guardians.

Plato's Republic: a vision of society ruled by philosopher-kings ❯

This utopian vision bears a certain resemblance to the social order of Sparta and is clearly a response to the failures of Athenian democracy in Plato's youth. But whether Plato himself believed in this system is open to interpretation. Indeed, the students of Socrates who are represented as discussing it voice many objections. The most obvious of these is "Who will guard the guardians?" For such a system presumes that properly educated rulers will never be corrupted by power or wealth, a proposition that has yet to be sustained in practice.

The more practical applications of philosophy would be the preoccupation of Plato's own student **Aristotle** (384–322 B.C.E.). Aristotle, son of a physician, stressed the importance of observing natural phenomena: understanding the workings of the world through the rational analysis of empirical knowledge—that is, information gained through sensory experience. In contrast to Plato, who taught that everything we experience is a pale reflection of some intangible ideal, Aristotle advocated the rigorous investigation of the natural universe and human beings' place within it. Unlike Socrates and Plato, whose dialogues were playful, Aristotle delivered lectures on which his students took detailed notes; eventually, these notes became treatises on politics, ethics, logic, metaphysics, and poetics. Aristotle also established rules for the syllogism, a form of reasoning in which certain premises inevitably lead to a valid conclusion, and categories that could be used to further philosophical and scientific analysis.

Main ideas in Aristotle's thinking: rational harmony and moderation ❯

Aristotle taught that the highest good consists in the harmonious functioning of the individual human mind and body. Since humans differ from animals because of their rational capacities, they find happiness by exercising these capacities appropriately. Good conduct is therefore rational conduct, and consists in acting moderately: showing courage rather than rashness or cowardice, temperance rather than excessive indulgence or self-denial.

Whereas Plato saw politics as a means to an end that could never be achieved in this life, Aristotle thought of politics as an end in itself: the collective exercise of moderation. But Aristotle also taught that some groups of people are not fully human and so intended by nature to be slaves. He also believed that women were not fully human and could never be participants in the public sphere of the polis. So when he asserted that "man is a political animal" (or, to be more faithful to the Greek, "a creature of the polis"), he meant only Greek men of privileged status. Like Plato, however, Aristotle saw democracy as a debased form of government. What he preferred was the polity, in which elements of monarchy, aristocracy, and representative governance are combined.

MEN OF THOUGHT AND ACTION

For all their brilliance, Plato and Aristotle offered few remedies for the ills of their own societies. But other intellectuals were considering more radical alternatives. One was Xenophon, that veteran of the Ten Thousand, who was another student

Aristotle (384–322 B.C.E.) Student of Plato whose philosophy was based on the rational analysis of the material world. In contrast to his teacher, he stressed the rigorous investigation of real phenomena, rather than the development of universal ethics.

Reconstructing an Ideal of Female Beauty

The lost statue known as the Aphrodite of Knidos was considered the most beautiful in the ancient world, but we can study it only by looking at later copies. It was the work of the fourth century's most renowned sculptor, Praxiteles, who was reputed to have modeled it after the Athenian courtesan known as Phryne, a renowned beauty who inspired several contemporary artists and a whole series of apocryphal stories. The most reliable of these tales concerns the riches she accrued. Apparently she became so wealthy that she offered to finance the rebuilding of Thebes in 336 B.C.E.—on the condition that the slogan "destroyed by Alexander, restored by Phryne the Courtesan" be prominently displayed on the new walls. (Her offer was rejected.)

Praxiteles' original statue is thought to have been the first monumental female nude fashioned in antiquity. According to one authority, Praxiteles initially received a commission from the island of Kos, for which he fashioned both clothed and naked versions of Aphrodite. Apparently, the scandalized citizens approved only the draped version and refused to pay for the nude. It was purchased instead by the city of Knidos on Cyprus, where it was displayed in an open-air temple so that it could be seen from all sides. It quickly became a tourist attraction and was widely copied and emulated. Two of the more faithful replicas, made by later artists working in Rome, are pictured here.

Questions for Analysis

1. As we have seen, the male nude was a favorite subject of Greek artists from the Archaic Period onward. Recall your knowledge of contemporary Greek culture and society. Why was it not until the fourth century B.C.E. that a life-size female nude could be publicly displayed? Were there any precedents for statues like this?

2. Compare and contrast the ideal of female beauty suggested by the Knidian Aphrodite with the male ideal discussed in Chapter 3. What can you conclude about the relationship between these ideals and the different expectations of male and female behavior in Greek society? Why, for example, would ancient sources insist that the model for this statue was a courtesan?

3. Among the Romans, a statue like the Knidian Aphrodite was called a *Venus pudica*, a "modest Venus" (image A). Yet the citizens of Kos were allegedly shocked by its indecency, and old photographs of the copy in the Vatican Museum (image B) show that it was displayed until 1932 with additional draperies made of tin. How do you account for these very different standards of decency? To what degree do they suggest that concepts of "beauty" or "modesty" are historically constructed?

A. Roman copy of the Aphrodite of Knidos.

B. Second century C.E. copy of the Aphrodite of Knidos.

of Socrates and an exact contemporary of Plato. After his return from Persia, he went to fight for the Spartan king Agesilaus (*ah-geh-si-LA-uhs*), who became a trusted friend. It is mostly thanks to Xenophon's admiring account that we know anything about the Spartiate system described in Chapter 3, which he intended as a rebuke to Athens. We also have his own view of Socrates' teaching, and his treatises on kingship and household management: the *Oikonomikos*, root of *economics*. He loved horses and dogs and wrote a treatise on training them for the hunt. All the while, he watched as the Theban leader Epaminondas crippled the Spartan state he so admired.

The Athenian orator Isocrates (436–338 B.C.E.) was another direct contemporary of Plato and was also convinced that something had gone horribly awry after the Peloponnesian War. Rather than imagining a reform of the polis, he proposed an invasion of Persia. This, he prophesied, would be led by a man of special vision and ability, someone who could unite the Greek world behind his cause. He even began to think that the man for the job was someone whom most Greeks considered no Greek at all: the king of Macedonia, Philip II.

The Rise of Macedonia

Until the fourth century, Macedonia (or Macedon) had been a weak kingdom, ruled by a royal dynasty in conflict with its own nobility, surrounded by even smaller kingdoms and predatory tribes. Despite some efforts to add a gloss of Hellenic culture to their royal court—one king had successfully entertained Euripides and Sophocles—the Greeks considered them nearly barbaric. The ancient Macedonian language was not Greek, although the royal family and some elites would have spoken Greek as a second language; and the Macedonians seem to have participated in the Olympic Games. But they were definitely perceived as dangerous outsiders. So when a young and energetic king consolidated the southern Balkans under his rule, many Greeks saw it as a troubling development.

THE REIGN OF PHILIP II (359–336 B.C.E.)

Philip II was not supposed to be a king. Born in 382 B.C.E., he was the third and youngest son of King Amyntas III and considered so dispensable that he was sent to Thebes as a hostage when he was fourteen. This turned out to be the making of him: he became the protégé of the brilliant Epaminondas and may even have trained with the general Pelopidas (*pel-OH-pi-das*) in the Sacred Band. When he returned to the Macedonian capital at Pella in 364 B.C.E., three years later, he had received a more thorough education than any Macedonian before him. He was also ambitious, and when both of his older brothers died in battle, one after the other, Philip was not content with the role of regent for an infant nephew. By 356 B.C.E., he had supplanted his nephew and was reigning as king. That same year, his queen, Olympias, bore him an heir. The boy was given the dynastic name Alexandros, "leader of men."

The first problem of Philip's reign was the fragility of Macedonia's northern borders. Through a combination of warfare and diplomacy, he subdued the tribes of the southern Balkans and incorporated their territory into his kingdom.

Philip II (382–336 B.C.E.) King of Macedonia and father of Alexander, he consolidated the southern Balkans and the Greek city-states under Macedonian domination.

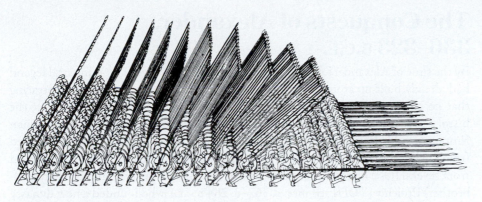

MACEDONIAN PHALANX. Philip of Macedonia's hoplite infantry—the model for Alexander's—was armed with two-handed pikes of graduated lengths, from thirteen to twenty-one feet, and was massed in squares sixteen rows deep and wide. Members of the phalanx were trained to wheel quickly in step formation and to double the width of their front rank as needed by filing off in rows of eight. The reach of their spears, called *sarissas*, extended the phalanx's fighting range.

His success had much to do with his reorganization of a hoplite infantry along Theban lines. The mineral resources of his conquered territories also helped to build a standing professional army; just one of his gold mines produced as much in one year as Athens had collected annually, at its height. Philip also organized an elite cavalry squad—the Companions—who fought with and beside the king. These young men were drawn from the nobility, whose loyalty Philip cultivated; in fact, he also gained valuable young hostages to ensure the good conduct of his rivals. Through a series of strategic marriages, Philip also managed to gain alliances with many neighboring kingdoms—although his open polygamy was, in Greek eyes, another barbarian trait.

Whereas Isocrates saw in Philip a potential savior of Greece, many Greeks believed that Philip's ultimate aim was to conquer them. In actuality, he was probably trying to forge an alliance with Athens, whose fleet could facilitate an invasion of Persia; in return, he promised to support Athens' old claim to dominance over Greece. But the Athenians refused to cooperate. This miscalculation ultimately led to war, which sent the Athenians scrambling to ally with Thebes and a number of smaller poleis. Their collective fate was sealed at the battle of Chaeronea (*kie-ROH-nee-ah*) in 338 B.C.E., when an army led by Philip and Alexander (aged seventeen) decimated the Athenian forces and the Theban Sacred Band. In the aftermath, Philip called delegates from around mainland Greece to Corinth, where he established a new political federation. This League of Corinth was to provide Greek forces for the invasion of Persia and maintain peace among rival poleis.

Philip never realized his dream of Persian conquest. Two years later, in 336 B.C.E., he was assassinated during a festival, purportedly by a former (male) lover. The kingship now fell to Alexander. Among the Greeks, he would be known as Alexander, Sacker of Cities. To the Romans, he would be **Alexander the Great**.

 Macedonians under Philip and Alexander defeat the Athenians and Thebans

The Conquests of Alexander, 336–323 B.C.E.

By the time of Alexander's early death at the age of thirty-two, a monumental legend had already built up around him. This makes it all the more ironic and frustrating that no contemporary account of his life has survived. When we reconstruct the history of his time, we are relying on men who lived and wrote under the Roman Empire, notably Plutarch (46–120 C.E.) and Arrian (c. 86–160 C.E.), both separated from their subject by 400 years. However, these historians used sources derived from several (lost) firsthand accounts, one by Alexander's general (and possibly half-brother) Ptolemy (*TOHL-eh-mee*; c. 367–c. 284 B.C.E.), who founded a new dynasty of Egyptian pharaohs. This is a reminder of how fragile the historical record of antiquity is, when sources for the life of such a famous man are so scarce.

THE CONQUEST OF PERSIA

When Alexander succeeded his father in 336 B.C.E., he had to put down the revolts that erupted immediately after Philip's death—notably at Thebes, which he punished by destroying its famous walls. Two years later, he was crossing the Hellespont at the head of a hoplite army to challenge the Great King of Persia, Darius III.

Darius was no match for Alexander. He was a minor member of the royal family who had been placed on the throne after a palace coup, at the relatively old age of forty-five, in the same year that Alexander became king at twenty. Darius and his advisers failed to take the Macedonian threat seriously, despite the Persians' past history of defeat at the hands of Greek armies—even on Persian soil and within living memory. Perhaps they assumed that the enormous forces of their empire would easily overwhelm a small army of forty-two thousand men; or perhaps they misunderstood Alexander's far-reaching aims.

In any event, the Persian army was made up of mercenaries or poorly paid conscripts under the command of inexperienced generals. As a result, Alexander achieved a series of extraordinary victories, beginning near the epic field of Troy and continuing down the Ionian coastline. In 333 B.C.E., Darius tried to engage Alexander personally, but the chosen site at Issus favored Alexander's fast-moving infantry, not the heavy cavalry and chariots of the Persians, which had no room to maneuver and were hampered by mud. Darius himself shamefully fled, abandoning his entire household, which included his wife and his mother. (They were captured by Alexander's troops, and treated by him with great respect.) Darius spent the remainder of his life running from Alexander's advancing army, until his defeat at Gaugamela (near Mosul, Iraq) in 331 B.C.E., when he was killed by a local chieftain who hoped to win Alexander's favor. Instead, Alexander—acting as the new Great King—had the chieftain executed for treason against his predecessor. The next spring, Alexander destroyed the royal capital of Persepolis, lest it serve as a rallying point for Persian resistance.

Within two years after Darius's humiliation at Issus, Alexander had completed his conquest. The cities of Syria and Palestine surrendered

MARBLE HEAD OF ALEXANDER. Alexander the Great was reported to have been very striking in appearance, although sources vary in their assessment of his physical beauty. This portrait bust was made in 180 B.C.E., about 150 years after his death. **› Given the trends in sculpture during that period (see page 118), is this likely to have been an accurate portrait? Why or why not?**

after Alexander made a powerful statement by destroying the wealthy Phoenician capital at Tyre. Following the example of Cyrus the Great, whose tactics he increasingly emulated, Alexander offered amnesty to cities that submitted peacefully—but dealt mercilessly with those that resisted. The fortified city of Gaza, the last Persian stronghold on the Egyptian border, provides a grim example: its commander not only refused to surrender but seemed determined to fight to the death, inflicting severe losses on Alexander's troops. When the city was finally taken, Alexander's troops slew all the adult males and enslaved the women and children. Alexander himself dragged the body of the commander around the city's walls behind his chariot, imitating Achilles' treatment of his fallen rival Hector.

ALEXANDER IN EGYPT

After this, Alexander marched into Egypt unopposed. In fact, he was welcomed: Egypt had been governed as a Persian satrapy (principality) since 525 B.C.E. Now Alexander himself was hailed as pharaoh and given the double crown of Upper and Lower Egypt (see Chapter 1). The "barbarian" chieftain of a backwater kingdom had become pharaoh of the oldest civilization on earth and heir to its immense riches and history.

While the Persians and (before them) the Medes had long been the Greeks' traditional enemies, the Egyptians had always been too far away to pose a threat; indeed, they were an object of awe. This may explain Alexander's response to the oracle of Ammon, the Egyptian sun god Amun-Ra, whom the Greeks identified with Zeus. At the oracle's desert oasis of Siwa, Alexander was told that he was the "son of Ammon" and a god himself. Ever mindful of historical precedent, Alexander seems to have decided at this point that Egypt should be the capital of his new empire. Persia had been the goal, but it was in Egypt that he would build his shining new city of Alexandria. Yet he had time only to lay out a plan for the streets and central spaces before he marched north to conquer other worlds. When he finally returned, he was in his sarcophagus.

ALEXANDER'S FINAL CAMPAIGNS

For five years, Alexander and his men campaigned in the mountainous regions of the Persian Empire that had been only loosely yoked to the more settled lands of Mesopotamia. This is the region encompassed today by Afghanistan, a terrain famous for defeating every attempt at conquest or control. In the mountains of Bactria, Alexander's army experienced hard fighting and never succeeded in gaining much ground, despite Alexander's marriage to Roxane, the daughter of a local chieftain. Thereafter, Alexander moved down through what is now Pakistan to the Indus Valley, meeting stiff resistance from its warlords but eventually defeating their leader, Porus, at the Battle of the Hydaspes (*heed-AH-spes*) in 326 B.C.E.

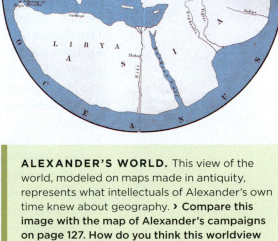

ALEXANDER'S WORLD. This view of the world, modeled on maps made in antiquity, represents what intellectuals of Alexander's own time knew about geography. › **Compare this image with the map of Alexander's campaigns on page 127. How do you think this worldview affected the planning of his route?** › **What similarities and differences do you find more generally, comparing this ancient map with the other maps that appear in this book?**

LESSER KINGS OF PERSIA APPROACH THE GREAT KING TO PERFORM *PROSKYNESIS*. › Why would Alexander's Greek and Macedonian soldiers have balked at the suggestion that they show their solidarity with the Persians by performing this ritual?

This was to be the last major battle of his career, the one in which his famous warhorse, Bucephalus ("Thunder-Head"), was killed. (He was buried nearby, and a city founded in his name.) It was here that Alexander's troops, exhausted, thousands of miles and eight years from home, refused to go on. Alexander decided against recrossing the mountains of the Hindu Kush, the forbidding range whose giant peaks stretch to the Himalayas. He and his army pressed southward to the shores of the Arabian Sea—what was then known as Ocean, and the end of the world. The ensuing march through the Gedrosian Desert weakened him and his army considerably.

But Alexander still had great plans. When he finally reached the royal palace of Susa, he began to indicate how he would have tried to combine his Greco–Macedonian Empire with that of Persia, had he lived. He announced a plan to train Persian youths to fight alongside Greeks and Macedonians. He arranged a mass marriage between hundreds of his officers and a corresponding number of Persian noblewomen. Most controversially, he showed respect for his Persian subjects by adopting Persian dress—considered by Greeks to be symbolic of their barbarism—and by encouraging the ritual performance of *proskynesis* (*pros-kin-EE-sis*). According to Herodotus, *proskynesis* was a gesture of bodily submission performed by all Persians—even those of royal rank—to honor the Great King. The person paying homage would bow deeply and kiss his hand to the emperor, in some cases prostrating himself entirely. To the Greeks, this practice was not only humiliating but blasphemous: it suggested that the Persians worshiped their emperor as a god. To Alexander, adopting *proskynesis* was probably intended to level cultural differences between Persians and Greeks. But it was not a success, and it fueled a mutiny among the Macedonians.

ALEXANDER'S DEATH

Apart from these attempts to create cross-cultural cohesion, Alexander took no realistic steps to create an administration for his vast empire. How he planned to

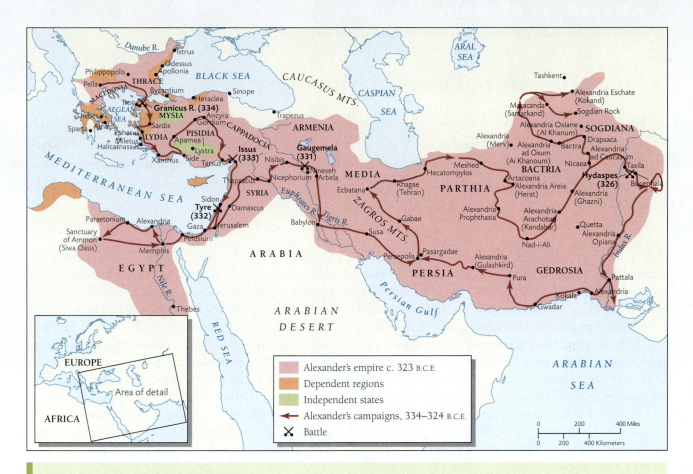

govern it effectively and bequeath it intact remains a mystery. Also mysterious is the cause of his death, and the fact that his body did not begin to decompose immediately. In 2019, a clinical physician published a report arguing that Alexander may have contracted Guillain-Barré syndrome, a rare autoimmune disorder that causes gradual paralysis and eventual unconsciousness. If so, he may have actually died later than the reported date of June 10 or 11, in 323 B.C.E. He was not yet thirty-three years old.

The Hellenistic Kingdoms

According to one Roman historian, Alexander's friends and officers gathered around his bed as he lay dying and asked to whom he wished to leave his empire. He had replied, "To the strongest." According to Plutarch and Arrian, though, he was actually incapable of speech. According to still other late sources, he

Alexander Puts Down a Mutiny

The following account comes from the history of Alexander's campaigns by the Greek-speaking Roman historian Arrian (c. 86–160 C.E.), who lived in the Roman province of Bithynia in northern Anatolia. This is the closest thing we have to a primary source, since histories written by Alexander's own contemporaries have not survived. The following passage describes Alexander's response to a mutiny among his troops after his return from India in 324 B.C.E.

"My countrymen, you are sick for home—so be it! I shall make no attempt to check your longing to return. Go wherever you will; I shall not hinder you. But if go you must, there is one thing I would have you understand—what I have done for you, and in what coin you have repaid me....

"[M]arching out from a country too poor to maintain you decently, [I] laid open for you at a blow, and in spite of Persia's naval supremacy, the gates of the Hellespont. My cavalry crushed the satraps of Darius, and I added all Ionia and Aeolia, the two Phrygias and Lydia to your empire.... I took them and gave them to you for your profit and enjoyment. The wealth of Egypt and Cyrene, which I shed no blood to win, now flows in your hands; Palestine and the plains of Syria and Mesopotamia are now your property; Babylon and Bactria and Susa are yours; you are the masters of the gold of Lydia, the treasures of Persia, the wealth of India—yes, and the seas beyond India, too. You are my captains, my generals, my governors of provinces.

"From all this that I have labored to win for you, what is left for me myself except the purple and the crown? I keep nothing for my own.... Perhaps you will say that, in my position as your commander, I had none of the labors and distress which you had to endure to win me what I have won.... Come now—if you are wounded, strip and show your wounds, and I will show mine. There is no part of my body but my back which does not have a scar; not a weapon a man may grasp or fling, the mark of which I do not carry on me ... and all for your sakes: for your glory and your gain. Over every land and sea, across river, mountain, and plain, I led you to the world's end, a victorious army. I marry as you marry, and many of you will have children related by blood to my own.... But you all wish to leave me. Go then! And when you reach home, tell them that Alexander your king, who vanquished the Persians and Medes and Bactrians ... tell them, I say, that you deserted him and left him to the mercy of barbarian men, whom you yourselves conquered...."

On the Macedonians, the immediate effect of Alexander's speech was profound.... But when they were told [three days later that] ... command was being given to Persian officers, foreign troops drafted into Macedonian units, a Persian corps of Guards called by a Macedonian name, Persian infantry units given the coveted title of Companions ... every man of them hurried to the palace ... and [they] swore they would not stir from the spot until Alexander took pity on them.

Source: Arrian, *The Campaigns of Alexander*, trans. Aubrey de Selincourt (New York: 1958), pp. 360–65 (slightly modified).

Questions for Analysis

1. What qualities of leadership does Alexander display in this speech? How do these qualities compare with those of Cyrus the Younger, in Xenophon's description of him (page 117)?

2. Given the circumstances that precipitated this mutiny, why does Alexander use the term *barbarians* to describe the Persians and other conquered peoples? What does he hope to convey by using this word and then by reorganizing his forces to replace Macedonians with Persians?

3. Histories written well into the nineteenth century of our era feature speeches that were allegedly spoken by historical characters on momentous occasions. How closely do you think Arrian's reconstruction of this speech reflects historical reality? How might you go about arguing that it is, in fact, an accurate reflection of what Alexander actually said?

silently gave his signet ring to a Macedonian general called Perdiccas, the leader of his cavalry.

Alexander's own son and heir was born to Roxane after his death, and it was eventually decided that the baby, Alexander IV of Macedonia, should rule jointly with Alexander's half-brother, Philip, the son of Philip II by one of his lesser wives. Philip III is reported to have suffered from a mental disability, but he was able to rule adequately for nearly six years, until he and his young nephew were murdered at the hands of Alexander's mother. Olympias had her own ambitions.

Meanwhile, the Persian satrapies that had been allotted to various leaders of Alexander's armies became the bases from which they attempted to seize control. The turmoil lasted for two generations, when three separate axes of military and political power emerged, each with a distinctive character but all headed by a Greco–Macedonian ruling class. Indeed, a striking feature of this period is the renewal of ancient political patterns. But more striking is the fact that a common culture continued to unite Alexander's fragmented empire in a **Hellenistic**, "Greek-like," world.

Hellenistic world
Describes the various Western civilizations of antiquity that were loosely united by shared Greek language and culture, especially around the eastern Mediterranean.

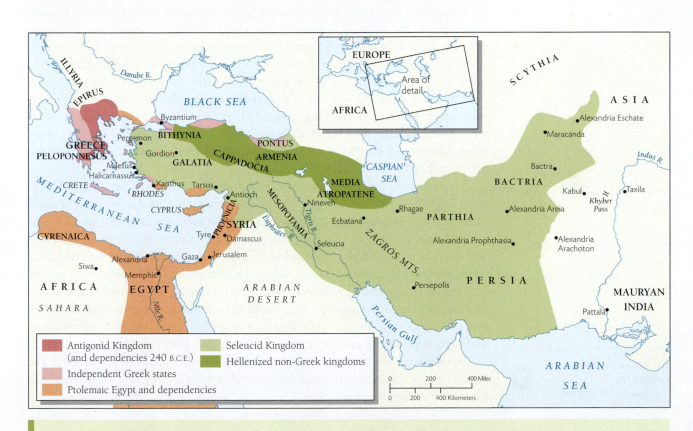

THE HELLENISTIC WORLD. Each of the three successor kingdoms to Alexander's empire was based in one of the three major civilizations we have studied so far: Egyptian, Mesopotamian, and Greek. › Based on the map above, what were the names of the three main successor states, and where were they located? › What might the division of Alexander's empire along such lines suggest about the lasting cultural differences among these regions? › What might it suggest about the likelihood of his forging a united empire, had he lived?

PTOLEMAIC EGYPT

Ptolemy strategically chooses Egypt to establish new independent monarchy

The most stable of the three successor states was Egypt, thanks in large part to the governance of Alexander's former general Ptolemy, possibly an illegitimate son of Philip II and certainly one of Alexander's most trusted advisers. Ptolemy decided to withdraw from the contest over the larger empire and asked only to be given Egypt as his satrapy. Clearly, he recognized Egypt's virtual invulnerability to attack. He also seems to have appreciated, as Alexander did, its historical cachet. And he may already have been planning to make Egypt an independent monarchy and a shrine to Alexander's memory. It was thanks to Ptolemy, in fact, that Alexander's embalmed body was returned to Egypt in 323 B.C.E. It was supposed to have gone to the royal burial ground of Aigai in Macedonia, but Ptolemy hijacked the funeral cortege and took it to the holy city of Memphis. Later, his son Ptolemy II moved the sarcophagus to Alexandria, where the tomb became a pilgrimage site, especially for Romans with imperial ambitions of their own (see Chapter 5).

The Ptolemaic Dynasty ruled for the next 300 years, until Egypt became a Roman province in 30 B.C.E.: the last of thirty-two dynasties stretching back to the fourth millennium B.C.E. The male heirs all took the name Ptolemy (hence the term *Ptolemaic Egypt*), and many of their sisters were called Cleopatra, the name of Alexander's own sister and a dynastic name among Macedonian royal women. Beginning in the reign of Ptolemy II Philadelphus ("sibling-lover"), the Ptolemies even began to follow ancient Egyptian custom by marrying their siblings. And in many other ways, they showed reverence for the culture of their kingdom while bringing it within the ambit of the wider Hellenistic world. They achieved this, in part, by ruling from the new city of Alexandria on the Mediterranean coast. There, they acted as Macedonian kings toward their Greek and Macedonian citizens; beyond Alexandria, they played the role of pharaohs. But only the last Ptolemaic ruler, Cleopatra VII (69–30 B.C.E.; see Chapter 5) ever bothered to learn the language spoken by her subjects.

In addition to being the most successful of the Hellenistic kingdoms, Ptolemaic Egypt was also the most influential, not only in its own day but now, because of its key role in preserving and transmitting the accumulated heritage of Egyptian, Mesopotamian, and Greek civilization. The Ptolemies used their wealth to patronize science and the arts, and their capital eventually displaced Athens as an intellectual and artistic center. Many breakthroughs in astronomy, mechanical engineering, and physics occurred in Alexandria. In particular, the study of medicine advanced greatly: freed from the taboos of their homeland, Greek researchers were permitted to perform autopsies on the bodies of dead criminals and vagrants, making anatomy a scientific discipline. It was also here that the texts of Greek poetry, drama, history, and philosophy were copied and preserved in the forms in which we know them. Even the Hebrew scriptures were translated into Greek for a wider audience.

Ptolemaic Egypt: cultural and technological legacies

SELEUCID ASIA

Alexander's Asian lands —both within the Persian Empire and beyond— fell to another Macedonian, Seleucus (*seh-LOO-kus*), who navigated the turmoil after Alexander's death successfully and cleverly exploited the connections he made

TWO PORTRAITS OF PTOLEMY I OF EGYPT. The Ptolemaic rulers of Egypt represented themselves as pharaohs to their Egyptian subjects (as in this bust) and as Greeks to their Macedonian and Greek subjects (as on this gold coin). › **Why would it have been important to project these two very different images?**

through his Persian wife. At his death in 281 B.C.E., his half-Persian son Antiochus (*an-TYE-oh-kuhs*) inherited an expansive realm centered on the city named after him, Antioch.

Indeed, this Seleucid dynasty struggled to keep the disparate parts of their realm together. Seleucus ceded much of the Indus Valley to the great Indian warrior-king Chandragupta, in exchange for peace and a squad of war elephants. The Seleucids had also lost control of Bactria, where a series of Indo-Greek states were emerging with a uniquely complex culture of their own. (One Greco-Bactrian king, Menander, is memorialized in Buddhist tradition.) The Seleucid heartland became northern Syria, parts of Anatolia, Mesopotamia, and the western half of Persia.

 The Seleucid dynasty struggles to unify a disparate realm

Like the Ptolemies, the Seleucids presented two faces to their subjects, one looking to ancient Mesopotamian traditions and the other looking to Greece. In his proclamations, Antiochus used terms reminiscent of Sargon, Hammurabi, and Cyrus: "I am Antiochus, Great King, legitimate king . . . king of Babylon, king of all countries." But on his coins, he wore his hair short in the Greek fashion and styled himself *basileus* (the Greek word for "king"). Although the Seleucids' bureaucracy was less organized than that of the Ptolemies, even haphazard tax collection could reap huge rewards in an empire of 30 million inhabitants. However, the Seleucids seldom converted their gains into public-works projects or capital investments. Instead, they hoarded their wealth in great state treasuries. It was not until the second century, when Antiochus III lost a costly war with the Romans, that he had to plunder temples and private wealth to pay off the indemnity imposed on him.

ANTIGONID MACEDONIA AND GREECE

Aetolian League and **Achaean League** Two alliances among Greek poleis formed during the Hellenistic period in opposition to the Antigonids of Macedonia.

The Macedonian homeland did not possess the vast wealth of the new kingdoms carved from Alexander's conquests. It also remained highly unstable until 276 B.C.E., when a general named Antigonus (*an-TIG-on-uhs*) was finally able to establish his own dynasty (known as the Antigonids). Thereafter, Macedonia drew its strength from considerable natural resources and its influence over Aegean trade, as well as its king's status as overlord of Greece.

Antigonus was influenced by a philosophical outlook called Stoicism (discussed later in this chapter) and viewed kingship as a form of noble servitude to be endured rather than enjoyed. This perspective, combined with modest resources, convinced him not to compete with the Seleucids and Ptolemies for dominance. Instead, Antigonid policy was to keep these other two powers at war with one another and away from the Macedonian sphere of influence.

The Greeks, however, were restive under the Antigonids, and two emergent powers became rallying points for those who resented "barbarian" rule. These two forces, the **Aetolian League** and the **Achaean League**, embodied a new form of Greek political organization. Unlike the defensive alliances of previous centuries, each of these two leagues constituted a true political entity, with some centralization of governance. Citizens of the member poleis participated in councils that dealt with foreign policy and military affairs, trials for treason, and the annual election of a league general and his deputy. All citizens of the various poleis enjoyed joint citizenship throughout the league. The same laws, weights and measures, coinage, and judicial procedures also applied throughout each federation. So impressive was this degree of cooperation that James Madison, John Jay, and Alexander Hamilton would employ the Achaean League as one of their models in advocating federalism in the United States.

From Polis to Cosmopolis

So what became of the polis, that building block of classical Greek civilization? As we have seen, the changes of the fourth century B.C.E. were already disrupting the traditional patterns of social and political life. If the conquests of Philip hastened this transformation, those of Alexander also opened up a wider world of opportunities. During the third century B.C.E., a common Hellenistic culture encompassed the eastern Mediterranean and western Asia, transcending political and geographical boundaries. The conditions that threatened Greek culture and identity in Greece, paradoxically, drove many Greeks to transplant that culture in the colonies Alexander had opened to them. Within just two generations, hundreds of thousands of migrants had joined a Greek diaspora ("dispersion") that reduced the population of mainland Greece by as much as 50 percent in the century between 325 and 225 B.C.E.

This exciting, urbane world was made up of interconnected cities whose scale dwarfed anything imaginable in Periclean Athens. During the fifth century B.C.E., direct participation in government had meant that every male citizen of a Greek polis had some share and stake in his society, its gods, its army, and its cultural life. In the huge and cosmopolitan Hellenistic city, by contrast, all these ways of defining oneself were no longer relevant. The individual male's intimate connection with the political life of the state was broken, as was his nexus of social and familial relationships. An average Greek in one of the Hellenistic cities might have only his immediate family to rely on; very often, he was alone. What resulted was a traumatic disjunction between the traditional values and assumptions of Greek life and the social and political realities of the day—and a host of entirely new opportunities.

COMMERCE AND URBANIZATION

The Hellenistic world was prosperous. Alexander's conquests had opened up a vast trading area stretching from Egypt to the Persian Gulf, dominated by Greek-speaking rulers and well-established merchant communities. These conquests also stimulated the economy by putting into circulation hoards of Persian gold and silver coins, jewelry, and other commodities acquired through plunder. Industries also benefited, because autocratic rulers found manufacturing to be a further means of increasing their revenues through trade and taxation.

New mercantile ventures were particularly encouraged in Ptolemaic Egypt and the Syrian heartland of the Seleucid realm. Harbors were improved, warships kept pirates at bay, roads and canals were built. The Ptolemies even employed geographers to discover new routes to distant lands and valuable markets. Into the port of Alexandria came spices from Arabia, gold from Ethiopia and India, tin from Britain, elephants and ivory from Nubia, silver from Spain, fine carpets from Anatolia, and even silk from China.

The Hellenistic kingdoms explore distant lands

The rapid growth of cities had both political and economic causes. Greek rulers imported Greek officials and especially Greek soldiers to maintain their control over non-Greek populations, making many new Greek settlements necessary. Alexander himself had founded some seventy cities as imperial outposts; over the next two centuries, his successors founded about two hundred more. Urbanization also increased, due to the expansion of commerce and industry. All of these factors created opportunities for adventurous men seeking to escape the harsh conditions of life in Greece. Both new and established cities needed artisans, merchants, teachers, and laborers of all kinds. But the most significant factor fueling rapid urban expansion was the mass migration of entire families of workers from rural areas. At Antioch, the population quadrupled during a single century. The new city of Seleucia on the Tigris grew from nothing to a metropolis of several hundred thousand in less than two centuries. Alexandria in Egypt had a half-million inhabitants. Only imperial Rome would surpass it in size, and not until the eighteenth century of our era did European cities such as London and Paris become as large.

HELLENISTIC EARRINGS. These exquisite pieces of jewelry illustrate the enormous wealth and extraordinary craftsmanship available to the elites of the Hellenistic world.

Problems faced by lower economic classes

Despite the overall growth of the Hellenistic economy, not everyone enjoyed prosperity. Agriculture remained the most common occupation, and small farmers in particular suffered severely from exploitative taxation. Although industrial production increased, it continued to be based on manual labor by individual artisans, most of whom lived in poverty. Among the teeming populations of Hellenistic cities, unemployment was a constant concern. Those who could not find work were forced to beg, steal, or sell themselves to survive.

Even those who prospered in the new economy were often subject to drastic fluctuations in their fortunes. A trader who did very well selling a luxury fabric might invest heavily in it, only to find that tastes had changed or that a ship full of his wares had sunk. An investor looking to make a fortune during an upward price spiral might go into debt to take advantage of the trend, only to find that supply exceeded demand, leaving him nothing. The economic landscape of the Hellenistic world was therefore one of contrasting extremes. In many ways, this was also the case with respect to its culture.

Hellenistic Worldviews

Life in the Hellenistic boomtowns produced new perspectives on the world and new philosophies that differed significantly from those of Plato and Aristotle. Two opposing trends ran almost parallel with one another. The first, exemplified by Stoicism (*STOH-iss-ism*) and Epicureanism (*eh-pih-CURE-ee-an-ism*), promoted rational thought as the key to alleviating the anxieties of modern life. The second trend, exemplified by the Skeptics and various religious cults, tended to deny the possibility of attaining truth through the exercise of human reason alone. Despite these stark differences, however, all forms of belief responded to the same need—to make human existence meaningful in a new age that lacked traditional civic structures and social values.

TWO PATHS TO TRANQUILITY: STOICISM AND EPICUREANISM

The two strains of philosophy that dominated the Hellenistic world both originated in Athens around 300 B.C.E. Their promoters were Epicurus and Zeno, and their teachings had several features in common. Both men were concerned with the well-being of the individual, not with the welfare of society as a whole. Both were also firmly rooted in the material world, denying the existence of any purely spiritual phenomena; they considered even the soul to be part of the mortal body. **Stoicism** and **Epicureanism** also responded to the new cosmopolitan age by promoting universal values: both taught that people are the same the world over and recognized no distinctions between Greeks and "barbarians."

But in other ways the two systems were radically different. The Stoics who followed Zeno of Citium (c. 335–c. 263 B.C.E.)—taking their name from the *stoa* ("colonnade") in which he regularly taught—believed that the cosmos is an ordered whole in which all contradictions are resolved for ultimate good. Evil is not absolute but relative, meaning that human misfortunes are merely incidents that will lead to the final perfection of the universe. Everything that happens is therefore predetermined, and people are free only to accept fate or rebel against it; that is, they are free to choose *how to respond* to adversity or prosperity. Through the exercise of reason and emotional restraint, the Stoics strove to adjust their expectations to the workings of fate and to purge their souls of all bitterness or regret. Stoicism therefore emphasized self-discipline and the fulfillment of one's duties. It taught tolerance and forgiveness, and urged participation in public affairs as a special responsibility for those with able minds. It condemned slavery and violence, although it took no real actions against these evils because it saw them as inevitable—and because extreme social change might be worse.

Stoic philosophy emphasizes discipline, duty, and tolerance

With some later modifications, Stoic philosophy became the driving force behind the values of the Roman Republic and even influenced early Christianity; it can be considered one of the most important products of the Hellenistic age. Even today, those who do not consciously embrace its tenets or its perspective may find that they have been influenced by its egalitarian and humanitarian ethos.

The second main philosophical trend derives from the teachings of Epicurus (341–270 B.C.E.). Epicurus was influenced by the atomic theory of an earlier Greek philosopher called Democritus (*dem-OH-kree-tuhs*), who lived in the latter part of the fifth century B.C.E. and is often called the "father of modern science." According to his central thesis, the universe is made up entirely of atoms, infinite in number, indestructible, and indivisible. Every individual object or organism is therefore the product of a combination of atoms.

Studying Democritus' writings, Epicurus and his followers reached a conclusion exactly opposite to that of the Stoics. They interpreted the atomic theory to mean that there is no ultimate purpose in the workings of the universe, and that these workings are entirely random. So the highest good cannot come of submitting oneself stoically to the endurance of hardship, because no hardship is part of a larger plan; it is merely the chance by-product of random atomic actions. The highest good, then, must be pleasure: the moderate satisfaction of bodily appetites, the intellectual pleasure of contemplating excellence and remembering past enjoyments, and serenity in the face of death. Indeed, an individual who understands that the soul itself is material and will not survive the death of the body, that the universe operates at random, and that no gods intervene in human affairs should have no fear of death or any other supernatural phenomena.

Epicurean philosophy emphasizes pleasure and happiness

The moral teachings and political goals of the Epicureans reflected this worldview. In contrast to the Stoics, they did not insist on virtue as an end in itself or on the fulfillment of one's duties. For an Epicurean, the only duty a person has is to the self, and the only reason to act virtuously is to increase one's own happiness. Similarly, Epicureans also denied that there is any such thing as absolute justice: laws and political institutions are "just" only insofar as they contribute to the welfare of the individual. Yes, every society has found certain rules to be necessary for the maintenance of order; but the state is, at best, a mere convenience. The wise man takes no active part in politics but, instead, withdraws to study philosophy and enjoy the fellowship of a few congenial friends. Modern libertarian movements share many characteristics with Epicureanism.

EXTREME DOUBT: SKEPTICISM

The most pessimistic philosophy generated by the Hellenistic era was propounded by the Skeptics, whose name derives from a Greek word meaning "those on the lookout" or "the spies." Skepticism reached the zenith of its popularity in the second century B.C.E. under the influence of Carneades (*kar-NEE-ah-dees*; c. 214–129 B.C.E.), a man born in the Greek city of Cyrene, in North Africa, and who spent his youth in Athens. The chief source of his inspiration was the teaching (derived from Aristotle) that all knowledge is based on sense perception and is therefore limited and relative. From this, the Skeptics concluded that no one can truly know or prove anything. Because the impressions of our senses can deceive us, we cannot even be certain about the truth of whatever empirical knowledge we think we have gained by observation of the world. All we can say is that things *appear* to be such and such; we do not know that they really *are* that way. It follows, furthermore, that we can have no definite knowledge of the supernatural, the meaning of life, or right and wrong.

The only sensible course for the Skeptic is therefore to suspend judgment: this alone can lead to happiness. If a person abandons the fruitless quest for truth and ceases to worry about good conduct and the existence of evil, he can at least attain a certain peace of mind. Needless to say, the Skeptics were even less concerned than the Epicureans with political and social problems, from which they felt wholly alienated. In some key respects, they anticipated modern existentialism and nihilism.

THE VARIETIES OF RELIGION

Like Epicureanism and Skepticism, Hellenistic religion tended to offer vehicles of escape from political commitments. When we think back to the link between Greek selfhood and politics—"man is a creature of the polis"—we can begin to appreciate what a radical change had occurred in just a few generations. In the classical age of the polis, as in all the societies we have studied so far, religion was wholly interconnected with politics. Divine worship centered on the gods who protected a community and furthered its interests. Hence, the most serious of the charges brought against Socrates was that he had "denied the gods of the polis" and thus committed treason. Religious crimes were political crimes, and piety was the same as patriotism.

Link between politics and religion

Although this sense of connection between a place and its gods persisted to a certain extent during the Hellenistic period, civic-oriented worship was compromised by the rootless multiculturalism of the third and second centuries B.C.E. In its place, some elite members of society gravitated toward one of the philosophies discussed above. Ordinary people, though, were more likely to embrace religious cults that offered emotional gratification or the diversion of colorful rituals, as well as some assurance of an afterlife—which the new philosophies did not.

In Greek-speaking communities especially, cults that stressed extreme methods of atonement for sin, ecstatic mystical union with the divine, or contact with supernatural forces attracted many followers. Among these mystery religions—so called because their membership was select and their rites secret—one of the most popular was the cult of Dionysos, which celebrated the cyclical death and resurrection of that Greek god. The Egyptian cult of Isis, drawing on the story of Osiris (see Chapter 1), also revolved around rituals of death and rebirth. So, too, did Zoroastrianism (see Chapter 2), which became increasingly dualistic: its magi taught that the material world was entirely evil and urged believers to adopt

A Jewish Response to Hellenization

Greek culture became a powerful force throughout the Hellenistic world, even among Jews. In the second century B.C.E., the Hellenized ways of the Jewish elites in Jerusalem led to a revolt by a native Hebrew dynasty known as the Maccabees, who decried the effects of Hellenization on Jewish life. These events are recorded in two apocryphal books of the Hebrew Bible. In the passage that follows, note that even the High Priest of the Temple bears a Greek name, Jason.

In those days, lawless men came forth from Israel and misled many, saying, "Let us go and make a covenant with the Gentiles [Greeks] round about us, for since we separated from them many disasters have come upon us." . . .

[This happened when] Antiochus [IV, 175–164 B.C.E.] who was called Epiphanes had succeeded to the kingdom, [and] Jason the brother of Onias obtained the high priesthood by corruption. . . . [H]e at once shifted his countrymen over to the Greek way of life . . . and he destroyed the lawful ways of living and introduced new customs contrary to the law. For with alacrity he founded a gymnasium right under the citadel, and he induced the noblest of the young men to wear the Greek hat [and not the traditional head covering]. There was such an extreme of Hellenization and increase in the adoption of foreign ways . . . that the priests were no longer intent upon the services of the altar. Despising the sanctuary and neglecting the sacrifices, they hurried to take part in the unlawful proceedings in the wrestling arena after the signal for the discus-throwing, disdaining the honors prized by their ancestors and putting the highest value upon Greek forms of prestige. . . . When the quadrennial games were being held at Tyre and the king was present, the vile Jason sent envoys . . . to carry three hundred silver drachmas for the sacrifice to Heracles. . . .

Not long after this, the king sent an Athenian senator to compel the Jews to forsake the laws of their fathers and cease to live by the laws of God, and also to pollute the temple in Jerusalem and call it the temple of Olympian Zeus. . . . Harsh and utterly grievous was the onslaught of evil. For the temple was filled with debauchery and reveling by the Gentiles, who dallied with prostitutes and had intercourse with women within the sacred precincts, and besides brought in things for sacrifice that were unfit. The altar was covered with abominable offerings that were forbidden by the laws. A man could neither keep the Sabbath nor observe the feasts of his fathers, nor so much as confess himself to be a Jew.

Source: Excerpted from 1 Maccabees 1:11; 2 Maccabees 4:10–18 and 6:1–6, *The New Oxford Annotated Bible* (Oxford: 1994).

Questions for Analysis

1. Given the history of their ancestors (see Chapter 2), why would Hellenistic culture be particularly threatening to the Jews?

2. What, specifically, are the offensive actions and activities described here? Why, for example, would the building of a gymnasium (a Greek academy and athletic facility) in Jerusalem be problematic?

ascetic practices that would purify their souls and prepare them for ethereal joy in the afterlife.

Like the peoples who worshiped them, the gods of the Hellenistic world were often immigrants from other lands. Temples to Greek gods and goddesses were dedicated throughout western Asia and Egypt; conversely, temples to Egyptian and Mesopotamian divinities were constructed in cities of the Greek homeland.

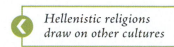

Hellenistic religions draw on other cultures

In Alexandria, scholars of religion collected anecdotes about exotic mythologies, which were recorded and reformulated for Greek-speaking audiences. The dazzling variety of religious choices included Buddhism, which flourished in the Greco-Indian kingdom that linked Afghanistan to Mesopotamia.

Even among the Jews, who resisted assimilation and the adoption of foreign customs, Hellenistic culture put down deep roots. This was especially true among Jewish elites and Jews of the diaspora living outside Palestine, who outnumbered the Palestinian population by a considerable margin. To meet the needs of these Greek-speaking Jews, and to satisfy the curiosity of Gentiles interested in Jewish beliefs, scholars working in Alexandria produced a Greek version of the Hebrew scriptures. It is known as the Septuagint, from the Greek word meaning "seventy": legend has it that seventy scribes, each working independently, produced individual translations from Hebrew to Greek that were identical in every respect. This story conveyed the message that the Septuagint was no less a product of divine inspiration than the original books that made up the Hebrew Bible and could be treated as an authoritative text in its own right. For Jews concerned about their social standing vis-à-vis their Greek neighbors, it was also proof of their cultivation and acceptance of Hellenistic values—although, ironically, many of the Jewish scriptures disapproved strongly of those values.

The Scientific Revolution of Antiquity

The Hellenistic period was the most brilliant age in the history of science before the seventeenth century of our era: the scientific revolution of antiquity. There are three major reasons for this. First, there was the enormous stimulus to intellectual inquiry caused by the fusion of Mesopotamian and Egyptian science with the philosophical methods of the Greeks. Second, as in the more famous scientific revolution (see Chapter 16), the use of a common language (in the seventeenth century it was Latin) and the ease of communication facilitated by quick, affordable travel also made the circulation of knowledge and sharing of ideas easier. (During the seventeenth century, ease of communication was increased by the printing press.) Finally, as in the seventeenth century, the competition among patrons of science was intense: every Hellenistic autocrat wanted to be thought enlightened and to be associated with new discoveries, and it might even be profitable to subsidize research that led to the development of new technologies, especially those with military applications. But most of all, the rulers who financed scientific endeavors did so primarily for motives of prestige and competition: they could show off a scientific gadget just as they could show off a sculpture. Even purely theoretical advances were so much admired that a Hellenistic prince who had bankrolled a breakthrough would share the glory of it.

The arts were also transformed by the economic and political conditions of the Hellenistic world. Writers and artists strove to demonstrate their mastery of difficult techniques and to attract the notice of potential patrons. New markets for art also changed *what* was being made, how, and for whom. In all of the civilizations we have studied so far, artists usually worked directly for individual or civic patrons. In the Hellenistic world, art became commodified. Sometimes a piece would be made expressly for a particular person, but many works of art were fashioned for the open market. They were designed to suit the tastes and lifestyles of urbane men and women who had disposable income and wanted to increase their social standing through conspicuous consumption. This was as true of literature as of sculpture or the decorative arts: we know the names of over a thousand Hellenistic authors, either because their work survives in multiple copies sold in bookshops, or because they are mentioned in other writings (letters, pamphlets) as being in fashion. Indeed, the number of texts and *objets d'art* that exist from this period is huge compared with those of earlier eras.

MEASURING AND MAPPING: ASTRONOMY, GEOGRAPHY, AND MATHEMATICS

Hellenistic scientists took a major interest in measurements and mapmaking, whether of the heavens (astronomy), the earth (geography), or the forms occurring in nature (geometry). The most renowned—and most wronged—of the Hellenistic astronomers was Aristarchus of Samos (310–230 B.C.E.), who deduced that the earth and other planets revolve around the sun. Unfortunately, however, his heliocentric model was not accepted by many of his contemporaries because it conflicted with the teachings of Aristotle and the Greek conviction that humanity, and therefore the earth, must be at the center of the universe. The sad fate of his discovery was sealed in the second century C.E., when the Alexandrian scholar Claudius Ptolemaeus (also known as Ptolemy) published an astronomical treatise, the *Almagest*, which unequivocally argued that Aristotle was correct. This misinformative book was then handed down to posterity as the authoritative work of ancient astronomy. It was not overturned until two thousand years later, when Copernicus and Galileo unwittingly reiterated the conclusions of Aristarchus.

Closely allied with astronomy were geography and mathematics. The most influential Hellenistic mathematician was Euclid, whose *Elements of Geometry* (c. 300 B.C.E.) codified the work of others, including pre-Socratic philosophers like Pythagoras (see Chapter 3). It remained the basic textbook for the study of geometry until the twentieth century of our era. Euclid's successor Hipparchus (second century B.C.E.) then laid the foundations of both plane and spherical trigonometry.

In the field of geography—and in a host of other pursuits, too—the most original thinker was Eratosthenes (*ehr-ah-TOS-then-ees*; c. 276–c. 196 B.C.E.) of Alexandria. Not only did he accurately calculate the circumference of the earth (within a tiny margin of error, less than two hundred miles), he also developed a system of latitude and longitude. He was the first to suggest the possibility of reaching eastern Asia by sailing west. In addition, he founded the science of chronology by attempting to establish the dates of major events reaching back to the siege of Troy. Students of history are forever in his debt.

MEDICINE AND MECHANICS: THE SCIENCES OF PHYSIOLOGY AND PHYSICS

Before the third century B.C.E., physics had been a branch of philosophy. It became a separate, experimental science thanks to the single-handed genius of one man, Archimedes of Syracuse (*ar-ki-MEE-dees*; c. 287–212 B.C.E.). It was he who discovered the law of floating bodies, or specific gravity, now known as "Archimedes' principle." According to legend, the idea came to him quite suddenly when he was in his bath, pondering possible theories. The stunning insight so excited him that he leaped from the water and dashed out naked into the street, shouting *Eureka!* ("I found it!"). He also established the principles of the lever, the pulley, and the screw, and invented both a compound pulley and a propeller. All of these discoveries had numerous practical uses in the construction of buildings, ships, and military machinery.

Other extraordinary advances of Hellenistic science were made in the field of medicine. Especially significant was the work of the Alexandrian scholar Herophilus of Chalcedon (c. 335–c. 280 B.C.E.), who was probably the first to practice human dissection. Many of his discoveries directly challenged the orthodoxy of Aristotelian teaching—and rightly, since Aristotle's understanding of physiology, like his knowledge of astronomical and natural science, has not stood the test of time so well as his grasp of logic. Herophilus' achievements included a detailed description of the brain, which allowed him to prove that it was the engine of human intellect (Aristotle thought that was the heart), as well as the discovery that the arteries contain blood alone (not, as Aristotle had taught, a mixture of blood and air) and that their function is to carry blood from the heart to all parts of the body. He also understood the significance of the pulse and its use in diagnosing illness.

His colleague Erasistratus (*ehr-ah-sis-STRAH-tus*) made allied discoveries, establishing that the heart was a pump and not an organ of emotion, explaining the working of its valves and distinguishing between motor and sensory nerves. Erasistratus also rejected the widely held theory of the physician Hippocrates (c. 460–c. 370 B.C.E.), who had posited that the body contains four "humors" that need to be kept in balance through bloodletting and other invasive practices. Unfortunately, this discovery went the way of the heliocentric universe posited by Aristarchus: another encyclopedist of the second century C.E., Galen, preferred the erroneous theory of Hippocrates. His baneful influence, and the practice of bloodletting, thus persisted into the nineteenth century of our era.

URBAN ARCHITECTURE AND SCULPTURE

Hellenistic architecture drew on Greek models, but it was also influenced by standards and tastes more characteristic of Egypt and Persia. The best-surviving example comes from Pergamon, a city on the coast of Anatolia that became the capital of a new kingdom wrested from the Seleucids' control in the second century B.C.E. It boasted an enormous altar dedicated to Zeus that crowned the heights of the city, below which an open-air theater was built into the steep slope of the hill. In Ephesus, not far away, the streets were not only paved, but paved with marble.

THE CITADEL OF PERGAMON. An artist's reconstruction of Pergamon in the second century B.C.E., based on the work of nineteenth-century German archaeologists. High atop the hill is the massive altar of Zeus (now in the Pergamon Museum in Berlin), and below it slope the tiers of the theater. Other features include fortifications, terraces, and artificial landscaping for public gardens. › **How does this complex of buildings compare with that of another citadel, the Acropolis of Athens (see page 91)?**

Perhaps the most influential of all Hellenistic arts was sculpture, which placed even more emphasis on realism than the fourth-century sculptures discussed earlier in this chapter. Sculptors now prided themselves on faithfully reproducing facial furrows, muscular distortions, and complex folds of drapery. Awkward human postures offered the greatest technical challenges, to such an extent that sculptors might prefer to show people stretching themselves or balancing on one leg in ways that hardly ever occur in real life.

Because monumental sculpture of this kind was executed for wealthy private patrons, it is clear that the goal was to create something unique in both conception and craftsmanship—something a collector could show off as the only one of its type. It is not surprising, therefore, that complexity came to be admired for its own sake, and extreme naturalism sometimes teetered on the brink of caricature. To our eyes, such works frequently appear familiar because of the influence they exerted on later sculptors like Michelangelo (see Chapter 12) and Auguste Rodin. Two of the most famous examples are pictured below, both exhibiting different aesthetic qualities and artistic techniques: *An Old Woman*, dating from around the second century; and *Laocoön and His Sons*, from the first century B.C.E.

***AN OLD WOMAN* (LEFT).** This marble statue is a Roman copy of Hellenistic work made in the second century B.C.E. It shows an elderly woman, probably an aged courtesan, on her way to a festival of Dionysos. Her elegant gown and sandals are ironic reminders of her past career success, and the drapery hangs awkwardly from her stooped body. She carries a basket of fruit and two chickens: either as gifts to the god or provisions for the feast. It is now in the Metropolitan Museum of Art in New York.

***LAOCOÖN AND HIS SONS* (RIGHT).** This famous sculpture group from the first century B.C.E. tells a story of divine retribution. According to legend, Laocoön warned the Trojans not to accept the wooden horse sent by the Greeks and was accordingly punished by the sea god Poseidon, who sent two serpents to kill him and his sons. The intense physicality of this work was an important influence on Michelangelo, a millennium and a half later. It is now in the Vatican Museum, Rome.

Debating the Education and Role of Women

The drastic political, social, and economic changes of the fourth century B.C.E. led philosophers to reimagine the traditional structures of the polis and to debate the proper role of women within these structures. Meanwhile, the cosmopolitan culture of the expanding Hellenistic world made it increasingly difficult to limit women's access to public spaces. The following excerpts represent two philosophical responses to these problems. The first comes from Plato's treatise on "Polis-matters" (Politeia), known to us as the Republic, *the longest of his philosophical dialogues and the most influential work of political thought in history. Its conceptual narrator and protagonist is Socrates, who engages in a series of debates with his pupils. The second excerpt is taken from a philosophical treatise attributed to a female follower of Pythagoras (see Chapter 3), but it was really written by a man around 200 B.C.E. in Hellenistic Italy.*

Plato, *The Republic*, c. 380 B.C.E.

SOCRATES: For men born and educated like our citizens, the only way, in my opinion, of arriving at a right conclusion about the possession and use of women and children is to follow the path on which we originally started, when we said that the men were to be the guardians and watchdogs of the herd.

GLAUCON: True.

SOCRATES: Let us further suppose the birth and education of our women to be subject to similar or nearly similar regulations; then we shall see whether the result accords with our design.

GLAUCON: What do you mean?

SOCRATES: . . . The education which was assigned to the men was music and gymnastic[s].

GLAUCON: Yes.

SOCRATES: Then women must be taught music and gymnastic[s] and also the art of war, which they must practice like the men?

GLAUCON: That is the inference, I suppose.

SOCRATES: I should rather expect . . . that several of our proposals, if they are carried out, being unusual, may appear ridiculous.

GLAUCON: No doubt of it.

SOCRATES: Yes, and the most ridiculous thing of all will be the sight of women naked in the palaestra, exercising with the men, especially when they are no longer young; they certainly will not be a vision of beauty, any more than the enthusiastic old men who in spite of wrinkles and ugliness continue to frequent the gymnasia. . . . . [Yet] not long ago, as we shall remind them, the Hellenes were of the opinion, which is still generally received among the barbarians, that the sight of a naked man was ridiculous and improper; and when first the Cretans and then the Lacedaemonians [Spartans] introduced the custom, the wits of that day might equally have ridiculed the innovation.

GLAUCON: No doubt. . . .

SOCRATES: First, then, whether the question is to be put in jest or in earnest, let us come to an understanding about the nature of woman: Is she capable of sharing either wholly or partially in the actions of men, or not at all? And is the art of war one of those arts in which she can or cannot share? That will be the best way of commencing the enquiry, and will probably lead to the fairest conclusion. . . .

GLAUCON: I suppose so. . . .

SOCRATES: And if . . . the male and female sex appear to differ in their fitness for any art or pursuit, we should say that such pursuit or art ought to be assigned to one or the other of them; but if the difference consists only in women bearing and men begetting children, this does not amount to a proof that a woman differs from a man in respect of the sort of education she should receive; and we shall therefore continue to maintain that our guardians and their wives ought to have the same pursuits.

GLAUCON: Very true.

SOCRATES: Next, we shall ask . . . how, in reference to any of the pursuits or arts of civic life, the nature of a woman differs from that of a man? . . .

GLAUCON: By all means.

SOCRATES: . . . [W]hen you spoke of a nature gifted or not gifted in any respect, did you mean to say that one man will acquire a thing easily, another with difficulty; a little learning will lead the one to discover a great deal; whereas the other, after much study and application, no sooner learns than he forgets? Or again, did you mean, that the one has a body which is a good servant to his mind, while the body of the other is a hindrance to him? Would not these be the sort of differences which distinguish the man gifted by nature from the one who is ungifted?

GLAUCON: No one will deny that.

SOCRATES: And can you mention any pursuit of mankind in which the male sex has not all these gifts and qualities in a higher degree than the female? Need I waste time in speaking of the art of weaving, and the management of pancakes and preserves, in which womankind does really appear to be great, and in which for her to be beaten by a man is of all things the most absurd?

GLAUCON: You are quite right . . . in maintaining the general inferiority of the female sex: although many women are in many things superior to many men, yet on the whole what you say is true.

Source: Excerpted from Plato, *The Republic*, Book V, trans. Benjamin Jowett (New York: 1982), pp. 170–76.

Treatise Attributed to Phintys, Third/Second Century B.C.E.

Now some people think that it is not appropriate for a woman to be a philosopher, just as a woman should not be a cavalry officer or a politician. . . . I agree that men should be generals and city officials and politicians, and women should keep house and stay inside and receive and take care of their husbands. But I believe that courage, justice, and intelligence are qualities that men and women have in common. . . . Courage and intelligence are more appropriately male qualities because of the strength of men's bodies and the power of their minds. Chastity is more appropriately female.

Accordingly, a woman must learn about chastity and realize what she must do quantitatively and qualitatively to be able to obtain this womanly virtue. I believe that there are five qualifications: (1) the sanctity of her marriage bed, (2) the cleanliness of her body, (3) the manner in which she chooses to leave her house, (4) her refusal to participate in secret cults . . . , (5) her readiness and moderation in sacrificing to the gods.

Of these, the most important quality for chastity is to be pure in respect of the marriage bed, and for her not to have affairs with men from other households. If she breaks the law in this way she wrongs the gods of her family and provides her family and home not with its own offspring but with bastards. . . . She should also consider the following: that there is no means of atoning for this sin; no way she can approach the shrines or the altars of the gods as a pure woman. . . . The greatest glory

a freeborn woman can have—her foremost honor—is the witness her own children will give to her chastity toward her husband, the stamp of the likeness they bear to the father whose seed produced them. . . .

As far as adornment of her body is concerned . . . [h]er clothes should not be transparent or ornate. She should not put on silken material, but moderate, white-colored clothes. In this way, she will avoid being over-dressed or luxurious or made-up, and not give other women cause to be uncomfortably envious. . . . She should not apply imported or artificial coloring to her face—with her own natural coloring, by washing only with water, she can ornament herself with modesty. . . .

Women of importance leave the house to sacrifice to the leading divinity of the community on behalf of their husbands and their households. They do not leave home at night nor in the evening, but at midday, to attend a religious festival or to make some purchase, accompanied by a single female servant or decorously escorted by two servants at most. . . . They keep away from secret cults . . . particularly because these forms of worship encourage drunkenness and ecstasy. The mistress of the house and head of the household should be chaste and untouched in all respects.

Source: From Mary R. Lefkowitz and Maureen B. Fant, eds. *Women's Life in Greece & Rome: A Source Book in Translation*, 2nd ed. (Baltimore, MD: 1992), pp. 163–64.

(continued from p. 143)

Questions for Analysis

1. Follow the steps of the argument made by Socrates. How does he go about proving that women and men are different and so should have different roles in society? Are there flaws in this argument? How would you refute it?

2. How does the author of the treatise seem to define "chastity," and why does she (or he) say that it corresponds to more masculine qualities of courage and intelligence? Why would this author have wanted to attribute these reflections to female members of the community founded by the philosopher Pythagoras (c. 570–c. 495) three centuries earlier? How might this treatise be a response to the changes brought about by the expansion of the Greek world in the fourth and third centuries B.C.E.?

3. What are the main points on which these two perspectives agree? How might ideas like those expressed here have influenced contemporary ideas of female beauty (see *Interpreting Visual Evidence* on page 121)?

LITERARY FANTASY AND HISTORICAL REALITY

In the sixth century B.C.E. it was the lyric, in the fifth century it was tragedy, and in the fourth century it was the novel; but in the Hellenistic era, the new literary genre was pastoral verse. These poems tapped into a strong vein of nostalgia for rural pastimes and simple pleasures, a make-believe world of shepherds and wood nymphs. The most important pastoral poet of the age was Theocritus (*thee-AW-krit-uhs*), who flourished around 270 B.C.E. in the big-city environment of Alexandria. Theocritus was a merchant of escapism. In the midst of urban bustle and within sight of overcrowded slums, he celebrated the charms of country life and lazy summer afternoons, putting into the mouths of his rustic characters unlikely sentiments expressed in ornate language. He thereby founded an enduring tradition that would be taken up by poets from the Roman Virgil to the Englishman (and classical scholar) A. E. Housman, and that has continuously provided a wealth of themes for the visual arts. Musical composers such as Beethoven and Debussy also owe a debt to Theocritus.

By contrast, Hellenistic prose literature was dominated by historians and biographers who consciously modeled their work on earlier pioneers, especially Thucydides. By far the most important was Polybius (*poh-LIB-ee-uhs*; c. 203–120 B.C.E.), a well-born Greek whose father was a prominent politician active in the Achaean League. Polybius himself was trained as a cavalry officer, and both his vocation and his family connections gave him ample opportunity to observe the workings of government, diplomacy, and military strategy. This was at a time when the Achaean League was trying to position itself favorably in ongoing wars between the rising republic of Rome and the various warring kingdoms of northern Greece. In 168 B.C.E., the Romans became suspicious of the Achaeans' declared neutrality and demanded that a thousand noble hostages be sent from Greece to Rome as a guarantee of the league's good behavior.

Polybius was one of those hostages, and he spent the next seventeen years living in Rome. There, he became a fervent admirer of Roman customs and especially of Rome's unique form of government. He also formed warm friendships with high-ranking Roman families, including the descendants of Scipio Africanus, a prominent Roman general. He kept up these contacts after his release, traveling to North Africa during the Third Punic War and witnessing firsthand the destruction of Carthage in 146 B.C.E. (see Chapter 5).

The result of this colorful career was a series of histories that glorified the achievements of Rome and its political system. Polybius also attempted to account for the patterns he discerned in the history of Greece since the Peloponnesian War. He argued that historical developments follow regular cycles, and that nations pass inevitably through stages of growth and decay. Hence, it should be possible to predict exactly where a given state is heading if one knows its history. Yet he also argued that the special character of Rome's constitution would allow it to break free from this cycle, because it combined all the different forms of government which Aristotle had outlined in his *Politics*. This view of history galvanized the framers of the U.S. Constitution, directly influencing their conception of our own political institutions.

Conclusion

Judged from the perspective of classical Greece, Hellenistic civilization seems alien and exotic. The autocratic governments of the age that followed Alexander's conquests would probably appear repugnant to a staunch proponent of Athenian democracy, and the Hellenistic love of extravagance can contrast strikingly with the tastes of the fifth century B.C.E. Yet Hellenistic civilization had its own achievements that make it, in some ways, more familiar to us. Most Hellenistic cities offered a greater range of public facilities, and the numerous advances in science and technology are astonishing when compared with anything that came before or even after.

But the most important contribution of the Hellenistic era to subsequent historical developments was its role as an intermediary between the nascent empire of Rome and the older civilizations of Mesopotamia, Egypt, and Greece. The example set by Alexander, in particular, was one that the Romans would emulate, while the economic and political infrastructures of those civilizations would undergird Roman imperial government. The Romans would also take advantage of the common language and cultural expectations that bound together the far reaches of the Greek-speaking world. Their own Latin language became acceptable for cultivated conversation and literary expression only toward the very end of the first century B.C.E., and it would never supplant Greek as the preeminent language of scholarship and administration in the eastern portions of their empire.

The Hellenistic era must also be recognized as the bridge that connects us to the earlier ages of antiquity: most of what is contained in the first four chapters of this textbook is known to us only because ancient texts and inscriptions and artifacts were collected and copied by the scholars of Alexandria and other Hellenistic cities. This era also bridges the gap between the ideals and customs of classical Greece and those that would be more characteristic of Rome. It was Hellenistic art and architecture, Hellenistic city planning and civic culture that the Romans strove to emulate and export to their own colonies, not those of Periclean Athens. The same can be said of drama and poetry.

For us, two further aspects of Hellenistic culture deserve special mention: its **cosmopolitanism** and its modernity. The word *cosmopolitan* itself comes from a Greek word meaning "universal city," and it was the Greeks of the Hellenistic period who came closest to turning this ideal of globalization into reality. Around 250 B.C.E., a Greek tourist could have traveled from Sicily to the borders of India—the two known ends of the earth—and never cease to be among people who spoke his language and shared his basic outlook. Nor would this tourist have identified himself in ethnic or nationalist terms, or felt any exclusive loyalty to a city-state

AFTER YOU READ THIS CHAPTER

CHRONOLOGY

404 B.C.E.	Sparta defeats Athens in the Peloponnesian War
401 B.C.E.	Xenophon and the Ten Thousand begin their Persian expedition
395–338 B.C.E.	The struggle for Greek dominance (Thebes, Athens, Sparta)
371 B.C.E.	Epaminondas of Thebes defeats the Spartans at Leuctra
356 B.C.E.	Philip II becomes king of Macedonia
338 B.C.E.	Macedonia defeats Thebes and Athens at Chaeronea
336–323 B.C.E.	Reign and campaigns of Alexander the Great
323–c. 275 B.C.E.	Formation of the Hellenistic kingdoms
323–c. 225 B.C.E.	The Greek diaspora
c. 300 B.C.E.	Formation of the Aetolian and Achaean Leagues
300–270 B.C.E.	Rise of Stoicism and Epicureanism
c. 300–200 B.C.E.	The Hellenistic scientific revolution
203–120 B.C.E.	Lifetime of the historian Polybius

REVIEWING THE OBJECTIVES

❯ Macedonia's successful conquest of the Greek poleis can be attributed to several factors. What are they?

❯ Alexander the Great's imperial policies were influenced by his own upbringing, the different cultures he encountered, and some key historical precedents. Give at least one example of each type of influence.

❯ Explain how the three Hellenistic kingdoms reflect the differences among the three main civilizations we have studied so far.

❯ Why is the Hellenistic world described as "cosmopolitan"? How did this urban culture differ from that of the Greek poleis?

❯ The philosophies of Plato and Aristotle both derive from the teachings of Socrates, but they diverge in some important ways. What are those main differences?

or kingdom; he would have considered himself a citizen of the world. He would also have considered himself a modern man, not bound by the old prejudices and superstitions of the past. It is for these reasons that Hellenistic civilization seems so closely related to our own. It was a world of stark contrasts and infinite possibilities, where economic instability, extremism, and authoritarian regimes existed side by side with unprecedented prosperity, rational inquiry, and extraordinary freedoms. In Chapter 5, we will see how this world adapted itself to the dominion of a single Italian city.

 Go to INQUIZITIVE to see what you've learned—and learn what you've missed—with personalized feedback along the way.

PEOPLE, IDEAS, AND EVENTS IN CONTEXT

> In what ways were the military strategies of **PHILIP II** of Macedonia variations on older forms of hoplite warfare? How did the rise of mercenary armies and of Thebes further change military strategies in the fourth century B.C.E.?

> How did the philosophies of **PLATO** and **ARISTOTLE** respond to the crisis of the polis?

> To what degree did the conquests of **ALEXANDER THE GREAT** unite Mesopotamia, Egypt, and Greece?

> Why and how did the three **HELLENISTIC KINGDOMS** emerge? How were the **AETOLIAN LEAGUE** and **ACHAEAN LEAGUE** new models for governance and cooperation in Greece?

> In what ways were **STOICISM**, **EPICUREANISM**, and other new philosophies a response to **COSMOPOLITANISM** and the breakdown of traditional societies and values?

> What were the driving forces behind the **SCIENTIFIC REVOLUTION OF ANTIQUITY**? What were its main achievements?

> What are some essential characteristics of **HELLENISTIC ART**? In what ways did it differ from that of the fifth century B.C.E. (see Chapter 3)?

THINKING ABOUT CONNECTIONS

> "The history of the world is but the biography of great men": so the Scottish historian Thomas Carlyle (1795–1881) summarized the impact of figures such as Alexander the Great. How would you construct an argument in support of this proposition, using what you've learned in this chapter? How would you refute it?

> In what ways do Alexander's actions demonstrate his own knowledge of history as well as a capacity to apply that knowledge to his own circumstances? Can you identify leaders of our own day who have mobilized their understanding of history in similar ways?

> In your view, which civilization more resembles our own: classical Athens or the Hellenistic world? Why? What characteristics make an era seem "modern"?

> In 2019, the leaders of Greece and Macedonia (formerly a part of Yugoslavia) ratified an official agreement designed to end a decades-long dispute over Macedonia's right to call itself by the name of Alexander's kingdom. It will now be known as "North Macedonia" to distinguish it from the Greek region of Macedonia. Given what you've learned, why would this have been such a contentious issue?

5

The Civilization of Ancient Rome

"**CAN ANYTHING BE MORE IMPORTANT** than understanding how the Romans brought nearly the whole inhabited world under their rule?" So the Greek soldier Polybius (c. 203–120 B.C.E.) addresses readers in a history celebrating the achievements of the Roman Republic. Polybius had witnessed some of these achievements firsthand: on the battlefield, in Rome itself as a hostage, and on a visit to newly conquered Carthage. What better testament could there be to a small Italian city than the admiration of a Greek aristocrat who, having been subjected to Roman authority, wholeheartedly embraced it? None, unless we cite the enthusiastic endorsement of the same Jews who had rebelled against Greek influence in 164 B.C.E. and who now willingly placed themselves under Roman protection:

> Those whom they wish to help and to make kings, they make kings, and those whom they wish they depose; and they have been greatly exalted. Yet not one of them has put on a crown or worn purple as a mark of pride, but they have built for themselves a senate chamber where senators constantly deliberate to govern the people well. (*1 Maccabees 8:12–15*)

To the Romans themselves, the enormous success of their empire meant that they were divinely chosen to colonize the world. This was the message conveyed by the poet Virgil (70–19 B.C.E.), commissioned by the emperor

BEFORE YOU READ THIS CHAPTER

STORY LINES

> The Romans were proud of their unique history, especially the legend that they had overthrown their kings. They clung to this story even when individual men came to wield kingly powers: especially Julius Caesar and his heir, Augustus.

> Roman identity, religion, and politics were intimately bound up in the worship of ancestors, especially male ancestors. As a result, fathers (living and dead) wielded extraordinary power in early Rome.

> Roman women enjoyed many more freedoms than women of ancient Greece, but were nevertheless subject to the authority of their male relatives.

> Paradoxically, the Romans celebrated their farming heritage even as they built a highly urbanized society. At the same time, they regarded Greek culture as both superior and dangerous.

> The Roman army had unprecedented strength and importance in this civilization, but the army's relationship to Roman politics and society changed drastically as Rome's empire grew.

CORE OBJECTIVES

> **IDENTIFY** the factors that influenced the formation of the Roman Republic.

> **UNDERSTAND** the basic elements of Roman identity.

> **ANALYZE** the competing interests of the different classes of people who struggled for power in Rome.

> **DESCRIBE** the impact of territorial expansion on Roman society.

> **TRACE** the events leading up to the establishment of the Principate and **UNDERSTAND** the significance of this new form of autocratic government.

Augustus to tell the story of Rome's rise to glory in a manner imitating the epics of Homer. In one key passage, the father of Aeneas "foretells" the future: "Remember, Roman, you whose power rules / all peoples, that these are your arts: plant peace, / make law, spare subjects, and put down the proud" (*Aeneid*, Book VI, lines 851–53).

While the Greeks struggled against the Persians and each other, a new civilization had emerged on the banks of the river Tiber in central Italy. By 300 B.C.E., Rome was the dominant power on the Italian peninsula. Two centuries later, it had conquered Greece itself. For the next three centuries after that, its power steadily increased. In the first century of our era, it ruled the former Hellenistic kingdoms as well as a vast region that Greek culture had never touched. Eventually, Rome's empire united the Mediterranean world and most of western Asia while embracing provinces that are now parts of France, Spain, Portugal, Britain, Belgium, Germany, Switzerland, and the Balkan states. Rome thus built a historical arc that joined Europe to the rich heritage of ancient Mesopotamia and Egypt. Without Rome, European culture as we know it would not exist, and neither would the political institutions that formed the United States. To echo Polybius: "Can anything be more important than understanding this?"

Rome's Early Influences

Etruscan influences on early Romans: architecture, sport, and religious practices >

When the Romans arrived in Italy, the dominant inhabitants of the peninsula were a people whom the Greeks called Tyrrhenians. To the Romans, they were **Etruscans**; to us, they remain mysterious because their language (not a branch of Indo-European) has never been fully deciphered. By the sixth century B.C.E., the Etruscans had established a confederation of independent city-states in north-central Italy. They were skilled metalworkers, artists, and architects, from whom the Romans later took their knowledge of the arch and the vault. They also took the love of blood sports and the practice of foretelling the future by studying the entrails of animals and the flight of birds.

The two most important foundation myths told by the Romans also derived from Etruscan tradition: the story of Aeneas's escape from Troy and the story of the infant twins Romulus and Remus, abandoned and then raised by a maternal wolf, afterward founding a city. Rome's historians mined both legends for their metaphorical significance. For example, the story of Aeneas's seduction and abandonment of Dido, queen of Carthage, reflected Rome's defeat of that powerful civilization. And for many Roman commentators, the murder of Remus at the hands of his brother Romulus epitomized an all-too-familiar pattern in Roman politics.

In marked contrast to women in Greek society, Etruscan women enjoyed very high status and played important roles in public life. They participated in politics, sports, and entertainments; wives even ate meals with their husbands. After death, devoted couples were buried together and their tombstones often emphasize their mutual affection. Some of these practices certainly affected the Romans, since Roman women were markedly less sequestered than their Greek counterparts. Yet they did not enjoy the same freedoms as Etruscan women until very late in Roman history, when these freedoms were condemned as signs of Rome's decadence.

Greek influences on early Romans: alphabet, religious beliefs, and art >

The Romans also borrowed ideas from the Greeks who had colonized southern Italy and Sicily: their alphabet, many of their religious beliefs, and much of their art. But the Romans downplayed Greek influence in their legends, emphasizing their alleged descent from the Trojans and an Italic people called the Sabines, whose women Romulus and his men had forcibly abducted in order to breed Roman children. This was a practice Romans would continue, in one form or another, as their legions planted new colonies and intermarried with indigenous populations from the Persian Gulf to the lowlands of Scotland.

THE FOUNDING OF ROME

The real founders of Rome were a tribe called the Latins, descendants of Indo-European–speaking peoples who crossed the Alps into Italy and settled on the banks of the Tiber by the tenth century B.C.E. This location was advantageous. Small trading ships (but not large war fleets) could navigate the river as far as the city, but no farther; thus Rome could be a commercial port but was not threatened by attack from the sea. Rome also sat astride the first good ford across the river, making it a major crossroads. The seven hills that ringed the early settlement also offered strategic advantages. Eventually, Rome's central marketplace—the *forum* or "open space"—would become the beating heart of the world's most populous and powerful city, with approximately a million people crowded into an area of five square miles.

The topography of Latium—a broad, flat plain with few natural obstacles—also influenced the Romans' relationships with outsiders because it lacked natural boundaries. At an early date, they and their neighbors negotiated a series of agreements collectively known as the Latin Right: a trading pact, provisions for intermarriage, and the *migratio*, which allowed a resident of one settlement to emigrate to another and, after a year's residence, have the full rights of a citizen there. These privileges contrast strongly with the mutual suspicion and hostility that divided the city-states of ancient Mesopotamia and Greece. Indeed, the Romans' later willingness to extend the Latin Right to colonies far beyond Latium was a key factor in the success of their empire.

The Romans' early government was a monarchy that mirrored the structure of Roman households, with a patriarchal king who exercised power checked only by a council of elders, the Senate (derived from the Latin *senex*, "old man"). Seven kings, beginning with Romulus, are said to have ruled in succession. The last, Tarquinius Superbus (Tarquin the Arrogant), is reputed to have been an Etruscan who dominated Latium and the agriculturally wealthy district of Campania to the south. But his power came at the price of Roman freedom, as was made clear when Tarquin's son raped a virtuous Roman wife, **Lucretia**, around 510 B.C.E. When she committed suicide to avoid dishonor, the Romans—led by Lucretia's kinsman, Brutus—rose up in rebellion, overthrowing not only the Etruscan dynasty but rejecting the very idea of kingship. Henceforth, any claim to royal authority in Rome was considered anathema, and the word *rex* ("king") became an insult. The Brutus who would be instrumental in the assassination of Julius Caesar nearly five centuries later was a descendant of the same Brutus who had driven out the Tarquin kings.

 The Latin Right

The Triumph of the Early Republic

The story of Lucretia was both a patriotic myth and a potent statement of Roman attitudes toward female chastity and family honor. And it coincided with a radical change to Roman governance—so radical, in fact, that it did not match any of Aristotle's

Roman Republic The Romans traced the founding of their republic to the overthrow of their last king and the establishment of a unique form of constitutional government, in which the power of the aristocracy (embodied by the Senate) was checked by the executive rule of the two elected consuls and the collective of the people.

political categories (see Chapter 4) but instead combined elements of all. The Romans themselves didn't know what to call their political system: they spoke of it merely as *res publica*, the "public thing."

THE TERRITORIAL EXPANSION OF ROME

The early **Roman Republic** was marked by almost constant warfare, aimed at stitching together a patchwork of valuable territories that could support a growing population. Gradually, the Romans came to control all the Latin hinterland and the valuable port of Ostia at the mouth of the Tiber, about twenty miles from their city. They also pushed northward toward Etruscan territory and southward to Naples, another good port. By 300 B.C.E., Romans had absorbed or allied themselves with all of central Italy and had begun to look even farther south, to the wealthy Greek colonies of Sicily.

CINCINNATUS, THE STATESMAN-FARMER. This bronze statue of Cincinnatus is prominent in Cincinnati, Ohio, which was named after the Roman hero (and in honor of George Washington) in 1790. In his right hand he holds the *fasces*, symbolizing his powers as dictator. In his left, he grasps the handle of a plow. **› Why would this figure have fired the imagination of Americans during their War of Independence?**

What was the secret of Roman success? For one thing, Romans did not impose heavy burdens of taxation or tribute; instead, they demanded that allies contribute soldiers to the Roman army. Rome also extended the Latin Right to many conquered territories, giving them a further stake in its continued political and military expansion. Rome thus gained a nearly inexhaustible reserve of fighting men. By the middle of the third century B.C.E., its army may have counted as many as three hundred thousand—a huge force even by modern standards, and all the more formidable due to rigorous training. Xenophon's army was ten thousand and Alexander's one hundred thousand. The Great King of Persia, at the height of his powers, could claim to muster a million men: but these were private or tribal militias, not a standing army. Romans, in contrast, devoted themselves to the discipline of warfare.

Although they originally borrowed the phalanx formation from the Greeks, the Romans eventually replaced it with smaller, more flexible divisions that could adjust to the varied geographical conditions of central Italy. Although the major unit of the army was the legion (five thousand men), the basic combat unit was the *maniple* ("handful"), a group of about a hundred and twenty infantrymen who trained together and often performed specialized tasks or used special weaponry. This made the army adaptable to climate, terrain, and the deployment of new military technologies.

The republic's early history reinforced not only the military character of the Roman state but also its commitment to agriculture as the only proper peacetime employment for a Roman. The acquisition of new lands made it possible for citizens to maintain themselves as farmers in the new colonies around Rome. By accommodating an increasing population in this way, the Romans were able to remain staunchly agricultural for a surprisingly long time. As a result, they developed an interest in shipping and commerce fairly late, compared with the Greeks or Phoenicians. And they would continue—even at the height of their empire—to valorize rural life over that of the city.

The paragon of Roman heroism in this era was Lucius Quinctius **Cincinnatus** (519–c. 430 B.C.E.), a citizen-farmer who reluctantly accepted political office when Rome was threatened by attack. According to legend, he was plowing his fields when a delegation of senators arrived to bring him to Rome where he was named *dictator*, a word that had positive connotations. This was a position of power to which the Romans temporarily elected one man during times of crisis. As legend has it, Cincinnatus dutifully performed this role, led Rome in its wars with hostile neighbors—and then went back to his farm. If Lucretia was the Roman epitome of womanly fortitude, Cincinnatus was the paradigm of manly virtue: willing to lead when necessary but preferring his plow.

Cincinnatus (519–c. 430 B.C.E.) Legendary citizen-farmer of Rome who reluctantly accepted an appointment as dictator.

THE CONSTITUTION OF THE EARLY REPUBLIC

Initially, the rejection of monarchy had resulted in only moderate changes: instead of a king, the Senate was headed by two elected officers called *consuls*. Although the consuls of the infant republic were supposedly chosen by all citizens, they were inevitably members of aristocratic families, known in Rome as *patricians* because they traced descent from a famous ancestor or "father" (*pater*). During his term of office, which lasted for one year, each consul exercised essentially the same power as a king: dealing justice, making law, and commanding the army. The only limit on consular power was the right of each consul to veto the actions of the other, which often led to stalemate or conflict. In such cases, the Senate might have to arbitrate. In times of grave emergency, like that resulting in Cincinnatus's election, a dictator might be appointed for a term not longer than six months.

Within a generation after the establishment of the republic, patrician dominance of the government began to be challenged by the *plebs* ("people"). This was the first stage in a centuries-long contest known as the Struggle of the Orders. The plebeian classes made up nearly 98 percent of the Roman population, and they were a diverse group. Some had grown wealthy through trade or agriculture, but most were smallholding farmers, artisans, or the urban poor. Although they were forced to serve in the army, they were nevertheless excluded from holding office. They were also victims of discriminatory decisions in civil trials, which were judged by patricians. They did not even know what legal rights they were supposed to enjoy, because Rome had as yet no established laws. The plebeians were also, like the poorer citizens of Greek poleis, threatened with debt slavery.

These wrongs prompted a rebellion in the early fifth century B.C.E., when plebeians refused to join in the military defense of Rome and instead seceded from the city, camping out on the Aventine Hill (see the map of Rome on page 178). This general strike forced the patricians to allow the people to elect their own officers, who were known as *tribunes* (tribal leaders). The job of each tribune was to protect his constituents from patrician injustice, and the plebeians guaranteed the safety of these officers by vowing to kill any person who hindered them from exercising their powers.

The plebs' victory also led to the codification of the Law of the Twelve Tables, proclaimed around 450 B.C.E. and inscribed on wooden tablets displayed in the forum.

 Diversity of the plebian classes

Plebeians were also made eligible to hold elected offices, and some gradually gained access to the Senate. A further victory came in 287 B.C.E., when the plebeians succeeded in passing a law that made decisions enacted in their own assembly binding on the Roman government—whether the Senate approved them or not. It was at this time that the phrase *Senatus Populusque Romanum* came into regular use, abbreviated *SPQR* and designating any decree or decision made by "the Senate and People of Rome." (Visitors to Rome will still find *SPQR* emblazoned on everything from public buildings to the manhole covers of Rome's sewers.)

These reforms had several important consequences. Successful plebeians could now work their way into the upper reaches of Roman society, which loosened the hold of patrician families. At the same time, laws preventing wealth from becoming a controlling factor in Roman politics barred senators from engaging directly in commerce. This restriction had the effect of creating a new social order, that of the equestrians ("horsemen" or knights): men whose wealth made it possible for them to own and equip warhorses for Rome's cavalry. But the equestrian and the senatorial classes were never wholly distinct. Often, some members of an equestrian family would underwrite the political careers of brothers or cousins. Those families who managed to win election by such means, generation after generation, became increasingly influential. Meanwhile, patricians who chose politics over wealth became impoverished and resentful. By the first century B.C.E., many such men felt excluded from power and pursued their political interests by representing themselves as champions of the people.

Later Roman patriots would regard this era as a golden age of shared government. But a republic differs from an aristocracy or oligarchy only in that power is exercised by men whose offices are not (at least in theory) hereditary. It is a political system designed to preserve the power of a privileged group, and to marginalize that of the people at large. The constitution that emerged in these key centuries therefore broadened and stabilized oligarchy by balancing competing governmental institutions: the people's assembly, the Senate, and executive officeholders. Thanks to this distribution of powers, no single individual or clique could become overwhelmingly strong; but neither could direct expressions of the popular will—that is, democracy.

For Polybius, this was an ideal system because it combined elements of a monarchy (executive officeholders, the consuls), an aristocracy (the Senate), and a polity (the people's assembly and tribune representatives). For the framers of the U.S. Constitution, it was a model for the three branches of a new government designed to prevent the vast majority of Americans from participating directly in politics, while allowing some citizens (originally, white men with sufficient property) a say in choosing their representatives. Polybius prophesied that such a system could last forever. He was wrong.

The Essence of Roman Identity

The early republic was a success, in part, because Romans were conservatives who accepted new things reluctantly. The prevailing principle behind their institutions was the **mos maiorum** (MOHS my-OR-um), "the code of the elders" or "the custom of the ancestors"—or even, to use the word derived from the Latin *mos*, "morality." This unwritten code was sacrosanct and essential to Roman identity, which was rooted in ancestor worship. The Latin word *pietas* ("piety") meant reverence for family traditions and for one's fathers—living and dead. What made the legendary **Aeneas** "pious Aeneas"

Connection between Roman religion and family

was his devotion to his father, Anchises (*an-KIE-sees*), whom he carried to safety on his back while Troy burned. In a metaphorical sense, this meant that Aeneas was the carrier of tradition, a man willing to shoulder the burdens of his ancestors forever.

This helps to explain why the Romans, in the ensuing centuries of their world domination, continued to identify so strongly with their homeland and its customs. In the Hellenistic world around them, as we have seen, the Greeks who emigrated to the new cosmopolitan kingdoms in Asia and Egypt were apt to adopt the customs, foods, and gods of these places. To a Roman, by contrast, "going native" in a foreign place was a terrible betrayal of the *mos maiorum*. Patriotism, after all, is dedication to the fatherland. This also explains the extraordinary maxim of *patria potestas* (*PAH-tree-a poh-TEST-ahs*; "fatherly power") upheld by the Twelve Tables. A Roman father, no matter what his social class, had absolute authority within his household, including the power of life and death. If he was too poor to raise a child, he could expose it or sell it into slavery. If his wife or child dishonored him, he could kill them with impunity.

These values set the Romans apart from the peoples with whom they came into contact. The Greeks, for example, never condoned anything like *patria potestas*: when a father kills his children in Greek mythology, he is inevitably revenged by another member of his own family, or by the gods. And although pride in one's ancestry is a very human attribute, and patriarchy common to every known civilization, the Romans' contemporaries were awed by their extreme devotion to these principles. Roman morality was what made them so admirable in the eyes of the Jews disgusted by the loose morals of Hellenistic civilization (see Chapter 4).

Although Roman religion resembled that of the Greeks in some respects, the Roman equation of religion with family meant that all gods were essentially family gods of the Roman state. The republic was essentially a giant, timeless household run by "elders" (senators) and "father figures" (patricians), some of whom traced their ancestry back to gods; the mother of Aeneas was Venus. Like a Roman household, the state could flourish only if these father- and mother-gods lent their continuing and active support. Committees of priests therefore functioned as branches of the government; and in stark contrast to priests in other ancient societies, these were not full-time professionals who formed a special caste but prominent senators. Their dual roles made religion even more integral to political life in Rome than it had been in Greece—similar in some ways to the integration of religion and politics in ancient Mesopotamia (see Chapter 1).

The all-important sense of ancestral duty is further reflected in Roman naming practices, another distinct custom. Most free men in other ancient cultures were known by a given name and their father's name: Alexander, before he was "Great," was "son of Philip." A free-born Roman, in contrast, had at least two names. The name that mattered was the name of his earliest ancestor. Gaius Julius Caesar, to take a famous example, would have entered public life as Julius, a member of the family of the Julii, who claimed ancestry from Iulus, the son of Aeneas. His forename, Gaius (*GUY-us*), was the most common name in Rome, the equivalent of "Joe" or "John." He would never be addressed by this name in public, except perhaps by very

A ROMAN PATRICIAN OF THE FIRST CENTURY B.C.E. This man, who wears the toga of an aristocrat, displays his piety by holding the busts of his ancestors. Busts, like the funerary masks described by Polybius (see page 156), commemorated the dead and were the focus for family worship in household shrines. › **How does the Roman attitude toward age and death differ from that of the Greeks (see the image on page 86)?** › **What do these differences suggest about the broader values of these two societies?**

Polybius Describes the Romans' Worship of Their Ancestors

The Law of the Twelve Tables forbade excessive display at funerals, especially displays of wealth and grief by women. Instead, funerals were supposed to be occasions for the display of family piety. In the following passage, the Greek historian Polybius—who had spent a formative fourteen years of his life in Rome—describes Roman burial customs and these rites' relationship to the strength of republican ideals.

I quote just one example to illustrate the pains taken by the Roman state to produce men who will endure anything to win a reputation for valor in their country. Whenever one of their celebrated men dies . . . his body is carried with every kind of honor into the Forum, . . . sometimes in an upright position so as to be conspicuous, or else, more rarely, recumbent. The whole mass of the people stand round to watch, and his son, if he has one of adult age who can be present, or if not some other relative, then . . . delivers an address which recounts the virtues and successes achieved by the dead man during his lifetime. By these means the whole populace . . . are involved in the ceremony, so that when the facts of the dead man's career are recalled . . . their sympathies are so deeply engaged that the loss seems . . . to be a public one which affects the whole people. Then, after the burial of the body and the performance of the customary rites, they place the image of the dead man in the most conspicuous position in the house, where it is enclosed in a wooden shrine. This image consists of a mask which is fashioned with extraordinary fidelity . . . to represent the features of these dead men. On occasions when public sacrifices are offered, these masks are displayed and decorated with great care. And when any distinguished member of the family dies, the masks are taken to the funeral, and are worn by men who are considered to bear the closest resemblance to the original, both in height and their general appearance and bearing. . . .

It would be hard to imagine a more impressive scene for a young man who aspires to win fame and practice virtue. For who could remain unmoved at the sight of the images of all these men who have won renown in their time, now gathered together as if alive and breathing? What spectacle could be more glorious than this?

Source: Polybius, *The Rise of the Roman Empire*, trans. Ian Scott-Kilvert (New York: 1979), pp. 346–47.

Questions for Analysis

1. Why does Polybius place so high a premium on the Romans' conduct at funerals? How can such rites be related to republican ideals?

2. Compare this analysis of Roman funerary rites with the image of a Roman patrician and his ancestors on page 155. How do they complement each other?

intimate friends. His third name, Caesar, which means "Hairy" (probably a joke), was a nickname he acquired in the course of his career. And because it was the most distinctive of his names, it became the name by which he was commonly known. The same goes for Marcus Tullius Cicero (Cicero means "chickpea"). The illustrious Cincinnatus was actually "Curly."

What's in a name? Everything, if you were a Roman man. And nothing, at least nothing of personal significance, if you were a Roman woman. Lucretia's name was not her own but her father's or forefather's: the feminine version of Lucretius. If she had a sister, they would both be called Lucretia, differentiated as Major and Minor ("big/elder" and "little/younger") Lucretia. If there were more girls, they would be Tertia and Quarta ("Third" and "Fourth") Lucretia, and so on. The only people in Rome who had personal names were slaves (who were named by their masters, like pets) or very low-born Romans and immigrants who had no lineage that mattered.

From Republic to Empire

For more than two centuries after the republic's founding, warfare and agriculture remained the chief occupations of most Romans. The fact that Rome had no standard system of coinage until 289 B.C.E. suggests strongly that commerce was an insignificant component of its economy. Romans didn't rely on portable wealth; when they weren't fighting, they wanted to be home on the farm. If they had money, they put it into real estate: land or slaves.

All of this changed rapidly when Romans began to look beyond Italy. In 265 B.C.E., they completed their absorption of Etruscan territory and controlled most of the peninsula. A year later, they were already embroiled in a war overseas. For a home-loving people this seems paradoxical. Indeed, historians continue to argue about the motives for Roman expansion. Did Rome constantly seek to extend its rule as a matter of policy, to feed a collective appetite for warfare and plunder? Or was it an accidental empire, built up in a series of reactions to changing pressures at home as well as in response to threats from abroad? No definitive answer is possible, but it was in this crucial period that the Roman Republic began to transform Western civilizations, and itself, into the Roman Empire.

THE PUNIC WARS, 264–146 B.C.E.

In 265 B.C.E., Roman territory extended to the tip of Italy's "boot," but there it ended. Just off its coast, the large islands of Corsica and Sardinia and the western half of Sicily were part of another state, much older and far wealthier. This was the great maritime empire of **Carthage**, which stretched along the northern coast of Africa from modern-day Tunisia through the Straits of Gibraltar and into modern Spain. Carthage itself was a vital port city at the northeastern tip of Africa, founded around 800 B.C.E. as a Phoenician colony (see Chapter 2). It had the largest and most effective navy of its day, and it commanded the vast resources of commercial networks that reached north to Britain and deep into Egypt. In almost every respect it was far superior to Rome. But although the Carthaginian fleet was unrivaled, it had no standing army. It relied on mercenaries bankrolled by the enormous profits of trade.

The epic struggle between Rome and Carthage lasted well over a century. It crystallized in three periods of concentrated warfare known as the **Punic Wars**, because the Romans called their enemies the Poeni ("Phoenicians"). The first began in 264 B.C.E. Twenty-three years of bitter fighting ensued, protracted because the Carthaginians needed to suffer only one defeat in a land battle before resolving to engage the Romans solely at sea. There they had the advantage—until the Romans built their own navy. In 241 B.C.E., Carthage was forced to cede all of its Sicilian lands to Rome

Carthage Great maritime empire that grew out of the Phoenician trading colonies in North Africa and eventually rivaled the power of Rome. Its wars with Rome ended in the destruction of Carthage in 146 B.C.E.

Punic Wars (264–146 B.C.E.) Three periods of warfare between Rome and Carthage, maritime empires that struggled for dominance of the Mediterranean.

First Punic War: Rome defeats Carthage in competition for Mediterranean dominance

and to pay reparations. Sicily thus became Rome's first overseas province; it was shortly followed by Corsica and Sardinia.

Thereafter, the Romans were determined not to let Carthage revive its maritime power. So when Carthage attempted to expand its presence in Spain, leaders of the Senate interpreted this as a threat to Roman interests and declared a new war that lasted for sixteen years: the Second Punic War. This time, however, Rome was thrown entirely off its guard by the brilliant exploits of the Carthaginian commander Hannibal (247–183 B.C.E.), who very nearly defeated the Romans on their own soil. Daringly, Hannibal raised an army in Spain, heavily manned by cavalry in order to counter the superior infantry of Rome, and equipped it with dozens of war elephants and siege engines. He then led this entire force across the Pyrenees into Gaul (now southern France) and then over the Alps into Italy. There, he harried Roman forces in their own territories for nearly sixteen years, from 218 to 202 B.C.E.

In the end, Hannibal was challenged more by the difficulty of supplying his army in hostile terrain than by the Romans themselves. He also seems to have counted on winning the support of the Italian territories that Rome had conquered, but Rome's generous treatment of its allies kept them loyal. As a result, Rome could call on vast resources while Hannibal had only his exhausted army, with no reserves forthcoming from Carthage. Nevertheless, he won several amazing victories in Italy before retreating—technically undefeated—in 202 B.C.E. He also won the admiration of the Romans themselves, whose own histories frankly acknowledge his tactical genius. Indeed, this phase of warfare ended only when a Roman general, Publius Cornelius Scipio, took a leaf out of Hannibal's book. He had been campaigning in Spain against the army of Hannibal's brother, Hasdrubal. In 201 B.C.E., having seized a number of key Carthaginian strongholds, he crossed into Africa and met Hannibal near Carthage. Scipio's victory ended the Second Punic War and won him a new name, "Africanus," in honor of his conquest.

Carthage was now compelled to abandon all of its possessions except the city itself and its immediate hinterlands, and to pay an indemnity three times greater than the reparations Rome had demanded after the First Punic War. Yet Roman suspicion of Carthage remained obsessive, and warmongers in the Senate read every sign of its recovery as a threat. By the middle of the second century, some hard-liners were urging a preemptive strike. Among the most vocal was an elderly patrician, Marcus Porcius Cato, famous for his stern obedience to Roman custom and his virulent xenophobia. Cato ended every speech he gave—no matter what the topic—with the words: "And furthermore, I strongly advise that Carthage be destroyed." This won him the nickname Cato the Censor, from the Latin verb meaning "to advise."

Eventually, the Senate was persuaded. In 149 B.C.E., it seized on a minor pretext to demand that the Carthaginians abandon their city and settle at least ten miles from the coast, where they would have no access to the sea. Of course, this absurd mandate amounted to a death sentence for a city dependent on commerce, and it was refused—as the Romans knew it would be. The result was the Third Punic War and the siege of Carthage, which ended in 146 B.C.E. when the Romans breached the walls and butchered the population. Those who survived the massacre were sold into slavery, and their once-magnificent city was razed to the ground. The legend that the Romans sowed the land with salt (to make it infertile) is not a real tactic but a poetic way of describing the successful eradication of an entire civilization. It would stand as a warning to Rome's other potential enemies.

Second Punic War: Romans surprised by Carthaginian army led by Hannibal

Third Punic War: Romans lay siege to, defeat, and raze Carthage

ROMAN CONTROL OF THE HELLENISTIC WORLD

Rome's victories over Carthage led to the creation of new colonial provinces in Sicily, North Africa, and Hispania (Spain). This not only brought great new wealth, it was also the beginning of the westward expansion that became Rome's defining influence on the history of Western civilizations.

At the same time, Rome's overseas expansion brought it into conflict with eastern Mediterranean powers. During the Second Punic War, Philip V of Macedonia had entered an alliance with Carthage; soon afterward, he moved aggressively into Greece and was rumored to have designs on Egypt. Rome sent an army to stop him and later foiled the plans of the Achaean League (see Chapter 4): this was when Polybius was sent to Rome as a hostage, where he became a guest-friend of the family descended from Scipio Africanus and later witnessed the destruction of Carthage. Rome also thwarted the Seleucid monarch Antiochus III. By 146 B.C.E., both Greece and Macedonia had become Roman provinces, the Seleucid kingdom had lost most of its territory, and Ptolemaic Egypt had become a pawn of Roman commercial and political interests.

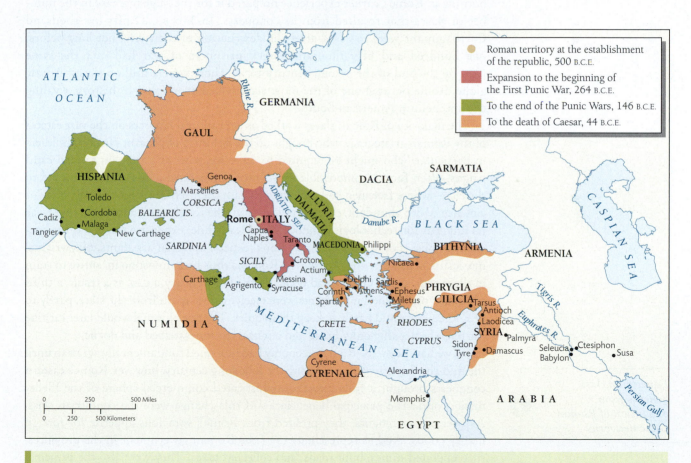

Roman territory at the establishment of the republic, 500 B.C.E.

Expansion to the beginning of the First Punic War, 264 B.C.E.

To the end of the Punic Wars, 146 B.C.E.

To the death of Caesar, 44 B.C.E.

THE FURTHER EXPANSION OF ROME, 264–44 B.C.E. The rapid increase of Rome's territories opened up new opportunities and challenges. › Examine the phases of expansion on this map. In what directions did Roman dominion move? › Why was this the case? › What particular problems might have been created by the eventual extension of Roman rule into Gaul, well beyond the "Roman lake" of the Mediterranean?

The Consequences of Imperialism

Rome's seemingly inadvertent conquest of Greece and western Asia transformed the economic, social, and cultural life of the republic. New wealth increased the inequalities within Roman society and challenged the traditional values of frugality and self-sacrifice. Small farmers were forced off their lands and swelled the impoverished urban population, unable to compete with the huge new plantations owned by aristocrats and worked by gangs of slaves. Slaves also played an increasing role in Roman cities as artisans, merchants, and household servants. Roman rule over the Hellenistic world had a particularly pervasive impact on cultural life—so much so that many Romans felt intellectually and culturally "conquered" by Greece. Hitherto self-assured, they now felt that their own language, history, and customs were uncouth and barbaric compared with those of their cultivated colonial subjects.

ECONOMIC CHANGE AND SOCIAL UPHEAVAL

Like all peoples of the ancient world, the Romans took **slavery** for granted. But nothing in Rome's earlier experience prepared it for the huge increase in the number of slaves that resulted from its conquests. In 146 B.C.E., fifty-five thousand Carthaginians were enslaved after the destruction of their city; not long before, one hundred and fifty thousand Greek prisoners of war had met the same fate. By the end of the second century B.C.E., there were a million slaves in Italy alone. Rome became one of the most slave-based economies in history, rivaling the antebellum American South.

The majority of Roman slaves worked as agricultural laborers on the vast estates of the Roman aristocracy, who bought up the holdings of peasant farmers. Soldiers in particular, who might be required to serve for years at a time on foreign campaigns, often found it impossible to maintain their farms. Instead, they moved to the city—where free men had no way to sustain themselves except through trade or violence. With abundant, cheap slaves to do all the rough work, moreover, there was no impetus for technological innovation. Meanwhile, expensive slaves did the specialized jobs: they were secretaries, bookkeepers, personal assistants, playwrights, musicians, sculptors, and artists. The Romans thus had almost no incentive to train in these arts, as the Greeks had done. By the first century B.C.E., as a result, a third of Rome's one million inhabitants were receiving free grain from the state, partly to keep them alive and partly to keep them quiet. The poet Juvenal would later satirize the plebs as needing only "bread and circuses" to stay satisfied and docile.

As we have seen, the Roman economy had remained fundamentally agrarian until the mid-third century B.C.E. During the following century, however, Rome's eastern conquests brought it fully into the sophisticated commercial sphere of the Hellenistic world. The principal beneficiaries of this change were the equestrian class. As overseas merchants, they profited from Rome's voracious appetite for foreign luxury goods. And as representatives of the Roman government in the provinces, they operated mines, built roads, and collected taxes. They were also the principal moneylenders to the Roman state and to distressed individuals.

Commoners who lost their lands suffered from these economic changes, but the principal victims of Rome's transformation were its slaves. Even though some were cultivated foreigners—mainly Greek-speaking—taken as prisoners of war, their

Equestrian class benefits from expansion of Roman trade networks

owners would get as much work out of them as possible until they died of exhaustion or were "freed" in old age to fend for themselves. The same irascible Cato the Censor who had demanded the destruction of Carthage even wrote a "how-to" book on this subject. This made Roman slavery a far more impersonal and brutal institution than it had been in many other ancient civilizations. While some domestic slaves were treated as trusted family members, and slave secretaries vital to Roman governance and the arts could even win fame or buy their freedom, the general lot of slaves was horrendous. Some businessmen owned slaves whom they trained as gladiators to be mauled by wild animals or by other gladiators for the amusement of a paying public. Dozens of slaves in every household were trapped in a cycle of menial tasks as doorkeepers, litter-bearers, couriers, valets, wet nurses, and childminders. In some great households, designated slaves had no other duties than to rub down the master after his bath or to keep track of the mistress's social engagements. It was a life that debased both slave and owner, according to many Roman critics, and undermined the republic.

NEW MONEY, NEW VALUES

In the early republic, as we have seen, Roman men had nearly absolute power over their households. During the second century B.C.E., two innovations greatly altered this pattern of patriarchal control. One was the introduction of new laws that allowed married women to manage their own property. Another allowed women to initiate divorce proceedings. These changes were intended to safeguard family wealth, but they eventually resulted in greater independence for women. A woman now had more authority within the household because she contributed to its upkeep. If her husband did not show respect, she could leave him and deprive him of income. It is ironic, too, that the growth of Rome's slave system gave women greater freedom, for slaves took over the traditional work of child-rearing, household maintenance, and the endless tasks of spinning and weaving. Women from well-to-do families now spent more time away from the home and began to engage in social, intellectual, and artistic activities. Indeed, women were among the chief consumers of the new Hellenistic fashions, commodities, and ideas available in Rome.

In earlier centuries, Romans had taken pride in the simplicity of their lives. Now, however, elite Romans began to cultivate Hellenistic habits as proof of their refinement. Bilingualism became increasingly common, and Greek literature became the standard against which Roman authors measured themselves. Latin was fine for politics or farming, but if one wanted to express lofty or beautiful thoughts one did so in Greek, which was far more flexible and sophisticated. Latin was not yet a literary language, and well-educated Greek slaves were therefore at a premium: to lend social cachet, to act as personal assistants, and to tutor Roman children.

But many Romans regarded these foreign influences with disgust. For them, the good old ways of paternal authority and military discipline were giving way to effeminacy and soft living. Conservative politicians passed laws that would regulate the conspicuous consumption, especially by women—but these measures were ineffectual. Rome was being transformed from a republic of self-reliant farmers into a complex metropolitan empire reliant on foreign slaves, foreign luxuries, and foreign ideas.

Roman simplicity gives way to Hellenistic refinement

PHILOSOPHY AND SPIRITUALITY IN THE LATE REPUBLIC

The late republic was deeply influenced by Hellenistic philosophy, and Stoicism found especially strong adherents in Rome. The most influential of these was Cicero (106–43 B.C.E.), an orator, statesman, and staunch defender of republican values. Cicero based his ethical teachings on the Stoic premises that virtue is happiness and tranquility of mind the highest good. Yet he diverged from many Stoics in his advocacy for an active, political life. His elegant prose style also advanced Latin's use as a language of eloquence and became the standard model for Latin composition: students learning Latin today still learn to read with Cicero.

Romans were also influenced by exotic mystery cults, which satisfied a need for more emotionally intense spiritual experiences than did traditional forms of Roman worship—again, especially for women, who were largely excluded from the patriarchal state religion. From Egypt came the cults of Isis and Osiris, while from Asia came the worship of the Great Mother: all emphasizing the power of female sexuality and reproduction. Yet Romans still continued to honor their traditional gods alongside these new deities. Roman polytheism could absorb them all, so long as the ancestor gods were paid due reverence.

"Restoring the Republic": The Struggle for Power

Within the city of Rome, the century after the Third Punic War was turbulent. Bloody competition among rival dictators and generals, civil disorder, and popular uprisings were common. Slave rebellions posed a particular threat. In 134 B.C.E., some seventy thousand slaves defeated a Roman army in Sicily before being put down by emergency reinforcements. In 73 B.C.E., a Thracian called Spartacus inspired a band of two hundred slaves to escape from a gladiatorial training camp at Capua (near Naples; see the map on page 159). Heavily armed, they took refuge on the slopes of Mount Vesuvius, where they attracted a huge host of other fugitives. For two years, this desperate force defeated two Roman legions and overran much of southern Italy before Spartacus himself was killed. The Senate, terrified by the near victory of the rebels, ordered six thousand of the captured slaves to be crucified along the road from Capua to Rome (about a hundred and fifty miles) as a warning to future insurgents. Crucifixion was a punishment reserved for slaves and non-Roman rebels: a slow, terrible, and public death from suffocation and exposure.

THE REFORMING EFFORTS OF THE GRACCHI

Meanwhile, the poorer classes of Rome were finding new champions among progressive aristocrats. In 133 B.C.E., Tiberius Gracchus was elected a tribune and proposed to close the growing rift between rich and poor by instituting major reforms, including the redistribution of property that had been amassed by large plantation owners. His motives were both populist and practical: the Roman army had been forced to expand its presence into far-reaching territories and needed more manpower to handle uprisings like that of Spartacus. Since a man had to meet certain property qualifications to serve in the Roman army, the available pool of citizen soldiers was shrinking along with the wealth of average citizens. Gracchus saw that the army could be strengthened if more Romans could qualify for citizenship.

With the support of his brother Gaius, Tiberius invoked an ancient law that limited landholdings to three hundred acres per citizen, plus a hundred and fifty acres for each child in his family. Since many aristocratic estates far exceeded these measures, the excess land could be divided among small farmers. But since most senators stood to lose from this legislation, they opposed it, accusing Gracchus of being a demagogue who had his sights set on a dictatorship. With this excuse, they murdered him and his closest supporters.

Ten years later, Gaius Gracchus was elected to the same office and renewed his older brother's proposals. Although some land reforms had been enacted by the Senate after the assassination of Tiberius, Gaius wanted to benefit the poor by stabilizing the price of grain in Rome and to check the abuses of senators by giving the equestrians greater powers. Controversially, he also proposed to extend full Roman citizenship to all the allied states of Italy: a move that would have created new citizens whose collective power would challenge existing elites. In the ensuing conflict, he and several thousand of his supporters became the victims of a violent political purge.

RIVALRY AMONG ROME'S GENERALS

The attempted reforms of the Gracchi exposed the corruption of the republic's constitution by a wealthy elite. And the brothers' popularity among the plebs suggested a new path to power for ambitious men, most of whom were former army commanders who traded on their military victories to win support. The first of these generals was Gaius Marius, who had fought a successful campaign against King Jugurtha of Numidia, a small kingdom in North Africa. In 107 B.C.E., Marius secured election to the office of consul, an office that he would hold six more times in the course of his career. This set a powerful precedent, because it showed that a man with no family connections or political experience could override opposition from older political elites if he had an army to help him intimidate those elites.

Marius shows how army command could be an alternative path to political power

Marius further influenced the future of Rome by reorganizing and expanding the army. Desperate for more men to fight in Africa and in Gaul, Marius abolished the property qualification that had limited military service to citizens; the potential pool of soldiers now included the urban poor and landless peasants. As a result, a career as a Roman legionnaire became an end in itself, rather than a matter of routine service to the state. This meant, further, that a soldier's loyalty was directed toward his commander, whose success would win rewards for his men, rather than to an abstract ideal of patriotism.

These changes also meant that discord between political rivals could lead to full-blown civil war, if legions loyal to one general were pitted against those of another. And indeed, this happened in Marius's own lifetime. An aristocratic general named Lucius Cornelius Sulla had fought with distinction in the so-called Social War of 91–88 B.C.E.: a conflict between Rome and its Italian allies. Sulla seemed the likely person to lead Rome's army to war in Anatolia, but Marius forced the Senate to deny his claim. Sulla's response was to rally the five victorious legions that had fought under his command and to march into Rome.

This was a disturbing move: strong taboos had long prevented any armed force from entering the city limits. But Sulla argued that his actions were in keeping with the *mos maiorum*, which Marius and the Senate had betrayed. When the intimidated Senate gave Sulla the coveted command, Marius seized control of the city with his own legions. When Marius died soon afterward, backlash against his popular rule led the aristocracy to appoint Sulla dictator—but not for the traditional six months, as under the early republic. Sulla's term had no limits, and he used his powers to exterminate his opponents and pack the Senate with men loyal to himself. Then, after three years of autocratic rule, he retired to a life of luxury on his country estate.

CAESAR'S TRIUMPH—AND HIS DOWNFALL

The effect of Sulla's dictatorship was to empower the aristocracy and terminally weaken the plebs. Soon, however, new leaders emerged to espouse the people's cause, once again using the army as their tool of influence. The most prominent of these generals were Gnaeus Pompeius Magnus (106–48 B.C.E.) and Gaius **Julius Caesar** (100–44 B.C.E.). Almost exact contemporaries, Pompeius (Pompey) and Caesar represented two very different branches of Roman society. Pompey was the son of an immigrant from central Italy who had made a fortune in Rome through questionable business practices. For Pompey, the army was a path toward gaining a political and social foothold. Caesar, by contrast, was descended from one of Rome's oldest patrician families, born to wealth and privilege. For him, the army was a stepping-stone toward greater power and influence.

Initially, Pompey and Caesar cooperated in a plot to "restore the republic" by forming an alliance with a third general, Marcus Licinius Crassus, the general who had finally defeated Spartacus. This alliance was known as a *triumvirate* (*tri-UM-vir-et*), meaning "rule of three men," but it soon dissolved into open rivalry. Pompey had won fame as the conqueror of Syria and Palestine; but Caesar had campaigned victoriously in Gaul, adding the territories encompassing modern France, Belgium, and western Germany to Rome's empire. Caesar's conquests secured his reputation at home and cemented the loyalty of his army.

Since the rise of Marius, it had become accepted that the best general should be the leader of Rome, while the example of Sulla had made it possible for that leader to be a dictator for life: a king in all but name. But it was Pompey, not Caesar, who was actually in Rome and able to influence the Senate. In the face of tremendous popular protest, and even some opposition from the aristocracy, Pompey managed to get himself elected sole consul. Using this authority, he declared that Caesar, who was still in Gaul, was an enemy of the republic.

The result was a widespread and deadly civil war. In 49 B.C.E., Caesar crossed the Rubicon River, the northern boundary of Rome's Italian territories, thereby signaling his intention to take Rome by force. Pompey fled to the east in the hope of gathering an army large enough to confront Caesar's legions. Caesar pursued him and, in 48 B.C.E., the two Roman armies met at Pharsalus in Greece. Pompey was defeated and fled to Alexandria, where he was murdered by a Roman officer attached to the court of Ptolemy XIII (62/61–47? B.C.E.). This young pharaoh, a descendant of Alexander's general Ptolemy, was then about fourteen years old and engaged in a civil war of his own—against his elder sister and co-ruler, Cleopatra VII (69–30 B.C.E.). Caesar threw his support on the side of the twenty-one-year-old queen. The two

BUST OF JULIUS CAESAR. Caesar's nickname meant "hairy," but it has come to be synonymous with imperial rule. It was the title preferred by the German kings of the late nineteenth and twentieth centuries, who called themselves *kaisers*, and by the tsars of Russia. In classical Latin, the "C" sound is hard, which means that the pronunciations of *caesar*, *kaiser*, and *tsar* are very similar.

must have become lovers soon after their first meeting, since their son Caesarion ("Little Caesar") was born just nine months later. After a brief struggle, Ptolemy was defeated. Cleopatra then ruled as pharaoh of Egypt in her own right, much as Hatshepsut had done nearly a millennium and a half before (see Chapter 2).

Caesar returned to Rome in triumph—literally. A *triumph* was a spectacular honor awarded to a victorious Roman general by the Senate and was the only occasion on which (unarmed) soldiers were allowed to parade in the streets of Rome. Triumphs had been celebrated since the earliest days of the republic, and they featured prisoners and spoils of war, chained captives (often enemy kings) led in humiliation to their public executions, floats commemorating the achievements of the triumphant man, and thousands of cheering Romans who received extra rations of grain and gathered up coins thrown by the handful. Through it all, Caesar would have ridden in a chariot with a golden wreath held above his head while a slave stood behind him, murmuring in his ear the words *Memento mori* ("Remember: you will die"). A triumph was so glorious and—under the republic—so rarely granted that those honored might forget their own mortality.

Caesar's power seemed absolute. In 46 B.C.E., he was named dictator for ten years; two years later, this was changed to a lifetime appointment. The Senate gave him full authority to make war and peace and to control the revenues of the state. He even governed the reckoning of time: in imitation of the Egyptian calendar (slightly modified by a Greek astronomer), Caesar revised the Roman calendar to make a 365-day year with an extra day added every fourth year. This Julian calendar (as adjusted by Pope Gregory XIII in 1582) is still observed, and the seventh month is still named after Julius.

Julius Caesar (100–44 B.C.E.) Roman general who conquered the Gauls, invaded Britain, and expanded Rome's territory in Asia Minor. He became the dictator of Rome in 46 B.C.E.

Caesar's dictatorship grows into lifetime rule with expanded powers

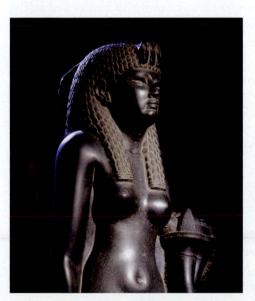

CLEOPATRA VII AS EGYPTIAN PHARAOH AND HELLENISTIC RULER. Like her ancestor Ptolemy I, Cleopatra represented herself as both enlightened Greek monarch and pharaoh. It was perhaps owing to her example that Julius Caesar was the first Roman leader to issue coins impressed with his own image. › **How does Cleopatra's self-representation compare with that of Hatshepsut (see page 46) or Ptolemy (see page 131)?**

Antony and Cleopatra

In his Parallel Lives, *the Greek intellectual Plutarch (c. 46–120 c.e.) paired the biographies of famous Greeks with those of famous Romans, always to the disadvantage of the latter. For example, Julius Caesar suffers in comparison with Alexander the Great, as Romulus does when set up against Theseus. The following excerpt is from Plutarch's* Life of Mark Antony, *in which the Hellenistic ruler of Egypt, Cleopatra, plays a starring role.*

Caesar and Pompey knew Cleopatra when she was still a girl, and ignorant of the world, but it was a different matter in the case of Antony, because she was ready to meet him when she had reached the time of life when women are most beautiful and have full understanding. So she prepared for him many gifts and money and adornment, of a magnitude appropriate to her great wealth and prosperous kingdom, but she put most of her hopes in her own magical arts and charms. . . . For (as they say), it was not because her beauty in itself was so striking that it stunned the onlooker, but the inescapable impression produced by daily contact with her: the attractiveness in the persuasiveness of her talk, and the character that surrounded her conversation was stimulating. It was a pleasure to hear the sound of her voice, and she tuned her tongue like a many-stringed instrument expertly to whatever language she chose, and only used interpreters to talk to a few foreigners. . . . She is said to have learned the languages of many peoples, although her predecessors on the throne did not bother to learn Egyptian, and some had even forgotten how to speak the Macedonian dialect.

She took such a hold over Antony that, while his wife Fulvia was carrying on the war in Rome against Octavian on his behalf, and the Parthian army . . . was about to invade Syria, Antony was carried off by Cleopatra to Alexandria, and amused himself there with the pastimes of a boy . . . and whether Antony was in a serious or a playful mood she could always produce some new pleasure or charm, and she kept watch on him by night and day and never let him out of her sight. She played dice with him and hunted with him and watched him exercising with his weapons and she roamed around and wandered about with him at night when he stood at people's doors and windows and made fun of people inside, dressed in a slave-woman's outfit; for he also attempted to dress up like a slave. He returned from these expeditions having been mocked in return, and often beaten, although most people suspected who he was. But the Alexandrians got pleasure from his irreverence . . . enjoying his humor and saying that he showed his tragic face to the Romans and his comic one to them.

Source: Plutarch, *Life of Marcus Antonius*, excerpted in *Women's Life in Greece and Rome: A Sourcebook in Translation*, eds. Mary R. Lefkowitz and Maureen B. Fant (Baltimore, MD: 1992), pp. 147–49.

Questions for Analysis

1. How do Cleopatra's behavior and accomplishments, in Plutarch's description of her, compare with those of Roman women?

2. Given what you have learned about the values of the Roman Republic, how would a Roman reader respond to this description of Antony's behavior under the influence of the Egyptian queen? What do you think were Plutarch's motives in portraying him in this light?

IDES OF MARCH COIN. This coin celebrates the assassination of Julius Caesar by Marcus Junius Brutus, who is shown on the face; on the reverse, a cap of liberty (customarily worn by freed slaves) is flanked by two daggers, and below it is the legend *EID-MAR*, the Latin abbreviation for "Ides of March."
› **Given that Caesar drew criticism for depicting himself on Roman coinage, what do you think is the significance of Brutus's image being shown in this way?**

Caesar also worked to eliminate the distinction between Italians and provincials by conferring citizenship on residents of Hispania (Spain) and the newly annexed provinces in Gaul. Moreover, by settling many of his army veterans in these lands, he furthered their colonization. Whereas Pompey, like Alexander, had gone east to gain fame and fortune, Caesar followed only the Phoenicians in recognizing the potential of the wild west.

In the eyes of many contemporaries, however, Caesar's achievements were signs that he actually did intend to make himself king: a hateful thought to those who still glorified the early republic. Indeed, it was a descendant of Lucretia's avenger, Brutus, who led the faction of senators who planned Caesar's assassination. On the Ides of March in 44 B.C.E.— according to his own calendar—Caesar was attacked on the floor of the Senate chamber and stabbed to death by a group of men. A later autopsy (the first forensic medical examination in recorded history) found that he had sustained twenty-three wounds.

The Principate and the *Pax Romana*, 27 B.C.E.–180 C.E.

In his will, Caesar had adopted his grandnephew Gaius Octavius (or Octavian; 63 B.C.E.–14 C.E.), a young man of eighteen serving in Illyria, across the Adriatic Sea. On learning of Caesar's death, Octavian hastened home to avenge his slain "father," whose name he took: Gaius Julius Caesar the Younger. But he had rivals among those supporters of Caesar, most notably Marcus Antonius (Mark Antony; 83–30 B.C.E.), who had served under Caesar's command in Gaul and had ambitions to make himself governor of that whole province.

Octavian engineered his own election to the office of consul (though he was far too young) and used his power to declare Caesar's assassins outlaws. He then pursued

OCTAVIAN. Caesar's adopted heir was later granted the title *augustus* ("worthy of honor") by the Senate and was also known as *princeps* ("first man"). He was worshiped as a god in Rome's provinces, and idealized statues like this one were erected in temples and public places throughout the empire.

Antony to Gaul, at the head of an army, where Antony's forces were overwhelmed. In 43 B.C.E., Antony and Octavian reconciled and formed an alliance, bringing in a third man, a senator named Marcus Aemilius Lepidus, to make up a second triumvirate. They then set about crushing the men responsible for Caesar's murder, and anyone else who opposed them. The most notable of these latter victims was Cicero, who was murdered by Antony's hired thugs. (This was to avenge Cicero's efforts to undermine Antony, whom he had branded a public enemy.) Meanwhile, the masterminds behind Caesar's assassination—Marcus Junius Brutus and Gaius Cassius—raised an army of legions from Greece and Anatolia. But they were defeated by the united forces of Antony and Octavian on a battlefield near the Macedonian town of Philippi (founded by Alexander's father, Philip II) in 42 B.C.E. Both Brutus and Cassius committed suicide. With their mutual enemies effectively destroyed, tensions mounted within the triumvirate. Antony and Octavian marginalized Lepidus, who was eventually exiled. Antony made an alliance with Cleopatra, plotting to use the resources of her realm against Octavian. Octavian reestablished himself in Rome, where he skillfully portrayed Antony as having been seduced and emasculated by his foreign lover, the Egyptian queen, whose son Caesarion threatened his own position as Caesar's heir. For ten years, Antony played the king in Egypt, fathering three of Cleopatra's children and making big plans for annexing Rome's eastern provinces. Eventually, Octavian had him declared a traitor while the Senate declared war on Cleopatra.

In 31 B.C.E., Octavian's superior forces defeated those of Antony and Cleopatra in the naval battle of Actium, off the coast of Greece. Soon afterward, Antony and Cleopatra committed suicide. But their children were taken back to Rome—Caesarion disappeared under suspicious circumstances—and paraded through the streets as captives. This marked the end of Egypt's independence: Cleopatra had been its last pharaoh. After more than three thousand years, it was just another province in Rome's empire.

THE GOVERNMENT OF AUGUSTUS

The victory at Actium marks a new period of Roman history. Octavian, or Gaius Julius Caesar the Younger, was now the only claimant to power. For the first time in over a century, Rome was not embroiled in civil war. But Rome was also no longer a republic. Even though Octavian maintained the fiction that he was a mere citizen, his rule was autocratic. In addition to being sole consul, he adopted the titles of *imperator* ("victorious commander") and *augustus* ("worthy of honor"). So although Rome had been an empire for centuries, it was not until now that it had a single emperor. To avoid confusion, historians therefore refer to this phase of Rome's history as the **Principate**, from the title Augustus himself preferred: *princeps*, "first man."

Augustus was determined not to be regarded as a tyrant or (worse) a king, so he left most of Rome's republican institutions in place—but he gradually emptied them of their power. In theory, the **emperor** served at the will of "the Senate and People of Rome." In practice, he controlled the army and the city. Fortunately, **Augustus** was an able ruler. He introduced a range of public services, including a police force and fire brigade. He instituted a new system of coinage and abolished the old, corrupt system that had allowed tax collectors to keep a portion of what they collected, which encouraged them to collect more than was due. Instead, Augustus appointed his own representatives and paid them regular salaries. He simultaneously conducted a census of the empire's population, and it was during one of these "enrollments" that the birth of Jesus took place, according to the Gospel of Luke (see Chapter 6).

Above all, Augustus represented himself as a stern defender of the *mos maiorum*. He rebuilt many of the city's ancient temples and prohibited the worship of foreign gods. In an attempt to increase the birthrate, he penalized men who failed to marry, required widows to remarry within two years of their husbands' deaths, and rewarded women who gave birth to more than two children. He also introduced laws punishing adultery and making divorces more difficult to obtain. To hammer the message home, Augustan propaganda portrayed the imperial family as a model of domestic virtue. Yet these portrayals were only moderately successful because the emperor's own extramarital affairs were notorious, while the sexual promiscuity of his daughter Julia eventually forced Augustus to have her exiled.

More territory was gained for Rome in the lifetime of Augustus than in all the previous centuries of its existence. His generals advanced farther and farther into central Europe, conquering the lands that are now Switzerland, Austria, and Bulgaria. Only in Germania did Roman troops meet defeat, when three legions were slaughtered in 9 C.E.: a devastating setback that convinced Augustus to hold the Roman borders at the Rhine and Danube Rivers. Augustus also encouraged the emigration of Rome's urban and rural poor to the new colonies. This not only alleviated social tensions but also promoted the integration of the Roman heartland with its far-flung hinterland. Augustus also allowed older cities and provinces more substantial rights of self-government than they had enjoyed before.

Principate Modern term for the centuries of autocratic rule by the successors of Augustus, who seized power in 27 B.C.E. and styled himself *princeps*, or Rome's "first man."

emperor Originally the term for any conquering commander of the Roman army whose victories merited celebration in an official triumph; after Augustus seized power in 27 B.C.E., it was the tittle borne by the sole ruler of the Roman Empire.

Augustus (63 B.C.E.–14 C.E.) Born Gaius Octavius, this grand-nephew and adopted son of Julius Caesar came to power in 27 B.C.E.

HADRIAN'S WALL. Stretching 73.5 miles across northern England, this fortification (begun in 122 C.E.) marked the frontier of the Roman province of Britannia as established by the emperor Hadrian. (A later wall, built farther north by Antoninus Pius in 142 C.E., was quickly abandoned.) Long stretches of the wall still exist, as do many of the forts built along it. The tree in this photograph stands on the site of a "mile castle," one of the smaller watchtowers built at intervals of a Roman mile and garrisoned by sentries.

THE LEGACY OF AUGUSTUS

When Augustus died in 14 C.E., he was not only *caesar*, *imperator*, and *augustus*; he was *pontifex maximus* ("high priest") and *pater patriae* ("father of the fatherland"). He was even deified by the Senate, which had also deified Julius Caesar. These titles were passed on to his successors, as was the system of government he had devised. And even those who mourned the passing of the republic had to admit that the system worked. Rome would enjoy nearly two centuries of peace, prosperity, and stability because of it. For the true test of any institution's strength is its capacity to survive incompetent officeholders. Aside from one brief period of civil war in 68 C.E., the transition of power between Augustan emperors was generally peaceful, and the growing imperial bureaucracy could manage affairs even when individual emperors proved vicious or ineffectual, like the notorious Caligula (r. 37–41 C.E.). Nevertheless, the fact that Rome had become an autocratic state became harder and harder to conceal.

THE ROMAN EMPIRE AT ITS GREATEST EXTENT, 97–117 C.E. › How much farther north and west does the empire now reach, compared with its earlier extent (see map on page 159)? › How did geography influence the process of expansion? › How did it dictate the limits of expansion? › For example, what role do major river systems seem to play?

The height of the Augustan system is generally considered to be the era between 96 and 180 c.e., often known as the reign of the "Five Good Emperors": Nerva (96–98 c.e.), Trajan (98–117 c.e.), Hadrian (117–138 c.e.), Antoninus Pius (138–161 c.e.), and Marcus Aurelius (161–180 c.e.). All were capable politicians, and since none but the last had a son that survived him, each adopted a worthy successor—a wise practice that allowed this generation of rulers to avoid the messy family dysfunctions of Augustus and his heirs. They also benefited from the fact that Rome had few external enemies left. The Mediterranean was under the control of a single power for the first (and only) time in history. On land, Roman officials ruled from Britain to Persia. The continual bloodshed of civil wars had ended and Augustus's own reign of terror had abated. Now was the time of the *Pax Romana*, the Roman Peace.

Making the World Roman

Occasionally, the Roman Peace was broken. In Britannia, Roman legions put down a rebellion led by the Celtic warrior queen Boudica (d. 60/61 c.e.), which ended in a massacre of indigenous tribes. Another rebellion was violently quashed in Judea, the most restive of all the Roman provinces, leading to the destruction of the Temple at Jerusalem in 70 c.e. In 135 c.e., a second Jewish rebellion completed the destruction of the city. Although it was refounded by Hadrian as Aelia Capitolina, a colony for veterans of Rome's army, Jews were forbidden to settle there (see Chapter 6).

Such rebellions were not the norm, however. Instead, Rome controlled its territories by offering incentives for assimilation. Local elites were encouraged to adopt Roman education, behavior, and dress in order to achieve political office. Local gods became Roman gods and were adopted into the Roman pantheon. And yet assimilation could work both ways. Tens of thousands of army veterans settled in the provinces, marrying local women and putting down roots. It was common for soldiers born in Syria or North Africa to end their days peacefully in northern Gaul or Pannonia (modern Hungary). In Camulodunum (now Colchester, England), the gravestone of a legionnaire called Longinus Sdapeze sketches a typical career: born in Serdica (modern Sofia, Bulgaria) to a local man named Matucus, he rose through the ranks to become a sergeant of the First Thracian Cavalry under Claudius and one of the first Roman colonists of Britannia.

Assimilation within Roman Empire works both ways

Rights of citizenship were also extended, and able provincials could rise far in the imperial government. Some, like the emperors Trajan and Hadrian—both raised in Hispania—came to control it. Even the outer fringes of the empire, areas not incorporated into provinces, need to be understood as part of Rome's orbit. Although we speak of the empire's "borders" for the sake of convenience, Roman influence reached far beyond these fluid frontiers. By the middle of the third century c.e., when some frontier garrisons were withdrawn to take part in wars within the empire itself, many of these peoples moved into the empire's settled provinces (see Chapter 6).

IMPERIAL INFRASTRUCTURE AND THE ENVIRONMENT

Augustus liked to boast that he had found Rome a city of clay and left it a city of marble. In reality, marble was too precious to be used in common construction. Instead, marble panels or ornaments were added to the facings of buildings made of concrete.

Two Views of Augustus's Rule

The emperor Augustus was a master propagandist with an unrivaled capacity for presenting his own actions in the best possible light. This list of his deeds was written by Augustus himself and was displayed on two bronze pillars set up in the Roman forum. The second excerpt is by the senatorial historian Tacitus (c. 56–117 C.E.). Writing in the first decades of the second century C.E., he began his chronicle of imperial rule, Annals, *with the death of Augustus a century earlier.*

Augustus Speaks for Himself

Below is a copy of the accomplishments of the deified Augustus by which he brought the whole world under the empire of the Roman people, and of the moneys expended by him on the state and the Roman people.

1. At the age of nineteen, on my own initiative and at my own expense, I raised an army by means of which I liberated the Republic, which was oppressed by the tyranny of a faction.

2. Those who assassinated my father I drove into exile, avenging their crime by due process of law.

3. I waged many wars throughout the whole world by land and by sea, both civil and foreign. . . .

* * *

5. The dictatorship offered to me . . . by the people and by the Senate . . . I refused to accept. . . . The consulship, too, which was offered to me . . . as an annual office for life, I refused to accept.

6. [T]hough the Roman Senate and people together agreed that I should be elected sole guardian of the laws and morals with supreme authority, I refused to accept any office offered me which was contrary to the traditions of our ancestors.

7. I have been ranking senator for forty years. . . . I have been *pontifex maximus*, augur, member of the college of fifteen for performing sacrifices, member of the college of seven for conducting religious banquets, member of the Arval Brotherhood, one of the *Titii sodales*, and a *fetial* [all priestly offices].

* * *

9. The Senate decreed that vows for my health should be offered up every fifth year by the consuls and priests. . . . [T]he whole citizen body, with one accord, . . . prayed continuously for my health at all the shrines.

* * *

17. Four times I came to the assistance of the treasury with my own money . . . providing bonuses for soldiers who had completed twenty or more years of service.

* * *

20. I repaired the Capitol and the theater of Pompey with enormous expenditures on both works, without having my name inscribed on them. I repaired . . . the aqueducts which were falling into ruin in many places. . . . I repaired eighty-two temples. . . . I reconstructed the Flaminian Way. . . .

* * *

34. [H]aving attained supreme power by universal consent, I transferred the state from my own power to the control of the Roman Senate and people. . . . After that time I excelled all in authority, but I possessed no more power than the others who were my colleagues in each magistracy.

35. At the time I wrote this document I was in my seventy-sixth year.

Source: "Res Gestae Divi Augusti," in *Roman Civilization, Sourcebook II: The Empire*, eds. Naphtali Lewis and Meyer Reinhold (New York: 1966), pp. 9–19.

The Historian Tacitus Evaluates Augustus's Reign

Intelligent people praised or criticized Augustus in varying terms. One opinion was as follows. Filial duty and a national emergency, in which there was no place for law-abiding conduct, had driven him to civil war—and this can be neither initiated nor maintained by decent methods. He had made many concessions to Antony and to Lepidus for the sake of vengeance on his father's murderers. When Lepidus grew old and lazy, and Antony's self-indulgence got the better of him, the only possible cure for the distracted country had been government by one man. However, Augustus had put the State in order not by making himself king or dictator but by creating the Principate. The empire's frontiers were on the ocean, or on distant rivers. Armies, provinces, fleets, the whole system was interrelated. Roman citizens were protected by the law. Provincials were decently treated. Rome itself had been lavishly beautified. Force had been sparingly used—merely to preserve peace for the majority.

The opposite view went like this. Filial duty and national crisis had been merely pretexts. In actual fact, the motive of Octavian, the future Augustus, was lust for power. Inspired by that, he had mobilized ex-army settlers by gifts of money, raised an army—while he was only a half-grown boy without any official status—won over a consul's brigade by bribery, pretended to support Sextus Pompeius [the son of Pompey], and by senatorial decree usurped the status and rank of a praetor. Soon both consuls . . . had met their deaths—by enemy action; or perhaps in the one case by the deliberate poisoning of his wound, and in the other at the hand of his own troops, instigated by Octavian. In any case, it was he who took over both their armies. Then he had forced the reluctant Senate to make him consul. But the forces given him to deal with Antony he used against the State. His judicial murders and land distributions were distasteful even to those who carried them out. True, Cassius and Brutus died because he had inherited a feud against them; nevertheless, personal enmities ought to be sacrificed to the public interest. Next he had cheated Sextus Pompeius by a spurious peace treaty, Lepidus by spurious friendship. Then Antony, enticed by treaties and his marriage with Octavian's sister, had paid the penalty of that delusive relationship with his life. After that, there had certainly been peace, but it was a blood-stained peace. . . . And gossip did not spare his personal affairs—how he had abducted [Livia] the wife of Tiberius Claudius Nero, and asked the priests the farcical question whether it was in order for her to marry while pregnant. Then there was the debauchery of his friend Publius Vedius Pollio. But Livia was a real catastrophe, to the nation, as a mother and to the house of the Caesars as a stepmother.

Source: Tacitus, *Annals* I.9–10. Based on *Tacitus: The Annals of Imperial Rome*, trans. Michael Grant (New York: 1989), pp. 37–39.

Questions for Analysis

1. How does Augustus organize his list, and why? What does he leave out, and what does he choose to emphasize?

2. Tacitus presents two contrasting views of Augustus's motives. Which does he himself seem to believe? How does his account complement or undermine that of Augustus himself?

3. Could you write a new account of Augustus's life, making use of both sources? How would you strike a balance between them? What would your own conclusion be?

The Romans had discovered how to make this reliable building material from a mixture of quicklime, volcanic ash, and pumice; and it was this—along with superior engineering skills—that allowed them to build massive structures such as the Colosseum, which could accommodate fifty thousand spectators.

Roman engineers also excelled in the building of roads and bridges, many of which were constructed by Rome's armies as they moved into new territories. Like the Persian Royal Road of the sixth century B.C.E. (or the German Autobahn of the 1930s and the interstate highways of the United States begun in the 1950s), roads have always been a device for moving armies and, secondarily, for moving goods and people. Many of these Roman roads still survive or form the basis for European highways. In Britain, the only major thoroughfares before the building of the modern motorways were Roman roads, to which the motorways now run parallel.

The inhabitants of Roman cities also enjoyed the benefits of a public water supply. By the early decades of the second century C.E., eleven aqueducts brought water into Rome from nearby hills and provided three hundred million gallons per day for drinking and bathing, and for flushing a well-designed sewage system. These amenities were common in cities throughout the empire, and the homes of the wealthy even had indoor plumbing and central heating. The emperor Nero built a famous Golden House with special pipes that sprinkled his guests with perfume, baths of medicinal waters, and a pond "like a sea."

But not all Roman cities would have had ready access to these resources, especially water. Depending on the local climate and landscape, the need to supply imperial subjects led to vast projects: swamps drained, forests felled, mountains leveled, and valleys filled in. In the process, Roman urban planners and engineers permanently altered the environment (see **Interpreting Visual Evidence** on page 178).

IMPERIAL ENTERTAINMENTS

Latin replaces Greek as dominant literary language

The cultural and intellectual developments of the Principate are richly reflected in its literature. For the first time, Latin began to replace Greek as a language of learning and poetry. Roman literature of this era is usually divided into the Golden Age of writings produced under the influence of Augustus, and the Silver Age of the first and early second centuries C.E. The poetry of Publius Vergilius Maro (Virgil; 70–19 B.C.E.) is typical of the former, and we have already noted his strategic use of "prophecy" to link the reign of Augustus to the story of Aeneas (see page 154). Other major poets included Quintus Horatius Flaccus (Horace; 65–8 B.C.E.) and Publius Ovidius Naso (Ovid; 43 B.C.E.–17 C.E.): the former was a master of the lovely, short lyric; the latter is our major source for Greek mythology, retold in the *Metamorphoses* ("Transformations"). Ovid was also a satirist, and his advice to readers on the best way to attract women and his own (probably fictional) strategy for conducting an adulterous affair are exemplary of the writings that resulted in his banishment.

After Augustus's death, Roman authors had more license and became incisive cultural critics. The tales of Petronius and Apuleius describe the bizarre and sometimes sordid aspects of Roman life, while Juvenal (60?–140 C.E.) wrote with savage wit about the moral degeneracy he saw in his contemporaries. A similar attitude

A BIRTHDAY INVITATION FROM ROMAN BRITAIN. The letter above was originally hinged in the middle, so that the two halves could be sealed shut. In it, Claudia Severa invites her friend, Sulpicia Lepida, to attend her birthday celebration and sends greetings to her family from her own husband and baby son. While most of the writing is that of a professional scribe, Claudia has added her own note in the three short lines on the bottom of the right-hand tablet: "I shall hope to see you, sister. / Take care, sister, dearest soul / and just as I prosper be well." Several of Claudia's notes survive, and are the earliest known Latin writings by a woman.

characterizes the writings of Tacitus (55?–117? C.E.), an aristocratic historian whose *Annals* offer a subtle but devastating portrait of the political system constructed by Augustus. In his account of Britain's colonization, a barbarian chieftain says, "They create a wilderness and call it peace." His *Germania* even contrasts the manly virtues of northern barbarians with the effeminate vices of decadent fellow Romans.

To many people today, the most repellent aspect of Roman culture is its spectacular cruelty, exhibited (literally) in the public arenas of every Roman town. Gladiatorial contests were presented in amphitheaters built to hold thousands, and they became increasingly brutal as people demanded more and more innovative violence. Individual gladiators fought to the death with the exotic weapons of their homelands. Teams of gladiators fought pitched battles, often reenacting historic Roman victories. Occasionally, a wealthy entrepreneur would fill an arena with water to stage a naval battle. Hundreds of men and women would die in organized slaughters. On other occasions, hundreds of half-starved animals imported from Africa, India, or Germania would tear each other (or human victims) apart. When a fighter went down with a disabling wound, the crowd would be asked to decide whether to spare his life or kill him.

ROMAN VISUAL ARTS

Like Latin literature, Roman art assumed a distinctive character during the Principate. Prior to this most artworks displayed in Roman homes and fora were imported from Hellenistic cities. Conquering armies also brought back statues, reliefs, and marble columns as plunder from Greece, Egypt, and western Asia. As the demand for such works increased, hundreds of copies were made by Roman artisans. In many cases, these copies proved more durable than their originals. (In Chapter 4, we were able to examine the lost Aphrodite of Knidos, courtesy of Roman sculptors.)

Encouraged by the patronage of Augustus and his successors, artists began to experiment with more distinctively Roman styles and subjects. The relief sculpture of this period is particularly notable for its delicacy and naturalism. On their coins, emperors were portrayed very much as they looked in real life; and since the matrices for coins were recut annually, we can trace on successive issues a ruler's receding hairline. Romans loved intense colors, and those who could afford it surrounded themselves with brilliant wall paintings and mosaics made of tiny fragments of glass and stone, which were often set into the floors of houses and public baths. Lavish mosaics have been found in the remains of Roman villas in all the territories of the empire, and similar design features indicate that many were mosaic "kits" that could be ordered from a manufacturer who would ship out all the necessary components, along with a team of workmen to assemble them.

A ROMAN FLOOR MOSAIC. This fine mosaic from the Roman city of Londinium (London) shows Bacchus (Dionysos), the god of wine and revelry, mounted on a tiger. Tigers, native to India, were prized by animal collectors and were also imported for gladiatorial shows.

THE REACH OF ROMAN LAW

Perhaps the most durable and useful of Rome's many legacies is its system of law. Over the course of several centuries, the primitive legal code of the Twelve Tables was largely replaced by a series of new precedents and principles. These reflect the changing needs of Rome's diverse and ever-growing population, the influence of new philosophies, the decisions of specific judges, and the edicts of magistrates called *praetors*, who had the authority to define and interpret law in particular cases.

During the Principate, the reach of Roman law had to match the reach of the empire. While governors sometimes asked the emperor's advice about legal matters, most of the cases they had to adjudicate could not wait for directives from Rome; there had to be administrative structures and guidelines already in place. These needs drove a rapid development in Roman legal thought and practice during these years. Augustus and his successors appointed a small number of professional jurists to deliver official opinions on common legal issues, in order to create a more standardized body of law. The five most prominent of these jurists flourished in the second century C.E.: Gaius (only this most common of names is known), Domitius Ulpianus (Ulpian), Modestinus, Aemelius Papinianus (Papinian), and Paulus. Taken together, their legal opinions constitute the foundation for all subsequent Western jurisprudence, a word derived from the Latin phrase meaning "legal wisdom."

As developed by the jurists, Roman law comprised three great branches: civil law, the law of nations, and natural law. Civil law was the law of Rome and its

> Jurists standardize laws with opinions on common legal issues ❯

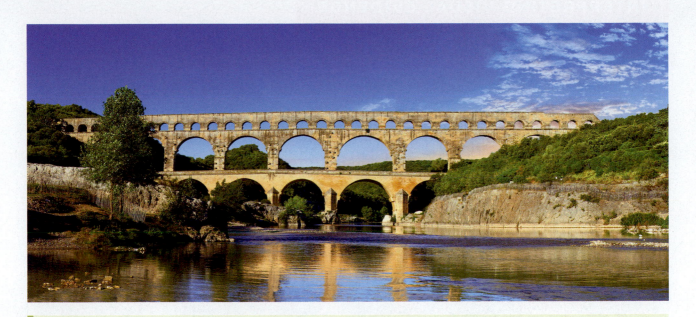

ROMAN AQUEDUCT IN SOUTHERN GAUL (PROVENCE). The massive arches shown here were originally part of a thirty-one-mile-long complex that supplied water to the city of Nemausus (Nîmes). It is now known as the Pont du Gard (Bridge of the Gardon), reflecting the use to which it was put after the aqueduct ceased to function, some eight centuries after its construction in the first century C.E. Some Roman aqueducts remained operational into the modern era: the one at Segovia, Spain, was still in use at the end of the twentieth century. **› What does the magnitude and longevity of such projects tell us about Roman power and technology?**

citizens, both written and unwritten. It included the statutes of the Senate, the decrees of the emperor, the edicts of magistrates, and ancient customs such as the *mos maiorum.* The law of nations extended to all people of the world regardless of their ethnicity and is the precursor of international law. This law authorized and regulated slavery; protected private ownership of property; and defined the mechanisms of purchase and sale, partnership, and contract. It applied especially to those inhabitants of the empire who were not citizens, as well as to all foreigners.

The most interesting—and in many ways the most important—branch was natural law. Roman Stoics, following in the footsteps of Cicero, had posited that nature itself is rationally ordered and that careful study will reveal the laws by which the world operates, including the nature of justice. All men are, by nature, equal and entitled to certain basic rights that governments have no authority to transgress. Accordingly, no person or institution has the authority to infringe on this law, repeal it, or ignore it. Although the practical law applied in Roman courts often bore little resemblance to the law of nature, the very concept of equal justice as a fundamental principle was one of the noblest achievements of Roman civilization. It gave us the doctrine of human rights—even if it did not end abuses of those rights.

Roman Urban Planning

Prior to Roman imperial expansion, most cities in the ancient world were not planned cities—with the exception of the new settlements established by Alexander the Great; notably, Alexandria in Egypt. Rome itself was not carefully planned but grew up over many centuries, expanding outward and up the slopes of its seven hills from the nucleus of the Forum. By the time of Augustus, it was a haphazard jumble of buildings

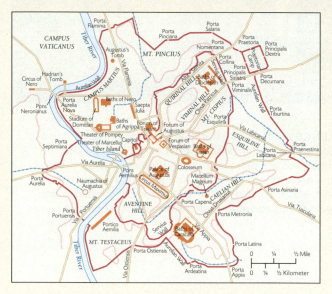

A. Imperial Rome.

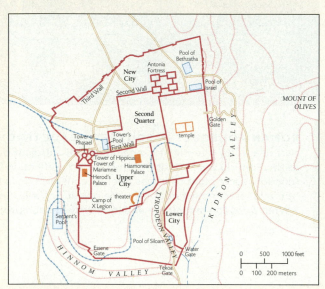

B. Roman settlement in Aelia Capitolina (Jerusalem) after 135 C.E.

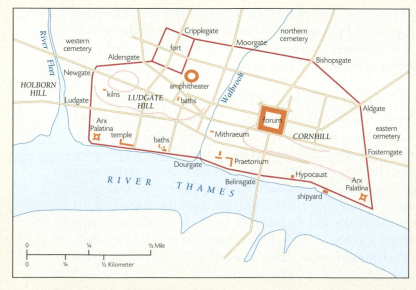

C. London under the Romans, c. 200 C.E.

and narrow streets. Outside of Rome, however, the efficiency of Roman government was in large part due to the uniformity of imperial urban planning. As their colonial reach expanded, the Romans sought to ensure that travelers moving within their vast domain would encounter the same amenities in every major city. They also wanted to convey, through the organization of the urban landscape, the ubiquity of Roman authority and majesty.

Questions for Analysis

1. Look closely at the map of Rome (map A). How did topographical features—such as the river Tiber and the seven hills—determine the shape and layout of the city? What are the major buildings and public areas?

What were the functions of these spaces? What do they reveal about Roman society and values?

2. Compare the plan of Rome with those of Roman London (map C) and Roman Jerusalem (map B). Which features do all three have in common, and why? Which features are unique to each place? What might these unique features reveal about the various regions of the empire and the needs of the various cities' inhabitants?

3. Given that all Roman cities share certain features, what message(s) were Roman authorities trying to convey to inhabitants and travelers through urban planning? Why, for example, would they have insisted on rebuilding Jerusalem as a Roman city after the rebellion of 135 C.E.?

Conclusion

The resemblances between Rome's history and those of Great Britain and the United States have often been noted. Like the British Empire, the Roman Empire was founded on conquest and its colonial subjects were regarded as beneficiaries of the metropole's "civilizing mission." Like America's, the Roman economy evolved from agrarianism to a complex system of domestic and foreign markets, leading to problems of unemployment, gross disparities of wealth, and vulnerability to financial crisis. And like both the British and the American empires, the Roman Empire justified itself by celebrating the peace its conquests allegedly brought to the world.

Yet Roman civilization also differed profoundly from any society of the modern world. It was not an industrialized society. Its government never pretended to be representative of all citizens. The Roman economy rested on slavery to a degree unmatched in any modern state. As a result, technological advances were not encouraged, social stratification was extreme, and gender relations were profoundly unequal. Religious practice and political life were inseparable.

Nevertheless, the civilization of ancient Rome continues to structure our everyday lives in ways so profound that they can go unnoticed. Our days are mapped onto the Roman calendar. The U.S. Constitution is modeled on that of the republic and Roman architecture survives in our public buildings. Roman law forms the basis of most European legal codes, and American judges still cite Gaius and Ulpian. Virtually all modern commemorative sculpture is inspired by Roman sculpture, and Roman authors continue to set the standards for prose composition.

Indeed, most European languages are either derived from Latin (Romance languages are "Roman-like") or have borrowed Latin grammatical structures (German, for example). The organization of the Roman Catholic Church can be traced back to the structure of the Roman state. Even today, the pope bears the title of Rome's high priest, *pontifex maximus*.

Perhaps the most significant of all Rome's contributions was its mediation between Europe and the civilizations of the ancient Mediterranean and

AFTER YOU READ THIS CHAPTER

CHRONOLOGY

753 B.C.E.	Legendary founding of Rome
c. 509 B.C.E.	Roman Republic established
c. 450 B.C.E.	Law of the Twelve Tables
287 B.C.E.	"Struggle of the Orders" ends
264–146 B.C.E.	Punic Wars
134–104 B.C.E.	Slave revolts in Sicily
133–122 B.C.E.	Reforms of the Gracchi
107–86 B.C.E.	Consulship of Marius
82–79 B.C.E.	Dictatorship of Sulla
73–71 B.C.E.	Rebellion of Spartacus
52–48 B.C.E.	Struggle of Pompey and Caesar
48–44 B.C.E.	Dictatorship of Caesar
44–30 B.C.E.	Rivalry of Octavian and Antony
27 B.C.E.–14 C.E.	Principate of the Emperor Augustus
27–180 C.E.	Flowering of the *Pax Romana*
79 C.E.	Eruption of Mount Vesuvius destroys (and preserves) Pompeii
117 C.E.	Roman Empire reaches its greatest territorial extent under Trajan

REVIEWING THE OBJECTIVES

❯ The founding of the Roman Republic was both a cherished myth and a series of events. What factors contributed to this unique system of government?

❯ The shared identity and values of the Roman people differed in many ways from those of other ancient civilizations. What were some of these major differences?

❯ Rome's population was divided among classes of people who often struggled with each other for power. Identify these classes and their points of contention.

❯ The expansion of Rome's empire had a profound impact on Roman society. Why?

❯ The establishment of the Principate ushered in a new era in the history of Rome. What events led to this change?

western Asia. Had Rome's empire not come to encompass much of Europe, there would be no such thing as the concept of Western civilization and no shared heritage to link us to those distant places and times. Although we will pursue the history of Rome's fragmentation and witness the emergence of three different civilizations in Chapter 6, we will see that they all shared a common cultural inheritance. In that sense, the Roman Empire did not collapse but was transformed.

 Go to **INQUIZITIVE** to see what you've learned—and learn what you've missed—with personalized feedback along the way.

PEOPLE, IDEAS, AND EVENTS IN CONTEXT

❱ In what ways were the early Romans influenced by their **ETRUSCAN** neighbors and by their location in central Italy?

❱ What were the components of the **ROMAN REPUBLIC**'s constitution? What was the relationship between **ROMAN CITIZENSHIP** and the **ROMAN ARMY** in this era?

❱ How do the stories of **AENEAS, LUCRETIA**, and **CINCINNATUS** reflect core Roman values? How did those values, summarized in the phrase *MOS MAIORUM*, set the Romans apart from the other civilizations we have studied?

❱ Why did the Romans come into conflict with **CARTHAGE**? How did the **PUNIC WARS** and Rome's other conquests change the balance of power in the Mediterranean?

❱ How did imperialism and contact with **HELLENISTIC CULTURE** affect the core values of Roman society, its economy, and its political system? What role did **SLAVERY** play in this civilization?

❱ What were the major crises of the late republic? What were the means by which ambitious men gained power? How did **JULIUS CAESAR** emerge triumphant, and why was he assassinated?

❱ In what ways did the **PRINCIPATE** differ from the **ROMAN REPUBLIC**? What were the new powers of the **EMPEROR**, and how did **AUGUSTUS** use these powers?

❱ How did the Romans consolidate their **EMPIRE** during the *PAX ROMANA*? By what means did they spread Roman culture?

THINKING ABOUT CONNECTIONS

❱ Polybius believed that the Roman Republic would last forever, because it fused together aspects of monarchy, aristocracy, and polity. What were the chief factors that led to its demise in the first century B.C.E.? Could these have been avoided? If so, how?

❱ In what ways does the Roman Empire share the characteristics of earlier empires, especially that of Alexander? In what ways does it differ from them?

❱ The Roman Empire could be said to resemble our own civilization in different ways. What features does the United States share with the republic today? With the Principate? What lessons can we draw from this resemblance?

6

The Transformation of Rome

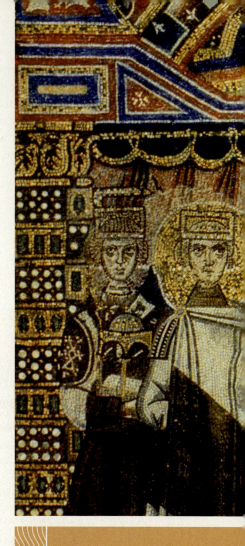

IN THE YEAR 203 C.E., Vivia Perpetua was brought before the Roman governor at Carthage. She was twenty-two years old, and from a respectable family. At the time of her arrest, she had an infant child, two brothers (one arrested with her), and a father who doted on her. She must have had a husband, too, but he is conspicuously absent from the firsthand account of her experiences. Perpetua says nothing about him, though she says a great deal about the efforts her father made to intercede on her behalf. Not only did he beg the judge for mercy, he begged his daughter to confess so that her life could be spared. He admitted to having loved her more than her brothers and blamed himself for the liberal education he had given her. Clearly, he had failed as a father: a Roman *paterfamilias* should never suffer humiliation through a daughter's conduct; he should kill her with his own hands if she disgraces the family. For Perpetua's crime was terrible: treason against the Roman state and an act of gross impiety toward her father and ancestors. Worse, it was punishable by a debasing death reserved for slaves, barbarians, and hardened criminals. It was inconceivable that a respectable Roman matron would be stripped naked before a holiday crowd and mauled by wild beasts in the arena of her own city. But that was the death Perpetua died. Perpetua was a Christian.

Early Christianity posed a challenge to the Roman Empire at almost every level, a challenge exemplified by Perpetua's defiance. Christians refused to venerate the emperor as the embodiment of Rome's gods. Moreover, the

BEFORE YOU READ THIS CHAPTER ❯

CONSTANTINVS MINOR IMPERATOR
HERACLII ET TIBERII IMPERATOR

AR
COP
VS

PRIVILEGIR

STORY LINES

> In a little over three centuries, Christianity grew from obscure beginnings in a small Roman province to become the official religion of the empire.

> Meanwhile, the Roman Empire was becoming too large and diverse to be governed by a single, centralized authority. Significant political, military, and economic changes occurred during the third century in response to these challenges.

> In the fourth century, the founding of a new capital at Constantinople shifted the focus of imperial administration to the eastern territories of the Roman Empire, while mass migrations of frontier peoples created new settlements within the western half of the empire.

> Christianity's eventual association with political power changed the religion in profound ways. At the same time, Christian intellectuals adapted Rome's traditional culture to meet Christian needs.

CORE OBJECTIVES

> **IDENTIFY** the historical factors that shaped early Christianity.

> **DESCRIBE** the pressures on Roman imperial administration during the third century.

> **TRACE** the ways that Christianity changed after it became a legal religion.

> **EXPLAIN** how barbarian migrations affected the empire.

> **UNDERSTAND** the difference between traditional Roman and Christian worldviews.

Christ whom Christians worshiped had himself been declared a criminal, a political insurgent, and had been duly put to death by the Roman state. Christians also flouted the conventions of Roman society. Perpetua was young, yet she disobeyed her aged father. She was well born, yet she chose a life of crime. She was a woman, yet she denied the authority of men and renounced her femininity, dying in the dust like a gladiator. If this was being a Christian, then being a Christian was incompatible with being a Roman.

How, then, did a Roman emperor become a Christian just a few centuries after Christ's death—and just a century or so after Perpetua's? What changes did both Rome and Christianity have to undergo for this to happen? The Rome in which Perpetua was raised stretched from central Asia to Britain, from the Rhine to her own province of North Africa. But the governance of this enormous state and its diverse population was straining the bureaucracy that had been built on the foundations of the old republic. By the third century C.E., it was increasingly obvious that Rome's western and eastern provinces could not be controlled by a single centralized authority. During the fourth century, Rome itself ceased to be the capital of the empire, sharing its prestige with the new city of Constantinople, named by the Christian emperor who founded it. Meanwhile, Rome's provinces were coming under increased pressure from groups of people moving from the periphery to the center.

The Challenge of Christianity

Like any religion, Christianity was—and is—the product of historical processes. It began with the teachings of Jesus, who lived among his fellow Jews until his death in 30 C.E. Christianity took root, however, in the Hellenistic world we studied in Chapter 4: the cosmopolitan, Greek-speaking cities that had now been absorbed into the Roman Empire.

THE CAREER OF JESUS

Yeshua bar Yosef (Joshua, son of Joseph), known to the Greeks as **Jesus**, is one of the few commoners in antiquity about whose life we know a great deal. The earliest writings that mention him specifically are the letters of his follower, Paul of Tarsus, a Hellenized Jew who was active during the 50s and 60s C.E. (see page 186). There are also many different narratives of Jesus' life and teachings, most written between c. 70 and 100 C.E. Four such accounts are included in the "New Testament," a collection of Christian scriptures appended to the Greek text of the Hebrew Bible, which Christians call the "Old Testament." In Greek, these accounts were called *evangelia* ("good messages"); we know them as *Gospels*, an Old English word that means the same thing.

Jesus was born around the year 4 B.C.E. When he was about thirty years old, he was ritually baptized by an influential Jewish reformer, John the Baptist, whom some considered to be a prophet. Jesus then began to travel around the rural areas of Galilee (his home province) and the Roman colony of Judea, teaching and displaying unusual healing powers. He accumulated a number of disciples, some of whom had political ambitions. Around the year 30 C.E., Jesus staged a ceremonial entry into Jerusalem during Passover, a major Jewish holy day. This move was interpreted, by the Roman colonial government and the Temple's priestly caste, as a bid for political power. Jesus also drew attention to himself by attacking merchants and moneychangers associated with the

Jesus (c. 4 B.C.E.–c. 30 C.E.) Jewish preacher and teacher in the rural areas of Galilee and Judea who was arrested for seditious political activity, tried, and crucified by the Romans.

Temple. The city's Jewish elite therefore arrested him and turned him over to the Roman governor, Pontius Pilatus (Pilate), for sentencing.

Pilate's main concern was to preserve peace during a volatile religious festival. He also needed to maintain good relations with local Jewish elites and with Herod Antipas, who ruled the province of Galilee as a client king of the empire. Because Jesus was a resident of Galilee, not a citizen of Roman Judea, Pilate sent Jesus to Herod for sentencing. But Herod sent him back, indicating that Jesus fell under Roman jurisdiction. This put Pilate in a difficult position: it had been rumored that Jesus planned to lead a rebellion, similar to that in the second century B.C.E., when a group of Jews had overthrown the Seleucid rule (Chapter 4) and established an autonomous state. Judea had come under Roman control only in 63 B.C.E., and many Jews resented Roman subjugation.

Pilate, mindful of all this, chose to make an example of Jesus and condemned him to death by crucifixion: the standard criminal penalty for non-Romans found guilty of sedition. And yet Jesus' followers asserted that he had risen from the dead and had then been taken up into heaven. They also said that Jesus would return again to judge all people, living and dead.

INTERPRETING THE LIFE AND DEATH OF JESUS

In 1947, an extraordinary cache of ancient scrolls was discovered in a cave near Qumran, near the Dead Sea. Eleven more caves have since been found, and more texts continue to be discovered. Written in Hebrew, Greek, and Aramaic at various times between 100 B.C.E. and 70 C.E., they have revolutionized our understanding of Judaism in the lifetime of Jesus: a period known as "Second Temple" Judaism, in reference to the reconstruction of the Temple at Jerusalem in the sixth century B.C.E. (see Chapter 2). These documents reveal the diversity of religious practice and the competition among Jews during this period.

When Jesus was born, many Jews had become content to live under Roman rule—especially the urban elite, who would have been Hellenized for generations and who reaped the rewards of participation in the Roman economy and administration. But many rural communities and the urban poor were disadvantaged by Roman rule and hoped for a *messiah*: a divinely inspired leader who would establish a new Jewish kingdom. A group of extremists, the Zealots, eventually led two armed revolts against Roman rule. The first, between 66 and 70 C.E. (a generation after Jesus' death), ended in the Romans' destruction of the Temple.

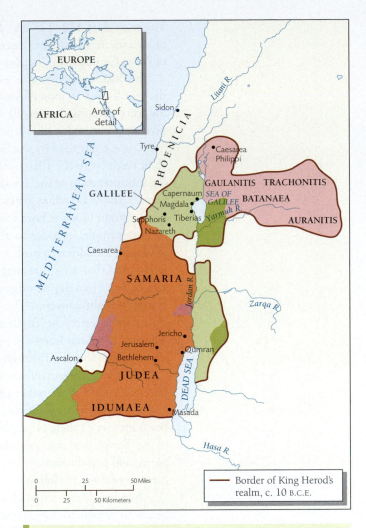

JUDEA AND GALILEE IN THE TIME OF JESUS. Judea was a Roman colony and Galilee was a province ruled by a client king, Herod, loyal to Rome. › **What were the major cities in first-century C.E. Judea?** › **What do they indicate about the effects of Roman occupation on the lives of Jews?** › Given what you have learned about their history, why do you think some Jews would resist Roman rule?

The second, in 132–135 C.E., led the Romans to expel the entire Jewish population of Jerusalem, which they razed to the ground. On its ruins, they built the colony of Aelia Capitolina (Chapter 5).

This historical context is essential to understanding the very different ways that the words and actions of Jesus were interpreted, since all written accounts of his life were composed after 70 C.E. It is also essential to understand the significant divisions within Jewish society. A powerful hereditary group, the Temple priesthood, was controlled by the Sadducees, who collaborated closely with Rome. Their chief rivals were the Pharisees. While the Sadducees claimed the right to control the interpretation of the Torah, the Pharisees argued that Yahweh had given Moses an oral Torah as well as a written one, and that this oral tradition, handed down to them, taught how the laws should be applied in daily life.

For example, in order to allow neighbors to eat together on the Sabbath, when Jews were forbidden to work and could not carry food outside their homes, the Pharisees ruled that an entire neighborhood could constitute a single household. They also believed in a day of judgment, looked forward to the arrival of the messiah, and actively sought converts. The Sadducees, determined to maintain their privileged status, interpreted the Torah more strictly and considered Judaism closed to anyone who had not been born a Jew. Countering both of these groups were the Essenes, who sought salvation through repentance, asceticism, and solitude.

Jesus may have been influenced by the Essenes, but his teachings also seem Pharisaic: his emphasis on ethics rather than the literal interpretation of law, his preaching on the coming "kingdom of God," and his outreach to people beyond the Jewish community. But Jesus carried these principles considerably further, deemphasizing the religious rites of the Temple and the importance of traditional practices such as circumcision, ritual purity, and prohibitions on the consumption of certain foods. But what made him most controversial was his followers' claim that he was the messiah.

After his death, these claims grew more assertive. And when Jesus' followers began to preach to non-Jewish audiences, they asserted that Jesus was not merely a Jewish messiah but the *Christos* ("anointed one" in Greek): the divine son of God who had suffered and died for the sins of all humanity. He had conquered death itself by rising from his tomb and would soon return to judge all the world's inhabitants. Those who believed in him would be given eternal life.

CHRISTIANITY IN THE HELLENISTIC WORLD

This understanding of Jesus' divinity was largely developed by his younger contemporary, **Paul of Tarsus** (c. 10 C.E.–c. 67 C.E.). Born in the capital city of Roman Cilicia (now south-central Turkey), Saul was a member of a family of Pharisees and was initially dedicated to stamping out the cult of Jesus. But at some point in his mid-twenties—within a decade of Jesus' death—he underwent a dramatic conversion experience. He changed his name to Paul and devoted the rest of his life to spreading the new faith to Greek-speaking communities throughout the eastern half of the Roman Empire. Taking advantage of imperial infrastructure and his own privileges as a Roman citizen, Paul traveled to preach the new faith in the old cities of the Hellenistic world.

Unlike Peter and the other disciples, Paul had never met Jesus. Instead, he claimed to have received a direct revelation of Jesus' teachings. This led to a number of major disputes, because Peter and his companions believed that followers of Jesus had to

Paul of Tarsus Originally known as Saul, Paul was a Greek-speaking Jew and Roman citizen who underwent a miraculous conversion experience and became the most important exponent of Christianity in the 50s and 60s C.E.

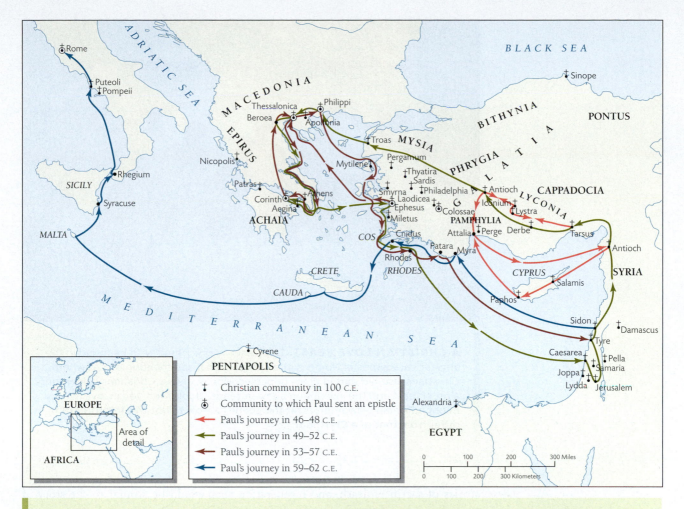

PAUL'S MISSIONARY JOURNEYS. Quite apart from its theological importance, Paul's career offers fascinating glimpses into the life of a Hellenized Roman citizen from one of the empire's eastern provinces. **› What were the main phases of Paul's travels in the eastern Mediterranean? › How were his itineraries shaped by geography and by various modes of transport? › What conclusions about his mission can you draw from the extent of his travels and his major destinations?**

be Jews, or converts to Judaism. Paul declared that Jewish law was now irrelevant; Jesus had made a new covenant possible between God and humanity, and the old covenant between God and the Jews no longer applied. This position was vehemently opposed by Peter and the disciples led by Jesus' brother, James. But after many difficult debates that took place around 49 C.E., Paul's position triumphed and a new community of Christian believers was formed: an *ekklesia*, the Greek word for an assembly. The Latinized form of this word is translated as "church."

The earliest converts to Christianity were Hellenized Jews like Paul himself, but the new faith was also attractive to cosmopolitan Greeks who saw Jesus as living by Stoic principles (Chapter 4) or as the embodiment of Ahura-Mazda, the good god of Zoroastrianism (Chapter 2). Devotees of mystery religions, like the cults of the Egyptian Isis (Chapter 1) or the Roman warrior god Mithras, already celebrated

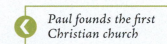

Paul founds the first Christian church

A CHRISTIAN LOVE FEAST. This fresco is one of many to be found in the ancient catacombs of Rome: subterranean burial and meeting places where Christians also hid during times of persecution. It shows Christians celebrating a ritual feast and the inscription above it reads, "I join with you in love." **› How might a Roman viewer interpret this scene? › How might this interpretation differ from that of a Christian?**

stories of sacrifice, death, and regeneration that would be similar to the story of Jesus. It was largely for the benefit of these converts that Christians began to practice baptism, a ritual purification rite common to many ancient religions.

However, while most mystery cults stressed the spiritual rebirth of the individual, Christianity emphasized the importance of community. By the middle of the second century, the Christian church at Rome had a recognizable structure, headed by a bishop (in Greek, *episcopos* or "overseer") and lesser officeholders, including priests and deacons. Women were extremely prominent in these churches, not only as benefactors but also as leaders. This was unusual. In other ancient religions, women could be priests—but only in cults open solely to women. Many cults, such as that of Mithras, denied them access entirely. The fact that Christians also represented a broad range of social classes was also distinctive. These unusual features were often distorted by Christianity's detractors, who alleged that Christians were political insurgents who engaged in illicit acts during "love feasts."

As both Christianity and Judaism redefined themselves during the second and third centuries c.e., they grew further apart. The mass exile of Jewish refugees from Jerusalem and surrounding provinces was forcing Jewish leaders to reshape the faith, and they largely ignored Christianity. Christians, however, could not ignore Judaism. Their religion rested on the belief that Jesus was the savior promised by God to Israel. For them, the heroes of Jewish scripture prefigured Jesus, while the major events of Hebrew history could be read, allegorically, as Christian paradigms. Christ

Community in early Christianity: unusually representative of women and people from various social classes

was the new Adam, reversing man's original sin; wood from the fateful Tree in Eden became the wood of the Cross. Christ, like Abel, had been slain by a brother. Christ was the new Noah, saving Creation from its sins. According to Christians, all the words of the Hebrew prophets point to Jesus, as do the Psalms and the Proverbs.

To Christians, the Hebrew Bible was therefore known as the Old Testament, superseded by the New Testament. At the Second Coming of Jesus, the Jews would see the error of their ways and convert. Until then, they existed to confirm the truth of Christianity by their very impiety, which had caused their exile from the Holy Land and would continue to bring suffering down on their descendants.

CHRISTIANITY AND THE ROMAN STATE

Judaism remained legally recognized and many Jews were further protected by their Roman citizenship. Indeed, the biblical book known as the Acts of the Apostles records how Paul, a Roman citizen, could not be summarily put to death (as Jesus had been) on charges of treason. It follows his progress through the Roman judicial system, until he is finally brought to trial at Rome and executed (by beheading) under Nero. Even after their rebellion, the Jews of the Diaspora were allowed to maintain the special status they had always had under Roman rule and were not required, as other subject peoples were, to offer sacrifices to the emperor.

Christianity, in contrast, was a novelty religion that raised suspicions on many levels: it encouraged women and slaves to hold office; it revolved around the worship of a condemned criminal; its secret meetings could be breeding grounds for rebellion. Nevertheless, the official attitude of the Roman state was largely one of indifference toward Christians. There were not enough of them to matter. During the first and second centuries, therefore, Christians were tolerated, except when local officials chose to make an example of someone who flouted authority—as Perpetua did.

The Challenge of Imperial Expansion

The emergence of Christianity coincided with the Roman Empire's most dramatic period of growth and a variety of accompanying challenges. For a long time, Rome's emperors and administrators clung to the methods of governance instituted by Augustus, based on a single centralized authority. In reality, however, Rome's empire was no longer centered on Rome, or even Italy. It embraced ecosystems, linguistic groups, ethnicities, cultures, and political systems of vastly different kinds. More and more people could claim to be Roman citizens, and this placed enormous stress on the imperial administration as the centrifugal forces of Rome's own making constantly pulled resources into far-flung provinces, where cities had to be built, people governed, and communications maintained. The fact that the empire had few defensible borders was another problem. Hadrian had attempted to establish one after 122 C.E. by building a wall between Roman settlements in southern Britannia and the badlands of northern tribes (see Chapter 5), but this act was more symbolic than effective.

For much of the second century, such stresses were masked by the peaceful transfer of power. Since none of emperors in this era had a surviving male heir, a custom developed whereby each adopted a young man of good family and trained him in the craft of government. But this sensible practice changed with the death of Marcus

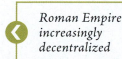

Roman Empire increasingly decentralized

The Prosecution of a Roman Citizen

The Acts of the Apostles was a continuation of Luke's Gospel, written by the same author. It recounts the adventures and ministry of Jesus' original disciples and also follows the career of Paul, a Hellenized Jew who became a missionary to the Gentiles throughout the Roman world. It offers fascinating glimpses into the workings of the Roman legal system because Paul, depicted here as a Roman citizen, had special rights under Roman law (as Jesus had not). In this passage, Paul—who has been accused of treason against the emperor by a group of Pharisees—has been sent to Felix, the governor of Judea. These events took place between 57 and 59 C.E.

So the soldiers, according to their instructions, took Paul and brought him by night to [the city of] Antipatris. The next day, they let the horsemen go on with him, while they returned to the barracks. When they came to Caesarea and delivered the letter to the governor, they presented Paul also before him. On reading the letter, he asked what province he belonged to, and when he learned that he was from Cilicia he said, "I will give you a hearing when your accusers arrive." Then he ordered that he be kept under guard in Herod's headquarters.

Five days later, the high priest Ananias came down with some elders and an attorney, a certain Tertullus, and they reported their case against Paul to the governor. When Paul had been summoned, Tertullus began to accuse him, saying: "Your Excellency, because of you we have long enjoyed peace, and reforms have been made for this people because of your foresight. We welcome this in every way and everywhere with utmost gratitude. But, to detain you no further, I beg you to hear us briefly with your customary graciousness. We have, in fact, found this man a pestilent fellow, an agitator among all the Jews throughout the world, and a ringleader of the sect of the Nazarenes. He even tried to profane the temple, and so we seized him. By examining him yourself you will be able to learn from him concerning everything of which we accuse him." The Jews also joined in the charge by asserting that all this was true.

Aurelius in 180 C.E. Although he was the closest Roman equivalent to Plato's ideal of the philosopher-king, Marcus was not wise enough to recognize that his own son, Commodus, lacked the capacity to rule. After his father's death, Commodus alienated the army by withdrawing from costly wars along the Danube. Unpopular with the Senate, Commodus's violent tendencies and scorn for the traditional norms of aristocratic conduct culminated in an alleged appearance as a gladiator in the Colosseum. In 192 C.E., a conspiracy was hatched inside his own palace, where he was strangled by his wrestling coach.

THE EMPIRE OF THE SEVERAN DYNASTY

Because Commodus had no obvious successor, the armies stationed in various provinces chose their own rival candidates. Civil war ensued, as it had during the crises of the late republic and in 68 C.E., when three men had struggled for imperial power. In this case, there were five major contenders. The eventual victor was a North African general, Septimius Severus (r. 193–211 C.E.).

When the governor motioned to him to speak, Paul replied: "I cheerfully make my defense, knowing that for many years you have been a judge over this nation. As you can find out, it is not more than twelve days since I went up to worship in Jerusalem. They did not find me disputing with anyone in the temple or stirring up a crowd either in synagogues or throughout the city. Neither can they prove to you the charge that they now bring against me. But this I admit to you, that according to the Way, which they call a sect, I worship the God of our ancestors, believing everything laid down according to the law or written in the prophets. I have hope in God—a hope that they themselves also accept—that there will be a resurrection of both the righteous and the unrighteous. Therefore I do my best always to have a clear conscience toward God and all people. . . ."

But Felix, who was rather well informed about the Way, adjourned the hearing with the comment, "When Lysias the tribune comes down, I will decide your case." Then he ordered the centurion to keep him in custody, but to let him have some liberty and not to prevent any of his friends from taking care of his needs.

When some days later Felix came with his wife Drusilla, who was Jewish, he sent for Paul and heard him speak concerning faith in Christ Jesus. And as he discussed justice and self-control and future judgment, Felix was alarmed and said, "Go away for the present; when I have an opportunity I will summon you." At the same time he hoped that money would be given him by Paul. So he sent for him often and conversed with him. But when two years had elapsed, Felix was succeeded by Porcius Festus; and desiring to do the Jews a favor, Felix left Paul in prison.

Source: Acts of the Apostles 23:31–24:27, in *The New Oxford Annotated Bible*, New Revised Standard Version, ed. Bruce M. Metzger and Roland E. Murphy (New York: 1994).

Questions for Analysis

1. According to this account, what legal procedures are in place for dealing with any Roman citizen accused of a crime?

2. What seems to be the relationship between the Jewish elite of Judea and the Roman governor? What is the role of their spokesman, Tertullus?

3. What is the nature of the accusation against Paul, and how does he defend himself?

Under Severus (*SEH-ver-uhs*) and his successors, the administration of Rome's empire changed to a greater extent than it had since the time of Augustus. In many respects, these changes were long overdue and reflected the new realities of colonial rule. Notably, Severus had been born and raised in the North African town of Leptis Magna (now in Libya) and identified strongly with his father's Punic (Afro-Phoenician) ancestors, more than with his mother's patrician family. Unlike Trajan and Hadrian, who had also grown up in the provinces, Severus did not regard Rome as the center of the universe. In fact, Severus represents the degree to which the Roman Empire had succeeded in making the world Roman—succeeded so well that Rome itself was becoming practically irrelevant. One could be as much a Roman in Britannia or Africa as in central Italy. Severus's second wife, Julia Domna, exemplifies this trend in a different way. Descended from the Aramaic aristocracy that ruled the Roman client kingdom of Emesa (Syria), her father was the high priest of its sun god, Ba'al. She was highly educated and proved an effective governor during her husband's almost perpetual absence from Rome.

The Development of an Imperial Policy toward Christians

It was not until the third century that the Roman imperial government began to initiate full-scale investigations into the activities of Christians. Instead, the official position was akin to a policy of "don't ask, don't tell." Local administrators handled only occasional cases, and they were often unsure as to whether the behavior of Christians was illegal or criminal. The following letter was sent to the emperor Trajan by Gaius Plinius Caecilius Secundus (Pliny the Younger), the governor of Bithynia-Pontus (Asia Minor), around 112 C.E. Pliny was anxious to follow proper procedures in dealing with the new sect and wanted advice about this. His letter indicates what Romans did and didn't know about early Christian beliefs and practices.

From Pliny to Trajan

It is my regular custom, my lord, to refer to you all questions which cause me doubt, for who can better guide my hesitant steps or instruct my ignorance? I have never attended hearings concerning Christians, so I am unaware what is usually punished or investigated, and to what extent. . . . In the meantime, this is the procedure I have followed in the cases of those brought before me as Christians. I asked them whether they were Christians. If they admitted it, I asked them a second and a third time, threatening them with execution. Those who remained obdurate I ordered to be executed, for I was in no doubt . . . that

their obstinacy and inflexible stubbornness should at any rate be punished. Others similarly lunatic were Roman citizens, so I registered them to be sent back to Rome.

Later in the course of the hearings, as usually happens, the charge rippled outwards, and more examples appeared. An anonymous document was published containing the names of many. Those who denied that they were or had been Christians and called upon the gods after me, and with incense and wine made obeisance to your statue . . . and who moreover cursed Christ . . . I ordered to be acquitted.

Severus largely ignored the politics of the Senate and slighted what remained of its powers. He preferred to rule through the army, which he reorganized and expanded. Two of his reforms had long-term consequences. The first was a drastic raise in army pay, probably as much as 100 percent, which had the effect of securing the soldiers' absolute loyalty and diminishing their need to augment their wages through plunder. The second was a relaxation of a long-standing rule forbidding soldiers to marry while in service. This encouraged younger men—not just veterans—to put down roots in local communities. At the same time, though, it made them reluctant to move when their legion was called up. On the one hand, this domesticated the army and may have made it less effective. On the other hand, it gave the army a stake in the peaceful governance of Rome's colonies and further contributed to the decentralization of power.

Severus died at Eboracum (York, England) in 211 C.E., after conducting a series of successful negotiations with Pictish tribes north of Hadrian's Wall. He is reported

> For Roman army, higher pay and ability to set down local roots in decentralized empire

Others, who were named by an informer, stated that they were Christians and then denied it. They said that they had been, but had abandoned their allegiance some years previously. . . . They maintained, however, that all that their guilt or error involved was that they were accustomed to assemble at dawn on a fixed day, to sing a hymn antiphonally to Christ as God, and to bind themselves by an oath . . . to avoid acts of theft, brigandage, and adultery. . . . When these rites were completed, it was their custom to depart, and then reassemble again to take food, which was, however, common and harmless. They had ceased, they said, to do this following my edict, by which in accordance with your instructions I had outlawed the existence of secret brotherhoods. So I thought it all the more necessary to ascertain the truth from two maidservants [i.e., slaves], who were called deaconesses, even by employing torture. I found nothing other than a debased and boundless superstition. . . .

From Trajan to Pliny

You have followed the appropriate procedures, my Secundus. . . . [N]o general rule can be laid down which would establish a definite routine. Christians are not to be sought out. If brought before you and found guilty, they must be punished, but in such a way that a person who denies that he is a Christian, and demonstrates this by his action . . . may obtain pardon for his repentance, even if his previous record is suspect. Documents published anonymously must play no role in any accusation, for they give the worst example, and are foreign to our age.

Source: Excerpted from *Pliny the Younger: The Complete Letters*, trans. P. G. Walsh (Oxford: 2006), pp. 278–79 (X. 96–97).

Questions for Analysis

1. How does Pliny's treatment of Christians differ according to their social class? How does it differ from Felix's treatment of Paul (pages 190–1)?

2. Why would Trajan insist that anonymous accusations, such as those Pliny mentions, not be used as evidence? Why was this "foreign to our age"?

3. What do you conclude from this exchange about the relationship between religion and politics under the Roman Empire?

to have said to his sons, "Get along together, keep the soldiers rich, and don't bother about anyone else." His elder son, Caracalla, didn't heed the first of these injunctions for long: by the end of the year, he had assassinated his brother, Geta. He then attempted to erase Geta from the historical record by declaring a *damnatio memoriae* (literally, "a condemnation of memory"), banning the mention of Geta's name and defacing his image on public monuments. The second of his father's orders he obeyed by extending the rights of Roman citizenship to everyone in the empire, including the entire army. Such a move was beneficial in some respects, but it also meant that Roman citizenship was no longer a prize to be won through service or the adoption of Roman values. His father's final piece of advice exacerbated Caracalla's already pronounced tendency to alienate everyone who disagreed with him. He was assassinated in 217 C.E.

Caracalla's true successor was his mother's sister, Julia Maesa, who ruled through his nominal heir, her adolescent grandson. This youth was known as Heliogabalus (or Elagabalus; r. 218–222 C.E.) because of his devotion to the sun god Ba'al. But when he attempted to replace Jupiter, Rome's patron god, with Sol Invictus ("Invincible Sun"), his own grandmother engineered his assassination. Another of her grandsons, Alexander Severus (r. 222–235 C.E.), took his place. Alexander, in turn, was ruled by his mother Julia Mamæa, the third in the succession of strong women behind the Severan dynasty. She even traveled with him on military campaigns, which eventually proved fatal for both. Many generals still aspired to imperial power and, in 235 C.E., both Alexander and his mother were murdered at Moguntiacum (Mainz, Germany) when the army turned against them. Fifty years of civil unrest ensued.

THE TEST OF ROME'S STRENGTH

Until 284 C.E., there were at least twenty-six "barracks emperors" in Rome: military commanders who, backed by a few loyal legions, struggled with each other. This period is sometimes called the "Third-Century Crisis," an era when the consequences of Roman expansion made themselves acutely felt. Inflation, caused by the devaluation of currency under Severus, drained Roman coinage of its value. Meanwhile, aspiring emperors levied exorbitant taxes in their provinces, as warfare among rival claimants destroyed crops and interrupted trade, causing food shortages. Because Rome itself was almost entirely dependent on Egyptian grain and other goods shipped in from the East, its inhabitants suffered. Poverty and famine even led to a new form of slavery in Italy, as free artisans, merchants, and small farmers were forced to labor on the estates of large landholders in exchange for protection and food.

In 251 C.E., a terrible plague, probably smallpox, swept through the empire's territories and recurred in some areas for almost two decades. With an estimated five thousand people dying every day in Rome alone, people sought local scapegoats and Christians were among those targeted. Beginning in the short reign of Decius (r. 249–251 C.E.), all Roman citizens were required to swear a public oath affirming their loyalty to Rome, which meant worshiping Rome's gods. Those who did so received a certificate, which they had to produce on demand. Large numbers of Christians were implicated when this edict was put into effect and the enlightened policies of earlier emperors abandoned.

THE EMPEROR SEPTIMIUS SEVERUS. This statue, carved during the emperor's lifetime, emphasizes his career as a military commander, showing him in the standard-issue uniform of a Roman legionnaire. How does this image of Severus compare with that of Augustus (see page 168)? › **What do these differences suggest about the emperor's new role in the third century?**

THE REORGANIZED EMPIRE OF DIOCLETIAN

Ironically, the most zealous persecutor of Christians was also responsible for reining in these destructive forces. **Diocletian** (*die-oh-KLEE-shan*; r. 284–305 C.E.) was a cavalry officer from the province of Dalmatia (modern Croatia) and could have been another "barracks emperor." Instead, he embraced the reality of Rome as a multicultural entity that could not be governed from one place by one person with one centralized bureaucracy. He appointed a fellow officer, Maximian, as co-emperor, putting him in charge of the western half of the empire and retaining the wealthier eastern half for himself. In 293 C.E., Diocletian delegated new authority to two junior emperors, or "caesars": Galerius and Constantius. The result was a **tetrarchy**, a "rule of four," with each man governing a quarter of the empire, further subdivided into administrative units called *dioceses*. This system not only responded to the challenges of imperial administration but was designed to secure a peaceful transfer of power, since the two young "caesars" were being groomed to take the place of the two senior "augusti."

Unlike Augustus and his successors, who had cloaked the reality of personal power in the trappings of the republic, Diocletian presented himself as an undisguised autocrat. His title was not *princeps* ("first man"), but *dominus* ("lord"). Gone were the days of republican simplicity and the scorn of kingly pomp. Diocletian wore a diadem of gold and a purple gown of silk, and he introduced Persian-style ceremonies at his court. Those lucky enough to gain an audience had to prostrate themselves, while a privileged few could kiss his robe. Under the Principate, the emperor's palace had been run like the household of any well-to-do Roman, only on a large scale. Diocletian, however, remained regally removed behind a maze of rooms and curtains.

Although Diocletian retained close personal control over the army, he took steps to separate military from civilian chains of command; never again would Roman armies make and unmake emperors. To control the devastating rates of inflation that were undermining the economy, Diocletian stabilized the currency, attempted to fix prices and wages, and reformed the tax system. He even moved the administrative center of the empire from Italy to Nicomedia in the Roman province of Bithynia (modern Turkey). Rome remained the symbolic capital of the empire, not least because the Senate continued to meet there, but the real power lay elsewhere.

THE TETRARCHY: DIOCLETIAN AND HIS COLLEAGUES. This grouping, carved from a valuable purple stone called porphyry, shows the two augusti, Diocletian and Maximian, embracing their younger caesars, Galerius and Constantius. › **Why do you think these rulers are portrayed with identical facial features and military regalia?** › **What message does this convey?**

Diocletian (245–316) As an emperor of Rome from 284 to 305, Diocletian recognized that the empire could not be governed by one man in one place. His solution was to divide the empire into four parts, each with its own imperial ruler, but he himself remained the dominant ruler of the resulting tetrarchy (rule of four).

tetrarchy The result of Diocletian's political reforms of the late third century C.E., which divided the Roman Empire into four quadrants.

The Conversion of Christianity

At the beginning of the fourth century, the number of Christians living within the empire was probably no more than 5 percent of the total population in the Latin West and possibly 10 percent of the Greek-speaking East. Still, one of Diocletian's methods for promoting unity was to suppress any group perceived as subversive. Those who could not show proof of their loyalty to Rome's gods were stripped of their rights as citizens. Christians who had been serving in the army or in government offices were dismissed. So were Manicheans, followers of the Persian prophet Mani (c. 216–276 C.E.), whose teachings paralleled Zoroastrianism in positing an eternal struggle between the forces of good and evil. Indeed, Christianity and Manichaeism

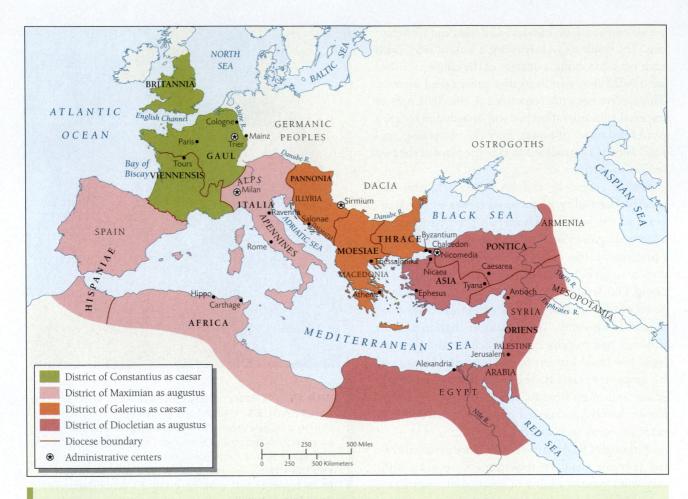

Legend:
- District of Constantius as caesar
- District of Maximian as augustus
- District of Galerius as caesar
- District of Diocletian as augustus
- Diocese boundary
- ✷ Administrative centers

0   250   500 Miles
0   250   500 Kilometers

DIOCLETIAN'S DIVISION OF THE EMPIRE, c. 304 c.e. › What areas did each of the four divisions of the empire cover? › What seems to be the strategy behind the location of the four major capitals, both within their respective quarters and in relation to each other? › What is the status of Rome itself, according to this map?

must have seemed very similar to outsiders, and both were implicated in a full-scale purge of religious dissidents in 303 c.e. This was the Great Persecution, a time when many became martyrs—from a Greek word meaning "witnesses"—for their faith.

CHRISTIANITY AND NEOPLATONISM

In time, the very crises that prompted Diocletian's persecution contributed to a growing interest in Christianity. Its message of social justice and equality before God was attractive to those suffering from hardship. It also appealed to followers of a new and influential philosophy called Neoplatonism ("New Platonism"), which drew on the more mystical aspects of Plato's thought (Chapter 4). Its founder was Plotinus (204–270 c.e.), a Hellenistic philosopher from Egypt who had many followers among the Roman elite. Plotinus taught that everything has its source in a single supreme being. But although the material world is part of this creation, it is merely the residue from which all spirituality has been drained. Human beings are thus composed of matter (bodies) and emanations of the divine (souls). This means that the individual soul, originally a part of God, is separated from its divine source by the fact of its embodiment. The highest goal of life is therefore to attain spiritual reunion with the divine, through contemplation and acts of asceticism (from the Greek word meaning "exercise" or "training") to liberate the soul from its bondage through fasting and other forms of self-denial.

Neoplatonism almost supplanted Stoicism, which did not hold out the hope of union with the divine. It also struck a blow at traditional Roman religion, including the worship of ancestors and devotion to the empire's gods. It was thus a natural ally of Christianity, and many important Christian theologians were influenced by it, while many educated Romans found their way to Christianity because of it. It was not, however, the path by which Christianity's first imperial convert reached the new faith.

CONSTANTINE'S VISION

In 305 c.e., Diocletian built a palace near his hometown of Split, on the Adriatic coast, and retired—the first time a Roman ruler had voluntarily removed himself from power since Sulla had resigned his dictatorship four centuries earlier (see Chapter 5). Maximian retired at the same time and the two caesars—Galerius and Constantius—moved up the ladder of succession, becoming augusti of the East and West, respectively.

But the transfer of power was not so orderly as Diocletian had intended. One of the candidates to fill the vacant post of caesar was Constantius's son, **Constantine**, who was being trained at Galerius's court. But Galerius had his own imperial agenda and did not promote Constantine, who left Nicomedia to join his father in Gaul. From there, father and son went to Britannia and campaigned on the northern borders until 306 c.e., when Constantius died and named Constantine his successor as augustus of the West. This infuriated Galerius, but with Constantine controlling the legions of Gaul and the Rhineland, as well as Britannia, he was forced to concede.

Meanwhile, war broke out among several other claimants to imperial authority. Constantine remained aloof from this struggle, which was waged mostly in Italy, and concentrated on securing his quarter of the empire. Beginning around 310 c.e., he began to promote himself as a favored devotee of the sun god Sol Invictus, whose cult had been revived by the emperor Aurelian (r. 270–275 c.e.). Increasingly, the "Invincible Sun" was associated not only with the Roman gods of light and war, Apollo and Mars, but also with Mithras, whose cult was popular with soldiers. It was increasingly popular in Rome as well, where the feast long dedicated to the sky god Saturn, the Saturnalia, was being celebrated as the rebirth of the sun after the winter solstice, on December 25.

From the worship of Sol Invictus to the worship of Christ was, at least for Constantine, a small step (see *Interpreting Visual Evidence* on page 199). In 312 c.e., Constantine decided to march on Italy, which was now in the hands of a man called Maxentius, who had declared himself emperor in the West and was trying to build up a coalition of supporters. Among those he courted was the Christian community of Rome, and this may have given Constantine the idea of currying favor in the same way. Or, as his Christian biographer insisted, it was divine inspiration that led him

From cult of Sol Invictus to Christ: a small step

Constantine conquers in name of Christ and issues Edict of Milan, cementing Christianity's new status

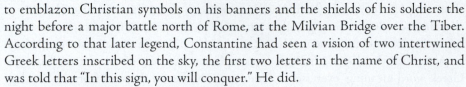

to emblazon Christian symbols on his banners and the shields of his soldiers the night before a major battle north of Rome, at the Milvian Bridge over the Tiber. According to that later legend, Constantine had seen a vision of two intertwined Greek letters inscribed on the sky, the first two letters in the name of Christ, and was told that "In this sign, you will conquer." He did.

In gratitude for his victory, Constantine showered benefits on the Christian church of Rome and patronized the construction of churches throughout the empire. He also forced Licinius, the new augustus of the East, to join him in promoting religious tolerance when they met at Milan (northern Italy) in 313 C.E. Their Edict of Milan guaranteed freedom of worship to all Rome's citizens, Christian and non-Christian. But because Christianity was the favored faith of the imperial family, and thus the pathway for anyone with political ambitions, Christians ceased to be members of an illegal and despised cult and became affiliates of a prestigious religion, one that was suddenly attractive to the ruling classes. The entire basis of Christianity's appeal had drastically changed.

FROM ILLEGAL SECT TO IMPERIAL INSTITUTION

In his letters, Paul of Tarsus addressed the small Christian assemblies he called churches; sometimes he even spoke of the whole Christian community as a church. But could Paul have imagined a day when representatives of an imperial church could meet openly, or a time when his letters to separate churches would be gathered together in a single book? Early Christianity had grown only sporadically, and it was not designed as a religious system. It had no absolute teachings, apart from the words of Jesus reported in the Gospels, which do not always agree on those teachings. And not all Christian communities had access to the same scriptures. Some churches had a few of Paul's letters; others had none. Some had bishops, priests, deacons, and other officeholders; some had only a handful of believers. Some counted women as their leaders; others disapproved of women in authority. Some had come under the influence of Neoplatonism or Manichaeism; others considered Neoplatonism and Manichaeism to be perversions.

In every respect, then, the Christianity that emerged after Constantine's conversion had to reinvent itself. Rituals and doctrines that had been formulated to suit the needs of small, scattered communities now had to be reconciled with one another to become a shared set of beliefs. An imperial church needed the same set of scriptures and a chain of command. All of these fundamental structures had to be hammered out in a painful process that never quite managed to forge a common understanding. This is hardly surprising: the varieties of Christianity were the products of the same diversity that made the Roman Empire hard to govern. Indeed, the degree to which the Christians of the fourth century were able to agree on so many things is remarkable, given these challenges.

THE HIERARCHY OF THE CHURCH

When it came to organization, Rome's administration provided practical models. Because the empire's basic unit of governance was the city, the city became the basic unit of ecclesiastical administration as well. Each major city now had a bishop who supervised all the churches and also the rural areas of his diocese, a term borrowed

The Power of the Invincible Sun

Roman emperors often linked their power to the powers of Rome's traditional gods, and emperors were also worshiped as gods in their own right. Look carefully at the following images and consider the visual language of power that came to be associated with Sol Invictus, the "Invincible Sun," and eventually with Jesus Christ.

Questions for Analysis

1. How did Constantine invoke the iconography of Sol Invictus (image A)? What messages does this image convey?

2. How might Constantine's use of this imagery—after his initial conversion to Christianity—have been interpreted by Christians? How might it have been interpreted by followers of Rome's other religions? Do you think it was designed to be ambiguous? Why or why not?

3. Scholars dispute both the dating and the significance of this mosaic, found beneath St. Peter's Basilica on the Vatican Hill in Rome (image B). Is it likely that this is a representation of Jesus as Sol Invictus? If not, how would you explain the association of this pagan deity with the Christian God?

B. This mosaic comes from a necropolis (cemetery) found beneath St. Peter's Basilica (the Vatican) in Rome. Its precise dating is in dispute, but it was made sometime between the mid-third and mid-fourth centuries. It shows Jesus with the halo of the sun god.

A. This coin issued by Constantine shows him with a halo, indicating his worship of Sol Invictus. The reverse features figures representing the Four Seasons.

from Diocletian's reorganization of the empire. Bishops of the largest cities were called *metropolitans*, and those who ruled over the oldest and most prestigious Christian communities were called *patriarchs*. These patriarchal cities also jockeyed for preeminence. Among the main contenders were Rome, whose inhabitants longed to be at the center of the world again; Alexandria, the capital of the Hellenistic world; and Constantinople, a new city founded by Constantine on the Hellespont between Europe and Asia.

CHRISTIAN SYMBOLS ON THE ROMAN FRONTIER. This stunning fresco is one of many found in the Cella Septichora, a series of decorated Christian burial chambers constructed in the Roman province of Pannonia (now in Hungary). Portraits of saints adorn the ceiling and wall, which also features the *chi-rho* monogram that Constantine claimed to have seen in the sky before his victory at the Milvian Bridge. *Chi* and *rho* are the first two letters in the Greek word *Christos*.

Which of these Roman cities should be the capital of the Roman Church? The patriarch of Rome's claim rested on several foundations. Rome was venerated as the place where both Peter and Paul were martyred. According to one of the Gospels (Matthew 16:18–19), Jesus had designated Peter as his earthly representative. Peter's successors, the bishops of Rome, claimed to exercise the same authority. And unlike the bishop of the new imperial capital at Constantinople, he could act with more freedom because he didn't have to deal directly with the emperor. But as far as eastern bishops were concerned, the patriarch of Constantinople should be the one to exercise control over the entire Church. This division—the product of cultural differences and contemporary politics—would continue to affect the development of Christian institutions. In time, it would lead to a very real division within Christianity, one that has never been resolved.

ORTHODOXY, HERESY, AND IMPERIAL AUTHORITY

Christian orthodoxy emerges as Constantine asserts imperial authority

Christianity's new prominence raised the stakes of disputes over its basic teachings, as well as its governance. Although followers of Jesus had disagreed about such matters since the time of his death, these disagreements were of little political consequence so long as Christianity remained an illegal movement. Under Constantine, however, doctrinal disputes had the potential to ignite riots and to undermine the credibility of the emperor. It was imperative, therefore, that these disputes be resolved.

The most divisive theological issue concerned the nature of God. Jesus had taught that he was the son of God and that, after his death, he would leave behind a comforting spirit that would also be an emanation of God. Accordingly, many Christians believed that God encompassed a Trinity of equal persons: Father, Son, and Holy Spirit. But other Christians, influenced by Neoplatonism, rejected the idea that Jesus could be equal with God. Instead, they maintained that Jesus was part of God's creation and shared in his divine essence; but he was not equal to God, or eternal like God. This latter school of thought was called Arianism, after the

Christian teacher Arius who espoused it. (It should not be confused with Aryanism, a modern racial concept.) After protracted struggles, Arianism was condemned as heresy, a word that comes from the Greek verb meaning "to choose for oneself." It became the Church's term for false beliefs punished with damnation. Yet many Christians continued to adhere to the Arian view.

This new emphasis on orthodoxy (Greek for "correct teaching") was another major consequence of Christianity's conversion. Christian intellectuals had to demonstrate that their beliefs could withstand intense philosophical scrutiny and that Christianity was superior to any pagan religion or Greek philosophy. Just as there were many different schools of Greek and Roman thought, so there arose many different interpretations of Christian doctrine. Before Christianity became a legal religion, any doctrinal disputes could only be addressed informally, by small groups of bishops meeting at local councils that had no power to enforce their decisions. In the fourth century, however, doctrinal disputes had real consequences.

As a result, the Roman state became increasingly enmeshed in the governance of the Church. Constantine began this process in 325 C.E., when he summoned Christian representatives to the first ecumenical ("worldwide") meeting of the Christian community, the Council of Nicaea, where Arianism was condemned and arguments over the books to be included in the Christian Bible were resolved. Constantine's successors carried this intervention much further. Gradually, they claimed to preside over Church councils as Christ's representatives. Some even violently suppressed Christian groups that refused to accept imperial mandates, labeled them heretical, and subjected them to ecclesiastical penalties—condemnation and excommunication from the Church—as well as criminal prosecution. It began to look as though secular and spiritual authority would be combined in the person of the emperor. But this would change in later centuries, as we shall see.

At Constantine's Council of Nicaea, secular and spiritual authority are further consolidated

NEW ATTITUDES TOWARD WOMEN AND THE BODY

Women were conspicuously absent from the new hierarchy of the Christian Church. Even though they had long been deacons and may even have performed priestly duties, women were now firmly excluded from any position of power.

This was an enormous change, more fundamental than any other aspect of Christianity's conversion. Jesus had included many women among his close followers—yet one of the early gospels rejected from the biblical canon was ascribed to Mary Magdalene. Paul had relied on women to organize and preside over churches and to finance his missionary journeys; he had declared in one letter (Galatians 3:28) that there should be no distinctions of gender, rank, or ethnicity among Christians. Women such as Perpetua were prominent among the martyrs and were often regarded as prophets. These strong roles had always set Christianity apart from the traditional values of Roman society—but that had also been one of Christianity's main attractions.

What accounts for this drastic change? Three factors can be clearly identified. When Christianity was absorbed into the staunch patriarchy of Rome, it could no longer promote the authority of women effectively. As the Church came to mirror the imperial administration, it had the capacity to exclude or censor writings that represented women as the companions of Jesus and as founders of the religion based on his teachings. These efforts were so successful that it was not until the very end of the nineteenth century that a gospel attributed to Mary Magdalene was known to exist.

The second factor was the growing identification of Christianity with Roman cults that emphasized masculinity, particularly the worship of Sol Invictus and the soldiers' god Mithras. This was a deliberate strategy on the part of the Church, because it is easier to convert people to a new set of beliefs and practices if they include elements of older religions. In common with these two cults, as well as with the worship of Osiris in Egypt, Christianity emphasized the heroic suffering and death of a male god and his eventual victory over death itself. As Christ became identified with Sol Invictus, his birthday came to be celebrated on December 25, the Roman holiday that marked the return of lengthening days.

The third factor contributing to women's exclusion from power was the Christian emphasis on asceticism and self-denial, which changed attitudes toward the body. As we noted previously, Neoplatonism taught that the goal of life was to liberate the soul from bodily desires, a teaching that it shared with Stoicism. But none of this was emphasized in the teachings of Jesus. Quite the contrary: the body was celebrated as God's creation, and Jesus had encouraged feasting, touching, bathing, and marriage. His followers insisted that he had been bodily resurrected, and that the bodies of all the faithful would be resurrected, too. Although early Christians had to be willing to sacrifice their lives for their faith, if need be, they were not required to renounce earthly pleasures.

SAINT SIMEON "THE STYLITE." This gold plaque dating from the sixth century depicts the exertions of the ascetic saint who defied the devil (shown as a huge snake) by abusing his own body. Admirers wishing to speak to the saint could climb the ladder shown on the left. › **What do you make of the relationship between the luxurious medium of this image (gold) and the message it conveys?**

After Christianity became legal, however, there were few opportunities to "bear witness" through martyrdom. Instead, some Christians began to practice asceticism as an alternative path to sanctity. This meant renunciation of the flesh, especially sex and eating: both associated with women, who were in charge of any household's food supply and who were (obviously) sexual partners. A new spiritual movement called *monasticism* took hold, providing an alternative lifestyle for men who wanted to reject the world entirely; the word for this movement comes from the Greek word *monos*, "alone." Early monks lived as hermits and practiced extraordinary feats of self-abasement. A monk named Cyriacus would stand for hours on one leg, like a crane. Another, Simeon "the Stylite," lived on top of a high pillar for thirty-seven years, punishing his lice-infested flesh while crowds gathered below to marvel.

This extreme denial of the body was a departure not only from most previous Christian practices but also from the practices of many civilizations up to this point—not to mention the realities of human existence. Ancient religions often celebrated sexuality as a delight, as well as a necessity. Even Greek and Roman religions had a place for priestesses. Moreover, marriage was so important a marker of social respectability that unmarried men were objects of deep suspicion. Furthermore, Romans had regarded citizens' bodies as being at the service of the state: men as soldiers and fathers, women as mothers and wives. Now, however, some Christians were asserting that their bodies belonged to God, and that to serve God fully meant no longer serving the state—or posterity—by bearing children. Virginity for both men and women was accordingly preached as the highest spiritual standard, with celibacy for those who had once been married valued almost as highly. Marriage remained acceptable for average people, the laity, but was often characterized as a second-best option to prevent weak-minded people from being consumed by desire. Moreover, because pseudoscientific theories stemming back to Aristotle posited that women were inherently more lustful than men, the denigration of sexuality had a disproportionately negative effect on attitudes toward women.

CHRISTIANS AND PAGANS

The urban focus of Christianity is reflected in the Latin word referring to a non-Christian: *paganus*, meaning someone who lives in the countryside. The implication is that only someone with a rustic outlook would cling to the old Roman religion and spoil his chances of social advancement. As Christians came to occupy positions of power, men with political ambitions were increasingly forced to convert—or at least conform—to Christian norms.

Constantine had retained both pagan and Christian officials in his court, but his successors were less inclined to tolerate competing faiths. An interesting exception was Constantine's nephew Julian "the Apostate" (r. 360–363 C.E.), who rejected Christianity and attempted to revive traditional Roman piety. But when Julian was killed in a battle with the Persians, his pro-pagan edicts were allowed to lapse. By 391 C.E., the emperor Theodosius (r. 379–395 C.E.) had prohibited pagan worship of any sort within the empire. Within three generations, Christianity had gone from being a persecuted faith to a persecuting religion. Theodosius even removed the sacred altar of the goddess Victory from the Senate chamber in Rome, prompting pagan loyalists to prophesy the end of the empire. Fifteen years later, Rome fell to a barbarian army.

> *Constantine's successors are increasingly less tolerant toward non-Christian pagans*

Shifting Centers and Moving Frontiers

In 324 C.E., Constantine broke ground for the capital city he named after himself, **Constantinople**. It was built on the site of a settlement called Byzantium, chosen for its strategic location at the mouth of the Black Sea and the crossroads between Europe and Asia: the Hellespont. This site gave Constantinople commanding advantages as a center for communications and trade. It also made the city readily defensible, because it was surrounded on three sides by water and protected by walls on land. It would remain the political and economic center of the Roman Empire until 1453, when the city was conquered by the Ottoman Turks (see Chapter 11).

EAST OR WEST?

The founding of Constantinople epitomizes the shift in Rome's center of gravity from western Europe to the eastern Mediterranean. It also signaled Constantine's intention to abandon the political precedents set by Diocletian. Instead, the imperial succession became hereditary. Constantine thus embraced a principle of dynastic monarchy that the Romans had rejected 800 years earlier. He also divided the empire among his three sons, resulting in a civil war, made more bitter because each of these men supported a different faction within the Church. The empire became more and more fragmented. The last ruler who could claim to govern a united Rome was the same Theodosius who outlawed its venerable religion; then he, too, divided the empire between his sons.

Constantinople City founded by the emperor Constantine on the site of a village called Byzantium; it became the new capital of the Roman Empire in 324 and continued to be the seat of imperial power after its capture by the Ottoman Empire in 1453.

Of course, there had always been complicated linguistic and cultural differences between the Greek- and Latin-speaking peoples under Roman rule. Now, however, these differences became heightened. The eastern empire was becoming more populous, prosperous, and central to imperial policy; the western provinces were becoming poorer and more peripheral. Many relied on funds from their eastern counterparts and suffered when communication failed, or Roman legions were transferred elsewhere. Rome itself, which had been demoted to provincial status under Diocletian, now lost even that nominal position. The Italian city of Ravenna on the Adriatic coast became the new capital of the region and a more convenient stopping place for travelers from Constantinople to the administrative centers of Milan and Trier (Germany). Only two of Constantine's successors ever visited Rome itself, and none of them lived there.

INTERNAL AND EXTERNAL PRESSURES

The shifting center of the empire and the widening gap between the eastern and western provinces were not the only fault lines emerging in this period. Beneath the surface of imperial autocracy, the fourth-century empire was slowly dissolving into its constituent parts. At the same time, it was also coming under renewed pressure from its frontiers. Since the third century, the growing power of a new Persian dynasty, the Sassanids, had prompted a shift of Roman military weight to the eastern borderlands, reducing the number of troops stationed elsewhere. Partly as a result of this, the northwestern territories were left vulnerable. While relations between assimilated Romans and their barbarian neighbors were generally peaceful, a new wave of settlers moved into the empire's oldest provinces during the early fifth century.

FROM THE PERIPHERY TO THE CENTER

"Barbarians": frontier peoples who didn't speak Greek or Latin

The peoples that lived along the empire's northern frontiers were barbarians in the pure sense of that (Greek) term: they did not speak either of the empire's civilized languages and did not live in cities. But in no sense were they savage; they were sophisticated agriculturalists and metalworkers who had enjoyed trading relationships with the Roman world for centuries. Many had been settled within Roman provinces for generations, and legionnaires from Germania were common recruits in Roman armies. In some frontier regions, entire tribes had become *foederati* (*feh-dor-AH-tee*): allied troops who reinforced or replaced Roman garrisons. One general of mixed descent, Flavius Stilicho (359–408 C.E.), was the military leader of the western empire under Theodosius. By the end of the fourth century, many of these tribes had even adopted the Arian form of Christianity. Although this made them heretics from the perspective of the Church, it tied them more closely to Roman civilization.

What altered this relatively peaceful coexistence? Our study of many previous civilizations has prepared us to answer this question: the arrival of new migrants and the subsequent struggle for land and resources. During the mid-fourth century, a group of nomadic herdsmen known as the Huns began to move westward from central Asia, into the region north and east of the Black Sea. Around 370 C.E., their arrival forced a number of other groups, notably the Goths, to migrate south and west.

The Goths had been clients of the Roman state for several centuries, but now they were refugees, too numerous and too desperate to repel by force. The Romans

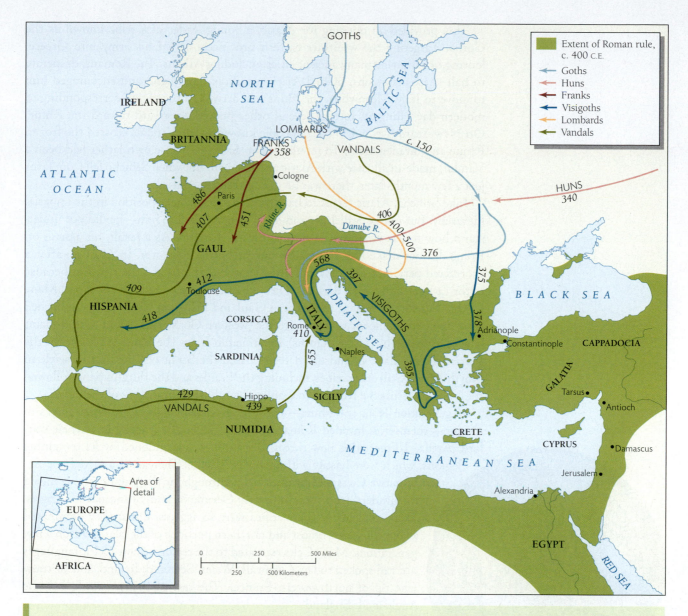

THE MIGRATIONS OF ROME'S FRONTIER PEOPLES. › What do the routes followed by these different peoples suggest about their destinations and motives? › Why did so many converge on Rome, although the city was no longer the capital even of the western Roman Empire? › Why did the Romans refer to these migrants as "barbarians"?

therefore permitted them to cross the Danube and settle within the empire. In return for food and other supplies, they were to guard the region against other migrant groups. Local officials, however, failed to uphold their end of the bargain. Instead, they forced the starving Goths to sell themselves and their children into slavery in return for food. In 378 C.E., the Goths revolted, and the army sent to suppress them was defeated at the Battle of Adrianople. Peace was restored when the empire accommodated the Goths' demands for farmland and enrolled them in the Roman army under their own military leaders.

This provided an opening for Alaric, a young leader of a tribe known as the Goths. Targeting the wealthier eastern provinces, he led his army into Greece, looting or capturing many ancient cities, including Athens. The Romans, desperate to halt these incursions, offered Alaric a military command and encouraged him to move to Italy. Meanwhile, the Huns had arrived in the region corresponding to modern-day Hungary, forcing several other peoples westward toward the Rhine. On New Year's Eve in 406 C.E., a people known as the Vandals crossed the frozen Rhine and invaded Gaul. To repulse them, Stilicho (whose own father had been a Vandal) made an alliance with Alaric and his men. But when Stilicho fell from favor just a few months later, there was no one to restrain Alaric.

Like Stilicho, Alaric seems to have wanted a permanent position in the imperial hierarchy. But unlike Stilicho—and many generals before him—he did not understand how to use violence as a means toward that end. As a result, his assault on Rome did not make him Rome's conqueror but its destroyer. In 410 C.E., after a protracted period of siege, Alaric's army captured and sacked the city. But because of the ravages of the siege, Rome had little to offer in the way of food or spoils. Many Goths therefore moved on to southern Gaul and Hispania, where they established what came to be known as the Visigothic (western Gothic) Kingdom. Others, later labeled Ostrogoths (eastern Goths), remained in Italy. The Vandals set out for the Iberian Peninsula, too, and ultimately crossed the Strait of Gibraltar to settle in North Africa. Still other tribes, including the Franks and the Burgundians, followed the Vandals across the Rhine into Gaul and established kingdoms of their own.

A generation later, the Huns—whose migration had set all of these forces in motion—themselves invaded Roman territory under the leadership of their warlord, Attila. To meet this new threat, Britannia was abandoned by its remaining legions, which were hastily withdrawn in 410 C.E. Thereafter, a mixed population of native Celts and peoples from throughout the empire intermingled with invaders from northwestern Germania and Scandinavia: Angles, Saxons, and Jutes. These tribes were so aggressive that they dominated all but the westernmost and northern portions of the island within a few generations. Many Celts retreated to the regions where Celtic languages are still spoken today: Cornwall, Wales, Scotland, Ireland, and Brittany (the tip of northwestern France). The rest of Britain would become Angle-land: England.

The last western Roman emperor was an ineffectual usurper derisively known as Romulus Augustulus ("Little Romulus Augustus"). In 476 C.E., he was deposed by Odovacar, a chieftain who headed a band of barbarians, Huns, and disgruntled Romans. From the perspective of Constantinople, this event was decisive: it was not only "New Rome," it was the only viable Rome left. The best way for its imperial agenda to be carried forward in the western provinces was through a strong barbarian ruler.

Luckily, the emperor Zeno (r. 474–491 C.E.) knew just the man: Theodoric, the son of a Gothic king who had been sent to Constantinople as a hostage and raised in the civilized surroundings of the imperial court. After a decade of fierce fighting, Theodoric and his imperially equipped Gothic army managed to drive the Huns northward from Italy and to establish a kingdom based in Ravenna. He ruled there—with imperial support from Constantinople—until his death in 526.

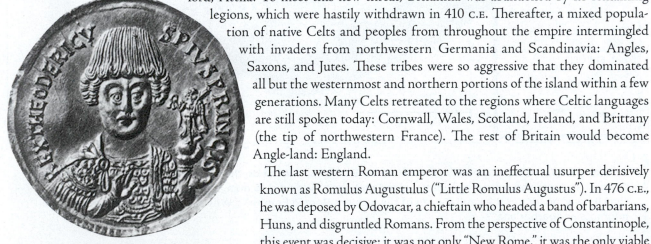

THEODORIC THE OSTROGOTH. This coin shows the king in Roman dress but with the long hair characteristic of a barbarian nobleman. The inscription reads *Rex Theodericvs pivs princis*, "King Theodoric, pious prince." › **How does this image compare with that of Constantine (see page 199)?**

THE IMPACT OF THE FIFTH-CENTURY MIGRATIONS

The events of the fifth century broke down the empire's northern frontiers and penetrated to its core provinces: Italy, Gaul, Hispania, and North Africa. Yet the migrant groups that moved into these territories were small war bands. Why couldn't long-established imperial cities defend themselves?

By the beginning of that century, as we just noted, many legions had already been withdrawn from frontier provinces to eastern ones. Those that remained tended to be integrated into the local communities, making it difficult to move troops even in an emergency. Furthermore, there was no mechanism for increasing the revenues needed to support the army. Even if the citizens of Rome's western provinces had been able to maintain a crack fighting force, they would have had little reason to think that such an expenditure was necessary. Their "barbarian" neighbors were often so Romanized that it is difficult to detect any differences between these groups in surviving archaeological evidence.

In the eastern Roman Empire, by contrast, a thriving economy made it easier and more necessary to maintain a strong fighting force. Cities remained centers of commerce and industry, and greater taxable wealth could sustain the burdens of the imperial bureaucracy. Moreover, potential invaders could be bribed or encouraged to direct their attention elsewhere—as Alaric had been. For all these reasons, the eastern empire prospered during the fifth century C.E., while the western empire floundered.

These differences were then exacerbated by the wave of fifth-century migrations. Every plundered territory resulted in the loss of tax revenues at an enormous scale: ten years after the Goths sacked Rome in 410 C.E., it produced only 15 percent of the revenues it had generated before. As the newcomers began to set up their own kingdoms in former provinces, they paid no taxes at all to imperial authorities. When the Vandals captured North Africa in 439 C.E., the richest of all Rome's provinces was lost.

As Rome's wealthy territories are sacked, the empire loses tax revenues and becomes further decentralized

The consequences were far-reaching. Around 400 C.E., the western Roman Empire was still known for the mass production of low-cost, high-quality consumer goods that circulated in massive quantities. But by 500 C.E., long-distance trade in bulk goods could be sustained only in the Mediterranean. As markets disappeared in northwestern provinces, skilled artisans had to find other work or had to emigrate. Standards of living declined, and so did the overall population. Indeed, the population of western Europe did not return to its fourth-century levels for a thousand years, until just before the Black Death (see Chapter 10).

Other aspects of Roman life in these regions changed, too—but more slowly. Roman bureaucracies often survived, with the proceeds of taxes going to the treasuries of new rulers or Christian bishops. Local Roman elites continued to dominate civic life, and Roman cities continued to dominate their surrounding regions, especially in southern Gaul and Hispania. Roman agricultural patterns continued in most areas, frequently under the same landlords. The invasions did not bring an end to Roman culture or the influence of Roman values. As King Theodoric the Ostrogoth was fond of remarking: "An able Goth wishes to be like a Roman; but only a poor Roman would want to be like a Goth."

The Shaping of a New Worldview

As the western territories of the empire sustained attacks from external forces, it seemed clear that a new age was beginning. Christ had promised to come again at

Jerome (c. 340–420) One of the early "fathers" of the Church; Jerome translated the Bible from Hebrew and Greek into a popular form of Latin—hence the name by which this translation is known: the Vulgate (i.e., "vulgar" or *popular*) Bible.

Ambrose (c. 340–397) One of the early "fathers" of the Church, he helped to define the relationship between the sacred authority of bishops and other Church leaders, and the secular authority of worldly rulers.

the end of time, when all human souls would be judged. How, then, should Christians live in this new world and prepare for that inevitable event?

The men who forged answers to this question were contemporaries who knew and influenced one another, though they did not always agree. They are now regarded as saints and "fathers" of the Church: Jerome (c. 340–420 C.E.), who came from northeastern Italy, near the port of Aquileia; Ambrose (c. 340–397), who grew up in Trier and was eventually named bishop of Milan; and Augustine (354–430), who was born and raised in North Africa, where he became a bishop in later life.

JEROME: TRANSLATING THE CHRISTIAN MESSAGE

Jerome's contribution to the culture of the Roman West was his translation of the Bible from Hebrew and Greek into Latin. Known as the Vulgate or "common" Bible, it remained the standard edition until the sixteenth century (see Chapter 13) and influenced all subsequent authors, worshipers, and artists in the Latin West. Jerome was also an influential commentator on the Bible, encouraging readings that emphasized a passage's moral or allegorical significance, as well as its literal or historical meanings.

Jerome was also among the first to argue that classical (non-Christian) texts could and should be studied by Christians so long as they were adapted to Christian aims. The perennial problem, of course, was that one was always tempted to appreciate classical literature for its own sake, and Jerome himself never succeeded in subordinating his love for ancient authors, especially Cicero, to his love for God. He liked to tell a story about a dream in which he arrived at the gates of heaven and was asked by God if he were a Christian. When he replied that he was, God retorted, "You're not a Christian; you're a Ciceronian." Perhaps to compensate for this, Jerome became a rigorous ascetic and promoter of monasticism. He also held a narrow view of women's roles that exercised a strong misogynistic influence on some later Christian teachers.

AMBROSE AND THE AUTHORITY OF THE CHURCH

Jerome was primarily a scholar; **Ambrose**, by contrast, was an aristocrat who helped to define the relationship between the sacred authority of the Church and the secular authority of rulers. As patriarch of the imperial administrative capital at Milan, he fearlessly rebuked the emperor Theodosius for his mismanaged massacre of innocent civilians in the Greek city of Thessalonica. Until Theodosius did penance for his sins, Ambrose refused to admit him into the communion of the Christian community. On matters of faith, he declared, "The emperor is within the Church, not above the Church." Eventually, Theodosius begged the forgiveness of God's representative, Ambrose, in his cathedral at Milan.

Ambrose was also an admirer of Cicero—but because of his Stoicism, not his elegant Latin. He drew heavily on Cicero's treatise *On Duties* for his ethics handbook, *On the Duties of Ministers*. Unlike Cicero, however, Ambrose argued that the goal of human conduct should be reverence for God, not social or political advancement. Ambrose argued that God assists all Christians by sharing the power of divine grace with them—but that he extends more grace to some Christians than to others. Ambrose's emphasis on the mystery of grace (Why does God give more to some than to others?) was refined and amplified by his disciple, Augustine.

THE SALVATION OF SAINT AUGUSTINE

Apart from Jesus and Paul, **Augustine** is often considered the greatest of all Christianity's founders, and may be the most important Christian thinker of all time. His theology is essential to the doctrines of the medieval Roman Church and thus to modern Roman Catholicism, and it also had a profound effect on Martin Luther and the development of Protestant Christianities (see Chapter 13). Today, many Christian philosophers of various denominations describe themselves as neo-Augustinians.

Augustine's understanding of Christianity was the result of a long process of self-discovery, which he described in a remarkable book called *Confessions*: a series of autobiographical reflections addressed to God. Augustine was not, as Jerome and Ambrose were, a Christian from the cradle. Although his mother was, he scorned her influence and refused baptism. Full of ambition, he left North Africa for Italy as a young man, winning early fame as a teacher and charismatic orator. All the while, he gravitated from one philosophy to another without finding intellectual or spiritual satisfaction. He regarded Christianity as a religion for fools, and only the appeal of Ambrose's teachings drove him to inquire further. After a spiritual epiphany described in *Confessions*, he decided to embrace Christianity at the significant age of thirty-three (the age when Jesus died). Yet his struggle to grasp and explain its paradoxes occupied him for the rest of his life. His skills as a preacher and commentator led to his rapid advancement in the Church hierarchy, and he returned to North Africa as the bishop of Hippo Regius in 395 C.E.

Although he led an extremely active life (when he died in 430, he was defending Hippo against the Vandals), Augustine still found time to write more than a hundred profound and powerful treatises analyzing the problems of Christian belief. All of these grapple with a basic question: If humanity is the creation of an omnipotent God whose nature is entirely good, why are human beings so profoundly sinful? Augustine was alarmed by humans' capacity for evil, and he believed this tendency was evident even in children. He adduced himself as a supreme example: in *Confessions*, he remembers that he and a few other boys once stole some pears from a neighbor's garden, not because they were hungry or even because the pears were beautiful, but simply for the sake of doing something bad. He also recounted his many sexual adventures as a young man and recalled that he had prayed, "O God, give me chastity—but not yet!" In short, he argued that the human inclination toward evil is innate. But how, if we are the creatures of a good God?

Augustine traced the origin of evil back to the story of the Garden of Eden, where God had given Adam and Eve, the first human couple, the freedom to follow either God's will or their own. He concluded that all the evils of the world are the result of human free will and the propensity to place one's own desires ahead of God's. This fact alone would justify God's condemnation of all mankind. But because God is merciful, he chose instead to save some human beings through the sacrifice of his son, Jesus.

But why only some? Because human beings are inherently sinful, Augustine reasoned, they cannot achieve salvation on their own; they need to be led to accept Jesus by an act of God's grace—hence the power of Augustine's own transformative experience, which led him to embrace Christianity *against his own will*. By granting grace to some and not to others, God chooses a portion of the human race for salvation and destines the rest to condemnation. If this seems unfair, Augustine would answer that strict fairness would condemn everyone to hell and that the basis for God's choice is a mystery far beyond the realm of human comprehension.

> **Augustine** (c. 354–400) One of the most influential theologians of all time, Augustine described his conversion to Christianity in his autobiographical *Confessions* and articulated a new Christian worldview in *The City of God*, among other works.

DEFENDING THE CITY OF GOD

After the sack of Rome in 410 C.E., Augustine knew that some staunchly traditional Romans blamed Christianity for this calamity. According to them, the attack on their city was the consequence of gross impiety toward Rome's traditional gods. In response, Augustine wrote one of his most famous works, *City of God*, to offer a new interpretation of human history. He argued that mankind has always been divided into two opposing societies: those who live for the world and those who seek eternal life. The former belong to the City of Man, and their rewards are riches, fame, and earthly power—all of which are tainted by sin. Only those predestined to salvation, members of the City of God, will be saved on Judgment Day.

Classical Learning and the Christian Life

Jerome, Ambrose, and Augustine were among the first generation to grow up in a world where Christianity was legal. For three centuries, there had been no such thing as a Roman Christian, which was a contradiction in terms. Now, however, many Romans *were* Christians. How could these identities be reconciled? None of these influential teachers wanted to discard the heritage of the past, but for all of them it posed serious challenges. Since the time of Socrates, philosophy had been characterized by its capacity to absorb and blend many competing ideas. Christian intellectuals wanted to be regarded as philosophers, but they also wanted to replace the doctrines of pagan philosophy with the doctrine of Christ. To do this, they needed to make classical learning applicable to a Christian way of life.

PRESERVING AND RECYCLING THE CLASSICS

Reinterpreting classical culture involved careful selection: something made easier by the fact that a gradual winnowing of Greek texts had already occurred in Alexandria and had continued under the Roman Empire.

Those pagan authors whose works were most immediately useful to Christians, such as Cicero and Virgil, therefore enjoyed continued celebrity. Texts that had long educated students in the liberal arts were also preserved, alongside major classics of Latin poetry and histories that recorded the errors of Rome's pagan past. But texts that could not be readily adapted to Christian purposes were subjected to careful editing. One of the men who undertook this task was Anicius Manlius Severinus **Boethius** (*boh-EE-thee-uhs*; c. 480–524 C.E.), an aristocrat attached to the court of Theodoric. Often described as the "last of the Romans," his goal was to preserve the best aspects of ancient learning by compiling a series of handbooks and anthologies that packaged and explained classical texts in ways appropriate for Christian readers.

Boethius devoted special attention to logic, translating several of Aristotle's treatises from Greek to Latin. Because Roman philosophers had never been much interested in logic, Boethius thus forged a crucial link between classical Greek thought and the new intellectual culture of Christianity. This is most evident in *The Consolation of Philosophy*, which he wrote in prison after Theodoric condemned him to death for treason. (The justice of the charge is unclear.) In this meditation, written in the form of a dialogue, Boethius concludes that happiness is not found in earthly rewards but in the "highest good," which is God. Yet he comes to this realization not through any reference to Christian revelation but through a series of imaginary conversations with "Lady Philosophy," the embodiment of wisdom. For the next millennium, Boethius's *Consolation* was one of the most read and imitated books in the West—the ultimate example of classical philosophy's absorption into the Christian worldview.

MONASTIC EDUCATION

The vital work of preserving the classics and interpreting their meaning was increasingly performed by monks, whose way of life had undergone some significant changes during the fourth century. Leaders of the monastic movement recognized that few men were capable of ascetic feats, and some disapproved of them. Rather, they advocated a more moderate approach and emphasized the benefits of communal life. In the Roman East, the most important figure in this new monasticism was Basil of Caesarea (c. 330–379). Basil's guidelines prohibited monks from engaging in prolonged fasts or extreme discipline of the flesh, and instead encouraged useful work and silent meditation.

In the Roman West, the most influential proponent of the monastic movement was a contemporary of Boethius, **Benedict of Nursia** (c. 480–c. 547). The son of a Roman aristocrat, Benedict founded a monastery at Monte Cassino, southeast of Rome, where he urged his followers to adopt a "simple rule for beginners." Benedict's *Rule* is notable for its brevity, flexibility, and practicality. It established a carefully defined cycle of daily prayers, lessons, and communal worship. It laid down guidelines for what monks should do and how the work of the monastery should be performed. Physical labor was encouraged—idleness, Benedict declared, was "an enemy of the soul"—but the monks also had time for private study and contemplation. In all such matters, Benedict left much to the discretion of the monastery's leader, whom all the monks were expected to obey without reserve. This man was the abbot, from the Syriac word *abba* ("father").

CASSIODORUS AND THE CLASSICAL CANON

Benedict was not really an admirer of classical pagan culture, but he did believe that monks must study the Bible in order to perform their daily cycle of prayers properly and to participate fully in the life of worship, which he called *Opus Dei*: "the work of God." He thus advocated that monks be educated along the lines prescribed by Augustine. And because many monks entered religious life as children, the monastery would need to provide schooling. Through this somewhat roundabout path, classical learning entered the monastic curriculum.

The man largely responsible for designing this curriculum was Flavius Magnus Aurelius **Cassiodorus** Senator (c. 490–c. 583), a younger contemporary of Benedict. Like Boethius, Cassiodorus

CASSIODORUS. This frontispiece from a Bible, produced in a monastery in Britain around the year 700, depicts Cassiodorus as a copyist and keeper of books. Monasteries were instrumental in changing the form of the book from the ancient scroll to the modern codex. Because their parchment pages were heavy, codices were customarily stored in cupboards, lying flat, as we see them here.

Roman or Barbarian?

These two letters from Sidonius Apollinaris (c. 430–c. 480) illustrate the ways in which cultural assimilation was rapidly blurring the distinctions between "Roman" and "barbarian" in the West. Sidonius was himself the descendant of an illustrious Roman provincial family in Gaul. He was one of the most admired Latin stylists of his day, and although he eventually became a bishop and was regarded as a saint, his letter collection (from which these extracts are taken) tells us much more about the literary culture of Romano-Visigothic Gaul than it does about Christianity. His two correspondents also exemplify this new hybrid culture: Arbogastes (ahr-bo-GAHS-tees) was the Frankish governor of the Roman city of Trier (in what is now Germany), and Syagrius (sigh-AG-ree-uhs) was from an ancient Roman family and became, effectively, the king of a large region now corresponding to northern France and Belgium.

Letter 4:17: Sidonius to His Friend Arbogastes

My honored Lord, your friend Eminentius has handed me a letter written by your own hand, a really literary letter, replete with the grace of a three-fold charm. The first of its merits is certainly the affection which prompted such condescension to my lowly condition, for if not a stranger I am in these days a man who courts obscurity; the second virtue is your modesty. . . . In the third place comes your urbanity, which leads you to make a most amusing profession of clumsiness, when as a matter of fact you have drunk deep from the spring of Roman eloquence and, dwelling by the Moselle, you speak the true Latin of the Tiber: you are intimate with the barbarians but are innocent of barbarisms, and are equal in tongue, as also in strength of arm, to the leaders of old, I mean those who were wont to handle the pen no less than the sword. Thus the splendor of the Roman speech, if it still exists anywhere, has survived in you, though it has long been wiped out from the Belgian and Rhenic lands: with you and your eloquence surviving, even though Roman law has ceased at our border, the Roman speech does not falter. For this reason . . . I rejoice greatly that at any rate in your illustrious breast there have remained traces of our vanishing culture. If you extend these by constant reading you will discover for yourself as each day passes that the educated are no less superior to the unlettered than men are to beasts.

(cass-ee-oh-DOHR-uhs) was attached to Theodoric's court and was for many years the secretary in charge of the king's correspondence. He also wrote a *History of the Goths*, which depicted Theodoric's people as part of Rome's history. After Theodoric's death, Cassiodorus founded an important monastery at Vivarium in southern Italy, where he composed his most influential work, the *Institutes*. Cassiodorus believed that the study of classical literature was an essential preliminary to a proper understanding of the Bible. The *Institutes* is essentially a syllabus, a list of readings arranged so that a student could begin with simpler, straightforward works before moving on to more difficult texts, and finally to the study of theology. Cassiodorus thereby defined a classical canon that formed the basis of Christian education in the Roman West.

In order to ensure that his monks had access to the necessary readings, Cassiodorus also encouraged the copying of books as precisely the sort of manual labor that Benedict had advocated in his Rule. Benedictine monasteries thus became engines for the collection, preservation, and transmission of knowledge. Nearly all the Greek

Letter 5:5: Sidonius to his Friend Syagrius

You are the great-grandson of a consul, and in the male line too—although that has little to do with the case before us; I say, then, you are descended from a poet, to whom his literary glory would have brought status had not his magisterial glories done so . . . and the culture of his successors has not declined one whit from his standard, particularly in this respect. I am therefore inexpressibly amazed that you have quickly acquired a knowledge of the German tongue with such ease.

And yet I remember that your boyhood had a good schooling in liberal studies and I know for certain that you often declaimed with spirit and eloquence before your professor of oratory. This being so, I should like you to tell me how you managed to absorb so swiftly into your inner being the exact sounds of an alien race, so that now after reading Virgil under the schoolmaster's cane and toiling and working the rich fluency of [Cicero] . . . you burst forth before my eyes like a young falcon from an old nest.

You have no idea what amusement it gives me, and others too, when I hear that in your presence the barbarian is afraid to perpetrate a barbarism in his own language. The bent elders of the Germans are astounded at you when you translate letters, and they adopt you as umpire and arbitrator in their mutual dealings. . . . And although these people are stiff and uncouth in body and mind alike, they welcome in you, and learn from you, their native speech combined with Roman wisdom.

Only one thing remains, most clever of men: continue with undiminished zeal, even in your hours of ease, to devote some attention to reading; and, like the man of refinement that you are, observe a just balance between the two languages: retain your grasp of Latin, lest you be laughed at, and practice the other, in order to have the laugh of them. Farewell.

Source: From *Sidonius: Volume II—Letters*, Loeb Classical Library, vol. 420, pp. 127–29, 181–83, Cambridge, MA: Harvard University Press.

Questions for Analysis

1. For what qualities does Sidonius praise Arbogastes? What might have been the motive behind his extravagant compliments?

2. For what different qualities does Sidonius praise Syagrius? Given that Syagrius controlled much of the former Roman province of northern Gaul, what would have been his reasons for learning the local language?

and Latin texts on which we rely for our study of Western civilizations survived because they were copied in monasteries.

Monasteries also developed and disseminated an important new information technology: the codex. For millennia, the standard book had been a scroll, a clumsy format that made searching for a particular passage difficult and confined the reader to one passage at a time. The codex facilitates indexing (from the Latin word for "pointing finger") because a reader can flip back and forth among various pages, with a finger in one place while looking at another. Codices also store information more safely and efficiently because they compress many hundreds of pages within protective bindings. They are less wasteful, too, because texts can be copied on both sides of a page. They even make finding a given book easier because titles can be written on the codex's spine. It's arguable, in fact, that the invention of the codex was more revolutionary than the invention of printing a thousand years later. Unless you are scrolling through a digital version of this book, your copy of *Western Civilizations* is a codex.

Conclusion

Since the English historian Edward Gibbon published the first volume of *The Decline and Fall of the Roman Empire* in 1776—a year when Britain's own empire suffered a notable setback—more has been written about the "fall of Rome" than on the passing of any other civilization. Gibbon himself blamed Christianity, depicting it as a debilitating disease that sapped the empire's strength. Others have accused the barbarians whose movements put pressure on Rome's frontiers. But even in the time of Julius Caesar, Roman moralists had already declared that Rome was in decline. Indeed, any self-respecting Roman republican would say that Rome fell when Augustus came to power.

More recent scholarship has argued that *transformation* is a more accurate way of understanding this period. No civilization is static and unchanging; human civilizations, like human beings, are living organisms. Therefore, any evidence of

AFTER YOU READ THIS CHAPTER

CHRONOLOGY

c. 4 B.C.E.–c. 30 C.E.	Lifetime of Jesus
46–67 C.E.	Paul's missionary career
66–70 C.E.	Jewish rebellion
132–135	Expulsion of Jews from Jerusalem
203	Death of Perpetua at Carthage
235–284	Rule of the "barracks emperors"
284–305	Diocletian divides the empire
312	Constantine's victory at the Milvian Bridge
313	Edict of Milan
325	Council of Nicaea convened
c. 370–430	Careers of Jerome, Ambrose, and Augustine
c. 376	Frontier migrations begin
391	Pagan religion outlawed
410	Goths sack Rome
476	Odovacar deposes Romulus Augustulus
493–526	Rule of Theodoric the Ostrogoth
c. 500–583	Careers of Boethius, Benedict, and Cassiodorus

REVIEWING THE OBJECTIVES

› A number of historical factors shaped the way Jesus' teachings were received. Describe the most important of these factors.

› The expansion of Rome and the strain on its central government posed significant challenges in the third century. How did Roman emperors respond?

› Christianity's legalization changed it in profound ways. Why was this?

› During the fourth and fifth centuries, a new wave of migrations penetrated to the very heart of the empire. What made this possible?

› The differences between traditional Roman and Christian cultures were gradually reconciled through the efforts of Christian intellectuals. Why was this considered necessary?

Rome's decline can also be read as evidence of adaptability. The imperial policies of Septimius Severus and Diocletian were responses to the realities of Rome's size and diversity. The settlement of frontier peoples in Rome's western provinces gave rise to hybrid polities that found new uses for Roman buildings, political offices, and laws. Through Christianity, the Latin language, administrative structures, and culture of ancient Rome were preserved and extended. The flexibility of the Roman political system made this possible, because it was inclusive to a degree no modern empire has ever matched.

Still, this transformation changed what it meant to be Roman, to the extent that historians now call this period "late antiquity" to distinguish it from the classical world that preceded it. By the seventh century, so much had changed that the contours of three distinctive civilizations can be discerned, each one exhibiting different aspects of Roman influence and crystallizing around different regions of the former empire. We will explore each of these civilizations in Chapter 7.

 Go to **INQUIZITIVE** to see what you've learned—and learn what you have missed—with personalized feedback along the way.

PEOPLE, IDEAS, AND EVENTS IN CONTEXT

❯ What were the main differences between **JESUS** and other Jewish leaders of his day?

❯ How did **PAUL OF TARSUS** reach out to the peoples of the Hellenistic world? How did his teachings influence the development of early Christianity?

❯ In what ways did **DIOCLETIAN**'s division of the empire and his institution of the **TETRARCHY** respond to longstanding problems?

❯ How and why was Christianity changed under **CONSTANTINE**? What effects did this have on attitudes toward women and their role in the church?

❯ How did the relocation of the imperial capital to **CONSTANTINOPLE** contribute to the growing divide between the **EASTERN** and **WESTERN ROMAN EMPIRE**? How did the mass migrations of frontier peoples transform the Latin West?

❯ What were the key contributions of **JEROME**, **AMBROSE**, and **AUGUSTINE** to the development of a specifically Christian outlook by the end of the fourth century C.E.?

❯ How did **BOETHIUS**, **BENEDICT**, and **CASSIODORUS** reshape classical culture in the fifth century C.E.?

THINKING ABOUT CONNECTIONS

❯ In your opinion, which phenomenon had a more profound impact on Rome: the overextension of imperial power, or the mass migration of peoples from Rome's frontier? Why?

❯ Few historians would now agree with the judgment of Edward Gibbon, who posited that Christianity destroyed the Roman Empire. But to what extent did Christianity alter the traditional values and infrastructure of the Roman state? Were these alterations inevitable? Why or why not?

7

Rome's Three Heirs, 500–950

AROUND THE YEAR 600, Anglo-Saxon tribes on the island of Britain were approached by missionaries sent from Rome. These Latin-speaking evangelists had to find a way to translate the central ideas of their Christian faith in ways that made sense in a new cultural context. They also needed to meld Roman practices with pagan ones. An account of these negotiations comes down to us in *The History of the English Church and People*, written by a monk named Bede (c. 672–735) several generations later. It describes how Celtic and Anglo-Saxon peoples were uneasily united under the Roman Church and how, in the process, Roman Christian ideals were changed and adapted to meet the needs of new converts.

This is just one example of how Rome's legacy was transmitted and transformed during an era known as the Middle Ages. This term is a problematic one for a pivotal, thousand-year period because it is a modern invention. In the seventeenth century, intellectuals began to argue that an intermediate "middle era" (*medium ævum*) separated their own "modern age" from classical Greece and ancient Rome, which many European states were trying to emulate. And yet the period between 500 and 1500 was actually the beginning of that "modern age," when three new civilizations became heirs of the Roman Empire: the new Rome of Byzantium; the Arabic empire, which promoted Islam; and the western European territories which looked to the Roman Church for leadership. Each of these interlocking cultures preserved and modified different aspects of their shared inheritance, and our world is still being shaped by the interactions among them.

BEFORE YOU READ THIS CHAPTER

› Emperor Justinian's attempt to reconquer the western territories of the Roman Empire was ultimately more destructive than the mass migrations of the previous centuries.

› The culture of the eastern Roman Empire (Byzantium) combined Roman legal and political systems with the learning of classical Greece but was most acutely shaped by Orthodox Christianity.

› Meanwhile, the rapid expansion of Islam was driven by the close connections among religious fervor, military conquest, and commercial opportunity.

› In western Europe, the disintegration of Roman political and economic infrastructures had a destabilizing effect, but this was countered by the success of the Frankish kingdom and the spread of monasticism.

› The empire of Charlemagne unified vast portions of northwestern Europe under a single centralized government, fostering important administrative, economic, and cultural developments.

CORE OBJECTIVES

› **DEFINE** the distinctive features of Byzantine culture.

› **EXPLAIN** the reasons for the rapid success of the Arab conquests and Islam's expansion.

› **DESCRIBE** the relationship between monasticism and secular power in early medieval Europe.

› **UNDERSTAND** the importance of the Carolingian Empire's role in stabilizing Western Europe after the fragmentation of Rome.

› **COMPARE** the cultures of the Roman Empire's "three heirs" and decide which (in your view) was the most important.

Justinian's Imperial Ambitions

As we observed in Chapter 6, the eastern and western territories of Rome's empire were becoming divided along linguistic, cultural, and economic lines; by the end of the fourth century, this division became political. The Ostrogothic kingdom of Italy under Theodoric (r. 493–526), supported by the imperial government, briefly enabled Constantinople to reestablish Roman rule in some regions of Italy and Gaul. But none of Theodoric's short-lived successors was able to rule this territory effectively and, in 535, the kingdom was overthrown in an attempt to reunify the entire Roman Empire.

The man responsible was Justinian (r. 527–565), the most ambitious emperor since Constantine and the last to come from a Latin-speaking province: Dardania (now Serbia). Although his efforts ultimately failed, they had a lasting influence on the entire Mediterranean world.

JUSTINIAN'S ATTEMPTED RECONQUEST

Justinian's initial efforts seemed successful. In 533, his general, Belisarius, conquered the Vandal kingdom of northwest Africa and led campaigns in Ostrogothic Italy and Visigothic Spain. By 536, he was poised to occupy Rome's old homeland, where he was welcomed as a savior. But these early victories were illusory: Belisarius's army was overextended, and Justinian's need to levy soldiers led to oppressive taxes on vitally important regions such as Egypt and Syria, undermining support for his imperial project. The Romans of Italy and North Africa, meanwhile, resented the costs of their own "liberation." When imperial armies were withdrawn from these regions to face the growing threat of Persia, North Africa was ripe for later conquest by the Arabs (see page 230).

PERSIA AND THE RISE OF RABBINIC JUDAISM

Although the Sassanid dynasty of Persia had long been Rome's rival, it had continued to expand its reach during the time when Rome's armies were contending with internal crises. And it was in Persia that many Palestinian Jews had found a home after the Romans' destruction of the Second Temple in Jerusalem (Chapter 6), where they joined older Jewish communities that had remained in Babylon since the conquests of Cyrus (Chapter 2). Here, a group of powerful *rabbis* (teachers) had kept Judaism flourishing, establishing schools (*yeshivas*) for the study of the Torah and presiding over the codification of the Talmud: writings that preserved and interpreted centuries of oral teachings. This new phase of Judaism's development is accordingly known as Rabbinic Judaism, and it influenced the establishment of similar schools in Jewish communities throughout the medieval world.

THE JUSTINIANIC PLAGUE

In addition to the challenge posed by Persia, Justinian's failed reconquest of Roman territories was complicated by a pandemic that broke out in 541–542. Known as the Justinianic Plague, recent findings by epidemiologists and geneticists have found that it was caused by a strain of the same virus that later caused the Black Death of the fourteenth century (see Chapter 10). Stretching from China (where

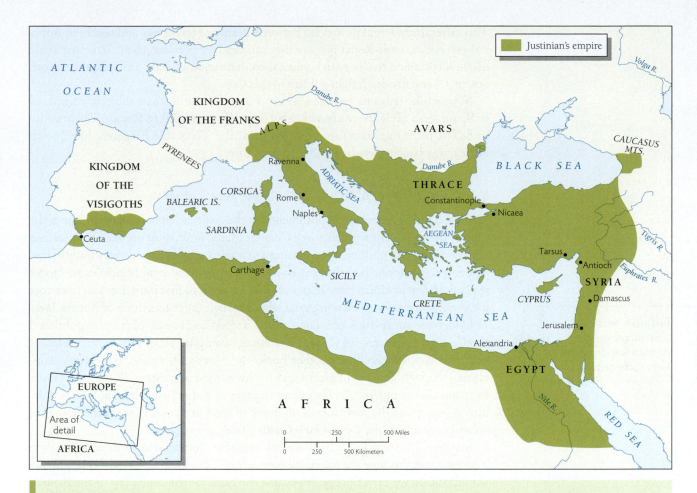

THE MEDITERRANEAN WORLD UNDER JUSTINIAN, 527–565. Compare this map with the one on page 196. Here, the green shading represents those regions controlled by Justinian. › What was the geographical extent of Justinian's empire? › Which areas of the former Roman Empire did Justinian not attempt to reconquer? › What may have been the strategy behind these campaigns?

it originated) to Scandinavia and into Africa and the Indian Ocean, it is estimated to have killed a large percentage of the world's population (some 25 million people). And it recurred in some places for the next two hundred years. Ironically, it spread so rapidly and so far because of the very efficient infrastructures—roads, bridges, and trading networks—that bound the Roman Empire together and linked it to its neighbors.

JUSTINIAN'S IMPACT ON THE WESTERN ROMAN EMPIRE

Justinian's wars proved more devastating than the previous incursions of barbarian peoples. Around Rome, the elaborate system of aqueducts, drainage ditches, and reservoirs was destroyed. Parts of the Italian countryside returned to marshland, and were not drained again until the twentieth century. In 568, a new group of migrants known as the Lombards began to settle the northern third of the peninsula.

Thereafter, Italy would be divided between Lombard territories and southern imperial territories, with Rome precariously sandwiched between them. This tripartite division remained the essential political configuration of Italy until the nineteenth century—and divides Italian politics to this day.

Meanwhile, tensions between Arian Visigoths and Roman subjects continued in Spain, even after the Visigothic king officially converted to Roman Christianity in 587. This mutual hostility persisted until the Visigothic kingdom, like North Africa, was largely absorbed under Islamic rule.

THE CODIFICATION OF ROMAN LAW

Justinian's most positive accomplishment was the codification of Roman law. Since the time of the third-century jurists (see Chapter 5), the number of imperial statutes and legal decisions had multiplied, producing a massive and self-contradictory body of law. Moreover, conditions had changed so radically that many legal principles no longer applied. When Justinian came to power in 527, one of his first initiatives was to restore the prestige and power of the imperial office through the rejuvenation of Roman law.

Justinian uses centralization of Roman law to revive imperial prestige

Under the supervision of a jurist called Tribonian, a team of lawyers published the Codex Justinianus, or Code, a systematic compilation of imperial statutes. It was then supplemented by another book, the Novels (*Novellae*, "new laws"), containing the legislation of Justinian and his immediate successors. A few years later, the team also completed the Digest, a summary of Rome's great legal authorities. Its final product was the Institutes, a textbook of legal principles. Together, these four volumes constitute the **Corpus Juris Civilis** ("body of civil law").

Justinian's *Corpus* was a brilliant achievement. In the eastern Roman Empire, it immediately became the foundation on which all subsequent legal developments would rest. In western Europe, it became the basis for the canon law of the Roman Church. Eventually, it influenced the legal systems of most European states and their American colonies. The *Corpus* also had a profound impact on political thought. Its maxim, that "what pleases the prince has the force of law," granted unlimited powers to the emperor and was later adopted by early modern rulers as a foundation for absolutism (see Chapter 15). But the *Corpus* also provided support for constitutional forms of government because it maintained that a sovereign's powers are delegated to him by the people, and that what is mandated by the people can also be taken away by them. Equally important is the fundamental principle that the state is a corporate body, not the extension of an individual's private property. The modern conception of the state as a public entity derives from the *Corpus*.

Justinian's *Corpus Juris Civilis* A systematic compilation of imperial statutes, legal writings and principles, and legislation that would form the basis of the legal system of the eastern Roman Empire and the Roman Church.

Byzantium Modern historians use this name to describe the eastern Roman Empire, which lasted in this region until 1453, though its inhabitants referred to themselves as Romans.

The Roman Empire of Byzantium

With the failure of Justinian's project of imperial reunification, the history of the eastern Roman Empire enters a new phase. Indeed, many historians regard it as a new entity, the Byzantine Empire, a name derived from the ancient port where Constantinople was situated. **Byzantium** thus became *one* of Rome's three heirs, not the sole heir of Roman authority, as Justinian had hoped. Yet according to its citizens, it never ceased to be Rome, and they were never anything but Romans who carried forward Roman traditions, values, and institutions.

As a result of Justinian's wars and outside pressures, however, this Rome was struggling for survival. By 610, the imperial dynasty that began with Heraclius (r. 610–641) was unable to extend its influence much farther west than the Adriatic. Meanwhile, the Persians had conquered almost all of the empire's eastern and southern territories in Syria and Palestine. They had even plundered Jerusalem. With an enormous effort, Heraclius rallied his remaining military powers and routed the Persians, recapturing Jerusalem in 627.

But these gains were short-lived. Arab armies, inspired by the new faith of Islam, profited from the empire's exhaustion. They soon occupied the recently reconquered Byzantine territories and claimed Jerusalem as a holy site for Muslims, as well as for Jews and Christians. They also absorbed the entire Persian Empire and rapidly made their way westward to Roman North Africa. They then took to the sea and, in 677, attempted a naval conquest of Constantinople. Repulsed with difficulty, they made another attempt in 717 by means of a concerted land and sea operation.

This new threat was countered by the emperor Leo III (r. 717–741), whose forces were able to defeat the Arabs by deploying a secret inflammatory mixture of chemicals that produced "Greek fire." Over the next few decades, his successors reconquered most of Anatolia, which remained the imperial heartland.

SOURCES OF STABILITY

In many ways, the internal politics of Byzantium were as challenging as its enemies. Because all power was concentrated in the imperial court at Constantinople, opposition to imperial authority could take the form of intrigue, treason, and violent plots: the very word *byzantine* has come to denote devious machinations or elaborate systems of bureaucracy. However, many able rulers wielded their powers very effectively through a strong, centralized government that continued to function even in times of upheaval. No western European state had anything resembling such effective mechanisms of government until a much later period.

Enduring political institutions thus constituted a major source of stability and sustained the extraordinary longevity of the empire's core provinces for nearly a thousand years. The imperial government oversaw the army and navy, the courts, and the diplomatic service, endowing these agencies with organizational strengths incomparable for their time. The imperial bureaucracy regulated prices and wages, maintained systems of licensing, and controlled exports and trade. Its educated officials also supervised many aspects of social and cultural life, including schools, the organization of the Orthodox Church, and the observance of religious rites. Even the popular sport of chariot racing was strictly regulated, as were the various teams' fiercely competitive fans.

Constantinople emerges as key trading link between Asia and western Europe >

Another source of stability was a well-integrated and sophisticated economy. Commerce and cities continued to flourish as they had done in late antiquity, which was not the case in western Europe at this time. Constantinople became a central emporium for eastern luxury goods and also nurtured and protected its own industries, most notably the manufacture and weaving of silk. According to legend, silkworms and the knowledge of cultivating them had been brought illegally to western Asia from China, where the industry was a carefully guarded secret among the women who dominated it—and who continued to do so in Byzantium.

Moreover, Constantinople was not Byzantium's only great urban center. The Hellenistic capital of Antioch and the bustling cities of Thessalonica and Trebizond were also large and prosperous when Paris was a village and Rome itself had only a few thousand people living among the ruins. In such cities, trade and industry produced most of the surplus wealth that sustained the state. But agriculture also lay at the heart of the Byzantine economy, and peasant farmers often struggled to maintain their independence from the large estates owned by wealthy aristocrats and monasteries. When these large landholders eventually gained control, during the eleventh century, many free peasants were transformed into impoverished tenant farmers, as had been the case in Italy during the third century C.E. This was one of the less positive ways in which the new Rome resembled its predecessor.

ORTHODOXY AND ICONOCLASM

Law, strong governance, and a thriving economy were the basis of Byzantine culture, but the identity of the eastern Roman Empire was also shaped by a passionate commitment to **Orthodox** Christianity, whose stakes were further heightened because emperors took an active role in doctrinal decisions and disputes.

The most contentious issue, and one that came to a head in the eighth century, was a violent and very public disagreement over the meaning and use of religious images, known as the **Iconoclast** ("image-breaking") **Controversy**. As we saw in Chapter 6, Christians had been accustomed to expressing their devotion to Christ and the saints through the veneration of images. There was even a legend that the author of Luke's Gospel had been a painter. However, some Christians argued that any representation of a holy person was a form of idolatry, something strongly condemned in the Jewish tradition that Christianity had inherited. Although both Roman and Orthodox theologians insisted that images were only *aids* to worship, not *objects* of worship, this fine line was easily crossed.

In Byzantium, the veneration of icons was an especially potent part of daily devotion. Any suggestion that such images should be suppressed or destroyed was therefore bound to be contentious—and that is precisely what the iconoclast movement advocated, arguing that honoring images was blasphemous. For their part, traditionalists argued that the images were windows through which a glimpse of heaven might be granted to human beings on earth.

Orthodox Refers to an adherence to traditional or conservative practice as it related to doctrinal decisions and disputes in the eastern Roman Empire.

Iconoclast Controversy A serious theological debate that raged in Byzantium after Emperor Leo III ordered the destruction of religious art on the grounds that any image representing a divine personage was blasphemous. Iconoclast means "breaker of icons."

The iconoclast movement initially triumphed through the support of Emperor Leo III, whose leadership had helped to save Constantinople from Arab invasion. By proclaiming a radical new religious doctrine, the emperor hoped to renew and strengthen control over the Orthodox Church and to combat the growing power of monasteries, which were the major producers of icons. When the monasteries rallied to the cause of images, they were strongly suppressed by Leo and his successors, who took this opportunity to confiscate much of their wealth.

THE LEGACY OF ICONOCLASM

The Iconoclast Controversy was resolved in favor of those who promoted religious imagery, the Iconodules ("image servants"). But it had many long-lasting effects. One was the destruction of many artworks produced or preserved in the eastern Roman Empire, which means that examples of Christian artistry from the first eight centuries after Jesus' death are preserved mainly in Italy, Palestine, Egypt, and Ethiopia—beyond the reach of iconoclastic emperors. A second consequence was the widening of the religious and political breach between the Greek East and the Latin West. Prior to Emperor Leo's iconoclastic initiatives, the patriarch of Rome—known as *"papa"* in Latin slang—had been a close ally of Byzantium's rulers. But iconoclasm called into question not only the veneration of images but also the veneration of the saints and, by extension, the Roman patriarch's claim to be Saint Peter's successor (see Chapter 6). This was not a position that the Roman *papa* (pope) could support.

The ultimate defeat of iconoclasm crystallized some aspects of belief and practice that came to be characteristic of Byzantium. One was a renewed emphasis on the Orthodox faith of the empire as the key to political unity and military success. This subsequently enforced the hegemony of Constantinople's own Christian traditions, marginalizing those of Syria and Armenia. Fear of heresy also tended to inhibit freedom of expression, and not just in religious matters.

DEVOTIONAL IMAGE—OR DANGEROUS IDOL?
This icon of the Virgin Mary, "the God-Bearer" (Theotokos), was painted in the sixth century and is one of the oldest such images in existence. Preserved at the Orthodox monastery of St. Catherine on Mount Sinai (Egypt), it shows the mother and child flanked by two warrior saints and protected by angels gazing upward at the hand of God emerging from heaven.
› How might such icons inspire devotion and shape viewers' ideas of femininity and motherhood? According to the proponents of iconoclasm, why would such an image be considered blasphemous?

TRADITION AND INNOVATION IN BYZANTIUM

Orthodox religion was central to the identity of Byzantine Romans, but so was their direct link with the Hellenistic past and heritage of ancient Greece. Byzantine schools based their instruction on classical Greek literature, in marked contrast to the more tentative attitude toward classical learning in western Europe (see Chapter 6). Educated men and women around the Byzantine court who quoted only a single line of Homer

Debating the Power of Icons

The Iconoclast Controversy of the eighth century divided Byzantine society and was a factor in the growing division between the Latin Church of Rome and the Greek Orthodox Church. The excerpts below are representative of the two main arguments voiced at the time. The first is from a treatise by John of Damascus (c. 675–749), a Christian in the service of the Muslim Umayyad caliphs. The second is an official report issued from the synod convened by the emperor Constantine V (r. 741–775) in 754. Constantine was carrying forward the iconoclastic policies of his father, Leo III.

John of Damascus on Holy Images

Our adversaries, the iconoclasts, say: "God's commands to Moses the law-giver were clear: 'Thou shalt adore the Lord thy God, and thou shalt worship him alone, and thou shalt not make any images of anything in the heaven above or in the earth beneath.'" But these laws were given to the Jews because they were apt to fall into idolatry. We, on the contrary, are no longer in need of such childish rules. We have grown up out of infancy and have reached the perfection of adulthood. We know how to distinguish between an image and something real or divine.

An image is only a likeness of the original and is therefore different from that original. It is not and cannot be an exact reproduction of the original. In just the same way, we know that Jesus Christ is the living, substantial, unchangeable Image of the invisible God: a Son equal to the Father in all things, but differing from Him because a Son is begotten of a Father. They are not the same. We can compare this divine example to a human one: a man who wishes to build a house first thinks and makes out a plan. The plan is an image of the house he will build, but it is not the same as the house. In the same way, things visible on earth are images of invisible and intangible things that we cannot see—but which help us to imagine the divine things in which we believe. Holy Scripture is itself an image of God, setting before us, in the imagery of words, the truths of God's justice and creation. It shows us what is otherwise unknowable, untouchable, making divine things imaginable and understandable. All the invisible workings of God since the creation of the world are made visible through images. We experience images of His creation which remind us of God, as when we admire the sun or a light, or feel burning rays, or drink from a running fountain or hear a full river, or see a rose tree or a sprouting flower, or smell a sweet fragrance.

Source: Excerpted and adapted from *St. John Damascene on Holy Images*, trans. Mary H. Allies (London: 1898), pp. 6–12.

could expect their listeners to recognize the entire passage from which it came. In the English-speaking world, only the King James Bible has ever achieved the same degree of cultural saturation. Indeed, Homeric epics were a kind of sacred text in Byzantium, as were the surviving tragedies of Athenian dramatists of the fifth century B.C.E.

Byzantine scholars also studied the philosophy of Plato and the historical prose of Thucydides. In contrast, Aristotle's works were less well known, and many other philosophical traditions of antiquity were deemed dangerous. Although Justinian had presided zealously over the codification of ancient Roman (and thus pagan) law, he registered his distrust of Greek (pagan) philosophy by shutting down the Athenian academies that had existed since Plato's day. The practice of Greek scientific inquiry and the advances of Hellenistic science were also neglected. Tradition

Canons of the Synod of 754

It is the unanimous doctrine of all the holy Fathers and of the six Ecumenical Synods, that no one may imagine any kind of separation or mingling in opposition to the unsearchable, unspeakable, and incomprehensible union of the two natures in the one *hypostasis* or person. What avails, then, the folly of the painter, who from sinful love of gain depicts that which should not be depicted—that is, with his polluted hands he tries to fashion that which should only be believed in the heart and confessed with the mouth? He makes an image and calls it Christ. The name *Christ* signifies *God and man.* Consequently it is an image of God and man, and consequently he has in his foolish mind, in his representation of the created flesh, depicted the Godhead which cannot be represented, and thus mingled what should not be mingled. Thus he is guilty of a double blasphemy—the one in making an image of the Godhead, and the other by mingling the Godhead and manhood . . . like the Monophysites, or he represents the body of Christ as not made divine and separate and as a person apart, like the Nestorians.

The only admissible figure of the humanity of Christ, however, is bread and wine in the holy Supper. This and no other form, this and no other type, has he chosen to represent his incarnation. Bread he ordered to be brought, but not a representation of the human form, so that idolatry might not arise. And as the body of Christ is made divine, so also this figure of the body of Christ, the bread, is made divine by the descent of the Holy Spirit; it becomes the divine body of Christ by the mediation of the priest who, separating the oblation from that which is common, sanctifies it.

Source: Excerpted from *The Seven Ecumenical Councils of the Undivided Church*, trans. H. R. Percival, in *Nicene and Post-Nicene Fathers*, 2nd Series, ed. P. Schaff and H. Wace (repr. Grand Rapids, MI: 1955), pp. 543–44.

Questions for Analysis

1. With what other things does John of Damascus compare the making of images? How do these comparisons help him make his argument in favor of them?

2. With what phenomena do the theologians of the synod compare the making of images? Why do they declare the bread and wine of the Eucharist to be the only legitimate representations of Christ?

3. What is the significance of the fact that John of Damascus did not live under the jurisdiction of the Byzantine emperor, but that of the Muslim Umayyad caliph? How might that have influenced his writing?

was more highly prized than originality, preservation over innovation. The benefit of this, for posterity, is that Byzantium rescued Greek and Hellenistic writings for later ages. The vast majority of ancient Greek texts known today survive only because they were copied by Byzantine scribes.

In further contrast to western Europe, as we shall see, the Byzantine educational system was inclusive, open to the laity and even to women. Although most girls from aristocratic or prosperous families were educated at home by private tutors, they nevertheless mingled with their male counterparts on social occasions, and many female intellectuals were praised for their erudition. There were even female physicians, another extraordinary departure from both ancient tradition and the practices of western Europe until the latter part of the nineteenth century.

BYZANTINE ART AND ARCHITECTURE

Byzantine achievements in the realms of architecture and art are exemplified by the church of Hagia Sophia ("Holy Wisdom") in Constantinople, constructed under the patronage of Justinian. Its purpose was not to express pride in human accomplishment but rather to symbolize the mysteries of the Christian faith and the holy knowledge imparted by Christ to the soul of the believer. For this reason, the architects paid little attention to the external appearance of the building. The interior, however, was decorated with rich mosaics, gold leaf, colored marble columns, and bits of tinted glass set on edge to refract rays of sunlight like sparkling gems. The magnificent dome over its central square was an unprecedented engineering feat, upheld by four great arches springing from pillars at the four corners of the square. The result was an architectural framework both marvelously strong and delicate. Its effect is heightened by the many windows placed around the dome's rim, which convey the impression that it floats in midair.

Many aspects of Byzantine arts and learning exerted strong influence on the artisans and scholars of western Europe through continued economic and cultural contact. St. Mark's Basilica in Venice (c. 1063) reflects this influence distinctly, as do medieval mosaics in such cities as Ravenna and Palermo. Greek-speaking monasteries in southeastern Italy maintained especially close ties with their counterparts in the eastern empire, and many were allowed to practice the rituals of the Orthodox Church; many Greek books, including the comedies of Aristophanes (Chapter 4), were copied and preserved there. Yet much of the heritage of Western civilizations that was cultivated in Byzantium was largely inaccessible elsewhere in Europe, because the knowledge of Greek became increasingly rare.

HAGIA SOPHIA. This great monument to the artistry, engineering skill, and spirituality of Byzantium was built during the reign of Justinian. The four minarets at its corners were added in 1453, after Constantinople (now Istanbul) was absorbed into the empire of the Ottoman Turks. Hagia Sophia is now a mosque and a museum.

Muhammad and the Teachings of Islam

The civilization that formed around the religion of Islam mirrors the Roman Empire in its global reach and longevity. Islam (Arabic for "submission") also calls to mind the early republic of Rome in that it demands loyalty—not just to common forms of worship, but also to certain social and cultural norms. But whereas the Roman Empire came to undergird Christianity, elevating it to the status of a major faith, the Muslim faith was itself an engine of imperial expansion.

THE REVELATIONS OF MUHAMMAD

Islam emerged in Arabia, a desert land so forbidding that neither the Romans nor the Persians had sought to conquer it. Arabian society did not revolve around urban settlements; most Arabs were tribal herdsmen, living off the milk of their camels and the produce of desert oases. But their very mobility, ingenuity, and pioneering spirit also made them daring explorers and long-distance traders. In the second half of the sixth century, when protracted wars between Byzantium and Persia made travel dangerous for merchants, Arabs established themselves as the couriers and guardians of transit routes between Africa and Asia.

As part of this process, towns began to emerge. The most prominent was Mecca, an ancient sacred site that lay at the crossroads of major caravan routes. Mecca was home to the Kaaba (*KAH-ah-bah*), a shrine housing the Black Stone venerated by many Arabian tribes. The Quraysh (*kur-AYSH*), the tribe that controlled this shrine, thus came to dominate the economic and religious life of the whole region, forming an aristocracy of traders and entrepreneurs.

Muhammad, the founder of Islam, was a member of this tribe. He was born in Mecca about 570. Orphaned early in life, he entered the service of a wealthy widow and successful merchant named Khadija, whom he married. She would be his closest confidant, first follower, and energetic proponent of his teachings.

At this time, the Arab tribes worshiped many gods. Yet, like the ancient Hebrews, they also acknowledged one god as more powerful. For the Hebrews, God was called Yahweh; for the Arabs, Allah. But whereas the Hebrews' embrace of monotheism was a long and gradual process, Muhammad's conversion was sudden: the immediate consequence of a revelation he experienced around 610. Thereafter, Muhammad received further revelations that persuaded him to accept the calling of a prophet and to proclaim the new faith of submission—Islam—to Allah alone.

THE BEGINNINGS OF ISLAM

But Muhammad was not immediately successful in gaining converts. In Mecca, leaders of the Quraysh feared that his teachings would diminish the importance of the Kaaba. The town of Yathrib, however, saw an opportunity to increase its prestige by inviting Muhammad to live there and to serve as judge and arbiter in local rivalries. Muhammad, mourning the recent death of Khadija, accepted this invitation in 622, along with a few loyal followers. Because this emigration—in Arabic, the *Hijra* (*HIJ-ruh*)—marks the beginning of Muhammad's wider influence, Muslims regard it as the beginning of time, just as Christians date all events according to the birth of Jesus.

Muhammad changed the name of Yathrib to Madinat an-nabi ("City of the Prophet") and established himself as the town's ruler. He did not, however, abandon his desire

Muhammad The founder of Islam, regarded by his followers as God's last and greatest prophet.

to exercise authority among his own people. He and his followers began a series of military raids on Quraysh caravans traveling beyond Mecca. Their success inspired more men to join Muhammad, but it also inspired further opposition: not only from Mecca, but from Jewish tribes in the region that joined forces with Muhammad's enemies. This led Muhammad to denounce the Jews as faithless to their own prophets and to expel all but one wealthy Jewish clan from Medina and its surrounding region.

In 627, the Quraysh assembled a large coalition force to attack Medina, hoping that the remaining Jews there—who had reason to distrust Muhammad—would join forces with them. In response, Muhammad risked a siege of the city and caused a deep defensive trench to be dug around it, slowing the enemy's advance. The Meccan army had not come equipped for an extended battle and eventually dispersed: an ignominious defeat. And even though the Jews of Medina had not joined forces with the Meccans, Muhammad's followers executed all the men and enslaved the women and children.

By 630, Muhammad's victories had persuaded his kinsmen to submit to his authority and teachings. Muhammad, in turn, ensured that the Kaaba's shrine would be revered as Islam's holiest place: a status it maintains today. And because Mecca had long been a pilgrimage site and gathering place for tribes throughout Arabia, many more people were now exposed to Muhammad's teachings and inspired by his military prowess, which promised prosperity for his people in the years to come. At the time of his death in 632, Muhammad's followers were committed to advancing the cause of Islam.

MUHAMMAD AND THE QUR'AN

Islam calls for submission to Allah, the universal God. (The Muslim saying "there is no god but Allah" is more accurately translated as "there is no god but God.") For Muslims, accordingly, the history and prophecies of the Jews are important components of their religion, as are the teachings of Jesus, who is regarded as a great prophet. But Muhammad is the greatest prophet, whose revelations established the rituals and teachings essential to Islam.

LEAVES FROM THE OLDEST EXTANT COPY OF THE QUR'AN. In 2015, scholars announced that two leaves of a Qur'an manuscript had been carbon dated to the years 568–645 C.E. This extraordinary discovery suggests that at least some of Muhammad's teachings were written down much earlier than had been previously thought— possibly even during his lifetime, and certainly within a decade or so of his death. The implications of this evidence will be debated by Arabic scholars and historians of Islam for years to come.

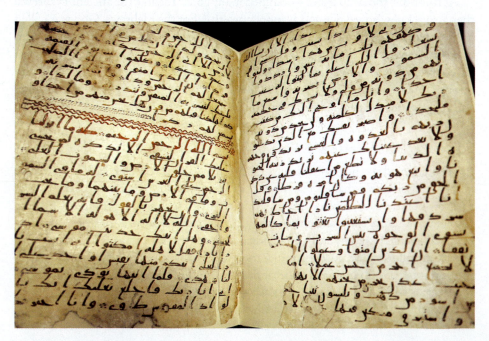

A Sura from the Qur'an

The Qur'an preserves the teachings of Muhammad in a series of suras, or chapters. Composed in verse forms that draw on much older traditions of Arabic poetry, they are meant to be sung or chanted. Indeed, the word Qur'an means "recitations," referring both to Muhammad's method of teaching and the Muslim practice of memorizing and repeating portions of scripture.

Sura 81: The Overturning

In the Name of God the Compassionate the Caring

When the sun is overturned

When the stars fall away

When the mountains are moved

When the ten-month pregnant camels are abandoned

When the beasts of the wild are herded together   5

When the seas are boiled over

When the souls are coupled

When the girl-child buried alive

is asked what she did to deserve murder

When the pages are folded out   10

When the sky is flayed open

When Jahím [the Day of Reckoning] is set ablaze

When the garden is brought near

Then a soul will know what it has prepared

I swear by the stars that slide,   15

stars streaming, stars that sweep along the sky

By the night as it slips away

By the morning when the fragrant air breathes

This is the word of a messenger ennobled,

empowered, ordained before the lord of the throne,   20

holding sway there, keeping trust

Your friend [Muhammad] has not gone mad

He saw him on the horizon clear

He does not hoard for himself the unseen

This is not the word of a satan struck with stones   25

Where are you going?

This is a reminder to all beings

For those who wish to walk straight

Your only will is the will of God lord of all beings   30

Source: From *Approaching the Qur'an: The Early Revelations*, trans. Michael Sells (Ashland, OR: 1999), pp. 48–50.

Questions for Analysis

1. What impressions of Arab culture emerge from this sura? What does the litany of unlikely or mystical events reveal about the values of Muhammad's contemporaries?

2. How does Muhammad speak of himself and his role in society?

These teachings are preserved in the sacred scripture of the **Qur'an** (*kuhr-AHN*), an Arabic word meaning "recitations" because Muhammad delivered his revelations in the form of oral poetry. These recitations were gathered together and transcribed through a process that continued after Muhammad's death. Unlike the Christian Gospels, which offer different perspectives on Jesus' ministry and which were recorded decades after his crucifixion, the Qur'an is considered to be a direct link with Muhammad.

Qur'an Islam's holy scriptures, comprising the prophecies revealed to Muhammad and redacted during his life and after his death.

Islam teaches that a day of judgment is coming—soon. On this day, the righteous will be granted eternal life in a paradise of delights, but wrongdoers will be damned to a realm of eternal fire. Therefore all people are offered a fundamental choice: to begin a new life of divine service or to follow their own paths. If they choose to follow God, they will be blessed; if they do not, God will turn away from them. Thus, the only sure means of achieving salvation is to observe the **Five Pillars** of the faith: submission to God's will as described in the teachings of Muhammad, frequent prayer, ritual fasting, giving alms, and at least one pilgrimage to Mecca (the *Hajj*) during the believer's lifetime.

Unlike Christianity, Islam is a religion without priests. In this, it resembles Rabbinic Judaism as it developed after the destruction of the Second Temple, which made a priesthood obsolete. As we noted previously, Jewish communities throughout the Diaspora gathered around a master teacher, a rabbi. Similarly, Muslims rely on a community leader or *imam*. Like Judaism, Islam also emphasizes the inextricable connection between religious observance and daily life, between spirituality and politics. There is no opposition of sacred and secular authority, as in Christianity. But in marked contrast to Judaism, Islam is a religion that aspires to unite the world in a shared faith. This means that Muslims, like Christians, consider it their duty to engage in missionary work and conversion.

The Widening Islamic World

As we have frequently noted, the death of any charismatic leader precipitates a series of crises. Muhammad and Alexander the Great represent different types of leadership, but both were visionaries whose military and political successes inspired intense loyalty; and neither designated his own successor, leaving behind a number of followers who disagreed as to the proper uses of the power they inherited.

THE ARAB CONQUEST OF THE WEST

Muhammad's closest followers were his father-in-law Abu Bakr (*ah-boo BAHK-uhr*) and an early disciple named Umar. After Muhammad's death, they took the initiative in providing a leader for the Muslims of Arabia by naming Abu Bakr *caliph*, the "deputy" or "representative" of Muhammad. But many tribes were unwilling to accept this aged man as Muhammad's successor, leading to a new phase of warfare. As armies loyal to Abu Bakr moved northward, their successes encouraged even more men to join the fight for Islam. When they came to the Arabian frontier they kept going, meeting only minimal resistance from the weakened Byzantine and Persian forces.

When Abu Bakr died two years later, Umar succeeded him as caliph. In the following years, Muslim victories were virtually continuous: in 636, Arabs routed a Byzantine army in Syria and then occupied the cities of Antioch, Damascus, and Jerusalem. In 637, they destroyed the main army of the Persians and took the capital of Ctesiphon. By 651, the Arabian conquest of Persia was virtually complete.

Arab forces, now increased by newer converts to Islam, then turned toward North Africa, capturing Roman Egypt by 646 and extending their control during the following decades. Only Ethiopia, far to the south, remained an independent Christian kingdom. Although attempts to capture Constantinople were not successful, as we saw previously, Arab and allied Muslim forces crossed from North Africa into Visigothic Spain in 711, quickly absorbing most of the Iberian Peninsula. In less than a century, followers of Islam had conquered the oldest civilizations of western Asia and much of the Roman Mediterranean. In the process, the desert-dwelling Arabs had transformed themselves into daring seafarers.

How can we explain this prodigious achievement? On a basic level, what motivated the Arabs had motivated all migrants before them: the search for richer territory and wealth. The Muslim identity that was bound up with military success also played a crucial role, as did the teachings of Muhammad and the shared study of the Qur'an, which forged common allegiances among many different groups. This Muslim identity must have been further strengthened by the absence of any organized opposition to its advancement: a mark of religious superiority.

Although there is little evidence that Muslims actively converted their new subjects to Islam at this time, they did establish themselves as a ruling class with a grasp of the sophisticated workings of governance and finance that matched their military acumen. This, in itself, would have inspired ambitious men to convert. So did the

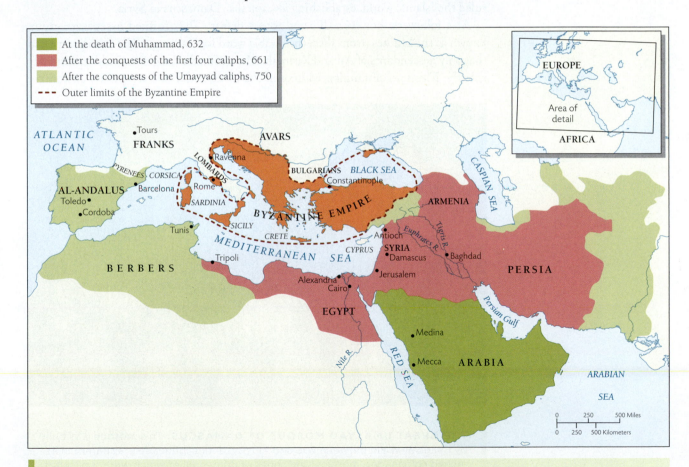

THE EXPANSION OF ISLAM TO 750. This map shows the steady advance of Islam through Arab conquests from the time of Muhammad to the middle of the eighth century. › **What was the geographical extent of Muslim rule in 750?** › **Compare this map to the map of Justinian's empire on page 219. Which of these territories had formerly belonged to Rome? What resources would have been available to the Muslim conquerors as they moved into these territories?**

fact that those living under Muslim rule were expected to pay the taxes that had been due to the previous Persian or Byzantine authorities, as well as a poll tax (*jizya*). In many places, indeed, those conquered by Muslims preferred their rule to that of their Byzantine and Persian predecessors.

THE SHI'ITE-SUNNI SCHISM

As conquest and settlement widened the reach of Islamic influence, disputes continued to divide the original Muslims of Mecca. When the caliph Umar died in 644, he was replaced by Uthman, a member of the Umayyad (*oo-MY-yad*) family: a wealthy clan that had long resisted Muhammad's authority. Opponents of Uthman accordingly rallied around Muhammad's cousin and son-in-law, Ali, whose marriage to Muhammad's only child, Fatimah, made him seem a more appropriate choice. When Uthman was murdered in 656, Ali's supporters declared him the new caliph—but Uthman's powerful family refused to accept him. When Ali, too, was murdered, another member of the Umayyad family replaced him. From 661 to 750, this **Umayyad caliphate** ruled the Islamic world, establishing its capital at Damascus in Syria.

Ali's followers, however, did not accept defeat. They formed a separate group known as the Shi'ites (from *shi'a*, the Arabic word for "faction"). The Shi'ites insisted that only descendants of Ali and Fatimah, Muhammad's daughter, could legitimately rule the Muslim community. Moreover, the Shi'ites did not accept the customary

THE GREAT UMAYYAD MOSQUE OF DAMASCUS. This mosque was built by Caliph al-Walid between 705 and 715. Byzantine influence is apparent in its arched colonnades, mosaics, and series of domes, all of which were replicated in many subsequent examples of Islamic architecture. The mosaic over the central doorway, shown here, indicates that the visitor is entering paradise. The mosque was constructed on the foundations of a Roman temple and also incorporates a later Christian shrine dedicated to Saint John the Baptist. **› Why would the caliph have chosen this site for his mosque?**

religious practices (*sunna*) that had developed under the first two caliphs who had succeeded Muhammad. Hence, those Muslims who supported the Umayyad family and who *did* regard these customs as binding were called Sunnis. This division between Shi'ites and Sunnis has lasted until the present day. Often persecuted by the Sunni majority as heretics, Shi'ites predominate in Iran and are the largest single Muslim group in Iraq, yet they constitute only one-tenth of the world's Muslims.

THE UMAYYAD AND ABBASID DYNASTIES

The political triumph of the Umayyads in 661 and the military conquests of their supporters created a strong state centered on Damascus, formerly an administrative capital of the Roman Empire. And in many ways, the Umayyad caliphate functioned as a Roman successor state: it even continued to employ Greek-speaking bureaucrats trained in the techniques of Roman governance.

Yet the failure of the Umayyads' two massive attacks on Constantinople checked their power, which was also challenged by a rival dynasty: the Abbasids, who claimed descent from one of Muhammad's uncles. In 750, the Abbasids led a successful rebellion, with the help of the Persians, forcing the Umayyads' retreat to al-Andalus (Muslim Spain: see the map on page 243).

In contrast with the Umayyads, the **Abbasid caliphate** stressed Persian elements over Roman ones. Symbolic of this change was the shift in capitals from Damascus to Baghdad, where the second Abbasid caliph, al-Mansur (r. 754–775), built a new city near the ruins of the old Persian capital. The Abbasid caliphs also modeled their rule on that of Persian princes, imposing heavy taxation to support a large professional army and presiding over an extravagant court. This is the world described in the *Arabian Nights*, a collection of stories written in Baghdad and glorifying the caliph Harun al-Rashid, who ruled from 786 to 809. His reign marked the height of Abbasid power.

Meanwhile, the Umayyad dynasty continued to rule in al-Andalus and continued to claim its legitimacy as Muhammad's successor. Relations between the Umayyads of Spain and the Abbasids of Persia were therefore very cold; but the hostility between them rarely erupted into war. Instead, the two courts competed for preeminence through literary and cultural patronage, much as the Hellenistic kingdoms had done. Philosophers, artists, and poets flocked to both. Not to be outdone by their rivals in Baghdad, the caliphate's capital in Córdoba amassed a library of more than four hundred thousand volumes—at a time when any Christian monastery that possessed even a hundred books qualified as a major center of learning.

COMMERCE AND INDUSTRY IN THE ISLAMIC WORLD

The transformation of tiny settlements into thriving metropolitan commercial centers is one of early Islam's most remarkable achievements. So is the Arabs' capacity to build on the long-established commercial infrastructures of Egypt, Syria, and Persia. By the tenth century, Arab merchants had penetrated into southern Russia and equatorial Africa, and had mastered the caravan routes to India and China. Islamic sailors established new trade routes across the Indian Ocean, the Persian Gulf, and the Caspian Sea.

Abbasid caliphate
Claiming to be descendants of Muhammad, the Abbasid family in 750 successfully seized from the Umayyads control of Muslim territories in Arabia, Persia, north Africa, and the Near East. They modeled their rule on that of the Persian Empire.

Arab merchants establish an astonishingly wide trade network

The growth of commerce during this period was driven by a number of important new industries. Mosul in Iraq was a center for the manufacture of cotton cloth; Baghdad specialized in glassware, jewelry, pottery, and silks; Damascus was famous for fine steel and the woven-figured silk known as "damask"; Morocco and al-Andalus were noted for leatherworking; Toledo produced excellent swords. Drugs, perfumes, carpets, tapestries, brocades, satins, metal goods, and a host of other products turned out by skilled artisans were carried throughout the Mediterranean world and into central Asia along the network known as the Silk Road—after the most prized Chinese commodity for which these goods were traded. With these precious goods went the Islamic faith, which took root among some peoples in places that are now India, Pakistan, and Afghanistan.

Arabs and Persians learn papermaking from the Chinese ❭

One commodity deserves special mention: paper. Both Arabs and Persians learned papermaking from the Chinese and became masters of the art. By the end of the eighth century, Baghdad alone had more than a hundred shops where blank paper or books written on paper were sold. Paper was cheaper to produce, easier to store, and far easier to use than papyrus (the chief writing material of antiquity) or parchment (widely used in northern Europe). As a result, it had replaced papyrus in the Islamic world by the early eleventh century—even in Egypt, the heartland of papyrus production for almost four thousand years.

The ready availability of paper brought about a revolution. Many of the characteristic features of Islamic civilization—bureaucratic record keeping, high levels of literacy, even the standard form of cursive Arabic script—were made possible by the widespread availability of paper. Europeans would continue to rely on the more durable parchment, made from animal hides, for the copying of most books and documents. It was not until the advent of print that paper began to replace parchment as the reading and writing material of western Europe (see Chapter 12).

MOBILITY, OPPORTUNITY, AND STATUS

As the reach of Islam was extended, Muslim culture became highly cosmopolitan, blending Arab customs with the civilizations of Byzantium and Persia. The ease of travel increased geographical mobility, and with it social mobility: careers were open to men of talent, regardless of birth or wealth. Because literacy was widespread, many could rise through education and achieve top offices; even slaves could achieve high status through these means. Slave women who bore male children to Muslim men often shared some of the privileges of their legitimate sons.

Meritocracy in Islamic world enabled by literacy, trade, and travel ❭

For those men wishing to embrace a more devout life, Islam offered two main alternatives. One was that of the *alim*, whose studies qualified him to offer advice on aspects of religious law and practice. Complementary to them were the *Sufis*, mystics who practiced contemplation and the cultivation of spiritual ecstasy. Sufis were usually organized into brotherhoods and eventually made many successful efforts to convert the peoples of Africa and India to Islam.

There were no comparable careers for religious women, although there are significant exceptions. Muhammad's favored wife, Aisha (*ah-EE-sha*; d. 678), played an important role in the creation and circulation of the *hadith* (Arabic for "narrative"): stories and sayings that shed light on the Prophet's life and teachings. But in general, women were considered valuable as indicators of a man's wealth and status. The Qur'an allowed any Muslim man to marry as many as four wives, which often meant that the number of women available for marriage was far smaller than the number of men who desired to marry.

This made for intense competition, and men who had wives and daughters needed to ensure that their prized assets were safeguarded. So women were usually kept from the sight of men who were not members of the family or trusted friends. Along with female servants and enslaved concubines, they were housed in a segregated part of the residence called the *haram* ("forbidden place"). Following Persian custom, they were often guarded by eunuchs (men, usually sold as slaves, who had been castrated prior to adolescence). Within these enclaves, women vied with each other for precedence and worked to advance the fortunes of their children—often the only form of power they could exercise.

ISLAM'S NEIGHBORS

The triumph of the Abbasid caliphate in the eighth century released Byzantium from the pressures of Umayyad expansion. Farther west, the Franks of Gaul also benefited from the advent of the Abbasids: because an Umayyad dynasty controlled al-Andalus, the great Frankish ruler Charlemagne (*SHAHR-leh-mayn*; r. 768–814) could counter these neighboring Muslims' power by maintaining strong diplomatic relations with the more distant Abbasid caliphate. A symbol of this connection was an elephant called Abul Abbas, a gift from Harun al-Rashid to Charlemagne.

More important, however, was the flow of silver that found its way from the Abbasid Empire north through the Baltic and into the Rhineland, where it was exchanged for Frankish exports of furs, wax, honey, leather, and especially slaves— Europeans, often Slavic peoples, who were captured and sold for profit by other Europeans. Through these channels, jewels, silks, spices, and other luxury goods from India and the Far East flowed into Frankish territory. These trading links funded the extraordinary achievements of Charlemagne's own empire, which had a lasting effect on the culture and politics of Europe.

The Conversion of Northwestern Europe

In the sixth century, the Frankish chronicler Gregory of Tours (c. 538–594) considered himself a Roman, proud of his family's senatorial rank that gave him (and his male relatives) the right to rule over Roman cities and the surrounding countryside. Like others of his class, Gregory still spoke and wrote Latin. And although he was aware that the western territories of the Roman Empire were now ruled by "barbarian" kings, he regarded at least some of these as Roman successors because they ruled in accordance with Roman models. His own Frankish king even ruled with the approval of the Roman emperor in Constantinople.

Two hundred years later, the greatest of all Frankish kings, Charlemagne (742–814), was crowned as a new kind of Roman emperor in the West. By this time, people no longer felt a sense of direct continuity with the earlier Roman world, or a sense of obligation to the Roman emperor in Byzantium. When intellectuals at Charlemagne's court set out to reform the political, religious, and cultural life of their time, their goal was to revive the Roman Empire from which they considered themselves estranged. They sought a *renovatio imperii Romanorum*: "a renewal of the Romans' empire." This awareness of a break with the Roman past developed during the seventh century as a consequence of profound changes.

ECONOMIC AND POLITICAL INSTABILITY

Even though the economy of the Roman Empire had become increasingly region-alized from the third century C.E. onward (see Chapter 6), the Mediterranean remained a crucial nexus of trade and communication. But in northwestern Europe, the inland cities of Italy, Gaul, and Hispania could no longer maintain their walls, public buildings, and urban infrastructure. Although Christian bishops and their kinsmen still governed from these cities, barbarian kings and their warriors were moving to the countryside, living from the produce of their own estates rather than purchasing their supplies in the marketplace. At the same time, much agricultural land was passing out of cultivation because the slaves or servile peasants who had farmed the large plantations had no Roman state to enforce their obedience. They were able to become more independent, if also less effective, working just a few acres by themselves. Productivity declined, as did revenues from tolls and taxes.

The systems of coinage that circulated in western Europe were also breaking down, which meant that wealth ceased to be readily portable. Gold coins from Muslim lands were too valuable to be useful in a local market economy; when we find evidence of such coins, they are more likely to have been plundered, hoarded, or given as gifts rather than used in commerce. Rulers who were still in a position to mint coins and guarantee their value had shifted from gold to silver. Indeed, Europe would remain a silver-based economy for the next thousand years, until the supply of gold from European conquests in Africa and America once again made a gold standard viable (see Chapter 12).

LORDSHIP AND ITS LIMITATIONS

As a result of these processes, most of Europe came to rely on a two-tier economy. Gold, silver, and luxury goods circulated among the very wealthy, but most people relied on barter to make transactions. Local lords collected rents in food or labor, but they then found it difficult to convert these in-kind payments into the weapons, jewelry, and silks that brought prestige in aristocratic society. This was problematic because the power of lords depended on their ability to bestow rich gifts on their followers (see *Interpreting Visual Evidence* on pages 238–239). When they could not acquire these items through trade, they had to win them through plunder, extortion, and violence.

The successful chieftains of this era tended to be those whose domains adjoined wealthy but poorly defended territories that could easily be attacked or blackmailed. Such "soft frontiers" provided warlords and kings alike with the land and booty their followers demanded, and brought more men to their service; so as long as more conquests were made, the process of amassing power and wealth would continue. But this power was inherently fragile: a few defeats might speedily reverse the fortunes of a warlord, whose men would seek service elsewhere.

It was also difficult to ensure the peaceful transfer of power from one leader to another. The kings who established themselves during the mass migrations of the fifth and sixth centuries faced opposition from many of their own warriors. Moreover, the groups that took possession of territories within the western Roman Empire during these years were rarely (if ever) composed of a single unified group; they were usually made up of many different tribes, including a sizable number of displaced Romans. Unity was largely the creation of a charismatic chieftain, and this charisma was not easily passed on.

THE PROSPEROUS KINGDOM OF THE FRANKS

Of all the European kingdoms that emerged during the fifth and sixth centuries, only the Franks succeeded in establishing a single dynasty from which leaders would be drawn for the next two hundred and fifty years. This dynasty reached back to Clovis (r. c. 481–511), a warrior king who established an alliance between his family and the powerful bishops of Gaul by converting to Roman Christianity—emulating the example of Constantine. Clovis's family came to be known as the **Merovingians**, after his legendary grandfather Merovech. Clovis's own name proved even longer lasting than the dynasty he founded: as the language of the Franks merged with the Latin of Gaul to become French, the name "Clovis" lost its hard C, and the pronunciation of the *v* was softened. Thus "Clovis" became "Louis," the name borne by French kings up to the time of the French Revolution (see Chapter 18).

The Merovingians were not the only family in Gaul with a claim to kingship, but they were more successful than their counterparts because of their capacity to transfer power from one generation to another. In early medieval Europe, the right of inheritance was not limited to the eldest male claimant of each competing royal family. When it came to property or power, all of a king's sons—and frequently all his male cousins and nephews, and even his daughters—could consider themselves rightful heirs. So even when the rule of any family was not threatened by outsiders, the transfer of power was almost always bloody.

The often brutal conflicts between rival Merovingian kings did not, however, disrupt the strength and sophistication of their governance. Many elements of Roman local administration survived and Latin literacy was fostered by a network of monasteries linked to the Frankish court. Indeed, the cultural revival associated with the reign of Charlemagne (see page 244) really began in the late seventh century at these monastic foundations, which became the engines that made Merovingian Gaul wealthier and more stable than any other region of northwestern Europe. Frankish bishops also prospered, along with their cities, amassing vast landed possessions from which their successors would continue to profit.

This massive redistribution and amassing of wealth reflected a fundamental shift in the economic center of gravity of the Frankish kingdom. In the year 600, the wealth of Gaul was still concentrated in the south; by 750, the economic center lay north of the Loire, in the territories that extended from the Rhineland to the North Sea. It was here that most of the new monastic foundations were established.

Behind this shift lay a long effort to bring under cultivation the rich, heavy soils of northern Europe. This effort was largely engineered by the new monasteries, which harnessed the peasant workforce and pioneered agricultural technologies adapted to the climate and terrain. The most important invention was a heavy, wheeled plow capable of cutting and turning grassland sod and clay: soils very different from those of the Mediterranean. This innovation in turn necessitated the development of more efficient devices for harnessing animals (particularly oxen) to these plows. A global warming period (see Chapter 8) also improved the fertility of the wet northern soils, lengthening the growing season and making crop rotation systems possible. As food became more plentiful, the birthrate and health of the population began to improve. All these developments would continue during the reign of Charlemagne, and beyond.

Merovingians A Frankish dynasty that claimed descent from a legendary ancestor called Merovech. They were the only powerful family to establish a lasting kingdom in western Europe during the fifth and sixth centuries.

New plow and livestock tools, amid favorable climate, drive a period of plentiful food and growing population

The Ship Burial of Sutton Hoo

Several of the most impressive finds in the history of British archaeology have been made by amateurs. A recent one, in the summer of 2009, was the largest hoard of worked gold and silver ever found in one place: more than 5 kilograms of gold and 2.5 kilograms of silver (image A). It was discovered by a man in Staffordshire walking over a neighbor's farm with a metal detector. The hoard's extraordinary value and range of artifacts—and their historical implications—can only be guessed at now; even the dating is inconclusive.

Another find, made in 1939, was a royal gravesite dating from the seventh century (image B). Many scholars believe it to be the tomb of King Redwald of East Anglia, described by Bede as a baptized Christian who refused to give up the worship of his ancestral gods. The king's body was placed in a wooden structure in the middle of a ninety-foot-long ship that had been dragged to the top of a bluff (a *hoo*) eleven miles from the English Channel. The ladder in the photograph of the original excavation reaches into the burial chamber.

The contents of the grave are extraordinarily varied and offer clues to values and contacts of the burial's occupant. They included the following items:

- A lamp and a bronze bucket once suspended from a chain

- A ceremonial helmet (image C) modeled on those worn by Roman cavalry officers just before the withdrawal of the legions from Britain in 410—but decorated like helmets found in eastern Sweden

- A sword and a large circular shield, resembling those found in Swedish burial sites

- Exquisitely crafted belt buckles (image D) and shoulder clasps made of gold and garnets and worked with designs

- A pair of silver spoons with long handles, possibly crafted in Byzantium, and inscribed in Greek with the names PAULOS and SAULOS (Paul and Saul)

A. The Staffordshire hoard, found in 2009.

B. The original excavation of the burial chamber at Sutton Hoo, found in 1939.

- A large silver dish (72 cm in diameter) made in Byzantium between 491 and 518

- A bronze bowl from the eastern Mediterranean

- A six-stringed lyre in a bag made of beaver skin, similar to lyres found in Germany

- A purse containing thirty-seven gold coins, each from a different Frankish mint, the most recent datable to the 620s

- Heaps of armor, blankets, cloaks, and other gear

Questions for Analysis

1. What do these artifacts, and the contexts in which they were found, reveal about the extent of Anglo-Saxon contact with the rest of the world? Which regions are represented, and why?

2. From this evidence, what conclusions can you draw about Anglo-Saxon culture and values?

3. Do any of these grave-goods indicate that the occupant was a Christian king? Why or why not?

C. Sutton Hoo helmet.

D. Sutton Hoo buckles.

THE POWER OF MONASTICISM

As we have just seen, the seventh century witnessed a rapid expansion of monastic houses in northwestern Europe. Although monasteries had existed in Gaul, Italy, and Hispania since the fourth century, most were located in highly Romanized areas. In the fifth century, a powerful monastic movement began in Ireland as well, eventually spreading to the Celtic regions of Britain and, from there, to the Continent. The Irish missionary Columbanus (540–615), for example, was the founder of Merovingian monasteries at Luxeuil (France) and Bobbio (Italy). Important Irish monasteries were also established on the island of Iona, off the western coast of Scotland, and at Lindisfarne, off Britain's northeastern coast. In all of these cases, close ties were forged between monks and local leaders or powerful families.

Most of these new monastic foundations were deliberately located in rural areas and at strategic trading crossroads, where they played a crucial role in trade and governance. Indeed, the material advantages of monastic innovation were a powerful incentive toward Christian conversion in the communities that benefited from improved living conditions. Prosperity was also a powerful advertisement for authority: a lord or chieftain who had the support of a monastery and the beneficent Christian God was obviously worthy of loyalty. Because monasteries played such a key role in economic development and political order, lords often granted them special privileges, helping to free them from the control of local bishops and giving them jurisdiction over their own lands. Thus, monasteries became politically powerful lordships in their own right.

Frequently, these new foundations accommodated women as well as men; often, they were established for women only. In either case, they were usually ruled by abbesses drawn from noble or royal families. Monasticism thus became a road to political power for women, too. It also gave women—commoners or queens—freedoms they did not have elsewhere, or at any other time in history up to this point.

> *Monasteries hold more than spiritual importance* ❯

ABBEY CHURCH, ISLAND OF IONA. This tiny island off Scotland's west coast is the site of many Iron Age forts and has been home to a monastic community since the sixth century. Missionaries from Iona were instrumental in converting the Celtic tribes of northern Britain to Christianity.

Within the monastery, women had control over their own minds and bodies. They could wield enormous influence, promoting their families' diplomatic and dynastic interests without the dangers and uncertainties of pregnancy. And they were guaranteed salvation, so that the prayers of holy women were regarded as particularly effective in securing divine support. This further enriched convents through donations of land and wealth, although it could not always safeguard them from violence.

Monasteries for women also served the interests of men, which is why kings and lords supported them. As dynastic repositories they also provided a dignified place of retirement for inconvenient but politically effective women, such as the sisters and daughters of rivals or the widow of a previous ruler. And by limiting the number of powerful women who could reproduce, monasteries also reduced the number of male claimants to power. Establishing aristocratic and royal women in such convents was thus an important way to control successions and manage disputes.

Monasticism played an important role in missionary activity, too. As noted previously, the work of Irish monks was crucial to the spread of Christianity in areas of northern Europe virtually untouched by the Roman Empire. Missionaries were also sponsored by the fledgling papacy in Rome and by the Merovingian royal family—especially its women. The best example of this is the conversion of Britain's Anglo-Saxon tribes, which we glimpsed in the opening paragraph of this chapter. In 597, forty Benedictine monks were sent by Pope Gregory I (r. 590–604) to the southeastern kingdom of Kent, where their efforts were assisted by Frankish translators—and the fact that the local king, Æthelbehrt (*ETH-el-behrt*), had married a Frankish princess who was already a Christian. This pattern of missionary influence, with powerful and pious women working behind the scenes, repeated itself all over southern and eastern Britain.

THE PAPACY OF GREGORY THE GREAT

Pope Gregory I, known as Gregory the Great, was the first bishop of Rome to envision a new role for the papacy. We have seen that the Roman *papa* had often tried to assert his authority over other Christian patriarchs; but in reality, he was subordinate to the emperor in Constantinople and the greater prestige of its patriarch. As Byzantine power in Italy declined, however, Gregory sought to create a more autonomous Latin Church by focusing attention on the taming of the wild West.

An influential theologian, Gregory greatly extended the teachings of earlier Church fathers (Chapter 6) to the world outside the Romanized Mediterranean. He emphasized the necessity of penance for the forgiveness of sins and introduced the concept of Purgatory as a place where the soul could be purified before being admitted into heaven—instead of being sent immediately to perpetual damnation. Gregory also emphasized the importance of pastoral care: the proper instruction and encouragement of laymen and laywomen, and sought to increase the affective power of worship through the performance of music. The very style of liturgical singing that emerged in this period is still known as Gregorian chant.

Gregory was also a statesman in the model of his Roman forebears. He protected Rome from Lombard invaders by clever diplomacy and the expert management of papal estates and revenues. He maintained good relations with Byzantium while asserting his authority over the other bishops of the Roman Church. His support of communities living under the *Rule* of Saint Benedict (see Chapter 6) helped to make **Benedictine monasticism** the predominant monastic force in the West. Yet

Benedictine monasticism
This form of monasticism was developed by Benedict of Nursia. Its followers adhere to a defined cycle of daily prayers, lessons, communal worship, and manual labor.

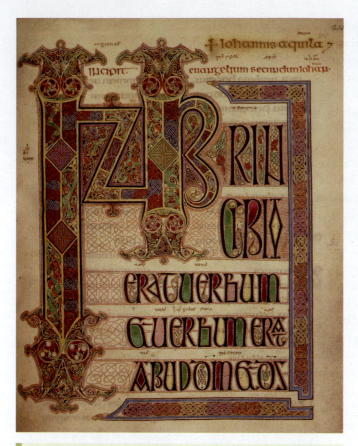

Gregory's influence was not always benign. He was the first prominent theologian to articulate the Church's official policy toward Jews, which became increasingly negative. Building on Gregory's example, later popes would insist that the Jews' alleged role in Christ's crucifixion and their denial of his divinity had deprived them of their rights in a Christian world.

The Empire of Charlemagne

Toward the end of the seventh century, tensions between the Merovingian heartland of Neustria and the Frankish border region of Austrasia were increasing (see map on page 243). Austrasian warlords had profited from their steady push into the "soft frontier" east of the Rhine, acquiring wealth and military power, while the Merovingians had no such easy conquests at their disposal. Moreover, the Merovingian dynasty had given a considerable portion of their land to monasteries, which decreased their wealth and capacity to attract followers. A succession of short-lived kings opened the door to a series of civil wars, and finally to a decisive challenge to the dynasty's royal power.

KINGS AND KINGMAKERS

In 687, an Austrasian nobleman called Pepin (635/45?–714) succeeded in making himself the Merovingian king's right-hand man. He took the title *maior domus* ("great man of the house") and began to exercise royal authority while maintaining the fiction that he was merely a royal servant. He did this effectively for more than twenty-five years. After his death, his illegitimate son Charles Martel ("the Hammer"; 688–741) further consolidated control over both the Merovingian homeland and the Frankish royal administration. He was also an effective warrior, leading a Frankish army against a small Muslim force from the Umayyad caliphate in al-Andalus, which was attempting to expand its reach across the Pyrenees and into the rich lands of Aquitaine (the Bordeaux region of modern France). Their defeat enabled Charles to advance Frankish power southward, toward the Muslim-held region of Narbonne.

At the same time, Charles fostered an alliance with Benedictine missionaries from England, who were attempting to convert the Low Countries and central Germany to Christianity. Charles's family had long been active in the drive to conquer and settle these areas, and he understood clearly how missionary work and Frankish expansion could go hand in hand. In return, the leader of the English Benedictines, Boniface (c. 672–754), brought him into contact with the papacy.

Although Charles never sought to become king himself, he was so clearly the effective ruler of Gaul that the Franks did not bother to choose a new king when the

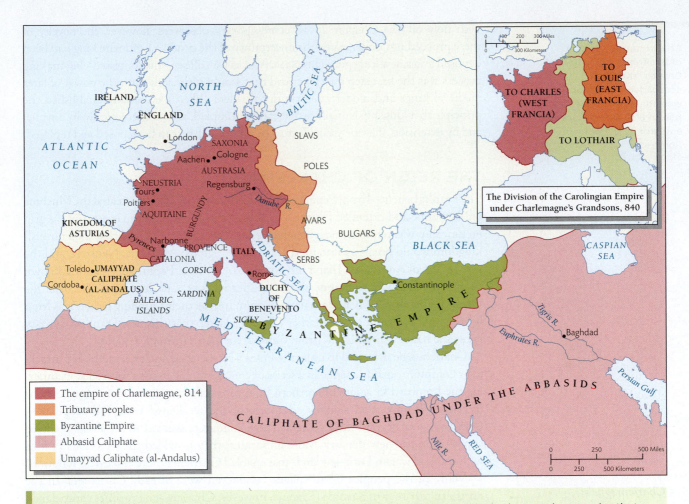

IRELAND

ENGLAND
London

SAXONIA
Aachen Cologne
AUSTRASIA
NEUSTRIA Regensburg
Tours
Poitiers
AQUITAINE
BURGUNDY
Danube R.
AVARS

SLAVS
POLES

BULGARS
SERBS

KINGDOM OF
ASTURIAS
Pyrenees
Narbonne
PROVENCE
CATALONIA
ITALY
CORSICA
Toledo UMAYYAD
CALIPHATE
Cordoba (AL-ANDALUS)
BALEARIC
ISLANDS
SARDINIA
Rome
DUCHY
OF
BENEVENTO
SICILY

NORTH
SEA

BALTIC SEA

ATLANTIC
OCEAN

ADRIATIC SEA

BLACK SEA

CASPIAN
SEA

Constantinople

BYZANTINE EMPIRE

Tigris R.
Euphrates R.
Baghdad

M E D I T E R R A N E A N   S E A

Persian Gulf

CALIPHATE OF BAGHDAD UNDER THE ABBASIDS

Nile R.
RED SEA

**The Division of the Carolingian Empire
under Charlemagne's Grandsons, 840**

TO CHARLES
(WEST
FRANCIA)

TO
LOUIS
(EAST
FRANCIA)

TO LOTHAIR

0   100   200   300 Miles
0   300 Kilometers

Legend:
- The empire of Charlemagne, 814
- Tributary peoples
- Byzantine Empire
- Abbasid Caliphate
- Umayyad Caliphate (al-Andalus)

0   250   500 Miles
0   250   500 Kilometers

THE EMPIRE OF CHARLEMAGNE IN 814. When Charlemagne died in 814, he had created an empire that embraced a large portion of the lands formerly united under the western Roman Empire. › **What were the geographical limits of his power?** › **How were these limits dictated by the historical forces we have been studying?** › **Along what lines was Charlemagne's empire divided after his death?**

reigning Merovingian ruler died in 737. But then Charles himself died in 741, and his sons Carloman and Pepin were forced to allow the election of a new king while they exercised power behind the scenes. This compromise did not last long, however. In 750, Carloman entered a monastery and Pepin decided to seize the throne.

This turned out to be harder than he may have expected. Even though the reigning king was ineffectual, Frankish tribal leaders were loyal to Clovis's descendants and reluctant to elect a new king. Pepin therefore turned to the Frankish bishops, who were also unwilling to support him without backing from Rome. Pepin therefore traded on his father's support of the monastic movement and of the papacy. The pope, for his part, saw that a powerful Frankish king could be an ally in his political struggle with the Byzantine emperors over iconoclasm, which the papacy opposed, and in his military struggle against the Lombards for control of central Italy.

So Boniface, acting as papal emissary, anointed Pepin king of the Franks in 751. Anointing was a new ritual, but it had a powerful biblical precedent: the ceremony by which the prophet Samuel had made Saul the first king of Israel, anointing his head

Charlemagne As king of the Franks (767–813), Charles "the Great" consolidated much of western Europe under his rule. In 800, he was crowned emperor by the pope in Rome.

with holy oil (see Chapter 2). To contemporary observers, however, the novelty of these proceedings underscored the uncertainty of the times: a legitimate king had been deposed and a new king put in his place. And as we will see, this contested king-making process was the first step on a long road that would ultimately limit the power of later medieval kings and modern constitutional rulers alike. It eventually established the principle that kingship is an office that can be occupied, at least theoretically, by anyone; and by extension, if a ruler is ineffectual or tyrannical, he can be deposed and replaced.

THE REIGN OF CHARLEMAGNE

The Franks benefited from Pepin's military leadership: in 759, he defeated the Muslims of Narbonne and extended Frankish control to the Mediterranean coast. But his grip on kingship was tenuous and, when he died in 768, it seemed likely that the Frankish kingdom would break up into mutually hostile regions: Austrasia, Neustria, and the new region of Aquitaine. That it did not was the work of Pepin's son, Charles: known to the French as **Charlemagne** and to the Germans as Karl der Grosse ("Charles the Great")—because both modern nations claim him as their founding father. It is from him, as well as from his grandfather Charles Martel, that this new Frankish dynasty takes the name "Carolingian" (from *Carolus*, the Latin form of "Charles").

Charlemagne managed to unite the Franks by the tried and true method of attacking a common, outside enemy. In a series of conquests, the Franks succeeded in annexing the Lombard kingdom of northern Italy, most of what is now Germany, portions of central Europe, and—taking advantage of the weakened Umayyad caliphate—Catalonia, just beyond the Pyrenees. These conquests seemed to set a seal of divine approval on the new dynasty. More important, they provided the victorious Franks with spoils of war and vast new lands that enabled Charlemagne to reward his followers.

Many of the peoples Charlemagne conquered were already Christians. In the northern territory of Saxonia (Saxony), however, Charlemagne's armies campaigned for twenty years before subduing the pagan inhabitants and forcing their conversion. This created a precedent that linked military conquest with religious conformity, and it would be repeated by Charlemagne's successors in Baltic and Slavic lands.

> *Charlemagne's conquests create a significant precedent: combining conquest with religious conformity*

To rule his new empire, Charlemagne enlisted the help of the Frankish warrior class he had enriched. These counts (*comites* in Latin, "followers") supervised local governance within their territories. Among their many duties were the administration of justice and the raising of armies. Charlemagne also established a network of local officials who convened courts, established tolls, administered royal lands, and collected taxes. To facilitate transactions and trade, he created a new coinage system based on a division of the silver pound into units of twenty shillings, each worth twelve pennies: this system lasted into the 1970s in parts of continental Europe and Britain.

Like Carolingian administration generally, this new monetary system depended on the regular use of written records, which means that the sources supporting historical research on Charlemagne's empire are unusually numerous and rich. But Charlemagne did not rely on the written word alone; periodically, his court sent special messengers, known as *missi*, on tours through the countryside to relay his instructions and report back on the conduct of local administrators. This was the most thorough system of governance in Europe since the height of the Roman Empire, reaching many parts of the Continent that the Romans had never occupied. It set a standard for royal administration that would be emulated and envied for centuries.

CHRISTIANITY AND KINGSHIP

Charlemagne took his responsibilities as a Christian king seriously. Moreover, as his empire expanded, he came to see himself as the leader of a unified Christian society, Christendom, which he was obliged to defend. Like his contemporaries in Byzantium and the Muslim world—as well as his Roman predecessors—he recognized no distinction between religion and politics. Indeed, he conceived kingship as a sacred office created by God to protect the Church and promote the salvation of Christian people. Religious reforms were therefore no less central to proper kingship than were justice and defense. In some ways, a king's responsibilities for his kingdom's spiritual welfare were more important than his other, secular responsibilities.

These ideas were not new, but they took on a new importance because of the extraordinary power Charlemagne wielded. Like other rulers of this period, Charlemagne was able to appoint and depose bishops and abbots, just as he did the counts and other officials who administered his realm. He extended his authority by changing the liturgy of Frankish churches, reforming the rules of worship in Frankish monasteries, declaring the tenets of Christian belief, ruthlessly prohibiting pagan practices, and forcibly imposing basic Christian observances on the conquered peoples of Saxony. As the dominant political power in central Italy, Charlemagne was also the protector of the papacy. Although he acknowledged the pope as the spiritual leader of Christendom, Charlemagne dealt with the bishop of Rome much as he did other bishops in his empire. He supervised papal elections and defended the pope from his many enemies.

THE CAROLINGIAN RENAISSANCE

Similar political and religious motivations lay behind the phenomenon known as the **Carolingian Renaissance**, a cultural and intellectual flowering that took place around the Carolingian court. Charlemagne and his son, Louis the Pious, considered it a crucial part of their role to be patrons of learning and the arts. In doing so, they created an ideal of the princely court that would profoundly influence western European cultural life until the First World War (see Chapter 24).

Behind the Carolingians' support for scholarship was the conviction that learning was essential to the salvation of God's people. Charlemagne therefore recruited intellectuals from all over Europe to further the cause of both Christian and **classical learning**. Foremost among these was the Anglo-Saxon scholar Alcuin, whose command of classical Latin established him as the leader of Charlemagne's educational project. Under Alcuin's direction, Carolingian authors produced original Latin poetry and an impressive number of theological and pastoral writings. They also devoted their efforts to collecting, correcting, and recopying ancient Latin texts, including the text of the Latin Bible, which had accumulated many generations of copyists' mistakes in the four hundred years since Jerome's translation (see Chapter 6).

To detect and amend these errors, Alcuin and his associates gathered as many different versions of the biblical text as they could find and compared them, word by word. After determining the correct version among all the variants, they made a new, corrected copy and destroyed the other versions. They also developed a new style of handwriting, with simplified letter forms and spaces inserted between words, making it much easier to read their new texts. Reading was further facilitated by the addition of punctuation. This new style of handwriting, known as Carolingian minuscule, is the foundation for the typefaces of most modern books—including this one.

Carolingian Renaissance A cultural and intellectual flowering that took place around the court of Charlemagne in the late eighth and early ninth centuries.

classical learning The study of ancient Greek and Latin texts. After Christianity became the only legal religion of the Roman Empire, scholars needed to find a way to make classical learning applicable to a Christian way of life. Christian monks played a significant role in resolving this problem by reinterpreting the classics for a Christian audience.

THE REVIVAL OF THE WESTERN ROMAN EMPIRE

On Christmas Day in the year 800, Charlemagne was crowned Emperor of the Romans by Pope Leo III. Centuries later, popes would cite this epochal event as precedent for the political superiority they claimed over the ruler of the "Holy Roman Empire," as it came to be called (see Chapter 9). In the year 800, however, Pope Leo was entirely under Charlemagne's control. And yet Charlemagne's biographer, Einhard, later claimed that the coronation was planned without the emperor's knowledge. Why, then, did he accept the title and, in 813, transfer it to his son Louis? For one thing, it was certain to anger the imperial government in Byzantium, with which Charlemagne had strained relations. For another, the imperial title tied Charlemagne more closely to the onerous task of defending a weak Roman papacy.

Historians still debate this question, but the symbolic significance of the action is clear. Although the Romans of Byzantium no longer influenced western Europe directly, they continued to regard it as an outlying province of their empire. Moreover, the emperor in Constantinople claimed to be the political successor of Caesar Augustus. Charlemagne's assumption of that title was therefore a clear slight to the reigning empress Irene (r. 797–802), whose occupation of the imperial throne was controversial because she was a woman. It also deepened Byzantine suspicion of Charlemagne's cordial relationship with Harun al-Rashid, the Abbasid caliph of Baghdad.

But for Charlemagne's successors—and all the medieval rulers who imitated him—the imperial title was a declaration of independence and superiority. With only occasional interruptions, western Europeans continued to crown Roman emperors until the nineteenth century. Meanwhile, medieval and modern territorial claims and concepts of national sovereignty would come to rest on Carolingian precedent. Whatever his own motives may have been, Charlemagne's revival of the western Roman Empire was crucial to the developing self-consciousness of western Europe.

Disputed Legacies and New Alliances

When Charlemagne died in 814, his empire descended intact to his only surviving son, Louis the Pious, who faced an impossible situation of a kind we have studied many times before: the task of holding together an artificial constellation of territories united by someone else. Charlemagne's empire had been built on successful conquests; however, he had pushed the borders of his empire beyond the practical limits of his administration. To the southwest, Louis now faced the Umayyad rulers of al-Andalus; to the north, the pagans of Scandinavia. In the east, his armies were too preoccupied with settling the territories they had already conquered to secure the Slavic lands that lay beyond. At the same time, the pressures that had driven these conquests—the need for land and plunder to ensure the allegiance of followers—had become ever more pronounced as a result of their very success. The number of counts had tripled, from approximately one hundred to three hundred, and each of them wanted more wealth and power.

Frustrated by the new emperor's inability to reward them, the Frankish aristocracy turned against Louis, and on each other. Smoldering hostilities among Austrasians, Neustrians, and Aquitanians flared up again. As centralized authority broke down, the vast majority of the empire's free inhabitants found themselves increasingly dominated by local lords who treated them like serfs. After Louis's death, the disintegrating empire was divided among his three sons: West Francia (the core of modern France) went to Charles the Bald; East Francia (which became key principalities of Germany) went to Louis the German; and a third kingdom (stretching from the Rhineland to Rome) went to Lothair, along with the imperial title. But when Lothair's line died out, in 856, this fragile compromise dissolved into open warfare, as the East and West Franks fought over Lothair's former territories and the imperial power that went with them. The heartland of this disputed domain, known to the Germans as Lotharingia and to the French as Alsace-Lorraine, would continue to be a site of bitter contention until the end of the Second World War (see Chapter 26).

THE IMPACT OF THE VIKING INVASIONS

As the Carolingian Empire collapsed, the weakening of the Abbasid caliphate in Baghdad caused a breakdown in the commercial networks through which Scandinavian traders had brought Abbasid silver into Carolingian domains. Deprived of their livelihood, these traders turned to *viking:* the Old Norse word for "raiding." Under these combined pressures, a new map of Europe began to emerge.

Scandinavian traders were already familiar figures in the North Sea and Baltic ports of Europe when Charlemagne came to power. They had begun to establish strategic settlements from which they navigated down the rivers to Byzantium (through the Black Sea) and the Abbasid caliphate (through the Caspian Sea). But when the power of the Abbasids declined, traders turned to plunder, ransom, and slaving. At first, these were small-scale operations; but soon, some Viking attacks involved organized armies numbering in the thousands. The small tribal kingdoms of the Anglo-Saxons and Celts made the British Isles easy targets, as were the divided kingdoms of the Franks.

By the tenth century, Vikings had established independent principalities in eastern England, Ireland, the islands of Scotland, and the region that is still called "Norseman land": Normandy. A Viking band known as the Rus' established the beginnings of a kingdom that would become Russia. At the end of the tenth century,

Vikings Scandinavian traders who began to establish colonies through a series of raids and invasions following the fall of the Abbasid caliphate.

Vikings ventured across the North Atlantic and colonized Iceland, Greenland, and a distant territory they called Vinland (Newfoundland, Canada).

Viking populations quickly assimilated into the cultural and political world of northwestern Europe. By 1066, when the "Norsemen" of Normandy conquered England, the English—many descended from Vikings themselves—perceived them to be French. Contributing to this rapid assimilation may have been the raids of the Magyars, a non-Indo-European people that crossed the Carpathian Mountains around 895 and carried out a number of devastating campaigns before settling in what is now Hungary. The disparate inhabitants of the new Viking colonies may have come to share a sense of common identity in the face of this common enemy.

The overall effect of the Viking diaspora continues to be a matter of scholarly debate. The destruction caused by raiding is undeniable, and many monasteries in Frankish, Anglo-Saxon, and Celtic lands were destroyed—along with countless precious books and artifacts. Yet the Vikings were not the only source of disorder: the civil wars and political rivalries that had replaced the centralized states of

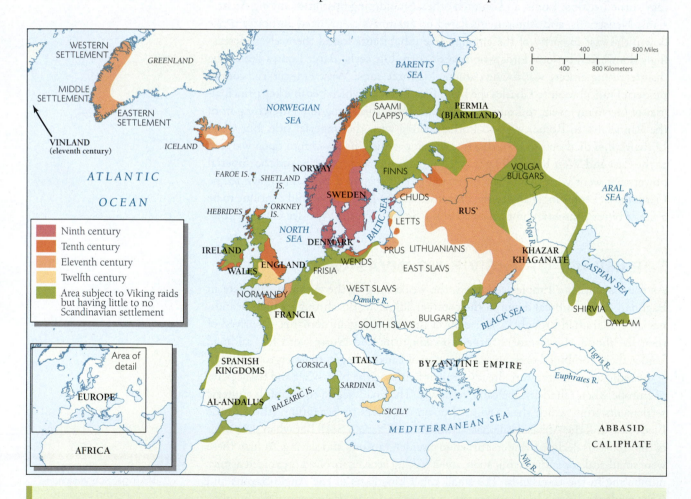

PATTERNS OF VIKING ACTIVITY AND SETTLEMENT, c. 800–1100. The Vikings were instrumental in maintaining commercial contacts among northern Europe, Byzantium, and Islam until the eighth century, when changing historical forces turned them into raiders and colonists. › **What area was the original homeland of the Vikings?** › **What geographic region did the Vikings first conquer, and why?** › **The areas marked in green show territories that were later targeted by pillagers. Why would the Vikings have avoided settlement in these areas?**

Charlemagne and the Islamic caliphates contributed mightily to the chaos and made the Vikings' successes easily won. Nor were the Vikings a source of disorder alone. In Ireland and eastern England, Vikings founded a series of new towns. And as long-distance traders, they transported large quantities of silver into western Europe, fueling the European economy.

ALFRED THE GREAT AND THE UNIFICATION OF ANGLO-SAXON ENGLAND

In those regions where people did succeed in fending off Viking attacks, the cohesive force of victory was strong. In England, which had remained divided into small kingdoms at war with one another—despite Bede's wishful history of an "English church and people"—response to the Viking threat led to the emergence of a loosely unified kingdom under Alfred the Great (r. 871–899). His success in defending his own small realm from Viking attacks allowed Alfred and his heirs to assemble effective armed forces, institute mechanisms of local government, found new towns, and codify English laws. In emulation of Charlemagne, Alfred also established a court school and fostered a distinctive literary culture. Although the Anglo-Saxon vernacular had been a written language since the time of the Roman missions, it now came to rival Latin as a language of administration, history, scholarship, and spirituality. Moreover, oral traditions of poetic composition and storytelling were preserved and extended, as exemplified by the epic *Beowulf*. Until the eleventh century, Anglo-Saxon was the only European vernacular used for regular written communication.

English institutions (laws, towns, and army) consolidate as Viking threat looms

THE DISINTEGRATION OF THE ISLAMIC WORLD

As noted previously, the declining power of the Abbasid dynasty was one of the forces that contributed to the escalation of Viking raids. A major cause of this decline was the impoverishment of the Abbasids' economic base in the ancient Tigris–Euphrates basin, caused by ecological crises and a devastating revolt by the enslaved African workforce there. Tax revenues also declined as provincial Muslim rulers in North Africa, Egypt, and Syria retained larger and larger portions of those revenues for themselves. Their sources of income depleted, the Abbasids were unable to support their large civil service and the mercenary army on which they relied for defense. Massively expensive building projects, including the construction of the Abbasid capital at Baghdad, further exacerbated the crisis.

Behind the Abbasid collapse lay two fundamental developments of great significance for the future of the Islamic world: the growing power of regional rulers and the sharpening religious divisions between Sunnis and Shi'ites, and among the Shi'ites themselves. In 909, regional and religious hostilities came together when a local Shi'ite dynasty known as the Fatimids seized control of the Abbasid province of North Africa. In 969, the Fatimids succeeded in conquering Egypt as well. Meanwhile, another Shi'ite group, rivals of both the Fatimids and the Abbasids, attacked Baghdad in 927 and Mecca in 930, seizing the Kaaba.

Although an Abbasid caliphate would continue to exist in Baghdad until 1258, when invading Mongol armies destroyed it (see Chapter 10), its empire had effectively disappeared by the 930s. In its place, a new order began to emerge, centered around an independent Egyptian kingdom and a new Muslim state in Persia, the ancestor of present-day Iran.

In al-Andalus, disputes over succession within the Umayyad dynasty were matched by external pressures: in the mid-ninth century, the small Christian kingdoms of northern and eastern Iberia began to encroach on Muslim territory. By the opening years of the eleventh century, the caliphate had dissolved, to be replaced by a host of smaller Muslim kingdoms, some of which paid tribute to the Christian rulers of the north.

Overall, the fractured political unity of the Islamic world deepened the religious divisions that had always existed among Muslim groups. Whereas Islamic rulers were relatively tolerant of religious and cultural differences when dealing with Jews and Christians, dissent within Islam itself was another matter. Under the strong rule of the caliphates, some different groups had learned to coexist; but with the disappearance of these centralized states, it became difficult to reconcile regional and ethnic differences.

Conclusion

Which of these three civilizations was the true heir of Rome? The answer depends on the criteria used to make this evaluation. If we argue that imperial Rome's most fundamental characteristics were the maintenance of legal and political institutions, the answer is Byzantium. If we are looking for a civilization that combines the rich

AFTER YOU READ THIS CHAPTER

CHRONOLOGY

481–511	Reign of Clovis, king of the Franks
527–565	Reign of Justinian
570–632	Lifetime of Muhammad and early Muslim conquests
590–604	Papacy of Gregory the Great
636–651	Arab conquests of Persia, Palestine, Egypt, and North Africa
661–750	Dominion of the Umayyad dynasty in the Islamic world
717–787	Iconoclast Controversy in Byzantium
717–751	The Carolingian dynasty shares power with Merovingian kings
730	The Venerable Bede completes his history of the English church
750–930	Dominion of the Abbasid and Umayyad dynasties
751	Pepin becomes king of the Franks
768–814	Reign of Charlemagne
800–1000	Period of Viking invasions
871–899	Reign of Alfred the Great in England

REVIEWING THE OBJECTIVES

› Byzantine culture was distinctive in many ways. What were some of its important features?

› The rapid expansion of Islam can be explained with reference to several historical factors. What were they?

› What accounts for the close relationship between monasticism and secular power in early medieval Europe?

› What was the Carolingian Empire? Why is it important?

› Based on your reading, which of Rome's three heirs was the most successful in carrying its legacy forward?

legacies of ancient Mesopotamia, Egypt, and the Hellenistic world, the answer is Islam, which also emulated Rome in promoting commerce and culture. If we associate Rome chiefly with the city itself and the Latin language of the first Romans, or with the Christian patriarchy of Rome, the answer is northwestern Europe.

There are also many connections to be drawn among these three successors. All had fruitful—if uneasy—relationships with each other, and many mutual dependencies. Italian traders were active in Constantinople, Muslim traders were common in the ports of southern Italy and Gaul; Anglo-Saxon merchants were regular visitors to the Mediterranean, Jewish merchants in the Rhineland traded with Muslim Egypt; Vikings opened trade routes from the Baltic to the Black Sea, founding cities from Novgorod to Dublin.

But the developments of the ninth and tenth centuries would disrupt these networks and create new centers of power. Western Europeans began to share a sense of common Christian identity: from the Baltic to the Mediterranean, from the Pyrenees to Poland. At the same time, western Europe became a society mobilized for war to a degree unmatched in either Byzantium or the Islamic world. In the centuries to come, this militarization would prove to be a decisive factor in the shifting relationship among Rome's heirs.

 Go to **INQUIZITIVE** to see what you've learned—and learn what you have missed—with personalized feedback along the way.

PEOPLE, IDEAS, AND EVENTS IN CONTEXT

› In what ways do **JUSTINIAN'S CODE OF ROMAN LAW** and the building of Hagia Sophia reflect his desire to revive the glories of ancient Rome?

› What were **BYZANTIUM**'s sources of stability, and how did the Byzantine Church promote **ORTHODOX** Christianity? What effect did the **ICONOCLAST CONTROVERSY** have on Byzantine society?

› What factors contributed to **MUHAMMAD**'s rise to power? What are the **FIVE PILLARS OF ISLAM**? What is the role of the **QUR'AN**?

› To what extent were the **UMAYYAD** and **ABBASID CALIPHATES** heirs of Rome? What made the Islamic culture of this period distinctive?

› How did the **MEROVINGIAN** kings of the Franks acquire and hold power? How did **BENEDICTINE MONASTICISM** contribute to the economy of western Europe? How was it linked to politics?

› How did **CHARLEMAGNE** build an empire? How did the **CAROLINGIAN RENAISSANCE** revive and extend **CLASSICAL LEARNING**?

› How did the **VIKINGS** contribute to the developments of the ninth and tenth centuries?

THINKING ABOUT CONNECTIONS

› How do the historical circumstances in which Islam emerged compare with those that shaped early Christianity? What are some key similarities and differences?

› The movement and resettlement of people is a major theme throughout the history of Western civilizations—and the upheavals of the sixth to tenth centuries created a series of refugee crises. How do those compare with similar crises in our own day? What might we learn from the historical comparison?

8

The Expansion of Europe, 950–1100

IN THE FICTIONAL HISTORY popularized by medieval minstrels, Charlemagne and his knights are campaigning on the mountainous borderlands of al-Andalus (Muslim Spain). Their remaining obstacle is the castle of a Muslim king whose courage commands their respect. So when the king's ambassadors promise his conversion to Christianity in exchange for the safety of his people, Charlemagne agrees. One of his men must now negotiate the terms of surrender. Roland, Charlemagne's nephew, suggests that his stepfather Ganelon be the chosen messenger. But Ganelon is furious, certain that the mission is too dangerous. Secretly, he betrays both his stepson—and his lord—by convincing the Muslim king that Charlemagne intends to trick him, and that the king should attack the Christians as they travel homeward through the mountain passes. Because Roland is the bravest knight, Ganelon knows that he will volunteer to command the rear guard.

When Roland's men are ambushed, his companion, Olivier, urges him to call for help by blowing his ivory horn. But Roland refuses to endanger his lord; instead, he will fight to the death. Then, with his last ounce of strength, he breaks his sword, to keep this sacred gift of Charlemagne— made holy by the relic in its pommel—from heathen hands. The worst thing imaginable is shame; the best, to become the hero of just such an epic.

Like Homer's *Iliad*, the *Song of Roland* is the product of an oral storytelling tradition that took shape over centuries. Written down

BEFORE YOU READ THIS CHAPTER

❯

> Around the year 1000, a warming climate and new agricultural technologies and social groupings transformed the economy and landscape of western Europe. New kingdoms also emerged in Scandinavia and eastern Europe.

> The rejuvenation of towns and trade created new opportunities. But at the same time, the decentralization of political power led to violent rule by lords who could harness human and material resources to their own advantage.

> Meanwhile, a new movement within the Roman Church increased the authority of the papacy, which attempted to assert its supremacy over secular rulers and to control violence.

> One manifestation of this Church-sanctioned violence was the First Crusade, which began when an attack by Muslim warriors on Byzantium became the pretext for a holy war.

> Crusading broadened cultural and economic contacts with the East, but also led to increased intolerance of "others," both outside and within Europe.

CORE OBJECTIVES

> **EXPLAIN** the reasons for the diffusion of political power throughout most of Europe during this period.

> **IDENTIFY** the most important outcomes of the medieval agricultural revolution.

> **DESCRIBE** the effects of the reforming movement within the Church.

> **UNDERSTAND** the motives behind the Crusades.

> **TRACE** the political, economic, intellectual, and cultural effects of the Crusades.

around the year 1100, it reveals how much the world had changed since the time of Charlemagne. Its very language was written not in the Frankish tongue of Charlemagne but in newer language we call French. In Charlemagne's day there were no such things as knighthood or chivalry, castles, or holy war against Muslims. All of these features were added to mirror a new reality: the ethos of the First Crusade (1095–1099).

This chapter begins to trace the processes that transformed western Europe from an economic and political backwater into the premier power among Rome's three successor civilizations. In this period, Christendom came to embrace Scandinavia, Hungary, Poland, and Bohemia. Christian colonists and missionaries also pushed into the Baltic and the Balkans. Allied Christian armies advanced into formerly Islamic territories in Spain and even established (and eventually lost) a kingdom centered on Jerusalem. This expansion would be accompanied by a revolution in agriculture, population growth, and urbanization. It would foster new monarchies, create a stratified new social order, and spur remarkable intellectual and cultural achievements.

A Tour of Europe around the Year 1000

This chapter is titled "The Expansion of Europe" for two main reasons. First, because the very idea of Europe as a geographical entity gained increasing coherence during this period; second, because Europeans' conquest of frontier territories led to an ongoing process of internal and external colonization. New kingdoms were being created by warfare and settlement within Europe, as well as beyond it, and Europeans were becoming the agents of imperialism, not its targets. This is a striking change. Western civilizations' center of gravity had always been the Mediterranean and adjacent lands in Anatolia, western Asia, and North Africa; it was from there that influences flowed to the less civilized lands of the farther West. But now, that trajectory was being reversed.

VIKING INITIATIVES

In the aftermath of the Viking invasions, new political entities began to emerge. Some were formed when the Vikings became colonists: Iceland, Greenland, and (briefly) Newfoundland. Indeed, Iceland can claim to be Europe's oldest state and the world's first parliamentary democracy: its political institutions date back to 930, when settlers formed a legislative assembly called the Althing, a Norse word with the same meaning as the Latin *res publica*. Icelanders would also produce fascinating and influential forms of entertainment, notably the *sagas*: family histories that unfold over generations, featuring diverse casts of characters, and ranging from the hilarious to the ruthless. Modern action films and television epics are heavily indebted to the sagas.

Iceland: the first parliamentary democracy

In regions where Vikings settled among more established groups—in Francia, the British Isles, Scandinavia, and the Low Countries—they both absorbed and affected these cultures. In Normandy, for example, the descendants of Vikings maintained marriage alliances and ties of kinship with the rest of the Norse world while intermarrying with the Franks and adopting their language.

THE RISE OF RUS' AND THE KINGDOMS OF EAST-CENTRAL EUROPE

One group of Vikings established a settlement in the heart of a region that still bears their name: Russia. Originally from Sweden, the Rus' were active raiders and traders in the Baltic, where they came to dominate the Finn and Slavic peoples who lived along the coast. Gradually, they extended their reach through Eurasian waterways, moving farther inland to Novgorod. By the year 1000, they had conquered the fortress of Kiev.

From Kiev, on the shores of the river Dnieper (now in western Ukraine), the Rus' had easy access to the Black Sea and so to Constantinople and Baghdad. They were thus in a position to trade directly with the eastern Roman Empire, as well as with Arabic, Persian, and Turkic peoples who had access to China. Through a series of strategic intermarriages, the Rus' also forged further connections with many of the royal and aristocratic dynasties of western Europe. This placed the new kingdom of Rus' at the heart of the medieval world.

The rise of Rus' was countered by the crystallization of independent Balkan and Slavic kingdoms. Serbia and Croatia, on the Adriatic, were long-settled Roman provinces. When the empire fractured along religious and cultural lines, the rulers of Croatia, who were neighbors of the Venetians, embraced the Latin Christianity of Rome. The Serbs, however, were loyal to the Orthodox Church of Byzantium.

Hungary, comprising the Roman province of Pannonia and stretching eastward to the Carpathian Mountains, had been conquered by the Huns in the late fourth century and had since attracted other immigrants. The most recent were the Magyars, a nomadic people from the Urals whose language, like that of the Finns, was not Indo-European. The Magyars were expert herdsmen and horsemen, and also served as mercenaries. Around 895, they united under a leader called Árpád and took control of the fertile Danube River basin, where they became farmers and cattle ranchers. Árpád's descendants embraced Latin Christianity and worked to integrate the kingdom of Hungary into western Europe through dynastic marriages and diplomacy.

Bohemia (now part of the Czech Republic) and Poland were also being actively courted by Rome. As in Anglo-Saxon England and the Frankish kingdom (Chapter 7), papal allegiance was advantageous for ambitious kings, who could legitimize their claims to power and tie the new towns of this region into the expanding web of overland and waterborne trade.

NEW SCANDINAVIAN KINGDOMS AND THE EMPIRE OF CNUT THE GREAT

With Rus' on the rise, other groups of Vikings were establishing control over parts of their Scandinavian homeland. By the year 1000, three kingdoms had emerged: Norway, Sweden, and Denmark. Each built on the legacy of powerful forebears who had already established Norse settlements in the lands of the Franks, the Anglo-Saxons, and the Irish: a reputation for fearlessness in battle, dominance of waterways, and canny practices of assimilation. The rulers of these new states blended this heritage with the strategic decision to convert their followers to Christianity and to the political conventions of the Continent. They simultaneously glorified their own distinctive culture and achievements while tying them to newer models of government. For these reasons, scholars often call this Europe's "Viking Age." On the one hand,

In the "Viking Age," Norse customs blend with political and religious customs of Christian Europe

older Western civilizations can be said to have colonized Scandinavia; on the other hand, it was really Scandinavians who were doing the colonizing.

The empire forged by Cnut (*kuh-NOOT*) the Great of Denmark is exemplary of this trend. At the time of his death in 1035, Cnut ruled over Norway, much of Sweden, and England, as well as his native land; he also had a controlling interest in large parts of Ireland and portions of the Low Countries; and he had diplomatic and family ties to the independent principalities of Flanders and Normandy, the new kingdom of Poland (through his mother, a Polish princess), and the imperial family of Germany (through his daughter, who became empress). Although Cnut's was, in many ways, a personal empire—like that of Alexander or Charlemagne—it had long-term effects on the political organization of northwestern Europe. Most notably, it set the stage for the Norman conquest of England (see *Interpreting Visual Evidence* on page 269).

MEDITERRANEAN MICROCOSMS

The new states of eastern Europe, Rus', and Scandinavia stand in contrast to the very different dynamics that governed relations around the medieval Mediterranean. If the map on the opposite page struggles to capture the patchwork of principalities within Europe's mainland, it fails utterly to convey the contours of political, religious, cultural, and economic interactions in this maritime world. Mediterranean coastal regions and islands were interlocking components of a complex contact zone. A community on the shores of North Africa—say, Muslim Tunis—would have more in common with Christian Barcelona than with another African Muslim community farther inland. In many places, it made little difference who the ostensible rulers were, especially since the persons and forms of rule changed so often.

Take Sicily, which had been part of the Phoenician empire of Carthage and, before that, a major Greek settlement (Chapters 2 and 3). It then became the first overseas colony of Rome (Chapter 5). All of those elements were part of Sicily's historical DNA when it was invaded by the Vandals in the fifth century, and afterward by the Goths. It was then reconquered by Justinian and became part of Byzantium—so important a part, in fact, that one emperor tried to move the capital from Constantinople to Palermo. In the tenth century, Sicily became an emirate of the Fatimid caliphate based in Egypt. In the eleventh, it was conquered by Norman mercenaries who eventually succeeded in establishing a kingdom there in 1072.

In such places, multiple influences, connections, and orbits of exchange mean more than borders or identities; indeed, this holds true of many areas of Europe during this period. Gaining "control" of any community meant harnessing its inherent complexity and commercial power, something not best done through violent conquest. A very light-handed interference was what enabled the Venetians to build a successful and long-lived trading empire in the Adriatic, and then in the eastern Mediterranean and Aegean Sea. By opening sea lanes and ports, the Venetians also became crucial to more militant forms of European expansion: the Crusades.

THE HEIRS OF CHARLEMAGNE

What had become of Europe's heartland, the empire of Charlemagne? The most powerful monarchs on the Continent were the Saxon kings of eastern Francia (in what is now Germany), who drew on aspects of **Carolingian rule**. Whereas England

Carolingian rule The rule of Charlemagne's dynasty, a term derived from the Latin form of the name Charles, *Carolus*. Though Charlemagne's father, Pepin, was the first member of that family to be crowned king of the Franks, his own father, Charles Martel, paved the way for the family's ascent.

EUROPE, c. 1000. This map shows the patchwork of political power in western Europe after the millennium, although it cannot accurately illustrate the degree of fragmentation within these major territories, especially those of the Holy Roman Empire. › **What factors account for the close relationship between Italy and the German principalities?** › **How are they related to the northwestern regions of the Continent and the British Isles?** › **Which geopolitical entities would you expect to emerge as dominant in the following centuries?**

was becoming an effective monarchy with a centralized bureaucracy, royal power on the Continent rested on the profits of continual expansion. Just as the Carolingians had built on the conquest of Saxony, the Saxons now built on the conquests of Slavic lands to the east. They also promoted their image as guardians of Christendom: in 955, when Otto I of Saxony defeated the pagan Magyars, he was carrying a sacred lance that had belonged to Charlemagne.

Otto I becomes emperor and deposes pope, laying foundation for his successors' imperial autonomy

In 962, Otto extended his claim to Charlemagne's legacy by accepting the imperial crown from Pope John XII, who hoped that Otto would defeat his own enemies. But Otto turned the tables, deposing John and selecting a new pope to replace him. Otto thereby claimed imperial autonomy, in imitation of the Byzantine emperors. He also practiced imperial patronage of the arts and learning, making the Saxon court a refuge for men and women of talent. The first known female playwright, Hrotsvitha of Gandersheim (c. 935–c. 1002), grew up there hearing the works of classical authors read aloud. When she entered a royal convent, she wrote plays blending Roman comedy with the stories of early Christian martyrs, for the entertainment and instruction of her fellow nuns. Otto also established cathedral schools and helped the bishops of his domain turn their own courts into cultural centers.

However, Otto could not maintain control over the papacy or the independent towns of northern Italy unless he had a permanent presence there. But if he remained in Italy too long, his authority in Saxony would break down. Balancing local realities with imperial ambitions thus presented a dilemma that neither he nor his successors could solve. The result was a gradually increasing rift between local elites and the king in his role as emperor. This alienation would accelerate in the eleventh century when the imperial crown passed to a new dynasty, the Salians, centered not in Saxony but in Franconia (see page 276).

Aspects of Charlemagne's legacy also survived in the Mediterranean world. In Catalonia, counts descended from Carolingian appointees continued to administer

EMPEROR OTTO THE GREAT. In this opening from a deluxe set of Gospels he commissioned for himself, Otto is shown seated on a throne, vested with the regalia of imperial and royal authority, and surrounded by clerical and secular counselors. On the left, a procession of deferential women offers him tribute, representing the four regions and peoples that Otto aspired to rule: Roma (Romans), Gallia (Franks), Germania (Germans), and Sclavinia (Slavs). **› What claims to power is Otto making through this iconography?**

justice in public courts of law, and to draw revenues from tolls and trade. The city of Barcelona grew rapidly as both a long-distance and a regional market under the protection of these counts. In Aquitaine also, the counts of Poitiers and Toulouse continued to rest their authority on Carolingian foundations.

In Charlemagne's own former kingdom, however, Carolingian rule collapsed under the combined weight of Viking raids, economic disintegration, and the rivalry of local lords. A few Carolingian institutions—such as public courts and a coinage—survived in new, autonomous principalities such as Anjou and Flanders. The Norse-Frankish rulers of Normandy also used these techniques effectively. But in the Franks' traditional heartland, even this modicum of authority disappeared. The local count, Hugh Capet, had managed to defend his territory against the Vikings and, in 987, this modest feat made him the new king of the Franks. Marooned on this Île-de-France (literally, "island of France"), a tiny territory around Paris, the Capetian kings clung to the fiction that they were the heirs of Charlemagne's greatness.

The Agricultural Revolution of the Medieval Warm Period

Prior to the late twentieth century, when human activity began to have a measurable effect on the global climate, the warmest period of the last two millennia occurred between 950 and 1250. It is known as the Medieval Warm Period or Medieval Climate Optimum, because it optimized the conditions for agricultural and economic growth. Archaeological evidence from the Americas to Europe to Asia shows similar patterns of human adaptation to this new environment, when average global temperatures rose by about 1°C or 2°C (3.6°F)—the same increment as anthropogenic warming to date. This made it possible to raise crops as far north as Greenland and to produce wine in southern England. Moreover, the warming climate benefited northern Europe by drying the soil and lengthening the growing season, with hotter summers and diminishing rainfall harming Mediterranean agriculture in equal measure.

NEW TECHNOLOGIES AND CONDITIONS FOR GROWTH

Europe's **agricultural revolution** had already begun in the eighth century, fostered by monastic inventions such as the new heavy plow that could cut and turn the rich soil of northern Europe (Chapter 7). Related improvements in harnessing made it possible for draft animals to pull heavy loads without choking. The development of iron horseshoes (around 900) and the tandem harnessing of paired teams (around 1050) also facilitated the transport of goods to new markets.

The widespread use of iron for hoes, pitchforks, shovels, and scythes made humans' work easier, too. The wheelbarrow was a crucial invention, as was the harrow, drawn over the field after plowing to level the earth and mix in the seed. Mills were another major innovation. The Romans had relied mainly on human- and animal-powered wheels to grind grain into flour or crush olives for oil, but

agricultural revolution One of the most significant occurrences in the history of Western civilizations, it began in the tenth century C.E. and increased the amount of land under cultivation as well as productivity of the land.

Smaller landholdings merged into common fields, allowing shared investments and experimentation ❯

the lack of slave labor led monastic engineers to experiment with various ways of harnessing water power. Landowners also recognized the mill as a source of economic and political power to which they could control access by demanding payment for its use.

HARNESSING PEOPLE

These new technologies became more widespread after the settlement of Viking and Magyar peoples decreased the threats of invasion. Left in relative peace, monasteries were able to develop these tools, which were then copied by local lords who saw the benefits of managing their own lands more efficiently—rather than raiding others'. Productivity was also linked to increased population, changes in settlement patterns, and the organization of the peasant workforce.

Most farmers in northern Europe lived on individual plots of land worked by themselves and their families. Starting in the ninth century, however, many of these individual holdings were merged into larger, common fields that could be farmed collectively by entire villages; the resulting complex was called a **manor** (from the Latin verb *manere*, "to dwell"). In many cases, the impetus came from the peasants themselves, because investment costs could be shared equally: a single plow and a few yokes of oxen obviated the need for every farmer to maintain his own equipment. Common fields were potentially more productive, too, allowing experimentation with new crops and supporting larger numbers of animals on common pastures. In time, a prosperous village could support a parish church, a communal oven, a blacksmith, a mill, even a tavern. In a difficult and demanding natural environment, these were important considerations.

In other cases, a manor could be created or co-opted by a local lord or monastery. Their greater productivity meant that lords could take a larger share of the peasants' surplus; it was also easier to control and exploit peasants who were bound to each other by ties of kinship and dependence. Over time, some lords were able to reduce formerly free peasants to **serfs** who could not leave the land without permission. Like slaves, serfs inherited their servile status; but unlike slaves, they could not be sold apart from the lands they worked. In practical terms, there may have been little difference between a serf and a free peasant. But, as we have seen, social mobility is often tied to geographical mobility; the inability of serfs to move freely prevented them from achieving the liberties of those who could (see pages 262–265).

THE CONQUEST OF THE LAND

Three-crop rotation system ❯

For centuries, farmers had known that sowing the same crop in the same field year after year would eventually exhaust the soil. The traditional solution was to divide the land, planting half in the fall to harvest in the spring, and leaving the other half to lie fallow. In the dry, thin soils of the Mediterranean, this remained the most common cropping pattern. In the more fertile soils of northern Europe, however, farmers slowly discovered that a three-field crop rotation plan could produce a sustainable increase in overall production. One-third of the land would lie fallow or be used as pasture, so that manure would fertilize the soil; one-third would be planted with winter wheat or rye, sown in the fall and harvested in the early summer; and one-third would be planted in the spring with another crop to be harvested in the fall. These fields were then rotated over a three-year cycle.

This system increased the amount of land under cultivation by over 50 percent, while the two separate growing seasons provided some insurance against natural disasters or inclement weather. It also produced higher yields per acre, particularly if legumes or fodder crops (such as oats) were sown to replace the nitrogen that wheat and rye leached out of the soil. Both humans and animals could eat oats, and legumes provided a source of protein to balance the intake of carbohydrates from bread and beer: the two main staples of the peasant diet in northern and central Europe. Additional fodder supported more and healthier animals, increasing the efficiency of plow beasts and providing additional sources of protein through meat and milk. The new crop rotation system also helped spread labor more evenly over the course of the year.

towns In the eleventh and twelfth centuries, an exploding population and opportunities for trade create the conditions for the emergence of new towns throughout Europe.

The Growth of Towns and Trade

As we observed in Chapter 7, the urban infrastructure of the western Roman Empire had weakened over the course of the fifth and sixth centuries. A few cities continued to thrive under the lordship of bishops, but many—including Rome itself—began to crumble as their depleted populations could no longer maintain public buildings, services, and defensive walls. In most areas, monasteries replaced cities as the nuclei of civilization. Then, under Charlemagne and his imitators, **towns** were planted as centers for markets and administration. In Anglo-Saxon England, too, King Alfred and his successors established new towns in strategic locations.

FOSTERING COMMERCE

Although many of these new towns were targeted by the Viking raids of the tenth century, the agricultural revolution helped to revitalize them—as did the influx of silver and gold set in circulation by the Vikings themselves. The rapid urbanization of Europe during the eleventh and twelfth centuries was also fostered by the initiatives of monasteries and lords who saw the economic advantages to be gained from providing safe havens for travelers and trade. This was especially true in the principalities of the Rhineland, the Low Countries, and the independent counties of Flanders and Champagne. Many towns grew up around monasteries, which provided protection and encouraged innovation. In southwestern Europe, existing towns prospered from their status as ports or their location along the overland routes connecting the Mediterranean with the Atlantic. In Italy, which had been decimated by five centuries of warfare and invasion, the growth of towns gave rise to especially dramatic changes.

The renewed prosperity of Italy initially depended on Byzantine suppression of piracy in the eastern Mediterranean. The most successful cities around the turn of the millennium were situated in the Byzantine-controlled areas: Venice in the northeast and Amalfi, Naples, and Palermo in the southwest. These were the trading posts that brought silks, spices, and other Eastern luxuries into western Europe. In the eleventh century, however, the Norman invasions of southern Italy frequently disrupted this trade, while Turkish invasions of Anatolia turned

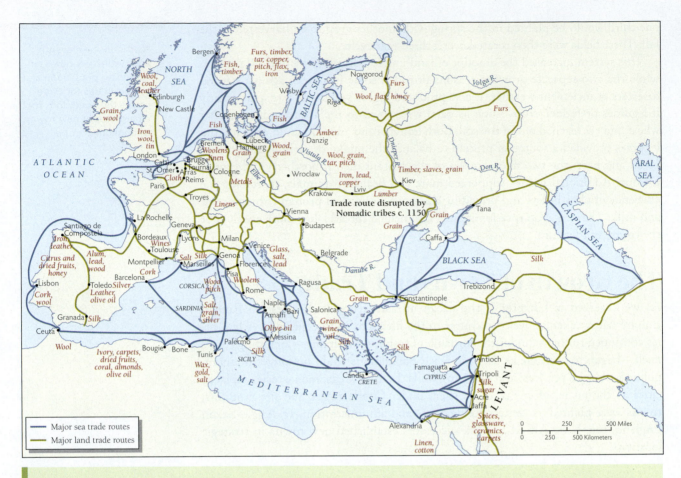

MEDIEVAL TRADE ROUTES. › What does this map reveal about the relationship between waterways and overland routes during the eleventh and twelfth centuries? › Which regions appear to be most extensively interconnected, and why? › How does the trade in certain specialized goods create certain commercial patterns?

attention to the empire's eastern frontier. This opened new opportunities for the northwestern ports of Genoa and Pisa, whose merchant navies took over policing the Mediterranean.

From these and other Mediterranean ports, exotic goods flowed northward to the towns of Flanders and the annual fairs—international markets convened at certain times of the year—that enriched the county of Champagne. Flemish towns, in turn, kept up a brisk trade in processing English wool into cloth, which was the staple commodity of medieval Europe. Older cities, including Paris and London, drew primarily on the wealth of their surrounding hinterlands for food, raw materials, and the bulk of their population.

"TOWN AIR MAKES YOU FREE"

To modern eyes, most medieval towns would still have seemed half rural. Streets were often unpaved, houses had vegetable gardens, and animals were everywhere: in the early twelfth century, the heir to the throne of France was killed when his horse

1. Cathedral
2. Alt St. Thomas
3. Alt St. Peter
4. Jung St. Peter
5. St. Nikolaus
6. St. Johann
7. St. Wilhelm
8. St. Stephen

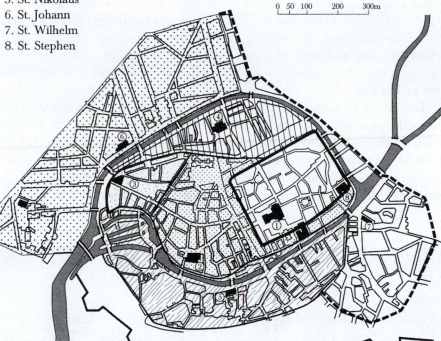

☐ Roman fortification, the 'city'

▦ Frankish settlement, called 'New City', walled at end of ninth century

▤ Extension of Frankish settlement before 1200 to include Alt St. Peter's parish

▥ Jung St. Peter's parish, walled 1202–1220

▨ St. Nikolaus parish, walled thirteenth and fourteenth centuries

▦ St. Johann Parish, walled 1374–1390

▪▪▪ St. Wilhelm parish, walled 1387–1441

THE METAMORPHOSIS OF A MEDIEVAL CITY. The city of Strasbourg, on the long-disputed border between modern Germany and France, exemplifies the multilayered dynamics of urban change throughout the Middle Ages. It began as a Roman settlement, which became the nucleus for an episcopal see—hence the cathedral (1), located in the ancient precinct. At the end of the ninth century, it was fortified with new walls as the Carolingian Empire was collapsing and the Vikings were on the move. It then responded to the renewed prosperity of the eleventh and twelfth centuries, far outgrowing its original bounds, and continued to expand for several centuries thereafter. › Note the scale of the map. What can you conclude from the scale about the density of settlement in a medieval city?

commune A community of individuals who have banded together in a sworn association, with the aim of establishing their independence and setting up their own form of representative government.

tripped over a pig running loose in Paris. Sanitary conditions were poor and the air reeked of excrement, animal and human. Under these conditions, disease could spread rapidly. Fire was another omnipresent danger because wooden and thatched buildings were clustered close together.

But these inconveniences were far outweighed by the advantages of urban life. As a German adage puts it, "Town air makes [you] free" (*Stadtluft macht frei*). This is because the citizens of most medieval towns were not subject to the arbitrary authority of a lord—or if they were, the lord realized that rewarding economic initiative with further freedoms fostered still more initiatives and wealth.

Many towns accordingly received charters of liberty from rulers and were given the right to govern themselves. Others seized that right: In 1127, the people of Arras, on the Franco-Flemish border, declared that they were no longer the serfs of the local monastery that had nurtured the growth of their town. They banded together to form a **commune**, swearing to maintain solidarity with one another and setting up their own representative government. The monastery was forced to free

THE MARKET SQUARE OF KRAKÓW (POLAND). This view of the *rynek* (or the main market square) of Kraków emphasizes the extraordinary scale of commercial activity that has taken place here since the eleventh century. Measuring around 430,000 square feet, it is one of the largest medieval town squares in Europe. Although the handsome Cloth Hall in the center was not built until the fifteenth century, it stands on the site of market stalls dating back to the foundation of the city. **›** Compare the scale of this market with the plan of Strasbourg on page 263. **›** What historical factors might account for the far more generous proportions of this newer medieval town?

them, and then was free to tax them. This arrangement was mutually beneficial; by the end of the century, Arras was the wealthiest and most densely populated town in northern Europe.

Urban areas further expanded through the constant immigration of free peasants and escaped serfs. Once a town had established its independence, newcomers could claim the status of citizens after a year and a day. For this reason, some powerful lords and rulers resisted the efforts of towns to claim independence. Almost inevitably, though, they paid a high price for this. In Rome, the pope's claim to authority over the city led to frequent uprisings. In the French city of Laon, the bishop who asserted his lordship over a newly formed commune was murdered in 1112. And in 1127, the count of Flanders was assassinated by a family of powerful officials who denied that they were his serfs.

For new residents of free towns, citizenship after a year and a day

PORTABLE WEALTH: MONEY AND CREDIT

The growth of towns and trade depends on more than surplus goods, initiative, and mobility; it also depends on a reliable supply of cash and the availability of credit. It is no accident that the earliest participants in the commercial revolution of the Middle Ages were cities located in regions whose rulers minted and regulated a strong currency: Byzantium, al-Andalus, the Christian kingdoms of Spain, the old Roman region of Provence (southern France), Anglo-Saxon England, and Flanders. Yet precisely because there were so many currencies in circulation, the economy also depended on moneychangers and bankers who could extend credit to merchants.

Most sophisticated financial mechanisms for extending credit had long been in place throughout the Islamic world and Byzantium. But in western Europe, much of this crucial activity was carried forward by Jewish bankers operating within the network of Jewish communities that connected Constantinople, Baghdad, and Córdoba to the burgeoning cities of the north. In many regions, Jews had a virtual monopoly on these activities, because Christians were technically forbidden to lend money at interest or make a profit from investments. Moneylending was called *usury* (from the Latin word for "interest"), and theologians cited various authorities that seemed to condemn it. But in practice, the Roman Church turned a blind eye to it. Indeed, many prominent bishops made fortunes lending money, as did many laymen—especially in towns such as Arras and Florence.

Still, the stigma attached to this necessary practice meant that Jews were often the ones targeted at times of crisis, just as they were the people to whom rulers would turn most readily when they needed funds—helping to explain why many kings, princes, and bishops protected the Jewish communities in their realms and extended special privileges to them in exchange for money. An unfortunate result of this was the circulation of conspiracy theories harmful to Jews, who were perceived as exercising control over Christians through secret channels of communication and maintaining a stranglehold on finance. Jewish communities' reliance on the protection of powerful men also made them vulnerable when those men withdrew their support or were incapable of controlling the violence unleashed by their own policies.

Jews, seen as key to finance, also targeted with hateful rumors

Violence, Lordship, and Monarchy

The new wealth of western Europe fostered social mobility, yet it also created a more stratified society. In the Carolingian period, the nobility comprised a relatively small number of families that counted each other as equals and married among themselves. During the tenth and eleventh centuries, however, new families began to produce territorial lords who rivaled and sometimes surpassed the old aristocracy in power and wealth. Some of these new families were descended from lesser office-holders in the Carolingian administration, men who used their public offices for private gain. Others were successful interlopers who had seized control of undefended manors and sustained war bands of treasure-hungry young men.

TOOLS OF POWER: CASTLES AND KNIGHTS

For rivaling lords, castles become key to territorial expansion and control

The predatory lords who emerged during this period protected their territories, families, and followers by building castles (from the Latin word *castellum*, "little fortress"). These structures, seldom known in Europe before the Viking invasions, came to dominate the landscape during the eleventh and twelfth centuries. A castle was both defensive and offensive. It rendered its owner more secure from arson and attack—though it was vulnerable to siege—and it enabled him to dominate the surrounding countryside. Sometimes, castles formed the nucleus of a new town by providing protection for the peasants and merchants who clustered their dwellings close to its walls. In case of attack, these outliers could move inside.

Although most early castles were modest structures built of wood, situated on earthwork mounds surrounded by a ditch or moat, stone walls and keeps (fortified towers) replaced wooden palisades as the level of competitive violence increased. In Italy, rival families even built castles and towers in the middle of towns. Eventually, some castellans ("castle-holders") acquired enough power and booty to challenge more established lords, laying claim not only to property but also to rank.

In addition to castle holding, both the older aristocracy and these self-made lords needed the help of warriors to enforce their claims to power. Accordingly, each lord maintained a private army of men heavily equipped with the weaponry and armor made possible by the widespread availability of iron, and new techniques for smelting it. These men fought on horseback, and were therefore called "horsemen" (in French, *chevaliers*; in English, *knights*). Knighthood was a career that embraced men of widely varying status. Some eleventh-century knights were the younger sons of lords who sought to increase their chances of winning wealth by attaching themselves to greater lords. Others were youths recruited from the peasantry. All that bound them together was the violent prosecution of their lord's interests. Gradually, though, knights came to regard themselves as belonging to a special military caste with its own rules of conduct. The beginnings of this process are discernible in the *Song of Roland*, and further developments would transform the meaning of *chivalry*, "horsemanship" (see page 280).

Emergence of knights as special military elite

KINGS AND LORDS

Despite the emergence of self-governing cities and new lordships, the idea of kingship was still a powerful one in Europe. For example, the weak Capetian rulers of Paris kept alive the pretense that everyone dwelling in the lands once ruled by their

more powerful Frankish predecessors still owed allegiance to them. The Ottonian dynasty claimed to be kings in northern Italy as well as in their own Saxon domain. In practice, however, neither was able to control the territories they claimed. Real political and military power lay in the hands of dukes, counts, castellans, and other local strongmen. From their castles, these lords (*domini*) constructed domains within which they exercised the rights to control property, mint money, judge legal cases, wage war, collect taxes, and impose tolls.

THE PROBLEM OF "FEUDALISM"

This highly diffused distribution of power is conventionally known as **feudalism**. But this vague term is unsatisfactory, for several reasons. First and foremost, it is a modern concept that would have puzzled anyone living in the period we are studying. Moreover, it has been used to mean very different things. Scholars influenced by the work of Karl Marx (1818–1883; see Chapter 20) use the term to describe an economic system in which wealth is entirely agricultural and cities have not yet formed; as we have seen, this does not reflect historical reality. For other scholars, feudalism means a system of landholding in which lesser men hold land from greater men in return for services of various kinds; but it was not always the greater men who held the most land or wealth. And because any such definition is anachronistic, most recent historians of the Middle Ages have challenged and abandoned the use of the term.

FIEF AND VASSALS

Although the people of this era would never have heard of "feudalism," they would have understood the word at its root: *feudum*, usually translated as "fief" (FEEF).

feudalism A problematic modern term that attempts to explain the diffusion of power in medieval Europe and the many kinds of political, social, and economic relationships that were forged through the giving and receiving of fiefs (*feoda*).

vassal A person who pledges to be loyal and subservient to a lord in exchange for land, income, or protection.

homage A ceremony in which an individual becomes the "man" (French: *homme*) of a lord.

A fief is a gift or grant that creates a kind of contractual relationship between the giver and receiver. A fief could be land, but it could also be revenues from a toll or a mill, or an annual sum of money. In return, the recipient owed the giver loyalty or services. In many cases, the gift implied that the recipient was subordinate to the giver and had in fact become the giver's **vassal** (from a Celtic word meaning "boy"). This relationship was dramatized in an act of **homage**, a powerful ceremony that made the vassal the *homme* ("man" in French) of his lord. Typically, the vassal would kneel and place his hands together in a position of prayer, and the lord would cover the clasped hands with his own. He would then raise up his new "man" and exchange a kiss with him. The symbolic importance of these gestures is clear: the lord (*dominus*) was literally the dominating figure. He could protect and raise up his man, but he could also discipline him. The role of the vassal, meanwhile, was to support the lord and do nothing to incur his displeasure.

In regions where no other form of authority existed, such personal relationships were essential to creating and maintaining order. However, these relationships were not understood in the same ways all over Europe. Many castellans and knights held their lands freely, owing no service whatsoever to the count or duke within whose territories their lands lay. Nor were these relationships neatly hierarchical: "feudalism" created no "feudal pyramids," in which knights held fiefs from counts, and counts held fiefs from kings, all in orderly fashion. Sometimes, kings would insist that the world *should* be structured this way, but they were seldom able to make this a reality.

A NEW TYPE OF MONARCHY: ENGLAND

The first place where we can observe a monarchy that successfully dominated other powerful lordships is England. In 1066, Duke William of Normandy claimed that he was the rightful successor of the English king, Edward the Confessor, who had just died. But the English elected a new king, Harold, ignoring William's claim. So William crossed the English Channel to take the kingdom by force, killing Harold at the Battle of Hastings (see *Interpreting Visual Evidence* on page 269). Now, William had to subjugate all the other chieftains who held power in England, many of whom also aspired to be king.

William accomplished this by asserting that he was king by imperial conquest as well as by succession, and that all the land of England thereby belonged to him. Then William rewarded his Norman followers with fiefs: extensive grants of land taken from their English holders. In return, William received their loyalty and a share of their revenues.

The Norman conquerors of England were already accustomed to holding land in return for service to their duke, back in Normandy. But in England, their subordination to the king was further enforced by the effective machinery of the Anglo-Saxon state and longstanding customs that had the force of law. As king of England, therefore, William was able to exercise a variety of public powers that he could not have enjoyed in Normandy. In England, only the king could coin money, and only the king's money was allowed to circulate. As kings of England, William and his successors also inherited the right to collect a national land tax, supervise justice in royal courts, and raise an army. They even retained the Anglo-Saxon officers of local government, known as sheriffs, to help them administer their rights.

The Graphic History of the Bayeux Tapestry

One of the most famous historical documents of all time is not a document at all, but an embroidered strip of linen 231 feet long (originally much longer) and 20 inches wide. It is also not an actual tapestry, as its name misleadingly implies, but an elaborate exercise in needlepoint. It tells the story of the Norman conquest of England and the events leading up to it. The circumstances of its making remain a mystery, but it was certainly commissioned by someone close to William the Conqueror (1027–1087), the Norman duke who claimed the throne of England in 1066. Indeed, its purpose was to demonstrate the truth of William's claim and to justify his invasion of England when Harold Godwinson (c. 1022–1066; image A) was crowned king of England in his place (image B). One likely patron was Queen Edith of England, the widow of the late King Edward (r. 1042–1066) and sister of Harold, who became a friend and adviser to William. Edith was noted for her skill in embroidery as well as for her political acumen, and she would have been able to oversee the making of this visual history by the women of her household. Two of its evocative scenes, with translations of accompanying Latin texts, are reproduced here.

A. Harold Sails the Sea. In this scene, from the first portion of the tapestry, Harold has been sent on an embassy by King Edward. He feasts with friends in a hall on the English coast before crossing the Channel.

B. Harold Is Seated, King of the English. Although Harold may have promised to relinquish his claim to the English throne in William's favor, the central scene of the tapestry is his coronation. Stigant, the archbishop of Canterbury, stands on his left. Outside the cathedral, the people of London look on curiously. Some appear to be surprised or alarmed.

Questions for Analysis

1. Like a graphic novel or a comic strip, the Bayeux Tapestry tells its story through images, and words (in very simple Latin) play a minor role. What do the tapestry's artists choose to express exclusively through visualization? When do they choose to state something verbally? What might be the motivation behind these choices? What is left out of the story, or left ambiguous? What might be the reason(s) for this ambiguity?

2. In addition to being a source for political and military historians, the Bayeux Tapestry provides us with fascinating glimpses into the daily life and material culture of the Middle Ages. What, for example, can you conclude about the necessary preparations for a voyage by sea? About the history of clothing, weaponry, or animals?

3. If Queen Edith was responsible for commissioning and helping to make the tapestry, it would constitute one of the few surviving historical accounts by a woman prior to the twentieth century. Would the creator's gender change your perception of this artifact or of these particular scenes? Why or why not?

In England, a new type of minority

William and his heirs thereby insisted that all the people of England owed ultimate loyalty to the king, even if they did not hold a scrap of land from him. Anglo-Norman kingship thus represented a powerful fusion of Carolingian traditions of imperial power with the new forms of lordship that had grown up in the tenth and eleventh centuries, bolstered by indigenous Anglo-Saxon forms of governance. It was a new type of monarchy.

THE STRUGGLE FOR IMPERIAL POWER

We can contrast the wide-ranging powers of the Anglo-Norman kings with those of German lands. No German king could claim to rule more than a single principality, and his authority as Emperor of the Romans was maintained only through a close alliance with the Church. For this reason, he relied heavily on his chief administrators: archbishops and bishops whom the emperor himself had appointed and installed in their offices, just as Charlemagne had done. The pope himself was frequently an imperial appointee. The fact that leading churchmen were often members of the imperial family also helped to counter the power of regional rulers.

But during the latter half of the eleventh century, this close cooperation between sacred and secular authority was fractured, as was the ultimate power of the German monarch, by this **Investiture Controversy**: a dispute over whether rulers could appoint their own bishops and invest them with their offices. It began in 1056, when the six-year-old Henry IV (1050–1106) succeeded his father as king and emperor. As we have frequently noted, political competition among the advisers of underage rulers often escalates into larger conflicts. In this case, German rulers of various regions tried to gain control of the royal government at the expense of Henry's regents. After Henry began to rule in his own right, these hostilities escalated into a civil war that broke out in 1073.

Meanwhile, the newly elected pope, Gregory VII (r. 1073–1085), began to insist that no layman—not even a king or emperor—should have any influence within the Church, and should certainly not be choosing and investing men who held Church offices. King Henry, of course, resisted any initiative that would prohibit him from selecting his own bishops, for these were key to the administration of his realm. So Pope Gregory allied himself with the rebellious German rulers, and together they moved to depose Henry.

To save his crown, Henry was forced to acknowledge the pope's superiority. Crossing the Alps into Italy in 1077, in the depths of winter, Henry found Gregory installed at the castle of Canossa under the protection of one of Europe's most powerful rulers, Matilda of Tuscany. Encouraged by Matilda, Henry performed an elaborate ritual of penance: standing for three successive days outside the gates of the castle, barefoot, stripped of his imperial trappings, clad in the sackcloth of a supplicant. This performance of subjection forestalled Henry's deposition, but it did not resolve his dispute with the nobility of German lands. And it also symbolically reversed the relationship between secular power and religious power. Since the time of Constantine, popes had been dependent on the rulers who protected them; but now, an emperor had been bested by a pope. For the other kings and lords of Europe, Henry's humiliation was a chilling example of what could happen when a king let himself be made a vassal.

Investiture Controversy
A series of disputes over the limitations of spiritual and secular power in medieval Europe. It came to a head when Pope Gregory VII and Emperor Henry IV of Germany both claimed the right to appoint and "invest" bishops with the regalia of office.

Religious Reform and Papal Power

The increased power of the papacy was a development that would have been hard to foresee at the time of Charlemagne's death. Yet, in the wake of the Viking invasions and the redistribution of power within the former Carolingian Empire, no ruler could maintain Charlemagne's hold on the Church. Many local churches had been abandoned or destroyed; those that survived were usually regarded as the personal property of some local family, whose responsibility for protecting parishioners could become an excuse to oppress them. Bishoprics, too, were regarded by certain powerful families as their private property.

Even monasteries underwent a process of privatization, becoming safe havens for aristocratic younger sons and daughters with little inclination for religious life. Meanwhile, the holders of papal office were its worst abusers. Most were the incompetent or corrupt sons of powerful Roman families. Many fathered sons who themselves succeeded to high ecclesiastical office, including that of pope. As the guardian of the tombs of Peter and Paul, the bishop of Rome had long occupied a privileged position in Christendom. Now, however, the papacy's very credibility had been compromised.

THE MONASTIC REFORM MOVEMENT

The first successful attempt to restore the spiritual authority of the Roman Church can be traced to the founding of a new kind of monastery in Burgundy (now southeastern France). In 910, a Benedictine abbey called Cluny freed itself from any obligation to local families by placing itself under the direct protection of the papacy. And although it had a wealthy benefactor, that benefactor relinquished control over Cluny's property; instead, Duke William of Aquitaine and his family gained the spiritual support and prayers of the monks, to save them from damnation.

This arrangement would set a new precedent for centuries to come, as Cluny began to sponsor other monasteries on the same model. Indeed, the foundation of these "daughter" houses was another innovation: prior to this, all Benedictine monasteries had been independent of each other, united only by their observance of Benedict's *Rule*. Now, Cluny established a network of Cluniac clones across Europe, all of which

MATILDA OF TUSCANY MEDIATES BETWEEN EMPEROR AND POPE. Matilda was one of the most powerful rulers in eleventh-century Europe, controlling many strategic territories in northern Italy. Fluent in German as well as Latin and Italian, she was a key mediator in the struggle between the emperor and the pope, and a supporter of the reforming movement within the Church. The Latin inscription accompanying this manuscript miniature reads: "The King entreats the Abbot [i.e., the pope] and even humbles himself before Matilda." › How does this image represent the relationships among these figures? › Which appears to be the most powerful, and why?

remained subordinate to the mother house. By 1049, there were sixty-seven such priories, each one performing the same elaborate round of worship for which Cluny became famous—and each one entirely free from the control of local lords.

Cluniac influence was strongest in the former Frankish territories and in Italy. In Germany and England, by contrast, fostering monastic reforms emerged as an essential responsibility of Christian rulers whose role model was the pious Charlemagne. These rulers, too, began to insist on the strict observance of poverty, chastity, and obedience within the monastery, and on the performance of liturgical prayer. Yet, because these rulers were the guarantors of the monasteries' freedom, it was they who appointed the abbots, just as they also appointed the bishops of their kingdoms. As a result, the kings of England would continue to have more direct control over Church lands than other European rulers. In Germany, as we have seen, a ruler's right to appoint spiritual leaders was the central cause of strife with the papacy.

> *Monastic life and tradition increasingly influence everyday people*

Despite their differences, these parallel reforming movements made monasticism the dominant spiritual model for Latin Christianity. Monasteries also had an important influence on the piety of ordinary people, because many monastic communities maintained parishes that ministered to the laity. The spiritual practices that had been unique to monks and nuns in earlier centuries, therefore, came to influence daily life outside the cloister.

RELICS AND PILGRIMS

One potent example of this new popular spirituality was the growing devotion to relics. Monasteries were often the repositories of cherished objects associated with saints, such as fragments of bone or pieces of cloth cut from the garments of some holy person. These souvenirs were believed to possess special protective and curative powers. Hence, a relic was always buried beneath the altar of a church during the ceremony of its consecration, to render the church building sacrosanct. Within the church, reliquaries made of precious metals and studded with jewels both reflected and augmented the value of the holy objects they contained.

Relics were so valuable that monasteries and cathedrals competed with one another for their acquisition and even plotted the "holy theft" of a particularly prized treasure. For instance, the relics of Nicholas, a fourth-century bishop of Myra (Turkey), were stolen from the saint's tomb during the eleventh century. These were brought to Bari in southeastern Italy, where Benedictine monks built a magnificent church to house them. It became a major—and lucrative—destination for pilgrims.

The possession and display of relics thus became a way for monasteries to generate revenue, since those who sought cures or favors at the shrine of a saint would make a donation to the monastery in the saint's honor. If a saint was especially famous for a particular type of miracle, pilgrims might travel thousands of miles to visit a shrine. Saint Nicholas was famous for increasing the wealth of his supplicants, and for bestowing gifts—hence his later incarnation as Santa Claus. The relics of Sainte Foy ("Saint Faith") of Conques (south-central France) were renowned for their power to rectify injustices, restore order, and heal the maladies of the poor. Those of the apostle James at Compostela (northern Spain) became the chief destination on a major pilgrimage route, rivaling even the holy sites of Rome and Jerusalem in its popularity.

Pilgrimage was another of the important ways in which the new patterns of Christian piety that developed in monasteries began to spread to the laity. Lay men and women from all social classes are represented in the records of the miracles recorded at shrines, many traveling in family groups or with neighbors. And because it was considered holy to house, feed, and care for pilgrims, many monasteries opened special hostels. As a result, even people of very humble means were able to make trips to shrines very far from home, increasing their sense of belonging to a shared Christian community.

Religious pilgrims and those hosting such travelers foster sense of Christian community

THE REFORM OF THE SECULAR CLERGY

By the eleventh century, the movement toward spiritual renewal in the monasteries of Europe began to embrace the sees of bishops. This was a major change. Bishops and the priests who served in their dioceses were secular clergy, living in the world (*saeculum*), and it had long been accepted that they would share some of the same worldly lifestyles. But as the values of reformed monasticism began to spread outward, abbots were more often appointed to episcopal offices. As a result, even nonmonastic bishops were forced to adopt stricter standards of personal conduct.

As their influence grew, the monasteries under the sway of Cluny began to lobby for even larger reforms, dismantling customs that reached back to the organization of the Church under Constantine. They centered their attacks on the practice of simony (*SIGH-mony*), a term describing any use of ecclesiastical office for personal gain, including the purchase or sale of a bishopric or a priest's living (house, goods, and annual salary). In other words, the reform movement targeted the very structure of the Church as a network of independent lordships held by powerful men in trust for their families.

Even more radical was the reformers' demand that secular clergy share the lifestyles of monks, taking vows of personal poverty and celibacy. Although some early councils of the Church had attempted to regulate the marriage of bishops and priests, none had been successful. And for good reason: ministering to the laity was a very different task from the monk's perpetual prayer and communal life. For a thousand years, it had been conceded that the demands of priestly celibacy were unreasonable, and would deprive parishioners of an additional resource and ministry—that of the priest's wife. In the year 1000, therefore, the vast majority of parish priests all across Europe were married, and in the eastern Orthodox Church they would remain so. Married bishops were more rare, but not unknown.

THE REFORM OF THE PAPACY

In Rome, the most powerful bishopric of all remained unreformed until 1046, when Emperor Henry III deposed three rival Roman nobles who claimed to be pope and appointed, instead, his own relative: a monk who adopted the name Leo IX (r. 1049–1054). Leo and his supporters took control of the papal court and began to promulgate decrees against simony and clerical marriage. They then took steps to enforce these decrees by traveling throughout Christendom, disciplining or removing from office priests deemed guilty of simony or reluctant to "put away" their wives—whom the reformers insisted on calling "concubines" as a way of discrediting legitimate relationships.

A Miraculous Reliquary

Although pilgrimages had been a part of Christian religious practice for centuries, they became much more central elements of popular piety from the tenth century on. Pilgrims brought money and spiritual prestige to the monasteries and cathedrals that housed miracle-working relics, and competition among monastic houses sometimes led one house to steal the relics of another. But some critics worried that these newly popular shrines were encouraging idolatry. Bernard of Angers (c. 960–1028) was one such critic. His account of a visit to the shrines of several saints, including that of Sainte Foy ("Saint Faith") at Conques, reveals the negative impression that ornate reliquaries made on him—and the power of wonder-working relics to correct that impression.

It is an ancient custom in all of Auvergne, Rodez, Toulouse, and the neighboring regions that the local saint has a statue of gold, silver, or some other metal . . . [that] serves as a reliquary for the head of the saint or for a part of his body. The learned might see in this a superstition and a vestige of the cult of demons, and I myself . . . had the same impression the first time I saw the statue of Saint Gerard . . . resplendent with gold and stones, with an expression so human that the simple people . . . pretend that it winks at pilgrims whose prayers it answers. I admit to my shame that turning to my friend Bernerius and laughing, I whispered to him in Latin, "What do you think of the idol? Wouldn't Jupiter or Mars be happy with it?" . . .

Three days later we arrived at [the shrine of] St. Faith. . . . We approached [the reliquary] but the crowd was such that we could not prostrate ourselves like so many others already lying on the floor. Unhappy, I remained standing, fixing my view on the image and murmuring this prayer, "St. Faith, you whose relics rest in this sham, come to my assistance on the day of judgment." And this time I looked at my companion . . . because I found it outrageous that all of these rational beings should be praying to a mute and inanimate object. . . .

Later I greatly regretted to have acted so stupidly toward the saint of God. This was because among other miracles [that] Don Adalgerius, at that time dean and later . . . abbot [of Conques], told me [was] a remarkable account of a cleric named Oldaric. One day when the venerable image had to be taken to another place, . . . he restrained the crowd from bringing offerings and he insulted and belittled the image of the saint. . . . The next

These reforming efforts promoted a new vision of the papacy as a type of monarchy, one that would severely limit the power of other ecclesiastical officeholders. It is not surprising, therefore, that Leo and his successors met considerable opposition from other powerful bishops within the Church. To counter this, Pope Nicholas II (r. 1059–1061) created a new legislative body, the College of Cardinals. Hitherto, Italian bishops around Rome had served the papacy as informal advisers, but now this body became the nexus for the creation of papal policy. It also ensured the continuity of the papal office by overseeing the selection of new popes, a role it still plays today.

THE INVESTITURE CONFLICT

This novel arrangement infuriated many bishops elsewhere in Europe, as well as many secular rulers because it denied the emperor's prerogative to oversee the process of papal selection himself and threatened all rulers' longstanding rights of night, a lady of imposing severity appeared to him: "You," she said, "how dare you insult my image?" Having said this, she flogged her enemy with a staff. . . . He survived only long enough to tell the vision in the morning.

Thus there is no place left for arguing whether the effigy of St. Faith ought to be venerated since it is clear that he who reproached the holy martyr nevertheless retracted his reproach. Nor is it a spurious idol where nefarious rites of sacrifice or of divination are conducted, but rather a pious memorial of a holy virgin, before which great numbers of faithful people decently and eloquently implore her efficacious intercession for their sins.

Source: Bernard of Angers, "The Procession of Saint Foy," in *Readings in Medieval History*, 5th ed, Patrick J. Geary, ed. (Toronto, Canada: 2016), pp. 290–91 (slightly modified).

Questions for Analysis

1. Why does Bernard initially object to the display of relics in ornate reliquaries? Why would he consider this practice blasphemous? How does he become reconciled to it?

2. Can you think of present-day practices that resemble the medieval fascination with collecting, displaying, and venerating relics? What do such practices reveal about any society?

The Reliquary of Saint Faith, Early Tenth Century.

choosing bishops within their own domains. The stage was already set for a conflict when the new College of Cardinals selected a Cluniac monk to become Pope Gregory VII. As we noted above, Gregory was a zealous promoter of the papacy's primacy over all Christian rulers, and the most visible sign of that primacy was, as we noted previously, **investiture**: the right to appoint bishops and to equip them with the regalia of office. According to Gregory, this practice smacked of simony, since a lay lord would obviously choose bishops who would be politically useful to him, regardless of their spiritual qualifications.

The real issue, however, was not the political power of bishops but the source of that power. The papal reform movement, as it developed under Gregory, was predicated (somewhat paradoxically) on liberating the Church from powerful worldly influences in order that the Church itself might become more powerful. This was the principle that lay behind discouraging clerical marriage, too: Church offices and Church property had to be protected by the Church for the Church; allowing priests

investiture the right to appoint bishops and to equip them with the regalia of office.

to marry might encourage the handing down of offices to sons, just as allowing rulers to appoint bishops encouraged these bishops to act as the rulers' agents. These practices threatened to alienate property and power that the papacy wanted to harness for its own purposes.

Gregory therefore took the reform movement to a new level, by insisting that adherence to these principles was not just a matter of policy but of religious dogma, defined as a "truth necessary for salvation." When Emperor Henry IV refused to accept Gregory's reforms and proceeded to select and invest the new archbishop of Milan, Gregory proclaimed that, as the successor of Saint Peter and the representative of Christ on earth, he himself had the power to save or damn all souls. To drive the point home, Gregory excommunicated a number of Henry's advisers, including several of the bishops who had participated in the investiture at Milan. Henry thereupon renounced his obedience to Gregory, calling on him to resign, to which Gregory responded by excommunicating Henry and his supporters.

In itself, the (temporary) excommunication of a king was not terribly unusual. Gregory, however, went much further by equating excommunication with deposition, declaring that since Henry was no longer a faithful son of the Church, he was no longer king either—and so his subjects had a sacred duty to rebel against him. It was this declaration that occasioned Henry's humiliating penance at Canossa in January of 1077. But the story does not end there, because Henry used his restored powers to crush Gregory's supporters among the German nobility and eventually to drive Gregory himself from Rome; in 1085, the aged pope died in exile in southern Italy. By then, however, he had established the principles on which papal governance would be based for the remainder of the Middle Ages.

Concordat of Worms resolves investiture controversy as Emperor Henry IV acknowledges free election of bishops and abbots

In 1122, the conflict over investiture was provisionally resolved at the Concordat of Worms (*Vohrms*) in Germany. Its terms declared that the emperor was forbidden to invest prelates with the *religious* symbols of their office but was allowed to invest them with the symbols of their rights as *temporal* or secular rulers. In practice, then, the rulers of Europe retained a great deal of influence over ecclesiastical appointments, but they also had to acknowledge that bishops were now part of a clerical hierarchy headed by the pope, and thus more loyal to the Church in Rome than to the ruler of the region in which they lived.

Crusading Causes and Outcomes

Gregory VII's equation of excommunication with deposition had given the pope a powerful new weapon, but his immediate successors would struggle to establish the credibility of his claims. In the end, it took the appeal of a Byzantine emperor and the preaching of a crusade against Muslims to unite western Christendom under the papal banner.

THE EXPANSION AND FRAGILITY OF BYZANTIUM

As Europe expanded, the eastern Roman Empire was undergoing its own series of transformations. The decline of the Abbasid caliphate in Baghdad had relieved some of the pressures on its borders, but Muslims from North Africa captured the Byzantine islands of Sicily and Crete. Meanwhile, the migration of pagan

Slavs into the Balkans was undermining Byzantine control of that region. And a formidable power had emerged in the north, where the Viking Rus' established themselves along the river systems that fed into the Black and Caspian Seas and sacked Constantinople.

The Byzantine response was to make these new enemies into allies. Greek-speaking missionaries began the process by converting some of the Balkan Slavs to Orthodox Christianity, devising for them a written language known as Old Church Slavonic and creating the Cyrillic alphabet still used today in Russia, Ukraine, Bulgaria, and Serbia. The empire also fostered a military and commercial alliance with the kingdom of Rus' centered around Kiev. In 911, hundreds of Rus' served with the Byzantine navy in an attack on Muslim Crete. In 957, a Kievan princess named Olga was lavishly entertained on a state visit to Constantinople. And in 989, Vladimir of Kiev helped Basil II win a civil war against an imperial rival; in return, Basil married him to his sister Anna, and Vladimir, along with his people, accepted baptism into the Orthodox Church.

At the same time, the eastern Roman Empire further strengthened its position by launching a series of successful campaigns against the Abbasids, reconquering territories that had been lost during the first wave of Muslim conquests in the seventh century. But although most of the peoples of this region had remained Christian through three centuries of Islamic rule, the Armenians and the Syrians in particular had their own distinctive Christian traditions that were at odds, both doctrinally and linguistically, with the Greek-speaking church at Constantinople. Reincorporating these "heretics" into the empire strained the limits of Orthodoxy to a considerable degree, and created centers of power that lay outside the imperial capital. Accordingly, rivalries divided the eastern nobility of the empire and the imperial court, eventually erupting into warfare after one aristocratic family attempted a coup.

All of these projects of reconquest and expansion were overextending the Byzantine military and treasury. In an effort to raise cash, some emperors began to debase the gold coinage that had kept the empire competitive with the Islamic caliphates, thus undermining Byzantine commerce at the very moment when Venice, Genoa, and Pisa were consolidating their control in the eastern Mediterranean and taking over the lucrative trade between Muslim North Africa and western Europe.

THE BYZANTINE EMPIRE, c. 1025. › According to the map, what political challenges faced the Byzantine Empire in the eleventh century? › How was the long-standing influence of Muslims in the Near East likely to affect the character of Byzantine culture? › How did the domain of Rus' potentially create additional economic and military pressure on Byzantium, directly as well as indirectly?

Preaching the First Crusade: Two Accounts

We owe the following account of Urban II's call for a crusade to Fulcher of Chartres, a priest who was present at the Council of Clermont in 1095 and later served as a chaplain to Baldwin, the first Norman king of Jerusalem. It forms part of Fulcher's contemporary chronicle of the First Crusade. The second account of the motives behind the Crusade comes from a biography of the Byzantine emperor Alexius Comnenus, written by his daughter Anna (1083–1153), who also lived through these events.

Pope Urban II's Call at Clermont, November 1095

Most beloved brethren: Urged by necessity, I, Urban, by the permission of God chief bishop and prelate over the whole world, have come into these parts as an ambassador with a divine admonition to you, the servants of God. . . .

Although, O sons of God, you have promised more firmly than ever to keep the peace among yourselves and to preserve the rights of the Church, there remains still an important work for you to do. Freshly quickened by the divine correction, you must apply the strength of your righteousness to another matter which concerns you as well as God. For your brethren who live in the east are in urgent need of your help, and you must hasten to give them the aid which has often been promised them. For, as most of you have heard, the Turks and Arabs have attacked them and have conquered the territory of Romania [the Byzantine Empire] as far west as the shore of the Mediterranean and the Hellespont. . . . They have occupied more and more of the lands of those Christians, and have overcome them in seven battles. They have killed and captured many, and have destroyed the churches and devastated the empire.

If you permit them to continue thus for a while with impunity, the faithful of God will be much more widely attacked by them. On this account I, or rather the Lord, beseech you as Christ's heralds to publish this everywhere and to persuade all people of whatever rank, footsoldiers and knights, poor and rich, to carry aid promptly to those Christians and to destroy that vile race from the lands of our friends. I say this to those who are present, but it is meant also for those who are absent. Moreover, Christ commands it.

All who die by the way, whether by land or by sea, or in battle against the pagans, shall have immediate remission of sins. This I grant them through the power of God with which I am invested. O what a disgrace, if such a despised and base race, which worships demons, should conquer a people which has the faith of omnipotent God and is made glorious with the name of Christ! With what reproaches will the Lord overwhelm us if you do not aid those who, with us, profess the Christian religion!

Let those who have been accustomed to wage unjust private warfare against the faithful now go against the infidels and end with victory this war which should have been begun long ago. Let those who for a long time have been robbers now become knights. Let those who have been fighting against their brothers and relatives now fight in a proper way against the barbarians. Let those who have been serving as mercenaries for

A failing economy, ongoing civil war, the weakening of the army, and uneasy relations with the new kingdoms of the Balkans proved nearly fatal to Byzantine sovereignty. And then, the empire was confronted with yet another threat: the Seljuk Turks, a powerful dynasty of Sunni Muslims who were building their own empire based in Persia, began to move westward in the latter part of the eleventh century.

small pay now obtain the eternal reward. Let those who have been wearing themselves out in both body and soul now work for a double honor. Behold! On this side will be the sorrowful and poor, on that, the rich; on this side, the enemies of the Lord, on that, his friends. Let those who go not put off the journey, but rent their lands and collect money for their expenses; and as soon as winter is over and spring comes, let them eagerly set out on the way with God as their guide.

Source: S. J. Allen and Emilie Amt, eds., *The Crusades: A Reader*, 2nd ed. (University of Toronto: 2014), pp. 34–35.

Anna Comnena Describes the Beginnings of the First Crusade

[Alexius] had no time to relax before he heard a rumour that countless Frankish armies were approaching. He dreaded their arrival, knowing as he did their uncontrollable passion, their erratic character and their irresolution, not to mention . . . their greed for money. . . . So far from despairing, however, he made every effort to prepare for war if need arose. What actually happened was more far-reaching and terrible than rumour suggested, for the whole of the West and all the barbarians who lived between the Adriatic and the Straits of Gibraltar migrated in a body to Asia, marching across Europe country by country with all their households. The reason for this mass movement is to be found more or less in the following events. A certain Kelt, called Peter [the Hermit] . . . left to worship at the Holy Sepulchre and after suffering much ill-treatment at the hands of the Turks and Saracens who were plundering the whole of Asia, he returned home with difficulty. Unable to admit defeat, . . . he worked out a clever scheme. He decided to preach in all the Latin countries. A divine voice, he said, commanded him to proclaim to all the counts in France that all should depart from their homes, set out to worship at the Holy Shrine, and . . . strive to liberate Jerusalem. . . . Surprisingly, he was successful. . . . Full of enthusiasm and ardour they thronged every highway, and with these warriors came a host of civilians, outnumbering the sand of the sea shore or the stars of heaven, carrying palms and bearing crosses on their shoulders. There were women and children, too, who had left their own countries. . . .

The upheaval that ensued as men *and* women took to the road was unprecedented within living memory. The simpler folk were in very truth led on by a desire to worship at Our Lord's tomb and visit the holy places, but the more villainous characters . . . had an ulterior purpose, for they hoped on their journey to seize the capital [Jerusalem] itself, looking upon its capture as a natural consequence of the expedition. . . .

Source: Excerpted from *The Alexiad of Anna Comnena*, trans. E. R. A. Sewter (New York: 1969), pp. 308–11.

Questions for Analysis

1. Given Urban II's explanation of the problems confronting the Byzantine Empire, how do you account for the fact that the Crusades were directed toward the Holy Land and not the relief of Byzantium?

2. How does Anna Comnena represent the motives of Peter the Hermit and the crusaders? What distinctions does she make among the participants?

3. Are there points of comparison between these two accounts? On what do they agree? How would you explain the differences between them?

In 1071, they captured Armenia and moved swiftly into the Byzantine heartland of Anatolia, where they destroyed a Byzantine army sent to deflect them.

At a blow, the wealthiest and most productive part of the empire fell into Muslim hands—and not those of the Abbasids, with whom the Byzantines had contended for centuries. In the same year, the Seljuks captured Jerusalem, which had been part of a Shi'ite caliphate based in Egypt, ruled by the Fatimids. By 1081, when the eastern nobility of Byzantium finally emerged triumphant in their ongoing bid for the imperial throne, the new emperor **Alexius Comnenus** (r. 1081–1118) found himself at the head of a crippled state.

THE CALL FOR A CRUSADE

In the first decade of his rule, Alexius managed to shore up the failing economy and secure his hold over the Balkans. He then began to plan a campaign against the Seljuks. But with what forces? The Byzantine army had been decimated in Greece by a far superior cavalry of Norman knights in 1085. For the Normans had established independent principalities in southern Italy and Sicily and were moving farther east, taking advantage of the power vacuum in the eastern Mediterranean and showcasing the effective tactics of chivalry. This encounter between the Byzantine army and western Europe's newly formidable warriors convinced Alexius that such heavily armed horsemen would be successful if pitted against the lightly armored Seljuks.

It was in the hopes of recruiting a mercenary force, therefore, that Alexius approached **Pope Urban II** (r. 1088–1099). This was a move that played into the hands of the papacy: Urban was struggling to realize some of the powerful claims that his recent predecessors had made on behalf of papal authority, and this seemed like a golden opportunity. By coming to the aid of the eastern Roman Empire, he would show the restive rulers of western Europe that the papacy was a force to be reckoned with. At the same time, he hoped to show that Latin military and spiritual might was greater than that of the weakened Greeks, thereby healing the schism between Orthodox and Roman Churches and realizing the centuries-old dream of a universal Christian Church based in Rome. In addition, Urban could support another reform that had gained momentum in recent years: a peace movement that was attempting to quell the cycles of violence unleashed by competitive bands of knights and their rapacious lords. What better way to defuse the situation than to ship those violent energies overseas, deploying them against a common enemy?

So Alexius received a favorable reply, but he got far more than he had asked for—or wanted. He had needed a few thousand knights to help him reconquer Anatolia. Instead, he got a vast army of a hundred thousand men, charged by Urban II to retake the holy city of Jerusalem for Christendom. For Urban decided to interpret Alexius's request very loosely (see *Competing Viewpoints* on pages 278–279). Speaking before an assembled crowd at an ecclesiastical council at Clermont (central France) in 1095, Urban announced that he fully supported the peace movement. He said, furthermore, that any knights who wished to fight, pillage, and wreak havoc could do so for a just and Christian cause by liberating the Holy Land from its Muslim rulers. At home, said Urban, most knights were riffraff and marauders, destined for hellfire and damnation; but abroad, by fighting or dying in the service of Christ, they would win absolution for their sins. By taking up the cross (*crux*, hence "crusade"), a warrior stood to win glory, booty, and salvation all at once.

THE MOTIVES OF CRUSADERS

The **First Crusade** was an irresistible lure for many ambitious or opportunistic men. Consequently, the ultimate response to Urban's call exceeded all expectations.

Indeed, his message was amplified by other preachers, including a zealous priest called Peter the Hermit, who claimed (falsely) that he had been prevented by the Seljuks from visiting the Holy Land. Within a year, tens of thousands of warriors, many of them new to battle, were on the march toward Constantinople, where they intended to gather before departing for Jerusalem. They were joined by thousands of women, even whole families, whose presence in the throng was noted by many chroniclers.

As with any large enterprise, the participants' motives must have varied. A few might have hoped to win principalities for themselves. Others were drawn by the prospect of adventure and the opportunity to escape the narrow confines of established social norms. Many were the dependents of greater men and had no choice but to accompany their lords; some hoped to free themselves from dependence by fighting. Most probably had no idea how long the journey would be or knew anything about the places for which they were destined.

Except for a few of the greatest lords—mostly Normans from Sicily and southern Italy—the prospect of winning new lands was both unlikely and undesired. Indeed, one of the greatest challenges facing the Christian kingdom that was established in Jerusalem after 1099 was the fact that crusaders so rarely wanted to stay. After fulfilling their vows, the vast majority went home. So why did they go in the first place? The risks of dying on such a journey were high, and the costs of embarking were enormous. Crusading knights needed a minimum of two years' revenues in hand to finance the journey; to raise such sums, most were forced to mortgage lands and borrow heavily from family, friends, monasteries, and merchants. They then had to find some way to pay back these loans if and when they returned home. By any rational assessment, the Crusade was a fool's errand.

The seeming irrationality of this endeavor underscores the importance of reckoning with the crusaders' piety, and even their desire to emulate legendary heroes such as Roland. Crusading was the ultimate pilgrimage, the holy places of Jerusalem the ultimate Christian shrines. If anyone could receive special blessings by traveling to Compostela, Conques, or Bari, how much more blessed would be those who fought through to the Holy Land! Urban II made this point explicit at Clermont, promising that crusaders would be freed from all penances imposed by the Church. Some zealots went even further, promising that crusaders would be entirely freed from all sins committed up to that point in their lives, and that the souls of those who died on a crusade would go straight to heaven.

Crusade preachers also emphasized the vengeance that Christ's soldiers should exact on his

ROLAND AS A CRUSADING KNIGHT. The association between knighthood and crusading helped to raise the social status of knights, and contributed to the refinement of a chivalric ethos. Here, Roland, as a crusading knight, dressed head to foot in expensive chain mail, is shown kneeling in homage to his lord, God.

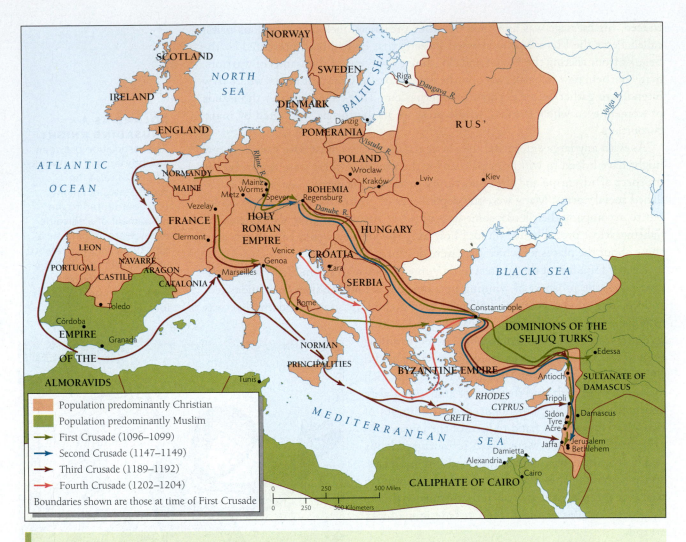

Population predominantly Christian
Population predominantly Muslim
→ First Crusade (1096–1099)
→ Second Crusade (1147–1149)
→ Third Crusade (1189–1192)
→ Fourth Crusade (1202–1204)
Boundaries shown are those at time of First Crusade

THE ROUTES OF THE CRUSADERS, 1096–1204. Compare the routes followed by the majority of participants in the first three Crusades. › What were the three main routes followed? › What geographical and political factors appear to be determining these trajectories? › Why was the Fourth Crusade so different?

pagan enemies. To some crusaders, accordingly, it seemed absurd to wait until they arrived in the Holy Land to undertake this aspect of their mission. Muslims might hold Jesus' property at Jerusalem, but Christians held Jews responsible for the death of Jesus himself. Assaults against Jewish communities therefore began in the spring of 1096 and quickly spread eastward with the crusading armies. Hundreds of Jews were massacred in the German towns of Mainz, Worms, Speyer, and Cologne, and hundreds more were forcibly baptized as the price for escaping death at the hands of crusading knights. Many individual rulers attempted to prevent these attacks, among them the bishops in whose dioceses Jews lived. But the Church's own negative propaganda thwarted these efforts, and pogroms (organized attacks) against Europe's Jews would remain a regular feature of Christian crusading.

THE CHRISTIAN CONQUEST OF JERUSALEM

Surprised by the nature and scale of the papal response to his appeal, Emperor Alexius did his best to move the crusaders quickly through Constantinople and into Anatolia. But differences in outlook between the crusaders and the Byzantine emperor quickly became apparent. Alexius had little interest in an expedition to Jerusalem, insisting that the crusaders promise to restore any territory they captured to his empire. To the crusaders—whose mission had been shaped by Pope Urban's policies, not those of Alexius—this seemed like treachery. The crusaders, furthermore, did not understand the Byzantine emperor's willingness to make alliances with some Muslim rulers (the Shi'ite Fatimids of Egypt and the Abbasids of Baghdad) against other Muslim rulers (the Sunni Seljuks). They ignorantly concluded that the Byzantines were working to undermine the crusading effort, perhaps even supporting the Muslims against them. Such suspicions contributed to their growing conviction that the eastern Roman Empire was itself an obstacle to the successful recovery of Jerusalem.

Viewed from the perspective of Alexius, the Crusade was a disaster; but from that of the crusaders, it was a triumph. In 1098, crusaders captured the old Hellenistic city of Antioch and with it most of the Syrian coast. At the end of 1099, they took Jerusalem, indiscriminately slaughtering its Muslim, Jewish, and Christian inhabitants. Their quick success stemmed mainly from the fact that their Muslim opponents were at that moment divided among themselves: the Fatimids had managed to recapture Jerusalem just months before the crusaders arrived, and the defeated Seljuks were at war with each other. Western military tactics, in particular the dominance of heavily armored knights, also played an important role in the crusaders' success. Equally critical was the naval support offered by Genoa and Pisa, whose merchant adventurers hoped—if their cause was successful—to control the Indian spice trade that passed through the Red Sea and on to Alexandria in Egypt. The Crusade thereby contributed to the further decline of Byzantine commerce and altered the balance of power between Byzantium and western Europe.

THE CONSEQUENCES OF CRUSADE

For Byzantium, then, the consequences of the First Crusade were tragic, and they would worsen in the course of the ensuing century (Chapter 9). On the Muslim world, however, its impact was more modest. The crusader kingdoms established by victorious warlords were never more than a sparsely settled cluster of colonies along the coastline of Syria and Palestine. Because the crusaders did not control the Red Sea, the main routes of Islamic commerce with India and the Far East were unaffected by the change in Jerusalem's religious allegiance.

In any case, those crusaders who settled in the region did not *want* to interfere with the overland caravan routes that wound through their new territories. Trade brokered by Arab, Persian, and Jewish merchants therefore continued and the greatest economic gains for western Europeans went to the Italian maritime republics of Venice and Genoa, and to other western markets now open to Muslim merchants and their goods. Both sides also gained in military terms: western Europeans learned new techniques of fortification, and Muslims learned new methods of siege warfare and new respect for the uses of heavy cavalry.

An Arab Aristocrat Encounters the Crusaders

Usama ibn Munqidh (1095–1188) was an Arab Muslim from Syria, whose family maintained a prominent place in the local administration even after the conquests of the Seljuks and the Christian crusaders. He traveled widely and worked in various Islamic cities as a diplomat and scholar. He ended his life in the service of Salah ad-Din (Saladin), the great Muslim leader who reconquered Jerusalem the year before Usama's death. The following excerpt is from Usama's memoir, which he called The Book of Contemplation. *The Templars mentioned in the account are the Christian military order of the Knights of the Temple, who dedicated themselves to protecting pilgrims in Jerusalem and guarding the holy sites. Their headquarters were in the main mosque of the city, which stood on the Temple Mount.*

Anyone who is recently arrived from the Frankish lands is rougher in character than those who have become acclimated and have frequented the company of Muslims. Here is an instance of their rough character (may God abominate them!):

Whenever I went to visit the holy sites in Jerusalem, I would go in and make my way up to the al-Aqsa Mosque, beside which stood a small mosque that the Franks had converted into a church. When I went into the al-Aqsa Mosque—where the Templars, who are my friends, were—they would clear out that little mosque so that I could pray in it. One day, I went into the little mosque, recited the opening formula "God is great!" and stood up in prayer. At this, one of the Franks rushed at me and grabbed me and turned my face towards the east, saying, "Pray like *this*!"

A group of Templars hurried towards him, took hold of the Frank and took him away from me. I then returned to my prayers. The Frank, that very same one, took advantage of their inattention and returned, rushing upon me and turning my face to the east, saying, "Pray like *this*!"

So the Templars came in again, grabbed him and threw him out. They apologized to me, saying, "This man is a stranger, just arrived from the Frankish lands sometime in the past few days. He has never before seen anyone who did not pray towards the east."

"I think I've prayed quite enough," I said and left. I used to marvel at that devil, the change of his expression, the way he trembled and what he must have made of seeing someone praying towards Mecca.

Source: Usama ibn Munqidh, *The Book of Contemplation: Islam and the Crusades*, trans. Paul M. Cobb (New York: 2008), p. 147.

Questions for Analysis

1. What does Usama's account reveal about the variety of relationships among Christians and Muslims in the crusader kingdom of Jerusalem?

2. Who is the true outsider in this scenario? What does Usama's treatment by the Templars suggest about the policy of Christian leaders toward the city's Muslim residents?

For those Europeans who remained in the Holy Land, it was necessary to adapt to a new way of life. Local languages, customs, and foods mingled with those the crusaders had brought with them, creating a hybrid culture that further enriched and complicated this long-settled, multicultural civilization. Men and women who had traveled alone, or who had lost their partners to violence, starvation, or disease, formed ties and intermarried with local families.

Perhaps the most lasting consequence of the First Crusade has also proved the deadliest in the long run. The Christian doctrine of holy war, which had developed in earlier centuries but which had never before been mobilized to such an extent, continues to be destructive in the twenty-first century. In the immediate aftermath of Jerusalem's conquest, crusading rhetoric would dictate the terms of western Europeans' attitudes toward the wider world and even toward each other, as we shall see in the following chapters. It fostered a new political and religious ethos that would drive the "reconquest" of the Iberian Peninsula by the Christian rulers of Spain and lead to the massacre or forced conversion of Muslims and Jews. Crusading rhetoric underlay English wars against the Welsh and the Scots, and justified the massacre and dispossession of "heretics" in southern France by northern French imperialists. It justified the conquest of the Baltic region and, later, the subsequent conquest of the Americas and the colonization of Asia, Africa, and Australia. And it has continued to exacerbate global animosities to this day.

Deadly legacy of the Crusades: Christian doctrine of "holy war"

The Culture of the Muslim West

Not all the consequences of the First Crusade were negative. Increased intellectual and cultural contact between the Latin West and the Islamic world had an enormous impact on western European learning, literature, music, and art. Moreover, the study and practical applications of mathematics were revolutionized when Europeans adopted Arabic numerals and the concept of zero—first promoted beyond the Islamic world, not surprisingly, by the son of a Pisan merchant who grew up in Algeria, Leonardo Fibonacci (c. 1170–c. 1250).

Even Christian theology was transformed by contact with Islam. For one thing, Muslim scholars had inherited, preserved, and developed not only Hellenistic medicine and science but the philosophy of Aristotle, which would form the basis of a new Christian philosophy in the twelfth and thirteenth centuries (see Chapter 9). For another, Europeans had been almost entirely ignorant of Islam prior to the Crusades, assuming that Muslims worshiped a god called Mahomet. But this began to change when Robert of Ketton (c. 1100–c. 1160), a scholar originally from a small town in England, completed a Latin translation of the Qur'an in 1143. In the 1130s, he and a friend, Hermann of Carinthia (in Slovenia), had traveled to Byzantium and the crusader kingdoms, where they became students of Arabic. They later helped to establish a school for translators in Toledo.

MUSLIM PHILOSOPHY AND CHRISTIAN THEOLOGY

The scholars of Byzantium had long taken a conservative approach to Greek philosophy. The dialogues of Plato and some works of Aristotle were copied and studied, but the latter's ideas were so hard to reconcile with Orthodox theology that Emperor Alexius Comnenus eventually banned the teaching of Aristotelian logic altogether. The cultures that provided the most direct access to Greek learning were Arabic-speaking, and it was through Arabic translations that western European intellectuals became acquainted with these ideas—thanks to the labor of pioneering scholars such as Robert and Hermann.

Ancient Greek texts reintroduced to western Europe via Arabic translations

Even before the rise of Islam, a number of Greek philosophical texts had been translated into Syriac, a Semitic language closely related to Arabic. Arabic translations soon followed, many sponsored by the Abbasid court at Baghdad, which established a special school for this purpose, known as the House of Wisdom. Even in the remote Persian city of Bukhara, the great Muslim philosopher and physician Avicenna (Ibn Sina; 980–1037) was able to read all of Aristotle's works before reaching the age of eighteen.

Like their counterparts in Byzantium, Muslim philosophers strove to reconcile Greek and Hellenistic philosophical traditions with each other and with the tenets of their theology. Reconciling Aristotelianism and Neoplatonism was the easier task. Many of the translations and commentaries of Aristotle from which Muslim philosophers worked had already been filtered through the philosophical traditions of Alexandria and Rome. Moreover, Aristotle and the Neoplatonists shared a number of common assumptions, including the eternity of the world and the rational capacity of the human mind. Both traditions also stressed the freedom of individual humans to choose between good and evil.

Combining Greek philosophy with Islamic theology was more difficult. Like Judaism and Christianity, Islam holds that a single omnipotent God created the world as an act of pure will and that the world will continue to exist only so long as

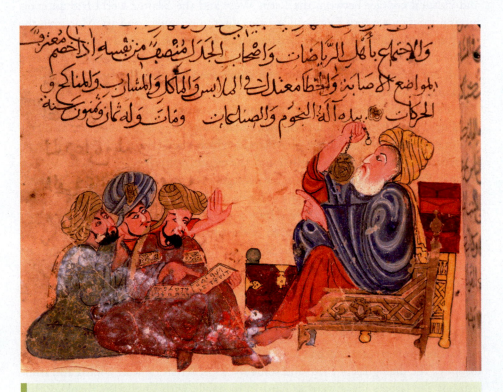

ARISTOTLE TEACHING ARAB ASTRONOMERS. In this Arabic manuscript from the thirteenth century, Aristotle is represented as a contemporary of the astronomers he is instructing. › **What does this illustration suggest about Muslims' attitude toward Greek philosophy?**

God wills it. This runs counter to the classical Greek view of the world as eternal. Moreover, both Christian and Islamic theology rest on the immortality of the individual human soul, another doctrine in conflict with Aristotelian and Neoplatonic thought. There were also conflicts over the concept of free will; and again, Muslims and Christians had more in common with one another than with the ancient Greek tradition. Although medieval theologians strongly emphasized the individual responsibility of believers to choose between good and evil, Muslims and Christians believed that nothing good could occur unless God actively willed it. Islamic philosophers adopted an array of different intellectual tactics to deal with these challenges and, in doing so, laid the groundwork for the Christian theologians who relied on them (see Chapter 9).

MUSLIM SCIENCE, MEDICINE, AND MATHEMATICS

Many Muslim philosophers were also distinguished physicians and scientists. The study of philosophy could bring a man renown but few tangible rewards, whereas successful physicians and astronomers might rise to positions of wealth and power. Both astronomy and medicine were applied sciences that relied on careful and accurate observation of natural phenomena. Indeed, Muslim observations of the heavens were so accurate that a few astronomers corroborated the findings of Hellenistic scientists (see Chapter 4), positing that the earth must rotate on its axis and revolve around the sun. But because these theories conflicted with the (mistaken) assumptions of Aristotle—that the earth remained stationary with the sun and planets revolving around it—they were not generally accepted in the Islamic world or in Europe. Yet they may have influenced Nicolaus Copernicus (1473–1543), who is usually credited as the first to suggest that the earth orbited the sun (see Chapter 16).

Muslim accomplishments in medicine were equally remarkable. Avicenna discovered the contagious nature of tuberculosis, described pleurisy, and noted that diseases could spread through contaminated water and soil. His *Canon of Medicine* remained an authoritative textbook in the Islamic world and western Europe until the seventeenth century. Later Islamic physicians learned the value of cauterization and styptic agents, diagnosed cancer of the stomach, prescribed antidotes in cases of poisoning, and made notable progress in treating eye diseases. They also recognized the infectious character of plague, pointing out that it could be transmitted by clothing.

Islamic physicians were pioneers in organizing hospitals and licensing medical practitioners. At least thirty-four great hospitals were located in the principal cities of Persia, Syria, and Egypt; each with separate wards for particular illnesses, a dispensary for giving out medicine, and a library. Chief physicians and surgeons lectured to students and graduates, examined them, and issued licenses to practice medicine. Even the owners of leeches (used for bloodletting, a standard medical practice of the day) had to submit their medicinal worms for inspection at regular intervals.

Islamic scientists made important advances in optics and chemistry, as well as mathematics. Using numerals they adopted from South Asia, mathematicians developed a decimal arithmetic based on place values and hinging on the concept of zero. Their work enabled fundamental advances in entirely new areas, both of which bear Arabic names: algebra and algorithms. Building on Greek geometry and their own astronomical observations, they also made great progress in spherical trigonometry.

Muslim mathematicians thus brought together and pushed forward all the areas of mathematical knowledge that were later adopted and developed in western Europe from the sixteenth century on. And they made an indispensable contribution to the burgeoning European economy, because the sophisticated accounting systems that supported commerce would have been impossible if merchants and bankers had continued to use the clumsy numerals adopted by the Romans. Thanks to Arabic mathematics, western Europeans could now add, subtract, divide, and multiply quickly and accurately, with or without the help of another Muslim invention, the abacus.

ISLAMIC LITERATURE AND ART

Poetry was integral to Islamic culture. It had been a highly developed art form long before the emergence of Islam and it then became even more important because it was the form of the Qur'an (see Chapter 7). Like medicine and astronomy, poetry was also a route to advancement. Around the Abbasid court, especially, poets writing in both Arabic and Persian enjoyed great renown. The best known of these is Umar Khayyam (d. 1123), whose Persian *Rubaiyat* was turned into a popular English verse cycle by the Victorian poet Edward Fitzgerald (1809–1883). Although Fitzgerald's translation distorts much, the lush sensuality of Umar's poetic imagery ("a jug of wine, a loaf of bread—and thou") faithfully reflects themes that were common to much Muslim poetry. Many such poems were addressed by men to other men, a fact that occasioned no concern within the elite circles in which they were composed and performed. Jews also participated in this elite literary world, especially in al-Andalus, where they wrote similarly sensuous, playful lyrics in both Hebrew and Arabic, praising wine, sexual intimacy, and their own songs. Muslim Spain saw a great flowering of Jewish intellectual life, which paralleled and intersected with that of the surrounding Muslim society.

Perhaps the most distinctive of Islamic arts are architectural and decorative, the arts that created the spaces in which poets and scientists interacted with their patrons. Many characteristic elements of Muslim architecture—the dome, the column, and the arch—were adapted from Byzantine models, but then combined with the intricate tracery and ambitious scale of Persian buildings to form a new architectural vocabulary. Building styles were further enriched by the many different cultures that embraced Islam, from Spain to Egypt to India and beyond. Muslim artistry was also expressed in the magnificent gardens

IVORY PYXIS FROM MEDINA AZAHARA. Fashioned in the year 964, this round box with a matching lid was made of elephant ivory imported from West Africa. Such intricately carved boxes usually held spices or incense. This one was made in the fortified town of Medina Azahara ("Shining City"), founded in the tenth century by the first Umayyad caliph of nearby Córdoba (Spain). Its decorative motifs remind us that Islam did not prohibit the representation of natural and fanciful creatures, as is often supposed.

and fountains that adorned palaces, and in the more portable magnificence of gorgeous carpets, tooled leather, brocaded silks and tapestries, inlaid metalwork, enameled glassware, and painted pottery—all decorated with Arabic script, interlacing geometric designs, plants, fruits, flowers, and fantastic animal figures (another Persian influence). These complex designs can often seem strikingly modern, precisely because they anticipate the abstract forms that were considered new in the twentieth century.

THE ISLAMIC INFLUENCE ON WESTERN EUROPE

Prior to the First Crusade, the cultural, economic, intellectual, and political achievements of Islamic civilization had completely overshadowed those of Christian Europe. Even the new Europe that emerged in the twelfth century would rely heavily on what it had learned from the Islamic world, as reflected in the large number of Arabic and Persian words that passed into European languages. Essential words for commerce include *traffic, tariff, alcohol, muslin, orange, lemon, alfalfa, saffron, sugar, syrup,* and *musk,* to name just a few. The word *admiral* also comes from Arabic (from the title *emir*), as do words that tell the story of Europe's reliance on Muslim science: *alchemy, algebra, algorithm, alkali, almanac, amalgam, cipher, soda, magazine,* and *zero*—not to mention the names of stars such as Aldebaran and Betelgeuse.

The Muslim world also had an enormous influence on the imagination and self-perception of Christian Europe. Latin Christians tended to look down on the Byzantine Greeks, but they respected and feared Muslims. Indeed, Islamic civilization at its zenith (to use another Arabic word) was one of the world's greatest. It brought Arabs, Persians, Turks, Egyptians, Africans, Indians, and Asians together in a common cultural and religious system, creating a diverse society and a splendid legacy of original discoveries and accomplishments that continue to shape the world today. The expanding Europe of the Middle Ages reaped the benefits of its interactions with this rich culture.

Conclusion

Before the year 1000, western Europe was the least powerful, least prosperous, and least sophisticated of the three civilizations that had emerged out of the Roman world. A hundred years later, it was a force to be reckoned with. This metamorphosis rested on economic foundations: increasingly efficient agriculture, a growing population, and expanding trade. These changes produced a dynamic, expansionist, and mobile society. Alongside them were the political and military developments that began to alter the map of Europe during these centuries. By 1100, the heavily armored, mounted knight had emerged as the most formidable military weapon of the day. Meanwhile, new conceptions of power—both spiritual and temporal—were being articulated and contested within Europe, and on crusade.

But Europe's rulers were not yet equipped to harness and control the energies of the workers, town dwellers, merchants, knights, and scholars whose endeavors were transforming their world. Up to this point, the civilizations of the West had rested on two basic types of government: city-states and empires. City-states were capable of mobilizing their citizens and, as a result, could sometimes win extraordinary victories against more powerful imperial rivals, as the Greek poleis did against the Persians (Chapter 3). But city-states were frequently divided by internal economic and social rivalries, and were not strong enough to defend themselves against sustained attack by foreign conquerors. Empires, by contrast, could win battles and

AFTER YOU READ THIS CHAPTER

CHRONOLOGY

900–1050	Monastic reform movement
911–989	The peoples of Rus' are converted by missionaries from Byzantium
930	Establishment of the Althing in Iceland
936–973	Reign of Otto I "the Great"
980–1037	Lifetime of Avicenna
1035	Death of Cnut the Great
1050	Medieval agricultural revolution at its height
1066–1087	Reign of William the Conqueror in England
1073–1085	Papacy of Gregory VII
1075–1122	Investiture Conflict
1081–1118	Reign of Alexius Comnenus in Byzantium
1095–1099	First Crusade
c. 1100	The *Song of Roland* is written down

REVIEWING THE OBJECTIVES

> The fragmentation of power in the ninth and tenth centuries created a world very different from that of Charlemagne. Describe some of the key changes. What were their causes?

> The agricultural revolution of the Middle Ages had far-reaching economic, social, and political consequences. What were they?

> The reforming movement within the Church changed the relationship between the papacy and the secular rulers of Christendom. Explain why.

> The motives behind the Crusades were political as well as religious. Why was this the case?

> The Crusades had profound effects on western Europe, Byzantium, and the Islamic world, as well as on the relationships among different groups within these societies. In what ways were these three civilizations transformed?

build powerful administrative bureaucracies, but they were generally too far-flung to maintain their stability.

Where, then, do the emerging kingdoms of medieval Europe fit in this picture? How would the struggle for the control of western Europe's expanding resources be carried forward in the wake of the First Crusade? And what cultural, spiritual, social, and intellectual innovations would result? These are the questions we address in Chapter 9.

 Go to **INQUIZITIVE** to see what you've learned—and learn what you've missed—with personalized feedback along the way.

PEOPLE, IDEAS, AND EVENTS IN CONTEXT

❯ How was Europe affected by Viking raids and settlements? Which territorial rulers imitated **CAROLINGIAN** models in the wake of these initiatives?

❯ What new technologies drove the **AGRICULTURAL REVOLUTION** of the Middle Ages? Why did the organization of labor on **MANORS** sometimes lead to **SERFDOM**?

❯ What conditions led to the growth of medieval **TOWNS**? Why did the formation of urban **COMMUNES** foster new types of liberty? How were money and credit essential to medieval commerce?

❯ Why is **FEUDALISM** a problematic concept? How did the ceremony of **HOMAGE** symbolize the relationship between a **VASSAL** and his lord?

❯ What were the causes of the **INVESTITURE CONFLICT**?

❯ Why did **ALEXIUS COMNENUS** ask **POPE URBAN II** for assistance? Why did the pope use this as a pretext for urging the **FIRST CRUSADE**?

❯ How and why did **MUSLIM LEARNING AND CULTURE** exercise a profound influence on western Europeans?

THINKING ABOUT CONNECTIONS

❯ In what ways does the Investiture Conflict reflect the unique historical circumstances of the late eleventh century? In what ways can it be viewed as an extension of longer-term phenomena?

❯ Judging by what we have learned about the relationship between political power and religious power in previous chapters, would you say that the clash between the papacy and the Holy Roman Empire was inevitable?

❯ Given the many negative aspects of the crusading movement—and its eventual failure—how might you explain the continuing appeal of crusading rhetoric down to the present day?

9

The Consolidation of Europe, 1100–1250

BEFORE YOU READ THIS CHAPTER ›

AT THE TURN OF THE TWELFTH CENTURY, the eldest son of a nobleman did something unusual: he traded lordship for scholarship. His name was **Peter Abelard**. After leaving his father's lands in Brittany and besting all the established teachers in Paris, he was appointed master of the cathedral school: one of the highest academic posts then available. There, he met a priest called Fulbert and his niece Heloise, who had received an excellent education in a nearby convent. Since the normal path of intellectual advancement—Abelard's school—was closed to her, Fulbert arranged for Heloise to become Abelard's private pupil. She soon became more than that: his intellectual partner, lover, and wife. This last step was particularly problematic, for marriage was now forbidden to clerics and would ruin Abelard's chances of a brilliant career. So it remained a secret, as had Heloise's pregnancy and the birth of their son. Yet her uncle found out and took revenge on Abelard, sending some local thugs to castrate him. Heloise and Abelard lived out the remainder of their lives apart from one another, and most of what we know about them comes from letters they exchanged years later, when Heloise was the leader of a new religious community and Abelard was laying the intellectual foundations of a university.

The developments of the twelfth and thirteenth centuries altered Europe in profound and lasting ways. This period witnessed the emergence of large, territorial monarchies and of the papacy as dominant forces, while cathedral schools and universities turned out the cohorts of professional

STORY LINES

❯ The power of Europe's new monarchies and of the papacy depended on new methods of oversight, administration, and documentation.

❯ Schools and universities were crucial to the development of these institutions, and they also provided ambitious men with unprecedented intellectual, social, and political opportunities.

❯ Crusading movements continued in the twelfth and thirteenth centuries, intensifying contacts between Latin Christendom and the Muslim world, while posing a threat to many minority groups within Europe, as well as to the Byzantine Empire.

❯ The Church's presence in the daily lives of the laity produced vibrant forms of spirituality, yet placed strict limitations on women, religious dissidents, and non-Christians.

❯ Meanwhile, Europe's princely courts, wealthy towns, universities, and cathedrals fostered new forms of entertainment, art, and architecture.

CORE OBJECTIVES

❯ **IDENTIFY** the differences among Europe's emerging monarchies.

❯ **DESCRIBE** the ongoing effects of crusading.

❯ **UNDERSTAND** the connections between new religious movements and the power of the papacy.

❯ **DEFINE** scholasticism and trace its development.

❯ **EXPLAIN** the changing meaning of *chivalry*.

men needed to run their bureaucracies. New opportunities for social advancement and new spiritual practices transformed daily life. As a result of the Crusades and medieval Europe's engagement with the Islamic world, both ancient texts and novel ideas generated the intellectual revolution in which Abelard and Heloise participated. Artistic and technological influences were galvanizing forces, too, financed by princely courts and wealthy towns engaged in an integrated and far-reaching economy. New literary forms took shape as the spoken vernaculars of Europe challenged Latin by becoming languages of learning, devotion, and entertainment. By the middle of the thirteenth century, the political institutions and cultural identities that still help to define Europe today had been formed.

The Making of Medieval Monarchies

As we learned in Chapter 8, independent medieval towns and powerful lords often refused to acknowledge royal authority. How, then, did some European rulers build states that continue to exist today? For crucially, the *idea* of a state that consolidates its people's sense of a shared identity and destiny was an idea forged in the twelfth and thirteenth centuries. It would endure to become the basis that still supports the political system of our world. Thereafter, it became so vital for modern European states to trace their origins to the medieval past that those states without a medieval pedigree would eventually have to invent one.

ENGLAND: FROM CONQUEST TO CONSOLIDATION

The imperial conquest of England in 1066 allowed the first Norman king, William, to experiment with a new type of kingship (Chapter 8). In theory, he commanded the allegiance of every person dwelling in his kingdom. In practice, he needed to impose his will in the form of violence and through the highly effective administrative structures of his Anglo-Saxon predecessors. This process was carried forward by William's sons, especially Henry I (r. 1100–1135), whose approach to kingship was unusual in its focus on effective governance rather than warfare. Henry strengthened the Anglo-Norman system of administration and centralized bureaucracy, and even instituted a system of traveling judges to administer justice. Yet Henry's hands-on approach was unpopular with lords who preferred to exercise power in their own domains. After his death, those negative reactions provoked a civil war—until the people of England began to long again for stable forms of governance.

A new form of kingship emerges based on governance, not warfare

They found their new ruler in Henry's grandson, Henry of Anjou (r. 1154–1189), who at the age of twenty-one was already the duke of Normandy. He also controlled the Aquitaine, thanks to his recent marriage to its powerful and brilliant ruler, Eleanor (1122–1204), who had annulled her first marriage to the French king Louis VII in order to marry Henry. As king of England, **Henry II** restored his grandfather's administration and began to extend its reach. He ordered reliable local juries (from the Latin *jus*, "law" and "oath") to report every major crime that occurred in their districts and also empowered them to investigate civil cases. Henry II also made it easier for common people to seek justice in the royal courts. Such innovations are the origin of the modern Anglo-American legal system and they brought an unprecedented number of average people into the exercise of government.

Yet these innovations also brought Henry into conflict with the Church, because the extension of royal justice impinged on ecclesiastical courts: bishops' tribunals that claimed the right to try and sentence clergy accused of committing crimes—even crimes such as murder. Henry had declared that clerics convicted of serious crimes should lose their clerical status and be handed over to the royal court for sentencing. The underlying principle aimed to promote a sense of shared identity and accountability: clerics should be English subjects before they were servants of the Roman Church.

Opposition to this policy came from an unexpected quarter: **Thomas Becket**, a longtime friend and supporter of Henry, and who was then the archbishop of Canterbury. Thomas was a self-made man, son of immigrants who had benefited from the social mobility of London, who had risen through the ranks of the Church. He feared that Henry's goal was to undermine the power of the clergy. Henry responded to his opposition by exiling Thomas for several years. Then, when Thomas returned to England in 1170, he was assassinated in his own cathedral by four of Henry's knights, allegedly acting on the king's orders. Thomas was quickly proclaimed a martyr and his tomb at Canterbury became an important pilgrimage site, and Henry was compelled to do penance at his tomb.

In the long run, Henry II did not win the right to sentence clerics in royal courts, but he did retain the right to nominate clerics to high office and thereby to exercise a large measure of control over those courts' personnel. The most concrete proof of his success is that his government continued to work efficiently even after his death—to the extent that his crusading son Richard "the Lionheart" (r. 1189–1199) could rule his father's empire for ten years while spending only about six months in England during that time.

THE MEANING OF MAGNA CARTA

Richard was succeeded by his brother John (r. 1199–1216), an efficient administrator. But by 1204, military losses had forced John to cede nearly all of his father's Continental possessions to the powerful young king of France, Philip II; only the Aquitaine—the inheritance of his mother, Eleanor—remained. This was politically disastrous for John, because all of the most powerful lords in England were of Norman descent and thus lost their ancestral lands when John lost Normandy. John attempted to recover these lost territories' revenue by raising taxes, which angered the nobility further. In 1215, they forced him to set his seal on **Magna Carta**, a "great charter" that defined the barons' rights while limiting those of the king.

Thomas Becket A longtime friend and supporter of Henry's who later became the archbishop of Canterbury.

Magna Carta The "Great Charter" of 1215, enacted during the reign of King John of England and designed to limit his powers.

THE MURDER OF THOMAS BECKET. In this illumination from a thirteenth-century prayer book, one of the knights has struck the archbishop so violently that he has broken his sword. **› How might a contemporary viewer have interpreted this symbolism?**

Key principles of *Magna Carta: taxation with consent, trial by jury, parliamentary representation*

>

Magna Carta established some important principles that would continue to shape the laws of England and, eventually, its modern colonies: the king could levy no taxes without the consent of the kingdom, no free man could be punished until he had been judged guilty by a jury of his peers, no one could be arrested without a warrant, and no unqualified person should hold public office. The charter also established a representative body of barons: Parliament (French for "talking together"). Above all, Magna Carta expressed the then-novel idea that a ruler is bound by the law.

We have frequently noted the achievements of various powerful lawgivers, starting with Hammurabi (Chapter 1). But those lawgivers held themselves to be above the law. Magna Carta thus sowed the seeds of the idea that the king must also be subject to laws and that a legislative body should help to govern the kingdom. And since Magna Carta demanded that no taxation be imposed without common consent, kings had to convene Parliament to explain why such taxation was necessary. Meetings of Parliament were also used to hear judicial cases, review complaints of injustice, and promulgate new laws. Gradually, England was changing from a conquered territory within a larger Norman empire into a constitutional monarchy.

THE EMERGENCE OF FRANCE

Compared with the king of England, the king of the Franks governed a minuscule territory around Paris over which he exercised little control. When Henry II's empire was at its height, the kingdom of Louis VII (r. 1137–1180)—who had lost both his wife, Eleanor, and her lands to that same Henry—was tiny and insignificant. But though small, this kingdom was a rich center of agriculture and trade, which provided a steadily increasing source of income. Its prestige was also enhanced by the new **University of Paris** founded by Abelard, which made the royal city the intellectual capital of Europe (see page 320). Beyond all this, many of Louis VII's successors proved to be shrewd politicians, husbanding their strengths while more powerful enemies overreached themselves.

The epitome was Louis VII's own son **Philip II** (r. 1180–1223), who styled himself "**Augustus**" and "king of France": king of a sovereign state, rather than "king of the Franks," a tribal people. Philip came to the throne at eighteen, having witnessed the struggles of his father. He knew that he could not win a direct confrontation with either Henry II or his son Richard; however, John—known as "Soft Sword" and "Lack Land"—was another matter. Philip declared that John owed him homage and allegiance in return for Normandy and its adjacent territories, and then undermined John's control over these lands. When John objected, Philip declared all John's lands forfeit to the French crown and backed this declaration with armies that won decisive victories in 1204 and 1214.

With Normandy and other former Angevin territories added to his domain, Philip had the means to build an effective system of local administration. He wisely chose to maintain the bureaucratic structures established by generations of Anglo-Norman rulers, but he appointed royal overseers who had full judicial, administrative, and military authority. Philip drew these men from among the needy knights and lesser nobility of his own domain and rotated them frequently from region to region, which prevented them from developing personal ties to the places they governed. This strategy recognized regional diversity while promoting centralized royal control, and it continued to characterize French royal government down to the time of the French Revolution (see Chapter 18).

University of Paris The reputation of Peter Abelard and his students attracted many intellectuals to Paris during the twelfth century. Some of them began offering instruction to aspiring scholars. By 1200, this loose association of teachers had formed itself into a *universitas*, or corporation.

Philip Augustus (1165–1223) The first French ruler to use the title "King of France" rather than "King of French." After he captured Normandy and its adjacent territories from the English, he built an effective system of local administration, which recognized regional diversity while promoting centralized royal control.

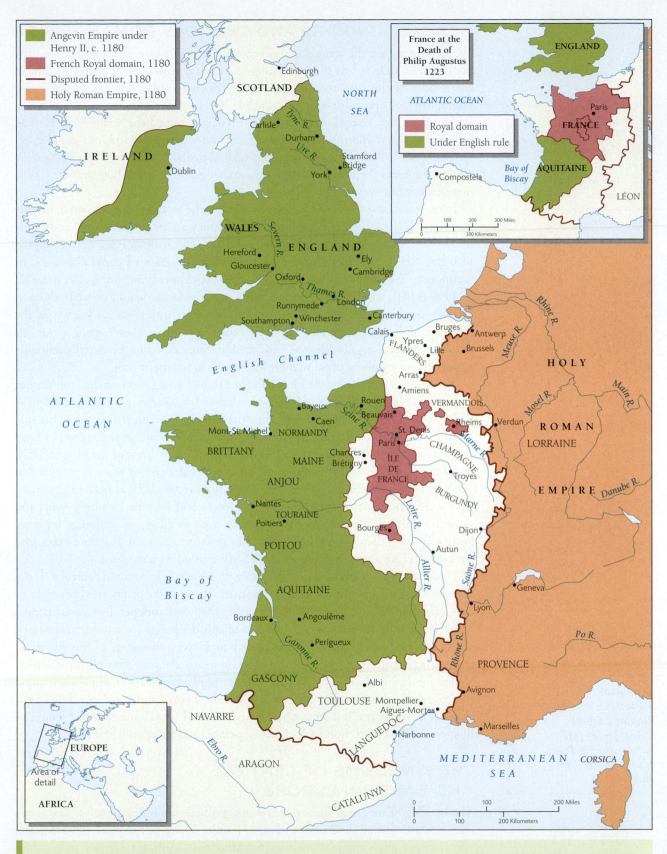

Legend (main map):

- Angevin Empire under Henry II, c. 1180
- French Royal domain, 1180
- Disputed frontier, 1180
- Holy Roman Empire, 1180

Inset map: France at the Death of Philip Augustus 1223

- Royal domain
- Under English rule

Labels on inset: ENGLAND, ATLANTIC OCEAN, Paris, FRANCE, AQUITAINE, Bay of Biscay, Compostela, LÉON

0 100 200 300 Miles
0 300 Kilometers

Main map labels:

Edinburgh, SCOTLAND, NORTH SEA, Carlisle, Tyne R., Durham, Ure R., Stamford Bridge, York, IRELAND, Dublin, WALES, ENGLAND, Hereford, Gloucester, Severn R., Ely, Cambridge, Oxford, Thames R., London, Runnymede, Winchester, Southampton, Canterbury, Calais

English Channel, ATLANTIC OCEAN

Bayeux, Rouen, Bruges, Antwerp, Rhine R., Meuse R., HOLY, Ypres, Lille, Brussels, FLANDERS, Caen, Seine R., Beauvais, Arras, Amiens, VERMANDOIS, Mont-St.-Michel, NORMANDY, St. Denis, Rheims, Verdun, ROMAN, BRITTANY, MAINE, Chartres, Paris, Mosel R., LORRAINE, Brétigny, ÎLE DE FRANCE, CHAMPAGNE, Marne R., ANJOU, Troyes, EMPIRE, Main R., Danube R., Nantes, TOURAINE, BURGUNDY, Poitiers, Bourges, Dijon, Loire R., POITOU, Autun, Saône R., Allier R., Geneva, Bay of Biscay, AQUITAINE, Lyon, Bordeaux, Angoulême, Garonne R., Perigueux, Rhône R., Po R., PROVENCE, GASCONY, Albi, Avignon, TOULOUSE, Montpellier, Aigues-Mortes, Marseilles, NAVARRE, LANGUEDOC, Narbonne, MEDITERRANEAN SEA, CORSICA, Ebro R., ARAGON, CATALUNYA

Locator inset: EUROPE, Area of detail, AFRICA

0 100 200 Miles
0 100 200 Kilometers

HENRY II'S EMPIRE AND THE KINGDOM OF FRANCE, 1180–1223. › What areas did Henry II's empire control in 1180? › What advantages would the king of France have when challenging English control over Continental territories—even though his own power was confined to the "island" (Île) of France around Paris?

GERMAN KINGSHIP AND THE HOLY ROMAN EMPIRE

We have seen that the struggles between the German emperor Henry IV and the papacy ultimately led to the weakening of imperial authority (Chapter 8). But in the middle of the twelfth century, a newly elected emperor made an ambitious attempt to free himself from papal control. This emperor was Frederick, known as Barbarossa ("Red Beard"; r. 1152–1190). Frederick coined the term "Holy Roman Empire" to assert that his rule derived from the blessing of God, not papal intervention. He also forged a close alliance with German princes by supporting their efforts to control their own territories. In exchange, he exacted their support for his imperial control over northern Italy.

Frederick uses term "Holy Roman Empire" to insist his rule is blessed by God without papal interference

In response, and with the blessing of the pope, the wealthy cities of northern Italy formed an alliance, the Lombard League, which put up a staunch resistance and finally forced Frederick to guarantee their independence. Meanwhile, Frederick attempted to bypass the power of the papacy by supporting a series of papal claimants, or "antipopes." This move was successfully countered by the reigning pope, Alexander III (r. 1159–1181), who drove a shrewd bargain: if Frederick would concede the sovereignty of the pope's rule within Rome and its territories—lands known as the Papal States—then Alexander would concede the emperor's sovereignty within his domains, even his overlordship of the Church in those domains. Frederick eventually agreed, thereby gaining papal support for his rule in northern Italy.

When Frederick left for the Holy Land in 1189—joining Richard the Lionheart of England and Philip Augustus of France on a doomed crusade to reconquer Jerusalem—he left his realm in a powerful position. Although he died on that venture, his son, Henry VI, succeeded to his father's throne without opposition and enjoyed a huge income from the northern Italian cities. Henry ultimately became the king of Sicily, too, which strengthened the empire's position even further. But when Henry died in 1197, he left only a three-year-old son, the future Frederick II, as his heir apparent. By the time he came of age, the German princes had become so autonomous and powerful that all he could do was recognize their privileges in exchange for their loyalty. In Italy, the cities of the Lombard League had ceased to pay their taxes, and the powerful administrative structure of Sicily had fallen into chaos.

Frederick tackled all these problems ably, and eventually restored control over the disparate territories of his empire. But he made the mistake of asserting the right to rule northern Italian cities directly, bypassing their own independent governments. The result was another Lombard League and another lengthy war, which continued until Frederick's death in 1250. The papacy took every advantage of this situation, even excommunicating Frederick and, after his death, denying the rights of his heirs. When Frederick's last legitimate son died in 1254, the prospect of effective imperial rule died with him. For the next five hundred years, until the founding of the modern German and Italian states, the lands of the Holy Roman Empire would be divided among several hundred territorial princes and independent cities.

After death of Frederick's son, Holy Roman Empire disintegrates into hundreds of independent principalities and cities.

THE KINGDOMS OF CENTRAL AND EASTERN EUROPE

The making of medieval monarchies was a gradual, nonlinear process. The states that formed, shifted, and reformed were fragile. Many of the most powerful and effective were cities and principalities, not kingdoms. However, the new monarchies

that were emerging in central and eastern Europe offer further instructive examples of state formation in this era.

Originally part of the Holy Roman Empire, Bohemia was a nonhereditary monarchy whose rulers were elected by powerful families. That changed at the end of the twelfth century, however, when Ottokar I (r. 1192–1230) secured papal and imperial support for the establishment of a dynasty. Bohemia also extended its rule into the province of Moravia, which it governed as a frontier principality. During the thirteenth century, when the Holy Roman Emperor's attention was fixed on fractious Italy, Bohemia emerged as one of the strongest states in central Europe.

The kings of Hungary, meanwhile, with their close ties to the papacy, cultivated a strong and relatively centralized royal authority. They also expanded Hungarian influence into the regions of Transylvania and Croatia, whose natural resources included rich silver mines. As a result, the wealth of King Béla III (r. 1172–1196) far exceeded that of his contemporaries elsewhere in Europe. He also adopted many of the bureaucratic techniques favored by these contemporaries, including the use of written records to aid in royal governance.

Poland, which had achieved a remarkable territorial unity at an early date (Chapter 8), was carved into several smaller dukedoms after 1138, when King Bolesław III (*BOHL-ess-wahv*; r. 1107–1138) divided these lands among his sons. This spurred the Polish dukes to seek out new ways of advancing their interests. Duke Conrad of Masovia (r. 1229–1232), for example, forged an alliance with the Teutonic Knights, crusaders who were conquering the pagan peoples of the Baltic (see page 306). Conrad's own northern frontier was subject to raids by the pagan Prussians, and he saw this as an expedient measure. Yet he could not prevent the knights from encroaching on his own territories, too.

Polish rulers encourage Jewish settlements >

Polish rulers also pursued more inclusive methods of strengthening their principalities. In the wake of the First Crusade, violent attacks against Jews were becoming increasingly common in northwestern Europe, while their legal rights were also being curtailed. But Polish dukes were eager to encourage Jewish settlements because their cities would benefit from the expertise of Jewish merchants and be woven into the banking networks that were crucial to the medieval economy. By the thirteenth century, thousands of Jews—entire communities—were making their way to Poland. The favorable conditions they sought are exemplified by the Statute of Kalisz (*KAH-leesh*), issued by Duke Bolesław the Pious in 1264. Regarded as a foundational document in the history of human rights, it granted Jews extensive privileges, including freedom of movement and worship; equal rights under the law; and the right to prosecute Christians who insulted, harmed, or stole from them. As a result of these initiatives, Poland became a magnet for Jews for the remainder of the Middle Ages, taking in still more refugees from the wave of expulsions suffered by the Jews of England, France, and Spain (see Chapters 10 and 12).

RUS' AND THE NOVGOROD REPUBLIC

The trading settlements established by the Viking Rus' in the eleventh century had benefited from kinship ties with many of Europe's royal families, and a close spiritual and political alliance with Byzantium. But as crusading movements weakened Byzantium and disrupted trade with the Islamic world (see page 307), the powerful position of Kiev was undermined. The center of gravity moved north, to the city of Novgorod, which was already economically powerful and ideally situated to trade with the Baltic and Scandinavia via the Volga and Dnieper Rivers. Novgorod functioned as a powerful city-state where the power of its prince and aristocracy was countered by merchant elites and a tradition of occasional public assemblies that gave voice to traders and craftsmen.

In 1204, however, when Constantinople was besieged and captured by crusaders (see page 307), many German and Scandinavian warlords began to make the Orthodox Christians of Rus' another target of crusading fervor. The Swedes invaded Novgorod's northern frontier, and there were constant skirmishes with the Danes and Germans as well. In 1240, a Swedish army attempted to gain control of the Neva River, a major trade route, but the invasion was routed by a young prince of Novgorod, Alexander (1221–1263), who thereafter took the surname Nevsky (victor of the Neva).

(see page 307)

THE "RECONQUEST" OF SPAIN

The small Christian kingdoms of the Iberian Peninsula were even more distinct from each other than the principalities of the Holy Roman Empire. And yet Christian rulers were beginning to forge effective alliances, in order to counter the power of their wealthy and well-governed Muslim neighbors. This process is somewhat misleadingly termed the *reconquista* ("reconquest") of Spain. In reality, the Roman

■	Christian territory, c. 900
■	Christian conquests, c. 900–1150
■	Christian conquests, c. 1150–1250
■	Muslim holdings, c. 1250

THE "RECONQUEST" OF SPAIN, 900–1250. › Where were the frontiers of the Christian kingdoms in 900? 1150? 1250? **›** What geographical factors might have helped to sustain these small kingdoms? **›** Why might Castile eventually have become the largest of the Christian kingdoms? **›** How could Aragon and Catalonia have maintained important positions as wealthy and significant powers?

LOARRE CASTLE, ARAGON. No single photograph can capture the size or setting of this massive castle complex in the foothills of the Pyrenees. Initially fortified in the eleventh century as a base for Christian expansion into Muslim territory, it was further enlarged in the twelfth century. The encircling wall and towers were added in the thirteenth and fourteenth centuries.

> *As in England, king of Aragon consolidates power through administration—not simply conquest*

province of Hispania had been only nominally Christian when the Visigoths settled there in the fifth century (Chapter 6), and the Visigoths themselves had only recently converted to Roman Christianity when the Muslims arrived in 711 (Chapter 7). But conceptualizing this struggle as a holy war to "reconquer" territory allowed Christian rulers to cast it as another crusade.

By the middle of the twelfth century, there were four major Christian kingdoms. In the far north was Navarre, which straddled the Pyrenees, and León-Castile, governed as a united kingdom after 1037. Beyond these kingdoms' southern frontier lay a broad swath of Muslim territory. Farther to the east was the Crown of Aragon, formed in 1137 when the count of Barcelona, who ruled Catalonia, married the queen of Aragon. Farthest west was the new kingdom of Portugal, the first territory gained by Christian conquests in the ninth century, which won independence from León-Castile in 1139.

Centuries of warfare between Muslims and Christians, and among competing Christian clans, had left the rocky landscape of Iberia sown with enormous castles. Even those nominally controlled by kings were the property and power bases of castellans (castle-keepers). A ruler seeking to establish effective control thus had to bring these rival powers to heel through conquest and the development of effective administrative structures: tactics we have already seen in England. In Iberia, this strategy is exemplified by King Alfonso II of Aragon (r. 1162–1196), who used documentation as the ultimate tool of power. Between 1192 and 1194, he presided over the compilation of a richly illuminated "big book of fiefs" (*Liber feudorum maior*: see **Interpreting Visual Evidence** on pages 304–305), which recounted property transactions and family lineages based on documents in the royal archives. Alfonso thereby grounded his authority on his command of history and written records.

Continuing the Crusades

When Pope Urban II urged the quarrelsome knights of northwestern Europe to take up the cross in 1095, he was responding to the Byzantine emperor's request for reinforcements in his war with the Seljuk Turks. But the pope's own conception of the crusaders' mission extended beyond the frontiers of Byzantium to the great Muslim cities of Antioch and Jerusalem. And, as we saw in Chapter 8, many crusaders acted on a still broader interpretation of their mission by attacking the Jewish communities of Europe.

From the first, then, crusading and its targets were ideologically malleable. Even though the papacy never approved violence against Jews, individual popes authorized the use of force against many different kinds of people who could be construed as "enemies of Christ." Although historians used to speak of crusading as divided into distinct phases (the Second Crusade, the Third Crusade, etc.), both aggressors and victims experienced crusading as a continuous, snowballing movement.

CRUSADER STATES AND CRUSADING ORDERS

The principalities known as the **Crusader States** added another layer to the diversity of peoples who inhabited the coastline of the eastern Mediterranean: an area formed by successive waves of migration and colonization over the course of millennia. Those Europeans who stayed and flourished were those who could adapt to this deep and complex culture. Some probably retained some aspects of their former identities—as Normans or Franks—but their descendants became intertwined with local populations, intermarrying and adopting their fashions, food, and outlook. In time, many had more in common with their neighbors—Syrian and Armenian Christians, Shi'ite and Sunni Muslims—than with their distant families "back home." Second- and third-generation settlers might never visit western Christendom in the course of their lives.

Because of these factors, the four principal Crusader States were very different from the states being consolidated in Europe. They were more like loosely configured and combative lordships; as such, they were mostly short-lived. The largest, the inland county of Edessa, was founded in 1098 and stretched as far east as the Tigris River; it had to be heavily fortified against constant internal uprisings

Crusader States The four fragile European principalities established on the eastern coast of the Mediterranean after the First Crusade (1096–1099).

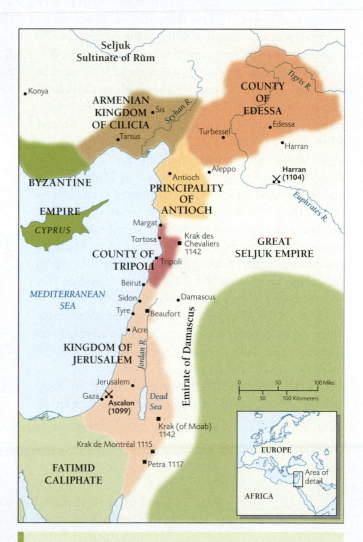

THE CRUSADER STATES. This map shows the fragile colonies known as the Crusader States at their greatest extent, around 1100. **› What geographical, political, and military factors would make these states vulnerable?**

Picturing Legal Transactions

Between the years 1192 and 1194, King Alfonso II of Aragon (r. 1162–1196) and his court scribes compiled a remarkable book. The codex known today as the "big book of fiefs" (*Liber feudorum maior*) may have been made to assist Alfonso and his descendants in legitimizing their authority over the many areas they controlled, but it was also a way of expressing that authority: its very existence represented a new claim to royal power. In its original form, it consisted of 888 parchment folios (1,776 pages) on which 903 separate documents were copied.

This "big book" represents a new trend in Europe. In most places, claims to property were made on the basis of custom and memory, not documentation. When property changed hands, the chief witnesses were people, and when questions arose, it was these people (or their heirs) whose testimony proved ownership. In Catalonia, the habit of documenting things had a long history, and it was not unusual for individual families to keep archives of documents. At the same time, however, documentation was never sufficient on its own: verbal exchanges of agreement and the public performance of transactions constituted legally binding ceremonies meaningful to the entire community, and the validity of these actions was not dependent on the making of a written record.

With all this in mind, it is striking that seventy-nine of the documents copied into the book are accompanied by images that convey important messages about documentation and its limitations.

On the book's opening frontispiece (image A), King Alfonso consults with his chief archivist, Ramón de Caldes. Ramón discusses one of the charters taken from a large pile at his elbow, while a scribe makes copies behind him—perhaps to aid in the compilation of the "big book." The king is backed by men who look on approvingly.

One of the charters copied into the "big book" is accompanied by another image (image B). It records that the Viscount of Nîmes betrothed his daughter, Ermengarde of Carcassonne, to the Count of Roussillon. Ermengarde, her flowing hair uncovered as a sign of her maidenhood, stands between her bearded father and her seated mother, Cecilia of Provence.

Questions for Analysis

1. Why would a book designed to document property transactions contain images, too? What functions could they have served?

2. Why would the artist of the "big book" have depicted the king consulting his archivist in the very first image? How does he depict the relationship between them? Why does he include a group of men as witnesses to their discussion?

3. Women figure prominently in many of the book's images, including image B. On what basis could you argue that their active presence is crucial to the transactions being described?

and external threats. But its European population was a tiny minority, and by 1150 it had been mostly subsumed into the Seljuk Empire. Although Antioch was named a patriarchate of the Roman Church, it also had a tiny European population and was largely dependent on Constantinople and Armenia for protection from the Seljuks.

The third major state, the county of Tripoli, was founded in 1109 and linked the northern states of Edessa and Antioch with the kingdom of Jerusalem. Tripoli's strategic commercial position exposed it to constant raids, which led

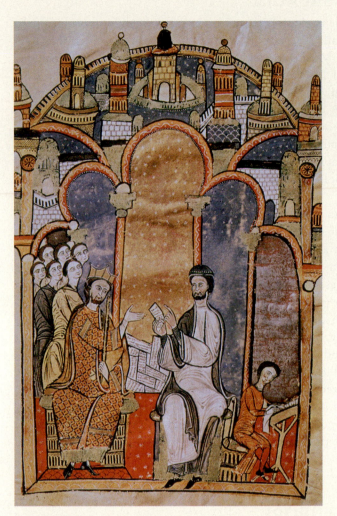

A. King Alfonso and Ramón de Caldes.

B. Betrothal of Ermengarde of Carcassonne to the Count of Roussillon.

to the formation of a new military order dedicated to perpetual crusading: the Knights Hospitaller. Originally charged with the care of pilgrims in the Hospital of St. John at Jerusalem, founded in 1023, members of this religious order became militarized after 1099. They controlled the islands of Rhodes and Malta, as well as many strategic fortifications in the eastern Mediterranean. Indeed, the Hospitallers long outlived the Crusader States, maintaining a sovereign presence in the region into the early nineteenth century; the order is now headquartered in Rome.

THE KINGDOM OF JERUSALEM AND THE CONQUEST OF SALADIN

The kingdom of Jerusalem, the fourth and most symbolically important of the Crusader States, was really a network of cities and fortresses: as much the target of rival crusaders as of Muslim raiders. Its cosmopolitan population included major concentrations of Muslims (both Sunni and Shi'ite), Orthodox Christians (Greek and Syrian), and smaller communities (Jews, Samaritans)—all of whom dwarfed the new European arrivals. Those who claimed kingship here were greatly dependent on support from another of the new crusading orders, the Knights Templar. Founded during the reign of King Baldwin II of Jerusalem (r. 1118–1131), the Templars were quartered in a wing of the captured al-Aqsa Mosque, part of King Solomon's original Temple complex (Chapter 2) and now the royal palace.

Although the kingdom of Jerusalem persisted in theory until 1291, it ceased to have any purchase on the city of Jerusalem after 1187. In this year, a remarkable Kurdish chieftain, Ṣalāḥ ad-Dīn (c. 1138–1193), the Sunni sultan of both Egypt and Syria, rallied Muslim opposition to the occupying crusaders and recaptured the Holy City. Saladin (as European admirers called him) became the target of a renewed crusading effort (the Third Crusade, 1189–1192), which, as we noted on page 298, included three kings: England's Richard the Lionheart, France's Philip Augustus, and the Holy Roman Empire's Frederick Barbarossa. Frederick was killed, Philip left early, and Richard was captured on the way home.

The victorious Saladin was celebrated not only by Muslims but also among crusaders, who considered him a paragon of chivalry. Richard even considered a marriage between his sister, Joan, and Saladin's brother, to establish allied rule in Jerusalem. This never happened, though, and the city of Acre (Akko, in northern Israel) became the new capital of the Christian kingdom until its fall in 1291.

Rationale for crusaders: both religious and political ❯

CRUSADING IN EUROPE

Once unleashed, the crusading ethos was not contained by efforts to liberate the Holy Land and almost immediately applied to a host of other initiatives that could open new lands for settlement and bring more peoples into the orbit of the Roman Church. By 1107, Flemish and German princes called for a crusade against the Slavs. In the 1160s, the rulers of Denmark and of Saxony began to colonize the Baltic coast with the aid of the Teutonic Knights. In 1202, they managed to carve out a new bishopric around Riga (present-day Latvia), where they set about the violent conversion of the indigenous inhabitants. We have already noted the Knights' subsequent clashes with the peoples of Poland and Rus'.

Meanwhile, the English were launching crusades against the "infidel" Irish and Welsh, who were actually Christian, on the grounds that Celts were barbarians who needed the civilizing influence of their superior overlords. It had been a short step from the calling of crusades against foreigners to those aimed at fellow Europeans and Christians.

THE CRUSADE AGAINST CONSTANTINOPLE AND THE REVENGE OF VENICE

The First Crusade had begun as an attempt to aid Constantinople; the Fourth Crusade (1202–1204) ended in its destruction. The object of this expedition, called by Pope **Innocent III** in 1198, was Egypt, where Saladin's successors continued to rally Muslim opposition to European colonial efforts. Because the remaining crusader outposts of the Holy Land had become too weak to enable the movement of armies by land, the attack was launched by sea. The natural embarkation point was Venice.

A major player in maritime trade since the ninth century, Venice had already benefited enormously from the Crusades, furnishing the ships and supplies that transported and sustained the waves of aspiring conquerors. It also forged close ties with Byzantium, with which it shared many interests. But relations with Constantinople worsened in the twelfth century, as crusaders increasingly damaged Byzantine trade and threatened its security. In 1182, citizens of Constantinople, seized by anticrusader sentiment, massacred enclaves of Italian merchants and seamen; those who were not killed were banished, the Venetians among them.

Venetians therefore had a reason to resent the Byzantines. And they were now overrun by an army of impoverished crusaders who could not pay for the passage to Cairo. So the crusaders paid the Venetians with the services they could render. Rather than sailing for Egypt, the crusading expedition was diverted to Zara on the Dalmatian coast of the Adriatic: a former Venetian port that had rebelled and sought the protection of the Hungarian king (it is now Zadar in Croatia). Despite the fact that Hungary was loyal to Rome, the city was attacked and taken.

From Zara, the crusaders moved on to Constantinople. After a terrible siege, the famished city was savagely overrun and sacked in 1204, its people killed or left homeless, its churches and public buildings destroyed, its books and artworks burned or looted. (The stolen porphyry statue of the Roman tetrarchs, shown on page 195, is still in Venice.) Thereafter, Venetians dominated the city itself, controlling shipping and ports on the island of Crete and many cities of the Greek mainland. By 1261, when Byzantine rule was reestablished in the capital, the empire had shrunk to a fraction of its former size.

INNOCENT III'S CRUSADE FOR A UNIFIED CHRISTENDOM

Pope Innocent III was an ambitious man. Elected at the age of thirty-seven, probably the youngest holder of the office in history, his goal was to unify all Christendom—and the wider world—under papal dominion. Unlike Gregory VII (Chapter 8), Innocent never questioned the right of kings and princes to rule in their own secular spheres. Instead, he saw the pope's role as regulatory and disciplinary: when rulers sinned, they should be reprimanded or excommunicated—thereby calling into question their legitimacy. Innocent also insisted on every Christian's obligation to obey the pope as Jesus Christ's representative.

Innocent sought to achieve this goal in many different ways. He made the papacy politically independent by expanding and consolidating papal territories

Pope Innocent III's ambitious goal: unite all Christians under the pope

in central Italy. (Vatican City still continues to function as an independent state.) He proclaimed his power as kingmaker by brokering the selection of the Holy Roman Emperor. He disciplined Philip Augustus (for marital misconduct) and John of England, who was compelled to recognize the pope as his overlord. He even levied the first income tax on the clergy, in order to support the crusade against Constantinople.

His crowning achievement was the ratification of his theological agenda at the Fourth Lateran Council of 1215: so called because it was held in the Roman palace of St. John Lateran. This council defined the newly central dogmas of the Church, including the acknowledgment of papal supremacy. Since a dogma is "a truth necessary for salvation," all Christians had to acknowledge the pope's ultimate power; those unwilling to do so were, by definition, heretics.

The Fourth Lateran Council regulates Christian education and discourages interreligious contact

To further unify the Church, the Fourth Lateran Council also took an unprecedented interest in the religious education of every Christian. It responded to urbanization by establishing free primary schools (for boys) in all major cities, requiring bishops to recruit effective preachers, and outlawing misbehavior on the part of the clergy. It also sought to increase animosity between Christians and their Muslim and Jewish neighbors by discouraging social relationships and intermarriage. Most disturbingly, Innocent's council mandated that "infidels" be distinguished from Christians by their distinctive clothing: the origins of the infamous "Jewish badge" (see Chapter 26).

THE CRUSADE AGAINST HERESY

Innocent's reign achieved the height of papal power, but it also fomented violence and dissent. Future popes would become enmeshed in political and military struggles that compromised the papacy's spiritual credibility. For example, when Innocent's successors came into conflict with the Holy Roman Emperor Frederick II, they called a crusade against him. Innocent also encouraged a new series of crusades against heretics, now defined as anyone who did not fall into line with the papal policy. The most notorious was the Albigensian (*al-bih-JEN-see-an*) Crusade, launched in 1209. Ostensibly, it was directed against a heretical sect called the Cathars; in reality, it justified the conquest and colonization of what is now southern France by land-hungry northern knights.

Although the Albigensian Crusade can be said to have ended by 1255, it created lasting tensions within the forcibly enlarged French kingdom. The inhabitants of this devastated region would later ally with the English during the Hundred Years' War (see Chapter 10) and would embrace Protestantism during the Reformation (Chapter 13). To this day, the language, culture, and political orientation of southern France are very different from those of Paris and its environs.

Unity and Dissent in the Western Church

Many regions of Europe supported the papacy's claim to supremacy, but others resisted its encroachment on centuries-old beliefs and social networks. It was customary for bishoprics to be controlled by certain families. Meanwhile, priests had been married men since the establishment of the first Christian churches; the wives of priests were not only their husbands' partners, they were ministers to their communities. When the papacy preached against "fornicating priests" and their "concubines," it delegitimized relationships that had been essential for generations.

On the one hand, the reforms of Pope Gregory VII and the canons of Innocent III gave the common people an important role to play, by educating them and urging them to embrace a more fervent Christian piety. Combined with the fervor whipped up by crusading, the result was a more widespread interest in spiritual matters and a greater participation in religious life. On the other hand, however, the new power of the papacy severely limited the ways in which the laity were allowed to express their spirituality or to participate meaningfully in the life of the Church.

THE NEW MONASTICISM AND THE MASS

The growth and diversification of monastic movements was one important driver of popular piety. The most successful of the new orders was founded at the monastery of Cîteaux in 1098, hence the name "Cistercian." Cistercian monks followed Benedict's *Rule*, but in the most austere way possible. They founded monasteries in remote areas, far from worldly temptations. They shunned all unnecessary decoration and elaborate rites. Instead, they practiced private prayer and hard manual labor. Under the charismatic leadership of Bernard of Clairvaux (1090–1153), a spellbinding preacher and one of the most influential men of his age, the Cistercian order grew exponentially, from five houses in 1115 to 343 by 1153. This astonishing increase meant that many more men were becoming monks, and that still more pious people were donating funds and lands to support monasteries and their life of devotion.

Another manifestation of popular piety was a new focus on the sacrament of the Mass: the ceremonial reenactment of Christ's last meal with his disciples. Also known as the Eucharist, this ritual had always been an important part of Christian practice (see Chapter 6); but only in the twelfth century did it become the central act of worship in the Roman Church. Bernard of Clairvaux was instrumental in this, by preaching the doctrine of transubstantiation. According to this doctrine, every Mass is a miraculous event because the priest's blessing transforms the bread and wine on the altar into the body and blood of Christ; hence the term *transubstantiation*, since earthly substances become the substance of Christ's divine body.

Not incidentally, this new theology of the Eucharist further enhanced the prestige of the priesthood by seeming to endow it with wonder-working powers. In later centuries, the Latin words spoken at the consecration of the Host, *Hoc est enim corpus meum* ("This is my body"), were understood as a magical formula, *hocus pocus*. Popular reverence for the Eucharist became so great that the Church initiated the practice of elevating the consecrated wafer of bread, known as the Host, so that the whole congregation could see it.

A new focus on the Eucharist makes priesthood more prestigious

HOLY WOMEN, HUMAN AND DIVINE

Popular devotion to the Eucharist was matched by another new religious practice: the veneration of Jesus' mother, Mary (in Hebrew, Miriam). In this development,

VIRGIN AND CHILD. This exquisite ivory sculpture (just over seven inches high) was carved in Paris in the mid- to late thirteenth century as an aid to private devotion and prayer. The mother of Jesus, Mary, was also regarded as the mother of all humanity, the *alma mater* ("nourishing mother") who could be relied on to protect and heal those who ask for her help.

too, Bernard of Clairvaux played an important role, promoting Mary as the very embodiment of the Church. Eventually, the Church would teach that Mary had not only given birth to Jesus while still a virgin, but that she had remained a virgin even after his birth; and, more radically, that she herself had been conceived without sin. This made Mary the exact opposite of Eve, whose disobedience had brought Original Sin into the world.

These new doctrines raised Mary from the position of God's humble handmaid to that of heaven's queen, with the power to intercede on behalf of even the worst sinners. Her soaring reputation as a miracle worker and advocate is amply testified by the thousands of devotional images created during this period, the many stories and hymns celebrating her virtues and miracles, and the fact that practically all of the magnificent new cathedrals of the age were dedicated to "Our Lady": the many churches of Notre Dame in France, the Frauenkirchen of Germany, and so on.

This burgeoning **cult of the Blessed Virgin** had two contradictory effects. It elevated a female figure to a prominent place in the Roman Church and thereby celebrated virtues associated with femininity: motherhood, healing, nourishment, mercy, kindness, and so on. Yet it also made Mary an unattainable model of female perfection: she alone could be both virgin and parent, Christ's mother and bride, God's maidservant and queenly consort. Real women, by contrast, were increasingly compared to Eve and perceived as weak, deceitful, and disobedient. Paradoxically, the veneration of a single, idealized woman coincided exactly with the suppression of most women's access to positions of power in the Church; as the cult of the Blessed Virgin grew, the opportunities for aspiring holy women shrank.

This paradox did not go unremarked at the time. As we noted on page 292, the career of **Heloise** (c. 1090–1164) exemplifies both the avenues of advancement for women as well as the blocking of those avenues by new constraints on women's activities. Heloise's exact contemporary, **Hildegard of Bingen** (1098–1179), was even more creative in her efforts to make a place for herself and her female followers, and more outspoken than Heloise in her criticism of male attempts to thwart them. Like Heloise, she was an abbess and a highly original thinker. But unlike Heloise, who was a scholar, Hildegard was a mystic who claimed to receive regular revelations from God.

Hildegard expressed these revelations in her own version of Latin, writings transcribed and illustrated under her close supervision. She also composed hymns and ambitious musical dramas for her nuns—music now widely available. Her advice was frequently sought by religious and secular authorities, including Bernard of Clairvaux and Frederick Barbarossa; she even received a special papal dispensation that allowed her to preach publicly.

Despite all these privileges, Hildegard had to fight constantly for her rights and those of her nuns; and after her death, efforts to have her recognized as a saint were thwarted by the papacy. Indeed, she was one of the first candidates for whom a new canonization process was instituted by the papal court, or curia, as a way of controlling the popular veneration of charismatic figures whom the Church considered threatening. It would take eight hundred years for Hildegard to be officially declared a saint, in 2012.

HERESY OR PIETY?

Christianity had been embraced by many different civilizations because it readily absorbs new influences. In the late twelfth and thirteenth centuries, however, the Roman Church began to lose its capacity to respond inclusively to challenges, preferring instead to crack down on "heresies" that undermined its power. Yet the more the papacy claimed to control every aspect of belief and practice, the more it made itself vulnerable to challenges. This resulted in large-scale movements of popular opposition to papal authority, as well as to more crusades aimed at harnessing popular devotion.

Consider Innocent III's very different responses to very similar popular movements. For example, Innocent labeled as "heretical" a religious movement known as Waldensianism, which originated in the teachings of a merchant named Peter Waldo (or Waldes). Waldensians were laypeople who wished to imitate the life of Christ to the fullest. They were active in the vernacular translation and study of the Gospels and dedicated to lives of poverty and preaching. None of this contradicted any contemporary doctrines, and for a while the Church did not interfere with the Waldensians' ministry. But when they began to preach without authorization, they were condemned as heretics. In response, they began to articulate a more radical opposition to the established hierarchy. Many of their leaders were women.

At the same time, however, Innocent embraced two other popular movements and turned them into new religious orders: the Dominicans and the Franciscans. Like the Waldensians, the friars ("brothers") of these orders imitated the life of Jesus and his apostles by wandering through the countryside and establishing missions in Europe's growing towns, preaching and offering spiritual and material assistance to the poor. They also embraced poverty and begged for a living, hence their categorization as *mendicants*, from the Latin verb *mendicare* ("to beg"). In the end, the only thing that separated them from the Waldensians was their willingness to subject themselves to papal authority.

Hildegard of Bingen
(1098–1179) A powerful abbess, theologian, scientist, musician, and visionary who claimed to receive regular revelations from God.

HILDEGARD OF BINGEN'S DIVINE INSPIRATION. This portrait of Hildegard and her male secretary, Volmar, appears in her book *Scivias* ("Know the Ways"). It shows Hildegard as the recipient of a divine vision (represented by tongues of heavenly fire), which she transcribes onto a wax tablet using a stylus—a common method for creating the first draft of a written work. Volmar is placed outside the frame in which her vision occurs, but he is prepared to copy it onto parchment. › **What does this image tell us about medieval ideas of authorship and authority?** › **What does it suggest about the relationship and status of the female and male figures?**

The Canons of the Fourth Lateran Council

In 1215, Innocent III presided over an ecumenical assembly of Church leaders in the papal palace and church of St. John Lateran in Rome. The resulting canons (rules) both reaffirmed older legislation and introduced a number of new laws in response to widespread social, economic, and cultural changes. Published in the same year as Magna Carta, they too became a standard set of principles and continued to be applied within the Church until they were modified by the Council of Trent in the sixteenth century.

Canon 1

. . . There is one Universal Church of the faithful, outside of which there is absolutely no salvation. In which there is the same priest and sacrifice, Jesus Christ, whose body and blood are truly contained in the sacrament of the altar under the forms of bread and wine; the bread being changed [*transubstantiation*] by divine power into the body, and the wine into the blood, so that to realize the mystery of unity we may receive of Him what He has received of us. And this sacrament no one can effect except the priest who has been duly ordained in accordance with the keys of the Church, which Jesus Christ Himself gave to the Apostles and their successors. . . .

* * *

Canon 3

We excommunicate and anathematize every heresy that rises against the holy, orthodox, and Catholic faith . . . condemning all heretics under whatever names they may be known, for while they have different faces they are nevertheless bound to each other by their tails, since in all of them vanity is a common element. Those condemned, being handed over to the secular rulers of their bailiffs, let them be abandoned, to be punished with due justice, clerics being first degraded from their orders.

* * *

Canon 9

Since in many places within the same city and diocese there are people of different languages having one faith but various rites and customs, we strictly command that the bishops of these cities and dioceses provide suitable men who will, according to the different rites and languages, celebrate the divine offices for them, administer the sacraments of the Church and instruct them by word and example.

Canon 10

. . . It often happens that bishops, on account of their manifold duties or bodily infirmities, or because of hostile invasions or other reasons, to say nothing of lack of learning, which must be absolutely condemned in them and is not to be tolerated in the future, are themselves unable to minister the word of God to the people, especially in large and widespread dioceses. Wherefore we decree that bishops provide suitable men, powerful in work and word, to exercise with fruitful result the office of preaching; who in place of the bishops, since these cannot do it, diligently visiting the people committed to them, may instruct them by word and example. . . .

Canon 11

Since there are some who, on account of the lack of necessary means, are unable to acquire an education or to meet opportunities for perfecting themselves, the Third Lateran Council in a salutary decree provided that in every cathedral church a suitable benefice be assigned to a master who shall instruct *gratis* the clerics of that church and other poor students, . . . we, confirming the aforesaid decree, add that, not only in every cathedral church but also in other churches where means are sufficient, a competent master be appointed . . . who shall instruct *gratis* and to the best of his ability the clerics of those and other churches in the art of grammar and in other branches of knowledge.

* * *

Canons 14–16

That the morals and general conduct of clerics may be better, let all strive to live chastely and virtuously, particularly those in sacred orders, guarding against every vice of desire . . .

. . . All clerics shall carefully abstain from drunkenness. . . .

We forbid hunting and fowling to all clerics; wherefore, let them not presume to keep dogs and birds for these purposes. . . .

Clerics shall not hold secular offices or engage in secular and, above all, dishonest pursuits. They shall not attend the performances of mimics and buffoons, or theatrical representations. They shall not visit taverns except in case of necessity, namely, when on a journey. They are forbidden to play games of chance or be present at them. They must have a becoming crown and tonsure and apply themselves diligently to the study of the divine offices and other useful subjects. Their garments must be worn clasped at the top and neither too short nor too long. They are not to use red or green garments or curiously sewed-together gloves, or beak-shaped shoes . . .

* * *

Canon 68

In some provinces a difference in dress distinguishes the Jews or Saracens [Muslims] from the Christians, but in certain others such a confusion has grown up that they cannot be distinguished by any difference. Thus it happens at times that through error Christians have relations with the women of Jews or Saracens, and Jews and Saracens with Christian women. Therefore, that they may not, under pretext of error of this sort,

excuse themselves in the future for the excesses of such prohibited intercourse, we decree that such Jews and Saracens of both sexes in every Christian province and at all times shall be marked off in the eyes of the public from other peoples through the character of their dress. . . .

Moreover, during the last three days before Easter and especially on Good Friday, they shall not go forth in public at all, for the reason that some of them on these very days, as we hear, do not blush to go forth better dressed and are not afraid to mock the Christians who maintain the memory of the most holy Passion by wearing signs of mourning. . . .

Source: Excerpted from H. J. Schroeder, *Disciplinary Decrees of the General Councils: Text, Translation, and Commentary* (St. Louis, MO: 1937), pp. 236–96.

Questions for Analysis

1. On the basis of this selection of canons, how would you characterize the main concerns of the Fourth Lateran Council? What is it attempting to regulate, and why? What changing historical circumstances do the canons reflect?

2. In what ways do the canons distinguish between clergy and laity? How does legislation work to maintain those distinctions?

3. Why do the canons place so much emphasis on clothing and appearance? Why would it be important for both clerics and "infidels" (Jews and Muslims) to dress in distinctive ways?

The **Dominican** order, formally known as the Order of Preachers, was founded by Dominic of Osma (1170–1221), a Castilian zealot. It was particularly dedicated to the persecution of heretics and the conversion of Jews and Muslims. The Dominicans hoped to achieve these ends by preaching and public debate, so many of its members pursued academic careers and thus contributed to the development of philosophy and theology in the nascent universities (see page 318). The most influential theologian of the Middle Ages, Thomas Aquinas (1225–1274), was a Dominican. But this order soon became associated with the use of other persuasive techniques through the Inquisition, formalized in the later thirteenth century. (It is now called the Congregation for the Doctrine of the Faith, and is still staffed by members of the order.)

The **Franciscans**, formally known as the Order of the Friars Minor ("Little Brothers"), were committed to the welfare of the poor and the cultivation of personal spirituality. Whereas Dominic was an ordained priest, the founder of the Franciscans was the ne'er-do-well son of an Italian merchant, Francis of Assisi (1182–1226), who rebelled against the materialistic values of his father. Stripping himself (literally) of all worldly possessions, he became a beggar and began to preach salvation in town squares. Initially, Francis did this without official approval, thereby risking rejection as a heretic. But when he submitted to papal obedience in 1209, Innocent granted Francis and his followers permission to preach.

Innocent did not, however, approve of this religious lifestyle for women. Francis's most important female follower, Clare of Assisi (1194–1253), had wanted to found an order along the same lines, the Order of Poor Ladies (also known as the Poor Clares). Yet its members were confined to cloisters and supported by charitable donations. Their more controversial counterparts in northern Europe were the Beguines (*beh-GHEENS*): communities of laywomen who lived in communal quarters and ministered directly to the poor. Their relationship with Church officials was strained, in part because the Beguines embraced many of the practices associated with the Waldensians, including the translation and study of the Bible. The fact that they were women made them even more suspect.

CHRISTIANS AGAINST JEWS

Officially, the Roman Church never explicitly endorsed the view that Jews were a threat to Christians—yet it did little to combat beliefs that Jews were agents of evil who routinely crucified Christian children and consumed their blood (a false charge known as blood libel), profaned the Eucharist, or spread disease by poisoning wells. Fanciful stories of Jewish wealth added an economic element to the development of anti-Semitism, as did the fact that the Jews' social and cultural networks were the engine of medieval trade.

Roots of anti-Jewish views

The precarious position of Europe's Jews worsened throughout the twelfth and thirteenth centuries, as both secular and ecclesiastical authorities devised more systematic mechanisms for policing them, alongside "heretics," the indigent poor, prostitutes, "sodomites," and lepers. The mandate that Jews be identified by a special badge or clothing made them visible targets in times of unrest. At the same time, the protections that Christian rulers had once extended to their Jewish subjects were gradually withdrawn. In Iberia, the "reconquista" had absorbed many of the Muslim kingdoms in which Jews had enjoyed a measure of tolerance, and these Jews were not always easily accommodated by the emerging Christian monarchies.

Starting in the 1280s, some European rulers even began to expel Jewish subjects from their kingdoms altogether, in most cases because they could no longer repay the enormous sums they had extorted from them; this was the case in Sicily (1288), England (1290), and France (1306). Jewish refugees from these realms settled either in the established communities of Spain or in those of the Rhineland. Others, as we noted on pages 298–300, started new settlements in Poland and other eastern European kingdoms.

An Intellectual Revolution

The Fourth Lateran Council responded to the urbanization of Europe by expanding the education of the laity and insisting on more rigorous training for all clergy. These opened new opportunities for advancement: the growth of towns had led to the growth of schools, founded by local bishops or monasteries. Meanwhile, the Crusades became conduits for the transmission of Muslim learning and, through Muslim mediation, the precepts of ancient Greek philosophy. The infusion of these new ideas created an extraordinary new forum for intellectual endeavor: the university. In much the same way that ease of travel and communication had fostered a scientific revolution in the cities of the Hellenistic world (Chapter 4), so the conditions that gave rise to the university sparked an intellectual revolution in Europe.

THE JEWISH BADGE. The distinctive apparel that marked Jews as different varied by from region to region. In some places it was pointed hats, like those worn by the Old Testament Jews in this manuscript illumination from a fourteenth-century Bible. This type of hat later became associated with witchcraft or idiocy, as in the dunce's cap or the witch's peaked hat. In other regions, Jews wore a distinctive patch on their clothing, often yellow to make it more visible.

ACCESS TO EDUCATION

Around 800, Charlemagne had ordered that primary schools be established in every city and monastery of his realm. But it was not until the economic revival of the late eleventh century that educational opportunities became more widely available. Then, in 1179, Pope Alexander III decreed that all cathedrals should have at least one schoolteacher who would accept all male pupils, rich or poor, without fee. He predicted, correctly, that this would increase the number of well-trained clerics to supply the growing bureaucracy of the Church. Thomas Becket had been an early beneficiary of such schooling.

The fundamental curriculum of these cathedral schools was known as the *trivium* ("three ways"): grammar, logic, and rhetoric. This meant a thorough grounding in the study of classical Latin authors, such as Cicero and Virgil, and training in the formulation of sound arguments. Students who mastered the trivium were fit to perform basic clerical tasks, but those who wanted to achieve higher office mastered the *quadrivium* ("four ways"): arithmetic, geometry, astronomy, and music. Together, these seven liberal arts—which liberated those who acquired them from menial labor—were the prerequisites for advanced study in philosophy, theology, law, and medicine.

Most students in urban schools belonged to the minor orders of the clergy, meaning that they took vows of obedience and were immune from prosecution by secular authorities—but not required to remain celibate, unlike priests and bishops, who belonged to major orders. Even men who hoped to become lawyers or bureaucrats

Two Conversion Experiences

Both Peter Waldo (or Waldes), later branded a heretic, and Francis of Assisi, later declared a saint, were moved to take up a life of preaching and poverty after undergoing a process of conversion. Their experiences exhibit some striking similarities despite their different fates. The first account is that of an anonymous chronicler in Peter's hometown of Lyon; the second is by Francis's contemporary and hagiographer, Thomas of Celano (c. 1200–c. 1260/70).

The Conversion of Peter Waldo

At about this time, in 1173, there was a citizen of Lyon named Peter Waldo, who had made a great deal of money by the evil means of usury. One Sunday he lingered by a crowd that had gathered round a traveling storyteller, and was much struck by his words. He took him home with him, and listened carefully to his story of how St. Alexis had died a holy death in his father's house. Next morning Waldo hastened to the schools of theology to seek advice about his soul. When he had been told of the many ways of coming to God he asked the master whether any of them was more sure and reliable than the rest. The master quoted to him the words of the Lord, "If thou wilt be perfect go sell what thou hast and give it to the poor and thou shalt have treasure in heaven. And come follow me."

Waldo returned to his wife and gave her the choice between having all his movable wealth or his property in land. . . . She was very upset at having to do this and chose the property. From his movable wealth he returned what he had acquired wrongly, conferred a large portion on his two daughters, whom he placed in the order of Fontevrault without his wife's knowledge, and gave a still larger amount to the poor.

At this time a terrible famine was raging through Gaul and Germany. . . . Waldo generously distributed bread, soup and meat to anyone who came to him. On the [Feast of the] Assumption of the Virgin [August 15] he scattered money among the poor in the streets saying, "You cannot serve two masters, God and Mammon." The people around thought he had gone out of his senses. Then he stood up on a piece of high ground and said, "Friends and fellow-citizens, I am not mad as you think. . . . I know that many of you disapprove of my having acted so publicly. I have done so both for my own sake and for yours: for my sake, because anybody who sees me with money in future will be able to say that I am mad; for your sake, so that you may learn to place your hopes in God and not in wealth." . . .

[In] 1177, Waldo, the citizen of Lyon whom we have already mentioned, who had vowed to God that he would possess neither gold nor silver, and take no thought for the morrow, began to make converts to his opinions. Following his example they gave all they had to the poor, and willingly devoted themselves to poverty. Gradually, both in public and in private they began to inveigh against both their own sins and those of others. . . .

[In] 1178, Pope Alexander III held a council at the Lateran palace. . . . The council condemned heresy and all those who fostered and defended heretics. The pope embraced Waldo, and applauded the vows of voluntary poverty which he had taken, but forbade him and his companions to assume the office of preaching except at the request of the priests. They obeyed this instruction for a time, but later they disobeyed, and affronted many, bringing ruin on themselves.

Source: Excerpted (with slight modifications) from *Chronicon universale anonymi Laudunensis*; trans. Robert I. Moore, ed, *The Birth of Popular Heresy* (London: 1975), pp. 111-13.

The Conversion of Francis of Assisi

There was a man by the name of Francis, who from his earliest years was brought up by his parents proud of spirit, in accordance with the vanity of the world. . . . These are the wretched circumstances among which the man whom we venerate today as a saint, for he is truly a saint, lived in his youth; and almost up to the twenty-fifth year of his age, . . . he outdid all his contemporaries in vanities and he came to be a promoter of evil and was more abundantly zealous for all kinds of foolishness. . . . And while, not knowing how to restrain himself, he was . . . worn down by a long illness, [he] began to think of things other than he was used to thinking upon. When he had recovered somewhat and had begun to walk about the house with the support of a cane to speed the recovery of his health, he went outside one day and began to look about at the surrounding landscape with great interest. But the beauty of the fields, the pleasantness of the vineyards, and whatever else was beautiful to look upon, could stir in him no delight. He wondered therefore at the sudden change that had come over him. . . . From that day on, therefore, he began to despise himself. . . .

Now since there was a certain man in the city of Assisi whom he loved more than any other because he was of the same age as the other, and since the great familiarity of their mutual affection led him to share his secrets with him; he often took him to remote places, places well-suited for counsel, telling him that he had found a certain precious and great treasure. This one rejoiced and, concerned about what he heard, he willingly accompanied Francis whenever he was asked. There was a certain grotto near the city where they frequently went and talked about this treasure. The man of God, who was already holy by reason of his holy purpose, would enter the grotto, while his companion would wait for him outside; and filled with a new and singular spirit, he would pray to his Father in secret. . . .

One day, however, when he had begged for the mercy of God most earnestly, it was shown to him by God what he was to do. . . . He rose up, therefore, fortified himself with the sign of the cross, got his horse ready and mounted it, and taking with him some fine cloth to sell, he hastened to the city called Foligno. There, as usual, he sold everything he had with him . . . and, free of all luggage, he started back, wondering with a religious mind what he should do with the money. . . . When, therefore, he neared the city of Assisi, he discovered a certain church . . . built of old in honor of St. Damian but which was now threatening to collapse because it was so old. . . . And when he found there a certain poor priest, he kissed his sacred hands with great faith, and offered him the money he had with him, . . . begging the priest to suffer him to remain with him for the sake of the Lord. . . .

When those who knew him . . . compared what he was now with what he had been . . . they began to revile him miserably. Shouting out that he was mad and demented, they threw the mud of the streets and stones at him. . . . Now . . . the report of these things finally came to his father . . . [who] shut him up mercilessly in a dark place for several days. . . . It happened, however, when Francis' father had left home for a while on business and the man of God remained bound in the basement of the house, his mother, who was alone with him and did not approve of what her husband had done, spoke kindly to her son . . . and loosening his chains, she let him go free. . . .

He [the father] then brought his son before the bishop of the city, so that, renouncing all his possessions into his hands, he might give up everything he had. . . . Indeed, he [Francis] did not wait for any words nor did he speak any, but immediately putting off his clothes and casting them aside, he gave them back to his father. Moreover, not even retaining his trousers, he stripped himself completely naked before all. The bishop, however, sensing his disposition and admiring greatly his fervor and constancy, arose and drew him within his arms and covered him with the mantle he was wearing. . . .

Source: Excerpted from Thomas of Celano, "The First Life of Saint Francis" in *Saint Francis of Assisi: Writings and Biographies*, ed. Marion A. Habig (Chicago: 1973), pp. 229–41.

continued on p. 318

(continued from p. 317)

Questions for Analysis

1. How do the conversions of Peter and Francis reflect the social and economic changes of the twelfth century? What new sources of tension and temptation are evident?

2. How do these two accounts describe the new converts' relationship(s) with their families, communities, and Church authorities? What are the similarities and differences? Why would these be important factors in determining the sanctity of either?

3. The story of Peter's conversion is written by an anonymous chronicler of Lyon, that of Francis by his follower and official biographer. How do these different perspectives shape the two accounts? Which is the more reliable, and why?

usually found it professionally advantageous to "take orders." Heloise tried to discourage Abelard from marrying her for this very reason, because it would destroy his chances of being appointed a bishop or papal legate. Abelard, a nobleman's son, was by no means typical of the men who rose to prominence through education. His contemporary and rival, Suger, was more representative: an orphan of obscure origins, he became abbot of the royal monastery of Saint-Denis and the chancellor of France.

Although formal schooling remained restricted to boys and men, many girls and women became highly educated, too, especially those reared in convents or princely courts. Heloise had an unusual degree of access to the educational milieu of Paris, but she had already received excellent training in the convent before she began her studies with Abelard. Most laywomen, however, were taught at home, sometimes by private tutors but more often by other women. In fact, laywomen were more likely to be literate than laymen, and it is for this reason that women were often the patrons of poets and the primary readers and owners of books. The effigy that **Eleanor of Aquitaine** commissioned for her own tomb shows her lying awake, reading, until Judgment Day.

THE TOMB OF ELEANOR OF AQUITAINE. Eleanor probably commissioned the tomb effigies representing herself, her husband Henry II, and her son Richard the Lionheart—both of whom died years before she did. She was eventually buried alongside them in the vault of the convent of Fontevrault in Anjou, where she spent the last years of her life. › Notice that Eleanor's effigy shows her reading a book. How does this reinforce or challenge what we have learned about women's access to education?

THE DEVELOPMENT OF SCHOLASTICISM

The educational revolution that began in the eleventh century led to the development of new critical methods for resolving complex theological and philosophical problems. These methods are collectively known as **scholasticism** because they had their origins in medieval schools. While scholastic methods are highly systematic and respectful of authority, they also rely on rigorous questioning and place great emphasis on evidence derived from reason. Indeed, scholasticism can be defined as a way of reconciling various forms of knowledge through logical debate, often called *dialectic*.

The earliest practitioner of the scholastic method is often considered to be Anselm of Canterbury (1033–1109), a Benedictine monk from northern Italy who became archbishop of Canterbury. Anselm's central premise was that the human mind can combine knowledge gained through education and experience with divine revelation. As he put it, "I believe in order to understand," so that belief can be enriched and strengthened by understanding. Building on the writings of Augustine and Boethius (Chapter 6), Anselm developed various rational proofs for the underlying truths of Christian doctrine. The most famous is his proof for the existence of God, known as the ontological proof ("proof from the fact of existence") because it reasons that human beings could not have ideas of goodness, truth, or justice unless some higher Being had instilled those ideas in us. He further reasoned that God, as the essence of all ideals, must be "that than which nothing greater can be conceived." As such, He must exist, or else God could not be the greatest thing conceivable.

Anselm's writings were influential, but it was Abelard who popularized the scholastic method and made Paris the intellectual capital of Europe. As a cathedral city and seat of the French monarchy, it already boasted a number of schools; but it was only after Abelard was appointed to the schoolmaster's chair at Notre Dame that Paris became a magnet for ambitious young men attracted to Abelard's unorthodox teaching style. We can glimpse it through his audacious treatise the *Sic et Non* ("Yes and No" or "So and Not So"). In this book, Abelard gathered a collection of contradictory statements from the Church fathers, organized around one hundred and fifty key theological problems. His ultimate ambition was to show that these divergent authorities could be reconciled through the skillful use of dialectic.

Yet Abelard did not propose any solutions in the *Sic et Non* itself, and the work therefore raised fears of heresy. More inflammatory still were Abelard's meditations on the doctrine of the Trinity, which circulated in a book denounced and burned in 1121. Eventually, Bernard of Clairvaux had Abelard brought up on another formal charge of heresy at the Council of Soissons, where he was condemned a second time. Luckily, Abelard's dedicated teaching had allowed him to train many pupils who eventually vindicated him. After his death, his student Peter Lombard asked the same fundamental questions, but he took care to resolve the tensions that the *Sic et Non* left open. His great work, known as the *Sentences*, became the standard theological textbook of the medieval university, and all doctoral candidates were required to comment on it.

THE INVENTION OF THE UNIVERSITY

The emergence of the university—a unique public forum for advanced study, the questioning of received ideas, and the creation of new knowledge—was an extension of Abelard's teachings. By 1200, the loose association of teachers that had gathered in Paris had formed into a *universitas* ("unity of diversity") and began to collaborate

Eleanor of Aquitaine (1122-1204) Ruler of the wealthy province of Aquitaine and wife of Louis VII of France, Eleanor had her marriage annulled in order to marry the young count Anjou, Henry Plantagenet, who became King Henry II of England a year later.

scholasticism The methods for resolving complex theological and philosophical problems that were born from the educational revolution that began in the eleventh century.

in the higher academic study of theology. At about the same time, students of law in Bologna came together in a *universitas* whose specialty was law.

Paris and Bologna provided the two models on which all medieval universities were based. In southern Europe, such universities as Montpellier, Salamanca, and Naples were patterned after Bologna, where the students themselves constituted a corporation: they hired teachers, paid their salaries, and fined or discharged them for poor instruction. The universities of northern Europe were like that of Paris: guilds of teachers who governed themselves and established rules of conduct and fees for tuition. They eventually embraced four faculties—liberal arts, theology, law, and medicine. By the end of the thirteenth century, the northern universities also expanded to include separate colleges that provided housing for poorer students and were often endowed by private benefactors. Over time, these colleges became centers of instruction as well as residences. The universities of Oxford and Cambridge still retain this pattern of organization.

Most of the degrees granted in our modern universities derive from those awarded in the Middle Ages, even though the courses of study are very different. No university curriculum included history or vernacular languages or anything like the social sciences prior to the nineteenth century. The medieval student was assumed to know Latin thoroughly before entering a university, which he would have learned in the primary ("grammar") schools discussed earlier. On admission, he spent about four years studying the basic liberal arts, which meant doing advanced work in Latin rhetoric and logic. If he passed his examinations, he received the degree bachelor of arts (from the Latin *baccalaureus*, "laurel crown"). He could also devote additional years to the advanced degrees of master of arts and doctor of laws, medicine, theology, or philosophy. University degrees of all grades were recognized as standards of attainment and became pathways to a variety of careers.

Student life in medieval universities was rowdy. Many students began their studies between the ages of twelve and fifteen, working through all the challenges of adolescence and early adulthood as they worked toward their degrees; this explains the many rules against drunkenness, gambling, and other pursuits mandated by the Fourth Lateran Council. Moreover, university students generally believed that they constituted an independent and privileged community, apart from the urban communities in which they lived. This often led to riots or even pitched battles between "town" and "gown."

That said, time devoted to actual study was intensive. Because books were expensive, the primary mode of instruction was the lecture (Latin for "reading"), in which a master would expound an authoritative work and comment on it, while students took notes. As students advanced in their disciplines, they were expected to develop their own skills of analysis and interpretation in formal, public disputations. Advanced disputations could become extremely complex and abstract, and sometimes might last for days. Often, they sparked public debates of great magnitude. The Ninety-Five Theses posted by Martin Luther in 1517 were actually a set of debating points organized along these lines (see Chapter 13).

CLASSICAL THOUGHT, MUSLIM LEARNING, AND SCHOLASTIC THEOLOGY

This intellectual revolution was hugely indebted to the intellectual legacy of Islam. As we saw in Chapter 8, Muslim philosophers had been honing an array of different techniques to deal with the challenge of reconciling classical thought with Islamic

CENTURY UNIVERSITY WAS FOUNDED

- ■ Twelfth century
- ■ Thirteenth century
- ■ Fourteenth century
- ■ Fifteenth century
- — Boundaries c. 1500

0   100   200   300 Miles
0   100   200   300 Kilometers

THE SPREAD OF UNIVERSITIES. This map shows the geographical distribution of Europe's major universities and their dates of foundation. › **Where were the first universities founded, and why?** › **Notice the number and location of universities founded in the fourteenth and fifteenth centuries. What pattern do you see in these later foundations?** › **What might explain this pattern?**

THE INFLUENCE OF AVERROÈS. This portrait of the Muslim polymath Averroès is featured in a fourteenth-century fresco celebrating the achievements of the Christian theologian Thomas Aquinas (c. 1225–1274).
> What does his inclusion in this context indicate about the relationship between Muslim and Christian intellectual traditions?

belief, and these techniques contributed fundamentally to the development of Christian theology in the wake of the First Crusade.

The most influential of these Muslim philosophers was Ibn Rushd, known to his Christian disciples as Averroès (*ah-VAIR-oh-ayz*; 1126–1198). Born in the Andalusian capital of Córdoba, Averroès single-handedly advanced the study of Aristotelian logic by publishing a series of commentaries that sought to purge the Greek philosopher's works of all later (and confusing) influences. Translated from Arabic into Latin, these commentaries were received in western Christendom alongside new translations of Aristotle's own texts, also conveyed to Latin readers via Arabic. The prestige of Averroès was so great that Christian intellectuals called him simply "the Commentator," just as they called Aristotle "the Philosopher."

Ironically, Averroès's learning was suppressed by the new Muslim dynasty that came to power in his lifetime, the Almohads, who demanded that all philosophical inquiry be subordinated to orthodox Muslim belief. After burning several of Averroès's works, they exiled him to Morocco. The greatest Jewish scholar of this period, Moses Maimonides (*my-MAHN-eh-dees*; c. 1137–1204), was also driven into exile by the Almohads. He traveled first to North Africa and then to Egypt, where he became a famous teacher, jurist, and physician. Like Averroès, he exercised great influence on Christian theologians through his systematic exposition of Jewish law in the *Mishneh Torah*.

Because many aspects of rabbinic tradition, Greek philosophy, and Arabic learning were not readily compatible with Christian faith, they had to be filtered through the dialectical methods pioneered by Abelard and his pupils. The greatest accomplishments in this endeavor were made by **Thomas Aquinas** (1225–1274), who became the leading theologian of Paris. A member of the Dominican order, Thomas was committed to the defense of the Church but he also believed that the study of the physical world was a legitimate way of gaining knowledge of the divine. Confident in the value of human reason and human experience, Thomas worked steadily on his two great summaries of theology, the *Summa contra Gentiles* (a compendium of the arguments for refuting non-Christian religions) and the comprehensive *Summa Theologiae*. The theology of the modern Roman Catholic Church still rests on Thomistic methods, doctrines, and principles.

Thomas Aquinas
(1225–1274) Dominican friar and theologian whose systematic approach to Christian doctrine was influenced by Aristotle.

Courts, Cities, and Cathedrals

In the eleventh century, it was possible to describe European society as divided among "those who worked, those who prayed, and those who fought." By 1200, such a description no longer bore much relationship to reality. New elites had emerged in the burgeoning cities of Europe. The wealthiest members of society were merchants and bankers, not aristocrats. The aristocracy still fought, but so did upwardly mobile peasants, urban archers, and citizen militias. Meanwhile, the pupils of the new schools and universities made up a growing professional class that further defied categorization. Careers in the Church or royal bureaucracies were particularly open to self-made, educated men, while medieval courts and cities also provided opportunities for advancement.

FROM *CHEVALERIE* TO CHIVALRY

The transformation of chivalry and the emergence of medieval court culture were connected to the growing wealth of Europe, the competition among states, and contemporary developments in military technology. In 1100, a knight could get by with a woolen tunic and leather corselet, a couple of horses, a groom, and a sword. A hundred years later, a knight needed full-body armor made of iron, a visored helmet, broadsword, lance, shield, and several warhorses capable of carrying all this gear. He also had to keep up appearances at tournaments, which meant sumptuous silk clothing for himself and caparisons for his steeds, and a retinue of liveried squires and servants. As the costs of a warrior's equipment rose, the number of men who could personally afford it dramatically declined, making knightly display something increasingly prized by nobles and upstart merchants alike. Knights who did not inherit or gain sufficient property to support themselves had to seek wealthy brides or the protection of a lord who could equip them.

Still other factors contributed to the prestige of knighthood. As part of a larger effort to control the violent competition for land and wealth, both secular and ecclesiastical rulers began to promote a new set of values that would come to redefine chivalry: bravery, loyalty, generosity, and civility. This new chivalry appealed to knights because it distinguished them from all the other "new men" who were emerging as powerful figures in this period, especially merchants and clerics. It also appealed to the nobility whose status in this socially mobile world no longer depended on descent from high-born ancestors; families who *did* have such ancestors did not necessarily have the wealth to maintain a noble lifestyle, whereas many families who posed as noble did not have noble ancestors.

A new sense of social mobility

THE ARISTOCRATIC LANDSCAPE AND ITS ENVIRONMENTAL EFFECTS

In previous centuries, warriors had hunted to supplement their diets or to protect their households from predators. But as more and more land was placed under cultivation, many species of wild animals (notably wolves, bears, and boar) were hunted to near extinction in Europe, and hunting ceased to be a necessity and became a symbol of noble status. Not only did hunting require a good horse, a pack of trained dogs, servants, and an array of weapons, it also required elites to enclose certain areas of protected land so that they could be stocked with game. These protected spaces were called forests—regardless of whether or not they were wooded—and they were governed by a "law of the forest," which stipulated that only the lord who controlled the forest could hunt (or allow others to hunt) there.

Forest law forbade peasants from hunting and prescribed heavy penalties for poaching (stealing). Such laws also prohibited foraging or cutting down trees for construction or as firewood. After the Norman Conquest, the kings of England had so increased the amount of land that was deemed "royal forest" that Magna Carta would contain a series of provisions demanding that this land be "disaforrested" and returned to common use. In 1217, the young King Henry III issued a companion document, the Charter of the Forest, to reestablish his subjects' rights to these lands.

As in so many other arenas, the Crusades had an impact on hunting and the environment, too. Crusaders were impressed and inspired by the elegance and elaborate engineering of the gardens and parks they saw in the Holy Land, North Africa, and Muslim Spain. So during the thirteenth century, many European aristocrats embarked on major projects designed to turn their own forests into hunting parks, creating habitats friendly to new species of birds and animals. The natural landscape of Europe was decisively altered as a result. Fallow deer (*Dama dama*), native only to Anatolia and brought to the Mediterranean by the Romans, were now introduced in England and France, where they were bred for hunting. Rabbits, originally native to Spain and North Africa, were also newcomers in northern Europe, prized for their meat and pelts but having an unexpectedly devastating effect on native plants and becoming invasive pests.

Crusaders return to western Europe with new species, sometimes invasive

Herons, although native to northern Europe, were now aggressively bred to stock heronries, which meant that many low-lying arable lands were removed from peasant control and artificially flooded to provide the proper habitat and sources of food. Herons, in turn, fed the new aristocratic mania for hunting: expensively trained hawks, falcons, and peregrines were loosed to catch and kill the large, graceful birds. Emperor Frederick II, having grown up in Sicily and the multicultural Mediterranean, drew on Arabic sources for his important treatise on falconry. He also maintained a menagerie of exotic animals. For him, as for his peers, control over the environment became a new source of aristocratic identity.

THE CULTURE OF THE COURT

Closely linked to the new ideology of chivalry was an emphasis on *courtoisie* ("courtliness"), the refined behavior appropriate to a court. This stemmed in part from practical necessity: those great lords who could support a knightly retinue had households full of energetic, lusty young men whose appetites had to be controlled. Hence, the emerging code of chivalry encouraged adherents to view noblewomen as objects of veneration who could be wooed and won only by polished manners, poetry, and valiant deeds; in other words, they had to be courted. (Nonnoble women, though, were fair game and could be taken by force if they did not yield willingly to a knight.)

Whole new genres of poetry, song, and storytelling emerged in the twelfth century to celebrate the allied cultures of chivalry and courtliness. These genres stand in marked contrast to the older entertainments of Europe's warrior class, the heroic epics that are often the earliest literary vernacular artifacts: the Anglo-Saxon *Beowulf*, the French *Song of Roland*, the Norse sagas, the German *Song of the Nibelungs*, and the Spanish *Poem of the Cid*. These epics portray a virile, violent society where gore flows freely; manly valor, honor, and loyalty are the major themes. If women are mentioned, it is usually as prizes to be won in battle.

The courtly entertainments introduced in the twelfth century were very different in style, subject, and authorship. Many were addressed to, and commissioned by, women. In some cases, they were even composed by women or in close collaboration with a female patron. An example of the former is the collection of *lais* (versified stories) by Marie de France, who was active during the reigns of Henry II and Eleanor of Aquitaine, and who may have been an abbess as well as a member of the Anglo-Norman aristocracy. An example of the latter are the Arthurian tales composed by Marie's contemporary, Chrétien de Troyes (*kray-tyan duh TWAH*; fl. 1165–1190), who worked under the patronage of Eleanor's daughter (by her first husband) Marie of Champagne.

Romances were engaging tales of love and adventure, often focusing on the exploits of King Arthur and his knights or some other heroic figure, such as Alexander the Great. But they were also attuned to the interests and concerns of women: threats to women's independence, enforced or unhappy marriages, disputed inheritances, fashion, and fantasies of power. The heroine of one anonymous romance is a woman who dresses as a knight and travels the world performing valiant deeds. Other heroines accompany their husbands on crusades or quests, defend their castles against attack, or have supernatural powers. Following in Chrétien's footsteps, the German poets Wolfram von Eschenbach and Gottfried von Strassburg vied to produce romances that retained the scope and complexity of heroic epics while featuring women in strong, central roles. Both Wolfram's *Parzival*, the story of the search for the Holy Grail, and Gottfried's *Tristan*, which retold the Celtic story of adulterous love between Tristan and Isolde, inspired the operatic masterpieces of Richard Wagner (1813–1883).

The poetic tradition initiated by the southern French troubadours and the northern French trouvères (from the verbs *trobar/trouver*, "to discover, to invent") also contributed to the culture of chivalry and inspired the work of German *Minnesänger* ("love singers"). Much troubadour poetry displays sensitivity to feminine beauty and the natural world, and pays eloquent tribute to the political and sexual powers of women. Other troubadour songs celebrate old-fashioned warlike virtues, bloodshed, and male friendships.

But to what extent do all of these courtly genres reflect the reality of noblewomen's status? Certainly, there were women throughout this period who wielded tremendous power, particularly in Scandinavia and parts of southern Europe, where women could inherit property, rule in their own right, and be treated as lords in fact

ON THE ART OF HUNTING WITH BIRDS. This beautifully illuminated manuscript of Frederick II's famous treatise on falconry was commissioned by his son Manfred shortly after his father's death in 1250. It is now in the Vatican Library in Rome. The artist's representations of various birds are so exact that researchers in Finland, in 2018, were able to identify one as a sulfur-crested cockatoo: a bird native to Australia and New Guinea.

and in name. For example, Queen Urraca of León-Castile ruled the combined king-dom from 1109 until 1126. Ermengarde of Narbonne (c. 1127–1197) governed her powerful county from early adolescence to the time of her death. Eleanor remained sole ruler of Aquitaine throughout her long life and played a crucial role in the government of England at various times. The strong-willed Blanche of Castile (1188–1252), Eleanor's granddaughter, ruled France during the minority of her son Louis IX, and again when he went on a crusade.

Queens are not typical, but their activities during this period reflect some of the opportunities open to other well-born women—and the freedoms that set most European women apart from their counterparts in the Byzantine and Muslim worlds. A striking symbol of this is the queen in a game of chess. In the Muslim courts where the game originated, the equivalent of the queen was a male figure, the king's chief minister, who could move only diagonally and one square at a time. In twelfth-century Europe, this piece became the queen: the only figure powerful enough to move all over the board.

URBAN OPPORTUNITIES AND INEQUALITIES

In 1174, a cleric named William FitzStephen wrote a biography of his late employer, Thomas Becket, who had recently been canonized. In it, William extolled the urban culture of London that had produced him and other "men of superior quality." Towns were crucibles of activity, and as such became cultural as well as economic powerhouses, the launching pads for the careers of ambitious men.

As we noted in Chapter 8, many of the towns that had emerged in the eleventh century were governed by associations of citizens. But urban governance was likely to fall into the hands of oligarchs, a trend that became increasingly marked during the thirteenth century, when the enormous wealth generated by some forms of commerce led to marked social inequalities. In Italy, some cities sought to control the resulting violence by turning to an outsider who would rule as an autocrat for a (supposedly) limited term. Other cities adopted the model of Venice and became formal oligarchies, casting off all pretense of shared governance. Some cities remained republics in principle, as did Florence, but became increasingly oligarchical in practice.

Guilds regulate industries to protect monopolistic interests

But even in places where town governance was controlled by a powerful few, there were many meaningful opportunities for collective activity. Urban manu-facturing was regulated by professional associations known as guilds or (in some regions) confraternities. Guilds promoted the interests of their members by trying to preserve monopolies and limit competition. To these ends, terms of employ-ment and membership were strictly regulated. If an apprentice or a journeyman worker (from the French *journée*, "day" and, by extension, "day's work") wished to become a master, he had to produce a "masterpiece" to be judged by the guild. Most guilds were closed to Jews and Muslims, and they also restricted the oppor-tunities available to women, who had little influence over the terms and conditions under which they worked.

Guilds and confraternities were therefore instruments of economic control, but they were also important social, political, and cultural institutions. Most combined the functions of religious association, drinking club, and benevolent society, look-ing after members and their families in hard times, supporting the dependents of

Illicit Love and the Code of Chivalry

Little is known about Marie de France, the author of a series of popular verse tales that are among the earliest chivalric romances. She may have been a nun or abbess living in the Anglo-Norman realm of Henry II and Eleanor of Aquitaine. The following excerpt is from her Lais, adapted from stories told in the Franco-Celtic county of Brittany (Abelard's home).

The Bretons, who lived in Brittany, were fine and noble people. In days gone by these valiant, courtly and noble men composed lays for posterity and thus preserved them from oblivion. . . . One of them, which I have heard recited, should not be forgotten. It concerns Equitan, a most courtly man, lord of Nantes, justiciary and king.

Equitan enjoyed a fine reputation and was greatly loved in his land. He adored pleasure and amorous dalliance: for this reason he upheld the principles of chivalry. Those who lack a full comprehension and understanding of love show no thought for their lives. Such is the nature of love that no one under its sway can retain command over reason. Equitan had a seneschal, a good knight, brave and loyal, who took care of his entire territory, governing it and administering its justice. Never, except in time of war, would the king have forsaken his hunting, his pleasures or his river sports, whatever the need might have been.

As his wedded wife the seneschal had a woman who was to bring great misfortune to the land. She was a lady of fine breeding and extremely beautiful with a noble body and good bearing. Nature had spared no pains when fashioning her: her eyes sparkled, her face and mouth were beautiful and her nose was well set. She had no equal in the kingdom, and the king, having often heard her praised, frequently sent her greetings and gifts. . . . He went hunting in her region on his own and on returning from his sport took lodging for the night in the place where the seneschal dwelt, in the very castle where the lady was to be found. He had ample occasion to speak with her, to express his feelings and display his fine qualities. He found her most courtly and wise, beautiful in body and countenance. . . .

That night he neither slept nor rested, but spent his time reproaching and reprimanding himself. "Alas," he said, "what destiny brought me to this region? Because of this lady I have seen, my heart has been overwhelmed by a pain so great that my whole body trembles. I think I have no option but to love her. Yet, if I did love her, I should be acting wrongly, as she is the seneschal's wife. I ought to keep faith with him and love him, just as I want him to do with me. . . ."

Source: From "Equitan," in *The Lais of Marie de France*, trans. Glyn S. Burgess and Keith Busby (Harmondsworth, UK: 1986), pp. 56–7.

Questions for Analysis

1. Despite the king's initial misgivings, he and the seneschal's wife eventually have an affair and plot to murder her husband, only to be caught in their own trap. Knowing this outcome, how would you interpret Marie's remarks about courtliness and "the code of chivalry"? What are the tenets of this code, according to the king?

2. What social tensions does this story reflect? How might it shed light on historical realities? What moral might contemporary readers draw from it?

members who died, and helping to finance funerals. Guilds also empowered their members in much the same way that unions do today, providing them with political representation and raising their social status. The wealthy town of Arras even had a guild of professional entertainers, the confraternity of *jongleurs*, which became the most powerful organization in the town by 1250.

VARIETIES OF VERNACULAR ENTERTAINMENT

Like courts, towns fostered the emerging vernacular languages of Europe and produced new kinds of entertainment. Even the genres of Latin poetry, song, and drama produced in this period can be considered "vernacular" because they made use of vernacular elements (such as rhyme, which is not a feature of classical Latin poetry), dealt with current events, and were popular with a wide audience. In one of Heloise's letters to Abelard, she recalls that he was so renowned for his love songs that "every street and tavern resounded with my name." It is possible that some of Abelard's songs were sung in French, but more probable that they used the edgy, colloquial Latin popular among student singer-songwriters known as "goliards," which means something like "daredevils." Their lyrics celebrated the carefree life of travel, the pleasures of drinking and dice, the joys of love, and the agonies of poverty.

Perhaps the genre most representative of urban culture is the *fabliau*, a rhymed "fable" or short story with a salacious, irreverent, or satirical twist. Fabliaux lampooned the different types of people striving to reinvent themselves in the permissive world of the town: the oafish peasant, the effete aristocrat, the corrupt priest, the sex-starved housewife, the wily student, the greedy merchant, the con man. Gender-bending and reversals of fortune are also common themes. In one fabliau, a young noblewoman is forced by her impoverished father to marry a buffoonish shopkeeper who thereby attains knighthood; to shame him, she dresses herself as a knight and beats her husband in a jousting match. In another, a priest tricks a poor peasant out of his cow by promising that God will reward him by doubling his "investment" in the Church; when the cow breaks out of the priest's pasture and runs for home—bringing the priest's cow, too—the peasant is delighted by the promised miracle.

THE MEDIEVAL CATHEDRAL

The cathedrals constructed in Europe's major cities during this period exemplify the ways in which the court, the schools, and the town came together. Although any cathedral-building campaign would have been spearheaded by a bishop looking to glorify his episcopal see, it could not be completed without the support of the nobility, the resources of the wealthy, the learning of trained theologians, and the talents of urban craftsmen. And cathedrals were not merely edifices: they were theaters for the performance of liturgy, music, drama, and preaching.

Cathedrals were not, in themselves, new: the seat of a bishop had long been known as his *cathedra*, his throne, and the church that housed it was the principal church of the diocese. But the size, splendor, and importance of cathedrals increased exponentially in the twelfth and thirteenth centuries, alongside the growing power of the Church, the population of cities, and the wealth and knowledge necessary for their construction. Indeed, the cathedrals of this period are readily distinguishable from their predecessors by their architectural style, which came to be called "Gothic," whereas the style of earlier buildings is known as "Romanesque."

As the term suggests, Romanesque buildings use the basic elements of public architecture under the Roman Empire: the rounded arch, massive stone walls, and sturdy

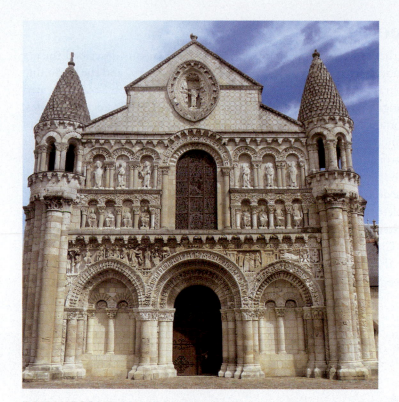

ROMANESQUE AND GOTHIC. Some distinguishing features of the Romanesque and Gothic styles are shown in these two churches, both dedicated to the Virgin Mary and built within a century of one another. On the left is the west front of the Church of Notre-Dame-la-Grande in Poitiers, the ancestral domain of Eleanor of Aquitaine. Constructed between 1135 and 1145, it featured rounded arches, strong stone walls, massive supporting pillars, and small windows. On the right is the cathedral of Notre-Dame at Reims in Champagne, built between 1220 and 1299. Here, the emphasis on stolid horizontal registers is replaced by soaring vertical lines. The gabled portals, pointed arches, and bristling pinnacles all accentuate the height of this structure, while the multitude of stained-glass windows—chiefly the enormous rose window—flood the vast interior with colored light.

supporting columns. These features made churches places of refuge that could be fortified and defended in troubled times. By contrast, the structural elements of Gothic architecture are the pointed arch, groined and ribbed vaulting, and the flying buttress: an external support that strengthened the much thinner stone walls and enormous stained-glass windows, whose light illuminated the church's elaborate decorative programs. The Gothic cathedral was a microcosm of the medieval world and an encyclopedia of medieval knowledge. They were manifestations of urban pride, expressions of practical and intellectual genius, and symbols of a triumphant and confident Church. Their builders would have been dismayed to learn that the modern term *gothic* was actually intended to be derogatory, the name for art forms that later Italian artists—who favored classical models—considered barbaric (see Chapter 12). They would have been still more shocked to learn that cathedrals were among the first monuments targeted for destruction during the Reformation, the revolutions of the eighteenth and nineteenth centuries, and the wars of the twentieth. One of the prime examples of Gothic architecture, the cathedral dedicated to the Virgin Mary at Reims (shown above), was largely destroyed during World War I; what visitors see today is a reconstruction.

Conclusion

A century ago, the American historian Charles Homer Haskins described the era we have been studying as the "Renaissance of the twelfth century" and the beginning of Europe's cultural prestige. A generation later, his student Joseph Strayer located the "medieval origins of the modern state" in this same period. In recent decades, the British historians R. I. Moore and Robert Bartlett have also argued that this era marks the beginning of the modern world—but not in positive ways. Moore sees the growth of strong institutions as leading to the "formation of a persecuting society," in which governmental and religious bureaucracies identify, control, and punish groups of people deemed threatening to those in power through a never-ending "war on heresy." Bartlett views this era as a brutal process of "conquest and colonization" visible in the eastern expansion of the Holy Roman Empire, the Norman conquest of England, the Crusades, and other movements.

Common to all of these paradigms is a recognition that, by 1250, Europe had taken on the geographic, political, linguistic, and cultural characteristics that we

AFTER YOU READ THIS CHAPTER

CHRONOLOGY

1079–1142	Lifetime of Peter Abelard
c. 1090–c. 1164	Lifetime of Heloise
1098–1179	Lifetime of Hildegard of Bingen
1099	First Crusade ends
1122–1204	Lifetime of Eleanor of Aquitaine
1152–1190	Reign of Frederick II Barbarossa
1180–1223	Reign of Philip II Augustus
1187	Muslim reconquest of Jerusalem
1192–1194	Alfonso II of Aragon compiles the *Liber feudorum maior*
1198–1216	Reign of Pope Innocent III
1204	Capture and sack of Constantinople
1209	Franciscan order established; beginning of the Albigensian Crusade
1215	Magna Carta and the canons of the Fourth Lateran Council are both formulated
1216	Dominican order established
1240	Battle of the Neva

REVIEWING THE OBJECTIVES

❯ The emerging monarchies of Europe shared certain features but differed from each other in significant ways. What were the major similarities and differences of kingship in England, France, and Iberia?

❯ How did the meaning and purposes of crusading change in the twelfth and thirteenth centuries?

❯ The growth of papal power made religion an important part of Christians' daily life in unprecedented ways, but how did it at the same time limit lay spirituality and the rights of non-Christians?

❯ Scholasticism was the method of teaching and learning fostered by medieval schools, but it was also a method of debating and resolving problems. How did scholasticism assist in the reconciliation of classical and Christian thought?

❯ Why did the meaning of chivalry change in the twelfth century? What new literary genres and art forms were fostered by courts, universities, and towns?

recognize today. Indeed, many European nations look to these centuries for their origins and for the monuments of their cultural heritage. Magna Carta is still cited as a foundational document of English law and constitutional monarchy. The territories united under the rule of the French kings still form the nation of France. The doctrines crystallized in medieval canon law and scholastic theology have become the core doctrines of the modern Roman Catholic Church, and devotion to the Virgin Mary is still central to the piety of millions. The religious orders that emerged to educate and curb a burgeoning medieval population continue their ministries. The houses of medieval monastic orders continue to proliferate in lands unknown to medieval Europeans: Japan, Australia, New Zealand, and the Americas. Students still pursue the degrees first granted in medieval universities, and those who earn them wear the caps and gowns of medieval scholars. Meanwhile, poets aspire to the eloquence of troubadours, singers record the music of Hildegard, and Hollywood films are based on chivalric romances and the tragic love of Abelard and Heloise. It is difficult to tell where the Middle Ages end and the modern world begins.

 Go to INQUIZITIVE to see what you've learned—and learn what you've missed—with personalized feedback along the way.

PEOPLE, IDEAS, AND EVENTS IN CONTEXT

› What was at stake in the clash between **HENRY II** of England and **THOMAS BECKET**?

› What was **MAGNA CARTA**? Why was it formulated? How did **PHILIP AUGUSTUS** consolidate royal authority in France? Why were the German emperors unable to do so?

› Why were the **CRUSADER STATES** short lived and fragile? How did the *RECONQUISTA* continue the Crusades?

› What were the main goals of **INNOCENT III**? How did the **FRANCISCANS** and the **DOMINICANS** advance his agenda?

› How do the **CULT OF THE BLESSED VIRGIN** and the careers of **HILDEGARD OF BINGEN** and **HELOISE** exemplify the ideals and realities of women's roles in the Church?

› What is **SCHOLASTICISM**? How did **THOMAS AQUINAS** respond to the influence of Classical and Muslim philosophies?

› Why were **PETER ABELARD**'s teachings condemned by the Church? In what sense can he be considered the founder of the **UNIVERSITY OF PARIS**?

› How did noblewomen such as **ELEANOR OF AQUITAINE** contribute to the emergence of a new vernacular culture? What types of entertainment were characteristic of medieval cities?

THINKING ABOUT CONNECTIONS

› The growth of towns, monarchies, and the Church increased the degree of control that those in power could exercise; yet this growth also increased access to education and new forms of social mobility. Is this a paradox, or are these two phenomena related?

› The U.S. Constitution is based on the legal principles and institutions that emerged in medieval England, but it also drew on Roman models. Which do you consider to be more influential, and why?

› Some historians have argued that the extent and methods of persecution discernible in the Middle Ages are unprecedented in the history of Western civilizations. How would you support or refute this thesis? For example, does the persecution of Jews in medieval Europe differ from their treatment under the neo-Assyrians and Chaldeans, or under the Roman Empire? Why or why not?

10

The Medieval World, 1250–1350

WHEN CHRISTOPHER COLUMBUS set out to find a new trade route to the East, he carried with him two influential books written centuries before his voyage. One was *The Book of Marvels*, composed around 1350 and attributed to John de Mandeville, an English adventurer (writing in French) who claimed to have reached the far horizons of the globe. The other was Marco Polo's *Description of the World*, an account of that Venetian merchant's journey through the vast Eurasian realm of the Mongols to the court of the Great Khan in China. He had dictated it to an author of popular romances in 1298, when both men were in prison—coincidentally, in Columbus's own city of Genoa. Both books reflect an extraordinary era of unprecedented interactions among the peoples of Europe, Asia, and the interconnected Mediterranean world. This was a time when ease of communication and commercial exchange made Western civilizations part of an interlocking network that had the potential to span the globe. Although this network would prove fragile in the face of a large-scale demographic crisis, the Black Death, it created a lasting impression of infinite possibilities. Indeed, it was only *because* of this network's connective channels that the Black Death wreaked such devastation in the years around 1350. Looking back, we can see the century leading up to this near-worldwide crisis as the beginning of a new global age.

Europeans' integration with this widening world not only put them into contact with unfamiliar cultures and commodities, it also changed the

BEFORE YOU READ THIS CHAPTER

›

da tenen genes q fan
ien hon fino los vls
efan aueqleaces al
es qui ben nom lemps
m les bones barguef

tagaza

GINYH

fudam

tenouch

autat de melly

cadia

tacozt

ASHARA

aqueft fenyor negre es apellat
muffe melly fenyor dels negres
de gineua aqueft rey es la pus
rich el pus noble fenyor detota
efta parda p la bondaçia de la el
qual ferseull en la fiua terra

buda

gougeu

maymia

STORY LINES

❯ The Mongol Empire widened channels of communication, commerce, and cultural exchange between Europe and the Far East. At the same time, Europeans were extending their reach into the Atlantic Ocean.

❯ Western civilizations' integration with this wider medieval world led to new ways of mapping, measuring, and describing that world.

❯ Despite these broadening horizons, most Europeans' lives were bounded by their communities and focused on the parish church.

❯ Meanwhile, the growing strength of the kings of France and England drew them into territorial disputes that led to the Hundred Years' War.

❯ As global climate change affected the ecosystems of Europe and caused years of famine, the integrated networks of the medieval world facilitated the rapid transmission of the Black Death.

CORE OBJECTIVES

❯ **DESCRIBE** the effects of the Mongol conquests.

❯ **IDENTIFY** the key characteristics of the medieval world system and the responses to it.

❯ **UNDERSTAND** the reasons for the papacy's loss of prestige and the rise of strong secular monarchs.

❯ **DEFINE** the concept of sovereignty and its importance.

❯ **EXPLAIN** the rapid spread of the Black Death in this historical context.

world they already knew and inspired novel artistic and intellectual responses. At the same time, involvement in this wider world placed new pressures on long-term developments within Europe, notably the growing tensions among territorial monarchies and between these secular powers and the papacy. The ensuing struggles for sovereignty would have a profound impact on the balance of power and further complicate Europeans' relationships with one another.

The Mongol Empire and the Reorientation of the West

Links between the Mediterranean world and the Far East reach back into antiquity, as we have often noted. But it was not until the mid-thirteenth century that Europeans were able to establish direct connections with India, China, and the so-called Spice Islands of the Indonesian archipelago. These connections would prove profoundly important, as much for their impact on the European imagination as for their economic significance. For the peoples of Asia, however, the more frequent appearance of Europeans was less consequential than the events that made their journeys possible: the rise of a new empire that encompassed the continent.

THE EXPANSION OF THE MONGOL EMPIRE

Although closely connected with the Turkish peoples of the central Asian steppes, the Mongols were herdsmen who spoke their own distinctive language and had their own homeland, in what is now known as Mongolia. They were also highly accomplished horsemen and raiders; indeed, it was to curtail their raids that the Chinese had fortified their Great Wall many centuries before. Primarily, though, China defended itself from the Mongols by ensuring that the various tribes turned their energies against each other.

In the late twelfth century, however, a Mongol chief named Temujin (c. 1162–1227) began to assert dominance over other tribal chiefs by incorporating their warriors into his own army. In 1206, his supremacy was reflected in a new title, **Genghis Khan** or "universal ruler," which revealed his wider ambitions. Taking advantage of China's division into three warring states, Genghis Khan launched an attack on the northern Chin Empire and penetrated deep into its interior by 1211. These initial attacks were probably looting expeditions rather than deliberate attempts at conquest, but their aims were soon sharpened under Genghis Khan's successors. Shortly after his death in 1227, a full-scale invasion of both northern and western China was under way. In 1234, these fell to the Mongols. By 1279, one of Genghis Khan's numerous grandsons, Kublai Khan, would complete the conquest of southern China, too.

For the first time in centuries, China was connected to western and central Asia in ways unprecedented in its long history, as Genghis Khan had brought crucial commercial cities and Silk Road trading posts into his empire. Building on these achievements, one of his sons, Ögedei (*EHRG-uh-day*), conquered the Rus' capital at Kiev between 1237 and 1240, and then launched a two-pronged assault on the rich lands of the European frontier. The smaller of two Mongol armies swept

Mongolian conquest under Ögedei spreads from China into central Asia and eastern Europe

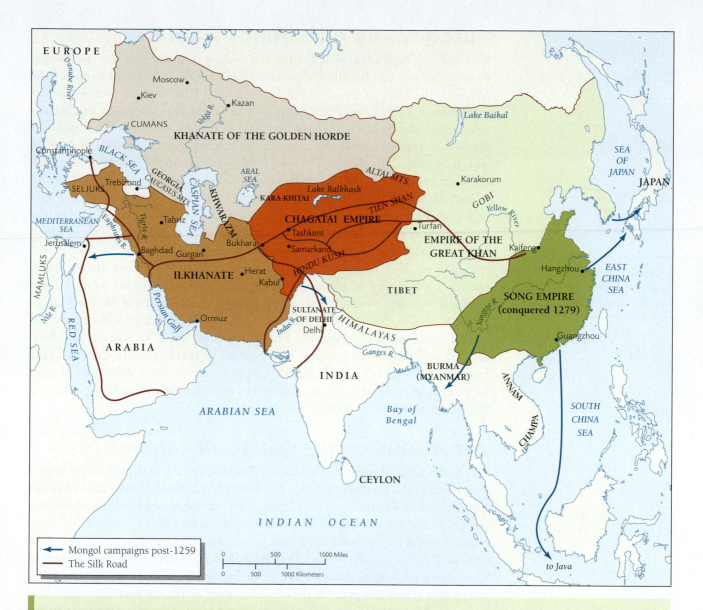

The Silk Road legend:
- Mongol campaigns post-1259
- The Silk Road

Map labels: EUROPE, Moscow, Kiev, Kazan, CUMANS, Danube River, Volga R., KHANATE OF THE GOLDEN HORDE, Lake Baikal, Constantinople, BLACK SEA, GEORGIA, CAUCASUS MTS., Trebizond, ARAL SEA, ALTAI MTS., SEA OF JAPAN, JAPAN, Karakorum, SELJUKS, KHWARIZM, CASPIAN SEA, KARA-KHITAI, Lake Balkhash, TIEN SHAN, GOBI, Yellow River, MEDITERRANEAN SEA, Tabriz, Bukhara, Tashkent, CHAGATAI EMPIRE, Turfan, EMPIRE OF THE GREAT KHAN, Kaifeng, EAST CHINA SEA, Jerusalem, Euphrates R., Tigris R., Baghdad, Gurgan, Samarkand, HINDU KUSH, Hangzhou, Herat, Kabul, ILKHANATE, MAMLUKS, Nile R., RED SEA, Persian Gulf, Ormuz, SULTANATE OF DELHI, Delhi, Indus R., HIMALAYAS, TIBET, Yangtze R., SONG EMPIRE (conquered 1279), Guangzhou, ARABIA, INDIA, Ganges R., BURMA (MYANMAR), ANNAM, CHAMPA, SOUTH CHINA SEA, ARABIAN SEA, Bay of Bengal, CEYLON, INDIAN OCEAN, to Java

Scale: 0 500 1000 Miles / 0 500 1000 Kilometers

THE STATES OF THE MONGOL EMPIRE. Like Alexander's, Genghis Khan's empire was swiftly assembled and encompassed vast portions of Europe and Asia. › How many different Mongol khanates were there after 1260, when Kublai Khan came to power? Were these domains mapped onto older divisions within Western civilizations? › How might the Mongol occupation of the Muslim world have aided the expansion of European trade? › At the same time, why would it have complicated the efforts of crusader armies in the Holy Land?

through Poland toward Germany; the larger went southwest toward Hungary. In April 1241, the smaller force met a hastily assembled army of Germans and Poles at the Battle of Legnica in southern Poland, where the Mongols were driven back. Two days later, the larger Mongol army annihilated a Hungarian army at the river Sajó. Its further advance into Europe was halted only when Ögedei Khan died in December of that year.

MUSCOVY AND THE MONGOL KHANATE

Kiev had long been a hub of diplomatic and trading relations with western Europe, Byzantium, and the Islamic Caliphate at Baghdad. But with the arrival of the Mongols, the locus of power in Rus' moved from Kiev to their own settlement on the lower Volga River. From there, they extended their dominion over terrain stretching from the Black Sea to central Asia. It became known as the Khanate of the Golden Horde, a name that captures the striking impression made by Mongol tents hung with cloth of gold. (The word *horde* derives from the Mongol word meaning "encampment" and the related Turkish word *ordu*, "army.")

Initially, the Mongols ruled Rus' directly, installing their own officials and requiring local princes to show their obedience by traveling in person to the Mongol court of the Great Khan in China. But after Kublai Khan's death in 1294, the Mongols began to tolerate the existence of several semi-independent principalities. Kiev never recovered its dominant position, but one of these principalities, the duchy of Moscow, gained prominence due to its strategic geographical location. Moscow became the tribute-collecting center for the Mongol Khanate, and its dukes were even encouraged to extend their lordship into neighboring territories. Eventually, the Muscovite dukes came to control the khanate's tax-collecting mechanisms. As a reflection of these extended powers, Duke Ivan I (r. 1325–1340) gained the title Grand Prince of Rus'. When the Mongol Empire began to disintegrate, the Muscovites were therefore in a strong position to supplant their former overlords.

> *Moscow becomes important financial and political center*

THE MAKING OF THE MONGOL ILKHANATE

As Ögedei Khan moved into the lands of Rus' and eastern Europe, Mongol armies also subdued the vast territory that had been encompassed by the former Persian Empire and its Roman successors. Indeed, the strongest state in this region was known as the sultanate of Rûm (the Arabic word for "Rome"), which had been founded by the Seljuk Turks in 1077 and consisted of Anatolian provinces formerly belonging to the eastern Roman Empire. It had successfully withstood waves of European crusading ventures while capitalizing on the misfortunes of Byzantium, taking over several key ports on the Mediterranean and Black Seas.

But in 1243, the Seljuks of Rûm surrendered to the Mongols, who had already occupied what is now Iraq, Iran, portions of Pakistan and Afghanistan, and the Christian kingdoms of Georgia and Armenia. Thereafter, the Mongols easily found their way into regions weakened by centuries of Muslim infighting and Christian crusading movements. The capitulation of Rûm left remaining Byzantine possessions in Anatolia open to the Mongols. In 1261, however, Emperor Michael VIII Palaeologus (r. 1259–1282) managed to regain control of Constantinople and its immediate hinterland from the Venetians. And although the crusader principality of Antioch succumbed to the Mongols in 1268, their advance into Palestine was halted by the Mamluk Sultanate of Egypt, established in 1250 and ruled by a powerful military caste.

All of these disparate territories came to be called the Ilkhanate, the "subordinate khanate," meaning that its Mongol rulers paid deference to the Great Khan. The first Ilkhan was Hulagu, a brother of China's Kublai Khan. His descendants would rule this realm for another eighty years, eventually converting to Islam.

در روزی بغایت مسعود آنرا براوراشت ومجلس را با انواع تجملات بیاراستند وملک فرطان از اسپهند ینه داشته مبارکی وطواف سد وطالعیند

وبسند کامکاری نشست وحوانین وثهزا دکان واورا که حاضر بودند وتمامت ارکان دولت واعیان حضرت ومهول وجحکام اطران کهد

رسول این نمین رسانیدند والنر

THE MONGOL RULER OF MUSLIM PERSIA, HIS CHRISTIAN QUEEN, AND HIS JEWISH HISTORIAN. Hulagu Khan (1217–1265) was a grandson of Genghis and a brother of Kublai. He consolidated Persia and its neighboring regions into the Ilkhanate. This image shows him with his wife, Dokuz Khatun, who was a Turkic princess and a Christian. The image comes from the *Compendium of Chronicles* by Rashid al-Din (1247–1318), a Jewish convert to Islam, whose work exemplifies the pluralistic culture encouraged by Mongol rule: written in Persian and often translated into Arabic, it embeds the achievements of the Mongol ruler within the long history of Islam. **› Why would Rashid al-Din have wanted to place the new Mongol dynasty in this historical context?**

THE PAX MONGOLICA AND ITS PRICE

Although the Mongols' expansion into Europe had been checked, their combined conquests stretched from the Black Sea to the Pacific: one-fifth of the earth's surface, the largest land empire in history. Yet no single Mongol ruler's power was absolute within this domain, and the distribution of authority made Mongol rule flexible and adaptable to local conditions. The Mongol khans were also highly tolerant of all religious beliefs, which was a further advantage in governing peoples who observed an array of Buddhist, Christian, and Muslim practices, not to mention Hindus, Jews, and many itinerant groups whose beliefs reflected a melding of many cultures.

 Mongol's massive empire characterized by religious toleration and cultural diversity

This acceptance of cultural and religious difference, alongside the Mongols' encouragement of trade and love of rich things, created ideal conditions for some merchants and artists. Hence, the term *Pax Mongolica* ("Mongol Peace") is often used to describe the century from 1250 to 1350, a period analogous to the one fostered by the Roman Empire at its greatest extent (Chapter 5). However, this peace was bought at a great price: the artists whose varied talents created the gorgeous textiles, utensils, and illuminated books prized by the Mongols were not all willing participants. Many were captives or slaves subject to ruthless relocation. The Mongols would often transfer entire families and communities of craftsmen

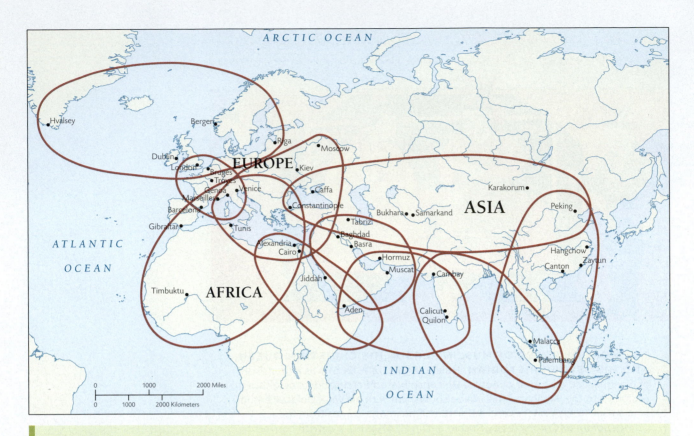

THE MEDIEVAL WORLD SYSTEM, c. 1300. At the turn of the fourteenth century, Western civilizations were more closely connected to each other and to the rest of the world than ever before: waterways and overland routes stretched from Greenland to the Pacific coast of Southeast Asia and down to West Africa. The interlocking regions and contact zones of this system are represented on this map. › How did Europe's relationship with its neighbors change as a result of its integration into this wider world? › How were seemingly marginal territories (such as Rus' or Hungary, Scotland, or Norway) central to one or more interlocking components of this system?

Pax Mongolica In imitation of the *Pax Romana* ("The Roman Peace," see Chapter 5), this phrase is used to describe the relatively peaceful century after the Mongol conquests, 1250–1350, which enabled an intensified period of trade, travel, and communication within the Eurasian landmass.

from one part of the empire to another, to encourage a fantastic blend of techniques, materials, and motifs. The result was an intensive period of cultural exchange that might combine Chinese, Persian, Venetian, and Hungarian influences (among many others) in a single work of art.

The Mongol Peace was also achieved at the expense of many flourishing Muslim cities that were devastated or crippled during the bloody process of Mongol expansion—cities that preserved the heritage of even older civilizations. The city of Heràt, situated in one of Afghanistan's few fertile valleys and described by a Persian poet as the "pearl in the oyster," was entirely destroyed by Genghis Khan in 1221. Baghdad, the splendid capital of the Abbasid Caliphate and a haven for artists and intellectuals since the eighth century (Chapter 8), was savagely besieged and sacked in 1258. Amid many other atrocities, this destroyed the House of Wisdom, the library and research center where Muslim scientists, philosophers, and translators had preserved classical knowledge and advanced cutting-edge scholarship in mathematics, astronomy, and medicine.

BRIDGING EAST AND WEST

To facilitate the movement of peoples and goods within their empire, the Mongols took control of caravan routes, policing bandits and making conditions safer for travelers. They also streamlined trade by funneling many exchanges through the Persian city of Tabriz, on which both land and sea routes from China converged. These measures accelerated and intensified the possible contacts between the Far East and the West. Prior to Mongol dominance, such networks had been inaccessible to most European merchants. The Silk Road was not a highway, but a tangle of trails and trading posts which few outsiders could navigate. Now travelers at all points of the route found their way smoothed.

Among the first travelers were Franciscan missionaries whose journeys were bankrolled by European rulers. In 1253, the friar William of Rubruck was sent by King Louis IX of France as his ambassador to the Mongol court, with letters of introduction and instructions to make a full report of his findings. Merchants quickly followed. The most famous are three Venetians: the brothers Niccolò and Matteo Polo, and Niccolò's son, Marco (1254–1324). **Marco Polo**'s account of his travels, which began when he was seventeen, reflects his twenty-four-year sojourn in

Mongols make long-distance trade easier, leading to increased cultural exchange

Marco Polo (1254–1324) Venetian merchant who traveled through Asia for twenty years and published his observations in a widely read memoir.

VENETIAN AMBASSADORS TO THE GREAT KHAN. Around 1270, the Venetian merchant brothers Niccolò and Matteo Polo returned to Europe after their first prolonged journey through the empire of the Great Khan, bearing with them an official letter to the Roman pope. This image, from a manuscript of Marco Polo's *Description of the World*, shows his father and uncle at the moment of their arrival in the Great Khan's court, to which they have seemingly brought a Christian cross and a Bible. › **Knowing what you've learned about the Mongols and the medieval world, do you think it is plausible that the Polo brothers would have carried these items with them?**

Two Travel Accounts

Two of the books that influenced Christopher Columbus and his contemporaries were travel narratives describing the exotic worlds that lay beyond Europe—worlds that may or may not have existed as they are described. The first excerpt below is taken from the account dictated by Marco Polo of Venice in 1298. The young Marco had traveled overland from Constantinople to the court of Kublai Khan in the early 1270s, together with his father and uncle. He became a gifted linguist and remained at the Mongol court until the early 1290s, when he returned to Europe after a journey through Southeast Asia and Indonesia, and across the Indian Ocean. The second excerpt is from the Book of Marvels, *attributed to John de Mandeville. This is an almost entirely fictional account of wonders that also became a source for European ideas about Southeast Asia. This particular passage concerns a legendary Christian figure named Prester ("Priest") John, who is alleged to have traveled to the East and become a great ruler.*

Marco Polo's Description of Java

Now know that when one leaves Champa[1] and went between south and southeast 1,500 miles, then one comes up to a very large island called Java which, according to what good sailors say who know it well, is the largest island in the world, for it is more than three thousand miles around. It has a great king; they are idolators and pay tribute to no man in the world. This island is one of very great wealth: they have pepper, nutmeg, spikenard, galangal, cubeb, cloves, and all the expensive spices you can find in the world. To this island come great numbers of ships and merchants who buy many commodities and make great profit and great gain there. On this island, there is such great treasure that no man in the world could recount or describe it. I tell you the Great Khan could never have it on account of the long and fearsome way in sailing there. Merchants from Zaytun[2] and Mangi[3] have already extracted very great treasure from this island, and continue to do so today.

[1] A collective name for the kingdoms of central Vietnam.
[2] The major port city of Quanzhou on southeastern coast of China.
[3] The kingdom of the Southern Song in China, south of the Huai River. The word *mangi* (or *manzi*) means "barbarians," which is what the northern Chinese called the people of the southern realm. When Marco Polo was in the service of the Great Khan, the Mongol conquest of the kingdom was still ongoing. It was completed in 1279.

Source: Marco Polo, *The Description of the World*, trans. Sharon Kinoshita, (Indianapolis/Cambridge, 2016), p. 149.

John de Mandeville's Description of Prester John

This emperor Prester John has great lands and has many noble cities and good towns in his realm and many great, large islands. For all the country of India is separated into islands by the great floods that come from Paradise, that divide the land into many parts. And also in the sea he has many islands. . . .

the service of the Great Khan, and the story of his journey home through the Spice Islands, India, and Persia. As we noted on page 332, this book had an enormous effect on the European imagination; Christopher Columbus's copy still survives.

Even more impressive in scope than Marco's travels are those of the Muslim adventurer Ibn Battuta (1304–1368), who left his native Morocco in 1326 to go on the sacred pilgrimage to Mecca—but then kept going. By the time he returned home

This Prester John has under him many kings and many islands and many varied people of various conditions. And this land is full good and rich, but not so rich as is the land of the Great Khan. For the merchants do not come there so commonly to buy merchandise as they do in the land of the Great Khan, for it is too far to travel to. . . .

[Mandeville then goes on to describe the difficulties of reaching Prester John's lands by sea.]

This emperor Prester John always takes as his wife the daughter of the Great Khan, and the Great Khan in the same way takes to wife the daughter of Prester John. For these two are the greatest lords under the heavens.

In the land of Prester John there are many diverse things, and many precious stones so great and so large that men make them into vessels such as platters, dishes, and cups. And there are many other marvels there that it would be too cumbrous and too long to put into the writing of books. But of the principal islands and of his estate and of his law I shall tell you some part.

This emperor Prester John is Christian and a great part of his country is Christian also, although they do not hold to all the articles of our faith as we do. . . .

And he has under him 72 provinces, and in every province there is a king. And these kings have kings under them, and all are tributaries to Prester John.

And he has in his lordships many great marvels. For in his country is the sea that men call the Gravelly Sea, that is all gravel and sand without any drop of water. And it ebbs and flows in great waves as other seas do, and it is never still. . . . And a three-day journey from that sea there are great mountains out of which flows a great flood that comes out of Paradise. And it is full of precious stones without any drop of water. . . .

He dwells usually in the city of Susa [in Persia]. And there is his principal palace, which is so rich and so noble that no one will believe the report unless he has seen it. And above the chief tower of the palace there are two round pommels of gold and in each of them are two great, large rubies that shine full brightly upon the night. And the principal gates of his palace are of a precious stone that men call sardonyxes [a type of onyx], and the frames and the bars are made of ivory. And the windows of the halls and chambers are of crystal. And the tables upon which men eat, some are made of emeralds, some of amethyst, and some of gold full of precious stones. And the legs that hold up the tables are made of the same precious stones. . . .

Source: Sir John Mandeville, *Mandeville's Travels*, ed. M. C. Seymour (Oxford: 1967), pp. 195–99 (language modernized from Middle English by R. C. Stacey).

Questions for Analysis

1. What does Marco Polo want his readers to know about Java, and why? What does this suggest about the interests of these intended readers?

2. What does Mandeville want his readers to know about Prester John and his domains? Why are these details so important?

3. Which of these accounts seems more trustworthy, and why? Even if we cannot accept one or both at face value, what insight do they give us into the expectations of Columbus and the other European adventurers who relied on these accounts?

in 1354, he had been to China and sub-Saharan Africa, as well as to the ends of both the Muslim and Mongolian worlds: a journey of over 75,000 miles.

The window of opportunity that made such journeys possible was relatively narrow, however. By the middle of the fourteenth century, hostilities among various components of the Mongol Empire were making travel more perilous. The Mongols of the Ilkhanate came into conflict with merchants from Genoa who were finally forced to abandon their settlement in Tabriz, breaking one of the major links in the commercial chain. In 1346, the Mongols of the Golden Horde besieged the Genoese colony at Caffa on the Black Sea, providing a conduit for the transmission of the Black Death (see pages 356–363). When the last Mongol rulers of China were overthrown in 1368, most Westerners were now denied access to its borders and the remaining Mongol warriors were restricted to cavalry service in the imperial armies of the new Ming dynasty. The conditions that had fostered an integrated trans-Eurasian cultural and commercial network were no longer sustainable.

Mongol rule disintegrates

The Extension of European Commerce and Settlement

The increased access of Western civilizations to the riches of the Far East ran parallel to a number of ventures that were extending the European presence in the Mediterranean and beyond. These endeavors were both mercantile and colonial, and in many cases resulted in the control of strategic trade routes that connected North Africa to the Silk Road as well as to the conduits of the sub-Saharan gold trade.

THE QUEST FOR AFRICAN GOLD

European commerce in African gold was not new. It had been going on for centuries, facilitated by Muslim traders whose caravans brought a steady supply from the Niger River to the North African ports of Algiers and Tunis. In the early thirteenth century, rival bands of merchants from Catalonia and Genoa had established trading colonies in Tunis to expedite this process, exchanging woolen cloth from northern Europe for both North African grain and sub-Saharan gold.

Gold—portable and newly plentiful—used for new currencies

But the medieval demand for gold accelerated during the late thirteenth and fourteenth centuries, because the luxuries coveted by Europeans were now too costly to be bought solely with bulk goods. Although precious textiles (usually silk) were a form of wealth the Mongols valued, the burgeoning economy of the medieval world demanded a reliable and abundant supply of more portable currency. Gold was therefore an obvious alternative currency for large transactions, and in the thirteenth century some European rulers began minting gold coins. But Europe itself had few natural gold reserves, and so maintaining and expanding these currencies required the exploitation of new sources.

The most obvious were in West Africa, especially Mali and Ghana. The sultan and emperor of that region, Mansa Musa (d. 1337), was the richest man in the world—and may have been the richest person in history. His sub-Saharan realm was also famed for its ivory, since the tusks of African elephants were especially prized by European artists, like the one who crafted the statue of the Virgin on page 311.

MODELS OF MEDITERRANEAN COLONIZATION: CATALONIA, GENOA, AND VENICE

The heightened European interest in the African gold trade, by the seafaring merchants of **Genoa** and **Catalonia** in particular, coincided with these merchants' creation of entrepreneurial empires in the western Mediterranean. During the thirteenth century, Catalan adventurers conquered and colonized a series of western Mediterranean islands, including Majorca, Ibiza, Minorca, Sardinia, and Sicily. Except in Sicily, which

Genoa Maritime city on Italy's northwestern coast; the Genoese were active in trading ventures along the Silk Road and in the establishment of trading colonies in the Mediterranean.

Catalonia Maritime region in northeastern Spain; during the thirteenth century, Catalan adventurers conquered and colonized a series of western Mediterranean islands.

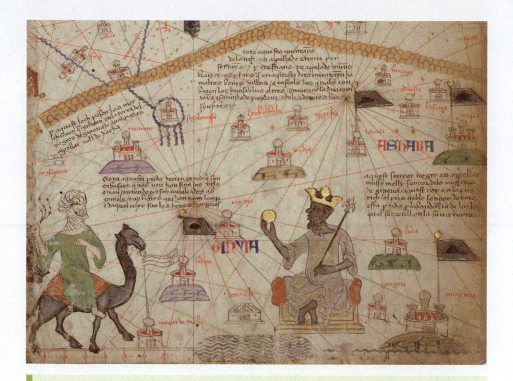

already had a large and diverse population that included many Christians (Chapter 8), the pattern of Catalan conquest was largely the same: expulsion or extermination of the existing population, usually Muslim; the encouragement of new settlers; and a heavy reliance on slave labor.

These Catalan colonial efforts were mainly carried out by private individuals or companies operating under royal charters. They therefore contrast strongly with the state-sponsored colonial practices of the Venetian maritime empire in the eastern Mediterranean, where the Venetians dominated the trade in spices and silks. Venetian colonies were administered directly by the city's rulers or by their appointed colonial governors. These colonies included long-settled civilizations such as Greece and Cyprus, meaning that Venetian administration laid just another layer on top of many older structures.

The Genoese, to take yet another case, also had extensive interests in the western Mediterranean, where they traded bulk goods such as cloth, hides, grain, timber, and sugar. They also established trading colonies, but these tended to consist of family networks that were closely integrated with the peoples of North Africa, Spain, and the shores of the Black Sea.

FROM THE MEDITERRANEAN TO THE ATLANTIC

For centuries, European maritime commerce had been divided between the Mediterranean and the northeastern Atlantic seaboard of northern France, the Low Countries, the British Isles, and Scandinavia. Starting around 1270, however, Italian merchants began to sail through the Straits of Gibraltar and up to the wool-producing regions of England and the Low Countries. This was a step toward the extension of Mediterranean commerce into the Atlantic. Another step was the European discovery of Atlantic island chains known as the Canaries and the Azores, which Genoese sailors reached in the fourteenth century.

Efforts to colonize the Canary Islands, and to convert and enslave their inhabitants, began almost immediately. Eventually, the Canaries would become the base for Portuguese voyages down the west coast of Africa. They would also be the point from which Christopher Columbus would sail westward across the Atlantic Ocean in the hope of reaching Asia (see Chapter 12).

There was also a significant European colonial presence in the northern Atlantic, and had been for centuries. Viking settlers had begun to colonize Greenland in the late tenth century, and had established a settlement in a place they called Vinland (the coast of Newfoundland in present-day Canada) around 1000. While North America did not become home to a permanent European population at this time, the Norse did build a viable community on Greenland, which eventually formed part of the kingdom of Norway. This settlement was facilitated by the warming of the earth's climate between 800 and 1300 (Chapter 8). For several centuries, favorable conditions made it possible to sustain some farming activities on the southern coastline of that huge island, supplemented by fishing, hunting, and foraging. But with the gradual cooling of the climate in the fourteenth century, which caused famines even in the rich farmlands of Europe, this fragile ecosystem was eroded and the Greenlanders died of starvation.

Ways of Knowing and Describing the World

European commercial expansion in this era both drove and depended on significant innovations in measuring and mapping. It also coincided with intellectual, literary, and artistic initiatives that aimed to capture and describe the workings of this wider world.

Europe–Asia contact, a legacy of Mongol expansion, leads to new innovations

BALANCE SHEETS, BANKS, CHARTS, AND CLOCKS

The integration of European and Asian commerce called for the refinement of existing business models and accounting techniques. New forms of partnership and the development of insurance contracts helped to minimize the risks associated with long-distance trading. Double-entry bookkeeping, widely used in Italy by the mid-fourteenth century, gave merchants a much clearer picture of their profits and losses by ensuring that both credits and debits were clearly laid out in parallel columns. The Medici family of Florence established branches of its bank in each of the major cities of Europe and were careful that the failure of one would not bankrupt the entire firm. Banks also experimented with advanced credit techniques borrowed from Muslim and Jewish financiers, allowing their clients to transfer funds without any real money changing hands. Such transfers were carried out by written receipts, the direct ancestors of the check.

Other late medieval technologies kept pace in different ways with the demands for increased efficiency. Eyeglasses, first invented in the 1280s, were perfected in the fourteenth century. The use of the magnetic compass helped ships to sail farther away from land, making longer-distance Atlantic voyages possible for the first time. And as more and more mariners began to sail waters less familiar to them, pilots began to make and use special charts that mapped the locations of ports; called *portolani* (**portolan charts**), they took note of prevailing winds, good harbors, and known perils.

Among the many implements of modern daily life invented in this era, the most familiar are clocks, which came into use shortly before 1300. They were too large and expensive for private purchase, but towns vied with each other to install them in prominent public buildings, thus advertising municipal wealth and good governance. Mechanical timekeeping had a profound effect on the regulation of daily life. Until the advent of clocks, time was flexible. Although days had been *theoretically* divided into hours, minutes, and seconds since the time of the Sumerians (Chapter 1), there was no way to map these temporal measurements onto an actual day. Now, clocks relentlessly divided time into exact units, giving rise to new expectations about labor and productivity. People were expected to start and end work "on time," and even to equate time with money. Like the improvements in bookkeeping, timekeeping made some kinds of work more efficient, but it also created new tensions and anxieties.

PORTOLAN CHART. The chart shown here is the oldest surviving example of a map used by mariners to navigate between Mediterranean ports: the word *portolan* is the term for such charts. It dates from the end of the thirteenth century, and its shape clearly indicates that it was made from an animal hide. Although parchment was extremely durable, it would slowly have worn away due to prolonged exposure to salt water and other elements—hence the rarity of this early example.

KNOWLEDGE OF THE WORLD AND OF GOD

In the mid-thirteenth century, Thomas Aquinas had argued that God's workings in the world are comprehensible to the inquiring human mind (Chapter 9). But a later philosopher, William of Ockham (d. c. 1348), an English Franciscan, denied that human reason could prove fundamental theological truths. Instead, he urged humans to investigate the natural world and better understand its laws—without positing any necessary connection between nature and divinity.

This philosophical position, known as nominalism, has had an enormous impact on modern thought. The distinction between the rational comprehensibility of the real world and the spiritual incomprehensibility of God encourages scientific investigation without reference to supernatural explanations. As such, it encourages empirical observation, since knowledge of the world should rest on sensory experience rather than abstract theories. These are the medieval foundations of the scientific method (see Chapter 16).

REPRESENTING GOD'S CREATION THROUGH ART

The artists of this era were also paying close attention to empirical evidence and creating realistic representations of the world. Carvings of plants and flowers are

portolani (**portolan charts**) These special charts were invented by medieval mariners during the fourteenth century and were used to map locations of ports and sea routes, while also taking note of prevailing winds and other conditions at sea.

THE MEETING OF JOACHIM AND ANNA BY GIOTTO. According to legend, Anna and Joachim were an aged and infertile couple who were able to conceive their only child, Mary, through divine intervention. Hence, this painting may portray the moment of her conception—but it also portrays the affection of husband and wife. › **What human characteristics and values does this painting convey to the viewer?**

clearly recognizable to botanists as distinct species. Statues of humans are realistic in their portrayals of facial expressions and bodily proportions. This trend toward naturalism extended to manuscript illumination and painting, as well. Indeed, painting itself was becoming realistically portable: while humans have been decorating walls since before the Neolithic Revolution, artists in the thirteenth century began to adapt the techniques used by icon painters in Byzantium, making freestanding pictures on pieces of wood or canvas using tempera (pigments mixed with water and natural gums) or oil paints. Because these devotional images and portraits were mobile, they were also more commercial. As long as artists could afford the necessary materials, they did not have to wait for specific commissions and chose their own subject matter, putting an individual stamp on their work—one of the reasons why we know the names of many more artists from this era.

One of these artists, Giotto di Bondone of Florence (c. 1267–1337), painted both walls and portable wooden panels. **Giotto** (*gee-OHT-toh*) was an especially keen observer of nature: not only do his human beings and animals look lifelike, they do natural things. When Christ enters Jerusalem on Palm Sunday, boys climb trees to get a better view; when the Virgin's parents meet after a long separation, they embrace and kiss one another tenderly. Although many of the artists who came after Giotto moved away from naturalism, this style would become the norm by 1400. For this reason, Giotto is often regarded as a painter who inspired the Italian Renaissance (see Chapter 11).

A VISION OF THE WORLD WE CANNOT SEE

An exact contemporary of Giotto's had a different way of capturing the spiritual world in a naturalistic way, and in a different medium. **Dante Alighieri** (1265–1321) of Florence pioneered what he called a "sweet new style" of poetry in his native Italian, which was now so different from Latin that it had become a new language. Yet, Dante also strove to make this Italian vernacular an instrument for serious political and social critique. His great work, known in his own day as the *Comedy* (called the *Divine Comedy* by later admirers), was composed during the years he spent in exile from his beloved city, after the political party he supported was ousted from power in 1301.

The *Comedy* describes the poet's imaginary journey through hell, purgatory, and paradise; a journey that begins in a "dark wood," a metaphor for the personal and political crises that threatened Dante's faith and livelihood. In the poem, the narrator is led out of this forest and through the first two realms by the Roman poet Virgil (Chapter 5), who represents the best of classical culture. But Dante can only

Dante's Comedy *elevates vernacular Italian from an everyday language to a literary one*

be guided toward knowledge of the divine by his deceased beloved, Beatrice, who symbolizes Christian wisdom. In the course of this visionary pilgrimage, Dante's narrator meets the souls of many historical personages and contemporaries, inviting them to explain why they met their fates. This was Dante's ingenious way of commenting on current events and passing judgment on his enemies. In many ways, this monumental poem is a fusion of classical and Christian cultures, Latin learning and vernacular artistry.

Papal Power and Popular Piety

Dante's *Comedy* was a creative response to the political turmoil that engulfed Italy during his lifetime, a situation that was transforming the papacy, too. Indeed, many of the men whom Dante placed in Hell were popes. Yet despite the weakening authority of the papal office, which caused violent divisions within the Church, popular piety arguably achieved its strongest expressions during this era.

THE LIMITS OF PAPAL POWER

As we saw in Chapter 9, the papacy reached new heights of power at the beginning of the thirteenth century, as holders of the office continued to centralize the government of the Church. But they extended their influence into the secular sphere, which led to protracted political struggles and the ultimate weakening of the papacy's credibility.

For example, the Italian territories under papal lordship shared a border with the kingdom of Sicily, which comprised all of southern Italy as well as Sicily itself. The ruler of these territories was also the German emperor Frederick II, who proved a formidable opponent. The reigning pope, therefore, called a crusade against him. But in order to implement this crusade, the pope needed to find a military champion willing to lead an army against a fellow Christian ruler: someone with little to lose and everything to gain.

This turned out to be Charles of Anjou, the youngest brother of the French king, who was eventually crowned king of Sicily. But he made matters in southern Italy worse by antagonizing his own subjects, who instead offered their allegiance to the king of Aragon. The papacy then made Aragon the target of yet another crusade, resulting in a disastrous war among Christian princes and their armies on European soil. In the wake of this debacle, the French king **Philip IV** (r. 1286–1314) resolved to punish the papacy for abusing its powers.

In 1300, **Pope Boniface VIII** (r. 1294–1303) called for the celebration of a papal jubilee, asserting that the Roman pope was the arbiter of all power. But just a few years later, there was no longer a Roman pope: the new capital of Christendom had moved to France, because Philip IV had challenged Boniface to prove that he could exercise real power—not just the power of propaganda. Following a heated dispute about the king's intervention in papal affairs, Philip sent thugs to the papal residence, where Boniface (then in his seventies) was so mistreated that he died a month later. Philip then pressed his advantage, forcing the new pope, Clement V, to thank him for his zealous defense of the faith and then, in 1309, moving the entire papal court to **Avignon** (*AH-vee-nyon*), a city in his own realm.

Giotto (c. 1266–1377) Florentine painter and architect who is often considered a forerunner of the Renaissance.

Dante Alighieri (c. 1265–1321) Florentine poet and intellectual whose *Divine Comedy* was a pioneering work in the Italian vernacular and a vehicle for political and religious critique.

Philip IV King of France from 1285 until his death, Philip's conflict with Pope Boniface VIII led to the transfer of the papal court to Avignon from 1309 to 1378.

Boniface VIII (r. 1294–1303) Pope whose repeated claims to papal authority were challenged by King Philip IV of France.

Avignon City in southeastern France that became the seat of the papacy between 1305 and 1377, a period known as the "Babylonian Captivity" of the Roman Church.

Seals: Signs of Identity and Authority

For much of human history, applying a seal to a document was the way to certify its legality and identify the people who had ratified it. During antiquity and the early Middle Ages, those people were only powerful men—kings, bishops, heads of monasteries—and occasionally powerful women. But as participation in documentary practices became more and more common, seals were increasingly used by corporations (such as universities and crusading orders), towns, and many individuals. The devices (images) and legends (writing) on these seals were carefully chosen to capture central attributes of their owners' personalities or status. A seal was made by pressing a deeply incised lead matrix onto hot wax or resin, which would quickly dry to form a durable impression. The images reproduced here are later engravings that make the features of the original seals easier to see.

A. Seal of the town of Dover, 1281. Dover has long been one of the busiest and most important port cities of England because of its strategic proximity to France; indeed, the Dover Strait that separates this town from Calais, just across the English Channel, is only twenty-one miles wide. In 1281, when this seal was used, ferries and other ships like the one depicted here made this crossing several times a day. The legend around the edges of the seal reads (in Latin) "Seal of the commune of barons of Dover." It reflects the high status accorded to the free men of Dover by the English crown: because of their crucial role in the economy and defense of the kingdom, they were considered a corporate body and entitled to representation in Parliament alongside individual barons.

B. Personal seal of Simon de Montfort, earl of Leicester, 1258. Simon de Montfort (c. 1208–1265) was a French nobleman who rose to a position of great power in England. In 1238, he married Eleanor, sister of King Henry III: a match that was opposed by England's great lords because it gave this foreigner a great deal of power. Indeed, Simon would later use that power to lead a rebellion against his royal brother-in-law, dying on the battlefield in 1265. This image was appended to a document made when Simon was fifty, but it shows him as a courtly youth, riding out with his favorite hound and blowing on a hunting horn. This means that Simon had continued to use a seal made for him when he was a much younger man, probably at the time when he was knighted, many years before, in France. The Latin legend, indeed, makes no mention of his English title: "Seal of Simon de Montfort."

Questions for Analysis

1. Medieval towns represented themselves in a variety of ways on their seals: sometimes showing a group portrait of town councilors, sometimes a local saint, sometimes a heraldic beast, and sometimes distinctive architectural features. Why would Dover choose this image? What messages does this seal convey?

2. Think carefully about the mystery of Simon de Montfort's seal. Usually, powerful men and women had new seals made to reflect their elevated status. What are all the possible reasons that the English earl would have continued to use a seal made for him so many years earlier, in France? What are the possible ramifications of this choice?

3. The seals of medieval women were almost always shaped like almonds (pointed ovals; the technical term is *vesica-shaped*). Yet Helwig's seal is round, like the seals of men and corporations. Why might that be the case?

4. In general, what is the value of seals for the study of history? What are the various ways in which they function as sources?

C. Seal of Helwig von Ysenburg, countess of Büdingen, 1274. Unlike the engravings of seals pictured on the facing page, this is an original wax impression of Helwig's seal and includes the silken cords that were used to fasten it to a document in 1274. It shows a slim young lady in a long, elegant gown and cape, pointed shoes, and an elaborate headdress. The falcon on her fist suggests that she is dressed to go hunting, but she is depicted against an interior background of diamond-shaped tiles: like her dress, a sign of wealth and status. The legend is difficult to decipher, but reads "Seal of Helwig von Ysen[burg]."

Babylonian Captivity
Refers both to Jews' exile in Babylon during the sixth century B.C.E. and the period from 1309 to 1378, when papal authority was subjugated to the French crown and the papal court was moved from Rome to the French city of Avignon.

Philip IV's legacy: political control over papacy ❯

THE BABYLONIAN CAPTIVITY OF THE PAPACY

The papacy's capitulation to French royal power illustrates the enormous gap between rhetoric and reality. Although Boniface was merely repeating the old claim that kings ruled by divine approval as recognized by the Church, the Church now exercised its authority only by bowing to the power of a king. The papacy would remain in Avignon for nearly seventy years (see Chapter 11): a period called the "**Babylonian Captivity**" of the papacy, recalling the Jews' exile in Babylon during the sixth century B.C.E. (Chapter 2). Even though the move was probably supposed to be temporary, it was not reversed after Philip IV's death in 1314. Perhaps many suppliants found that doing business in Avignon was easier than in Rome. Not only was Avignon closer to the major centers of power in northwestern Europe, it was removed from the tumultuous politics of Italy. Moreover, all the popes elected there were natives of the region, as were nearly all the cardinals whom they appointed. This further cemented their loyalty to the French king.

Although the Avignon popes never abandoned claims to the lordship of Rome and the Papal States, making good on these claims required a great deal of money. The Avignon popes accordingly imposed new taxes and obligations on the wealthy dioceses of France, England, Germany, and Spain. Judicial cases from ecclesiastical courts also brought large revenues into the papal coffers. Most controversially, the Avignon popes claimed the right to appoint bishops and priests to vacant offices anywhere in Christendom, bypassing the rights of individual dioceses and collecting huge fees from successful appointees.

By these and other measures, the Avignon popes further strengthened administrative control while further weakening the papacy's moral authority. Stories of the

THE PAPAL PALACE AT AVIGNON. The work on this great fortified palace was begun in 1339 and symbolizes the apparent permanence of the papal residence in Avignon. ❯ **Why was it constructed as a fortress as well as a palace?**

court's unseemly luxury circulated widely, especially during the reign of the notoriously corrupt Clement VI (r. 1342–1352), who openly sold spiritual benefits for money (he would appoint a jackass to a bishopric if it would turn a profit, he boasted) and who insisted that his sexual transgressions were therapeutic. His reign also coincided with the Black Death, which did not improve his reputation for leadership.

UNITING THE FAITHFUL: THE POWER OF SACRAMENTS

Despite the centralizing power of the papacy, most medieval Christians experienced the Church at a local level, within their community's parish. In these churches, parish priests not only taught the elements of Christian doctrine but also administered the **sacraments**: rituals that conveyed the grace of God by marking significant moments in the life cycle of every person and significant times in the Christian calendar.

Medieval piety came to revolve around these sacraments, which included baptism, confession of sins (also known as Penance), Extreme Unction (last rites for the dying), the ordination of priests, and the Eucharist or Mass. Baptism, which had been administered to adults in the early centuries of Christianity (Chapter 6), had become a sacrament given to infants as soon as possible after birth, to safeguard their souls in case of an early death. Periodic confession of sins to a priest was thought to guarantee God's forgiveness, for if a sinner did not perform appropriate acts of penance, he or she would have to complete atonement in Purgatory—the netherworld between Paradise and Hell, whose existence was confirmed as a doctrine for the first time in 1274. Another sacrament, marriage, was very seldom practiced as a formal ceremony; in reality, it required only the exchange of promises and was often formed simply by an act of sexual intercourse.

sacraments Sacred rites. In the Roman Catholic tradition, the administration of the sacraments is considered necessary for salvation.

"THIS IS MY BODY": THE ELEVATION OF THE HOST. This fresco from a chapel in Assisi was painted by Simone Martini in the 1320s. It shows the moment in the Mass when the priest raises the eucharistic host so that it can be seen by the faithful. The Latin phrase spoken at this moment, *Hoc est enim corpus meum* ("This is my body"), was regarded as transforming the substance of bread into the divine substance of Christ's body. › Since medieval Christians believed that the sight of the host was just as powerful as ingesting it, how would they have responded to this life-size image of the elevation? › What does the appearance of angels (above the altar) signify?

THE MIRACLE OF THE EUCHARIST

Of these sacraments, the one most central to the religious lives of medieval Christians was the Eucharist, or Mass. As we noted in Chapter 9, the ritual power of the Mass was greatly enhanced in the twelfth century, when the Church began promoting the doctrine of transubstantiation. Christians attending Mass were taught that when the priest spoke Christ's ritual words "This is my body" and "This is my blood," the substances of bread and wine on the altar were miraculously transformed into the body and blood of Jesus. To consume one or both of these substances was to ingest holiness. So powerful was this idea that most Christians received the sacramental bread just once a year, at Easter.

But to share in the miracle of the Eucharist, one did not even have to consume it. One had only to witness the elevation of the Host: the wafer of bread raised up by the priest, which "hosted" the real presence of Jesus Christ. Daily attendance at Mass simply to view the consecration of the Host was a common form of devotion, as was the practice of displaying a consecrated wafer in a special reliquary called a monstrance ("showcase") set up on an altar or carried through the streets.

THE PURSUIT OF HOLINESS

The fundamental theme of preachers in this era, that salvation lay open to any Christian who strove for it, helps to explain the central place of the Mass and other sacraments in daily life. It also compelled many to seek out new paths that could lead to God. But, as we noted in Chapter 9, some believers who sought to achieve a mystical union with God were ultimately condemned for heresy because they did not subordinate themselves to Church authority. Even less radical figures might find themselves on dangerous ground, especially if they published their ideas.

For example, the German preacher Master Eckhart (c. 1260–1327), a Dominican friar, taught that there is a "spark" deep within every human soul, and that God lives in this spark. Through prayer and self-renunciation, any person could retreat into this inner recess of his or her being, and access divinity. This conveyed the message that laypeople could attain salvation through their own efforts, without the intervention of a priest or any of the sacraments he alone could perform. As a result, many of Eckhart's teachings were condemned. But very similar views continued to find support in the teachings of popular preachers.

Struggles for Sovereignty

When the French king Philip IV transplanted the papal court to Avignon, he was not just responding to papal abuses of power; he was bolstering his own. By the middle of the thirteenth century, the growth of strong territorial monarchies, combined with the increasing sophistication of royal justice, taxation, and propaganda, had given some secular rulers greater power than any European ruler had wielded since the time of Charlemagne. Although a king still needed to be anointed with holy oil at the time of his coronation—a rite that required a bishop and, by extension, papal support—a king's authority in his own realm rested on the consent of the aristocracy and the popular perception of his reputation for justice, piety, and regard for his subjects' prosperity. On the wider stage of the medieval world, it also rested on his successful assertion of his kingdom's sovereignty.

THE PROBLEM OF SOVEREIGNTY

Sovereignty can be defined as an inviolable authority over a defined territory. In Chapter 9, we learned that Philip Augustus was the first monarch to call himself "king of France" and not "king of the Franks." In other words, he was defining his kingship in geographical terms, claiming that there was an entity called France and that he was king within that area.

sovereignty An inviolable authority over a defined territory.

But what was France? Was it the tiny "island" (Île-de-France) around Paris, which had been Philip's father's domain? If so, France was very small—and very vulnerable, lacking in sovereignty. Or did France include any region, such as Champagne or Normandy, whose lord was willing to do homage to the French king? In that case, the king would need to enforce his rights of lordship constantly and, if necessary, exert his rule directly.

But what if some of France's neighboring lords ruled in their own right, as did the independent counts of Flanders, thus threatening the security of France's borders? In that case, the king would need either to forge an alliance with these borderlands or deny their independence. He would need to assert his sovereignty by absorbing these regions into an ever-growing kingdom.

The problem of sovereignty, then, is a zero-sum game: one state's sovereignty is won and maintained by diminishing that of other states. Although many French citizens today would assert that France has, in some mystical way, always existed in its present form, in fact, France and many other European states were being cobbled together during the medieval period through a process of annexation and colonization—just as the United States was assembled at the expense of the empires that had colonized North America and through the killing or displacement of autonomous native peoples.

Sovereignty as a "zero-sum game": one state asserts authority at expense of others

The process of achieving sovereignty is thus an aggressive and often violent one. In Spain, the "reconquest" of Muslim lands, which had accelerated in the twelfth century, continued apace in the thirteenth and fourteenth centuries, to the detriment of these regions' Muslim and Jewish inhabitants. German princes continued to push northward into the Baltic, where they responded with brutal force to native resistance. Meanwhile, the Scandinavian kingdoms that had been forming in the eleventh and twelfth centuries fought among themselves and their neighbors for the control of contested regions and resources. Italy and the Mediterranean became a constant battleground, as we have observed.

Among these emerging states, the two most strident in their assertion of sovereignty were France and England.

THE PRESTIGE OF FRANCE: THE SAINTLY KINGSHIP OF LOUIS IX

After the death of Philip Augustus, the heirs to the French throne continued to pursue an expansionist policy, pushing the boundaries of the kingdom to the east and south. There were significant pockets of resistance, though, notably from the independent towns of Flanders. In 1302, citizen militias from several of these towns, fighting on foot with farming implements and other unconventional weapons, managed to defeat the heavily armed French cavalry. This victory at the Battle of Courtrai (Kortrijk in Flemish) is still celebrated as a national holiday by Flemish-speaking Belgians.

This defeat was a setback for Philip IV of France, much of whose power derived from his grandfather, **Louis IX** (r. 1226–1270). Louis was famous for his piety and his conscientious exercise of kingship. Unlike most princes, Louis not only pledged to go on a crusade—he actually went. And although both of his campaigns were notorious failures (he died on the second, in 1270), they cemented his saintly reputation and political clout.

Louis IX King of France from 1226 to his death on crusade in 1270, Louis was renowned for his piety and for his close attention to the administration of law and justice in his realm.

First, Louis's willingness to risk his life (and those of his brothers) in the service of the Church would give him tremendous influence in papal affairs—a key factor in making his youngest brother, Charles of Anjou, the king of Naples and Sicily. Second, ensuring the good administration of his kingdom during his years of absence prompted Louis to invent or reform many key aspects of royal governance, which made France the bureaucratic rival of England for the first time. Third, Louis's crusading ventures were seen as confirmation that the king of France had inherited the mantle of Charlemagne as the protector of the Church.

The prestige of the French monarchy found artistic expression in the Sainte-Chapelle (Holy Chapel), a gorgeous jewel box of a church that Louis built in Paris for his collection of relics thought to have been used for the torture and crucifixion of Christ. The most important of these was the Crown of Thorns, intended by Pilate as a mocking reference to "the king of the Jews" (see Chapter 6). Now that this holy crown belonged to Louis and was housed in Paris, it was a sign that Paris was the new Jerusalem.

Widely regarded as a saint in his lifetime, Louis was formally canonized in 1297 by the same Pope Boniface VIII who was brought down by Philip IV, Louis's grandson. Indeed, Boniface partly intended this gesture as a rebuke, but Philip turned it to his advantage. He even used his grandfather's pious reputation as a cloak for his frankly rapacious treatment of the Knights Templar, whose military order he suppressed in 1314 so that he could confiscate its wealth and dissolve his own debts. He had expelled the Jews from his realm in 1306 for similar reasons.

CASTLES AND CONTROL: EDWARD I AND THE EXPANSION OF ENGLISH RULE

The expulsion of Jews who depended on a king's personal protection had been a precedent set by Philip's contemporary and kinsman, **Edward I** of England (r. 1272–1307). Unlike Philip, Edward had to build up the sovereignty of his state almost from scratch—for his father, Henry III (r. 1216–1272), had a long but

Edward I King of England from 1272 to his death in 1307, Edward presided over the creation of new legal and bureaucratic institutions in his realm, violently subjugated the Welsh, and attempted to colonize Scotland. He expelled English Jews from his domain in 1290.

troubled reign. Henry inherited the throne as a young boy, shortly after his father John's loss of Normandy and capitulation to Magna Carta (Chapter 9), and he had to contend with rebellions among the restive barons of his realm. When Edward himself became king in 1272, he took steps to ensure that there would be no further revolts by tightening his control on the aristocracy's lands, diffusing their power by strengthening that of Parliament and reforming the administration of the realm.

Edward then looked to England's borders. Since Welsh chieftains had been major backers of the rebel barons, he was determined to bring "wild Wales" within the orbit of English sovereignty. Edward accordingly embarked on an ambitious and ruthless campaign of castle building, ringing the hilly country with enormous fortifications on a scale not seen in most of Europe—these were, in fact, crusader castles—and treating the Welsh (his fellow Christians) as infidels. Indeed, he treated Wales like a conquered state, making it a settler colony and subjecting the Welsh to the lordship of his own men. When his son, the future Edward II, was born in 1284 at the great castle he had built at Caernarvon, he gave the infant the title "Prince of Wales": a title usually borne by a Welsh chieftain.

Edward then turned to England's final frontier. Until now, control of Scotland had not been an English concern. The Scottish border had been peaceful for many years, and the Scottish kings did homage to the English king for some of their lands. In 1290, however, the succession to the Scottish throne was disputed among rival claimants, and Edward intervened to press his own claim and threatened to take Scotland by

CAERNARVON CASTLE. One of many massive fortifications built by Edward I, this castle was the birthplace of the first English Prince of Wales and the site where the current Prince of Wales, Charles, was formally invested with that title in 1969. › Castles of this size and strength had been constructed in the Crusader States and on the disputed frontiers of Muslim and Christian Spain, but never before in Britain (see the photos on page 302). What does their construction reveal about Edward's attitude toward the Welsh?

A Declaration of Scottish Independence

In April 1320, a group of powerful Scottish lords gathered at the abbey of Arbroath to draft a letter to Pope John XXII in Avignon. The resulting Declaration of Arbroath petitioned the exiled pope (a Frenchman loyal to the French king) to recognize the Scots as a sovereign nation and to support their right to an independent kingdom that would be free from encroachment by the English. The Scots' elected king, Robert the Bruce, had been excommunicated by a previous pope who had upheld English claims to lordship in Scotland. The letter therefore makes a number of different arguments for the recognition of the Scots' right to self-governance.

We know, most Holy Father and lord, and have gathered from the deeds and books about men in the past, that . . . the nation of the Scots has been outstanding for its many distinctions. It journeyed from the lands of Greece and Egypt by the Tyrrhenian Sea and the Pillars of Hercules, . . . but could not be subdued anywhere by any peoples however barbaric. . . . It took possession of the settlements in the west which it now desires, after first driving out the Britons and totally destroying the Picts, and although often attacked by the Norwegians, Danes and English. Many were its victories and innumerable its efforts. It has held these places always free of all servitude, as the old histories testify. One hundred and thirteen kings of their royal lineage have reigned in their kingdom, with no intrusion by a foreigner.

If the noble qualities and merits of these men were not obvious for other reasons, they shine forth clearly enough in that they were almost the first to be called to his most holy faith by the King of Kings and Lord of Lords, our Lord Jesus Christ, after his Passion and Resurrection, even though they were settled on the most distant boundaries of the earth. . . .

Thus our people lived until now in freedom and peace . . ., until that mighty prince Edward [I] king of England (the father of the present king) in the guise of a friend and ally attacked our kingdom in hostile fashion, when it had no head and the people were not harbouring any evil treachery, nor were they accustomed to wars or attacks. His unjust acts, killings, acts of violence, pillagings, burnings, imprisonments of prelates, burnings of monasteries, robbings and killings of regular clergy, and also innumerable other outrages, which he committed against the said people, sparing none on account of age or sex, religion or order—no one could write about them or fully comprehend them who had not been instructed by experience.

From these countless ills we have been set free, with the help of Him who follows up wounds with healing and cures, by our most energetic prince, king and lord Sir Robert [the Bruce; r. 1306–1329]. . . . By divine force. To avoid this, the Scots forged an alliance with the French, but could not prevent Edward's army from fighting its way through to Scone Abbey in 1296.

Scone was a symbolic target: the site of the Stone of Destiny on which Scottish kings were traditionally enthroned. So Edward seized this potent symbol, brought it back to Westminster Abbey in London, and embedded it in the coronation chair of his namesake, Edward the Confessor, the last Anglo-Saxon king of England (Chapter 8). Save for a brief hiatus in 1950, when the stone was stolen from the abbey by students at the University of Glasgow, it would remain there until 1996, after which it was returned to Scotland. (It will be temporarily loaned to London when the next British monarch is crowned.)

Edward considered the subjugation of Scotland to be England's manifest destiny. He called himself the "Hammer of the Scots" and, before he died, charged his son providence his succession to his right according to our laws and customs which we intend to maintain to the death, together with the due consent and assent of us all, have made him our prince and king. . . . But if he should give up what he has begun, seeking to subject us or our kingdom to the king of the English, . . . we would immediately strive to expel him as our enemy and a subverter of his right and ours, and we would make someone else our king, who is capable of seeing to our defence. For as long as a hundred of us remain alive, we intend never to be subjected to the lordship of the English, in any way. For it is not for glory in war, riches or honours that we fight, but only for the laws of our fathers and for freedom, which no good man loses except along with his life.

Therefore, most Holy Father and lord, we implore your holiness with all vehemence in our prayers that you . . . look with paternal eyes on the troubles and difficulties brought upon us and the Church of God by the English. And that you deign to admonish and exhort the king of the English, who ought to be satisfied with what he has (since England was formerly enough for seven kings or more), to leave us Scots in peace, living as we do in the poor country of Scotland beyond which there is no dwelling place, and desiring nothing but our own. . . .

It is important for you, Holy Father, to do this, since you see the savagery of the heathen raging against Christians (as the sins of Christians require), and the frontiers of Christendom are being curtailed day by day, and you have seen how much it detracts from your holiness's reputation if (God forbid!) the Church suffers eclipse or scandal in any part of it during your time. Let it then rouse the Christian princes who are covering up their true motivation when they pretend that they cannot go to the assistance of the Holy Land on account of wars with their neighbours. The real reason that holds them back is that in warring with their smaller neighbours they anticipate greater advantage to themselves and weaker resistance. . . .

But if your Holiness too credulously trusts the tales of the English fully, or does not leave off favouring the English to our confusion, then we believe that the Most High will blame you for the slaughter of bodies. . . . Dated at our monastery at Arbroath in Scotland 6 April 1320 in the fifteenth year of our said king's reign.

Source: Walter Bower. *Scotichronicon*, Vol. 7, ed. A. B. Scott and D. E. R. Watt (Aberdeen, Scotland: 1996).

Questions for Analysis

1. On what grounds does this letter justify the political independence of the Scots? What different arguments does it make? Which in your view is the most compelling?

2. Why does this letter mention crusading? What are the Scottish lords implying about the relationship between Europe's internal conflicts and the ongoing wars with external adversaries?

3. Imagine that you are an adviser to the pope. Applying your knowledge of the papacy's situation at this time, would you advise him to do as this letter asks? Why or why not?

Edward II (r. 1307–1327) with the completion of his task. But the younger Edward was not a ruthless advocate of English expansion; he had to contend, instead, with a rebellion led by his own queen, Isabella of France, who eventually engineered his abdication and murder. Their son, Edward III (r. 1327–1377), did renew his grandfather's expansionist policies, but his main target was not Scotland—it was France.

THE OUTBREAK OF THE HUNDRED YEARS' WAR

The **Hundred Years' War** was the longest and widest-ranging military conflict since Rome's wars with Carthage in the third and second centuries B.C.E. (Chapter 5). Although England and France were its principal antagonists, almost all major

European powers became involved at some stage. Active hostilities began in 1337 and lasted until 1453, interrupted by truces of varying lengths. We will continue tracing its developments in Chapter 11.

The most fundamental source of conflict was the fact that the kings of England held the duchy of Gascony as vassals of the French king; this had been part of Eleanor of Aquitaine's domain, added to the Anglo-Norman Empire in 1154 (Chapter 9). In the thirteenth century, when the French kings had not yet absorbed this region into their domain, this fact had seemed less of an anomaly. But as the French monarchy began to claim sovereignty within the "natural" boundaries of their domains, the English presence in Gascony became more and more problematic. The fact that England also had close commercial and cultural ties to Flanders—which consistently resisted annexation by France—added fuel to the fire; as did the French alliance with the Scots.

Complicating this volatile situation was the disputed French succession. In 1328, the last of Philip IV's three sons died without leaving a son to succeed him: the Capetian dynasty, founded by the Frankish warlord Hugh Capet in 987 (Chapter 8), had finally exhausted itself. A new dynasty, the Valois, came to the throne—but only by insisting that women could neither inherit royal power nor pass it on. For otherwise, the heir to France was Edward III of England, whose ambitious mother, Isabella, was Philip IV's only daughter. Initially, when his mother's claim was passed over, Edward was only fifteen and in no position to protest. In 1337, however, when the disputes over Gascony and Scotland erupted into war, Edward raised the stakes by claiming to be the rightful king of France.

Although France was richer and more populous than England by a ratio of at least three to one, the English crown was more effective in mobilizing the entire population, for reasons we discussed in Chapter 9. Edward III was therefore able to levy an army of seasoned and well-disciplined soldiers, cavalrymen, and archers. The huge but virtually leaderless armies assembled by the French proved no match

THE DISPUTED FRENCH SUCCESSION IN 1328

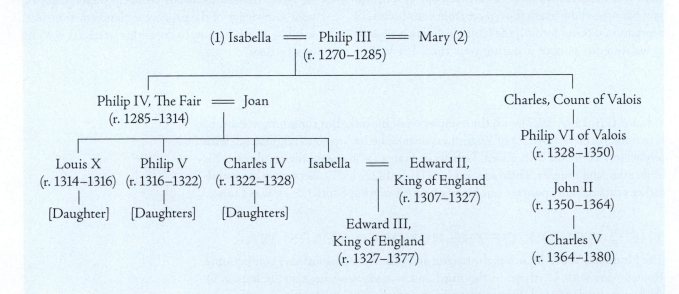

for the tactical superiority of these smaller English forces. English armies pillaged the French countryside at will, while civil wars broke out between embattled French lords. A decade after the declaration of war, French knights were defeated in two humiliating battles at Crécy (1346) and Calais (1347). The English seemed invincible—but they were no match for a new and unexpected adversary approaching from the East.

From the Great Famine to the Black Death

By 1300, Europe was connected to Asia by an intricate network that fostered connections of all kinds. At the same time, Europe was reaching its own ecological limits. Between 1000 and 1300, the population had tripled; a sea of grain fields stretched, almost unbroken, from Ireland to Ukraine; forests had been cleared, marshes drained, and pastureland reduced by generations of peasants performing lifetimes of labor. But still, Europe was barely able to feed its people. At the same time, the Medieval Warm Period (Chapter 8) was ending, and with it the favorable climatic conditions that had enabled the agricultural revolution of the previous three centuries. Even a reduction of 1 or 2°C is enough to cause substantial changes in rainfall patterns, shorten growing seasons, and decrease agricultural productivity. So it did in Europe, with disastrous consequences.

EVIL TIMES: THE SEVEN YEARS' FAMINE

Between the years 1315 and 1322, the cooling climate caused continuous adverse weather conditions in northern Europe. Winters were extraordinarily severe: in 1316, the Baltic Sea froze over and ships were trapped in the ice. Rains prevented planting in spring or summer; when a crop did struggle through, it would be dashed by rain and hail in autumn. Amid these natural calamities, dynastic warfare continued in the sodden wheat fields, as the princes of Scandinavia and the Holy Roman Empire fought for supremacy and succession. In the once-fertile fields of Flanders, French armies slogged through mud in continued efforts to subdue the Flemish population. On the Scottish and Welsh borders, uprisings were ruthlessly suppressed and the peasantry pillaged to feed the English raiders.

The result was human suffering more devastating than that caused by any European famine since that time; hence the name "**Great Famine**" to describe this terrible crisis. Weakened by malnutrition, between 10 and 15 percent of the northern population perished. Many starved, while others fell victim to epidemic diseases. In southern Europe, around the shores of the Mediterranean, the effects of climate change were more muted and food could be distributed through different channels. Nonetheless, the overall health of this region also suffered from the disruption of trade and the shortage of staple goods, as well as from the highly unstable political situation we have discussed.

As food grew scarcer, prices climbed unpredictably, making most goods unobtainable by the poor. Plans for future crops, which kept hope alive, would be dashed when flooded fields prevented seeds from germinating. People then spent cold summers and autumns foraging for food. Hunting was restricted to the nobility (Chapter 9), but even those who risked the death penalty for poaching found little game. Wages did not keep pace with rising costs, so those who lived in towns and depended on markets had less to spend on scarce provisions. Only a year after the famine began, townspeople were dying of ailments that would not have been fatal in good years.

Great Famine Period of terrible hunger and deprivation in Europe that peaked between 1315 and 1317, caused by a cooling of the climate and by environmental degradation due to overfarming. It is estimated to have reduced the population of Europe by 10 to 15 percent.

The effects of the famine were especially devastating for children, since even those who survived were highly susceptible to disease, owing to the severe impairment of their immune systems. It may have been the Great Famine, then, that paved the way for the even more horrific destruction of the Black Death.

A CRISIS OF CONNECTIVITY: TRACKING THE BLACK DEATH

The **Black Death** is the name given to a deadly global pandemic—an epidemic affecting "all people" (Greek: *pan + demos*)—that spread from Mongolia to China, northern India, and western Asia during the 1330s and 1340s. By 1346, the plague had reached the Black Sea, where it was transmitted to the Genoese colonists at Caffa. From there, in 1347, Genoese ships inadvertently took it to Sicily, North Africa, and northern Italy. From Italy, it spread rapidly along trade routes, striking seaports and then turning inland with the travelers who carried it. By 1350, it had reached Scandinavia and northern Russia, then spread southward again until it linked up with the original waves of infection that had taken it from central Asia to the Black Sea. In Europe, it continued to erupt in local epidemics until the eighteenth century. In Asia and Africa, it was still causing devastating losses of life into the nineteenth century.

Although the *absolute* (total) mortality caused by other global pandemics has been greater—including the influenza pandemic of 1918–1919 and the ongoing HIV/AIDS pandemic—the *percentage* of the population affected by the Black Death was higher. In the space of a few decades, 40 to 70 percent of all people in these affected areas had died. The tremendous consequences of this catastrophe and the survivors' responses to the world left behind will be explored in Chapter 11. But what caused it?

In 2011, scientists confirmed that the Black Death bacterium was the deadly microbe *Yersinia pestis* and that it originated on the Tibetan-Qinghai Plateau. In 2013, another team of scientists proved that this medieval pandemic was actually the *second* plague caused by *Y. pestis*; an earlier strain had resulted in the Justinianic Plague of the sixth century C.E. (Chapter 7). This microbe is especially virulent because it can be contracted and manifested in so many ways, including bubonic plague and its even deadlier cousins, septicemic plague and pneumonic plague.

In its *bubonic* form, the plague microbe is carried by fleas that can live and travel on the backs of many kinds of animals, including rats, marmots, hamsters, rabbits, camels, dogs, and birds. Humans bitten by an infected flea or animal contract the plague through their lymphatic systems, resulting in the eruption of enormous and painful swellings (buboes) in the lymph nodes of the groin, neck, and armpits. *Septicemic* plague occurs when an infected flea introduces the microbe directly into the human bloodstream, causing death within hours, usually before any symptoms of disease are obvious. *Pneumonic* plague, perhaps the most frightening variation, results when *Y. pestis* infects the lungs, allowing the contagion to spread silently and invisibly, in the same ways as the common cold.

One of the things that made the Black Death so terrifying, therefore, was that it was mysteriously inconsistent. Those afflicted by the hideous bubonic plague might actually recover, whereas others—seemingly untouched—might die suddenly, from no apparent cause. Observers quickly realized that the plague was contagious, but precisely how it spread remained unknown. Some believed that it was caused by breathing "bad air" and so urged people to flee from stricken areas, which caused

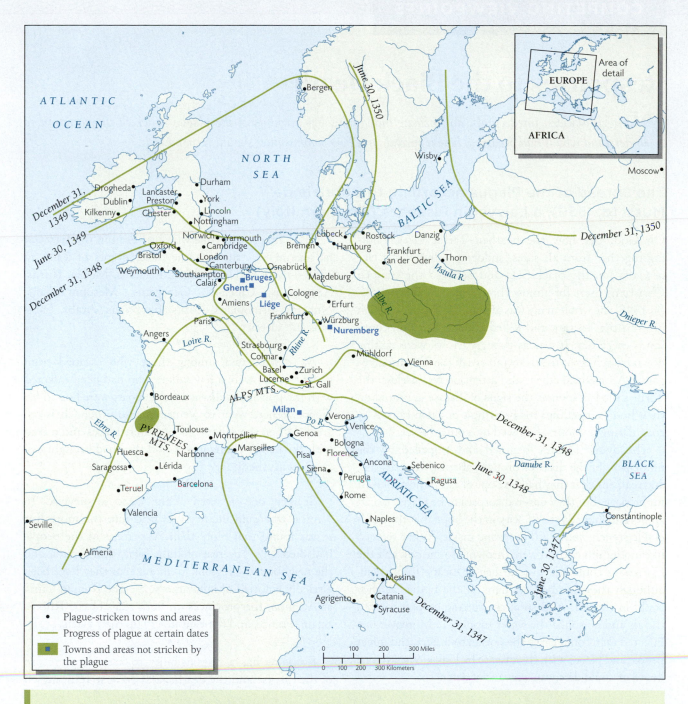

Plague-stricken towns and areas

Progress of plague at certain dates

Towns and areas not stricken by the plague

EUROPEAN OUTBREAKS OF THE BLACK DEATH, 1347–1350. › What trajectories did the Black Death follow once it arrived in Europe? › How might the growth of towns, trade, and travel have contributed to the spread of the Black Death? › Would such a rapid advance have been likely during the early Middle Ages or even in the ancient world? Why or why not?

Responses to the Black Death

Many chroniclers, intellectuals, and private individuals left accounts of the plague in which they attempt to understand why it had occurred, how it spread, and how communities should respond to it.

The Spread of the Plague according to Gabriele de' Mussi (d. 1356), a Lawyer in Piacenza (Northern Italy)

Oh God! See how the heathen Tartar races, pouring together from all sides, suddenly infested the city of Caffa [on the Black Sea] and besieged the trapped Christians there for almost three years. . . . But behold, [in 1346] the whole army was affected by a disease which overran the Tartars and killed thousands upon thousands every day. It was as though arrows were raining down from heaven to strike and crush the Tartars' arrogance. All medical advice and attention was useless; the Tartars died as soon as the signs of disease appeared on their bodies: swellings in the armpit or groin caused by coagulating humours, followed by a putrid fever.

The dying Tartars, stunned and stupefied by the immensity of the disaster brought about by the disease, and realising that they had no hope of escape, lost interest in the siege. But they ordered corpses to be placed in catapults and lobbed into the city in the hope that the intolerable stench would kill everyone inside. What seemed like mountains of dead were thrown into the city, and the Christians could not hide or flee or escape from them, although they dumped as many of the bodies as they could in the sea. And soon the rotting corpses tainted the air and poisoned the water supply. . . . Moreover one infected man could carry the poison to others, and infect people and places with the disease by look alone. No one knew, or could discover, a means of defence.

Thus almost everyone who had been in the East . . . fell victim . . . through the bitter events of 1346 to 1348—the Chinese, Indians, Persians, Medes, Kurds, Armenians, Cilicians, Georgians, Mesopotamians, Nubians, Ethiopians, Turks, Egyptians, Arabs, Saracens and Greeks. . . .

* * *

As it happened, among those who escaped from Caffa by boat were a few sailors who had been infected with the poisonous disease. Some boats were bound for Genoa, others went to Venice and to other Christian areas. When the sailors reached these places and mixed with the people there, it was as if they had brought evil spirits with them. . . .

* * *

Scarcely one in seven of the Genoese survived. In Venice, where an inquiry was held into the mortality, it was found that more than 70 percent of the people had died. . . . The rest of Italy, Sicily and Apulia and the neighbouring regions maintain that they have been virtually emptied of inhabitants. . . . The Roman Curia at Avignon, the provinces on both sides of the Rhône, Spain, France, and the Empire cry up their griefs. . . .

* * *

Everyone has a responsibility to keep some record of the disease and the deaths, and because I am myself

the disease to spread even faster. Another response was the flagellant movement, so called because of the whips (*flagella*) with which traveling bands of penitents lashed themselves in order to appease the wrath of God. The unruly and sometimes hysterical mobs that gathered around the flagellants aroused the concern of both ecclesiastical and secular authorities, and the movement was suppressed by papal order.

Still others looked for scapegoats and revived old conspiracy theories that implicated Jews in the poisoning of communal water sources. Scores of Jewish communities from Piacenza I have been urged to write more about what happened there in 1348. . . .

I don't know where to begin. Cries and laments arise on all sides. Day after day one sees the Cross and the Host being carried about the city, and countless dead being buried. . . . The living made preparations for their [own] burial, and because there was not enough room for individual graves, pits had to be dug in colonnades and piazzas, where nobody had ever been buried before. It often happened that man and wife, father and son, mother and daughter, and soon the whole household and many neighbours, were buried together in one place. . . .

Source: From Rosemary Horrox, ed. and trans., *The Black Death* (Manchester, 1994), pp. 16–21, 219–20.

A Letter from the Town Council of Cologne to the Town Council of Strasbourg (Germany), 12 January 1349

Very dear friends, all sorts of rumours are now flying about against Judaism and the Jews prompted by this unexpected and unparalleled mortality of Christians. . . . Throughout our city, as in yours, many-winged Fame clamours that this mortality was initially caused, and is still being spread, by the poisoning of springs and wells, and that the Jews must have dropped poisonous substances into them. When it came to our knowledge that serious charges had been made against the Jews in several small towns and villages on the basis of this mortality, we sent numerous letters to you and to other cities and towns to uncover the truth behind these rumours, and set a thorough investigation in train. . . .

If a massacre of the Jews were to be allowed in the major cities (something which we are determined to prevent in our city, if we can, as long as the Jews are found to be innocent of these or similar actions) it could lead to the sort of outrages and disturbances which would whip up a popular revolt among the common people— and such revolts have in the past brought cities to misery and desolation. In any case we are still of the opinion that this mortality and its attendant circumstances are caused by divine vengeance and nothing else. Accordingly we intend to forbid any harassment of the Jews in our city because of these flying rumours, but to defend them faithfully and keep them safe, as our predecessors did—and we are convinced that you ought to do the same. . . .

Questions for Analysis

1. How does Gabriele de' Mussi initially explain the causes of the plague? How does his understanding of it change as he traces its movements from East to West, and closer to Italy?

2. Why does the Council of Cologne wish to quell violence against the Jews? How does this reasoning complement or challenge what we have learned so far about the treatment of Jews in medieval Europe?

3. In your view, do these two perspectives display a rational approach to the horrors of the Black Death? Why or why not?

were attacked and thousands of their inhabitants massacred in parts of the Rhineland, southern France, and the Christian kingdoms of Spain. For example, an important archaeological and forensic study published in 2014 reveals that hundreds of Jews— including children, the elderly, and the disabled—were brutally clubbed and hacked to death by their Christian neighbors in the small Catalonian town of Tàrrega. The papacy and some local authorities tried to halt such attacks, but these efforts usually came too late.

Conclusion

The century between 1250 and 1350 was a time of significant change within all Western civilizations. The growing power of some monarchies led to encroachments on territories and cities that had once been independent, fueling resistance. The papacy, whose power had seemed so secure at the turn of the thirteenth century, would itself become a pawn in the keeping of the French king by the beginning of the fourteenth. Rome thereby lost its last source of authority while the New Rome, Constantinople, struggled to rebuild its prestige in the face of Mongol expansion. Yet for the Mongol khans and the merchants they favored, for seafaring cities such as Venice and Genoa, for ambitious students at the universities, and for men on the make, the opportunities for advancement and mobility were great.

But even in good times, Europe's population had outgrown its capacity to produce food; and when the climate grew cooler, years of cold summers and heavy rainfall took an enormous toll. Those regions most closely tied to the new global networks were densely settled and urban, which made the shortage of food and the spread of disease more acute there. In short, the benefits and drawbacks of increased globalization were already beginning to manifest themselves in the early fourteenth

AFTER YOU READ THIS CHAPTER

CHRONOLOGY

1206–1260	Rapid expansion of the Mongol Empire under Genghis Khan and his heirs
1240	The territory of Rus' is dominated by the Mongols
	Mongol Khanate of the Golden Horde established
1260–1294	Reign of Kublai Khan, Great Khan, and emperor of China
1271–1295	Travels of Marco Polo
1309	"Babylonian Captivity" of the papacy in Avignon begins
1315–1322	The Great Famine in Europe
1320	The Declaration of Arbroath proclaims Scotland's independence from England
1326–1354	The travels of Ibn Battuta
1337	Beginning of the Hundred Years' War
1347–1353	Spread of the Black Death
1352	Circulation of Mandeville's *Book of Marvels*

REVIEWING THE OBJECTIVES

› How did the conquests of the Mongols significantly impact Europe?

› The expansion of commerce and communication between eastern and western civilizations created a new world system. What were some key characteristics of this system? What kinds of exchange did it enable?

› What is *sovereignty*? What were the effects of competition for sovereignty among European rulers?

› What were the short- and long-term causes for the papacy's loss of prestige? Why was the papal court moved to Avignon?

› What caused the Black Death? In what sense can it be seen as a product of the new world system that began with the Mongol conquests?

century—700 years ago. The Black Death can be understood as the ultimate example of such connectivity.

The scale of mortality caused by this pandemic is almost unimaginable, to us as to those who survived it; at least a third, and probably over half, of Europe's people died between 1347 and 1353. In the countryside, entire villages disappeared. Cities and towns, overcrowded and unsanitary, were particularly vulnerable to plague and, thereafter, to outbreaks of violence. The immediate social consequences were profound, as were the economic ones. Crops rotted in the fields, manufacturing ceased, and trade came to a standstill in affected areas. Basic commodities became scarcer and prices rose higher, prompting ineffectual efforts to control prices and to force the remaining able-bodied laborers to work.

These were the short-term effects. How did the Black Death matter to those who survived it—including ourselves? According to Ibn Khaldun (1332–1406), a Muslim historian who is considered one of the founders of modern historical methods, it marked the end of the old world and the beginning of a new one that would require new systems of government, bodies of knowledge, and forms of art. Was he right? We will begin to answer that question in Chapter 11.

Go to **INQUIZITIVE** to see what you've learned—and learn what you've missed—with personalized feedback along the way.

PEOPLE, IDEAS, AND EVENTS IN CONTEXT

› What accounts for the success of **GENGHIS KHAN** and his successors? What circumstances enabled **MARCO POLO**'s travels to China? To what extent does the term *PAX MONGOLICA* describe this era in history?

› How did seafaring communities such as **GENOA** and **CATALONIA** rise to prominence in this era? Why were new navigational aids such as **PORTOLAN CHARTS** necessary?

› How do the paintings of **GIOTTO** capture contemporary attitudes toward the world? How does **DANTE**'s artistry respond to the religious and political trends of his day?

› What was at stake in the controversy between **BONIFACE VIII** and **PHILIP IV**? Why was the papacy's residency at **AVIGNON** called the **BABYLONIAN CAPTIVITY**? What is a **SACRAMENT**? Why were these rites so important?

› In what different ways did **LOUIS IX** of France and **EDWARD I** of England contribute to the **SOVEREIGNTY** of their respective kingdoms? What was the relationship between claims to sovereignty and the causes of the **HUNDRED YEARS' WAR**?

› How did climate change contribute to the outbreak of the **GREAT FAMINE**?

› What were the long- and short-term causes of the **BLACK DEATH**?

THINKING ABOUT CONNECTIONS

› If the Mongol khan Ögedei had not died in 1241, the Mongols could conceivably have continued their westward movement into Europe. Knowing what you have learned about Mongol rule, how do you think this might have changed the history of the world?

› How do the patterns of conquest and colonization discussed in this chapter compare with those of earlier periods, particularly those of antiquity? How many of these developments were new in 1250–1350?

› We live in a world in which the global circulation of people, information, goods, and bacteria is rapid—hence the dangers of emerging viruses such as Ebola and Zika. How does the medieval system compare with ours? What features seem familiar?

11

Rebirth and Unrest, 1350–1453

BEFORE YOU READ THIS CHAPTER

❯

IN JUNE 1381, thousands of laborers from rural England rose up in rebellion against local authorities. Most were peasants or village artisans who were dismissed as ignorant by contemporary chroniclers. Yet the revolt was carefully coordinated. Plans were spread in coded messages circulated by word of mouth and by the followers of a renegade Oxford professor, John Wycliffe, who had called for the redistribution of Church property and taught that common people should be able to read the Bible in their own language.

The rebellion's immediate catalyst had been a series of exorbitant taxes levied by Parliament for the support of the ongoing war with France. But its more fundamental cause was an epidemic that had occurred thirty years earlier. The Black Death had reduced the entire population of Europe by 60 to 70 percent and drastically altered the world of those who survived it. In this new world, workers were valuable and could stand up to those who paid them poorly or treated them like slaves. Indeed, Parliament had immediately responded to this new reality by enacting the Statute of Laborers in 1351, in a futile attempt to prohibit the movement of workers and their demands for higher wages.

During that fateful summer of 1381, the peasants of England even vowed to kill representatives of both the Church and the government and destroy all the documents that had been used to keep them in subjection. It was a revolution, and it partly succeeded. Although the leaders were eventually captured and executed, the rebellion had made the strength of the common people known to all.

> The Black Death altered Europe in profound ways. The opportunities and challenges of this era are dynamically reflected in an array of developments.

> Some of these developments were associated with a new artistic and cultural movement known as the Renaissance, which began in Italy.

> Here, renewed appreciation of the classics and of Greek was facilitated by the flight of Greek-speaking intellectuals from Byzantium, as the Ottoman Turks absorbed the remaining lands of the eastern Roman Empire.

> Meanwhile, the competing territorial claims of Europe's sovereign powers led to large-scale warfare.

> Even after the papacy's return to Rome from Avignon, the failure of internal reform efforts led to the further decline of papal credibility. Consequently, a number of influential religious leaders sought more radical reforms.

> **TRACE** the economic and social effects of the Black Death.

> **EXPLAIN** the relationship between the concepts of the Middle Ages and the Renaissance.

> **DESCRIBE** the intellectual, cultural, and technological innovations of this era.

> **DEFINE** the concept of national monarchy and summarize its implications.

> **UNDERSTAND** the significance of the conciliar movement and its defeat by the papacy.

The fourteenth century is often seen as a time of crisis: famine and plague cut fearful swaths through the population; war was a brutally recurrent fact of life; and the papacy spent seventy years in continuous exile from Italy, only to see its prestige decline further after its return to Rome. But this was also a time of extraordinary opportunity and achievement. The exhausted land of Europe recovered from centuries of overfarming. Workers gained the economic edge; and eventually, some even gained social and political power. Meanwhile, popular and intellectual movements sought to reform the Church. A host of intellectual, artistic, and scientific innovations contributed to all of these phenomena.

This era of rebirth and unrest has been called by two different names: the later Middle Ages and the Renaissance. But these are not two separate historical periods; rather, these two terms reflect two different ways of naming an era that is the immediate precursor of modernity. To understand it, we need to study it holistically.

Life after the Black Death

By 1353, when the **Black Death** began to loosen its death grip on Europe, the Continent had lost at least half its population from famine and disease in the space of two generations (see Chapter 10). In the following century, recurring outbreaks of the plague and frequent warfare resulted in further reductions. Life was therefore radically different for those who survived, because massive depopulation affected every aspect of existence, from nutrition to spirituality.

THE ENVIRONMENTAL IMPACT OF THE PLAGUE

This devastating mortality had significant environmental implications. In central Europe, some four hundred towns and villages became depopulated and disappeared. Around Paris, more than half the farmland became wasteland or pasture due to the absence of workers and decreased demand for food. In many regions, fields returned to woodland, increasing forested areas for the first time in centuries. This reestablished a healthier ecological balance, replenishing nutrients in the exhausted soil and providing habitats for animals in danger of extinction. Meanwhile, the smaller population reduced demand for grain, so farmers began to diversify their crops and establish livestock herds.

At the same time, the environment continued to be affected by the plague because *Yersinia pestis* became endemic (that is, permanently embedded) in some locales. This bacterium thrives in cool, upland climates, where it can lie dormant for many years. But a sudden change in temperature can activate it, as can intensified interactions between humans and the animals who act as hosts. To take one example, remote villages in the Alps suffered repeated outbreaks of the plague harbored by local fauna, including marmots and other rodent species. The plague would spread still farther if a villager exposed to plague traveled to a city or brought animal skins there for sale.

THE SOCIAL IMPACT OF THE PLAGUE

Smaller population in wake of Black Death leads to better nourishment and wages

The relative abundance of food meant that the price of bread—the staple of the medieval diet—fell. At the same time, the scarcity of workers made labor more valuable and some peasants and artisans could negotiate higher wages. Ordinary people could now afford a better diet, including dairy products, meat, fish, and vegetables.

As a result, Europeans became better nourished than they had ever been—better than many are today. The improved health of the population also caused improved fertility and birthrates.

Survivors of the Black Death also experienced tremendous social and economic changes—even small farmers, who were able to increase the size of their holdings and achieve a higher social status. However, large landholders often responded to the labor shortage by forcing their peasants to perform additional, unpaid labor; in parts of eastern Europe, formerly free workers became serfs for the first time.

In France and the Low Countries, by contrast, peasants were able to exercise more freedoms than in the past. In England, where peasant bondage had been more common than in France, serfdom disappeared altogether. Although the Peasants' Revolt of 1381 was unsuccessful, increased economic opportunity led to increased geographic mobility, as workers moved either to towns or to the lands of a lord who offered lower rents, fewer work requirements, and greater freedoms. As we have often noted, geographical mobility and social mobility are intertwined. In the cities affected by the plague, mortality rates were high; but some populations recovered relatively quickly due to emigration from the countryside. In Florence, for example, the population rebounded rapidly but was eventually depleted by civil unrest (see page 370).

As a result, a far larger number of people were living in towns by 1500: approximately 20 percent, as opposed to about 5 percent prior to the Black Death. Also fueling this growth was the increasing specialization of the economy. With farmers under less pressure to produce grain in bulk, they could diversify their crops and sell produce more efficiently on the open market. Towns with links to trading networks grew exponentially. In northern Europe, a group of cities formed a coalition called the Hanseatic League, which came to control commerce from Britain and Scandinavia to the Baltic. In northern Italy, the increased demand for luxury goods brought renewed wealth to the spice- and silk-trading city of Venice. Milan's armaments industry also prospered, supplying its warring neighbors and the large armies of Europe's growing monarchies.

THE PLAGUE CLAIMS A VICTIM. A priest gives the last rites to a bedridden plague victim as a smiling devil pierces the dying man with a spear and Christ looks mercifully down from heaven. › **What are the possible meanings of this image?** › **What does it reveal about contemporary attitudes toward death by the plague?**

POPULAR REVOLTS AND REBELLIONS

Yet Europeans did not adjust easily to these changes. Established elites, in particular, resisted the demands of newly powerful workers; as a result, hundreds of popular rebellions challenged the status quo in many regions. In 1358, peasants

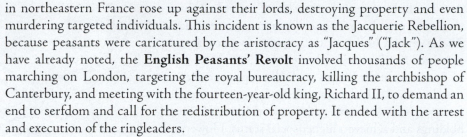

English Peasants' Revolt
In this violent 1381 uprising, thousands of people marched on London to demand an end to serfdom and called for the redistribution of property. It ended with the arrest and execution of the ringleaders.

> *In Ciompi rebellion, cloth workers seize control of Florence, demanding economic and political reforms*

in northeastern France rose up against their lords, destroying property and even murdering targeted individuals. This incident is known as the Jacquerie Rebellion, because peasants were caricatured by the aristocracy as "Jacques" ("Jack"). As we have already noted, the **English Peasants' Revolt** involved thousands of people marching on London, targeting the royal bureaucracy, killing the archbishop of Canterbury, and meeting with the fourteen-year-old king, Richard II, to demand an end to serfdom and call for the redistribution of property. It ended with the arrest and execution of the ringleaders.

In Florence, workers in the cloth industry, known as the Ciompi (*chee-OHM-pee*), were more successful in the short term. Their rebellion began in 1378, when guild members protested high unemployment and mistreatment by the manufacturers, who also ran the Florentine government. They seized control of the city, demanding tax relief, full employment, and political representation. Remarkably, the Ciompi regime remained in power for nearly four years, before it was suppressed by the urban elite.

The local circumstances behind each of these revolts were unique, but there are certain common features. Those who took part were empowered by the new economy and wanted to leverage their position to enact larger changes. Some rebellions were touched off by resistance to higher taxes; others targeted unpopular governments weakened by factionalism. In all cases, rural and urban laborers were taking advantage of their new status and importance.

ARISTOCRATIC LIFE IN THE WAKE OF THE PLAGUE

The rural aristocracies of Europe did not adapt easily to this "world turned upside down." Although many great families became wealthier, they now had to compete with an upwardly mobile population and enriched urban elites. Noble families traditionally derived revenue from vast land holdings, but some now tried to increase their income through investment in trading ventures. In Catalonia, Italy, Germany, and England, this became common. In France and Castile, however, involvement in commerce was regarded as socially demeaning and avoided by established families. Commerce could be a route to higher status in these kingdoms, but once a merchant achieved wealth he was expected to adopt an appropriate lifestyle: living in a rural castle or urban palace surrounded by a lavish household, embracing the values and conventions of chivalry, and serving his ruler at court and in warfare.

> *Social distinctions between nobles and nonnobles become increasingly blurry*

What it meant to be "noble" became, as a result, even more difficult to define than during the twelfth and thirteenth centuries. In regions where noble rank entailed certain legal privileges, proven descent from aristocratic ancestors might be necessary. Fundamentally, however, nobility was expressed and epitomized by land ownership, political influence, deference from social inferiors, courtly manners, and ostentatious display. This means that, in practice, distinctions between noble and nonnoble families were very hard to discern. Even on the battlefield, where the mark of nobility was to fight on horseback, the supremacy of the mounted knight was being threatened by the growing importance of professional soldiers, archers, crossbowmen, and artillery experts. There were even hints of a more radical critique of the aristocracy's claims to superiority. As the English rebels put it in 1381, "When Adam dug and Eve spun, who then was a gentleman?" In other words, social distinctions are not innate but artificial.

Precisely because nobility was contested, those who claimed it took elaborate measures to assert their right to this status through what we would call conspicuous consumption. This helps to explain the extraordinary number, variety, and richness of the artifacts and artworks that survive from this period. Aristocrats, or those who wanted to be classed as such, vied with each other in hosting lavish banquets that required numerous costly utensils, specially decorated chambers, legions of servants, and the most exotic foods. They also dressed in rich and extravagant clothing—close-fitting doublets and hose with long, pointed shoes for men; multilayered silk dresses with ornate headdresses for women. Some noble households were enormous: in France, for example, the Duke of Berry had four hundred matched pairs of hunting dogs and a thousand servants. Aristocrats also took part in elaborately staged tournaments, in which participants dressed as the heroes of chivalric romances. All of these activities supported a growing number of artists and artisans.

Across Europe, kings and princes also competed for status by founding chivalric orders, such as the Knights of the Garter in England. These orders exalted the nobility as a special class, strengthening the links that bound powerful families to their sovereign lords. These bonds were further strengthened by the gifts, offices, and marriage prospects that rulers could bestow. Indeed, the alliance forged in the fifteenth century between kings and their noble supporters would become one of the most characteristic features of Europe's ruling class.

CAPTURING THE NEW REALITY IN WRITING

The writings of those who survived the Black Death, or who grew up in the decades following it, are characterized by intense observations of the world—and were read by a larger and more diverse audience than ever before. The vernacular languages that were becoming powerful vehicles for literary expression (Chapter 9) were now being used to advance critical perspectives on changing social norms, political developments, and religious beliefs. We can see these innovations at work in the writings of three major authors: Giovanni Boccaccio, Geoffrey Chaucer, and Christine de Pizan.

Giovanni Boccaccio (*bohk-KAHT-chee-oh*; 1313–1375) is best known for *The Decameron*, a collection of stories about sex, adventure, and trickery told over a period of ten days (hence the title of the book: "ten days") by a sophisticated party of young women and men who have taken residence in a country villa outside Florence to escape the Black Death. Whereas Dante had used the Florentine dialect to evoke the awesome landscape of sacred history in the *Divine Comedy* (Chapter 10), Boccaccio used it to capture in plain-spoken prose the foibles of human beings.

The poet **Geoffrey Chaucer** (c. 1340–1400) was among the first to pioneer a form of English that readers today can understand with just a little effort. Known as Middle English, it blended Anglo-Saxon (Old English) with the French dialect of the Norman conquerors to create a new language. Chaucer's masterpiece, *The Canterbury Tales*, was influenced by Boccaccio's *Decameron*: it, too, is a collection of stories held together by a framing narrative. In this case, the stories are in verse and are told by a diverse group of people traveling together on a pilgrimage to the shrine of Saint Thomas Becket at Canterbury. Each character tells a story that is particularly suited to his or her own occupation and outlook, forming a kaleidoscopic human comedy.

Vernacular languages are now common vehicles for social and political commentary

Giovanni Boccaccio (c. 1313–1375) Italian writer best known for *The Decameron*.

Geoffrey Chaucer (c. 1340–1400) English poet and author who was among the first to pioneer Middle English, which blended Anglo-Saxon (Old English) with the French dialect of the Norman conquerors to create a new language.

CHRISTINE DE PIZAN. One of the most prolific authors of the Middle Ages, Christine used her influence to uphold the dignity of women and to celebrate their history and achievements. Here we see her describing the prowess of an Amazon warrior who could defeat men effortlessly in armed combat.

Christine de Pizan (c. 1365–c. 1431) The first lay woman to earn her living by writing. She is the author of treatises in warfare and chivalry, as well as of books and pamphlets that challenge longstanding misogynistic claims.

In the generation or so after the Black Death, we find professional authors who could make their living through aristocratic patronage and broader publication networks. One of the first was a woman, **Christine de Pizan** (c. 1365–c. 1434). Born in northern Italy, Christine spent her adult life in France, where her husband was a member of the king's household. When he died, Christine wrote to support herself and her children, mastering a wide variety of genres that include treatises on chivalry and warfare as well as many works celebrating the capacities and history of women. Indeed, Christine took part in a vigorous pamphlet campaign that condemned the misogynistic claims made by male authors such as Boccaccio. This debate became so famous that it was given a name: the *querelle des femmes* ("the debate over women"). Remarkably, Christine even wrote a song in praise of Joan of Arc—though she did not live long enough to see her younger contemporary put to death for behaving too much like a man (see pages 386–388).

VISUALIZING THE NEW REALITY

The desire to capture real experiences was also a dominant trait of the visual arts produced after the Black Death. This is evident both in the older arts of manuscript illumination and in the new kinds of painting and sculpture we discussed in Chapter 10. A further innovation was the technique of painting in oils: a medium pioneered in Flanders, where artists found a ready market for their works among wealthy merchants. Oil paints were revolutionary because they do not dry so quickly as water-based pigments, so a painter can work more slowly, taking time with more difficult techniques and making corrections. Masterly practitioners included Rogier

Why a Woman Can Write about Warfare

Christine de Pizan (c. 1365–c. 1434) was one of the West's first professional writers, best known today for her Book of the City of Ladies *and* The Treasure of the City of Ladies, *works that aimed to provide women with an honorable and rich history and to combat generations of institutionalized misogyny. But in her own time, Christine was probably best known for the work excerpted here,* The Book of Deeds of Arms and of Chivalry, *a manual of military strategy and conduct written in 1410, at the height of the Hundred Years' War.*

As boldness is essential for great undertakings, and without it nothing should be risked, I think it is proper in this present work to set forth my unworthiness to treat such exalted matter. I should not have dared even to think about it, but although boldness is blameworthy when it is foolhardy, I should state that I have not been inspired by arrogance or foolish presumption, but rather by true affection and a genuine desire for the welfare of noble men engaging in the profession of arms. I am encouraged, in the light of my other writings, to undertake to speak in this book of the most honorable office of arms and chivalry. . . . So to this end I have gathered together facts and subject matter from various books to produce this present volume. But inasmuch as it is fitting for this matter to be discussed factually, diligently, and sensibly . . . and also in consideration of the fact that military and lay experts in the aforesaid art of chivalry are not usually clerks or writers who are expert in language, I intend to treat the matter in the plainest possible language. . . .

As this is unusual for women, who generally are occupied in weaving, spinning, and household duties, I humbly invoke . . . the wise lady Minerva [Athena], born in the land of Greece, whom the ancients esteemed highly for her great wisdom. Likewise the poet Boccaccio praises her in his *Book of Famous Women*, as do other writers praise her art and manner of making trappings of iron and steel, so let it not be held against me if I, as a woman, take it upon myself to treat of military matters. . . .

O Minerva! goddess of arms and of chivalry, who, by understanding beyond that of other women, did find and initiate among the other noble arts and sciences the custom of forging iron and steel armaments and harness both proper and suitable for covering and protecting men's bodies against arrows slung in battle—helmets, shields, and protective covering having come first from you—you instituted and gave directions for drawing up a battle order, how to begin an assault and to engage in proper combat. . . . In the aforementioned country of Greece, you provided the usage of this office, and insofar as it may please you to be favorably disposed, and I in no way appear to be against the nation from which you came, the country beyond the Alps that is now called Apulia and Calabria in Italy, where you were born, let me say that like you I am an Italian woman.

Source: From Christine de Pizan, *The Book of Deeds of Arms and of Chivalry*, ed. Charity Cannon Willard and trans. Sumner Willard (University Park, PA: 1999), pp. 11–13.

Questions for Analysis

1. Christine very cleverly deflects potential criticism for her "boldness" in writing about warfare. What tactics does she use?

2. The Greco-Roman goddess Athena (Minerva) was the goddess of wisdom, weaving, and warfare. Why does Christine invoke her aid? What parallels does she draw between her own attributes and those of Minerva?

van der Weyden (c. 1400–1464), who communicated deep spiritual messages against a backdrop of everyday life (see *Interpreting Visual Evidence* on page 377). This conveyed the message that Biblical events are constantly present, here and now.

The same immediacy is also evident in drama, because medieval plays were often devotional exercises that involved the entire community. In the English city of York, for example, an annual series of pageants reenacted the history of human salvation from the Creation to the Last Judgment in a single summer day, beginning at dawn and ending late at night. Each pageant was produced by a particular craft guild and showcased that guild's special talents: "The Last Supper" was performed by the bakers, whose bread became the first Eucharist, whereas "The Crucifixion" was performed by the nail makers and painters, whose wares were instrumental in Christ's bloody death on the cross.

In Italy, guilds and confraternities (brotherhoods) competed to honor local saints with songs and processions. In many regions of Spain, there were elaborate dramas celebrating the life and miracles of the Virgin. One of these is still performed every year in the Basque town of Elche, making it the oldest European play in continuous production. In northern France, the Low Countries, and German-speaking lands, civic spectacles were performed over a period of several days, celebrating the community's connection to the sacred history of the Bible. But not all plays were pious; some honored visiting kings, while others celebrated the flouting of social conventions through cross-dressing and the reversal of hierarchies: appropriate for the topsy-turvy world after the Black Death.

The Beginnings of the Renaissance in Italy

Rummaging through the books in a cathedral library, an Italian bureaucrat at the papal court in Avignon was surprised to find a manuscript of Cicero's letters, which he had not known to exist. They had probably been copied in the time of Charlemagne and then forgotten for centuries. How many other great works of antiquity had been lost to posterity? Clearly, thought Francesco Petrarca (1304–1374), he was living in an age of ignorance. A great gulf seemed to open up between his own time and that of the ancients.

PETRARCH'S COPY OF VIRGIL. Petrarch's devotion to the classics of Roman literature prompted him to commission this new frontispiece for his treasured volume of Virgil's poetry. It was painted by the Sienese artist Simone Martini, who (like Petrarch) was attached to the papal court at Avignon. It is an allegorical depiction of Virgil (top right) and his poetic creations: the hero Aeneas, wearing armor (top left); and the farmer and shepherd, whose humble labors are celebrated in Virgil's lesser-known works. The figure next to Aeneas is the fourth-century scholar Servius, who wrote a famous commentary on Virgil. He is shown drawing aside a curtain to reveal the poet in a creative trance. The two scrolls proclaim (in Latin) that Italy was the country that nourished famous poets, and that Virgil helped it to achieve the glories of classical Greece. **› How does this image encapsulate and express Petrarch's devotion to the classical past?**

For centuries, Christian intellectuals had regarded the "dark ages" as the time between Adam's expulsion from Eden and the birth of Christ. But now, Petrarch (the anglicized form of Petrarca) redefined that concept. According to him, this "dark age" was not the pagan past but the time that separated him from direct communion with the classics. "I would have written to you long ago," he said in a Latin letter to the Greek poet Homer (dead for over two thousand years), "had it not been for the fact that we lack a common language." Petrarch was famous in his own day as an Italian poet, a Latin stylist, and a tireless advocate for the resuscitation of antiquity. The values that he and his followers espoused would give rise to a new intellectual and artistic movement in Italy, a movement strongly critical of the present and admiring of a past that had disappeared with the fragmentation of Rome's empire and Italy's greatness.

We know this movement as the **Renaissance**, from the French word for "rebirth": a term invented in the eighteenth century and popularized in the nineteenth, when the term *medieval* was also invented. It has since become shorthand for the epoch *following* the Middle Ages—but it was actually part of that same era.

Renaissance From the French word "rebirth," this term came to be used in the nineteenth century to describe the artistic, intellectual, and cultural movement that emerged in Italy after 1300, and which sought to recover and emulate the heritage of the classical past.

RENAISSANCE CLASSICISM

Talking about "the Renaissance," then, is a way of talking about some significant changes in education and artistic outlook that began in northern Italy during the late fourteenth century—and that eventually influenced the rest of Europe, too. Yet the term should not be taken literally, as though antiquity had ceased to be appreciated in earlier centuries: we have been tracing the enduring influence of classical civilization through many chapters, and have constantly noted the reverence accorded to the heritage of antiquity, not to mention the persistence of Roman law and institutions.

That said, the concept of "renaissance" does help to explain some new developments. For example, the ancient texts that had long been preserved in monastic libraries now came to be more widely available to secular scholars such as Petrarch. Their "discovery" of works by Livy, Tacitus, and Lucretius expanded the classical canon considerably, supplementing the well-studied works of Virgil, Ovid, and Cicero.

Even more important was scholars' expanded access to ancient Greek literature. As we noted in Chapters 8 and 9, Greek scientific and philosophical works became available to Europeans in the twelfth and thirteenth centuries thanks to increased contact with Islam, via Latin translations of Arabic translations of the original Greek. And yet no Greek poems or plays were yet available in Latin translations, and neither were the major dialogues of Plato. Moreover, only a handful of Europeans could read the language of classical Greece. But as the Mongols and, after them, the Ottoman Turks put increasing pressure on the shrinking borders of Byzantium (see pages 379–381), more and more Greek-speaking intellectuals fled to Italy, bringing their books and knowledge with them.

Contact with Muslim world enables more Europeans access to ancient Greek literature

Some Italian scholars not only had increased access to more classical texts, they also used these texts in new ways. For centuries, Christian teachers had worked to bring ancient writings and values into line with their own beliefs (Chapter 6). But the new reading methods of Petrarch and his circle fostered an increased awareness of the conceptual gap that separated their contemporary world from that of antiquity. This awareness awakened a determination to recapture truly ancient worldviews.

In the second half of the fifteenth century, especially, classical models also shaped the distinctive artistic style that is most strongly associated with the Renaissance, which we will address in Chapter 12.

Another distinguishing feature of this new perspective on the classical past was its commercialization. Competition among and within Italian states fostered a culture that used the symbols and artifacts of ancient Rome as pawns in an endless power game. Meanwhile, the relative weakness of the Church contributed to the growth of claims to power based on classical models—even by Italian bishops and Church-sponsored universities. When the papacy eventually returned to Rome, it also had to compete in this Renaissance arena.

RENAISSANCE HUMANISM

A crucial feature of this new intellectual and cultural movement is summarized in the term **humanism**. This was a program of study that aimed to replace the scholastic emphasis on logic and theology—central to the curriculum of universities—with the study of ancient literature, rhetoric, history, and ethics. The goal of a humanist education was the understanding of the human experience through the lens of the classical past. In contrast, a scholastic education filtered human experience through the teachings of scripture and the Church Fathers, with human salvation as the ultimate goal.

Humanists accordingly preferred ancient writings to those of more recent authors. And although some humanists wrote in Italian as well as Latin, most regarded vernacular literature as a lesser diversion; serious scholarship and praiseworthy poetry could be written only in Latin or Greek. Proper Latin, moreover, had to be the classical Latin of Cicero and Virgil, not the evolving language common to universities, international diplomacy, law, and the Church. Renaissance humanists therefore condemned the living Latin of their day as a barbarous departure from "correct" standards. And ironically, their determination to revive this older language eventually killed the lively Latin that had continued to flourish: for by insisting on outmoded standards of grammar, syntax, and diction, they turned Latin into a fossilized discourse that ceased to have any relevance to daily life. They thus contributed, unwittingly, to the ultimate triumph of Europe's vernaculars and the demise of Latin as a common medium of communication.

Because humanism was an educational program designed to produce virtuous citizens and able public officials, it also excluded women, who were largely denied any role in Italian public life. In a political context, humanism could be made to serve either the ideals of citizenship as exemplified by the Roman Republic, or the authoritarian agendas of autocratic rulers who wanted to emulate Roman imperial power.

WHY ITALY?

These new attitudes toward education and the ancient past were fostered in northern Italy for historically specific reasons. After the Black Death, this was the most densely populated part of Europe; other urban areas, notably northeastern France and Flanders, had been decimated by the Great Famine as well as by the plague. Northern Italy also differed from the rest of urbanized Europe because aristocratic families lived in cities rather than in rural castles; consequently, they became more

Realizing Devotion

These two paintings by the Flemish artist Rogier van der Weyden (*FAN der VIE-den*; c. 1400–1464) capture some of the most compelling characteristics of late medieval art, particularly the trend toward realistic representations of holy figures and sacred stories. In image A, the artist depicts himself as the evangelist Luke, regarded in Christian tradition as a painter of portraits. He is sketching the Virgin nursing the infant Jesus in a townhouse overlooking a Flemish city. In image B, van der Weyden imagines the entombment of the body of Christ by his followers, including the Virgin (left), Mary Magdalene (kneeling), and the disciple John (right). Here he makes use of a motif that became increasingly prominent in the later Middle Ages: Christ as the Man of Sorrows, displaying his wounds and inviting the viewer to share in his suffering. In both paintings, van der Weyden emphasizes the humanity of his subjects rather than their iconic status (see Chapter 7), and places them in the urban and rural landscapes of his own world.

Questions for Analysis

1. How are these paintings different from the sacred images of the earlier Middle Ages (see, for example, pages 225 and 346)? What messages does the artist convey by setting these events in his own immediate present?

2. In what ways do these paintings reflect broad changes in popular piety and medieval devotional practices? Why, for example, would the artist display the dead body of Christ, covered with wounds, rather than depicting him as resurrected and triumphant, or as an all-seeing creator and judge?

3. In general, how would you interpret these images as evidence of the worldview of the fifteenth century? What do they tell us about people's attitudes, emotions, and values?

A. *Saint Luke Drawing the Virgin.*

B. *The Lamentation of Christ.*

fully involved in public affairs. Moreover, many town-dwelling aristocrats were engaged in banking or mercantile enterprises, while many rich mercantile families imitated the aristocracy: a prime example of the latter is the Florentine ruling family, the Medici, who originally made their fortune in commerce.

These developments help to explain the emergence of humanist education. Newly wealthy families were not content to have their sons learn only the skills necessary for business; they sought teachers who would impart the knowledge and finesse that would enable them to cut a figure in society, mix with their noble neighbors, and speak with authority on public affairs. Consequently, Italy produced and attracted a large number of independent intellectuals who were not affiliated with monasteries, cathedral schools, or universities. Many served as schoolmasters for wealthy young men while acting as cultural consultants and secretaries for their families. And they advertised their learning by producing political and ethical treatises and works of literature that would attract the attention of wealthy patrons. As a result, Italian schools and private tutors turned out the best-educated laymen in Europe, men who constituted a new generation of wealthy, knowledgeable patrons ready to invest in new forms of literary and artistic expression.

In ancient Roman past, Italians find a source of heritage and pride >

A second reason was that late-medieval Italy was politically disjunctive and competitive. Unlike France and England, or the kingdoms of Spain, Scandinavia, and eastern Europe, Italy had no unifying political institutions. Italians therefore looked to the classical past for their time of glory, dreaming of a day when Rome would be, again, the center of the world. They boasted that ancient Roman monuments were omnipresent in their landscape and that classical Latin literature referred to cities and sites they recognized as their own. By reappropriating their classical heritage, Italians particularly sought to establish an independent cultural identity that could oppose the intellectual and political supremacy of France. The removal of the papacy to Avignon had heightened antagonism toward the powerful monarchy beyond the Alps. This also explains humanists' rejection of scholasticism, since ancient Roman models were an intellectual alternative to the dominant university in Paris.

Finally, this Italian Renaissance could not have occurred without the underpinning of Italian wealth gained through the commercial ventures described in Chapter 10. This wealth meant that talented men seeking employment and patronage also fueled the artistic and intellectual competition that arose from the intensification of urban pride and the concentration of individual and family wealth in urban areas. Cities themselves became among the primary patrons of art and learning.

FLORENTINE CIVIC IDEALS

Petrarch's personal goal was a solitary life of contemplation. But for subsequent Italian intellectuals, especially those of Florence, the goal of classical education was civic enrichment. Humanists such as Leonardo Bruni (c. 1370–1444) and Leon Battista Alberti (1404–1472) taught that man's nature equips him for action, for usefulness to his family, and for serving the state. In their view, worldly ambitions were noble impulses that ought to be encouraged and channeled toward these ends. They also refused to condemn the accumulation of material possessions, arguing that the history of human progress is inseparable from the human dominion of the earth and its resources.

Many of the Florentine humanists' civic ideals are expressed in Alberti's treatise *On the Family* (1443), in which he presents the nuclear family as the fundamental unit of the city-state. Alberti accordingly argued that women—who, in reality, governed the household—should be relegated to childbearing, child rearing, and subservience to men even within this domestic realm. He asserted, furthermore, that women should play no role whatsoever in the public sphere. Although actual women fiercely resisted such dismissals of their abilities, Renaissance humanism was characterized by a pervasive denigration of them—a misogyny often mirrored in the works of classical literature that the humanists so much admired.

NEW WAYS OF READING ANCIENT TEXTS

The humanists were aided by a number of Byzantine immigrants to northern Italy who gave instruction in the ancient form of their own language. Wealthy, well-connected men increasingly aspired to acquire Greek masterpieces, which often involved journeys back to Constantinople. In 1423, one adventurous bibliophile managed to bring back 238 manuscript books, among them rare works of Sophocles, Euripides, and Thucydides. These were quickly paraphrased in Latin and so made accessible to medieval Europeans for the first time.

Byzantine immigrants bring to Italy knowledge of ancient Greek texts

This influx of classical texts spurred a new interest in the critical reading of ancient sources. A pioneer in this activity was Lorenzo Valla (1407–1457). Born in Rome and active as a secretary to the king of Naples, Valla had no allegiance to the civic ideals of the Florentine humanists. Instead, he turned his skills to the painstaking analysis of Greek and Latin writings to show how the historical study of language could discredit old assumptions and even unmask some texts as forgeries. For example, papal propagandists were arguing that the papacy's claim to secular power in Europe derived from rights granted to the bishop of Rome by Constantine in the fourth century, as enshrined in a document known as the "Donation of Constantine." By analyzing the language of this text, Valla proved that it could not have been written in the time of Constantine because it contained more recent Latin usages and vocabulary.

This demonstration not only threatened to discredit more traditional scholarly methods, it alerted scholars to the necessity of avoiding anachronism in the study of history—that is, the intellectual vigilance needed to avoid projecting present values and expectations onto the past. Valla even applied his expert knowledge of Greek to elucidate the meaning of Saint Paul's letters, which he believed had been mangled by Jerome's Latin translation (Chapter 6). Valla's work was to prove an important link between Renaissance humanism and the Christian humanism that fueled the Reformation (see Chapter 13).

The End of the Eastern Roman Empire

The Greek-speaking refugees who arrived in Italy after the Black Death were responding to a succession of calamities that had reduced the once-proud eastern Roman Empire to a scattering of provinces. When Constantinople fell to papal crusaders in 1204, the surrounding territories of Byzantium were severed from the capital (Chapter 9). When the Latin presence in Constantinople was finally expelled, in 1261, imperial power had been so weakened that it extended only into the immediate hinterlands of the city and to parts of the Greek Peloponnese. The rest of the empire had become a collection of small principalities in precarious alliance with the Mongols, on whom they depended for survival (Chapter 10). Then, with the coming of the Black Death, the imperial capital suffered a loss of population and shrank still further. Meanwhile, the disintegration of the Mongol Empire laid the larger region open to a new set of invaders.

THE RISE OF THE OTTOMAN TURKS

When the Mongols arrived in northwestern Anatolia, the Turks—originally a nomadic people—were already being converted to Islam by the resident Muslim powers of the region: the Seljuk sultanate of Rûm and the Abbasid caliphate of Baghdad. But when the Mongols toppled these older powers, they eliminated the two traditional authorities that had kept the Turkish chieftains in check. So now the Turks were free to raid, unhindered, along the soft frontiers of Byzantium. At the same time, the Turks remained far enough from the centers of Mongol power to avoid being destroyed themselves. One of their chieftains, Osman Gazi (1258–1326), even managed to establish his own kingdom; over time, his name became that of the Turkish dynasty known as the **Ottomans**.

By the mid-fourteenth century, Osman's successors had solidified their preeminence by capturing a number of important cities. These successes brought the Ottomans to the attention of the Byzantine emperor, who hired a contingent as mercenaries in 1345. They were extraordinarily successful, but the eastern Roman Empire could not control them. The Turks struck out on their own and began to extend their control westward. By 1370, their holdings stretched all the way to the Danube. In 1389, they defeated a powerful coalition of Serbian forces at the Battle of Kosovo and began subduing Bulgaria, the Balkans, and eventually Greece. In 1396, the Ottoman army attacked Constantinople itself, although it withdrew to repel an ineffectual crusading force that had been hastily sent by the papacy.

In 1402, another attack on Constantinople was deflected—this time, by a more potent foe. Timur the Lame (Tamerlane, as he was called by European admirers) was born to a family of small landholders in the Mongol Khanate of Chagatai. While still a young man, he rose to prominence as a military leader and gained a reputation for tactical genius. He never officially assumed the title of khan in any of the territories he dominated, but instead moved ceaselessly from conquest to conquest, becoming the master of lands stretching from the Caspian Sea to the Volga River, as well as most of Persia. For a time, it looked briefly as if the Mongol Empire might be reunited under his reign. But Timur died in 1405, on his way to invade China, and his various conquests fell to local rulers. In Anatolia, the Ottoman Turks were able to regain their dominant position.

THE FALL OF CONSTANTINOPLE

As Ottoman pressure increased on Constantinople during the 1420s and 1430s, monasteries and schools that had been established since the time of Constantine found themselves in the path of an advancing army. A steady stream of scholars fled westward, carrying a millennium's worth of books preserving the heritage of ancient Greece and the Hellenistic world. Then, in 1451, the Ottoman sultan Mehmet II turned his full attention to the conquest of the imperial city. In 1453, after a

Ottoman Empire (c. 1300–1923) During the thirteenth century, the Ottoman dynasty established itself as leader of the Turks. From the fourteenth to sixteenth centuries, they conquered Anatolia, Armenia, Syria, and North Africa as well as parts of southeastern Europe, the Crimea, and areas along the Red Sea.

brilliantly executed siege, his army succeeded in breaching its walls. The Byzantine emperor was killed in the assault, the city was violently plundered, and its remaining population killed or sold into slavery.

The Ottoman conquest of Constantinople administered an enormous intellectual shock to Europeans, yet its wider political and economic impact was minor. Ottoman control may have reduced European access to the Black Sea, but the bulk of the Eastern luxury trade had never passed through Black Sea ports in the first place. Europeans got most of their spices and silks through Venice, from Alexandria and Beirut, which did not fall to the Ottomans until the 1520s. Moreover, as we saw in Chapter 10, Europeans already had colonial settlements in West Africa and the eastern Atlantic that connected them to far-reaching networks.

But if the practical effects on Europe were modest, the effects on the Turks themselves were transformative. Vast new wealth poured into Anatolia, which the Ottomans increased by carefully tending the industrial and commercial interests of their new capital city, which they called Istanbul: the Turkish pronunciation of the Greek phrase *eis tan polin* ("in the city"). Trade routes were redirected to feed the capital, and the Ottomans became a naval power in the eastern Mediterranean as well as in the Black Sea. As a result, Istanbul's population grew from fewer than a hundred thousand in 1453 to more than half a million. By 1600, it was the largest city in the world outside of China.

SLAVERY AND SOCIAL ADVANCEMENT IN THE OTTOMAN EMPIRE

To manage its continual expansion, the Ottoman army and administration grew exponentially, drawing manpower from conquered territories. And because both army and bureaucracy were largely composed of slaves, the demand for more soldiers and administrators could best be met through further conquests that would yield yet more slaves. Those conquests, however, required a still larger army and an even more extensive bureaucracy—and so the cycle continued. It mirrors, in many respects, the dilemma of the Roman Empire in the centuries of its rapid expansion (Chapter 5).

Not only were slaves the backbone of the Ottoman state, they were also critical to the lives of the Turkish upper class. An important measure of status was the number of slaves in one's household, with some elites maintaining households in the thousands. By the sixteenth century, the sultan alone possessed more than twenty thousand slave attendants, not including his bodyguard and elite infantry units, both of which also comprised slaves.

Where did all of these slaves come from? Many were captured in war and many others were taken during raiding forays into Poland and Ukraine, then sold to slave merchants

SULTAN MEHMET II, "THE CONQUEROR" (r. 1451–1481). This portrait, executed by the Ottoman artist Siblizade Ahmed, exhibits stylistic features characteristic of both central Asia and Europe. The sultan's pose—his aesthetic appreciation of the rose, his elegant handkerchief—are indicative of the former, as is the fact that he wears the white turban of a scholar and the thumb ring of an archer. But the subdued coloring and three-quarter profile may reflect the influence of Italian portraits. › **What did the artist achieve through this blending of styles and symbols?** › **What messages does this portrait convey?**

who shipped them from the Crimea to the markets of Istanbul. But slaves were also recruited from rural areas of the Ottoman Empire itself. Most were coerced, but some may have gone willingly: because the vast majority of slaves were household servants and administrators rather than laborers, rural laborers believed that they would be better off as slaves in Istanbul than as impoverished peasants. In the Balkans, especially, many people were enslaved as children, handed over by their families to pay the "child tax" which the Ottomans imposed on areas too poor to pay a monetary tribute. Although an excruciating experience for families, this practice opened up some opportunities for social advancement. Special academies were created at Istanbul to train the ablest of the enslaved boys to act as administrators and soldiers, some of whom then rose to become powerful figures.

For this reason, slavery carried relatively little social stigma in the Ottoman Empire. The sultans themselves were most often the sons of enslaved women. And

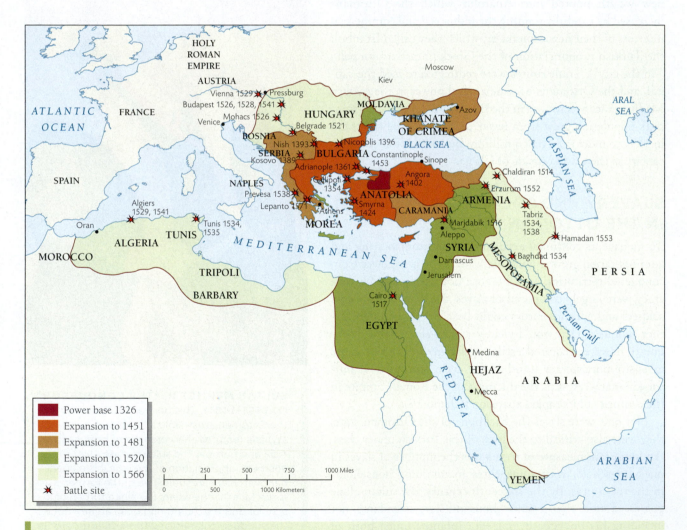

THE GROWTH OF THE OTTOMAN EMPIRE. Consider the patterns of Ottoman expansion revealed in this map. › Where is Constantinople (Istanbul), and how might its capture in 1453 have facilitated further conquests? › Compare the extent of the Ottoman Empire in 1566 with that of the Byzantine Empire under Justinian (see the map on page 218). How would you account for their similarities?

because Muslims were not permitted to enslave other Muslims, the vast majority of Ottoman slaves were Christian, many of whom held elite positions within the government. The paradoxical result was that Muslims, including the Turks, were effectively excluded from the main avenues of social and political influence in the Ottoman Empire.

Commerce also remained largely in the hands of non-Muslims, most frequently Greeks, Syrians, and Jews who had found a welcome refuge from the persecutions and expulsions that had characterized their lives in Europe. The Ottoman sultans accommodated their fellow monotheists, Christians and Jews, who were organized into legally recognized units and were permitted some rights of self-government. The authority of the Greek Orthodox patriarch of Constantinople was also tolerated. But because the Turks were Sunni Muslims, they often dealt harshly with other Muslim sects, and they did not tolerate any forms of polytheism.

Warfare and Nation Building

War has always been an engine for the development of new technologies. But in the era after the Black Death, the pace and scale of warfare escalated to an unprecedented degree—as did the deployment of new weapons. Explosives had been invented in China, for use in fireworks displays, but they were now used to destructive effect in Europe. Although the earliest cannons were as dangerous to those who fired them as to those they targeted, they revolutionized the nature of warfare. In 1453, heavy artillery played a leading role in the outcomes of two crucial conflicts: the Ottoman Turks' breach of Constantinople's ancient defenses and the French capture of the English-held city of Bordeaux, which brought an end to the **Hundred Years' War**.

Thereafter, cannons made it more difficult for rebellious aristocrats to hole up in their stone castles, and so consequently aided in the consolidation of monarchies. Cannons placed aboard ships made Europe's developing navies more effective agents of empire. A handheld firearm, the pistol, was also invented during the fourteenth century; and around 1500, the musket ended forever the military dominance of armored cavalry, giving the advantage to foot soldiers recruited from the ranks of average citizens.

Indeed, there is a symbiotic relationship between warfare and nation building, as well as between warfare and technology. Because Europeans were almost constantly at war from the fourteenth century to the middle of the twentieth, governments claimed new powers to tax their subjects and to recruit them as soldiers. Armies became larger and military technology deadlier. Wars became more destructive and society more militarized. As a result, the most successful European states were aggressively expansionist, and they aggressively engaged in creating an idea of national identity that would bind their peoples together against a common enemy.

THE HUNDRED YEARS' WAR RESUMES

The Hundred Years' War can be divided into three main phases (see the map on page 385). The first phase dates from the initial declaration of war in 1337 (see Chapter 10), after which the English won a series of startling military victories before the Black Death put a temporary halt to hostilities. The war then

Prevalence of warfare leads to new relationship between governments and citizens

Hundred Years' War (1337–1453) A series of wars between England and France, fought mostly on French soil and prompted by the territorial and political claims of English monarchs.

resumed in 1356, with another English victory at Poitiers. Four years later, in 1360, Edward III decided to leverage his strong position and renounced his larger claim to the French throne, in return for full sovereignty over a greatly enlarged duchy in southwestern France.

But the terms of that treaty were never honored, nor did the treaty resolve the underlying issues that had led to war: namely, the problem of making any claim to sovereignty in contested territory and the question of the English king's place in the French royal succession. The French king continued to treat the English king as his vassal, while Edward and his heirs quickly renewed their claim to the throne of France.

Although there were no pitched battles in France itself for two decades after 1360, a destabilizing proxy war developed during the 1360s and 1370s, which spread violence to neighboring regions. Both English and French soldiers organized themselves into "Free Companies" of mercenaries and hired themselves out in the service of hostile factions in Castile and competing city-states in northern Italy. By 1376, when the conflict reignited, the Hundred Years' War had become a Europe-wide phenomenon.

THE BRIEF VICTORY OF HENRY V

During this second phase, the tide quickly shifted in favor of France. The new king, Charles V (r. 1364–1380), imposed a series of taxes to fund an army, restored order by disbanding the Free Companies, and hired the leader of one as the commander of his army. He thereby created a professional military that could match the English in discipline and tactics. By 1380, English territories in France had been reduced to a core area around the southwestern city of Bordeaux and the port of Calais in the extreme northeast.

Meanwhile, the aging Edward III had been succeeded by his nine-year-old grandson, Richard II (r. 1377–1399), who was too young to resume armed conflict. This was problematic because the war had been extremely popular in England. Moreover, mismanagement by Richard's advisers had triggered the Peasants' Revolt in 1381. But when Richard came of age and showed no signs of warlike ambition, many of his own relatives turned against him. Richard retaliated against the ringleader of this faction, his cousin Henry of Lancaster, sending him into exile and confiscating his property. Henry's supporters rebelled and, in 1399, Richard was deposed and eventually murdered.

As a usurper whose legitimacy was always in doubt, Henry IV (r. 1399–1413) struggled to maintain his authority in the face of further rebellions and challenges to his kingship. The best way to unite the country would have been to renew the war against France, but Henry was frequently ill. However, when his son Henry V succeeded him in 1413, the young king immediately began to prepare for an invasion. His timing was excellent: the French royal government was foundering, owing to the insanity of the reigning king, Charles VI (r. 1380–1422). A brilliant diplomat as well as a capable soldier, Henry V sealed an alliance with the powerful Duke of Burgundy, who was nominally loyal to France but stood to gain from its defeat. Henry also made a treaty with the German emperor, who agreed not to come to France's aid.

When he crossed the English Channel with his troops in the autumn of 1415, Henry thus faced a much-depleted French army that could not rely on reinforcements.

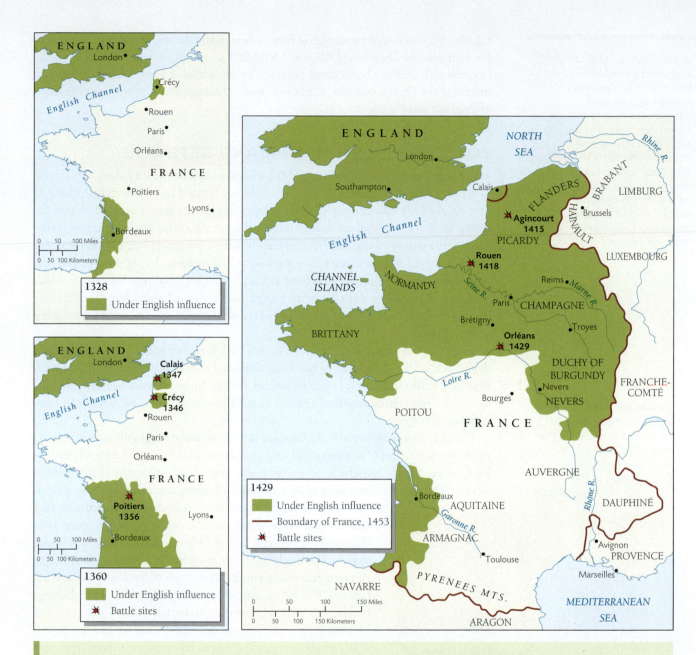

THE PHASES OF THE HUNDRED YEARS' WAR. Here we see three snapshots of the political geography of France during the Hundred Years' War. › In what areas of France did England make its greatest territorial gains before 1360? › How and why did this change in the period leading up to 1429? › What geographic and strategic advantages did the French monarchy enjoy after 1429 that might help explain its success in recapturing the French kingdom from the English?

Although it was still vastly larger, with hundreds of mounted knights, it was undisciplined. It was also severely hampered by bad weather and deep mud when the two armies clashed at Agincourt on October 25 of that year—conditions that favored the lighter English infantry. Henry's men managed to win a crushing victory. Then, over the next five years, Henry conquered most of northern France. In 1420, the ailing

Charles VI was forced to recognize him as heir to the throne, thereby disinheriting his own son, the Dauphin (*DOE-fah*, "dolphin"), a ceremonial title derived from the heraldic device of the borderland province he controlled. Henry sealed the deal by marrying the French princess, Catherine, and fathering an heir to the joint kingdom of England and France.

JOAN OF ARC'S TRIUMPH AND BETRAYAL

Unlike his great-grandfather Edward III, who had claimed the French throne largely as a bargaining chip, Henry V honestly believed himself to be the rightful king of France. And his astonishing success in capturing the kingdom seemed to put the stamp of divine approval on that claim. But Henry's successes in France also transformed the nature of the conflict, turning it from a profitable war of conquest and plunder into an extended and expensive military occupation. It might have been sustainable had Henry been as long-lived as his predecessors, but he died early in 1422, just short of his thirty-sixth birthday. King Charles VI died only a few months later, leaving the infant Henry VI (r. 1422–1461) to be crowned the first—and last—king of both realms.

The Dauphin was now determined to win back his inheritance. Yet French confidence in his right to the throne had been shattered by his own mother's declaration that he was illegitimate. It began to look as though England would once again rule an empire comprising much of France, as it had for a century and a half after the Norman Conquest.

But in 1429, a peasant girl from Lorraine (a territory only marginally part of France) made her way to the Dauphin's court and announced that an angel had told her that he, Charles, was the rightful king, and that she, Joan, should drive the English out of France. The very fact that **Joan of Arc** even got a hearing underscores the hopelessness of the Dauphin's position—as does the extraordinary fact that he gave her a contingent of troops. With this force, Joan liberated the strategic city of Orléans (*OR-lay-ah*), then under siege by the English. She then led her army to a series of victories that culminated in the coronation of the Dauphin as King Charles VII in the cathedral of Reims, where French kings had been crowned for nearly a thousand years.

Despite her miraculous successes, Charles and his aristocratic generals regarded Joan as an embarrassment: a peasant leading nobles, a woman dominating men, and a commoner who claimed divine inspiration. Her very charisma made her dangerous. So when the Burgundians captured her in battle a few months later, and handed her over to the English as a prisoner of war, the king she had helped to crown did nothing to save her. Accused of witchcraft, condemned by the theologians of Paris, and tried for heresy by an English ecclesiastical court, Joan was burned to death in the market square at Rouen in 1431. She was nineteen years old.

The French forces whom Joan had inspired, however, continued on the offensive. In 1435, the duke of Burgundy withdrew his alliance with the English, whose young king,

JOAN OF ARC.
A contemporary sketch of Joan was drawn in the margin of this register, documenting official proceedings at the Parlement of Paris in 1429.

The Condemnation of Joan of Arc by the University of Paris, 1431

After Joan's capture by the Burgundians, she was handed over to the English and tried for heresy at an ecclesiastical court set up in Rouen. It was on this occasion that the theology faculty of Paris pronounced the following verdict on her actions.

You, Joan, have said that, since the age of thirteen, you have experienced revelations and the appearance of angels, of St. Catherine and St. Margaret, and that you have very often seen them with your bodily eyes, and that they have spoken to you. As for the first point, the clerks of the University of Paris have considered the manner of the said revelations and appearances. . . . Having considered all . . . they have declared that all the things mentioned above are lies, falsenesses, misleading and pernicious things and that such revelations are superstitions, proceeding from wicked and diabolical spirits.

Item: You have said that your king had a sign by which he knew that you were sent by God, for St. Michael, accompanied by several angels, some of which having wings, the others crowns, with St. Catherine and St. Margaret, came to you at the chateau of Chinon. All the company ascended through the floors of the castle until they came to the room of your king, before whom the angel bearing the crown bowed. . . . As for this matter, the clerks say that it is not in the least probable, but it is rather a presumptuous lie, misleading and pernicious, a false statement, derogatory of the dignity of the Church and of the angels. . . .

Item: You have said that, at God's command, you have continually worn men's clothes, and that you have put on a short robe, doublet, shoes attached by points, also that you have had short hair, cut around above the ears, without retaining anything on your person which shows that you are a woman, and that several times you have received the body of Our Lord dressed in this fashion, despite having been admonished to give it up several times, the which you would not do. You have said that you would rather die than abandon the said clothing, if it were not at God's command, and that if you were wearing those clothes and were with the king, and those of your party, it would be one of the greatest benefits for the kingdom of France. You have also said that not for anything would you swear an oath not to wear the said clothing and carry arms any longer. And all these things you say you have done for the good and at the command of God. As for these things, the clerics say that you blaspheme God and hold him in contempt in his sacraments; you transgress Divine Law, Holy Scripture, and canon law. You err in the faith. You boast in vanity. You are suspected of idolatry and you have condemned yourself in not wishing to wear clothing suitable to your sex, but you follow the custom of Gentiles and Saracens.

Source: Carolyne Larrington, ed. and trans., *Women and Writing in Medieval Europe* (New York: 1995), pp. 183–84.

Questions for Analysis

1. Paris was in the hands of the English when this condemnation was issued. Is there any evidence that its authors were coerced into making this pronouncement?

2. On what grounds was Joan condemned for heresy?

3. In what ways does Joan's behavior highlight larger trends in late medieval spirituality and popular piety?

Henry VI, proved to be first incompetent and then insane. Finally, a series of French victories culminated in the capture of Bordeaux. After 1453, English control over French territory was limited to the port of Calais on the French coast of the English Channel.

THE LONG SHADOW OF THE HUNDRED YEARS' WAR

The Hundred Years' War challenged the very existence of France. The disintegration of that kingdom—first during the 1350s and 1360s, and again between 1415 and 1435—glaringly revealed the fragility of the bonds that tied the king to his people and the royal capital to the kingdom's outlying regions. Yet the king's power had increased by the war's end, laying the foundations on which the power of the French state would be built.

The Hundred Years' War also had dramatic effects on the English monarchy. When English armies in France were successful, the king rode a wave of popularity that fueled an emerging sense of English identity. When the war turned against them, defeats abroad undermined support for the monarch at home. This was a consequence of England's peculiar form of kingship, whose strength depended on the king's ability to mobilize popular support through Parliament while maintaining the support of his nobility through successful wars. Failure to maintain this balance was even more destabilizing in England than it would have been elsewhere, precisely because royal power was so centralized.

In France, the nobility could endure the insanity of Charles VI because his government was not powerful enough to threaten them. In England, by contrast, neither the nobility nor the nation could afford the weak kingship of Henry VI. The result was an aristocratic rebellion that led to a full-blown civil war: the Wars of the Roses, so called because of the floral emblems (red and white) adopted by the two competing noble families, Lancaster and York. It ended only when a Lancastrian claimant, Henry Tudor (r. 1485–1509), resolved the dynastic feud by marrying Elizabeth of York and ruling as Henry VII, establishing a new dynasty whose symbol was a rose with both white and red petals. His second son would become Henry VIII (see Chapter 13).

In spite of England's ultimate defeat, the Hundred Years' War strengthened English identity in several ways. First, it equated national belonging with the power of the state and its king. Second, it fomented a strong anti-French sentiment that led to the triumph of the English language over French for the first time since the Norman Conquest, over 300 years earlier; the first royal court to speak English was that of Richard II, a patron of Geoffrey Chaucer. And having lost its continental possessions, England became a self-contained island nation that looked to the sea for defense and opportunity—not to the Continent.

CONFLICT IN ITALY AND THE HOLY ROMAN EMPIRE

Elsewhere, the perpetual warfare that began to characterize the history of Europe during this period was even more destructive. In northern and central Italy, the second half of the fourteenth century was marked by incessant conflict. With the papacy based in Avignon, Rome was torn by factional violence. Warfare

An emerging sense of English identity built on (1) power of state and king and (2) dominance of English language

among northern Italian city-states was constant. Finally, around 1400, Venice, Milan, and Florence succeeded in stabilizing their differing forms of government: Venice was now ruled by an oligarchy of merchants; Milan by a family of despots; and Florence was ruled as a republic but dominated by the influence of a few wealthy clans, especially the Medici banking family. These three cities then began to expand their influence by subordinating other cities to their rule.

Italian city-states consolidate rule and expand territorial control

Eventually, almost all the towns of northern Italy were allied with one or another of these powers. An exception was Genoa, which had its own trading empire in the Mediterranean and Atlantic (Chapter 10). The papacy, meanwhile, reasserted its control over central Italy after its return to Rome in 1377. The southern kingdom of Naples persisted as a separate entity, but a constantly unstable one. After 1453, when the Hundred Years' War had ended and Ottoman expansion had temporarily halted, an uneasy peace was achieved.

In the lands of the Holy Roman Empire, meanwhile, armed conflict among territorial princes significantly weakened all combatants. Periodically, a powerful emperor would emerge to play a role, but the dominant trend was toward the continuing disintegration of power, with German princes dividing their territories among their heirs while free cities and local lords strove to shake off the princes' rule. Only in the eastern regions of the empire were the rulers of Bavaria, Austria, and Brandenburg-Prussia able to strengthen their authority, by supporting the nobility's efforts to subjugate the peasants and colonizing new territories on their eastern frontiers.

In German lands, political power mostly fragmentary

THE FLOURISHING OF EASTERN EUROPE

During the thirteenth century (Chapter 9), Poland had been culturally and economically enriched by its willingness to welcome the Jewish communities that were being expelled from other parts of Europe. In the fourteenth century, Polish towns also benefited from a wave of German immigrants, mostly merchants, with ties to the Hanseatic League and to independent cities in the Holy Roman Empire. In order to attract and accommodate these newcomers, the rulers of Poland and other eastern European kingdoms granted special charters to the towns in which they settled. These charters granted citizens the rights of self-governance, collectively known as Magdeburg Law (named after a major German city).

In the centuries after the Black Death, more and more towns and villages were able to take advantage of these privileges, promoting the rapid urbanization of the once rural region of eastern Europe and creating a web of prosperous and diverse cities that generated enormous wealth. Lviv, now in western Ukraine, is a splendid example: ruled by Polish kings and governed by German town law, it fostered a large population of Armenians, Jews, Serbians, and Hungarians, among many others.

Alongside the commercial benefits of these burgeoning towns were the intellectual benefits. Just as medieval universities flourished in western Europe during the economic boom of the twelfth century, they now came to be established in central and eastern Europe, too. The first was founded in the Bohemian capital of Prague in 1347, by Emperor Charles IV. The Polish king Casimir III (r. 1333–1370) followed his lead by establishing a fledgling university in Kraków in 1364. Universities in Vienna and Pécs (Hungary) were also established in the next few years. The university at Kraków soon came to be known as the Jagiellonian University, after the new dynasty that endowed it as a permanent institution.

KING JADWIGA OF POLAND AND THE JAGIELLONIAN DYNASTY

The Jagiellonian dynasty was formed when the young female ruler of Poland, Jadwiga (*yahd-VEE-gah*), married the Grand Duke of Lithuania, Jagiello (*yahg-ee-EL-oh*). It was an extraordinary match. Jadwiga had been crowned king (not queen) in 1384, when she was barely ten years old. The Polish lords who acted as her advisers had insisted on the title because they did not want to see her eventual husband ruling over them. In search of a suitable match, they turned their gaze to the neighboring northern territory of Lithuania, which would give Poland more access to the Baltic Sea and more support against ongoing encroachments from the east by the Teutonic Knights of Prussia. Jadwiga agreed to the match, even though Duke Jagiello was thirty years her senior—and the last pagan ruler in Europe. They were married after Jagiello's acceptance into the Roman Church in 1386, when he received the baptismal name Wladyslaw (*VWAD-is-laff*).

Jadwiga and Wladyslaw II Jagiello ruled their realms jointly, tripling the size of Poland-Lithuania and making it the largest and most powerful state in central Europe. Their patronage of the new university at Kraków turned it into one of Europe's intellectual powerhouses: it would later nurture such great Polish scholars as Nicolaus Copernicus (1473–1543) (see Chapter 16). Jadwiga also promoted Polish as a literary language, encouraging the translation of the Bible into the vernacular. When she died in 1399, in the course of a difficult childbirth, her husband married the wife she had chosen for him. In 1997, she was canonized as a saint of the Catholic Church.

THE ROYAL CHAPEL OF KING WLADYSLAW II JAGIELLO. This image captures only some of the hundreds of magnificent paintings that decorate the walls of the chapel in Lublin (Poland). This cycle of frescoes, which depict scenes from the Bible, was commissioned by King Jagiello after the death of his royal wife Jadwiga. The paintings, completed in 1418, were executed by a team of master artists from Ukraine, who combined eastern Orthodox imagery and styles with those of western Europe. › **Based on what you have learned about Jagiello, why would he have chosen to decorate his chapel in this way?**

THE EMERGENCE OF NATIONAL MONARCHIES

In France, England, Poland, Hungary, and in smaller kingdoms such as Scotland and Portugal, the later Middle Ages saw the growth of more cohesive states than any that had existed before. The political patterns established in the formative twelfth and thirteenth centuries had made this possible, yet the active construction of a sense of shared identity in these territories, and the fusion of that identity with kingship, were new phenomena. Fueled by the growing cultural importance of vernacular languages, this fusion produced a new type of political organization: the national monarchy.

The advantages of a national monarchy over older forms of political organization—such as the empire, the principality, or the city-state—are significant. But the new national monarchies brought significant disadvantages, too. They guaranteed the prevalence of warfare in Europe as they continued their struggles for sovereignty and territory. Eventually, they would export their rivalry through imperial ventures in Africa and the New World. While a shared feeling of belonging to a nation can be extremely positive, it can also be poisoned or undermined if one ethnic group, or one region, claims superiority over others.

Challenges to the Roman Church

The century after the Black Death witnessed the papacy's return to Rome, but it also witnessed changes that would have far-reaching consequences. After almost seventy years of exile, the Church was now riven by a debilitating forty-year schism and faced a protracted battle with reformers who sought to reduce the pope's role in Church governance. While the papacy won this battle in the short term, the renewed abuse of papal power would, in the long run, bring about the permanent schism of the Reformation (see Chapter 13).

THE GREAT WESTERN SCHISM

In the decades after the plague, calls for the papacy's return to Rome grew more insistent. It was eventually brought about by the letter-writing campaign of the nun and mystic Catherine of Siena (1347–1380), whose teasing but pious missives to Gregory XI (r. 1370–1378) alternately shamed and coerced him. In 1377, he was persuaded to make the move.

But the papacy's restoration in Rome was short-lived. A year after Gregory's return, he died. His cardinals—many of them Frenchmen—then struggled to interpret the wishes of the volatile Romans, whose habit of expressing themselves through violence was unsettling to outsiders. Later, the cardinals would claim that they had unwillingly capitulated to the Roman mob when they elected an Italian candidate, Urban VI. When Urban fell out with them, the cardinals fled the city and, from a safe distance, declared his reign invalid because they had elected him under duress. They then elected a new pope, a Frenchman who took the name Clement VII. Urban retaliated by naming a new and entirely Italian College of Cardinals. The French pope and his cardinals withdrew ignominiously to the papal palace in Avignon, while the Italian pope remained in Rome.

The resulting rift is known as the **Great Schism** (or, more specifically, the Great Western Schism, to distinguish it from the East–West Schism between the Roman and Orthodox Churches). Between 1378 and 1417, the Roman Church was divided between two—and, ultimately, three—competing papacies, each claiming to be legitimate and each denouncing the heresy of the others. Europe's religious allegiances largely fractured along political lines drawn by the ongoing Hundred Years' War: France and its allies Scotland, Castile, Aragon, and Naples recognized the pope in Avignon; England, Germany, northern Italy, Scandinavia, Bohemia, Poland, and Hungary recognized the Roman pope.

There was no obvious way to end this impasse, and the two rival Colleges of Cardinals continued to elect successors every time a pope died, perpetuating the problem. Finally, in 1409, some cardinals from both camps met at Pisa, where they ceremonially declared the deposition of both popes and named a new one from among their number. But neither of the popes reigning in Rome and Avignon accepted that decision, and there were now three rival popes excommunicating each other instead of two.

Great Schism (1378–1417) Also known as the Great Western Schism, to distinguish it from the longstanding rupture between the Greek East and Latin West. During the schism, the Roman Church was divided between two (and, ultimately, three) competing popes. Each pope claimed to be legitimate and each denounced the heresy of the others.

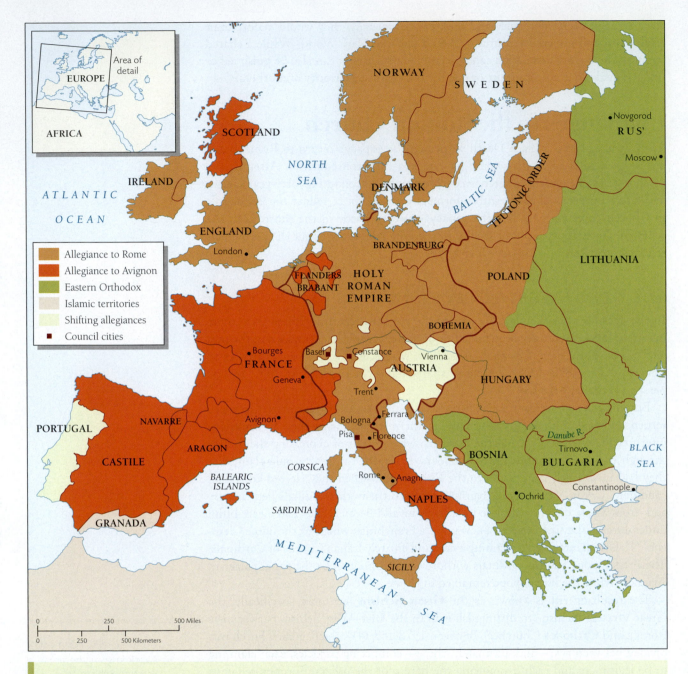

THE GREAT SCHISM, 1378–1417. During the Great Western Schism, the various territories of Europe were divided in their allegiances. › **According to the map key, what choices were the peoples of these regions making?** › **What common interests would have united the supporters of the Avignon pope or of the Roman pope?** › **Why would areas such as Portugal and Austria waver in their support?**

THE COUNCIL OF CONSTANCE AND THE FAILURE OF THE CONCILIAR MOVEMENT

This debacle was ultimately addressed between 1414 and 1418 at the **Council of Constance**, the largest and longest ecclesiastical gathering since the Council of Nicaea more than a thousand years before (Chapter 6). Its chief mission was to remove all rival claimants for papal office before agreeing on the election of a new pope, an Italian who took the name Martin V. But many of the council's delegates had even farther-reaching plans for the reform of the Church, ambitions that stemmed from the legal doctrine that gave the council the power to depose and elect popes in the first place.

This doctrine, known as **conciliarism**, holds that supreme authority within the Church rests not with the pope but with a representative general council. The delegates at Constance thus decreed that general councils should meet regularly to oversee the governance of the Church and to act as a check on the unbridled abuse of papal power. Had conciliarism triumphed, the Reformation of the following century might not have occurred.

But, perhaps predictably, Martin V and his successors did everything they could to undermine this doctrine, precisely because it limited their power. When the next general council met at Siena in 1423, Pope Martin duly sent representatives—who then turned around and went back to Rome. (The Council of Constance had specified that councils must meet frequently, but had not specified how long they should last.) A lengthy struggle for power ensued between the advocates of papal monarchy and the conciliarists. Twenty-five years later, in 1449, the Council of Basel dissolved itself, bringing an end to a radical experiment in conciliar government—and dashing the hopes of an internal reformation that would keep the Roman Church intact.

SPIRITUAL CHALLENGES

The spiritual and social lives of medieval Christians were inextricably intertwined; indeed, any distinction between the two would have made little sense to most people of the time. The parish church stood literally at the center of their lives. Churchyards were communal meeting places, sometimes even the sites of markets; church buildings were a refuge from attack and a gathering place for parish business; church's holidays marked the passage of the year; and church's bells marked the hours of the day. The church was holy, but it was also essential to daily life.

Yet, in the wake of the Black Death, many parishes ceased to exist because so many communities were decimated. And increasingly, medieval Christians were not satisfied with the conventional practices and forms of piety. As Joan of Arc's predicament reveals, medieval women found it particularly challenging to find outlets for their faith that would not earn them the condemnation of the Church. Executed as a heretic, Joan was officially exonerated a generation later; but she would not be canonized as a saint until 1920.

Many women therefore internalized their devotional practices or confined them to the domestic sphere—sometimes to the inconvenience of their families and communities. The young Catherine of Siena, the one who later convinced the pope to return to Rome, refused to help with the housework or to support her working-class family; instead, she took over one of the house's two rooms for her private prayers, confining her parents and a dozen siblings to the remaining room. Julian of Norwich (1342–1416) withdrew from the world into a small cell built next to her local church, where she spent the rest of her life in prayer and contemplation. Her younger contemporary, the housewife Margery Kempe (c. 1372–c. 1439), resented the fact that she could not take such a step because she had a husband, numerous children, and a household to support. In later life, she renounced her domestic duties and devoted

Council of Constance (1414–1418) A meeting of clergy and theologians in an effort to resolve the Great Schism within the Roman Church. The council deposed all rival papal candidates and elected a new pope, Martin V, but it also adopted the doctrine of conciliarism.

conciliarism Adopted during the Council of Constance, this legal doctrine decreed that the supreme authority within the Church rests not with the pope but with a representative general council.

In medieval Europe, the church was an engine of holy life

Council or Pope?

The Great Schism spurred a fundamental and far-reaching debate about the nature of authority within the Church. Arguments for papal supremacy rested on traditional claims that the popes were the successors of Saint Peter, to whom Jesus Christ had delegated his own authority. Arguments for the supremacy of a general council had been advanced by many intellectuals throughout the fourteenth century, but it was only during the circumstances of the schism that these arguments found a wide audience. The following documents trace the history of the controversy, from the declaration of conciliar supremacy at the Council of Constance (Haec Sancta Synodus), to the council's efforts to guarantee regular meetings of general councils thereafter (Frequens), to the papal condemnation of appeals to the authority of general councils issued in 1460 (Execrabilis).

Haec Sancta Synodus (1415)

This holy synod of Constance . . . declares that being lawfully assembled in the Holy Spirit, constituting a general council and representing the Catholic Church Militant, it has its power directly from Christ, and that all persons of whatever rank or dignity, even a Pope, are bound to obey it in matters relating to faith and the end of the Schism and the general reformation of the church of God in head and members.

Further, it declares that any person of whatever position, rank, or dignity, even a Pope, who contumaciously refuses to obey the mandates, statutes, ordinances, or regulations enacted or to be enacted by this holy synod, or by any other general council lawfully assembled, relating to the matters aforesaid or to other matters involved with them, shall, unless he repents, be . . . duly punished.

Source: L. R. Loomis, ed. and trans., *The Council of Constance* (New York: 1961), p. 229.

Frequens (1417)

The frequent holding of general councils is the best method of cultivating the field of the Lord, for they root out the briars, thorns, and thistles of heresies, errors, and schisms, correct abuses, make crooked things straight, and prepare the Lord's vineyard for fruitfulness and rich fer-tility. Neglect of general councils sows the seeds of these evils and encourages their growth. This truth is borne in upon us as we recall times past and survey the present.

Therefore by perpetual edict we . . . ordain that henceforth general councils shall be held as follows:

her life to performing acts of histrionic piety that alienated many of those who came into contact with her. For example, she was so moved by the contemplation of Jesus' sufferings on the cross that she would cry hysterically for hours, disrupting the Mass; and when on a pilgrimage in Rome, she cried at the sight of babies that reminded her of the infant Jesus or young men whom she thought resembled him.

The extraordinary piety of such individuals could be inspiring, but it could also threaten the Church's control and the links that bound individuals to their communities. It could, therefore, be regarded as dangerous. More safely orthodox was the practical mysticism preached by Thomas à Kempis, whose *Imitation of Christ* (c. 1427) the first within the five years immediately following the end of the present council, the second within seven years from the end of the council next after this, and subsequently every ten years forever. . . . Thus there will always be a certain continuity. Either a council will be in session or one will be expected at the end of a fixed period.

Source: L. R. Loomis, ed. and trans., *The Council of Constance* (New York: 1961), pp. 246–47.

Execrabilis (1460)

An execrable abuse, unheard of in earlier times, has sprung up in our period. Some men, imbued with a spirit of rebellion and moved not by a desire for sound decisions but rather by a desire to escape the punishment for sin, suppose that they can appeal from the Pope, Vicar of Jesus Christ—from the Pope, to whom in the person of blessed Peter it was said, "Feed my sheep" and "whatever you bind on earth will be bound in heaven"—from this Pope to a future council. How harmful this is to the Christian republic, as well as how contrary to canon law, anyone who is not ignorant of the law can understand. For . . . who would not consider it ridiculous to appeal to something which does not now exist anywhere nor does anyone know when it will exist? The poor are heavily oppressed by the powerful, offenses remain unpunished, rebellion against the Holy See is encouraged, license for sin is granted, and all ecclesiastical discipline and hierarchical ranking of the Church are turned upside down.

Wishing therefore to expel this deadly poison from the Church of Christ, and concerned with the salvation of the sheep committed to us . . . with the counsel and assent of our venerable brothers, the Cardinals of the Holy Roman Church, together with the counsel and assent of all those prelates who have been trained in canon and civil law who follow our Court, and with our own certain knowledge, we condemn appeals of this kind, reject them as erroneous and abominable, and declare them to be completely null and void. And we lay down that from now on, no one should dare . . . to make such an appeal from our decisions, be they legal or theological, or from any commands at all from us or our successors.

Source: Reprinted by permission of the publisher from Gabriel Biel, *Defensorium Obedientiae Apostolicae et Alia Documenta*, ed. and trans. Heiko A. Oberman, Daniel E. Zerfoss, and William J. Courtenay (Cambridge, MA: 1968), pp. 224–27. Copyright © 1968 by the President and Fellows of Harvard College.

Questions for Analysis

1. On what grounds does *Haec Sancta Synodus* establish the authority of a council? Why would this be considered a threat to papal power?

2. Why did the Council of Constance consider it necessary for councils to meet regularly (*Frequens*)? What might have been the logical consequences of such regular meetings?

3. On what grounds does *Execrabilis* condemn the appeals to future councils that have no specified meeting date? Why would it not have condemned the conciliar movement altogether?

taught readers how to appreciate aspects of the divine in their everyday lives. Originally written in Latin, it was quickly translated into many vernacular languages and is now more widely read than any other Christian book except the Bible.

POPULAR AND INTELLECTUAL REFORMERS

For the most part, the threat of dissenting movements was less dangerous to the Church than the corruption of the papacy. But in the kingdoms of England, Bohemia (the modern Czech Republic), and Poland,

WYCLIFFE'S ENGLISH BIBLE. Although John Wycliffe was not directly responsible for this translation of the Bible, it was made in the later fourteenth century by his followers. Written in the same Middle English vernacular that Geoffrey Chaucer used for his popular works, it was designed to be accessible to lay readers who did not understand Latin. This page shows the beginning of the Gospel of Mark: "The byg*yn*-/nyng of Þe gos-/pel of Ihesu Crist/Þe sone of god. . . ." (Note that the old English letter Þ stands for *th*.) › **What might have been the impact of this translation on readers and listeners in the late fourteenth century? › How would this English Bible have helped to further the reforming efforts of Wycliffe and his disciples?**

some reform movements posed serious challenges because they were galvanized by respected intellectuals. In Poland, a professor at the new Jagiellonian University in Kraków, Paulus Vladimiri (Pawel Wlodkowic; c. 1370–1435), wrote a treatise that criticized papal and imperial efforts to convert the peoples of eastern Europe and the Baltic by force, through their support of the Teutonic Knights. He argued that the violence could not be justified, and that pagans and Christians could coexist in peace. He advanced these radical arguments as the Polish representative to the Council of Constance.

The Oxford theologian **John Wycliffe** (c. 1330–1384) was a central figure in both the English and Bohemian reform movements. A survivor of the Black Death and an outspoken critic of the papacy, he asserted that the empty sacraments of a corrupt Church could not save anyone, and therefore urged the English king to confiscate ecclesiastical wealth and to replace decadent priests and bishops with men who would live according to apostolic standards of poverty and piety.

Some of Wycliffe's followers went even further, dismissing the sacraments as fraudulent attempts to extort money from the faithful. These preachers advocated for direct access to the scriptures and promoted an English translation of the Bible sponsored by Wycliffe himself. Wycliffe's teachings also played an important role in the Peasants' Revolt of 1381, and his movement was even supported by a number of aristocratic families. But after a failed uprising in 1414, both the movement and its supporters went underground.

In Bohemia and other regions of central Europe, Wycliffe's ideas lived on and put down even deeper roots. They were powerfully adopted by **Jan Hus** (c. 1373–1415), a charismatic teacher at the Charles University in Prague. In contrast to English followers of Wycliffe, Hus emphasized the centrality of the Eucharist to Christian piety. Indeed, he demanded that the laity be allowed to receive not only the consecrated bread but also the consecrated wine, which was usually reserved for priests. This demand became a rallying cry for the Hussite movement. Influential nobles also supported Hus, partly in the hope that reforms might restore revenues they had lost to the Church over the previous century.

Accordingly, most of Bohemia was behind him when Hus traveled to the Council of Constance to publish his views and urge the assembled delegates to undertake sweeping reforms. But instead, the other delegates convicted Hus of heresy and had him burned at the stake. Back home, Hus's supporters raised the banner of open revolt, and the aristocracy took advantage of the situation to seize Church property. Between 1420 and 1424, armed bands of fervent Hussites resoundingly defeated several armies, as priests, artisans, and peasants rallied to pursue Hus's goals of religious reform and social justice.

These victories increased popular fervor, but they also made radical reformers increasingly volatile. Accordingly, in 1434, a more conservative arm of the Hussite movement was able to negotiate a settlement with the Bohemian church. By the terms of this settlement, Bohemians could receive both the bread and the wine of the Mass, which thus placed them beyond the pale of Latin orthodoxy and effectively separated the Bohemian national church from the Church of Rome.

English and Czech reforming efforts exhibit a number of striking similarities. Both began in universities and then spread to the countryside, both called for the clergy to live in simplicity and poverty, and both attracted noble support. Both movements also employed their own vernacular languages (English and Czech), and both relied on vernacular preaching and social activism. In all these respects, they established patterns that would emerge again in the vastly larger currents of the Protestant Reformation (see Chapter 13).

THE TEACHINGS OF JAN HUS. An eloquent religious reformer, Jan Hus was burned at the stake in 1415 after he was found guilty of heresy at the Council of Constance. This lavishly illustrated booklet of his teachings was published over a century later in his native Bohemia and includes texts in the Czech vernacular and in Latin. › **What does this booklet's later publication suggest about how Hus's image and theology were put to use during the Protestant Reformation?**

Jan Hus (c. 1373–1415) A Czech reformer who adopted many of the teachings of the English theologian John Wycliffe, and who also demanded that the laity be allowed to receive both the consecrated bread and wine of the Eucharist.

Conclusion

The century after the Black Death was a period of tremendous creativity and revolutionary change. The effects of the plague were catastrophic, but the resulting food surpluses, opportunities, and experimentation opened up broad avenues for advancement. Europe's economy diversified and expanded, while increasing wealth and access to education produced new forms of art and new ways of looking at the world. Women were still excluded from formal schooling, but nevertheless they became active—and in many cases dominant—participants in literary endeavors, cultural life, and religious movements. Average men and women not only became more active in cultivating their own worldly goals, they also took control of their spiritual destinies at a time when the institutional Church provided little inspiring leadership.

Meanwhile, some states were growing stronger and more competitive, whereas other regions remained deeply divided. The rising Ottoman Empire eventually absorbed many of the oldest territories of Western civilizations, including the venerable Muslim caliphate at Baghdad, the western portions of the former Mongolian Empire, the Christian Balkans and Greece, and—above all—the surviving core of the eastern Roman Empire at Constantinople. As a result, Greek-speaking refugees streamed into

AFTER YOU READ THIS CHAPTER

CHRONOLOGY

1304–1374	Lifetime of Petrarch
1351	Black Death at its height
	The English Parliament passes the Statute of Laborers
1377	The papacy returns to Rome from Avignon
1378	The Great Schism begins
1381	Rebellions culminate in the English Peasants' Revolt
1414–1418	The Council of Constance is convened to end the Great Schism
	Jan Hus burned at the stake in 1415
1429–1431	The career of Joan of Arc
1431–1449	The Council of Basel fails to check papal power
1440	Lorenzo Valla debunks "The Donation of Constantine"
1453	The Hundred Years' War ends
	Constantinople falls to the Ottoman Turks

REVIEWING THE OBJECTIVES

› The Black Death had short- and long-term effects on the economy and societies of Europe. What were some of the most important changes?

› The later "Middle Ages" and the "Renaissance" are often perceived to be two different periods, but the latter was actually part of the former. Explain why.

› What were some of the intellectual, cultural, and artistic innovations of this era in Italy and elsewhere in Europe?

› How did some European kingdoms become stronger and more centralized during this period? What were some examples of national monarchies?

› How did the conciliar movement seek to limit the power of the papacy? Why was this movement unsuccessful?

Italy, many bringing with them classic works of Greek philosophy and literature hitherto unknown in western Europe. Fueled by new ideas and a fervid nostalgia for the ancient past, Italians began to experiment with new ways of reading ancient texts, advocating a return to classical models while at the same time trying to counter the political and cultural authority of the more powerful kingdoms north of the Alps.

In contrast to Italy, these emerging national monarchies cultivated shared identity through the promotion of a common vernacular language and allegiance to a strong, more centralized state. These tactics allowed kingdoms such as Poland and Scotland to increase their territories and influence, and also led France and England into an epic battle for sovereignty and hegemony. The result, in all cases, was the escalation of armed conflict as incessant warfare drove more powerful governments to harvest a larger percentage of their subjects' wealth through taxation, which they proceeded to invest in ships, guns, and the standing armies made possible by new technologies and more effective administration.

In short, the generations that survived the calamities of famine, plague, and warfare seized the opportunities their new world presented. In the latter half of the fifteenth century, they stood on the verge of an extraordinary period of expansion and conquest that enabled them to dominate the globe.

 Go to **INQUIZITIVE** to see what you've learned—and learn what you've missed—with personalized feedback along the way.

PEOPLE, IDEAS, AND EVENTS IN CONTEXT

› Compare and contrast the **BLACK DEATH**'s effects on rural and urban areas.

› In what ways do rebellions such as the **ENGLISH PEASANTS' REVOLT** reflect the changes brought about by the plague? How do the works of **GIOVANNI BOCCACCIO, GEOFFREY CHAUCER**, and **CHRISTINE DE PIZAN** exemplify the culture of this era?

› What was **HUMANISM**? How was it related to the artistic and intellectual movement known as the **RENAISSANCE**?

› How did the **OTTOMAN EMPIRE** come to power? What were some of the consequences of its rise?

› What new military technologies were deployed during the **HUNDRED YEARS' WAR**? How did this conflict affect other parts of Europe, beyond England and France? What role did **JOAN OF ARC** play?

› How did the **COUNCIL OF CONSTANCE** respond to the crisis of the **GREAT SCHISM**?

› Why did **CONCILIARISM** fail? How did **JOHN WYCLIFFE** and **JAN HUS** seek to reform the Church?

THINKING ABOUT CONNECTIONS

› In the year 2000, a group of historians was asked to identify the most significant historical figure of the past millennium. Rather than selecting a person (e.g., Martin Luther, Shakespeare, Napoleon, Adolf Hitler), they chose the microbe *Yersinia pestis,* which caused the Black Death. Do you agree with this assessment? Why or why not?

› In your view, which was more crucial to the formation of the modern state: the political and legal developments surveyed in Chapter 9 or the emergence of national identities discussed in this chapter? Why?

› Given what we have learned about the history of the Roman Church, do you think the conciliar movement was doomed to fail? Why or why not? How far back do we need to go to trace the development of disputes over ecclesiastical governance?

12

Innovation and Exploration, 1453–1533

WHAT IF EXACT COPIES of an idea could circulate quickly, all over the world? What if the same could be done for the latest news, the most beautiful poems, or the most exciting discoveries? It would do for knowledge what the invention of coinage did for wealth, making it portable and easier to disseminate. Indeed, it's no accident that the man who developed such a technology, **Johannes Gutenberg** of Mainz (c. 1398–1468), was the son of a goldsmith who made coins: metal disks stamped with identical words and images impressed by a reusable matrix. In similar fashion, the pages of the first printed books were stamped with ink spread on rows of movable type (lead or cast-iron letter forms and punctuation marks) slotted into frames to form lines of words. Once a set of pages was ready, a **printing press** could make hundreds of copies in a matter of hours, many hundreds of times faster than the same page being copied by hand.

A major stimulus for this invention was the availability of paper, which became more widespread in Europe during the late thirteenth century. Made from rags turned into pulp by mills, paper was both cheaper and far easier to use than parchment. Accordingly, books became cheaper and written communication even more common. Growing levels of literacy then led to a growing demand for books, which in turn led to Gutenberg's breakthrough of the 1450s. By 1455, his workshop had printed multiple copies of the Latin Bible (of which forty-eight complete or partial volumes survive).

BEFORE YOU READ THIS CHAPTER

❯ The invention of the printing press enabled the widespread dissemination of information, including reports on the riches of the New World.

❯ Competition for power in Italy led to increased violence as well as to increased artistic patronage, providing opportunities to a new breed of Renaissance men.

❯ The humanist approach to education that had developed in Italy spread to other parts of Europe, influencing new approaches to biblical scholarship and new political philosophies.

❯ Spain, the newest and most powerful European state, completed its "reconquest" of the Iberian Peninsula in 1492 and then looked to counter the successful colonial ventures of the Portuguese. This led to the early beginnings of a Spanish Empire in the Americas.

CORE OBJECTIVES

❯ **UNDERSTAND** the relationship between Renaissance ideals and the political and economic realities of Italy.

❯ **IDENTIFY** the key characteristics of Renaissance arts and learning during this period.

❯ **DEFINE** the term *reconquista* and its meaning in Spain.

❯ **DESCRIBE** the methods and motives of European colonization during this period.

❯ **EXPLAIN** why Europeans were able to dominate the peoples of the New World.

Refugees from Ottoman conquest bring ancient Greek texts to Europe

Although printing never entirely replaced traditional modes of manuscript publication, it revolutionized the spread of information.

In fact, the printing press played a crucial role in many of the developments that we will study in this chapter. The artistic and intellectual experiments of the Italian Renaissance were rapidly exported to other parts of Europe. Plans for innovative weapons were printed on the same presses that churned out humanist writings. News of Columbus's first voyage and the subsequent conquests of the Americas would spread via the same medium. Printing not only increased the volume and rapidity of communication, it made it more difficult for those in power to censor dissenting opinions. The printing press also made it possible for rulers to govern growing empires abroad and increasingly centralized states at home. The "reconquest" of Spain and the extension of Spanish imperialism to the New World were both facilitated by printed propaganda. Printing even helped standardize languages by enabling governments to promote one official dialect over others: hence "the king's English," the language spoken around London, was imposed throughout the English realm and contributed to the growth of a common linguistic and national identity.

Renaissance Ideals—and Realities

The intellectual movement that began in Italy during the fourteenth century was, as we noted in Chapter 11, characterized by an intense interest in the classical past and a new type of educational program known as humanism. This movement was extended and diversified in the later fifteenth century: by the time the Ottoman conquest of Constantinople was complete, just a year or so before Gutenberg's invention, hundreds of refugees had brought precious manuscripts of Greek texts to Europe, such as the epics of Homer and the dialogues of Plato. Prior to the invention of print, such manuscripts could be owned and studied by only a very few. Now, printers in Venice and other cities rushed to produce cheap editions of classical texts, as well as Greek grammars and glossaries that could facilitate reading them.

Within a few decades, an informal "Platonic Academy" had formed in Florence, fostered by the patronage of the wealthy Cosimo de' Medici. Based on his reading of Plato, the philosopher Marsilio Ficino (1433–1499) moved away from the focus on civic life that had been such a feature of earlier humanist thought. Instead, he taught that the individual man should work to free his immortal soul from its "always miserable" mortal body—a Platonic idea very compatible with late-medieval Christian piety. Ficino's translation of Plato's works into Latin made them widely accessible—again, thanks to the medium of print. His disciple, Giovanni Pico della Mirandola (1463–1494), also rejected the everyday world of public affairs and took an even more exalted view of man's intellectual and artistic capacities, arguing that man (but not woman) could aspire to union with God through the exercise of his unique talents.

THE POLITICS OF ITALY AND THE PHILOSOPHY OF MACHIAVELLI

But not all Florentines were galvanized by Platonic ideals. The most influential author of this era was a thoroughgoing realist who spent more time studying ancient Roman history than Greek philosophy: **Niccolò Machiavelli** (1469–1527).

THE SPREAD OF PRINTING

Area of detail
EUROPE
AFRICA

NORWAY

SWEDEN

Stockholm
1483

TEUTONIC
ORDER

BALTIC SEA

SCOTLAND

Edinburgh
1507

NORTH
SEA

DENMARK

Copenhagen
1490

Odense
1482

Danzig
1499

Elbe R.

Vistula R.

Warsaw
1580

Dublin
1551

ENGLAND

POLAND

Thames R.

London
1492

Westminster
1476

Utrecht
1470

Brussels
1475

Cologne
1465

Rhine R.

Leipzig
1481

Prague
1487

Wrocław
1475

Kraków
1474

Lviv
1593

HOLY ROMAN EMPIRE

Dniester R.

ATLANTIC
OCEAN

Paris
1470

Seine R.

Eltville
1467

Mainz
1450

Bamberg
1460

Pilsen
1468

Nuremberg
1470

Strasbourg
1458

Danube R.

Basel
1468

Beromünster
1470

Augsburg
1468

AUSTRIA

Vienna
1482

Buda
1472

HUNGARY

FRANCE

SWITZERLAND

Loire R.

Lyons
1473

Milan
1471

Venice
1469

VENETIAN EMPIRE

ADRIATIC SEA

OTTOMAN
EMPIRE

Rhône R.

Florence
1482

PAPAL
STATES

CORSICA

Rome
1467

PORTUGAL

SPAIN

Valencia
1474

SARDINIA

Naples
1471

KINGDOM
OF TWO
SICILIES

Lisbon
1489

Seville
1478

BALEARIC ISLANDS

MEDITERRANEAN
SEA

0   100   200   300 Miles
0 100 200 300 Kilometers

THE SPREAD
OF PRINTING

■ Up until 1470
■ 1471–1500
■ 1501–1600

THE SPREAD OF PRINTING. This map shows how quickly the technology of printing spread throughout Europe between 1470 and 1600. › In what regions were printing presses most heavily concentrated? › What factors may have led to their proliferation in the Low Countries, northern Italy, and central Europe—compared with France, Spain, and England? › Why would so many presses have been located along waterways?

Printing, Patriotism, and the Past

The printing press helped to create new communities of readers by standardizing national languages and even promoting patriotism. And even as it enabled authors of new works to reach larger audiences, it also allowed printers to popularize older writings that had previously circulated in manuscript. The two sources presented here exemplify two aspects of this trend. The first is a preface by William Caxton of London, a printer who specialized in publishing books that glorified England's history and heritage. The preface is to a version of the legend of King Arthur, originally written by the English soldier Sir Thomas Malory, who completed it in 1470. It was printed for the first time in 1485 and quickly became a bestseller. The second excerpt is from the concluding chapter of Machiavelli's treatise The Prince. *Like the book itself, these remarks were originally addressed to Lorenzo de' Medici, head of Florence's most powerful family. But when* The Prince *was printed in 1532, five years after Machiavelli's death, the author's passionate denunciation of foreign "barbarians" and his lament for Italy's lost glory resonated with a wider Italian-speaking public.*

William Caxton's preface to Thomas Malory's *Le Morte d'Arthur* ("The Death of Arthur"; printed 1485)

After I had accomplished and finished diverse histories, both of contemplation and of other historical and worldly acts of great conquerors and princes, . . . many noble and diverse gentlemen of this realm of England came and demanded why I had not made and imprinted the noble history of the Holy Grail, and of the most renowned Christian king and worthy, King Arthur, which ought most to be remembered among us Englishmen before all other Christian kings. . . . The said noble gentlemen instantly required me to imprint the history of the said noble king and conqueror King Arthur, and of his knights, with the history of the Holy Grail . . . considering that he was a man born within this realm, and king and emperor of the same: and that there be, in French, diverse and many noble volumes of his acts, and also of his knights. To whom I answered that diverse men hold opinion that there was no such Arthur, and that all such books as have been made of him be feigned and fables, because some chronicles make of him no mention. . . . Whereto they answered, and one in special said, that in him that should say or think that there was never such a king called Arthur might well be accounted great folly and blindness. . . . For in all places, Christian and heathen, he is reputed and taken for one of the Nine Worthies, and the first of the three Christian men. And

also, he is more spoken of beyond the sea, and there are more books made of his noble acts than there be in England, as well in Dutch, Italian, Spanish, and Greek, as in French. . . . Wherefore it is a marvel why he is no more renowned in his own country. . . .

Then all these things aforesaid alleged, I could not well deny but that there was such a noble king named Arthur, reputed one of the Nine Worthies, and first and chief of the Christian men. And many noble volumes be made of him and of his noble knights in French, which I have seen and read beyond the sea, which be not had in our maternal tongue. . . . Wherefore, among all such [manuscript] books as have late been drawn out briefly into English I have . . . undertaken to imprint a book of the noble histories of the said King Arthur, and of certain of his knights, after a copy unto me delivered—which copy Sir Thomas Malory did take out of certain books of French, and reduced it into English. And I, according to my copy, have done set it in print, to the intent that noble men may see and learn the noble acts of chivalry, the gentle and virtuous deeds that some knights used in those days, by which they came to honor, and how they that were vicious were punished and oft put to shame and rebuke; humbly beseeching all noble lords and ladies (with all other estates of what estate or degree they be) that shall see and read in this said book and work, that they take the good and honest acts to their remembrance, and follow the same. . . . For herein may be seen noble chivalry, courtesy, humanity, friendliness, hardiness, love, friendship, cowardice, murder, hate, virtue, and sin. Do after the good and leave the evil, and it shall bring you to good fame and renown.

Source: Sir Thomas Malory, *Le Morte d'Arthur* (London: 1485) (text and spelling slightly modernized).

From the conclusion of Niccolò Machiavelli, *The Prince* (completed 1513; printed 1532)

Reflecting in the matters set forth above and considering within myself where the times were propitious in Italy at present to honor a new prince and whether there is at hand the matter suitable for a prudent and virtuous leader to mold in a new form, giving honor to himself and benefit to the citizens of the country, I have arrived at the opinion that all circumstances now favor such a prince, and I cannot think of a time more propitious for him than the present. If, as I said, it was necessary in order to make apparent the virtue of Moses, that the people of Israel should be enslaved in Egypt, and that the Persians should be oppressed by the Medes to provide an opportunity to illustrate the greatness and the spirit of Cyrus, and that the Athenians should be scattered in order to show the excellence of Theseus, thus at the present time, in order to reveal the valor of an Italian spirit, it was essential that Italy should fall to her present low estate, more enslaved than the Hebrews, more servile than the Persians, more disunited than the Athenians, leaderless and lawless, beaten, despoiled, lacerated, overrun and crushed under every kind of misfortune. . . . So Italy now, left almost lifeless, awaits the coming of one who will heal her wounds, putting an end to the sacking and looting in Lombardy and the spoliation and extortions in the Realm of Naples and Tuscany, and cleanse her sores that have been so long festering. Behold how she prays God to send her someone to redeem her from the cruelty and insolence of the barbarians. See how she is ready and willing to follow any banner so long as there be someone to take it up. Nor has she at present any hope of finding her redeemer save only in your illustrious house [the Medici] which has been so highly exalted both by its own merits and by fortune and which has been favored by God and the church, of which it is now ruler. . . .

This opportunity, therefore, should not be allowed to pass, and Italy, after such a long wait, must be allowed to behold her redeemer. I cannot describe the joy with which he will be received in all these provinces which have suffered so much from the foreign deluge, nor with what thirst for vengeance, nor with what firm devotion, what solemn delight, what tears! What gates could be closed to him, what people could deny him obedience, what envy could withstand him, what Italian could withhold allegiance from him? THIS BARBARIAN OCCUPATION STINKS IN THE NOSTRILS OF ALL OF US. Let your illustrious house then take up this cause with the spirit and the hope with which one undertakes a truly just enterprise. . . .

Source: Niccolò Machiavelli, *The Prince*, ed. and trans. Thomas G. Bergin (Arlington Heights, IL: 1947), pp. 75–76, 78.

Questions for Analysis

1. What do these two sources reveal about the relationship between patriotism and the awareness of a nation's past? Why do you think Caxton looks back to a legendary medieval king, whereas Machiavelli's references are all to ancient examples? What do both excerpts reveal about the value placed on history in the popular imagination?

2. How does Caxton describe the process of printing a book? What larger conclusions can we draw from this about the market for printed books in general?

3. Why might Machiavelli's treatise have been made available in a printed version nearly twenty years after its original appearance in manuscript? How might his new audience have responded to its message?

Machiavelli's writings reflect the unstable politics of his home city, as well as his aspirations for a unified Italy that could revive the glory of Rome. We have observed that Italy had been in political disarray for centuries, a situation exacerbated by the "Babylonian Captivity" of the papacy and the controversies raging after its return to Rome (Chapters 10 and 11). Now, Italy was becoming the arena where bloody international struggles were being played out: the kings of France and Spain both had claims to territory there, and both sent invading armies into the peninsula while busily competing for the allegiance of various city-states, which in turn were torn by internal dissension.

In 1498, Machiavelli became a prominent official in a new Florentine republic, founded after a French invasion led to the expulsion of the ruling Medici family. His duties largely involved diplomatic missions to other Italian city-states. He became fascinated by the career of Cesare Borgia (1475–1507), illegitimate son of Pope Alexander VI, who was attempting to create his own principality in central Italy. Machiavelli noted Borgia's ruthlessness and his complete subordination of personal ethics to political ends. In 1512, when the Medici returned to overthrow the Florentine republic, Machiavelli was imprisoned, tortured, and exiled. He thereafter devoted his energies to the articulation of a political philosophy suited to the times and the tactics of the family that had ousted him.

On the surface, Machiavelli's two great works of political analysis appear to contradict each other. In his *Discourses on Livy*, which drew on the works of that Roman historian (Chapter 5), he praised the Roman Republic as a model for his own contemporaries, lauding constitutional government and equality among citizens. There is little doubt, in fact, that Machiavelli was a committed believer in the free city-state as the ideal form of human government. Yet Machiavelli also wrote *The Prince*, a "handbook for tyrants" in the eyes of his critics, and dedicated this work to Lorenzo, the son of Piero de' Medici, whose family had overthrown the Florentine republic.

Because *The Prince* has been much more widely read, it has often been interpreted as an endorsement of power for its own sake. But Machiavelli's real position was quite different: in the political chaos of his time, he saw the likes of Cesare Borgia as the only hope for revitalizing the spirit of independence and thus making Italy fit, eventually, for self-governance. Machiavelli never ceased to hope that his contemporaries would rise up, expel the French and Spanish, and restore ancient traditions of liberty and equality. He regarded a period

THE STATES OF ITALY, c. 1494. This map shows the divisions of Italy on the eve of the French invasion in 1494. Contemporary observers often described Italy as being divided among five great powers: Milan, Venice, Florence, the Papal States, and the united kingdoms of Naples and Sicily. › Which of these powers seems most capable of expanding their territories? › Which neighboring states would be most threatened by such attempts at expansion? › Why would Florence and the Papal States so often find themselves in conflict with each other?

of despotism as a necessary step toward that end, not as a permanently desirable form of government. Accordingly, Machiavelli insisted that a prince's actions must be judged by their consequences and not by their intrinsic moral quality. He argued that the "necessity of preserving the state will often compel a prince to take actions which are opposed to loyalty, charity, humanity, and religion." As we shall see in later chapters, many subsequent political philosophers would go even further than Machiavelli in arguing that the avoidance of political chaos does indeed warrant the exercise of absolute power (see Chapters 14 and 15).

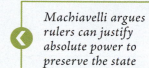

Machiavelli argues rulers can justify absolute power to preserve the state

THE IDEAL OF THE COURTIER

Machiavelli's political theories were informed by years of diplomatic service in the courts of Italy, and so was his engaging literary style. Indeed, he never ceased writing courtly poems, and plays. In this he resembled another poet-courtier, Ludovico Ariosto (1474–1533), who undertook diplomatic missions for the Duke of Ferrara and some of Rome's most powerful prelates. Ariosto's lengthy verse narrative, *Orlando Furioso* ("The Madness of Roland"), was a retelling of the heroic exploits celebrated in the French *Song of Roland* (Chapter 8)—but without the heroism. Although very different in form and tone from *The Prince*, it shared that work's skepticism of political or chivalric ideals. It emphasized the comedy of its lovers' passionate exploits and sought to charm an audience that found consolation in pleasure and beauty.

Thus a new Renaissance ideal was born: the ideal of the courtier, personified by the diplomat and nobleman Baldassare Castiglione (*bahl-dahs-SAH-re kah-stig-lee-OH-neh*; 1478–1529). His handbook, *The Book of the Courtier*, stands in sharp contrast to the treatises on public virtue composed in the previous century. Whereas Bruni and Alberti (Chapter 11) had lauded the sober virtues of service to the city-state, Castiglione taught how to attain the elegant and seemingly effortless skills necessary for advancement in princely courts. Many of these talents are still associated with the "Renaissance man": accomplished in many different pursuits, witty, cultured, and stylish. But in many ways, Castiglione's courtiers—women as well as men—represent a *rejection* of the older ideals associated with humanism's emphasis on classical education for public men. Castiglione also rejected the misogyny of the humanists by showing how court ladies could rise to influence and prominence through the graceful and wily exercise of their womanly powers.

THE DILEMMA OF THE ARTIST

Without question, the most enduring legacy of the Italian Renaissance has been the contributions of its artists, particularly those who embraced new media and new attitudes toward the human body. The creative and economic opportunities afforded by painting on canvas or wood panels freed artists from having to work on site and entirely on commission. We have also noted (Chapter 11) that the use of oil paints, pioneered in Flanders, further revolutionized painting styles. To these benefits, the artists of Italy added an important technical ingredient: mastery of a vanishing (one-point) perspective, which gave an illusion of three-dimensional space. They also experimented with effects of light and shade, and intently studied anatomy and bodily proportions: techniques that also influenced sculptors. Just as Petrarch and other early humanists had urged a return to classical poetry and rhetoric, artists now recaptured the symmetry of classical art and placed the human subject at the center of artistic experience.

But behind all their beautiful artworks lie some harsh realities. Increasing private wealth and political jockeying had created a huge demand for commodities that could increase the status of men grappling for prestige. The development of portraiture was a direct result, because princes and merchants alike sought to glorify themselves and their families, to compete with neighbors and rivals. An artist therefore had to study the techniques of the courtier, and not just the new artistic techniques, in order to win patrons. He also had to perform services for which he needed other talents: overseeing the building and decoration of palaces; designing tableware, furniture, and liveries (uniforms) for servants and soldiers; even decorating firearms. Some artists were prized as much for their capacity to invent deadly weapons as for their paintings.

THE CAREER OF LEONARDO

The most adventurous and versatile artist of this period was **Leonardo da Vinci** (1452–1519). Leonardo personifies the Renaissance ideal: he was a painter, architect, musician, mathematician, engineer, and inventor. The illegitimate son of a notary, he had set up an artist's shop in Florence by the time he was twenty-five and gained the patronage of the Medici ruler Lorenzo the Magnificent. Yet Leonardo had a weakness: he worked slowly and had difficulty finishing anything. This naturally displeased Lorenzo and other Florentine patrons, who regarded artists as crafts-men who worked on their patrons' time, not their own. Leonardo, however, strongly objected to this view, considering himself to be an inspired, independent innovator. He therefore left Florence in 1482 and went to work for the Sforza dictators of Milan, whose favor he courted by emphasizing his skills as a maker of bombs, cannons, and siege engines. He remained there until the French invasion of 1499, and then wandered about until finally accepting the patronage of the French king.

Paradoxically, considering his skill in fashioning weapons, Leonardo believed in the essential divinity of all living things. He was a vegetarian—unusual at the time—and went to the marketplace to buy caged birds only to release them once he had finished observing them. He made careful drawings of grass, cloud formations, a waterfall; he obtained human corpses for dissection to study the minutest features of the body. This knowledge he poured into his paintings: *The Virgin of the Rocks* typifies not only his technical skill but also his passion for nature. In *The Last Supper*, Leonardo displayed his equally keen studies of human psychology. In this image, a serene Christ has just announced that one of his gathered disciples will betray him. Leonardo succeeds in portraying the mingled emotions of surprise, horror, and guilt on their faces. He also implicates the painting's viewers in this dramatic scene, since they, too, dine alongside Christ in the very same room.

Renaissance artists drawn into intense political and social competition of era

THE VIRGIN OF THE ROCKS. This painting reveals Leonardo's interest in the variety of human faces and facial expressions, and in natural settings.

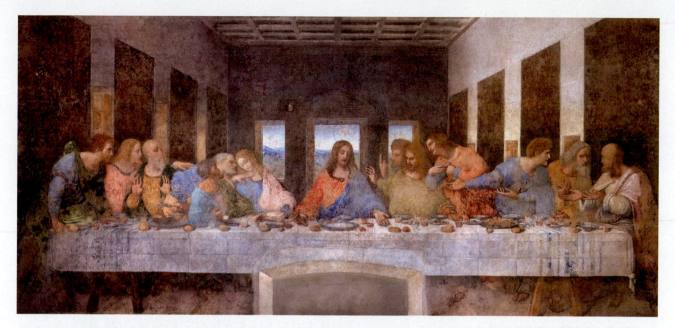

THE LAST SUPPER. This fresco on the refectory wall of the monastery of Santa Maria delle Grazie in Milan is a testament to both the powers and the limitations of Leonardo's artistry. It skillfully employs the techniques of one-point perspective to create the illusion that Jesus and his disciples are actually dining at the monastery's head table; but because Leonardo had not mastered the techniques of fresco painting, he applied tempera pigments onto a dry wall that had been coated with a sealing agent. As a result, the painting's colors began to fade just years after its completion. By the middle of the sixteenth century, it had seriously deteriorated, and large portions of it were invisible prior to recent restoration work.

ARTISTS AND PATRONS

The innovations of Florentine artists were widely imitated by Venetian painters, whose sumptuous portraits of the rich and powerful mirrored the tastes of the patrons for whom they worked. Rome, too, became a major artistic center in this era. Among its eminent painters was Raffaello Sanzio, or Raphael (1483–1520). Although influenced by Leonardo, Raphael cultivated a more philosophical approach: as we noted in Chapter 4, his fresco *The School of Athens* depicts both the harmony and the differences of Platonic and Aristotelian thought (see page 119). It also includes a number of Raphael's contemporaries as models: the image of Plato is actually a portrait of Leonardo, the architect Donato Bramante (c. 1444–1514) stands in for Euclid, and Michelangelo for the philosopher Heraclitus.

Michelangelo Buonarroti (1475–1564), who spent many decades in the service of the papacy, was another native of Florence. Like Leonardo, he was a polymath: painter, sculptor, architect, and poet. But whereas Leonardo was a naturalist, Michelangelo was an idealist. At the center of all his work, as at the center of Renaissance humanism, is the male figure: the embodied masculine mind. Michelangelo's greatest achievements in painting appear in a single location: the Sistine Chapel of the Vatican palace. As products of two different periods in the artist's life, they exemplify two different artistic styles and outlooks on the human condition. More famous are the extraordinary frescoes painted on the ceiling during

Leonardo da Vinci (1452–1519) Florentine inventor, sculptor, architect, and painter whose breadth of interests typifies the ideal of the "Renaissance man."

Michelangelo Buonarroti (1475–1564) A virtuoso Florentine sculptor, painter, and poet who spent much of his career in the service of the papacy. He is best known for the decoration of the Sistine Chapel and for his monumental sculptures.

the years between 1508 and 1512, depicting scenes from the book of Genesis. Of all the panels in this series, *The Creation of Adam* exemplifies the young artist's commitment to classical artistic principles and affirms the heroic qualities of mankind.

But a quarter of a century later, when Michelangelo returned to work in the Sistine Chapel, both his style and mood had changed dramatically. In the enormous *Last Judgment*, a fresco completed on the chapel's altar wall in 1536, Michelangelo repudiated classical restraint and represented humans racked with fear, guilt, and frailty. He even included himself in it via a grotesque self-portrait on the flayed flesh of Saint Bartholomew, who was martyred by being skinned alive. One wonders whether Michelangelo intended this as a reflection on the challenges of working for the papal court.

SELF-PORTRAIT OF THE ARTIST AS A YOUNG MAN: DETAIL FROM *THE SCHOOL OF ATHENS*. We already analyzed aspects of Raphael's famous group portrait of the Greek philosophers, with Plato and Aristotle at center (see page 419). In addition to featuring his own contemporaries as models—including the artists Leonardo and Michelangelo and the architect Bramante—Raphael put himself in the picture.
› **What messages does this choice convey?**

THE RENAISSANCE OF SCULPTURE

Although sculpture was not a new medium for artists, as oil painting was, it became an important area of Renaissance innovation. For the first time since late antiquity, monumental statues became figures "in the round" rather than sculptural elements incorporated into buildings or featured on tombs. By freeing sculpture from its bondage to architecture, the Renaissance reestablished it as a separate art form.

THE CREATION OF ADAM. This is one of a series of frescoes Michelangelo painted on the ceiling of the Sistine Chapel in the Vatican palace in Rome. He executed them over a period of many years and under circumstances of extreme physical hardship. It has since become an iconic image. › **How might it be said to capture Renaissance ideals?**

Leonardo da Vinci Applies for a Job

Few sources illuminate the tensions between Renaissance ideals and realities better than the résumé of accomplishments submitted by Leonardo da Vinci to a prospective employer, Ludovico Sforza of Milan. In the following letter, Leonardo explains why he deserves to be appointed chief architect and military engineer in the duke's household administration. He got the job and moved to Milan in 1481.

1. I have the kind of bridges that are extremely light and strong, made to be carried with great ease, and with them you may pursue, and, at any time, flee from the enemy; . . . and also methods of burning and destroying those of the enemy.

2. I know how, when a place is under attack, to eliminate the water from the trenches, and make endless variety of bridges . . . and other machines. . . .

3. . . . I have methods for destroying every rock or other fortress, even if it were built on rock, etc.

4. I also have other kinds of mortars [bombs] that are most convenient and easy to carry. . . .

5. And if it should be a sea battle, I have many kinds of machines that are most efficient for offense and defense. . . .

6. I also have means that are noiseless to reach a designated area by secret and tortuous mines. . . .

7. I will make covered chariots, safe and unattackable, which can penetrate the enemy with their artillery. . . .

8. In case of need I will make big guns, mortars, and light ordnance of fine and useful forms that are out of the ordinary.

9. If the operation of bombardment should fail, I would contrive catapults, mangonels, trabocchi [trebuchets], and other machines of marvelous efficacy and unusualness. In short, I can, according to each case in question, contrive various and endless means of offense and defense.

10. In time of peace I believe I can give perfect satisfaction that is equal to any other in the field of architecture and the construction of buildings. . . . I can execute sculpture in marble, bronze, or clay, and also in painting I do the best that can be done, and as well as any other, whoever he may be.

Having now, most illustrious Lord, sufficiently seen the specimens of all those who consider themselves master craftsmen of instruments of war, and that the invention and operation of such instruments are no different from those in common use, I shall now endeavor . . . to explain myself to your Excellency by revealing to your Lordship my secrets.

Source: Excerpted from Leonardo da Vinci, *The Notebooks*, in *The Italian Renaissance Reader*, eds. Julia Conaway Bondanella and Mark Musa (Harmondsworth, UK: 1987), pp. 195–96.

Questions for Analysis

1. Judging from the qualifications Leonardo highlights in this letter, what can you conclude about the political situation in Milan and the priorities of its duke? What can you conclude about the state of military technologies during this period and the conduct of warfare?

2. What do you make of the fact that Leonardo mentions his artistic endeavors only at the end of the letter? Does this fact alter your opinion or impression of him? Why or why not?

THE POWER AND VULNERABILITY OF THE MALE BODY. Donatello's *David* (left) was the first freestanding nude executed since antiquity. It shows the Hebrew leader as an adolescent youth and is a little over five feet tall. In contrast, Michelangelo's *David* (center) stands thirteen feet high and was placed prominently in front of Florence's city hall to proclaim the city's power and humanistic values. Michelangelo's *Descent from the Cross* (right), which shows Christ's broken body in the arms of the elderly Nicodemus (the sculptor himself), was made for Michelangelo's own tomb. (The Gospels describe Nicodemus as a Pharisee who became a follower of Jesus, and who was present at his death.) › **Why would Michelangelo choose to represent himself as Nicodemus?** › **How does his representation of David, and the context in which this figure was displayed, compare with that of Donatello's sculpture?**

The first great master of Renaissance sculpture was the Florentine known as Donatello (c. 1386–1466). His bronze statue of David, triumphant over the head of the slain Goliath, is the first freestanding nude of the period. Yet this *David* is clearly an agile adolescent rather than the muscular Greek athlete of Michelangelo's *David*, which was executed in 1501 as a public expression of Florentine civic life. Michelangelo regarded sculpture as the most exalted of the arts because it allowed the artist to imitate God most fully in re-creating human forms. He also insisted on working in marble—the "noblest" sculptural material—and creating figures twice as large as life.

By sculpting a serenely confident young man at the peak of physical fitness, Michelangelo celebrated the Florentine republic's own determination to resist tyrants and uphold ideals of civic justice. Yet in the sculptures of Michelangelo's later life, as in his painting, he began to explore the use of anatomical distortion to create emotional intensity. The culmination of this trend is his unfinished but intensely moving *Descent from the Cross*, a depiction of an old man (the sculptor himself) grieving over the distorted, slumping body of the dead Christ.

RENAISSANCE ARCHITECTURE

Renaissance architecture had its roots in the classical past to an even greater extent than either sculpture or painting. The Gothic style pioneered in northern France (see Chapter 9) had not found a welcome reception in Italy. Most of the buildings constructed there were Romanesque, and the great architects generally adopted their building plans from these structures. They also copied decorative devices from the authentic ruins of ancient Rome and studied the writings of Vitruvius (fl. c. 60–15 B.C.E.), the Roman architect and engineer. The principles laid out by Vitruvius were popularized by Leon Battista Alberti in his book *On the Art of Building*, which began to circulate in manuscript around 1450.

In keeping with these classical models, Renaissance buildings emphasized geometrical proportion inspired by Platonic philosophy, which taught that certain mathematical ratios reflect the harmony of the universe. For example, the proportions of the human body are the basis for the proportions of the quintessential Renaissance building: St. Peter's Basilica in Rome. Designed by some of the most celebrated architects of the time, including Bramante and Michelangelo, it is still one of the largest buildings in the world. Yet it seems smaller than a Gothic cathedral because it is built to human scale. The same artful proportions are evident in smaller-scale buildings too, as in the aristocratic country houses later designed by the northern Italian architect Andrea Palladio (1508–1580), who created secular miniatures of ancient temples to glorify his patrons.

The Renaissance North of the Alps

It was not until the very end of the fifteenth century that the innovative artistry and learning of Italy began to be exported across the Alps into northern Europe and across the Mediterranean into Spain. For beyond Italy, intellectual life was dominated by universities such as those of Paris, Oxford, Kraków, and Prague, whose scholastic curricula still focused on logic, dialectic, and theology. Universities in Italy, by contrast, were more often professional schools specializing in law and medicine, and were more integrally tied to the interests of urban elites. In northern Europe, scholars who *were* influenced by Italian ideas usually worked outside the university system, under the private patronage of kings and princes.

In Italy, as we have seen, such patronage was an important arena for competition between political rivals. Elsewhere in Europe, however, political units were larger and political rivals fewer; it was therefore less necessary to promote art for political purposes than in the small principalities and city-states of Italy. But as royal courts became more firmly established in royal capitals—and so became showcases for royal power—kings increasingly needed to impress their own subjects and to display their power to foreign courtiers and visitors. Consequently, they relied more and more on artists and intellectuals to advertise their wealth and taste.

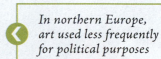

In northern Europe, art used less frequently for political purposes

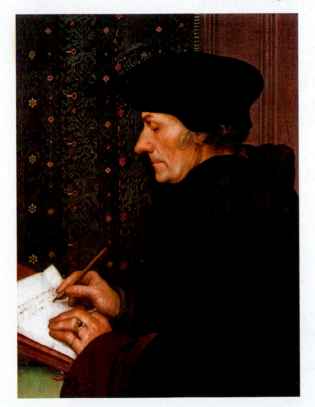

ERASMUS, **BY HANS HOLBEIN THE YOUNGER.** This is generally regarded as the most evocative portrait of the preeminent Christian humanist.

CHRISTIAN HUMANISM AND THE CAREER OF ERASMUS

In general, then, the Renaissance movement in northern Europe differed from that of Italy because it grafted certain Italian ideals onto preexisting traditions, rather than sweeping away older forms of knowledge and artistry. This can be seen very clearly in the case of a hybrid development known as Christian humanism. Although Christian humanists shared the Italian humanists' scorn for scholasticism's limitations and applied new critical methods to ancient texts, these northern scholars were more committed to seeking ethical guidance from biblical and religious precepts, as well as from Cicero or Virgil. Like their Italian counterparts, these scholars embraced the wisdom of antiquity, but the antiquity they favored was Christian as well as classical: the antiquity of the New Testament and the early Church.

Chief among them was **Desiderius Erasmus** (c. 1469–1536). The illegitimate son of a priest, Erasmus was born near Rotterdam in the Netherlands. Forced to enter a monastery when he was a teenager, the young Erasmus found little useful instruction there—but plenty of freedom to read widely. He devoured all the classics he could get his hands on, alongside the writings of the Church Fathers (Chapter 6). When he was about thirty years old, he obtained permission to leave the monastery and to enroll in the University of Paris, where he completed the requirements for a bachelor's degree in divinity.

But Erasmus subsequently rebelled against what he regarded as the arid learning of Parisian scholasticism, and he never served actively as a priest. Instead, he made his living from teaching, writing, and the proceeds of various ecclesiastical offices that required no pastoral duties. Ever on the lookout for new patrons, he traveled often to England, stayed for three years in Italy, and resided in several different cities in Germany and the Low Countries before settling, toward the end of his life, in Basel (Switzerland). Through these travels, as well as a voluminous correspondence with learned friends, Erasmus became the humanist leader of northern Europe.

As a Latin prose stylist, Erasmus was often compared to Cicero. Extraordinarily eloquent and witty, he reveled in tailoring his mode of discourse to fit his subject, creating dazzling verbal effects and coining puns that took on added meaning if the reader knew Greek as well. But although Erasmus's urbane style and humor earned him a wide audience, he intended everything he wrote to promote the "philosophy of Christ." He believed that the society of his day had lost sight of the Gospels' teachings. Accordingly, he offered his contemporaries three different kinds of writings: clever satires in which people could recognize their own foibles, serious moral treatises meant to offer guidance toward proper Christian behavior, and new editions of basic Christian texts.

In the first category belong works that are still widely read today: *The Praise of Folly* (1511), in which Erasmus ridiculed pedantry, ignorance, and gullibility—even within the Church; and the *Colloquies* (1518), in which he subjected contemporary religious practices to keen examination, couching a serious message in an ironic tone. In these books, Erasmus let fictional characters do the talking, so his own views on any given topic can only be determined by inference. But in his second category of writings, Erasmus spoke clearly in his own voice. In *Handbook of the Christian Knight* (1503), he used the language of chivalry to encourage a life of inward piety; in *Complaint of Peace* (1517), he argued movingly for Christian pacifism.

The third set of writings, which Erasmus himself considered his greatest achievement, were critical editions of works by Augustine, Jerome, and Ambrose. He also used his extraordinary command of Latin and Greek to produce a more accurate edition of the New Testament. After reading Lorenzo Valla's *Notes on the New Testament* in 1504, Erasmus became convinced that nothing was more imperative than divesting the Christian scriptures of the myriad errors in transcription and translation that had piled up over the course of preceding centuries. He therefore spent ten years comparing all the early Greek biblical manuscripts he could find in order to establish an authoritative text. When it finally appeared in 1516, Erasmus's Greek New Testament—published together with explanatory notes and his own new Latin translation—became one of the most important scholarly landmarks of all time. It would play a critical role in the early stages of the Reformation (see Chapter 13).

THE INFLUENCE OF ERASMUS

One of Erasmus's closest friends was another prominent Christian humanist, Sir **Thomas More** (1478–1535). In later life, following a successful career as a lawyer and speaker of the House of Commons in Parliament, More was appointed lord chancellor of England in 1529. However, he lost that post when he opposed King Henry VIII's plan to establish a national church under royal control, in order to deny the supremacy of the pope (see Chapter 13). He was executed in 1535 and is now revered as a Catholic martyr.

In 1516, More published his most famous book, *Utopia* (Greek for *No Place*). Written in Latin and purporting to describe an ideal community on an imaginary island, the book is really a satirical critique of contemporary culture. In contrast to Europeans, the inhabitants of the fictional Utopia hold all their goods in common, work only six hours a day (so that all may have leisure for intellectual pursuits), and practice the virtues of wisdom, moderation, fortitude, and justice. Although More did not advance explicit arguments in favor of Christianity, he may have meant to imply that if the Utopians could manage their society so well without the benefit of Christian revelation, Europeans who knew the Gospels ought to be able to do even better.

Erasmus and More head a long list of energetic and eloquent northern humanists who made signal contributions to the collective enterprise of revolutionizing the study of early Christianity, and their achievements had a direct influence on

SIR THOMAS MORE, **BY HANS HOLBEIN THE YOUNGER.** Holbein's skill in rendering the gravity and interiority of his subject is matched by his masterful representation of the sumptuous chain of office, furred mantle, and velvet sleeves that indicate the political and professional status of Henry VIII's lord chancellor.

Protestant reformers (as we will see in the next chapter). Yet very few of these men were willing to join Luther and other Protestant leaders in rejecting the fundamental principles on which the power of the Roman Church was based. Most tried to remain within its fold while still espousing an ideal of inward piety and scholarly inquiry. But as the leaders of the Church grew less and less tolerant of dissent, even mild criticism came to seem like heresy. Erasmus died early enough to escape persecution, but several of his less fortunate followers did not.

THE LITERATURE OF THE NORTHERN RENAISSANCE

Alongside Christian humanism, a literary Renaissance also flourished in northern Europe. Poets in France and England vied with one another to adapt the elegant lyric forms pioneered by Petrarch and popularized by many subsequent poets, including Michelangelo. The sonnet was particularly influential and would become one of the verse forms embraced by William Shakespeare (1564–1616) (see Chapter 14). Another English poet, Edmund Spenser (c. 1552–1599), drew on the literary innovation of Ariosto's *Orlando Furioso*: his *Faerie Queene* is a similarly long chivalric romance that revels in sensuous imagery.

Meanwhile, the more satirical side of humanism was embraced by the French writer François Rabelais (*RAH-beh-lay*; c. 1494–1553). Like Erasmus, Rabelais began his career in the Church but soon left the cloister to study medicine. A practicing physician, Rabelais interspersed his professional activities with literary endeavors, the most enduring of which are the twin books *Gargantua* and *Pantagruel*: a series of "chronicles" describing the lives and times of giants whose fabulous size and gross appetites serve as vehicles for much lusty humor. Like Erasmus, too, Rabelais also satirized religious hypocrisy, pedantry, superstition, and bigotry. But unlike Erasmus, who wrote in a highly cultivated Latin style comprehensible only to very learned readers, Rabelais addressed a wider audience by writing in extremely crude French and glorifying human foibles as natural and healthy.

NORTHERN ARCHITECTURE AND ART

Although many architects in northern Europe continued to build in the flamboyant Gothic style of the later Middle Ages, the classical values of Italian architects can be seen in some of the splendid new castles constructed in France's Loire valley— châteaux too elegant to be defensible—and in the royal palace of the Louvre in Paris (now the museum), which replaced an old twelfth-century fortress. The influence of Renaissance ideals is also visible in the work of the German artist Albrecht Dürer (*DIRR-er*; 1471–1528). Dürer was the first northerner to master the techniques of proportion and perspective, and he shared with contemporary Italians a fascination with nature and the human body. He also took advantage of the printing press to circulate his work to a wide audience, making his delicate pencil drawings into engravings that could be mass produced.

But Dürer never really embraced classical subjects, as his Italian counterparts did; instead, he drew inspiration from Christian legends and the humanism of

Erasmus. For example, Dürer's serenely radiant engraving of Saint Jerome seems to express the scholarly absorption that Erasmus himself would have enjoyed while working in his study. Indeed, Dürer aspired to immortalize Erasmus himself in a major portrait, but the paths of the two men crossed only once. Instead, the accomplishment of capturing Erasmus's pensive spirit in art was left to another northern artist, the German Hans Holbein the Younger (1497–1543). Holbein also painted an acute portrait of Erasmus's friend, Sir Thomas More. These two portraits, in themselves, exemplify a Renaissance emphasis on the making of naturalistic likenesses that express human individuality.

TRADITION AND INNOVATION IN MUSIC

Like the visual arts, the lovely music produced during this era was nourished by patrons' desire to surround themselves with beauty. Yet unlike painting and sculpture, musical practice did not reach back to classical antiquity, but instead drew on well-established medieval conventions. Even before the Black Death, a musical movement called *ars nova* ("new art") was already flourishing in France and spread to Italy during the lifetime of Petrarch; its outstanding composers were Guillaume de Machaut (*mah-SHOH*; c. 1300–1377) and Francesco Landini (c. 1325–1397).

The part-songs and ballads composed by these musicians and their successors expanded on earlier genres of secular music, but their greatest achievement was a highly complicated yet delicate contrapuntal style adapted for the liturgy of the Church. Machaut's polyphonic (multivoiced and harmonized) setting of the major sections of the Mass is the earliest by a single composer. In the fifteenth century, the dissemination of this new musical aesthetic combined with a host of French, Flemish, and Italian elements in the multicultural courts of Europe, particularly that of Burgundy. By the beginning of the sixteenth century, Franco-Flemish composers dominated many important cathedrals, too, creating a variety of new forms and styles that bear a close affinity to Renaissance art and poetry.

Throughout Europe, the general level of musical proficiency during this era was very high. The singing of part-songs was a popular pastime in homes and at informal social gatherings, and the ability to read a part at sight was considered part of an elite education. Aristocratic women, in particular, were expected to display mastery of the new musical instruments that had been developed to add nuance and texture to existing musical forms, including the lute, the viol, the violin, and a variety of woodwind and keyboard instruments such as the harpsichord.

Although most composers of this period were men trained in the service of the Church, they rarely made sharp distinctions between sacred and secular music. Like sculpture, music was coming into its own as a serious, independent art. As such,

***SAINT JEROME IN HIS STUDY*, BY DÜRER.** Jerome, the biblical translator of the fourth century (Chapter 6), was a hero to both Dürer and Erasmus, and the paragon of inspired Christian scholarship. Note how the scene exudes contentment, even down to the sleeping lion, which seems more like an overgrown tabby cat than a symbol of Christ.

it would become an important medium for the expression of both Catholic and Protestant ideals during the Reformation, and also one of the few art forms equally acceptable to all.

The Politics of Christian Europe

We have already observed how the intellectual and artistic activity of the Renaissance was both fueled and hindered by the political developments of the later fifteenth century—within Italy, and throughout Europe. In 1453, France had emerged victorious in the Hundred Years' War, whereas England plunged into three decades of bloody civil conflict that touched every corner of that kingdom. The French monarchy, therefore, was able to rebuild its power and prestige while at the same time extending its control over regions once controlled by the English, but now part of an enlarged French kingdom.

In 1494, the French king Charles VIII expanded his reach even farther, into Italy. Leading an army of thirty thousand well-trained troops across the Alps, and aided by an alliance with the duchy of Milan, he intended to press his ancestral claim to the kingdom of Naples. This effort solidified Italian opposition to French occupation—as we noted in our discussion of Machiavelli.

The rulers of Spain, whose territorial claims on Sicily also extended to Naples, were spurred by Charles's expansionism to forge an uneasy alliance with the Papal States, some principalities of the Holy Roman Empire, Milan, and Venice. But the respite was brief, for Charles's successor, Louis XII, launched a second French invasion in 1499. For more than a generation, until 1529, warfare in Italy was virtually uninterrupted. Alliances and counteralliances among city-states became further catalysts for violence and made Italy a magnet for mercenaries who could barely be kept in check by the generals who employed them.

Meanwhile, the northern Italian city-states' virtual monopoly on trade with Asia, which had been one of the chief economic underpinnings of artistic and intellectual patronage, was being gradually eroded by the shifting of trade routes from the Mediterranean to the Atlantic (Chapters 10 and 11). It was also hampered by the increasing power of the Ottoman Empire, and even by the imperial pretensions of a new Russian ruler.

THE POWER OF IVAN THE GREAT

In Chapter 10, we saw that Moscow had emerged as an administrative capital under the Mongols, and had then become the center of an independent principality, the Grand Duchy of Muscovy. In the fifteenth century, its exponential growth was driven by its ruler Ivan III (r. 1462–1505), also known as **Ivan the Great**, the first Muscovite prince to adopt a distinctive imperial agenda.

Ivan launched a series of conquests that annexed all the independent principalities between Moscow and the border of Poland-Lithuania. After invading Lithuania in 1492 and 1501, he also succeeded in bringing parts of that domain (portions of modern Belarus and Ukraine) under his control, although this did not sever the region's strong cultural ties to Poland or its religious allegiance to Rome. Meanwhile, Ivan married the niece of the last Byzantine emperor: an alliance that inspired

Ivan the Great
(1440–1505) Russian ruler who annexed neighboring territories and consolidated his empire's position as a European power.

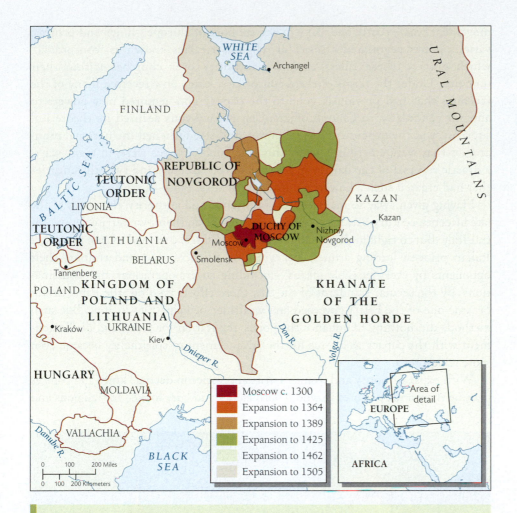

THE EXPANSION OF MUSCOVITE TERRITORY TO 1505. The Grand
Duchy of Moscow (also known as Muscovy) was the heart of what would
become an empire. › **With what other empires and polities did the Muscovites
have to compete during this period of expansion?**

later Russian rulers to claim that Moscow was the "third Rome" while they were
heirs of the Caesars—hence the title *czar* or **tsar**. Ivan also rebuilt his fortified
Moscow residence, known as the Kremlin, in magnificent Italianate style. By the
time of his death in 1505, Muscovy was firmly established as a dominant power on
the frontier of Europe.

THE GROWTH OF NATIONAL CHURCHES

At the same time that Muscovy laid claim to the mantle of Roman imperial
power, the papacy was pouring resources into the glorification of the original
Rome and the aggrandizement of the papal office. But neither the city nor its
rulers could keep pace with their political and religious rivals. Following the
Council of Constance (Chapter 11), the papacy's victory over the conciliar

tsar Russian word for
"emperor," derived from the
Latin *caesar* and similar to
the German word *Kaiser*.
This was the title claimed
by the rulers of medieval
Muscovy and of the later
Russian Empire.

In a series of concordat treaties, popes cede political power and revenues to kings and princes

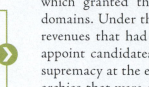

movement was a costly one. To win the support of Europe's kings and princes, various popes negotiated a series of religious treaties known as "concordats," which granted these rulers extensive authority over churches within their domains. Under the terms of these concordats, kings now received many of the revenues that had previously gone to the papacy and acquired new powers to appoint candidates to Church offices. The papacy thus secured its theoretical supremacy at the expense of its real power, and strengthened the national monarchies that were emerging during this era. Such changes were, in many ways, a drastic reversal of the hard-won reforms of the eleventh and twelfth centuries that had created such a powerful papacy in the first place.

Having given away so many sources of revenue and authority, the popes of the late fifteenth century became even more dependent on their own territories in central Italy. But to tighten their hold on the Papal States, they had to rule like other Italian princes: leading armies, jockeying for alliances, and undermining their opponents by every possible means—including covert operations and assassinations. By the secular standards of the day, these efforts paid off: the Papal States became one of the better-governed and wealthier principalities in Italy. But such methods did nothing to enhance the popes' reputation for piety, and disillusionment with the papacy as a force for the advancement of spirituality became even more widespread.

With papal authority and Rome's spiritual prestige in decline, kings and princes became the primary figures to whom both clergy and laity looked for religious and

AN ITALIAN RENAISSANCE CATHEDRAL IN MUSCOVITE RUS'. Ivan the Great commissioned the Italian architect Aristotele Fioravanti to build this cathedral, dedicated to the Blessed Virgin and honoring her Assumption into heaven. It is now part of the Kremlin palace complex in Moscow. **› Why would Ivan choose to build this cathedral and commission this particular architect? › What messages might he have been trying to convey?**

moral guidance. Many secular rulers responded to such expectations aggressively, closing scandal-ridden monasteries, suppressing alleged heretics, and prohibiting the lower classes from dressing like the nobility. By these and other such measures, rulers could present themselves as champions of moral reform even as they strengthened their political power. The result was an increasingly close link between national monarchies and national churches, a link that would become even stronger after the Reformation.

THE TRIUMPH OF THE *RECONQUISTA*

The kingdoms of the Iberian Peninsula were also in constant conflict during this period. In Castile, civil war and incompetent governance allowed the Castilian nobility to gain greater control over the peasantry and greater independence from the monarchy. In Aragon, royal government benefited from the extended commercial influence of Catalonia, which was under Aragonese rule. But after 1458, Aragon also became enmeshed in a civil war that involved both France and Castile.

The solution to the disputed succession that had caused this war ultimately lay in the blending of two powerful royal families. In 1469, Prince **Ferdinand of Aragon** was recognized as the undisputed heir to that throne and, in the same year, secured this position by marrying **Isabella**, the heiress of **Castile**. Isabella became queen in 1474 and Ferdinand became king in 1479. Although Castile and Aragon continued to be ruled as separate kingdoms until 1714—there are tensions between the two former kingdoms even now—their marriage enabled Isabella and Ferdinand to pursue several ambitious policies. In particular, their combined resources went to the creation of Europe's most powerful army, which was employed to conquer the last remaining Muslim principality of what had been al-Andalus, Muslim Spain. That principality, Granada, fell in 1492.

THE END OF THE *CONVIVENCIA* AND THE EXPULSION OF THE JEWS

For more than seven centuries, many of Spain's Jewish communities had enjoyed certain privileges extended by their Muslim rulers, who were also relatively tolerant of their Christian subjects. Scholars often refer to this period of Spain's history as a time of *convivencia*, "living together" or "coexistence." Although relations among various religious and ethnic groups were not always peaceful or positive, the policies of Muslim rulers in al-Andalus had enabled an extraordinary hybrid culture to flourish.

The aims of the Spanish *reconquista* were diametrically opposed to those of "living together." The "reconquest" sought to forge a single, homogeneous community based on the fiction that Spain had once been entirely Christian and should be restored to its former purity. The year 1492, therefore, marks not only the end of Muslim rule in medieval Spain but also the culmination of Jewish exclusion, a process that had accelerated in the late thirteenth century (Chapter 9). Within this history, the Spanish expulsion of the Jews stands out for the staggering scope of

Ferdinand of Aragon (1452–1516) In 1469, he married the heiress to Castile, Isabella. Their union allowed them to pursue several ambitious policies, including the conquest of Granada, the last Muslim principality in Spain, and the expulsion of Spain's large Jewish community.

Isabella of Castile (1451–1504) The heiress to Castile, she married Ferdinand of Aragon. In 1492, she granted three ships to Christopher Columbus of Genoa (Italy), who went on to claim portions of the new world for Spain.

reconquista A period of "reconquest" in medieval Spain that sought to forge a single, homogeneous community based on the fiction that Spain had once been entirely Christian and should be restored to its former purity.

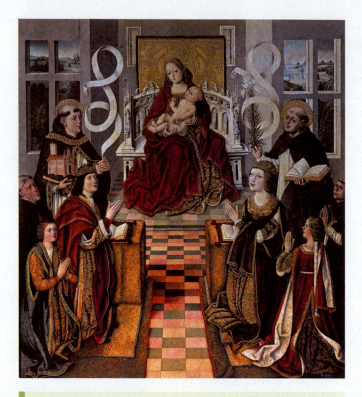

FERDINAND AND ISABELLA HONORING THE VIRGIN. In this contemporary Spanish painting, the royal couple are shown with two of their children and two household chaplains, in the company of the Blessed Virgin, the Christ Child, and saints from the Dominican order. (The Dominicans were instrumental in conducting the affairs of the Spanish Inquisition.) › How clear is the distinction between these holy figures and the royal family? › What message is conveyed by their proximity?

the displacements and destruction it entailed: at least a hundred thousand (and possibly as many as two hundred thousand) men, women, and children were forced from their homes as refugees.

The Christian monarchs' motives for ordering this expulsion are still debated. Tens of thousands of Spanish Jews had already converted to Christianity between 1391 and 1420, many as a result of coercion. And for a generation or so, it seemed possible that these converts, known as *conversos*, might successfully assimilate into Christian society. But the same civil wars that led to the union of Ferdinand and Isabella made the *conversos* targets of discrimination. Conflicts may also have fueled popular suspicions that these converts remained Jews in secret. To make "proper" Christians out of the *conversos*, the "Most Catholic" monarchs (as they were now called) may have concluded that they needed to remove any potentially seditious influences that might stem from the continuing presence of a Jewish community in Spain.

What became of the Spanish Jews? Some traveled north, to the towns of Germany and the Low Countries or to Poland and eastern Europe. But most settled in Muslim regions of the Mediterranean, where many found a haven in the Ottoman Empire. As we already noted, there were many opportunities for advancement in the Ottoman imperial bureaucracy, while the Ottoman economy benefited from the highly skilled labor of Jewish artisans and the vast trading networks of Jewish merchants. In time, new forms and expressions of Jewish culture would emerge, but the descendants of these Spanish Jews—known as Sephardic Jews, or Sephardim—still treasured the traditions and customs formed in Spain over a thousand years.

THE EXTENSION OF THE *RECONQUISTA*

The Christian conquest of Granada and the expulsion of the Jews in 1492 were watershed events. They mark the beginning of a sweeping initiative to construct a unified kingdom that could transcend rival regional identities. Like other contemporary monarchs, Ferdinand and Isabella strengthened their emerging nation-state by constructing an exclusively Christian identity for its people, attaching that new identity to the crown, and promoting a single national language: Castilian Spanish. They also succeeded in capturing and redirecting another language: the rhetoric of crusade.

The crusading ethos, as we have seen, always seeks new outlets. With the creation of a new Christian kingdom through the defeat of all external enemies and internal threats, where could the energies harnessed by the *reconquista* be directed? The answer came from an unexpected quarter. Just a few months after Ferdinand and Isabella marched victoriously into Granada, the queen granted three ships to a Genoese adventurer who promised to reach India by sailing westward across the Atlantic Ocean, and to claim any new lands he found for Spain. Columbus never reached India, but he did help to extend the traditions of reconquest and crusading to the New World—with far-reaching consequences.

New Targets and Technologies of Conquest

The Spanish monarchs' decision to underwrite a voyage of exploration was spurred by their desire to counter the successful Portuguese ventures of the past half century. It was becoming clear that the tiny kingdom on the northwestern tip of the Iberian Peninsula would soon dominate the sea lanes if rivals did not find alternate routes and establish equally lucrative colonies. This competition with Portugal was another reason that Isabella turned to a Genoese sea captain—not to a Portuguese one—when she sought to expand Spain's wealth and global influence.

PRINCE HENRY THE NAVIGATOR AND PORTUGUESE COLONIAL INITIATIVES

Although Portugal had been an independent Christian kingdom since the twelfth century (Chapter 9), it was never able to compete effectively with its more powerful neighbors on land. But when the focus of European economic expansion began to shift toward the Atlantic (Chapter 10), Portuguese mariners were well placed to take advantage of this trend.

A central figure in this maritime history is **Prince Henry** (1394–1460), later called "**the Navigator**," a son of King João I of Portugal and his English queen Philippa, the sister of England's Henry IV. Prince Henry was fascinated by the sciences of cartography and navigation, and he helped to ensure that Portuguese sailors had access to the latest charts and technologies. He was also inspired by the stories told by Marco Polo and other travel writers—particularly the legend of Prester John, a mythical Christian king whom Europeans believed would be their ally against the Muslims (if only they could find him). Indeed, Prince Henry was Grand Master of a new crusading order, the Order of Christ, whose mission was to drive the Muslims out of Africa. He also had ambitions to extend Portuguese control into the Atlantic, to tap into the burgeoning market for slaves in the Ottoman Empire and to establish direct links with sources of African gold.

Prince Henry played an important part in organizing the Portuguese colonization of Madeira, the Canary Islands, and the Azores. He also pioneered the Portuguese slave trade, which almost entirely eradicated the population of the Canaries before targeting West Africa. By the 1440s, Portuguese explorers had reached the Cape Verde Islands. In 1444, they landed on the African mainland, in the area that became known as the Gold Coast, where they began to collect cargoes of gold and slaves for export.

Prince Henry the Navigator (1394–1460) A member of the Portuguese royal family, Henry encouraged the exploration and conquest of western Africa and the trade in gold and slaves.

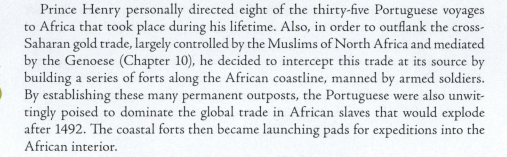

Portuguese under leadership of Henry establish permanent trading outposts in Africa

Prince Henry personally directed eight of the thirty-five Portuguese voyages to Africa that took place during his lifetime. Also, in order to outflank the cross-Saharan gold trade, largely controlled by the Muslims of North Africa and mediated by the Genoese (Chapter 10), he decided to intercept this trade at its source by building a series of forts along the African coastline, manned by armed soldiers. By establishing these many permanent outposts, the Portuguese were also unwittingly poised to dominate the global trade in African slaves that would explode after 1492. The coastal forts then became launching pads for expeditions into the African interior.

FROM AFRICA TO INDIA AND BEYOND: AN EMPIRE OF SPICES

By the 1470s, Portuguese sailors had rounded the western coast of Africa and were exploring the Gulf of Guinea. In 1483, they reached the mouth of the Congo River. In 1488, the Portuguese captain Bartolomeu Dias was inadvertently blown around the southern tip of Africa by a gale, after which he named the point "Cape of Storms." But King João II (r. 1481–1495), taking a more optimistic view, renamed it the Cape of Good Hope and began planning a naval expedition to India. In 1497–1498, Vasco da Gama rounded the cape and then, with the help of a Muslim navigator named Ibn Majid, crossed the Indian Ocean to Calicut, on the southwestern coast of India.

This voyage opened a viable sea route between Europe and the Far Eastern spice trade for the first time. Although da Gama lost half his fleet and one-third of his men on this two-year voyage, his cargo of spices was so valuable that these losses were deemed insignificant. His heroism became the basis for the Portuguese national epic, the *Lusiads*.

Now masters of the quickest route to riches in the world, the Portuguese swiftly capitalized on their decades of accomplishment. Not only did their trading fleets sail regularly to India, they attempted to monopolize the entire spice trade. In 1509, the Portuguese defeated an Ottoman fleet and blockaded the mouth of the Red Sea, attempting to cut off one of the traditional routes by which spices traveled to Alexandria. By 1510, Portuguese forces had established a series of forts along the western Indian coastline, with headquarters at Goa. In 1511, Portuguese ships seized Malacca, a center of the spice trade on the Malay Peninsula. By 1515, they had reached the Spice Islands (Indonesia) and the coast of China.

NAVAL TECHNOLOGY AND NAVIGATION

The Portuguese caravel—the workhorse ship of those first voyages to Africa—was based on ship and sail designs that had been in use among Portuguese fishermen since the thirteenth century. Starting in the 1440s, however, Portuguese shipwrights began building larger caravels of about 50 tons' displacement and equipped with two masts, each carrying a triangular (lateen) sail. Columbus's *Niña* was a ship of this design, although it was refitted with two square sails in the Portuguese Canary Islands, to help it sail more efficiently before the Atlantic wind. Such ships required much smaller crews than did the multi-oared galleys still commonly used in the Mediterranean. By the end of the fifteenth century, even larger caravels of around 200 tons were being constructed, with a third mast and a combination of square and lateen sails.

New navigational instruments also made these voyages possible. Quadrants, which could be used to calculate latitude by the height of the North Star above the horizon, were in widespread use by the 1450s. As sailors approached the equator, however, the quadrant became less and less useful, so navigators instead used astrolabes to reckon latitude by the height of the sun. Although both of these techniques had been in use for centuries, it was not until the 1480s that they became practical instruments for seaborne navigation, thanks to the preparation of standardized tables for the calculation of latitude. Compasses, too, were coming into more widespread use. The accurate calculation of longitude, however, remained impossible until the eighteenth century, when the invention of the marine chronometer made it possible to keep accurate time at sea. In this prior age, sailors had to rely on their skill at dead reckoning to determine how far east or west they were.

New technologies enable surge of long-distance naval exploration

These sailors also benefited from new maps and navigational charts. Printed books known as *rutters* or *routiers* contained detailed sailing instructions and descriptions of the coastal landmarks a pilot could expect to encounter en route to a variety of destinations. Mediterranean sailors had relied on similar information recorded on portolan charts since the thirteenth century (see Chapter 10). During the fifteenth century, mapmaking was extended to the Atlantic Ocean. By the end of the sixteenth, rutters spanned the globe.

ARTILLERY AND EMPIRE

Larger, more maneuverable ships and improved navigational aids enabled Europeans to reach West Africa, Southeast Asia, and—eventually—the Americas. But fundamentally, the lasting empires established in these regions were military achievements that extended what Europeans had learned in their wars against each other. Perhaps the most critical military advance was the increasing sophistication of artillery, a development made possible not only by gunpowder but also by improved metallurgical techniques for casting cannon barrels. By the middle of the fifteenth century, as we observed in Chapter 11, the use of artillery pieces had rendered the stone walls of medieval castles and towns obsolete, a fact brought home in 1453 by the successful French siege of Bordeaux (which ended the Hundred Years' War), and by the Ottoman siege of Constantinople (which ended the Byzantine Empire).

Indeed, the new ship designs were important in part because their larger size made it possible to carry effective artillery pieces: scores of guns mounted in fixed positions along their sides and swivel guns mounted fore and aft. These guns and ships were vastly expensive, but they made it possible to back mercantile ventures with military power. Although Vasco da Gama had sailed to the Indian Ocean in 1498, the Portuguese did not control that ocean until 1509, when they defeated Ottoman and Indian naval forces. Without this essential military component, the European maritime empires that were emerging in this period could not have existed.

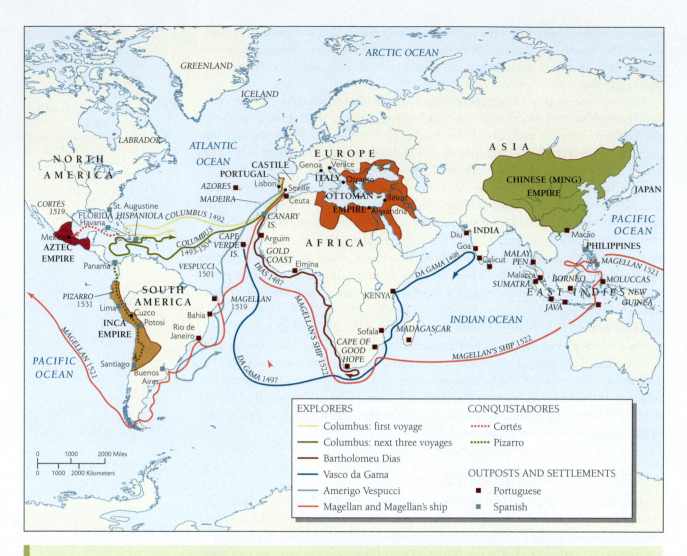

OVERSEAS EXPLORATION IN THE FIFTEENTH AND SIXTEENTH CENTURIES. › What were the major routes taken by European explorers of the fifteenth and sixteenth centuries? **›** What appear to have been the explorers' main goals? **›** How might the establishment of outposts in Africa, the Americas, and the East Indies have radically altered the balance of power in the Old World, and why?

A NEW KIND OF SLAVERY

Although slavery had effectively disappeared in much of northwestern Europe by the early twelfth century, it continued in parts of the Mediterranean world and had been introduced into many regions of central and eastern Europe after the Black Death. But this slavery existed on a very small scale; there were no slave-powered factories or large-scale agricultural systems in this period. The only major slave economies were in the Ottoman Empire, where slaves ran the vast bureaucracy and staffed the army. In all these cases, as in antiquity, no aspect of slavery was racially based. Most Ottoman slaves were European Christians. In the early Middle Ages, Germanic and Celtic peoples had been widely enslaved. In antiquity, slaves had come from every part of the known (and unknown) world.

What was new about the slavery of the late fifteenth century was its increasing racialization—an aspect of modern slavery that has made an indelible impact on our own society. To Europeans, African slaves were visible in ways that other slaves were not, and it became convenient for those who dealt in them to justify the mass deportation of entire populations by claiming their racial inferiority and their "natural" fitness for a life of bondage. This nefarious ideology has had long-lasting and tragic consequences that still afflict the civilizations of our own world.

Europeans justify slavery by claiming racial superiority over Africans

In Lisbon, which became a significant market for enslaved Africans during Prince Henry's lifetime, something on the order of fifteen to twenty thousand African captives were sold within a twenty-year period. In the following half century, by about 1505, the numbers amounted to a hundred and fifty thousand. For the most part, the purchasers of these slaves regarded them as status symbols; it became fashionable to have African footmen, pageboys, and ladies' maids. In the Atlantic colonies—Madeira, the Canaries, the Azores—land was still worked mainly by European settlers or native sharecroppers. Slave labor, if employed at all, was generally used only in sugar mills. On Madeira and the Canaries, where sugar became the predominant cash crop during the last quarter of the fifteenth century, some slaves were introduced as agricultural laborers. But even sugar production did not lead to the widespread use of slavery on these islands.

However, a new kind of slave-based sugar plantation began to emerge in Portugal's Cape Verde Islands in the 1560s, and then extended southward into the Gulf of Guinea. These islands were not populated when the Portuguese began to settle them, and their climate generally discouraged Europeans from living there. They were ideally located, however, along the routes of slave traders venturing outward from the nearby West African coast. It is this plantation model that would be exported to Brazil by the Portuguese and to the Caribbean islands of the Americas by their Spanish conquerors, with incalculable negative consequences for the indigenous peoples of Africa and the Americas (see Chapter 14).

Europeans in a New World

Like his contemporaries, **Christopher Columbus** (1451–1506) understood that the world was a sphere; but he also thought it was much smaller. (As we saw in Chapter 4, the accurate calculation of the globe's circumference, done in ancient Alexandria, had been later suppressed by Roman geographers.) Furthermore, it had long been accepted that there were only three continents: Europe, Asia, and Africa; hence the hypothesis that one could reach Asia by sailing west.

The "discovery" of the Canary Islands and the Azores further suggested that the Atlantic was dotted with similar lands all the way to Japan. This emboldened Columbus's royal patrons, who were convinced that the Genoese mariner could reach China in about a month, after a stop for provisions on the Canaries. So when Columbus reached the Bahamas and the island of Hispaniola after only a month, he thought that he had reached the outer islands of Asia.

Christopher Columbus (1451–1506) A Genoese sailor who persuaded King Ferdinand and Queen Isabella of Spain to fund his expedition across the Atlantic, with the purpose of discovering a new trade route to Asia. His miscalculation landed him in the Bahamas and the island of Hispaniola in 1492.

THE SHOCK OF DISCOVERY

Of course, Columbus was not the first European to set foot on an American continent. Viking sailors had briefly settled present-day Newfoundland, Labrador, and perhaps even portions of New England around the year 1000 (Chapter 8). But knowledge of these landings had been forgotten or unknown outside of Iceland for hundreds of years. It wasn't until the 1960s that the stories of these expeditions were corroborated by archaeological evidence. (In 2016, a new site of Norse settlement was identified on the coast of Baffin Island.) Moreover, the tiny Norwegian colony on Greenland—technically part of the North American landmass—had been abandoned in the fifteenth century, when the cooling of the climate (Chapter 10) destroyed the fragile ecosystems that barely sustained the lives of settlers there.

Although Columbus did not return with spices to prove that he had found an alternate route to Asia, he did return with some small samples of gold and a few indigenous people—whose existence gave promise of entire tribes that might be enslaved or "saved" by conversion to Christianity, and whose lands could provide homes for Spanish settlers seeking new frontiers after the *reconquista*. This provided sufficient incentive for the "Most Catholic" monarchs to finance three more expeditions by Columbus and many more by adventurers, missionaries, and colonists.

Gold, land, and indigenous peoples (to enslave or convert) justify further Spanish exploration

Meanwhile, the Portuguese, who had already obtained a papal decree granting them (theoretical) ownership of all lands south of the Canaries, rushed to establish their own claims. After two years of wrangling and conflicting papal pronouncements, the Treaty of Tordesillas (1494) sought to demarcate Spanish and Portuguese possession of as-yet-undiscovered lands. The Spanish would ultimately emerge as the big winners in this game of blind-man's bluff: within a decade, the coasts of two hitherto unknown continents were identified, as were clusters of new islands, most on the Spanish side of the meridian.

Gradually, Europeans reached the conclusion that the voyages of Columbus and his successors had revealed an entirely "New World." And, shocking to Europeans, this world had not been foretold by either the teachings of Christianity or the wisdom of the ancients. Among the first to champion the fact of two new continents' existence was the Italian explorer and geographer Amerigo Vespucci (1454–1512), whose name was soon adopted as a descriptor for them. Eventually, those who came to accept this fact were forced to question the reliability of the key sources of knowledge on which Western civilizations had hitherto hinged (see Chapter 14).

At first, the realization that the **Americas** were not an outpost of Asia came as a disappointment to the Spanish, because it meant that two major land masses and two vast oceans disrupted their plans to beat the Portuguese to the Spice Islands. But new possibilities quickly became clear. In 1513, the Spanish explorer Vasco Núñez de Balboa first viewed the Pacific Ocean from the Isthmus of Panama, and news of the narrow divide between two vast oceans prompted Ferdinand and Isabella's grandson to renew their dream. This young monarch, Charles V (1500–1556), ruled not only Spain but also a huge patchwork of territories encompassed by the Holy Roman Empire. In 1519, he accepted Ferdinand Magellan's proposal to see whether a route to Asia could be found by sailing around South America.

Yet Magellan's voyage demonstrated beyond question that the world was simply too large for any such plan to be feasible at that time. Of the five ships that left Spain under his command, only one returned, three years later, having been forced to circumnavigate the globe. Out of a crew of 265 sailors, only 18 survived, most having died of scurvy or starvation. Magellan himself had been killed in a skirmish with native peoples in the Philippines. This fiasco ended all hope of discovering

Americas The name given to the two great landmasses of the New World, derived from the name of the Italian geographer Amerigo Vespucci.

America as an Object of Desire

Under the influence of popular travel narratives that had circulated in Europe for centuries, Columbus and his fellow voyagers were prepared to find the New World full of cannibals. They also assumed that the indigenous peoples' custom of wearing little or no clothing—not to mention their "savagery"—would render their women sexually available. In a letter sent back home in 1495, one of Columbus's men recounted a notable encounter with a "cannibal girl" whom he had taken captive in his tent and whose naked body aroused his desire. He was surprised to find that she resisted his advances so fiercely that he had to tie her up—which of course made it easier for him to "subdue" her. In the end, he cheerfully reports, the girl's sexual performance was so satisfying that she might have been trained, as he put it, in a "school for whores."

The Flemish artist Jan van der Straet (1523–1605) would have heard many such reports of the encounters between (mostly male) Europeans and the peoples of the New World. This engraving, based on one of his drawings, is among the thousands of mass-produced images that circulated widely in Europe, thanks to the invention of printing. It imagines the first encounter between a male "Americus" (such as Columbus or Amerigo Vespucci himself) and the New World "America," depicted as a voluptuous, available woman. The Latin caption reads: "America rises to meet Americus; and whenever he calls her, she will always be aroused."

Questions for Analysis

1. Study the details of this image carefully. What does each detail symbolize? How do they work together as an allegory of conquest and colonization?

2. On what stereotypes of indigenous peoples does this image draw? Notice, for example, the cannibalistic campfire of the group in the background and the posture of "America."

3. Why is the New World itself ("America") imagined as female in this image? What messages might this—and the suggestive caption—have conveyed to a European viewer?

Americen Americus retexit, & . . . . Semel vocauit inde semper excitam .

AMERICA.

"America rises to meet Americus; and whenever he calls her, she will always be aroused."

an easy southwest passage to Asia—although the deadly dream of a northwest passage survived and motivated many European explorers of North America into the twentieth century. It has been revived today, in our age of global warming. The retreat of Arctic pack ice has led to the opening of new shipping lanes and, in 2019, a meeting of the Arctic Council in Finland revealed competing plans for a new round of colonial ventures.

THE DREAM OF GOLD AND THE DOWNFALL OF EMPIRES

Europeans were quick to capitalize on the sources of wealth that the New World could offer. What chiefly fired the imagination were those small samples of gold that Columbus had initially brought back to Spain. Although rather paltry in themselves, they nurtured hopes that gold might lie piled in ingots somewhere in these vast new lands. Rumor fed rumor, until a few freelance Spanish soldiers really did strike it rich beyond their most avaricious imaginings.

Their success, though, had little to do with their own efforts. After Columbus's first landing, European diseases had spread rapidly among the indigenous peoples of the Caribbean and the American coastlines. These diseases—especially measles and smallpox—were not fatal to those who carried them, because Europeans had developed immunities over many generations. But to the peoples of this New World, they were extremely deadly: of the two hundred and fifty thousand people living on Hispaniola when Columbus arrived, 70 percent had perished from disease within a generation.

> *Disease and brutality decimate indigenous population in Central and South America*

The ambitions of Spanish *conquistadores* (conquerors) were also assisted by the complex political, economic, and military rivalries that already existed among the sophisticated societies they encountered. The Aztec Empire of Mexico rivaled any European state in its power, culture, and wealth—and like any successful empire it had subsumed many neighboring territories in the course of its own conquests. Its capital, Tenochtitlán (*ten-och-tit-LAN*; now Mexico City), amazed its European assailants, who had never seen anything like the height and grandeur of its buildings or the splendor of its public works. This splendor was itself evidence of the Aztecs' imperial might, which was resisted by many of the peoples from whom they demanded tribute.

The Aztecs' eventual conqueror, Hernán Cortés (1485–1547), arrived in Hispaniola as a young man, in the wake of Columbus's first landing. He had received a land grant from the Spanish crown and acted as magistrate in one of the new towns established there. In 1519, he headed an expedition to the mainland, which had been the target of some earlier exploratory missions rebuffed by the Aztecs. But Cortés had the advantage of insider knowledge, having formed an intimate relationship with a native woman known as La Malinche. She became his interpreter in the Nahua language, the lingua franca among the many different ethnic groups within the empire. With her help, he discovered that some subjugated peoples were rebellious, and so he began to form strategic alliances with their leaders.

These alliances were crucial. Although Cortés and his small force had potentially superior weapons—guns and horses—these were more effective for their novelty than their utility: gunpowder dampened by the humid climate had a tendency to misfire or fail to ignite. So Cortés adopted the tactics and weaponry of his native

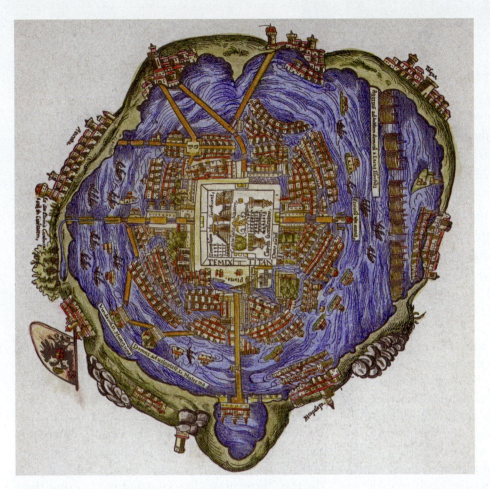

THE AZTEC CITY OF TENOCHTITLÁN. The Spanish conquistador Bernal Díaz del Castillo (1492–1585) took part in Hernán Cortés's conquest of the Aztec Empire and later wrote an account of his adventures. His admiring description of the Aztec capital at Tenochtitlán records that the Spaniards were amazed to see such a huge city built in the midst of a vast lake, with gigantic buildings arranged in a meticulous urban plan around a central square and broad causeways linking the city to the mainland. This hand-colored woodcut was included in an early edition of Cortés's letters to Emperor Charles V, printed at Nuremberg (Germany) in 1524.

allies in his dealings with the Aztec king Montezuma II (r. 1502–1520) and in his assaults on the fortifications of Tenochtitlán. In the end, though, it was European bacteria, not European technology, that secured his victory: the Aztecs were devastated by an outbreak of the plague that had arrived with Cortés and his men. In 1521, the Aztec Empire fell.

In 1533, another lucky conquistador, Francisco Pizarro, would manage to topple the highly centralized empire of the Incas, based in what is now Peru, by similar means. In this case, he took advantage of an ongoing civil war that had weakened the reigning dynasty; he was also assisted by an epidemic of smallpox. Like Cortés, Pizarro promised his native allies liberation from an oppressive regime. But the former subjects of the Aztecs and Incas would soon be able to judge how sincere these promises were.

A Spanish Critique of New World Conquest

Not all Europeans approved of European imperialism or its "civilizing" effects on the peoples of the New World. One of the most influential contemporary critics was Bartolomé de las Casas (1484–1566) of Spain. In 1502, when Bartolomé was eighteen years old, he and his father joined an expedition to Hispaniola. In 1510, he became the first ordained priest in the Americas and eventually bishop of Chiapas (Mexico). Although he was a product of his times—he owned many slaves—he was also prescient in discerning the devastating effects of European settlement in the West Indies and Central America, and he particularly deplored the exploitation and extermination of indigenous populations. The following excerpt is from one of the many eloquent manifestos he published in an attempt to gain the sympathies of the Spanish crown and to reach a wide readership. It was printed in 1542, but it draws on the impressions and opinions he had formed since his arrival in New Spain as a young man.

God made all the peoples of this area, many and varied as they are, as open and as innocent as can be imagined. The simplest people in the world—unassuming, long-suffering, unassertive, and submissive—they are without malice or guile, and are utterly faithful and obedient both to their own native lords and to the Spaniards in whose service they now find themselves. . . . They are innocent and pure in mind and have a lively intelligence, all of which makes them particularly receptive to learning and understanding the truths of our Catholic faith and to being instructed in virtue; indeed, God has invested them with fewer impediments in this regard than any other people on earth. . . .

It was upon these gentle lambs . . . that from the very first day they clapped eyes on them the Spanish fell like ravening wolves upon the fold, or like tigers and savage lions who have not eaten meat for days. The pattern established at the outset has remained unchanged to this day, and the Spaniards still do nothing save tear the natives to shreds, murder them and inflict upon them untold misery, suffering and distress, tormenting, harrying and persecuting them mercilessly. . . .

When the Spanish first journeyed there, the indigenous population of the island of Hispaniola stood at some three million; today only two hundred survive. The

THE PRICE OF CONQUEST

In Mexico and Peru, the *conquistadors* had access to hoards of gold and silver that had been accumulated for centuries by Aztec and Inca rulers. And almost immediately, a search for the sources of these metals was launched by agents of the Spanish crown. The first gold deposits were discovered in Hispaniola, where surface mines were speedily established using native laborers who were already dying in appalling numbers from disease, and who were now further decimated by brutality. The population soon dwindled to a mere 10 percent of its pre-Columbian strength.

The loss of so many workers made the mines of Hispaniola uneconomical to operate, so European colonists turned instead to livestock and sugar production. Modeling their sugarcane plantations on those of the Cape Verde Islands and St. Thomas (São Tomé) in the Gulf of Guinea, colonists began to import thousands of African slaves to labor in the new industry. Sugar production was, by its nature, a island of Cuba, which extends for a distance almost as great as that separating Valladolid from Rome, is now to all intents and purposes uninhabited; and two other large, beautiful and fertile islands, Puerto Rico and Jamaica, have been similarly devastated. Not a living soul remains today on any of the islands of the Bahamas . . . even though every single one of the sixty or so islands in the group . . . is more fertile and more beautiful than the Royal Gardens in Seville and the climate is as healthy as anywhere on earth. The native population, which once numbered some five hundred thousand, was wiped out by forcible expatriation to the island of Hispaniola, a policy adopted by the Spaniards in an endeavour to make up losses among the indigenous population of that island. . . .

At a conservative estimate, the despotic and diabolical behaviour of the Christians has, over the last forty years, led to the unjust and totally unwarranted deaths of more than twelve million souls, women and children among them. . . .

The reason the Christians have murdered on such a vast scale and killed anyone and everyone in their way is purely and simply greed. . . . The Spaniards have shown not the slightest consideration for these people, treating them (and I speak from first-hand experience, having been there from the outset) not as brute animals—indeed, I would to God they had done and had shown them the consideration they afford their animals—so much as piles of dung in the middle of the road. They

have had as little concern for their souls as for their bodies, all the millions that have perished having gone to their deaths with no knowledge of God and without the benefit of the Sacraments. One fact in all this is widely known and beyond dispute, for even the tyrannical murderers themselves acknowledge the truth of it: the indigenous peoples never did the Europeans any harm whatever.

Source: Bartolomé de las Casas, *A Short Account of the Destruction of the Indies*, trans. Nigel Griffin (Harmondsworth, UK: 1992), pp. 9–12.

Questions for Analysis

1. Given his perspective on the behavior of his countrymen, how might Bartolomé de las Casas have justified his own presence in New Spain (Mexico)? What do you think he may have hoped to achieve by publishing this account?

2. What comparisons does Bartolomé make between New Spain (Mexico) and the Old, and between indigenous peoples and Europeans? What is he trying to convey?

3. Compare this account with the contemporary print on page 429. What new light does this excerpt shine on that visual allegory? How might a reader-viewer of the time have reconciled these two very different pictures of European imperialism?

capital-intensive undertaking and the need to import slave labor added further to its costs. This guaranteed that control over the new industry would fall into the hands of a few extremely wealthy planters and financiers.

Despite the establishment of Caribbean plantations and Mexican cattle and sheep ranching—whose devastating effects on the fragile ecosystem of Central America will be discussed in Chapter 14—it was mining that would shape the Spanish colonies most fundamentally in this period. If gold was the lure that had inspired the conquest, silver became its most lucrative export. Even before the discovery of vast silver deposits, the Spanish crown had assumed direct control over all colonial exports. It was therefore to the Spanish crown that the profits of the empire were channeled. Europe's silver shortage, which had been acute for centuries, came to an end.

Yet this massive infusion of silver created more problems than it solved, because it accelerated the monetary inflation that had already begun in the late fifteenth century. Initially, it had been driven by the renewed growth of the European population, an expanding economy, and a relatively fixed supply of food. Thereafter, thanks to the influx of New World silver, inflation was driven by the vastly increased supply of coinage, which led to the doubling and quadrupling of prices in the course of the sixteenth century and the collapse of the European economy—which paradoxically drove a wave of impoverished refugees to settle in the New World in ever greater numbers.

Conclusion

The growing connection between the Mediterranean and the Atlantic, which had begun in the thirteenth century, was the essential preliminary to the rise of European empires in West Africa, India, and the Americas. Other events and innovations we have surveyed in this chapter played a key role, too: the rapid communications fueled by the printing press; the struggles for power that led to the development of ever deadlier weapons; the navigational and colonial initiatives of the Portuguese; and the Spanish *reconquista*, which drove Spanish rulers and adventurers to seek their fortunes overseas.

AFTER YOU READ THIS CHAPTER

CHRONOLOGY

1454–1455	Gutenberg's printed Bible completed
1488	Bartolomeu Dias rounds the Cape of Good Hope (Africa)
1492	Christopher Columbus reaches the West Indies
1494	Treaty of Tordesillas divides the New World
	Charles VIII of France invades Italy
1498	Vasco da Gama reaches India
1511	Erasmus publishes *The Praise of Folly*
1511	The Portuguese venture to Indonesia
1512	Michelangelo completes painting the ceiling of the Sistine Chapel
1513	Niccolò Machiavelli completes *The Prince*
	Vasco Núñez de Balboa reaches the Pacific Ocean
1516	Thomas More publishes *Utopia*
1519–1521	Aztec wars enable Cortés's conquest of Mexico
1519–1522	Magellan's fleet circumnavigates the globe
1531– 1533	Pizarro's conquest of the Inca Empire

REVIEWING THE OBJECTIVES

❯ The artists of Italy were closely tied to those with political and military power. How did this relationship affect the kinds of work these artists produced?

❯ Which aspects of Renaissance artistry and learning were adopted in northern Europe?

❯ What was the *reconquista*, and how did it lead to a new way of thinking about Spanish identity?

❯ Europeans, especially the Portuguese, developed new technologies and techniques that enabled exploration and colonial ventures in this period. What were they?

❯ The "discovery" of the New World had profound effects on the indigenous peoples and the environment of the Americas. Describe some of these effects.

For the indigenous peoples of Africa and the Americas, the results were cataclysmic. Within a century of Europeans' arrival, between 50 and 90 percent of some native populations had perished from disease, massacre, and enslavement. Moreover, competing imperial ventures profoundly destabilized Europe's already warring territories.

The ideals of the humanists and the artistry associated with the Renaissance therefore stand in sharp contrast to the harsh realities in which they were rooted. Artists could thrive in the atmosphere of competition and one-upmanship that characterized this period, but they were also compelled to subordinate their artistry to the demands of warfare, espionage, and slavery. Some humanists may have wanted to revive the principles of the Roman Republic, but many of them worked for ambitious despots who modeled themselves on Rome's dictators. Meanwhile, the theories that undergirded European politics and colonial expansion were being used to legitimize a newly racialized industry of enslavement. All of these trends would be carried forward into the sixteenth century, and would play a role in the upheaval that shattered Europe's fragile religious unity. It is to this upheaval—the Reformation—that we turn in Chapter 13.

 Go to **INQUIZITIVE** to see what you've learned—and learn what you've missed—with personalized feedback along the way.

PEOPLE, IDEAS, AND EVENTS IN CONTEXT

❯ Why was **GUTENBERG**'s invention of the **PRINTING PRESS** such a significant development?

❯ How did **NICCOLÒ MACHIAVELLI** respond to Italy's political situation within Europe? In what ways do artists such as **LEONARDO DA VINCI** and **MICHELANGELO BUONARROTI** exemplify the ideals and realities of the Renaissance?

❯ How did northern European scholars such as **DESIDERIUS ERASMUS** and **THOMAS MORE** apply humanist ideas to Christianity? How were these ideas expressed in art?

❯ What is significant about **IVAN THE GREAT**'s use of the title **TSAR**?

❯ How did **ISABELLA OF CASTILE** and **FERDINAND OF ARAGON** succeed in creating a unified Spain through the *RECONQUISTA*?

❯ How does **PRINCE HENRY THE NAVIGATOR** exemplify the motives for pursuing overseas expansion? Why were the Portuguese so successful in establishing colonies during this period?

❯ What were the expectations that launched **COLUMBUS**'s voyage? What enabled the Spanish *CONQUISTADORS* to subjugate the peoples of the **AMERICAS**?

THINKING ABOUT CONNECTIONS

❯ Phrases such as "Renaissance man" and "Renaissance education" are still part of our common vocabulary. Given what you have learned in this chapter, how has your understanding of such phrases changed? How would you explain their true meaning to others?

❯ How do the patterns of conquest and colonization discussed in this chapter compare with those of earlier periods, such as the era of the Crusades or the empires of antiquity? How many of these developments were new?

❯ Although the growth of the African slave trade resulted in a new racialization of slavery in the Atlantic world, the justifications for slavery had very old roots. How might Europeans have used Greek and Roman precedents in defense of these new ventures (see Chapters 4 and 5)?

13

The Age of Dissent and Division, 1500–1564

IN 1517, ON THE NIGHT before the Feast of All Saints—All Hallows' Eve (or Halloween)—a professor of theology at a small university in northern Germany posted a list of debating points on the door of Wittenberg's Castle Church. Technically part of the princely palace of the local ruler, the elector of Saxony, the church also served as the university's chapel. Despite its timing, the professor's action was not a prank; it was the usual method of announcing a scholarly disputation. Yet Martin Luther's choice of an evening associated with mischief-making was appropriate, because the posting of these Ninety-Five Theses was a subversive act. For one thing, the sheer number of propositions that Dr. Luther offered to debate was unusual. But what really caught the attention of fellow scholars was their unifying theme: the corruption of the Roman Church and, in particular, the office of the pope. It was a topic very much in vogue at the time, but it had seldom been dissected so clearly by a licensed theologian who was also a monk, an ordained priest, and a charismatic teacher.

This document, and the wider controversy it stimulated, soon spread far beyond Wittenberg. By the time the papacy formally retaliated in 1520, religious dissent was mounting—and not only among academics. Many of Europe's rulers saw the political advantages of either defying or defending the pope, and they chose sides accordingly. Luther's own lord, Frederick III of Saxony, would spend the rest of his life shielding the man who had first expounded those theses in his own church.

BEFORE YOU READ THIS CHAPTER ❯

STORY LINES

> The movement catalyzed by Martin Luther's challenge to the Roman Church grew out of much earlier attempts at reform, but it was also a response to more recent religious and political developments.

> Within a decade of Luther's excommunication, religious dissent was widespread and a number of different Protestant faiths were taking hold in various regions of Europe.

> Forms of Protestantism transformed not only the political landscape of Europe but also basic structures of the family and attitudes toward marriage and sexuality that still shape our lives today.

> These changes also affected the structures and doctrine of the Roman Catholic ("universal") Church, which reemerged as an institution different in many ways from the medieval Church, and more similar to that of today.

CORE OBJECTIVES

> **DEFINE** the main premises of Lutheranism.

> **EXPLAIN** why some rulers and/or regions embraced forms of Protestant Christianity and why others did not.

> **IDENTIFY** the ways in which family structures and values changed during the Reformation.

> **UNDERSTAND** the reasons behind England's unusual Protestant faith.

> **DESCRIBE** the Roman Catholic Church's response to the challenge of Protestantism.

Reformation Sixteenth-century religious and political movement that led to a break between dissenting forms of Christianity and the Roman Catholic Church.

Martin Luther (1483–1546) A German monk and professor of theology whose critique of the papacy launched the Protestant Reformation.

Indulgences Grants exempting Catholic Christians from the performance of penance, either in life or after death.

Luther had grown up in a largely peaceful Europe. The economy was expanding, cities were growing, and major monarchies were secure. Meanwhile, the Church had weathered the storms of the Avignon captivity and the Great Schism, and alleged heresies had been suppressed or contained. At the local level, the devotion of ordinary Christians was strong and the parish was a crucial site of community identity. In short, few could have predicted that Europe's religious and political coherence would be irreparably shattered in the course of a generation, or that the next century would witness an appallingly destructive series of wars. Moreover, no one could have foreseen that the catalyst for these extraordinary events would be an obscure professor.

The debate ignited by Martin Luther (1483–1546) set off a chain reaction we know as the **Reformation**. Although initially intended as a call for another phase in the Church's long history of internal reforms, Luther's teachings instead launched a religious revolution that splintered western Christendom into a variety of Protestant ("dissenting") faiths, and prompted the Roman Church to reaffirm its status as the only true Catholic ("universal") faith. The result was a profound transformation of the religious, social, and political landscape that affected the lives of everyone in Europe—and in the new European colonies.

Martin Luther and the Reformation in Germany

Although Luther began as a reformer seeking to change the Church from within, he quickly became an uncompromising opponent of it, and many of his followers were even more radical. The movement that began with Luther therefore went beyond "reformation," and instead dismantled religious, political, and social institutions that had been in place for a thousand years.

MARTIN LUTHER. This portrait by Lucas Cranach the Elder (1472–1553), the court painter to the electors of Brandenburg and a friend of Luther, was made late in Luther's life.

LUTHER'S QUEST FOR SPIRITUAL JUSTICE

Martin Luther was the son of a German peasant who had prospered through business ventures. Eager to see his clever son rise still further, the elder Luther sent Martin to the University of Erfurt to study law. In 1505, however, Martin shattered his father's hopes by becoming a monk of the Augustinian order. But he never lost touch with his peasant roots and, indeed, his later literary successes owed a great deal to the earthy German dialect he had learned in the cradle.

As a monk, Luther zealously pursued all the traditional means for achieving holiness. Not only did he fast and pray continually, he also confessed his sins so often that his exhausted confessor reportedly joked that he should wait until he did something really bad. Still, Luther regarded himself as deeply sinful and feared that he could never perform enough good deeds to deserve salvation. But then he had an insight that led to a new understanding of God's justice.

For years, Luther had worried that it seemed unfair for God to issue commandments he knew humans could not observe, and then punish them with eternal damnation. Yet, upon further study of the Bible, he realized that God's justice lay not in his power to punish, but in his mercy. As Luther later wrote, "I began to understand the justice of God as that by which God makes *us* just . . . and at this I felt as though I had been born again, and had gone through open gates into paradise."

Lecturing at Wittenberg in the years immediately following this realization, which occurred around 1515, Luther reached his central doctrine of "justification by faith" as he pondered a passage in Paul's letter to the Romans: "[T]he just shall live by faith" (1:17). He concluded that God's justice does not demand endless pious works and religious rituals, because humans can never attain salvation through their own weak efforts. Rather, humans are saved by God's grace—that is, by the unconditional and benevolent love of the divine being, manifested on earth by the sacrifice of Jesus Christ. God offers this grace as an utterly undeserved gift to those whom he has predestined (selected) for salvation. Men and women are therefore "justified"—made worthy of salvation—by their faith in God's grace. Works of piety and charity are signs of that faith, but they are not what saves the soul. They are merely visible signs of each believer's invisible spiritual state, which is known to God alone.

The essence of this doctrine was not original to Luther, and had been central to the thought of Augustine (see Chapter 6), the patron saint of Luther's own monastic order. During the twelfth and thirteenth centuries, however, theologians such as Peter Lombard and Thomas Aquinas (see Chapter 9) had developed a very different understanding of salvation through their own readings of scripture. Though not discounting the importance of faith, they emphasized the crucial role that the Church and its sacraments played in the process of salvation. In subsequent centuries, the Church had increasingly represented the process of salvation in quantitative terms, teaching that a believer could reduce the penance owed for sins—and thus the soul's time in purgatory (Chapter 10)—by a specific number of days through performing specific actions, such as making a pilgrimage or a pious donation. These actions earned the "indulgence" of God to the degree merited by the piety of the action.

When **indulgences** were first conceptualized in the late eleventh century, they could be earned only through performing demanding spiritual exercises, such as joining a crusade. But by the end of the fourteenth century, indulgences were for sale. And a century later, when Luther was a child, the papacy had begun to claim that the purchase of indulgences could even benefit the dead, meaning that faithful men and

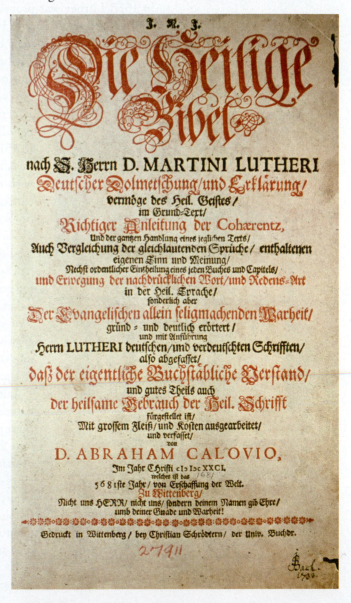

women could purchase multiple indulgences for deceased family members or friends to reduce the number of days or years they spent in purgatory.

Long before Luther, critics of this practice argued that the sale of indulgences was scandalous, even heretical. The sin of exchanging God's grace for cash was a heresy known as simony, which had been loudly condemned by Wycliffe and his followers (Chapter 11) and later by Erasmus (Chapter 12). But Luther's objections to indulgences had much more radical consequences because they rested on a set of theological premises that, taken to their logical conclusion, resulted in dismantling much of contemporary religious practice—not to mention the authority of the Church. Luther himself does not appear to have realized this at first, but as the implications of his ideas became clear, he did not withdraw them. Instead, he pressed on.

> *Luther's central doctrine: salvation through personal faith, not ritual or doctrine*

THE SCANDAL OF INDULGENCES

In 1517, Luther was provoked to action by a local abuse of spiritual power. The worldly Bishop Albert of Hohenzollern had paid a large sum for papal permission to hold the lucrative bishoprics of Magdeburg and Halberstadt concurrently: even though, at twenty-three, he was not old enough to be a bishop at all. When the prestigious archbishopric of Mainz fell vacant the following year, Albert bought that, too, by taking out loans from a German banking firm. He then struck a bargain with Pope Leo X (r. 1513–1521): Leo would authorize the sale of indulgences in Albert's ecclesiastical territories—where Luther lived—with the understanding that half of the income would go to Rome, where it would finance the building of the new St. Peter's Basilica; the other half would go to Albert.

Luther did not know the sordid details of this bargain, but he did know that a Dominican friar named Tetzel was soon hawking indulgences throughout the region, deliberately giving people the impression that an indulgence was an automatic ticket to heaven for oneself or one's loved ones in purgatory. Not only was Tetzel violating Luther's conviction that people are saved by God's grace alone, he was also misleading people into thinking that they no longer needed to confess their sins to a priest. In essence, he was putting innocent souls at risk.

Luther therefore focused his Ninety-Five Theses on dismantling the doctrine of indulgences. He originally wrote up these points for debate in Latin, but they were soon translated into German and published more widely. As this hitherto obscure academic gained widespread notoriety, Tetzel and his allies demanded that Luther withdraw his charges against the Church. But Luther grew bolder. In 1519, at a public disputation in Leipzig attended by throngs of people, he defiantly maintained that all clerics, even the pope, were merely fallible men and that the highest authority was the truth of scripture.

In 1520, building on this argument, Luther composed a series of pamphlets setting forth his three primary premises:

ST. PETER'S BASILICA, ROME. The construction of a new papal palace and monumental church began in 1506. This enormous complex replaced a modest, dilapidated Romanesque basilica that had replaced an even older church built on the site of the apostle Peter's tomb. **› How might contemporaries have interpreted this building project depending on their attitudes toward the papacy?**

justification by faith, the authority of scripture, and the "priesthood of all believers." We have already examined the meaning of the first premise. His second premise meant that the Bible took precedence over all other Church traditions, including the teachings of theologians and the sacraments, and that any beliefs (such as purgatory) or practices (such as the veneration of saints) not explicitly grounded in scripture should be rejected as human inventions. Finally, Luther declared that Christian believers were spiritually equal before God, which meant that priests, monks, and nuns had no special authority—hence the "priesthood of all believers."

From these premises, a host of practical consequences logically followed: because works could not lead to salvation, fasting, pilgrimages, and the veneration of relics were spiritually valueless. Luther called for the dissolution of all monasteries and convents, and advocated that religious rites be simplified, proposing the substitution of German (and other vernacular languages) for Latin and calling for a reduction in the number of sacraments from seven to two. In his view, the only true sacraments were Baptism and the Eucharist, both of which had been instituted by Christ. (He included Penance later.) Although Luther continued to believe that Christ was really present in the consecrated bread and wine of the Lord's Supper, he insisted that it was only through the faith of the individual believer that this sacrament could lead to God; it was not a miraculous act performed by a priest.

Luther's doctrines (personal salvation and the importance of the Bible over traditions) lead to argument for Church simplification

To further emphasize that those who served the Church had no supernatural authority, Luther insisted on calling them "ministers" or "pastors," rather than priests. He also proposed to abolish the entire ecclesiastical hierarchy, from pope to bishops on down. Finally, on the principle that no distinction existed between clergy and laity, he argued that ministers could and should marry. In 1525, he himself took a wife, Katharina von Bora, one of a dozen nuns whom he had helped to escape from a convent.

THE BREAK WITH ROME

Widely disseminated by the printing press, Luther's polemical pamphlets gained him passionate popular support and touched off a religious revolt against the papacy. Whereas the average press run of a printed book before 1520 had been a thousand copies, the first run of Luther's letter *To the Christian Nobility* (1520) was four thousand—and it sold out in a few days; many thousands of copies quickly followed. Even more popular were woodcut illustrations mocking the papacy and exalting Luther; these sold in the tens of thousands and could be readily understood even by those who could not read. (See *Interpreting Visual Evidence* on page 442.)

Luther's denunciations reflected widespread public dissatisfaction with the corruption of the papacy. Pope Alexander VI (r. 1492–1503) had bribed cardinals to gain his office and then used the money raised from the papal jubilee of 1500 to support the military campaigns of his illegitimate son, Cesare Borgia (1475–1507). His successor, Julius II (r. 1503–1513), devoted his reign to enlarging the Papal States in a series of wars. Leo X (r. 1513–1521) was a self-indulgent member of the Medici family of Florence.

In *The Praise of Folly*, first printed in 1511 and frequently reprinted (Chapter 12), Erasmus had declared that the popes of his day were incapable of leading Christlike lives. But his Latin writings reached only a select audience. In Germany, resentment of the papacy ran especially high because there were no special agreements (concordats) limiting papal authority in its principalities, as there were in Spain,

Split into principalities, Germany has weaker control over papacy than France, Spain, and Italy

Decoding Printed Propaganda

The printing press has been credited with helping to spread the teachings of Martin Luther and thus securing the success of the Protestant Reformation. But even before Luther's critiques were published, reformers were using the new technology to disseminate images that attacked the corruption of the Church. After Luther rose to prominence, both his supporters and detractors vied to disseminate propaganda that appealed visually to a lay audience and could be understood even by those who could not read.

The first pair of images below is really a single printed artifact dated to around 1500, an early example of a "pop-up" card. It shows Pope Alexander VI (r. 1492–1503) as a stately pontiff (image A) whose true identity is concealed by a flap, but when the flap is raised, he is revealed as a devil (image B). The Latin texts read: "Alexander VI, *pontifex maximus*" and "I am the pope," respectively.

The other two examples represent both sides of the debate as it had developed by 1530, and they do so with

A. Pope Alexander VI as pontiff.

B. Pope Alexander VI as a devil.

reference to the same image: the seven-headed beast mentioned in the Book of Revelation. Image C, a Lutheran engraving, shows the papacy as the beast with seven heads, representing seven orders of Catholic clergy. The sign on the cross (referring to the sign hung over the head of the crucified Christ) is in German, and reads: "For money, a sack full of indulgences"; the Latin words on either side say "Reign of the Devil." By contrast, image D, a Catholic engraving produced in Germany, shows Luther as Revelation's beast, with its seven heads labeled: "Doctor–Martin–Luther–Heretic–Hypocrite–Fanatic–Barabbas," the last alluding to the thief who should have been executed instead of Jesus, according to the Gospels.

Questions for Analysis

1. Given that the attack on Pope Alexander VI precedes Martin Luther's critique of the Church by nearly two decades, what can you conclude about its intended audience? To what extent can it be read as a barometer of popular disapproval? What might have been the reason(s) for using the concealing flap?

2. What do you make of the fact that both Catholic and Protestant propagandists used the same imagery? What do you make of the key differences, such as the fact that the seven-headed papal beast sprouts out of an altar on which a eucharistic chalice is displayed, while the seven-headed Martin Luther is reading a book?

3. All of these printed images make use of words. Would the message of each image be clear without the texts? Why or why not?

C. The seven-headed papal beast.

D. The seven-headed Martin Luther.

France, Bohemia, and England (Chapter 12). German princes complained that papal taxes were draining the country of its wealth, and yet Germans had almost no influence over papal policy. Frenchmen, Spaniards, and Italians dominated the College of Cardinals and the papal bureaucracy, and the popes were almost invariably Italian (as they would continue to be until 1978, when the Polish John Paul II was elected). As a result, graduates from the rapidly growing German and central European universities almost never found employment in Rome; instead, many joined the throngs of Luther's supporters, to become leaders of the new religious movement.

EMPEROR CHARLES V AND THE CONDEMNATION AT WORMS

In 1520, Pope Leo X issued a papal edict condemning Luther's publications as heretical and threatening him with excommunication. Luther was defiant: rather than acquiescing to the pope, he staged a public burning of the edict. His heresy confirmed, he was formally given over for punishment to his lay overlord, Frederick III "the Wise" of Saxony. Frederick, however, proved a critic of the papacy, too. Rather than burning him at the stake, he declared that Luther had not yet received a fair hearing. Early in 1521, he therefore brought Luther to the city of Worms (*VORMS*) to be examined by a select assembly known as a "diet."

At Worms, the diet's presiding officer was the newly elected Holy Roman Emperor Charles V, a member of the Habsburg family who had been born and bred in his ancestral holding of Flanders. By 1521, through the unpredictable workings of dynastic inheritance, marriage, and election, he had become not only the ruler of the Netherlands but also the king of Germany, Holy Roman emperor, duke of Austria, duke of Milan, and ruler of the Franche-Comté. And as the grandson of Ferdinand and Isabella on his mother's side, he was also the king of Spain; king of Naples, Sicily, and Sardinia; and ruler of all the Spanish possessions in the New World.

Governing such an extraordinary combination of territories posed enormous challenges, especially since this empire had no centralized administrative institutions and shared no common language or geographically contiguous borders. Because of this diversity, Charles could not tolerate threats to the fundamental force that held it together: Catholicism, as the religion of Rome was coming to be called.

There was, therefore, little doubt that the **Diet of Worms** would condemn Martin Luther for heresy. And when Luther refused to back down, Frederick the Wise intervened once more, arranging for him to be "kidnapped" and hidden for a year at the elector's castle of the Wartburg. Although Charles proclaimed Luther an outlaw, this edict was never enforced.

THE EMPEROR CHARLES V. This portrait by the Venetian painter Titian depicts Europe's most powerful ruler sitting quietly in a chair, dressed in simple clothing of the kind worn by judges or bureaucrats. › **Why might Charles have chosen to represent himself this way, rather than in the regalia of his many royal, imperial, and princely offices?**

THE EUROPEAN EMPIRE OF CHARLES V, c. 1526. Charles V ruled a variety of widely dispersed territories in Europe and the New World, and as Holy Roman emperor he was also the titular ruler of Germany. › **What were the main countries and kingdoms under his control? › Which regions were most threatened by Charles's extraordinary power, and where might the rulers of these regions turn to for allies? › How might the expansion of the Ottoman Empire have complicated the political and religious struggles within Christian Europe?**

A year later, in 1522, Luther returned in triumph to Wittenberg, where the changes he had called for had already been put into practice by his supporters. When several German princes formally converted to Lutheranism, they brought their territories with them. In a little over a decade, a new form of Christianity had been established.

Spread of Lutheran religion depends on support of German princes

THE GERMAN PRINCES AND THE LUTHERAN CHURCH

Ensconced in Wittenberg under princely protection, Luther began to express his political and social views more vehemently. In a treatise of 1523, he insisted that "godly" (Protestant) rulers must be obeyed in all things and that even "ungodly" ones should never be targets of dissent, because tyranny "is not to be resisted but endured." In 1524, when peasants throughout Germany rebelled against their landlords, Luther initially called for a peaceful resolution; but when the rebellion turned violent, he responded with intense hostility. In his vituperative pamphlet *Against the Thievish, Murderous Hordes of Peasants*, he urged readers to hunt the rebels down as though they were mad dogs. After the ruthless suppression of this revolt, which may have cost as many as a hundred thousand lives, the firm alliance of Lutheranism with state power helped preserve and sanction the existing social order. The decision of some German princes to embrace Lutheran religious practices is an important development, because popular support for Luther would not have been enough to ensure the success of his teachings. Indeed, it was only in those territories where Lutheranism was formally established that the new religion prevailed. Elsewhere in Germany, Luther's sympathizers were forced to flee, face death, or conform to Catholicism.

A long tradition of political control over religious practice

The power of individual lords to control the practice of religion in their lands reflects developments we have noted in previous chapters. Rulers had long sought to control appointments to Church offices, to restrict the flow of money to Rome, and to limit the reach of ecclesiastical courts. But in Germany, neither the emperor nor the princes had been strong enough to secure such privileges—until Luther provided a new justification for their independence: in one of the pamphlets published in 1520, Luther explicitly encouraged German princes to confiscate the wealth of the Church. Personal convictions surely played a role in individual cases of conversion, but political and economic considerations were generally more decisive. Protestant princes could consolidate authority by naming their own religious officials, cutting off fees to Rome, and curtailing the jurisdiction of Church courts. No longer would a rival ecclesiastical prince (such as a bishop or archbishop) be able to use his spiritual office to undermine a secular prince's sovereignty.

Similar considerations also moved a number of free cities to adopt Lutheranism. Acting independently, town councils could establish themselves as the supreme governing authorities within their jurisdictions, cutting out local bishops or powerful monasteries. Given the added fact that, under Lutheranism, monasteries and convents could be shut down and their lands appropriated by the newly sovereign secular authorities, the practical advantages of the new faith were overwhelming.

The Many Forms of Protestantism

Originating as a term applied to Lutherans who "protested" Catholic rule, the word **Protestant** was soon applied to a much wider range of dissenting forms of Christianity. Lutheranism planted lasting roots in northern Germany and Scandinavia, where it became the state religion of Denmark, Norway, and Sweden as early as the 1520s. Elsewhere in Europe, competing forms of Protestantism soon emerged from the seeds Luther had sown.

A LABORATORY OF DISSENT: PROTESTANTISM IN SWITZERLAND

Protestantism The name given to the many dissenting varieties of Christianity that emerged during the Reformation in sixteenth-century western Europe.

Switzerland offers a particularly useful case study because religious affiliations differed from one independent city to another, with three main forms of Protestantism emerging between 1520 and 1550: Zwinglianism, Anabaptism, and Calvinism.

Legend:
- Church of England
- Calvinist
- Eastern Orthodox
- Lutheran
- Roman Catholic
- Hussite
- Anabaptist
- Islamic
- Boundary of the Holy Roman Empire

CONFESSIONAL DIFFERENCES, c. 1560. The religious affiliations (confessions) of Europe's territories had become very complicated by the year 1560, roughly a generation after the adoption of Lutheranism in some areas. › Which major countries and kingdoms had embraced a form of Protestantism by 1560? › To what extent do these divisions conform to political boundaries? › To what extent did the divisions complicate the political situation? › Why might Lutheranism have spread north into Scandinavia, but not south into Bavaria or west across the Rhine?

Zwinglianism, founded in Zurich by **Ulrich Zwingli** (*TSVING-lee*; 1484–1531), was the most theologically moderate form. Zwingli had begun his career as a Catholic priest, but his humanist study of the Bible convinced him that Catholic theology conflicted with the Gospels. This eventually led him to condemn religious images and hierarchical authority. In 1522, Zwingli began attacking Rome directly, and soon some northern Swiss communities had accepted his religious leadership.

Although Zwingli's reforms closely resembled those of Luther, Zwingli differed regarding the theology of the Eucharist. Whereas Luther believed in the real presence of Christ's body in the sacrament, Zwingli taught that the Eucharist was simply a reminder and celebration of Christ's historic sacrifice on the cross. This fundamental disagreement prevented Lutherans and Zwinglians from uniting in a common Protestant front.

A more radical form of Protestantism was embraced by the **Anabaptists**. Initially, these were members of Zwingli's circle in Zurich, but they broke from him on the issue of infant baptism: Anabaptists were convinced that the sacrament of Baptism was effective only when administered to willing adults who understood its significance. They accordingly required those who had been baptized as infants to be baptized again as adults (the term *Anabaptism* means "rebaptism"). This doctrine reflects the Anabaptists' fundamental belief that the true church was a small community of believers whose members had to make a deliberate, inspired decision to join it.

THE ANABAPTISTS' CAGES, THEN AND NOW. After the three Anabaptist leaders of Münster were executed in 1535, their corpses were prominently displayed in cages hung from a tower of the marketplace church. As can be seen from the photo on the right, their bones are gone, but the iron cages remain. › **What would be the purpose of keeping these cages on display?** › **What different messages might this sight convey?**

No other Protestant groups went so far in rejecting the medieval view of the Church as a single vast body to which all Christian members of society belonged from birth. And because almost everyone assumed that religious and secular authority were inextricably connected, Anabaptism was rejected by all established powers, both Protestant and Catholic. It was a movement that appealed to sincere religious piety in calling for strict personal morality and extreme simplicity of worship.

This changed when a group of Anabaptist extremists managed to gain control of the German city of Münster in 1534. These zealots were driven by millenarianism: the belief that God intends to institute a completely new order throughout the world before the end of time. Determined to help God bring about this goal, the extremists attempted to turn Münster into a new Jerusalem. A former tailor named John of Leyden assumed the title "king of the New Temple" and proclaimed himself the successor of the Hebrew king David. Under his leadership, Anabaptist religious practices were made obligatory, private property was abolished, and even polygamy was permitted, based on Old Testament precedents. Such practices were deeply shocking to Protestants and Catholics alike. Accordingly, Münster was besieged and captured by Catholic forces little more than a year after the Anabaptist takeover. The new "David," together with two of his lieutenants, was put to death by torture, and the three bodies were displayed in iron cages in the town square.

Thereafter, even moderate Anabaptists throughout Europe were ruthlessly persecuted on all sides. The few who survived banded together in the Mennonite sect, named after its founder, the Dutchman Menno Simons (c. 1496–1561). This sect, dedicated to pacifism and the simple "religion of the heart" of original Anabaptism, is still particularly strong in the central United States.

JOHN CALVIN'S REFORMED THEOLOGY

A year after the events in Münster, a twenty-six-year-old Frenchman, **John Calvin** (1509–1564), published the first version of his *Institutes of the Christian Religion*, the most influential formulation of Protestant theology ever written. Born in northern France, Calvin had originally trained for the law; by 1533, he was studying the Greek and Latin classics while living off the income from a priestly benefice. As he later wrote, he was "obstinately devoted to the superstitions of popery" until he experienced a miraculous conversion. He became a Protestant theologian and propagandist, eventually fleeing to the Swiss city of Basel to escape persecution.

Although some aspects of Calvin's early career resemble those of Luther, the two men were very different. Luther was a volatile personality and a lover of controversy. He responded to theological problems as they arose, or as the impulse struck him, and never attempted to systematize his beliefs. Calvin, however, was a cool-headed legal analyst who resolved to set forth Protestant principles comprehensively, logically, and systematically. After several revisions and enlargements, the definitive edition of *Institutes* appeared in 1559.

Calvin's austere and stoical theology starts with the omnipotence of God: the entire universe depends on the will of the Almighty, who knows all things present and to come. Because of man's original fall from grace, all human beings are sinners by nature, yet God (for reasons of his own) predestines some for eternal salvation and damns the rest. There is nothing, then, that individuals can do to alter their fate. And yet Christians cannot be indifferent to their conduct, for if they are among

John (Jean) Calvin
(1509–1564) French-born theologian and reformer whose radical form of Protestantism was adopted in many Swiss cities, notably Geneva.

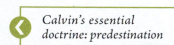

Calvin's essential doctrine: predestination

JOHN CALVIN. This recently discovered portrait by an anonymous artist shows the young Protestant reformer as a serene and authoritative figure. It places the grotesque caricature of Calvin (right) in perspective.

CALVIN AS SEEN BY HIS ENEMIES. In this image, which circulated among Calvin's Catholic detractors, the reformer's facial features are a disturbing composite of fish, toad, and chicken.

the elect God will implant in them the desire to live according to his laws. Upright conduct is thus a sign that an individual has been chosen, as is membership in the Reformed Church (as Calvinist churches are known). Most of all, true Christians will show themselves to be chosen instruments of God, actively fulfilling his purposes on earth and doing all that they can to prevent sin.

Calvin's religious teachings therefore diverged from those of Luther in several essentials. For Luther, a Christian should endure the trials of life through suffering; for Calvin, the world was to be mastered through unceasing labor. Calvin's religion was also more controlling: although Luther insisted that his followers attend church on Sunday, he did not demand that they refrain from all pleasure or work during the remainder of the day. Calvin, however, issued stern strictures against worldliness of any sort on the Sabbath and forbade all sorts of minor self-indulgences even on non-Sabbath days.

The two men also differed on fundamental matters of church governance and worship. Although Luther broke from the Catholic system of hierarchical church government, Lutheran district superintendents exercised some of the same powers as bishops. Luther also retained many features of traditional Christian worship, including music and ritual. Calvin, however, rejected everything that smacked of "popery" and argued for the elimination of all traces of hierarchy; each congregation should elect its own ministers, and assemblies of ministers and "elders" should govern the Reformed Church as a whole. He also insisted on the utmost simplicity in worship, prohibiting (among much else) vestments, processions, instrumental music, and religious images of any sort. He also dispensed with all remaining vestiges of Catholic sacramental theology by making the sermon, rather than the Eucharist, the centerpiece of reformed worship. As a sign of this change, pulpits were frequently moved to the center of the church sanctuary.

CALVINISM IN GENEVA

Calvin was intent on putting his religious teachings into practice. Sensing an opportunity in the French-speaking Swiss city of Geneva—then in the throes of political and religious upheaval—he moved there in 1536 and immediately began to preach and organize. In 1538, his activities caused him to be expelled by the city council, but he returned in 1541.

With Calvin's influence, Geneva's laws make Protestant ideals into law

With Calvin's guidance, Geneva's government became a theocracy: a society under the "rule of God." Supreme authority was vested in a "consistory," or assembly composed of twelve lay elders and between ten and twenty pastors whose weekly meetings Calvin dominated. In addition to passing legislation, the consistory's main function was to supervise morality, public and private. To this end, Geneva was divided into districts and a committee of the consistory visited every household, without prior warning, to check on the behavior of its members. Dancing, card playing, attending the theater, and working or playing on the Sabbath were all outlawed as works of the devil. Innkeepers were forbidden to allow anyone to consume food or drink without first saying grace, or to permit any patron to stay up after nine o'clock. Adultery, blasphemy, and heresy all became capital crimes, and penalties even for lesser crimes were severe. During the first four years after Calvin gained control, there were fifty-eight executions in a city whose total population was only sixteen thousand.

As rigid as such a regime may seem today, Geneva was a beacon of light to thousands of Protestants throughout Europe. Calvin's disciple John Knox (c. 1514–1572), who brought the reformed religion to Scotland, declared Geneva the "most perfect school of Christ that ever was on earth since the days of the apostles." Converts such as Knox flocked to Geneva for refuge or instruction, and then returned home to become ardent proselytizers. Geneva thus became the center of an international movement dedicated to spreading reformed religion to the rest of Europe.

By the end of the sixteenth century, Calvinists were a majority in Scotland (where they were known as Presbyterians) and Holland (where they founded the Dutch Reformed Church). They were also influential in England, where the Church of England adopted aspects of reformed theology but not reformed worship. (Calvinists who sought further reforms were known as Puritans.) There were also substantial Calvinist minorities in France (where they were called Huguenots), Germany, Hungary, Lithuania, and Poland. By the end of the sixteenth century, Calvinism had spread to the New World.

THE BEGINNINGS OF RELIGIOUS WARFARE IN DIVIDED EUROPE

Less than a generation after Luther's challenge to the Church, wars between Catholic and Protestant rulers began. In Germany, Charles V launched a military campaign against several German princes who had instituted Lutheran worship; but despite several notable victories, his efforts to defeat the Protestant princes failed because their Catholic counterparts worked against him, fearing that any suppression of Protestant princes might diminish their own independence. Meanwhile, the French were also at war with Charles and looked beyond Christian Europe to form a powerful alliance with the Muslim sultan Suleiman the Magnificent (r. 1520–1566), who brought the Ottoman Empire into the military and diplomatic sphere of Europe.

Religious warfare in various regions was intermittent until a compromise settlement was reached via the Peace of Augsburg in 1555. Its governing principle was *cuius regio, eius religio* ("as the ruler, so the religion"). This meant that, in those principalities where Lutherans ruled, Lutheranism would be the sole state religion; where Catholic princes ruled, the people of their territories would be Catholic. In some regions, this rule was not needed or enforced, because local rulers permitted religious diversity. In Transylvania, a province under the overlordship of Hungary (now in Romania), Catholics lived alongside three different Protestant groups in relative peace. In Poland, Lithuania, and Ukraine, Eastern Orthodox Christianity expanded its influence alongside Catholicism and was eventually tolerated. But these were rare exceptions.

For better and for worse, the Peace of Augsburg was a historical milestone. For the first time since Luther had been excommunicated, Catholic rulers were forced to acknowledge the legality of Protestantism. Yet the peace set a dangerous precedent, because it seemed to establish the premise that no sovereign state can tolerate religious diversity. Moreover, it excluded Calvinism entirely and thus spurred German and Scottish Calvinists to become aggressive opponents of the status quo. As a result, Europe was riven by religious warfare for another century and exported that sectarian violence to the New World (see Chapter 14).

Peace of Augsburg guarantees political rulers could determine state religion

The Domestication of Reform

Within two decades, Protestantism had become a diverse revolutionary movement whose underlying claims for the spiritual equality of all Christians had the potential to undermine the political, social, and even gender hierarchies on which European society rested. Luther himself did not anticipate that his ideas might have such implications, and most other prominent Protestant leaders were also reluctant to relinquish the support of existing elites by embracing more radical reforms. As a result, the Reformation movement was speedily "domesticated" in two senses: its revolutionary potential was toned down, and there was an increasing emphasis on the patriarchal family as the central institution of Protestant life.

REFORM AND DISCIPLINE

As we have seen, injunctions to lead a more disciplined and godly life had been a frequent message of previous religious reform movements, especially after the Black Death (Chapter 11). Many of these efforts had been actively promoted by princes and town councils, most famously perhaps in Florence, where the Dominican preacher Girolamo Savonarola led the city on an extraordinary but short-lived campaign of puritanism and moral reform between 1494 and 1498. And there are numerous other examples of rulers legislating against sin. When Erasmus called on secular authorities to think of their territories as giant monasteries, he was sounding an already familiar theme.

Protestant rulers, however, took the need to enforce godly discipline with particular seriousness because the depravity of human nature was a fundamental tenet of Protestant belief. Like Saint Augustine at the end of the fourth century (Chapter 6), they believed that people would inevitably turn out to be bad unless they were compelled to be good. It was therefore the responsibility of secular and religious leaders to control and punish the misbehavior of their people, because otherwise their evil deeds would anger God and destroy human society.

Protestant godliness began with the discipline of children. Luther himself wrote two catechisms (instructional tracts) designed to teach children the tenets of their faith and the obligations—toward parents, masters, and rulers—that God imposed on them. Luther also insisted that all children, boys and girls alike, be taught to read the Bible in their own languages. Schooling thus became a characteristically Protestant preoccupation and rallying cry. Even the Protestant family was designated a "school of godliness," in which fathers were expected to instruct and discipline their wives, children, and household servants.

But family life in the early sixteenth century still left much to be desired in the eyes of Protestant reformers. Drunkenness, domestic violence, illicit sexual relations, dancing, and blasphemous swearing were frequent topics of reforming discourse. Various methods of discipline were attempted, including public confessions of wrongdoing, public penance and shaming, exclusion from church services, and even imprisonment. All of these efforts met with varying, but generally modest, success. Creating godly Protestant families and enforcing discipline within entire communities were going to require the active cooperation of the authorities.

Protestant reformers target family life in moral crusade to create godly discipline

NEW REGIMES OF RELIGIOUS DISCIPLINE

The domestication of the Reformation took place principally in the free towns of Germany, Switzerland, and the Netherlands. Here, Protestant attacks on monasticism and clerical celibacy also found a receptive audience because citizens resented the immunity of monastic houses from taxation and regarded clerical celibacy as a subterfuge for the seduction of their own wives and children. Protestant emphasis on the depravity of the human will also resonated powerfully with guilds and town governments, which were anxious to maintain and increase the control exercised by urban elites (merchants and master craftsmen) over the apprentices and journeymen who made up the majority of the male population. Protestant town governments could thus consolidate all public authority into their own hands.

Meanwhile, Protestant authorities reinforced the domestic power of men by emphasizing the family as the basic unit of religious education. In place of a priest, an all-powerful father figure was expected to assume responsibility for instructing and disciplining his household according to the precepts of reformed religion. At the same time, Protestant regimes introduced a new religious ideal for women. No longer was the virginal nun the exemplar of female holiness; in her place stood the obedient Protestant "goodwife." As one Lutheran prince wrote in 1527, "Those who bear children please God better than all the monks and nuns singing and praying." To some extent, then, Protestantism resolved the tensions between piety and sexuality that had long characterized Christian teachings, by declaring the holiness of marital sex.

But this did not promote a progressive view of women's spiritual potential or elevate their social and political status. Quite the contrary: Luther regarded women as

Marriage and Celibacy: Two Views

These two selections illustrate strong contrasting views on the spiritual value of marriage versus celibacy as embraced by Protestant and Catholic religious authorities. The first selection is part of Martin Luther's more general attack on monasticism, which emphasizes his contention that marriage is the natural and divinely intended state for all human beings. The second selection, from the canons of the Council of Trent (1545–1563), restates traditional Church teaching on the holiness of marriage but also emphasizes the spiritual superiority of virginity to marriage and the necessity of clerical celibacy. Celibacy for all clergy (not only monks and nuns) had been instituted for the first time in the eleventh century (Chapter 8), but it had never been fully accepted, especially in Britain and Scandinavia, or universally practiced.

Luther's Views on the Impossibility of Celibacy (1535)

Listen! In all my days I have not heard the confession of a nun, but in the light of Scripture I shall hit upon how matters fare with her and know I shall not be lying. If a girl is not sustained by great and exceptional grace, she can live without a man as little as she can without eating, drinking, sleeping, and other natural necessities. Nor, on the other hand, can a man dispense with a wife. The reason for this is that procreating children is an urge planted as deeply in human nature as eating and drinking. That is why God has given and put into the body the organs, arteries, fluxes, and everything that serves it. Therefore what is he doing who would check this process and keep nature from running its desired and intended course? He is attempting to keep nature from being nature, fire from burning, water from wetting, and a man from eating, drinking, and sleeping.

Source: E. M. Plass, ed., *What Luther Says*, vol. 2 (St. Louis, MO: 1959), pp. 888–89.

Church Canons on the Sacrament of Matrimony (1563)

CANON 1: If anyone says that matrimony is not truly and properly one of the seven sacraments . . . instituted by Christ the Lord, but has been devised by men in the Church and does not confer grace, let him be anathema [cursed]. . . .

CANON 9: If anyone says that clerics constituted in sacred orders or regulars [monks and nuns] who have made solemn profession of chastity can contract marriage . . . and that all who feel that they have not the gift of chastity, even though they have made such a vow, can contract marriage, let him be anathema, since God does not refuse that gift to those who ask for it rightly, neither does he suffer us to be tempted above that which we are able.

CANON 10: If anyone says that the married state excels the state of virginity or celibacy, and that it is better and happier to be united in matrimony than to remain in virginity or celibacy, let him be anathema.

Source: H. J. Schroeder, *Canons and Decrees of the Council of Trent* (St. Louis, MO: 1941), pp. 181–82.

Questions for Analysis

1. On what grounds does Luther attack the practice of celibacy? Do you agree with his basic premise? Why or why not?

2. How do the canons of the Catholic Church respond to Protestant views such as Luther's? What appears to be at stake in this defense of marriage and celibacy?

even more sexually depraved than men, and less capable of controlling their desires. His opposition to convents rested on his belief that it was impossible for women to remain chaste, so sequestering them simply made illicit behavior inevitable. To prevent sin, it was necessary that all women be married, preferably at a young age, and placed under the governance of a godly husband.

For the most part, Protestant town governments were happy to cooperate in shutting down female monasteries, since a convent's property went to the town. But conflicts did arise between Protestant reformers and town fathers over marriage and sexuality, especially over the reformers' insistence that both men and women should marry young as a restraint on lust. In many towns, men were traditionally expected to delay marriage until they had achieved the status of master craftsman—an expectation that had become increasingly difficult to meet, as guilds sought to restrict the number of journeymen permitted to become masters. In theory, then, apprentices and journeymen were not supposed to marry, but instead were expected to frequent brothels and taverns—a legally sanctioned outlet for extramarital sexuality long viewed as necessary to men's physical well-being—which Protestant reformers now deemed morally abhorrent.

Towns responded to these opposing pressures in various ways. Some instituted special committees to police public morals, as in Calvin's Geneva. Some abandoned the legislation of Protestant reforms altogether. And others, such as the German town of Augsburg, alternated between Protestant and Catholic governance for several decades. Yet regardless of a town's religious allegiance, a revolution had taken place with respect to public morality by the end of the sixteenth century. For in their competition with each other, neither Catholics nor Protestants wished to be seen as soft on sin. The result was the widespread closing of publicly licensed brothels, the outlawing of prostitution, and far stricter supervision of many other aspects of private life than had ever been the case in any Western civilization.

THE CONTROL OF MARRIAGE

Protestant reforming movements also increased parents' control over their children's choice of marital partners. The medieval Church had defined marriage as a sacrament, but one that did not require the involvement of a priest: the mutual consent of two individuals, even if exchanged without witnesses or parental approval, was enough to constitute a legally valid marriage. Opposition to this doctrine had long come from wealthy families, because marriage involved rights of inheritance to property; it was regarded as too important to be left to the choice of unsupervised adolescents. Instead, elite parents wanted the power to prevent unsuitable matches and, in some cases, to force their children to accept the marriage arrangements their families might negotiate on their behalf. For such elites, Protestantism offered an opportunity to obtain this control. Luther had declared marriage to be a purely secular matter, not a sacrament at all, and one that could be regulated however governing authorities thought best. Calvin largely followed suit.

Even the Catholic Church was eventually forced to give way. Although it never abandoned its insistence that both members of a couple must freely consent, the Church's new doctrine required formal public notice of intent to marry and insisted on the presence of a priest at the wedding ceremony. Both rules were efforts to prevent clandestine marriages and to allow families time to intervene before an unsuitable match was concluded. Individual Catholic countries sometimes went even further in asserting parental control: in France, for example, couples who married without parental consent forfeited their rights to inherit property.

In somewhat different ways then, both Protestantism and Catholicism moved to strengthen the control parents could exercise over their children, and husbands over their wives. Both confessions also empowered the state to exercise an unprecedented degree of control over the bodies and individual choices of all people.

The Reformation in England

In England, the Reformation took a rather different course than it did in continental Europe. Although a long tradition of popular dissent paved the way for Protestant ideas, England was not particularly oppressed by the papal abuses that roiled Germany, and English monarchs already exercised a great deal of control over Church appointments and received the lion's share of papal taxes. Even the power of ecclesiastical courts did not inspire any particular resentments; on the contrary, these courts would continue to function in Protestant England until the eighteenth century. Why, then, did England become a Protestant country at all?

"THE KING'S GREAT MATTER"

In 1527, King **Henry VIII** of England (r. 1509–1547) had been married to Ferdinand and Isabella's daughter, Catherine of Aragon, for eighteen years. Yet all the offspring of this union had died in infancy, with the exception of a daughter, Mary. Because Catherine was now past childbearing age and Henry needed a male heir to preserve the peaceful succession to the throne, he had political reasons to propose a change of wife. He also had a more personal motive, having become infatuated with a courtier named Anne Boleyn.

HENRY VIII OF ENGLAND. Hans Holbein the Younger executed several portraits of the English king. This one depicts him in middle age, confident of his powers.

Henry therefore appealed to Rome to annul his marriage to Catherine, arguing that because she had previously been married to his older brother Arthur, who had died in adolescence, his marriage to Catherine had been invalid from the beginning. As Henry's representatives pointed out, the Bible pronounced it "an unclean thing" for a man to marry his brother's wife and cursed such a marriage with childlessness (Leviticus 20:21). Even a papal dispensation, which Henry and Katherine had obtained, could not exempt them from such a clear prohibition—as their childless marriage proved.

Henry's petition put Pope Clement VII (r. 1523–1534) in an awkward position. Popes had long granted annulments to reigning monarchs on far weaker grounds. But if the pope granted Henry's annulment, he would cast doubt on the validity of all papal dispensations. More seriously, he would provoke the wrath of Emperor Charles V, Catherine of Aragon's nephew, whose armies were in firm command of Rome and who at that moment held the pope himself in captivity. Clement was trapped; all he could do was procrastinate and hope that the matter would resolve itself. For two years, he allowed Henry's case to proceed in England without reaching a verdict. Then, suddenly, he transferred the case to Rome, where the legal process began all over again.

Exasperated by these delays, Henry began to increase pressure on the pope. In 1531, he compelled an assembly of English clergy to declare him "protector and only supreme head" of the Church in England. In 1532, he encouraged Parliament to produce an inflammatory list of grievances against the English clergy and used this threat to force their concession to his right, as king, to approve or deny all Church legislation. In January 1533, Henry married Anne Boleyn (already pregnant) even though his marriage to Catherine had still not been annulled. The new archbishop of Canterbury, Thomas Cranmer, later provided the required annulment in May, acting on his own authority.

Henry declares new Church of England with himself as spiritual leader

In September, Princess Elizabeth was born; her father, disappointed again in his hopes for a son, refused to attend her christening. Nevertheless, Parliament settled the succession to the throne on the children of Henry and Anne, redirected all papal revenues from England into the king's hands, prohibited appeals to the papal court, and formally declared the "King's Highness to be Supreme Head of the Church of England." In 1535, Henry executed his former tutor and chancellor, Sir Thomas More (Chapter 12), for his refusal to endorse this declaration of supremacy, and he took steps toward dissolving England's many monasteries. By the end of 1539, these monasteries and convents were emptied and their lands and wealth confiscated by the king, who distributed their properties and revenues to reward his supporters and appease his potential enemies.

These measures, masterminded and engineered by Henry's Protestant adviser Thomas Cromwell (c. 1485–1540), broke the bonds that linked the English Church to Rome. But they did not make England a wholly Protestant country. Although certain traditional practices (such as pilgrimages and the veneration of relics) were prohibited, the **Church of England** remained overwhelmingly Catholic in organization, doctrine, ritual, and language. The Six Articles promulgated by Parliament in 1539 at Henry VIII's behest left no room for doubt as to the official orthodoxy: confession to priests, masses for the dead, and clerical celibacy were all confirmed; the Latin Mass continued; and Catholic eucharistic doctrine was not only confirmed but its denial was made punishable by death. To most English people, only the disappearance of the monasteries and the king's own continuing matrimonial adventures (he married six women in all) were evidence that their Church was no longer in communion with Rome.

THE BRIEF REIGN OF EDWARD VI AND THE RETURN TO CATHOLIC RULE UNDER MARY

For truly committed Protestants, the changes Henry VIII enforced on the English Church did not go nearly far enough. And in 1547, the accession of the nine-year-old king Edward VI (Henry's son by his third wife, Jane Seymour) gave them the opportunity to finish the task of reform. Henry's last wife, Catherine Parr, was a Lutheran sympathizer and, as the teacher of the royal children, contributed greatly to further reforms that stripped many Roman practices from the English Church. Edward's government permitted priests to marry; English services replaced Latin ones; the veneration of images was discouraged and the images themselves were defaced or destroyed; prayers for the dead were declared useless, and endowments for such prayers confiscated; and new articles of belief repudiated all sacraments

Church of England
Founded by Henry VIII in the 1530s as a consequence of his break with the authority of the Roman pope.

The Six Articles of the English Church

Although Henry VIII withdrew the Church of England from obedience to the papacy, he continued to reject most Protestant theology. Some of his advisers, most notably Thomas Cromwell, were committed Protestants, and the king allowed his son and heir, Edward VI, to be raised as a Protestant. But even after several years of rapid (and mostly Protestant) change in the English Church, Henry reasserted a set of traditional Catholic doctrines in the Six Articles of 1539. These remained binding on the Church of England until the king's death in 1547.

First, that in the most blessed sacrament of the altar, by the strength and efficacy of Christ's mighty word, it being spoken by the priest, is present really, under the form of bread and wine, the natural body and blood of our Savior Jesus Christ, conceived of the Virgin Mary, and that after the consecration there remains no substance of bread or wine, nor any other substance but the substance of Christ, God and man;

Secondly, that communion in both kinds is not necessary for salvation, by the law of God, to all persons, and that it is to be believed and not doubted . . . that in the flesh, under the form of bread, is the very blood, and with the blood, under the form of wine, is the very flesh, as well apart as though they were both together;

Thirdly, that priests, after the order of priesthood received as afore, may not marry by the law of God;

Fourthly, that vows of chastity or widowhood by man or woman made to God advisedly ought to be observed by the law of God. . . .

Fifthly, that it is right and necessary that private masses be continued and admitted in this the king's English Church and congregation . . . whereby good Christian people . . . do receive both godly and goodly consolations and benefits; and it is agreeable also to God's law;

Sixthly, that oral, private confession is expedient and necessary to be retained and continued, used and frequented in the church of God.

Source: *Statutes of the Realm*, vol. 3 (London: 1810–1828), p. 739 (modernized).

Questions for Analysis

1. Three of these six articles focus on the sacrament of the Eucharist (the Mass). Given what you have learned in this chapter, why would Henry have been so concerned about this sacrament? What does this reveal about his values and those of his contemporaries?

2. Given Henry's insistence on these articles, why might he have allowed his son to be raised a Protestant? What does this suggest about the political situation in England?

except Baptism and Communion, affirming the Protestant creed of justification by faith alone. Most important, *The Book of Common Prayer* by Archbishop Cranmer, considered one of the great landmarks of English literature, defined precisely how the new English-language services of the church were to be conducted.

Yet Edward's reign was brief and his successor was his much older half-sister Mary (r. 1553–1558): a committed Catholic and granddaughter of the "Most Catholic" Ferdinand and Isabella. Mary speedily reversed her half-brother's religious policies, restoring the Latin Mass and requiring married priests to give up their wives. She even prevailed on Parliament to vote for England's return to papal allegiance. Hundreds of Protestant leaders fled abroad, many to Geneva; others, including Archbishop Cranmer, were burned at the stake for refusing to abjure their

QUEEN MARY AND QUEEN ELIZABETH. The two daughters of Henry VIII, Queen Mary (left) and Queen Elizabeth (right), were the first two queens regnant of England; that is, the first women to rule in their own right. Despite the similar challenges they faced, they had strikingly different fates and have been treated very differently in popular histories. **› How do these two portraits suggest differences in the queens' personalities and their self-representation as rulers?**

Protestantism. News of the martyrdoms shocked Protestant Europe, but Mary's policies sparked relatively little resistance. After two decades of religious upheaval, most English men and women were probably hoping that Mary's reign would bring some stability to their lives.

This, however, Mary could not do. The executions she ordered were insufficient to wipe out religious resistance; instead, Protestant propaganda about "Bloody Mary" caused widespread unease, even among those who welcomed the return of traditional religious forms. She also could not restore monasticism, because too many leading families had profited from Henry VIII's dissolution for her to reverse this policy. Mary's marriage to her cousin Philip, Charles V's son and heir to the Spanish throne, was another miscalculation. Although the marriage treaty stipulated that Philip could not succeed her, in the event of her death, her English subjects never trusted him. When she allowed herself to be drawn by Philip into a war with France on Spain's behalf—in which England lost Calais, its last foothold on the European continent—many became highly disaffected.

Ultimately, however, what doomed Mary's policies was an accident of biology: she was unable to conceive an heir. When she died after only five years of rule, her throne passed to her Protestant half-sister, Elizabeth.

THE ELIZABETHAN SETTLEMENT

The daughter of Henry VIII and Anne Boleyn, Elizabeth (r. 1558–1603) was predisposed in favor of Protestantism by the circumstances of her parents' marriage as well as by her upbringing. But Elizabeth also recognized that supporting radical Protestantism in England might provoke bitter sectarian strife. Accordingly, she presided over what is often known as the "Elizabethan settlement" or compromise. By a new Act of Supremacy (1559), she repealed Mary's Catholic legislation, prohibiting foreign religious powers (the pope) from exercising any authority within England and declaring herself "supreme governor" of the English Church—a more Protestant title than Henry VIII's "supreme head," since most Protestants believed that Christ alone was the head of the Church. She also adopted many of the Protestant liturgical reforms instituted by her half-brother Edward, including Cranmer's revised version of *The Book of Common Prayer*.

In Act of Supremacy, Elizabeth brings back Anglican Church in a slightly more Protestant form

But Elizabeth retained vestiges of Catholic practice, too, including the hierarchy of bishops, church courts, and many liturgical rites. Still, religious tensions persisted, not only between Protestants and Catholics but also between moderate and more extreme Protestants. On the one hand, the queen was obliged to continue Mary's practice of persecuting notorious heretics—in this case, Catholics who refused to practice their faith discreetly—and executing them for treason. On the other hand, her attempts to promote a "middle way" among competing forms of Christianity caused dissatisfaction among hard-liners of all stripes.

In the long run, what preserved the "Elizabethan settlement" was the extraordinary length of the queen's reign and the fact that, for much of that time, Protestant England was at war with Catholic Spain. Under Elizabeth, Protestantism and English forms of nationalism gradually fused into a potent conviction that God himself had chosen England for greatness. After 1588, when English naval forces won an improbable victory over the Spanish Armada (see Chapter 14), Protestantism and Englishness became nearly indistinguishable. Laws against Catholic practices became increasingly severe, and although an English Catholic tradition survived, its adherents were a small minority. In Ireland, where the vast majority of people remained Catholic despite the government's efforts to impose Protestantism, Irishness would be as firmly identified with Catholicism as was Englishness with Protestantism—but it was the Protestants who were in power in both countries.

The Rebirth of the Roman Catholic Church

Counter-Reformation The movement to counter the Protestant Reformation, initiated by the Catholic Church at the Council of Trent in 1545.

So far, our account of Protestantism has cast the spotlight on dissident reformers such as Luther and Calvin. But there was also a powerful reform movement within the Church during the same decades, which resulted in the birth (or rebirth) of a Catholic ("universal") faith. For some, this movement is the "Catholic Reformation"; for others, it is the "**Counter-Reformation**." Those who prefer the former term emphasize that the Church was continuing significant reforming movements that can be traced back to the eleventh century (Chapter 8) and that gained new momentum in the wake of the Great Schism (Chapter 11). Others insist that most Catholic reformers of this period were reactionaries, inspired primarily by the urgent need to resist Protestantism and strengthen the power of the Roman Church in opposition.

CATHOLIC REFORMS

Even before Luther's challenge, there was a strong movement for moral and institutional reform within the Church, as we have seen. And while the papacy showed little interest in these efforts, they were receiving new support from several secular rulers. In Spain, for example, reforming activities directed by Cardinal Francisco Jiménez de Cisneros (1436–1517) were designed to eliminate abuses prevalent among the clergy. Jiménez (*he-MEN-ez*) also helped to regenerate the spiritual life of the Spanish Church. In Italy, earnest clerics labored to make the Italian Church more worthy of its prominent position despite the poor example set by the papal court. Some new religious orders, dedicated to high ideals of piety and social service, were also emerging. In northern Europe, Christian humanists such as Erasmus and Thomas More played a role in this Catholic reform movement (Chapter 12).

These internal measures were inadequate, however, as a response to the concerted challenges of Protestantism. Starting in the 1530s, therefore, a more aggressive phase of reform began to gather momentum under a new style of vigorous papal leadership. The Counter-Reformation popes Paul III (r. 1534–1549), Paul IV (r. 1555–1559), Pius V (r. 1566–1572), and Sixtus V (r. 1585–1590) were the most zealous reformers of the Church since the eleventh century. All led upright lives; some, indeed, were so grimly ascetic that contemporaries longed for the bad old days. And these Counter-Reformation popes were not merely holy men but also accomplished administrators, reorganizing papal finances and filling ecclesiastical offices with bishops and abbots who were no less renowned for austerity and holiness than the popes themselves.

Papal reform efforts were consolidated at the **Council of Trent**, a general meeting of the entire Church convened in 1545 and continuing at intervals until 1563. The decisions made at Trent, a provincial capital of the Holy Roman Empire (Trento in modern-day Italy), provided the foundations on which a new Roman Catholic Church would be erected. Although the council began by debating some form of compromise with Protestantism, it ended by reaffirming all the Catholic tenets challenged by Protestant critics. "Good works" were affirmed as necessary for salvation and all seven sacraments were declared indispensable, without which salvation was impossible. Transubstantiation, purgatory, the

Council of Trent
The name given to a series of meetings held in the Italian city of Trent (Trento) between 1545 and 1563, when leaders of the Roman Church reaffirmed Catholic doctrine and instituted internal reforms.

THE INSPIRATION OF SAINT JEROME, BY GUIDO RENI (1635). The Council of Trent declared Saint Jerome's Latin translation of the Bible, the Vulgate, to be the Catholic Church's official version. Biblical scholars had known since the early sixteenth century that Saint Jerome's translation contained numerous mistakes, so Catholic defenders of the Vulgate insisted that even his mistakes had been divinely inspired. **› How does this painting attempt to make this point?**

invocation of saints, and the discipline of celibacy for the clergy were all confirmed as dogmas—essential elements—of the Catholic faith. The Bible, in its imperfect Vulgate translation (not the critical edition of Erasmus: Chapter 12), and the traditions of apostolic teaching were held to be of equal authority. Papal supremacy over every bishop and priest was expressly maintained, and the supremacy of the pope over any Church council was declared outright, signaling a final defeat of the still-active conciliar movement (Chapter 11). The Council of Trent even reaffirmed the doctrine of indulgences that had touched off the Lutheran revolt, although it condemned the worst abuses connected with their sale.

The decrees issued at Trent were not confined to matters of doctrine. To improve pastoral care of the laity, bishops and priests were forbidden to hold more than one spiritual office. To address concerns that priests were not sufficiently prepared for their tasks, a theological seminary was to be established in every diocese. The council also suppressed a variety of local religious practices and saints' cults, replacing them with new cults authorized and approved by Rome. To prevent heretical ideas from corrupting the faithful, the council further decided to censor or suppress dangerous books.

In 1564, a specially appointed commission published the first Index of Prohibited Books, an official list of writings forbidden to Catholics. It is ironic that all of Erasmus's works were immediately placed in the Index, even though he had been a champion of the Church against Martin Luther only forty years before. A permanent agency known as the Sacred Congregation of the Index was later set up to revise the list, which was maintained until 1966, when it was abolished after the Second Vatican Council (1962–1965). For centuries, it symbolized the doctrinal intolerance that characterized much of sixteenth-century Christianity, in both Catholic and Protestant varieties.

Seeking to maintain purity of Catholic doctrine, Council of Trent turns to censorship

IGNATIUS LOYOLA AND THE SOCIETY OF JESUS

Another force propelling the Counter-Reformation was the foundation of the **Society of Jesus** (commonly known as the Jesuits) by **Ignatius Loyola** (1491–1556). In the midst of a career as a mercenary, this young Spanish nobleman had been wounded in battle in 1521: the same year in which Luther defied authority at the Diet of Worms. While recuperating, he turned from the reading of chivalric romances to a romantic retelling of the life of Jesus. The impact of this experience convinced him to become a spiritual soldier of Christ.

For ten months, Ignatius lived as a hermit in a cave near the town of Manresa, where he experienced ecstatic visions and worked out the principles of his subsequent guidebook, the *Spiritual Exercises*. This manual, completed in 1535 and first published in 1541, offered practical advice on how to master one's will and serve God through a systematic program of meditations on sin and on the life of Christ. It eventually became the basic handbook for all Jesuits and has been widely studied by Catholic laypeople, as well. Indeed, Loyola's *Spiritual Exercises* ranks alongside Calvin's *Institutes* as the most influential religious text of the sixteenth century.

The Jesuit order originated as a group of six disciples who gathered around Loyola during his belated career as a student in Paris. Vowing to serve God in

Society of Jesus The religious order commonly known as the Jesuits, founded in 1540 by Ignatius Loyola to combat the spread of Protestantism.

Ignatius Loyola (1491–1556) Founder of the Society of Jesus (commonly known as the Jesuits), whose members vowed to serve God through poverty, chastity, and missionary work.

The Demands of Obedience

The necessity of obedience in the spiritual formation of monks and nuns can be traced back to the Rule *of Saint Benedict in the early sixth century. In keeping with the mission of its founder, Ignatius of Loyola (1491–1556), the Society of Jesus brought renewed fervor to this old ideal, dedicating its members to superior intellectual achievements, teaching, and missionary work. Below are excerpts from two of the order's founding texts, the* Spiritual Exercises *of Ignatius and the* Jesuit Constitutions.

Rules for Thinking with the Church

1. Always to be ready to obey with mind and heart, setting aside all judgment of one's own, the true spouse of Jesus Christ, our holy mother, our infallible and orthodox mistress, the Catholic Church, whose authority is exercised over us by the hierarchy.

2. To commend the confession of sins to a priest as it is practised in the Church; the reception of the Holy Eucharist once a year, or better still every week, or at least every month, with the necessary preparation....

* * *

4. To have a great esteem for the religious orders, and to give the preference to celibacy or virginity over the married state....

* * *

6. To praise relics, the veneration and invocation of Saints: also the stations, and pious pilgrimages, indulgences, jubilees, the custom of lighting candles in the churches, and other such aids to piety and devotion....

* * *

9. To uphold especially all the precepts of the Church, and not censure them in any manner; but, on the contrary, to defend them promptly, with reasons drawn from all sources, against those who criticize them.

10. To be eager to commend the decrees, mandates, traditions, rites, and customs of the Fathers in the Faith or our superiors....

11. That we may be altogether of the same mind and in conformity with the Church herself, if she shall have defined anything to be black which to our eyes appears to be white, we ought in like manner to pronounce it to be black. For we must undoubtingly believe, that the Spirit of our Lord Jesus Christ, and the Spirit of the Orthodox Church His Spouse, by which Spirit we are governed and directed to salvation, is the same....

From the Constitutions of the Jesuit Order

Let us with the utmost pains strain every nerve of our strength to exhibit this virtue of obedience, firstly to the Highest Pontiff, then to the Superiors of the Society; so that in all things . . . we may be most ready to obey his voice, just as if it issued from Christ our Lord . . . leaving any work, even a letter, that we have begun and have not yet finished; by directing to this goal all our strength and intention in the Lord, that holy obedience may be made perfect in us in every respect, in performance, in will, in intellect; by submitting to whatever may be enjoined on us with great readiness, with spiritual joy and perseverance; by persuading ourselves that all things [commanded] are just; by rejecting with a kind of blind obedience all opposing opinion or judgment of our own.

Source: Henry Bettenson, ed., *Documents of the Christian Church,* 2nd ed. (Oxford: 1967), pp. 259–61.

Questions for Analysis

1. How might Loyola's career as a soldier have inspired the language used in his "Rules for Thinking with the Church"?

2. In what ways do these Jesuit principles respond directly to the challenges of Protestant reformers?

poverty, chastity, and missionary work, they were formally constituted by Pope Paul III in 1540. By the time of Loyola's death, the Society of Jesus already numbered some one thousand five hundred members. It was by far the most militant of the religious orders fostered by the Catholic reform movements of the sixteenth century: not merely a monastic society but a company of soldiers sworn to defend the faith through eloquence, persuasion, and correct instruction. Their activities consisted primarily of proselytizing and establishing schools, which meant that they were ideal emissaries for the Counter-Reformation. Accordingly, Jesuits were soon dispatched to preach and teach in India, China, and the Spanish colonies in the Americas. One of Loyola's closest associates, Francis Xavier (*ZAY-vyer*; 1506–1552), baptized thousands of people and traveled thousands of miles in South and East Asia.

Although Loyola had not conceived of his society as a battalion of "shock troops" in the fight against Protestantism, that is what it became. Through preaching and diplomacy—sometimes at the risk of their lives—Jesuits in the second half of the sixteenth century helped to colonize the world. In many places, they were instrumental in keeping rulers and their subjects loyal to Catholicism; in others, they met martyrdom; and in still others, notably Poland and parts of Germany and France, they succeeded in regaining territory previously lost to followers of Luther and Calvin. Wherever they were allowed to settle, they set up schools and colleges on the grounds that only a vigorous Catholicism nurtured by widespread literacy and education could combat Protestantism.

> *After Loyola's death, his Society of Jesus has global impact*

A NEW CATHOLIC CHURCH

The greatest achievement of these reform movements was the revitalization of the Roman Church. Had it not been for such determined efforts, Catholicism would not have swept over the globe during the seventeenth and eighteenth centuries—or reemerged in Europe as a vigorous spiritual force.

The reforms had other consequences, such as the rapid advancement of lay literacy in Catholic countries and the growth of intense concern for acts of charity. Because Catholicism continued to emphasize good works as well as faith, charitable activities took on an extremely important role.

There was also a renewed emphasis on the role of religious women. While Catholicism did not exalt marriage as a route to holiness to the same degree as Protestantism, it did encourage the piety of female religious elites. For example, it embraced the mysticism of Saint Teresa of Ávila (1515–1582) and her renewal of religious women's spirituality through new orders of nuns, such as the Ursulines and the Sisters of Charity. Both Protestants and Catholics continued to exclude women from the priesthood or ministry, but Catholic women could pursue religious lives with at least some degree of independence; the convent thus continued to be a route toward spiritual and even political advancement.

The reformed Catholic Church did not, however, embrace the tolerant Christianity of Erasmus. Instead, Christian humanists lost favor with the papacy, and even scientists such as Galileo were regarded with suspicion (see Chapter 16). Yet contemporary Protestantism was just as intolerant and sometimes even more hostile to the cause of rational thought. Indeed, because Catholic theologians turned for guidance to the scholasticism of Thomas Aquinas (Chapter 9), they tended to be much more committed to the dignity of human reason than some of their Protestant counterparts, who emphasized the literal interpretation of the Bible and the importance of unquestioning faith. It is no coincidence that René Descartes, one of the pioneers of rational philosophy ("I think, therefore I am"), was educated by Jesuits.

It would be wrong, therefore, to claim that the Protestantism of this era was more forward-looking or progressive than Catholicism. Both were, in fact, products of the same troubled time. Each variety of Protestantism responded to specific historical conditions and the needs of specific peoples in specific places, while carrying forward certain aspects of the Christian tradition considered valuable by those communities. The Catholic Church also responded to new spiritual, political, and social realities—to such an extent that it must be regarded as distinct from either the early Church of the later Roman Empire or the ever-evolving Church of the Middle Ages. That is why the phrase "Roman Catholic Church" has not appeared in this book prior to this chapter; the Roman Catholic Church as we know it emerged in the sixteenth century.

Conclusion

The Reformation grew out of the complex historical processes that we have been tracing in the last few chapters. Foremost among these was the increasing power of Europe's sovereign states. As we have seen, the German princes who embraced Protestantism were moved to do so by their desire for sovereignty. The kings of Denmark, Sweden, and England followed suit for many of the same reasons. Protestantism bolstered state power because Protestant leaders preached absolute obedience to godly rulers, and the state in Protestant countries assumed direct control of its churches. Yet the power of the state had been growing for a long time prior to the Reformation, especially in such countries as France and Spain, where Catholic kings already exercised most of the same rights that were seized by Lutheran authorities and by Henry VIII of England. Those rulers who aligned themselves with Catholicism, then, had the same need to bolster their sovereignty and power.

Ideas of national identity, too, were already influential and available for manipulation by Protestants and Catholics alike. Religion thus became a new source of both identity and disunity. Prior to the Reformation, peoples in different regions of Germany spoke such different dialects that they had difficulty understanding each other. But Luther's Bible gained such currency that it eventually became the linguistic standard for all these disparate regions, which began to conceive of themselves as part of a single nation. Yet religion alone could not achieve the political unification of Germany, which did not occur for another three hundred years (see Chapter 21); and, indeed, it contributed to existing divisions by cementing the opposition of Catholic princes and peoples. Elsewhere in Europe—as in the Netherlands, where Protestants fought successfully against a foreign, Catholic overlord—religion created a shared identity where politics could not. In England, where it is arguable that a certain sense of nationalism had already been fostered before the Reformation (Chapter 12), membership in the Church of England became a new, if not uncontested, attribute of "Englishness."

Ideals characteristic of the Renaissance also contributed something to the Reformation and the Catholic responses to it. The criticisms of Christian humanists helped to prepare Europe for the challenges of Lutheranism, and close textual study of the Bible led to the publication of the newer, more accurate editions used by Protestant reformers. For example, Erasmus's improved edition of the Latin New Testament enabled Luther to reach some crucial theological conclusions and became the foundation for Luther's own translation of the Bible. However, Erasmus was not a supporter of Lutheran principles and most other Christian humanists shunned Protestantism as soon as it became clear to them what Luther was actually teaching. Indeed, in certain basic respects, Protestant doctrine was completely at odds with the principles, politics, and beliefs of most humanists, who mostly became staunch supporters of the Catholic Church.

AFTER YOU READ THIS CHAPTER

CHRONOLOGY

1517	Luther posts the Ninety-Five Theses
1520s	Lutheranism becomes the official religion of Scandinavian countries
1521	Luther is excommunicated at the Diet of Worms
1525	German peasants' revolt
1529	Luther breaks with Zwingli
1534	Henry VIII establishes the Church of England
1534	Ignatius Loyola founds the Society of Jesus (the Jesuits)
1541	Geneva adopts a theocratic government based on Calvinism
1545–1563	Council of Trent is convened
1555	Peace of Augsburg
1553–1558	Mary Tudor attempts to restore the Catholic faith in England
1559	Elizabeth reestablishes Protestantism in England
1564	Papal Index of Forbidden Books is published for the first time

REVIEWING THE OBJECTIVES

❯ The main premises of Luther's theology had religious, political, and social implications. What were they?

❯ Switzerland fostered a number of different Protestant movements. Why was this the case?

❯ The Reformation had a profound effect on the basic structures of family life and on the attitudes toward marriage and morality. Describe these changes.

❯ The Church of England was established in response to what specific political situation?

❯ How did the Catholic Church respond to the challenge of Protestantism?

In the Americas and Asia, both Protestantism and Catholicism became forces of imperialism and new catalysts for competition. The race to secure colonies and resources now became a race for converts, too, as missionaries of both faiths fanned out over the globe. In the process, the confessional divisions of Europe were mapped onto these regions, often with violent results. Over the course of the ensuing century, newly sovereign nation-states would struggle for hegemony at home and abroad, setting off a series of religious wars that would cause as much destruction as any plague. Meanwhile, Western civilizations' extension into the Atlantic would create new ecosystems, forms of wealth, and types of bondage.

 Go to **INQUIZITIVE** to see what you've learned—and learn what you've missed—with personalized feedback along the way.

PEOPLE, IDEAS, AND EVENTS IN CONTEXT

> How did **MARTIN LUTHER**'s attack on **INDULGENCES** tap into a more widespread criticism of the papacy? What role did the printing press and the German vernacular play in the dissemination of his ideas?

> Why did many German principalities and cities rally to Luther's cause? Why did his condemnation at the **DIET OF WORMS** not lead to his execution on charges of heresy?

> How did the Protestant teachings of **ULRICH ZWINGLI, JOHN CALVIN**, and the **ANABAPTISTS** differ from one another and from those of Luther?

> What factors made some of Europe's territories more receptive to **PROTESTANTISM** than others? What was the meaning of the principle *cuius regio, eius religio*, established by the Peace of Augsburg?

> How did the **REFORMATION** alter the status and lives of women in Europe? Why did it strengthen male authority in the family?

> Why did **HENRY VIII** break with Rome? How did the **CHURCH OF ENGLAND** differ from other Protestant churches in Europe?

> What decisions were made at the **COUNCIL OF TRENT**? What were the founding principles of **IGNATIUS LOYOLA**'s **SOCIETY OF JESUS**, and what was its role in the **COUNTER-REFORMATION** of the Catholic Church?

THINKING ABOUT CONNECTIONS

> Our study of Western civilizations has shown that reforming movements are nothing new, and Christianity has been continually reformed throughout its long history. What made this Reformation so different?

> Was a Protestant break from the Catholic Church inevitable? Why or why not?

> The political, social, and religious structures put in place during this era continue to shape our lives in such profound ways that we scarcely notice them—or we assume them to be inevitable and natural. In your view, what is the farthest-reaching consequence of this age of dissent and division? Why? In what ways has it formed your own values and assumptions?

Europe in the Atlantic World, 1550–1660

THE ATLANTIC OCEAN THRASHES the western shores of Europe and Africa with waves that have traveled thousands of miles from the American coasts. It links continents shaped by a wide variety of climates and ecologies. For most of human history, the limited movement of peoples across the ocean meant that each region nurtured its own forms of plant and animal life, and its own unique microbes and pathogens.

But in the sixteenth century, the Atlantic world became an arena of cultural and economic exchange that broke down the isolation of these ecosystems. Populations of humans, animals, and plants on once-remote shores came into frequent and intense contact. Europeans brought diseases that devastated the peoples of the Americas, along with gunpowder and a hotly divided Christianity. Meanwhile, the huge influx of silver from South America transformed (and eventually exploded) the cash-starved European economy, along with the arrival of American stimulants such as tobacco, sugar, and chocolate. The need for slaves to power the plantations that supplied these consumer products fostered a vast industry of human trafficking and caused the violent removal of nearly eleven million people from Africa over the course of three centuries. Colonial ventures in North and South America also created new social hierarchies and forms of inequality, which unsettled even long-established structures in Europe, too. The indigenous peoples of the Americas were forced to deal with newly arrived settlers and the meddling interference of distant imperial bureaucracies.

BEFORE
YOU
READ
THIS
CHAPTER
>

> By the middle of the sixteenth century, the Atlantic Ocean had become a central space for colonization, migration, and settlement, as the peoples of this Atlantic world confronted each other.

> In the wake of the Reformation, Europe itself remained politically unstable, and devastating religious wars were waged on the Continent. In England, mounting pressures caused a crisis that resulted in civil war and the execution of the reigning king.

> At the same time, competition in the wider Atlantic world exported these political and religious conflicts to the new European colonies.

> This widening world and its pervasive violence caused many Europeans to question the beliefs of earlier generations. Intellectuals and artists sought new sources of authority and new ways of explaining the complex circumstances of their time.

CORE OBJECTIVES

> **TRACE** the new linkages between Western civilizations and the Atlantic world, and **EXPLAIN** their consequences.

> **DESCRIBE** the various forms of unfree labor that developed in European colonies during this period.

> **IDENTIFY** the monarchies that dominated Europe and the Atlantic world and the newer powers whose influence was expanding.

> **EXPLAIN** the reasons for Europe's religious and political instability and its consequences for Europe's monarchies and the Atlantic world.

> **UNDERSTAND** how artists and intellectuals responded to the crises and uncertainties of this era.

Meanwhile, European states were riven by dissent and deadly competitions among themselves. Galvanized by the crisis of the Reformation (Chapter 13), the Roman Catholic Church sought to spread its influence to the Americas and Asia through the work of new missionary orders. Attempts by the Catholic Habsburg monarchy to enforce religious uniformity among the varied territories of central Europe led to the Thirty Years' War, one of the longest and bloodiest conflicts in history. These deadly disputes pushed persecuted minorities to emigrate, replanting and propagating religious rivalries throughout the Atlantic world.

Religion was not the only cause of conflict. Tension was growing between powerful monarchs and landowning elites who disputed the right of rulers to raise revenues through increased taxation. As notions of kingship were strained, political and moral philosophers struggled to redefine the role of government in a world of religious pluralism and to articulate new ideologies that did not necessitate violence among peoples of different faiths. Intellectuals and artists also strove to reassess the place of Europe in an expanding world, and to make sense of the profound changes that were occurring in daily life.

The Emergence of the Atlantic World

By the middle of the sixteenth century, Spanish and Portuguese ventures into Africa, the Caribbean, and South America were galvanizing other European kingdoms to launch imperial experiments of their own. In 1497–1498, the Italian-born explorer John Cabot was hired by the English crown to explore the mouth of the St. Lawrence River; but it was nearly a century later, in 1585, that Walter Raleigh attempted to start an English colony just north of Spanish Florida. The settlement at Roanoke Island (present-day North Carolina) was intended to solidify English claims to the territory of Virginia, named for the "Virgin Queen" Elizabeth. It originally encompassed the North American seaboard from South Carolina to Maine, including Bermuda.

However, this bold experiment ended with the disappearance of the first colonists. It was followed by Christopher Newport's expedition to the Chesapeake Bay in 1606: a voyage funded by a private London firm, the Virginia Company. Newport and his followers did not conceive of themselves as empire builders. They were "gentleman planters" whose goal was to provide agricultural goods for the European market and so make their fortunes before returning home. Nevertheless, Newport's band was prepared to subdue any indigenous peoples who proved uncooperative. So when the Powhatan tribe killed one-third of the settlers during a raid in 1622, the colonists responded by crushing the tribe and seizing their lands.

For decades thereafter, the native populations of North America remained capable of both threatening and nurturing the fragile European settlements on the coast. Especially in the early years of colonization, when the number of European immigrants was small, some Native American peoples sought to take advantage of these contacts to trade for goods otherwise unavailable to them. European settlers, for their part, often behaved with a combination of paternalism and contempt for the peoples they encountered. Some hoped to make converts to Christianity, others sought laborers. Ultimately, however, the balance was tipped by environmental, biological, and demographic factors.

Chief motivations for English colonists: fortune from trade

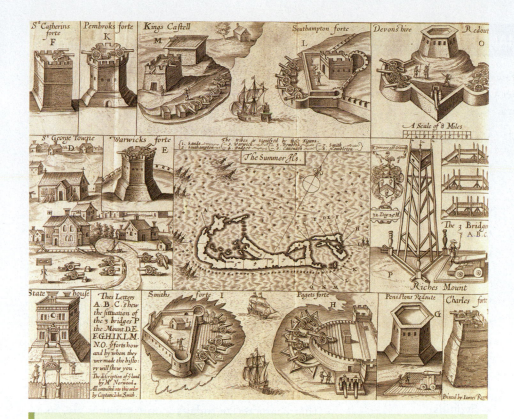

THE ISLAND OF BERMUDA. This map of the "Summer Isle" of Bermuda and the accompanying images of its major fortifications and sites were drawn by Captain John Smith and published in *The Generall Historie of Virginia, New-England, and the Summer Isles* (1624). **› Why would such features be of interest to readers of this pamphlet?**

THE COLUMBIAN EXCHANGE AND ITS ENVIRONMENTAL EFFECTS

The accelerating rate of global connections in the sixteenth century precipitated the unprecedented movement of peoples, plants, animals, and bacteria. This movement is known as the "**Columbian exchange**," and it soon came to encompass lands that lay far beyond the purview of Columbus and his contemporaries, including Australia and the Pacific Islands.

Because of its profound consequences, the Columbian exchange is a fundamental turning point in both human history and the history of the earth's ecology. It put new agricultural products into circulation, introduced new species of animals, and accidentally encouraged the spread of diseases and the devastating invasions of nonnative plants and animals. For example, the introduction of pigs and dogs to islands in the Atlantic and Pacific resulted in the extinction of indigenous animals and birds. The landscapes of Central America and southwestern North America were denuded of vegetation after Spanish settlers attempted large-scale herding and ranching operations. European honeybees displaced native insect populations and fostered harmful plant species. Gray squirrels and raccoons from North America

Columbian exchange The widespread exchange of peoples, plants, animals, diseases, goods, and culture between the African and Eurasian landmasses (on the one hand) and the region that encompasses the Americas, Australia and the Pacific Islands (on the other); precipitated by Christopher Columbus.

THE COLUMBIAN EXCHANGE

The following are just a few of the commodities and contagions that moved between the Old World and the New World in this era.

Old World → New World	New World → Old World
• Wheat	• Corn
• Sugar	• Potatoes
• Bananas	• Beans
• Rice	• Squash
• Wine grapes	• Pumpkins
• Horses	• Tomatoes
• Pigs	• Avocados
• Chickens	• Chili peppers
• Sheep	• Pineapples
• Cattle	• Cocoa
• Smallpox	• Tobacco
• Measles	• Syphilis
• Typhus	

found their way to Britain and the European Continent, and brown rats and even some species of earthworms were transported to the Americas. Insects from all over the world traveled to new environments and spread unfamiliar forms of bacteria and pollen.

The mass transfer—voluntary or violent—of human populations accelerated this process. Entire peoples were wiped out by force, resettlement, or disease. As much as 90 percent of the pre-Columbian population of the Americas died of smallpox, cholera, influenza, typhoid, measles, malaria, and bubonic plague—all brought from Europe. Syphilis, in contrast, appears to have been brought to Europe from the Americas, possibly by Columbus's own sailors.

Meanwhile, the importation of foodstuffs from one part of the world to another, and their cultivation in new habitats, revolutionized the diets of local populations. The American potato, which could be grown in substandard soil and stored for long periods, eventually became the staple diet of the European poor. Indeed, the foods and flavors that characterize today's iconic cuisines are, to an extraordinary degree, the result of the Columbian exchange. Who can imagine an English meal without potatoes? Switzerland or Belgium without chocolate? Thai food without chili peppers? On the other side of the Atlantic, Florida without oranges? Colombia without coffee? Hawaii without pineapples? Of the ingredients that make up the quintessential American hamburger—ground-beef patties on a bun with lettuce, tomato, pickles, onion, and (if you like) cheese—only one component is indigenous to America: tomato. Everything else is Old World. Even the name is European, a reference to Hamburg in Germany.

EARLY COLONIAL POPULATIONS

Most newcomers to the Americas are Africans forced into enslavement

Compared with the seven million Africans forced to labor and die on plantations across the Atlantic, only about 1.5 million Europeans immigrated to the Americas in the sixteenth and seventeenth centuries. Most of them were men, and they were subject to high mortality rates. Rulers did what they could to encourage fresh waves of settlement, but the number of those who chose to seek their fortunes abroad remained relatively small during this period.

In the Spanish colonies, by 1570, some hundred and fifty thousand settlers were largely concentrated in the military and administrative centers of the empire. Even the owners of plantations lived in cities, with foremen to manage their estates. Only those who had been granted *encomiendas* tended to live on the lands entrusted to them by the crown (the Spanish verb *encomendar* means "to entrust"). The *encomienda* system was an extension of the earlier "reconquista" of Spain (Chapter 12), originally set up to manage Muslim populations in territories captured by Christian crusaders.

In the American version of the system, the lands overseen by *encomenderos* were still technically owned by native peoples; but in practice, settlers exploited the land for their own profit, treating native workers like serfs. Some *encomenderos* were descendants of the first conquistadors. Others were drawn from Aztec and Inca elites, many of whom were women—including the daughters of the Aztec emperor Montezuma.

In North America, by contrast, English colonies in New England and the Chesapeake Bay were tiny and rural. Yet they grew more quickly, with settlers numbering about a quarter of a million by 1700. Part of the reason for this growth was the greater impetus for emigration caused by overpopulation in the British Isles. The persecution of radical Protestant groups also played an important role in driving immigration, especially to the New England colonies, where relocation of entire families and even communities was common. The colonies in Virginia offered additional incentives by granting a hundred acres to each settler.

The numbers of migrants was also swelled by indentured servitude, a practice that brought thousands of "free" European laborers across the Atlantic under terms that made them temporary slaves. The term "indenture" refers to the contract that bound a servant to a master for a set period of time: copied in duplicate on a single sheet of paper or parchment, the two halves would be cut apart in such a way as to leave jagged edges that looked like teeth (in Latin, *dentes*) and which could be fitted together to prove the contract's validity. As much as 80 percent of the people who arrived in the Chesapeake colony were indentured servants, nearly a quarter of them women.

 Indentured servitude: a different form of unfree labor

NEW SOCIAL HIERARCHIES IN NEW SPAIN

After the conquests of the Aztec and Inca Empires (Chapter 12), the Spanish established colonial governments in Mexico and Peru. Overseen by a bureaucracy in Madrid, these colonies were highly centralized—but only because they built on the administrative structures of indigenous governments. For the most part, native peoples already lived in large, well-regulated villages and towns, so the Spanish government worked closely with local elites to maintain order. Indeed, the *encomienda* system was so effective because it also built on these existing structures and did not attempt to uproot or eliminate existing native cultures; it focused, instead, on exploiting native labor, especially for extracting mineral resources. Although farming and ranching were encouraged, mining dominated the Spanish colonial economy in this era.

 Spanish colonizers partner with Aztec and Inca elites in efficient, yet exploitative, rule

While the Spanish worked to convert native peoples to Catholicism, they did not attempt to change basic patterns of life. The result was widespread cultural assimilation by the relatively small numbers of (usually male) European settlers, who mostly intermarried with their colonial subjects. This pattern gave rise to a complex and distinctive caste system in New Spain, with a few "pure-blooded" immigrants at the top, a large number of creoles (peoples of mixed descent) in the middle, and Native Americans at the bottom. In theory, these racial categories also corresponded to class distinctions; but in practice, race and class did not always coincide. Racial concepts were extremely flexible, and prosperous families of mixed descent often found ways to establish their "pure" Spanish ancestry by adopting the social practices of colonial elites. The lingering effects of this complicated stratification can still be seen in Latin America today.

Enslaved Native Laborers at Potosí

The Spanish crown received one-fifth of all revenues from the mines of New Spain, as well as maintained a monopoly over the mercury used to refine the silver ore into silver, so it had an important stake in ensuring the mines' productivity. To this end, the crown granted colonial mine owners the right to conscript native peoples and gave them considerable freedom in the treatment of their workers. This account, dated to about 1620, describes the conditions endured by these native laborers at Potosí (discussed in Chapter 12).

According to His Majesty's warrant, the mine owners on this massive range [at Potosí] have a right to the conscripted labor of 13,300 Indians in the working and exploitation of the mines, both those [mines] which have been discovered, those now discovered, and those which shall be discovered. It is the duty of the *Corregidor* [municipal governor] of Potosí to have them rounded up and to see that they come in from all the provinces between Cuzco . . . and as far as the frontiers of Tarija and Tomina. . . .

The conscripted Indians go up every Monday morning to the . . . foot of the range; the *Corregidor* arrives with all the provincial captains or chiefs who have charge of the Indians assigned him for his miner or smelter; that keeps him busy till 1 P.M., by which time the Indians are already turned over to these mine and smelter owners.

After each has eaten his ration, they climb up the hill, each to his mine, and go in, staying there from that hour until Saturday evening without coming out of the mine; their wives bring them food, but they stay constantly underground, excavating and carrying out the ore from which they get the silver. They all have tallow candles, lighted day and night; that is the light they work with, for as they are underground, they have need for it all the time. . . .

These Indians have different functions in the handling of the silver ore; some break it up with bar or pick, and dig down in, following the vein in the mine; others bring it up; others up above keep separating the good and the poor in piles; others are occupied in taking it down from the range to the mills on herds of llamas; every day they bring up more than 8,000 of these native beasts of burden for this task. These teamsters who carry the metal are not conscripted, but are hired.

Source: Antonio Vázquez de Espinosa, *Compendium and Description of the West Indies*, trans. Charles Upson Clark (Washington, DC: 1968), p. 62.

Questions for Analysis

1. From the tone of this account, what do you think was the narrator's purpose in writing it? Who is his intended audience?

2. Reconstruct the conditions in which these laborers worked. What would you estimate to be the human costs of a week's labor? Why, for example, would a fresh workforce be needed every Monday?

SUGAR, SLAVES, AND THE TRANSATLANTIC TRIANGLE

European settlers in the Americas faced a major problem: labor. Mining and agriculture required many workers, and the indigenous labor supply had already been decimated by disease. Indeed, the recurrence of plague in Europe, along with the loss of life in wars of religion, meant that Europe could not satisfy labor needs either. Colonial agents thus imported slaves from Africa in ever greater numbers, to

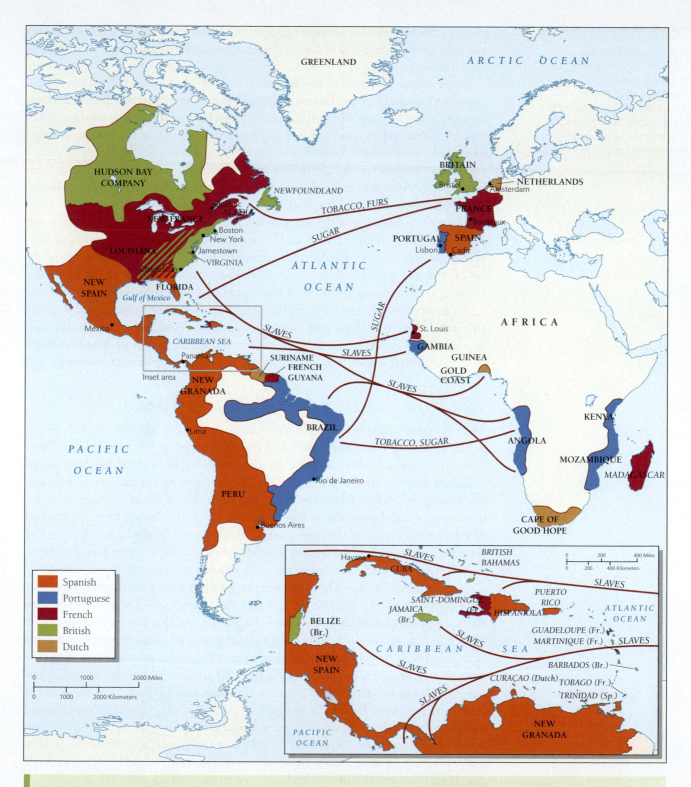

The map legend reads:

- Spanish
- Portuguese
- French
- British
- Dutch

Map labels include: GREENLAND, ARCTIC OCEAN, HUDSON BAY COMPANY, NEWFOUNDLAND, BRITAIN, Bristol, NETHERLANDS, Amsterdam, NEW FRANCE, ACADIA, Quebec, FRANCE, Bordeaux, Boston, New York, Jamestown, VIRGINIA, PORTUGAL, SPAIN, LOUISIANA, Charleston, Lisbon, Cadiz, NEW SPAIN, FLORIDA, Gulf of Mexico, ATLANTIC OCEAN, AFRICA, Mexico, CARIBBEAN SEA, Panama, SLAVES, St. Louis, GAMBIA, GUINEA, GOLD COAST, Inset area, NEW GRANADA, SURINAME, FRENCH GUYANA, Lima, BRAZIL, KENYA, ANGOLA, MOZAMBIQUE, MADAGASCAR, PACIFIC OCEAN, Rio de Janeiro, PERU, Buenos Aires, CAPE OF GOOD HOPE

Trade route labels: TOBACCO, FURS; SUGAR; SLAVES; TOBACCO, SUGAR

Inset map labels: Havana, CUBA, SLAVES, BRITISH BAHAMAS, BELIZE (Br.), NEW SPAIN, SAINT-DOMINGUE (Fr.), JAMAICA (Br.), HISPANIOLA, PUERTO RICO, ATLANTIC OCEAN, CARIBBEAN SEA, GUADELOUPE (Fr.), MARTINIQUE (Fr.), SLAVES, BARBADOS (Br.), CURAÇAO (Dutch), TOBAGO (Fr.), TRINIDAD (Sp.), PACIFIC OCEAN, NEW GRANADA

Scale bars: 2000 Miles / 2000 Kilometers; 400 Miles / 400 Kilometers

THE ATLANTIC WORLD AND THE TRIANGULAR TRADE. › Trace the routes of the triangular trade. What products did French and British colonies in North America provide to the European market? › Which colonies were most dependent on slave labor and what products did they produce? › How did these products enter into the triangle?

triangular trade The commercial Atlantic shipping pattern that took rum from New England to Africa, traded it for slaves taken to the West Indies, and bought sugar back to New England to be processed into rum.

produce the wealth they so avidly sought. And overwhelmingly, that wealth was not gold or silver but a new commodity for which Europeans had an insatiable appetite: sugar.

Sugar was at the center of the "**triangular trade**" that linked markets in Africa, the Americas, and Europe. For example, slave ships that transported African slaves to the Caribbean might trade their human cargo for molasses made on sugar plantations. These ships would proceed to New England, where the molasses would be traded to make rum. Loaded up with rum, the slavers would return to Africa and repeat the process. An alternative triangle brought manufactured goods from England to Africa, traded for slaves shipped to Virginia and exchanged for tobacco, which was shipped back to England.

Many other branches of the Atlantic world economy were tied to the slave trade: investors in Amsterdam, London, and Lisbon financed the slave ships; insurance brokers negotiated complex formulas for protecting investments in human flesh; bankers offered a range of credit options to new slave traders. And in myriad ways, the everyday lives of average people were also bound to slavery: all who bought the commodities produced by slave labor, or who manufactured the implements and weapons that enabled it, were implicated. The enslavement of Africans created wealth and prestige for every sector of European society, not merely for those who had direct contact with it. It was the engine that created the modern globalized economy.

THE HUMAN COST OF THE SLAVE TRADE

The Portuguese were the first to bring African slaves to sugarcane plantations in Brazil, in the 1540s. By this time, slavery had become crucial to the economies of West African kingdoms. In the following decades, however, the demand for slaves would cause the disintegration of political order in this region by fomenting war and raiding among rival tribes. Moreover, the increased traffic in human beings called for more systematized methods for corralling, sorting, and shipping them. By the end of the sixteenth century, the Portuguese government established a fortified trading outpost on an island off the central African coast (near what is now Angola). Additional posts were established along the coast to assist with processing captives.

On board ships, enslaved humans were shackled below decks in spaces barely wider than their own bodies, without sanitary facilities of any kind. The mortality rate on these voyages was relatively low, probably 10 percent, but this was only because those chosen for transport were healthy to begin with, and already the toughened survivors of unimaginable hardships. To place that statistic in a larger context, we need to consider that of a hundred people captured in the African interior, thirty-six would perish in the six-month-long forced march to the coast, and another dozen or so would die in prisons there. Eventually, perhaps fifty-seven of the original hundred would be taken aboard ship, and some fifty-one would survive the journey and be sold into slavery. If the destination was Brazil's sugar plantations, only forty would still be alive after two years. In other words, the actual mortality rate of enslaved people was closer to 60 percent—and this doesn't begin to account for their life expectancy.

The people consigned to this fate were those who shaped the emerging Atlantic world. When opportunity arose, they banded together in revolt—a perpetual possibility that led to draconian regimes of violence and punishment. They also resorted to other forms of resistance, among them suicide and infanticide. Above all, slaves sought to liberate themselves, and communities of fugitives sprang up throughout the Americas. Some were large enough to assert and defend their autonomy. One such community, founded in 1603 in the hinterlands of Brazil, persisted for more than a century and had as many as twenty thousand inhabitants. Most others were much smaller and more ephemeral, but their existence testifies to the limits of imperial authority and the power of human ingenuity.

Conflict and Competition in Europe and the Atlantic World

Most of Europe had enjoyed steady economic growth since the middle of the fifteenth century, and colonization of the Americas seemed to promise further prosperity. But the prolonged political, religious, and economic crises of the sixteenth century were devastating. And inevitably, these European conflicts spread to European colonies.

NEW WORLD SILVER AND OLD WORLD ECONOMIES

In the latter half of the sixteenth century, unprecedented price inflation profoundly destabilized the European economy and caused widespread panic. There were two underlying developments for what historians have termed a "**price revolution**." The first was demographic: after the Black Death (Chapter 11), Europe's population had grown from roughly fifty million people in 1450 to ninety million in 1600: an increase of nearly 80 percent in a short span of time. Yet Europe's food supply remained nearly constant, causing food prices to rise steeply due to the high demand for basic commodities. Meanwhile, the enormous influx of silver and gold from Spanish America flooded a previously cash-poor economy (Chapter 12), and the sudden availability of ready coin drove prices higher still.

About ten million ducats' worth of silver, roughly equivalent to ten billion U.S. dollars in today's currency, passed through the Spanish port of Seville in just four years, from 1556 to 1560. Yet the high worth of these coins was quickly downgraded due to the large amount of money in circulation; and as more silver poured in, the value of coinage decreased even more. By 1580, the amount of imported silver doubled; by 1595, it more than quadrupled. And because most of this money was used by the Spanish crown to pay its armies and its many creditors, this huge volume of debased coinage was circulated through European banks, making inflation even more widespread. Since some people suddenly had more money to pay for goods and services, those who supplied these commodities charged higher and higher prices. But at the same time, the value of the coinage itself was plummeting. "I learned a proverb here," said a French traveler in Spain in 1603. "Everything costs a lot, except silver."

THE NEW EUROPEAN POOR

In this economic climate, aggressive entrepreneurs profited from financial speculation, landholders from the rising prices of agricultural produce, and merchants from the demand for luxury goods. But workers were caught in a vise: wages were not keeping pace with rising prices because the population boom kept labor cheap. As the cost of food rose, poor people had to spend an ever-greater percentage of their

price revolution An unprecedented inflation in prices during the latter half of the sixteenth century, resulting in part from the enormous influx of silver bullion from Spanish America.

Causes of rapid inflation: (1) explosive population growth outstrips limited food supply

Causes of rapid inflation: (2) an influx of gold and silver from the Americas lowers real value of currency

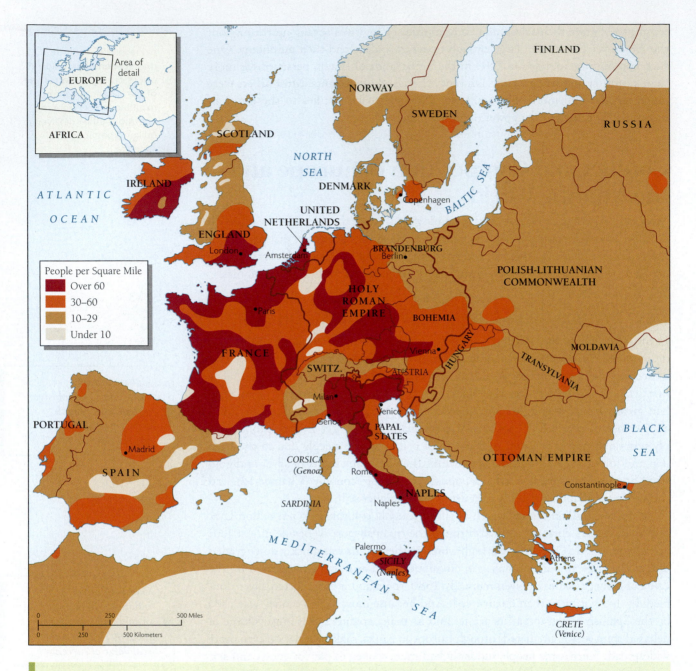

› In what regions was the population most dense? › The largest gains in population were on the coasts; why might that be? › How would urbanization affect patterns of life and trade?

incomes on necessities. The overall cost of living in England, for example, more than doubled in William Shakespeare's lifetime. When disasters such as wars or bad harvests drove grain prices higher still, the poor starved to death.

The price revolution also placed new pressures on European states. Inflation depressed the value of money, so income derived from fixed taxes and rents yielded less actual wealth. Governments were forced to raise taxes just to keep revenues constant;

yet most states needed even more revenue because they were engaging in more wars, and warfare was increasingly expensive. When taxes rose, governments also faced continuous threats of defiance and even armed resistance from citizens.

Although population growth and the flood of silver began to slow after 1600, the ensuing decades were a time of economic stagnation. A few areas—notably the Netherlands (see pages 480–481)—still thrived, and the rich were usually able to hold their own, but the laboring poor made no advances. Indeed, the plight of the poor deteriorated further, as helpless civilians were plundered by tax collectors, looting soldiers, or sometimes both. Peasants who had been dispossessed of property or driven off once-common lands were branded as vagrants, and vagrancy itself became a criminal offense. It was this population of newly impoverished men and women who became the indentured servants or deported criminals of Europe's colonies.

Many of Europe's peasants, dispossessed and sometimes criminalized, find new lives in colonies

WARS OF RELIGION IN FRANCE

Compounding these economic problems were the wars that erupted within many European states. As we began to observe in Chapter 9, most medieval kingdoms were created through the colonization of smaller, traditionally autonomous territories—either by conquest or through marriage alliances with ruling families. Now these enlarged but disunited states began to make ever-greater claims on their citizens while at the same time demanding religious uniformity. The result was regional and civil conflict, as local populations and even elites rebelled against the centralizing demands of monarchs who often embraced a different religion than their subjects.

France was the first to be enflamed by religious warfare. Calvinist missionaries from Geneva had made significant headway there, assisted by the conversion of many aristocratic Frenchwomen who in turn converted their husbands. By the 1560s, French Calvinists, known as Huguenots (*HEW-guh-nohz*), made up between 10 and 20 percent of the population. Although there was no open warfare, political rivalries led factions within the government to break down along religious lines, pitting the (mostly southern) Huguenots against the (mostly northern) Catholic aristocracy. While the Huguenots were not strong enough to threaten Catholic dominance, they were too many to be ignored.

In 1572 the two sides almost brokered a truce: the presumptive heir to the throne, Prince Henry of Navarre—who had become a Protestant—was to marry the Catholic sister of the reigning king, Charles IX. But this compromise was undone by the Queen Mother, Catherine de' Medici, whose faction plotted to kill all the Huguenot leaders assembled in Paris for her daughter's wedding. In the early morning of Saint Bartholomew's Day (August 24), most of these Protestant aristocrats were murdered in their beds and thousands of humble Protestants were slaughtered in the streets or drowned in the river Seine. When word of the massacre spread to the provinces, local massacres proliferated.

HENRY IV OF FRANCE. The reign of Henry of Navarre (r. 1589–1610) founded the Bourbon dynasty that would rule France until 1792, and ended the bitter civil war between Catholic and Huguenot factions.

Henry of Navarre escaped, along with his bride, but the war continued for more than two decades. In 1589, when Catherine's death was followed by that of her son, who had produced no heir, Henry of Navarre became **Henry IV** and renounced his Protestant faith to placate the Catholic majority. In 1598, Henry made a landmark effort to end the conflict by issuing the Edict of Nantes, which recognized Catholicism as the official religion of the realm but permitted Protestants to practice their religion in specified places.

With Edict of Nantes, France retains official Catholic religion but tolerates Protestants

This was an important step toward a policy of religious tolerance. For the first time, Protestants in France were allowed to hold public office and enroll in universities. And because the religious divide was also a regional one, the edict reinforced a tradition of local autonomy in southwestern France, countering the monarchy's centralized power. The success of this effort can be measured by the fact that peace was maintained even after Henry IV was assassinated by a Catholic in 1610.

THE REVOLT OF THE NETHERLANDS AND THE DUTCH TRADING EMPIRE

Warfare between Catholics and Protestants also broke out in the Netherlands during this period. Controlled for almost a century by the same Habsburg family that ruled Spain and its overseas empire, the Netherlands had prospered through intense involvement with Atlantic world trade. The Dutch had the highest per capita wealth in Europe, and the city of Antwerp (now in Belgium) was northern Europe's leading financial center. So when the Spanish king **Philip II** (r. 1556–1598) attempted to tighten his hold there in the 1560s, the fiercely independent Dutch cities resented his imperial intrusion and were ready to fight it.

This conflict became a religious one because Calvinism had spread to the Netherlands from France, while Philip was an ardent Catholic. When crowds began ransacking and desecrating Catholic churches throughout the country, Philip dispatched an army of ten thousand Spanish soldiers to wipe out Protestantism in his Dutch territories. A reign of terror ensued, which further catalyzed the Protestant opposition.

In 1572, a Dutch aristocrat, William of Orange, emerged as the anti-Spanish leader and sought help from religious allies in France, Germany, and England. Organized fleets of Protestant privateers (privately owned ships) began harassing the Spanish navy in the North Atlantic. William's Protestant army then seized control of the Netherlands' northern provinces. Although William was assassinated in 1584, his efforts were instrumental in forcing the Spanish crown to recognize the independence of a northern Dutch Republic in 1609. Once united, these seven provinces became wholly Calvinist; the southern region, still largely Catholic, remained under Spanish rule.

This new Dutch Republic emerged as the most prosperous European commercial empire of the seventeenth century, extending beyond the Atlantic to the Indian Ocean and East Asia. The Dutch colonial project owed more to the strategic "fort and factory" model favored by the Portuguese than to the Spanish model of conquest and settlement. Many early initiatives were spurred by the establishment of the Dutch East India Company, a private mercantile corporation that came to control Sumatra, Borneo, and the Moluccas (the so-called Spice Islands). The company also secured an exclusive right to trade with Japan, and maintained military and trading outposts in China and India.

Henry of Navarre
(1553–1610) Crowned King Henry IV of France, he renounced his Protestantism but granted limited toleration to Huguenots (French Protestants) through the Edict of Nantes in 1598.

Philip II King of Spain from 1556 to 1598 and briefly king of England and Ireland during his marriage to Queen Mary I of England.

PROTESTANTS RANSACKING A CATHOLIC CHURCH IN THE NETHERLANDS. Protestant destruction of religious images provoked a stern response from Philip II. **› Why would Protestants have smashed statuary and other devotional artifacts?**

The Dutch also established an outpost in North America, the colony known as New Amsterdam until it was surrendered to the English in 1667, and renamed New York. Their remaining territorial holdings in the Atlantic were Dutch Guyana (present-day Surinam) on the coast of South America and the islands of Curaçao and Tobago in the Caribbean. The establishment of a second mercantile enterprise, the Dutch West India Company, allowed them to dominate the African slave trade after 1621.

In constructing this transoceanic empire of slaves and spices, the Dutch pioneered a new investment mechanism: the joint-stock company. The Dutch East and West India Companies raised cash by selling shares to individual investors whose liability was limited to the sum of their investments. While not part of the company's management, these investors were entitled to a proportionate share in the profits. Originally, the Dutch East India Company had intended to pay off its investors within ten years; but when that period was up, it convinced those investors who wanted to realize their profits immediately to sell their shares on the open market. The creation of a market in shares of stock, which we now call a stock market, was a major innovation. Stock markets now control the world's economy.

 The joint-stock company, a Dutch invention, drives a surge in investment

THE PROTESTANT SETTLEMENT OF IRELAND AND STRUGGLE BETWEEN ENGLAND AND SPAIN

Religious strife could spark civil war (as in France) or political rebellion (as in the Netherlands), and could also provoke warfare between sovereign states, as

THE NETHERLANDS AFTER 1609. › What were the two main divisions of the Netherlands? › Which was Protestant and which was Catholic? › How could William of Orange and his allies use the geography of the northern Netherlands against the Spanish?

in the struggle between England and Spain. In this case, religious conflict was entangled with both dynastic claims and economic competition in the Atlantic world.

The dynastic competition came from the English royal family's division along confessional lines. The Catholic queen Mary (r. 1553–1558), eldest daughter of Henry VIII and granddaughter of Ferdinand and Isabella of Spain (Chapter 13), had married her cousin Philip II of Spain in 1554, and she ruled at a time of great strife between Catholics and Protestants in England. After Mary's death, her Protestant half-sister Elizabeth (r. 1558–1603) came to the throne, and relations with Spain rapidly declined. They declined further when Catholic Ireland—an English colony—rebelled in 1569 with Spain's support. Although it took almost thirty bloody years, English forces eventually suppressed the Irish. Elizabeth then cemented the defeat by encouraging Protestant occupation of their lands. She did so in conscious imitation of Spanish colonial policy in the Americas, in hopes of creating a new state with a largely English identity. Instead, these measures created the deep ethnic and religious conflicts that trouble Ireland to this day.

England's conflict with Spain was worsened by the fact that English economic interests were directly opposed to those of Spain. English traders were making steady inroads into Spanish commercial networks in the Atlantic, as English sea captains such as Sir Francis Drake and Sir John Hawkins plundered Spanish vessels on the high seas. In a particularly dramatic exploit lasting from 1577 to 1580, prevailing winds and a lust for booty propelled Drake all the way around the world, to return with stolen Spanish treasure worth twice as much as Queen Elizabeth's annual revenue.

After suffering numerous such attacks over a period of two decades—and after Elizabeth's government openly supported the Dutch revolt in 1585—King Philip finally resolved to fight back. In 1588, he dispatched an enormous fleet, confidently called the "Invincible Armada," whose mission was to invade England. But after an indecisive initial encounter between the two fleets, a fierce storm—hailed as a "Protestant wind" by the lucky English—drove the Spanish galleons off course, wrecking many off the Irish coast. Elizabeth took credit for her country's miraculous escape.

ENGLAND'S COLONIAL AMBITIONS

Unlike New Spain, England's North American colonies had no significant mineral wealth; instead, English colonists sought to profit from the establishment of

THE "ARMADA PORTRAIT" OF ELIZABETH. This is one of several royal portraits that commemorated the defeat of the Spanish Armada in 1588. Through the window on the left, an English flotilla sails serenely on sunny seas; on the right, Spanish ships are wrecked by a "Protestant wind." Elizabeth's right hand rests protectively—and commandingly—on the globe. › **How would you interpret this image?**

large-scale plantations in North America and the Caribbean. The first permanent colony was founded at Jamestown, Virginia, in 1607. More than twenty autonomous settlements were established over the next forty years, by a total of about eighty thousand immigrants.

Many were religious refugees—hence the name given to the Pilgrims who landed at Plymouth, Massachusetts, in 1620. These radical Calvinists, known as Puritans, were also political dissidents and were almost as unwelcome as Catholics in England. Yet even these committed Christians showed little interest in converting Native American peoples. Missionizing played a much larger role in Spanish Central and South America, and in French efforts to penetrate the North American wilderness.

Another difference between Spanish and English colonialism is the fact that English colonies did not begin as royal enterprises. They were private ventures, either by individual landholders (as in Maryland and Pennsylvania) or managed by joint-stock companies (as in Virginia and the Massachusetts Bay Colony). Because most land in Europe was owned by royal and aristocratic families, the accumulation of wealth through the control of land was a new and exciting prospect for small- and medium-scale landholders in the new English colonies. This helps to

PLIMOTH PLANTATION. An English settlement was established at Plimoth (now Plymouth) in the Massachusetts Bay Colony in 1620. This image shows a reconstruction of the village as it might have looked in 1627. Although speculative, this reconstruction captures the plantation's diminutive fragility and isolation.

explain the colonies' rural, agricultural character—in contrast to the great cities of New Spain. But the focus on agriculture was also due to the demographic catastrophe that had decimated the native population; a great deal of rich land had been abandoned by Native American farmers because there were so few of them to till it. As more colonists arrived, and competition for land increased, indigenous peoples who had survived European diseases were now under threat from Europeans who wanted complete and exclusive control over these lands.

English colonists expel and massacre Native Americans in fierce competition over land

To this end, the English soon set out to eliminate, through expulsion and massacre, the former inhabitants of the region. There were a few exceptions, such as in the Quaker colony of Pennsylvania, where colonists and Native Americans maintained friendly relations for more than half a century. In the Carolinas, by contrast, there was widespread enslavement of native peoples, either for sale to the West Indies or for work on the rice plantations along the coast. In another contrast to the Spanish and French colonies, intermarriage between English colonists and native populations was rare, which also created the sense of an unbridgeable racial divide in North America.

The Thirty Years' War and Its Outcomes

With the promulgation of the Edict of Nantes in France, the end of open hostilities between England and Spain, and the truce between Spain and the Dutch Republic, religious warfare in Europe came briefly to an end. In 1618, however, a new series of wars broke out in central Europe, in the German-speaking lands that had felt the first divisive effects of the Reformation. This period of warfare was one of the longest in history, and one of the bloodiest, engulfing most of the Continent before it ended thirty years later, in 1648. Although it began as a religious conflict, it quickly became an international struggle for dominance that claimed some eight million lives, with entire regions devastated by the rapacity of crisscrossing armies.

THE BEGINNINGS OF THE THIRTY YEARS' WAR AND THE DOWNFALL OF BOHEMIA

Like the variety of combatants involved, the causes of the **Thirty Years' War** are complicated. On one level, it was an outlet for aggressions and tensions that had been building up since the Peace of Augsburg in 1555. On another level, it grew out of longer-standing disputes among rulers and territories in the patchwork of provinces that made up the Holy Roman Empire. On still another level, it was an opportunity for players on the fringes of power to rise to prominence.

The catalyst came in 1618, when the Austrian Habsburg (Catholic) prince Ferdinand, who also ruled Hungary and the united Polish-Lithuanian Commonwealth, was named heir to the throne of Protestant Bohemia. This prompted a rebellion among the Bohemian aristocracy. A year later, the complex dynastic politics of Europe also resulted in Ferdinand's election as Holy Roman Emperor, a title that gave him access to an imperial (Catholic) army, which he sent to crush the Protestant revolt. The Bohemians, meanwhile, were bolstered by the support of some Austrian nobility—many also Protestant—who saw a way to recover power from the Habsburg ruling family.

In 1620, the war escalated when the Ottomans threw their support behind the Protestants and touched off a war with staunchly Catholic Poland, whose borders the Muslim army needed to cross. The Poles won, and the Ottomans retreated. Meanwhile, Ferdinand's Habsburg cousin, the Spanish king Philip IV, had renewed his war against the Dutch Republic—thus forming an alliance between the two Habsburg rulers. This led to a major pitched battle between united Protestant forces and the Spanish-led Catholic army just outside of Prague. The Habsburgs were victorious, and the Czechs of Bohemia were forced to accept Ferdinand's Catholic rule. As a result, the kingdom of Bohemia, a powerful force in the region and an early cradle of Protestant reform (Chapter 12), ceased to exist.

THE TANGLED POLITICS AND PRICE OF WAR

The conflict should have ended there, but it did not. Instead, it metastasized when tensions between Catholics and Protestants in other parts of central Europe erupted into war. French Catholics and Protestants, who had enjoyed relatively peaceful relations since 1598, came into violent contact once again. Protestant Denmark, fearing that Catholic victories in neighboring parts of the Holy Roman Empire might threaten its sovereignty, was also drawn in.

In this new phase of the war, political expediency soon outweighed either religious or dynastic allegiances. When a confederation of Catholic princes seemed close to uprooting Protestantism in Germany in 1630, other German Catholic princes allied with Protestants to preserve their autonomy. Joining them was the Protestant king of Sweden, Gustavus Adolphus (r. 1611–1632), who championed both the German Lutheran states and his own nation's sovereignty in the wake of Denmark's territorial losses. Yet his Protestant army was secretly subsidized by Catholic France, which sought to avoid being surrounded by a strong Habsburg alliance on its borders.

Gustavus, who had become king at age seventeen, was one of the great military commanders of all time. Like another young general, Alexander the Great (Chapter 4), he was not only an expert tactician but also a charismatic leader. His army became the best-trained and best-equipped fighting force of the era—the first modern army. By the time he died in battle, in 1632, a month before his thirty-eighth

An alliance of two Catholic Habsburg rulers

The Devastation of the Thirty Years' War

The author of the following excerpt, Hans Jakob Christoffel von Grimmelshausen (GRIM-mill-show-sen; 1621–1676), barely survived the horrors of the Thirty Years' War. His parents were killed, probably when he was thirteen years old, and he himself was kidnapped the following year and forced into the army. By age fifteen, he was a soldier. His darkly satiric masterpiece, Simplicissimus *("The Simpleton"), drew heavily on these experiences and, although technically a fictional memoir, portrays with brutal accuracy the terrible realities of this era.*

Although it was not my intention to take the peaceloving reader with these troopers to my dad's house and farm, seeing that matters will go ill therein, yet the course of my history demands that I should leave to kind posterity an account of what manner of cruelties were now and again practised in this our German war: yes, and moreover testify by my own example that such evils must often have been sent to us by the goodness of Almighty God for our profit. For, gentle reader, who would ever have taught me that there was a God in Heaven if these soldiers had not destroyed my dad's house, and by such a deed driven me out among folk who gave me all fitting instruction thereupon? . . .

The first thing these troopers did was, that they stabled their horses: thereafter each fell to his appointed task: which task was neither more nor less than ruin and destruction. For though some began to slaughter and to boil and to roast so that it looked as if there should be a merry banquet forward, yet others there were who did but storm through the house above and below stairs. Others stowed together great parcels of cloth and apparel and all manner of household stuff, as if they would set up a frippery market. All that they had no mind to take with them they cut in pieces. Some thrust their swords through the hay and straw as if they had not enough sheep and swine to slaughter: and some shook the feathers out of the beds and in their stead stuffed in bacon and other dried meat and provisions as if such were better and softer to sleep upon. Others broke the stove and the windows as if they had a never-ending summer to promise. Houseware of copper and tin they beat flat, and packed such vessels, all bent and spoiled, in with the rest. Bedsteads, tables, chairs, and benches they burned, though there lay many cords of dry wood in the yard. Pots and pipkins must all go to pieces, either because they would eat none but roast flesh, or because their purpose was to make there but a single meal.

Our maid was so handled in the stable that she could not come out, which is a shame to tell of. Our man they laid bound upon the ground, thrust a gag into his mouth, and poured a pailful of filthy water into his body: and by this, which they called a Swedish draught, they forced him to lead a party of them to another place where they captured men and beasts, and brought them back to our farm, in which company were my dad, my mother, and our Ursula.

And now they began: first to take the flints out of their pistols and in place of them to jam the peasants' thumbs in and so to torture the poor rogues as if they had been about the burning of witches: for one of them they had taken they thrust into the baking oven and there lit a fire under him, although he had as yet confessed no crime: as for another, they put a cord round his head and so twisted it tight with a piece of wood that the blood gushed from his mouth and nose and ears. In a word each had his own device to torture the peasants, and each peasant his several tortures.

Source: Hans Jakob Christoph von Grimmelshausen, *Simplicissimus*, trans. S. Goodrich (New York: 1995), pp. 1–3, 8–10, 32–35.

Questions for Analysis

1. The first-person narrator here recounts the atrocities committed "in this our German war," in which both perpetrators and victims are German. How believable is this description? What lends it credibility?

2. Why would Grimmelshausen have chosen to publish his account as a satirical fiction rather than as a straightforward historical narrative or an autobiography? How would this choice have affected readers' response to scenes such as he describes?

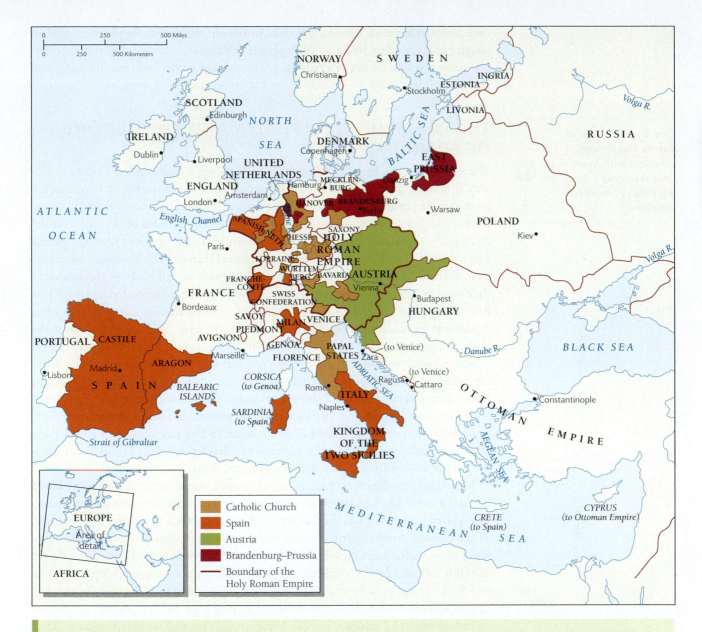

birthday, Sweden had become a global power rivaling Spain and Russia in size and prestige.

In 1635, with Gustavus dead, France was compelled to join Sweden in declaring war on the Spanish and Austrian Habsburgs. In the middle lay central Europe, already weakened by seventeen years of war and now a helpless battleground. In the next thirteen years, this region suffered more from warfare than at any other time until the twentieth century. Several cities were besieged and sacked nine or ten times over. Soldiers from all nations, who had to sustain themselves by plunder, gave no quarter to defenseless civilians. With plague and disease adding to the toll of butchery, some towns were nearly eradicated. The carnage continued into the war's final years, even after peace negotiators arrived at broad areas of agreement.

Peace of Westphalia favors France and Sweden, with Spanish and Austrian Hapsburgs markedly weakened

THE PEACE OF WESTPHALIA AND THE DECLINE OF SPAIN

The adoption of the Peace of Westphalia in 1648 was a watershed in European history. It marked the emergence of a new Swedish empire and the rise of France as the predominant power on the Continent, a position it would hold for the next two centuries. The greatest losers in the conflict (aside from the millions of victims) were the Austrian Habsburgs, who were forced to surrender all the territory they had gained and to abandon their hopes of dominating central Europe. The Spanish Habsburgs were also substantially weakened, and no longer able to fall back on the wealth of their empire. Large portions of the Atlantic trade had been infiltrated by merchants from other countries, while the expansion of colonial economies made them less dependent on trade with Spain itself. In 1600, the Spanish Empire had been the mightiest power in the world; a half-century later, it had begun to fall apart.

Moreover, as we have noted, New Spain's great wealth had proven a liability when the infusion of silver spiked inflation and slowed economic development at home. Lacking both agricultural and mineral resources of its own, Spain could have developed its own industries and a balanced trading pattern, as some of its Atlantic rivals were doing. But instead, it used imperial silver to buy manufactured goods from other parts of Europe, offering no incentives to develop exports of its own. So when the river of silver abated, Spain was plunged into debt.

Meanwhile, the Spanish crown's commitment to supporting the Catholic Church involved it into costly wars, as did attempts to maintain Spain's international dominance. The Thirty Years' War was the last straw: the strains of warfare drove the kingdom, with its power base in Castile, to raise more money and soldiers from the other Iberian provinces, leading to revolts in Catalonia and Portugal (incorporated into Spain in 1580), followed by the southern Italians' rebellion against their viceroys in Naples and Sicily. It was only by chance that Spain's greatest external enemies, France and England, could not act to take advantage of its plight. By 1652, the Castilian government had brought Catalonia to heel, but Portugal regained its independence. After the Peace of Westphalia, Spain was isolated, weakened, and without European allies.

THE SWEDISH EMPIRE AND THE INVASION OF POLAND-LITHUANIA

In the decades after 1648, the power of Sweden continued to rise. With its mighty and disciplined army, Sweden colonized the Baltic in the course of the Thirty Years' War. But a richer prize lay to the south: the wealthy Polish-Lithuanian Commonwealth, with its prosperous commercial centers, rich agricultural lands, and mineral deposits. As Sweden's fortunes rose, Poland-Lithuania was in conflict with Russia for dominance of Ukraine, while also struggling to put down rebellions by Cossacks and Ukrainian peasants along its eastern frontier. Moreover, the reigning king, John II Casimir (r. 1648–1668), was unpopular with many factions within the Polish aristocracy, some of whom urged Charles Gustav of Sweden, the king's cousin, to claim the Polish crown.

In the summer of 1655, two Swedish armies marched into Poland from the north, supported by forces from Transylvania and Brandenburg-Prussia. Over the next five years, the formerly peaceful commonwealth suffered losses nearly as devastating as those of World War II (see Chapter 26), fighting on multiple fronts with only shaky support from its allies and more harm than help from the Russians. By 1660, when a peace treaty was negotiated, the capital of Warsaw had been destroyed, cities looted or torched, castles razed, and churches desecrated.

FRENCH POWER IN EUROPE AND NORTH AMERICA

France emerged from the crisis of the Thirty Years' War with a stronger state, more dynamic economy, and increased influence. Like Spain, France had grown over the course of previous centuries by absorbing formerly independent principalities whose inhabitants cherished traditions of local independence. The fact that France became more powerful as a result of this process, whereas Spain did not, can be attributed in part to France's more significant natural resources and in part to the greater prestige of the French monarchy. Most subjects of the French king, including the Protestants whose welfare had been cultivated by Henry IV, were loyal to the crown. Moreover, France had enormous economic resiliency, thanks to its rich and varied agricultural productivity. Unlike Spain, which had to import food, France was able to feed itself. Furthermore, Henry IV's ministers had financed the construction of roads, bridges, and canals to facilitate the flow of goods, supporting royal factories that manufactured luxury goods such as crystal, glass, and tapestries. Henry also supported the production of silk, linen, and wool throughout the kingdom.

Henry's patronage had enabled the explorer Samuel de Champlain to claim parts of Canada as France's first foothold in the New World. In 1608, Champlain founded the colony of Québec in the Saint Lawrence River Valley. Whereas the English had limited their colonial settlements to regions along the Atlantic coastline, the French set out to dominate the interior of the continent. French traders ranged far up and down the Canadian rivers that led inland, exchanging furs and goods with the Native American groups they encountered; French missionaries, meanwhile, used the same arteries to spread Catholic Christianity from Québec to Louisiana. Eventually, French imperial ventures spread via the Great Lakes and the great river systems along the Mississippi to the prairies of America's Midwest.

These far-flung French colonies were established and administered as royal enterprises, like those of Spain: a fact that distinguished them from the private commercial ventures of the English and the Dutch. Also, like New Spain, the colonies of New France were overwhelmingly populated by men. The elite of French colonial society were military officers and administrators sent from Paris; below their ranks were fishermen, traders, small farmers, and commoners. Because the fishing and fur trades relied on cooperative relationships with native peoples, a mutual economic interdependence grew up between the French colonists and the peoples of the surrounding regions; intermarriage between French traders and native women was common.

Yet in contrast to both Spanish and English colonies, these French colonies remained dependent on the wages and supplies sent to them from the mother country; only rarely did they become truly self-sustaining. Indeed, their financial

Unlike English and Dutch private ventures, French colonies administered by crown

rewards were modest: only furs, fish, and tobacco were exported to European markets. It was not until the late seventeenth century that some French colonists began to realize large profits by establishing sugar plantations on the Caribbean islands of Hispaniola (the French portion of this large island, now Haiti, was known as Saint-Domingue), Guadeloupe, and Martinique. By 1750, half a million slaves were laboring on Saint-Domingue under extraordinarily harsh conditions to produce 40 percent of the world's sugar and 50 percent of its coffee (see Chapter 15).

THE POLICIES OF CARDINAL RICHELIEU

This expansion of French power can be credited, in part, to Henry IV's de facto successor: Armand Jean du Plessis, **Cardinal Richelieu** (*REESH-eh-lyuh*). The real king of France, Henry's son Louis XIII (r. 1610–1643), had come to the throne at the age of nine. Richelieu, as his chief minister of state, dominated his reign, centralizing royal bureaucracy while exploiting opportunities to foster French influence abroad.

Within France, Richelieu amended the Edict of Nantes so that it no longer supported the military and political rights of Huguenots. He also prohibited French Protestants from settling in Québec. Yet the fact that he allowed the edict to stand at all reflects his larger interest in fostering a sense of French identity centered on the monarchy. In keeping with this policy, he imposed direct taxation on powerful provinces that had long retained their financial autonomy. Later, to ensure that taxes were efficiently collected, Richelieu instituted a new system of local government that empowered royal officials to put down provincial resistance.

These measures made the French royal government more powerful than any in Europe. It also doubled the crown's income. But this increased centralization of royal authority also provoked challenges from aristocratic elites and popular factions in the years after Richelieu's death—eventually, leading to the French Revolution (see Chapter 18).

Cardinal Richelieu
(1585–1642) First minister to King Louis XIII, he is considered by many to have ruled France in all but name, centralizing political power and suppressing dissent.

Cardinal Richelieu on the Common People of France

Armand Jean du Plessis, duke of Richelieu and cardinal of the Roman Catholic Church, was the effective ruler of France from 1624 until his death in 1642. His Political Testament was assembled after his death from historical sketches and from memoranda of advice he had prepared for King Louis XIII, the ineffectual monarch whom he served. This book was eventually published in 1688, during the reign of Louis XIV.

All students of politics agree that when the common people are too well off it is impossible to keep them peaceable. The explanation for this is that they are less well informed than the members of the other orders in the state, who are much more cultivated and enlightened, and so if not preoccupied with the search for the necessities of existence, find it difficult to remain within the limits imposed by both common sense and the law.

It would not be sound to relieve them of all taxation and similar charges, since in such a case they would lose the mark of their subjection and consequently the awareness of their station. Thus being free from paying tribute, they would consider themselves exempted from obedience. One should compare them with mules, which being accustomed to work, suffer more when long idle than when kept busy. But just as this work should be reasonable, with the burdens placed upon these animals proportionate to their strength, so it is likewise with the burdens placed upon the people. If they are not moderate, even when put to good public use, they are certainly unjust. I realize that when a king undertakes a program of public works it is correct to say that what the people gain from it is returned by paying the *taille* [a heavy tax imposed on the peasantry]. In the same fashion it can be maintained that what a king takes from the people he returns to them, and that they advance it to him only to draw upon it for the enjoyment of their leisure and their investments, which would be impossible if they did not contribute to the support of the state.

Source: *The Political Testament of Cardinal Richelieu*, trans. Henry Bertram Hill (Madison, WI: 1961), pp. 31–32.

Questions for Analysis

1. According to Cardinal Richelieu, why should the state work to subjugate the common people? What assumptions about the nature and status of "common people" underlie this argument?

2. What theory of the state emerges from this argument? According to Richelieu, what is the relationship between the king and the state and between the king and the people?

THE CHALLENGE OF THE *FRONDE*

An immediate response to these policies was a series of revolts known collectively as the *Fronde* (from the French for "slingshot"). In 1643, just after the death of Richelieu, Louis XIII was succeeded by his five-year-old son, Louis XIV. The young king's regents were his mother, Anne of Austria, and her alleged lover, Cardinal Jules Raymond Mazarin. Both were foreigners—Anne was a Habsburg and Mazarin an Italian—and both were despised by many powerful nobles, who also hated the way that Richelieu's government had curtailed their authority in their own ancestral provinces. Popular resentments were aroused as well, because the costs of the ongoing Thirty Years' War had combined with several consecutive years of bad harvests. So when the nobles expressed their disgust for Mazarin, they found much popular support.

In 1648, the levy of a new tax sent protesters out on the streets of Paris, armed with slings and projectiles. Neither the aristocratic leaders of the Fronde nor the commoners who joined them claimed to be resisting the young king; their targets were the corruption and mismanagement of Mazarin. But years later, when Louis XIV began to rule in his own right, the memory of these early turbulent years haunted him, and he resolved never to let the aristocracy or their provinces get out of hand. With this aim, he became the most effective absolute monarch in Europe (see Chapter 15).

The Crisis of Kingship in England

Of all the crises that shook Europe in this era, the most radical in its consequences was the English Civil War. The causes of this conflict were similar to those that had sparked trouble in other countries: regional hostilities, religious animosities, struggles among competing aristocratic factions, and a fiscal system that could not keep pace with the increasing costs of government. But in England, these developments led to the unprecedented criminal trial and execution of a king: an event that sent shock waves throughout the world.

THE ORIGINS OF THE CIVIL WAR

The chain of events that led to civil war can be traced to the last decades of Queen Elizabeth's reign. The expenses of England's defense against Spain, rebellion in Ireland, widespread crop failures, and the inadequacies of the antiquated English taxation system drove the queen's government deeply into debt. In 1603, when Elizabeth died and was succeeded by her cousin, James Stuart—King James VI of Scotland, James I of England—bitter disputes at court were complicated by the financial crisis. When the English Parliament rejected James's demands for more taxes, he raised what revenues he could without parliamentary approval, imposing new tolls and selling trading monopolies to favored courtiers. These measures aroused resentment against the king and made voluntary grants of taxation from Parliament even less likely.

James also struggled with religious divisions among his subjects. His own kingdom of Scotland had been firmly Calvinist since the 1560s. England, too, was Protestant—but of a very different kind, because the Church of England retained many of the rituals, hierarchies, and doctrines of the medieval Church (Chapter 13). Indeed, a significant number of English Protestants, the Puritans, wanted to bring this church more firmly into line with Calvinist principles. Although James was largely successful in mediating these conflicts, he stirred up trouble in staunchly Catholic Ireland by encouraging thousands of Scottish Calvinists to settle in the northern Irish province of Ulster, exacerbating a situation that had already become violent under Elizabeth.

PARLIAMENT VERSUS THE KING

The situation became more volatile in 1625, when James was succeeded by his surviving son, **Charles**. Charles alarmed his Protestant subjects by marrying the Catholic sister of France's Louis XIII; he then launched a new war with Spain, straining his already slender financial resources. When Parliament refused to grant

Charles I (r. 1625–1649) The second Stuart king of England, Ireland, and Scotland, Charles attempted to rule without the support of Parliament, sparking a controversy that erupted into civil war in 1642.

him funds, he demanded forced loans from his subjects and punished those who refused by lodging soldiers in their homes and imprisoning others without trial. Parliament responded in 1628 by imposing the Petition of Right, which declared that taxes not voted by Parliament were illegal, condemned arbitrary imprisonment, and prohibited the quartering of soldiers in private houses. Thereafter, Charles tried to rule England without Parliament—something that had not been attempted since the establishment of that body 400 years earlier (Chapter 9). He also ran into trouble with his Calvinist subjects in Scotland because he began to favor the most Catholic-leaning elements in the English Church. The Scots rebelled in 1640, and a Scottish army marched south into England to demand the withdrawal of Charles's "Catholicizing" measures.

Conflict sparks as Charles declares war without financial support of Parliament

To meet the Scottish threat, Charles was forced to summon Parliament, whose members were determined to impose radical reforms on the king's government before they would consider granting him funds for an army. The Scottish Calvinists even found support among some Puritans in Parliament. To avoid dealing with this difficult political situation, Charles tried to arrest Parliament's leaders and force his own agenda. When this failed, he withdrew from London to raise his own army. Parliament responded by mustering a separate military force and voting itself the taxation to pay for it. By the end of 1642, open warfare had erupted between the English king and the English government: something inconceivable in neighboring France, where king and government were inseparable.

Arrayed on the king's side were most of England's aristocrats and largest landowners, many of whom owned lands in the Atlantic colonies as well. The parliamentary forces were made up of smaller landholders, tradesmen, and artisans, many of whom were Puritan sympathizers. The king's royalist supporters were commonly known by the aristocratic name of Cavaliers. They derisively called their opponents, who cut their hair short in contempt for the fashionable custom of wearing long curls, Roundheads. After 1644, when the parliamentary army was efficiently reorganized, the royalist forces were badly beaten; and in 1646, the king was compelled to surrender. Soon thereafter, the episcopal hierarchy of the Church of England was abolished and a Calvinist-style church was mandated throughout England and Wales.

The struggle might have ended here had not a quarrel developed within the parliamentary party. The majority of its members were ready to restore Charles to the throne as a limited monarch, under an arrangement whereby a uniformly Calvinist faith would be imposed on both Scotland and England as the state religion. But a radical minority of Puritans, known as Independents, insisted on religious freedom for themselves and all other Protestants. Their leader was Oliver Cromwell (1599–1658), who had risen to command the Roundhead army, which he reconstituted as the "New Model Army."

CHARLES I. King Charles I of England was a connoisseur of the arts and a patron of artists. He was adept at using portraiture to convey the magnificence of his tastes and the grandeur of his conception of kingship. **› How does this portrait by Anthony van Dyck compare with the engravings of the "martyred" king in Interpreting Visual Evidence on page 498?**

OLIVER CROMWELL AS PROTECTOR OF THE COMMONWEALTH. This coin, minted in 1658, shows the Lord Protector wreathed with laurel garlands like a classical hero or a Roman consul. It also proclaims him to be "by the Grace of God Protector of the Commonwealth." › **What mixed messages does this imagery convey?**

THE FALL OF CHARLES STUART AND THE ESTABLISHMENT OF OLIVER CROMWELL'S COMMONWEALTH

Taking advantage of the dissension within the ranks of his opponents, Charles renewed the war in 1648. But he was forced to surrender after a brief campaign, and Cromwell seized control of the government. To ensure that the Puritan agenda would be carried out, Cromwell ejected all the moderates from Parliament by force. This "Rump" (remaining) Parliament then proceeded to put the king on trial and eventually to condemn him to death for treason against his own subjects.

Charles Stuart was publicly beheaded on January 30, 1649—marking the first time in history that a reigning king had been legally deposed and executed. Europeans reacted to his death with horror, astonishment, or rejoicing, depending on their political convictions (see *Interpreting Visual Evidence* on page 498).

After the king's execution, his son Charles and his royalist supporters fled to France. Cromwell and his supporters then abolished Parliament's hereditary House of Lords and declared England a Commonwealth: an English translation of the Latin *res publica*. Technically, the Rump Parliament continued as the legislative body; but Cromwell, with the army at his command, possessed the real power. By 1653 the "Commonwealth" had become the "Protectorate," a thinly disguised autocracy established under a constitution drafted by officers of the army. Called the *Instrument of Government*, this text is the nearest approximation to a written constitution that England has ever had. Extensive powers were given to Cromwell as Lord Protector for life, and his office was made hereditary.

THE RESTORATION OF THE MONARCHY

By this time, though, Cromwell's Puritan military dictatorship was growing unpopular, not least because it prohibited public recreation on Sundays and closed London's theaters. Many became nostalgic for the milder and more tolerant Church of England and began to hope for the restoration of a royalist regime.

The opportunity came with Cromwell's death in 1658. His son Richard had no sooner succeeded to the office of Lord Protector when a faction within the army removed him from power. As groups of royalists plotted an uprising, a new Parliament was organized. In April 1660, it declared that King Charles II had been the ruler of England since his father's execution in 1649. Almost overnight, England became a monarchy again.

Charles II (r. 1660–1685) revived the Church of England but was careful not to revive the provocative policies of his father. Quipping that he did not wish to "resume his travels," he agreed to respect Parliament and to observe the Petition of Right. He also accepted all the legislation passed by Parliament immediately before the outbreak of civil war in 1642, including the requirement that Parliament be summoned at least once every three years. England thus emerged from its civil war as a limited monarchy, in which power was exercised by "the king in Parliament." It remains a constitutional monarchy to this day.

Under Charles II monarchy is restored, but with new powers for Parliament

THE ENGLISH CIVIL WAR AND THE ATLANTIC WORLD

These tumultuous events had a significant influence on the development of a new political sensibility within England's Atlantic colonies. The landed aristocracy had sided with the king during this conflict, but many in the colonies had sympathized with Parliament and its claims to protect the liberties of small landowners. Even after the Restoration of the monarchy in 1660, many colonial leaders maintained an antimonarchist and antiaristocratic bias. Moreover, twelve years of civil war had given the colonies a large degree of independence. As a result, efforts to extend royal control over the colonies caused increasing friction (see Chapter 15). The bitter religious conflicts that had divided the more radical Puritans from the Church of England also forced the colonies to come to grips with the problem of religious diversity. Some colonies, like Massachusetts, took the opportunity to impose their own brand of Puritanism on settlers, while others experimented with forms of religious toleration that went beyond the freedoms that existed in England.

Paradoxically, though, the spread of ideas about the protection of liberties and citizens' rights coincided with a rapid and considerable expansion of unfree labor in the colonies. Prior to the 1640s, English colonies in North America and the Caribbean had been assured of a steady stream of immigrants. But the civil war and subsequent triumph of the Puritans under Cromwell caused a drop in migration. In the colonies, the decline was so sudden that it caused a depression in local economies: the demand for labor was increasing rapidly owing to the expansion of tobacco plantations in Virginia and sugar plantations in Barbados and Jamaica, which the British captured from the Spanish in 1655. These plantations, with their punishing conditions and high mortality rates, were insatiable in their demand for workers. Plantation owners thus sought to meet this demand by investing ever more heavily in indentured servants and African slaves. The social and political crisis unleashed by the English Civil War also led to the forced migration of paupers and political prisoners, especially from Scotland, Wales, and Ireland.

These immigrants, many without resources, swelled the ranks of the unfree and the very poor in England's Atlantic colonies. As earlier arrivals sought to distance themselves from more recent immigrants, whom they regarded as inferiors, new social hierarchies formed. The crisis of kingship in England thus led to a substantial increase in the African slave trade and a sharpening of social and economic divisions in the colonies.

> *After independence during civil war, English colonies resent growing authority*

An Age of Doubt and the Art of Being Human

On the first day of November in 1611, a new play by **William Shakespeare** premiered in London. *The Tempest* takes place on a remote island, where an exiled duke from the Italian city of Milan has used his magical arts to subjugate the island's inhabitants. The plot drew on reports from the Caribbean, where slaves were called Caribans—hence the name of the play's rebellious slave, Caliban, who seeks revenge on the magician Prospero, his oppressive master. Reminded that he owes his knowledge of English to the teaching of Prospero's daughter, Miranda, Caliban retorts, "You taught me language, and my profit on't is, I know how to curse." The benefits of a European education could not outweigh the evils of colonization—but could be used to resist it.

William Shakespeare
(1564–1616) An English playwright who flourished during the reigns of Elizabeth I and James I.

Debating the English Civil War

The English Civil War raised fundamental questions about political rights and responsibilities, many of which are addressed in the two excerpts below. The first comes from a lengthy debate held within the General Council of Cromwell's army in October 1647. The second is taken from the speech given by King Charles I, moments before his execution in 1649.

The Army Debates, 1647

COLONEL RAINSBOROUGH: Really, I think that the poorest man that is in England has a life to live as the greatest man, and therefore truly, sir, I think it's clear, that every man that is to live under a government ought first by his own consent to put himself under that government, and I do think that the poorest man in England is not at all bound in a strict sense to that government that he has not had a voice to put himself under . . . insomuch that I should doubt whether I was an Englishman or not, that should doubt of these things.

GENERAL IRETON: Give me leave to tell you, that if you make this the rule, I think you must fly for refuge to an absolute natural right, and you must deny all civil rights, and I am sure it will come to that in the consequence. . . . For my part, I think it is no right at all. I think that no person has a right to an interest or share in the disposing of the affairs of the kingdom, and in determining or choosing those that shall determine what laws we shall be ruled by here, no person has a right to this that has not a permanent fixed interest in

this kingdom, and those persons together are properly the represented of this kingdom who, taken together, and consequently are to make up the representers of this kingdom. . . .

We talk of birthright. Truly, birthright there is. . . . [M]en may justly have by birthright, by their very being born in England, that we should not seclude them out of England. That we should not refuse to give them air and place and ground, and the freedom of the highways and other things, to live amongst us, not any man that is born here, though he in birth or by his birth there come nothing at all that is part of the permanent interest of this kingdom to him. That I think is due to a man by birth. But that by a man's being born here he shall have a share in that power that shall dispose of the lands here, and of all things here, I do not think it is a sufficient ground.

Source: David Wootton, ed., *Divine Right and Democracy: An Anthology of Political Writing in Stuart England* (New York: 1986), pp. 286–87 (language modernized).

The doubt and uncertainty caused by Europe's extension into the Atlantic world were primary themes and motivators of this era's creative arts, which both documented and critiqued contemporary trends. Another artistic response is the novel *Don Quixote*, which Miguel de Cervantes (*sehr-VAHN-tehs*; 1547–1616) composed largely in prison. It recounts the adventures of an idealistic Spanish gentleman, Don Quixote of La Mancha, who becomes deranged by his reading of chivalric romances and sets out to have delusional adventures of his own. His sidekick, Sancho Panza, is his exact opposite: a plain, practical man content with modest pleasures. *Don Quixote* is both a devastating satire of Spain's decline and a sincere celebration of human optimism.

Charles I on the Scaffold, 1649

I think it is my duty, to God first, and to my country, for to clear myself both as an honest man, a good king, and a good Christian.

I shall begin first with my innocence. In truth I think it not very needful for me to insist long upon this, for all the world knows that I never did begin a war with the two Houses of Parliament, and I call God to witness, to whom I must shortly make an account, that I never did intend to incroach upon their privileges. . . .

As for the people—truly I desire their liberty and freedom as much as anybody whatsoever. But I must tell you that their liberty and freedom consists in having of government those laws by which their lives and goods may be most their own. It is not for having share in government. That is nothing pertaining to them. A subject and a sovereign are clean different things, and therefore, until they do that—I mean that you do put the people in that liberty as I say—certainly they will never enjoy themselves.

Sirs, it was for this that now I am come here. If I would have given way to an arbitrary way, for to have all laws changed according to the power of the sword, I needed not to have come here. And therefore I tell you

(and I pray God it be not laid to your charge) that I am the martyr of the people.

Source: Brian Tierney, Donald Kagan, and L. Pearce Williams, eds., *Great Issues in Western Civilization* (New York: 1967), pp. 46–47.

Questions for Analysis

1. What fundamental issues are at stake in both excerpts? How do the debaters within the parliamentary army (first excerpt) define "natural" and "civil" rights?

2. How does Charles defend his position? What is his theory of kingship? How does it compare with that of Cardinal Richelieu (see page 491)? How does it conflict with the ideas expressed in the army's debate?

3. It is interesting that none of the participants in these debates seems to have recognized the implications that their arguments might have for the political rights of women. Why would that have been the case?

Throughout the long century between 1550 and 1660, Europeans confronted a world in which all that they had once taken for granted was cast into confusion. Vast continents had been discovered, populated by millions of people whose very existence challenged Western civilizations' former parameters and Europeans' most basic assumptions. Not even religion seemed an adequate foundation on which to build new certainties, for European Christians now disagreed about the fundamental truths of their faith. Political allegiances were similarly under threat, as intellectuals and common people alike asserted the right to resist princes with whom they disagreed. The very notions of morality and custom were beginning to seem arbitrary. There was a sometimes desperate search for new bases on which to construct some measure of certainty.

The Execution of a King

This allegorical engraving (image A) accompanied a pamphlet called *Eikon Basilike* ("The Kingly Image"), which began to circulate in Britain just weeks after the execution of King Charles I. It was purported to be an autobiographical account of the king's last days, and a justification of his royal policies. It was intended to arouse widespread sympathy for the king and his exiled heir, Charles II; and it succeeded admirably, as the cult of Charles "King and Martyr" became increasingly popular. Here, the Latin inscription on the shaft of light suggests that Charles's piety will beam "brighter through the shadows," while the scrolls on the left proclaim "virtue grows beneath weight" and "unmoved, triumphant." Charles's earthly crown (on the floor at his side) is "splendid and heavy," whereas the crown of thorns he grasps is "bitter and light"; this heavenly crown is "blessed and eternal." Even people who could not read these and the other Latin mottoes would have known that Charles's last words were: "I shall go from a corruptible to an incorruptible Crown, where no disturbance can be."

At the same time, broadsides showing the moment of execution (image B) circulated in various European countries with explanatory captions. This one was printed in Germany, with almost identical versions surviving from the Netherlands. It shows members of the crowd fainting and turning away at the sight of blood spurting from the king's neck while the executioner holds up the severed head.

Questions for Analysis

1. How would you interpret the message of image A? How might it have been read differently by Catholics and Protestants within Britain and Europe?

2. What might have been the political motives underlying the publication and display of these images? For example, would you expect the depiction of the king's execution to be supportive of monarchy or antiroyalist? Why?

3. Given what you have learned about the political and religious divisions in Europe at the time of the king's execution, where do you think image A would have found the most sympathetic audiences? Why might it be significant that image B circulated more widely in Germany and the Netherlands than in France or Spain?

A. King Charles I as a martyr.

B. The execution of King Charles I.

WITCHCRAFT AND THE POWER OF THE STATE

Contributing to the anxiety was the widespread conviction that witchcraft was an increasing threat. Although belief in magic was not new, it was not until the late fifteenth century that authorities began to insist that such powers could derive only from some kind of satanic bargain. In 1484, Pope Innocent VIII had ordered papal inquisitors to use all means at their disposal to detect and eliminate witchcraft. Predictably, torture increased the number of accused witches who "confessed" to their alleged crimes; and as more accused witches "confessed," more witches were "discovered," tried, and executed—even in places such as England and Scotland, where torture was not legal and the Catholic Church had no influence. For both Luther and Calvin had urged that accused witches be tried and sentenced with less leniency than ordinary criminals.

It was through this fundamental agreement between Catholics and Protestants, and with the complicity of secular states, that an early modern "**witch craze**" claimed tens of thousands of victims. The final death toll will never be known, but the vast majority of the victims were women. When accusations of witchcraft diminished in Europe they became endemic in some European colonies, such as at the English settlement of Salem in the Massachusetts Bay Colony.

The obsession with witches resulted in part from fears that traditional religious remedies (prayer, the sacraments) were no longer adequate to guard against evil. It also reflected Europeans' growing conviction that only the state had the power to protect them. Even in Catholic countries, where witchcraft prosecutions began in Church courts, these cases were transferred to the state for final judgment and punishment because Church courts could not carry out capital penalties. In most Protestant countries, the entire process of identifying, prosecuting, and punishing suspected witches was carried out under state supervision.

Obsession with witchcraft comes from anxieties of age: religious change and growing state power

THE SEARCH FOR A SOURCE OF AUTHORITY

The crisis of religious and political authority in Europe also spurred more rational approaches to the problem of uncertainty. The French nobleman **Michel de Montaigne** (*mohn-TEHN-yeh*; 1533–1592), the son of a Catholic father and a Huguenot mother of Jewish ancestry, applied a searching skepticism to all traditional ways of knowing and adopted a practice of profound introspection. His *Essays* (from the French for "attempts") were composed during the French wars of religion and proceed from one basic question: *Que sais-je?* ("What do I know?"). Their first premise is that every human perspective is limited: what may seem true and moral to one group of people may seem absolutely false to another. From this follows Montaigne's second main premise: the need for moderation. Because all people think they follow the true religion or have the best form of government, he concludes that no religion or government is really perfect, and consequently no belief is worth fighting or dying for.

Another French philosopher, **Blaise Pascal** (*pahs-KAHL*; 1623–1662), confronted the problem of doubt by embracing an extreme form of puritanical Catholicism known as Jansenism, named after its Flemish founder, Cornelius Jansen. Until his death, he worked on a highly ambitious philosophical-religious project meant to establish the truth of Christianity by appealing simultaneously to the intellect and the emotions. In his posthumous work, *Pensées* ("Thoughts"), Pascal argued that only faith could resolve the contradictions of the world because "the heart has its reasons, of which reason itself knows nothing." Pascal's own awe in the face of evil

witch craze The rash of prosecutions that took place in both Catholic and Protestant countries of early modern Europe and their colonies, facilitated by secular governments and religious authorities.

Michel de Montaigne (1533–1592) French philosopher and social commentator, best known for his *Essays*.

Blaise Pascal (1623–1662) A Catholic philosopher who wanted to establish the truth of Christianity by appealing simultaneously to intellect and emotion.

and uncertainty is presented as evidence for the existence of God. His hope was that some measure of confidence in humanity and its capacity for self-knowledge could be rediscovered through faith.

THE SCIENCE OF POLITICS

The French jurist **Jean Bodin** (*boh-DAN*; 1530–1596) found a solution to uncertainty in the power of the state. Like Montaigne, Bodin was troubled by the upheavals of the religious wars. He had witnessed the Saint Bartholomew's Day Massacre of 1572 and, in response, developed a theory of absolute sovereignty that would (he surmised) put an end to such catastrophes. In his monumental *Six Books of the Commonwealth* (1576), he argued that the state has its origins in the needs of family-oriented communities, and its paramount duty is to maintain order.

Bodin defined sovereignty as the "most high, absolute, and perpetual power over all subjects," meaning that a sovereign head of state could make and enforce laws without the consent of those governed: precisely what King Charles of England later argued when he tried to dispense with Parliament—and precisely what his subjects ultimately rejected. Even if the ruler proved a tyrant, Bodin insisted that subjects had no right to resist, for any resistance would open the door to anarchy, "which is worse than the harshest tyranny in the world."

In England, experience of civil war led **Thomas Hobbes** (1588–1679) to propose a different theory of sovereignty in his treatise *Leviathan* (1651). Whereas Bodin assumed that sovereign power should be vested in a monarch, Hobbes argued that any form of government capable of protecting its subjects' lives and property might act as an all-powerful sovereign. Hobbes's conviction of the need for a strong state arose from his view of human nature. The "state of nature" before government, he wrote, was "war of all against all." Because any man naturally behaves as "a wolf" toward other men, life without government is "solitary, poor, nasty, brutish, and short." To escape such consequences, people must surrender their liberties to a sovereign state, in exchange for the state's obligation to keep the peace.

Hobbes and Bodin developed such theories in response to their firsthand experience of political and social upheavals. Their different philosophies thus reflect a practical preoccupation with the observation and analysis of actual occurrences (empirical knowledge) rather than abstract or theological arguments. Because of this practical bent, they are seen as early examples of a new kind of discipline: what we now call political science.

POETRY AND THEATER

In the late sixteenth century, the construction of public playhouses (enclosed theaters) made drama an especially effective mass medium for the formation of public opinion and the dissemination of ideas. Theater was an especially influential artform in England during the last two decades of Elizabeth's reign and that of her successor, James, and it fostered the very different talents of three particularly innovative playwrights.

Christopher Marlowe (1564–1593), who may have been a spy for Elizabeth's government and who was mysteriously murdered in a tavern brawl, was extremely popular in his day. In plays such as *Tamburlaine*, about the life of the Mongolian warlord Timur the Lame (Chapter 12), and *Doctor Faustus*, he created heroes who pursue larger-than-life ambitions only to be felled by their limitations. In contrast to the heroic tragedies of Marlowe, Ben Jonson (c. 1572–1637) wrote dark comedies that

Montaigne on Cannibals

The Essays *of Michel de Montaigne (1533–1592) reflect his attempts to grapple with the contradictions of his own time. In this famous passage, he contrasts the barbarism of the European wars of religion and conquest with the reported behavior of peoples in the New World.*

I had with me for a long time a man who had lived ten or twelve years in that other world which has been discovered in our time. . . . This discovery of so vast a country seems to me worth reflecting on. I should not care to pledge myself that another may not be discovered in the future, since so many greater men than we have been wrong about this one. . . .

[And] I do not believe, from what I have been told about [the] people [of this land] that there is anything barbarous or savage about them, except that we call barbarous anything that is contrary to our own habits. Indeed we seem to have no other criterion of truth and reason than the type and kind of opinions and customs current in the land where we live. . . . These people are wild in the same way . . . that fruits are wild, when nature has produced them by herself and in her ordinary way; whereas, in fact, it is those that we have artificially modified, and removed from the common order, that we ought to call wild. . . .

These [people], then, seem to me barbarous in the sense that they have received very little moulding from the human intelligence, and are still very close to their original simplicity. . . . They are in such a state of purity that it sometimes saddens me to think that we did not learn of them earlier . . . when there were men who were better able to appreciate them than we. . . .

[For example,] they have their wars against the people who live further inland, on the other side of the mountains; and they go to them quite naked, with no other arms but their bows or their wooden swords, pointed at one end. . . . [And after] treating a prisoner well for a long time, and giving him every attention he can think of, his captor assembles a great company of his acquaintances. He then ties a rope to the prisoner's arms, holding him by the other end, at some yards' distance for fear of being hit, and gives his best friend the man's other arm, to be held in the same way; and these two, in front of the whole assembly, dispatch him with their swords. This done, they roast him, eat him all together, and send portions to their absent friends. . . .

I am not so anxious that we should note the horrible savagery of these acts as concerned that, whilst judging their faults so correctly, we should be so blind to our own. I consider it more barbarous to eat a man alive than to eat him dead; to tear by rack and torture a body still full of feeling, to roast it by degrees, and then give it to be trampled and eaten by dogs and swine—a practice which we have not only read about but seen within recent memory, not between ancient enemies, but between neighbours and fellow-citizens and, what is worse, under the cloak of piety and religion—than to roast and eat a man after he is dead.

Source: Michel de Montaigne, *Essays*, trans. J. M. Cohen (Harmondsworth: 1958), pp. 105–13.

Questions for Analysis

1. How does Montaigne regard the "barbarous" people of the New World? How does he (re)define that concept?

2. How does Montaigne critique the assumptions and values of his own time in this passage?

3. Montaigne compares the reported behavior of cannibals with the behavior of Europeans during the ongoing wars of religion. What is he trying to achieve by making this comparison?

expose human vices and foibles. In *The Alchemist*, he balanced an attack on pseudo-scientific quackery with admiration for resourceful lower-class characters who take advantage of their supposed betters.

William Shakespeare (1564–1616) was born into a family of a tradesman in the provincial town of Stratford-upon-Avon, where he attained a modest education before moving to London around the age of twenty. There, he composed or collaborated on an unknown number of plays, of which some forty survive in whole or in part. They owe their longevity to the author's unrivaled gifts of verbal expression, humor, and psychological insight. Those written during the playwright's early years reflect the upheavals of the late sixteenth century, including many history plays that recount episodes from England's medieval past and the struggles that established the Tudor dynasty. They also include the lyrical tragedy *Romeo and Juliet* and a number of comedies that explore fundamental problems of identity, honor and ambition, love and friendship. The plays from Shakespeare's second period, like other contemporary artworks, are characterized by a troubled search for the mysteries and meaning of human existence; they showcase the perils of indecisive idealism (*Hamlet*) and the abuse of power (*Macbeth* and *King Lear*). The plays composed toward the end of his career emphasize the possibilities of reconciliation and peace, even after years of misunderstanding and violence: *The Tempest* is one of these.

THE ARTISTS OF SOUTHERN EUROPE

The ironies and tensions inherent in this age also found expression in the visual arts. In Italy and Spain, many painters cultivated a highly dramatic style sometimes known as Mannerism. The most unusual of these artists was El Greco ("the Greek"; c. 1541–1614), a pupil of the Venetian master Tintoretto (1518–1594). Born Doménikos Theotokópoulos on the island of Crete, El Greco absorbed some of the stylized elongation characteristic of Byzantine icon painting (Chapter 7) before traveling to Italy and then settling in Spain. Many of his paintings were too strange to be truly appreciated in his day, and even now appear so avant-garde as to be almost surreal. His *View of Toledo*, for example, is a transfigured landscape, mysteriously lit from within.

In the seventeenth century, the dominant artistic style of southern Europe was the Baroque, whose name has become a synonym for elaborate, highly wrought sculpture and architectural details. This style originated in Rome during the Counter-Reformation and promoted a

VIEW OF TOLEDO, **BY EL GRECO.** This is one of El Greco's many landscape paintings depicting the hilltop city that became his home in later life. Its supple style almost defies historical periodization.

glorified Catholic worldview. Its most imaginative and influential figure was the architect and sculptor Gianlorenzo Bernini (1598–1680), a frequent employee of the papacy who created a magnificent celebration of papal grandeur in the sweeping colonnades leading up to St. Peter's Basilica. Breaking with the more serene classicism of Renaissance styles (Chapter 12), Bernini's work drew inspiration from the restless motion and artistic bravado of Hellenistic statuary (Chapter 4).

Characteristics of this Baroque style can also be found in paintings, such as those of the great Spanish master Diego Velázquez (*vay-LAH-skez;* 1599–1660), who served the Spanish Habsburg court in Madrid. Although many of his canvases display a Baroque attention to motion and drama, those most characteristic are more conceptually thoughtful and daring. An example is *The Maids of Honor (Las Meniñas),* a masterpiece of self-referentiality, completed around 1656. It shows the artist himself at work on a double portrait of the Spanish king and queen, but the scene is dominated by the children and servants of the royal family.

DUTCH PAINTING IN THE GOLDEN AGE

Southern Europe's main rival in the visual arts was the Netherlands. Pieter Bruegel the Elder (*BROO-ghul;* c. 1525–1569) exulted in portraying the busy, elemental life of the peasantry. But late in his career, Bruegel became appalled by the intolerance and bloodshed he witnessed during the Calvinist riots and the Spanish repression of the Netherlands. He expressed his criticism in works such as *The Massacre of the Innocents:* from a distance, this painting looks like a snug scene of village life; but, in fact, soldiers are methodically breaking into homes and slaughtering helpless

THE MASSACRE OF THE INNOCENTS, BY PIETER BRUEGEL THE ELDER. This painting shows how effective art can be as a means of political and social commentary. Here, Bruegel depicts the suffering of the Netherlands at the hands of the Spanish in his own day, with reference to the biblical story of Herod's slaughter of Jewish children after the birth of Jesus—thereby collapsing the two historical incidents.

infants—as Herod's soldiers allegedly did after the birth of Jesus, and as warring armies did in Bruegel's own day.

Another Dutch painter, Peter Paul Rubens (1577–1640), was inspired by very different politics. A native of Antwerp, part of the Spanish Netherlands, Rubens was a staunch Catholic who glorified the Roman Church and the local aristocrats who supported the Habsburg regime. Even when his intent was not propagandistic, Rubens reveled in the sumptuous extravagance of the Baroque style. (He is most famous today for the pink and rounded flesh of his well-nourished nudes.) Although he celebrated martial valor for most of his career, his late painting *The Horrors of War* movingly captures what he called "the grief of unfortunate Europe, which, for so many years now, has suffered plunder, outrage, and misery."

In some ways a blend of Bruegel and Rubens, Rembrandt van Rijn (*vahn REEN*; 1606–1669) defies all attempts at easy characterization. Living in the staunchly Calvinist Dutch Republic, Rembrandt managed to put both realistic and Baroque traits to new uses. Early in his career, he gained fame and fortune as a painter of

biblical scenes and portraits for wealthy patrons. But as personal tragedies mounted in middle age, his art gained dignity, subtlety, and mystery. His later self-portraits are highly introspective and suggest that only part of the story is being told. Equally frank and fearless is the gaze of Rembrandt's slightly younger contemporary, Judith Leyster (1609–1660), who looks out of her own self-portrait with a refreshingly good-humored expression.

SELF-PORTRAITS. Self-portraits became common during the sixteenth and seventeenth centuries, reflecting the intense introspection of the period. Rembrandt painted more than sixty self-portraits; this one on the left, dating from around 1660, captures the artist's creativity, theatricality (note the costume), and honesty of self-examination. Judith Leyster, shown on the right, was a contemporary of Rembrandt who pursued a successful career during her early twenties before she married. Respected in her own day, she was all but forgotten for centuries thereafter, but is once again the object of much attention.

Conclusion

It would take centuries for Europeans to adapt themselves to the changes brought about by their integration into the Atlantic world. Finding new lands and cultures unknown to the ancients and unmentioned in the Bible had exposed the limitations of Western civilizations' accumulated knowledge and called for new ways of knowing and explaining the world. The Columbian exchange of people, plants, animals, and pathogens that had previously been isolated from each other had a profound and lasting effect on populations and ecosystems throughout the globe. The transatlantic

AFTER YOU READ THIS CHAPTER

CHRONOLOGY

1562–1598	French wars of religion
1566–1609	Dutch wars with Spain
1588	Destruction of the Spanish Armada
1598	Henry IV issues the Edict of Nantes
1607	English colony of Jamestown founded
1608	French colony in Québec founded
1611	William Shakespeare's play *The Tempest* performed in London
1618	Thirty Years' War begins
1621	Dutch West India Company founded
1642–1649	English Civil War
1648	Beginning of the Fronde rebellions
	Thirty Years' War ends
1660	Restoration of the English monarchy

REVIEWING THE OBJECTIVES

> How were the peoples and ecosystems of the Americas, Africa, and Europe intertwined during this period? What were some of the consequences of these new linkages?

> Why did the colonies of the Spanish, the English, and the Dutch differ from each other? How did these differences affect the lives and labor of colonists, both free and unfree?

> Which European powers came to dominate the Atlantic world? What factors led to the decline of Spain and the rise of France?

> What forms did religious and political conflict take in France, the Netherlands, and Germany? What were the causes of the English Civil War? What impact did this event have on the English colonies?

> How do the arts and the political philosophies of this period reflect the turmoil of Europe and the Atlantic world?

slave trade, which made all this possible, brought Africans and their cultures into a world of growing global connections under the worst possible circumstances—yet this did not prevent them from actively shaping this new world.

Meanwhile, the influx of silver from New Spain precipitated the great price revolution of the sixteenth and seventeenth centuries, which contributed to the atmosphere of crisis in a post-Reformation Europe already riven by religious and civil warfare. The response was a trend toward stronger centralized states, justified by theories of absolute government. Led by the French monarchy of Louis XIV, these absolutist regimes would reach their apogee in the coming century.

Go to **INQUIZITIVE** to see what you've learned—and learn what you've missed—with personalized feedback along the way.

PEOPLE, IDEAS, AND EVENTS IN CONTEXT

❯ What was the **COLUMBIAN EXCHANGE**? How did it affect relations among the peoples of the Americas, Africa, and Europe during this period?

❯ What circumstances led to the development of the **TRIANGULAR TRADE**?

❯ What were the main sources of instability in Europe during the sixteenth century? How did the **PRICE REVOLUTION** exacerbate this instability?

❯ How did **HENRY IV** of France and **PHILIP II** of Spain deal with the religious conflict that beset Europe during these years?

❯ What were the origins of the **THIRTY YEARS' WAR**? Was it primarily a religious conflict? Why or why not?

❯ How did the policies of **CARDINAL RICHELIEU** strengthen the power of the French monarchy?

❯ What policies of England's **CHARLES I** were most detested by his subjects? Why was his execution so momentous?

❯ In what ways did the **WITCH CRAZE** of early modern Europe reveal the religious and social tensions of the sixteenth and seventeenth centuries?

❯ What were the differences between **JEAN BODIN**'s theory of absolute sovereignty and that of **THOMAS HOBBES**?

❯ How did philosophers such as **MONTAIGNE** and **PASCAL** respond to the uncertainties of the age? How were contemporary trends reflected in the works of **SHAKESPEARE** and in the visual arts?

THINKING ABOUT CONNECTIONS

❯ The emergence of the Atlantic world can be seen as the *cause* of new developments as well as the *result* of historical processes. What long-term political, economic, and demographic circumstances drove the expansion of European influence into the Atlantic? What subsequent historical developments can be attributed to the creation of this interconnected world?

❯ The political crises of this era reveal the tensions produced by sectarian religious disputes as well as by a growing rift between powerful centralizing monarchies and landholding elites who are unwilling to surrender their authority and independence. What other periods in history are marked by similar tensions? How do those periods compare with the one we have studied in this chapter?

❯ The intellectual currents of this era reveal that a new generation was challenging the assumptions of its predecessors. In what other historical eras do we find similar phenomena? What social and political circumstances tend to produce consensus, and what tend to produce dissent, skepticism, and doubt?

15

European Monarchies and Absolutism, 1660–1725

BEFORE YOU READ THIS CHAPTER

❯

IN THE MOUNTAINOUS REGION of central France known as the Auvergne, the Marquis of Canillac had a notorious reputation. His noble title gave him the right to collect minor taxes on special occasions, but he insisted that these privileges be converted into annual tributes. To collect these payments, he housed twelve accomplices in his castle whom he called his apostles. Their other nicknames—one was known as Break Everything—gave a more accurate sense of their activities in local villages. The marquis imprisoned those who resisted and forced their families to buy their freedom. In an earlier age, the marquis might have gotten away with this profitable arrangement. In 1662, however, he ran up against the authority of a king, **Louis XIV**, who was determined to demonstrate that the power of the central monarch was absolute. The marquis was brought up on charges before a special court of judges from Paris, was found guilty, and was forced to pay a large fine. The king then confiscated his property and had his castle destroyed.

Louis XIV's special court in the Auvergne heard nearly a thousand civil cases over four months in 1662. It convicted 692 people, many of whom, like the Marquis of Canillac, were noble. The verdicts were an extraordinary example of Louis XIV's ability to project his authority into the remote corners of his realm. During his long reign (1643–1715), Louis XIV systematically asserted his power over the nobility, the clergy, and the provincial courts. These elites were forced to look to the crown to guarantee their

> After 1660, many European rulers invoked an absolutist definition of sovereignty in order to expand the power of the monarchy. The most successful absolutist kings, such as Louis XIV of France or Peter the Great of Russia, limited the power of traditional aristocratic elites and the independence of religious institutions.

> Absolutism was not universally successful. Efforts by English monarchs to create an absolutist regime in England after the Civil War were resisted by political opponents of the Crown in Parliament. Other regimes in Europe that found alternatives to absolutism included the Dutch Republic and the Polish-Lithuanian Commonwealth.

> Absolutism reinforced the imperial ambitions of European monarchies and led to frequent wars that were increasingly fought both in Europe and in colonial spaces in other parts of the world. The pressures of war favored dynasties capable of building strong centralized states with reliable sources of revenue from trade and taxation.

CORE OBJECTIVES

> **DEFINE** *absolutism,* **UNDERSTAND** its central principles as a theory of government, and **IDENTIFY** the major absolutist rulers in Europe during this period.

> **DEFINE** *mercantilism* and its relation to absolutist rule.

> **EXPLAIN** the alternatives to absolutism that emerged, most notably in England, the Dutch Republic, and Poland-Lithuania.

> **DESCRIBE** how the wars between 1661 and 1715 changed the balance of power in Europe and in the colonial spheres of the Atlantic world.

> **UNDERSTAND** the reforms undertaken by Peter the Great in Russia and **COMPARE** his regime with the absolutist kingdoms of western and central Europe.

interests, and their own power became closely connected with the monarchy. Louis XIV's model of kingship was known as *absolute monarchy*—a system of government that invested all authority in the king. In recognition of the influence of Louis XIV's political system, the period from around 1660 (when the English monarchy was restored and Louis XIV began his personal rule in France) to 1789 (when the French Revolution erupted) is traditionally known as the age of absolutism. This is a crucial period in the development of modern, centralized, bureaucratic states in Europe.

Absolutism was a political theory that encouraged rulers to claim complete sovereignty within their territories. An absolute monarch could make law, dispense justice, create and direct a bureaucracy, declare war, and levy taxation without the approval of any other governing body. Absolutist rulers claimed to govern by divine right, just as fathers ruled over their households (see **Competing Viewpoints** on page 516). After the chaos and religious wars of the previous century, many Europeans believed that only absolute rulers could bring order to European life.

European monarchs also projected their power abroad. By 1660, the French, Spanish, Portuguese, English, and Dutch had established colonies in the Americas and Asia. These colonies brought profitable new consumer goods such as sugar, tobacco, and coffee to a wide public in Europe. They also relied on slavery to produce these goods. Rivalry among colonial powers to control the trade in slaves and consumer goods was intense, leading to wars fought both in Europe and in contested colonies. These wars, in turn, drove absolutist rulers to extract more revenue from their subjects and to develop the armies, navies, tax systems, and trade controls that enhanced their power.

Absolutism was not universally successful. The English monarchy, restored in 1660 after the turbulent years of the Civil War, attempted to impose absolutist rule but met resistance from parliamentary leaders. After 1688, England, Scotland, the Dutch Republic, Switzerland, Venice, Sweden, and Poland-Lithuania were all either limited monarchies or republics. In Russia, on the other hand, an extreme autocracy emerged that gave the tsar a degree of political control far beyond anything imagined by western European absolutists. Even in Russia, however, absolutism was never unlimited in practice. Absolute monarchs could rule effectively only with the consent of their subjects, particularly the nobility. When serious opposition erupted, even powerful kings were forced to back down. King George III of Britain discovered this when his North American colonies declared their independence in 1776, forming the United States of America. In 1789, a more sweeping revolution began in France, and the entire structure of absolutism came crashing to the ground (see Chapter 18).

Population and Climate in the Absolutist Age

A period of disorder and war drives Europeans to seek stability and order

Absolutism's promise of stability was an appealing alternative to the disorder of the previous century. Religious persecution and war put large populations on the move before 1650 as religious minorities were expelled from various regions during a long period of conflict over questions of faith. The expulsion of Jews from Spain (between 1420 and 1520) was followed by similar expulsions of Jews from Geneva, areas of southern France, southern Italy, and some German cities. Many French Protestants, known as Huguenots, emigrated in the last decades of the sixteenth century during France's wars of religion.

These population movements were dwarfed by the catastrophe of the Thirty Years' War (1618–1648), which killed one-third of the town dwellers in German territories of central Europe, and 40 percent of the rural population from hunger, disease, and murder. Many Europeans scrambled to meet basic security and subsistence needs. This problem was magnified by the Little Ice Age, a period of much lower temperatures in Europe and North America in the mid-seventeenth century that brought colder winters, a shorter growing season, and more frequent crop failures. For populations living on the edge of subsistence—the vast majority of people in Europe—famine was an ever-present threat.

Even in times of peace, European populations were highly mobile. This movement of people challenges myths of a "traditional" Europe where people were born and died in a single village. Regions that could not support their own population sent laborers annually to more fertile areas where larger farms paid higher wages. Tens of thousands of migrant workers went every summer to eastern England, to the farms of the Paris basin in northern France, and to Castile and Galicia in Spain to harvest grain. Similar numbers moved annually to southern France to pick grapes and to northern Italy to harvest rice.

Itinerant traders accompanied labor migrants. Commercial travelers built enduring networks: by the 1700s, for example, forty villages on the border between the Netherlands and present-day Belgium sent five hundred to eight hundred traders every year on routes that reached from the Atlantic coast to western Russia, selling textiles, copper products, and women's hair for the wig industry. Other mobile trades included chimney sweeps, stonemasons, and construction workers who moved seasonally from rural areas to cities to seek work. This mobility of people within Europe was just as important for economic development as the broader movement of peoples in the Atlantic world (see Chapter 14).

WINTER LANDSCAPE WITH ICE SKATERS, c. 1608, HENDRICK AVERCAMP. During the "Little Ice Age" more frequent cold winters regularly froze rivers and canals in northern Europe. Dutch painters frequently depicted winter village scenes, which provide a vivid portrait of daily life, work, and leisure during this period.

Absolutism's Goals and Opponents

Absolutist monarchs sought control of the state's armed forces and its legal system, and demanded the right to collect and spend the state's financial resources at will. To do this, they needed an efficient bureaucracy that owed its allegiance to the monarch. Creating such a bureaucracy was expensive but necessary to weaken the authority of other bodies that hindered the free exercise of royal power. The nobility and the clergy, with their traditional legal privileges; the political authority of semiautonomous regions; and representative assemblies such as parliaments, diets, or estates-general were all obstacles—in the eyes of absolutists—to strong, centralized monarchical government. The history of absolutism is the history of kings who attempted to bring such institutions to heel.

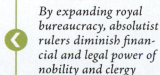

By expanding royal bureaucracy, absolutist rulers diminish financial and legal power of nobility and clergy

In most Protestant countries, the church had already been subordinated to the state when the age of absolutism began. Even where Roman Catholicism remained the state religion, such as in France, Spain, and Austria, absolutist monarchs worked to bring the Church under royal control. Louis XIV took an active role in religious matters, appointing his own bishops and encouraging the repression of religious dissidents. Unlike his predecessors, however, he rarely appointed members of the clergy to offices within his administration.

The most important opponents of royal absolutism were nobles. Louis XIV deprived the French nobility of political power but increased their social prestige by making them live at his court at Versailles (*vuhr-SY*). **Peter the Great** of Russia (1682–1725) forced his nobles into lifelong government service. Successive monarchs in Brandenburg-Prussia co-opted the aristocracy by granting them immunity to taxation and giving them the right to enserf their peasants; in exchange, they ceded administrative control to the Prussian state. In most European monarchies, including Spain, France, Prussia, and England, the nobility retained their role within the military. Absolutist monarchies of the eighteenth century continued to trade privileges for allegiance, so that nobles came to see their own interests as tied to those of the crown. For this reason, wary cooperation between kings and nobles was more common than open conflict during the eighteenth century.

The Absolutism of Louis XIV

In Louis XIV's state portrait, it is almost impossible to discern the human being behind the facade of the absolute monarch dressed in his coronation robes and surrounded by the symbols of his authority. Louis and his successors staged theatrical demonstrations of their sovereignty to enhance their position as rulers endowed with godlike powers.

PERFORMING ROYALTY AT VERSAILLES

Louis's most elaborate staging of his authority took place at his palace at Versailles, outside Paris. The building's front was a third of a mile in length. Inside, tapestries and paintings celebrated French military victories, and mirrors reflected light throughout the building. In the vast gardens outside, statues of the Greek god of the sun, Apollo, recalled Louis's claim to be the "Sun King" of France. Noblemen vied to attend him when he arose from bed, ate his meals (usually stone cold after having traveled the distance of several city blocks from kitchen to table), strolled in his gardens (even the way the king walked was choreographed by the royal dancing master), or rode to the hunt. France's leading nobles were required to reside with Louis at Versailles for a portion of the year; the splendor of Louis's court was calculated to blind them to the possibility of disobedience (see *Interpreting Visual Evidence* on pages 514–515).

But the nobility did not surrender all their power. They retained enormous privileges and rights over local peasants within their jurisdiction. The absolutist system forced the nobility to depend on the crown, but it did not seek to undermine their superior place in a deeply hierarchical society. In this sense, the relationship between Louis XIV and the nobility was more of a negotiated settlement than a complete victory of the king. In their own way, absolutists still depended on the consent of other powerful elites in their kingdom.

ADMINISTRATION AND FINANCE

Absolutist rulers concentrated power in fewer hands, diminishing the ability of local elites to shape policy. Under Louis, the French administration was run by thirty-three royal intendants appointed to each of France's regions. Members of regional *parlements* (law courts) that refused to approve his laws were exiled. The Estates General, the French representative assembly that met at the king's pleasure, was last summoned in 1614 and did not meet at all in Louis's long reign. It was not convened again until 1789.

Louis's most able official was Jean-Baptiste Colbert, finance minister from 1664 to 1683. Before Louis XIV's reign, the tax system was notoriously inefficient: the nobility was exempt from the land tax (*taille*), and collection of indirect taxes on salt, wine, tobacco, and other goods was difficult. Colbert eliminated the practice of tax farming, which permitted collection agents to retain a percentage of taxes they gathered for the king. When Colbert assumed office, only about 25 percent of collected taxes reached the treasury. By the time he died, this figure reached 80 percent. Colbert raised additional funds through the sale of public offices, including judgeships and mayoralties, and he forced guilds to pay for the enforcement of trade regulations.

Colbert was a **mercantilist**—he believed that France's wealth would grow if it reduced its imports and increased its exports. He imposed tariffs on foreign goods, and used state money to promote the domestic manufacture of imports like silk, lace, tapestries, and glass. To encourage trade he improved France's roads, bridges, and waterways. But Colbert's efforts to increase royal revenues fell short of the insatiable demands of Louis XIV's wars (see pages 522–523). By the end of Louis's reign, his aggressive foreign policy lay in ruins, and his country's finances had been shattered by the unsustainable costs of war.

LOUIS XIV'S RELIGIOUS POLICIES

Louis was determined to impose religious unity on France. The majority of the French population was Roman Catholic, but Louis vigorously persecuted dissenting movements within the Church, especially the Quietists and the Jansenists. Quietists emphasized a personal mysticism that believed in a direct relationship between God and the individual. Louis and the Church hierarchy disliked Quietism because it implied that believers did not need the intermediary services of the clergy. Jansenism—a movement named for its founder, Cornelius Jansen, a seventeenth-century bishop of Ypres—held to an Augustinian doctrine of predestination that sounded like a kind of Catholic Calvinism. Louis offered Quietists and Jansenists a stark choice between recanting and prison or exile. At the same time, he supported the Jesuits in their efforts to create a Counter-Reformation Catholic Church in France. Louis's support for the Jesuits upset the traditional Gallican Catholics of France, however, who desired a French church independent of papal, Jesuit, and Spanish influence. As a result of this dissension among Catholics, the religious aura of Louis's kingship diminished during the course of his reign.

Against the Protestant Huguenots Louis waged unrelenting war. Protestant churches and schools were destroyed, and Protestants were banned from many professions. In 1685, Louis revoked the Edict of Nantes, the legal foundation of the toleration the Huguenots had enjoyed since 1598. Protestant clerics were exiled, laymen were sent to the galleys as slaves, and their children were forcibly

mercantilism A theory and policy for directing the economy of monarchial states between 1600 and 1800, based on the assumption that wealth and power depended on a favorable balance of trade and the accumulation of precious metals.

Colbert's mercantilist policy: protecting domestic industries through tariffs and favorable trade policies

The Performance and Display of Absolute Power at the Court of Louis XIV

Historians studying the history of absolutism and the court of Louis XIV in particular have emphasized the Sun King's brilliant use of symbols and display to demonstrate his personal embodiment of sovereignty. Royal portraits, such as that painted by Hyacinthe Rigaud in 1701 (shown below), vividly illustrate the degree to which Louis's power was based on a studied performance. His pose, with his exposed and shapely calf, was an important indication of power and virility, necessary elements of legitimacy for a hereditary monarch. In the elaborate rituals of court life at Versailles, Louis often placed his own body at the center of attention, performing in one instance as the god Apollo in a ballet before his assembled courtiers. His movements through the countryside, accompanied by a retinue of soldiers, servants, and aristocrats, were another occasion for highly stylized ritual demonstrations of his quasi-divine status. Finally, of course, the construction of his palace at Versailles, with its symmetrical architecture and sculpted gardens, was a demonstration that his power extended over the natural world as easily as it did over the lives of his subjects.

Questions for Analysis

1. Who was the intended audience for the king's performance of absolute sovereignty?

2. Who were Louis's primary competitors in this contest for eminence through the performance of power?

3. What possible political dangers might lie in wait for a regime that invested so heavily in the sumptuous display of semidivine authority?

A. Hyacinthe Rigaud's 1701 portrait of Louis XIV.

B. Louis XIV as the Sun King.

C. *A Cavalcade*, by Adam Frans van der Meulen (1664).

D. *The Palace of Versailles*, by Pierre Patel (c. 1668).

Absolutism and Patriarchy

These selections show how two political theorists justified royal absolutism by deriving it from the absolute authority of a father over his household. Bishop Jacques-Bénigne Bossuet (1627–1704) was a famous French preacher and the tutor to the son of King Louis XIV of France before becoming bishop of Meaux. Sir Robert Filmer (1588–1653) was an English political theorist. Filmer's works attracted particular attention in the 1680s, when John Locke directed the first of his Two Treatises of Government *to refute Filmer's views on the patriarchal nature of royal authority.*

Bossuet on the Nature of Monarchical Authority

There are four characteristics or qualities essential to royal authority. First, royal authority is sacred; Secondly, it is paternal; Thirdly, it is absolute; Fourthly, it is subject to reason. . . . All power comes from God. . . . Thus princes act as ministers of God, and his lieutenants on earth. It is through them that he exercises his empire. . . . In this way . . . the royal throne is not the throne of a man, but the throne of God himself. . . .

We have seen that kings hold the place of God, who is the true Father of the human race. We have also seen that the first idea of power that there was among men, is that of paternal power; and that kings were fashioned on the model of fathers. Moreover, all the world agrees that obedience, which is due to public power, is only found . . . in the precept which obliges one to honor his parents. From all this it appears that the name "king" is a father's name, and that goodness is the most natural quality in kings. . . .

Royal authority is absolute. In order to make this term odious and insupportable, many pretend to confuse absolute government and arbitrary government.

But nothing is more distinct, as we shall make clear when we speak of justice. . . . The prince need account to no one for what he ordains. . . . Without this absolute authority, he can neither do good nor suppress evil: his power must be such that no one can hope to escape him. . . . [T]he sole defense of individuals against the public power must be their innocence. . . .

One must, then, obey princes as if they were justice itself, without which there is neither order nor justice in affairs. They are gods, and share in some way in divine independence. . . . It follows from this that he who does not want to obey the prince . . . is condemned irremissibly to death as an enemy of public peace and of human society. . . . The prince can correct himself when he knows that he has done badly; but against his authority there can be no remedy. . . .

Source: Jacques-Bénigne Bossuet, *Politics Drawn from the Very Words of Holy Scripture*, trans. Patrick Riley (Cambridge: 1990), pp. 46–69, 81–83.

Religious persecution causes massive migration, with human and economic effects

baptized as Catholics. Many families converted, but two hundred thousand Protestant refugees fled to England, Holland, Germany, and America, taking with them their professional and artisanal skills. This emigration was an enormous loss to France. Huguenots fleeing Louis XIV's persecution, for example, established the silk industries of Berlin and London.

FRENCH COLONIALISM UNDER LOUIS XIV

Colbert regarded overseas expansion as an integral part of the monarchy's economic policy and with his guidance, France emerged as a major colonial power. Colbert encouraged the development of sugar-producing colonies in the West Indies,

Filmer on the Patriarchal Origins of Royal Authority

The first government in the world was monarchical, in the father of all flesh, Adam being commanded to multiply, and people the earth, and to subdue it, and having dominion given him over all creatures, was thereby the monarch of the whole world; none of his posterity had any right to possess anything, but by his grant or permission, or by succession from him. . . . Adam was the father, king and lord over his family: a son, a subject, and a servant or a slave were one and the same thing at first. . . .

I cannot find any one place or text in the Bible where any power . . . is given to a people either to govern themselves, or to choose themselves governors, or to alter the manner of government at their pleasure. The power of government is settled and fixed by the commandment of "honour thy father"; if there were a higher power than the fatherly, then this commandment could not stand and be observed. . . .

All power on earth is either derived or usurped from the fatherly power, there being no other original to be found of any power whatsoever. For if there should be granted two sorts of power without any subordination of one to the other, they would be in perpetual strife which should be the supreme, for two supremes cannot agree. If the fatherly power be supreme, then the power of the people must be subordinate and depend on it. If the power of the people be supreme, then the fatherly power must submit to it, and cannot be exercised without the licence of the people, which must quite destroy the frame and course of nature. Even the power which God himself exercises over mankind is by right of fatherhood: he is both the king and father of us all. As God has exalted the dignity of earthly kings . . . by saying they are gods, so . . . he has been pleased . . . [t]o humble himself by assuming the title of a king to express his power, and not the title of any popular government.

Source: Robert Filmer, "Observations upon Aristotle's Politiques," in *Divine Right and Democracy: An Anthology of Political Writing in Stuart England*, ed. David Wootton (Harmondsworth, UK: 1986), pp. 110–18. First published 1652.

Questions for Analysis

1. Bossuet's definition of *absolutism* connected the sacred power of kings with the paternal authority of fathers within the household. What consequences does he draw from defining the relationship between king and subjects in this way?

2. What does Filmer mean when he says, "All power on earth is either derived or usurped from the fatherly power"? How many examples does he give of paternal or monarchical power?

3. Bossuet and Filmer make obedience the basis for order and justice in the world. What alternative political systems did they most fear?

---

the largest of which was Saint-Domingue (present-day Haiti). Sugar, virtually unknown in Christian Europe during the Middle Ages, became a popular luxury item in the late fifteenth century (see Chapter 14). It took the brutal slave plantations of the Caribbean to turn sugar into a mass-market product. By 1750, slaves in Saint-Domingue produced 40 percent of the world's sugar (and 50 percent of its coffee), exporting more sugar than Jamaica, Cuba, and Brazil combined. The sugar plantations of the Caribbean had their own social structure, with slaves at the bottom, people of mixed African and European descent forming the middle layer, and wealthy European plantation owners at the top. Well over half of the sugar and coffee sent to France was resold to markets throughout Europe. Historians estimate that as many as one million of the twenty-five million inhabitants of

France in the eighteenth century lived off the money flowing through this colonial trade, making the slave colonies of the Caribbean a powerful force for economic change in France. The wealth generated from these colonies added to the prestige of France's absolutist government.

By 1700, France also dominated the interior of the North American continent, where French traders traded with Native Americans and missionaries preached Christianity in a vast territory that stretched from Québec to Louisiana. Like the earlier Spanish colonies (see Chapter 14), the French colonies were established and administered as direct crown enterprises. French colonial settlements in North America served as military outposts and trading centers, and they were overwhelmingly populated by men. The elite were military officers and administrators sent from Paris. Below their ranks were fishermen, fur traders, small farmers, and common soldiers who constituted the majority of French settlers in North America. Because the fishing and the fur trades relied on cooperative relationships with native peoples, a mutual economic interdependence grew between the French colonies and the peoples of the surrounding region. Intermarriage, especially between French traders and native women, was common. The financial returns from North America were never large, however. Furs, fish, and tobacco were exported to European markets but never matched the profits from the Caribbean sugar colonies or from trading posts in India.

Alternatives to Absolutism

Absolutism did not take root everywhere in Europe. A republican oligarchy continued to rule in Venice. In the Polish-Lithuanian Commonwealth, the monarch was elected by the nobility and governed alongside a parliament that met every two years. England, which had suffered through violent civil war between 1642 and 1651, followed by Oliver Cromwell's Commonwealth and the Protectorate (see Chapter 14), arrived at a constitutional settlement that gave a larger role to Parliament and allowed the participation of nonnobles in the affairs of state. Arriving at this settlement was not easy, however. The end of the civil wars had made it clear that England would be a monarchy and not a republic, but what sort of monarchy England would be remained an open question. Two issues were paramount: religion and the relationship between Parliament and the king.

THE RESTORATION MONARCHY IN ENGLAND

Following the restoration of the Stuarts in 1660, **Charles II** (r. 1660–1685) showed his affinity for Catholicism by bringing bishops back to the Church of England, but he also declared limited religious freedom for Protestant "dissenters." He promised to observe the Magna Carta and he accepted legislation stating that Parliament be summoned at least once every three years. England thus emerged from its civil war as a limited monarchy, with power exercised by the "king in Parliament." During the 1670s, however, Charles began openly to model his kingship on the absolutism of Louis XIV. England's elites became divided between Charles's supporters (known as "Tories," a nickname for Irish Catholic bandits) and his opponents (called "Whigs," a nickname for Scottish Presbyterian rebels). In fact, both sides feared absolutism and the prospect of renewed civil war. What they could not agree on was which possibility frightened them more.

Colbert's mercantilist financial policy drives growth of colonial expansion

French colonists cooperate economically and socially with native peoples

Charles II (r. 1660–1685) Nominally king of England, Ireland, and Scotland after his father Charles I's execution in 1649, Charles II lived in exile until he was restored to the throne in 1660.

James II King of England, Ireland, and Scotland from 1685 to 1688, whose commitment to absolutism and Catholic Zealotry led to his exile to France after the Glorious Revolution of 1688.

Charles's known sympathy for Roman Catholicism and his claim that he had the right to ignore parliamentary legislation worked to the advantage of his Whig opponents, who won a series of electoral victories between 1679 and 1681. Charles responded by moving aggressively against Whig leadership, executing several on charges of treason. Charles died in 1685 with his power enhanced, but his divisive legacy was the undoing of his less able successor, his Roman Catholic brother **James II**.

James's admiration of the French monarchy's Gallican Catholicism led him to look for ways to develop an absolutist state in England. His commitment to absolutism led him to build up the English army and navy, which required increased taxation and generated resentment in towns required to quarter troops. He took control over the country's new post office, making domestic surveillance routine, and prosecutions of seditious speech frequent. For the Whigs, James's policies were all that they had feared. The Tories, meanwhile, remained loyal to the Church of England and were alienated by James's Catholicism. When a son was unexpectedly born to the royal couple, and it was announced that he was to be raised a Catholic, events moved swiftly to a climax. A delegation of Whigs and Tories crossed the channel to Holland to invite James's Protestant daughter Mary Stuart and her Protestant husband, William of Orange, to cross to England with an invading army to preserve English Protestantism and English liberties by summoning a new Parliament.

THE GLORIOUS REVOLUTION

Following the invasion, James fled for exile in France. Parliament declared the throne vacant, allowing William and Mary to succeed him as joint sovereigns in 1688. Parliament passed a Bill of Rights, which reaffirmed civil liberties, such as trial by jury, *habeas corpus* (a guarantee that no one could be imprisoned unless charged with a crime), and the right to petition the monarch through Parliament. The Bill of Rights also declared that the monarchy was subject to the law. The Act of Toleration granted Protestant dissenters the right to worship freely, and in 1701, the Act of Settlement ordained that every future English monarch must be a member of the Church of England.

The English referred to the events of 1688–1689 as the "**Glorious Revolution**," because it established England as a mixed monarchy governed by the "king in Parliament" according to the rule of law. After 1688, no English monarch attempted to govern without Parliament, which has met annually ever since. The House of Commons also strengthened its control over taxation and expenditure. Although Parliament never codified the legal provisions of this form of monarchy into one constitutional document, historians consider the settlement of 1688 as a founding moment in the development of a constitutional monarchy in Britain.

CHARLES II OF ENGLAND (r. 1660–1685) *IN HIS CORONATION ROBES.* This full frontal portrait of the monarch, holding the symbols of his rule, seems to confront the viewer personally with the overwhelming authority of the sovereign's gaze. Compare this classic image of the absolutist monarch with the very different portraits of William and Mary, who ruled after the Glorious Revolution of 1688 (page 520). › **What had changed between 1660, when Charles II came to the throne, and 1688, when the more popular William and Mary became the rulers of England?**

Glorious Revolution The overthrow of King James II of England and the installation of his Protestant daughter, Mary Stuart, and her husband, William of Orange, to the throne in 1688 and 1689. It is widely regarded as the founding moment in the development of a constitutional monarchy in Britain.

WILLIAM AND MARY. In 1688, William of Orange and his wife, Mary Stuart, became Protestant joint rulers of England in a coup that took power from her father, the Catholic James II. Compare this contemporary print with the portraits of Louis XIV (page 514) and Charles II (page 519). › What relationship does this portrait seem to depict between the royal couple and their subjects? › What is the significance of the gathered crowd in the public square in the background? › How is this different from the spectacle of divine authority projected by Louis XIV or the image of Charles II looking straight at the viewer?

Yet the revolution of 1688 was not all glory. It was not "bloodless" and was accompanied by violence in many parts of England, Scotland, and Ireland. The revolution consolidated the position of large property holders, whose control over local government had been threatened by the absolutist policies of Charles II and James II. It reinforced the power of a wealthy class of English elites who would soon become even wealthier from government patronage and the profits of war. It also brought misery to the Catholic minority in Scotland and to the Catholic majority in Ireland. After 1690, power in Ireland would lie firmly in the hands of a "Protestant Ascendancy," whose dominance over Irish society would last until modern times.

The Glorious Revolution nevertheless favored the growth and political power of the English commercial classes, especially the urban populations whose livelihood depended on trade with the Atlantic world and beyond. In the decades to come, trade became a political issue, and merchants' associations began to lobby Parliament for favorable legislation. Whigs in Parliament became the voice of this newly influential pressure group of commercial entrepreneurs, and they called for revisions to the tax code that would benefit those engaged in manufacturing and trade. In 1694, the Whigs succeeded in establishing the Bank of England, inaugurating a financial revolution that would make London the center of a vast network of international banking and investment in the eighteenth century.

JOHN LOCKE AND THE CONTRACT THEORY OF GOVERNMENT

The Glorious Revolution was the product of unique circumstances, but it also reflected antiabsolutist theories of politics that were taking shape in the late seventeenth century. Chief among these opponents of absolutism was the Englishman **John Locke** (1632–1704), whose *Two Treatises of Government* were written before the Glorious Revolution but published for the first time in 1690.

Locke's **contract theory of government** was based on a parable about the origins of human society. According to Locke's story, humans had originally lived in a state of nature characterized by absolute freedom and equality, with no government of any kind. The only law was the law of nature, by which individuals enforced for themselves their natural rights to life, liberty, and property. Soon, however, humans perceived that the inconveniences of the state of nature outweighed its advantages. Accordingly, they agreed to establish a civil society based on absolute equality, and then to set up a government to arbitrate the disputes that might arise within this civil society. Locke considered this agreement to be the founding contract that gave government its legitimacy through the consent of the people. The contract did not make government's powers absolute. All powers not expressly surrendered to the government were reserved to the people themselves; as a result, governmental authority was conditional. If a government exceeded or abused the authority granted to it, society had the right to dissolve it and create another.

Locke condemned absolutism in every form. He denounced absolute monarchy, but he was also critical of claims for the sovereignty of parliaments. Government, he argued, had been instituted to protect life, liberty, and property; no political authority could infringe these natural rights. The law of nature was therefore an automatic and absolute limitation on every branch of government.

In the late eighteenth century, Locke's ideas would resurface as part of the intellectual background of both the American and French Revolutions. Between 1690 and 1720, however, they served a far less radical purpose. The landed gentry who replaced James II with William and Mary read Locke as a defense of their conservative revolution. Rather than protecting their liberty and property, James II had threatened both; hence, the magnates were entitled to overthrow the tyranny he had established and replace it with a government that would defend their interests by preserving these natural rights. English government after 1689 was dominated by Parliament; Parliament in turn was controlled by a landed aristocracy that was firm in the defense of its common interests, and that perpetuated its control by determining that only men possessed of substantial property could vote or run for office. During the beginning of the eighteenth century, then, both France and Britain had solved the problem of political dissent and social disorder in their own way. The emergence of a limited monarchy in England after 1688 contrasted vividly with the absolutist system developed by Louis XIV, but both systems, in fact, worked well enough to balance the competing interests of royal authority and powerful landed nobles.

THE DUTCH REPUBLIC

Another exception to absolutist rule in Europe was the Dutch Republic of the United Provinces, which had gained its independence from Spanish rule in 1648 (see Chapter 14). The seven provinces of the Dutch Republic preserved their autonomy with a federal legislature known as the States General, with delegations from each province. This flexible structure was intended to prevent the reestablishment of hereditary monarchy. Instead of a king, the republic delegated the title of *stadtholder*, or steward, to the princes of the House of Orange. The *stadtholder* had no power to make laws, though they had some military authority.

By 1670, the prosperity of the Dutch Republic was strongly linked to trade: grain and fish from eastern Europe and the Baltic Sea; spices, silks, porcelains, and tea from the Indian Ocean and Japan; and slaves, silver, coffee, sugar, and tobacco from the Atlantic world. With a population of nearly two million and a capital, Amsterdam, that was an international hub for goods and finance, the Dutch Republic's commercial network was global (see Chapter 14). Trade brought with it an extraordinary diversity of peoples and religions, as Spanish and Portuguese Jews, French Huguenots, English Quakers, and Protestant dissidents all sought to take advantage of the relative spirit of toleration that existed in the Netherlands. This toleration did have limits, however. Jews were not required to live in segregated neighborhoods, as in

John Locke (1632–1704) English philosopher and political theorist known for his contributions to liberalism.

contract theory of government Posits that government authority is both contractual and conditional; therefore, if a government has abused its given authority, society has the right to dissolve it and create another.

Through global trade network and tolerant policies, Dutch Republic becomes home to diverse population— with some limits many other European capitals, but they were prohibited from joining guilds or trade associations. Tensions between Calvinists and Catholics were also a perennial issue.

The last quarter of the seventeenth century witnessed a decline in Dutch power. The turning point came in 1672, when the French king, Louis XIV, put together a coalition that quickly overran all but two of the Dutch provinces. Popular anger at the failures of Dutch leadership turned violent, and in response, the panicked assemblies named William of Orange the new stadtholder of Holland, giving him the power to organize the defense of the Republic and quell internal dissent. William opened the dikes that held back the sea from the Republic's low-lying territories, and the French armies were forced to retreat in the face of rising waters. After the Glorious Revolution of 1688 in England, which brought William of Orange to the English throne, the Dutch joined an alliance with the English against the French. This alliance protected the Republic against further aggression from France, but it also forced the Dutch into heavy expenditures on fortifications and defense and involved them in a series of costly wars (see the next section). As a result, the dynamic and flexible political institutions that had been part of the strength of the Dutch Republic became more rigid and inflexible over time. In the eighteenth century, the Dutch no longer exercised the same influence abroad.

English alliance draws Dutch into costly wars ❯

THE POLISH-LITHUANIAN COMMONWEALTH

The Commonwealth of Poland and Lithuania was a vast state that ruled over much of present-day Poland, Lithuania, Latvia, Estonia, Belarus, and Ukraine between 1569 and 1795. At its greatest extent, in the early seventeenth century, the Commonwealth reached from the Baltic coast nearly to the Black Sea. The Commonwealth had a tradition of limits to royal authority, making it an important exception to the trend toward absolutist rule in seventeenth-century Europe.

The limits to the king's power in Poland-Lithuania were enforced by the relatively numerous landowning gentry. These nobles elected members to seats in smaller provincial assemblies and in a parliament known as the Sejm (*SAY-m*). It was generally accepted that the king could not outfit an army or raise taxes without consulting the Sejm. After 1569, the Chamber and the Senate met for a six-week session at least every two years. When the king died, the Sejm supervised the process by which the landowning aristocracy elected a new ruler. Parliamentary authority was not at all complete, however, and the crown retained considerable power. One-sixth of the land in the Commonwealth remained under the direct control of the king.

In the Restoration monarchy of England after 1688, the Dutch Republic, and the Polish-Lithuanian Commonwealth, therefore, circumstances allowed for greater power to remain in the hands of the gentry. In France, Prussia, and Russia (see the next section), on the other hand, absolutist rulers eventually succeeded in imposing their will on the aristocrats who remained their most powerful rivals for authority.

War and the Balance of Power, 1661–1715

By the beginning of the eighteenth century, Europe was being reshaped by wars whose effects were also felt far beyond Europe's borders. These wars were rooted in the French monarch's efforts to challenge his main European rivals: the Habsburg powers in Spain, the Spanish Netherlands, and the Holy Roman Empire. Louis XIV's personal rule began in 1661 (he had come to the throne as a child in 1643), and he first invaded the Spanish Netherlands in 1667. In successive campaigns, he expanded his territory, eventually taking Strasbourg (1681), Luxembourg (1684), and Cologne (1688). In response, William of Orange organized the League of Augsburg, which eventually included Holland, England, Spain, Sweden, Bavaria, Saxony, the Rhine Palatinate, and the Austrian Habsburgs. The resulting Nine Years' War between France and the League extended from Ireland to India to North America (where it was known as King William's War), demonstrating the broadening imperial reach of European dynastic regimes and the increasing significance of French and English competition in the Atlantic world.

These wars were signs of both the heightening power of Europe's absolutist regimes and their growing vulnerability. Financing costly wars was a central challenge faced by all of Europe's absolutist regimes, and the pressure to raise revenues from their subjects through taxation would eventually strain European society to a breaking point. By the end of the eighteenth century, popular unrest and political challenges to absolutist and imperial states were widespread, both on the European continent and in the colonies of the Atlantic world.

FROM THE LEAGUE OF AUGSBURG TO THE WAR OF THE SPANISH SUCCESSION

The League of Augsburg reflected the emergence of a new diplomatic goal in western and central Europe: the preservation of a **balance of power**. This goal animated European diplomacy for two hundred years, until the balance-of-power system collapsed with the outbreak of the First World War. The main proponents of balance-of-power diplomacy were England, the United Provinces (Holland), Prussia, and Austria. By 1697, the League forced Louis XIV to make peace, because France was exhausted by war and famine. Louis gave back many of his recent gains but kept his eyes on the real prize: a French claim to succeed to the throne of Spain and so control the Spanish Empire in the Americas, Italy, the Netherlands, and the Philippines.

In the 1690s, both Louis XIV of France and Leopold I of Austria (r. 1658–1705) pushed for their own relatives to succeed King Charles II of Spain, threatening the balance of power in Europe. When Charles II died, Louis XIV's grandson Philip (r. 1700–1746) was proclaimed King Philip V of Spain, and Louis XIV rushed troops into the Spanish Netherlands while also sending French merchants into the Spanish Americas to challenge Spain's monopoly on trade. Immediately the War of the Spanish Succession broke out, pitting England, the United Provinces, Austria, and Prussia against France, Bavaria, and Spain. English generals marched their armies deep into the European continent, inflicting a devastating defeat on the French and their Bavarian allies at Blenheim (1704). Soon after, the English captured Gibraltar, establishing a commercial foothold in the Mediterranean. The costs of the campaign nevertheless created a chorus of complaints from English and Dutch merchants, who feared the damage that was being done to trade and commerce. Queen Anne of England (Mary's sister and William's successor) grew disillusioned with the war, and her government sent out peace feelers to France.

In 1713, the war finally came to an end with the **Treaty of Utrecht**. Its terms were reasonably fair to all sides. Philip V, Louis XIV's grandson, remained on the throne of Spain and kept Spain's colonial empire intact. In return, Louis agreed that France and Spain would never be united under the same ruler. Austria gained

balance of powers The principle that no one country should be powerful enough to destabilize international relations.

Treaty of Utrecht (1713) Resolution to the War of the Spanish Succession that reestablished a balance of power in Europe, to the benefit of Britain and in ways that disadvantaged Spain, Holland, and France.

 France's motivation to control Spanish succession is tied to its colonial holdings

THE TREATY OF UTRECHT, 1713. This illustration from a French royal almanac depicts the treaty that ended the War of the Spanish Succession and reshaped the balance of power in western Europe in favor of Britain and France.

After Treaty of Utrecht, Britain emerges as dominant power in slave trade ❯

territories in the Spanish Netherlands and Italy, including Milan and Naples. The Dutch were guaranteed protection of their borders against future invasions by France, but the French retained both Lille and Strasbourg. The most significant consequences of the settlement, however, were played out in the Atlantic world, as the balance of powers among Europe's colonial empires underwent a profound shift.

IMPERIAL RIVALRIES AFTER THE TREATY OF UTRECHT

The fortunes of Europe's colonial empires changed dramatically owing to the wars of the late seventeenth and early eighteenth centuries. Habsburg Spain proved unable to defend its early monopoly over colonial trade, and by 1700, although Spain still possessed a substantial empire, it lay at the mercy of its more dynamic rivals. Portugal, too, found it impossible to prevent foreign penetration of its colonial empire. In 1703, the English signed a treaty with Portugal allowing English merchants to export woolens duty free into Portugal and allowing Portugal to ship its wines duty free into England. Access to Portugal also led British merchants to trade with the Portuguese colony of Brazil, an important sugar producer and the largest of all the American markets for African slaves.

The 1713 Treaty of Utrecht opened a new era of colonial rivalries. The French retained Québec and other territories in North America, as well as their small foothold in India. The biggest winner by far was Great Britain, as the combined kingdoms of England and Scotland were known after 1707. The British kept Gibraltar and Minorca in the Mediterranean and also acquired large chunks of French territory in the New World, including Newfoundland, mainland Nova Scotia, the Hudson Bay, and the Caribbean island of St. Kitts. Even more valuable, however, Britain also extracted from Spain the right to transport and sell African slaves in Spanish America. As a result, the British were now poised to become the principal slave merchants and the dominant colonial and commercial power of the eighteenth-century world.

The Treaty of Utrecht thus reshaped the balance of power in the Atlantic world in fundamental ways. Spain's collapse was already precipitous, and by 1713 it was complete. Spain would remain the "sick man of Europe" for the next two centuries. The Dutch decline was more gradual, but by 1713, the inability of Dutch merchants to compete with the British in the slave trade diminished their economic clout. In the Atlantic, Britain and France were now the dominant powers. Although they would duel for another half century for control of North America, the balance of colonial power tilted decisively in Britain's favor after Utrecht. Within Europe, the myth of French military supremacy had been shattered. Britain's navy, not France's army, would rule the new imperial and commercial world of the eighteenth century.

The Remaking of Central and Eastern Europe

The decades between 1680 and 1720 also were decisive in reshaping the balance of power in central and eastern Europe. As Ottoman power waned, the Austro-Hungarian Empire of the Habsburgs emerged as the dominant power in central and southeastern Europe. To the north, Brandenburg-Prussia was also a rising power. The most dramatic changes, however, occurred in Russia, which emerged from a long war with Sweden as the dominant realm in the Baltic Sea and would soon threaten the combined kingdom of Poland-Lithuania. Within these regimes, the main tension came from ambitious monarchs who sought to increase the power of the centralized state at the expense of other elites, especially aristocrats and the Church. In Brandenburg-Prussia and in tsarist Russia, these efforts were largely successful, whereas in Habsburg Austria, regional nobilities retained much of their influence.

THE AUSTRIAN HABSBURG EMPIRE

In the second half of the seventeenth century, as Louis XIV of France demonstrated the power of absolutism in western Europe, the Austrian Habsburg Empire, with its capital in Vienna, must have seemed like a holdover from a previous age. Habsburg Austria was the largest state within what remained of the medieval Holy Roman Empire, a complex federal association of nearly three hundred nominally autonomous dynastic kingdoms, principalities, duchies, and archbishoprics that had been created to protect and defend the papacy. Each Holy Roman emperor was chosen by seven "electors" who were either of noble rank or archbishops—but in practice, the emperor was always from the Habsburg family. Through strategic marriages with other royal lines, earlier generations of Habsburg rulers had consolidated their control over a substantial part of Europe, including Austria, Bohemia, Moravia, and Hungary in central Europe; the Netherlands and Burgundy in the west; and, if one included the Spanish branch of the Habsburg family, Spain and its vast colonial empire as well. After 1648, when the Treaty of Westphalia granted individual member states within the Holy Roman Empire the right to conduct their own foreign policy, the influence of the Austrian Habsburgs waned, at precisely the moment when they faced challenges from France to the west and the Ottoman Empire to the east.

The complicated structure of the Holy Roman Empire limited the extent to which a ruler such as Leopold I of Austria could emulate the absolutist rule of Louis XIV in France. Every constituent state within the empire had its own political institutions and its own entrenched nobilities. Each state had a strong incentive to resist any centralization of tax collection or the raising of armies. Even if direct assertion of absolutist control was impossible, Habsburg rulers found ways to increase their authority. In Bohemia and Moravia, the Habsburgs encouraged landlords to produce crops for export by forcing peasants to provide three days of unpaid work per week to their lords. In return, the landed elites of these territories permitted the emperors to reduce the political independence of their traditional legislative estates. In Hungary, however, the powerful and independent nobility resisted such compromises. In 1679, when the Habsburgs began a campaign against Hungarian Protestants, an insurrection broke out that forced Leopold to grant concessions to Hungarian nobles in exchange for their assistance in restoring order. When the

Limitations to absolutist rule within Habsburg states

Ottoman Empire sought to take advantage of this disorder to press an attack against Austria from the east, the Habsburgs survived only by enlisting the help of a Catholic coalition led by the Polish king John Sobieski (r. 1674–1696).

In 1683, the Ottomans launched their last assault on Vienna, but after their failure to capture the Habsburg capital, Ottoman power in southeastern Europe declined. By 1699, Austria had reconquered most of Hungary from the Ottomans, and by 1718, it controlled Hungary, Transylvania, and Serbia. With these victories, Austria became one of the arbiters of the European balance of power. The same obstacles to the development of centralized absolutist rule persisted, however, and Austria was increasingly overshadowed in central Europe by the rise of another German-speaking state: Prussia.

EUROPE AFTER THE TREATY OF UTRECHT (1713). › What were the major Habsburg dominions? › What geographical disadvantage faced the kingdom of Poland as Brandenburg-Prussia grew in influence and ambition? › How did the balance of power change in Europe as a result of the Treaty of Utrecht?

THE RISE OF BRANDENBURG-PRUSSIA

After the Ottoman defeat, the main threat to Austria came from the rising power of Brandenburg-Prussia. Like Austria, Prussia was a composite state made up of several geographically divided territories acquired through inheritance by a single royal family, the Hohenzollerns. Their two main holdings were Brandenburg, centered on its capital city, Berlin, and the duchy of East Prussia. Between these two territories lay Pomerania (claimed by Sweden) and an important part of the kingdom of Poland, including the port of Gdańsk (Danzig). The Hohenzollerns' aim was to unite their state by acquiring these intervening territories. Over the course of more than a century of steady state building, they finally succeeded. In the process, Brandenburg-Prussia became a dominant military power and a key player in the balance-of-power diplomacy of the mid-eighteenth century.

The foundations for Prussian expansion were laid by Frederick William, the "Great Elector" (r. 1640–1688). He obtained East Prussia from Poland in exchange for help in a war against Sweden. Behind the elector's diplomatic triumphs lay his

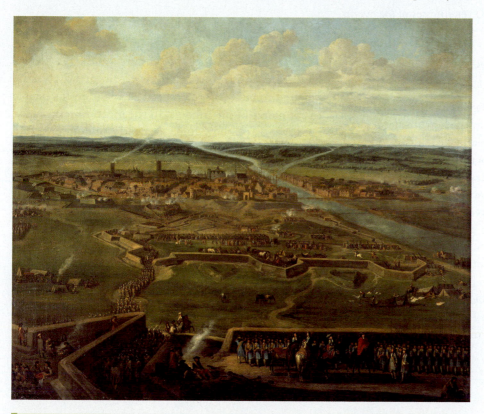

THE CITY OF STETTIN UNDER SIEGE BY THE GREAT ELECTOR FREDERICK WILLIAM IN THE WINTER OF 1677–1678 (c. 1680). This painting depicts the growing sophistication and organization of military operations under the Prussian monarchy. Improvements in artillery and siege tactics forced cities to adopt new defensive strategies, especially the zones of battlements and protective walls that became ubiquitous in central Europe during this period. › **How might these defensive developments have shaped the layout of Europe's growing towns and cities? › How might this emphasis on the military and its attendant bureaucracy have affected the relationship between the monarchy and the nobility, or between the king and his subjects?**

The Siege of Vienna (1683)

In 1683, the armies of the Ottoman Empire besieged the city of Vienna, the capital of the Austrian Habsburg monarchy, which was defended by forces of the Holy Roman Empire of the German Nations, led by King John III Sobieski of the Polish-Lithuanian Commonwealth. The battle marked the high point of Ottoman expansion into southeastern Europe, and the Ottoman defeat was celebrated by many in Europe as a victory of Christianity over Islam. The reality was more complicated, however, as Protestant armies in Hungary that allied with anti-Habsburg forces had received arms and support from the Ottoman Empire in the years before the battle, apparently in exchange for a promise that Hungary would control Vienna in the event of an Ottoman victory. This source, published in 1684 in English in Cologne and London, contains enough details to allow one to assume that it was, at least in part, informed by eyewitnesses of the events.

Emperor Leopold I Flees Vienna for Passau

The Emperor who had receiv'd a fierce alarm by the suddain irruption of the Infidels, and who consider'd that after the revolt of the Hungarians, he could no longer remain at Vienna in surety, bethought himself at the same time of leaving it. But first augmented the privileges of the Scholars, which were already very great, and considerable, that having receiv'd them as a recompence of their Courage which they shew'd heretofore against Solyman [the Ottoman Emperor Suleiman the Magnificent], when he besieg'd the City [in 1529] this should be a fresh incitement to defend it with the same resolution. He gave also to the Shoomakers Apprentices their Freedom, who were to the number of about 1500, in case they took Arms, and did any thing considerable for the Country.

* * *

Every one wept at his departure, and this Prince had much ado to forbear himself. So greatly was he afflicted to be thus constrained to abandon his people to the mercy of the Infidels. In the mean time each one endeavor'd to follow him, to avoid the being expos'd to those mischiefs which they represented. In fine, there being not Coaches enough to carry all those that offer'd 'emselves, several Women of Quality got behind like Lacques [servants]; so that one might have seen the first Prince in the World, follow'd by all the flower of the German Nobility, to go as an exul [exile] amidst the screeches and lamentations of his people, who presented 'emselves in his passage with showr's of tears. . .

* * *

The Emperor all this while marched with a countenance sad and dejected like his fortune. Others kept a mournful silence, and although each had left their estates behind 'em 'twas not known whether their own mishap or that

Frederick William gains support of Junker nobles in exchange for financial privileges and wealth

success in building an army and mobilizing the resources to pay for it. He gave the powerful nobles of his territories, known as "Junkers" (*YUN-kurs*), the right to enserf their peasants and guaranteed immunity from taxation. In exchange, they staffed the officer corps of his army and supported his highly autocratic taxation system. Secure in their estates and made increasingly wealthy in the grain trade, the Junkers surrendered management of the Prussian state to the elector's newly reformed bureaucracy, which set about its main task of increasing the size and strength of the Prussian army.

By supporting Austria in the War of the Spanish Succession, the Great Elector's son, Frederick I (r. 1688–1713), earned the right to call himself king of Prussia of the Prince was to be most lamented. In fine, this march much resembled a Funeral Pomp, when another spectacle encreas'd the dolour and compassion. For they beheld the other side of the *Danube* all in fire, and the Emperor having caused his Coach to stop, knowing not at first what it was, soon perceived 'twas the *Turks*, who shew'd there new testimonies of their barbarous cruelty. He could not withhold his tears at the sight of a thing so much needing his compassion, and although he did all he could to refrain his grief, he could not effect it.

Disease Afflicts the Defenders of Vienna

And having made his retreat, and taken great care of the wounded, [Stahrenberg, the military commander of Vienna] made a review of those Forces he had left him; which he found diminish'd by a third part, not so much by Sallies, and in this last occasion, as by the Dysentery or Flux which began to rage in the Town, as well amongst the Citizens and Soldiers. In effect the fatigues together with the bad food they eat, had so heated the bloud of most of 'em, that they fell sick every day. And it being impossible for 'em after this to do service, the rest, whose weariness increased as fast as the number of the others diminish'd, were soon in the same condition, or at least so tir'd out with labour and watching, that they were all ready to drop down as they march'd. . . .

* * *

But that which contributed to render this malady more incurable was the Airs being so infected by the stench of the dead Bodies which lay unburied, that it could not be more dangerous in a time of Plague. The cause of this stench was that Stahrenberg would not yield to any terms of a Truce propos'd by the Visier [Vizier], to take away those of his party, who had been kild in so many several skirmishes, hoping that besides the displeasure he would receive thereby, this would be a spectacle to damp the Courage of the Soldiers, when in marching up to the Charge, they should see before their Eyes the fortune of their Companions, which would be a presage to them of the like. Howsoever whether 'twas this infection or something else, which brought this grievous sickness into the Town, they were so greatly incommodated [*sic*] by it, that they would willingly have been deliver'd from of it at the cost of a greater danger from the enemy. Yet did this distemper rage as well in the Camp of the Turks, of which there dyed every day near 300, but which was scarce perceivable, because they continually receiv'd fresh supplies, which made up their losses.

Source: Anonymous, *The History of the late war with the Turks, during the siege of Vienna, and the great victory obtain'd against them at the raising of the siege* (Cologne and London, 1684), pp. 33–86.

Questions for Analysis

1. How did Emperor Leopold encourage the people of the city to defend themselves even as he retreated to a safer location?

2. What is the significance of the term *Infidels*, which the author uses to describe the Ottomans?

3. What does this description tell us about the effects of the siege on military and civilian populations? What explanation does the author give for the spread of disease in the city and among the attacking armies?

from the Austrian emperor. He too was a crafty diplomat, but his main attention was devoted to developing the cultural life of his new royal capital, Berlin. His son, Frederick William I (r. 1713–1740), however, focused on building the army like his grandfather. During his reign, the Prussian army grew from thirty thousand to eighty-three thousand men, becoming the fourth largest army in Europe, after those of France, Austria, and Russia. To support his army, Frederick William I increased taxes and shunned the luxuries of court life. For him, the theater of absolutism was not the palace but the office, where he personally supervised his army and the growing bureaucracy that sustained it. Frederick William's son, known as Frederick the Great, would use this Prussian army and the bureaucracy that sustained it to transform the kingdom into a major power in central Europe after 1740 (see Chapter 17).

Thus, in both Prussia and Habsburg Austria, the divided nature of the respective realms and the entrenched strength of local nobilities forced the rulers of each to grant significant concessions to noble landowners in exchange for incremental increases in the power of the centralized state. Whereas the nobility in France increasingly sought to maximize their power by participating in the system of absolutist rule at the court of Louis XIV, and wealthy landowners in England sought to exercise their influence through Parliament, the nobilities of Prussia and Habsburg Austria had more leverage to demand something in return for their cooperation. Often, what they demanded was the right to enserf or coerce labor from the peasantry in their domains. In both eastern and western Europe, therefore, the state became stronger. In eastern Europe, however, this increase in state power often came at the expense of an intensification of feudal obligations that the peasantry owed to their local lords.

> *In Prussia and Habsburg Austria, nobles defer to growing state power in exchange for tightened grip over peasantry*

Autocracy in Russia

An even more dramatic transformation took place in Russia under Tsar Peter I (r. 1682–1725). Peter's official title was "autocrat of all the Russias," but he was soon known as Peter the Great. His imposing height (six feet eight inches) and his mercurial personality (jesting one moment, raging the next) added to the outsize impression he made on his contemporaries. Peter was not the first tsar to bring his country into contact with western Europe, but his policies were decisive in making Russia a great European power.

THE EARLY YEARS OF PETER'S REIGN

Like Louis XIV of France, Peter came to the throne as a young boy, and his minority was marked by political dissension and court intrigue. In 1689, however, at the age of seventeen, he overthrew the regency of his half-sister Sophia and assumed personal control of the state. Determined to make Russia into a great military power, the young tsar traveled to Holland and England during the 1690s to study shipbuilding and to recruit skilled foreign workers to help him build a navy. But while he was abroad, his elite palace guard (the *streltsy*) rebelled, attempting to restore Sophia to the throne. Peter quickly returned home from Vienna and crushed the rebellion with striking savagery. About 1,200 suspected conspirators were summarily executed, many of them gibbeted outside the walls of the Kremlin, where their bodies rotted for months as a graphic reminder of the fate awaiting those who dared challenge the tsar's authority.

THE TRANSFORMATION OF THE TSARIST STATE

Peter is most famous as the tsar who attempted to westernize Russia by imposing a series of social and cultural reforms on the traditional Russian nobility: ordering noblemen to cut off their long beards and flowing sleeves; publishing a book of manners that forbade spitting on the floor and eating with one's fingers; encouraging polite conversation between the sexes; and requiring noblewomen to appear, together with men, in Western garb at weddings, banquets, and other public occasions. The children of Russian nobles were sent to western European courts for their education. Thousands of western European experts were brought to Russia to staff the new schools and academies Peter built; to design the new buildings he constructed; and to serve in the tsar's army, navy, and administration.

These measures were important, but the tsar was not motivated primarily by a desire to modernize or westernize Russia. Peter's policies transformed Russian life in fundamental ways, but his real goal was to make Russia a great military power, not to remake Russian society. For example, while his new taxation system (1724), which assessed taxes on individuals rather than on households, rendered many of the traditional divisions of Russian peasant society obsolete, it was created to raise more money for war. His Table of Ranks, imposed in 1722, had similar impact on the nobility. By insisting that all nobles must work their way up from the (lower) landlord class to the (higher) administrative class and to the (highest) military class, Peter reversed the traditional hierarchy of Russian noble society, which had valued landlords by birth above administrators and soldiers who had risen by merit. This created a powerful new incentive to lure his nobility into administrative and military service to the tsar.

As "autocrat of all the Russias," Peter the Great was the absolute master of his empire to a degree unmatched elsewhere in Europe. After 1649, Russian peasants were legally the property of their landlords; by 1750, half were serfs and the other half were state peasants who lived on lands owned by the tsar himself. (In contrast, many peasants in western Europe owned their own land, and very few were serfs.) State peasants could be conscripted to serve as soldiers in the tsar's army, as workers in his factories (whose productive capacity increased enormously during Peter's reign), or as forced laborers in his building projects. Serfs could also be taxed by the tsar and summoned for military service, as could their lords. All Russians, of whatever rank, were expected to serve the tsar, and all Russia was considered in some sense to belong to him. Russia's autocracy thus went even further than the absolutism of Louis XIV.

To consolidate his power further, Peter replaced the Duma—the tsar's hand-picked council of noble elites—with a smaller handpicked senate, a group of nine administrators who supervised military and civilian affairs. In religious matters, he took direct control over the Russian Orthodox Church by appointing an imperial official to manage its affairs. To cope with the demands of war, he also fashioned a new, larger, and more efficient administration, for which he recruited both nobles

PETER THE GREAT CUTS THE BEARD OF AN OLD BELIEVER. This woodcut depicts the Russian emperor's enthusiastic policy of westernization, as he pushed everybody in Russia who was not a peasant to adopt western styles of clothes and grooming. The Old Believer (a member of a religious sect in Russia) protests that he has paid the beard tax and should therefore be exempt. › Why would an individual's choices about personal appearance be so politically significant in Peter's Russia? › What customs were the target of Peter's reforms?

The Revolt of the *Streltsy* and Peter the Great

The streltsy were four regiments of Moscow guards that became involved in a conspiracy in support of Peter the Great's older sister Sophia, who had earlier made claim to the throne while Peter was still a child. Approximately four thousand of the rebels were defeated in June 1698 by troops loyal to Peter. Peter himself was abroad during the fighting, and although his officers had already tortured many of the streltsy to determine the involvement of other nobles, he ordered further-reaching investigation on his return. One thousand of the streltsy were executed after being tortured again. Afterward, their bodies were put on display in the capital. Johann Georg Korb, an Austrian diplomat in Moscow, recorded his observations of the power wielded by the Russian autocrat.

How sharp was the pain, how great the indignation to which the Czar's Majesty was mightily moved, when he knew of the rebellion of the Strelitz [*streltsy*], betrayed openly a mind panting for vengeance. [*sic*] . . . Going immediately to Lefort (the only person almost that he condescended to treat with intimate familiarity), he thus indignantly broke out: "Tell me, Francis, son of James, how I can reach Moscow, by the shortest way, in a brief space, so that I may wreak vengeance on this great perfidy of my people, with punishments worthy of their flagitious crime. Not one of them shall escape with impunity. Around my royal city, of which, with their impious efforts, they meditated the destruction, I will have gibbets and gallows set upon the walls and ramparts, and each and every of them will I put to a direful death." . . .

His first anxiety, after his arrival [in Moscow] was about the rebellion. In what it consisted? What the insurgents meant? Who had dared to instigate such a crime? And as nobody could answer accurately upon all points, and some pleaded their own ignorance, others the obstinacy of the Strelitz, he began to have suspicions of everybody's loyalty, and began to cogitate about a fresh investigation. The rebels that were kept in custody . . . were all brought in by four regiments of the guards, to a fresh investigation and fresh tortures. Prison, tribunal, and rack, for those that were brought in, was in Bebraschentsko. No day, holy, or profane, were the inquisitors idle; every day was deemed fit and lawful for torturing. As many as there were accused there were knouts, and every inquisitor was a butcher. Prince Feodor Jurowicz Romadonowski showed himself by so much more fitted for his inquiry, as he surpassed the rest in cruelty. He

put the interrogatories, he examined the criminals, he urged those that were not confessing, he ordered such Strelitz as were more pertinaciously silent, to be subjected to more cruel tortures; those that had already confessed about many things were questioned about more; those who were bereft of strength and reason, and almost of their senses, by excess of torment, were handed over to the skill of the doctors, who were compelled to restore them to strength, in order that they might be broken down by fresh excruciations. The whole month of October was spent in butchering the backs of the culprits with knout and with flames: no day were those that were left alive exempt from scourging or scorching, or else they were broken upon the wheel, or driven to the gibbet, or slain with the axe—the penalties which were inflicted upon them as soon as their confessions had sufficiently revealed the heads of the rebellion.

Source: Johann Georg Korb, *Diary of an Austrian Secretary of Legation at the Court of Czar Peter the Great*, trans. Count MacDonnell (London: 1863), vol. 2, pp. 85–87.

Questions for Analysis

1. Why was it important for Korb to begin this account with a description of the monarch's pain?

2. What does this episode reveal about Peter's conception of his own person and of the loyalty that his subjects owed him? Does it show that his power was fragile, immense, or both?

3. What does it mean to describe torture as an "investigation" even while also describing it as "vengeance"?

and nonnobles. The rank in the new bureaucracy did not depend on birth. One of his principal advisers, Alexander Menshikov, began his career as a cook and finished as a prince. This degree of social mobility would have been impossible in any contemporary western European country. In Russia, more so than in western Europe, noble status depended on government service, with all nobles expected to participate in Peter's army or administration. Peter was not entirely successful in enforcing this requirement, but the administrative machinery he devised furnished Russia with its ruling class for the next two hundred years.

Peter creates new noble hierarchy with emphasis on military merit and government service

RUSSIAN IMPERIAL EXPANSION

The goal of Peter's foreign policy was to secure year-round ports for Russia on the Black Sea and the Baltic Sea. In the Black Sea, his enemy was the Ottoman Empire. Here, however, he had little success, and Russia would not secure its position in the Black Sea until the end of the eighteenth century. Nevertheless, Peter continued to push against the Ottoman Empire in the northern Caucasus region throughout his reign. This mountainous area on Russia's southern flank became an important site for Russia's experiments in colonial expansion into central Asia, which began during the sixteenth century and would later mirror the process of colonial conquest undertaken by European powers and the United States in North and South America. Like those of France and Britain, the Russian state bureaucracy was built during a period of ambitious colonialism; and as in Spain, the monarchy's identity was shaped by a long contest with Muslim power on its borders.

Since the late sixteenth century, successive Russian leaders had extended their control over bordering territories of central Asia. Although merchants helped fund early expeditions into Siberia, this expansion was primarily motivated by geopolitical concerns; the tsar sought to gain access to the populations of Russia's border areas and bring them into the service of the expanding Russian state. In this sense, Russian colonialism during this period differed from western European expansion into the Atlantic world, which had primarily been motivated by hopes of commercial gain.

In its early stages, as successive Russian emperors moved Russian troops eastward into Asia, they relied on a process of indirect rule, often seeking to co-opt local elites. Later in the eighteenth century, they had more success settling Russians in border regions to rule directly over local populations. Religion also provided a cover for expansion, and Peter and his successors funded missionary work by Georgian Christians among Muslims in the Caucasus. Efforts to convert Muslim populations to Orthodox Christianity had little effect, and in fact the opposite occurred: the region's commitment to Islam was continuously renewed through contact with different strains of Islamic practice coming from neighboring Ottoman lands and Persia.

Peter could point to more concrete success to the north. In 1700, he began what would become a twenty-one-year war with Sweden, then the dominant power in the Baltic Sea. By 1703, Peter had secured a foothold on the Gulf of Finland and immediately began to build a new capital city there, which he named St. Petersburg. After 1709, when Russian armies decisively defeated the Swedes at the battle of Poltava, work on Peter's new capital city accelerated. An army of serfs was now conscripted to build the new city, whose centerpiece was a royal palace designed to imitate and rival Louis XIV's Versailles. Conditions for the laborers were grueling and

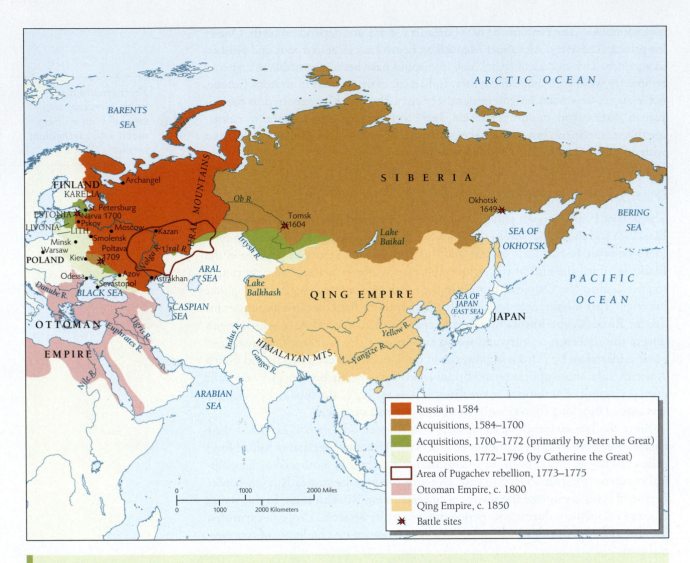

Russia in 1584
Acquisitions, 1584–1700
Acquisitions, 1700–1772 (primarily by Peter the Great)
Acquisitions, 1772–1796 (by Catherine the Great)
Area of Pugachev rebellion, 1773–1775
Ottoman Empire, c. 1800
Qing Empire, c. 1850
✳ **Battle sites**

THE GROWTH OF THE RUSSIAN EMPIRE. › How did Peter the Great expand the territory controlled by Russia? › What neighboring dynasties were most affected by Russian expansion? › How did the emergence of a bigger, more powerful Russia affect the European balance of power?

Peter's building sites required armed guards to maintain order. In 1714, he forced one thousand aristocrats to move into the new capital with their families, ignoring their protests. Peter's model city was equipped with remarkable amenities: street lighting, regular waste collection, and a fire brigade. But resentment at his autocratic methods remained for generations afterwards.

The Great Northern War with Sweden ended in 1721 with the Peace of Nystad. This treaty marked a realignment of power in eastern Europe comparable to the Treaty of Utrecht in the West. Sweden lost its North Sea territories to Hanover, and its Baltic German territories to Prussia. Its eastern territories, including the entire Gulf of Finland, Livonia, and Estonia, passed to Russia. Poland-Lithuania survived but only as a declining power. By the end of the eighteenth century, this kingdom would disappear altogether, its territories swallowed up by its more powerful neighbors (see Chapter 17). The victors at Nystad were the Prussians and the Russians.

Peter's accomplishments came at enormous cost. Direct taxation in Russia increased 500 percent during his reign, and in the 1720s, his army numbered more than three hundred thousand men. Peter made Russia a force to be reckoned with on the European scene, but in so doing, he aroused great resentment, especially among his nobility. Peter's only son and heir, Alexis, became the focus for conspiracies against the tsar, and Peter had him arrested and executed in 1718. As a result, when Peter died in 1725, he left no son to succeed him. A series of ineffective tsars followed, and resentful nobles reversed many of Peter the Great's reforms. In 1762, however, the crown passed to Catherine the Great, a ruler whose ambitions and determination were equal to those of her great predecessor (see Chapter 17).

Conclusion

By the time of Peter the Great's death in Russia in 1725, the power of Europe's absolutist realms to reinvigorate European political institutions was visible to all. Government was more bureaucratic; state service was more professionalized; and administrators loyal to the kings had become more numerous, more efficient, and more demanding. Despite the increasing scope of government, the principles of royal authority changed relatively little. Apart from Great Britain, the Dutch Republic, and Poland-Lithuania, the great powers of eighteenth-century Europe were still governed by rulers who styled themselves as absolutist monarchs in the mold of Louis XIV, who claimed an authority that came directly from God and ruled over a society in which social hierarchies based on birth were taken for granted.

However, these absolutist regimes could not hide the fact that their rule depended on a kind of negotiated settlement with other powerful elites within European society, in particular with landed aristocrats and religious leaders. Louis XIV used his power to curb the worst excesses of nobles who abused their position, and to defend Catholic orthodoxy against dissident Catholics and Protestants. Nevertheless, his power depended on a delicate exchange of favors: French aristocrats surrendered their political authority to the state in exchange for social and legal privileges and immunity from many (but not all) forms of taxation, and the Church made a similar bargain. Peter the Great's autocratic rule in Russia worked out a slightly different balance of powers between his state and the Russian aristocracy, one that tied aristocrats more closely to an ideal of state service, a model that also worked well for the rulers of Brandenburg-Prussia. Even in England, the establishment of a limited constitutional monarchy and a king who ruled alongside Parliament was not really a radical departure from the European absolutist model. It was merely a different institutional answer to the same problem: What relationship should the monarchical state have with other elites within society?

The demands of state building during this period required kings to raise enormous revenues—for the sumptuous displays of their sovereignty in royal residences such as Louis XIV's palace at Versailles, for the sponsorship of royal academies and the patronage of artists, but most of all, for war. Expanding territory within Europe and holding on to colonial empires in the Atlantic world were costly. Distributing the burden of taxation to pay for these endeavors became an intensely fraught political issue for European monarchs during this period, and the financing of royal debt became an increasingly sophisticated art. Colbert's mercantilist policy was an attempt to harness the full power of the economy for the benefit of royal government; and the competition among Spain, Holland, England, and France to control the revenue flows coming from the Atlantic world forced Europe's monarchs to recognize that the balance of power was increasingly being played out on a global stage.

These themes—the expansion of state powers; conflicts between the monarchy and the aristocracy or with religious dissidents; the intensification of the tax burden on the population; and the opening up of Europe to ever more frequent interactions with other peoples in the Atlantic world, the Indian Ocean, and eventually, the Pacific—prompted many in eighteenth-century Europe to reflect on the consequences of these developments. What were the limits to state power, and by

AFTER YOU READ THIS CHAPTER

CHRONOLOGY

1643–1715	Reign of Louis XIV of France
1660	Restoration of the Stuart kings in England
1682–1725	Reign of Peter the Great of Russia
1683	Ottoman siege of Vienna
1685	Revocation of the Edict of Nantes
1688	Glorious Revolution in England
1688–1697	War of the League of Augsburg
1690	Publication of John Locke's *Two Treatises of Government*
1702–1713	War of the Spanish Succession
1713	Treaty of Utrecht

REVIEWING THE OBJECTIVES

> Absolutist rulers claimed a monopoly of power and authority within their realms. What was absolutism? Who were the most successful absolutist monarchs?

> Mercantilism was an economic doctrine that guided the policies of absolutist rulers. What did mercantilists believe?

> Alternatives to absolutist government emerged in England, Holland, and Poland-Lithuania. What forms of government did these regimes develop? How did they differ from the absolutist and autocratic regimes of France, Prussia, and Russia?

> The wars begun by Louis XIV after 1680 drove his opponents to ally with each other to achieve a balance of power. What was the result of these conflicts in Europe and in the Atlantic world?

> Peter the Great embarked on an ambitious program of reform and territorial expansion in Russia. How did his autocratic government compare with absolutist regimes in western and central Europe?

what criteria were the actions of rulers to be judged? What was the proper measure of economic prosperity, and who was it for? Could a well-ordered society tolerate religious diversity? Given Europe's growing awareness of cultures in other parts of the world with different religions, different political systems, and different ways of expressing their moral and ethical values, how might Europeans justify or measure their own beliefs and customs? The intellectuals who looked for answers to these questions were similar to earlier generations of scientific researchers in their respect for reason and rational thought, but they turned their attention beyond problems of natural philosophy and science to the messy world of politics and culture. Their movement—known as the Enlightenment—reached its peak in the middle decades of the eighteenth century and created the basis for a powerful critique of Europe's absolutist regimes. The Enlightenment itself emerged slowly from a revolution in scientific thinking that had begun earlier in the early modern period, and it is to this history that we now turn.

Go to **INQUIZITIVE** to see what you've learned—and learn what you've missed—with personalized feedback along the way.

PEOPLE, IDEAS, AND EVENTS IN CONTEXT

❯ What did **LOUIS XIV** of France and **PETER THE GREAT** of Russia have in common? How did they deal with those who resisted their attempts to impose absolutist rule?

❯ Compare the religious policies of **LOUIS XIV** of France with the religious policies of the English Stuart kings **CHARLES II** and **JAMES II**. In what way did religious disagreements limit their ability to rule effectively?

❯ How did European monarchies apply the economic theory known as **MERCANTILISM** to strengthen the power and wealth of their kingdoms? How did this theory influence French colonialism?

❯ What was the **CONTRACT THEORY OF GOVERNMENT** according to the English political thinker **JOHN LOCKE**?

❯ What limits to royal power were recognized in Great Britain as a result of the **GLORIOUS REVOLUTION**?

❯ What was significant about the new **BALANCE OF POWER** that developed in Europe as a result of **LOUIS XIV**'s wars?

❯ What does the **TREATY OF UTRECHT** (1713) tell us about the diminished influence of Spain and the corresponding rise of Britain and France as European and colonial powers?

❯ What was different about the attempts by rulers in Habsburg Austria and Brandenburg-Prussia to impose **ABSOLUTISM** in central Europe?

❯ What innovations did **PETER THE GREAT** bring to Russia?

THINKING ABOUT CONNECTIONS

❯ What makes absolutism different from older models of kingship in earlier periods?

❯ Was the absolutist monarchs' emphasis on sumptuous displays of their authority something new? Explain how the display of power under absolutism is different from the way that political power is represented in democratic societies today.

16

The New Science of the Seventeenth Century

Doubt thou the stars are fire,
Doubt that the sun doth move,
Doubt truth to be a liar,
But never doubt I love.

Shakespeare, *Hamlet*, II.2

BEFORE YOU READ THIS CHAPTER

❯

"DOUBT THOU THE STARS ARE FIRE" and "that the sun doth move." Was Shakespeare alluding to controversial ideas about the cosmos that contradicted the teachings of medieval scholars? *Hamlet* (c. 1600) was written more than fifty years after the Polish astronomer Nicolaus Copernicus suggested that the earth revolved around the sun. Shakespeare probably knew of such theories, although they circulated only among small groups of learned Europeans. As Hamlet's speech to Ophelia makes clear, they were considered conjecture—or strange mathematical hypotheses. These theories were not exactly new: a heliocentric (sun-centered) universe had been proposed as early as the second century B.C.E. by ancient Greek astronomers. But they contradicted the consensus that had set in after Ptolemy proposed an earth-centered universe in the second century C.E. To Shakespeare's contemporaries, they defied common sense.

Still, a small handful of thinkers did doubt. Shakespeare was born in 1564, the same year as Galileo. By the time they were adults, scientific observers were discovering a new set of rules that explained how the

> After about 1550, new sciences in Europe questioned older beliefs about the physical universe. New methods of inquiry led to the development of astronomy, physics, biology, chemistry, geology, and new institutions that supported scientific research and education.

> The scientific revolution gave rise to theoretical breakthroughs in explaining the physical universe as well as advances in the practical knowledge of artisans who built mechanical devices such as telescopes or microscopes. This combination of scientific inquisitiveness and craft techniques encouraged technological developments that would later be useful in industrialization.

> The new sciences did not mark a clean rupture with older traditions of religious thinking. Most scientists of the 1600s remained essentially religious in their worldview. In any case, their work was accessible only to a small, literate minority who had access to books.

> **DEFINE** *scientific revolution* and **EXPLAIN** what is meant by *science* in this historical context.

> **UNDERSTAND** the older philosophical traditions that were important for the development of new methods of scientific investigation during the seventeenth century.

> **IDENTIFY** the sciences that made important advances during this period and **UNDERSTAND** what technological innovations encouraged a new spirit of investigation.

> **EXPLAIN** the differences between the Ptolemaic view of the universe and the new vision of the universe proposed by Nicolaus Copernicus.

> **UNDERSTAND** the different definitions of *scientific method* that emerged from the work of Francis Bacon and René Descartes.

universe worked. A hundred years later, the building blocks of the new view had been put in place. This intellectual transformation brought sweeping changes to European philosophy and to Western views of the natural world and of humans' place in it.

"Science": several interrelated meanings

Science entails at least three things: a body of knowledge, a method or system of inquiry, and a community of practitioners and the institutions that support their work. The *scientific revolution* of the seventeenth century involved each of these three realms. First, the scientific revolution saw the confirmation of a heliocentric view of the planetary system, which displaced the earth—and humans—from the center of the universe. Even more fundamental, it brought a new mathematical physics that gave precision to this view. Second, the scientific revolution established a method of inquiry for understanding the natural world, a method that emphasized the role of observation, experimentation, and the testing of hypotheses. Third, *science* emerged as a distinctive branch of knowledge. During the period covered in this chapter, people referred to the study of matter, motion, optics, or the circulation of blood as natural philosophy (the more theoretical term), experimental philosophy, medicine, and—increasingly—science. The growth of institutions dedicated to what we now commonly call scientific research was central to the changes at issue here. Science required not only brilliant thinkers but also patrons, states, and communities of researchers; the scientific revolution was thus embedded in other social, religious, and cultural transformations.

The scientific revolution was not an organized effort. Brilliant hypotheses sometimes led to dead ends, discoveries were often accidental, and artisans grinding lenses for telescopes played as big a role as did great abstract thinkers. Educated women also claimed the right to participate in scientific debate, but their efforts were met with opposition or indifference. Old and new worldviews often overlapped as individual thinkers struggled to make their theories—about the movement of bodies in the heavens, or the age of the earth, for instance—consistent with their faith or received wisdom. It did not necessarily undermine religion, and it certainly did not intend to (figures such as Isaac Newton thought their work confirmed and deepened their religious beliefs). Science worked its way into popular understanding slowly. But as the new method started to produce radical new insights into the workings of nature, it eventually came to be accepted beyond the small circles of experimenters and philosophers with whom it had begun.

The Intellectual Origins of the Scientific Revolution

The scientific breakthroughs of the sixteenth and seventeenth centuries were rooted in earlier developments. Artists and intellectuals had been observing the natural world with great precision since at least the twelfth century. Medieval sculptors accurately carved plants, animals, and human forms. The link among observation, experimentation, and invention was not new. The magnetic compass had been known in Europe since the thirteenth century; gunpowder since the early fourteenth; and printing—which opened new possibilities for disseminating ideas quickly and building libraries—since the middle of the fifteenth. A fascination with light encouraged the study of optics. Lens grinders laid the groundwork for the invention of the telescope and microscope, creating reading glasses along the way. Astrologers were also active in the later Middle Ages, charting the heavens in the firm belief that the stars controlled the fates of human beings.

Behind these efforts to understand the natural world lay a nearly universal conviction that the natural world had been created by God. Religious belief spurred scientific study. One school of thinkers, the **Neoplatonists**, argued that nature was a book written by its creator to reveal the ways of God to humanity. Convinced that God's perfection must be reflected in nature, Neoplatonists searched for the perfect structures they believed must lie behind the "shadows" of the everyday world. Mathematics, particularly geometry, were important tools in this quest.

Renaissance humanism provided a foundation for the scientific revolution. Humanists revered the authority of the ancients. The energies the humanists poured into recovering and translating classical texts about the natural world made many of those important works available for the first time to a wider audience. Previously, Arabic sources had provided Europeans with the main route to ancient Greek learning. Greek authors such as Ptolemy were translated into Arabic by Islamic scholars, who often knew them better than Europeans. Later these texts returned to Europe through the work of late medieval scholars in Spain and Sicily. The humanists' return to the original texts—and the fact that they could be printed and circulated in larger numbers—encouraged study and debate. The humanist rediscovery of works by Archimedes—the great Greek mathematician who had proposed that the natural world operated on the basis of mechanical forces, like a great machine, and that these forces could be described mathematically—profoundly impressed important late-sixteenth- and seventeenth-century thinkers.

The Renaissance also encouraged collaboration between artisans and intellectuals. Twelfth- and thirteenth-century thinkers had observed the natural world, but they had little contact with the artisans who constructed machines for practical use. During the fifteenth century, however, these two worlds began to come together. Renaissance artists such as Leonardo da Vinci were accomplished craftsmen; they investigated the laws of perspective and optics, they worked out geometric methods for supporting the weight of enormous architectural domes, they studied the human body, and they devised new and more effective weapons for war. Wealthy amateurs built observatories, measured the courses of the stars, and published work in astrology and alchemy. This fusion of intellectual curiosity and skilled handiwork created new possibilities for research and encouraged the creation of new fields of knowledge.

Sixteenth-century observers often linked the exploration of the globe to new knowledge of the cosmos. An admirer wrote to Galileo that he had kept the spirit of exploration alive: "The memory of Columbus and Vespucci will be renewed through you, and with even greater nobility, as the sky is more worthy than the earth." The parallel does not work quite so neatly, however. Columbus had not been driven by an interest in science. Moreover, it took centuries for European thinkers to realize the New World's implications for different fields of study, and the links between the voyages of discovery and breakthroughs in science were largely indirect. The discoveries of new lands made the most immediate impact in the field of natural history, which was vastly enriched by travelers' detailed accounts of the flora and fauna of the Americas. Finding new lands and cultures in Africa and Asia and the revelation of the Americas—a world unknown to the ancients and unmentioned in the

Neoplatonism A school of thought based on the teachings of Plato, which had a profound effect on the formation of Christian theology. Believing the natural world was a divine creation, Neoplatonists searched nature for proof of God's perfection.

Renaissance humanism An intellectual movement that stressed the study and debate of ancient Greek and Roman texts.

Renaissance legacies: (1) increased circulation of classical texts, including those by ancient scientists and mathematicians

(2) closer relationship between intellectual curiosity and skilled handiwork

Bible—also laid bare gaps in Europeans' inherited body of knowledge. In this sense, the exploration of the New World dealt a blow to the authority of the ancients.

In sum, the late medieval recovery of ancient texts long thought to have been lost, the expansion of print culture and reading, turmoil in the Church after the Reformation, and the encounter with the Americas all shook the authority of older ways of thinking in Europe. What we call the scientific revolution was part of the intellectual excitement that surrounded these challenges.

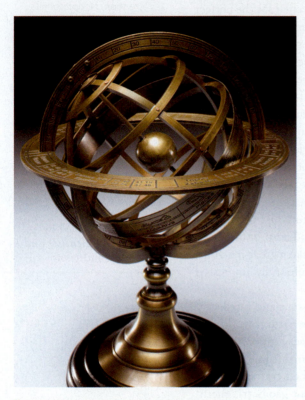

PTOLEMAIC ASTRONOMICAL INSTRUMENT. Armillary sphere, 1560s, built to facilitate the observation of planetary positions relative to the earth, in support of Ptolemy's theory of an earth-centered universe. In the sphere, seven concentric rings rotated about different axes. When the outermost ring was set to align with a north–south meridian, and the next ring was set to align with the celestial pole (the North Star, or the point around which the stars seem to rotate), the user could determine the latitude where the instrument was located. The inner rings were used to track the angular movements of the planets, key measurements in validating the Ptolemaic system. › **What forms of knowledge were necessary to construct such an instrument?** › **How do they relate to the breakthrough that is known as the scientific revolution?**

The Copernican Revolution

Medieval cosmologists, like their ancient counterparts, wrestled with the contradictions between ancient texts and the evidence of their own observations. Their view of an earth-centered universe was influenced by the teachings of Aristotle (384–322 B.C.E.) and by Ptolemy of Alexandria (100–170 C.E.). Ptolemy's vision of an earth-centered universe contradicted an earlier proposal by Aristarchus of Samos (310–230 B.C.E.), who had deduced that the earth and other planets revolve around the sun. Ptolemy's medieval followers used astronomical observations to support their theory, but the persuasiveness of this model for medieval scholars also derived from the ways that it fitted with their Christian beliefs (see Chapter 4). According to Ptolemy, the heavens orbited the earth in a hierarchy of spheres. Earth and the heavens were made of fundamentally different matter and subject to different laws of motion. The sun, moon, stars, and planets were formed of a perfect unchanging ether. The earth, by contrast, was composed of four elements (earth, water, fire, and air), and each of these elements had its natural place: the heavy elements (earth and water) toward the center and the lighter ones farther out. The heavens—first the planets, then the stars—traced perfect circular paths around the stationary earth. The motion of these celestial bodies was produced by a prime mover, whom Christians identified as God. The view fitted Aristotelian physics, according to which objects could move only if acted on by an external force. This Ptolemaic view confirmed the belief in the purposefulness of God's universe.

By the late Middle Ages astronomers knew that this **"Ptolemaic system"** did not correspond exactly to what many had observed. Orbits did not conform to the Aristotelian ideal of perfect circles. Certain planets, Mars in particular, sometimes appeared to loop backward. Ptolemy accounted for these irregularities with complicated mathematics, but efforts to make the observed motions of the planets fit into the model of perfect circles in an earth-centered cosmos produced bewildering complexity. Most importantly, the Ptolemaic system proved unable to solve serious difficulties with the calendar. That practical crisis precipitated Nicolaus Copernicus's intellectual leap forward.

By the early sixteenth century, the old Roman calendar was significantly out of alignment with the movements of the heavenly bodies. The major saints' days, Easter, and the other holy days were sometimes weeks off where they should have been according to the stars. Catholic authorities tried to correct this problem, consulting mathematicians and astronomers all over Europe. One of these was a Polish church official and astronomer, **Nicolaus Copernicus** (1473–1543), a devout Catholic who did not believe that God's universe could be as messy as Ptolemy's model. His proposed solution, based on mathematical calculations, was simple and radical: Ptolemy was mistaken. The earth was not stationary; it rotated on its axis and orbited with the other planets around the sun. Reordering the Ptolemaic system simplified the geometry of astronomy and made the orbits of the planets comprehensible.

Copernicus was in many ways a conservative thinker. He did not consider his work to be a break with either the Church or the authority of ancient texts. He believed, rather, that he had restored a pure understanding of God's design. Still, the implications of his theory troubled him. His ideas contradicted centuries of astronomical thought, and they were hard to reconcile with the observed behavior of objects on earth. If the earth moved, why was that movement imperceptible? Copernicus calculated the distance from the earth to the sun to be at least six million miles. Even by Copernicus's very low estimate, the earth was hurtling around the sun at the dizzying rate of many thousands of miles an hour. How did people and objects remain standing? (The earth is actually about 93 million miles from the sun, moving through space at 67,000 miles an hour and spinning on its axis at about 1,000 miles an hour!)

Copernicus was not a physicist. He tried to refine, rather than overturn, traditional Aristotelian physics, but his effort to reconcile that physics with his new model of a sun-centered universe created new problems that he could not resolve. These frustrations dogged Copernicus's later years, and he hesitated to publish his findings. Just before his death, he consented to the release of his major treatise, *On the Revolutions of the Heavenly Spheres* (*De Revolutionibus Orbium Coelestium*), in 1543. To fend off scandal, the Lutheran scholar who saw his manuscript through the press added an introduction to the book declaring that Copernicus's system should be understood as an abstraction, a set of mathematical tools for doing astronomy and not a dangerous claim about the nature of heaven and earth. For decades after 1543,

NON PAREM PAVLO GRATIĀ·REQVIRO VENIAM PETRI NEQ·POSCO,SED QVAM IN CRVCIS LIGNO DEDERAS LATRONI SEDVLVS ORO

NICOLAUS COPERNICUS. This anonymous portrait of Copernicus characteristically blends his devotion and his scientific achievements. His scholarly work (behind him in the form of an early planetarium) is driven by his faith (as he turns toward the image of Christ triumphant over death). › **What relationship between science and religion is evoked by this image?**

Ptolemaic system In Ptolemy's vision of cosmology, influenced by Aristotle, the heavens orbit the earth in an organized hierarchy of spheres. The earth and the heavens are made of different matter and subject to different laws of motion. A prime mover (usually understood to be God) produces the motion of the celestial bodies.

Copernicus's ideas were taken in just that sense—as useful but not realistic mathematical hypotheses. In the long run, however, Copernicanism represented the first systematic challenge to the Ptolemaic conception of the universe.

Tycho's Observations and Kepler's Laws

Within fifty years, Copernicus's cosmology was revived and modified by two astronomers also critical of the Ptolemaic model of the universe: **Tycho Brahe** (*TI-koh BRAH-hee*; 1546–1601) and **Johannes Kepler** (1571–1630). Tycho was born into the Danish nobility, but he abandoned his family's military and political legacy to pursue his passion for astronomy. Like Copernicus, he sought to correct the contradictions in traditional astronomy. But unlike Copernicus, who was a theoretician, Tycho championed observation. He first made a name for himself by observing a completely new star, a "nova," that flared into sight in 1572. The Danish king Frederick II granted him the use of a small island, where Brahe built a castle specially designed to house an observatory he called Uraniborg. For over twenty years, Tycho meticulously charted the movements of each significant object in the night sky, compiling the finest set of astronomical data in Europe.

Tycho suggested that the planets orbited the sun and that the whole system orbited a stationary earth. This picture of cosmic order, though clumsy, seemed to fit the observed evidence better than the Ptolemaic system, and avoided the upsetting physical and theological implications of the Copernican model. In the late 1590s, Tycho moved his work and his huge collection of data to Prague, where he became the court astronomer to the Holy Roman emperor Rudolf II. In Prague, he was assisted by a young mathematician from a troubled family, Johannes Kepler. Kepler

TYCHO BRAHE'S EARTH-CENTERED UNIVERSE. This image of Tycho's heliocentric (Earth-centered) vision is from a 1660 star atlas published by a Dutch-German cartographer. Note the geometric renderings of planetary orbits accompanied by astrological symbols on the outer ring of the image. In the foreground are images of people using instruments to make astronomical observations alongside young people being taught about the physical characteristics of the terrestrial globe. Tycho himself is portrayed in the lower right corner.

was more impressed with the Copernican model than was Tycho, and he combined the study of Copernicus's work with his own interest in mysticism, astrology, and the religious power of mathematics.

Kepler published his revolutionary work on planetary motion, *Astronomia Nova*, in 1609. He believed that everything in creation, from human souls to the orbits of the planets, had been created according to mathematical laws. Understanding those laws would allow humans to share God's wisdom and penetrate the inner secrets of the universe. Mathematics was God's language. After Tycho's death, Kepler had inherited Tycho's position in Prague as well as his trove of observations and calculations. Those data demonstrated to Kepler that two of Copernicus's assumptions about planetary motion simply did not match observations. Copernicus, in keeping with Aristotelian notions of perfection, had believed that planetary orbits were circular. Kepler, however, calculated that the planets traveled in elliptical orbits around the sun (this finding became the first of Kepler's three laws of planetary motion). Copernicus held that planetary motion was uniform. But Kepler stated that the speed of the planets varied with their distance from the sun (consequences of his second and third laws). Kepler also argued that magnetic forces between the sun and the planets kept the planets in orbital motion, an insight that paved the way for Newton's law of universal gravitation nearly eighty years later. Kepler's version of Copernicanism fitted with remarkable accuracy the best observations of the time (which were Tycho's). Kepler's search for rules of motion that could account for the earth's movements in its new position was also significant. More than Copernicus, Kepler broke down the distinction between the heavens and the earth that had been at the heart of Aristotelian physics.

Drawing on Tycho's data, Kepler corrects Copernican model and develops laws of planetary motion

New Heavens, New Earth, and Worldly Politics: Galileo

Kepler had a friend deliver a copy of *Cosmographic Mystery* to the "mathematician named Galileus Galileus," then teaching mathematics and astronomy at Padua, near Venice. **Galileo Galilei** (1564–1642) thanked Kepler in a letter that nicely illustrates the Italian's views at the time (1597):

> So far I have only perused the preface of your work, but from this I gained some notion of its intent, and I indeed congratulate myself of having an associate in the study of Truth who is a friend of Truth. . . . I adopted the teaching of Copernicus many years ago, and his point of view enables me to explain many phenomena of nature which certainly remain inexplicable according to the more current hypotheses. I have written many arguments in support of him and in refutation of the opposite view—which, however, so far I have not dared to bring into the public light. . . . I would certainly dare to publish my reflections at once if more people like you existed; as they don't, I shall refrain from doing so.

Kepler replied, urging Galileo to "come forward!" Galileo did not answer.

At Padua, Galileo couldn't teach what he believed; Ptolemaic astronomy and Aristotelian cosmology were the established curriculum. By the end of his career, however,

Galileo Galilei (1564–1642) Italian physicist and inventor; the implications of his ideas raised the ire of the Catholic church, and he was forced to retract most of his findings.

Galileo had provided powerful evidence in support of the Copernican model and laid the foundation for a new physics. What was more, he wrote in the vernacular (Italian) as well as in Latin, and his writings were widely translated and read, raising awareness of changes in natural philosophy across Europe. His discoveries made him the most famous scientific figure of his time, but his work put him on a collision course with Aristotelian philosophy and the authority of the Catholic Church.

In 1609, Galileo heard reports from Holland of a lens grinder who had made a spyglass that could magnify very distant objects. Excited, Galileo quickly devised his own telescope. He trained it first on earthly objects to demonstrate that it worked, and then dramatically pointed it at the night sky. Galileo studied the surface of the moon, finding mountains, plains, and other features of an earthlike landscape. His observations suggested that celestial bodies resembled the earth, a view at odds with the concept of the heavens as an unchanging sphere of heavenly perfection, inherently and necessarily different from the earth. He saw moons orbiting Jupiter, evidence that earth was not at the center of all orbits. And he saw spots on the sun. Galileo published these results, first in *The Starry Messenger* (1610) and then in *Letters on Sunspots* (1613). *The Starry Messenger*, with its amazing reports of Jupiter's moons, was short, aimed at a wide reading audience, and bold. It only hinted at Galileo's Copernicanism, however. The *Letters on Sunspots* declared it openly.

As a professor of mathematics, Galileo chafed at the power of university authorities who were subject to Church control. Princely courts offered an inviting alternative. The Medici family of Tuscany, like others, burnished its reputation and bolstered its power by surrounding itself with intellectuals as well as artists. Persuaded he would be freer at its court than in Padua, Galileo took a position as tutor to the Medicis and flattered and successfully cultivated the family. He addressed *The Starry Messenger* to them, and named the newly discovered moons of Jupiter the "Medicean stars." He was rewarded with the title of chief mathematician and philosopher to Cosimo II de' Medici, the grand duke of Tuscany. Now well positioned in Italy's networks of power and patronage, Galileo was able to pursue his goal of demonstrating that Copernicus's heliocentric (sun-centered) model of the planetary system was correct.

This pursuit, however, was a high-wire act, for he could not afford to antagonize the Catholic Church. In 1614, an ambitious and outspoken Dominican monk denounced Galileo's ideas as dangerous deviations from biblical teachings. Disturbed by the murmurings against Copernicanism, Galileo penned a series of letters to defend himself. He addressed the relationship between natural philosophy and religion, and argued that one could be both a sincere Copernican and a sincere Catholic (see *Analyzing Primary Sources* on page 550). The Church, Galileo said, did the sacred work of teaching scripture and saving souls, but accounting for the workings of the physical world was a task better left to natural philosophy, grounded in observation and mathematics. For the Church to take a side in controversies over natural science might compromise its spiritual authority and credibility. Galileo envisioned natural philosophers and theologians as partners in a search for truth, but with very different roles: the purpose of the Bible, he said, was to "teach us how to go to heaven, not how heaven goes."

Nevertheless, in 1616, the Church moved against Galileo. The Inquisition ruled that Copernicanism was "foolish and absurd in philosophy and formally heretical." Copernicus's *De Revolutionibus Orbium Coelestium* was placed on the Index of Prohibited Books, and Galileo was warned not to teach Copernicanism.

Galileo provides proof for Copernicus's theoretical model

For Galileo, scientific and theological inquiry not mutually exclusive

For a while, he did as he was asked. But when his Florentine friend and admirer Maffeo Barberini was elected pope as Urban VIII in 1623, Galileo believed the door to Copernicanism was (at least half) open. He drafted one of his most famous works, *A Dialogue Concerning the Two Chief World Systems*, which was published in 1632. The *Dialogue* was a hypothetical debate between supporters of the old Ptolemaic system, represented by a character he named Simplicio (simpleton) on the one hand, and proponents of the new astronomy on the other. Galileo gave the best lines to the Copernicans throughout. However, at the very end, to satisfy the letter of the Inquisition's decree, he had them capitulate to Simplicio.

The Inquisition banned the *Dialogue* and ordered Galileo to stand trial in 1633. Pope Urban, provoked by Galileo's scorn and needing support from Church conservatives during a difficult stretch of the Thirty Years' War, refused to protect his former friend. The verdict of the secret trial shocked Europe. The Inquisition forced Galileo to repent his Copernican position, banned him from working on or even discussing Copernican ideas, and placed him under house arrest for life. According to a story that began to circulate shortly afterward, as he left the court for house arrest he stamped his foot and muttered defiantly, looking down at the earth, "Still, it moves."

The Inquisition could not put Galileo off his life's work. He proposed an early version of the theory of inertia, which held that an object's motion stays the same until an outside force changes it. He calculated that objects of different weights fall at almost the same speed and with a uniform acceleration. He argued that the motion of objects follows regular mathematical laws. The same laws that govern the motions of objects on earth (which could be observed in experiments) could also be observed in the heavens—an important step toward a coherent physics based on a sun-centered model of the universe. Compiled under the title *Two New Sciences* (1638), this work was smuggled out of Italy and published in Protestant Holland.

Galileo believed that Copernicanism and natural philosophy in general need not subvert theological truths, religious belief, or the authority of the Church. But his trial seemed to show the contrary: that natural philosophy and Church authority could not coexist. Galileo's trial silenced Copernican voices in southern Europe, and the Church's leadership retreated into conservative reaction. It was therefore in northwest Europe that the new philosophy Galileo had championed would flourish.

Despite the Inquisition's house arrest, Galileo continued to make breakthrough discoveries in physics

Determining the Age of the Earth: The Origins of Geology and the Environmental Sciences

In retrospect, it is not surprising that the Church perceived Galileo's teachings to be a threat. At the same time, the split between religion and the new science was not absolute. The modern science of geology, for example, emerged out of a long debate that juxtaposed evidence from religious and secular texts on the one hand, and data gathered by those who made observations about the physical landscape and stones found in the countryside. The debate that fostered this discussion revolved around a fundamental question that had long provoked theologians: How old was the earth?

In 1654, **James Ussher** (1581–1656), the archbishop of Armagh in Ireland, published an account of the earth's creation, using both biblical and secular sources.

James Ussher (1581-1656)
An Irish archbishop who attempted to reconcile natural and biblical events in a later discredited chronology of the world.

Astronomical Observations and the Mapping of the Heavens

One (often-repeated) narrative about the scientific revolution is that it marked a crucial break, separating modern science from an earlier period permeated by an atmosphere of superstition and theological speculation. But, in fact, medieval scholars tried hard to come up with empirical evidence for beliefs that their faith told them must be true, and without these traditions of observation, scientists like Copernicus would never have been led to propose alternative cosmologies (see "Ptolemaic Astronomical Instruments" on page 542).

The assumption that the "new" sciences of the seventeenth century marked an extraordinary rupture with a more ignorant or superstitious past is thus not entirely correct. It would be closer to the truth to suggest that works such as that of Copernicus or Galileo provided a new context for assessing the relationship between observations and knowledge that came from other sources. Printed materials provided opportunities for early modern scientists to learn as much from each other as from more ancient sources.

A. The Ptolemaic universe, as depicted in Peter Apian, *Cosmographia* (1524).

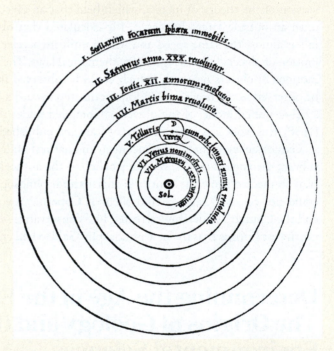

B. The Copernican universe (1543).

Ussher declared that the world had been created on Saturday, October 22, 4004 B.C. Often ridiculed as an extreme example of biblical literalism, Ussher's thinking was very much rooted in the culture of his time, and his estimate differed little from the assertions of many of his contemporaries. Ussher's chronology was part of a larger intellectual attempt to construct a timeline for the history of the world that

The illustrations here are from scientific works on astronomy both before and after the appearance of Copernicus's work. All of them were based on some form of observation and claimed to be descriptive of the existing universe. Compare the abstract illustrations of the Ptolemaic (image A) and Copernican (image B) universes with Tycho Brahe's (image C) attempt to reconcile heliocentric observations with geocentric assumptions, or with Galileo's illustration of sunspots (image D) observed through a telescope.

Questions for Analysis

1. What do these illustrations tell us about the relationship between knowledge and observation in sixteenth- and seventeenth-century science? What kinds of knowledge were necessary to produce these images?

2. Are the illustrations A and B intended to be visually accurate, in the sense that they represent what the eye sees? Can we say the same of illustration D? What makes Galileo's illustration of sunspots different from the others?

3. Are the assumptions about observation in Galileo's drawing of sunspots (image D) applicable to other sciences such as biology or chemistry? If yes, how so?

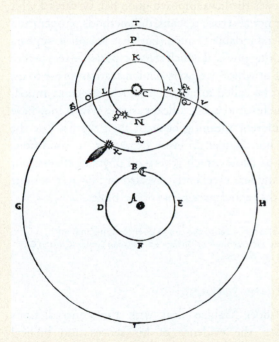

C. Tycho Brahe's universe (c. 1572). A, earth; B, moon; C, sun.

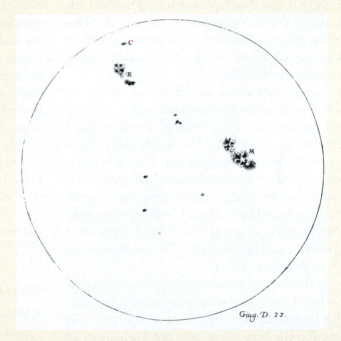

D. Galileo's sunspots, as observed through a telescope (1612).

recorded both material events such as the appearance of comets, volcanic eruptions, or solar and lunar eclipses as well as sacred dates. His decision to treat the Bible as one source among many was in fact a significant departure from a purely religious approach, and his desire to divide the history of the earth into "epochs" or "eras" marked an important step toward a more historical approach to the earth's past.

Galileo on Nature, Scripture, and Truth

One of the clearest statements of Galileo's convictions about religion and science comes from his 1615 letter to the grand duchess Christina, the mother of Galileo's patron, Cosimo II de' Medici, and a powerful figure in her own right. Galileo knew that others objected to his work. The Church had warned him that Copernicanism was inaccurate and impious, that it could be disproved scientifically, and that it contradicted the authority of those who interpreted the Bible. Thoroughly dependent on the Medicis for support, he wrote to the grand duchess to explain his position. In this section of the letter, Galileo sets out his understanding of the parallel but distinct roles of the Church and natural philosophers. He walks a fine line between acknowledging the authority of the Church and standing firm in his convictions.

Possibly because they are disturbed by the known truth of other propositions of mine which differ from those commonly held, and therefore mistrusting their defense so long as they confine themselves to the field of philosophy, these men have resolved to fabricate a shield for their fallacies out of the mantle of pretended religion and the authority of the Bible. . . .

Copernicus never discusses matters of religion or faith, nor does he use arguments that depend in any way upon the authority of sacred writings which he might have interpreted erroneously. He stands always upon physical conclusions pertaining to the celestial motions, and deals with them by astronomical and geometrical demonstrations, founded primarily upon sense experiences and very exact observations. He did not ignore the Bible, but he knew very well that if his doctrine were proved, then it could not contradict the Scriptures when they were rightly understood. . . .

I think that in discussions of physical problems we ought to begin not from the authority of scriptural passages, but from sense-experiences and necessary demonstrations; for the holy Bible and the phenomena of nature proceed alike from the divine Word, the former as the dictate of the Holy Ghost and the latter as the observant executrix of God's commands. It is necessary for the Bible, in order to be accommodated to the understanding of every man, to speak many things which appear to differ from the absolute truth so far as the bare meaning of the words is concerned. But Nature, on the other hand, is inexorable and immutable; she never transgresses the laws imposed upon her, or cares a whit whether her abstruse reasons and methods of operation are understandable to men. For that reason it appears that nothing physical which sense-experience sets before our eyes, or which necessary demonstrations prove to us, ought to be called in question (much less condemned) upon the testimony of biblical passages which may have some different meaning beneath their words. For the Bible is not chained in every expression to conditions as strict as those which govern all physical effects; nor is God any less excellently revealed in Nature's actions than in the sacred statements of the Bible. . . .

Source: Galileo, "Letter to the Grand Duchess Christina," in *Discoveries and Opinions of Galileo*, ed. Stillman Drake (Garden City, NY: 1957), pp. 177–83.

Questions for Analysis

1. How does Galileo deal with the contradictions between the evidence of his senses and biblical teachings?

2. For Galileo, what is the relationship between God, man, and nature?

3. Why did Galileo need to defend his views in a letter to Christina de' Medici?

CABINET OF CURIOSITIES. This illustration was the frontispiece of a book on natural history by a Danish doctor, Ole Wurm, who taught medicine, Latin, and Greek in Copenhagen after studying in Marburg. Wurm was a celebrated collector of objects, ranging from fossils and specimens of animals to artifacts of ethnographic interest. Such collections provided the principal data for those engaged in debates about the origins of fossils and the age of the earth.

Ussher, like other early seventeenth-century writers, assumed that the earth's history and human history covered roughly the same length of time: following the story of Genesis, they assumed that humans appeared on earth soon after its creation. They also assumed that the stories told in the Bible—including the story of Noah and the Flood—had some basis in historical fact. A German Jesuit, Athanasius Kircher (1602–1680), suggested that the Flood story could be analyzed historically, and he attempted to calculate the amount of water that would have been required to cover the earth's mountains. He assumed that the physical landscape of the earth would have been transformed as the floodwaters drained away. Only later did natural philosophers realize the vast expanse of earth's history that predated human society, but they were already beginning to imagine that this history was accessible to human knowledge through observation.

Such speculation was fueled by the work of natural philosophers who asked questions about fossils found throughout the European countryside. As interest in natural philosophy developed, scholars assembled large collections of what they called "curiosities"—images and forms of animals and plants found in stones and seashells collected on mountaintops far from the ocean, as well as the bones and antlers of animals both recognizable and unknown. Some of these objects could be explained in terms of accepted biblical histories. Religious believers, for example, asserted that seashells on mountaintops could have been deposited by Noah's Flood. A Danish physician, Niels Stensen (more frequently referred to by his Latin name, **Nicolas Steno**), began a more systematic compilation of this evidence that pointed the way toward the science of geology. The key breakthrough was a paper he published in 1667 that demonstrated that shark's teeth, obtained through the

Nicolas Steno Danish scientist whose studies of rock layers and fossils was foundational to the development of geological sciences.

dissection of a recently caught animal, were structurally similar, though smaller in size, to petrified teeth found bound in stone on land far from the sea. Steno began to believe that the physical landscape of Tuscany (where he was living at the time) constituted a visible record of a historical sequence that could be reconstructed through observation. He noted a tendency of broken hillsides to reveal strata of different stones, as if one layer had been laid down over the previous one. An English natural philosopher, Robert Hooke, writing at the same time in England, came to the same conclusion, asserting that the rocks and fossils were "documents" to be read in the book of nature.

The debate on the age of the earth continued into the eighteenth and nineteenth centuries, but the line from Steno's and Hooke's remarks to modern geological research is a direct one. In the space of little more than one or two generations in the seventeenth century, the earth sciences had emerged in a form that is recognizable to modern readers: the earth's landscape constituted a legible "monument" pointing to a distant past accessible to our understanding through observation.

Methods for a New Philosophy: Bacon and Descartes

Advances in the new sciences eventually became concentrated in northwest Europe, where thinkers began to spell out standards of practice and evidence. Sir **Francis Bacon** (1561–1626) and **René Descartes** (*deh-KAHRT*) loom especially large in this development, setting out the methods or the rules that should govern modern science.

"Knowledge is power." This phrase is Bacon's and captures the new confidence in the potential of human thinking. Bacon trained as a lawyer, serving in Parliament and briefly as the lord chancellor to James I of England. His abiding concern was with the assumptions, methods, and practices he believed should guide natural philosophers. The authority of the ancients should not constrain modern thinkers, and deference to accepted doctrines could block innovation or obstruct understanding. Pursuing knowledge did not mean thinking abstractly and leaping to conclusions; it meant observing, experimenting, confirming ideas, or demonstrating assertions. If thinkers will be "content to begin with doubts," Bacon wrote, "they shall end with certainties." We thus associate Bacon with the gradual separation of scientific investigation from philosophical argument.

Bacon advocated an *inductive* approach to knowledge: amassing evidence from specific observations to draw general conclusions. In Bacon's view, many philosophical errors arose from beginning with assumed first principles. The traditional view of the cosmos, for instance, rested on the principles of a prime mover and the perfection of circular motion for the planets and the stars. The inductive method required accumulating data (as Tycho had done) and then, after careful review and experiment, drawing appropriate conclusions about the motions of heavenly bodies. Bacon argued that scientific knowledge was best tested through the cooperative efforts of researchers performing experiments that could be repeated and verified.

Bacon's vision of science and progress is vividly illustrated by two images. The first, more familiar, is the title page of Bacon's *Novum Organum* (1620), shown on the right, with its bold ships sailing out beyond the Straits of Gibraltar, formerly the limits of the West, into the open sea, in pursuit of unknown but great things to come. The second is of Bacon's imagined factory of discovery, "Solomon's house," at the end of his utopian *New Atlantis* (1626). Inside the factory, "sifters" would examine and conduct experiments, passing on findings to senior researchers who would draw conclusions and develop practical applications. The work of these scholars would be supplemented by accounts sent by their emissaries abroad, traveling ambassadors of science who would gather data and information about the natural world and human societies in other places. Bacon's utopian image of patient researchers and experimenters anticipated the modern university.

René Descartes (1596–1650) was French, though he lived all over Europe. His *Discourse on Method* (1637), for which he is best known, began simply as a preface to three essays on optics, geometry, and meteorology. It is personal, recounting Descartes's dismay at the "strange and unbelievable" theories he encountered in his traditional education. His first response, as he described it, was to doubt systematically everything he had ever known or been taught. Better to clear the slate, he believed, than to build an edifice of knowledge on received assumptions. His first rule was "never to receive anything as a truth which [he] did not clearly know to be such." He took the human ability to think as his point of departure, summed up in his famous and enigmatic *Je pense, donc je suis*, later translated into Latin as *Cogito, ergo sum* and into English as "I think, therefore I am." As the phrase suggests, Descartes's doubting led (quickly, by our standards) to self-assurance and truth: the thinking individual existed, reason existed, God existed. For Descartes, then, doubt was a ploy, or a piece that he used in an intellectual chess game to defeat skepticism. Certainty, not doubt, was the centerpiece of the philosophy he bequeathed to his followers.

Unlike Bacon, however, Descartes emphasized *deductive* reasoning, proceeding logically from one certainty to another. "So long as we avoid accepting as true what is not so," he wrote in *Discourse on Method*, "and always preserve the right order of deduction of one thing from another, there can be nothing too remote

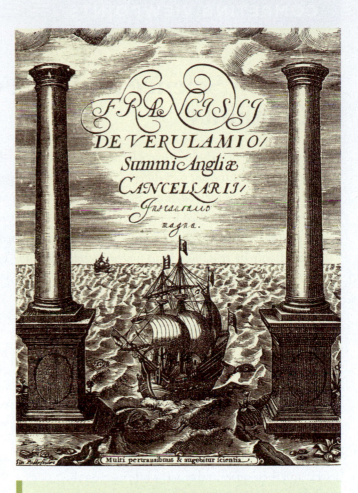

FRONTISPIECE TO BACON'S *NOVUM ORGANUM* (1620). This illustration suggests that scientific work is like a voyage of discovery, similar to a ship setting out through uncharted waters. Compare this image with the representation of Tycho Brahe's earth-centered universe on page 544. Pay particular attention to the imagery and symbols surrounding the geometric model. **› What metaphors and allegorical imagery did scientists use during this period to characterize the significance of their work?**

In deductive reasoning, thinker begins with one self-evident truth and uses reason to test hypotheses and build understanding

The New Science and the Foundations of Certainty

Francis Bacon (1561–1626) and René Descartes (1596–1650) were both enthusiastic supporters of science in the seventeenth century, but they differed in their opinions regarding the basis for certainty in scientific argumentation. Bacon's inductive method emphasized the gathering of particular observations about natural phenomena, which he believed could be used as evidence to support more general conclusions about causes, regularity, and order in the natural world. Descartes, on the other hand, defended a deductive method. He believed that certainty could be built only by reasoning from first principles that one knew to be true, and he was less certain of the value of evidence that came from the senses alone.

Aphorisms from *Novum Organum*

XXXI It is idle to expect any advancement in science from the super-inducing and engrafting of new things upon old. We must begin anew from the very foundations, unless we would revolve forever in a circle with mean and contemptible progress. . . .

XXXVI One method of delivery alone remains to us which is simply this: we must lead men to the particulars themselves, and their series and order; while men on their side must force themselves for a while to lay their notions by and begin to familiarize themselves with facts. . . .

XLV The human understanding of its own nature is prone to suppose the existence of more order and regularity in the world than it finds. And though there be many things in nature which are singular and unmatched, yet it devises for them parallels and conjugates and relatives which do not exist. Hence the fiction that all celestial bodies move in perfect circles. . . . Hence too the element of fire with its orb is brought in, to make up the square with the other three which the sense perceives. . . . And so on of other dreams. And these fancies affect not dogmas only, but simple notions also. . . .

XCV Those who have handled sciences have been either men of experiment or men of dogmas. The men of experiment are like the ant, they only collect and use; the reasoners resemble spiders, who make cobwebs out of their own substance. But the bee takes a middle course: it gathers its material from the flowers of the garden and of the field, but transforms and digests it by a power of its own. Not unlike this is the true business of philosophy; for it neither relies solely or chiefly on the powers of the mind, nor does it take the matter which it gathers from natural history and mechanical experiments and lay it up in the memory whole . . . but lays it up in the understanding altered and digested. Therefore, from a closer and purer league between these two faculties, the experimental and the rational (such as has never yet been made), much may be hoped. . . .

Source: Michael R. Matthews, ed., *The Scientific Background to Modern Philosophy: Selected Readings* (Indianapolis, IN: 1989), pp. 47–48, 50–52.

From *Discourse on Method*

Just as a great number of laws is often a pretext for wrongdoing, with the result that a state is much better governed when, having only a few, they are strictly observed; so also I came to believe that in the place of the great number of precepts that go to make up logic, the following four would be sufficient for my purposes, provided that I took a firm but unshakeable decision never once to depart from them.

The first was never to accept anything as true that I did not *incontrovertibly* know to be so; that is to say, carefully to avoid both *prejudice* and premature conclusions; and to include nothing in my judgments other than that which presented itself to my mind so *clearly* and *distinctly*, that I would have no occasion to doubt it.

The second was to divide all the difficulties under examination into as many parts as possible, and as many as were required to solve them in the best way.

The third was to conduct my thoughts in a given order, beginning with the *simplest* and most easily understood objects, and gradually ascending, as it were step by step, to the knowledge of the most *complex*; and *positing* an order even on those which do not have a natural order of precedence.

The last was to undertake such complete enumerations and such general surveys that I would be sure to have left nothing out.

The long chain of reasonings, every one simple and easy, which geometers habitually employ to reach their most difficult proofs had given me cause to suppose that all those things which fall within the domain of human understanding follow on from each other in the same way, and that as long as one stops oneself taking anything to be true that is not true and sticks to the right order so as to deduce one thing from another, there can be nothing so remote that one cannot eventually reach it, nor so hidden that one cannot discover it. . . .

[B]ecause I wished . . . to concentrate on the pursuit of truth, I came to think that I should . . . reject as completely false everything in which I could detect the least doubt, in order to see if anything thereafter remained in my belief that was completely indubitable. And so, because our senses sometimes deceive us, I decided to suppose that nothing was such as they lead us to imagine it to be. And because there are men who make mistakes in reasoning, even about the simplest elements of geometry, and commit logical fallacies, I judged that I was as prone to error as anyone else, and I rejected as false all the reasoning I had hitherto accepted as valid proof. Finally, considering that all the same thoughts which we have while awake can come to us while asleep without any one of them then being true, I resolved to pretend that everything that had ever entered my head was no more true than the illusions of my dreams. But immediately afterwards I noted that, while I was trying to think of all things being false in this way, it was necessarily the case that I, who was thinking them, had to be something; and observing this truth: *I am thinking therefore I exist*, was so secure and certain that it could not be shaken by any of the most extravagant suppositions of the sceptics, I judged that I could accept it without scruple, as the first principle of the philosophy I was seeking.

Source: René Descartes, *A Discourse on the Method*, trans. Ian Maclean (New York: 2006), pp. 17–18, 28.

Questions for Analysis

1. Descartes's idea of certainty depended on a "long chain of reasonings" that departed from certain axioms that could not be doubted and rejected evidence from the senses. What science provided him with the model for this idea of certainty? What was the first thing that he felt he could be certain about? Did he trust his senses?

2. Bacon's idea of certainty pragmatically sought to combine the benefits of sensory knowledge and experience (gathered by "ants") with the understandings arrived at through reason (cobwebs constructed by "spiders"). How would Descartes have responded to Bacon's claims? According to Bacon, was Descartes an ant or a spider?

3. What do these two thinkers have in common?

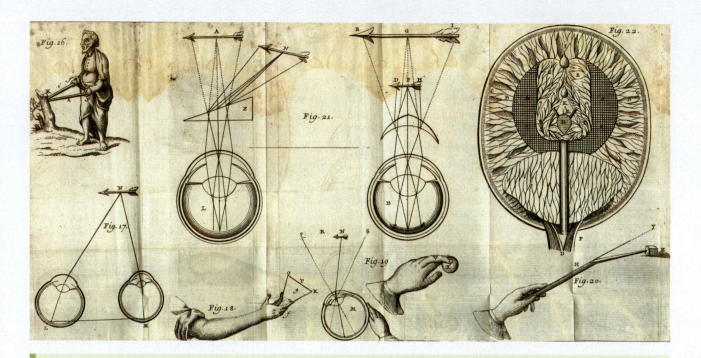

to be reached in the end, or too well hidden to be discovered." For Descartes, mathematical thought expressed the highest standards of reason, and his work contributed greatly to the authority of mathematics as a model for scientific reasoning.

Descartes's mechanical philosophy

Descartes made a particularly forceful statement for *mechanism*, a view of the world shared by Bacon and Galileo and one that came to dominate seventeenth-century scientific thought. As the name suggests, mechanical philosophy proposed to consider nature as a machine. It rejected the traditional Aristotelian distinction between the works of humans and those of nature, and the view that nature, as God's creation, necessarily belonged to a different—and higher—order. In the new picture of the universe that was emerging from the discoveries and writings of the early seventeenth century, it seemed that all matter was composed of the same material and that all motion obeyed the same laws. Descartes sought to explain everything, including the human body, mechanically. As he put it firmly, "There is no difference between the machines built by artisans and the diverse bodies that nature alone composes." Nature operated according to regular and predictable laws and thus was accessible to human reason. This belief guided, indeed inspired, much of the scientific experiment and argument of the seventeenth century.

THE POWER OF METHOD AND THE FORCE OF CURIOSITY: SEVENTEENTH-CENTURY EXPERIMENTERS

For nearly a century after Bacon and Descartes, most of England's natural philosophers were Baconian, and most of their colleagues in France, Holland, and elsewhere in northern Europe were Cartesians (followers of Descartes). The Cartesians turned toward mathematics and logic. Descartes himself pioneered analytical geometry. Blaise Pascal (1623–1662) worked on probability theory and invented a calculating machine before applying his intellectual skills to theology. A Dutch Cartesian, Baruch Spinoza (1632–1677), applied geometry to ethics and believed he had proved that the universe was composed of a single substance that was both God and nature.

English experimenters pursued a different course. They began with practical research, putting the alchemist's tool, the laboratory, to new uses. They also sought a different kind of conclusion: empirical laws or provisional generalizations based on evidence rather than absolute statements of deductive truth. Among the many English laboratory scientists of this era were the physician William Harvey (1578–1657), the chemist Robert Boyle (1627–1691), and the inventor and experimenter Robert Hooke (1635–1703).

Harvey observed human and animal bodies and explained that blood circulated through the arteries, heart, and veins. Boyle performed experiments and established a law (known as Boyle's law) showing that at a constant temperature the volume of a gas decreases in proportion to the pressure placed on it. Hooke introduced the microscope to the experimenter's tool kit. The compound microscope had been invented in Holland early in the seventeenth century, but it was not until the 1660s that Hooke and others demonstrated its potential by using it to study the cellular structure of plants. Like the telescope before it, the microscope revealed an unexpected dimension of material phenomena. Examining even the most ordinary objects revealed detailed structures of perfectly connected smaller parts, and this persuaded many that with improved instruments they would uncover even more of the world's intricacies.

The microscope also provided what many regarded as new evidence of God's existence. The minute structure of a living organism, viewed under a microscope, corresponded to its purpose and testified not only to God's existence but also to God's wisdom. The mechanical philosophy did not exclude God but in fact could be used to confirm his presence. If the universe was a clock, there must be a clockmaker. Hooke himself declared that only imbeciles would believe that what they saw under the microscope was "the production of chance" rather than of God's creation.

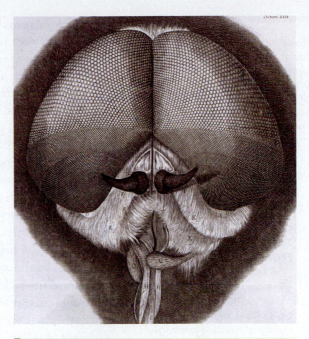

ROBERT HOOKE'S *MICROGRAPHIA*.
Hooke's diagram of a fly's eye as seen through a microscope seemed to reveal just the sort of intricate universe the mechanists predicted.
> **Compare this image with that of Galileo's sunspots (page 549). What do these two images have in common?**

In "clockmaker" theory, advances in observational sciences seen as further evidence of the glory of God's creation

THE STATE, SCIENTIFIC ACADEMIES, AND WOMEN SCIENTISTS

Seventeenth-century state building (see Chapter 14) helped secure the rise of science. In 1660, the newly crowned King Charles II granted a group of natural

OBSERVING THE TRANSIT OF VENUS (1673). Elisabetha (1647–1693) and Johannes Hevelius (1611–1687) believed that precise observations about the timing of Venus's passage across the face of the sun when observed from different parts of the earth could be used to calculate the distance from the earth to the sun. This husband-and-wife astronomy team worked together on many of their projects.

philosophers a royal charter (1662) to establish the **Royal Society** of London, for the "improvement of natural knowledge." The Royal Society would pursue Bacon's goal of collective research, in which members would conduct formal experiments, record the results, and share them with other members. These members would in turn study the methods and attempt to reproduce the experiment. This enterprise would give England's natural philosophers a common sense of purpose and a system to reach reasoned, gentlemanly agreement on "matters of fact." By separating systematic scientific research from the dangerous language of politics and religion that had marked the English Civil War, the Royal Society could help restore a sense of order and consensus to intellectual life.

The French **Academy of Sciences** was founded in 1666, and it was also tied to seventeenth-century state building, in this case, Bourbon absolutism (see Chapter 15). Royal societies, devoted to natural philosophy as a collective enterprise, provided a state- (or prince-)sponsored framework for science, and an alternative to the important but uncertain patronage of religious (and largely conservative, Aristotelian) universities. Scientific societies reached rough agreements about what constituted legitimate research; they established the modern scientific custom of crediting discoveries to those who were the first to publish results; and they enabled the easier exchange of information and theories across national boundaries. Science began to take shape as a discipline.

The early scientific academies did not have explicit rules barring women, but with few exceptions they consisted only of men. This did not mean that women did not practice science, though their participation in scientific research and debate remained controversial. In some cases, the new science could itself become a justification for women's inclusion, as when the Cartesian philosopher François Poullain de la Barre used anatomy to declare in 1673 that "the mind has no sex." Since women possessed the same physical senses as men and the same nervous systems and brains, Poullain asserted that they might occupy the same roles in society as men. In fact, historians have discovered more than a few women who taught at European universities in the sixteenth and seventeenth centuries, above all in Italy. Elena Cornaro Piscopia received her doctorate of philosophy in Padua in 1678, the first woman to do so. **Laura Bassi** became a professor of physics at the University of Bologna after receiving her doctorate there in 1733, and on the merits of her exceptional contributions to mathematics, she became a member of the Academy of Science in Bologna. Her papers—such as "On the Compression of Air" (1746), "On the Bubbles Observed in Freely Flowing Fluid" (1747), and "On Bubbles of Air That Escape from Fluids" (1748)—gained her a stipend from the academy.

Italy appears to have been an exception in allowing women to win formal recognition for their education and research in established institutions. Elsewhere, elite women could educate themselves by associating with learned men. The aristocrat **Margaret Cavendish** (1623–1673), a natural philosopher in England, gleaned the information necessary to start her career from her family and their friends, a network that included Thomas Hobbes and René Descartes. These connections were not enough to overcome the isolation she felt working in a world of letters that was still largely the preserve of men, but this did not prevent her from developing her own speculative natural philosophy and using it to critique those who would exclude her from scientific debate. The "tyrannical government" of men over women, she wrote, "hath so dejected our spirits, that we are become so stupid, that beasts being but a degree below us, men use us but a degree above beasts. Whereas in nature we have as clear an understanding as men, if we are bred in schools to mature our brains."

The construction of observatories in private residences enabled some women living in such homes to work their way into the growing field of astronomy. Between 1650 and 1710, 14 percent of German astronomers were women, the most famous of whom was **Maria Winkelmann** (1670–1720). Winkelmann had collaborated with her husband, Gottfried Kirch, in his observatory, and when he died she had already done significant work, discovering a comet and preparing calendars for the Berlin Academy of Sciences. When Kirch died, she petitioned the academy to allow her to take her husband's place in that prestigious body but was rejected. Gottfried Leibniz, the academy's president, explained, "Already during her husband's lifetime the society was burdened with ridicule because its calendar was prepared by a woman. If she were now to be kept on in such capacity, mouths would gape even wider." In spite of this rejection, Winkelmann continued to work as an astronomer, training both her son and two daughters in the discipline.

Like Winkelmann, the entomologist **Maria Sibylla Merian** (1647–1717) was able to carve out a space for her scientific work by exploiting the precedent of guild women who learned their trades in family workshops. Merian was a daughter of an engraver and illustrator in Frankfurt and served as his informal apprentice before beginning her own career as a scientific illustrator, specializing in detailed engravings of insects and plants. Traveling to the Dutch colony of Surinam, Merian supported herself and her two daughters by selling exotic insects and animals she collected and brought back to Europe. She fought the colony's sweltering climate and malaria to publish her most important scientific work, *Metamorphosis of the Insects of Surinam*, which detailed the life cycles of Surinam's insects in sixty ornate illustrations. Merian's *Metamorphosis* was well received in her time; in fact, Peter I of Russia proudly displayed her portrait and books in his study.

"And All Was Light": Isaac Newton

Sir Isaac Newton's work marks the culmination of the scientific revolution. Galileo had come to believe that the earth and the heavens were made of the same material and he proposed theories of inertia. But it was Newton who articulated the laws of motion and presented a coherent, unified vision of how the universe worked. One set of forces, which could be expressed mathematically, explained why planets orbited in ellipses and why (and at what speed) apples fell from trees. There was only one universe, and Newton claimed to have discovered its laws.

Academy of Sciences
French institute of scientific industry founded in 1666 by Louis XIV. France's statesmen exerted control over the academy and sought to share in the rewards of any discoveries its members made.

Laura Bassi (1711–1778)
Admitted to the Academy of Science in Bologna for her work in mathematics, which made her one of the few women to be accepted into a scientific academy in the seventeenth century.

Margaret Cavendish
(1623–1673) English natural philosopher who developed her own speculative natural philosophy. She used this philosophy to critique those who excluded her from scientific debate.

Maria Winkelmann
(1670–1720) German astronomer who discovered a comet and prepared calendars for the Berlin Academy of Sciences

Maria Sibylla Merian
(1647–1717) A scientific illustrator and an important early entomologist.

Gassendi on the Science of Observation and the Human Soul

Pierre Gassendi (1592–1655) was a seventeenth-century French Catholic priest and philosopher. A contemporary of Descartes, Gassendi was part of a group of intellectuals in France who sought a new philosophy of nature that could replace the traditional teachings of Aristotle that Copernicus and his followers had so severely criticized. Gassendi had no doubt that his faith as a Christian was compatible with his enthusiasm for the new sciences of observation, but in order to demonstrate this to his contemporaries, he had to show that the mechanical explanations of the universe and the natural world did not necessarily lead to a heretical materialism or atheism. In the following passage, taken from his posthumously published work Syntagma Philosophicum *(1658), Gassendi attempted to demonstrate that one might infer the existence of the human soul, even if it was not accessible to the senses.*

There are many such things for which with the passage of time helpful appliances are being found that will make them visible to the senses. For example, take the little animal the mite, which is born under the skin; the senses perceived it as a certain unitary little point without parts; but since, however, the senses saw that it moved by itself, reason had deduced from this motion as from a perceptible sign that this little body was an animal and because its forward motion was somewhat like a turtle's, reason added that it must get about by the use of certain tiny legs and feet. And although this truth would have been hidden to the senses, which never perceived these limbs, the microscope was recently invented by which sight could perceive that matters were actually as predicted. Likewise, the question had been raised what the galaxy in the sky with the name of the Milky Way was. Democritus, concerning whom it was said that even when he did not know something he was knowing, had deduced from the perceptible sign of its filmy whiteness that it was nothing more than an innumerable multitude of closely packed little stars which could not be seen separately, but produced that effect of spilt milk when many of them were joined together. This truth had become known to him, and yet had remained undisclosed to the senses until our day and age, until the moment that the telescope, recently discovered, made it clear that things were in fact what he had said. But there are many such things which, though they were hidden from the ancients, have now been made manifest for our eyes. And who knows but a great many of those which are concealed in our time, which we perceive only through the intelligence, will one day also be clearly perceived by the senses through the agency of some helpful appliance thought up by our descendants? . . .

Isaac Newton (1642–1727)
An English mathematician and physicist; he is noted for his development of calculus, work on the properties of light, and theory of gravitation.

Isaac Newton (1642–1727) entered Trinity College in Cambridge University in 1661, where he would remain for the next thirty-five years, first as a student and then as the Lucasian Professor of Mathematics. His first great burst of creativity came at Cambridge from 1664 to 1666, where he broke new ground in three areas. The first was optics. Using prisms he had purchased at a local fair, Newton showed that white light was composed of different-colored rays (see image on page 562). Newton's work on the composite nature of white light led him to make a reflecting telescope, which used a curved mirror rather than lenses. The telescope earned him

Secondly, if someone wonders whether a certain body is endowed with a soul or not, the senses are not at all capable of determining that by taking a look as it were at the soul itself; yet there are operations which when they come to the senses' notice, lead the intellect to deduce as from a sign that there is some soul beneath them. You will say that this sign belongs to the empirical type, but it is not at all of that type, for it is not even one of the indicative signs since it does not inform us of something that the senses have ever perceived in conjunction with the sign, as they have seen fire with smoke, but informs us instead of something that has always been impenetrable to the senses themselves, like our skin's pores or the mite's feet before the microscope.

You will persist with the objection that we should not ask so much whether there is a soul in a body as what its nature is, if it is the cause of such operations, just as there is no question that there is a force attracting iron in a magnet or that there is a tide in the sea, but there are questions over what their nature is or what they are caused by. But let me omit these matters which are to be fully treated elsewhere, and let it be enough if we say that not every truth can be known by the mind, but at least some can concerning something otherwise hidden, or not obvious to the senses themselves. And we bring up the example of the soul both because vital action is proposed by Sextus Empiricus as an example of an indicative sign and because even though it pertains not so much to the nature of the soul as to its existence, still a truth of existence of such magnitude as this, which it is most valuable for us to know, is made indisputable. For when among other questions we hear it asked if God is or exists in the universe, that is a truth of existence which it would be a great service to establish firmly even if it is not proven at the same time what he is or what his nature is. Although God is such that he can no more come under the perusal of the senses than the soul can, still we infer that the soul exists in the body from the actions that occur before the senses and are so peculiarly appropriate to a soul that if one were not present, they would not be either. In the same way we deduce that God exists in the universe from his effects perceived by the senses, which could not be produced by anything but God and which therefore would not be observed unless God were present in the world, such as the great order of the universe, its great beauty, its grandeur, its harmony, which are so great that they can only result from a sovereignly wise, good, powerful, and inexhaustible cause. But these things will be treated elsewhere at greater length.

Source: Craig B. Brush, ed., *The Selected Works of Pierre Gassendi* (New York: 1972), pp. 334–36.

Questions for Analysis

1. What is the relationship between new knowledge and new scientific tools (the microscope and the telescope) in Gassendi's examples of the mite and the Milky Way? Is he a Baconian or a Cartesian?

2. What are the limitations of the senses when it comes to questions of the human soul, according to Gassendi?

3. Given these limitations, does Gassendi conclude that science will never be able to say anything about his religious faith?

election to the Royal Society in 1672. The second area was in mathematics. In a series of brilliant insights, Newton invented both integral calculus and differential calculus, providing mathematical tools to model motion in space. The third area of his creative genius involved his early work on gravity. Newton later told different versions of the same story: the idea about gravity had come to him when he was in a "contemplative mood" and was "occasioned by the fall of an apple." Why did the apple "not go sideways or upwards, but constantly to the earth's center? . . . Assuredly the reason is, that the earth draws it. There must be a drawing power in matter."

NEWTON'S EXPERIMENTS WITH LIGHT (1672). Earlier scientists had explained the color spectrum, which they produced by shining sunlight through a prism, by insisting that the colors were a by-product of contaminating elements within the prism's glass. Newton disproved this theory by shining the sunlight through two consecutive prisms. The first produced the characteristic division of light into a color spectrum. When one of these colored beams passed through a second prism, however, it emerged on the other side unchanged, demonstrating that the glass itself was not the cause of the dispersal.

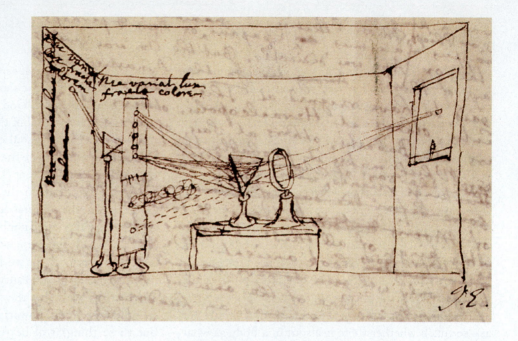

His theory of gravity rested on mathematical formulations, and Newton did not work it out fully until the *Principia*, more than twenty years later.

Newton's *Principia Mathematica* (Mathematical Principles of Natural Philosophy) was published in 1687. It was prompted by a question being discussed at the Royal Society: Was there a mathematical basis for the elliptical orbits of the planets? This question inspired Newton to expand his earlier calculations into an all-encompassing theory of celestial—and terrestrial—dynamics. *Principia* was long and difficult—purposefully so, for Newton said he did not want to be "baited by little smatterers in mathematics." Its central proposition was that gravitation was a universal force that could be expressed mathematically. Newton built on Galileo's work on inertia, Kepler's findings concerning the elliptical orbits of planets, the work of Boyle and Descartes, and even on his rival Robert Hooke's work on gravity. But Newton's theory of gravity formulated something entirely new, offering a single, descriptive and mathematical account of mass and motion. His theory was, literally, universal.

By 1713, pirated editions of *Principia* were being published in Amsterdam for distribution throughout Europe. And by the time Newton died, in 1727, he had become an English national hero and was given a funeral at Westminster Abbey. The poet Alexander Pope expressed the awe that Newton inspired in some of his contemporaries in a famous couplet:

> Nature and nature's law lay hid in night;
> God said, "Let Newton be!" and all was light.

Voltaire, the French champion of the Enlightenment (discussed in the next chapter), was largely responsible for Newton's reputation in France. In this, he was helped by a woman who was a brilliant mathematician in her own right, Emilie du Châtelet. She coauthored a book with Voltaire introducing Newton to a French audience; and she translated *Principia*, a daunting scientific and mathematical task and one well beyond Voltaire's mathematical abilities. Newton's French admirers and publicists disseminated Newton's findings. In their eyes, Newton exemplified a cultural transformation, a turning point in the history of knowledge.

SCIENCE AND CULTURAL CHANGE

From the seventeenth century on, science stood at the heart of what it meant to be "modern." It grew increasingly central to the self-understanding of Western culture, and scientific and technological power became one of the justifications for the expansion of Western empires and the subjugation of other peoples. At the same time, however, the break was not as sudden as the idea of a scientific "revolution" seems to indicate. To begin with, the transformation we have considered in this chapter involved elite knowledge. Ordinary people inhabited a very different cultural world. Second, natural philosophers' discoveries—Tycho's mathematics and Galileo's observations, for instance—did not undo the authority of the ancients in one blow, nor did they seek to do so. Third, science did not subvert religion. Even when traditional concepts collapsed in the face of new discoveries, natural philosophers seldom gave up on the project of restoring a picture of a divinely ordered universe. Science was thoroughly compatible with belief in God's providential design, at least through the seventeenth century.

Like his predecessors, Newton saw the world as God's message to humanity, a text to be deciphered, and close reading and study would unlock its mysteries. This same impulse led Newton to read accounts of magic, investigate alchemy's claims that base metals could be turned into gold, and immerse himself in the writings of the Church Fathers and the Bible, which he knew in intimate detail. If these activities sound unscientific from the perspective of the present, it is because the strict distinction between rational inquiry and belief in the occult or religious traditions simply did not exist in his time. Such a distinction is a product of a long history of scientific developments after the eighteenth century.

What, then, did the scientific revolution change? Seventeenth-century natural philosophers had produced new answers to fundamental questions about the physical world. Age-old questions about astronomy and physics had been recast. This process brought about a new approach to amassing and integrating information in a systematic way, an approach that helped yield more insights into the workings of nature as time went on. During this period, the most innovative scientific work moved out of the restrictive environment of the Church and the universities. Natural philosophers began talking to and working with each other in lay organizations that developed standards of research. England's Royal Society spawned imitators in Florence and Berlin, and later, in Russia. The French Academy of Sciences had a particularly direct relationship with the monarchy and the French state. France's statesmen exerted control over the academy and sought to share in the rewards of any discoveries made by its members.

Finally, rather than simply confirming established truths, the new methods were designed to explore the unknown and provide means to discover new truths. As Kepler wrote to Galileo, "How great a difference there is between theoretical speculation and visual experience, between Ptolemy's discussion of the Antipodes and Columbus's discovery of the New World." In the older model, to learn was to read: reason logically, argue, compare classical texts, and absorb a finite body of knowledge. In the newer one, to learn was to discover, and what could be discovered was boundless.

Conclusion

The pioneering natural philosophers remained circumspect about their abilities. Some sought to lay bare the workings of the universe, while others believed humans could only catalog and describe the regularities observed in nature. By unspoken but seemingly mutual agreement, the question of first causes was left aside. The new science did not say *why*, but *how*. Newton, for one, worked toward explanations that would reveal the logic of creation laid out in mathematics. Yet, in the end, he settled for theories explaining motions and relationships that could be observed and tested.

AFTER YOU READ THIS CHAPTER

CHRONOLOGY

1543	Nicolaus Copernicus (1473–1543) publishes *On the Revolutions of the Heavenly Spheres*
1576	Tycho Brahe sets up Uraniborg observatory
1609	Johannes Kepler (1571–1630) publishes *Astronomia Nova*
1610	Galileo (1564–1642) publishes *The Starry Messenger*
1620	Francis Bacon (1561–1626) publishes *Novum Organum*
1632	Galileo publishes *Dialogue Concerning the Two Chief World Systems*
1633	Galileo's trial
1637	René Descartes (1596–1650) publishes *Discourse on Method*
1660	Royal Society of London founde*d*
1666	French Academy of Sciences founded
1687	Isaac Newton (1642–1727) publishes *Principia Mathematica*

REVIEWING THE OBJECTIVES

❯ The scientific revolution marked a shift toward new forms of explanation in descriptions of the natural world. What made the work of scientists during this period different from earlier forms of knowledge or research?

❯ The scientific revolution nevertheless depended on earlier traditions of philosophical thought. What earlier traditions proved important in fostering a spirit of scientific investigation?

❯ Observations of natural processes both in the heavens and on the earth played a central role in the scientific revolution. What technological innovations made new astronomical work possible? What questions led to the development of geology and the earth sciences?

❯ Central to the scientific revolution was the rejection of the Ptolemaic view of the universe and its replacement by the Copernican model. What was this controversy about?

❯ Francis Bacon and René Descartes held contrasting ideas about scientific method. What approach to science did each of these natural philosophers defend?

The eighteenth-century heirs to Newton were much more daring. Laboratory science and the work of the scientific societies largely stayed true to the experimenters' rules and limitations. But as we will see in the next chapter, the natural philosophers who began investigating the human sciences cast aside some of their predecessors' caution. Society, technology, government, religion, even the individual human mind seemed to be mechanisms or parts of a larger nature waiting for study. The scientific revolution overturned the natural world as it had been understood for a millennium; it also inspired thinkers more interested in revolutions in society.

 Go to **INQUIZITIVE** to see what you've learned—and learn what you've missed—with personalized feedback along the way.

PEOPLE, IDEAS, AND EVENTS IN CONTEXT

❯ How did the traditions of **NEOPLATONISM** and **RENAISSANCE HUMANISM** contribute to a vision of the physical world that encouraged scientific investigation and explanation?

❯ In what way did the work of **NICOLAUS COPERNICUS**, **TYCHO BRAHE, JOHANNES KEPLER**, and **GALILEO GALILEI** undermine the intellectual foundations of the **PTOLEMAIC SYSTEM**? Why did their work largely take place outside the traditional centers of learning in Europe, such as universities?

❯ What was the significance of **JAMES USSHER**'s claim that the earth was created in 4004 B.C.? How did **NICOLAS STENO** demonstrate that the different layers of the earth's surface were visible signs of the earth's history?

❯ What differences in scientific practice arose from **FRANCIS BACON**'s emphasis on observation and **RENÉ DESCARTES**'s insistence that knowledge could be derived only from unquestionable first principles?

❯ What were **ISAAC NEWTON**'s major contributions to the scientific revolution? Why have some suggested that Newton's interests and thinking were not all compatible with modern conceptions of scientific understanding?

❯ What was important about the establishment of institutions such as the British **ROYAL SOCIETY** or the French **ACADEMY OF SCIENCES** for the development of scientific methods and research?

❯ What prevented women from entering most of Europe's scientific academies? How did educated women such as **LAURA BASSI, MARGARET CAVENDISH, MARIA WINKELMANN**, and **MARIA SIBYLLA MERIAN** gain the skills necessary to participate in scientific work?

THINKING ABOUT CONNECTIONS

❯ How did ideas about the value of ancient scholarship and philosophy change after the development of new sciences of observation during the seventeenth century?

❯ What possible connections might be made between the intellectual developments in scientific thinking during the seventeenth century and the Reformation of the sixteenth century? Was the new science incompatible with religious faith?

Appendix

Rulers of Principal States

THE CAROLINGIAN DYNASTY

Pepin of Heristal, mayor of the palace, 687–714
Charles Martel, mayor of the palace, 715–741
Pepin III, mayor of the palace, 741–751; king, 751–768
Charlemagne, king, 768–814; emperor, 800–814
Louis the Pious, emperor, 814–840

West Francia

Charles the Bald, king, 840–877; emperor, 875–877
Louis II, king, 877–879
Louis III, king, 879–882
Carloman, king, 879–884

Middle Kingdoms

Lothair, emperor, 840–855
Louis (Italy), emperor, 855–875
Charles (Provence), king, 855–863
Lothair II (Lorraine), king, 855–869

East Francia

Ludwig, king, 840–876
Carloman, king, 876–880
Ludwig, king, 876–882
Charles the Fat, emperor, 876–887

HOLY ROMAN EMPERORS

Saxon Dynasty

Otto I, 962–973
Otto II, 973–983
Otto III, 983–1002
Henry II, 1002–1024

Franconian Dynasty

Conrad II, 1024–1039
Henry III, 1039–1056
Henry IV, 1056–1106
Henry V, 1106–1125
Lothair II (Saxony), 1125–1137

Hohenstaufen Dynasty

Conrad III, 1138–1152
Frederick I (Barbarossa), 1152–1190
Henry VI, 1190–1197
Philip of Swabia, 1198–1208 } Rivals
Otto IV (Welf), 1198–1215

Frederick II, 1220–1250
Conrad IV, 1250–1254

Interregnum, 1254–1273

Emperors from Various Dynasties

Rudolf I (Habsburg), 1273–1291
Adolf (Nassau), 1292–1298
Albert I (Habsburg), 1298–1308
Henry VII (Luxemburg), 1308–1313
Ludwig IV (Wittelsbach), 1314–1347
Charles IV (Luxemburg), 1347–1378
Wenceslas (Luxemburg), 1378–1400
Rupert (Wittelsbach), 1400–1410
Sigismund (Luxemburg), 1410–1437

Habsburg Dynasty

Albert II, 1438–1439
Frederick III, 1440–1493

A1

Maximilian I, 1493–1519
Charles V, 1519–1556
Ferdinand I, 1556–1564
Maximilian II, 1564–1576
Rudolf II, 1576–1612
Matthias, 1612–1619
Ferdinand II, 1619–1637
Ferdinand III, 1637–1657

Leopold I, 1658–1705
Joseph I, 1705–1711
Charles VI, 1711–1740
Charles VII (not a Habsburg), 1742–1745
Francis I, 1745–1765
Joseph II, 1765–1790
Leopold II, 1790–1792
Francis II, 1792–1806

RULERS OF FRANCE FROM HUGH CAPET

Capetian Dynasty

Hugh Capet, 987–996
Robert II, 996–1031
Henry I, 1031–1060
Philip I, 1060–1108
Louis VI, 1108–1137
Louis VII, 1137–1180
Philip II (Augustus), 1180–1223
Louis VIII, 1223–1226
Louis IX (Saint Louis), 1226–1270
Philip III, 1270–1285
Philip IV, 1285–1314
Louis X, 1314–1316
Philip V, 1316–1322
Charles IV, 1322–1328

Valois Dynasty

Philip VI, 1328–1350
John, 1350–1364
Charles V, 1364–1380
Charles VI, 1380–1422
Charles VII, 1422–1461
Louis XI, 1461–1483
Charles VIII, 1483–1498
Louis XII, 1498–1515
Francis I, 1515–1547

Henry II, 1547–1559
Francis II, 1559–1560
Charles IX, 1560–1574
Henry III, 1574–1589

Bourbon Dynasty

Henry IV, 1589–1610
Louis XIII, 1610–1643
Louis XIV, 1643–1715
Louis XV, 1715–1774
Louis XVI, 1774–1792

After 1792

First Republic, 1792–1799
Napoleon Bonaparte, first consul, 1799–1804
Napoleon I, emperor, 1804–1814
Louis XVIII (Bourbon dynasty), 1814–1824
Charles X (Bourbon dynasty), 1824–1830
Louis Philippe, 1830–1848
Second Republic, 1848–1852
Napoleon III, emperor, 1852–1870
Third Republic, 1870–1940
Pétain regime, 1940–1944
Provisional government, 1944–1946
Fourth Republic, 1946–1958
Fifth Republic, 1958–

RULERS OF ENGLAND

Anglo-Saxon Dynasty

Alfred the Great, 871–899
Edward the Elder, 899–924
Ethelstan, 924–939
Edmund I, 939–946
Edred, 946–955
Edwy, 955–959
Edgar, 959–975

Edward the Martyr, 975–978
Ethelred the Unready, 978–1016
Canute, 1016–1035 (king of Denmark)
Harold I, 1035–1040
Hardicanute, 1040–1042
Edward the Confessor,
    1042–1066
Harold II, 1066

House of Normandy

William I (the Conqueror), 1066–1087
William II, 1087–1100
Henry I, 1100–1135
Stephen, 1135–1154

House of Plantagenet

Henry II, 1154–1189
Richard I, 1189–1199
John, 1199–1216
Henry III, 1216–1272
Edward I, 1272–1307
Edward II, 1307–1327
Edward III, 1327–1377
Richard II, 1377–1399

House of Lancaster

Henry IV, 1399–1413
Henry V, 1413–1422
Henry VI, 1422–1461

House of York

Edward IV, 1461–1483
Edward V, 1483
Richard III, 1483–1485

House of Tudor

Henry VII, 1485–1509
Henry VIII, 1509–1547
Edward VI, 1547–1553
Mary I, 1553–1558
Elizabeth I, 1558–1603

House of Stuart

James I, 1603–1625
Charles I, 1625–1649

Commonwealth and Protectorate, 1649–1659

Oliver Cromwell, Lord protector, 1653–1658

House of Stuart Restored

Charles II, 1660–1685
James II, 1685–1688
William III and Mary II, 1689–1694
William III alone, 1694–1702
Anne, 1702–1714

House of Hanover

George I, 1714–1727
George II, 1727–1760
George III, 1760–1820
George IV, 1820–1830
William IV, 1830–1837
Victoria, 1837–1901

House of Saxe-Coburg-Gotha

Edward VII, 1901–1910
George V, 1910–1917

House of Windsor

George V, 1917–1936
Edward VIII, 1936
George VI, 1936–1952
Elizabeth II, 1952–

RULERS OF AUSTRIA AND AUSTRIA-HUNGARY

*Maximilian I (archduke), 1493–1519
*Charles V, 1519–1556
*Ferdinand I, 1556–1564
*Maximilian II, 1564–1576
*Rudolf II, 1576–1612
*Matthias, 1612–1619
*Ferdinand II, 1619–1637
*Ferdinand III, 1637–1657
*Leopold I, 1658–1705
*Joseph I, 1705–1711
*Charles VI, 1711–1740
Maria Theresa, 1740–1780

*Joseph II, 1780–1790
*Leopold II, 1790–1792
*Francis II, 1792–1835 (emperor of Austria as Francis I after 1804)
Ferdinand I, 1835–1848
Francis Joseph, 1848–1916 (after 1867 emperor of Austria and king of Hungary)
Charles I, 1916–1918 (emperor of Austria and king of Hungary)
Republic of Austria, 1918–1938 (dictatorship after 1934)
Republic restored, under Allied occupation, 1945–1956
Free Republic, 1956–

*Also bore title of Holy Roman emperor

RULERS OF PRUSSIA AND GERMANY

*Frederick I, 1701–1713
*Frederick William I, 1713–1740
*Frederick II (the Great), 1740–1786
*Frederick William II, 1786–1797
*Frederick William III, 1797–1840
*Frederick William IV, 1840–1861
*William I, 1861–1888 (German emperor after 1871)
Frederick III, 1888

*kings of Prussia

*William II, 1888–1918
Weimar Republic, 1918–1933
Third Reich (Nazi dictatorship), 1933–1945
Allied occupation, 1945–1952
Division into Federal Republic of Germany in west
    and German Democratic Republic in east,
    1949–1991
Federal Republic of Germany (united), 1991–

RULERS OF RUSSIA

Ivan III, 1462–1505
Vasily III, 1505–1533
Ivan IV, 1533–1584
Theodore I, 1584–1598
Boris Godunov, 1598–1605
Theodore II, 1605
Vasily IV, 1606–1610
Michael, 1613–1645
Alexius, 1645–1676
Theodore III, 1676–1682
Ivan V and Peter I, 1682–1689
Peter I (the Great), 1682–1725
Catherine I, 1725–1727
Peter II, 1727–1730

Anna, 1730–1740
Ivan VI, 1740–1741
Elizabeth, 1741–1762
Peter III, 1762
Catherine II (the Great), 1762–1796
Paul, 1796–1801
Alexander I, 1801–1825
Nicholas I, 1825–1855
Alexander II, 1855–1881
Alexander III, 1881–1894
Nicholas II, 1894–1917
Russian Revolution and Civil War, 1917–1922
Union of Soviet Socialist Republics, 1922–1991
Russian Federation, 1991–

RULERS OF UNIFIED SPAIN

Ferdinand { and Isabella, 1479–1504
and Philip I, 1504–1506
and Charles I, 1506–1516
Charles I (Holy Roman Emperor Charles V), 1516–1556
Philip II, 1556–1598
Philip III, 1598–1621
Philip IV, 1621–1665
Charles II, 1665–1700
Philip V, 1700–1746
Ferdinand VI, 1746–1759
Charles III, 1759–1788
Charles IV, 1788–1808
Ferdinand VII, 1808

Joseph Bonaparte, 1808–1813
Ferdinand VII (restored), 1814–1833
Isabella II, 1833–1868
Republic, 1868–1870
Amadeo, 1870–1873
Republic, 1873–1874
Alfonso XII, 1874–1885
Alfonso XIII, 1886–1931
Republic, 1931–1939
Authoritarian nationalist dictatorship under Francisco
    Franco, 1939–1975
Juan Carlos I, 1975–2014
Felipe VI, 2014–

RULERS OF ITALY

Victor Emmanuel II, 1861–1878
Humbert I, 1878–1900
Victor Emmanuel III, 1900–1946

Fascist dictatorship under Benito Mussolini, 1922–1943
   (maintained in northern Italy until 1945)
Humbert II, May 9–June 13, 1946
Republic, 1946–

PROMINENT AND RECENT POPES

Silvester I, 314–335
Leo I, 440–461
Gelasius I, 492–496
Gregory I, 590–604
Nicholas I, 858–867
Silvester II, 999–1003
Leo IX, 1049–1054
Nicholas II, 1058–1061
Gregory VII, 1073–1085
Urban II, 1088–1099
Paschal II, 1099–1118
Alexander III, 1159–1181
Innocent III, 1198–1216
Gregory IX, 1227–1241
Innocent IV, 1243–1254
Boniface VIII, 1294–1303
John XXII, 1316–1334
Nicholas V, 1447–1455
Pius II, 1458–1464
Alexander VI, 1492–1503

Julius II, 1503–1513
Leo X, 1513–1521
Paul III, 1534–1549
Paul IV, 1555–1559
Sixtus V, 1585–1590
Urban VIII, 1623–1644
Gregory XVI, 1831–1846
Pius IX, 1846–1878
Leo XIII, 1878–1903
Pius X, 1903–1914
Benedict XV, 1914–1922
Pius XI, 1922–1939
Pius XII, 1939–1958
John XXIII, 1958–1963
Paul VI, 1963–1978
John Paul I, 1978
John Paul II, 1978–2005
Benedict XVI, 2005–2013
Francis, 2013–

Further Readings

CHAPTER 1

Baines, J., and J. Málek. *Atlas of Ancient Egypt*. Rev. ed. New York, 2000. A reliable, well-illustrated survey, with excellent maps.

Bottéro, Jean. *Everyday Life in Ancient Mesopotamia*. Trans. Antonia Nevill. Baltimore, 2001. A wide-ranging, interdisciplinary account.

Bottéro, Jean. *Religion in Ancient Mesopotamia*. Chicago, 2001. An accessible, engaging survey.

Broodbank, Cyprian. *The Making of the Middle Sea: A History of the Mediterranean from Its Beginning to the Emergence of the Classical World*. Oxford, 2013. A landmark study of the Mediterranean world, beautifully written.

Foster, Benjamin R., and Karen Polinger Foster. *Civilizations of Ancient Iraq*. Princeton, NJ, 2011. A critically acclaimed survey that charts the history of this region from the earliest Sumerian civilization to the Arab conquests of the seventh century C.E.

Geller, Markham J. *Ancient Babylonian Medicine: Theory and Practice*. Malden, MA, 2010. Makes use of previously unstudied cuneiform sources to tell a new story about the relationship between medicine and magic.

George, Andrew, trans. *The Epic of Gilgamesh: A New Translation. The Babylonian Epic Poem and Other Texts in Akkadian and Sumerian*. New York and London, 1999. A reliable translation that carefully distinguishes the chronological "layers" of this famous text; also includes many related texts.

Hodder, Ian. *The Leopard's Tale: Revealing the Mysteries of Çatalhöyük*. London and New York, 2006. The most up-to-date account of this fascinating archaeological site, written for general readers by the director of the excavation.

Leick, Gwendolyn. *The Babylonians: An Introduction*. London and New York, 2002. A wide-ranging survey of Babylonian civilization across the centuries.

McDowell, A. G. *Village Life in Ancient Egypt: Laundry Lists and Love Songs*. Oxford, 1999. A fascinating collection of translated texts recovered from an Egyptian peasant village, dating from 1539 to 1075 B.C.E.

McGregor, Neil. *A History of the World in 100 Objects*. London, 2011. Based on an acclaimed BBC Radio program, this book features a range of artifacts from the collections of the British Museum, embeds them in their historical contexts, and explores the ways that they still hold meaning today.

Mithen, Steven, with Sue Mithen. *Thirst: Water and Power in the Ancient World*. Cambridge, MA, 2013. A new comparative history of water management and consumption throughout the ancient world.

Redford, Donald B., ed. *The Oxford Encyclopedia of Ancient Egypt*. 3 vols. New York, 2001. An indispensable reference work, intended for both specialists and beginners.

Richardson, Seth. "Early Mesopotamia: The Presumptive State." *Past and Present* 215 (2012): 3–49. A powerful summary of the new methodologies and research questions that are challenging the traditional narrative of state building and urban life in Mesopotamia.

Robins, Gay. *The Art of Ancient Egypt*. London, 1997. An excellent survey.

Rutherford, Adam. *A Brief History of Everyone Who Ever Lived: The Stories in Our Genes*. New York, 2017. A compelling and entertaining study of Homo sapiens and our shared DNA.

Scott, James C. *Against the Grain: A Deep History of the Earliest States*. New Haven, 2017. A daring account of the ways that all settled societies depend on grain agriculture, unfree labor, and the control of women's productivity.

Shafer, Byron E., ed. *Religion in Ancient Egypt: Gods, Myths, and Personal Practice*. London, 1991. A scholarly examination of Egyptian belief and ritual, with contributions from leading authorities.

Shaw, Ian, ed. *The Oxford History of Ancient Egypt*. Oxford, 2000. An outstanding collaborative survey of Egyptian history from the Stone Age to c. 300 C.E., with excellent bibliographical essays.

Shryock, Andrew, and Daniel Lord Smail. Berkeley, 2012. *Deep History: The Architecture of Past and Present*. A fascinating fusion of historical, anthropological, and scientific research on what it means to be human.

Smail, Daniel Lord. *On Deep History and the Brain*. Berkeley, 2008. A pioneering introduction to the historical uses of neuroscience and evolutionary biology.

Snell, Daniel C., ed. *A Companion to the Ancient Near East*. Oxford, 2005. A topical survey of recent scholarly work, particularly strong on society, economy, and culture.

Wengrow, David. *The Archaeology of Early Egypt: Social Transformations in North-East Africa, 10,000 to 2650 B.C.* Cambridge, 2006. An authoritative account of archaeological evidence and its interpretation.

CHAPTER 2

Aubet, Maria Eugenia. *Phoenicia and the West: Politics, Colonies, and Trade.* Trans. Mary Turton. Cambridge, 1993. An intelligent and thought-provoking examination of Phoenician civilization and its influence.

Blenkinsopp, Joseph. *David Remembered: Kingship and National Identity in Ancient Israel.* Cambridge, 2013. An accessible history of King David, his dynasty, and his historical legacy, authored by a noted biblical scholar.

Boardman, John. *Persia and the West.* London, 2000. A great book by a distinguished scholar, with a particular focus on art and architecture as projections of Persian imperial ideologies.

Boyce, Mary. *Textual Sources for the Study of Zoroastrianism.* Totowa, NJ, 1984. An invaluable collection of documents.

Bryce, Trevor. *The Kingdom of the Hittites.* Oxford, 1998; and *Life and Society in the Hittite World.* Oxford, 2002. An extraordinary synthesis, now the standard account of Hittite political, military, and daily life.

Collins, John J., and Daniel C. Harlow, eds. *The Eerdmans Dictionary of Early Judaism.* Cambridge, 2010. A comprehensive tool for students and researchers.

Cooney, Kara. *The Woman Who Would Be King: Hatshepsut's Rise to Power in Ancient Egypt.* New York, 2014. A blend of historical scholarship and informed, imaginative reconstruction.

Curtis, John. *Ancient Persia.* Cambridge, MA, 1990. Concise, solid, reliable.

Dever, William. *Who Were the Early Israelites and Where Did They Come From?* Grand Rapids, MI, 2003. A balanced, fair-minded account with excellent bibliographical guidance to recent work.

Dickinson, O. T. P. K. *The Aegean Bronze Age.* Cambridge, 1994. An excellent summary of archaeological evidence and scholarly argument concerning Minoan, Mycenaean, and other cultures of the Bronze Age Aegean basin.

Dothan, Trude, and Moshe Dothan. *Peoples of the Sea: The Search for the Philistines.* New York, 1992. The essential starting point for understanding Philistine culture and its links to the Aegean basin.

Drews, Robert. *The End of the Bronze Age: Changes in Warfare and the Catastrophe ca. 1200 B.C.* Princeton, NJ, 1993. A stimulating analysis and survey, with excellent bibliographies.

Finkelstein, Israel, and Nadav Na'aman, eds. *From Nomadism to Monarchy: Archaeological and Historical Aspects of Early Israel.* Jerusalem, 1994. Scholarly articles on the Hebrews' transformation from pastoralists to a sedentary society focused on the worship of Yahweh.

Fitton, J. Lesley. *Minoans: Peoples of the Past.* British Museum Publications. London, 2002. A careful, reliable debunking of myths about the Minoans, written for nonspecialists.

Hamblin, William J. *Warfare in the Ancient Near East to 1600 BC: Holy Warriors at the Dawn of History.* Routledge, 2006. A wide-ranging study of military technologies, practices, and motives.

Kamm, Antony. *The Israelites: An Introduction.* New York, 1999. A short, accessible history of the land and people of Israel up to 135 C.E., aimed at students and general readers.

Kemp, Barry. *The City of Akhenaten and Nefertiti: Amarna and Its People.* London, 2012. A cutting-edge study of this ancient site, based on decades of archaeological research.

Kuhrt, Amélie. *The Ancient Near East, c. 3000–330 B.C.* 2 vols. London and New York, 1995. An outstanding survey, written for students, that includes Egypt and Israel as well as Mesopotamia, Babylonia, Assyria, and Persia.

Marinatos, Nannos. *Minoan Kingship and the Solar Goddess: A Near Eastern Koine.* Champaign, IL, 2010. A rich new interpretation of Minoan culture and its wider connections and influence within the world of the late Bronze Age.

Metzger, Bruce M., and Michael D. Coogan, eds. *The Oxford Companion to the Bible.* New York, 1993. An outstanding reference work, with contributions by leading authorities.

Niditch, Susan. *Ancient Israelite Religion.* New York, 1997. A short introduction designed for students, emphasizing the diversity of Hebrew religious practices.

Prezioso, Donald, and Louise A. Hitchcock. *Aegean Art and Architecture.* Oxford, 2000. Archaic Greek artistic forms in their broader geographic and cultural context, from the fourth millennium to 1000 B.C.E.

Redford, Donald B. *Egypt, Canaan, and Israel in Ancient Times.* Princeton, NJ, 1992. An overview of the interactions between these peoples from about 1200 B.C.E. to the beginning of the Common Era.

Renfrew, Colin. *Archaeology and Language: The Puzzle of Indo-European Origins.* Cambridge, 1987. A masterful but controversial work by one of the most creative archaeologists of the twentieth century.

Sandars, Nancy K. *The Sea Peoples: Warriors of the Ancient Mediterranean.* Rev. ed. London, 1985. An introductory account for students and scholars.

Tubb, Jonathan N., and Rupert L. Chapman. *Archaeology and the Bible.* London, 1990. A good starting point for students that clearly illustrates the difficulties in linking archaeological evidence to biblical accounts of early Hebrew history and society.

Wood, Michael. *In Search of the Trojan War.* New York, 1985. Aimed at a general audience, this carefully researched and engagingly written book is an excellent introduction to the late–Bronze Age context of the Trojan War.

CHAPTER 3

Penguin Classics and the Loeb Classical Library both offer reliable translations of Greek literary, philosophical, and historical texts.

Beard, Mary. *The Parthenon*. Cambridge, MA, 2003. Traces the successive stages of this monument's construction, deconstruction, reconstruction, and restoration.

Brunschwig, Jacques, and Geoffrey E. R. Lloyd. *Greek Thought: A Guide to Classical Knowledge*. Trans. Catherine Porter. Cambridge, MA, 2000. An outstanding work of reference.

Buckley, Terry, ed. *Aspects of Greek History, 750–323 B.C.: A Source-Based Approach*. London, 1999. A good collection of source materials.

Cartledge, Paul A. *The Spartans: An Epic History*. New York, 2003. A lively and authoritative history of Sparta from its origins to the Roman conquest.

Fantham, Elaine, Helene Foley, Natalie Kampen, Sarah B. Pomeroy, and H. A. Shapiro. *Women in the Classical World: Image and Text*. Oxford, 1994. Wide-ranging analysis drawing on both visual and written sources, covering both the Greek and the Roman periods.

Garlan, Yvon. *Slavery in Ancient Greece*. Ithaca, NY, 1988. Now the standard account.

Havelock, Eric A. *The Literate Revolution in Greece and Its Cultural Consequences*. Princeton, 1982. A now-classic account of the wide-ranging effects of writing on Greek society.

Jones, Nicholas F. *Ancient Greece: State and Society*. Upper Saddle River, NJ, 1997. A concise survey from the Minoans up to the end of the Classical period.

Krentz, Peter. *The Battle of Marathon*. New Haven, 2011. A fresh analysis of this landmark battle, paying special attention to the conditions in which hoplite warriors fought.

Lee, Mireille M. *Body, Dress, and Identity in Ancient Greece*. Cambridge, 2015. A major interdisciplinary contribution to our understanding of personal adornment, class, and gender identity.

Lefkowitz, Mary, and Maureen Fant. *Women's Life in Greece and Rome: A Source Book in Translation*. 3rd ed. Baltimore, 2005. A remarkably wide-ranging collection, topically arranged, invaluable to students.

Malkin, Irad. *A Small Greek World: Networks in the Ancient Mediterranean*. Oxford, 2011. A study showing how a Panhellenic identity developed during and because of widespread Greek settlement throughout the ancient world.

Manning, J. G. *The Open Sea: The Economic Life of the Ancient Mediterranean World from the Iron Age to the Rise of Rome*. Princeton, 2018. An ambitious study of interconnected cultures, commercial exchanges, and climate.

Nevett, Lisa C. *Domestic Space in Classical Antiquity*. Cambridge, 2010. Reassesses what we can know about the architecture of households in antiquity through a fresh assessment of archaeological evidence and material culture.

Pomeroy, Sarah. *Goddesses, Whores, Wives, and Slaves: Women in Classical Antiquity*. New York, 1995. The first historical survey of antiquity to place women at the center of the narrative, and still unrivaled in scope.

Price, Simon. *Religions of the Ancient Greeks*. Cambridge, 1999. Concise and authoritative, this survey extends from the Archaic Period up to the fifth century C.E.

Pritchard, David M., ed. *War, Democracy and Culture in Classical Athens*. Cambridge, 2010. A collection of scholarly essays on the close relationship between Athenian politics, culture, and military technology.

Robinson, Eric W. *Democracy beyond Athens: Popular Government in the Greek Classical Age*. Cambridge, 2011. An important contribution to the history of Greek political institutions in poleis other than Athens.

Seaford, Richard. *Money and the Greek Mind: Homer, Philosophy, Tragedy*. Cambridge, 2004. A provocative study of portable wealth and its far-reaching effects.

Simpson, St. John and Svetlana Pankiva, eds. *Scythians: Warriors of Ancient Siberia*. London, 2018. The catalogue of a major exhibition at the British Museum devoted to the nomadic people who fascinated and terrified the ancient Greeks.

Strassler, Robert B., ed. *The Landmark Thucydides*. New York, 1996. Reprints the classic Richard Crawley translation with maps, commentary, notes, and appendices by leading scholars.

Thomas, Rosalind. *Oral Tradition and Written Record in Classical Athens*. Cambridge, 1989. A fascinating look at how oral epic, lyric, and drama were transmitted over time.

CHAPTER 4

Penguin Classics and the Loeb Classical Library both offer reliable translations of scores of literary and historical texts from this period. Particularly important are historical works by Arrian (*Anabasis of Alexander*), Plutarch (*Life of Alexander*), and Polybius (*The Histories*).

Austin, M. M. *The Hellenistic World from Alexander to the Roman Conquest: A Selection of Ancient Sources in Translation*. Cambridge, 1981. A good collection of primary documents.

Aylward, William, ed. *Excavations at Zeugma*. 3 vols. Oxford, 2013. Available free online: http://zeugma.packhum. org. The results of a massive scholarly effort (undertaken between 1987 and 1988) to excavate and analyze the remains of Samosata and the palace of Antiochus I, the best-preserved royal palace in the Hellenistic world, before the site was submerged beneath a Turkish dam in 1989.

Borza, Eugene N. *In the Shadow of Olympus: The Emergence of Macedon*. Princeton, NJ, 1990. The standard account of the rise of Macedon up to the accession of Philip II.

Bosworth, A. B. *Conquest and Empire: The Reign of Alexander the Great*. Cambridge, 1988. A political and military analysis of

Alexander's career that strips away the romance, maintaining a clear vision of the ruthlessness and human cost of his conquests.

————. *The Legacy of Alexander: Politics, Warfare, and Propaganda under the Successors.* Oxford, 2002. The most recent survey of the half century following Alexander's death and of the people who created the Hellenistic kingdoms of Egypt, Persia, and Macedon.

Burstein, Stanley M., ed. and trans. *The Hellenistic Age from the Battle of Ipsos to the Death of Kleopatra VII.* Cambridge, 1985. An excellent collection, with sources not found elsewhere.

Cartledge, Paul. *Agesilaus and the Crisis of Sparta.* Baltimore, 1987. A thorough but readable analysis of the social and political challenges besetting Sparta in the fourth century B.C.E.

————. *Alexander the Great: The Hunt for a New Past.* Woodstock, NY, 2004. A compelling account of Alexander's life, times, and influences.

Green, Peter. *Alexander of Macedon, 356–323 B.C.* Berkeley, 1991. Revised edition of the author's earlier biography; entertainingly written, rich in detail and insight.

————. *The Hellenistic Age: A Short History.* New York, 2007. An authoritative synthesis that carries the history of Greek influence into the fourth century C.E.

Hansen, Mogens H. *The Athenian Democracy in the Age of Demosthenes.* Oxford, 1991. An examination of the political institutions of Athens in the fourth century B.C.E.

Holt, Frank. L. *Into the Land of Bones: Alexander the Great in Afghanistan.* Repr. ed. Berkeley, 2012. A vivid, charged narrative that places the beginning of a current war in the distant past.

Johnstone, S. "A New History of Libraries and Books in the Hellenistic Period." *Classical Antiquity* 33 (2014): 347–93. A revolutionary and accessible review of the ancient evidence for the first public libraries.

Lloyd, Geoffrey, and Nathan Sivin. *The Way and the Word: Science and Medicine in Early China and Greece.* New Haven, 2002. An extraordinary comparative study.

McGing, Brian. *Polybius' Histories.* Oxford, 2010. A critical dissection of this influential ancient historian's techniques and historical philosophy.

Nicholas, G. L. *The Genius of Alexander the Great.* Chapel Hill, NC, 1998. A clear, authoritative, admiring account, distilling a lifetime of research on the subject.

Ober, Josiah. *Mass and Elite in Democratic Athens: Rhetoric, Ideology, and the Power of the People.* Princeton, NJ, 1989. An excellent study of the ideology of democracy in Athens that borrows from the insights of modern social science.

Pollitt, Jerome J. *Art in the Hellenistic Age.* New York, 1986. The standard account, blending cultural history with art history.

Sherwin-White, Susan, and Amélie Kuhrt. *From Samarkhand to Sardis: A New Approach to the Seleucid Empire.* London, 1993. A stimulating examination of the relationship between rulers and ruled in the vast expanses of the Seleucid Empire.

Shipley, Graham. *The Greek World after Alexander, 323–30 B.C.* New York and London, 2000. A study of the social, intellectual, and artistic changes in the Hellenistic era.

Thomas, Carol G. *Alexander the Great in His World.* Oxford and Malden, MA, 2007. A study of the contexts—familial, political, and social—that shaped Alexander's career.

Tripolitis, Antonia. *Religions of the Hellenistic-Roman Age.* Grand Rapids, MI, 2002. Survey of the variety of religious experience, ritual, and belief in the centuries before the emergence of Christianity.

Tritle, Lawrence A., ed. *The Greek World in the Fourth Century: From the Fall of the Athenian Empire to the Successors of Alexander.* New York, 1997. A wide-ranging collection of scholarly essays.

CHAPTER 5

Translations of Roman authors are available in both the Penguin Classics series and in the Loeb Classical Library.

Alston, Richard. *Rome's Revolution: Death of the Republic and Birth of the Empire.* Oxford, 2015. A clear and compelling narrative of the events surrounding the rise and assassination of Julius Caesar, and reign of Augustus.

Arnason, Johann P., and Kurt A. Raaflaub, eds. *The Roman Empire in Context: Historical and Comparative Perspectives.* Malden, MA, 2011. One of the few books to place the formation of the Roman Empire in a comparative, global perspective.

Barker, Graeme, and Tom Rasmussen. *The Etruscans.* Oxford and Malden, MA, 1998. A fine survey, from the Blackwell *Peoples of Europe* series.

Beard, Mary. *SPQR: A History of Ancient Rome.* New York, 2015. A masterful narrative and critical history of the shift from republic to Principate.

————. *Pompeii: The Life of a Roman Town.* New York, 2010. A fascinating, cutting-edge study of daily life and of the archaeological work that uncovered it.

Cornell, T. J. *The Beginnings of Rome: Italy and Rome from the Bronze Age to the Punic Wars (c. 1000–264 B.C.).* London, 1995. An ambitious survey of the archaeological and historical evidence for early Rome.

Crawford, Michael. *The Roman Republic,* 2nd ed. Cambridge, MA, 1993. A lively, fast-paced survey of republican Rome. An excellent place to start.

Fantham, Elaine, Helene Peet Foley, Natalie Boymel Kampen, Sarah B. Pomeroy, and H. Alan Shapiro. *Women in the Classical World.* Oxford, 1994. An expert survey of both Greece and Rome.

Harris, William V. *War and Imperialism in Republican Rome, 327–70 B.C.* Oxford, 1979. A challenging study arguing that Rome's need for military conquest and expansion was deeply embedded in the fabric of Roman life.

Hartnett, Jeremy. *The Roman Street: Urban Life and Society in Pompeii, Herculaneum, and Rome.* Cambridge, 2017. An illuminating study of public life and culture.

Hayes, Ian. *Blood of the Provinces: The Roman Auxilia and the Making of Provincial Society from Augustus to Severus.* Oxford, 2013. A new history of Roman warfare and its role in expanding imperial power, showing how archaeological evidence challenges written sources.

Krebs, Christopher. *A Most Dangerous Book: Tacitus's "Germania" from the Roman Empire to the Third Reich.* A history of this ancient ethnography's transmission and reception, and especially the political uses to which it was put in Nazi Germany.

Lancel, Serge. *Carthage: A History.* Trans. Antonia Nevill. Oxford, 1995. An account of Rome's great rival for control of the Mediterranean world.

Millar, Fergus G. B. *The Emperor in the Roman World, 31 B.C.–A.D. 337.* London, 1977. A classic work that showed (among much else) the importance of emperor worship to the religious outlook of the Roman Empire.

————. *The Crowd in Rome in the Late Republic.* Ann Arbor, MI, 1999. A revisionist account that emphasizes the reality of Roman democracy in the late republic, against those who would see the period's politics as entirely under the control of aristocratic families.

Watkin, David. *The Roman Forum.* London, 2009. A history of the successive buildings and archaeological excavations of this central Roman space.

Wells, Colin. *The Roman Empire,* 2nd ed. Cambridge, MA, 1992. An easily readable survey from the reign of Augustus to the mid–third century C.E., particularly useful for its treatment of the relationship between the Roman central government and its Italian provinces.

Wiseman, T. P. *Remembering the Roman People.* Oxford, 2009. A collection of studies devoted to popular politics in the late republic.

Woolf, Greg. *Becoming Roman: The Origins of Provincial Civilization in Gaul.* Cambridge, 1998. An exemplary study of how provincial elites made themselves "Roman."

————. *Rome: An Empire's Story.* Oxford, 2012. A masterful account of Rome's reconfiguration of the ancient world and its enduring impact; critically acclaimed by scholars and general readers.

————. *Tales of the Barbarians: Ethnography and Empire in the Roman West.* Malden, MA, 2011. Applies modern ethnographic methodologies to a dissection of how Romans applied their own ethnographic theories to contemporary "others."

CHAPTER 6

Augustine. *The City of God.* Trans. Henry Bettenson. Baltimore, 1972.

————. *Confessions.* Trans. Henry M. Chadwick. Oxford, 1991.

————. *On Christian Doctrine.* Trans. D. W. Robertson Jr. New York, 1958.

Boethius. *The Consolation of Philosophy.* Trans. R. Green. Indianapolis, 1962.

Bowersock, G. W., Peter Brown, and Oleg Grabar. *Late Antiquity: A Guide to the Postclassical World.* Cambridge, MA, 1999. An authoritative compilation. The first half is devoted to essays on the cultural features of the period; the second half is organized as an encyclopedia.

Brown, Peter. *Augustine of Hippo.* Berkeley, 1967. A great biography by the great scholar of late antiquity.

————. *The Body and Society: Men, Women and Sexual Renunciation in Early Christianity.* New York, 1988. A revealing study of the fundamental transformations wrought by Christianity in the late antique world.

————. *The Rise of Western Christendom: Triumph and Diversity, 200–1000,* 2nd ed. Oxford, 2002. An evocative picture of Christianity's spread eastward and northward from the Mediterranean world.

————. *The World of Late Antiquity.* New York, 1971. Still the best short survey of the period, with excellent illustrations.

————. *Through the Eye of a Needle: Wealth, the Fall of Rome, and the Making of Christianity in the West, 350–550 A.D.* Princeton, NJ, 2012. The most recent of this historian's magisterial dissections of late antiquity, focused on the relationship between religion, culture, power, and wealth (or its lack).

Cameron, Averil. *The Later Roman Empire, A.D. 284–430.* London, 1993. Now the standard account of its period, with an emphasis on imperial politics.

————. *The Mediterranean World in Late Antiquity, A.D. 395–600.* London, 1993. Masterful, with succinct bibliographical essays.

Cassiodorus. *An Introduction to Divine and Human Readings.* Trans. L. W. Jones. New York, 1946.

Chadwick, Henry M. *Boethius.* Oxford, 1981. An intellectual biography of this important thinker.

Clark, Gillian. *Christianity and Roman Society.* Cambridge, 2004. A short, stimulating survey that places early Christianity firmly in its Roman social context.

————. *Women in Late Antiquity.* Oxford, 1993. A clear, compact account of an important subject.

Ehrman, Bart D. *The New Testament: A Historical Introduction to the Early Christian Writings,* 4th ed. Oxford, 2008. The standard textbook by a leading authority.

Ehrman, Bart D., and Zlatko Pleše, eds. *The Aprocryphal Gospels: Texts and Translations* Oxford, 2011. The first scholarly edition and translation of all the apocryphal gospels, including Latin, Greek, and Coptic texts.

Eusebius. *The History of the Church*. Trans. G. A. Williamson. Baltimore, 1965. A contemporary account of Constantine's reign, written by one of his courtier-bishops.

———. *Eusebius' Life of Constantine*. Trans. Averil Cameron and Stuart Hall. Oxford, 1999. An admiring biography that reflects Constantine's own vision of his religious authority.

Grig, Lucy, and Gavin Kelly, eds. *Two Romes: Rome and Constantinople in Antiquity*. Oxford, 2015. A set of comparative essays by noted scholars.

Hopkins, Keith. *A World Full of Gods: The Strange Triumph of Christianity*. New York, 1999. An imaginative study of religious pluralism in the Roman world and the context in which Christianity emerged.

Kulikowski, Michael. *Imperial Triumph: The Roman World from Hadrian to Constantine*. Profile Books, 2018. A sweeping and engaging history of Rome's power at its height.

———. *Rome's Gothic Wars: From the Third Century to Alaric*. Cambridge, 2007. An authoritative and critical account.

Lane Fox, Robin. *Augustine: Conversions to Confessions*. New York, 2015. A beautifully written reconstruction of Augustine's early life in its historical context.

Lawrence, Clifford Hugh. *Medieval Monasticism*. 3rd ed. London, 2000. Concise, perceptive survey of monasticism from its beginnings to the end of the Middle Ages.

Pagels, Elaine. *The Gnostic Gospels*. New York, 1979. A pathbreaking study of the noncanonical gospels and the history of their exclusion from the Bible.

Potter, David. *The Roman Empire at Bay*, A.D. 180–395. London and New York, 2004. The most up-to-date account of the empire's reorganization and transformation in this era.

Rebillard, Éric. *Christians and Their Many Identities in Late Antiquity, North Africa, 200–450 C.E.* Ithaca, NY, 2012. In this book, as in his earlier works, the author argues that there was no special importance attached to being a "Christian" in late antiquity, and that religious identities are better understood as fluid and hybrid.

Sanders, E. P. *The Historical Figure of Jesus*. London and New York, 1993. A fine study of Jesus in his first-century Jewish context.

Shanks, Hershel, ed. *Christianity and Rabbinic Judaism: A Parallel History of Their Origins and Early Development*. Washington, DC, 1992. Accessible chapters written by top authorities, describing both Jewish and Christian developments from the first to the sixth centuries C.E.

Sherwin-White, A. N. *Roman Society and Roman Law in the New Testament*. Oxford, 1963. A fascinating reading of the New Testament in its historical context.

Traina, Giusto. *428 A.D.: An Ordinary Year at the End of the Roman Empire*. Princeton, NJ, 2011. An enlightening glimpse into the world of late antiquity, from the vantage point of a single "average" year.

Whittaker, C. R. *Frontiers of the Roman Empire: A Social and Economic Study*. Baltimore, 1994. A convincing picture of the frontiers of the Roman Empire as zones of intensive cultural interaction.

Williams, Stephen. *Diocletian and the Roman Recovery*. New York, 1997. Thorough and authoritative.

CHAPTER 7

Translations of Arabic sources are now available in the *Library of Arabic Literature* series from New York University Press.

Arnold, Jonathan J. *Theoderic and the Roman Imperial Restoration*. Cambridge, 2014. An ambitious new reading of Theodoric's reign, arguing for the thoroughly Roman identity and ambitions of this Gothic ruler.

Bede. *A History of the English Church and People*. Trans. Leo Sherley-Price. Baltimore, 1955. The fundamental source for early Anglo-Saxon history.

Campbell, James, ed. *The Anglo-Saxons*. Oxford, 1982. An authoritative and splendidly illustrated volume.

Conant, Jonathan. *Staying Roman: Conquest and Identity in Africa and the Mediterranean, 439–700*. Cambridge, 2012. An exploration of what it meant to be "Roman" and the sources of identity in this tumultuous period.

Einhard and Notker the Stammerer. *Two Lives of Charlemagne*. Trans. Lewis Thorpe. Baltimore, 1969. Lively and entertaining works of contemporary biography.

Geanakoplos, Deno John, ed. *Byzantium: Church, Society and Civilization Seen through Contemporary Eyes*. Chicago, 1984. An outstanding source book.

Gregory, Timothy E. *A History of Byzantium*. Malden, MA, and Oxford, 2005. An accessible textbook and an excellent place to start.

Herrin, Judith. *Byzantium: The Surprising Life of a Medieval Empire*. Princeton, NJ, 2009. An accessible and comprehensive history of the eastern Roman Empire.

———. *The Formation of Christendom*. Princeton, NJ, 1987. A synthetic history of the Christian civilizations of Byzantium and western Europe from 500 to 800, written by a prominent historian.

Hodges, Richard, and David Whitehouse. *Mohammed, Charlemagne and the Origins of Europe*. London, 1983. A critical analysis of the "Pirenne thesis," reexamining the relationship between the Mediterranean world and northern Europe.

Hourani, Albert. *A History of the Arab Peoples*. New York, 1992. A sympathetic and clear survey written for nonspecialists.

Hoyland, Robert G. *In God's Path: The Arab Conquests and the Creation of the Islamic Empire*. Oxford, 2014. A highly acclaimed new study of Islam's rapid expansion as a product of Arab imperial ambitions.

Kennedy, Hugh. *The Prophet and the Age of the Caliphates*. 2nd ed. Harlow, UK, 2004. A lucid introduction to the political history of the Islamic world from the sixth through the eleventh centuries.

Krautheimer, Richard. *Early Christian and Byzantine Architecture.* 4th ed. New York, 1986. A classic work by one of the greatest Byzantine art historians of the twentieth century.

Little, Lester K., ed., *Plague and the End of Antiquity: The Pandemic of 541–750.* Cambridge, 2006. The first full-length scholarly history of the first global pandemic.

Mango, Cyril, ed. *The Oxford History of Byzantium.* Oxford and New York, 2002. Full of sharp judgments and attractively illustrated.

McCormick, Michael. *The Origins of the European Economy: Communications and Commerce A.D. 300–900.* Cambridge, 2002. An astonishing reinterpretation of the evidence for the myriad contacts between Christian Europe and Islam.

McKitterick, Rosamond. *Charlemagne: The Formation of a European Identity.* Cambridge, 2008. A history of Charlemagne's career and its lasting impact by an eminent scholar of the Carolingian world.

———, ed. *The Uses of Literacy in Early Medieval Europe.* New York, 1990. A superb collection of essays.

McNamara, Jo Ann, and John E. Halborg, eds. *Sainted Women of the Dark Ages.* Durham, NC, 1992. Translated saints' lives from Merovingian and Carolingian Europe.

Murray, A. C., ed. *From Roman to Merovingian Gaul: A Reader.* Toronto, 2000. An excellent collection of sources.

Pelikan, Jaroslav. *The Christian Tradition.* Vol. 2, *The Spirit of Eastern Christendom.* Chicago, 1974. An outstanding synthetic treatment of the doctrines of Byzantine Christianity.

Procopius. *The Secret History.* Trans. G. A. Williamson. Baltimore, 1966. An "unauthorized" account of Justinian's reign, written by the emperor's offical historian.

Reuter, Timothy. *Germany in the Early Middle Ages, 800–1056.* New York, 1991. The best survey in English.

Sardar, Ziauddin. *Reading the Quran.* Hachette, 2011. A readable guide to Muslim scripture and the many controversies over its interpretation.

Sijpesteijn, Petra M. *Shaping a Muslim State: The World of a Mid-Eighth-Century Egyptian Official.* Oxford, 2013. Based on a cache of papyrus letters sent to a Muslim administrator, this book reveals how an Arab/Muslim state was established in a former province of the eastern Roman Empire.

Treadgold, Warren. *A History of the Byzantine State and Society.* Stanford, CA, 1997. A massive, encyclopedic narrative of the political, economic, and military history of Byzantium from 284 until 1461.

Wallace-Hadrill, John Michael. *Early Germanic Kingship in England and on the Continent.* Oxford, 1971. A classic analysis of changing ideas about kingship in early medieval Europe, emphasizing the links between Anglo-Saxon and Carolingian cultures.

———. *The Frankish Church.* Oxford, 1983. A masterful account that links the Merovingian and Carolingian churches.

Watt, W. Montgomery. *Islamic Philosophy and Theology.* 2nd ed. Edinburgh, 1985. The standard English account.

Wemple, Suzanne Fonay. *Women in Frankish Society: Marriage and the Cloister, 500–900.* Philadelphia, 1981. An influential account of changing attitudes toward marriage among the early Franks.

Whittow, Mark. *The Making of Orthodox Byzantium, 600–1025.* London, 1996. Emphasizes the centrality of orthodoxy in shaping Byzantine history. Particularly good on Byzantine relations with the peoples outside the empire.

Wickham, Chris. *Framing the Middle Ages: Europe and the Mediterranean, 400–800.* Oxford, 2007. An eye-opening history that spans the transitional periods of late antiquity and the early Middle Ages, paying careful attention to regional differences.

Wood, Ian. *The Merovingian Kingdoms, 450–751.* New York, 1994. A detailed study, but difficult for beginners.

CHAPTER 8

Amt, Emily, ed. *Women's Lives in Medieval Europe: A Sourcebook.* New York, 1993. An excellent collection of primary texts.

The Song of Roland. Trans. Robert Harrison. New York, 1970. A lively translation.

Arnold, Benjamin. *Princes and Territories in Medieval Germany.* Cambridge and New York, 1991. The best such survey in English.

Berend, Nora, Przemysław Urbańczyk, and Przemysław Wisewski. *Central Europe in the High Middle Ages: Bohemia, Hungary and Poland, c. 900–c. 1300.* Cambridge, 2013. An accessible introduction to the medieval history of this region.

Boswell, John E. *Christianity, Social Tolerance, and Homosexuality: Gay People in Western Europe from the Beginning of the Christian Era to the Fourteenth Century.* Chicago, 1980. A pioneering account, hotly debated but highly respected.

Burman, Thomas E. *Reading the Qur'ān in Latin Christendom, 1140–1560.* Philadelphia, 2007. A fascinating account of the Qur'an's reception in medieval Europe.

Dunbabin, Jean. *France in the Making, 843–1180.* 2nd ed. Oxford and New York, 2000. An authoritative survey of the disparate territories that came to make up the medieval French kingdom.

Dyer, Christopher. *Making a Living in the Middle Ages: The People of Britain 850–1520.* New Haven, 2002. A splendid new synthesis that combines social, economic, and archaeological evidence.

Fossier, Robert. *The Ax and the Oath: Ordinary Life in the Middle Ages.* Princeton, NJ, 2010. A quirky, personal, and often insightful look at the daily lives and worldview of this era by a leading French historian.

Frankopan, Peter. *The First Crusade: The Call from the East.* Cambridge, MA, 2012. Analyzes the causes and catalysts of the crusading movement.

Hartnell, Jack. *Medieval Bodies: Life, Death, and Art in the Middle Ages.* New York, 2019. A rich and beautifully written cultural history.

Hicks, Carola. *The Bayeux Tapestry: The Life Story of a Masterpiece.* London, 2006. An art historian's engrossing account of the making, reception, and interpretation of this amazing artifact.

Horden, Peregrine, and Nicholas Purcell. *The Corrupting Sea: A Study of Mediterranean History.* Malden, MA, 2000. An extraordinary attempt to encompass the history of the Mediterranean world over a span of three millennia.

Leyser, Henrietta. *Medieval Women: A Social History of Women in England, 440–1500.* New York, 1995. Although limited to one country, this is the best of the recent surveys treating medieval women.

McLaughlin, Megan. *Sex, Gender, and Episcopal Authority in an Age of Reform, 1000–1122.* Cambridge, 2010. A new interpretation of gendered discourse and politics during the Investiture Controversy.

Martin, Janet. *Medieval Russia, 980–1584.* 2nd ed. Cambridge, 2007. A concise history with a wide reach.

Miller, Maureen C. *Power and the Holy in the Age of the Investiture Conflict: A Brief History with Documents.* Boston, 2005. A stimulating approach to the eleventh-century conflicts over temporal and spiritual power, with many newly translated sources.

Moore, Robert I. *The First European Revolution, c. 970–1215.* Oxford and Cambridge, MA, 2000. A remarkable description of the ways in which European society was fundamentally reshaped during the eleventh and twelfth centuries.

Raffensperger, Christian. *Reimagining Europe: Kievan Rus' in the Medieval World.* Cambridge, MA, 2012. An exciting new study of early Rus' and its neighbors.

Reynolds, Susan. *Fiefs and Vassals: The Medieval Evidence Reinterpreted.* Oxford and New York, 1994. A detailed revisionist history of "feudalism."

Rubenstein, Jay. *Armies of Heaven: The First Crusade and the Quest for Apocalypse.* New York, 2011. An accessible narrative of the First Crusade, written for a general audience and arguing for a new interpretation of the crusaders' motives.

Sawyer, Peter, ed. *The Oxford Illustrated History of the Vikings.* Oxford, 1997. The best one-volume account, lavishly illustrated.

Sheingorn, Pamela, trans. *The Book of Sainte Foy.* Philadelphia, 1995.

Stow, Kenneth R. *Alienated Minority: The Jews of Medieval Latin Europe.* Cambridge, 1992. An excellent survey.

Throop, Susanna A. *The Crusades: An Epitome.* Kismet Press, 2018. This extremely brief but hugely insightful introduction is also available in an Open Access format.

Winroth, Anders. *The Conversion of Scandinavia: Vikings, Merchants, and Missionaries in the Remaking of Northern Europe.* New Haven, 2012. Argues that the peoples of Scandinavia were active participants in the cultural, economic, and political processes that accompanied their conversion to Christianity.

CHAPTER 9

Abelard and Heloise. *The Letters and Other Writings.* Trans. William Levitan. Indianapolis, 2007. A beautiful and accurate translation of the correspondence and related documents, with a full introduction and notes.

Abulafia, David. *Frederick II: A Medieval Emperor.* London and New York, 1988. A reliable biography that strips away much of the legend that has hitherto surrounded this monarch.

Baldwin, John W. *The Government of Philip Augustus.* Berkeley and Los Angeles, 1986. A landmark scholarly account.

Barber, Malcolm. *The Crusader States.* New Haven, 2012. A new and comprehensive history by an esteemed historian.

Bartlett, Robert. *The Making of Europe: Conquest, Colonization and Cultural Change, 950–1350.* Princeton, NJ, 1993. A wide-ranging examination of the economic, social, and religious expansion of Europe, full of stimulating insights.

Bisson, Thomas N. *The Crisis of the Twelfth Century: Power, Lordship, and the Origins of European Government.* Princeton, NJ, 2009. A new interpretation of the evidence.

Bynum, Caroline Walker. *Holy Feast and Holy Fast: The Religious Significance of Food to Medieval Women.* Berkeley and Los Angeles, 1988. One of the most influential and important works of scholarship published in the late twentieth century.

Camille, Michael. *Gothic Art: Glorious Visions.* New York, 1996. A succinct and beautifully illustrated introduction to the art of the twelfth through fifteenth centuries in Europe.

Catlos, Brian. *Kingdoms of Faith: A New History of Islamic Spain.* Basic Books, 2018. A masterful and nuanced study of the forces shaping and threatening the Muslim states of Iberia.

Chrétien de Troyes. *Arthurian Romances.* Trans. W. W. Kibler. New York, 1991.

Clanchy, Michael T. *Abelard: A Medieval Life.* Oxford and Cambridge, MA, 1997. A great biography.

———. *From Memory to Written Record: England, 1066–1307.* Oxford, 1992. A fascinating and hugely influential account of a revolutionary shift toward documentation.

Fassler, Margot. *Gothic Song: Victorine Sequences and Augustinian Reform in Twelfth-Century Paris.* Cambridge, 1993. The emergence of new musical genres and their cultural context.

Gillingham, John. *The Angevin Empire.* 2nd ed. Oxford and New York, 2001. The best treatment by far of its subject, brief but full of ideas.

Gottfried von Strassburg. *Tristan.* Trans. A. T. Hatto. Baltimore, 1960.

Hallam, Elizabeth, and Judith Everard. *Capetian France, 987–1328.* 2nd ed. New York, 2001. A clear and well-organized account.

Jones, P. J. *The Italian City-State: From Commune to Signoria.* Oxford and New York, 1997. A fundamental reinterpretation of the evidence.

Jordan, William C. *Europe in the High Middle Ages.* Vol. 3 of the Penguin History of Europe. New York and London, 2003. An outstanding survey.

Kaeuper, Richard W. *Chivalry and Violence in Medieval Europe.* Oxford and New York, 1999. A darker view of chivalry than Keen's.

Keen, Maurice. *Chivalry.* New Haven, 1984. A comprehensive treatment of chivalry from its origins to the sixteenth century.

Lawrence, Clifford Hugh. *The Friars: The Impact of the Early Mendicant Movement on Western Society.* London and New York, 1994. The best short introduction to the early history of the Franciscans and the Dominicans.

Leclerq, Jean. *The Love of Learning and the Desire for God.* 3rd ed. New York, 1982. A beautiful interpretation of twelfth-century monastic culture and the influence of Bernard of Clairvaux.

Little, Lester. *Religious Poverty and Profit Economy in Medieval Europe.* Ithaca, NY, 1978. A fascinating study of the relationship between religious practice and economic reality.

Lopez, Robert S., and Irving W. Raymond, eds. *Medieval Trade in the Mediterranean World.* New York, 1990. A useful collection of source material.

Madden, Thomas F. *The New Concise History of the Crusades.* New York, 2005. An acclaimed and accessible survey for students.

Marie de France. *Lais.* Trans. Glyn S. Burgess and Keith Busby. Harmondsworth, UK, 1999. A compelling and entertaining prose translation.

Moore, R. I. *The War on Heresy.* Cambridge, MA, 2012. A courageous and searching revisionist history, based on decades of research and reflection. Moore argues for a radical reassessment of what "heresy" consisted of, and why those branded as "heretics" were persecuted during the Middle Ages.

Morris, Colin. *The Papal Monarchy: The Western Church from 1050 to 1250.* Oxford, 1989. An excellent scholarly survey, part of the Oxford History of the Christian Church series.

Newman, Barbara, ed. *Voice of the Living Light: Hildegard of Bingen and Her World.* Berkeley and Los Angeles, 1998. An introduction to Hildegard's life and work.

Nirenberg, David. *Neighboring Faiths: Christianity, Islam and Judaism in the Middle Ages and Today.* Chicago, 2014. A thoughtful and powerful study of interfaith relations and the challenges of coexistence, then and now.

Otto, Bishop of Freising. *The Deeds of Frederick Barbarossa.* Trans. C. C. Mierow. New York, 1953. A contemporary chronicle interesting enough to read from start to finish.

Smalley, Beryl. *The Study of the Bible in the Middle Ages.* 3rd ed. Oxford, 1983. The standard work, gracefully written and illuminating.

Strayer, Joseph R. *On the Medieval Origins of the Modern State.* With new forewords by Charles Tilly and William Chester Jordan. Princeton, NJ, 2005. This new edition of Strayer's series of lectures places them in their scholarly context.

Swanson, R. N. *The Twelfth-Century Renaissance.* Manchester, UK, 1999. An updated survey of the intellectual developments of the twelfth century.

Symes, Carol. *A Common Stage: Theater and Public Life in Medieval Arras.* Ithaca, NY, 2007. A study of a vibrant cultural hub.

Wakefield, Walter, and Austin P. Evans, eds. and trans. *Heresies of the High Middle Ages.* New York, 1969, 1991. A comprehensive collection of sources.

Wei, Ian. *Intellectual Culture in Medieval Paris: Theologians and the University, c. 1100–1330.* Cambridge, 2012. A fresh and compelling new history of medieval intellectual culture that ranges beyond Paris and pays attention to the contributions of medieval women.

Wolfram von Eschenbach. *Parzival.* Trans. H. M. Mustard and C. E. Passage. New York, 1961.

CHAPTER 10

Abu-Lughod, Janet L. *Before European Hegemony: The World System A.D. 1250–1350.* Oxford and New York, 1989. A now classic study of the trading links among Europe, the Middle East, India, and China, with special attention to the role of the Mongol Empire; extensive bibliography.

Allsen, Thomas T. *Culture and Conquest in Mongol Eurasia.* Cambridge and New York, 2001. A synthesis of the author's earlier studies, emphasizing Mongol involvement in the cultural and commercial exchanges that linked China, Central Asia, and Europe.

Cole, Bruce. *Giotto and Florentine Painting, 1280–1375.* New York, 1976. A clear and stimulating introduction.

Crummey, Robert O. *The Formation of Muscovy, 1304–1613.* New York, 1987. The standard account.

Dante Alighieri. *The Divine Comedy.* Trans. Mark Musa. 3 vols. Baltimore, 1984–1986.

Dunn, Ross E. *The Adventures of Ibn Battuta: A Muslim Traveler of the Fourteenth Century.* Rev. ed. Berkeley, 2005. Places the writings and experiences of this far-reaching Muslim traveler in their historical and geographical contexts.

Dyer, Christopher. *Standards of Living in the Later Middle Ages: Social Change in England, c. 1200–1520.* Cambridge and New York, 1989. Detailed but highly rewarding.

Fancy, Hussein. *The Mercenary Mediterranean: Sovereignty, Religion, and Violence in the Medieval Crown of Atagon.* Chicago, 2018. An acclaimed archival study of the complicated relationship between religion and politics in medieval Spain.

Foltz, Richard. *Religions of the Silk Road: Premodern Patterns of Globalization.* 2nd ed. New York, 2010. A compelling and thought-provoking study of the varieties of religious experience and cross-cultural interaction in medieval Eurasia.

Green, Monica, ed. *Pandemic Disease in the Medieval World: Rethinking the Black Death.* Special inaugural issue, *The Medieval Globe*, 1, no. 1 (2014). Available online in an open-access format: http://scholarworks.wmich.edu/tmg/vol1/iss1/. A pathbreaking collection of articles synthesizing the most recent research in the history, epidemiology, microbiology, and archaeology of the plague.

Horrox, Rosemary, ed. *The Black Death.* New York, 1994. A fine collection of documents reflecting the impact of the Black Death, especially in England.

Jackson, Peter. *The Mongols and the West, 1221–1410.* Harlow, UK, 2005. A well-written survey that emphasizes the interactions among the Mongol, Latin Christian, and Muslim worlds.

Jordan, William Chester. *The Great Famine: Northern Europe in the Early Fourteenth Century.* Princeton, NJ, 1996. An outstanding social and economic study.

Keen, Maurice, ed. *Medieval Warfare: A History.* Oxford and New York, 1999. The most attractive introduction to this important subject, lively and well illustrated.

Kitsikopoulos, Harry, ed. *Agrarian Change and Crisis in Europe, 1200–1500.* London, 2011. An up-to-date collection of scholarly essays that addresses a classic and complicated set of historical questions.

Komaroff, Linda, and Stefano Carboni, eds. *The Legacy of Ghenghis Khan: Courtly Art and Culture in Western Asia, 1256–1353.* New York, 2002. An informative and lavishly illustrated catalog of an acclaimed exhibition.

Larner, John. *Marco Polo and the Discovery of the World.* New Haven, 1999. A study of the influence of Marco Polo's *Travels* on Europeans.

Memoirs of a Renaissance Pope: The Commentaries of Pius II. Abridged ed. Trans. Florence A. Gragg, ed. Leona C. Gabel. New York, 1959. Remarkable insights into the mind of a particularly well-educated mid-fifteenth-century pope.

Morgan, David. *The Mongols.* 2nd ed. Oxford, 2007. An accessible introduction to Mongol history and its sources, written by a noted expert on medieval Persia.

Onon, Urgunge, trans. *The History and the Life of Chinggis Khan: The Secret History of the Mongols.* Leiden, 1997. A newer version of *The Secret History*, now the standard English version of this important Mongol source.

Polo, Marco. *The Description of the World.* Trans. Sharon Kinoshita. Indianapolis, 2016. A faithful and accessible new translation of the text, with authoritative notes and commentary.

Rossabi, Morris. *Khubilai Khan: His Life and Times.* Berkeley, 1988. The standard English biography.

Seymour, M. C., ed. *Mandeville's Travels.* Oxford, 1968. An edition of the *Book of Marvels* based on the Middle English version popular in the fifteenth century.

Swanson, R. N. *Religion and Devotion in Europe, c. 1215–c. 1515.* Cambridge and New York, 1995. An excellent study of late-medieval popular piety; an excellent complement to Oakley.

Vaughan, Richard. *Valois Burgundy.* London, 1975. A summation of the author's four-volume study of the Burgundian dukes.

CHAPTER 11

Alberti, Leon Battista. *The Family in Renaissance Florence (Della Famiglia).* Trans. Renée Neu Watkins. Columbia, SC, 1969.

Allmand, Christopher T., ed. *Society at War: The Experience of England and France during the Hundred Years' War.* Edinburgh, 1973. An outstanding collection of documents.

Boccaccio, Giovanni. *The Decameron.* Trans. Mark Musa and P. E. Bondanella. New York, 1977.

Brucker, Gene. *Florence: The Golden Age, 1138–1737.* Berkeley and Los Angeles, 1998. A classic account of the city at the height of its influence.

Bruni, Leonardo. *The Humanism of Leonardo Bruni: Selected Texts.* Trans. Gordon Griffiths, James Hankins, and David Thompson. Binghamton, NY, 1987. Excellent translations, with introductions, to the Latin works of a key Renaissance humanist.

Burkhardt, Jacob. *The Civilization of the Renaissance in Italy.* There are many editions of this nineteenth-century study, which influentially crystallized the concept of the "Renaissance."

Cassirer, Ernst, et al., eds. *The Renaissance Philosophy of Man.* Chicago, 1948. Excerpts from important original works by Petrarch, Ficino, and Pico della Mirandola, among others.

Castor, Helen. *Joan of Arc: A History.* London, 2015. An accessible and highly readable account of the ways that Joan was understood in her own time, and her changing reputation up to the present day.

Chaucer, Geoffrey. *The Canterbury Tales.* Trans. Nevill Coghill. New York, 1951. A modern English verse translation, lightly annotated.

Cohn, Samuel K., Jr. *Lust for Liberty: The Politics of Social Revolt in Medieval Europe, 1200–1425. Italy, France, and Flanders.* Cambridge, MA, 2006. An important and provocative study of social movements before and after the Black Death.

Coles, Paul. *The Ottoman Impact on Europe*. London, 1968. An excellent introductory text, still valuable despite its age.

Dobson, R. Barrie. *The Peasants' Revolt of 1381*. 2nd ed. London, 1983. A comprehensive source collection, with excellent introductions to the documents.

Fernández-Armesto, Felipe. *Before Columbus: Exploration and Colonisation from the Mediterranean to the Atlantic, 1229–1492*. London, 1987. An indispensible study of the medieval background to the sixteenth-century European colonial empires.

Froissart, Jean. *Chronicles*. Trans. Geoffrey Brereton. Baltimore, 1968. A selection from the most famous contemporary account of the Hundred Years' War to about 1400.

Frost, Robert. *The Oxford History of Poland-Lithuania. Volume One: The Making of the Polish-Lithuanian Union*, 1385–1569. Oxford, 2018. A magisterial study of this powerful medieval state.

Goffman, Daniel. *The Ottoman Empire and Early Modern Europe*. Cambridge and New York, 2002. A revisionist account that presents the Ottoman Empire as a European state.

Hankins, James. *Plato in the Italian Renaissance*. Leiden and New York, 1990. A definitive study of the reception and influence of Plato on Renaissance intellectuals.

———, ed. *Renaissance Civic Humanism: Reappraisals and Reflections*. Cambridge and New York, 2000. An excellent collection of scholarly essays reassessing republicanism in the Renaissance.

Hobbins, Daniel, ed. and trans. *The Trial of Joan of Arc*. Cambridge, MA, 2007. An excellent translation of the transcripts of Joan's trial.

Inalcik, Halil. *The Ottoman Empire: The Classical Age, 1300–1600*. London, 1973. The standard history by the dean of Turkish historians.

———, ed. *An Economic and Social History of the Ottoman Empire, 1300–1914*. Cambridge, 1994. An important collection of essays, spanning the full range of Ottoman history.

John Hus at the Council of Constance. Trans. M. Spinka, New York, 1965. The translation of a Czech chronicle with an expert introduction and appended documents.

Kafadar, Cemal. *Between Two Worlds: The Construction of the Ottoman State*. Berkeley and Los Angeles, 1995. An important study of Ottoman origins in the border regions between Byzantium, the Seljuk Turks, and the Mongols.

Kaldellis, Anthony. *A New Herodotos: Laonikos Chalkokondyles on the Ottoman Empire, the Fall of Byzantium, and the Emergence of the West*. Washington, DC, 2014. This volume is the first full-length study of Laonikos Chalkokondyles, a historian from Athens who wrote a classical Greek history of his own times, tracing the fall of Constantinople.

Kempe, Margery. *The Book of Margery Kempe*. Trans. Barry Windeatt. New York, 1985. A fascinating personal narrative by an early fifteenth-century Englishwoman who hoped she might be a saint.

Lane, Frederic C. *Venice: A Maritime Republic*. Baltimore, 1973. An authoritative account.

Ormrod, W. Mark. *Edward III*. New Haven, 2012. A new biography of this English monarch by a leading social historian.

Normore, Christina. *A Feast for the Eyes: Art, Performance, and the Late Medieval Banquet*. Chicago, 2015. A fascinating study of the aristocratic feast and its meanings.

Shirley, Janet, trans. *A Parisian Journal, 1405–1449*. Oxford, 1968. A marvelous panorama of Parisian life recorded by an eyewitness.

Sumption, Jonathan. *The Hundred Years' War*. Vol. 1, *Trial by Battle*. Vol. 2, *Trial by Fire*. Philadelphia, 1999. The first two volumes of a massive narrative history of the war, carrying the story up to 1369.

CHAPTER 12

Baxandall, Michael. *Painting and Experience in Fifteenth-Century Italy*. Oxford, 1972. A classic study of the perceptual world of the Renaissance.

Castiglione, Baldassare. *The Book of the Courtier*. Many editions. The translations by C. S. Singleton (New York, 1959) and by George Bull (New York, 1967) are both excellent.

Cellini, Benvenuto. *Autobiography*. Trans. George Bull. Baltimore, 1956. This Florentine goldsmith (1500–1571) is the source for many of the most famous stories about the artists of the Florentine Renaissance.

Columbus, Christopher. *The Four Voyages of Christopher Columbus*. Trans. J. M. Cohen. New York, 1992. Columbus's own self-serving account of his expeditions to the Indies.

Erasmus, Desiderius. *The Praise of Folly*. Trans. J. Wilson. Ann Arbor, MI, 1958.

Fernández-Armesto, Felipe. *1492: The Year the World Began*. London, 2010. A panoramic view of the world in a pivotal year, putting the voyage of Columbus in a broad historical perspective.

Flint, Valerie I. J. *The Imaginative Landscape of Christopher Columbus*. Princeton, NJ, 1992. A short, suggestive analysis of the intellectual influences that shaped Columbus's geographical ideas.

Fox, Alistair. *Thomas More: History and Providence*. Oxford, 1982. A balanced account of a man too easily idealized.

Grafton, Anthony, and Lisa Jardine. *From Humanism to the Humanities: Education and the Liberal Arts in Fifteenth- and Sixteenth-Century Europe*. London, 1986. An account that presents Renaissance humanism as the elitist cultural program of a self-interested group of pedagogues.

Grendler, Paul, ed. *Encyclopedia of the Renaissance*. New York, 1999. A valuable reference work.

Jardine, Lisa. *Worldly Goods*. London, 1996. A revisionist account that emphasizes the acquisitive materialism of Italian Renaissance society and culture.

Kanter, Laurence, Hilliard T. Goldfarb, and James Hankins. *Botticelli's Witness: Changing Style in a Changing Florence.* Boston, 1997. This catalog for an exhibition of Botticelli's works, at the Gardner Museum in Boston, offers an excellent introduction to the painter and his world.

King, Margaret L. *Women of the Renaissance.* Chicago, 1991. Deals with women in all walks of life and in a variety of roles.

Kristeller, Paul O. *Renaissance Thought: The Classic, Scholastic, and Humanistic Strains.* New York, 1961. Very helpful in defining the main trends of Renaissance thought.

Machiavelli, Niccolò. *The Discourses* and *The Prince.* Many editions. These two books must be read together if one is to understand Machiavelli's political ideas properly.

Mallett, Michael, and Christine Shaw. *The Italian Wars, 1494–1559: War, State, and Society in Early Modern Europe.* Boston, 2012. Argues that the endemic warfare of this period within Italy revolutionized European military tactics and technologies.

Mann, Charles. C. *1491: New Revelations of the Americas before Columbus.* New York, 2006.

———. *1493: Uncovering the New World Columbus Created.* New York, 2012. Written for a popular audience, these are also engaging and well-informed syntheses of historical research.

Martines, Lauro. *Power and Imagination: City-States in Renaissance Italy.* New York, 1979. Insightful account of the connections among politics, society, culture, and art.

More, Thomas. *Utopia.* Many editions.

Olson, Roberta. *Italian Renaissance Sculpture.* New York, 1992. The most accessible introduction to the subject.

Parker, Geoffrey. *The Military Revolution: Military Innovation and the Rise of the West (1500–1800).* 2nd ed. Cambridge and New York, 1996. A work of fundamental importance for understanding the global dominance achieved by early modern Europeans.

Perkins, Leeman L. *Music in the Age of the Renaissance.* New York, 1999. A massive study that needs to be read in conjunction with Reese.

Phillips, J. R. S. *The Medieval Expansion of Europe.* 2nd ed. Oxford, 1998. An outstanding study of the thirteenth- and fourteenth-century background to the fifteenth-century expansion of Europe. Important synthetic treatment of European relations with the Mongols, China, Africa, and North America. The second edition includes a new introduction and a bibliographical essay; the text is the same as in the first edition (1988).

Phillips, William D., Jr., and Carla R. Phillips. *The Worlds of Christopher Columbus.* Cambridge and New York, 1991. The first book to read on Columbus: accessible, engaging, and scholarly. Then read Fernández-Armesto's biography.

Rabelais, François. *Gargantua and Pantagruel.* Trans. J. M. Cohen. Baltimore, 1955. A robust modern translation.

Reese, Gustave. *Music in the Renaissance.* Rev. ed. New York, 1959. A great book; still authoritative, despite the more recent work by Perkins, which supplements but does not replace it.

Rice, Eugene F., Jr., and Anthony Grafton. *The Foundations of Early Modern Europe, 1460–1559.* 2nd ed. New York, 1994. The best textbook account of its period.

Rowland, Ingrid D. *The Culture of the High Renaissance: Ancients and Moderns in Sixteenth-Century Rome.* Cambridge and New York, 2000. Beautifully written examination of the social, intellectual, and economic foundations of the Renaissance in Rome.

Russell, Peter. *Prince Henry "The Navigator": A Life.* New Haven, 2000. A masterly biography by a great historian who has spent a lifetime on the subject. The only book one now needs to read on Prince Henry.

Scammell, Geoffrey V. *The First Imperial Age: European Overseas Expansion, 1400–1715.* London, 1989. A useful introductory survey, with a particular focus on English and French colonization.

Waltom, Nicholas. *Genoa, "La Superba": The Rise and Fall of a Merchant Pirate Superpower.* London, 2015. A history of the maritime city-state that shaped the career of Columbus and other adventurers.

CHAPTER 13

Bainton, Roland. *Erasmus of Christendom.* New York, 1969. A classic biography in English of the Dutch reformer and intellectual.

Benedict, Philip. *Christ's Churches Purely Reformed: A Social History of Calvinism.* New Haven, 2002. A wide-ranging recent survey of Calvinism in both western and eastern Europe.

Bossy, John. *Christianity in the West, 1400–1700.* Oxford and New York, 1985. A brilliant, challenging picture of the changes that took place in Christian piety and practice as a result of the sixteenth-century reformations.

Bouwsma, William J. *John Calvin: A Sixteenth-Century Portrait.* Oxford and New York, 1988. The best biography of this magisterial reformer.

Duffy, Eamon. *The Stripping of the Altars: Traditional Religion in England, c. 1400–c. 1550.* A brilliant study of religious exchange at the parish level.

———. *The Voices of Morebath: Reformation and Rebellion in an English Village.* New Haven, 2003. How the crises of this period affected and are reflected in the history of a single parish.

Hart, D. G. *Calvinism: A History.* New Haven, 2013. A new survey of this leading Protestant movement from its beginnings to the present day.

John Calvin: Selections from His Writings. Ed. John Dillenberger. Garden City, NY, 1971. A judicious selection, drawn mainly from Calvin's *Institutes*.

Jouanna, Arlette. *The St. Bartholomew's Day Massacre: The Mysteries of a Crime of State*. Translated from the French by Joseph Bergin. Manchester, 2015. A new interpretation of the events and motives surrounding the slaughter of Protestants in Paris on August 24, 1572.

Koslofksy, Craig. *The Reformation of the Dead: Death and Ritual in Early Modern Germany*. Basingstoke, UK, 2000. How essential rituals and responses to death were reshaped during this period.

Loyola, Ignatius. *Personal Writings*. Trans. by Joseph A. Munitiz and Philip Endean. London and New York, 1996. An excellent collection that includes Loyola's autobiography, his spiritual diary, and some of his letters, as well as his *Spiritual Exercises*.

MacCulloch, Diarmaid. *Reformation: Europe's House Divided, 1490–1700*. London and New York, 2003. A definitive new survey; the best single-volume history of its subject in a generation.

Marshall, Peter, ed. *The Oxford Illustrated History of the Reformation*. Oxford, 2015. A compendium of new perspectives on the religious upheavals of the sixteenth century.

Martin Luther: Selections from His Writings, ed. John Dillenberger. Garden City, NY, 1961. The standard selection, especially good on Luther's theological ideas.

McGrath, Alister E. *Reformation Thought: An Introduction*. Oxford, 1993. A useful explanation, accessible to non-Christians, of the theological ideas of the major Protestant reformers.

Mullett, Michael A. *The Catholic Reformation*. London, 2000. A sympathetic survey of Catholicism from the mid-sixteenth to the eighteenth century that presents the mid-sixteenth-century Council of Trent as a continuation of earlier reform efforts.

Murray, Linda. *High Renaissance and Mannerism*. London, 1985. The place to begin a study of fifteenth- and sixteenth-century Italian art.

O'Malley, John W. *The First Jesuits*. Cambridge, MA, 1993. A scholarly account of the origins and early years of the Society of Jesus.

———. *Trent: What Happened at the Council*. Cambridge, MA, 2012. A clear and comprehensive narrative of the Church council that gave birth to the modern Catholic Church.

Pettegree, Andrew. *Brand Luther: How an Unheralded Monk Turned His Small Town into a Center of Publishing, Made Himself the Most Famous Man in Europe—and Started the Protestant Reformation*. Penguin, 2016. The title says it all.

Pelikan, Jaroslav. *Reformation of Church and Dogma, 1300–1700*. Vol. 4 of *A History of Christian Dogma*. Chicago, 1984. A masterful synthesis of Reformation theology in its late-medieval context.

Roper, Lyndal. *The Holy Household: Women and Morals in Reformation Augsburg*. Oxford, 1989. A pathbreaking study of Protestantism's effects on a single town, with special attention to its impact on attitudes toward women, the family, and marriage.

Ryrie, Alex. *Being Protestant in Reformation Britain*. Oxford, 2015. A vivid portrait of daily life in a turbulent time.

Shagan, Ethan H. *Popular Politics and the English Reformation*. Cambridge, 2002. Argues that the English Reformation reflects an ongoing process of negotiation, resistance, and response.

Tracy, James D. *Europe's Reformations, 1450–1650*. 2nd ed. Lanham, MD, 2006. An outstanding survey, especially strong on Dutch and Swiss developments, but excellent throughout.

Williams, George H. *The Radical Reformation*. 3rd ed. Kirksville, MO, 1992. Originally published in 1962, this is still the best book on Anabaptism and its offshoots.

CHAPTER 14

Bonney, Richard. *The European Dynastic States, 1494–1660*. Oxford and New York, 1991. An excellent survey of continental Europe during the "long" sixteenth century.

Briggs, Robin. *Witches and Neighbors: The Social and Cultural Context of European Witchcraft*. New York, 1996. An influential recent account of Continental witchcraft.

Cervantes, Miguel de. *Don Quixote*. Trans. Edith Grossman. New York, 2003. A splendid new translation.

Clarke, Stuart. *Thinking with Demons: The Idea of Witchcraft in Early Modern Europe*. Oxford and New York, 1999. By placing demonology into the context of sixteenth- and seventeenth-century intellectual history, Clarke makes sense of it in new and exciting ways.

Cochrane, Eric, Charles M. Gray, and Mark A. Kishlansky. *Early Modern Europe: Crisis of Authority*. Chicago, 1987. An outstanding source collection from the University of Chicago Readings in Western Civilization series.

Cook Harold. *The Young Descartes: Nobility, Rumor, and War*. Chicago, 2018. A new biography that firmly embeds the philosopher in his historical context.

Elliot, J. H. *The Old World and the New, 1492–1650*. Repr. ed. Cambridge, 1992. A brilliant and brief set of essays on the ways that the discovery of the Americas challenged European perspectives on the world and themselves.

———. *Empires of the Atlantic World: Britain and Spain in America, 1492–1830*. An illuminating comparative study. New Haven, 2007.

Geschwend, Annemarie Jordan, and K. J. P. Lowe, eds. *The Global City: On the Streets of Renaissance Lisbon*. London, 2015. A beautifully illustrated collection of essays by leading scholars.

Hibbard, Howard. *Bernini*. Baltimore, 1965. The basic study in English of this central figure of Baroque artistic activity.

Hirst, Derek. *England in Conflict, 1603–1660: Kingdom, Community, Commonwealth*. Oxford and New York, 1999. A complete revision of the author's *Authority and Conflict* (1986), this is an up-to-date and balanced account of a period that has been a historical battleground over the past twenty years.

Hobbes, Thomas. *Leviathan*. Ed. Richard Tuck. 2nd ed. Cambridge and New York, 1996. The most recent edition, containing the entirety of *Leviathan*, not just the first two parts.

Holt, Mack P. *The French Wars of Religion, 1562–1629*. Cambridge and New York, 1995. A clear account of a confusing time.

Ipsen, Pernille.*Daughters of the Trade: Atlantic Slavers and Interracial Marriage on the Gold Coast*. Philadelphia, 2014. A study that puts women and families at the heart of the story of African slavery.

Kors, Alan Charles, and Edward Peters. *Witchcraft in Europe, 400–1700: A Documentary History*. 2nd ed. Philadelphia, 2000. A superb collection of documents, significantly expanded in the second edition, with up-to-date commentary.

Kingdon, Robert. *Myths about the St. Bartholomew's Day Massacres, 1572–1576*. Cambridge, MA, 1988. A detailed account of this pivotal moment in the history of France.

Kochanowski, Jan. *Laments*. Translated by Stanislaw Baranczak and Seamus Heaney. New York, 1995. A moving rendition of works by the great poet of Renaissance Poland.

Levack, Brian P. *The Witch-Hunt in Early Modern Europe*, 2nd ed. London and New York, 1995. The best account of the persecution of suspected witches; coverage extends from Europe in 1450 to America in 1750.

Levin, Carole. *The Heart and Stomach of a King: Elizabeth I and the Politics of Sex and Power*. Philadelphia, 1994. A provocative argument for the importance of Elizabeth's gender for understanding her reign.

Limm, Peter, ed. *The Thirty Years' War*. London, 1984. An outstanding short survey, followed by a selection of primary-source documents.

Lynch, John. *Spain, 1516–1598: From Nation-State to World Empire*. Oxford and Cambridge, MA, 1991. The best book in English on Spain at the pinnacle of its sixteenth-century power.

MacCaffrey, Wallace. *Elizabeth I*. New York, 1993. An outstanding traditional biography by an excellent scholar.

Martin, Colin, and Geoffrey Parker. *The Spanish Armada*. London, 1988. Incorporates recent discoveries from undersea archaeology with more traditional historical sources.

Mattingly, Garrett. *The Armada*. Boston, 1959. A great narrative history that reads like a novel; for more recent work, however, see Martin and Parker.

McGregor, Neil. *Shakespeare's Restless World*. London, 2013. Based on an acclaimed BBC Radio program, this book illuminates Shakespeare's life, times, and plays with reference to specific objects in the British Museum.

Newson, Linda A., and Susie Minchin. *From Capture to Sale: The Portuguese Slave Trade to Spanish South America in the Early Seventeenth Century*. London, 2007. Makes use of slave traders' own rich archives to track the process of human trafficking.

Parker, Geoffrey. *The Dutch Revolt*. 2nd ed. Ithaca, NY, 1989. The standard survey in English.

Pascal, Blaise. *Pensées* (French-English edition). Ed. H. F. Stewart. London, 1950.

Pestana, Carla. *Protestant Empire: Religion and the Making of the British Atlantic World*. Philadelphia, 2010. How the Reformation helped to drive British imperial expansion.

Roberts, Michael. *Gustavus Adolphus and the Rise of Sweden*. London, 1973. Still the authoritative English-language account.

Russell, Conrad. *The Causes of the English Civil War*. Oxford, 1990. A penetrating and provocative analysis by one of the leading "revisionist" historians of the period.

Schmidt, Benjamin. *Innocence Abroad: The Dutch Imagination and the New World, 1570–1670*. Cambridge, 2006. A cultural history of Europeans' encounter with the Americas that highlights the perspective and experience of Dutch merchants, colonists, and artists.

Strum, Daniel. *The Sugar Trade: Brazil, Portugal, and the Netherlands (1595–1630)*. Translated by Colin Foulkes, Roopanjali Roy, and H. Sabrina Gledhill. Stanford, CA, 2013. A close examination of the merchants, seafarers, and slaves who drove the economy of the Atlantic world.

CHAPTER 15

Beik, William. *A Social and Cultural History of Early Modern France*. Cambridge, 2009. A broad synthesis of French history from the end of the Middle Ages to the French Revolution, by one of the world's foremost authorities on absolutism.

Clark, Christopher. *Iron Kingdom: The Rise and Downfall of Prussia, 1600–1947*. Cambridge, MA, 2009. A definitive account of Prussian history over nearly four centuries.

Jones, Colin. *The Great Nation: France From Louis XV to Napoleon*. New York, 2002. An excellent and readable scholarly account that argues that the France of Louis XV in the eighteenth century was even more dominant than the kingdom of Louis XIV in the preceding century.

Kishlansky, Mark A. *A Monarchy Transformed: Britain, 1603–1714*. London, 1996. An excellent survey that takes seriously its claim to be a "British" rather than merely an "English" history.

Klein, Herbert S. *The Atlantic Slave Trade*. Cambridge and New York, 1999. An accessible survey by a leading quantitative historian.

Lewis, William Roger, gen. ed. *The Oxford History of the British Empire*. Vol. I: *The Origins of Empire: British Overseas Enterprise to the Close of the Seventeenth Century*, ed. Nicholas Canny. Vol. II: *The Eighteenth Century*, ed. Peter J. Marshall. Oxford and New York, 1998. A definitive, multiauthor account.

Locke, John. *Two Treatises of Government*. Ed. Peter Laslett. Rev. ed. Cambridge and New York, 1963. Laslett has revolutionized our understanding of the historical and ideological context of Locke's political writings.

Massie, Robert. *Peter the Great, His Life and World*. New York, 1980. Prize-winning and readable narrative account of the Russian tsar's life.

Monod, Paul K. *The Power of Kings: Monarchy and Religion in Europe, 1589–1715*. New Haven, 1999. A study of the seventeenth century's declining confidence in the divinity of kings.

Page Moch, Leslie. *Moving Europeans: Migration in Western Europe since 1650*. Bloomington, Indiana, 2003.

Quataert, Donald. *The Ottoman Empire, 1700–1822*. Cambridge and New York, 2000. Well balanced and intended to be read by students.

Riasanovsky, Nicholas V., and Steinberg, Mark D. *A History of Russia*. 7th ed. Oxford and New York, 2005. Far and away the best single-volume textbook on Russian history: balanced, comprehensive, and intelligent, with full bibliographies.

Saint-Simon, Louis. *Historical Memoirs*. Many editions. The classic source for life at Louis XIV's Versailles.

Snyder, Timothy. *The Reconstruction of Nations: Poland, Ukraine, Lithuania, Belarus, 1569–1999*. New Haven, 2004. Essential account of nation building and state collapse in eastern Europe with significant relevance to the region's contemporary situation.

Thomas, Hugh. *The Slave Trade: The History of the Atlantic Slave Trade, 1440–1870*. London and New York, 1997. A survey notable for its breadth and depth of coverage and for its attractive prose style.

Tracy, James D. *The Rise of Merchant Empires: Long-Distance Trade in the Early Modern World, 1350–1750*. Cambridge and New York, 1990. Important collection of essays by leading authorities.

White, Richard. *The Middle Ground: Indians, Empires and Republics in the Great Lakes Region, 1650–1815*. Cambridge, 1991. A path-breaking account of interactions between Europeans and Native Americans during the colonial period.

CHAPTER 16

Biagioli, Mario. *Galileo, Courtier*. Chicago, 1993. Emphasizes the importance of patronage and court politics in Galileo's science and career.

Cohen, I. B. *The Birth of a New Physics*. New York, 1985. Emphasizes the mathematical nature of the revolution; unmatched at making the mathematics understandable.

Daston, Lorraine, and Elizabeth Lunbeck, eds. *Histories of Scientific Observation*. Chicago, IL, 2011. Field-defining collection of essays on the history of scientific observation from the seventeenth to the twentieth centuries.

Daston, Lorraine. *Wonders and the Order of Nature, 1150–1750*. Cambridge, MA, 2001. Erudite, sweeping account of the history of science in the early modern period, emphasizing the natural philosopher's awe and wonder at the marvelous, the unfamiliar, and the counterintuitive.

Dear, Peter. *Revolutionizing the Sciences: European Knowledge and Its Ambitions, 1500–1700*. Princeton, NJ, 2001. Among the best short histories.

Drake, Stillman. *Discoveries and Opinions of Galileo*. Garden City, NY, 1957. The classic translation of Galileo's most important papers by his most admiring modern biographer.

Feingold, Mardechai. *The Newtonian Moment: Isaac Newton and the Making of Modern Culture*. New York, 2004. An engaging essay on the dissemination of Newton's thought, with excellent visual material.

Gaukroger, Stephen. *Descartes: An Intellectual Biography*. Oxford, 1995. Detailed and sympathetic study of the philosopher.

Gleick, James. *Isaac Newton*. New York, 2003. A vivid and well-documented brief biography.

Grafton, Anthony. *New Worlds, Ancient Texts: The Power of Tradition and the Shock of Discovery*. Cambridge, MA, 1992. Accessible essay by one of the leading scholars of early modern European thought.

Jacob, Margaret. *Scientific Culture and the Making of the Industrial West*. Oxford, 1997. A concise examination of the connections between developments in science and the Industrial Revolution.

Kuhn, Thomas. *The Structure of Scientific Revolutions*. Chicago, 1962. A classic and much-debated study of how scientific thought changes.

Pagden, Anthony. *European Encounters with the New World*. New Haven and London, 1993. Subtle and detailed on how European intellectuals thought about the lands they saw for the first time.

Rudwick, Martin J. S. *Earth's Deep History: How It Was Discovered and Why It Matters* (Chicago, 2014). A fascinating account of the origins of the geological sciences and awareness of the earth's long history before the advent of human civilizations.

Scheibinger, Londa. *The Mind Has No Sex? Women in the Origins of Modern Science*. Cambridge, MA, 1989. A lively and important recovery of the lost role played by women mathematicians and experimenters.

Shapin, Steven. *The Scientific Revolution*. Chicago, 1996. Engaging, accessible, and brief—organized thematically.

Shapin, Steven, and Simon Schaffer. *Leviathan and the Air Pump*. Princeton, NJ, 1985. A modern classic, on one of the most famous philosophical conflicts in seventeenth-century science.

Stephenson, Bruce. *The Music of the Heavens: Kepler's Harmonic Astronomy*. Princeton, NJ, 1994. An engaging and important explanation of Kepler's otherworldly perspective.

Thoren, Victor. *The Lord of Uraniborg: A Biography of Tycho Brahe*. Cambridge, 1990. A vivid reconstruction of the scientific revolution's most flamboyant astronomer.

Westfall, Richard. *The Construction of Modern Science*. Cambridge, 1977.

———. *Never at Rest: A Biography of Isaac Newton*. Cambridge, 1980. The standard work.

Wilson, Catherine. *The Invisible World: Early Modern Philosophy and the Invention of the Microscope*. Princeton, NJ, 1995. An important study of how the "microcosmic" world revealed by technology reshaped scientific philosophy and practice.

Zinsser, Judith P. *La Dame d'Esprit: A Biography of the Marquise Du Châtelet*. New York, 2006. An excellent cultural history. Issued in paperback as *Emilie du Châtelet: Daring Genius of the Enlightenment* (2007).

Glossary

1973 OPEC oil embargo Some leaders in the Arab-dominated Organization of the Petroleum Exporting Countries (OPEC) wanted to use oil as a weapon against the West in the Arab-Israeli conflict. After the 1972 Arab-Israeli war, OPEC instituted an oil embargo against Western powers. The embargo increased the price of oil and sparked spiraling inflation and economic troubles in Western nations, triggering in turn a cycle of dangerous recession that lasted nearly a decade. In response, Western governments began viewing the Middle Eastern oil regions as areas of strategic importance.

Abbasid caliphate (750–930) The Abbasid family claimed to be descendants of Muhammad, and in 750 they successfully led a rebellion against the Umayyads, seizing control of Muslim territories in Arabia, Persia, North Africa, and the Near East. The Abbasids modeled their behavior and administration on those of the Persian princes and their rule on that of the Persian Empire, establishing a new capital at Baghdad.

Peter Abelard (1079–1142) Highly influential philosopher, theologian, and teacher, often considered the founder of the University of Paris.

absolutism Form of government in which one person or body, usually the monarch, controls the right to make war, tax, judge, and coin money. The term was often used to refer to the state monarchies in seventeenth- and eighteenth-century Europe.

abstract expressionism The mid-twentieth-century school of art based in New York that included Jackson Pollock, Willem de Kooning, Franz Kline, and Helen Frankenthaler. It emphasized form, color, gesture, and feeling instead of figurative subjects.

Academy of Sciences This French institute of scientific inquiry was founded in 1666 by Louis XIV. France's statesmen exerted control over the academy and sought to share in the rewards of any discoveries its members made.

Aeneas Mythical founder of Rome, Aeneas was a refugee from the city of Troy whose adventures were described by the poet Virgil in the *Aeneid*, which was modeled on the oral epics of Homer.

Aetolian and Achaean Leagues These two alliances among Greek poleis were formed during the Hellenistic period in opposition to the Antigonids of Macedonia. Unlike the earlier defensive alliances of the classical period, each league was a real attempt to form a political federation.

African National Congress (ANC) Multiracial organization founded in 1912 whose goal was to end racial discrimination in South Africa.

Afrikaners Descendants of the original Dutch settlers of South Africa; formerly referred to as Boers.

agricultural revolution Numerous agricultural revolutions have occurred in the history of Western civilizations. One of the most significant began in the tenth century C.E. and increased the amount of land under cultivation as well as the productivity of the land. This revolution was made possible through the use of new technology, a rise in global temperatures, and more efficient methods of cultivation.

AIDS Acquired Immunodeficiency Syndrome. The final phase of HIV, AIDS first appeared in the 1970s and has developed into a global health catastrophe; it is spreading most quickly in developing nations in Africa and Asia.

Akhenaten (r. 1352–1336 B.C.E.) Pharaoh whose attempt to promote the worship of the sun god, Aten, ultimately weakened his dynasty's position in Egypt.

Alexander the Great (356–323 B.C.E.) The Macedonian king whose conquests of the Persian Empire and Egypt created a new Hellenistic world.

Alexander II (1818–1881) After the Crimean War, Tsar Alexander embarked on a program of reform and modernization, which included the emancipation of the serfs. A radical assassin killed him in 1881.

Alexius Comnenus (1057–1118) This Byzantine emperor requested Pope Urban II's help in raising an army to recapture Anatolia from the Seljuk Turks. Instead, Pope Urban II called for knights to go to the Holy Land and liberate it from its Muslim captors, launching the First Crusade.

Algerian War (1954–1962) The war between France and Algerians seeking independence. Led by the National Liberation Front (FLN), guerrillas fought the French army in the mountains and desert of Algeria. The FLN also initiated a campaign of bombing and terrorism in Algerian cities that led French soldiers to torture many Algerians, attracting world attention and international scandal.

Dante Alighieri (c. 1265–1321) Florentine poet and intellectual whose *Divine Comedy* was a pioneering work in the Italian vernacular and a vehicle for political and religious critique.

Allied Powers The First World War coalition of Great Britain, Ireland, Belgium, France, Italy, Russia, Portugal, Greece, Serbia, Montenegro, Albania, and Romania.

al Qaeda The radical Islamic organization founded in the late 1980s by former mujahidin who had fought against the Soviet Union in Afghanistan. Al Qaeda carried out the 9/11 terrorist attacks and is responsible as well for attacks in Africa, Southeast Asia, Europe, and the Middle East.

Ambrose (c. 340–397) One of the early church fathers, he helped define the relationship between the sacred authority of bishops and other Church leaders and the secular authority of worldly rulers. He believed that secular rulers were a part of the Church and therefore subject to it.

Americanization The fear of many Europeans, since the 1920s, that U.S. cultural products, such as film, television, and music, exerted too much influence. Many of the criticisms centered on America's emphasis on mass production and organization. Fears about Americanization were not limited to culture but extended to corporations, business techniques, global trade, and marketing.

Americas The name given to the two great landmasses of the New World, derived from the name of the Italian geographer Amerigo Vespucci. In 1492, Christopher Columbus reached the Bahamas and the island of Hispaniola, which began an era of Spanish conquest in North and South America. Originally, the Spanish had sought a route to Asia. Instead they discovered two continents whose wealth they decided to exploit. They were especially interested in gold and silver, which they either stole from indigenous peoples or mined, using indigenous peoples as labor. Silver became Spain's most lucrative export from the New World.

Amnesty International Nongovernmental organization formed in 1961 to defend "prisoners of conscience"—those detained for their beliefs, color, sex, ethnic origin, language, or religion.

Anabaptism Protestant movement that emerged in Switzerland in 1521; its adherents insisted that only adults could be baptized Christians.

anarchism In the nineteenth century, a political movement with the aim of establishing small-scale, localized, and self-sufficient democratic communities that could guarantee a maximum of individual sovereignty. Renouncing parties, unions, and any form of modern mass organization, the anarchists fell back on the tradition of conspiratorial violence.

Anatolia A region consisting of the peninsula linking Asia to Europe and reaching northward to the Black Sea, southward to the Mediterranean, and westward to the Aegean; often called "Asia Minor."

Anthropocene A term coined by geographers, geologists, and climate scientists to describe the era when human activities began to reshape earth's environment. Although some scholars contend that this epoch dates only as far back as the Industrial Revolution of the mid-nineteenth century, others date it from the Neolithic Revolution and the emergence of the earliest civilizations.

Anti–Corn Law League This organization successfully lobbied Parliament to repeal Britain's Corn Laws in 1846. The Corn Laws of 1815 had protected British landowners and farmers from foreign competition by establishing high tariffs, which kept bread prices artificially high for British consumers. The league saw these laws as unfair protection of the aristocracy and pushed for their repeal in the name of free trade.

anti-Semitism Anti-Semitism refers to hostility toward Jewish people. Religious forms of anti-Semitism have a long history in Europe, but during the nineteenth century anti-Semitism emerged as a potent ideology for mobilizing new constituencies in the era of mass politics. Playing on popular conspiracy theories about alleged Jewish influence in society, anti-Semites effectively rallied large bodies of supporters in France during the Dreyfus Affair, and then again during the rise of National Socialism in Germany after the First World War. The Holocaust would not have been possible without the acquiescence or cooperation of many thousands of people who shared anti-Semitic views.

apartheid The racial segregation policy of the Afrikaner-dominated South African government. Legislated in 1948 by the Afrikaner National Party, it existed in South Africa for many decades.

appeasement The policy pursued by Western governments in the face of German, Italian, and Japanese aggression leading up to the Second World War. The policy, which attempted to accommodate and negotiate peace with the aggressive nations, was based on the belief that another global war like the First World War was unimaginable, a belief that Germany and its allies had been mistreated by the terms of the Treaty of Versailles, and a fear that fascist Germany and its allies protected the West from the spread of Soviet communism.

Thomas Aquinas (1225–1274) Dominican friar and theologian whose systematic approach to Christian doctrine was influenced by Aristotle.

Arab-Israeli conflict Between the founding of the state of Israel in 1948 and the present, a series of wars has been fought between Israel and neighboring Arab nations: the war of 1948 when Israel defeated attempts by Egypt, Jordan, Iraq, Syria, and Lebanon to prevent the creation of the new state; the 1956 war between Israel and Egypt over the Sinai Peninsula; the 1967 war, when Israel gained control of additional land in the Golan Heights, the West Bank, the Gaza strip, and the Sinai; and the Yom Kippur War of 1973, when Israel once again fought with forces from Egypt and Syria. A particularly difficult issue in all of these conflicts has been the situation of the 950,000 Palestinian refugees made homeless by the first war in 1948 and the movement of Israeli settlers into the occupied territories (outside of Israel's original borders). In the late 1970s, peace talks between Israel and Egypt inspired some hope of peace, but an ongoing cycle of violence between Palestinians and the Israeli military has made a final settlement elusive.

Arab nationalism During the period of decolonization, secular forms of Arab nationalism, or pan-Arabism, found a wide following in many countries of the Middle East, especially in Egypt, Syria, and Iraq.

Arianism A variety of Christianity condemned as a heresy by the Roman Church, it derives from the teaching of a fourth-century priest named Arius, who rejected the idea that Jesus could be the divine equal of God.

aristocracy From the Greek word meaning "rule of the best." By 1000 B.C.E., the accumulated wealth of successful traders in Greece had created a new type of social class, which was based on wealth rather than warfare or birth. These men saw their wealth as a reflection of their superior qualities and aspired to emulate the heroes of old.

Aristotle (384–322 B.C.E.) A student of Plato, he based his philosophy on rational analysis of the material world. In contrast to his teacher, he stressed the rigorous investigation of real phenomena, rather than the development of universal ethics. He was, in turn, the teacher of Alexander the Great.

Armenian genocide The Ottoman government's attempt to exterminate the Armenian people with the Ottoman Empire during the First World War, resulting in the deaths of 1.5 million Armenians between 1914 and 1923.

Asiatic Society A cultural organization founded in 1784 by British Orientalists who lauded native culture but believed in colonial rule.

Assyrians A Semitic-speaking people that moved into northern Mesopotamia around 2400 B.C.E.

Athens Athens emerged as the Greek polis with the most markedly democratic form of government through a series of political struggles during the sixth century B.C.E. After its key role in the defeat of two invading Persian forces, Athens became the preeminent naval power of ancient Greece and the exemplar of Greek culture. But it antagonized many other poleis, and became embroiled in a war with Sparta and its allies in 431 B.C.E. Called the Peloponnesian War, this bloody conflict lasted until Athens was defeated in 404 B.C.E.

atomic bomb In 1945, the United States dropped atomic bombs on Hiroshima and Nagasaki in Japan, ending the Second World War. In 1949, the Soviet Union tested its first atomic bomb, and in 1953 both superpowers demonstrated their new hydrogen bombs. Strategically, the nuclearization of warfare polarized the world. Countries without nuclear weapons found it difficult to avoid joining either the Soviet or American military pacts. Over time, countries split into two groups: the superpowers with enormous military budgets and those countries that relied on agreements and international law. The nuclearization of warfare also encouraged "proxy wars" between clients of superpowers. Culturally, the hydrogen bomb came to symbolize the age as well as both humanity's power and its vulnerability.

Augustine (c. 354–397) One of the most influential theologians of all time, Augustine described his conversion to Christianity in his autobiographical *Confessions* and articulated a new Christian worldview in *The City of God*, among other works.

Augustus (63 B.C.E.–14 C.E.) Born Gaius Octavius, this grandnephew and adopted son of Julius Caesar came to power in 27 B.C.E. His reign signals the end of the Roman Republic and the beginning of the Principate, the period when Rome was dominated by autocratic emperors.

Auschwitz-Birkenau The Nazi concentration camp in Poland that was designed for the systematic murder of Jews and Gypsies. Between 1942 and 1944 over one million people were killed in Auschwitz-Birkenau.

Austro-Hungarian Empire The dual monarchy established by the Habsburg family in 1867; it collapsed at the end of the First World War.

authoritarianism A centralized and dictatorial form of government, proclaimed by its adherents to be superior to parliamentary democracy. Authoritarian governments claim to be above the law, do not respect individual rights, and do not tolerate political opposition. Authoritarian regimes that have developed a central ideology such as fascism or communism are sometimes termed "totalitarian."

Avignon A city in southeastern France that became the seat of the papacy between 1305 and 1377, a period known as the "Babylonian Captivity" of the Roman Church.

Aztecs An indigenous people of central Mexico; their empire was conquered by Spanish conquistadors in the sixteenth century.

baby boom (1950s) The post–Second World War upswing in U.S. birth rates; it reversed a century of decline.

Babylon An ancient city between the Tigris and Euphrates Rivers, which became the capital of Hammurabi's empire in the eighteenth century B.C.E. and continued to be an important administrative and commercial capital under many subsequent imperial powers, including the Neo-Assyrians, Chaldeans, Persians, and Romans. It was here that Alexander the Great died in 323 B.C.E.

Babylonian captivity Refers both to the Jews' exile in Babylon during the sixth century B.C.E. and the period from 1309 to 1378, when papal authority was subjugated to the French crown and the papal court was moved from Rome to the French city of Avignon.

Francis Bacon (1561–1626) British philosopher and scientist who pioneered the scientific method and inductive reasoning. In other words, he argued that thinkers should amass many observations and then draw general conclusions or propose theories on the basis of these data.

balance of powers The principle that no one country should be powerful enough to destabilize international relations. Starting in the seventeenth century, this goal of maintaining balance influenced diplomacy in western and central Europe for two centuries until the system collapsed with the onset of the First World War.

Balfour Declaration A letter dated November 2, 1917, by Lord Arthur J. Balfour, the British foreign secretary, that promised a homeland for the Jews in Palestine.

Laura Bassi (1711–1778) She was accepted into the Academy of Science in Bologna for her work in mathematics, which made her one of the few women to be accepted into a scientific academy in the seventeenth century.

Bastille The Bastille was a royal fortress and prison in Paris. In June 1789, a revolutionary crowd attacked the Bastille to show support for the newly created National Assembly. The fall of the Bastille was the first instance of the people's role in revolutionary change in France.

Bay of Pigs invasion (1961) The unsuccessful invasion of Cuba by Cuban exiles, supported by the U.S. government. The rebels intended to incite an insurrection in Cuba and overthrow the communist regime of Fidel Castro.

Cesare Beccaria (1738–1794) An influential writer during the Enlightenment who advocated for legal reforms. He believed that the only legitimate rationale for punishments was to maintain social order and to prevent other crimes. He argued for the greatest possible leniency compatible with deterrence and opposed torture and the death penalty.

Thomas Becket (1118–1170) Archbishop of Canterbury whose opposition to King Henry II's innovations to the court system led to his exile and later assassination by the king's knights. Beckett was later proclaimed a martyr and saint, and his tomb at Canterbury became one of the most important pilgrimage sites in Europe.

Beer Hall Putsch (1923) An early attempt by the Nazi party to seize power in Munich; Adolf Hitler was imprisoned for a year after the incident.

Benedict of Nursia (c. 480–c. 547) Benedict's rule for monks formed the basis of Western monasticism and is still observed in monasteries all over the world.

Benedictine monasticism This form of monasticism was developed by Benedict of Nursia. Its followers adhere to a defined cycle of daily prayers, lessons, communal worship, and manual labor.

Jeremy Bentham (1748–1832) Influential British liberal philosopher who proposed in his major work, *The Principles of Morals and Legislation* (1789), that society adopt the organizing principle of utilitarianism.

Berlin airlift The transport in 1948 of vital supplies to West Berlin by air, primarily under U.S. auspices, in response to a blockade of the city that had been instituted by the Soviet Union to force the Allies to abandon West Berlin.

Berlin Conference At this conference in 1884, the leading colonial powers met and established ground rules for the partition of Africa by European nations. By 1914, 90 percent of African territory was under European control. The Berlin Conference ceded control of the Congo region to a private company run by King Leopold II of Belgium. The company agreed to make the Congo valleys open to free trade and commerce, to end the slave trade in the region, and to establish a Congo Free State. In reality, King Leopold II's company established a regime that was so brutal in its treatment of local populations that an international scandal forced the Belgian state to take over the colony in 1908.

Berlin Wall The wall built in 1961 by the East German Communists to prevent citizens of East Germany from fleeing to West Germany; it was torn down in 1989.

birth control pill This oral contraceptive became widely available in the mid-1960s. For the first time, women had a simple method of birth control that they could take themselves.

Otto von Bismarck (1815–1898) The prime minister of Prussia and later the first chancellor of a unified Germany, Bismarck was the architect of German unification and helped to consolidate the new nation's economic and military power.

Black Death The epidemic of bubonic plague that ravaged Europe, Asia, and North Africa during the fourteenth century, killing one third to one half of the population.

Blackshirts The troops of Mussolini's fascist regime; the squads received money from Italian landowners to attack socialist leaders.

Black Tuesday October 29, 1929, the day on which the U.S. stock market crashed, plunging the U.S. and international trading systems into crisis and leading to the Great Depression.

William Blake (1757–1827) Romantic writer who criticized industrial society and factories. He championed the imagination and poetic vision, seeing both as transcending the limits of the material world.

Blitzkrieg The German "lightning war" strategy used during the Second World War; the Germans invaded Poland, France, Russia, and other countries with fast-moving and well-coordinated attacks using aircraft, tanks, and other armored vehicles, followed by infantry.

Bloody Sunday On January 22, 1905, the Russian tsar's guards killed 130 demonstrators who were protesting the tsar's mistreatment of workers and the middle class.

Jean Bodin (1530–1596) A French political philosopher whose *Six Books of the Commonwealth* advanced a theory of absolute sovereignty, on the grounds that the state's paramount duty is to maintain order and that monarchs should therefore exercise unlimited power.

Giovanni Boccaccio (1313–1375) Florentine author best known for his *Decameron*, a collection of prose tales about sex, adventure, and trickery written in the Italian vernacular after the Black Death.

Boer War (1898–1902) Conflict between British and ethnically European Afrikaners in South Africa, with terrible casualties on both sides.

Boethius (c. 480–524) A member of a prominent Roman family, he sought to preserve aspects of ancient learning by compiling a series of handbooks and anthologies appropriate for Christian readers. His translations of Greek philosophy provided a crucial link between classical Greek thought and the early intellectual culture of Christianity.

Bolsheviks Former members of the Russian Social Democratic Party who advocated the destruction of capitalist political and economic institutions and started the Russian Revolution. In 1918, the Bolsheviks changed their name to the Russian Communist Party. Prominent Bolsheviks included Vladimir Lenin and Joseph Stalin. Leon Trotsky joined the Bolsheviks late but became a prominent leader in the early years of the Russian Revolution.

Napoleon Bonaparte (1769–1821) Corsican-born French general who seized power and ruled as dictator and emperor from 1799 to 1814. After the successful conquest of much of Europe, he was defeated by Russian and Prussian forces and died in exile.

Boniface VIII During his pontificate (1294–1303), repeated claims to papal authority were challenged by King Philip IV of France. When Boniface died in 1309 (at the hands of Philip's thugs), the French king moved the papal court from Rome to the French city of Avignon, where it remained until 1378.

Sandro Botticelli (1445–1510) An Italian painter devoted to the blending of classical and Christian motifs by using ideas associated with the pagan past to illuminate sacred stories.

bourgeoisie Term for the middle class, derived from the French word for a town dweller, *bourgeois.*

Boxer Rebellion (1899–1900) Chinese peasant movement that opposed foreign influence, especially that of Christian missionaries; it was finally put down after the Boxers were defeated by a foreign army composed mostly of Japanese, Russian, British, French, and American soldiers.

Tycho Brahe (1546–1601) Danish astronomer who believed that the careful study of the heavens would unlock the secrets of the universe. For over twenty years, he charted the movements of significant objects in the night sky, compiling the finest set of astronomical data in Europe.

Brexit A public referendum in June 2016 in which the population of the United Kingdom, by a slim majority, voted to leave the European Union (EU). This marked the first time that a member nation chose to retreat from the goal of increased integration with other members of the EU. The Brexit vote was controversial in Scotland and Northern Ireland, because in these areas of the United Kingdom, a majority expressed a wish to remain in the EU.

British Commonwealth of Nations Formed in 1926, the Commonwealth conferred dominion status on Britain's white settler colonies in Canada, Australia, and New Zealand.

Bronze Age (3200–1200 B.C.E.) The name given to the era characterized by the discovery of techniques for smelting bronze (an alloy of copper and tin), which was then the strongest known metal.

Brownshirts Troops of young German men who dedicated themselves to the Nazi cause in the early 1930s by holding street marches, mass rallies, and confrontations. They engaged in beatings of Jews and anyone who opposed the Nazis.

Edmund Burke (1729–1797) Conservative Anglo-Irish writer and member of the British Parliament who was critical of the French Revolution and its goal of radical political change.

George Gordon, Lord Byron (1788–1824) Writer and poet whose life helped give the Romantics their reputation as rebels against conformity. He was known for his love affairs, his defense of working-class movements, and his passionate engagement in politics, which led to his death in the war for Greek independence.

Byzantium A small settlement located at the mouth of the Black Sea and at the crossroads between Europe and Asia, it was chosen by Constantine as the site for his new imperial capital of Constantinople in 324. Modern historians use this name to refer to the eastern Roman Empire, which lasted in this region until 1453, but the inhabitants of that empire referred to themselves as Romans.

Julius Caesar (100–44 B.C.E.) The Roman general who conquered the Gauls, invaded Britain, and expanded Rome's territory in Asia Minor. He became the dictator of Rome in 46 B.C.E. His assassination led to the rise of his grand-nephew and adopted son, Gaius Octavius Caesar, who ruled the Roman Empire as Caesar Augustus.

caliphs Islamic rulers who claim descent from the prophet Muhammad.

John Calvin (1509–1564) French-born theologian and reformer whose radical form of Protestantism was adopted in many Swiss cities, notably Geneva.

Canary Islands Islands off the western coast of Africa that were colonized by Portugal and Spain in the mid-fifteenth century, after which they became bases for further expeditions around the African coast and across the Atlantic.

Carbonari An underground organization that opposed the Concert of Europe's restoration of monarchies. They held influence in southern Europe during the 1820s, especially in Italy.

Carolingian Derived from the Latin name Carolus (Charles), this term refers to the Frankish dynasty that began with the rise to power of Charlemagne's grandfather, Charles Martel (688–741). At its height under Charlemagne (Charles "the Great"), this dynasty controlled what are now France, Germany, northern Italy, Catalonia, and portions of central Europe. The Carolingian Empire collapsed under the combined weight of Viking raids, economic disintegration, and the growing power of local lords.

Carolingian Renaissance A cultural and intellectual flowering that took place around the court of Charlemagne in the late eighth and early ninth centuries.

Carthage The great maritime empire that grew out of Phoenician trading colonies in North Africa and rivaled the power of Rome. Its wars with Rome, collectively known as the Punic Wars, ended in its destruction in 146 B.C.E.

Cassidorus (c. 490–c. 583) Member of an old senatorial family, he was largely responsible for introducing classical learning into the monastic curriculum and for turning monasteries into centers for the collection, preservation, and transmission of knowledge. His *Institutes*, an influential handbook of classical literature for Christian readers, was intended as a preface to more intensive study of theology and the Bible.

Catalonia Maritime region in northeastern Spain; during the thirteenth century, Catalan adventurers conquered and colonized a series of western Mediterranean islands.

Catholic Church The "universal" (catholic) church based in Rome, which was redefined in the sixteenth century, when the Counter-Reformation resulted in the rebirth of the Catholic faith at the Council of Trent.

Margaret Cavendish (1623–1673) English natural philosopher who developed her own speculative natural philosophy. She used this philosophy to critique those who excluded her from scientific debate.

Camillo Benso di Cavour (1810–1861) Prime minister of Piedmont-Sardinia and founder of the Italian Liberal party; he played a key role in the movement for Italian unification under the Piedmontese king, Victor Emmanuel II.

Central Powers The First World War alliance between Germany, Austria-Hungary, Bulgaria, and Turkey.

Charlemagne (742–814) As king of the Franks (767–813), Charles "the Great" consolidated much of western Europe under his rule. In 800, he was crowned emperor by the pope in Rome, establishing a problematic precedent that would have wide-ranging consequences for western Europe's relationship with the eastern Roman Empire in Byzantium and for the relationship between the papacy and secular rulers.

Charles I (r. 1625–1649) The second Stuart king of England, Ireland, and Scotland, Charles attempted to rule without the support of Parliament, sparking a controversy that erupted into civil war in 1642. The king's forces were ultimately defeated and Charles himself was executed by act of Parliament, the first time in history that a ruling king was legally deposed and executed by his own government.

Charles II Nominally king of England, Ireland, and Scotland after his father Charles I's execution in 1649, Charles II lived in exile until he was restored to the throne in 1660. Influenced by his cousin, King Louis XIV of France, he presided over an opulent royal court until his death in 1685.

Chartism A working-class movement in Britain that called for reform of the British political system during the 1840s. The Chartists were supporters of the "People's Charter," which had six demands: universal white male suffrage, secret ballots, an end to property qualifications as a condition of public office, annual parliamentary elections, salaries for members of the House of Commons, and equal electoral districts.

Geoffrey Chaucer (1340–1400) English poet whose collection of versified stories, *The Canterbury Tales*, features characters from a variety of classes.

Christendom A term used to denote an ideal vision of Christian unity—political and cultural, as well as spiritual—promoted by powerful Christian rulers, beginning with Charlemagne. The "Holy Roman Empire," a term coined by Frederick I Barbarossa, was an outgrowth of this idea. Christendom was never a united entity, but it was a powerful vision.

Christine de Pizan (c. 1364–c. 1431) Born in Italy, Christine spent her adult life attached to the French court and, after her husband's death, became the first laywoman to earn her living by writing. She was the author of treatises on warfare and chivalry as well as of books and pamphlets that challenged long-standing misogynistic claims.

Church of England Founded by Henry VIII in the 1530s, as a consequence of his break with the authority of the Roman pope.

Winston Churchill (1874–1965) British prime minister who led the country during the Second World War. He also coined the phrase "Iron Curtain" in a speech at Westminster College in 1946.

Marcus Tullius Cicero (106–43 B.C.E.) Influential Roman senator, orator, Stoic philosopher, and prose stylist. His published writings still form the basis of instruction in classical Latin grammar and usage.

Lucius Quinctius Cincinnatus (519–c. 430 B.C.E.) A legendary citizen-farmer of Rome who reluctantly accepted an appointment as dictator. After defeating Rome's enemies, he allegedly left his political office and returned to his farm.

Civil Constitution of the Clergy Issued by the French National Assembly in 1790, the Civil Constitution of the Clergy decreed that all bishops and priests should be subject to the authority of the state. Their salaries were to be paid out of the public treasury, and they were required to swear allegiance to the new state, making it clear that they served France rather than Rome. The Assembly's aim was to make the Catholic Church of France a truly national and civil institution.

civilizing mission The basis of an argument made by Europeans to justify colonial expansion in the nineteenth century. Supporters of this idea believed that Europeans had a duty to impose Western ideas of economic and political progress on the indigenous peoples they ruled over in their colonies. In practice, the colonial powers often found that ambitious plans to impose European practices on colonial subjects led to unrest that threatened the stability of colonial rule. By the early twentieth century most colonial powers were more cautious in their plans for political or cultural transformation.

civil rights movement The Second World War increased African American migration from the American South to northern cities, intensifying a drive for rights, dignity, and independence. By 1960, civil rights groups had started organizing boycotts and demonstrations directed at discrimination against blacks in the South. During the 1960s, civil rights laws passed under President Lyndon B. Johnson did bring African Americans some equality with regard to voting rights and, to a much lesser degree, school desegregation. However, racism continued in areas such as housing, job opportunities, and the economic development of African American communities.

Civil War (1861–1865) Conflict between the northern and southern states of America that cost over 600,000 lives; this struggle led to the abolition of slavery in the United States.

classical learning The study of ancient Greek and Latin texts. After Christianity became the only legal religion of the Roman Empire, scholars needed to find a way to make classical learning applicable to a Christian way of life. Christian monks played a significant role in resolving this problem by reinterpreting the classics for a Christian audience.

Cluny A powerful Benedictine monastery founded in 910 whose enormous wealth and prestige derived its independence from secular authorities as well as from its wide network of daughter houses (priories).

Cold War (1945–1991) Ideological, political, and economic conflict in which the USSR and Eastern Europe opposed the United States and Western Europe in the decades after the Second World War. The Cold War's origins lay in the breakup of the wartime alliance between the United States and the Soviet Union in 1945 and resulted in a division of Europe into two spheres: the West, committed to market capitalism; and the East, which sought to build socialist republics in areas under Soviet control. The Cold War ended with the collapse of the Soviet Union in 1991.

collectivization Stalin's plan for nationalizing agricultural production, begun in 1929. Twenty-five million peasants were forced to give up their land and join 250,000 large collective farms. Many who resisted were deported to labor camps in the Far East, and Stalin's government cut off food rations to those areas most marked by resistance to collectivization. In the ensuing human-caused famines, millions of people starved to death.

Columbian exchange The widespread exchange of peoples, plants, animals, diseases, goods, and culture between the African and Eurasian landmass (on the one hand) and the region that encompasses the Americas, Australia, and the Pacific Islands (on the other); precipitated by Christopher Columbus's voyage in 1492.

Christopher Columbus (1451–1506) A Genoese sailor who persuaded King Ferdinand and Queen Isabella of Spain to fund his expedition across the Atlantic, with the purpose of discovering a new trade route to Asia. His miscalculations landed him in the Bahamas and the island of Hispaniola in 1492.

commercial revolution A period of economic development in Europe lasting from c. 1500 to c. 1800. Advances in agriculture and handicraft production, combined with the expansion of trade networks in the Atlantic world, brought new wealth and new kinds of commercial activity to Europe. The commercial revolution prepared the way for the Industrial Revolution of the 1800s.

Committee of Public Safety Political body during the French Revolution that was controlled by the Jacobins, who defended the revolution by executing thousands during the Reign of Terror (September 1793–July 1794).

commune A community of individuals who have banded together in a sworn association, with the aim of establishing their independence and setting up their own form of representative government. Many medieval towns originally founded by lords or monasteries gained their independence through such methods.

The Communist Manifesto Radical pamphlet by Karl Marx (1818–1883) that predicted the downfall of the capitalist system and its replacement by a classless, egalitarian society. Marx believed that this revolution would be accomplished by the workers (the proletariat).

Compromise of 1867 Agreement between the Habsburgs and the peoples living in Hungarian parts of the empire that the Habsburg state would be officially known as the Austro-Hungarian Empire.

Concert of Europe (1814–1815) The body of diplomatic agreements designed primarily by the Austrian minister Klemens von Metternich between 1814 and 1848 and supported by other European powers until 1914. Its goal was to maintain a balance of power on the Continent and to prevent destabilizing social and political change in Europe.

conciliarism A doctrine developed in the thirteenth and fourteenth centuries to counter the growing power of the papacy, conciliarism holds that papal authority should be subject to a council of the Church at large. Conciliarists emerged as a dominant force after the Council of Constance (1414–1418) but were eventually outmatched by a rejuvenated papacy.

Congress of Vienna (1814–1815) International conference to reorganize Europe after the downfall of Napoleon and the French Revolution. European monarchies restored the Bourbon family to the French throne and agreed to respect each other's borders and to cooperate in guarding against future revolutions and war.

conquistador Spanish term for "conqueror," applied to the mercenaries and adventurers who campaigned against indigenous peoples in central and South America.

conservatives In the nineteenth century, conservatives aimed to legitimize and solidify the monarchy's authority and the hierarchical social order. They believed that change had to be slow, incremental, and managed so that the structures of authority were strengthened and not weakened.

Constantine (275–337 C.E.) The first emperor of Rome to convert to Christianity, Constantine came to power in 312 C.E. In 324 C.E., he founded a new imperial capital, Constantinople, on the site of a maritime settlement known as Byzantium.

Constantinople Founded by the emperor Constantine on the site of a village called Byzantium, Constantinople became the new capital of the Roman Empire in 324 C.E. and continued to be the seat of imperial power after its capture by the Ottoman Turks in 1453. It is now known as Istanbul.

contract theory of government A theory of government written by Englishman John Locke (1632–1704) that posits that government authority is both contractual and conditional; therefore, if a government has abused its given authority, society has the right to dissolve it and create another.

Nicolaus Copernicus (1473–1543) Polish astronomer who advanced the idea that the earth revolves around the sun.

cosmopolitanism Stemming from the Greek word meaning "universal city," the culture characteristic of the Hellenistic world challenged and transformed the narrower worldview of the Greek polis.

cotton gin Invented by Eli Whitney in 1793, this device mechanized the process of separating cotton seeds from cotton fibers, which sped up the production of cotton and reduced its price. This change made slavery profitable in the United States.

Council of Constance (1417–1420) A meeting of clergy and theologians in an effort to resolve the Great Schism within the Roman Church. The council deposed all rival papal candidates and elected a new pope, Martin V, but it also adopted the doctrine of conciliarism, which holds that the supreme authority within the Church rests with a representative general council and not with the pope. However, Martin V himself was an opponent of this doctrine and refused to be bound by it.

Council of Trent The name given to a series of meetings held in the Italian city of Trent (Trento) between 1545 and 1563, when leaders of the Roman Church reaffirmed Catholic doctrine and instituted internal reforms.

Counter-Reformation The movement to counter the Protestant Reformation, initiated by the Catholic Church at the Council of Trent in 1545.

coup d'état French term for the overthrow of an established government by a group of conspirators, usually with military support.

Crimean War (1854–1856) War waged by Russia against Great Britain and France. Spurred by Russia's encroachment on Ottoman territories, the conflict revealed Russia's military weakness when Russian forces fell to British and French troops.

Crusader States The four fragile European principalities established on the eastern coast of the Mediterranean after the First Crusade (1096–1099): the county of Edessa (which effectively disappeared by 1150), the principality of Antioch (until 1268), the county of Tripoli (until 1291), and the kingdom of Jerusalem (which lost control of Jerusalem itself in 1187 and fell in 1291).

Cuban missile crisis (1962) Diplomatic standoff between the United States and the Soviet Union that was provoked by the Soviet Union's attempt to base nuclear missiles in Cuba; it brought the world closer to nuclear war than ever before or since.

cuius regio, eius religio A Latin phrase meaning "as the ruler, so the religion." Adopted as a part of the settlement of the Peace of Augsburg in 1555, it meant that those principalities ruled by Lutherans would have Lutheranism as their official religion and those ruled by Catholics must practice Catholicism.

cult of domesticity Concept associated with Victorian England that idealized women as nurturing wives and mothers.

cult of the Blessed Virgin The beliefs and practices associated with the veneration of Mary, the mother of Jesus, which became increasingly popular in the twelfth century.

cuneiform An early writing system that began to develop in Mesopotamia during the fourth millennium B.C.E. By 3100 B.C.E., its distinctive markings were impressed on clay tablets using a wedge-shaped stylus.

Cyrus the Great (c. 585–529 B.C.E.) As architect of the Persian Empire, Cyrus extended his dominion over a vast territory stretching from the Persian Gulf to the Mediterranean and incorporating the ancient civilizations of Mesopotamia. His successors ruled this Persian Empire as "Great Kings."

Darius (521–486 B.C.E.) The Persian emperor whose conflict with Aristagoras, the Greek ruler of Miletus, ignited the Persian Wars. In 490 B.C.E., Darius sent a large army to punish the Athenians for their intervention in Persian imperial affairs, but this force was defeated by Athenian hoplites on the plain of Marathon.

Charles Darwin (1809–1882) British naturalist who wrote *On the Origin of Species* and developed the theory of natural selection to explain the evolution of organisms.

D-Day (June 6, 1944) Date of the Allied invasion of Normandy, under General Dwight Eisenhower, to liberate Western Europe from German occupation.

Decembrists Nineteenth-century Russian army officers who were influenced by events in France and formed secret societies that espoused liberal governance. They were put down by Nicholas I in December 1825.

Declaration of Independence (1776) Historic document stating the principles of government on which the United States was founded.

Declaration of the Rights of Man and of the Citizen (1789) French charter of liberties formulated by the National Assembly during the French Revolution. The seventeen articles later became the preamble to the new constitution, which the assembly finished in 1791.

democracy In ancient Greece, this form of government allowed a class of propertied male citizens to participate in the governance of their polis; but it excluded women, slaves, and citizens without property from the political process. As a result, the ruling class amounted to only a small percentage of the entire population.

René Descartes (1596–1650) French philosopher and mathematician who emphasized the use of deductive reasoning.

Denis Diderot (1713–1784) French philosophe and author who was the guiding force behind the publication of the first encyclopedia. His *Encyclopedia* showed how reason could be applied to nearly all realms of thought and aimed to be a compendium of all human knowledge.

Dien Bien Phu (1954) Defining battle in the war between French colonialists and the Viet Minh that secured North Vietnam for Ho Chi Minh and his army and left the south to form its own government, which was supported by France and the United States.

Diet of Worms The select council of the Church that convened in the German city of Worms and condemned Martin Luther on a charge of heresy in 1521.

Diocletian (245–316 C.E.) As emperor of Rome from 284 to 305 C.E., Diocletian recognized that the empire could not be governed by one man in one place. His solution was to divide the empire into four parts, each with its own imperial ruler, but he himself remained the dominant ruler of the resulting tetrarchy ("rule of four"). He also initiated the Great Persecution, a time when many Christians became martyrs to their faith.

Directory (1795–1799) Executive committee that governed after the fall of Robespierre and held control until the coup of Napoleon Bonaparte.

Discourse on Method Philosophical treatise by René Descartes (1596–1650) proposing that the path to knowledge was through logical deduction, beginning with one's own self: "I think, therefore I am."

Dominican order Also called the Order of Preachers, it was founded by Dominic of Osma (1170–1221), a Castilian preacher and theologian, and approved by Innocent III in 1216. The order was dedicated to the rooting out of heresy and the conversion of Jews and Muslims. Many of its members held teaching positions in European universities and contributed to the development of medieval philosophy and theology. Others became the leading administrators of the Inquisition.

dominion in the British Commonwealth Status granted to Canada after its promise to maintain fealty to the British crown, even after gaining independence in 1867; later applied to Australia and New Zealand.

Dreyfus Affair The 1894 French scandal surrounding accusations that a Jewish captain, Alfred Dreyfus, sold military secrets to the Germans. Convicted, Dreyfus was sentenced to solitary confinement for life. However, after a public outcry, it was revealed that the trial documents were forgeries, and Dreyfus was pardoned after a second trial in 1899. In 1906, he was fully exonerated and reinstated in the army. The affair revealed the depths of popular anti-Semitism in France.

Alexander Dubček (1921–1992) Communist leader of the Czechoslovakian government who advocated for "socialism with a human face." He encouraged debate within the party, academic and artistic freedom, and less censorship, which led to the "Prague spring" of 1968. People in other parts of Eastern Europe began to demonstrate in support of Dubček and demanded their own reforms. When Dubček tried to democratize the Communist party and did not attend a meeting of the Warsaw Pact, the Soviets sent tanks and troops into Prague and ousted Dubček and his allies.

Duma The Russian parliament, created in response to the revolution of 1905.

Dunkirk The French port on the English Channel where British and French forces retreated after sustaining heavy losses against the German military. Between May 27 and June 4, 1940, the Royal Navy evacuated over 300,000 troops in commercial and pleasure boats.

Eastern Front Battlefront between Berlin and Moscow during the First and Second World Wars.

East India Company (1600–1858) British charter company created to outperform Portuguese and Spanish traders in the Far East; in the eighteenth century the company became, in effect, the ruler of a large part of India. There was also a Dutch East India Company.

Edict of Nantes (1598) Issued by Henry IV of France in an effort to end religious violence. The edict declared France to be a Catholic country but tolerated some forms of Protestant worship.

Edward I King of England from 1272 to his death in 1307, Edward presided over the creation of new legal and bureaucratic institutions in his realm, violently subjugated the Welsh, and attempted to colonize Scotland. He expelled English Jews from his domain in 1290.

Eleanor of Aquitaine (1122–1204) Ruler of the wealthy province of Aquitaine and wife of Louis VII of France, Eleanor had her marriage annulled in order to marry the young count of Anjou, Henry Plantagenet, who became King Henry II of England a year later. The mother of two future kings of England, she was an important patron of the arts.

Elizabeth I (1533–1603) The Protestant daughter of Henry VIII and his second wife, Anne Boleyn, Elizabeth succeeded her sister Mary as the second queen regnant of England (1558–1603).

emancipation of the serfs (1861) The abolition of serfdom was central to Tsar Alexander II's program of modernization and reform, but it produced a limited amount of change. Former serfs now had legal rights. However, farmland was granted to village communes instead of to individuals. The land was of poor quality, and the former serfs had to pay installments for it to the village commune.

emperor Originally the term for any conquering commander of the Roman army whose victories merited celebration in an official triumph. After Augustus seized power in 27 b.c.e., it was the title borne by the sole ruler of the Roman Empire.

empire A centralized political entity consolidated through the conquest and colonization of other nations or peoples in order to benefit the ruler and/or his homeland.

Enabling Act (1933) Emergency act passed by the Reichstag (German parliament) that helped transform Hitler from Germany's chancellor, or prime minister, into a dictator, following the suspicious burning of the Reichstag building and a suspension of civil liberties.

enclosure Long process of privatizing what had been public agricultural land in eighteenth-century Britain; it helped to stimulate the development of commercial agriculture and forced many people in rural areas to seek work in cities during the early stages of industrialization.

Encyclopedia Joint venture of French philosophe writers, led by Denis Diderot (1713–1784), which proposed to summarize all modern knowledge in a multivolume illustrated work with over 70,000 articles.

Friedrich Engels (1820–1895) German social and political philosopher who collaborated with Karl Marx on many publications.

English Civil War (1642–1649) Conflicts between the English Parliament and King Charles I erupted into civil war, which ended in the defeat of the royalists and the execution of Charles on charges of treason against the crown. A short time later, Parliament's hereditary House of Lords was abolished and England was declared a Commonwealth.

English Navigation Act of 1651 Act stipulating that only English ships could carry goods between the mother country and its colonies.

English Peasants' Revolt Violent 1381 uprising in London, during which thousands of people marched on London to demand an end to serfdom and called for the redistribution of property. It ended with the arrest and execution of the ringleaders.

Enlightenment Intellectual movement in eighteenth-century Europe with a belief in human betterment through the application of reason to solve social, economic, and political problems.

Epicureanism A philosophical position articulated by Epicurus of Athens (c. 342–270 b.c.e.), who rejected the idea of an ordered universe governed by divine forces; instead, he emphasized individual agency and proposed that the highest good is the pursuit of pleasure.

Desiderius Erasmus (c. 1469–1536) Dutch-born scholar, social commentator, and Catholic humanist whose new translation of the Bible influenced the theology of Martin Luther.

Estates General The representative body of the three estates in France. In 1789, King Louis XVI summoned the Estates General to meet for the first time since 1614 because it seemed to be the only solution to France's worsening economic crisis and financial chaos.

Etruscans Settlers of the Italian peninsula who dominated the region from the late Bronze Age until the rise of the Roman Republic in the sixth century B.C.E.

Euclid Hellenistic mathematician whose *Elements of Geometry* (c. 300 B.C.E.) forms the basis of modern geometry.

eugenics A Greek term, meaning "good birth," referring to the project of "breeding" a superior human race. It was popularly championed by scientists, politicians, and social critics in the late nineteenth and early twentieth centuries.

Eurasia The preferred term for the geographical expanse that encompasses both Europe and Asia.

European Common Market (1957) The Treaty of Rome established the European Economic Community (EEC), or Common Market. The original members were France, West Germany, Italy, Belgium, Holland, and Luxembourg. The EEC sought to abolish trade barriers between its members and it pledged itself to common external tariffs, the free movement of labor and capital among the member nations, and uniform wage structures and social security systems to create similar working conditions in all member countries.

European Union (EU) Successor organization to the European Economic Community or European Common Market, formed by the Maastricht Treaty, which took effect in 1993. Currently twenty-eight member states compose the EU, which has a governing council, an international court, and a parliament. Over time, member states of the EU have relinquished some of their sovereignty, and cooperation has evolved into a community with a single currency, the euro.

Exclusion Act of 1882 U.S. law prohibiting nearly all immigration from China to the United States; fueled by animosity toward Chinese workers in the American West.

existentialism Philosophical movement that arose out of the Second World War and emphasized the absurdity of human condition. Led by Jean-Paul Sartre and Albert Camus, existentialists encouraged humans to take responsibility for their own decisions and dilemmas.

expulsion of the Jews European rulers began to expel their Jewish subjects from their kingdoms beginning in the 1280s, mostly due to their inability to repay the money they had extorted from Jewish moneylenders but also as a result of escalating anti-Semitism in the wake of the Crusades. Jews were also expelled from the Rhineland during the fourteenth century and from Spain in 1492.

fascism The doctrine formulated by Benito Mussolini, which emphasized three main ideas: statism ("nothing above the state, nothing outside the state, nothing against the state"), nationalism, and militarism. Its name derives from the Latin *fasces*, a symbol of Roman imperial power adopted by Mussolini.

Fashoda Incident (1898) Disagreements between the French and the British over land claims in North Africa led to a standoff between armies of the two nations at the Sudanese town of Fashoda. The crisis was solved diplomatically. France ceded southern Sudan to Britain in exchange for a stop to further expansion by the British.

Federal Republic of Germany Nation founded from the Allied zones of occupation of Germany after the Second World War; also known as West Germany.

The Feminine Mystique Groundbreaking book by the feminist Betty Friedan (1921–2006), who tried to define *femininity* and explored how women internalized those definitions.

Franz Ferdinand (1863–1914) Archduke of Austria and heir to the Austro-Hungarian Empire; his assassination led to the beginning of the First World War.

Ferdinand (1452–1516) **and Isabella** (1451–1504) In 1469, Ferdinand of Aragon married the heiress to Castile, Isabella. Their union allowed them to pursue several ambitious policies, including the conquest of Granada, the last Muslim principality in Spain, and the expulsion of Spain's large Jewish community. In 1492, Isabella granted three ships to Christopher Columbus of Genoa (Italy), who went on to claim portions of the New World for Spain.

Fertile Crescent An area of fertile land comprising what are now Syria, Israel, Turkey, eastern Iraq, and western Iran that was able to sustain settlements due to its wetter climate and abundant natural food resources. Some of the earliest known civilizations emerged there between 9000 and 4500 B.C.E.

feudalism A problematic modern term that attempts to explain the diffusion of power in medieval Europe and the many different kinds of political, social, and economic relationships that were forged through the giving and receiving of fiefs (*feoda*). But because it is anachronistic and inadequate, this term has been rejected by most historians of the medieval period.

financial crisis of 2008 A global economic crisis following the sudden collapse of real estate prices in many parts of the world in 2008. The effects of this crisis were magnified by the increased level of globalization in the world economy, particularly in banking and the financial industry. In order to prevent a complete collapse of the global economy, governments in the United States and in Europe provided bailouts to cash-strapped banks and financial institutions, funded by taxpayers.

First Crusade (1095–1099) Launched by Pope Urban II in response to a request from the Byzantine emperor Alexius Comnenus. Alexius had asked for a small contingent of knights to assist him in fighting Turkish forces in Anatolia, but Urban instead directed the crusaders' energies toward the Holy Land and the recapture of Jerusalem, promising those who took the cross (*crux*) that they would merit eternal salvation if they died in the attempt. This crusade prompted attacks against Jews throughout Europe and resulted in six subsequent—and unsuccessful—military campaigns.

First World War A total war from August 1914 to November 1918, involving the armies of Britain, France, and Russia (the Allies) against Germany, Austria-Hungary, and the Ottoman Empire (the Central Powers). Italy joined the Allies in 1915, and the United States joined them in 1917, helping to tip the balance in favor of the Allies, who also drew on the populations and raw materials of their colonial possessions. Also known as the Great War.

Five Pillars of Islam The Muslim teaching that salvation is assured only through observance of five basic precepts: submission to God's will as described in the teachings of Muhammad, frequent prayer, ritual fasting, the giving of alms, and an annual pilgrimage to Mecca (the Hajj).

Five-Year Plan Soviet effort launched under Stalin in 1928 to replace the market with a state-owned and state-managed economy in order to promote rapid economic development over a five-year period and thereby "catch and overtake" the leading capitalist countries. The First Five-Year Plan was followed by the Second Five-Year Plan (1933–1937) and so on, until the collapse of the Soviet Union in 1991.

fly shuttle Invented by John Kay in 1733, this device sped up the process of weaving.

Charles Fourier (1772–1837) French philosopher and thinker who sought to organize utopian societies.

Fourteen Points President Woodrow Wilson proposed these points as the foundation on which to build peace in the world after the First World War. They called for an end to secret treaties, "open covenants, openly arrived at," freedom of the seas, the removal of international tariffs, the reduction of arms, the "self-determination of peoples," and the establishment of a League of Nations to settle international conflicts.

Franciscan Order Also known as the Order of the Friars Minor. The earliest Franciscans were followers of Francis of Assisi (1182–1226) and strove, like him, to imitate the life and example of Jesus. The order was formally established by Pope Innocent III in 1209. Its special mission was the care and instruction of the urban poor.

Frankfurt Assembly (1848–1849) Failed attempt to create a unified Germany under constitutional principles. In 1849, the assembly offered the crown of the new German nation to Frederick William IV of Prussia, but he refused the offer and suppressed a brief protest. The delegates went home disillusioned.

Frederick I "Barbarossa" ("Red Beard"; r. 1155–1190) was the first of Charlemagne's successors to call his realm the Holy Roman Empire, thereby claiming its spiritual and political independence from Rome. He spent his long reign struggling with the papacy and the rebellious towns of northern Italy. He died during the Third Crusade.

Frederick the Great (1712–1786) Prussian ruler (1740–1786) who engaged the nobility in maintaining a strong military and bureaucracy and led Prussian armies to notable military victories. He also encouraged Enlightenment rationalism and artistic endeavors.

French Revolution of 1789 In 1788, a severe financial crisis forced the French monarchy to convene the Estates General, an assembly representing the three estates of the realm: the clergy, the nobility, and the commons (known as the Third Estate). When the Estates General met in 1789, representatives of the Third Estate demanded major constitutional changes. When the king and his government proved uncooperative, the Third Estate broke with the other two estates and renamed itself the National Assembly, demanding a written constitution. The position of the National Assembly was confirmed by a popular uprising in Paris, forcing the king to accept the transformation of France into a constitutional monarchy. This constitutional phase of the revolution lasted until 1792, when the pressures of foreign invasion and the emergence of a more radical revolutionary movement caused the collapse of the monarchy and the establishment of a Republic in France.

French Revolution of 1830 The French popular revolt against Charles X's July Ordinances of 1830, which dissolved the French Chamber of Deputies and restricted suffrage to exclude almost everyone except the nobility. After several days of violence, Charles abdicated the throne and was replaced by a constitutional monarch, Louis Philippe.

French Revolution of 1848 Revolution overthrowing Louis Philippe in February 1848, leading to the formation of the Second Republic (1848–1852). Initially enjoying broad support from both the middle classes and laborers in Paris, the new government became more conservative after elections in which the French peasantry participated for the first time. A workers' revolt was violently repressed in June 1848. In December 1848, Napoleon Bonaparte's nephew, Louis-Napoleon Bonaparte, was elected president. In 1852, Louis-Napoleon declared himself emperor and abolished the republic.

Sigmund Freud (1856–1939) Austrian physician who founded the discipline of psychoanalysis and suggested that human behavior was largely motivated by unconscious and irrational forces.

Galileo Galilei (1564–1642) Italian physicist and inventor; the implications of his ideas raised the ire of the Catholic Church, and he was forced to retract most of his findings.

Gallipoli (1915) During the First World War, a combined force of French, British, Australian and New Zealand troops tried to invade the Gallipoli Peninsula, in the first large-scale amphibious attack in history, and seize it from the Turks. After seven months of fighting, the Allies had lost 200,000 soldiers. Defeated, they withdrew.

Mohandas K. (Mahatma) Gandhi (1869–1948) The Indian leader who advocated nonviolent noncooperation to protest colonial rule and helped win home rule for India in 1947.

Giuseppe Garibaldi (1807–1882) Italian revolutionary leader who led the fight to free Sicily and Naples from the Habsburg Empire; those lands were then peaceably annexed by Sardinia to produce a unified Italy.

Gaul The region of the Roman Empire that was home to the Celtic people of that name, comprising modern France, Belgium, and western Germany.

Geneva Peace Conference (1954) International conference to restore peace in Korea and Indochina. The chief participants were the United States, the Soviet Union, Great Britain, France, the People's Republic of China, North Korea, South Korea, Vietnam, the Viet Minh party, Laos, and Cambodia. The conference resulted in the division of North and South Vietnam.

Genoa Maritime city on Italy's northwestern coast. The Genoese were active in trading ventures along the Silk Road and in the establishment of trading colonies in the Mediterranean. They were also involved in the world of finance and backed the commercial ventures of other powers, especially Spain.

German Democratic Republic Nation founded from the Soviet zone of occupation of Germany after the Second World War; also known as East Germany.

German Social Democratic party Founded in 1875, it was the most powerful socialist party in Europe before 1917.

Gilgamesh Sumerian ruler of the city of Uruk around 2700 B.C.E., Gilgamesh became the hero of one of the world's oldest epics, which circulated orally for nearly a millennium before being written down.

Giotto (c. 1266–1337) Florentine painter and architect who is often considered a forerunner of the Renaissance.

glasnost Introduced by the Soviet leader Mikhail Gorbachev in June 1987, glasnost was one of the five major policies that constituted *perestroika* ("reform" or "restructuring"). Often translated into English as "openness," it called for transparency in Soviet government and institutional activities by reducing censorship in mass media and lifting significant bans on the political, intellectual, and cultural lives of Soviet civilians.

globalization The term used to describe political, social, and economic networks that span the globe. These global exchanges are not limited by nation-states and in recent decades have become associated with new technologies, such as the Internet. Globalization is not new, however; human cultures and economies have been in contact with each other for centuries.

Glorious Revolution The overthrow of King James II of England and the installation of his Protestant daughter, Mary Stuart, and her husband, William of Orange, to the throne in 1688 and 1689. It is widely regarded as the founding moment in the development of a constitutional monarchy in Britain. It also established a more favorable climate for the economic and political growth of the English commercial classes.

Mikhail Gorbachev (1931–) Soviet leader who attempted to reform the Soviet Union through his programs of glasnost and perestroika in the late 1980s. He encouraged open discussions in other countries of the Soviet bloc, which helped inspire the velvet revolutions throughout Eastern Europe. Eventually the political, social, and economic upheaval he had unleashed led to the breakup of the Soviet Union.

Gothic style A type of graceful architecture emerging in twelfth- and thirteenth-century England and France. This style is characterized by pointed arches, delicate decoration, and large windows.

Olympe de Gouges (1748–1793) French political radical and feminist whose *Declaration of the Rights of Woman* demanded an equal place for women in France.

Great Depression Global economic crisis following the U.S. stock market crash on October 29, 1929, and ending with the onset of the Second World War.

Great Famine A period of terrible hunger and deprivation in Europe that peaked between 1315 and 1317, caused by a cooling of the climate and by soil exhaustion due to over-farming. It is estimated to have reduced the population of Europe by 10 to 15 percent.

Great Fear (1789) Following the outbreak of revolution in Paris, fear spread throughout the French countryside, as rumors circulated that armies of brigands or royal troops were coming. Some peasants and villagers organized into militias; others attacked and burned the manor houses in order to destroy the records of manorial dues.

Great Schism (1378–1417) Also known as the Great Western Schism, to distinguish it from the long-standing rupture between the churches of the Greek East and the Latin West. During the Great Schism, the Roman Church was divided between two (and, ultimately, three) competing popes. Each pope claimed to be legitimate, and each denounced the heresy of the others.

Great Terror (1936–1938) The systematic murder of nearly a million people and the deportation of another million and a half to labor camps by Stalin's regime in an attempt to consolidate power and remove perceived enemies.

Greek East After the founding of Constantinople, the eastern Greek-speaking half of the Roman Empire grew more populous, prosperous, and central to imperial policy. Its inhabitants considered themselves to be the true heirs of Rome and their own Orthodox Church to be the true manifestation of Jesus's ministry.

Greek independence Nationalists in Greece revolted against the Ottoman Empire and fought a war that ended in Greek independence in 1827. They received crucial help from British, French, and Russian troops as well as widespread sympathy throughout Europe.

Pope Gregory I (r. 590–604) Also known as Gregory the Great, he was the first bishop of Rome to successfully negotiate a more universal role for the papacy. His political and theological agenda widened the rift between the western Latin (Catholic) Church and the eastern Greek (Orthodox) Church in Byzantium. He also articulated the Church's official position on the status of Jews, promoted effective approaches to religious worship, encouraged the Benedictine monastic movement, and sponsored missionary expeditions.

Guernica The Basque town bombed by German planes in April 1937 during the Spanish Civil War. It is also the subject of Pablo Picasso's famous painting from the same year.

guilds Professional organizations in commercial towns that regulated business and safeguarded the privileges of those practicing a particular craft. Often identical to confraternities ("brotherhoods").

Gulag The vast system of forced labor camps under the Soviet regime. It originated in 1919 in a small monastery near the Arctic Circle and spread throughout the Soviet Union. Penal labor was required of both ordinary criminals and those accused of political crimes. Tens of millions of people were sent to the camps between 1928 and 1953; the exact figure is unknown.

Gulf War (1991) Armed conflict between Iraq and a coalition of thirty-two nations, including the United States, Britain, Egypt, France, and Saudi Arabia. The seeds of the war were planted with Iraq's invasion of Kuwait on August 2, 1990.

Johannes Gutenberg European inventor of the printing press. His shop in Mainz produced the first printed book—a Bible—between the years 1453 and 1455.

Habsburg Dynasty A powerful European dynasty that came to power in the eleventh century in a region now part of Switzerland. Early generations of Habsburgs consolidated their control over neighboring German-speaking lands. Through strategic marriages with other royal lines, later rulers eventually controlled a substantial part of Europe—including much of central Europe, the Netherlands, and even Spain and all its colonies for a time. In practice, the Holy Roman Emperor was chosen from a member of the Habsburg lineage. By the latter half of the seventeenth century, the Austrian Habsburg Empire was made up of nearly 300 nominally autonomous dynastic kingdoms, principalities, duchies, and archbishoprics.

Hagia Sophia The enormous church dedicated to "Holy Wisdom," built in Constantinople at the behest of the emperor Justinian in the sixth century C.E. When Constantinople fell to Ottoman forces in 1453, it became an important mosque.

Haitian Revolution (1791–1804) In 1802, Napoleon sought to reassert French control of Saint-Domingue, but stiff resistance and yellow fever crushed the French army. In 1804, Jean-Jacques Dessalines, a general in the army of former slaves, declared the independent state of Haiti (see **slave revolt in Saint-Domingue**).

Hajj The annual pilgrimage to Mecca; an obligation for Muslims.

Hammurabi Ruler of Babylon from 1792 to 1750 B.C.E., Hammurabi issued a collection of laws that were greatly influential in the Near East and that constitute the world's oldest surviving law code.

Harlem Renaissance Cultural movement in the 1920s that was based in Harlem, a part of New York City with a large African American population. The movement gave voice to black novelists, poets, painters, and musicians, many of whom used their art to protest racial subordination.

Hatshepsut (1479–1458 C.E.) As a pharaoh during the New Kingdom, she launched several successful military campaigns and extended trade and diplomacy. She was an ambitious builder who probably constructed the first tomb in the Valley of the Kings. Though she never pretended to be a man, she was routinely portrayed with a masculine figure and a ceremonial beard.

Hebrews Originally a pastoral people divided among several tribes, they were briefly united under the rule of David and his son, Solomon, who promoted the worship of a single god, Yahweh, and constructed the first temple at the new capital city of Jerusalem. After Solomon's death, the Hebrew tribes were divided between the two kingdoms of Israel and Judah, which were eventually conquered by the Neo-Assyrian and Chaldean empires. It was in captivity that the Hebrews came to define themselves through worship of Yahweh and to develop a religion, Judaism, that could exist outside of Judea. They were liberated by the Persian king Cyrus the Great in 539 B.C.E.

Hellenistic art The art of the Hellenistic period bridged the tastes, ideals, and customs of classical Greece and those that became more characteristic of Rome. The Romans strove to emulate Hellenistic city planning and civic culture, thereby exporting Hellenistic culture to their own far-flung colonies in western Europe.

Hellenistic culture The "Greek-like" culture that dominated the ancient world in the wake of Alexander's conquests.

Hellenistic kingdoms Following the death of Alexander the Great, his vast empire was divided into three separate states: Ptolemaic Egypt, under the rule of the general Ptolemy and his successors; Seleucid Asia, ruled by the general Seleucus and his heirs; and Antigonid Greece, governed by Antigonus of Macedonia. Each state maintained its independence, but the shared characteristics of Greco-Macedonian rule and a shared Greek culture and heritage bound them together in a united cosmopolitan world.

Hellenistic world The various Western civilizations of antiquity that were loosely united by shared Greek language and culture, especially around the eastern Mediterranean.

Heloise (c. 1090–1164) One of the foremost scholars of her time, she became the pupil and the wife of the philosopher and teacher Peter Abelard. In later life, she was the founder of a new religious order for women.

Henry II (1133–1189) Also known as Henry of Anjou, he was King of England from 1154 to 1189. Thanks to his marriage to Eleanor of Aquitaine, who had annulled her first marriage to the French king Louis VII in order to marry him, he was also able to control the Aquitaine.

Henry IV King of Germany and Holy Roman Emperor from 1056—when he ascended the throne at the age of six—until his death in 1106. Henry's reign first was weakened by conflict with the Saxon nobility and later was marked by the Investiture Controversy with Pope Gregory VII.

Henry VIII (1491–1547) King of England from 1509 until his death, Henry rejected the authority of the Roman Church in 1534 when the pope refused to annul his marriage to his queen, Catherine of Aragon; Henry became the founder of the Church of England.

Henry of Navarre (1553–1610) Crowned King Henry IV of France, he renounced his Protestantism but granted limited toleration to Huguenots (French Protestants) through the Edict of Nantes in 1598.

Prince Henry the Navigator (1394–1460) A member of the Portuguese royal family, Henry encouraged the exploration and conquest of western Africa and the trade in gold and slaves.

hieroglyphs The writing system of ancient Egypt, based on a complicated series of pictorial symbols. It fell out of use when Egypt was absorbed into the Roman Empire and was deciphered only after the discovery of the Rosetta Stone in the early nineteenth century.

Hildegard of Bingen (1098–1179) A powerful abbess, theologian, scientist, musician, and visionary who claimed to receive regular revelations from God. Although highly influential in her own day, she was never officially canonized by the Church, in part because her strong personality no longer matched the changing ideal of female piety.

Hiroshima Japanese port devastated by an atomic bomb on August 6, 1945.

Adolf Hitler (1889–1945) The author of *Mein Kampf* and leader of the Nazis who became chancellor of Germany in 1933. Hitler and his Nazi regime started the Second World War and orchestrated the systematic murder of over 6 million Jews, hundreds of thousands of people with disabilities living in institutions, tens of thousands of Roma, and thousands of homosexuals.

Hitler-Stalin Pact (1939) Treaty between Stalin and Hitler that promised Stalin a share of Poland, Finland, the Baltic states, and Bessarabia in the event of a German invasion of Poland, which began shortly thereafter, on September 1, 1939.

HIV-AIDS epidemic The first cases of HIV (human immunodeficiency virus) infection appeared in the late 1970s. It swiftly became a global crisis as those infected passed away from its late stages, AIDS, or acquired immunodeficiency syndrome.

Thomas Hobbes (1588–1679) English political philosopher whose *Leviathan* argued that any form of government capable of protecting its subjects' lives and property might act as an all-powerful sovereign. This government should be allowed to trample over both liberty and property for the sake of its own survival and that of his subjects. Hobbes argued that in his natural state, man was like "a wolf" toward other men.

Holy Roman Empire The loosely allied collection of lands in central and eastern Europe ruled by German kings from the twelfth century until 1806. Its origins are usually identified with the empire of Charlemagne, the Frankish king who was crowned emperor of Rome by the pope in 800. The term itself was promoted by Frederick I "Barbarossa" in the mid-twelfth century.

homage A ceremony in which an individual becomes the "man" (French: *homme*) of a lord.

Homer (fl. eighth century B.C.E.) A Greek rhapsode ("weaver" of stories) credited with merging centuries of poetic tradition in the epics known as the *Iliad* and the *Odyssey*.

hoplite A Greek foot-soldier armed with a spear or short sword and protected by a large round shield (*hoplon*). In battle, hoplites stood shoulder to shoulder in a close formation called a phalanx.

Huguenots French Protestants who endured severe persecution in the sixteenth and seventeenth centuries.

humanism A program of study associated with the movement known as the Renaissance, humanism aimed to replace the scholastic emphasis on logic and philosophy with the study of ancient languages, literature, history, and ethics.

human rights The rights of all people to legal equality, freedom of religion and speech, and the right to participate in government. Human rights laws prohibit torture, cruel punishment, and slavery.

David Hume (1711–1776) Scottish writer who applied Newton's method of scientific inquiry and skepticism to the study of morality, the mind, and government.

Hundred Years' War (1337–1453) A series of wars between England and France, fought mostly on French soil and prompted by the territorial and political claims of English monarchs.

Jan Hus (c. 1373–1415) A Czech reformer who adopted many of the teachings of the English theologian John Wycliffe, and who also demanded that the laity be allowed to receive both the consecrated bread and wine of the Eucharist. The Council of Constance burned him at the stake for heresy. In response, his supporters, the Hussites, revolted against the Church.

Saddam Hussein (1937–2006) The dictator of Iraq who invaded Iran in 1980 and started the eight-year-long Iran-Iraq war; invaded Kuwait in 1990, which led to the Gulf War of 1991; and was overthrown when the United States invaded Iraq in 2003. Involved in Iraqi politics since the mid-1960s, Hussein became the official head of state in 1979.

Iconoclastic Controversy (717–787) A serious and often violent theological debate that raged in Byzantium after Emperor Leo III ordered the destruction of religious art on the grounds that any image representing a divine or holy personage was likely to promote idol worship and blasphemy. *Iconoclast* means "breaker of icons." Those who supported the veneration of icons were called iconodules, "adherents of icons."

Il-khanate Mongol-founded dynasty in thirteenth-century Persia.

Inca Empire The highly centralized South American empire that was toppled by the Spanish conquistador Francisco Pizarro in 1533.

Indian National Congress Formed in 1885, this Indian political party worked to achieve Indian independence from British colonial control. The Congress was led by Gandhi during the 1920s and 1930s.

Indian Rebellion of 1857 This uprising began near Delhi, when the military disciplined a regiment of Indian soldiers employed by the British for refusing to use rifle cartridges greased with pork fat—unacceptable to either Hindus or Muslims. Rebels attacked law courts and burned tax rolls, protesting debt and corruption. The mutiny spread through large areas of northwest India before being violently suppressed by British troops.

Indo-Europeans A group of people speaking variations of the same language and who moved into the Near East and Mediterranean region shortly after 2000 B.C.E.

indulgences Grants exempting Catholic Christians from the performance of penance, either in life or after death. The abusive trade in indulgences was a major catalyst of the Protestant Reformation.

Innocent III (1160/61–1216) As pope, he wanted to unify all of Christendom under papal hegemony. He furthered this goal at the Fourth Lateran Council of 1215, which defined one of the Church's dogmas as the acknowledgment of papal supremacy. The council also took an unprecedented interest in the religious education and habits of every Christian.

Inquisition Formalized in the thirteenth century, this tribunal of the Roman Church aims to enforce religious orthodoxy and conformity.

International Monetary Fund (IMF) Established in 1945 to ensure international cooperation regarding currency exchange and monetary policy, the IMF is a specialized agency of the United Nations.

Investiture Controversy The name given to a series of debates over the limitations of spiritual and secular power in Europe during the eleventh and early twelfth centuries, it came to a head when Pope Gregory VII and Emperor Henry IV of Germany both claimed the right to appoint and invest bishops with the regalia of office. After years of diplomatic and military hostility, it was partially settled by the Concordat of Worms in 1122.

Irish potato famine Period of agricultural blight from 1845 to 1849 whose devastating results produced widespread starvation and led to mass immigration to the United States.

Iron Curtain Term coined by Winston Churchill in 1946 to refer to the borders of Eastern European nations that lay within the zone of Soviet control.

Islamic State (Daesh) In 2014, following the outbreak of the civil war in Syria, a militant group of Muslim fundamentalists seized territory in northeastern Syria and northwestern Iraq and proclaimed themselves a new *caliphate*, the authority over all Muslims. Known as the Islamic State of Iraq and Syria (ISIS) or the Islamic State of Iraq and the Levant (ISIL), they are also called Daesh by Arabic-speaking critics of their violence and brutality. ("Daesh" is an Arabic acronym for the group's name, but it also sounds like a word that means to trample or crush something.) They have been designated a terrorist organization by the United Nations and many countries of the world, both for their actions in the Middle East and for their encouragement of terrorist acts in Europe, Africa, and North and South America.

Italian invasion of Ethiopia (1896) Italy invaded Ethiopia, the last major independent African kingdom. Menelik II, the Ethiopian emperor, soundly defeated the Italian forces.

Ivan III, the Great (1440–1505) Russian ruler who annexed neighboring territories and consolidated his empire's position as a European power.

Jacobins Radical French political group during the French Revolution that took power after 1792, executed the French king, and sought to remake French culture.

Jacquerie Violent 1358 peasant uprising in northern France, incited by disease, war, and taxes.

James I (1566–1625) Monarch who ruled Scotland as James VI and who succeeded Elizabeth I as king of England in 1603. He supervised the English vernacular translation of the Bible known by his name.

James II King of England, Ireland, and Scotland from 1685 to 1688 whose commitment to absolutism and Catholic zealotry led to his exile to France after the Glorious Revolution of 1688.

Janissaries Corps of enslaved soldiers recruited as children from the Christian provinces of the Ottoman Empire and trained to display intense personal loyalty to the Ottoman sultans, who used these forces to curb local autonomy and as their personal bodyguards.

January Rising Failed attempt by Polish nationalists to reestablish the Polish-Lithuanian Commonwealth in 1863–1864.

Jerome (c. 340–420 C.E.) One of the early church fathers, he translated the Bible from Hebrew and Greek into a popular form of Latin—hence the name by which this translation is known: the Vulgate, or "vulgar" (popular), Bible.

Jesuits The religious order formally known as the Society of Jesus, founded in 1540 by Ignatius Loyola to combat the spread of Protestantism. The Jesuits became active in politics, education, and missionary work.

Jesus (c. 4 B.C.E.–c. 30 C.E.) A Jewish preacher and teacher in the rural areas of Galilee and Judea who was arrested for seditious political activity, tried, and crucified by the Romans. After his execution, his followers claimed that he had been resurrected from the dead and taken up into heaven. They began to teach that Jesus had been the divine representative of God, the Messiah foretold by ancient Hebrew prophets, and that he had suffered for the sins of humanity and would return to judge all the world's inhabitants at the end of time.

Joan of Arc (c. 1412–1431) A peasant girl from the province of Lorraine who claimed to have been commanded by God to lead French forces against the English occupying army during the Hundred Years' War. Successful in her efforts, she was betrayed by the French king and handed over to the English, who condemned her to death for heresy. Her reputation underwent a process of rehabilitation, but she was not officially canonized as a saint until 1920.

Judaism The religion of the Hebrews as it developed in the centuries after the establishment of the Hebrew kingdoms under David and Solomon, especially during the period of Babylonian Captivity.

June Days Uprising of workers in Paris against the Second Republic in June 1848, over the government's decision to curtail economic support for the unemployed.

Justinian (527–565) Emperor of Rome who unsuccessfully attempted to reunite the eastern and western portions of the empire. Also known for his important codification of Roman law, in the *Corpus Juris Civilis.*

Justinian's Code of Roman Law Formally known as the *Corpus Juris Civilis,* or "Body of Civil Law," this compendium consisted of a systematic compilation of imperial statutes, the writings of Rome's great legal authorities, a textbook of legal principles, and the legislation of Justinian and his immediate successors. As the most authoritative collection of Roman law, it formed the basis of canon law (the legal system of the Roman Church) and became essential to the developing legal traditions of every European state as well as of many countries around the world.

Das Kapital ("Capital") The 1867 book by Karl Marx that outlined the theory behind historical materialism and attacked the socioeconomic inequities of capitalism.

Johannes Kepler (1571–1630) Mathematician and astronomer who elaborated on and corrected Copernicus's theory and is chiefly remembered for his discovery of the three laws of planetary motion that bear his name.

Keynesian Revolution Postdepression economic ideas developed by the British economist John Maynard Keynes, whereby the state took a greater role in managing the market economy through monetary policy in order to maintain levels of unemployment during periods of economic downturn.

KGB Soviet political police and spy agency, first formed as the Cheka not long after the Bolshevik coup in October 1917. It grew to more than 750,000 operatives with military rank by the 1980s.

Genghis Khan (c. 1167–1227) "Oceanic Ruler," the title adopted by the Mongol chieftain Temujin, founder of a dynasty that conquered much of southern Asia.

Khanate The major political unit of the vast Mongol Empire. There were four Khanates, including the Yuan Empire in China, forged by Chingiz Khan's grandson Kubilai in the thirteenth century.

Ruhollah Khomeini (1902–1989) Iranian Shi'ite religious leader who led the revolution in Iran that resulted in the abdication of the shah in 1979. His government allowed some limited economic and political populism combined with strict constructions of Islamic law, restrictions on women's public life, and the prohibition of ideas or activities linked to Western influence.

Nikita Khrushchev (1894–1971) Leader of the Soviet Union during the Cuban missile crisis, Khrushchev came to power after Stalin's death in 1953. His reforms and criticisms of the excesses of the Stalin regime led to his fall from power in 1964.

Kremlin Once synonymous with the Soviet government, this word refers to Moscow's walled city center and the palace originally built by Ivan the Great.

Kristallnacht Organized attack by Nazis and their supporters on the Jews of Germany following the assassination of a German embassy official by a Jewish man in Paris. Throughout Germany, thousands of stores, schools, cemeteries, and synagogues were attacked on November 9, 1938. Dozens of people were killed, and tens of thousands of Jews were arrested and held in camps, where many were tortured and killed in the ensuing months.

Labour party Founded in Britain in 1900, this party represented workers and was based on socialist principles.

Latin West After the founding of Constantinople, the western Latin-speaking half of the Roman Empire became poorer and more peripheral, but it also fostered the emergence of new barbarian kingdoms. At the same time, the Roman pope claimed to have inherited both the authority of Jesus and the essential elements of Roman imperial authority.

League of Nations International organization founded after the First World War to solve international disputes through arbitration; it was dissolved in 1946 and its assets were transferred to the United Nations.

Leonardo da Vinci (1452–1519) Florentine inventor, sculptor, architect, and painter whose breadth of interests typifies the ideal of the "Renaissance man."

Vladimir Lenin (1870–1924) Leader of the Bolshevik Revolution in Russia (1917) and the first leader of the Soviet Union.

Leviathan A book by Thomas Hobbes (1588–1679) that recommended a ruler have unrestricted power.

liberalism Political and social theory that judges the effectiveness of a government in terms of its ability to protect individual rights. Liberals support representative forms of government, free trade, and freedom of speech and religion. In the economic realm, liberals believe that individuals should be free to engage in commercial or business activities without interference from the state or their community.

lithograph Art form that involves drawing or writing on stone and producing printed impressions.

John Locke (1632–1704) English philosopher and political theorist known for his contributions to liberalism. Locke had great faith in human reason and believed that just societies were those that infringed the least on the natural rights and freedoms of individuals. This led him to assert that a government's legitimacy depended on the consent of the governed, a view that had a profound effect on the authors of the United States' Declaration of Independence.

Louis IX King of France from 1226 to his death on crusade in 1270, Louis was famous for his piety and for his close attention to the administration of law and justice in his realm. He was officially canonized as Saint Louis in 1297.

Louis XIV (1638–1715) Called the "Sun King," he was known for his success at strengthening the institutions of the French absolutist state.

Louis XVI (1754–1793) Well-meaning but ineffectual king of France, finally deposed and executed during the French Revolution.

Louis-Philippe (1773–1850) King of France from 1830 to 1848, during a period known as the July Monarchy, after the July Revolution of 1830 that brought him to the throne. Abdicated during the Revolution of 1848.

Toussaint L'Ouverture (1743–1803) A former slave who, after 1791, led the slaves of the French colony of Saint-Domingue in the largest and most successful slave insurrection in world history. After his capture and death in 1803, his followers succeeded in establishing an independent Haiti in 1804.

Ignatius Loyola (1491–1556) Founder of the Society of Jesus (commonly known as the Jesuits), whose members vowed to serve God through poverty, chastity, and missionary work. He abandoned his first career as a mercenary after reading an account of Christ's life written in his native Spanish.

Lucretia According to Roman legend, Lucretia was a virtuous Roman wife who was raped by the son of Rome's last king and who virtuously committed suicide in order to avoid bringing shame on her family.

Luftwaffe Literally "air weapon," this is the name of the German air force, which was founded during the First World War, disbanded in 1945, and reestablished when West Germany joined NATO in 1950.

Lusitania The British passenger liner that was sunk by a German U-boat (submarine) on May 7, 1915. Public outrage over the sinking contributed to the U.S. decision to enter the First World War.

Martin Luther (1483–1546) A German monk and professor of theology whose critique of the papacy launched the Protestant Reformation.

ma'at The Egyptian term for the serene order of the universe, with which the individual soul (*ka*) must remain in harmony. The power of the pharaoh was linked to *ma'at*, insofar as it ensured the prosperity of the kingdom. After the upheavals of the First Intermediate Period, the perception of the pharaoh's relationship with *ma'at* was revealed to be conditional, something that had to be earned.

Niccolò Machiavelli (1469–1527) As the author of *The Prince* and the *Discourses on Livy*, he looked to the Roman past for paradigms of greatness, at the same time hoping to win the patronage of contemporary rulers who would restore Italy's political independence.

Magna Carta The "Great Charter" of 1215, enacted during the reign of King John of England and designed to limit his powers. It is regarded now as a landmark in the development of constitutional government. In its own time, its purpose was to restore the power of great lords.

Magyar nationalism Lajos Kossuth led this national movement in the Hungarian region of the Habsburg Empire, calling for national independence for Hungary in 1848. With the support of Russia, the Habsburg army crushed the movement and all other revolutionary activities in the empire. Kossuth fled into exile.

Moses Maimonides (c. 1137–1204) Jewish scholar, physician, and scriptural commentator whose *Mishneh Torah* is a fundamental exposition of Jewish law.

Thomas Malthus (1766–1834) British political economist who believed that populations inevitably grew faster than the available food supply. Societies that could not control their population growth would be checked only by famine, disease, poverty, and infant malnutrition. He argued that governments could not alleviate poverty. Instead, the poor had to exercise "moral restraint," postpone marriage, and have fewer children.

Nelson Mandela (1918–2013) The South African opponent of apartheid who led the African National Congress and was imprisoned from 1962 until 1990. After his release from prison, he worked with Prime Minister Frederik Willem De Klerk to establish majority rule. Mandela became the first black president of South Africa in 1994.

Manhattan Project The secret U.S. government research project to develop the first nuclear bomb. The vast project involved dozens of sites across the United States, including New Mexico, Tennessee, Illinois, California, Utah, and Washington. The first test of a nuclear bomb was near Alamogordo, New Mexico, on July 16, 1945.

manors Common farmland worked collectively by the inhabitants of entire villages, sometimes on their own initiative, sometimes at the behest of a lord.

Mao Zedong (1893–1976) The leader of the Chinese Revolution who defeated the Nationalists in 1949 and established the Communist regime in China.

Marne A major battle of the First World War in September 1914; halted the German invasion of France and led to protracted trench warfare on the Western Front.

Marshall Plan Economic aid package given to Europe by the United States after the Second World War to promote reconstruction and economic development and to secure European countries from a feared communist takeover.

Karl Marx (1818–1883) German philosopher and economist who believed that a revolution of the working classes would overthrow the capitalist order and create a classless society. Author of *Das Kapital* and *The Communist Manifesto*.

Marxists Followers of the socialist political economist Karl Marx, who called for workers everywhere to unite and create an independent political force. Marxists believed that industrialization brought about an inevitable struggle between laborers and the class of capitalist property owners. This struggle would culminate in a revolution that would abolish private property and establish a society committed to social equality.

Mary See **cult of the Virgin**.

Mary I (1516–1558) Catholic daughter of Henry VIII and his first wife, Catherine of Aragon, Mary Tudor was the first queen regnant of England. Her attempts to reinstitute Catholicism in England met with limited success. After her early death, she was labeled "Bloody Mary" by the Protestant supporters of her half sister and successor, Elizabeth I.

mass culture The spread of literacy and public education in the nineteenth century created a new audience for print entertainment and a new class of media entrepreneurs to cater to this audience. The invention of radio, film, and television in the twentieth century carried this development to another level, as millions of consumers were now accessible to the producers of news, information, and entertainment. The rise of this "mass culture" has been celebrated as an expression of popular tastes but also criticized as a vehicle for the manipulation of populations through clever and seductive propaganda.

Maya Native American people whose culturally and politically sophisticated empire encompassed lands in present-day Mexico and Guatemala.

Giuseppe Mazzini (1805–1872) Founder of Young Italy and an ideological leader of the Italian nationalist movement.

Mecca Center of an important commercial network of the Arabian Peninsula and birthplace of the prophet Muhammad. It is now considered the holiest site in the Islamic world.

Medici A powerful dynasty of Florentine bankers and politicians whose ancestors were originally apothecaries ("medics").

Meiji Empire Empire created under the leadership of Mutsuhito, emperor of Japan from 1868 until 1912. During the Meiji period, Japan became a world industrial and naval power.

Mensheviks Within the Russian Social Democratic Party, the Mensheviks advocated slow changes and a gradual move toward socialism, in contrast to the Bolsheviks, who wanted to push for a proletarian revolution. The Mensheviks believed that a proletarian revolution in Russia was premature and that the country needed to complete its capitalist development first.

mercantilism A theory and policy for directing the economy of monarchical states between 1600 and 1800 based on the assumption that wealth and power depended on a favorable balance of trade (more exports and fewer imports) and the accumulation of precious metals. Mercantilists advocated forms of economic protectionism to promote domestic production.

Maria Sibylla Merian (1647–1717) A scientific illustrator and an important early entomologist. She conducted research on two continents and published the well-received *Metamorphosis of the Insects of Surinam*.

Merovingian dynasty A Frankish dynasty that claimed descent from a legendary ancestor called Merovic, the Merovingians were the only powerful family to establish a lasting kingdom in western Europe during the fifth and sixth centuries.

Mesopotamia The "land between the Tigris and the Euphrates rivers," where the civilization of Sumer, the first urban society, flourished.

Klemens von Metternich (1773–1859) Austrian foreign minister whose primary goals were to bolster the legitimacy of monarchies and, after the defeat of Napoleon, to prevent another large-scale war in Europe. At the Congress of Vienna, he opposed social and political change and wanted to check Russian and French expansion.

Michelangelo Buonarroti (1475–1564) A virtuoso Florentine sculptor, painter, and poet who spent much of his career in the service of the papacy. He is best known for the decoration of the Sistine Chapel and for his monumental sculptures.

Middle East Like "Near East," this term was invented in the nineteenth century. It usually describes a region stretching from North Africa and Egypt to the Arabian Peninsula and Anatolia.

Middle Kingdom of Egypt (2055–1650 B.C.E.) The period following the First Intermediate Period of dynastic warfare, which ended with the reassertion of pharaonic rule under Mentuhotep II.

Miletus A Greek polis and Persian colony on the Ionian coast of Asia Minor. Influenced by the cultures of Mesopotamia, Egypt, and Lydia, it produced several of the ancient world's first scientists and sophists. Thereafter, a political conflict between the ruler of Miletus, Aristagoras, and the Persian emperor, Darius, sparked the Persian Wars with Greece.

John Stuart Mill (1806–1873) English liberal philosopher whose faith in human reason led him to support a broad variety of civic and political freedoms for men and women, including the right to vote and the right to free speech.

Slobodan Milosevic (1941–2006) The Serbian nationalist politician who became president of Serbia and whose policies during the Balkan wars of the early 1990s led to the deaths of thousands of Croatians, Bosnian Muslims, Albanians, and Kosovars. After leaving office in 2000, he was arrested and tried for war crimes at the International Court in The Hague. The trial ended before a verdict with his death in 2006.

Minoan Crete A sea empire based at Knossos on the Greek island of Crete and named for the legendary King Minos. The Minoans dominated the Aegean for much of the second millennium B.C.E.

modernism There were several different modernist movements in art and literature, but they shared three key characteristics. First, modernists believed that the world had radically changed and that this change should be embraced. Second, they believed that traditional aesthetic values and assumptions about creativity were ill suited to the present. Third, they developed a new conception of what art could do that emphasized expression over representation and insisted on the value of novelty, experimentation, and creative freedom.

Mongol people A nomadic people from the steppes of Central Asia who were united under the ruler Genghis Khan. His conquest of China was continued by his grandson Kubilai and his great-grandson Ogedei, whose army also seized southern Russia and then moved through Hungary and Poland toward eastern Germany. The Mongol armies withdrew from eastern Europe after the death of Ogedei, but his descendants continued to rule his vast empire for another half century.

Michel de Montaigne (1533–1592) French philosopher and social commentator, best known for his *Essays*.

Baron de Montesquieu (1689–1755) An Enlightenment philosophe whose most influential work was *The Spirit of Laws*. In this work, he analyzed the structures that shaped law and categorized governments into three types: republics, monarchies, and despotisms. His ideas about the separation of powers among the executive, the legislative, and the judicial branches of government influenced the authors of the U.S. Constitution.

Thomas More (1478–1535) Christian humanist, English statesman, and author of *Utopia*. In 1529, he was appointed lord chancellor of England but resigned because he opposed King Henry VIII's plans to establish a national church under royal control. He was eventually executed for refusing to take an oath acknowledging Henry to be the head of the Church of England and has since been canonized by the Catholic Church.

mos maiorum Literally translated as the "code of the elders" or the "custom of ancestors." This unwritten code governed the lives of Romans under the Republic and stressed the importance of showing reverence to ancestral tradition. It was sacrosanct and essential to Roman identity and an important influence on Roman culture, law, and religion.

Wolfgang Amadeus Mozart (1756–1791) Austrian composer, famous at a young age as a concert musician and later celebrated as a prolific composer of instrumental music and operas that are seen as the apogee of the Classical style in music.

Muhammad (570–632 c.e.) The founder of Islam, regarded by his followers as God's last and greatest prophet.

Munich Conference (1938) Hitler met with the leaders of Britain, France, and Italy and negotiated an agreement that gave Germany a major slice of Czechoslovakia. The British prime minister Neville Chamberlain believed that the agreement would bring peace to Europe, but instead Germany invaded and seized the rest of Czechoslovakia.

Muscovy The duchy centered on Moscow whose dukes saw themselves as heirs to the Roman Empire. In the early fourteenth century, Moscow was under the control of the Mongol Khanate. After the collapse of the Khanate, the Muscovite grand duke, Ivan III, conquered all the Russian principalities between Moscow and the border of Poland-Lithuania, and then Lithuania itself. By the time of his death, Ivan had established Muscovy as a dominant power.

Muslim learning and culture The Crusades brought the Latin West in contact with the Islamic world, which influenced European culture in myriad ways. Europeans adapted Arabic numerals and mathematical concepts as well as Arabic and Persian words. Through Arabic translations, Western scholars gained access to Greek learning, which had a profound influence on Christian theology. European scholars also learned from the Islamic world's accomplishments in medicine and science.

Benito Mussolini (1883–1945) The Italian founder of the Fascist party who came to power in Italy in 1922 and allied himself with Hitler and the Nazis during the Second World War.

Mycenaean Greece (1600–1200 b.c.e.) The term used to describe the civilization of Greece during the late Bronze

Age, when territorial kingdoms such as Mycenae formed around a king, a warrior caste, and a palace bureaucracy.

Nagasaki Second Japanese city on which the United States dropped an atomic bomb. The attack took place on August 9, 1945; the Japanese surrendered shortly thereafter, ending the Second World War.

Napoleon III (1808–1873) The nephew of Napoleon Bonaparte, Napoleon III was elected president of the French Second Republic in 1848 and made himself emperor of France in 1852. During his reign (1852–1870), he rebuilt the French capital of Paris. Defeated in the France-Prussian War of 1870, he went into exile.

Napoleonic Code Legal code drafted by Napoleon in 1804 and based on Justinian's *Corpus Iuris Civilis*. It distilled different legal traditions to create one uniform law. The code confirmed the abolition of feudal privileges of all kinds and set the conditions for exercising property rights.

Napoleon's military campaigns In 1805, the Russians, Prussians, Austrians, Swedes, and British attempted to contain Napoleon, but he defeated them. Out of his victories, Napoleon created a new empire and affiliated states. In 1808, he invaded Spain, but fierce resistance prevented him from achieving a complete victory. In 1812, he invaded Russia, and his army was decimated as it retreated from Moscow during the winter. After the Russian campaign, the united European powers defeated Napoleon and forced him into exile. He escaped and reassumed command of his army, but the European powers defeated him for the final time at the Battle of Waterloo.

Gamal Abdel Nasser (1918–1970) President of Egypt and the most prominent spokesman for secular pan-Arabism. He became a target for Islamist critics, such as Sayyid Qutb and the Muslim Brotherhood, angered by the Western-influenced policies of his regime.

National Assembly Governing body of France that succeeded the Estates General in 1789 during the French Revolution. It was composed of, and defined by, the delegates of the Third Estate.

National Association for the Advancement of Colored People (NAACP) Founded in 1910, this U.S. civil rights organization is dedicated to ending inequality and segregation for black Americans.

National Convention The governing body of France from September 1792 to October 1795. It declared France a republic and then tried and executed King Louis XVI. The Convention also confiscated the property of the enemies of the revolution, instituted a policy of de-Christianization, changed marriage and inheritance laws, abolished slavery in its colonies, placed a cap on the price of necessities, and ended the compensation of nobles for their lost privileges.

nationalism Movement to unify a country under one government based on perceptions of the population's common history, customs, and social traditions.

nationalism in Yugoslavia In the 1990s, Slobodan Milosevic and his allies reignited Serbian nationalism in the former Yugoslavia, which led non-Serb republics in Croatia and Slovenia to seek independence. The country erupted into war, with the worst violence taking place in Bosnia, a multiethnic region with Serb, Croatian, and Bosnian Muslim populations. European diplomats proved powerless to stop attempts by Croatian and Serbian military and paramilitary forces to claim territory through ethnic cleansing and violent intimidation. Atrocities were committed on all sides, but pro-Serb forces were responsible for the most deaths.

NATO The North Atlantic Treaty Organization, a 1949 military agreement among the United States, Canada, Great Britain, and eight Western European nations, which declared that an armed attack against any one of the members would be regarded as an attack against all. Created during the Cold War in the face of the Soviet Union's control of Eastern Europe, NATO continues to exist today. Its twenty-eight countries include former members of the Warsaw Pact as well as Albania and Turkey.

Nazi party Founded in the early 1920s, the National Socialist German Workers' Party (NSDAP) gained control over Germany under the leadership of Adolf Hitler in 1933 and continued in power until Germany was defeated in 1945.

Nazism The political movement in Germany led by Adolf Hitler that advocated a violent anti-Semitic, anti-Marxist, pan-German ideology.

Near East Like "Middle East," a geographical term coined during the nineteenth century to describe western Asia and the eastern Mediterranean—that is, the parts of Asia nearest to Europe.

Neo-Assyrian Empire (883–859 B.C.E. to 612–605 B.C.E.) Assurnasirpal II laid the foundations of the Neo-Assyrian Empire through military campaigns against neighboring peoples. Eventually, the empire stretched from the Mediterranean Sea to western Iran. A military dictatorship governed the empire through its army, which it used to frighten and oppress both its subjects and its enemies. The empire's ideology was based on waging holy war in the name of its principal god, Assur, and the exaction of tribute through terror.

neoliberalism Neoliberals believe that free markets, profit incentives, and restraints on both budget deficits and social welfare programs are the best guarantee of individual liberties. Beginning in the 1980s, neoliberal theory was used to structure the policy of financial institutions such as the International Monetary Fund and the World Bank, which turned away from interventionist policies in favor of market-driven models of economic development.

Neolithic Revolution The "New" Stone Age, which began around 11,000 B.C.E., saw new technological and social developments, including managed food production, the beginnings of permanent settlements, and the rapid intensification of trade.

Neoplatonism A school of thought based on the teachings of Plato. Prevalent in the Roman Empire, it had a profound effect on the formation of Christian theology. Neoplatonists argued that nature is a book written by its creator to reveal the ways of God to humanity. Convinced that God's perfection must be reflected in nature, the Neoplatonists searched for the ideal and perfect structures that they believed must lie behind the "shadows" of the everyday world.

New Deal President Franklin D. Roosevelt's package of government reforms that were enacted during the depression of the 1930s to provide jobs for the unemployed, social welfare programs for the poor, and security to the financial markets.

New Economic Policy In 1921, the Bolsheviks abandoned war communism in favor of the New Economic Policy (NEP). Under the NEP, the state still controlled all major industry and financial concerns, while individuals could own private property, trade freely within limits, and farm their own land for their own benefit. Fixed taxes replaced grain requisition. The policy successfully helped Soviet agriculture recover from the civil war but was later abandoned in favor of collectivization.

Isaac Newton (1642–1727) One of the foremost scientists of all time, Newton was an English mathematician and physicist; he is noted for his development of calculus, work on the properties of light, and theory of gravitation.

Nicholas II (1868–1918) The last Russian tsar, who abdicated the throne in 1917. He and his family were executed by the Bolsheviks on July 17, 1918.

Friedrich Nietzsche (1844–1900) The German philosopher who denied the possibility of knowing absolute "truth" or "reality," since all knowledge comes filtered through linguistic, scientific, or artistic systems of representation.

He also criticized Judeo-Christian morality for instilling a repressive conformity that drained civilization of its vitality.

nongovernmental organizations (NGOs) Private organizations such as the Red Cross that play a large role in international affairs.

novel A fictional work typically written in narrative prose, that recounts the actions and circumstances of individuals and their social lives. The novel as a literary form first emerged in the 18th century and was particularly popular among women readers.

Novum Organum Work by the English statesman and scientist Francis Bacon (1561–1626) that advanced a philosophy of study through observation.

October Days (1789) The high price of bread and the rumor that the king was unwilling to cooperate with the assembly caused the women who worked in Paris's large central market to march to Versailles along with their supporters to address the king. Not satisfied with their initial reception, they broke through the palace gates and called for the king to return to Paris from Versailles, which he did the following day.

offensives of 1916–1917 A series of costly but unsuccessful offensive operations initiated by the Allies and the Germans to break the stalemate on the western front, including the battles of Verdun, the Somme, and Passchendaele (also known as the Third Battle of Ypres).

Old Kingdom of Egypt (c. 2686–2160 B.C.E.) During this period, the pharaohs controlled a powerful and centralized bureaucratic state whose vast human and material resources are exemplified by the pyramids of Giza. This period came to an end as the pharaoh's authority collapsed, leading to a period of dynastic warfare and localized rule.

OPEC (Organization of the Petroleum Exporting Countries) Organization created in 1960 by oil-producing countries in the Middle East, South America, and Africa to regulate the production and pricing of crude oil.

Operation Barbarossa The code name for Hitler's invasion of the Soviet Union in 1941.

Opium Wars (1839–1842, 1856–1860) Wars fought between the British and Qing China to protect the British trade in opium; resulted in the ceding of Hong Kong to the British.

Oracle at Delphi The most important shrine in ancient Greece. The priestess of Apollo who attended the shrine was believed to have the power to predict the future.

Orthodox Refers to an adherence to traditional or conservative practice as it related to doctrinal decisions and disputes in the eastern Roman empire.

Ottoman Empire (c.1300–1923) During the thirteenth century, the Ottoman dynasty established itself as leader of the Turks. From the fourteenth to sixteenth centuries, the Ottomans conquered Anatolia, Armenia, Syria, and North Africa as well as parts of southeastern Europe, the Crimea, and areas along the Red Sea. Portions of the Ottoman Empire persisted up to the time of the First World War, but it was dismantled in the years following the war.

Robert Owen (1771–1858) Welsh industrialist and reformer who made efforts to improve factory conditions for workers in Scotland.

Mohammad Reza Pahlavi (1919–1980) The West-friendly shah of Iran who was installed during a 1953 coup supported by Britain and the United States. After a lengthy economic downturn, public unrest, and personal illness, he retired from public life under popular pressure in 1979.

Pan-African Conference A 1900 assembly in London that sought to draw attention to the sovereignty of African people and their mistreatment by colonial powers.

Panhellenism The "all-Greek" culture that allowed ancient Greek colonies to maintain a connection to their homeland and to each other through their shared language and heritage. These colonies also exported their culture into new areas and created new Greek-speaking enclaves, which permanently changed the cultural geography of the Mediterranean world.

pan-Slavism Cultural movement that sought to unite native Slavic peoples within the Russian and Habsburg Empires under Russian leadership.

Partition of India (1947) At independence, British India was partitioned into the nations of India and Pakistan. The majority of the population in India was Hindu, and the majority of the population in Pakistan was Muslim. The process of partition brought brutal religious and ethnic warfare. More than 1 million Hindus and Muslims died, and 12 million became refugees.

Blaise Pascal (1623–1662) A Catholic philosopher who wanted to establish the truth of Christianity by appealing simultaneously to intellect and emotion. In his *Pensées*, he argued that faith alone can resolve the world's contradictions and that his own awe in the face of evil and uncertainty must be evidence of God's existence.

Paul of Tarsus Originally known as Saul, Paul was a Greek-speaking Jew and Roman citizen who underwent a miraculous conversion experience and became the most important proponent of Christianity in the 50s and 60s C.E.

Pax Mongolica In imitation of the *Pax Romana* ("The Roman Peace": Chapter 5), this is the phrase used to describe the relatively peaceful century after the Mongol conquests, which enabled an intensified period of trade, travel, and communication within the Eurasian landmass.

Pax Romana (27 B.C.E.–180 C.E.) Literally translated as the "Roman Peace." During this time, the Roman world enjoyed an unprecedented period of peace and political stability.

Peace of Augsburg A settlement negotiated in 1555 among factions within the Holy Roman Empire, it formulated the principle *cuius regio, eius religio* ("he who rules, his religion"): the inhabitants of any given territory should follow the religion of its ruler, whether Catholic or Protestant.

Peace of Paris The 1919 Paris Peace Conference established the terms to end the First World War. Great Britain, France, Italy, and the United States signed five treaties with each of the defeated nations: Germany, Austria, Hungary, Turkey, and Bulgaria. The settlement is notable for the territory that Germany had to give up, including large parts of Prussia to the new state of Poland, and Alsace and Lorraine to France; the disarming of Germany; and the "war-guilt" provision, which required Germany and its allies to pay massive reparations to the victors.

Peace of Westphalia (1648) An agreement reached at the end of the Thirty Years' War that altered the political map of Europe. France emerged as the predominant power on the Continent. The Austrian Habsburgs had to surrender all the territories they had gained and could no longer use the office of the Holy Roman Emperor to dominate central Europe. Spain was marginalized, and Germany became a volatile combination of Protestant and Catholic principalities.

Pearl Harbor The American naval base in Hawaii that was bombed by the Japanese on December 7, 1941, bringing the United States into the Second World War.

peasantry Term used in continental Europe to refer to rural populations that lived from agriculture. Some peasants were free and could own land. Serfs were peasants who were legally bound to the land and subject to the authority of the local lord.

Peloponnesian War The name given to the series of wars fought between Sparta (on the Greek Peloponnesus) and Athens from 431 B.C.E. to 404 B.C.E., which ended in the defeat of Athens and the loss of its imperial power.

perestroika Introduced by Soviet leader Mikhail Gorbachev in June 1987, *perestroika* was the name given to economic and political reforms begun earlier in his tenure. It restructured the state bureaucracy, reduced the privileges of the political elite, and instituted a shift from the centrally planned economy to a mixed economy, combining planning with the operation of market forces.

Periclean Athens Following his election as strategos in 461 B.C.E., Pericles pushed through political reforms in Athens that gave poorer citizens greater influence in politics. He promoted the Athenians' sense of superiority through ambitious public works projects and lavish festivals to honor the gods, thus ensuring his continual reelection. But eventually, Athens' growing arrogance and aggression alienated it from the rest of the Greek world.

Pericles (c. 495–429) Athenian politician who occupied the office of strategos for thirty years and who presided over a series of civic reforms, building campaigns, and imperialist initiatives.

Persian Empire Consolidated by Cyrus the Great in 559, this empire eventually stretched from the Persian Gulf to the Mediterranean and also encompassed Egypt. Persian rulers were able to hold their empire together through a policy of tolerance and a mixture of local and centralized governance. This imperial model of government was adopted by many future empires.

Persian Wars (490–479 B.C.E.) In 501 B.C.E., a political conflict between the Greek ruler of Miletus, Aristagoras, and the Persian emperor, Darius, sparked the first of the Persian Wars when Darius sent an army to punish Athens for its intervention on the side of the Greeks. Despite being heavily outnumbered, Athenian hoplites defeated the Persian army at the plain of Marathon. In 480 B.C.E., Darius's son Xerxes invaded Greece but was defeated at sea and on land by combined Greek forces under the leadership of Athens and Sparta.

Peter the Great (1682–1725) Energetic tsar who transformed Russia into a leading European country by centralizing government, modernizing the army, creating a navy, and reforming education and the economy.

Francesco Petrarca (Petrarch) (1304–1374) Italian scholar who revived interest in classical writing styles and was famed for his vernacular love sonnets.

pharaoh A term meaning "household," which became the title borne by the rulers of ancient Egypt. The pharaoh was regarded as the divine representative of the gods and the embodiment of Egypt itself. The powerful and centralized bureaucratic state ruled by the pharaohs was more stable and long lived than any other civilization in world history, lasting (with few interruptions) for approximately 3,000 years.

Pharisees A group of Jewish teachers and preachers who emerged in the third century b.c.e. They insisted that all of Yahweh's (God's) commandments were binding on all Jews.

Philip II (382–336 b.c.e.) King of Macedonia and father of Alexander, he consolidated the southern Balkans and the Greek city-states under Macedonian domination.

Philip II King of Spain from 1556 to 1598 and briefly king of England and Ireland during his marriage to Queen Mary I of England. As a staunch Catholic, Philip responded with military might to the desecration of Catholic churches in the Spanish Netherlands in the 1560s. When commercial conflict with England escalated, Philip sent the Spanish Armada to conquer England in 1588, but it was largely destroyed by stormy weather.

Philip II Augustus (1165–1223) The first French ruler to use the title "king of France" rather than "king of the French." After he captured Normandy and its adjacent territories from the English, he built an effective system of local administration, which recognized regional diversity while promoting centralized royal control. This administrative pattern would characterize French government until the French Revolution.

Philip IV (1268–1314) King of France from 1285 until his death. Philip's conflict with Pope Boniface VIII led to the transfer of the papal court to Avignon from 1309 to 1378.

Philistines Descendants of the Sea Peoples who fled to the region that now bears their name, Palestine, after their defeat at the hands of the pharaoh Ramses III. They dominated their neighbors the Hebrews, who used writing as an effective means of discrediting them. (The Philistines themselves did not leave a written record to contest the Hebrews' views.)

philosophe During the Enlightenment, this word referred to a person whose reflections were unhampered by the constraints of religion or dogma.

Phoenicians A Semitic people known for their trade in exotic purple dyes and other luxury goods, they originally settled in present-day Lebanon around 1200 b.c.e. and from there established commercial colonies throughout the Mediterranean, notably Carthage.

Plato (429–349 b.c.e.) A student of Socrates, Plato dedicated his life to transmitting his teacher's legacy through the writing of dialogues on philosophical subjects in which Socrates himself plays the major role. The longest and most famous of these, known as the *Republic*, describes an idealized polis governed by a superior group of individuals chosen for their natural attributes of intelligence and character, and who rule as philosopher-kings.

Plotinus (204–270 c.e.) A Neoplatonist philosopher who taught that everything in existence has its ultimate source in the divine and that the highest goal of life should be the mystic reunion of the soul with this divine source, something that can be achieved through contemplation and asceticism. This outlook blended with that of early Christianity and was instrumental in the spread of that religion within the Roman Empire.

polis One of the major political innovations of the ancient Greeks was the *polis*, or city-state (plural *poleis*). These independent social and political entities began to emerge in the ninth century b.c.e., organized around an urban center and fostering markets, meeting places, and religious worship. Frequently, poleis also controlled some surrounding territory.

Polish nationalism Movement to reestablish an independent Polish nation after the partitions of the late eighteenth century divided the former Polish-Lithuanian Commonwealth between the Prussian, Austrian, and Russian empires.

Marco Polo (1254–1324) Venetian merchant who traveled throughout Asia for twenty years and published his observations in a widely read memoir.

population growth In the nineteenth century, Europe experienced a dramatic increase in population. During this period, the spread of rural manufacturing allowed men and women to marry younger and raise families earlier, which increased the size of the average family. As the population increased, the proportion of young and fertile people also increased, which reinforced population growth. By 1900, population growth was strongest in Britain and Germany and slower in France.

portolan charts Also known as *portolani*, these special charts were invented by medieval mariners during the fourteenth century and were used to map locations of ports and sea routes, while also taking note of prevailing winds and other conditions at sea.

Potsdam Conference (1945) At this conference, Truman, Churchill, and Stalin met to discuss their options at the conclusion of the Second World War, including making territorial changes to Germany and its allies and the question of war reparations.

Prague spring A period of political liberalization in Czechoslovakia between January and August 1968 that was initiated by Alexander Dubček, the Czech leader. This period of expanding freedom and openness in this Eastern-bloc nation ended on August 20, when the USSR and Warsaw Pact countries invaded with 200,000 troops and 5,000 tanks.

pre-Socratics A group of philosophers in the Greek city of Miletus who raised questions about humans' relationship with the natural world and the gods and who formulated rational theories to explain the physical universe they observed. Their name reflects the fact that they flourished prior to the lifetime of Socrates.

Price Revolution An unprecedented inflation in prices during the latter half of the sixteenth century, resulting in part from the enormous influx of silver bullion from Spanish America.

Principate Modern term for the centuries of autocratic rule by the successors of Augustus, who seized power in 27 B.C.E. and styled himself Rome's *princeps* (or "first man"). See **Roman Republic**.

printing press Developed in Europe by Johannes Gutenberg of Mainz in 1453–1455, this new technology quickly revolutionized communication and played a significant role in political, religious, and intellectual movements.

Protestantism The name given to the many dissenting varieties of Christianity that emerged during the Reformation in sixteenth-century western Europe. Although Protestant beliefs and practices differed widely, all were united in their rejection of papal authority and the dogmas of the Roman Catholic Church.

provisional government After the collapse of the Russian monarchy in February 1917, leaders in the Duma organized a government and hoped to establish a democratic system under constitutional rule. They also refused to concede military defeat in the First World War. It was impossible to institute domestic reforms and fight a war at the same time. As conditions worsened, the Bolsheviks gained support. In October 1917, they attacked the provisional government and seized control.

Claudius Ptolomeus, called Ptolemy (c. 100–170 C.E.) A Greek-speaking geographer and astronomer active in Roman Alexandria, he rejected the findings of previous Hellenistic scientists in favor of the erroneous theories of Aristotle, publishing highly influential treatises that promulgated these errors and suppressed, for example, the accurate findings of Aristarchus, who had discovered the heliocentric universe, and Erathosthenes, who had calculated the circumference of the earth.

Ptolemaic system Ptolemy of Alexandria promoted Aristotle's understanding of cosmology. In this system, the heavens orbit the earth in an organized hierarchy of spheres, and the earth and the heavens are made of different matter and subject to different laws of motion. A prime mover produces the motion of the celestial bodies.

Ptolemy (c. 367–c. 284 B.C.E.) One of Alexander the Great's trusted generals (and possibly his half brother), he became pharaoh of Egypt and founded a new dynasty that lasted until that kingdom's absorption into the Roman Empire in 30 B.C.E.

public sphere Between the official realm of state activities and the private realm of the household and individual lies the public sphere. The public sphere has a political dimension—it is the space of debate, discussion, and expressions of popular opinion. It also has an economic dimension—it is where business is conducted, where commercial transactions take place, where people enter into contracts, search for work, or hire employees.

Punic Wars (264–146 B.C.E.) Three periods of warfare between Rome and Carthage, two maritime empires that struggled for dominance of the Mediterranean. Rome emerged as the victor, destroyed the city of Carthage, and took control of Sicily, North Africa, and Hispania (Spain).

pyramid Constructed during the third millennium B.C.E., the pyramids were monuments to the power and divinity of the pharaohs entombed inside them.

Qur'an (often Koran) Islam's holy scriptures, comprising the prophecies revealed to Muhammad and redacted during his life and after his death.

Raphael (Raffaelo Sanzio) (1483–1520) Italian painter active in Rome. His works include *The School of Athens*.

realism Artistic and literary style that sought to portray common situations as they would appear in reality.

Realpolitik Political strategy based on advancing power for its own sake.

reason The human capacity to solve problems and discover truth in ways that can be verified intellectually. Philosophers distinguish the knowledge gained from reason from the teachings of instinct, imagination, and faith, which are verified according to different criteria.

reconquista The process during which Christian rulers in Spain were beginning to forge effective alliances, in order to counter the power of their wealthy and well-governed Muslim neighbors.

Reformation Religious and political movement in sixteenth-century Europe that led to a break between dissenting forms of Christianity and the Roman Catholic Church; notable figures include Martin Luther and John Calvin.

Reich A term for the German state. The First Reich corresponded to the Holy Roman Empire (ninth century to 1806), the Second Reich lasted from 1871 to 1919, and the Third Reich lasted from 1933 through May 1945.

Reign of Terror (1793–1794) Campaign at the height of the French Revolution in which violence, including systematic executions of opponents of the revolution, was used to purge France of its "enemies" and to extend the revolution beyond its borders. Radicals executed as many as 40,000 people who were judged enemies of the state.

Renaissance From the French word meaning "rebirth," this term came to be used during the nineteenth century to describe the artistic, intellectual, and cultural movement that emerged in Italy after 1300 and that sought to recover and emulate the heritage of the classical past.

Restoration (1815–1848) European movement after the defeat of Napoleon to restore Europe to its pre–French Revolution status and to prevent the spread of revolutionary or liberal political movements.

Cardinal Richelieu (1585–1642) First minister to King Louis XIII, he is considered by many to have ruled France in all but name, centralizing political power and suppressing dissent.

Roman army Under the Republic, the Roman army was made up of citizen-soldiers who were required to serve in wartime. As Rome's empire grew, the need for more fighting men led to the extension of citizenship rights and, eventually, to the development of a vast, professional, standing army that numbered as many as 300,000 by the middle of the third century B.C.E. By that time, however, citizens were not themselves required to serve, and many legions were made up of paid conscripts and foreign mercenaries.

Roman citizenship The rights and responsibilities of Rome's citizens were gradually extended to the free (male) inhabitants of other Italian provinces and later to most provinces in the Roman world. In contrast to slaves and non-Romans, Romans had the right to be tried in an imperial court and could not be legally subjected to torture.

Roman Republic The Romans traced the founding of their republic to the overthrow of their last king and the establishment of a unique form of constitutional government, in which the power of the aristocracy (embodied by the Senate) was checked by the executive rule of two elected consuls and the collective will of the people. For hundreds of years, this balance of power provided the Republic with a measure of political stability and prevented any single individual or clique from gaining too much power.

Romanticism Beginning in Germany and England in the late eighteenth century and continuing until the end of the nineteenth century, Romanticism was a movement in art, music, and literature that countered the rationalism of the Enlightenment by placing greater value on human emotions and the power of nature to stimulate creativity.

Jean-Jacques Rousseau (1712–1778) Philosopher and radical political theorist whose *Social Contract* attacked privilege and inequality. One of the primary principles of Rousseau's political philosophy is that politics and morality should not be separated.

Royal Society The goal of this British society, founded in 1660, is to pursue collective research. Members would conduct experiments, record the results, and share them with their peers, who would study the methods, reproduce the experiment, and assess the results. This arrangement gave English scientists a sense of common purpose as well as a system for reaching a consensus on facts.

Russian Revolution of 1905 After Russia's defeat in the Russo-Japanese War, Russians began clamoring for political reforms. Protests grew over the course of 1905, and the autocracy lost control of entire towns and regions as workers went on strike, soldiers mutinied, and peasants revolted. Forced to yield, Tsar Nicholas II issued the October Manifesto, which pledged individual liberties and provided for the election of a parliament (called the Duma). The most radical of the revolutionary groups were put down with force, and the pace of political change remained very slow in the aftermath of the revolution.

Russo-Japanese War (1904–1905) Japanese and Russian expansionist goals collided in Manchuria and Korea. Russia was humiliated after the Japanese navy sank its fleet, which helped provoke a revolt in Russia and led to an American-brokered peace treaty.

sacrament A sacred rite. In the Catholic tradition, the administration of the sacraments is considered necessary for salvation.

Saint Bartholomew's Day Massacre The mass murder of French Protestants (Huguenots) instigated by Queen Catherine de' Medici of France and carried out by Catholics.

It began in Paris on August 24, 1572 (Saint Bartholomew's day) and spread to other parts of France, continuing into October of that year. More than 70,000 people were killed.

salon Informal gathering of intellectuals and aristocrats that allowed discourse about Enlightenment ideas.

Sappho (c. 620–c. 550 B.C.E.) One of the most celebrated Greek poets, she was revered as the "Tenth Muse" and emulated by many male poets. Ironically, though, only two of her poems survive intact, and the rest must be pieced together from fragments quoted by later poets.

Sargon the Great (r. 2334–2279 B.C.E.) The Akkadian ruler who consolidated power in Mesopotamia.

SARS epidemic (2003) The successful containment of severe acute respiratory syndrome (SARS) is an example of how international health organizations can effectively work together to recognize and respond to a disease outbreak. The disease itself, however, is a reminder of the dangers that exist in a globalized economy with a high degree of mobility of both populations and goods.

Schlieffen Plan Devised by the German general Alfred von Schlieffen in 1905 to avoid the dilemma of a two-front war against France and Russia. The Schlieffen Plan required that Germany attack France first through Belgium and secure a quick victory before wheeling to the east to meet the slower armies of the Russians on the Eastern Front. The Schlieffen Plan was put into operation on August 2, 1914, at the outset of the First World War.

scholasticism The methods for resolving complex theological and philosophical problems that were born from the educational revolution that began in the eleventh century.

scientific revolution of antiquity The Hellenistic period was the most brilliant age in the history of science before the seventeenth century C.E. Aristarchus of Samos posited the existence of a heliocentric universe. Eratosthenes of Alexandria accurately calculated the circumference of the earth. Archimedes turned physics into its own branch of experimental science. Hellenistic anatomists became the first to practice human dissection, which improved their understanding of human physiology. Ironically, most of these discoveries were suppressed by pseudoscientists who flourished under the Roman Empire during the second century C.E., notably Claudus Ptolomeus (Ptolemy) and Aelius Galenus (Galen).

second industrial revolution The technological developments in the last third of the nineteenth century, which included new techniques for refining and producing steel; increased availability of electricity for industrial, commercial, and domestic use; advances in chemical manufacturing; and the creation of the internal combustion engine.

Second World War Worldwide war that began in September 1939 in Europe, and even earlier in Asia (the Japanese invasion of Manchuria began in 1931), pitting Britain, the United States, and the Soviet Union (the Allies) against Nazi Germany, Italy, and Japan (the Axis). The war ended in 1945 with Germany and Japan's defeat.

Seleucus (d. 280 B.C.E.) The Macedonian general who ruled the Persian heartland of Alexander the Great's empire.

Semitic language The Semitic language family has the longest recorded history of any linguistic group and is the root of most languages of the Middle and Near East. Ancient Semitic languages include those of the ancient Babylonians and Assyrians, Phoenician, the classical form of Hebrew, early dialects of Aramaic, and the classical Arabic of the Qur'an.

Sepoy Mutiny of 1857 See **Indian Rebellion of 1857**.

serfdom Peasant labor. Unlike slaves, serfs are "attached" to the land they work and are not supposed to be sold apart from that land.

William Shakespeare (1564–1616) An English playwright who flourished during the reigns of Elizabeth I and James I. Shakespeare received a basic education in his hometown of Stratford-upon-Avon and worked in London as an actor before achieving success as a dramatist and poet.

Shi'ites An often-persecuted minority within Islam, Shi'ites, from the Arabic word *shi'a* ("faction"), believe that only descendants of Muhammad's successor Ali and his wife Fatimah, Muhammad's daughter, can have any authority over the Muslim community. Today, Shi'ites constitute the ruling party in Iran and are numerous in Iraq but otherwise comprise only 10 percent of Muslims worldwide.

Abbé Sieyès (1748–1836) In 1789, he wrote the pamphlet "What Is the Third Estate?" in which he posed fundamental questions about the rights of the Third Estate and helped provoke its secession from the Estates General. He was a leader at the Tennis Court Oath, but he later helped Napoleon seize power.

Sinn Féin The Irish revolutionary organization that formed in 1900 to fight for Irish independence.

Sino-Japanese War (1894–1895) Conflict over the control of Korea; China was forced to cede the province of Taiwan to Japan.

slave revolt in Saint-Domingue (1791–1804) In September of 1791, the largest slave rebellion in history broke out in Saint-Domingue, an important French colony in the Caribbean. In 1794, the revolutionary government in France abolished slavery in the colonies, though this act essentially only recognized the liberty that the slaves had seized by their own actions. Napoleon reestablished slavery in the French Caribbean in 1802 but failed in his attempt to reconquer Saint-Domingue. Armies commanded by former slaves succeeded in winning independence for a new nation, Haiti, in 1804, making the revolt in Saint-Domingue the first successful slave revolt in history.

slavery The practice of subjugating people to a life of bondage and of selling or trading these unfree people. For most of human history, slavery had no racial or ethnic basis and was widely practiced by all cultures and civilizations. Anyone could become a slave, for example, by being captured in war or by being sold for the payment of a debt. It was only in the fifteenth century, with the growth of the African slave trade, that slavery came to be associated with particular races and peoples.

Adam Smith (1723–1790) Scottish economist and liberal philosopher who proposed that competition between self-interested individuals led naturally to a healthy economy. He became famous for his influential book *The Wealth of Nations* (1776).

Social Darwinism Belief that Charles Darwin's theory of natural selection (evolution) was applicable to human societies and justified the right of the ruling classes or countries to dominate the weak.

social democracy The belief that democracy and social welfare go hand in hand and that diminishing the sharp inequalities of class society is crucial to fortifying democratic culture.

socialism Political ideology that calls for a classless society with collective ownership of all property.

Society of Jesus See **Jesuits**.

Socrates (469–399 B.C.E.) The Athenian philosopher and teacher who promoted the careful examination of all inherited opinions and assumptions on the grounds that "the unexamined life is not worth living." A veteran of the Peloponnesian War, he was tried and condemned by his fellow citizens for engaging in allegedly seditious activities and was executed in 399 B.C.E. His most influential pupils were the philosopher Plato and the historian and social commentator Xenophon.

Solidarity Polish trade union that organized a series of strikes across Poland in 1980.

Solon (d. 559 B.C.E.) Elected archon in 594 B.C.E., this Athenian aristocrat enacted a series of political and economic reforms that formed the basis of Athenian democracy.

Somme (1916) During this battle of the First World War, Allied forces attempted to take entrenched German positions from July to mid-November of 1916. Neither side was able to make any real gains despite massive casualties: 500,000 Germans, 400,000 British, and 200,000 French.

sovereignty An inviolable authority over a defined territory.

Soviet bloc International alliance that included the East European countries of the Warsaw Pact as well as the Soviet Union; it also came to include Cuba.

soviets Local councils elected by workers and soldiers in Russia. Socialists started organizing these councils in 1905, and the Petrograd soviet in the capital emerged as one of the centers of power after the Russian monarchy collapsed in 1917 in the midst of World War I. The soviets became increasingly powerful, pressing for social reform and the redistribution of land, and calling for Russian withdrawal from the war effort.

Spanish-American War (1898) War between the United States and Spain in Cuba, Puerto Rico, and the Philippines. It ended with a treaty whereby the United States took over the Philippines, Guam, and Puerto Rico; Cuba won partial independence.

Spanish Armada The supposedly invincible fleet of warships sent against England by Philip II of Spain in 1588 but vanquished by the English fleet and bad weather in the English Channel.

Sparta Around 650 B.C.E., after the suppression of a slave revolt, Spartan rulers militarized their society in order to prevent future rebellions and to protect Sparta's superior position in Greece, orienting their society toward the maintenance of their army. Sparta briefly joined forces with Athens and other poleis in the second war with Persia in 480–479 B.C.E., but these two rivals ultimately fell out again in 431 B.C.E. when Sparta and its Peloponnesian allies went to war against Athens and its allies. This bloody conflict lasted until Athens was defeated in 404 B.C.E., after Sparta received military aid from the Persians.

Spartiate A full citizen of Sparta, hence a professional soldier of the hoplite phalanx.

spinning jenny Invention of James Hargreaves (c. 1720–1774) that revolutionized the British textile industry by allowing a worker to spin much more thread than was possible on a hand spinner.

SS (Schutzstaffel) Formed in 1925 to serve as Hitler's personal security force and to guard Nazi party (NSDAP) meetings, the SS grew into a large militarized organization that became notorious for its participation in carrying out Nazi policies.

Joseph Stalin (1879–1953) The Bolshevik leader who succeeded Lenin as leader of the Soviet Union and ruled until his death in 1953.

Stalingrad (1942–1943) The turning point on the Eastern Front during the Second World War came when the German army tried to take the city of Stalingrad in an effort to break the back of Soviet industry. The German and Soviet armies fought a bitter battle, in which more than a half million German, Italian, and Romanian soldiers were killed and the Soviets suffered over a million casualties. The German army surrendered after over five months of fighting. After Stalingrad, the Soviet army launched a series of attacks that pushed the Germans back.

Nicolas Steno (1638–1686) Danish scientist whose studies of rock layers and fossils was foundational to the development of geological sciences.

Stoicism An ancient philosophy derived from the teachings of Zeno of Athens (fl. c. 300) and widely influential within the Roman Empire; it also influenced the development of Christianity. Stoics believe in the essential orderliness of the cosmos and that everything that occurs happens for the best. Since everything is determined in accordance with rational purpose, no individual is master of his or her fate, and the only agency that human beings have consists in their response to good fortune or adversity.

Sumerians The ancient inhabitants of southern Mesopotamia (modern Iraq and Kuwait) whose sophisticated civilization emerged around 4000 B.C.E.

Sunnis Proponents of Islam's customary religious practices (*sunna*) as they developed under the first two caliphs to succeed Muhammad: his father-in-law Abu-Bakr and his disciple Umar. Sunni orthodoxy is dominant within Islam but is opposed by the Shi'ites.

syndicalism A nineteenth-century political movement that embraced a strategy of strikes and sabotage by workers. The syndicalists hoped that a general strike of all workers would bring down the capitalist state and replace it with workers' syndicates, or trade associations. Their refusal to participate in politics limited their ability to command a wide influence.

Syrian civil war (2011–) Sparked when protestors called for reform to Syria's dictatorial government in 2011, the conflict has since escalated, with two chief camps: Assad's government backed by Russia and Iran, and rebel groups backed by the United States, Turkey, Saudi Arabia, and other powers in the region.

tabula rasa Latin for "clean slate." Term used by John Locke (1632–1704) to describe people's minds before they acquired ideas as a result of experience.

Battle of Tannenberg German victory over Russian armies in August 1914, leading to the almost complete destruction of Russia's offensive capacity in the first months of the war.

Tennis Court Oath (1789) Oath taken by representatives of the Third Estate in June 1789, pledging to form a National Assembly and write a constitution limiting the powers of the king.

tetrarchy The result of Diocletian's political reforms of the late third century C.E., which divided the Roman Empire into four quadrants.

Theban Hegemony The term describing the period when the polis of Thebes dominated the Greek mainland, which reached its height after 371 B.C.E., under leadership of the Theban general Epaminondas. It was in Thebes that the future King Philip II of Macedon spent his youth. Macedonian hegemony was forcefully asserted in the defeat of Thebes and Athens at the hands of Philip and Alexander at the Battle of Chaeronea in 338.

theory of evolution Darwin's theory linking biology to history. Darwin believed that competition among different organisms and their struggle with the environment were fundamental and unavoidable facts of life. In this struggle, those individuals who were better adapted to their environment survived, whereas the weak perished. This produced a "natural selection," or the favoring of certain adaptive traits over time, leading to a gradual evolution of different species.

Third Estate The population of France under the Old Regime was divided into three estates, corporate bodies that determined an individual's rights or obligations under royal law. The nobility constituted the First Estate, the clergy the Second, and the commoners (the vast majority of the population) made up the Third Estate.

Third Reich The German state from 1933 to 1945 under Adolf Hitler and the Nazi party.

Third World Those nations—mostly in Asia, Latin America, and Africa—that are not highly industrialized.

Thirty Years' War (1618–1648) Beginning as a conflict between Protestants and Catholics in Germany, this series of skirmishes escalated into a general European war fought on German soil by armies from Sweden, France, and the Holy Roman Empire.

Timur the Lame (1336–1405) Also known as Tamerlane, he was the last ruler of the Mongol Khans' Asian empire.

Josip Broz Tito (1892–1980) This Yugoslavian communist and resistance leader became the leader of Yugoslavia and fought to keep his government independent of the Soviet Union. In response, the Soviet Union expelled Yugoslavia from the communist countries' economic and military pacts.

town A center for markets and administration. Towns existed in a symbiotic relationship with the countryside. They provided markets for surplus food from outlying farms as well as produced manufactured goods. In the Middle Ages, towns tended to grow up around a castle or monastery that afforded protection.

transatlantic triangle The trading of African slaves by European colonists to address labor shortages in the Americas and the Caribbean. Slaves were treated like cargo, loaded onto ships and sold in exchange for molasses, tobacco, rum, and other precious commodities.

Treaty of Brest-Litovsk (1918) Separate peace between imperial Germany and the new Bolshevik regime in Russia. This treaty acknowledged the German victory on the Eastern Front and withdrew Russia from the war.

Treaty of Utrecht (1713) Resolution to the War of Spanish Succession that reestablished a balance of power in Europe, to the benefit of Britain and in ways that disadvantaged Spain, Holland, and France.

Treaty of Versailles Signed on June 28, 1919, this peace settlement ended the First World War and required Germany to surrender a large part of its most valuable territories and to pay huge reparations to the Allies.

trench warfare Weapons such as barbed wire and the machine gun gave tremendous advantages to defensive positions in the First World War, leading to prolonged battles between entrenched armies in fixed positions. The trenches eventually consisted of 25,000 miles of tunnels and ditches that stretched across the Western Front in northern France, from the Atlantic coast to the Swiss border. On the Eastern Front, the large expanse of territories made trench warfare less significant.

triangular trade The eighteenth-century commercial Atlantic shipping pattern that took rum from New England to Africa, traded it for slaves taken to the West Indies, and brought sugar back to New England to be processed into rum.

Triple Entente Alliance developed before the First World War that eventually included Britain, France, and Russia.

Truman Doctrine (1947) Declaration promising U.S. economic and military intervention to counter any attempt by the Soviet Union to expand its influence. Often cited as a key moment in the origins of the Cold War.

tsar Russian word for "emperor," derived from the Latin *caesar* and similar to the German *kaiser*. This was the title claimed by the rulers of medieval Muscovy and of the later Russian Empire.

Ubaid culture An early civilization that flourished in Mesopotamia between 5500 and 4000 B.C.E., it was characterized by large village settlements and temple complexes: a precursor to the more urban civilization of the Sumerians.

Umayyad caliphate (661–930) The Umayyad family resisted the authority of the first two caliphs who succeeded Muhammad but eventually placed a member of their own family in that position of power. The Umayyad caliphate ruled the Islamic world from 661 to 750, modeling its administration on that of the Roman Empire. But after a rebellion led by the rival Abbasid family, the power of the Umayyad caliphate was confined to its territories in al-Andalus (Spain).

Universal Declaration of Human Rights (1948) United Nations declaration that laid out the rights to which all human beings are entitled.

University of Paris The reputation of Peter Abelard and his students attracted many intellectuals to Paris during the twelfth century. Some of them began offering instruction to aspiring scholars. By 1200, this loose association of teachers had formed itself into a *universitas*, or corporation. The teachers began collaborating in the higher academic study of the liberal arts, with a special emphasis on theology.

Urban II (1042?–1099) Instigator of the First Crusade (1096–1099), this pope promised that anyone who fought or died in the service of the Church would receive absolution from sin.

urban population During the nineteenth century, urban populations in Europe increased sixfold. For the most part, urban areas had medieval infrastructures, which new populations and industries overwhelmed. As a result, many European cities became overcrowded and unhealthy.

James Ussher (1581–1656) An Irish archbishop who attempted to reconcile natural and biblical events in a later discredited chronology of the world.

Utilitarianism Theory based on the idea that social institutions and laws should be measured according to their social usefulness, which is equated to the amount of happiness it produced.

Utopia A semisatirical social critique by the English statesman Sir Thomas More (1478–1535); the title derives from the Greek "best place" or "no place."

Utopian Socialists A body of writers and intellectuals in western Europe who supported social reforms and economic planning that would mitigate what they saw as the devastating effects of industrialization on European society.

Lorenzo Valla (1407–1457) One of the first practitioners of scientific philology (the historical study of language). Valla's analysis of the so-called Donation of Constantine showed that this document could not possibly have been written in the fourth century C.E. but must have been forged centuries later.

vassal A person who pledges to be loyal and subservient to a lord in exchange for land, income, or protection.

velvet revolutions The peaceful political revolutions against the Soviet Union throughout Eastern Europe in 1989.

Verdun (1916) This battle between German and French forces lasted for ten months during the First World War. The Germans saw the battle as a chance to break French morale through a war of attrition, and the French believed the battle to be a symbol of France's strength. In the end, over 400,000 lives were lost, and the German offensive failed.

Versailles Conference (1919) Peace conference of the victors of the First World War, it resulted in the Treaty of Versailles, which forced Germany to pay reparations and to give up its colonies to the victors.

Victoria (1819–1901) Influential queen of Great Britain, who reigned from 1837 until her death. Victoria presided over the expansion of the British Empire as well as the evolution of English politics and social and economic reforms.

Viet Cong Vietnamese communist group formed in 1954; committed to overthrowing the government of South Vietnam and reunifying North and South Vietnam.

Vikings (800–1000) The collapse of the Abbasid caliphate disrupted Scandinavian commercial networks and turned traders into raiders. (The word *viking* describes the activity of raiding.) These raids often escalated into invasions that contributed to the collapse of the Carolingian Empire, resulted in the devastation of settled territories, and ended with the establishment of Viking colonies. By the tenth century, Vikings controlled areas of eastern England; Scotland;

the islands of Ireland, Iceland, and Greenland; and parts of northern France. They had also established the beginnings of the kingdom that became Russia and made exploratory voyages to North America, founding a settlement in Newfoundland (Canada).

A Vindication of the Rights of Woman Noted work of Mary Wollstonecraft (1759–1797), an English republican who applied Enlightenment political ideas to issues of gender.

Virgil (70–19 B.C.E.) An influential Roman poet who wrote under the patronage of the emperor Augustus. His *Aeneid* was modeled on the ancient Greek epics of Homer and told the mythical tale of Rome's founding by the Trojan refugee Aeneas.

Visigoths The tribes of "west" Goths who sacked Rome in 410 C.E. and later established a kingdom in the Roman province of Hispania (Spain).

Voltaire Pseudonym of French philosopher and satirist François Marie Arouet (1694–1778), who championed the cause of human dignity against state and Church oppression. Noted deist and author of *Candide*.

Lech Wałęsa (1943–) Leader of the Polish labor movement Solidarity, which organized a series of strikes across Poland in 1980. The strikers protested working conditions, shortages, and high prices. Above all, they demanded an independent labor union. Solidarity's leaders were imprisoned and the union banned, but they launched a new series of strikes in 1988 that led to the legalization of Solidarity and open elections.

war communism The Russian civil war forced the Bolsheviks to take a more radical economic stance. They requisitioned grain from the peasantry and outlawed private trade in consumer goods as "speculation." They also militarized production facilities and abolished money.

Wars of the Roses Fifteenth-century civil conflict between the English dynastic houses of Lancaster and York, each of which was symbolized by the heraldic device of a rose (red and white, respectively). It was ultimately resolved by the accession of the Lancastrian king Henry VII, who married Elizabeth of York.

Warsaw Pact (1955–1991) Military alliance between the USSR and other communist states that was established in response to the creation of the NATO alliance.

The Wealth of Nations 1776 treatise by Adam Smith, whose laissez-faire ideas predicted the economic boom of the Industrial Revolution.

Weimar Republic The government of Germany between 1919 and the rise of Hitler and the Nazi party in 1933.

Western Front During the First World War, the military front that stretched from the English Channel through Belgium and France to the Alps.

Whites Refers to the "counterrevolutionaries" of the Bolshevik Revolution (1918–1921) who fought the Bolsheviks (the "Reds"); included former supporters of the tsar, Social Democrats, and large independent peasant armies.

William the Conqueror (1027–1087) Duke of Normandy who laid claim to the throne of England in 1066, defeating the Anglo-Saxon king Harold at the Battle of Hastings. William and his Norman followers imposed imperial rule in England through a brutal campaign of military conquest, surveillance, and the suppression of the indigenous Anglo-Saxon language.

William of Ockham (d. 1349) An English philosopher and Franciscan friar, he denied that human reason could prove fundamental theological truths, such as the existence of God. Instead, William argued that there is no necessary connection between the observable laws of nature and the unknowable essence of divinity. His theories, derived from the work of earlier scholastics, form the basis of the scientific method.

Woodrow Wilson (1856–1924) U.S. president who requested and received a declaration of war from Congress so that America could enter the First World War. After the war, his prominent role at the Paris Peace Conference signaled the rise of the United States as a world power. He also proposed the Fourteen Points, which influenced the peace negotiations.

Maria Winkelmann (1670–1720) German astronomer who worked with her husband in his observatory. Although she discovered a comet and prepared calendars for the Berlin Academy of Sciences, the academy would not let her take her husband's place within the body after he died.

witch craze The rash of persecutions that took place in both Catholic and Protestant countries of early modern Europe and their colonies, facilitated by secular governments and religious authorities.

women's associations Because European women were excluded from the workings of parliamentary and mass politics, some women formed their own organizations to press for political and civil rights. Some groups focused on establishing educational opportunities for women; others campaigned energetically for the vote.

women's suffrage movement Nineteenth- and early twentieth-century campaigns led by women to gain the right to vote and run for office.

William Wordsworth (1770–1850) Romantic poet whose central themes were nature, simplicity, and feeling. He considered nature to be the most trustworthy teacher and the source of sublime power that nourished the human soul.

World Bank International agency established in 1944 to provide economic assistance to war-torn nations and countries in need of economic development.

John Wycliffe (c. 1330–1384) A professor of theology at the University of Oxford, Wycliffe urged the English king to confiscate ecclesiastical wealth and to replace corrupt priests and bishops with men who would live according to the apostolic standards of poverty and piety. He advocated direct access to the scriptures and promoted an English translation of the Bible. His teachings played an important role in the Peasants' Revolt of 1381 and inspired the still more radical initiatives of a group known as Lollards.

Xerxes (519?–465 B.C.E.) Xerxes succeeded his father, Darius, as Great King of Persia. Seeking to avenge his father's shame and eradicate any future threats to Persian hegemony, he launched his own invasion of Greece in 480 B.C.E. An allied Greek army defeated his forces in 479 B.C.E.

Yalta conference Meeting among U.S. president Franklin D. Roosevelt, British prime minister Winston Churchill, and Soviet premier Joseph Stalin that occurred in the Crimea in 1945 shortly before the end of the Second World War in which the three leaders planned for the postwar order.

Young Turks The 1908 Turkish reformist movement that aimed to modernize the Ottoman Empire, restore parliamentary rule, and depose Sultan Abdul Hamid II.

ziggurats Temples constructed under the Dynasty of Ur in what is now Iraq, beginning around 2100 B.C.E.

Zika virus A mosquito-borne virus, originally identified in Africa.

Zionism A political movement dating to the end of the nineteenth century holding that the Jewish people constitute a nation and are entitled to a national homeland. Zionists rejected a policy of Jewish assimilation and advocated the reestablishment of a Jewish homeland in Palestine.

Zollverein In 1834, Prussia started a customs union, which established free trade among the German states and a uniform tariff against the rest of the world. By the 1840s, the union included almost all of the German states except

German Austria. It is considered an important precedent for the political unification of Germany, which was completed in 1870 under Prussian leadership.

Zoroastrianism One of the three major universal faiths of the ancient world, alongside Judaism and Christianity, it was derived from the teachings of the Persian Zoroaster around 600 B.C.E. Zoroaster redefined religion as an ethical practice common to all, rather than as a set of rituals and superstitions that cause divisions among people. Zoroastrianism teaches that there is one supreme god in the universe, Ahura-Mazda (Wise Lord), but that his goodness will be constantly assailed by the forces of evil until the arrival of a final "judgment day." Proponents of this faith should therefore help good to triumph over evil by leading a good life and by performing acts of compassion and charity. Zoroastrianism exercised a profound influence over many early Christians, including Augustine.

Ulrich Zwingli (1484–1531) A former priest from the Swiss city of Zurich, Zwingli joined Luther and Calvin in attacking the authority of the Roman Catholic Church.

Text Credits

CHAPTER 1

Nels M. Bailkey (ed.): From *Readings in Ancient History: Thought and Experience from Gilgamesh to St. Augustine, 5th Edition.* © 1996 Wadsworth, a part of Cengage Learning, Inc. Reproduced by permission. www.cengage.com/permissions.

Bible. New Revised Standard Version: Scripture quotations from Genesis 6–9 from the New Revised Standard Version of the Bible, copyright © 1989 National Council of the Churches of Christ in the United States of America. Used by permission. All rights reserved.

Maureen Gallery Kovacs (trans.): Excerpt from *The Epic of Gilgamesh*, with an Introduction and Notes by Maureen Gallery Kovacs, translator. Copyright © 1985, 1989 by the Board of Trustees of the Leland Stanford Junior University. All rights reserved. Reprinted by permission of the publisher, Stanford University Press, www.sup.org.

Martha T. Roth (ed.): Excerpts from "The Code of Hammurabi" from *Law Collections from Mesopotamia and Asia Minor*, edited by Martha T. Roth, pp. 76–135. © 1995 Society of Biblical Literature. Reprinted by permission of Society of Biblical Literature.

CHAPTER 2

James B. Pritchard (ed.): "Cyrus." From *Ancient Near Eastern Texts Relating to the Old Testament—Third Edition with Supplement.* © 1950, 1955, 1969, renewed 1978 by Princeton University Press. Reprinted by permission of Princeton University Press.

CHAPTER 3

Aristophanes: Excerpt from *The Clouds* from *Lysistrata and Other Plays* by Aristophanes, translated with an introduction by Alan H. Sommerstein (Penguin Classics, 1973). Copyright © Alan H. Sommerstein, 1973. Reproduced by permission of Penguin Books Ltd.

Homer: From *The Odyssey* by Homer, translated by Emily Wilson. Copyright © 2018 by Emily Wilson. Used by permission of W. W. Norton & Company, Inc.

Plato: Excerpts from *The Last Days of Socrates* by Plato, translated with an introduction by Hugh Tredennick (Penguin Classics 1954, Third edition 1969). Copyright © Hugh Tredennick, 1954, 1959, 1969. Reproduced by permission of Penguin Books Ltd.

Sappho: "Fragment 16" from *The Poetry of Sappho*, translated and notes by Jim Powell, pp. 6–7. Copyright © 2007 by Jim Powell. Reprinted by permission of Jim Powell. "Sappho to Her Pupils," translated by Lachlan Mackinnon, *The Times Literary Supplement*, July 15, 2005. © Lachlan Mackinnon/The Times Literary Supplement/News International Trading Ltd. Reprinted with permission.

CHAPTER 4

Arrian: Excerpts from *The Campaigns of Alexander* by Arrian, translated by Aubrey de Sélincourt, revised with an introduction and notes by J. R. Hamilton (Penguin Classics 1958, Revised edition 1971). Copyright © the Estate of Aubrey de Sélincourt, 1958. Introduction and Notes copyright © J. R. Hamilton, 1971. Reproduced by permission of Penguin Books Ltd.

Phintys: From Lefkowitz, Mary R., and Maureen B. Fant, eds., *Women's Life in Greece and Rome: A Source Book in Translation, Second Edition*, pp. 163–164. © 1982, 1992 M. B. Fant & M. R. Lefkowitz. Reprinted with permission of Johns Hopkins University Press and Bristol Classical Press, an imprint of Bloomsbury Publishing Plc.

CHAPTER 5

Plutarch: From Lefkowitz, Mary R., and Maureen B. Fant, eds., *Women's Life in Greece and Rome: A Source Book in Translation*, Second Edition, pp. 147–149. © 1982, 1992 M. B. Fant & M. R. Lefkowitz. Reprinted with permission of Johns Hopkins University Press and Bristol Classical Press, an imprint of Bloomsbury Publishing Plc.

Polybius: Excerpts from *The Rise of the Roman Empire* by Polybius, translated by Ian Scott-Kilvert, selected with an introduction by F. W. Walbank (Penguin Classics, 1979). Copyright © Ian Scott-Kilvert, 1979. Reproduced by permission of Penguin Books Ltd.

Tacitus: Excerpts from *The Annals of Imperial Rome* by Tacitus, translated with an introduction by Michael Grant (Penguin Classics 1956, Sixth revised edition 1989). Copyright © Michael Grant Publications Ltd, 1956, 1959, 1971, 1973, 1975, 1977, 1989. Reproduced by permission of Penguin Books Ltd.

CHAPTER 6

Bible. New Revised Standard Version: Scripture quotations from Acts of the Apostles 23–24 from the New Revised Standard Version of the Bible, copyright © 1989 National Council of the Churches of Christ in the United States of America. Used by permission. All rights reserved.

Sidonius: Reprinted from *Sidonius: Volume II—Letters*, translated by W. B. Anderson, Loeb Classical Library Volume 420, pp. 127–129, 181–183, Cambridge, Mass.: Harvard University Press, Copyright © 1965 by the President and Fellows of Harvard College. Loeb Classical Library ® is a registered trademark of the President and Fellows of Harvard College. Reprinted with permission.

P. G. Walsh (trans.): Letters from Book Ten of *Pliny the Younger: Complete Letters*, translated by P. G. Walsh. Copyright © P. G. Walsh 2006. Reprinted by permission of Oxford University Press.

CHAPTER 7

H. R. Loyn and John Percival: "Capitulary concerning the parts of Saxony" from *The Reign of Charlemagne: Documents on Carolingian Government and Administration* (New York: St. Martin's Press, 1976), edited and translated by H. R. Loyn and John Percival. Reprinted by permission of the Estate of H. R. Loyn.

Michael Sells (trans.): "Sura 81: The Overturning" from *Approaching the Qur'an: The Early Revelations*, translated by Michael Sells, pp. 48, 50. Copyright © 1999 by Michael A. Sells. Reprinted by permission of White Cloud Press.

CHAPTER 8

Bernard of Angers: "Miracles of Saint Foy" from *Readings in Medieval History*, 5th Edition, edited and translated by Patrick J. Geary, © University of Toronto Press 2016. Reprinted by permission of the publisher.

Anna Comnena: Excerpts from *The Alexiad of Anna Comnena*, translated by E. R. A. Sewter (Penguin Classics, 1969). Copyright © E. R. A. Sewter, 1969. Reproduced by permission of Penguin Books Ltd.

Pope Urban II: "Urban II's Call for a Crusade," from *The Crusades: A Reader*, 2nd edition, edited by S. J. Allen and Emilie Amt, © University of Toronto Press 2014. Reprinted by permission of the publisher.

CHAPTER 9

Marie de France: "Equitan" from *The Lais of Marie de France*, translated by Glyn S. Burgess and Keith Busby (Penguin Classics 1986, Second edition 1999). Copyright © Glyn S. Burgess and Keith Busby, 1986, 1999. Reproduced by permission of Penguin Books Ltd.

Robert I. Moore (ed. & trans.): "The Conversion of Peter Waldo" from *The Birth of Popular Heresy*, edited and translated by Robert I. Moore (London: Edward Arnold, 1975). Copyright © 1975, Edward Arnold Publishers. Reproduced by permission of Robert I. Moore.

St. Francis of Assisi: Excerpts from Marion A. Habig, editor, *St. Francis of Assisi: Omnibus of Sources* (Cincinnati: Franciscan Media, 2012) are used by permission. All rights reserved.

CHAPTER 10

Walter Bower: "A Declaration of Scottish Independence," from *Scotichronicon*, Volume 7, by Walter Bower. Edited by B. Scott and D. E. R. Watt. Copyright © University of St. Andrews 1996. Reprinted by permission of Birlinn Ltd.

Rosemary Horrox (ed.): Excerpts from *The Black Death*, translated and edited by Rosemary Horrox. © Rosemary Horrox 1994. Reprinted by permission of Manchester University Press, Manchester, UK.

Marco Polo: From *The Description of the World*, by Marco Polo, translated by Sharon Kinoshita. © 2016 by Hackett Publishing Company, Inc. Reprinted by permission of Hackett Publishing Company, Inc. All rights reserved.

M. C. Seymour (ed.): "The Legend of Prester John" from *Mandeville's Travels*, pp. 195–199. Copyright © 1967 Clarendon Press. Reprinted by permission of Oxford University Press.

CHAPTER 11

Gabriel Biel: "Execrabilis." Reprinted by permission of the publisher from *Defensorium Obedientiae Apostolicae et alia Documenta* by Gabriel Biel, edited and translated by Heiko A. Oberman, Daniel E. Zerfoss and William J. Courtenay, pp. 224–227, Cambridge, Mass.: The Belknap Press of Harvard University Press, Copyright © 1968 by the President and Fellows of Harvard College.

Christine de Pizan: Excerpt from pages 11–13, in *The Book of the Deeds of Arms and of Chivalry*, edited by Charity Cannon Willard and translated by Sumner Willard, 1999. Copyright © 1999 by The Pennsylvania State University Press. Reprinted by Permission of The Pennsylvania State University Press.

Carolyne Larrington (trans.): "The Condemnation of Joan of Arc by the University of Paris" from *Women and Writing in Medieval Europe: A Sourcebook*, by Carolyne Larrington, Copyright © 1995 Routledge. Reproduced with permission of Taylor & Francis Books UK.

L. R. Loomis (ed. and trans.): "Haec Sancta Synodus" and "Frequens" from *The Council of Constance: The Unification of the Church*, by L. R. Loomis pp. 229, 246–247. Copyright © 1961 Columbia University Press. Reprinted by permission of the publisher.

CHAPTER 12

Bartolome de las Casas: Excerpts from *A Short Account of the Destruction of the Indies* by Bartolome de las Casas, edited and translated by Nigel Griffin, introduction by Anthony Pagden (Penguin Classics, 1992). Translation and Notes copyright © Nigel Griffin, 1992. Introduction copyright © Anthony Pagden 1992. Reproduced by permission of Penguin Books Ltd.

Niccoló Machiavelli: From *The Prince* by Niccoló Machiavelli, translated and edited by Thomas G. Bergin, pp. 75–76, 78. Copyright © 1947 by F. S. Crofts & Co., Inc., copyright © renewed 1975 by Thomas G. Bergin. Reprinted by permission of John Wiley & Sons, Inc.

CHAPTER 13

Henry Bettenson (ed.): "Rules for Thinking with the Church" and "Obedience of the Jesuits" from *Documents of the Christian Church*, 2nd Edition (1967). Reprinted by permission of Oxford University Press.

E. M. Plass (ed.): From *What Luther Says, Vol. II*, (pgs. 888–889) © 1959, 1987 Concordia Publishing House. Used with permission of CPH. All rights reserved.

CHAPTER 14

Michel de Montaigne: Excerpts from *Montaigne: Essays* by Michel de Montaigne, translated by J. M. Cohen (Penguin Classics, 1958). Copyright © J. M. Cohen, 1958. Reproduced by permission of Penguin Books Ltd.

Armand Jean du Plessis: From Henry Bertram Hill (trans.), *The Political Testament of Cardinal Richelieu*, pp. 31–32. © 1961 by the Board of Regents of the University of Wisconsin System. Reprinted by permission of The University of Wisconsin Press.

CHAPTER 15

Robert Filmer: "Observations upon Aristotle's Politiques" (1652), in *Divine Right and Democracy: An Anthology of Political Writing in Stuart England*, edited by David Wootton, pp. 110–18. Copyright © 1986. Reproduced by permission of Hackett Publishing.

CHAPTER 16

René Descartes: From *A Discourse on the Method*, translated by Ian Maclean. Copyright © Ian Maclean 2006. Reprinted by permission of Oxford University Press.

Galileo Galilei: Excerpts from *Discoveries and Opinions of Galileo* by Galileo, translated by Stillman Drake, copyright © 1957 by Stillman Drake. Used by permission of Doubleday, an imprint of the Knopf Doubleday Publishing Group, a division of Penguin Random House LLC. All rights reserved.

Pierre Gassendi: From *The Selected Works of Pierre Gassendi*, edited by Craig B. Brush. (New York: Johnson Reprint Corporation, 1972), pp. 334–336.

Photo Credits

Collection/Alamy Stock Photo; **p. 448:** (**left**): akg-images; (**right**): Erich Lessing/Art Resource, NY; **p. 450:** (**both**): Erich Lessing/Art Resource, NY; **p. 456:** PRISMA ARCHIVO/Alamy Stock Photo; **p. 459:** (**left**): Niday Picture Library/Alamy Stock Photo; (**right**): Scala/Art Resource, NY; **p. 461:** Peter Horree/Alamy Stock Photo.

CHAPTER 14

p. 469: Archivart/Alamy Stock Photo; **p. 471:** Virginia Historical Society, Richmond/Bridgeman Images; **p. 479:** Heritage Image Partnership Ltd/Alamy Stock Photo; **p. 481:** akg-images; **p. 483:** Archivart/Alamy Stock Photo; **p. 484:** Andreas Juergensmeier/Shutterstock; **p. 490:** Granger, NYC; **p. 493:** The National Trust Photolibrary/Alamy Stock Photo; **p. 494:** Military History Collection/Alamy Stock Photo; **p. 498:** (**left**): Pictorial Press Ltd/Alamy Stock Photo; (**right**): Interfoto/Alamy Stock Photo; **p. 502:** Heritage Image Partnership Ltd/Alamy Stock Photo; **p. 503:** PAINTING/Alamy Stock Photo; **p. 504:** Peter Horree/Alamy Stock Photo; **p. 505:** (**top**): classicpaintings/Alamy Stock Photo; (**left**): The Iveagh Bequest, Kenwood House, London, UK/Bridgeman Images; (**right**): The Artchives/Alamy Stock Photo.

CHAPTER 15

p. 509: IanDagnall Computing/Alamy Stock Photo; **p. 511:** Courtesy Rijksmuseum, Amsterdam; **p. 514:** (**left**): FORGET Patrick/SAGAPHOTO.COM/Alamy Stock Photo; (**right**): The Picture Art Collection/Alamy Stock Photo; **p. 515:** (**top**): Edinburgh University Library, Scotland/With kind permission of the University of Edinburgh/Bridgeman Images; (**bottom**): Erich Lessing/Art Resource, NY; **p. 519:** IanDagnall Computing/Alamy Stock Photo; **p. 520:** Pictorial Press Ltd/Alamy Stock Photo; **p. 524:** Dagli Orti/REX/Shutterstock; **p. 527:** Bpk, Berlin/Jörg P. Anders. Stiftung Preussische Schlösser und Gärten/Art Resource, NY; **p. 531:** Courtesy Dr. Alexander Boguslawski, Professor of Russian Studies, Rollins College.

CHAPTER 16

p. 539: Private Collection/Bridgeman Images; **p. 542:** Jeffrey Coolidge/Getty Images; **p. 543:** Album/Alamy Stock Photo; **p. 544:** Science History Images/Alamy Stock Photo; **p. 548:** (**left**): Granger, NYC; (**right**): Science History Images/Alamy Stock Photo; **p. 549:** (**left**): Universal History Archive/UIG/Bridgeman Images; (**right**): Royal Astronomical Society/Science Source; **p. 551:** Photos 12/Alamy Stock Photo; **p. 553:** Look and Learn/Bridgeman Images ; **p. 556:** Courtesy of Historical Collections & Services, Claude Moore Health Sciences Library, University of Virginia; **p. 557:** Universal History Archive/UIG/Bridgeman Images; **p. 558:** SSPL/Getty Images; **p. 562:** Courtesy of the Warden and Scholars of New College, Oxford/Bridgeman Images.

Index

Note: Page numbers in *italics* refer to illustrations, maps, and tables.

Abbasid dynasty
  Baghdad as capital, 233, 246, 247, 249, 286, 289, 338, 380
  declining power, 247, 249, 276, 277
  poetry, 288
  trade with Charlemagne and Franks, 235, 246, 247
  translations of Greek authors, 286
  Umayyads and, 232, 233, 235
Abbey Church (Cluny), 271–72
Abbey Church (Island of Iona), *240*
Abelard, Heloise, 292, 294, 310, 318, 328
Abelard, Peter, 292, 294, 296, 318, 319, 322, 328
abortion, 63
absolutism, 508–37
  absolute monarchy, defined, 510
  alternatives to, 518–22
  appeal and justification of, 510, 516–17
  autocracy in Russia, 530–35, *531*
  centralized bureaucracy and, 510, 511, 528, 529–30, 533
  chronology, 510, *536*
  defined, 510
  of Louis XIV, 491–92, 508, 510–18, *514–15*, 521, 525, 530
  nobility and, 512, 525, 528, 530–31
  overview, 508–10
  patriarchy and, 516–17
  population and climate in absolutist age, 510–11, *511*
  remaking of Central and Eastern Europe, 525–30
  war and balance of power (1661–1715), 522–24
  see also monarchies
Abu Bakr, 230
Abul Abbas (elephant), 235
Abydos (Egypt), 24, 26
Academy (Athens), 119, *119*
Academy of Sciences (France), 558, 559, 563
Achaean League, 132, 144, 159
Achilles (Greek hero), 40, 80, 89, 114, 125

Acre, as capital of kingdom of Jerusalem, 306
acropolis, 82, *91*, 92
Actium, battle of, 168
Act of Settlement, 519
Act of Supremacy (1559), 460
Act of Toleration (England), 519
Acts of the Apostles, 189, 190–91
Adam (biblical character), 71, 189, 209, 516
Aegean civilization
  Minoan Crete, 51, 52, 52–53, 53, 54
  Mycenaean Greece, 51, 53–54, *54*, 55, 57, 80, 81, 103
  overview, 51
  Sea Peoples and end of Bronze Age, 54–56, 62
Aelia Capitolina, 171, *178*, 186
  see also Jerusalem
Aeneas (Roman epic hero), 150, 154–55, 174, *374*
Aeneid (Virgil), 148, 150
Aeschylus (Greek playwright), 101
Aetolian League, 132
Afghanistan
  Alexander the Great in, 125
Africa
  Cape of Good Hope, 424
  early humans in, 5
  medieval demand for gold in, 342–43
  slave trade
    fifteenth-century exploration and, 423–24, 426–27, 432
    sixteenth–seventeenth century colonialism and, 472, 474–76, *475*, 481, 495
  Stone Age societies in, 5
  Vandals' capture of North Africa, 206, 207, 209
  see also individual countries
Against the Thievish, Murderous Hordes of Peasants (Luther), 446
Agamemnon (legendary Mycenaean king), 51, 80, 89
Agesilaus (Spartan king), 122

Agincourt, battle of, 385
agora, 81, 82, *91*
agriculture
  in ancient Athens, 89
  in ancient Egypt, 21
  ancient Rome and, 152–53, 157, 160
  Black Death impact on, 368
  Columbian exchange and effects on, *472*
  crop-rotation systems, 260–61
  of early civilizations, 4, 6–8, 7
  Early Middle Ages in Europe, 236, 237
  feudalism and, 267
  Great Famine (1315–1322), 359–60, 376
  during Hellenistic period, 134
  hunter-gatherer societies and, 4, 6
  irrigation in ancient Egypt, 35
  irrigation in Mesopotamia, 8, 9, 16, 22, 65
  Medieval Climate Optimum, 259–61, 344
  Medieval Warm Period and agricultural revolution, 237, 259–61, 359
  plows, for farming, *17*, *36*, *152*, 237, 259
  seed drills (Sumerian), 16, *17*
  Ubaid culture, 9
  see also serfs/serfdom
Ahhotep (queen of Egypt), 45
Ahmose (pharaoh of Egypt), 45
Ahriman (Zoroastrianism counter-deity), 69
Ahura-Mazda (Zoroastrianism god), 68, *68*, 69, 187
Aisha (wife of Muhammad), 234
Akhaiwoi (Achaeans), 57
Akhenaten (pharaoh of Egypt), 48, 48–49
Akhetaten (Egypt), 48, 49
Akkadian Realm, 17–18
al-Andalus (Muslim Spain). *see* Spain
al-Aqsa Mosque, 284, 306
Alaric (leader of the Goths), 206, 207
Alberti, Leon Battista, 378–79, 407, 413
Albert of Hohenzollern, 440
Albigensian Crusade, 308
Alchemist, The (Jonson), 502
Alcuin (Anglo-Saxon monk), 245

Alexander III (pope), 298, 315, 316
Alexander IV (Alexander the Great's son),
129
Alexander VI (pope), 406, 441, 442, *442*
Alexander the Great
    admiration of Cyrus the Great, 67, 125
    admiration of Cyrus the Younger,
        114, 117
    Aristotle and, 114
    attempted mutiny against, 128
    cities founded by, 125, 126, 133
    conquest of Persia by, 124–25, *126*
    death of, 126–27
    in Egypt, 24, 125
    final campaigns of, 125–26, *127*
    legacy of, 132, 485
    marble head of, *124*
    overview, 114, 116
    Philip II and, 122, 123
    Ptolemy and, 124, 130
    successor kingdoms to Alexander's
        empire, 127, 129, 129–32
    world of Alexander, maps, *125, 127*
    see also Macedonia
Alexandria (Egypt), 125, 130, 133,
    138, *178*
Alexis, Saint, 316
Alexius Comnenus (Byzantine emperor),
    278, 279, 280, 283, 285
Alfonso II (king of Aragon), 302, 304, *305*
Alfred the Great (king of England), 249, 261
Ali (caliph), 232
Alkibiades, 106–7
Allah, 228
Almagest (Ptolemy), 139
Almohads, 322
alphabet(s)
    Cyrillic, 277
    demotic, 27, *29*
    evolution of, *59*
    Greek, 59, *59*, 150
    Hebrew, *59*
    Linear A (Minoan script), 53, *53*
    Linear B (Mycenaean Greek script),
        53, 54, 80, 81
    Phoenician, 59, *59*, 81
    Roman, *59*, 150
    Ugaritic alphabet, 51, 59
Ambrose, Saint, 208, 209, 210, 415
Amenemhet (pharaoh of Egypt), 36, 37
Amenhotep II (pharaoh of Egypt), 46–47
Amenhotep III (pharaoh of Egypt), 54
Amenhotep IV (pharaoh of Egypt).
    see Akhenaten

American Revolution of 1776, 510
Ammonites, 61
Ammon, oracle of, 125
Amon (Egyptian god), 47–49
Amon-Ra (Egyptian god), 48
Amorites, 19
    see also Hammurabi
Amos (Hebrew prophet), 74
Amun-Ra (Egyptian god), 125
Amyntas III (king of Macedonia), 123
Anabaptists and Anabaptism, *448,*
    448–49
Anabasis, "The Inland Expedition"
    (Xenophon), 114, 117
analytical geometry, 557
Anatolia
    Byzantine Empire, 221, 261, 279, 336
    Çatalhöyük, 4, 8
    before civilization, 4
    Greek culture in, 81, 85, 95–96, 140
    Hittites in, 44, 49, 57
    Indo-European immigrants in, 44
    Mongol Empire and, 336, 380
    Mycenaean Greeks and, 51, 54, 57
    Ottoman Turks, 380, 381
    sultanate of Rûm, 336
    Turkish invasions, 261–62, 279
    see also Turkey
Anavyssos (Attica), 87
Anchises, 155
Andalus, Al- (Muslim Spain). *see* Spain
Andromache (wife of Hector), 89
Angles, 206
Anglo-Norman system, 268–70, 294, 296
Anglo-Saxons, 216, 241, 249, 268
animals, domestication of, 4, 6
Anna Comnena (daughter of Alexius
    Comnenus), 278, 279
Annals (Tacitus), 172, 173, 175
Anne of Austria, 491
Anne (queen of England), 523
Anselm of Canterbury, 319
Anthropocene epoch, 7
Antigonids, 132
Antigonus (Macedonian ruler), 132
Antioch (Turkey), 131, 133, 222, 230, 283,
    303, 304, 336
Antiochus (Seleucid ruler), 131
Antiochus III (Seleucid ruler), 131, 159
Antiochus IV (Seleucid ruler), 137
anti-Semitism
    development of, 314–15
    see also Judaism
Antoninus Pius (Roman emperor), *169,* 171

Antony, Mark (Marcus Antonius), 166,
    167–68, 173
Anubis (Egyptian god), 32, 34
apella, 93
Aphrodite (Greek goddess), 90
Aphrodite of Knidos, 121, *121*, 176
Apian, Peter, *548*
Apollo (Greek god), 85, 87, 197, 512, 514
Apuleius (Roman author), 174
aqueducts, Neo-Assyrian Empire, 65
aqueducts, Roman Empire, 172, 174,
    177, 219
Aquitaine, 242, 244, 247, 259, 294, 295, 326
Arabian Nights, 233
Arabs
    art and literature, 233
    Byzantine Empire and, 221
    commerce and industry, 233–34
    conquest of West by, 230–32
    revelations of Muhammad, 227
    see also Islam; *individual countries*
Aragon
    "big book of fiefs" (Alfonso II of
        Aragon), 302, 304, *305*
    Middle Ages, 302, *302,* 304, *305*
    Renaissance in, 421
    see also individual leaders
Arbogastes, 212
Arbroath, abbey of, 356
Archaic Greece (800–500 B.C.E.),
    80–100
    aristocracy, tyranny, and democracy
        in, 80, 87–88, 89, 91–92
    cavalry, 86
    colonization and Panhellenism, *84,*
        84–85
    culture of, overview, 83–89
    hoplites and political system, 87, 88,
        91, 100, 103
    hoplite warfare, *86,* 86–87, 88, 93, 97,
        99, *100*
    importance of horses to, 85–86, *86*
    male beauty as ideal, 87
    Persian Wars, 67–68, 97–100, *99, 100*
    poetry of, 88–89, 90
    poleis of, overview, 89–96
    population growth, 81
    rise of Greek poleis, 81–82
    sculpture, 87, *87*
    trade and seafaring, 80, 81, 84–85
    Xerxes' invasion, 68, 98–100, *99*
    see also specific locations and topics
Archaic or Early Dynastic Period (ancient
    Egypt), 26

Archilochus of Paros, 89
Archimedes of Syracuse, 139–40, 541
architecture
        of Byzantine Empire, 226, *226*
        of classical Greece, 103
        Gothic style, 328–29, *329*, 413, 416
        Hellenistic period, 140, *140*
        Medieval cathedrals, 328–29, *329*
        Muslim, Middle Ages, 288–89
        of northern European Renaissance,
            416, *420*
        public works projects of Roman
            Empire, 171, 174, *177*
        Renaissance, 413, 416, *420*
        Romanesque style, 328–29, *329*, 413
        wall and tower of Jericho, 8
archons, 89, 91, 92
Areopagus, 89
Ares (Greek god), 87
Arianism, 200–201, 204, 220
Ariosto, Ludovico, 407, 416
Aristagoras, 97
Aristarchus of Samos, 139, 140
aristocracy
        of Archaic Greece, 80, 87–88, 89, 91
        Black Death impact on, 370–71
        environmental effects, 324
        hunting and, 323–24, *325*, 359
        of Middle Ages, 323–24
        ostentatious display of wealth, 371
        see also class; nobility
Aristophanes (playwright), 101–2, 106,
        110–11, 118, 226
Aristotle
        Alexander the Great and, 114
        astronomy and, 139, *286*, 287,
            542, 545
        birth and death, 84, 120
        on democracy, 88, 120
        legacy of, 210, 224, 285–87, *286*, 322
        on man as political animal, 81
        philosophy of, *119*, 120, 285
        on physiology, 140
        on slavery, 120
        on tragedy, 101
        on women, 120, 203
Ark of the Covenant, 60, 61, 62
"Armada Portrait" (Elizabeth I), *483*
Armenia
        Assyrians and, 63
        capture by Seljuk Turks, 279
        Christian traditions, 223, 277
        Crusader States and, 304
armillary sphere, 542

Árpad (Magyar leader), 255
Arras, France, 264–65, 327
Arrian (Roman), 124, 127, 128
art
        in ancient Egypt, 23, 28, 32, 34, 46–47
        following Black Death, 372, 374
        Byzantine Empire, 226
        classical Greece, 103, *118*, 118–19,
            121, *121*
        Dutch painting, seventeenth century,
            503–5, *504*, *505*, *511*
        entertainment in Middle Ages, 328
        of fourth century B.C.E., *118*, 118–19,
            121, *121*
        Hellenistic period, *133*, 138–39, 141, *141*
        Late Middle Ages, 345–46, *346*
        Muslim, Middle Ages, *288*, 288–89
        naturalism in, 103, 141, 345–46, 417
        northern European Renaissance, *414*,
            415, 416–17, *417*
        papermaking, 234
        perspective in Renaissance art,
            407, 417
        portraiture of Renaissance, 408
        Renaissance, 407–13, *408*, *409*, *412*,
            416–17, *417*
        Roman Empire, 175–76, *176*
        southern Europe, seventeenth century,
            502, 502–3, *503*
        see also painting; sculpture
Artaxerxes II (Persian emperor), 117
artillery, 383, 425
Aryan (Indo-European) race, concept of, 201
asceticism, 197, 202
Ashdod (Philistine citadel), 59
Asherah (Canaanite goddess), 70, *74*
Ashkelon (Philistine citadel), 59
Asia
        European explorers' search for routes
            to, 424, *426*, *427*, *428*, 430
        see also individual countries
Assur (Assyrian god), 63, 64, 72, 74
Assurbanipal (Neo-Assyrian king), *65*,
        65–66
Assurnasirpal II (king of Assyria), 63
Assyrian Empire. *see* Neo-Assyrian
        Empire
Assyrians
        chariots, 44, 64
        migrations, 42–43
        Sea Peoples and, 56, 62
        transnational trade networks in
            Bronze Age, 42–43, 49, 56, 62
        see also Neo-Assyrian Empire

astrolabes, 425
astrology, 541, *544*, 545
Astronomia Nova (Kepler), 545
astronomy
        Aristotle, 139, *286*, 287, 542, 545
        Copernican revolution, 139,
            542–44, *543*
        education in Middle Ages, 315
        heliocentric universe concept, 139,
            287, 538, *543*, 543–44, 545,
            546–47
        Hellenistic period, 139
        Kepler, 544–45, 562, *563*
        Muslim scientists in Middle Ages,
            286, 287–88
        Ptolemaic system, 139, 538, 542,
            542–44, 545, *547*, 548
        Tycho Brahe, *544*, 544–45, 549,
            552, *563*
        women and seventeenth-century
            astronomy, 558, *559*
asty, 81, 82
Aten, 48, *48*
Æthelbehrt (king of Kent), 241
Athena (Greek goddess), 89, *91*, 103, *103*
Athens
        Academy, 119, *119*
        acropolis, 82, *91*, 92
        archons, 89, 91, 92
        Areopagus, 89
        classical Greek culture and life, 103–5
        colonization, 84
        destruction of Melos, 106, 108, 109
        downfall of poleis and, 116, 118
        failure of Athenian democracy, 107,
            108–12
        Hellenic League and Xerxes' invasion,
            98–100, *99*
        ostracism, 92, 101
        overview, 89, 91–92
        Parthenon, 103, *103*
        Peloponnesian War, 106–7,
            106–9, *107*
        Periclean Athens, 100–101, 103, 105,
            132, 145
        Pnyx, *91*, 92
        rise of poleis and, 82
        slavery in, 104–5
        theater, 101–2
        Thirty Tyrants, 108
        trireme warships, 98, *98*, 100
Attila, 206
Augustine, Saint, 208, 209–10, 211, 319,
        439, 453

Augustinian order, 438, 439
Augustus (Octavian, Roman emperor)
    infrastructure and public works, 171,
        172, 174
    legacy of, 170–71
    patronage of artists and writers, 148,
        150, 174, 176
    as *pontifex maximus*, 170, 172
    Principate, 168–71, 173, 174, 176, 195
    reign of, 168–69, 171, 172–73, 195
    rise to power, 167–68
    Roman law and, 169, 176
    statue, *168*
Aurelian (Roman emperor), 197
Austrasia, 242, 244, 247
Austria
    absolutism, 512
    Habsburg Empire, 525–26, 528
    League of Augsburg, 523
    Ottoman expansion into Europe and,
        526, 528–29
    siege of Vienna, 526, 528–29
    Treaty of Utrecht, 523–24
    see also Habsburg dynasty
Austria-Hungary
    dominance as Ottoman power
        waned, 526
    see also Austria; Hungary
Avercamp, Hendrick, *511*
Averroès (Ibn Rushd), 322, *322*
Avesta (Zoroastrianism), 70
Avicenna, 286, 287
Avignon, papacy in, 347, 350, *350*–52,
    356, 374, 378, 388, 391
Azores, 344, 423, 427
Aztec Empire of Mexico, *431*, 473

Ba'al (Canaanite god), 70, 74, 191, 194
Babylon
    Babylonian Captivity of Jews, 66, 74,
        75, 351
    captured and sacked by Hittites,
        21, 44
    captured by Cyrus and Persians, 66,
        72–73, 75, 218
    Hammurabi's rule of, 19–21
    hanging gardens, 65, *65*
    Kassite rule, 44, 49, 56
    rebuilt by Neo-Assyrians, 65, *65*
"Babylonian Captivity" of papacy,
    350–51, 406
    see also Avignon, papacy in
Bacchus (Roman god), *176*
Bacon, Francis, 552–54, *553*, 556, 557, 558

Baconians, 557
Baghdad
    as Abbasid capital, 233, 246, 247, 249,
        276, 289
    Mongol destruction of, 249, 338
    papermaking, 234
Balboa, Vasco Núñez de, 428
Baldwin (king of Jerusalem), 278
Baldwin II (king of Jerusalem), 306
Balkans
    Slavs' migration to, 276–77
Balzac, Honoré de, 337
Bank of England, 520
baptism, 188, 351, 448
barbarians
    Greek concept, 78, 204
    migrations of Rome's frontier peoples,
        204–6, *205*, 207
    Roman concept, 212–13
Barbarossa (Frederick I, Holy Roman
    Emperor), 298, 306
Barberini, Maffeo, 547
    see also Urban VIII (pope)
"barracks emperors" (Roman), 194
Bartlett, Robert, 330
Basil II (Byzantine emperor), 277
Basil of Caesarea, 211
Bassi, Laura, 558, 559
Bayeux Tapestry, 269, *269*
Becket, Thomas, 295, *295*, 315, 326
Bede (monk), 216, 238, 249
Beethoven, Ludwig van, 144
Before the Common Era (B.C.E.), 4
Beguines, 314
Béla III (king of Hungary), 300
Belarus, 418, 522
Belgium
    Battle of Courtrai, 353
Belisarius (Byzantine general), 219
Benedictine monasticism, 211, 212–13,
    241, 242, 271–72
Benedict of Nursia (saint), 210, 211, 212, 241
Benedict's *Rule*, 210, 211, 212, 241, 271,
    309, 463
Beowulf, 249, 324
Berlin Academy of Sciences, 559
Bermuda, colonization, *471*
Bernard of Angers, 274–75
Bernard of Clairvaux, Saint, 309, 310, 319
Bernini, Gianlorenzo, 503
Berry, duke of, 370
bibloi (books), 58
"big book of fiefs" (Alfonso II of Aragon),
    302, 304, *305*

Bill of Rights (England), 519
birds, hunting of (Middle Ages), 324, *325*
birthday invitation from Roman Britain, *175*
Black Death
    challenges to Roman Church follow-
        ing, 391, 393–95
    European outbreaks of, 360–63, *361*
    impact of, 332, 368–74, *369*
    Mongol siege of Genoese at Caffa,
        342, 360
    population loss from, 360, 365,
        367, 368
    Yersinia pestis, 360, 368
Black Stone, 227
Blanche of Castile, 326
Blessed Virgin, cult of, 310, *310*
Boccaccio, Giovanni, 371
Bodin, Jean, 500
Boethius, Anicius Manlius Severinus,
    210–11, 319
Bohemia
    conversion to Christianity, 255
    in Middle Ages, 299–300
    reform movements, Late Middle Ages,
        395–97
    Thirty Years War, 485
Bołeslaw III (king of Poland), 300
Bołeslaw the Pius (Polish duke), 300
Boleyn, Anne, 456, 457, 460
Boniface VIII (pope), 347, 350, 354
Boniface, Saint, 242, 243
Book of Common Prayer, The (Cranmer),
    458, 460
Book of Contemplation, The (Usama), 284
Book of Deuteronomy, 74
Book of Marvels, The (Mandeville), 332,
    340–41
Book of the City of Ladies (Christine de
    Pizan), 373
Book of the Courtier, The (Castiglione), 407
*Book of the Deeds of Arms and of Chivalry,
    The* (Christine de Pizan), 373
books
    bibloi, 58
    censorship and, 462
    codex invention, 211, 213
    rutters/routiers, 425
    see also Christian Bible; Hebrew Bible;
        printing; *individual titles of books*
books of the dead, 32
Borgia, Cesare, 406, 441
Borneo, 480
Bossuet, Jacques-Bénigne, 516
Boudica (Celtic warrior queen), 171

Bourbon dynasty
absolutism, 558
Henry of Navarre and, *479*, 480
Boyle, Robert, 557, 562
Bramante, Donato, 409, *410*, 413
Brandenburg-Prussia, 512, 525,
527–30, 535
Brazil
fugitive slave community in, 477
Bretons, 327
Bronze Age
chronology, *38*, 76
maps of, *43*, *50*, *54*
migrations of, 42–44, *43*
Mycenaean Greece, 51, 53–54, *54*, 55,
57, 80, 81, 103
overview, 15
Sea Peoples and end of, 54–56, 62
transnational diplomacy in Late
Bronze Age, 49, 57
transnational trade networks in late
Bronze Age, 42–44, 49–51, 56, 80
see also Hammurabi; Middle Kingdom
bronze, defined, 16, 49
Bruegel, Pieter the Elder, 503–4, *504*
Bruni, Leonardo, 378, 407
Brutus, Lucius Junius, 151, 167
Brutus, Marcus Junius, 151, 167, *167*,
168, 173
bubonic plague, 360–63, *361*, 368, 431
see also Black Death
Bucephalus (Alexander the Great's
warhorse), 126
bull-leaping fresco (Minoan), *52*
bureaucracy
absolutism and, 510, 511, 528,
529–30, 533
of ancient Egypt, 24, 26
in tsarist Russia, 533
Burgundians, 206, 386
Burgundy, duke of, 384, 386
Byzantine Empire
art and architecture of, 226, *226*
Byzantium and, 220
consequences of First Crusade, 283
economic decline in eleventh century,
277–78
education system, 223–25
end of eastern Roman Empire,
379–83
expansion and fragility of, 276–80, *277*
Greek fire, 221, *221*
iconoclasm, 222–23, 224–25, 243
Islam and, 221, 230, *231*, 235

map (1025), *277*
piracy issues of, 261
religious orthodoxy, 222–23
stability of, 221–22
tradition and innovation in, 223–25
see also Roman Empire

Cabinet of Curiosities (Wurm), *551*
Cabot, John, 470
Cadmus, 59
Caernarvon Castle, 355, *355*
Caesar, Augustus (Octavian). *see* Augustus
(Octavian, Roman emperor)
Caesar, Gaius Julius, 35, 151, 155–56, *164*,
164–65, *165*, 167, 170
Caesarion, 165, 168
calendars
Anno Domini (A.D.), concept, 11
Before the Common Era (B.C.E.),
concept, 4
Common Era (C.E.), concept, 11
Julian, 35, 165
lunar, 17, 35
solar, 35
Caligula (Roman emperor), 170
caliph, defined, 230
Calvinism
in Geneva, 451, 455, 479
inception of, 449–51
in Netherlands, 451, 480, *481*, 503, 504
in Scotland, 451, 492, 493
Calvin, John, 448, 449–51, *450*, 455, 499
Cambridge University, 320, 560
Cambyses (king of Persia), 73
Cambyses II (king of Persia), 67
Camulodunum, 171
Canaanites, *50*, 56, 60, 61, 72
see also Phoenicians
Canada
French exploration of, 489
Québec, 489, 490, 524
Canary Islands, 344, 423, 424, 427
Canillac, Marquis of, 508
cannons, 383, 425
Canon of Medicine (Avicenna), 287
Canterbury Tales, The (Chaucer), 371
Cape of Good Hope, 424
Capetian dynasty, 259, 266–67, 358
Cape Verde Islands, 423, 427, 432
Caracalla (Roman emperor), 193
caravels, 424–25
Caribbean
Louis XIV (king of France) and
colonization of, 516–18

Carloman (son of Charles Martel), 243
Carneades (Greek Skeptic), 136
Carolingian Empire, 242–48, *243*, 256–59
Carolingian minuscule, 245, *246*
Carolingian Renaissance, 245
Carolingian rule, 256
Cartesians, 557
Carthage
maritime empire, 157
as Phoenician colony, 59, 157
Punic Wars and, 145, 157–58,
158, 159
Casas, Bartolomé de las, 432–33
Casimir III (king of Poland), 389
Cassiodorus Senator, Flavius Magnus
Aurelius, 210, *211*, 211–12
Cassius, Gaius, 168, 173
castellans, 266–67, 268, 302
Castiglione, Baldassare, 407
Castile, 302, 306, 370, 384, 421
Castle Church (Wittenberg), 436
castles of Middle Ages, 266, *267*, 302, *302*,
354, *354*
catacombs, *188*
Catalan Atlas, *343*
Çatalhöyük, 4, 8
Catalonia
colonies, 342–43
Middle Ages, 244, 258–59, 302
Renaissance, 421
revolt after Thirty Years' War, 488
Cathars, 308
cathedrals, medieval, 328–29, *329*
Catherine of Aragon, 456–57
Catherine of Siena, Saint, 391, 393
Catherine the Great (empress of Russia), 535
Catholicism
Catholic, defined, 438, 460
Catholic reforms at time of Protestant
Reformation, 461–62
challenges in Late Middle Ages,
391–97
conciliar movement, 392–93, 394–95,
419–20, 462
Council of Constance, 392–93,
394–95, 397, *397*, 419, 462
Fourth Lateran Council of 1215, 308,
312–13, 315, 316, 320
Great East–West Schism, 391
Great Schism, 391, 392, 392–93
Mass, 309, 351–52
monastic reform movement, 271–72
popular and intellectual reformers,
Late Middle Ages, 395–97, *397*

religious reform and papal power, 271–76, 280, 308–9, 347, 350–51

sacraments, 351–52, 439, 441

spiritual challenges, Middle Ages, 393–95

unity and dissent in western Church, 308–15

see also papacy; Roman Catholic Church

Cato, Marcus Porcius (Cato the Censor), 158, 161

Cavalcade, A (van der Meulen), *515*

Cavaliers, 493

Cavendish, Margaret, 559

cave paintings, of Lascaux, 5, *5–6*

Caxton, William, 404–5

Cecilia of Provence, 304, *305*

celibacy
  asceticism and, 202
  Gregory VII's reforms, 275–76, 309
  Leo IX's reforms, 273
  Protestant Reformation and Council of Trent on, 454
  reform of secular clergy (eleventh century), 273

Cella Septichora, *200*

Celts
  Abbey Church (Island of Iona), *240*
  Boudica (Celtic warrior queen), 171
  Christianity, 216, 306
  English crusades against, 306
  impact of migrations and invasions, 206, 248
  monasticism of Early Middle Ages, 240

censorship
  by Council of Trent, 462

Central Europe
  absolutism and, 525–30
  map, c. 1200, *299*
  medieval monarchies of, 298–300
  new kingdoms in Middle Ages, 255
  see also individual countries

Cervantes, Miguel de, 496

Chadwick, John, 123

Chaeronea, battle of, 123

Chaldeans, 66–67, 68, 70, 74–75

Champlain, Samuel de, 489

Champollion, Jean François, 27

Chandragupta (Indian warrior-king), 131

chariots
  Archaic Greece and, 86, *86*
  Assyrians, 64
  Byzantine Empire, 222
  Hittites, 44

Mycenaean Greeks, 53

Persians, *68*, 100, 124

Roman Empire, 86

Sumerian, 16

Charlemagne (Holy Roman Emperor)
  Abbasid caliphate and, 235, 246, 247
  access to education during reign of, 315
  Carolingian Empire of, 242–46, *243,* 256–59
  Carolingian Renaissance and, 245
  Christianity and kingship, 245
  coronation as emperor, 246
  death of, 247, 271
  legacy of, 256–59
  Merovingians and, 237
  overview, 235
  reign of, 244–45

Charles I (Charles Stuart; king of England), 492–94, *493,* 496, 497, 498, *498,* 500

Charles II (king of England), 494, 498, 518–19, *519,* 520, 523, 557

Charles II (king of Spain), 523

Charles IV (Holy Roman Emperor), 389

Charles V (Holy Roman Emperor, king of Spain), 428, 444, *444,* 451–52, 456

Charles V (king of France), 384

Charles VI (king of France), 384, 386, 388

Charles VII (king of France), 386

Charles VIII (king of France), 418

Charles IX (king of France), 479–80

Charles Gustav (king of Sweden), 489

Charles Martel, 242–43, 244

Charles of Anjou, 347, 354

Charles (Prince of Wales), *355*

Charles the Bald (Charles II; Holy Roman Emperor), 247

Charter of the Forest (Henry III), 324

Chaucer, Geoffrey, 371, 388, *396*

Chauvet (France), cave paintings of, 5–6

children
  enslavement of, in Ottoman Empire, 382
  Protestant Reformation on discipline of, 453

China
  Black Death origin and, 360
  exploration of fifteenth century and, 424
  explosives, invention of, 383
  Great Wall of, 334
  Mongol Empire and, 332, 334, 336, 342
  see also Mongol Empire

chivalry, code of, 266, 323, 324, 327

Chrétien de Troyes, 325

Christian Bible

Council of Nicea, 201

Erasmus's translation of, 208, 415

Gutenberg's printing press and, 400, 402

Jerome's translation of, 208, 245, 379, *417, 461*

King James Bible, 224

Luther's translation of, *439*

Vulgate, 208, *461,* 462

Wycliffe's English Bible, *396,* 397

see also Gospels

Christian humanism, 379, *414,* 414–17, 464

Christianity, 182–215
  Augustine's influence on, 209
  background, 182–84
  as challenge to Roman Empire and its values, 182–84
  Christ (*Christos*), defined, 186
  chronology, *214*
  classical learning and, 210–13, *211*
  conversion of Northwestern Europe, 216, 235–42
  conversion to, in Roman Empire, 195–203
  early Islam and, 230
  Eucharist, 309, 351–52, 397
  in Hellenistic world, 186–89, *187, 188*
  hierarchy and structure of church, 188, 198–200
  Innocent III's crusade for a unified Christendom, 307–8
  Jesus' life and death, 184–86
  Judaism and inception of, 185–89
  Justinian and, 226, *226*
  Mass, focus on, 309, 351–52
  as minority religion in Roman Empire, 188, 189, 192–93, 194, 195–98
  missionary activity, Early Middle Ages, 216, 240, 241, 242
  monastic reform movement, 271–72
  orthodoxy in, 201
  persecution of, *188,* 194–95, 196
  Roman Church religious reform and papal power, 271–76, 280, 308–9, 347, 350–51
  Rome's legacy and, 216
  sacraments ("holy rites"), 351–52, 439, 441
  worldview, fourth–fifth centuries C.E., 207–10
  see also Catholicism; Crusades; Protestantism; Roman Catholic Church

Christina (grand duchess, Medici family), 550

Christine de Pizan, 372, *372*, 373
chronology
    absolutism, *536*
    Bronze Age, *38, 76*
    Christianity, early history, *214*
    colonialism (sixteenth–seventeenth
      centuries), *506*
    early civilizations, *38*
    European–Atlantic world integration
      (1550–1660), *506*
    Greece (ancient), *112, 146*
    Iron Age, *76*
    Middle Ages, *250, 290, 330, 364, 398*
    peoples, gods, and empires (1700–500
      B.C.E.), *76*
    Reformation, *466*
    Renaissance, *398, 434*
    Roman Republic and Roman
      Empire, *180*
    scientific revolution, *564*
Church of England
    Calvinism influence on, 451
    Civil War (England) and, 492, 493, 494
    Edward VI and, 457–58
    Elizabeth I and, 460
    English nationalism and, 465
    Henry VIII and, 457, 458
    Six Articles, 457, 458
Cicero, Marcus Tullius, 156, 162, 168,
    177, 208, 374, 375
Cimon, 101
Cincinnatus, Lucius Quinctius, *152*,
    153, 156
Ciompi rebellion, 370
Cistercian order, 309
citadels
    Mycenaean Greek citadels, 51, 53–54,
      56, 59, 80
    Pergamon, *140*
    Philistine citadels, 59
citizenship
    Roman Empire, 163, 167, 171,
      190–91, 193
    towns of eleventh century and, 265
City of God (Augustine), 210
City of Man, 210
City of Stettin Under Siege, The, 527
civilization, defined, 2, 4
civil law, of Roman Empire, 176–77
Civil War (England)
    Cromwell's Commonwealth and
      Protectorate, 494, 496, 518
    debates about political rights and,
      496–97

    effect on Atlantic colonies, 495
    fall of Charles I, 494, 497, 498
    origins and overview, 492
    Parliament *versus* Charles I, 492–93,
      497, 500
    restoration of monarchy, 494, 495,
      510, 518–19
    taxes and, 493
Clare of Assisi, 314
class
    in Babylonian society, 20–21
    in classical Greece, 100–101
    mobility, opportunity, status in
      Islamic world, 234
    in Roman Republic, 153, 154, 160, 162
    see also aristocracy; peasantry; serfs/
      serfdom
classical Greece (500–323 B.C.E.),
    100–113, 114–27
    art and architecture, 103, *118*, 118–19,
      121, *121*
    Athenian theater, 101–2
    daily life in Athens, 103–5
    downfall of Greek poleis, 116, 118
    Golden Age of, 100–105
    Herodotus and, 78
    hoplite warfare, 99, 100, 116
    Marathon, battle of, 67–68, 97,
      98–100, 101
    Peloponnesian War, 106–8, *107*
    Pericles, 100–101, 103, 105, 106
    Persian Wars, 67–68, 97–100, *99*, *100*
    rise of Macedonia and, 116
    Xerxes' invasion, 68, 98–100, *99*
    see also specific locations and topics
classical learning
    in Byzantine Empire, 223–25
    in Carolingian empire, 245
    Christianity and, 210–13, *211*
    defined, 245
    Middle Ages, 320, 322
    during Renaissance, 375–76, 402
Claudius Ptolemaeus, 139
Claudius (Roman emperor), 171
Cleisthenes, 92
Clement V (pope), 347
Clement VI (pope), 351
Clement VII (pope), 391, 456–57
Cleon (Athenian leader), 106
Cleopatra (use of name, in Ptolemaic
    Egypt), 130
Cleopatra VII (Egyptian pharaoh), 130,
    164–65, *165*, 167, 168
Clifford, Roger, *267*

climate
    in absolutist age, 511, *511*
    Great Famine, 359–60
    Little Ice Age, 511, *511*
    Medieval Climate Optimum
      (Medieval Warm Period), 237,
      259–61, 344, 359
    Neolithic Revolution and, 6
clocks, invention of, 345
cloth of gold, 336
Clouds, The (Aristophanes), 110–11
Clovis (warrior-king of Franks), 237, 243
Clunaic monasticism, 271–72, 273
Cluny, 271–72, 273
Cnut the Great (king of Denmark), 256
Code of Hammurabi, 20–21, 22–23,
    23, 63
Code of Justinian, 220
codex, invention of, 211, 213
coffee trade
    Louis XIV and colonization of
      Caribbean, 517
    Saint-Domingue, 490, 517
coffin texts, 32
coins/coinage
    African gold for, 342
    Byzantine Empire, 277
    of Charlemagne, 244
    Egyptian, *131*
    invention of, 95
    Lydian, 66, *66*, 95
    Oliver Cromwell, *494*
    Renaissance, 400
    Roman, 157, *165*, *167*, 168, 176, *199*
    Seleucids, 131
    Spanish American gold for, 477
    Theodoric the Ostrogoth, *206*
    western Europe in Middle Ages,
      236, 239
Colbert, Jean-Baptiste, 513, 516, 518
College of Cardinals, 274, 275,
    391, 444
Colloquies (Discussions) (Erasmus),
    414–15
Cologne, Town Council of, 363
colonialism
    Atlantic Ocean, Late Middle Ages,
      344, 381, 423
    Civil War (England) and effect on
      Atlantic colonies, 495
    extension of Crusades into European
      colonialism, 306
    under Louis XIV (king of France),
      516–18

Russian imperial expansion (sixteenth to eighteenth centuries), 533–35
    see also colonialism (1550–1660); imperialism
colonialism (1550–1660), 468–77
    chronology, *506*
    colonial populations compared, 472–73
    Columbian exchange and environmental effects, 471–72, *472*
    European colonialism and conflict, overview, 477
    European poverty and, 477–79
    Europe in Atlantic world (1550–1660), overview, 468–70
    slavery and triangular trade, 474–76, *475*
    social hierarchies of New Spain, *473*
colonization by Archaic Greece, 84, *84–85*
color spectrum, Newton on, 560, *562*
Colosseum (Rome), 174, 190
Columbanus (Irish missionary), 240
Columbian exchange, 471–72, *472*
Columbus, Christopher
    Canary Islands, 344, 427
    Ferdinand and Isabella and, 421, 423, 428
    printing presses and, 402
    and traditions of reconquest and crusading, 423
    travel books carried on voyage, 332, 340–41
    voyages, 344, 427–28, *429*, 541
Comedy (Dante), 346–47, 371
commerce
    extension of European commerce and settlement, Late Middle Ages, 342–44, *343*
    founding of Rome, 151
    growth of towns and trade in Middle Ages, 261–65, *263*, *264*
    Hellenistic period, 133–34
    Islamic world during Early Middle Ages, 233–34
    Ottoman Empire, 383
    by Phoenicians, 84
    Sparta and, 94
    see also economic issues; trade
Commodus (Roman emperor), 190
Common Era (C.E.), 11
communes, 264
Companions (Macedonia), 123
compass, magnetic, 345, 425, 540
Complaint of Peace (Erasmus), 415

conciliarism, 392–93, 394–95, 419–20, 462
Concordat of Worms, 276
concordats, 420, 441
concrete, discovery by Romans, 171, 174
confession of sins, 351
Confessions (Augustine), 209
confraternities, 326–27, 374
Congregation for the Doctrine of the Faith, 314
conquistadors, 430–32, *431*
Conrad (duke of Masovia), 300
Consequences of War, The (Rubens), *505*
Consolation of Philosophy, The (Boethius), 210–11
Constantine (Roman emperor)
    attack by Arabs, 221
    Church governance and, 200, 201, 270, 273, 379
    Constantinople founding, 184, 199, 203
    conversion to Christianity, 197–98, *200*, 237
    Council of Nicaea, 201
    "Donation of Constantine," 379
    early career, 197
    Sol Invictus and, 197, *199*
    successors, 203
Constantine V (Byzantine emperor), 224
Constantinople
    Arab attempts to capture, 221, 223, 230–31, 233
    Byzantine Empire and, 220, 222, 223
    Byzantium and, 197, 203, 220
    capture during Crusades, 301, 307, 379
    establishment of, 184, 199–200, 203–7
    fall to Ottoman Turks, 203, 226, 380–81, 383, 402, 425
    sack by Rus', 277
    see also Byzantine Empire; Istanbul; Ottoman Empire
Constantius (Roman emperor), 195, *195*, 197
constitutions
    Constitutions of the Jesuit Order, 463
    Instrument of Government (English Protectorate), 494
    Roman Republic, 153–54, 163
consuls, 152, 153, 154
contract theory of government, 520–21
conversos, 422
convivencia, 421
Copernicus, Nicolaus, 139, 287, 538, *543*, 543–44, 545, 546–47, 548

copper, 16, 44
Coptic language, 29
Corinth
    colonization, 84, 85
    Hellenic League and Xerxes' invasion, 98–100, *99*
    hoplite warfare, *86*
    Peloponnesian League, 105–6
Corpus Juris Civilis (Justinian), 220
Corsica, 157, 158
Cortés, Hernán, 430–31, *431*
Cosmographia (Apian), *548*
Cosmographic Mystery (Kepler), 545
cosmopolis, polis transition to, 132–34
cosmopolitanism, 146
Cossacks, 488
Council of Basel, 393
Council of Constance, 392–93, 394–95, 397, *397*, 419, 462
Council of Nicaea, 201, 392
Council of Siena, 393
Council of Trent, 312, 454, 460, 461–62
Counter-Reformation (Catholic Church), 460–65, 513
counts (comites) in Carolingian empire, 244, 245, 247, 258–59
courtier, as ideal, 407
courtoisie ("courtliness"), 324–25
Courtrai, Battle of, 353
Cranach, Lucas "the Elder," *438*
Cranmer, Thomas (archbishop of Canterbury), 457, 458, 460
Crassus, Marcus Licinius, 164
Creation of Adam, The (Michelangelo), 410, *410*
creation story
    Adam (biblical character), 71, 189, 209, 516
    The Creation of Adam (Michelangelo), 410, *410*
    Genesis, 2, 15, 71, 551
    myths and, 2
    scientific revolution and, 547–49, 551
Crete
    Minoan Crete, 51, *52*, 52–53, *53*, 54
    Muslim capture of, 276
Crito (dialogue with Socrates), 110–11
Croatia
    Middle Ages, 255, 300
Croesus (king of Lydia), 66, *66*, 85
Cromwell, Oliver, 493–94, *494*, 495, 518
Cromwell, Richard, 494
Cromwell, Thomas, 457, 458
Crown of Aragon, 302

Crown of Thorns, 354, *354*
crucifixion, 162
Crusades
    Albigensian Crusade, 308
    background, 278–79
    Christian conquest of Jerusalem, 283
    consequences of First Crusade, 283–85
    against Constantinople, 301, 307, 308
    Crusader States, 281, 283, 285, *303*, 303–5
    crusading orders, 305
    expansion and fragility of Byzantium, 276–80, *277*
    extension of, against fellow Europeans, 306
    First Crusade, 254, 278–79, 280–83, 303, 307
    Fourth Crusade, 307
    Innocent III and, 307–8
    intellectual revolution in Europe following, 294, 315–22
    motives of crusaders, 280–82, 303
    revenge of Venice and, 307
    routes of, *282*
    Third Crusade, 298, 306
    Urban II, 278–79, 280, 281, 283, 303
csar/tsar, terminology, 419
cuneiform, *11*, 11–12, 17, 23, 27, 51
Curaçao, 481
Cyriacus (monk), 202
Cyrillic alphabet, 277
Cyrus the Great (king of Persia), 66–67, 72–73, 75, 125, 131, 218
Cyrus the Younger, 114, 117, 118
Czechoslovakia
    reform movements, Late Middle Ages, 397

Daedalus, 51
da Gama, Vasco, 424, 425
Damascus, as capital of Islam, 232, 233
Damian, Saint, 317
Dante Alighieri, 346–47, 371
Darius the Great (king of Persia), 67–68, *68*, 69, 97–98
Darius III (king of Persia), 124, 128
Dauphin (French royal title), 386
    see also Charles VII (king of France)
David (Donatello), 412, *412*
David (king of Israel), 60, 61, 62, 71
David (Michelangelo), 412, *412*
Dead Sea Scrolls, 185
Death of Arthur, The (Malory), 404–5

Debussy, Claude, 144
Decameron, The (Boccaccio), 371
Decius (Roman emperor), 194
Declaration of Arbroath, 356–57
Decline and Fall of the Roman Empire, The (Gibbon), 214
deductive reasoning, 553, 554–55
de Fer, Nicolas, *490*
Delian League, 100, 105
Delilah, 60
democracy
    of ancient Greece, 54, 88
    Aristotle on, 88, 120
    demos, defined, 88
    failure of Athenian democracy, 107, 108–12
    Pericles and, 101
    Plato on, 120
    republic compared to, 154
Democritus (Greek philosopher), 135
demotic script, 27, 29
Denmark
    Cnut the Great, 256
    European colonialism, 306
    Lutheranism as state religion (sixteenth century), 446
    Middle Ages, 255–56
    Thirty Years' War and, 485
Descartes, René, 465, 552, 554–55, *556*, 559, 562
Descent from the Cross (Michelangelo), *412*, 413
Description of the World (Polo), 332, *339*, 339–40
Deucalion, 40
dialectic methods of debate, 319, 322
Dialogue Concerning the Two Chief World Systems, A (Galileo), 547
Dias, Bartolomeu, 424
diaspora, Greek, 132
Diaspora, Jewish, 138, 189, 230
diaspora, Viking, 248
Díaz del Castillo, Bernal, *431*
dictator (Roman), 153
Diet of Worms, 444–45, 462
Digest (Roman law), 220
Din, Rashid al-, 337
dioceses, defined, 195
Diocletian (Roman emperor), 194–96, *195*, *196*, 197, 199, 203, 204
Dionysos (Greek god), 54, 101, 136, *176*
Discourse on Method (Descartes), 553, 554–55, *556*
Discourses on Livy (Machiavelli), 402, 406

disease
    bubonic plague, 360–63, *361*, 368, 431
    colonialism of seventeenth century and, 484
    Columbian exchange and, 471–72, *472*
    HIV-AIDS, 360
    influenza pandemic of 1918–1919, 360
    Justinianic Plague, 218–19, 360
    pandemics, 218–19, 360–63
    plague in Roman Empire (smallpox), 194
    pneumonic plague, 360
    septicemic plague, 360
    spread by European explorers, 430, 431
    see also Black Death
Divine Comedy (Dante), 346–47, 371
divorce
    ancient Egypt, 35
    ancient Rome, 161, 169
    Hammurabi's code, 21, 23, 63
    see also marriage
Djoser (pharaoh of Egypt), 29, *30*, 36
DNA
    analysis from Griffin Warrior tomb, 53
Doctor Faustus (Marlowe), 500
documentation
    "big book of fiefs" (Alfonso II of Aragon), 302, 304, *305*
    development of writing, 10–12, *11*
    library of Nineveh, 65
    printing press invention, 400, 402, *403*, 404–5, 540
    seals, 68, 348, *348–49*
    see also books; language; printing
dogma, defined, 276
Dokuz Khatun, 337
Dominican order, 311, 314, 322, 422
Dominic of Osma, 314
Donatello, 412, *412*.
"Donation of Constantine," 379
Don Quixote (Cervantes), 496
double-entry bookkeeping, Middle Ages, 344
Dover, seal of, *348*
Drake, Francis, 482
Drakon, 91
du Châtelet, Emilie, 562–63
Duma (Russia), 531
Dürer, Albrecht, 416–17, *417*
Dutch East and West India Companies, 480–81
Dutch Guyana (Surinam), 481
Dutch Reformed Church, 451

Dutch Republic
    commercial empire, 480, 521
    independence of (1609), 480
    invasion by Louis XIV, 522
    stadtholder, 521–22
    States General, 521
    Thirty Years War, 485
    United Provinces, 521, 523
    see also Holland; Netherlands

early civilizations, 2–39
    Akkadian Realm, 17–18
    chronology, 38
    Egyptian civilization, 21, 24–31
    Egyptian culture and society, 31–37
    emergence of towns and villages, 8
    empire of Hammurabi, 19–23
    Mesopotamia, early empires in, 17–21
    Neolithic Revolution, 6–8
    overview, 2–4
    rise of trade, 4, 6, 8, 9, 10
    stories about great flood, 14–15, 40,
        60, 71
    Sumerian culture, 9–17
    Ubaid culture, 9–10
    Ur, 18–19, 19
    urban development in Mesopotamia,
        10, 12
Early Dynastic Period (Sumer), 12–13, 14
Early Middle Ages (500–950), 216–51
    see also Middle Ages
earth, debate about age of, 547–49, 551–52
Eastern Europe
    absolutism and, 529–30
    flourishing of, in Late Middle Ages, 389
    map, c. 1200, 299
    medieval monarchies of, 298–300
    new kingdoms in Middle Ages, 255
eastern Roman Empire. see Byzantine
    Empire; Roman Empire
Eckhart, Master, 352
economic issues
    banking in Middle Ages, 344–45
    Black Death impact on, 368–69
    of colonialism in sixteenth–seventeenth
        centuries, 477–79
    downfall of poleis and economic
        crisis, 118
    of European exploration, 432–34
    feudalism concept and, 267
    during Hellenistic period, 133–34
    Italian wealth and Renaissance
        beginning, 378
    of Late Middle Ages, 344–45

money and credit in Middle Ages, 265
    price revolution, sixteenth century,
        477, 478
    in Roman Republic, 160–61
    silver and gold from Spanish America
        (sixteenth century), 432–34, 474,
        477, 479, 488
    of triangular trade, 474–76, 475
    see also specific topics
Ecumenical Synods, 225
Edessa, as Crusader State, 303–4
Edict of Milan, 198
Edict of Nantes, 480, 484, 490, 513
Edith (queen of England), 269
education
    Byzantine Empire, 223–25
    Canons of the Fourth Lateran Council
        on, 308, 312–13, 315
    cathedral schools, 258, 292, 315
    classical cannon of Cassiodorus,
        211–12
    liberal arts concept, 315, 320
    Middle Ages, 308, 312–13, 315, 318,
        319–20, 321
    monastic education, 211–12
    primary education in Middle Ages,
        308, 315, 320
    Protestant Reformation and, 453
    quadrivium, 315
    during reign of Charlemagne, 315
    Renaissance in Italy, 375, 376, 378
    role of women, fourth–second
        centuries B.C.E., 142–43
    trivium, 315
    in tsarist Russia, 531
Edward I (king of England), 354–57
Edward II (king of England), 355, 357
Edward III (king of England), 357, 358,
    384, 386
Edward VI (king of England), 457–58
Edward the Confessor (king of England),
    268, 269, 269, 356
Egypt
    Mamluk Sultanate, 336
    Rosetta Stone, 27, 29
Egypt (ancient)
    agriculture in, 21
    Alexander the Great in, 24, 125
    Archaic or Early Dynastic Period, 26
    beliefs about life and death, 32, 34,
        34, 36
    civilization development in, 21,
        24–31, 25
    culture and society, 31–37

Eighteenth Dynasty, 45–49
    First Intermediate Period, 31
    Hebrews and, 60
    Imhotep and Step Pyramid, 29, 30
    irrigation by, 35
    kingdoms and periods, defined, 24
    language, 29
    maps of, 25, 50
    Middle Kingdom, 34, 36–37, 44, 52
    Narmer Palette, 28, 28
    New Kingdom, 44–49
    Old Kingdom, 26–36, 33
    overview, 21, 24, 25
    palace bureaucracy, 24, 26
    power of pharaohs, 24, 26
    Predynastic Egypt, 24–25
    Ptolemaic Egypt, 27, 130, 133
    Sea Peoples and, 54–56, 60
    Second Intermediate Period, 44–45
    social pyramid of, 35
    Step Pyramid, 29
    urban planning of Alexandria, 125, 178
    writing in, 27, 27, 29, 29
Eighteenth Dynasty (ancient Egypt),
    45–49
Eikon Basilike, 498
Einhard (Frankish scholar), 246
ekklesia, 91, 92, 187
Ekron (Philistine citadel), 59
El (Canaanite god), 70, 74
Elche, Spain, 374
Eleanor of Aquitaine
    descendants, 295, 325, 326
    domain, 295, 296, 319, 326, 327,
        329, 358
    marriages, 294, 296, 319, 325
    tomb, 318, 318
Eleanor of England, 348
Elements of Geometry (Euclid), 139
El Greco, 502, 502
Elizabeth I (queen of England), 457, 459,
    460, 482, 483, 492, 500
Elizabethan settlement, 460
Elizabeth of York, 388
emperor, defined, 169
encomienda system, 472–73
England
    Black Death impact on, 369
    colonialism in sixteenth–seventeenth
        centuries, 482–84, 484
    as Commonwealth under Cromwell,
        494, 496, 518
    crisis of kingship (sixteenth–seventeenth
        centuries), 492–95

England (*Continued*)
Elizabethan settlement, 460
expansion of, Late Middle Ages, 354–57
expulsion of Jews, 300, 315, 354
Hundred Years' War, 357–59, 383–88, *385*
Hundred Years' War consequences, 388, 418
League of Augsburg, 523
Magna Carta, 295–96, 312, 324, 355
medieval monarchies, 268–70, 294–96, *297*
Norman conquest of, 256, 268–70, 294
Peasants' Revolt in 1381, 367, 369, 370, 384, 397
poverty in sixteenth–seventeenth centuries, 478
Protestant Reformation, 456–60
queens regnant of England, 458–60, *459*
reform movements, Late Middle Ages, 395–97
religious conflict with Spain (sixteenth century), 481–82, *483*
restoration of monarchy, 494, *495*, 510, 518–19
Treaty of Utrecht, 524, *524*
unification under Alfred the Great, 249
Vikings and, 247, *248*, 249
see also Civil War (England); Great Britain
English Peasants' Revolt, 367, 369, 370, 384, 397
Enheduanna of Akkad, 18
Enkidu (Epic of Gilgamesh character), 13
environmental issues
Black Death impact on, 368
Columbian exchange, 471–72, *472*
environmental sciences during scientific revolution, 547–49, 551–52
Neolithic Revolution effects, 7–8
Epaminondas (Theban leader), 116, 122
Ephesus (Ionia), 140
ephors, 93
Epic of Gilgamesh, 12–15, 65, 80
Epicureanism, 134, 135, 136
Epicurus, 134, *135*
Epidauros, theater at, *102*
equestrian class (Roman), 154, 160, 163
Erasistratus, 140
Erasmus, Desiderius
career, 414–15
Christian humanism, *414*, 414–17, 452, 461, 464

Index of Prohibited Books and, 462
influence of, 415–16, 441, 461
portrait, *414*, 417
simony condemned by, 440
Eratosthenes, 139
Eretria, 98
Ermengarde of Carcassonne, 304, *305*
Ermengarde of Narbonne, 326
Esarhaddon (Assyrian king), 72
Essays (Montaigne), 499, 501
Essenes, 186
Estates General (France), 513
Estonia, 522
ethics
Aristotle on, 120
Stoicism and Christianity, 135, 187, 202
Stoicism, Hellenistic, 132, 134–35
Stoicism, Roman, 135, 162, 177, 197, 202, 208
see also philosophy
Ethiopia, 230
Etruscans, 150–51
Eucharist, 309, 351–52, 397
Euclid (Hellenistic mathematician), 139, 409
Euphrates river, 9, *13*, 17
Euripides (Greek playwright), 101, 102, 122, 379
Europe
confessional differences, c. 1560, 447
consolidation of (1100–1250), 292–331
empire of Charles V, 444, *445*
expansion of (950–1100), 252–91, *257*
extension of commerce and settlement in Late Middle Ages, 342–44, *343*
impact of Crusades on western Europe, 285
map of Europe (c. 1000), *257*
"Viking Age," 255–56
see also Europe in the Atlantic world (1550–1660); *individual countries*
Europe in the Atlantic world (1550–1660), 468–507
age of doubt and, 495–500
arts, 495–96, 498, 502, 502–5, *503*, *504*, *505*
chronology, *506*
colonialism, 468–77
competition and economics in Europe, 477–79, 480–84
crisis of kingship in England, 492–95
overview, 468–70

population growth in sixteenth–seventeenth centuries, 477, *478*
religious wars in Europe, 479–82, *481*, 484–92
Thirty Years' War, 484–92, *487*
Evans, Arthur, 51
Eve (biblical character), 71, 209, 311
excommunication, 276, 298, 307, 312, 356, 391
Execrabilis (Council of Constance), 394, *395*
Exodus, 71
expansion of Europe in Middle Ages (950–1100), 252–91, *257*
see also Middle Ages
exploration (fifteenth–sixteenth centuries)
by Columbus, 427–28, *429*
consequences of, 432–34
gold as goal of, 423–24, 428, 430–31, 432–33
map, *426*
by Portugal, 423–27, 428
scientific revolution and, 541–42
slavery and, 423–24, 426–27, 432–33
Spanish *conquistadors*, 430–32, *431*
eyeglasses, invention of, 345, 541
Ezekiel (Hebrew prophet), 74, *75*
Ezra (Hebrew prophet), 75

fables (*fabliau*) in Middle Ages, 328
Faerie Queene (Spenser), 416
fairs in Middle Ages, 262
Faith, Saint (Saint Foy of Conques), 272, 274–75, *275*
falconry, 324, *325*
fallow deer (*Dama dama*), 324
family life
nuclear family concept, 379
Protestant Reformation and patriarchy, 453
see also divorce; marriage
faqirs, 234
Fatimah (Muhammad's daughter), 232
Fatimids, 249, 256, 280, 283
female beauty, as ideal, 121, *121*
Ferdinand VII (king of Spain), 421, *422*, 422–23, 427
Ferdinand (Holy Roman Emperor), 485
Ferdinand of Aragon, 421
Ferrara, duke of, 407
Fertile Crescent, *13*, 25
feudalism, 267–68
Fibonacci, Leonardo, 285
Ficino, Marsilio, 402
fiefs/fiefdoms, 267–68, 302, 304, *305*

Fifth Dynasty (ancient Egypt), 30
Filmer, Robert, 516, 517
Fioravanti, Aristotele, *420*
First Cataract (Nile River), 24, 31
First Intermediate Period (ancient Egypt), 31
First Punic War, 157
Fitzgerald, Edward, 288
FitzStephen, William, 326
Five Good Emperors, 171
Five Pillars, 230
flagellation and flagellants, 362
Flanders
    Middle Ages trade in, 261, 262
    sovereignty in Middle Ages, 256, 259,
        261, 353, 358
Florence
    Black Death impact on, 369
    Ciompi rebellion, 370
    civic ideals in Renaissance, 378–79
    Middle Ages in, 265, 326
    puritanism and reform in, 452
    Renaissance in, 378–79, 402, 406
    as republic or oligarchy, 389, 406
    see also Medici family; Renaissance
foederati, 204
forest law, in Middle Ages, 323–24
Fourth Dynasty (ancient Egypt), 29, 31, *32*
Fourth Lateran Council of 1215, 308,
    312–13, 315, 316, 320
France
    Albigensian Crusade, 308
    Alsace-Lorraine, 247
    Black Death impact on, 369
    Cardinal Richelieu and, 490–91
    Charles V (Holy Roman Emperor)
        and, 452
    colonial rivalries after Treaty of
        Utrecht, 524
    colonies in North America, 489–90, 518
    disputed succession in 1328, 358, *358*
    emergence of, 296, *297*
    expulsion of Jews, 300, 315, 354, 511
    Fronde, 491–92
    Hundred Years' War, 357–59,
        383–88, *385*, 425
    Hundred Years' War consequences,
        388, 418
    Jacquerie Rebellion, 369–70
    Joan of Arc, 372, 386, *386*, 387, 393
    Lascaux cave paintings, 5, *5*–6
    Louis XIV and absolutism, 491–92,
        508, 510–18, *514–15*, 521, 525
    sovereignty in Middle Ages, 352–53
    Thirty Years' War, 485, 487, 489

Thirty Years' War consequences, 488,
    489, 491
    Treaty of Utrecht, 523, 524, *524*
    wars of religion (sixteenth–seventeenth
        centuries), 479–80, 485, 487
Franciscan order, 311, 314, 339, 345
Francis of Assisi, Saint, 314, 317
Franks
    Abbasids and, 235, 246, 247
    Merovingian dynasty, 237, 241,
        242–43
    migration, 206
    prosperity of, 237
Frederick I (Barbarossa; Holy Roman
    Emperor), 298, 306, 310
Frederick I (king of Prussia), 528–29
Frederick II (Holy Roman Emperor), 298,
    308, 324, *325*, 347
Frederick II (king of Denmark), 544
Frederick II (the Great; king of Prussia)
    Prussia transformation into major
        power, 529–30
Frederick III (Frederick the Wise, elector
    of Saxony), 436, 444
Frederick William I (king of Prussia), 529
Frederick William (Great Elector of
    Prussia), 527, *527*–28
French Academy of Sciences, 558, 559, 563
Frequens (Council of Constance), 394–95
fresco paintings
    Averroès in Thomas Aquinas fresco, *322*
    from catacombs, *188*
    Cella Septichora, *200*
    Last Supper, The (Leonardo da Vinci),
        408, *409*
    Minoan frescoes, 52, *52*
    School of Athens, The (Raphael), *119*,
        409, *410*
    Sistine Chapel, Vatican, 410–11, *411*
    "This Is My Body," *351*
Fronde rebellions, 491–92
Fulcher of Chartres, 278
funerary masks (Roman), *155*, 156

Gaius (Roman jurist), 176
Galen (second-century scientist), 140
Galerius (Roman emperor), 195, *195*, 197
Galilee, 184–85, *185*
Galileo Galilei
    birth of, 538, 545
    Church challenge to, 545, 546–47, 550
    Inquisition and, 546–47
    scientific theories of, 139, 541,
        545–47, 549, 550, 556, 559

Gallican Catholics, 513, 519
garden design (Muslim, Middle Ages),
    288–89
Garden of Eden, 209
Gargantua (Rabelais), 416
Gassendi, Pierre, 560–61
Gath (Philistine citadel), 59
Gaul
    Hannibal in, 158
    Merovingian kings, 237, 241, 242–43
    Merovingian monasteries, 237, 240
    migrations in fifth century, 206, 207
    Roman aqueduct in, *177*
    in Roman Empire, 164, 167, 197,
        212–13, 218
    trade with eastern provinces, 235
    see also France; Franks
Gaza (Philistine citadel), 59, 125
gender
    Roman cults and masculinity, 202
    see also sex; women's roles/rights
Genesis, 2, 15, 71, 551
genetics
    DNA analysis from ancient Greece, 53
Geneva, Calvinism in, 451, 455, 479
Genghis Khan, 334, *335*, 338
Genoa
    colonies, 342, 343, 360
    maritime navy, 262, 283
    Mongol Empire and, 341–42
    trade and commerce, 262, 277, 283,
        341–42, 389
geology, 547–49, 551–52
George III (king of England), 510
Germania (Tacitus), 175
Germany
    Anglo-Norman kings of England
        compared to kings of, 270
    German kingship and Holy Roman
        Empire, 298, 299
    German princes and Lutheran
        Church, 445–46, 451–52
    Lotharingia, 247
    Protestant Reformation in, 436,
        438–46, 451–52
gerousia, 93
Geta (Roman emperor), 193
Ghana, 342
Gibbon, Edward, 214
Gilgamesh (Epic of Gilgamesh), 12–15,
    65, 80
Giotto di Bondone, 346, *346*, 347
Giza, pyramids at, 29
gladiators, 161, 162, 175

Glorious Revolution, 518, 519–20, 522
gold
    cloth of gold, 336
    colonialism in sixteenth–seventeenth
        centuries and, 477
    exploration (fifteenth–sixteenth
        centuries) and, 423–24, 428,
        430–31, 432–33
    medieval demand for gold of Africa,
        342–43, 343
    Portuguese pursuit of African gold,
        423–24
    Vikings and, 261
Gold Coast (Ghana), 423
gold standard, 236
Goliath, 60
Gospels
    about, 184, 229
    accounts of Jesus's life, 184, 198
    Acts of the Apostles and, 189, 190–91
    Gospel of Luke, 169, 190, 222
    Gospel of Mark, 396
    Gospel of Matthew, 200
    Mary Magdalene, 201
Gothic architecture, 328–29, 329, 413, 416
Goths, 204–5, 206, 207
Gottfried von Strassburg, 325
Gracchi, reform efforts, 162–63
Gracchus, Gaius, 163
Gracchus, Tiberius, 162–63
Granada (Spain), 421, 423
Grand Duchy of Muscovy, 418, 419
gravity, theory of, 561–62
Great Britain
    American Revolution of 1776, 510
    battle of Hastings, 268, 269
    birthday invitation from Roman
        Britain, 175
    Hadrian's Wall, 169, 189, 192
    imperial and commercial dominance
        after Treaty of Utrecht, 524, 524
    name of, 524
    see also specific locations and people
Great East–West Schism, 391
Great Famine (1315–1322), 359–60, 376
Great Khan (Kublai Khan), 332, 334, 336,
    339, 340–41
Great Northern War, 533–35
Great Pyramid of Khufu, 29–30
Great Schism (Great Western Schism),
    391, 392, 392–93
Great Umayyad Mosque, 232
Great Wall, 334
Greece, 78–113, 114–47

Archaic Greece, 80–100
    chronology, 112, 146
    classical Greece, 100–113, 114–27
    at end of Bronze Age, 80
    Hellenistic Greece, 127–45
    literature of, rediscovered during
        Renaissance, 375
    Mycenaean Greece, 51, 53–54, 54, 55,
        57, 80, 81, 103
Greek fire, 221, 221
Greek Orthodox Church, 222–23, 224, 383
    see also Orthodox Christianity
Greenland
    Medieval Warm Period in, 259, 344
    Vikings and, 248, 254, 344, 428
Gregorian chant, 241
Gregory I (the Great; pope), 241–42
Gregory VII (pope), 270, 271, 275–76,
    307, 309
Gregory XI (pope), 391
Gregory XIII (pope), 35, 165
Gregory of Tours, 235
Griffin Warrior (tomb), 53, 54
Grimmelshausen, Hans Jacob Christoffel
    von, 486
Guadeloupe, 490
guest friendship, 81, 82
guild system
    inception of, 326–27
    medieval drama, 374
    during Protestant Reformation,
        453, 455
    rebellion by guilds in 1378 (Italy), 370
gunpowder, 425, 430, 468, 540
Gustavus Adolphus (king of Sweden),
    485, 487
Gutenberg, Johannes of Mainz, 400, 402

habeas corpus, 519
Habsburg dynasty
    absolutism and, 525–26
    in Austria, 485, 487, 488, 525–26, 528
    Holy Roman Empire and, 444, 522,
        525, 528
    Hungary and, 525–26, 528
    Ottoman Empire and, 526, 528–29
    in Spain, 480, 485, 487, 488, 503
    Thirty Years' War, 470, 485, 487
    war and balance of power (1661–1715),
        522–24
hadith stories, 234
Hadrian (Roman emperor), 169, 171,
    189, 191
Hadrian's Wall, 169, 189, 192

Haec Sancta Synodus (Council of
    Constance), 394
Hagia Sophia (church), 226, 226
Hajj, 230
Hamilton, Alexander, 132
Hamlet (Shakespeare), 502, 538
Hammurabi (king of Babylon), 19–23,
    23, 131
Handbook of the Christian Knight
    (Erasmus), 415
Hannibal (Carthaginian leader), 158
Hanseatic League, 369, 389
haram, 235
Harold Godwinson (king of England),
    268, 269, 269
Harvey, William, 557
Hasdrubal (Carthaginian leader), 158
Haskins, Charles Homer, 330
Hastings, battle of, 268, 269
Hatshepsut (queen of Egypt), 45–47, 46,
    47, 165
Hattusilis (king of Hittites), 44
Hattusilis III (king of Hittites), 57
Hawkins, John, 482
Hebrew Bible
    Book of Deuteronomy, 74
    Garden of Eden, 209
    Genesis, 2, 15, 71, 551
    historical books of, 60
    on Maccabees, 137
    as "Old Testament," 60, 184, 189
    Ten Commandments, 71
    Torah (first five books), 60, 75, 186, 218
    translation into Greek language, 138
Hebrews
    Babylonian Captivity and, 66, 74, 75
    development of Hebrew monotheism,
        70–75, 227
    early Judaism, 74–75
    King Solomon's reign, 62, 70, 73
    old polytheistic religion, 70
    Philistines and, 59, 60, 61
    scriptures of, 60–61
    struggle for unity in Early Iron Age, 61
    tribes of Judah and Israel, 61, 62, 62,
        63, 74
    see also Judaism
Hecataeus (Milesian philosopher), 95
Hector (Iliad character), 80, 89, 125
Helen (Iliad character), 80, 90
heliocentric universe concept, 139, 287,
    538, 543, 543–44, 545, 546–47
Heliogabalus (Roman emperor), 193–94
Hellenic League, formation of, 98

Hellenistic Greece (323–31 B.C.E.), 127–45
    Greek diaspora, 132
    Greek poleis transition to cosmopolis,
        132–34
    Hellenistic kingdoms and, 127, *129*,
        129–32
    Hellenistic world, map, *129*
    Hellenistic worldviews, 134–38
    as Roman province, 159
Hellenistic period
    architecture and sculpture, 138–39,
        140, 140–41, *141*
    Christianity in, 186–89, *187*, *188*
    culture, 132–34
    Epicureanism, 134, 135, 136
    Greek poleis transition to cosmopolis,
        132–34
    Hellenistic kingdoms, 127, *129*,
        129–32
    literature, 144–45
    religious variety during, 136–38
    Roman control following, 159
    science, 138–41, 144–45
    Skepticism, 135–36
    Stoicism, 132, 134–35
    worldviews, overview, 134–38
    see also Alexander the Great;
        Hellenistic Greece
Heloise, 292, 294, 310, 318, 328
helots, 92, 93–94, 105, 106, 116
Helwig von Ysenburg (countess of
    Büdingen), seal of, *349*
henotheists, 64
Henry I (king of England), 294
Henry II (Henry of Anjou; king of
    England), 294–95, 296, *297*, *318*, 319,
    325, 327
Henry III (Holy Roman Emperor), 273
Henry III (king of England), 324, *348*,
    354–55
Henry IV (Henry of Navarre, king of
    France), *479*, 479–80, 489, 490
Henry IV (Holy Roman Emperor), 270,
    271, 276, 298
Henry IV (king of England), 384, 423
Henry V (king of England), 384–86
Henry VI (Holy Roman Emperor), 298
Henry VI (king of England and France),
    386, 388
Henry VII (king of England), 388
Henry VIII (king of England), 388, 415,
    415, *456*, 456–57, 458, 459, 460
Henry "the Navigator" (prince of
    Portugal), 423–24, 427

Heraclius (Byzantine emperor), 221
Herât, Afghanistan, 338
heresy
    Arianism, 200–201, 205, 220
    in early Christianity, 200–201
    Great Schism, 391
    Innocent III and, 308, 311
    Jan Hus, 397, *397*
    Joan of Arc, 386, 387
    Martin Luther and, 444
    Peter Abelard, 319
    simony, 273, 275, 440
Hermann of Carinthia, 285
Herod Antipas, 185, *185*
Herodotus of Halicarnassus
    on Alexander the Great, 126
    on civilization of Greece, 78, 83–84,
        97, 104
    on Egyptian pyramids, 30, 78
    historic works of, 102
    Ionian Revolt and, 97–98
    on Persian Empire, 66, 78, 126
    on Phoenician colonies, 58
heroic tradition, Homer and, 80–81
herons, 324
Herophilus of Chalcedon, 140
Hesiod, 40, 42, 51, 53–54, 80
Hevelius, Elisabetha, *558*
Hevelius, Johannes, *558*
hieratic script, 27, *27*
hieroglyphs and hieroglyphics, 27, *27*, 29
High Middle Ages (950–1250), 252–91,
    292–331
    see also Middle Ages
Hijra, 227
Hildegard of Bingen, Saint, 310, 311, *311*
Hipparchus, 139
Hippocrates, 140
Hispaniola, 427, 430, 432, 490
*History of the English Church and People,
    The* (Bede), 216
History of the Goths (Cassiodorus), 212
Hittites, 44, 49, 51, 52, 54, 55–56, 57
HIV-AIDS, 360
Hobbes, Thomas, 500, 559
Hohenzollern family, 440, 527
Holbein, Hans (the Younger), *414*, *415*,
    417, *456*
holiness, pursuit of, 352
Holland
    League of Augsburg, 523
    see also Dutch Republic; Netherlands
Holy Roman Empire
    Charlemagne crowned as emperor, 246

defined, 298
    German kingship and Holy Roman
        Empire, 298, 299
    Habsburg dynasty and, 444, 522,
        525, 528
    Late Middle Ages conflict in, 388–89
    map, c. 1200, *299*
    Thirty Years' War, 485
holy war, doctrines of, 64, 254, 285, 302
homage, 268
Homer (Greek poet), 80–81, 101,
    223–24, 402
Homme, L' (Descartes), 556
Homo sapiens, defined, 4
homosexuality
    in ancient Greece, 88
    male beauty as Greek ideal, 87
    Theban Sacred Band, 116, 122, 123
Hooke, Robert, 552, 557, *557*, 562
hoplites
    Macedonian warriors, 123, *123*, 124
    and political system, 87, 88, 91, 100, 103
    Theban Sacred Band, 116, 122, 123
    warfare, Archaic Greece, *86*, 86–87,
        88, 93, 97, 99, *100*
    warfare, classical Greece, 99, *100*, 116
hoplon shields, 86, *86*, 88
Horace (Quintus Horatius Flaccus), 174
Horemheb (pharaoh of Egypt), 49
Horrors of War, The (Rubens), 504
horses, 85–86, *86*, 126
Horus (Egyptian god), 28, 31, 32
Hosea (Hebrew prophet), 74
Hospital of St. John at Jerusalem, 305
Host (Eucharist), 309, *351*, 351–52
House of Wisdom, 286, 338
Housman, A. E., 144
Hrotsvitha of Gandersheim, 258
hubris, 80
Hugh Capet, 259, 358
Huguenots, 451, 479, 490, 511, 513, 516
Hulagu Khan, 336, *337*
human body, asceticism and, 202–3
humanism
    Castiglione on, 407
    Christian humanism, *414*, 414–17, 464
    defined, 376
    northern European Renaissance and,
        414–17
    Renaissance, 376, 378–79, 402, 407,
        409, 414, 541
humanitas, 113
human rights
    during Roman Empire, 177

Hundred Years' War
    Albigensian Crusade legacy and, 308
    Black Death and, 383
    cannons of fifteenth century, 383, 425
    challenges to Roman Church during, 391
    consequences of, 388, 418
    disputed French succession in 1328,
        358, *358*, 384
    end of, 358, 383, 388, 418, 425
    Free Companies of mercenaries, 384
    Joan of Arc and, 386, 387, 393
    outbreak of, 357–59, 383–84
    phases of, 383–84, *385*
Hungary
    Habsburg dynasty and, 525–26, 528
    Huns' conquest of, 206, 255
    Magyars' conquest of, 248, 255
    in Middle Ages, 300
Huns, 204, 206, 255
hunter-gatherer societies, 4, 6
Hus, Jan, 397, *397*
Hussites, 397
Hydaspes, battle of, 125
Hyksos, 44–45, 48

Ibn Battuta, 340–41
Ibn Khaldun, 365
Ibn Majid, 424
Ibn Rushd (Averroès), 322, *322*
Iceland and Vikings, 248, 254, 428
iconoclasm, 222–23, 243
Iconoclast Controversy, 222–23,
    224–25, 243
Iconodules, 223
iconography, of Egyptian pharaohs, 46
Ides of March, 167, *167*
Ignatius of Loyola, 462–64
Iliad (Homer), 51, 80, 81, 89, 114, 252
Ilkhanate, 336, *337*, 341
Illinois Indians, *490*
imams, 230
Imhoteph, 29, *30*
Imitation of Christ (Thomas à Kempis),
    394–95
immigration
    Bronze Age immigrants in Anatolia,
        42–44
imperialism
    consequences of Roman imperialism,
        160–62
    see also colonialism entries; *specific
        countries*
Inanna (Sumerian goddess), 13, 18
Incas, 16, 431, 473

indentured servants, 473, 479, 495
Index of Prohibited Books, 462
India
    Alexander the Great in, 116, 128
    Portuguese exploration and, 424
indirect rule, 533
Indo-European languages and peoples,
    42–44, *43*, 53
Indonesia, 334, 340
inductive method, 552, 554
indulgences, 439–40, 443, 462
inflation
    in Europe, fifteenth–seventeenth
        centuries, 433–34, 477–78, 488
    price revolution and, 477, 478
    in Roman Empire, 194, 195
influenza pandemic of 1918–1919, 360
"Inland Expedition, The," *Anabasis*
    (Xenophon), 114, 117
Innocent III (pope), 307–8, 309, 311,
    312, 314
Innocent VIII (pope), 499
Inquisition, 314, *422*, 546–47
Inspiration of Saint Jerome (Reni), *461*
Institutes (Cassiodorus), 212
Institutes of the Christian Religion (Calvin),
    449, 462
Institutes (Roman law), 220
Instruction of Ptah-Hotep, The (ancient
    Egypt), 33, 37
Instrument of Government (England), 494
intellectualism
    Christianity's worldview, 207–10
    intellectual revolution in Middle Ages,
        294, 315–22
    Middle Ages, 315–22, *321*
    origins of scientific revolution, 540–42
    philosophy of Plato and Aristotle, *119*,
        119–20
    reform during Middle Ages, 395–97, *397*
    Renaissance humanism, 376, 378–79,
        402, 407, 409, 414, 541
investiture, 270, 274–76
Investiture Controversy, 270, 274–76
Ionia, 67, 81, 95–96, *96*, 97–98, 108
    see also Miletus
Ionian League, 95
Ionian Revolt, 97–98
Iran (ancient). *see* Persian Empire
Iraq
    Ubaid culture, 9–10
Ireland
    Elizabeth I and Elizabethan
        settlement in, 460

Protestant Ascendancy dominance
    after 1690, 520
rebellion of 1569, 482
Vikings and, 247, 249
Irene (Byzantine empress), 246
Iron Age
    chronology, 76
    Early Iron Age states, 56, 58–62
    Hebrew monotheism, 70–75
    Late Bronze Age and transition to,
        42, 56
    Neo-Assyrian Empire, 62–66, *64*, *65*
    Neo-Assyrian smelting techniques,
        16, 64
    overview, 42
    Persian Empire, 66–70, *68*, *69*
Isabella (queen of Aragon and Castile),
    421, 422, *422*–23, 427
Isabella (queen of France), 356, 358
Isaiah (Hebrew prophet), 74
Ishtar (Akkadian goddess), 18
Isis (Egyptian goddess), 32, 136, 162, 187
Islam
    ancient Egyptian pyramids and, 30
    Byzantine Empire and, 221, 230,
        231, 235
    Canons of the Fourth Lateran Council
        on, 313
    commerce and industry, 233–34
    conversion of Muslims to Christianity,
        Middle Ages, 285, 314
    culture of Muslim west in Middle
        Ages, 285–89, *286*
    disintegration of Islamic World in
        tenth century, 249–50
    end of Muslim rule in Spain, 421
    expansion of, 230–32, *231*
    Five Pillars, 230
    Hijra, 227
    intellectualism in Middle Ages, 315,
        320, 322
    mobility, opportunity, status, 234
    Mongol Empire and, 338, 380
    monotheism, 227, 286, 383
    Muslim philosophy and Christian
        theology, 285–87
    papermaking and, 234
    Pepin's defeat of, at Narbonne, 244
    Persian Empire absorbed by, 221, 230
    Qur'an, *228*, 228–30, 231, 234,
        285, 288
    Shi'ite-Sunni schism, 232–33, 249
    Sunna (Sunnah), 233
    teachings of, 228–30, 286–87

Umayyad dynasty, 224, 232–33, 235, 242, 244, 247, 248
see also Abbasid dynasty; Crusades; Shi'ite Muslims; Sunni Muslims
Isocrates (Athenian orator), 122, 123
Israel, ancient
conquered by Sargon II, 63, 74
kingdom of, 61–62, 62, 63, 71–74
tribes of Israel, 60–61, 63
see also Hebrews; Judaism
Istanbul, 226, 381
see also Constantinople
Italy
art, seventeenth century, 502–3
Black Death impact on, 369, 376
Gregory the Great and, 241
growth of towns and trade in Middle Ages, 261–62
Justinian's impact on western Roman Empire, 219–20
Late Middle Ages conflict in, 388–89
Magna Graecia in, 85
medieval drama in, 374
papal power, Middle Ages, 347
rebellion by guilds in 1378, 370
Renaissance beginning in, 374–79, 402
Renaissance politics of, and philosophy of Machiavelli, 402, 404–7, 406
Roman expansion in, 152–53, 157
states of Italy (c. 1494), 406
tripartite division in Middle Ages, 220
women scientists of scientific revolution in, 558
"I think, therefore I am," 553
Ivan I (Grand Prince of Rus'), 336
Ivan III (the Great; tsar of Russia), 418–19, 420

Jacquerie Rebellion, 369–70
Jadwiga (female king of Poland), 390
Jagiello (grand duke of Lithuania), 390, 390
Jagiellonian dynasty, 390
Jagiellonian University (Kraków), 389, 396
James I (king of England), 492, 500, 552
James II (king of England), 518, 519, 520, 521
James, Saint, 187, 272
Jansen, Cornelius, 499, 513
Jansenism, 499, 513
Jason (High Priest), 137
Java, 340
Jay, John, 132
Jeremiah (Hebrew prophet), 71, 74
Jericho, 8, 9

Jerome, Saint, 209, 210, 245, 379, 417, 417, 461
Jerusalem
Arab conquest of, 221
capture by Seljuk Turks, 279
Christian conquest of, 283
Crusades and, 280, 281, 283, 303
destruction by Romans, 171, 186
first Temple, 62, 66, 70, 75, 306
Jesus in, 184–85
King David and, 61
kingdom of Jerusalem as Crusader State, 281, 304, 306
Muslim occupation of, 230
Persian conquest of, 221
rule by Fatimids, 279–80
second Temple, 75, 171, 184–85, 186, 218, 230
urban planning during Roman Empire, 178
see also Aelia Capitolina
Jesuit order (Society of Jesus), 462–64, 513
Jesus of Nazareth
birth of, 169, 184
crucifixion, 185, 354
life and death of, 184–86
women's status in Christianity and, 201
Jiménez de Cisneros, Francisco, 461
Joan of Arc, 372, 386, 387, 393
Joan of Sicily, 306
João I (king of Portugal), 423
João II (king of Portugal), 424
John II Casimir (king of Poland), 488
John III Sobieski (king of Poland), 526, 528
John XII (pope), 258
John XXII (pope), 356
John (king of England), 295, 296, 308, 355
John of Damascus, 224
John of Leyden, 449
John Paul II (pope), 444
John the Baptist, 184, 232
joint-stock companies, 481, 483
Jones, William, 42
Jonson, Ben, 500, 502
Jordan, 8
Josiah (king of Judah), 74–75
journeymen, 326
Judah, kingdom of, 62, 62, 63, 73–74
Judaism
Babylonian Captivity and, 66, 74, 75, 350
Black Death blamed on Jews, 362–63
Canons of the Fourth Lateran Council on, 308, 313

Christianity inception and, 185–89
conversion of Jews to Christianity, Middle Ages, 282, 285, 314, 422
Crusades and attacks on Jews, 282, 285, 300, 303
early Islam and, 228
early monotheism and, 70–75, 227
expulsion from Europe, Middle Ages, 300, 315, 354, 383, 510–11
expulsion from Spain, 300, 421–22, 510
Hellenistic period and, 137, 138, 148, 155, 185–86
idolatry condemned by, 222
inception of, 42, 75
intellectualism in Middle Ages, 322
"Jewish badge," 308, 314, 315
Jewish Diaspora, 138, 189, 230
Jews as money lenders in Middle Ages, 265, 315
literature and poetry, Middle Ages, 288
pogroms, 282
Rabbinic Judaism, 218, 322
Roman rule and, 148, 155, 171, 185–86, 188–89
Sephardic Jews, defined, 422
Talmud, 218
Torah, 60, 75, 186, 218
see also anti-Semitism; Hebrew Bible; Hebrews
Judea, 75, 171, 184–85, 185, 190
Jugurtha of Numidia, 163
Julia Domna (Roman empress), 191
Julia Maesa (Roman empress), 193–94
Julia Mamæa (Roman empress), 194
Julian calendar, 35, 165
Julian of Norwich, 393
Julian the Apostate (Roman emperor), 203
Julius II (pope), 441
Julius Caesar (Gaius Julius Caesar), 35, 151, 155–56, 164, 164–65, 165, 167, 170
Junkers, 528
Jupiter (Roman god), 194
jurists, during Roman Empire, 176–77
justification by faith doctrine, 439, 441, 458
Justinian (eastern Roman emperor)
attempt to reunify the Roman Empire, 218, 220–21, 256
Christianity and, 226, 226
codification of Roman Law, 220, 224
Corpus Juris Civilis, 220
impact on Western Roman Empire, 219–20
regions controlled by, 219

Justinianic Plague, 218–19, 360
Jutes, 206
Juvenal (Roman satirist), 160, 174

ka, 28, 29, 32, 34, 36
Kaaba (shrine), 227, 228, 249
Kadesh, battle of, 51
Kassites, 44, 49, 56
katharsis (catharsis), 101
Kempe, Margery, 393–94
Kepler, Johannes, 544–45, 562, 563
Khadija (wife of Muhammad), 227
Khamerernebty II (queen of Egypt), *32, 36*
Khanate of the Golden Horde, 336, 342
khora, 81–82
Khufu (Cheops, pharaoh of Egypt), 29
Kiev, 255, 277, 300, 334, 336
"king in Parliament" (England), 494,
    518, 519
King James Bible, 224
King Lear (Shakespeare), 502
"king's English," 402
King William's War, 523
Kircher, Athanasius, 551
Kirch, Gottfried, 559
Knights Hospitaller, 305
knights/knighthood, 266, 268, 323
Knights of the Garter, 371
Knights Templar, 284, 306, 354
Knossos (palace), 51, 52, *52,* 53, 54
"knowledge is power," 552
Knox, John, 451
Koran. *see* Qur'an
Korb, Johann Georg, 532
Kosovo, battle of (1389), 380
kouros, 87, *87,* 103
Kraków, Poland, market square of, *264*
Kremlin, 419, *420*
krypteia, 93
Kublai Khan (Great Khan), 332, 334, 336,
    339, 340–41
Kurds
    Saladin (Sala ah-Din), 284, 306
Kush (Nubian kingdom), 45, 72

Labyrinth, 51, 52
Lancastrian dynasty, 388
Landini, Francesco, 417
language
    of Akkadians, 18
    of ancient Egypt, 29
    Anglo-Saxon vernacular, 249
    English usage in Church of England, 457
    Etruscan, 150–51

Greek used in Roman Republic, 161
Indo-European languages and peoples,
    42–44, 53
Islamic influence on western Europe,
    289
"king's English," 402
Latin used in Roman Empire, 162, 174
Linear A (Minoan script), 53, *53*
Meroitic language, 37, *37,* 45
Old Church Slavonic, 277
printing press effect on, 402, 404
Rosetta Stone, 27, 29
Sumerian, 11, 18
Syriac, 286
see also alphabet(s)
Laocoön and His Sons (sculpture), 141, *141*
Laon, France, 265
Lascaux, cave paintings of, 5, *5–6*
Last Judgment (Michelangelo), 410
Last Supper, The (Leonardo da Vinci),
    408, *409*
Late Bronze Age
    transnational diplomacy, 49, 57
    transnational trade networks, 42–44,
        49–51, 56, 80
Late Middle Ages (1250–1453), 332–65,
    366–99
    see also Middle Ages
Latin Right, 151, 152
Latins, 151
Latium, 151
Latvia, 522
law of nations, in Roman Empire, 177
Law of the Twelve Tables, 153, 155, 156, 176
League of Augsburg, 523–24
League of Corinth, 123
legal issues
    "big book of fiefs" (King Alfonso II of
        Aragon), 302, 304, *305*
    Code of Hammurabi, 20–21, 22–23,
        23, 63
    codification of Roman law, 220
    forest law, in Middle Ages, 323–24
    Henry II and English legal system,
        294–95
    Law of Moses, 74
    Law of the Twelve Tables, 153, 155,
        156, 176
    legal code of Ur, 18
    Neo-Assyrian laws, 63
    Roman Empire and reach of Roman
        law, 176–77
    see also constitutions; slavery; women's
        roles/rights

Legnica, battle of, 335
Leibniz, Gottfried, 559
Leo III (Byzantine emperor), 221, 222,
    223, 224
Leo III (pope), 246
Leo IX (pope), 273–74
Leo X (pope), 440, 441, 444
Leonardo da Vinci, 408, *408,* 409, *409,*
    411, 541
León-Castile, 302, 326
Leopold I of Austria (Holy Roman
    Emperor), 523, 525, 528–29
Lepidus, Marcus Aemilius, 168, 173
Letters on Sunspots (Galileo), 546
Levant, Early Iron Age states, 56, 58–62
    see also Israel, ancient; Neo-Assyrian
        Empire; Syria
Leviathan (Hobbes), 500
Levites, 71
Leyster, Judith, 505, *505*
liberal arts concept, 315, 320
library of Nineveh, 65
Licinius, 198
light, Newton on, 560, 562
Lindisfarne Gospels, *242*
Linear A (Minoan script), *53*
Linear B (Mycenaean Greek script), 53,
    54, 80, 81
literature
    classical learning and Christianity,
        210–13, *211*
    emergence of prose, 119
    Hellenistic period, 139, 144–45
    of Middle Ages, 324–25, 328, 346–47
    Muslim, Middle Ages, 233, 288
    of northern European Renaissance,
        414–15, 416
    reading ancient texts during
        Renaissance, 375, 376, 379, 541, 542
    Renaissance, 404–5, 406–7
    Roman Empire, 174–75
    seventeenth century, 495–96
    use of rhyme in Middle Ages, 328
    writing following Black Death,
        371–72, *372*
    see also poetry
Lithuania
    Ivan the Great, 418
    Jagiello (grand duke), 390, *390*
    Poland-Lithuania and Great Northern
        War, 534
    Polish-Lithuania Commonwealth,
        488–89, 518, 522, 528
    Thirty Years War, 485, 488

Little Ice Age, 511, *511*

Livia (wife of Nero), 173

Livy (historian), *246*, 375, 406

Loarre Castle, Aragon, *302*

Locke, John, 516, 520–21

logic, Descartes on, 554–55, 557

Lombard League, 298

Lombard, Peter, 319, 439

Lombards, 219–20, 241, 243, 244

Longinus Sdapeze (legionnaire), 171

lordships in Middle Ages, 236, 266–67

Lorenzo the Magnificent (Medici ruler), 404, 406, 408

Lothair (Holy Roman Emperor), 247

Louis as name of French kings, 237

Louis VII (king of France), 294, 296, 319

Louis IX (Saint Louis; king of France), 326, 339, 353–54

Louis XII (king of France), 418

Louis XIII (king of France), 490, 491

Louis XIV (king of France)
    absolutism, 491–92, 508, 510–18, *514–15*, 521, 525, 530
    administration and finance, 513
    colonialism under, 516–18
    Fronde rebellion and, 491–92
    invasion of Dutch Republic, 522
    League of Augsburg and War of the Spanish Succession, 523–24
    Nine Years' War, 523
    religious policies of, 512, 513, 516
    Royal Academy of Sciences, 559
    staging of authority by, 512, *514–15*
    as Sun King, 510, 512, 514, *514*

Louis the German, 247

Louis the Pious, 245, 246, 247

"love feasts," 188, *188*

Lower Egypt, 24–25, 26, 28, 44–45

Lucretia (Roman), 151, 153, 156–57, 167

Lucretius (Roman writer), 375

lugals, 12, 14–15, 17, 20, 35

Luke (Gospel), 169, 190, 222

lunar calendar, 17

Lusiads (Portuguese epic), 424

Luther, Martin
    on accused witches, 499
    Augustine's effect on, 209, 439
    biographical information, 438–39
    break with Rome, 441–44, 450
    Calvinism and, 449, 450
    Charles V and condemnation at Worms, *444*, 444–45, 462
    German princes and Lutheran Church, 445–46

justification by faith doctrine of, 439, 441

on marriage and celibacy, 441, 453, 454, 455

Ninety-Five Theses of, 320, 436, 440

pamphlet publication and effect of printing press, *439*, 440–41, *442–43*, 446

portrait, *438*

primary premises, 440–41

on religious education, 453

translation of the bible, *439*

Lydia, kingdom of, 66, 85, 95

ma'at, 33, 34, 37, 44

Macbeth (Shakespeare), 502

Maccabees, 137, 148

Macedonia
    Antigonid Macedonia, 132
    Companions, 123
    hoplite infantry, 123, *123*, 124
    Philip II, 116, 122–23, 124, 132
    rise of, overview, 116, 122–23
    as Roman province, 159
    see also Alexander the Great

Machaut, Guillaume de, 417

Machiavelli, Niccolò, 37, 402, 404, 405, 406–7

Madeira, 423, 427

Madison, James, 132

Magdeburg Law, 389

Magellan, Ferdinand, 428

magi, 69, 136

Magna Carta, 295–96, 312, 324, 355, 518

Magna Graecia, 85

Magyars, 248, 255, 257, 260

Maids of Honor, The (*Las Meniñas*) (Velázquez), 503, *503*

Maimonides, Moses, 322

Mali, 342, *343*

Malinche, La, 430

Malory, Thomas, 404

Mamluk Sultanate of Egypt, 336

Mandeville, John de, 332, 340–41

Manetho, 26

Manichaeism, 195–96, 198

Mani (Persian prophet), 195

Mannerism, 502

manors, 260

Mansa Musa, 342, *343*

Mansur, al- (caliph), 233

Marathon, battle of, 67–68, 97, 98–100, 101

Marcus Aurelius (Roman emperor), 171, 189–90

Marduk (Babylonian god), 19, 22, 72–73

Marie de France, 325, 327

Marie of Champagne, 325

Marius, Gaius, 163–64

Mark (Gospel), *396*

Marlowe, Christopher, 500

marriage
    in ancient Rome, 169
    asceticism and, 202–3
    in Athens, 104
    Code of Hammurabi on, 21, 22, 63
    Henry VIII and Protestant Reformation, 456–57
    Luther and, 441, 453, 454, 455
    mass marriage arranged by Alexander the Great, 126
    by priests, 273, 275–76, 308–9
    Protestant Reformation and Council of Trent on, 454
    Protestant Reformation and patriarchy, 453, 455–56
    reform of secular clergy (eleventh century), 273, 275–76
    Renaissance in Italy, 379
    as sacrament, 351, 454, 455
    during Severan dynasty, 192
    in Sparta, 93
    see also divorce; family life

Mars (Roman god), 197

Martin V (pope), 393

Martinique, 490

Martini, Simone, *351, 374*

Marx, Karl
    feudalism concept and, 267

Mary I (Bloody Mary, Mary Tudor, queen of England), 456, 458–59, *459*, 460, 482

Mary Magdalene, 201, *377*

Mary Stuart (queen of England), 519, *520*, 521, 523

Mary (Virgin), 223, 309–10, *310*

Mass
    doctrine of transubstantiation, 309, 312, *351*, 351–52
    Middle Ages, 309, 351–52

Massachusetts Bay Colony, 483, *484*, 499

Massacre of the Innocents, The (Bruegel the Elder), 503–4, *504*

mastaba, 29

mathematics
    analytical geometry, 557
    Arabic numerals, 285, 287
    education in Middle Ages, 315
    Galileo and, 545
    geometry, 109, 139

mathematics (*Continued*)
Hellenistic period, 139
integral calculus and differential calculus, 561
Kepler and, 545
Muslim mathematicians, Middle Ages, 287–88
Newton and, 561–63
Pythagorean theorem, 109
Matilda of Tuscany, 270, *271*
Matthew (Gospel), 200
Maxentius, 197
Maximian (Roman emperor), 194, *195*, 197
Mazarin, Jules Raymond (cardinal), 491–92
measles, spread by European explorers, 430
Mecca, 227, 228, 249
mechanism view, 556, *556*, 557, *557*, 560
Medes, 63, 66, 125
Medici family
Catherine de' Medici, 479–80
Cosimo de' Medici, 402
Cosimo II de' Medici, 546, 550
economic power, 344, 389
expulsion from Florence, 406
Galileo and, 546, 550
Leo X (pope), 440, 441, 444
Lorenzo the Magnificent, 404, 406, 408
overthrow of Florentine republic, 406
Piero de' Medici, 406
The Prince (Machiavelli), 404, 406
medicine
Hellenistic period, 140
Muslim physicians, Middle Ages, 287
see also disease
Medieval Climate Optimum (Medieval Warm Period), 237, 259–61, 344, 359
medieval monarchies
Central and Eastern Europe, 298–300, *299*
emergence of France, 296, *297*
England, 268–70, 294–96, *297*
German kingship and Holy Roman Empire, 298, *299*
Magna Carta and, 295–96, 312, 324, 355
overview, 294
"reconquest" of Spain, *301*, 301–2, 353
Rus' and Novgorod Republic, 300–301
struggles for sovereignty during Middle Ages, 352–59
see also monarchies
Medieval Warm Period, 237, 259–61, 344, 359

Medina, 227–28
Medina Azahara, *288*
Mediterranean world
commerce and settlement, Late Middle Ages, 342–44
diverse microcosms (1000), 256, *257*
see also individual countries
Meeting of Joachim and Anna, The (Giotto), 346
Mehmet II (the Conqueror; Ottoman sultan), 380–81, *381*
Melos, destruction of, 106, 108, 109
Menander (Greco-Bactrian king), 131
mendicants, 311
Menelaus (*Iliad* character), 80
Menkaure (pharaoh of Egypt), 32
Menshikov, Alexander, 533
Mentuhotep II (pharaoh of Egypt), 36
mercantilism, defined, 513
Merian, Maria Sibylla, 559
Meroitic language, 37, *37*, 45
Merovech, 237
Merovingian dynasty, 237, 241, 242–43
Mesopotamia
about, 9
early empires in, 17–21
Fertile Crescent, *13*, 25
urban development in, 9–10
writing in, 10–12, *11*, 17, 27
see also Sumer
messiah, 185, 186
Metamorphoses (Ovid), 174
Metamorphosis of the Insects of Surinam (Merian), 559
metropolitans, 199
Mexico
Aztec Empire of Mexico, 430–31, *431*, 473
cattle and sheep ranching, 432
Michael VIII Palaeologus (Byzantine emperor), 336
Michelangelo Buonarroti, 141, 409–10, *410*, 412, *412*, 413, 416
Micrographia (Hooke), 557
microscope, invention of, 541, 557
Middle Ages, 216–51, 252–91, 292–331, 332–65, 366–99
agricultural revolution of Medieval Warm Period, 237, 259–61, 359
Carolingian Empire, 242–46, *243*, 256–59
Christian conversion of Northwestern Europe, 216, 235–42
chronology, *250*, *290*, *330*, *364*, *398*

conflict in Italy and Holy Roman Empire, 388–89
consolidation of Europe (1100–1250), 292–331
courts, cities, cathedrals, 322–29
culture of Muslim west, 285–89, *286*
defined, 216
early Islam and, 227–35
Early Middle Ages (500–950), 216–51
economic and political instability in Europe, 236
end of eastern Roman Empire, 379–83
Europe, 235–50
European expansion (950–1100), 252–91
Europe around the year 1000, 254–59, *257*
expansion of Europe (950–1100), 252–91, *257*
extension of European commerce and settlement, 342–44, *343*
First Crusade, 254, 278–79, 280–83
Great Famine, 359–60, 376
Great Schism, 391, *392*, 392–93
growth of towns and trade, 261–65, *263*, *264*, 315
High Middle Ages (950–1250), 252–91, 292–331
Hundred Years' War, 357–59, 383–88, 425
intellectualism, 294, 315–22, *321*
Jagiellonian dynasty in Poland, 390
Justinian and, 218–20, 224
kingdoms of Central and Eastern Europe, 298–300, *299*
Late Middle Ages (1250–1453), 332–65, 366–99
lordship and its limitations in western Europe, 236
Magna Carta, 295–96, 312, 324, 355
Medieval world (1250–1350), overview, 333–34, *338*
Mongol Empire and reorientation of West, 334–42
new kingdoms of Europe, 255–59
popular piety in, 272, *273*, *274*, 309, 351–52
"reconquest" of Spain, 285, *301*, 301–2, 353
reformers in Late Middle Ages, 395–97
Renaissance beginning in Italy, 374–79
Roman Church religious reform and papal power, 271–76, 280, 308–9, 350–51

Roman Empire of Byzantium, 220–26
Rome's legacy and Christianity, 216
Scandinavian kingdoms and Cnut the Great, 255–56
spiritual challenges of, 393–95
struggles for sovereignty during, 352–59
warfare and nation building in Late Middle Ages, 383–91
see also specific topics
Middle Kingdom (ancient Egypt), 34, 36–37, 44, 52
migratio, 151
Milan
    armaments industry, 369
    government by family of despots, 389, 408
    Roman Empire administrative capital, 204, 208
Milesian philosophy, 95–96, 108, 109, 111
Miletus, 57, 95–96, *96*, 97
military
    chivalry, 266, 323
    exploration of fifteenth century and, 425
    hoplite warfare, Archaic Greece, *86*, 86–87, 88, 93, 97, 99, *100*
    hoplite warfare, classical Greece, 99, *100*, 116
    hoplite warfare, Macedonian warriors, 123, *123*, 124
    of Philip II and Alexander the Great, 122–27, *123*, *127*, 128
    Roman Republic, 152–53, 163–64
    of Sparta, 93
    trireme warships, 98, *98*, 100
    see also imperialism; weapons
millenarianism, 449
mills (water mills), 259–60
Miltiades (Athenian general), 98
Minnesänger, 325
Minoan Crete, 51, 52, *52–53*, 53, 54
Minos (king of Crete), 51, 52
Minotaur, 51, 52
Mishneh Torah (Maimonides), 322
missi, 244
Mitanni, 44
Mithraism, 187–88, 197, 202
Moabites, 61
Modestinus (Roman jurist), 176
monarchies
    absolute monarchy, defined, 510
    Carolingian Empire, 242–46, *243*, 256–59
    Christianity and kingship, during Carolingian Empire, 245

crisis of kingship in England (sixteenth–seventeenth centuries), 492–95
csar/tsar, 419
Dauphin (French royal title), 386
feudalism and, 268
growth of national monarchies, Middle Ages, 390–91
Hammurabi's changes to kingship, 21
Hundred Years' War and effect on British monarchy, 388
limited monarchy, 493, 494, 510, 518, 521
Merovingian dynasty, 237, 241, 242–43
Middle Ages monarchy of western Europe, 266–67, 268–70
monarchy rejected by early Romans, 151, 153
queens of Middle Ages, 326
restoration of monarchy in England, 494, 495, 510, 518–19
sovereignty, defined, 352
western European lordship in the Early Middle Ages, 236
see also absolutism; medieval monarchies; *individual monarchs*
monasticism
    asceticism and, 202
    Benedictine order, 211, 212–13, 241, 242, 271–72
    Cistercian order, 309
    crusading orders, 305
    Dominican order, 311, 314, 322, 422
    Franciscan order, 311, 314, 345
    Luther on, 441, 446, 454, 455
    monastic education, 211–12
    monastic reform movement, 271–72
    secular clergy and reform (eleventh century), 273
    of Western Europe in Early Middle Ages, 237, 240–41
Mongol Empire
    bridging East and West, 339–42
    China and, 332, 334, 336, 342
    expansion, 334–35, *335*, 336, 338
    Grand Duchy of Muscovy, 418, *419*
    Khanate of the Golden Horde, 336, 342
    Mongol Ilkhanate, 336, *337*, 341
    Muscovy and Mongol Khanate, 336
    overview, 334
    Pax Mongolica, 337–38
    tolerance of cultural and religious difference, 337

monolatry, 71
monotheism
    Hebrew/Judaic, 70–75, 227
    of Islam, 227, 286, 383
monstrances, 352
Montaigne, Michel de, 499, 500, 501
Montezuma II, 431
Moore, R. I., 330
More, Thomas, 415, 415–16, 417, 457, 461
Morte d'Arthur, Le (Malory), 404–5
mosaics
    medieval mosaics, 226, *232*
    Roman Empire, 176, *176*, *199*
Moscow
    cathedral in, *420*
    Grand Duchy of Muscovy, 418, *419*
    Ivan the Great, 418, *420*
    Mongol Empire and, 418
    see also Russia
Moses (Hebrew prophet), 60, 71, 186, 224
mos maiorum (code of the elders), 154–55, 164, 169, 177
Muhammad, 227–30, 288
mummies, of ancient Egypt, 32
Münster (Germany), Anabaptists of, *448*, 449
music
    ars nova ("new art"), 417
    education in Middle Ages, 315
    Gregorian chant, 241
    of northern European Renaissance, 417–18
Mussi, Gabriele de', 362–63
Mycenaean Greece, 51, 53–54, *54*, 55, 57, 80, 81, 103
mystery cults, 136, 162, 187–88

naming practices of Romans, 155–57
Naples
    Charles VII (king of France) and, 418
Naram-Sin of Akkad, 18
Narmer (king of Egypt), 26, 28, *28*, 31, 45
Narmer Palette, 28, *28*
Native Americans
    colonialism of sixteenth–seventeenth centuries and, 471, 483–84
    English colonialism and, 483–84
    European explorers' treatment of, 428, 429, 430–31, 432–33
    Illinois Indians, *490*
    slaves at Potosí, 474
naturalism in art, 103, 141, 345–46, 417
natural law, of Roman Empire, 177
Nausicaa, 81, 82–83

naval technology/navigation of fifteenth century, 424–25

Navarre, 302

navigation equipment, 345, 424–25

Neanderthals, 5

Near East, early civilizations of, 4–5

Nebuchadnezzar (Chaldean king), 75

Nefertiti (queen of Egypt), 48, *48*

Neferure (Egyptian princess), 45, 47

Nehemiah (governor of Judea), 75

Nekhen, 28, 31

Neo-Assyrian Empire
Assyrian military-religious ethos, *64*, 64–65
atrocities, *64*, 64
government and administration, 63
iron-smelting techniques, 16, 64
legacy of Neo-Assyrian power, *65*, 65–66
overview, 62–63, 72
see also Assyrians

Neolithic Era, defined, 5

Neolithic Revolution, 6–8

Neoplatonism, 196–97, 198, 200, 202, 286–87, 541

Nero (Tiberius Claudius Nero, Roman emperor), 173, 174, 189

Nerva (Roman emperor), 171

Netherlands
Calvinism, 451, 480, *481*
prosperity in sixteenth–seventeenth centuries, 479, 480
religious divisions, 480, *481*
revolt of (sixteenth century), 480, *481*, 482
see also Dutch Republic; Holland

Neustria, 242, 244, 247

Nevsky, Alexander, 301

New Atlantis (Bacon), 553

New France, 489–90

New Kingdom of Egypt
Akhenaten's reign in, *48*, 48–49
Hatshepsut's legacy, 45–47, *47*
pharaohs of Eighteenth Dynasty, 45–49, *46*, *47*, *48*
religious change and political change in, 47–49
treaty with Hittites, 51
Tutankhamun and, 49

New Model Army, 493

Newport, Christopher, 470

New Spain
slaves at Potosi, 474
social hierarchies in, 473

Thirty Years' War and, 488
see also Europe in the Atlantic world (1550–1660); Mexico

New Testament, 184, 189, 415

Newton, Isaac, 540, 545, 559–63, *562*

New World
exploration/conquests, 427–34
Thirty Years War and French power in, 489–90
see also Europe in the Atlantic world (1550–1660); exploration (fifteenth–sixteenth centuries)

Nicholas II (pope), 274

Nicholas, Saint, 272

Nikias (Athenian leader), 106

Nile River, 23–25, *25*

Nimaathap (queen of Egypt), 36

Niña (Columbus' ship), 424

Nineteenth Dynasty (ancient Egypt), 49

Ninety-Five Theses (Luther), 320, 436, 440

Nineveh, *64*, 65–66

Nine Years' War, 523

Noah (biblical character), 14, 15, 40, 71, 189

nobility
absolutism and, 512, 525, 528, 530–31
clothing of, Middle Ages, 371
defined, 370
following Black Death, 370–71
Junkers, 528
Table of Ranks (Russia), 531
in tsarist Russia, 512, 530–31
see also aristocracy

nominalism, 345

Normandy
loss by John to Philip II, 295, 296, 355
Vikings and, 247, 248, 254, 259
see also Anglo-Norman system

Norseman-land. *see* Normandy

North America. *see specific topics and locations*

northern European Renaissance
architecture and art of, *414*, *415*, 416–17, *417*, *420*
Christian humanism, 379, *414*, 414–17
Erasmus, *414*, 414–16, 417
literature of, 414–15, 416
music of, 417–18
overview, 413
Thomas More and, *415*, 415–16, 417, 457, 461
see also Renaissance

northwestern Europe in the Middle Ages, 216, 235–42

northwest passage to Asia, 430

Norway, 255–56, 446
see also Vikings

Notes on the New Testament (Valla), 415

Notre-Dame-la-Grande, Poitiers, 329

Notre-Dame, Reims, 329, *329*

Novels (Justinian legislation), 220

Novgorod Republic, 300–301

Novum Organum (Bacon), 553, *553*, 554

Nubia and Nubians, 31, 36–37, *37*, 45

nuclear family concept, 379

obedience, Ignatius Loyola on, 463

Octavian (Augustus Caesar). *see* Augustus (Octavian, Roman emperor)

Odovacar (barbarian chieftain), 206

Odysseus (Greek hero), 40, 51, 80–81, 82–83

Odyssey, The (Homer), 51, 80, 82–83

Oedipus at Colonus (Sophocles), 101

Ögedei Khan, 334–35, 336

Oikonomikos (Xenophon), 122

oil paints, in Middle Ages, 346, 372, 407

Old Babylonian Empire, 19–20

Old Believer, *531*

Old Church Slavonic (language), 277

Old Kingdom (ancient Egypt), 26–36

Old Woman, An (sculpture), 141, *141*

Olga (Kievan princess), 277

oligarchy, defined, 92

Olympias (queen of Macedonia), 122, 129

Olympic Games, 51, 85, 86, *86*

"On Bubbles of Air That Escape from Fluids" (Bassi), 558

"On Cannibals" (Montaigne), 501

On Duties (Cicero), 208

On the Art of Building (Alberti), 413

On the Art of Hunting with Birds (Frederick II), 325

"On the Bubbles Observed in Freely Flowing Fluid" (Bassi), 558

"On the Compression of Air" (Bassi), 558

On the Duties of Ministers (Ambrose), 208

On the Family (Alberti), 379

On the Revolutions of the Heavenly Spheres (Copernicus), 543, 546

ontological proof, 319

oracles
Alexander and oracle of Ammon, 125
at temple of Apollo at Delphi, 66, 85

Order of Christ, 423

Order of Preachers, 314

Order of the Friars Minor, 314

Orlando Furioso (Ariosto), 407, 416

Orthodox Christianity
    early Christian emphasis on
        orthodoxy, 201
    Great East–West Schism, 391
    Greek Orthodox Church, 222–23,
        224, 383
    iconoclasm and, 222–23, 224–25
    Reformation and Eastern Orthodox
        Christianity, 452
    reform of secular clergy (eleventh
        century), 273
Osiris (Egyptian god), 32, 34, *34*, 136,
    162, 202
Osman Gazi, 380
ostracism, 92, 101
Ostrogoths, 206, 207, 218
Otto I of Saxony (Otto the Great),
    257–58, *258*
Ottokar I (king of Bohemia), 299
Ottoman Empire
    attempted expansion into southeastern
        Europe, 526, 528–29
    Christians and Jews in, 383
    commerce and trade, 383
    fall of Constantinople and, 203,
        380–81, 383, 402, 425
    growth of, 380–81, *382*
    Habsburg dynasty and, 526, 528–29
    Mongols and, 380
    Protestant Reformation and, 452
    Renaissance politics and increasing
        power of, 418
    rise of Ottoman Turks, 380–81
    slavery in, 381–83, 423, 426
    social advancement in, 382–83
    Thirty Years' War, 485
    see also Turkey
Ovid (Publius Ovidius Naso), 174, 375
Oxford University, 320

pagans, 203
painting
    Baroque style, 502–3, *503*
    in Late Middle Ages, 346, *346*
    Mannerism, 502
    oil paints in Middle Ages, 346, 372, 407
    Renaissance painting techniques, 407–8
    tempera, 346, *409*
    see also art; fresco paintings
Pakistan, Alexander the Great in, 125
Paleolithic Era, 5
Palestine
    Alexander the Great and, 124–25
    ancient Egypt and, 37

    Hellenistic culture among Jews, 138
    Philistines and, 54, 60
    Roman rule, 164, 185–86
Palladio, Andrea, 413
Panhellenism, 84–85
panoply, 86–87
Pantagruel (Rabelais), 416
papacy
    in Avignon, 347, *350*, 350–52, 356,
        374, 378, 388, 391
    "Babylonian Captivity" of, 350–51, 406
    challenges to Roman Church, Late
        Middle Ages, 391–97
    conciliarism and, 392–93, 394–95,
        419–20, 462
    Council of Constance, 392–93,
        394–95, 397, *397*, 419, 462
    Fourth Lateran Council of 1215, 308,
        312–13, 316
    German emperors and, 270, *271*, 298
    Luther's break with Rome, 441–44
    reform and papal power, Middle Ages,
        271–76, 280, 308–9, 347, 350–51
    reform of (eleventh century), 273–74,
        275–76
    Renaissance and growth of national
        churches, 419–21
    return to Rome in 1377, 376, 389, 391
    as Saint Peter's successors, 200, 223, 395
    see also Catholicism; Roman Catholic
        Church
Papal States, 298, 350, *406*, 418, 420
papermaking, early, 234
paper, printing press invention and, 234, 400
Papinian (Aemelianus Papinianus; Roman
    jurist), 176
papyrus
    in Byblos, 56, 58
    funerary scrolls, *34*
    production of, 27, 29, 234
    Sappho of Lesbos poetry, 90
Parallel Lives (Plutarch), 166
Paris (*Iliad* character), 80, 81
parlements (France), *386*, 513
Parliament (British)
    Civil War (England), 492–93, 494,
        497, 500
    establishment of, 296
    "king in Parliament," 494, 518, 519
    Oliver Cromwell and Rump
        Parliament, 494
Parr, Catherine, 457
Parthenon, 103, *103*
Parzival (Wolfram), 325

Pascal, Blaise, 499–500, 557
Passion, relics of, 354, *354*
Patel, Pierre, *515*
patria potestas, 155
patricians, 153, *155*
Paul III (pope), 461, 464
Paul IV (pope), 461
Paul of Tarsus (Saint Paul)
    conversion, 187–88
    development of early Christianity and,
        187–88, 201
    missionary journeys, *187*
    prosecution and death, 189,
        190–91, 200
    writings and letters, 184, 198, 201,
        379, 439
Paulus (Roman jurist), 176
Pax Mongolica (Mongol Peace), 337–38
Pax Romana (Roman Peace), 171
Peace of Augsburg, 452, 485
Peace of Nystad, 534–35
Peace of Westphalia, *487*, 488, 525
peasantry
    in ancient Egypt, 35, 36
    English Peasants' Revolt, 367, 369,
        370, 384, 397
    German peasant revolt (1524),
        445–46
    in tsarist Russia, 531
Peasants' Revolt (England), 367, 369, 370,
    384, 397
pedagogy, 113
Peisistratos (Greek aristocrat), 92
Pelopidas (Theban general), 122
Peloponnesian War
    destruction of Melos, 106, 108, 109
    downfall of Greek poleis and, 116
    failure of Athenian democracy and,
        107, 108
    inception of, 105–7, *107*
    map of colonies and alliances, *107*
    overview, 101
    Peloponnesian League, 105–6
Peloponnesus, 85, 92, *94*, 106
Pensées (Pascal), 499
Pentapolis (Philistine citadels), 59
Pepin (Austrasian nobleman), 242
Pepin (king of Franks), 243–44
Perdiccas (Macedonian general), 129
Pergamon (Anatolia), 140, *140*
Pericles, 100–101, 103, 105, 106
perioikoi, 94
Perpetua, Vivia, 182–84, 189, 201
Persepolis (Persian Empire), 67, 124

Persia
Abbasid caliphate in, 233
Byzantine Empire and, 221
Rabbinic Judaism in, 218
Sassanid dynasty, 204, 218
Persian Empire
Alexander the Great's conquest of, 124–25, *126*
Arab conquest of, 221, 230
cavalry, 98, 100, 124
consolidation of Persian rule, 67–68
Cyrus the Great, 66–67, 72–73, 75
map, *69, 96*
Mongol rule of, 336, *337*
overview, 66
Persian Wars, 67–68, 97–100, *99, 100*
Royal Road, 67, *69,* 174
seals, *68*
wars with Greece, 67–68, 97–100, *99, 100*
Zoroastrianism, 68–70
see also Seleucids
Persians (Aeschylus), 101
Persian Wars, 67–68, 97–100, *99, 100*
perspective in Renaissance art, 407–8
Peter I ("the Great;" tsar of Russia), 512, 530–35, *531,* 559
Peter, Saint, 186–87, 200
Peter the Hermit, 281
Petition of Right, 493, 494
Petrarch (Francesco Petrarca), *374,* 374–75, 378, 407, 416, 417
Petronius (Roman author), 174
phalanx, *86,* 86–87, 88, 116, *123,* 152
pharaohs, power of, 24, 26
see also Egypt (ancient)
Pharisees, 186, 190, *412*
Philip II (king of Macedonia), 116, 122–23, 124, 132, 168
Philip II (king of Spain), 459, 480, *481,* 482
Philip III of Macedonia, 129
Philip IV (king of France), 347, 350, 352, 353, 354, 358
Philip IV (king of Spain), 485
Philip V (Philip of Anjou, king of Spain), 523
Philip V of Macedonia, 159
Philip Augustus (Philip II; king of France), 295, 296, 298, 306, 308, 352, 353
Philippa (queen of Portugal), 423
Philippines
Magellan death in, 428
Philistines, 54, 56, 59–60, 61

philosophia, 95
philosophy
classical learning and Christianity, 210–11
Epicureanism, 134, 135, 136
inception of Greek *philosophia,* 95
of Late Roman Republic, 162
mechanical philosophy, 556, 557
Milesian philosophy, 95–96, 108, 109, 111
Muslim philosophy and Christian theology, 285–87
Neoplatonism, 196–97, 198, 200, 202, 286–87
nominalism, 345
"philosopher-kings," 120
Pythagorean, 108–9, 111
schools of Plato and Aristotle, *119,* 119–20
seventeenth century, 499–500, 501
Skepticism, 135–36
Socratic, 108, 109–12
Sophist, 108–9, 110–11
Stoicism and Christianity, 135, 187, 202
Stoicism, Hellenistic, 132, 134–35
Stoicism, Roman, 135, 162, 177, 197, 202, 208
see also ethics
Phintys (Hellenistic writer), 143
Phoenicians
alphabet, 59, *59,* 81
colonies, 56, *58,* 58–59, 157
overview, 56, 58
pottery, 85
seafaring, 58, 81
trade and commerce, 84
Tyre (capital), 59, 62, 125
see also Canaanites
phonemes, 11
Phryne (Athenian courtesan), 121
Pico della Mirandola, Giovanni, 402
pictograms, 11, *11,* 27
Pilate (Pontius Pilatus), 185, 354
pilgrimages and pilgrims (Christian), 272–73, 274–75, 281
Pilgrims (Plymouth, Massachusetts), 483, *484*
piracy and medieval trade, 261–62
Pisa, 262, 277, 283
Piscopia, Elena Cornaro, 558
Pius V (pope), 461
Pizarro, Francisco, 431
Plataea, 98

Plato
birth and death, 84, 119
dialogues, 110–11, 119–20, 142–43, 285, 375, 402
philosophy of, 112, *119,* 119–20, 224, 413
Republic, The, 120, 142–43
on Socrates' philosophy, 110–11, 119–20
on true love, 89
"Platonic Academy," 402
plebeians ("plebs"), 153–54
Pliny the Younger (Gaius Plinius Caecilius Secundus), 192–93
Plotinus (Hellenistic philosopher), 195
plows, for farming, *17, 36, 152,* 237, 259
Plutarch (Roman historian), 124, 127, 166
Plymouth (Massachusetts), Pilgrims of, 483, *484*
pneumonic plague, 360
see also Black Death
Pnyx, *91,* 92
poaching, 324
Poem of the Cid, 324
poetry
of Archaic Greece, 88–89, 90
Muslim, Middle Ages, 229, 288
seventeenth century, 500, 502
sonnets, 416
use of rhyme in Middle Ages, 328
pogroms, 282
Poland
battle of Legnica, 335
conversion to Christianity, 255
encouragement of Jewish settlements, 300, 315, 389
Great Northern War and, 534
Jadwiga (female king of Poland), 390
Jagiellonian dynasty, 390
Kraków market square, *264*
Middle Ages, 300
Mongol Empire and, 334–35
Polish-Lithuania Commonwealth, 488–89, 518, 522, 528
reform movements, Late Middle Ages, 395–96
Thirty Years War, 485, 488
poleis (ancient Greece, singular polis)
artistic/intellectual response to downfall of, 118–22
defined, 81
downfall of, 116, 118
rise of, 81–82
transition to cosmopolis, 132–34

polis. *see* poleis

Political Testament (Richelieu), 491

political theory
contract theory of government, 520–21
Epicureanism and, 135
oligarchy, 92
res publica, 152, 254
science of, in seventeenth century, 500

Politics (Aristotle), 145

polity, defined, 88, 120, 154

Polo, Marco, 332, *339*, 339–40, 423

Polo, Matteo, 339, *339*

Polo, Niccolò, 339, *339*

Poltava, battle of, 533

Polybius (Greek historian), 144–45, 148, 150, 154, *155*, 156, 159

Pompeius, Sextus, 173

Pompey (Gnaeus Pompeius Magnus), 164, 166, 167, 173

pontifex maximus, 170, 172

Poor Ladies, Order of (Poor Clares), 314

Pope, Alexander, 562

population growth
of Archaic Greece, 81
in early civilizations, 7–8
in Europe in sixteenth–seventeenth centuries, 477, 478

portolan charts (*portolani*), 345, *345*, 425

portraits
portraiture of Renaissance, 408
self-portraiture of seventeenth century, 505, *505*

Portugal
in Canary Islands, 344
colonialism (sixteenth–seventeenth centuries), 476, 480
colonial rivalries after Treaty of Utrecht, 524
exploration by (fifteenth–sixteenth centuries), 423–27, 428
independence after Thirty Years' War, 488
medieval kingdom, 302
slave trade, 423–24, 427, 476

Porus (Indus Valley leader), 125

Poseidon (Greek god), 54

Potosi, slaves at, 474

pottery
of early civilizations, 4, 8, 16
Greek pottery, 50, 80, 91
Phoenician pottery, 85
wheel invention and, 16

Poullain de la Barre, François, 558

poverty
European poverty in sixteenth–seventeenth centuries, 477–79

Powhatan tribe, 470

praetors, 176

Praise of Folly, The (Erasmus), 414, 441

Praxiteles (sculptor), 118, *118*, 121

Predynastic Egypt, 24–25
see also Egypt (ancient)

Presbyterians, 451

Prester John (*Description of the World* character), 340–41, 423

price revolution, 477, 478

Prince, The (Machiavelli), 37, 404, 405, 406–7

Principate (Roman Empire), 168–71, 173, 174, 176, 195

Principia Mathematica (Newton), 562–63

printing
invention of printing press, 400, 402, 403, 404–5, 540
Luther and, *439*, 441, 442–43

prose
emergence of, 119
of Hellenistic period, 144–45

proskynesis, 126, *126*

prostitution
Protestant Reformation and, 455

Protagoras, 109

Protestantism
absolutism and, 512
forms of, 446–52
Hungary and Habsburg dynasty, 525, 528
Protestant, defined, 446
see also Reformation; *specific churches*

Protestant Reformation. *see* Reformation

proxy wars, 384

Prussia
Brandenburg-Prussia and absolutism, 512, 525, 527–30, 535
Great Northern War, 534–35
Junkers, 528

Ptah-Hotep (official of ancient Egypt), 33, 37

Ptolemaic Egypt, 27, 130, 133, 159

Ptolemaic system, 139, 538, *542*, 542–44, 545, 547, 548

Ptolemy I (Egyptian satrap and pharaoh), 124, 130, *131*, 164

Ptolemy II (Egyptian ruler), 130

Ptolemy II Philadelphus (Egyptian ruler), 130

Ptolemy XIII (Egyptian pharaoh), 164

Ptolemy of Alexandria (Claudius Ptolemaeus), 139, 538, 541, 542, 563

public works projects, of Roman Empire, 171, 174, *177*

Punic Wars
First Punic War, 157
overview, 157–58, *158*
Second Punic War, 158, 159
Third Punic War, 145, 158

purgatory, 241, 351, 439–40

Puritans
in Atlantic colonies, 495
Calvinism and, 451, 483, 492
Civil War (England) and, 492, 493, 494, 495

Pylos (grave), 53, 54

Pythagoras, 108, 139

Pythagorean theorem, 109

pyxis, *288*

quadrants (instrument), 425

quadrivium, 315

Québec (Canada), 489, 490, 524

querelle des femmes, 372

Quietists, 513

Qur'an (Koran), *228*, 228–30, 231, 234, 285, 288

Quraysh, 227–28

Ra (Egyptian god), 31, 44, 48

Rabbinic Judaism, 218, 322

rabbis, 218, 230

Rabelais, François, 416

race/racial prejudice
racialization and slavery, 427
see also anti-Semitism

Raleigh, Walter, 470

Ramón de Caldes, 304, *305*

Ramses (pharaoh of Egypt), 49

Ramses II (pharaoh of Egypt), 51

Ramses III (pharaoh of Egypt), 54, 59, 60

Raphael (Raffaello Sanzio), *119*, 409, *410*

Rashid, Harun al-, 233, 235, 246

Ravenna, Italy, 204, 206, 226

reconquista, 301–2, 314, 421, 422–23, 472

Redwald of East Anglia (king), 238

Reformation, 436–67
Albigensian Crusade legacy and, 308
Catholic Reformation and rebirth, 460–65
chronology, *466*
domestication of reform, 452–56
enforcement of godly discipline, 451, 453
in England, 456–60

Reformation, (*Continued*)
  events leading to, 397
  forms of Protestantism, 446–52, *447*
  government role in public morality,
    451, 453, 455–56
  Luther and reformation in Germany,
    436, *438*, 438–46, 451–52
  overview, 436–38
  Protestant, defined, 446
  religious affiliations (confessions) in
    Europe, c. 1560, *447*
  religious education, 453
  religious warfare, 451–52
Reformed Church, 450
relics/reliquaries, 272, 274–75, *275*, 352,
  354, *354*
religion
  absolutism and, 512
  of ancient Egypt, 24–25, 31, 32
  of ancient Greece, 85, 136–38
  Assyrian religious ethos, 64–65
  Civil War (England) and, 492–95
  of early civilizations, 9, 10
  Galileo and, 464, 545, 546–47, 550
  gods and religion of ancient Rome,
    155, 156, 162, 171, 203
  great flood accounts, 14–15, 40, 60, 71
  Hammurabi's use of, 19
  Hebrew monotheism, 70–75, 227
  Hellenistic period, 136–38
  myths and, 2
  New Kingdom of Egypt, religious
    change, 47–49
  Persian Empire and, 68–70
  popular piety in Middle Ages, 272,
    273, 274, 309, 352
  pursuit of holiness, Late Middle Ages,
    352
  Renaissance and growth of national
    churches, 419–21
  Roman Church reform and papal
    power, 271–76, 280, 308–9, 347,
    350–51
  scientific revolution and, 540, 541,
    550, 560–61, 563
  spiritual challenges, in Middle Ages,
    393–95
  Sumerian, 14–15, 18
  wars of religion in sixteenth–seventeenth
    centuries, 479–82, *481*, 484–92
  Xenophanes on images of god, 95–96
  see also individual religions
Rembrandt van Rijn, 504–5, *505*
Remus, 150

Renaissance, 374–79, 400–435
  architecture, 413, 416, *420*
  art, 407–13, *408*, *409*, *412*, 416–17, *417*
  beginning of, in Italy, 374–79, 402
  chronology, *398*, *434*
  classicism, 375–76, 402
  defined, 368
  Europeans in New World, 427–34
  in Florence, 378–79, 402, 406
  humanism, 376, 378–79, 402, 407,
    409, 414, 541
  ideal of courtier, 407
  ideals of, overview, 402
  overseas exploration during, 423–30,
    426, *429*
  politics of Christian Europe during,
    418–23
  politics of Italy and philosophy of
    Machiavelli, 402, 404–7
  printing during, 400, 402, *403*,
    404–5, 540
  reading ancient texts during, 375, 376,
    379, 541, 542
  "Renaissance man" ideal, 407
  scientific revolution and, 541
  sculpture, 410, *412*, 412–13
  see also northern European
    Renaissance
Renaissance, Carolingian, 245
Reni, Guido, *461*
Republic, The (Plato), 120, 142–43
res publica, 152, 254
rex, 151
rhapsodes, 80
Rhine Palatinate, League of Augsburg, 523
rhyme in Middle Ages, 328
Richard I (the Lionheart; king of
  England), 295, 296, 298, 306, *318*
Richard II (king of England), 370, 384, 388
Richelieu, Cardinal (Armand Jean du
  Plessis), 490–91
Riga, bishopric of, 306
Rigaud, Hyacinthe, 514, *514*
Roanoke Island (North Carolina), 470
Robert of Ketton, 285
Robert the Bruce, 356
Rodin, Auguste, 140
Roman alphabet, 59, 150
Roman Catholic Church
  absolutism and, 512
  Catholic reforms at time of Protestant
    Reformation, 461–62
  Council of Trent, 312, 454, 460,
    461–62

Counter-Reformation, 460–65, 513
  Galileo and, 464, 545, 546–47, 550
  Ignatius Loyola and Society of Jesus,
    462–64
  Index of Prohibited Books, 462
  Jansenism, 499, 513
  Louis XIV (king of France) and, 513
  on marriage as sacrament, 351, 454, 455
  Protestant Reformation and rebirth
    of, 460–65
  reformed Catholic Church of
    seventeenth and eighteenth
    centuries, 464–65
  sacraments, 351–52, 439, 441
  witchcraft accusations and, 499
  see also Catholicism; papacy
Roman Empire, 148–81, 182–215
  arts of, 121, *121*
  Christianity and Rome's legacy, 216
  Christianity as challenge to, 182–84
  Christianity as minority religion in,
    188, 189, 192–93, 194, 195–98
  Christianity conversion in, 195–203
  chronology, *180*
  consequences of imperialism, 160–62
  Constantinople establishment and,
    184, 203–7
  end of eastern Roman Empire, 379–83
  Five Good Emperors, 171
  founding of Rome and, 151
  infrastructure and public works, 171,
    174, *177*
  Justinian's impact on western Roman
    Empire, 219–20
  kings and early history of Rome, 151
  literature, 174–75
  maps, *159*, *170*
  migrations of Rome's frontier peoples,
    204–6, *205*, *207*
  overview, 148–50
  Pax Romana (Roman Peace), 171
  Polybius' written accounts of, 145, 150
  Principate, 168–71, 173, 174, 176, 195
  Roman Empire of Byzantium, 220–26
  Roman foundation myths, 150–51
  Roman Republic transition to Roman
    Empire, 157–59
  Rome as symbolic capital, under
    Diocletian, 195
  sacking of Rome, 206, 207, 210
  during Severan dynasty, 190–94
  shifting centers of, 203–7
  territorial expansion, challenges of,
    189–95

territorial expansion of, 152–53, 159, *159*, 169, *170*

"Third-Century Crisis," 194

transformation and decline of, 182–215

urban planning in Roman Empire, 174, *178*, 178–79

see also Byzantine Empire; Holy Roman Empire; Roman Republic; *individual emperors*

Romanesque architecture, 328–29, *329*, 413

Roman Forum, 151

Roman Republic, 151–68

  chronology, *180*

  consequences of imperialism, 160–62

  constitution of early Roman Republic, 153–54, 163

  defined, 152

  economic issues, 160–61

  founding of Rome and, 151

  kings and early history of Rome, 151

  Law of the Twelve Tables, 153, 155, 156, 176

  monarchy rejected by early Romans, 151, 153

  overview, 148–50

  Polybius' written accounts of, 145

  "restoring Republic" and struggle for power, 162–67

  Roman identity and, 154–57

  slavery in, 160–61

  territorial expansion, 152–53, 159, *159*

  transition to Roman Empire, 157–59

  triumphs of early Roman Republic, 151–54

  see also Roman Empire

Rome

  foundation myths, 150–51

  founding and early history, 151

  pope's claim to secular authority, 265

  Renaissance art in, 409–10

  sack by Goths, 206, 207, 210

  urban planning during Roman Empire, *178*, 178–79

  see also Roman Empire; Roman Republic

Romeo and Juliet (Shakespeare), 502

Romulus, 150, 151, 166

Romulus Augustulus (Roman emperor), 206

Rosetta Stone, 27, *29*

Roundheads, 493

Roxane (wife of Alexander the Great), 125, 129

Royal Society of London, 558, 561, 563

Rubaiyat (Umar Khayyam), 288

Rubens, Peter Paul, 504, *505*

Rubicon River, 164

Rudolf II (Holy Roman Emperor), 544

Rule of Saint Benedict, 210, 211, 212, 241, 271, 309, 463

Rûm, sultanate of, 336, 380

Rus', 247–48, 255, 276, 300–301, 334, 336

Russia

  absolutism and, 510, 530–35, *531*

  expansion into Siberia, 533

  Great Northern War, 533–35

  imperial expansion (sixteenth to eighteenth centuries), 533–35, *534*

  taxes in tsarist Russia, 531, 535

  Viking Rus', 247–48, 255, 276, 300–301, 334, 336

  see also Moscow

rutters/routiers (books), 425

Sabines, 151

sacraments, 351–52, 439, 441

Sacred Congregation of the Index, 462

Sadducees, 186

Saint Bartholomew's Day Massacre, 479, 500

Saint-Domingue, 490, 517

Sainte-Chapelle (Holy Chapel), 354, *354*

Saint Jerome in His Study (Dürer), *417*, 417

St. Mark's Basilica in Venice, 226

Saladin (Sala ah-Din), 284, 306

Salamis, battle of, 100, *101*

Salian dynasty, 258

Samuel (Hebrew tribal judge), 61, 243

Sappho of Lesbos, 89, 90

Sarcophagus of the Muses, *109*

Sardinia, 157, 158

Sardis (Lydia), 67, 98

Sargon II (Assyrian king), 63, 65, 72, 74

Sargon the Great (king of Akkadians), 17–18, 26, 60, 63, 131

Sassanids, 204, 218

"Satire of the Trades, The" (ancient Egypt), 27

satraps, 67, 117, 125, 128, 129, 130

Saturnalia, 197

Saturn (Roman god), 197

Saul (king of Israel), 61, 243

Savonarola, Girolamo, 452

Saxons, 206, 244, 245, 256–58

Saxony

  conquest by Charlemagne, 244, 245

  European colonialism, 306

Scandinavia

  new kingdoms and Cnut the Great, 255–56

  new kingdoms in Middle Ages, 255–56

  sovereignty in Middle Ages, 353

Schliemann, Heinrich, 51

scholasticism, 318–19, 320, 322, 376, 378, 464

School of Athens, The (Raphael), *119*, 409, *410*

science

  of ancient Egypt, 34–35

  defined, 540

  geography of Hellenistic period, 139

  Hellenistic period, 138–41, 144–45

  innovation of Middle Ages, 344–45

  Muslim scientists, Middle Ages, 286, 287–88

  naval technology/navigation and exploration of fifteenth century and, 424–25

  patrons of, 546, 550, 558

  Sumerian, 16–17

  see also scientific revolution

scientific revolution, 538–65

  chronology, *564*

  Copernican revolution, 139, 542–44, *543*

  cultural change and, 563

  Descartes, 465, 552, 554–55, *556*, 559, 562

  Francis Bacon, 552–54, *553*, 556, 557, 558

  Galileo and, 464, 545–47

  geology and environmental sciences, 547–49, 551–52

  intellectual origins of, 540–42

  Newton, 540, 545, 559–63, *562*

  observations of natural processes, 544–45, 548–49, 551, 560–61

  overview, 138, 538–40

  Ptolemaic system and, 538, *542*, 542–44, 545, 547, *548*

  religion and, 540, 541, 550, 560–61, 563

  science, defined, 540

  seventeenth-century experimenters, 557

  state, scientific academies, and women scientists during, 557–59

  Tycho's observations and Kepler's laws, *544*, 544–45

Scipio, Publius Cornelius (Scipio Africanus), 145, 158, 159

Scivias (Hildegard of Bingen), *311*

Scone Abbey, 356

Scorpion (king of Egypt), 26
Scotland
    Abbey Church (Island of Iona), *240*
    Calvinism, 451, 492, 493, 503, 504
    Civil War (England) and, 492, 493
    John Knox and Presbyterians, 451
    monasticism of seventh century,
        240, *240*
    sovereignty in Middle Ages, 355–57
    subjugation by England, 355–57
    union with England (1707), 524
    Vikings and, 247
    "Whigs" name and, 518
sculpture
    Archaic Greece, 87, *87*
    classical Greece, 103, *103*, 118, *118*,
        121, *121*
    fourth century B.C.E., 118, *118*,
        121, *121*
    Hellenistic period, 138–39, 141, *141*
    Renaissance, 410, *412*, 412–13
    see also art
seals, *68*, *348*, 348–49
Sea Peoples, 54–56, 59, 60, 62
Second Dynasty (ancient Egypt), 26
Second Intermediate Period (ancient
    Egypt), 44–45
Second Punic War, 158, 159
Second Vatican Council, 462
secular clergy, reform of (eleventh
    century), 273
seed drills (Sumerian), 16, *17*
Sejm (Commonwealth of Poland and
    Lithuania), 522
Seleucids, 130–31, 133, 159
Seleucus (Persian ruler), 130–31
self-portraiture, of seventeenth century,
    505, *505*
Seljuk Turks, 278–79, 280, 281, 283, 284,
    303–4, 336, 380
Semitic peoples
    Akkadians, 18
    Amorites, 19
    Chaldeans, 66–67, 68, 70, 74–75
    languages of, 56
    migrations, 43
Senate (Roman)
    altar of the goddess Victory removed
        from, 203
    crucifixion used by, 162
    in early republic, 153, 154
    inception of, 151
    Julius Caesar's assassination, 167
    Punic Wars and, 158

statutes written by, 177
    Sulla and, 163–64
Sennacherib (Neo-Assyrian king), *64*, 65, 72
Sentences (Lombard), 319
Sephardic Jews, 422
septicemic plague, 360
    see also Black Death
Serbia
    Middle Ages, 255
serfs/serfdom
    after the Black Death, 369
    in Middle Ages, 260, 264–65
    in Russia under Tsar Peter I, 531, 533
Seth (Egyptian god), 32
"seven-headed papal beast"/"seven-headed
    Martin Luther," 443
Seven Years Famine, 359–60
Severan dynasty, 190–94
Severus, Alexander (Roman emperor), 194
Severus, Septimus (Roman emperor),
    190–93, 194, *194*
sex
    asceticism and, 202–3
    homosexuality in ancient Greece, 88, 116
    prostitution, 455
Seymour, Jane (queen of England), 457
Sforza dictators, of Milan, 408
Shakespeare, William
    about, 478, 495, 502, 538
    plays, 495, 502, 538
    sonnets, 416
Shamash (Babylonian god), 20, *23*
Shi'ite Muslims
    Fatimids, 249, 256, 280
    Shi'ite-Sunni schism, 232–33, 249
Shiloh, 60
shipping
    naval technology/navigation of
        fifteenth century, 424–25
Shulgi (king of Ur), 18
Sic et Non (Abelard), 319
Sicily
    Black Death, 360, 362
    in Byzantine Empire, 256
    Charles of Anjou and, 347, 354
    as colony of Rome, 157–58, 159, 256
    Emperor Frederick II and, 298, 324, 347
    expulsion of Jews, 315, 421–22, 510
    Fatimid caliphate and, 256, 276
    Greek settlement of, 85, 106, 118,
        150, 256
    invasion by Vandals and Goths, 256
    Norman kingdom in, 256
Sidonius Apollinaris, 212–13

siege of Vienna, 526, 528–29
Silk Road, 234, 334, 335, 339, 340
silver
    from Abbasid Empire, 235, 247
    colonialism in sixteenth–seventeenth
        centuries and, 434, 474, 477, 479, 488
    European exploration for, 432–33
    Vikings and, 249, 261
Simeon "the Stylite," Saint, 202, *202*
Simon de Montfort (earl of Leicester), seal
    of, *348*
simony, 273, 275, 440
Simplicissimus (Grimmelshausen), 486
Sisters of Charity, 464
Sistine Chapel, Vatican, 410–11, *411*
Six Articles, Church of England, 457, 458
Six Books of the Commonwealth (Bodin), 500
Sixth Dynasty (ancient Egypt), 30, 31
Sixtus V (pope), 461
Skepticism, 135–36
slavery
    in ancient Egypt, 35, 45
    in ancient Greece, 91
    Aristotle on, 120
    in Babylonian society, 20–21
    Caribans, 495
    Civil War (England) and, 495
    of classical Greece, 104–5
    colonization of New World and, 472,
        474–76, *475*, 481
    debt slavery, 21, 91, 105, 114, 153
    defined, 160
    Dutch West India Company, 481
    European exploration (fifteenth century)
        and, 423–24, 426–27, 432–33
    fears of violence, 476
    fugitive slave communities in New
        World, 477
    Goths and, 205
    human cost of the slave trade, 476–77
    Islam and, 234, 235, 249
    in Ottoman Empire, 381–83, 423, 426
    plantation model of, 427, 432–33, 476,
        484, 490, 495
    Portuguese slave trade, 423–24, 427, 476
    racialization of in fifteenth century, 427
    in Roman Republic, 160–61, 162
    in Sumerian culture, 12
Slavs
    conversion to Orthodox Christianity,
        277
    migration to Balkans, 276–77
smallpox, spread by European explorers,
    430, 431

Smith, John, *471*
Sobieski, John III (king of Poland), 526, 528
social pyramid, of ancient Egypt, 35
Social War (Roman Republic), 163
Society of Jesus (Jesuits), 462–64, 513
Socrates
    The Clouds (Aristophanes), 110–11
    dialogues, 109, 110–11, 119–20, 142–43
    image of, *109*
    legacy of, 119–20
    philosophy and, 108, 109–12
    Republic (Plato), 120, 142–43
    trial and execution of, 96, 112, 118, 119, 136
solar calendar, of ancient Egypt, 35
Sol Invictus, 194, 197, 199, *199*, 202
Solomon (king of Israel), 62, 70, 73
Solon, 91–92
Song of Roland, 252, 254, 266, 281, *281*, 324, 407
Song of the Nibelungs, 324
Sophia, rebellion of streltsy and, 530, 532
Sophists, 108–9, 110–11
Sophocles (Greek playwright), 101, 122, 379
sovereignty
    defined, 352, 500
    struggles for, during Middle Ages, 352–59
    see also individual rulers
Spain
    Arab conquest of, 231
    art, seventeenth century, *502*, 502–3, *503*
    Christian kingdoms of Iberian Peninsula in Middle Ages, *301*, 301–2
    colonial rivalries after Treaty of Utrecht, 524
    Columbus and, 423, 427–28
    conquistadors, 430–32, *431*
    end of *convivencia*, 421
    end of Muslim rule in, 421
    expulsion of Jews, 300, 421–22
    League of Augsburg and War of the Spanish Succession, 523–24
    literature and poetry, Middle Ages, 288
    medieval drama in, 374
    Naples and Charles VII (king of France), 418
    "reconquest" of, 285, *301*, 301–2, 353
    reconquista, 301–2, 314, 421, 472
    silver and gold from Spanish America (sixteenth century), 432–34, 474, 477, 479, 488

Spanish Armada and conflict with England, 460, 481–82, *483*
    Thirty Years' War and, 488
    Treaty of Utrecht, 523
    Umayyad caliphate in, 233, 235, 242, 244, 247, 250
    see also specific individuals and topics
Sparta
    downfall of Greek poleis and, 116, 118
    government in, 92, 93–94
    Hellenic League and Xerxes' invasion, 98–100, *99*
    helots, 92, 93–94, 105–6, 116
    low birthrate, 93, 95
    marriage in, 93
    militarized life in, 93
    overview, 92–95
    Peisistratid tyranny ousted by, 94
    Peloponnesian War, 106–8, 116
    Peloponnesus and, 92, 94, 106
    rise of poleis and, 81
Spartacus (Thracian slave), 162
Spenser, Edmund, 416
Spice Islands, 334, 340, 424, 428, 480
spice trade, 283, 343, 381, 424, 481
Spinoza, Baruch, 557
Spiritual Exercises (Ignatius of Loyola), 462, 463
SPQR (Senatus Populusque Romanum), 154
stadtholder, 521–22
Staffordshire hoard, 238, *238*
Starry Messenger, The (Galileo), 546
Statute of Kalisz, 300
steles
    Code of Hammurabi, 20, *23*
    of Hatshepsut and Thutmose, 46, *47*
    of King Esarhaddon at Senjirli, *72*
    Nubian stele, *37*
    Rosetta Stone, 27, *29*
Steno, Nicolas (Niels Stensen), 551–52
Step Pyramid, 29, *30*
Stilicho, Flavius, 204, 206
stock markets, creation of, 481
Stoicism
    Christianity and, 135, 187, 202
    Hellenistic Stoicism, 132, 134–35
    Roman Stoicism, 135, 162, 177, 197, 202, 208
Stone Age societies, 5–6
Stone of Destiny, 356
St. Peter's Basilica, 198, *198*, 413, 440, *440*, 503
St. Petersburg (Russia), building of, 533–34
Strasbourg, *263*, 363, 523, 524

strategos, 100–101, 116
Stratford-upon-Avon (England), Shakespeare and, 502
Strayer, Joseph, 330
streltsy, revolt of, 530, 532
Struggle of the Orders, 153
St. Thomas (São Tomé), 432
stylus, development of, 11
Sufis, 234
sugar
    Civil War (England) and, 495
    French colonialism and, 490, 516–18
    slavery and, 427, 432–33, 474–76, 490, 516–18
Suger, Abbot, 318
Suleiman the Magnificent (sultan), 452, 528
Sulla, Lucius Cornelius, 163–64, 197
Sumatra, 480
Sumer, 9–17
    culture of Sumer, 12–17
    development of writing, 10–12, *11*, 27
    Early Dynastic Period, 12–13, 14
    religion, 14–15
    science and technology, 16–17, *17*
    timekeeping, 17, 345
    trade, 10, 16, 17
    Ubaid culture, 9–10
    Uruk, 10, *10*
Summa contra gentiles (Thomas Aquinas), 322
Summa Theologiae (Thomas Aquinas), 322
Sun King, Louis XIV (king of France) as, 510, 512, 514, *514*
Sunna (Sunnah), 233
Sunni Muslims
    rise of Ottoman Empire and, 383
    Seljuk Turks, 278–79, 280, 281, 283, 284, 303–4, 336, 380
    Shi'ite-Sunni schism, 232–33, 249
sunspots, discovery of, 546, 549
suras (Qur'an), 229
Susa (Persian Empire), 67, 126
Sutton Hoo Ship Burial, 238–39, *238–39*
Sweden
    Great Northern War, 533–34
    invasion of Poland-Lithuania, 488–89
    League of Augsburg, 523
    Lutheranism as state religion (sixteenth century), 446
    Middle Ages, 255–56
    Thirty Years' War, 485, 487, 488
Switzerland
    Calvinism in Geneva, 451, 455
    Protestantism in (sixteenth century), 446, 448–49

Syagrius, 212, 213
syllogism, 120
symposium (symposia), 88
Synod of 754, Canons of, 224, 225
Syntagma Philosophicum (Gassendi), 560–61
Syria
     Alexander the Great and, 124–25
     ancient Egypt and, 37, 45
     Bronze Age immigrants, 44
     Christian traditions, 223, 277
     Minoans and, 52
     Roman rule, 164
     Seleucids, 131, 133
     see also Assyrians
Syriac, 286

Table of Ranks (Russia), 531
Tabriz, 339, 342
Tacitus (Roman historian), 172, 173,
     175, 375
Talmud, 218
Tamburlaine (Marlowe), 500
Tarquinius Superbus (Tarquin the
     Arrogant), 151
taxes
     Early Middle Ages, 233, 236, 249
     Louis XIV (king of France) and, 513
     in tsarist Russia, 531, 535
technology
     Middle Ages agricultural innovation,
          237, 259–60
     naval technology/navigation of
          fifteenth century, 424–25
     Sumerian, 16–17, *17*
     see also weapons
telescope, invention of, 541, 546, 560
tempera, 346, *409*
Tempest, The (Shakespeare), 495, 502
Templars, 284, 306, 354
Temujin. *see* Genghis Khan
Tenochtitlán, 430, 431, *431*
Ten Thousand, 114, 117, 118, 120, 152
Teresa of Ávila, Saint, 464
tetrarchy, 195, *195*
Tetzel (Dominican friar), 440
Teutonic Knights, 300, 306, 390, 396
textiles
     of classical Greece, 104, *104*
     cloth of gold, 336
     of early civilizations, 4, 12, *20*
thalassocracy, 52
theater
     of classical Greece, 101–2, *102*,
          118–19

plays of Middle Ages, 374
     seventeenth century, 495, 500, 502
Thebes (Egypt)
     First Intermediate Period, 31
     Middle Kingdom, 36
     New Kingdom, 47–48
     Second Intermediate Period, 44
Thebes (Greece)
     Alexander the Great and, 121, 124
     downfall of Greek poleis and, 116, 122
     Peloponnesian War, 108
     rebuilding of, 121
     rise of poleis and, 81
     Theban Hegemony, 116
     Theban Sacred Band, 116, 122, 123
Themistocles (Athenian politician), 98, 100
theocracy, defined, 451
Theocritus (Hellenistic poet), 144
Theodoric the Ostrogoth (king of Goths),
     206, *206*, 207, 210, 212, 218
Theodosius (Roman emperor), 203, 204, 208
Theotokos, 223
Thermopylae, battle of, 99–100
Theseus (Greek hero), 40, 51, 53, 166
thetes, 100–101
Third Dynasty (ancient Egypt), 27, 29
Third Punic War, 145, 158
Thirtieth Dynasty (ancient Egypt), 34
Thirty Tyrants, 108
Thirty Years' War
     beginning of, 484, 485
     devastation of, 484, 486, 487–88, 511
     downfall of Bohemia, 485
     overview, 484, *487*
     Peace of Westphalia, 487, 488, 525
     politics and consequences of,
          485–88, *487*
     scientific revolution and, 547
     Sweden and invasion of
          Poland-Lithuania, 488–89
"This Is My Body" (fresco), *351*
Thomas à Kempis, 394
Thomas Aquinas, Saint, 314, 322, *322*,
     345, 439, 464
Thomas of Celano, 316, 317
Thracians, 95–96
Thucydides, 52, 84, 102, 103, 106, 144,
     224, 379
Thutmose I (pharaoh of Egypt), 45
Thutmose II (pharaoh of Egypt), 45
Thutmose III (pharaoh of Egypt), 46, 47
Tiber River, 150, 151, 152
Tigris river, 9, *13*, 17
timekeeping, Sumerian, 17, 345

time, measurement in Middle Ages, 345
Timur the Lame (Tamurlane), 380, 500
Tintoretto, 502
Tirhakah (king of Egypt and Kush), 72
Titian (Tiziano Vecellio), *444*
tobacco plantations, 495
Tobago, 481
toleration
     Act of Toleration (England), 519
Torah, 60, 75, 186, 218
Tories (Great Britain), 518, 519
torture, instruments of, *558*
Tory Party (Great Britain), 518, 519
To the Christian Nobility (Luther), 441
Tower of Babel, 2, 9, 42
"Town air makes you free" (German
     adage), 262–65
towns, emergence in early civilizations, 8
trade
     in Archaic Greece, 80, 84–85, 92
     Atlantic Ocean, Late Middle Ages,
          344, 381, 418, 424
     by Dutch Republic (seventeenth
          century), 521
     early civilizations, rise of trade, 4, 6,
          8, 9, 10
     Early Middle Ages, 227, 233–34, 236,
          247, 249
     growth of towns and trade in Middle
          Ages, 261–65, *263*, *264*
     Hellenistic period, 133–34
     medieval trade routes, *262*
     Mongol Empire and, 334, 337, 339–42
     by Phoenicians, 84
     slavery and triangular trade, 474–76, *475*
     spice trade, 283, 343, 381, 424, 481
     Sumerian, 10, 16, 17
     transnational trade of Late Bronze
          Age, 42–44, 49–51, 56, 80
     see also commerce
Trajan (Roman emperor), 171, 191,
     192–93
transnational diplomacy in Late Bronze
     Age, 49, 57
transubstantiation, doctrine of, 309, 312,
     351, 351–52
Transylvania, 300, 452
Treasure of the City of Ladies, The (Christine
     de Pizan), 373
Treaty of Tordesillas, 428
Treaty of Utrecht, 523–24, *524*, 526
Treaty of Westphalia, 487, 488, 525
triangular trade, 474–76, *475*
Tribonian (jurist), 220

tribunes, 153, 154
Trier, Germany, 204, 212
Tripoli, 304
trireme warships, 98, *98*, 100
Tristan (Gottfried), 325
triumph (Roman Republic), 165
triumvirate, 164, 168
trivium, 315
Trojan war, 51, 80–81
Trojan Women, The (Euripides), 101
troubadour songs, 325
trouvères, 325
Troy (Ilium), 51, 54, 57, 80, 89, 139, 150
Tudor dynasty, 388
Turkey
    Çatalhöyük, 4, 8
    see also Anatolia; Ottoman Empire
Tutankhamun (pharaoh of Egypt), 49
Twelfth Dynasty (ancient Egypt), 36–37
Two New Sciences (Galileo), 547
Two Treatises of Government (Locke),
    516, 520
Tycho Brahe, 544, 544–45, 549, 552, 563
tyranny in Archaic Greece, 88
Tyre (Phoenician capital), 59, 62, 125
Tyrrhenians, 150

Ubaid culture, 9–10
Ugaritic alphabet, 51, 59
Ugarit (Syria), 50, 56, 59
Ukraine
    Ivan the Great, 418
    Jagiellonian dynasty, 390
    Polish-Lithuanian Commonwealth,
        488, 522
ulamas, 234
Ulpian (Domitius Ulpianus; Roman
    jurist), 176
Uluburun, Turkey, shipwreck, 50
Umar (caliph), 230, 232
Umar Khayyam, 288
Umayyad dynasty, 224, 232–33, 235, 242,
    244, 247, 248, 250
United Provinces, 521, 523
United States
    American Revolution of 1776, 510
universities
    establishment in central and eastern
        Europe, 389
    inception of, 292, 296, 314, 319–20, *321*
    in northern Europe and Italy, con-
        trasted, 320, 413
University of Bologna, 320, 558
University of Paris, 296, 319–20, 387, 414

Upper Egypt, 24–25, 26, 28, 44–45
Ur, 18–19, *19*
Urban II (pope), 278–79, 280, 281, 283,
    303
Urban VI (pope), 391
Urban VIII (pope), 547
urbanization
    advantages of in Middle Ages, 264–65
    Black Death impact on, 369, 376, 378
    cities of Middle Ages, 326–27
    in Eastern Europe, Late Middle Ages,
        389
    emergence of towns and villages in
        early civilizations, 8
    governance of towns in Middle Ages,
        261–65, *263, 264*, 315, 326–27
    growth of towns and trade in Middle
        Ages, 261–65, *263, 264*
    Hellenistic period, 133–34
    in Mesopotamia, 9–10, 12
    Roman urban planning, 174, *178*,
        178–79
    "Town air makes you free," 262–65
    see also poleis
Ur-Nammu (king of Ur), 18, 26
Urraca (queen of León-Castile), 326
Ursulines, 464
Uruk (Sumerian city), 10, *10*, 12–13, 18, 24
Usama ibn Munqidh, 284
Ussher, James, 547–49, 551
usury, 265, 316
Uthman (caliph), 232
Utnapishtim (Sumerian hero), 14–15, 40
Utopia (More), 415

Valla, Lorenzo, 379, 415
Valois dynasty, 358
Vandals, 206, 207, 209, 218, 256
van der Meulen, Adam Frans, *515*
van der Straet, Jan, 429, *429*
van der Weyden, Rogier, 372, 374, 377
vassals, 268, 270
Velázquez, Diego, 503, *503*
Venice
    Black Death impact on, 369
    commerce and settlement, Middle
        Ages, 343
    oligarchy in, 326, 389, 518
    revenge of, 307
    trading empire, 256, 261, 277, 283, 343
Venus pudica, 121
Venus (Roman goddess), 155
vernacular entertainment in Middle
    Ages, 328

Versailles
    absolutism and, 512, 514, *515*
    Peter the Great's emulation of, 533
Vespucci, Amerigo, 428, 429, 541
Victory, altar removed from Roman
    Senate, 203
Vienna, siege of, 526, 528–29
View of Toledo (El Greco), 502, *502*
Vikings
    assimilation and intermarriage, 248,
        254, 255
    Greenland and, 248, 254, 344, 428
    Iceland and, 248, 254, 428
    invasions by, 247–49, *248*
    in North America, 248, 254, 344,
        427–28
    Novgorod Republic, 300–301
    Rus', 247–48, 255, 276, 300–301,
        334, 336
    settlements and colonization by, *248*,
        248–49, 254, 255
    trading by, 247, 249
Vinland (Newfoundland), 248, 254, 344
Virgil (Publius Virgilius Maro; Roman
    poet)
    Aeneid, 148, 150, 174
    in Dante's *Comedy*, 346
    influence of Theocritus, 144
    Petrarch and, *374*, 375
Virginia
    colonization of, 470, 483, 484
Virgin of the Rocks, The (Leonardo da
    Vinci), 408, *408*
Visigoths, 206, 218, 220, 231, 302
Vitruvius, 413
Vladimiri, Paulus, 396
Vladimir (prince of Kiev), 277
Volmar, *311*
Voltaire (François-Marie Arouet)
    Newton and, 562–63
von Bora, Katharina, 441
Vulgate, 208, *461*, 462

Wagner, Richard, 325
Waldensianism, 311, 314
Waldo, Peter, 311, 316
Wales, 355
Walid, al- (caliph), *232*
Warm Period, Medieval, 237,
    259–61, 344
War of the Spanish Succession,
    523–24, *524*
Wars of the Roses, 388
Wartburg (castle), 444

weapons
artillery, 383, 425
cannons, pistols, and muskets, invention of, 383, 425
Leonardo da Vinci and, 408, 411
see also military; technology
wheel, invention of, 16
Whig Party (Great Britain), 518–19, 520
White Temple (Uruk), 10, *10*
William of Aquitaine, 271
William of Ockham, 345
William of Orange (king of England), 480, 519–20, *520*, 521, 522, 523
William of Rubruck, 339
William the Conqueror (king of England; William of Normandy), *267*, 268–70, 294
Winkelmann, Maria, 559
Winter Landscape with Ice-Skaters (Avercamp), *511*
winter solstice, celebration of, 197
witchcraft, 499
witch craze, 499
Wittenberg, Luther at, 436, 439, 445
Wladyslaw II Jagiello (king of Poland), 390, *390*
Wlodkowic, Pawel, 396
Wolfram von Eschenbach, 325
women's roles/rights
access to education in Middle Ages, 318
in ancient Egypt, 35–36
in ancient Nubia, 37
of ancient Rome, 150, 151, 161
of Archaic Greece, 88
Byzantine Empire, 223, 225
of classical Greece, 103–4, *104*

Code of Hammurabi and, 21, 23, 63
court culture of Middle Ages, 324–26
in the Crusades, 281
early Christianity and, 188, 201–3, 208
early Islam and, 234–35
education and role of women, fourth–second centuries B.C.E., 142–43
in Etruscan culture, 150
European explorers' treatment of indigenous women, 429
female beauty as ideal, 121, *121*
Jadwiga (female king of Poland), 390
medieval women with religious ambition, 393–94
monasticism and, 240–41
Mycenaean Greece, 103
Protestant Reformation and, 453, 455
queens of Middle Ages, 326
queens regnant of England, 458–60, *459*
querelle des femmes, 372
in reformed Catholic Church of seventeenth–eighteenth centuries, 464
Renaissance in Italy, 379, 407
of Roman Republic, 161
status of Mary, 309–10, *310*
witchcraft accusations against women, 499
women scientists during scientific revolution, 540, 558, 558–59
Worms, Diet of, 444–45, 462
writing
in ancient Egypt, 27, *27*, 29
Carolingian minuscule, 245, *246*
cuneiform, *11*, 11–12, 17, 23, 27, 51
demotic script, 27, 29

development of, 10–12, *11*
hieratic script, 27, *27*
hieroglyphs and hieroglyphics, 27, *27*, 29
Wurm, Ole, 551
Wycliffe, John, 366, *396*, 396–97, 440

Xavier, Francis, 464
Xenophanes, 95–96
xenophobia, 158
Xenophon (Athenian author), 84, 114, 117, 118, 120, 122, 152
Xerxes (king of Persia), 68, 98–100, *99*, 101

Yahweh (Hebrew/Judaic god), 61–62, 70–75, 186, 227
Yersinia pestis, 360, 368
yeshivas, 218
York Castle (England), *267*
York dynasty, 388
York (England), medieval drama in, 374

Zagros Mountains (Ur), 18
Zara, Fourth Crusade and, 307
Zarathustra (Zoroaster), 68–69, 70
Zealots, 185
Zeno (eastern Roman emperor), 206
Zeno of Citium, 134
"Zero Dynasty" (ancient Egypt), 26
Zeus (Greek god), 85, 89, 125
Ziggurat of Ur, 18, *19*
Zoroastrianism, 42, 68–70, 136–37, 187, 195
Zwinglianism, 448
Zwingli, Ulrich, 448